**Abkürzungen** der Informationsverarbeitung
**Abbreviations** of Data Processing Terms
**Abréviations** du Traitement de l'Information

Amkreutz

# Abkürzungen
### der Informationsverarbeitung

# Abbreviations
### of Data Processing Terms

# Abréviations
### du Traitement de l'Information

**A–Z**

aus allen Bereichen
der Daten- und
Informationsverarbeitung

deutsche · englische · französische
spanische und italienische
Abkürzungen

DATAKONTEXT~VERLAG

CIP-Kurztitelaufnahme der Deutschen Bibliothek

**Amkreutz, Johann J.:**
Abkürzungen der Informationsverarbeitung von A–Z / Amkreutz. – Köln: Datakontext-Verlag, 1986.
  ISBN 3-921899-66-4

NE: HST

ISBN 3-921899-66-4

Alle Rechte vorbehalten
© 1986 by DATAKONTEXT-VERLAG GmbH
Aachener Straße 1052, D-5000 Köln 40

Ohne ausdrückliche Genehmigung des Verlages ist es nicht gestattet, das Buch oder Teile daraus in irgendeiner Weise zu vervielfältigen.
Lizenzausgaben sind nach Vereinbarung möglich.

Druck: J. P. Bachem Druckerei, Köln

Printed in Germany

# Vorwort

In einer Welt, in der der ökonomische Umgang mit dem wertvollsten Gut des Menschen überhaupt – der Zeit – jedem als Notwendigkeit plastisch vor Augen geführt wird (indem die Menschen nämlich alle erdenklichen Wege nutzen, die Zeit zu sparen), ist die Herausgabe eines Wörterbuchs, das Abkürzungen eines bestimmten Fachgebiets über drei bzw. fünf Sprachen hinweg erklärt, sicherlich keine „sprachverarmende", den Gebrauch von Abkürzungen fordernde Maßnahme, sondern ebenfalls ein Instrument der „Zeitökonomie". Jeder, der mit dem in den letzten Jahren stark verbreiterten Gebiet der Informationsverarbeitung zu tun hat – möglicherweise grenzüberschreitend oder fremdsprachige Literatur nutzend –, weiß, daß Abkürzungen nicht auszurotten sind; im Gegenteil: Manche Texte würden geradezu unlesbar, wenn nicht endlose Wurmgebilde von Begriffen für das Auge zu rasch erkennbaren Abkürzungen zusammengefaßt würden.

Dieses Werk, das auf dem 1982 erschienenen Wörterbuch „Abkürzungen der Datenverarbeitung" aufbaut, hat den damaligen Wissensstand fortgeschrieben, vor allem Anwendungsgebiete integriert, die über die „klassische" Datenverarbeitung hinausgehen, und damit Aspekte der automatisierten Kommunikation aufgearbeitet. Verlag und Autor ist deshalb zu danken, daß sie einen gut eingeführten Titel aufgaben – also keine wesentlich erweiterte Ausgabe des alten Wörterbuchs, sondern eine Neuauflage unter einem dem neuen Inhalt angepaßten Titel unternommen haben.

Dem Leser sei aber nicht nur der Umgang mit diesem Wörterbuch empfohlen, sondern auch ans Herz gelegt, dem Verlag neue Begriffsverbindungen und -abkürzungen mitzuteilen, wenn er ihnen begegnet. Der rasche technische Fortschritt der Informationsverarbeitung läßt für die kommenden Jahre durchaus eine Weiterentwicklung auch der Fachsprache der Informatik erwarten. Künftigen Neuauflagen kämen daher Anregungen aus der Leserschaft sehr zugute.

Bonn, Januar 1986

Hans Gliss,
Fachjournalist

Abkürzungen der Informationsverarbeitung

Die Abkürzungen wurden kritisch ausgewählt, um sie der Fachöffentlichkeit in Form eines Nachschlagewerks als Arbeitshilfe zugänglich zu machen. Es mag durchaus sein, daß nicht alle Dialekte und nicht jeder DV-Slang mit den damit verbundenen Abkürzungen in dieses Werk Eingang gefunden haben. Es wäre auch nicht fair, den Benutzer dieses Nachschlagewerks mit Begriffen zu überfrachten, die ihm voraussichtlich nie in seinem Leben begegnen werden. Die allgemein wichtigen Abkürzungen hingegen sind dokumentiert; angesichts einer weltweit raschen Weiterentwicklung der Daten- und Textverarbeitung sammelt der Autor auch weiterhin neue Abkürzungsbegriffe und kündigt jetzt schon eine Fortschreibung des vorliegenden Nachschlagewerkes an.
Um die Herkunft der Abkürzungen zu verdeutlichen, wurden im Gegensatz zur geltenden Grammatik alle Anfangsbuchstaben, aus denen sich die Abkürzung zusammensetzt, groß geschrieben.
Mit drei Punkten (. . .) versehene Abkürzungen verweisen auf Namen von Firmen, die diese Abkürzungen für die Bezeichnung ihrer Produkte verwenden.
Das Buch selbst ist ein Produkt der Textverarbeitung, was für Benutzer den Vorteil hat, daß zwischen Redaktionsschluß und Erscheinen ein nur geringer Zeitraum lag. Dies sichert dem Käufer eine hohe Aktualität an verfügbaren Abkürzungen der Informationsverarbeitung.
An dieser Stelle sei insbesondere Herrn Wilhelm Carl BDÜ, Mitautor des dreisprachigen „Wörterbuch der Datenverarbeitung" – in Fachkreisen als „Roter Amkreutz" bekannt –, gedankt, der durch Rat und Tat am Aufbau des Stammsatzes in den Jahren 1971 bis 1981 mitgewirkt hat.

Köln, im März 1986

Autor und
Herausgeber

# Preface

In a world where the economical use of man's most valuable asset of all – time – is vividly brought to everyone's attention as a necessity (by using all conceivable ways to save time), the publishing of a dictionary explaining abbreviations in three resp. five languages within a particular field is by no means a step towards "language impoverishment", encouraging the use of abbreviations, but rather a "time saving" instrument. Anyone who has anything to do with data processing intensified so greatly in recent years, knows – possibly through border crossing or through the use of foreign language literature – that abbreviations are not to be eradicated; on the contrary: some texts would be unreadable unless the endless chaining of terminology could be summarized into the form of abbreviations that are easily recognizable visually.

This work, based on the 'Abbreviations of Data Processing Terms' dictionary published in 1982, has updated the level of knowledge, above all integrating fields of application beyond 'classical' data processing, thus incorporating aspects of automated communication. The publishers and author should therefore be thanked for dispensing with a well-known title – not presenting a substantially extended edition of the old dictionary, but rather a new edition with a title adapted to the new contents.

The reader is not only recommended to use this dictionary, but is also warmly recommended to inform the publishers of any new terminological associations and abbreviations they encounter. As technology advances more rapidly one can definitely expect the specialist language of information technology to develop further. Future editions can only profit from suggestions made by the readership.

Bonn, January 1986

Hans Gliss,
Professional journalist

## Abbreviations of Data Processing Terms

The abbreviations were carefully selected so that they are accessible to the specialist reader as a working aid in the form of a reference work. It may well be that not all dialects and DP-slang and the abbreviations associated with them have found their way into this reference work. It also would not be fair to burden the user of this work with terminology that he will probably never encounter. The abbreviations of general importance are documented; as data processing is such a fast growing field, the author is continually collecting new abbreviation terms and is already announcing the updating of the current reference work.
In order to clarify the origin of the abbreviations, all the first letters were capitalized, contrary to the current rules of grammar.
Abbreviations marked with three dots (. . .) refer to the names of companies using these abbreviations to describe their products.
The current work would be incomplete if the reader was not given the opportunity to make a separate note of abbreviations important to him and add new ones encountered in specialist literature. This is why the reader has a few blank pages at his disposal.
The book itself is a product of word processing, giving the user the advantage of a short period of time between the copy deadline and publication. This ensures the buyer that the abbreviations of data processing terms in the work are very up-to-date.
At this point, thanks should go to Mr. Wilhelm Carl BDÜ especially, co-author of the work called 'Dictionary of Data Processing', who, actively contributed to the composition of the source data between 1971 and 1981.

Cologne, March 1986

Author
and publisher

Avant-propos

Dans un monde où chacun ressent la nécessité d'économiser ce que l'homme a de plus précieux – le temps – et utilise tous les moyens qui le lui permettent, l'édition d'un dictionnaire expliquant en trois resp. cinq langues la signification des abréviations usitées dans un domaine technique bien précis n'est certes ni un facteur d'appauvrissement de la langue ni une mesure d'encouragement à l'usage d'abréviations, mais bel et bien un moyen de plus d'économiser du temps. Quiconque est confronté à ce secteur en forte expansion qu'est l'informatique et doit par exemple consulter des ouvrages en langues étrangères ou correspondre avec des interlocuteurs étrangers sait que loin d'être superflues, les abréviations sont devenues indispensables dans bien des cas: certains textes seraient en effet parfaitement incompréhensibles s'il n'y avait pas les abréviations pour saisir d'emblée la signification de termes souvent juxtaposés à l'infini.

Cet ouvrage élaboré à partir du dictionnaire «Abréviations du traitement de l'information» paru en 1982 le réactualise en y intégrant à fois les connaissances acquises depuis et les domaines d'application dépassant le cadre du traitement classique de l'information, et en touchant donc à certains aspects de la communication automatisée. C'est la raison pour laquelle la maison d'édition et l'auteur renoncèrent à reprendre le titre bien connu de l'ancien dictionnaire pour lui en préférer un autre mieux adapté à la teneur de ce nouvel ouvrage qui est plus qu'une simple édition remise à jour du précédent.

Nous invitons nos lecteurs non seulement à consulter ce dictionnaire, mais aussi à communiquer à son éditeur les nouvelles combinaisons terminologiques et abréviations qu'ils peuvent être amenés à rencontrer. Vu l'évolution rapide de la technologie de l'informatique, il faut s'attendre à ce que le «jargon» informatique continue, lui aussi, de progresser dans les années à venir. Les suggestions de nos lecteurs ne peuvent donc que profiter aux futurs remaniements de cet ouvrage.

Bonn, janvier 1986

Hans Gliss,
Journaliste professionnel

Abréviations usitées en informatique

Les abréviations de cet ouvrage ont été choisies avec méthode et regroupées en un aide-mémoire destiné à faciliter la tâche de son utilisateur. Il est tout à fait possible que cet ouvrage ne comporte pas toutes les abréviations plus ou moins abitraires et ne reflète pas tous les jargons informatiques qui ont cours. Ce ne serait, il est vrai, pas aider l'utilisateur de cet ouvrage que de le submerger d'une foule de termes qu'il ne rencontrera peut-être jamais dans sa vie. Cet ouvrage se concentre donc sur la documentation des abréviations importantes et d'usage courant. Vu la rapidité avec laquelle l'informatique évolue, l'auteur continue de recueillir de nouvelles abréviations et annonce d'ores et déjà qu'il complétera le présent recueil.
En dépit des règles grammaticales, toutes les premières lettres composant chaque abréviation ont été écrites en majuscules pour en faire ressortir l'origine.
Les abréviations accompagnées de trois points (...) se réfèrent aux noms des firmes utilisant ces abréviations pour désigner leurs produits.
Plusieurs pages ont été réservées aux annotations du lecteur, car le présent ouvrage ne saurait être complet s'il ne donnait à son lecteur l'occasion d'en retenir les abréviations qui lui importent et d'y rajouter celles qu'il peut rencontrer dans les revues et documentations techniques.
Ce dictionnaire étant lui-même un produit du traitement des textes, son acheteur peut être sûr que les abréviations qui le composent sont de la dernière actualité puisqu'il ne fallut pas longtemps pour le publier une fois rédigé.
Nous nous permettons ici de remercier tout particulièrement Monsieur Wilhelm Carl BDÜ, coauteur de l'ouvrage trilingue intitulé «Dictionnaire du Traitement de l'Information» qui, de 1971 à 1981, participa activement à la constitution du répertoire de base et nous aida toujours de ses conseils.

Cologne, Mars 1986

Auteur
et éditeur

# Büro kommunikation

## manager-info-reihe:

Günter Darazs - Manager-Info 1/2 -
**Neue Bürokommunikationssysteme und -netze**
Kurzeinführung für das
Management in die Bürolandschaft von morgen,
83 S., 3-921899-43-5, DM 35,–

Gerhard Dieterle - Manager-Info 3 -
**Local Area Networks (LAN)**
Schlüssel zur Kommunikation
von heute und morgen,
85 S., 3-921899-50-8, DM 45,–

3-921899-50-8

Widdel/Krawulsky - Manager-Info 4 -
**Technologische Elemente
der Büroautomation**
Wegweiser für das Büro von heute
90 S., 3-921899-51-6, DM 45,–

Bornheim/Voßbein - Manager-Info 5 -
**Entscheidungshilfen beim
Bürocomputer-Einsatz**
Betriebswirtschaftliche und
Datensicherheitskriterien zur
Auswahl und Bewertung von
PC's und Bürocomputern
132 S., 3-921899-61-3, DM 40,–

3-921899-61-3

Dworatschek/Büllesbach/Koch u.a.
**Personalcomputer und
Datenschutz** - Manager-Info 6 -
– Leitfaden für die Praxis –
80 S., 3-921899-76-1, DM 35,–

Edgar Pohle - Manager-Info 7 -
**Praktikable Datensicherung
bei Kleincomputern**
– Vom Pocket Computer bis zur
mittleren Datentechnik –
Ausführliche Anleitungen,
112 S., 3-921899-77-X, DM 38,–

3-921899-77-X

**DATAKONTEXT-VERLAG**
Aachener Straße 1052 · D-5000 KÖLN 40
Tel. 0221/486503 · Telex 8881833 data d

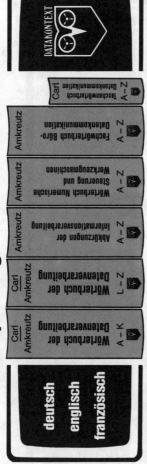

# A

| | | | |
|---|---|---|---|
| A | Abbreviation | A-ADU | Amplituden-Analog/Digital-Umsetzer |
| A | Abfrage | | |
| A | Abrechnungsart | A-O AMPL | And-Or Amplifier |
| A | Abrechnungsautomat | A-P | Arithmetic and Program |
| A | Abschnitt | A-REG | Akkumulator-Register |
| A | Absolutadresse | A-W | Audible Warning |
| A | Absolute | A/D | Analog to Digital |
| A | Absolute Address | A/D | Analog/Digital |
| A | Abstracting Automatic | A/E | Architectural/Engineering firm |
| A | Abteilung | | |
| A | Access Address | A/E | Ausgabe/Eingabe |
| A | Account | A/EF | Architectural/Engineering Firm |
| A | Accounting Automation | | |
| A | Accumulator | A/M | Auto-Manual |
| A | Active Accounts | A/N | Analogique/Numérique |
| A | Actual Address | A/N | Alphanumerics |
| A | Additional | A/N | Alphnumerisch |
| A | Address | A/O | Answer/Originate |
| A | Administration | A/P MCU | Autopilot Monitor and Control Unit |
| A | Aggregat | | |
| A | Alarm | A/P MON | Autopilot Monitor |
| A | Alphabet | A/P TSTPG | Autopilot Test Programmer |
| A | Ammeter | | |
| A | Ampere | A/S | Adder/Subtracter |
| A | Amplification | A/T | Action Time |
| A | Amplifier | A/T | Alignment Technique |
| A | Amplitude | A/W | Aufnahme/Wiedergabe |
| A | Analog | AA | Absolute Altitude |
| A | Analysis | AA | Actual Argument |
| A | Analyzer | AA | Add Address |
| A | Angström | AA | Additional Addressing |
| A | Anode | AA | Address Accumulator |
| A | Anpassung | AA | Address Adder |
| A | Anschluß | AA | Address Algorithm |
| A | Answer | AA | Address Allocation |
| A | Anweisung | AA | Address Appendix |
| A | Arbeit | AA | Address Arithmetic |
| A | Area | AA | Address Array |
| A | Arithmetic | AA | Address Assignment |
| A | Aspect Ratio | AA | Adressenänderung |
| A | Assembly | AA | Advanced Algebra |
| A | Asymmetric | AA | Advice of Allotment |
| A | Aufgabe | AA | Air-to-Air |
| A | Aufzeichnung | AA | Alarm Apparatus |
| A | Ausgabe | AA | Algebraic Adder |
| A | Ausgang | AA | Algebraic Addition |
| A | Auslösung | AA | Alphanumeric Address |
| A | Aussteuerung | AA | Alphanumerische Adressendatei |
| A | Austastsignal | | |
| A | Auswahlprüfung | AA | Alternate Area |
| A | Auswertung | AA | Analog Adder |
| A | Automatic | AA | Anfangsadresse |
| A | Auxiliary | AA | Annual Audit |
| A | Availability | AA | Arbeitsanweisung |
| A TOT | After Total | AA | Arbitrary Access |

# A

| | | | |
|---|---|---|---|
| AA | Argument Association | AADC | Advanced Avionics Digital Computer |
| AA | Arithmetic Algorithm | AADC | All Application Digital Computer |
| AA | Arithmetic Average | | |
| AA | Audible Alarm | AADIS | Automatic Air Defense Information System |
| AA | Auftragsart | | |
| AA | Ausführungsanweisung | AADR | Alternate Address |
| AA | Ausgangsanzeige | AADS | Area Air Defense System |
| AA | Automatic Abstracting | AADS | Automatic Aircraft Diagnostic System |
| AA | Automatic Account | | |
| AA | Automatic Acquisition | AAE | Auto-Answer Equipment |
| AA | Automatic Answer | AAE | Automated Analysis Equipment |
| AA | Automatic Approval | | |
| AA | Automatikbefehl Aus | AAE | Automatic Answering Equipment |
| AA | Auxiliary Accumulator | | |
| AA | Auxiliary Address | AAE | Automatische Anrufbeantwortungseinrichtung |
| AA | Auxiliary Algorithm | | |
| AA | Änderungsauftrag | | |
| AAA | Active Acquisition Aid | AAE | Automatische Anrufeinrichtung |
| AAA | Automatic Accounting Apparatus | | |
| AAAI | American Association for Artificial Intelligence | AAE | Automatische Anschalteinheit |
| | | AAE | Automatische Anschalteinrichtung |
| AAAS | American Association for Advancement of Science | AAE | Automatische Antworteinheit |
| AAAS | Automated Attendance Accounting System | AAES | American Association of Engineering Societies |
| AAB | Allgemeine Ausführungsbestimmungen | AAH | Adressenanhang |
| | | AAI | Automatic Attendant Identifier |
| AAB | Automatische Angebots- und Auftragsbearbeitung | AAID | Arithmetic Array Identification |
| AAC | Acquisition Advice Code | AAID | Arithmetic Array Identifier |
| AAC | Advanced Airborne Computer | AAIM | American Association of Industrial Management |
| AAC | Alphanumeric Accounting Computer | AAIS | Administrative Analysis, Information and Statistics |
| AAC | Ampere Alternating Current | | |
| AACC | American Automatic Control Council | AAK | Amplituden-Adreß-Kodesystem |
| AACFD | Automatic Account Card Feed Device | AAL | Absolute Assembly Language |
| AACL | Affect Adjective Check List | AALUE | Asymptotically Admissible Linear Unbiased Estimator |
| AACS | Advanced Automatic Compilation System | AAM | Amplitude and Angle Modulation |
| AACS | Airborne Astrographic Camera System | AAM | Additional Addressing Module |
| AAD | Address Adder | | |
| AAD | Auftastimpuls-Auslösediode | AAM | Alphabetical Accounting Machine |
| AADC | Advanced Airborne Digital Computer | AAM | Automatic Accounting Machine |

# A

| | | | |
|---|---|---|---|
| AAM | Automatic Address Modification | AAVD | Automatic Alternate Voice Data |
| AAMS | Airborne Auxiliary Memory System | AB | Absorbed Burden |
| | | AB | Accumulator Bit |
| AAN | Ausstattungsanweisung | AB | Accumulator and Buffer |
| AAO | Advanced Arithmetical Operations | AB | Adapter Booster |
| | | AB | Add Binary |
| AAP | Advise if Able to Proceed | AB | Additional Bit |
| AAP | Agribusiness Accountability Project | AB | Address Base |
| | | AB | Address Bit |
| AAP | Algorithm for Arithmetic Operation | AB | Address Blank |
| | | AB | Address Byte |
| AAP | Automatischer Arbeitsplatz | AB | Airborne |
| | | AB | Algorithmic Block |
| AAPL | An Additional Programming Language | AB | Allgemeine Bedingungen |
| | | AB | Alphabetical Block |
| AAR | A Address Register | AB | Amplitudenbegrenzer |
| AAR | Address Addend Register | AB | Anfangsbedingung |
| AAR | Anfangsadreßregister | AB | Anfangsbestand |
| AAR | Association of American Railroads | AB | Arbeitsbereich |
| | | AB | Arbeitsbewertung |
| AAR | Auxiliary Address Register | AB | Argument Byte |
| | | AB | Arithmetic Bit |
| AARS | Automated Attendance Reporting System | AB | Arithmetic Bus |
| | | AB | Ausfallspeicherbank |
| AAS | Advanced Administrative System | AB | Ausführungsbestimmung |
| | | AB | Ausgangsblock |
| AAS | Advanced Aerial System | AB | Ausnahmebedingung |
| AAS | Advanced Antenna System | AB | Aussetzender Betrieb |
| AAS | Allgemeines Auskunftssystem | AB | Automated Bibliography |
| | | ABA | Active Buffer Address |
| AAS | Annual Average Score | ABA | American Bankers Association |
| AAS | Arithmetic Assignment Statement | ABA | Annual Budget Authorization |
| AAS | Ausnutzung des Arbeitsspeichers | ABA | Audio/Visual Annunciator |
| AAS | Automated Accounting System | ABAC | A Basic Coursewriter |
| | | ABACUS | Architecture and Building Aids Computer Unit of Strathclyde University |
| AAS | Automatic Address Selector | | |
| AAS | Automatic Address Substitution | | |
| AAS | Automatic Array Scaling | ABACUS | Automatic Block-schematic Advanced Control User-oriented System |
| AAS | Azimuth Alignment System | | |
| AAT | Aktionsanzeigeteil | | |
| AAT | Attitude Acquisition Technique | ABACUS | Automatic Business And Control United System |
| AAT | Automatic Answer Trunk | ABAR | Advanced Battery Acquisition Radar |
| AAT | Average Access Time | | |
| AATS | Automatic Anti-Theft System | ABAR | Alternate Battery Acquisition Radar |
| AAVCS | Automatic Aircraft Vectoring Control System | ABAS | Ablaufanforderungsauswahlsteuerung |

# A

| | | | |
|---|---|---|---|
| ABAS | Ablaufanforderungssteuerung | ABIIS | Automated Blood Inventory Information System |
| ABB | Automatic Back Bias | | |
| ABBR | Abbreviate | ABK | Arbeitsbegleitkarte |
| ABBR | Abbreviation | ABK | Auftragsbegleitkarte |
| ABC | Abrechnungscomputer | ABL | Atlas Basis Language |
| ABC | Advanced Ballistic Computer | ABLE | Activity Balance Line Evaluation |
| ABC | Airborne Computer | ABLE | Agricultural Biological Literature Evaluation |
| ABC | Anwendungs- und Bedienungsorientiertes Computersystem | ABLE | Agricultural Biological Literature Exploitation |
| ABC | Approach By Concept | ABLS | Atlas Biomedical Literature System |
| ABC | Automatic Background Control | ABM | Asynchronous Balanced Mode |
| ABC | Automatic Bandwidth Control | ABM | Automated Batch Mixing |
| ABC | Automatic Bass Control | ABM | Automatic Batch Mixing |
| ABC | Automatic Beam Control | ABM | Automatic Billing Machine |
| ABC | Automatic Bias Control | | |
| ABC | Automatic Binary Computer | ABME | Asynchronous Balanced Mode Extended |
| ABC | Automatic Blank Character | ABO | Advanced Byte-Oriented |
| | | ABO | Astable Blocking Oscillator |
| ABC | Automatic Branch Control | ABP | Active Bandpass |
| ABC | Automatic Brightness Control | ABP | Actual Block Processor |
| ABC | Automation of Bibliography through Computerization | ABP | Alphanumeric Block Printer |
| | | ABP | Assumed Binary Point |
| ABCB | Air Blast Circuit Breaker | ABPLM | Asynchronous Bipolar Pulse Length Modulation |
| ABCD | Accelerated Business Collection and Delivery | ABR | Abbreviation |
| | | ABR | Abréviation |
| ABCD | Automated Biological and Chemical Data | ABR | Ausgabebaugruppe Register |
| ABCL | As-Built Configuration Lists | ABR | Automatic Backup and Recovery |
| ABCU | Association of Burroughs Computer Users | ABR | Automatic Bit Rate |
| | | ABS | Absent Subscriber |
| ABD | Alloy Bulk Diffusion | ABS | Absolute |
| ABD | Automated Block Diagramming | ABS | Advanced Business Systems |
| ABDL | Automatic Binary Data Link | ABS | Allied Business Systems |
| | | ABS | Anodenbasisschaltung |
| ABE | Arithmetic Building Element | ABS | Anschlußsteuerung Bildschirmeinheit |
| ABE | Automatic Block End | ABS | Auftragsfreigabe mit Belastungsschranke |
| ABEL | Auftragsbelegerstellung | | |
| ABEND | Abnormal End | ABS | Ausgabebaugruppe Steuerung |
| ABEST | Auftragsbestand | | |
| ABF | Arbeitszeiterfassung, Betriebsdatenerfassung und Fertigungssteuerung | ABS | Ausgabe-Blattschreiber |
| | | ABS | Automatic Beam-current Stabilizing |

# A

| | | | |
|---|---|---|---|
| ABS VM | Absolute Voltmeter | AC | Adding Counter |
| ABS... | Allied Business | AC | Additional Code |
| | System Ltd. | AC | Address Calculation |
| ABSAP | Airborne Search and | AC | Address Card |
| | Attack Plotter | AC | Address Carry |
| ABT | Acetate Base Tape | AC | Address Chain |
| ABT | Automatic Block Transfer | AC | Address Character |
| ABT | Automatic Block | AC | Address Check |
| | Transport | AC | Address Code |
| ABTICS | Abstract and Book Title | AC | Address Comparing |
| | Index Card Service | AC | Address Complete |
| ABU | Advanced Business Unit | AC | Address Computation |
| ABU | Answer-Back Unit | AC | Address Constant |
| ABV | Absolute Value | AC | Address Conversion |
| ABV | Automatischer | AC | Address Counter |
| | Blockierverhinderer | AC | Addressable Clock |
| ABW | Abschlußsteuerung | AC | Addressed Core |
| | Blockdruckwerk | AC | Adjacent Channel |
| ABW | Automated Batch | AC | Alert Condition |
| | Weighting | AC | Algebraic Calculation |
| AC | AND Circuit | AC | Algebraic Curve |
| AC | Absence Card | AC | Algorithm Control |
| AC | Absolute Code | AC | Allocation Counter |
| AC | Absolute Coding | AC | Alphabetic Character |
| AC | Absolute Convergence | AC | Alphabetic Code |
| AC | Absolute Counter | AC | Alphabetic Coding |
| AC | Abstract Code | AC | Alphabetic Collator |
| AC | Abstract Computer | AC | Alphanumeric Character |
| AC | Acceptance | AC | Alphanumeric Code |
| AC | Access Coding | AC | Alphanumeric Coding |
| AC | Access Control | AC | Alphanumeric Command |
| AC | Access Cycle | AC | Alteration Cancellation |
| AC | Account | AC | Alternate Code |
| AC | Account Card | AC | Alternate Current |
| AC | Account Code | AC | Alternating Current |
| AC | Account Current | AC | Amortized Cost |
| AC | Accounting Calculation | AC | Analog Channel |
| AC | Accounting Card | AC | Analog Circuit |
| AC | Accounting Carriage | AC | Analog Computation |
| AC | Accounting Computer | AC | Analog Computer |
| AC | Accumulateur | AC | Analog Computing |
| AC | Accumulating Counter | AC | Anisotropic Constant |
| AC | Accumulator | AC | Answer Construct |
| AC | Accumulator Contents | AC | Antenna Current |
| AC | Accuracy Check | AC | Anti-Clutter |
| AC | Accuracy Control | AC | Anwendungscode |
| AC | Action Chart | AC | Aperture Card |
| AC | Action Code | AC | Application Control |
| AC | Active Computer | AC | Application Controller |
| AC | Actual Cost | AC | Approach Coupler |
| AC | Adaptive Control | AC | Approximate Calculation |
| AC | Add Carry | AC | Approximate Computation |
| AC | Adder Carry | AC | Approximation Calculus |
| AC | Adder Circuit | AC | Arithmetic Check |

# A

| | | | |
|---|---|---|---|
| AC | Arithmetic Computation | ACARD | Advisory Council for Applied Research and Development |
| AC | Arithmetic and Controls | | |
| AC | Array Calculation | | |
| AC | Aspect Card | ACAS | Automatic Component Assembly System |
| AC | Assembler Code | | |
| AC | Astable Circuit | ACASS | Automated Credit Authorization Subsystem |
| AC | Asynchronous Computer | | |
| AC | Attention Command | | |
| AC | Attenuation Characteristics | ACAU | Automatic Calling and Answering Unit |
| AC | Autocoder | ACB | Access Control Block |
| AC | Autocorrelation | ACB | Access method Control Block |
| AC | Automatic Calculator | | |
| AC | Automatic Carriage | ACB | Adapter Control Block |
| AC | Automatic Check | ACB | Align Control Box |
| AC | Automatic Checking | ACB | Allocate Control Block |
| AC | Automatic Clearing | ACB | Application Control Block |
| AC | Automatic Code | | |
| AC | Automatic Coding | ACBS | Accrediting Commission for Business Schools |
| AC | Automatic Computer | | |
| AC | Automatic Control | ACBT | Automatic Circuit Board Tester |
| AC | Automatic Controller | | |
| AC | Automation Center | ACC | Acceleration |
| AC | Availability Check | ACC | Acceptance |
| AC-AMDF | Auto-Correlation-Average Magnitude Difference Function | ACC | Access |
| | | ACC | Accumulate |
| | | ACC | Accumulator-shift Circuit |
| AC-CT | Access Control | | |
| ACA | Accounts Control Area | ACC | Acknowledge Control |
| ACA | Adjacent Channel Attenuation | ACC | Adaptive Control Constraint |
| ACA | Advanced Calculator Attachment | ACC | Additive Card Code |
| | | ACC | Airborne Control Computer |
| ACA | American Communications Association | | |
| | | ACC | Alternating Current Circuit |
| ACA | Asynchronous Communication Adapter | ACC | Application Control Code |
| ACA | Automatic Circuit Analyzer | | |
| | | ACC | Area Control Center |
| ACA | Automatic Clinical Analyzer | ACC | Automatic Carrier Control |
| ACA | Automatisches Code-Auswertungssystem | ACC | Automatic Chroma Control |
| | | ACC | Automatic Chrominance Control |
| ACAM | Apollo Computer Address Matrix | | |
| | | ACC | Automatic Console Control |
| ACAM | Augmented Content-Addressed Memory | | |
| | | ACC | Automatic Contrast Control |
| ACAMPS | Automated Communications And Message Processing System | | |
| | | ACC T | Access Time |
| | | ACC-MD | Accumulator/Multiplicand Divisor |
| ACAP | Automatic Circuit Analysis Program | | |
| ACAPE | Aerospace Computer Automatic Program Evaluator | ACCA | Asynchronous Communications Control Attachment |

- 6 -

# A

| | | | |
|---|---|---|---|
| ACCAP | Autocoder to COBOL Conversion And Program | ACD | Alphabetic Collating Device |
| ACCD | Access Denied | ACD | Automatic Call Distributor |
| ACCEL | Automated Circuit Card Etching Layout | ACD | Automatic Circuit Design |
| ACCESS | Air Canada Cargo Enquiry and Service System | ACDC | Alternating Current/Direct Current |
| ACCESS | Aircraft Communication Control and Electronic Signalling System | ACDL | Asynchronous Circuit Design Language |
| | | ACDMS | Automated Control of a Document Management System |
| ACCESS | Argonne Code Center Exchange and Storage System | ACDP | Automatic Centralized Data Processing |
| ACCESS | Automatic Card Control Entrance Security System | ACDPS | Automated Cartographic Drafting and Photogrammetric System |
| ACCESS | Automatic Checking and Control for Electrical Systems Support | ACDS | Advanced Command Data System |
| | | ACDS | Automatic Comprehensive Display System |
| ACCESS | Automatic Computer-Controlled Electronic Scanning System | ACDTR | Airborne Central Data Tape Recorder |
| ACCG | Accumulating | ACE | Accelerated Cathode Excitation |
| ACCN | Accumulation | | |
| ACCORD | Analog Computer Checkout Routine Digitally | ACE | Acceptance Checkout Equipment |
| ACCPAC | Accounting Package | ACE | Acknowledge Enable |
| ACCPT | Acceptance | ACE | Add Command Execution |
| ACCR | Accumulator | ACE | Altimeter Control Equipment |
| ACCRY | Accessory | | |
| ACCS | Access | ACE | Analytic Computer Equipment |
| ACCS | Automatic Checkout & Control System | ACE | Animated Computer Education |
| ACCT | Access Time | | |
| ACCT | Account | ACE | Association of Computer Educators |
| ACCT | Accounting | | |
| ACCT | Ad hoc Committee for Competitive Telecommunications | ACE | Attitude Control Electronics |
| | | ACE | Automated Computing Engine |
| ACCTG | Accounting | | |
| ACCU | Accumulator | ACE | Automated Cost Estimating |
| ACCUGRAF | Accurate Graphics | | |
| ACCUM | Accumulate | ACE | Automatic Calling Equipment |
| ACCUM | Accumulator | | |
| ACCUR | Accurate | ACE | Automatic Card Ejection |
| ACCY | Accessory | ACE | Automatic Checkout Equipment |
| ACCY | Accuracy | | |
| ACD | Accessory Control Document | ACE | Automatic Circuit Exchange |
| ACD | Advanced Circuit Design | ACE | Automatic Computer Evaluation |
| ACD | Aerial Control Display | | |
| ACD | Alphabetic Coding Device | ACE | Automatic Computing Engine |

- 7 -

# A

| | |
|---|---|
| ACE | Automatic Computing Equipment |
| ACEMIS | Army Communications and Electronics Management Information System |
| ACES | Automated Code Evaluation System |
| ACES | Automatic Checkout and Evaluation System |
| ACESA | Australian Commonwealth Engineering Standards Association |
| ACF | Absolute Cumulative Frequency |
| ACF | Accelerated Card Feeding |
| ACF | Access Control Facility |
| ACF | Access Control Field |
| ACF | Account Card Feeding |
| ACF | Address Code Format |
| ACF | Advanced Communications Function |
| ACF | Alternate Communications Facility |
| ACF | Analog Computer Facility |
| ACF | Area Computing Facilities |
| ACF | Autocorrelation Function |
| ACF | Automatic Card Feeding |
| ACF | Availability Control File |
| ACF/NCP | Advanced Communication Function for Network Control Program |
| ACFD | Account Card Feeding Device |
| ACFF | Alternating Current Flip Flop |
| ACFG | Automatic Continuous Function Generation |
| ACG | Address Coding Guide |
| ACG | Adjacent Charging Group |
| ACG | Automatic Character Generation |
| ACG | Automatic Correlation Guidance |
| ACH | Acknowledge Hold |
| ACH | Automated Clearing House |
| ACH | Automatic Cartridge Handler |
| ACHS | Automatic Checkout System |
| ACI | Address Compilation Instruction |
| ACI | Address Computation Instruction |
| ACI | Alteration Cancellation Installation |
| ACI | Asynchronous Communications Interface |
| ACI | Automatic Car Identification |
| ACI | Automation Center International |
| ACIA | Asynchronous Communications Interface Adapter |
| ACIB | Arithmetic Checker In Bus |
| ACID | Automatic Circuit Design |
| ACID | Automatic Classification and Interpretation of Data |
| ACIP | Active Certificate Information Program |
| ACIR | Adder Center Input Register |
| ACIS | Academic Information System |
| ACIS | Advanced Credit Information System |
| ACK | Acknowledge |
| ACK | Acknowledge character |
| ACK | Acknowledgment |
| ACK | Alternate Coding Key |
| ACKI | Acknowledge Input |
| ACKO | Acknowledge Output |
| ACL | Administration Communication Language |
| ACL | Analytical and Computer Laboratory |
| ACL | Application Control Language |
| ACL | Association for Computational Linguistics |
| ACL | Atlas Commercial Language |
| ACL | Automatic Cartridge Loader |
| ACL | Automatic Coding Language |
| ACL | Automatic Current Limiting |

# A

| | | | |
|---|---|---|---|
| ACM | Active Counter Measures | ACORN | Automatic Checkout and Recording Network |
| ACM | Addressable Core Memory | | |
| ACM | Amplitude Comparison Monopulse | ACORN | Automatic Coder of Report Narrative |
| ACM | Association for Computing Machinery | ACOS | Automatic Checkout Set |
| | | ACP | Abnormal Condition Program |
| ACM | Association of Computer Manufacturers | ACP | Acceptance Checkout Procedure |
| ACM | Association of Computing Machinery | ACP | Adaptive Control Process |
| ACM | Automatic Calculating Machine | ACP | Advanced Circuits Program |
| ACM | Automatic Clutter Mapper | ACP | Advanced Computational Processor |
| ACME | Attitude Control and Maneuvering Electronics | ACP | Aerospace Computer Program |
| | | ACP | Airline Control Program |
| ACME | Automatic Correction of Multiple Errors | ACP | Alarm Control Panel |
| | | ACP | Align Control Panel |
| ACMRU | Audio Commercial Message Repeating Unit | ACP | All Cards Printed |
| | | ACP | Allied Communications Procedures |
| ACN | Assignment Control Number | ACP | Alphabetical Code Punching |
| ACN | Authorized Code Number | ACP | Alternating Current Probe |
| ACNA | Analog Computer for Net Adjustment | ACP | Analog Computer Program |
| ACNMR | Alternating Current Normal-Mode Rejection | ACP | Analytical Computer Program |
| ACO | Adaptive Control Optimization | ACP | Automated Chemistry Program |
| ACO | Assembly and Checkout | ACP | Automatic Command Processing |
| ACO | Automatic Call Originate | | |
| ACO | Average Calculating Operation | ACPA | Association of Computer Programmers and Analysts |
| ACO-NET | Akademisches Computernetz | ACPDP | Alternating Current Plasmadisplay Panel |
| ACOB | Arithmetic Checker Out Bus | ACPI | Automatic Cable Pair Identification |
| ACOE | Automatic Checkout Equipment | ACPT | Accept |
| | | ACPTD | Accepted |
| ACOM | Automatic Coding Machine | ACPU | Auxiliary Computer Power Unit |
| ACOMA | Automatische Codiermaschine | ACPX | Advanced Circuit Packaging Extended |
| ACON | Akademisches Computernetz | ACPX | Advanced Computer Program Experimental |
| ACOPP | Abbreviated COBOL Pre-Processor | ACQ | Acquisition |
| ACORD | Automatic Component Ordering | ACQSN | Acquisition |
| | | ACR | Access Control Register |
| ACORN | Associative Content Retrieval Network | ACR | Accumulator |
| | | ACR | Accumulator Register |
| ACORN | Automated Conversion Routine | ACR | Adaptive Character Reader |

- 9 -

# A

| | | | |
|---|---|---|---|
| ACR | Address Conversion Register | ACS | Analog Computer System |
| ACR | Advanced Capabilities Radar | ACS | Analysis Computer System |
| ACR | Alternate CPU Recovery | ACS | Application Customizer Service |
| ACR | Alternate Recovery | ACS | Applied Computer Sciences Limited |
| ACR | Antenna Coupling Regulator | ACS | Assembler Control System |
| ACR | Approach Control Radar | ACS | Assembly Control System |
| ACR | Audio Cassette Recorder | ACS | Assembly Cost System |
| ACR | Automatic Call Recording | ACS | Attitude Control System |
| ACR | Automatic Card Reader | ACS | Australian Computer Society |
| ACR | Automatic Carriage Return | ACS | Automated Communications Set |
| ACR | Automatic Character Reader | ACS | Automatic Call Selector |
| ACR | Automatic Character Recognition | ACS | Automatic Checkout System |
| ACR | Auxiliary Computer Room | ACS | Automatic Cheque Sorter |
| ACRD | Anticipated Card Release Date | ACS | Automatic Coding System |
| ACRE | APAR Control Remote Entry | ACS | Automatic Control System |
| ACRIT | Automatic Crystal Resistivity Indexing Tester | ACS | Automatic Counter System |
| ACROM | Associative-Capacitive Read-Only Memory | ACS | Auxiliary Control Station |
| ACS | Access | ACS | Auxiliary Core Storage |
| ACS | Accounting Control System | ACS | Auxiliary Core Store |
| ACS | Accumulator Switch | ACS | Average Calculating Speed |
| ACS | Accuracy Control System | ACS... | Applied Computer Sciences Ltd. |
| ACS | Acoustic Computer Signal | ACSAP | Automated Cross-Section Analysis Program |
| ACS | Adaptive Control System | ACSC | Army Computer Systems Command |
| ACS | Additional Core Storage | ACSF | Association des Centres Serveurs Français |
| ACS | Addressable Core Store | ACSL | Advanced Continuous Simulation Language |
| ACS | Administrative Control System | ACSP | Alternating Current Spark Plug |
| ACS | Advance Communications Service | ACSS | Analogue Computer Subsystem |
| ACS | Advance Communications System | ACST | Access Time |
| ACS | Advanced Computer System | ACSV | Automatische Computergesteuerte Schneideeinrichtung für Videobänder |
| ACS | Advice Called Subscriber | ACT | ABEND Control Table |
| ACS | Along Computer System | ACT | Account Control Table |
| ACS | Alternating Current Synchronous | ACT | Accumulateur Temporaire |
| ACS | American Chemical Society | ACT | Acting |
| ACS | Analog Computer Simulation | ACT | Action |
| | | ACT | Activated |

- 10 -

# A

| | | | |
|---|---|---|---|
| ACT | Activation | ACTRAN | Autocoder-to-COBOL Translating service |
| ACT | Activator | | |
| ACT | Active | ACTRS | Agence Commerciale de la Téléinformatique et des Réseaux Spécialisés |
| ACT | Activity | | |
| ACT | Actual | | |
| ACT | Actuate | | |
| ACT | Actuating | ACTS | Acoustic Control and Telemetry System |
| ACT | Actuator | | |
| ACT | Address Conversion Table | ACTS | Acquisition, Cataloguing, Technical System |
| ACT | Advanced Communications Technology | | |
| ACT | Advanced Computer Technique | ACTS | Advanced Channel Testing System |
| ACT | Air Cooled Triode | ACTS | Airline Computer Tracing System |
| ACT | Algebraic Compiler and Translator | ACTS | Analog Conditioning and Test System |
| ACT | Alternating Current Trigger | ACTS | Automatic Computer Telex Services |
| ACT | Analogical Circuit Technique | ACTS | Automatic Computer Telex System |
| ACT | Anti-Comet Tail | | |
| ACT | Applied Computer Techniques Limited | ACTV | Activate |
| | | ACTV | Activation |
| ACT | Automated Contingency Translator | ACTV | Activity |
| | | ACTVT | Activate |
| ACT | Automated Continuity Tester | ACTVTR | Activator |
| | | ACTY | Activity |
| ACT | Automatic Capacitance Testing | ACU | Address Control Unit |
| | | ACU | Align Control Unit |
| ACT | Automatic Code Translation | ACU | Analog Calibration Unit |
| | | ACU | Automatic Call Unit |
| ACT | Automatic Code Translator | ACU | Automatic Calling Unit |
| | | ACU | Automatic and Control Unit |
| ACT | Automatic Component Tester | ACUT | Automatic Calling Unit Terminator |
| ACT | Average Calculating Time | ACUTE | Accountant Computer Users Technical Exchange |
| ACT... | Advanced Computer Technique Corp. | | |
| ACTA | Automatic Computerized Transverse Axial | ACV | Access Control Verification |
| ACTE | Actuate | ACV. | Address Control Vector |
| ACTE | Automatic Checkout Test Equipment | ACV | Alarm Check Value |
| | | ACV | Alternating Current Volt |
| ACTG | Acting | | |
| ACTG | Actuating | ACVC | ADA Compiler Validation Capability |
| ACTIVE | Advanced Computer Training In a Versatile Environment | ACVM | Adaptive Control Voltage Module |
| ACTN | Action | ACVT | Activate |
| ACTO | Automatic Computing Transfer Oscillator | ACVTY | Activity |
| | | ACW | Alternating Continous Wave |
| ACTP | Advanced Computer Technology Project | ACW | Ausgabecodewandler |
| ACTR | Actuator | ACW | Access Control Word |

# A

| | | | |
|---|---|---|---|
| AD | Abbreviated Dialling | ADA | Adresse für Ausgabegerät |
| AD | Ablaufdiagramm | ADA | Advance Deposit Agreement |
| AD | Absolute Delay | | |
| AD | Absolute Determination | ADA | Advance Design Aids |
| AD | Absolute Deviation | ADA | Airborne Data Automation |
| AD | Accelerated Depreciation | ADA | Alphanumeric Data Acquisition |
| AD | Account Distribution | | |
| AD | Accounting Department | ADA | Analog Driver Amplifier |
| AD | Accounts Department | ADA | Analog-Digital-Analog |
| AD | Acquisition Data | ADA | Angle Data Assembly |
| AD | Adapt | ADA | Automated Dispensing Analyzer |
| AD | Adapted | | |
| AD | Adapter | ADA | Automated Document Analysis |
| AD | Adaptor | | |
| AD | Add Decimal | ADA | Automatic Data Acquisition |
| AD | Adder | | |
| AD | Additional Data | ADAAC | Automatic Data Acquisition And Computer |
| AD | Address Decoding | | |
| AD | Address Defined | ADABAS | Adaptable Data Base-management system |
| AD | Addressable Data | | |
| AD | Adressed Device | ADABAS | Adaptable Database System |
| AD | Adressendefinition | | |
| AD | Advanced Design | ADABAS | Adaptierbares Datenbanksystem |
| AD | Alarm Device | | |
| AD | Alphabetic Data | ADABAS | Allgemeines Datenbanksystem |
| AD | Alphanumeric Data | | |
| AD | Alphanumeric Device | ADAC | Acoustic Data Analysis Center |
| AD | Amplifier Detector | | |
| AD | Amplitudendiskriminator | ADAC | Analog-Digital-Analog Converter |
| AD | Analog Data | | |
| AD | Analog Device | ADAC | Astrodata Data Acquisition and Control |
| AD | Application Definition | | |
| AD | Application Documentation | ADAC | Automated Direct Analog Computer |
| AD | Arbeitsplatzdatei | ADAC | Automatic Data Automatic Correction |
| AD | Architectural Design | | |
| AD | Archivdatei | ADACC | Automatic Data Acquisition and Computer Complex |
| AD | Area Discriminator | | |
| AD | Arithmetic Device | | |
| AD | Array Declaration | ADACS | Automatic Data Acquisition and Control System |
| AD | Array Declarator | | |
| AD | Assembler Deck | | |
| AD | Attention Display | ADACX | Automatic Data Acquisition and Computer complex |
| AD | Authorized Distributor | | |
| AD | Automatic Detection | | |
| AD | Automatic Dictionary | | |
| AD | Automatic Display | ADAE | Asociacion De Aplicationes de la Electricidad |
| AD | Automatic Divide | | |
| AD | Available Data | | |
| AD | Average Devation | ADAI | Agence pour Développement des Applications Informatiques |
| AD... | Applied Dynamics Ltd. | | |
| ADA | Action Data Automation | | |
| ADA | Actuarial Data Assembly | ADALINE | Adaptive Linear |
| ADA | Address Adder | ADAM | A Data Management |

# A

| | | | |
|---|---|---|---|
| ADAM | Advanced Data Access Method | ADAR | Advanced Design Array Radar |
| ADAM | Advanced Data Management | ADAR | Analog-to-Digital-to-Analog Recording |
| ADAM | Allgemeine Dialog-Anwendungs-Methode | ADAR | Appareil Distributeur par Agent Receveur |
| ADAM | Assoсiometrics Data Management | ADARCO | Advise Date of Reporting in Compliance with Orders |
| ADAM | Automated Data Management | ADARS | Airborne Data Acquisition and Recording System |
| ADAM | Automatic Distance and Angle Measurement | ADAS | Action Data Automation System |
| ADAMS | Application Development And Management System | ADAS | Adaptive Digital Acquisition Sampling |
| ADAP | Advanced computer for Array Processing | ADAS | Airborne Data Acquisition System |
| ADAP | Adapted | ADAS | Automatic Data Acquisition System |
| ADAP | Adapter | ADAS | Auxiliary Data Annotation Set |
| ADAPS | Armament Delivery Analysis Programming System | ADASP | Automatic Data And Select Program |
| ADAPS | Automatic Display And Platting System | ADAT | Automatic Data Accumulation and Transfer |
| ADAPSO | Association of Data Processing Service Organizations | ADAT | Automatic Data Accumulator and Transfer |
| ADAPT | Adaptable | ADAT | Automatisierte, Dateigesteuerte Testabwicklung |
| ADAPT | Adaption | ADATE | Automatic Digital Assembly Test Equipment |
| ADAPT | Adaption of Automated Programmed Tools | ADAU | Auxiliary Data Acquisition Unit |
| ADAPT | Adaption of Automatically Programmed Tools | ADAWS | Action Data Automation Weapon System |
| ADAPT | Advanced Data Adapter/Processor Tester | ADB | Apollo Data Bank |
| ADAPT | Aerospace Data Adapter Programmable Tester | ADBS | Advanced Data Base System |
| ADAPT | Analog Digital Automatic Program Tester | ADBS | Association française des Documentalistes et Bibliothécaires Spécialisés |
| ADAPT | Arizona Data Accessing Programming and Training | ADC | Accounting Detail Card |
| ADAPT | Automated Data Analysis and Planning Technique | ADC | Action Delay Character |
| ADAPT | Automated Data Analysis using Patternrecognition Techniques | ADC | Actual Device Code |
| ADAPTS | Analog/Digital/Analog Process and Test System | ADC | Advanced Display Computer |
| ADAPTS | Automatic Data Acquisition and Processing for Transportation System | ADC | Air Data Computer |
| | | ADC | Air Data Computing |
| | | ADC | Air Data Converter |
| | | ADC | Air Defense Computer |

# A

| | |
|---|---|
| ADC | Airborne Digital Computer |
| ADC | Ampex Disk Controller |
| ADC | Analog Derived Clock |
| ADC | Analog-Digital Computer |
| ADC | Analog-Digital Control |
| ADC | Analog-Digital Converter |
| ADC | Analog-to-Digital Conversion |
| ADC | Analog-to-Digital Converter |
| ADC | Antenna Disk Control |
| ADC | Applied Data Communications |
| ADC | Area Data Center |
| ADC | Assembler Card Deck |
| ADC | Asynchronous Digital Combiners |
| ADC | Audio/Data Communications |
| ADC | Authorized Data Chain |
| ADC | Automated Data Center |
| ADC | Automatic Data Channel |
| ADC | Automatic Data Coding |
| ADC | Automatic Data Collection |
| ADC | Automatic Data Computing |
| ADC | Automatic Digital Calculator |
| ADC | Automatic Digital Computer |
| ADCAD | Airways Data Collection And Distribution |
| ADCAT | Automatic Data Correction And Transfer |
| ADCC | Air Defense Command Computer |
| ADCC | Asynchronous Data Communication Controller |
| ADCCP | Advanced Data Communications Control Procedure |
| ADCIS | Association for Development of Computer-based Instructional Systems |
| ADCOM | Association of Data Center Owners and Managers |
| ADCON | Address Constant |
| ADCON | Advanced Concepts |
| ADCON | Analog-to-Digital Converter |
| ADCP | Advanced Control Programmer |
| ADCR | All Digital Control Run |
| ADCS | Advanced Data Communication for Stores |
| ADCS | Air Data Computing System |
| ADCS | Automatic Data Collecting System |
| ADCU | Analog-to-Digital Conversion Unit |
| ADD | Adder |
| ADD | Addiere |
| ADD | Addieren |
| ADD | Addierer |
| ADD | Addition |
| ADD | Address |
| ADD | Address Defined |
| ADD | Adressendecoder |
| ADD | Aerospace Digital Development |
| ADD | Airborne Digital Decoder |
| ADD | Analog Data Digitizer |
| ADD | Analog Digital Designer |
| ADD | Analog-Digital Display |
| ADD | Arbeitskreis Dezentrale Datenverarbeitung |
| ADD | Arbeitskreis Digitale Datensysteme |
| ADD | Architectural Design Document |
| ADD | Automatic Data Distribution |
| ADD | Automatic Digit Display |
| ADD | Automatic Digital Depth |
| ADD | Automatic Drawing Device |
| ADDA | Automatic Decentral Data Acquisition |
| ADDAC | Analog Data Distributor And Computer |
| ADDAC | Analog Data Distributor And Control |
| ADDACE | Analog-to-Digital, Digital-to-Analog Conversion Equipment |
| ADDAR | Automatic Digital Data Acquisition and Recording |
| ADDAS | Airborne Digital Data Acquisition System |

# A

| | | | |
|---|---|---|---|
| ADDAS | Automatic Digital Data Assembley System | ADE | Approved Data Element |
| ADDDS | Automatic Direct Distance Dialling System | ADE | Authorized Data Element |
| | | ADE | Automated Design Engineering |
| ADDER | Automatic Digital Data Error Recorder | ADE | Automated Draughting Equipment |
| ADDER | Automatic Digital Data Error Recording | ADE | Automatic Data Encoding |
| | | ADE | Automatic Data Evaluation |
| ADDG | Adding | ADE | Automatic Design Engineering |
| ADDL | Additional | | |
| ADDM | Addendum | ADE | Automatic Drafting Equipment |
| ADDN | Addition | | |
| ADDNS | Additions | ADE | Automatic Drawing Equipment |
| ADDPEP | Aerodynamic Deployable Decelerator Performance Evaluation Program | ADE | Automatisation des Dossiers d'Etudes |
| | | ADEBUG | Assembly language symbolic Debug |
| ADDR | Adder | | |
| ADDR | Address | ADEC | Address Decoding |
| ADDRESOR | Analog-to-Digital Data-Reduction System for Oceanographic Research | ADEC | Aiken Dahlgren Electronic Calculator |
| | | ADEG | Auxiliary Display Equipment Group |
| ADDS | Advanced Data Display System | ADEK | Allgemeiner Datenerhebungskatalog |
| ADDS | Applied Digital Data Systems | ADELE | Automatische Datenerfassung durch Lochkarteneingabe |
| ADDS | Automatic Data Digitizing System | ADELI | Association pour le Développement de la Logique Informatique |
| ADDS | Automatic Data Distribution System | | |
| ADDS | Automatic Digital Design System | ADEM | Anwendungs-Datenerfassungs-Matrix |
| ADDT | All Digital Data Tape | ADEM | Automatically Data-Equalized Modem |
| ADDT | Angulate Distribution Data Tape | ADEMS | Automated Data Entry Measurement System |
| ADE | ADA Development Environment | ADEPA | Association pour le Développement de la Production Automatisée |
| ADE | Address Enable | | |
| ADE | Adresse für Eingabegerät | | |
| ADE | Allgemeine Datenerfassung | ADEPA | Association pour le Développement de la Programmation Automatique |
| ADE | Allgemeines Datenerfassungsprogramm | | |
| ADE | Alphanumeric Display Equipment | ADEPA | Agence nationale pour le Développement de la Production Automatisée |
| ADE | Analog-to-Digital Encoder | | |
| ADE | Anschlußeinheit für Datenerfassung und/-ausgabe | ADEPO | Automatic Dynamic Evaluation by Programmed Organizations |
| ADE | Anschlußeinheit für Datenendplätze | | |

# A

| | | | |
|---|---|---|---|
| ADEPT | A Display Expedited Processing and Tutorial | ADIAF | Association pour le Développement de l'Informatique dans l'Administration Française |
| ADEPT | A Distinctly Empirical Prover of Theorems | | |
| ADEPT | Advanced Development Prototype | ADIC | Analog-to-Digital Conversion |
| ADEPT | Analog Data Extractor and Plotting Table | ADIC | Analog-to-Digital Converter |
| ADEPT | Automated Direct-Entry Packaging Technique | ADIE | Acquisition Data Input Equipment |
| ADEPT | Automatic Data Extractor and Plotting Table | ADIGE | Association pour le Développment de l'Information de Gestion |
| ADEPT | Automatic Dynamic Evaluation by Programmed Testing | | |
| ADES | Automated Data Entry System | ADIJ | Association pour le Développement de l'Informatique Juridique |
| ADES | Automatic Digital Encoding System | | |
| ADF | Adaptives Digitalfilter | ADIK | Aussprache, Daten, Instruktionen, Konstanten |
| ADF | Advanced Disk File | | |
| ADF | Airborne Direction Finder | ADIOS | Automatic Digital Input/Output System |
| ADF | Application Design Factor | | |
| ADF | Application Development Facility | ADIP | Alternating Direction Implicit Procedure |
| ADF | Automatic Direction Finder | ADIRA | Association pour le Développement de l'Informatique dans la Région Rhône-Alpes |
| ADF | Automatische Datenverarbeitung in der Fertigungsindustrie | | |
| | | ADIRS | ADIS Drug Information Retrieval System |
| ADFG | Arbitrary Diode Function Generator | ADIS | A Data Interchange System |
| ADFSC | Automatic Data Field System Command | ADIS | Airborne Digital Instrumentation System |
| ADG | Attitude Display Group | | |
| ADH | A-Digit Hunter | ADIS | Automatic Data Interchange System |
| ADH | Automatic Data Handling | | |
| ADHA | Analog Data Handling Assembly | ADISP | Automated Data Interchange Systems Panel |
| ADHS | Analog Data Handling System | ADIT | Analog to Digital Integrating Translator |
| ADI | Agence De l'Informatique | ADITAS | Außenwerbungs-, Dispositions- und Tafelabrechnungssystem |
| ADI | Alternate Digit Inversion | | |
| ADI | American Documentation Institute | ADJ | Adjust |
| | | ADJ | Adjustable |
| ADI | Anwenderverband Deutscher Informationsverarbeiter e.V. | ADJ | Adjusted |
| | | ADJ | Adjusting |
| | | ADJ | Adjustment |
| ADI | Arbeitsgemeinschaft für Informationsverarbeitung e.V. | ADJD | Adjusted |
| | | ADL | Airborne Data Link |
| | | ADL | Arbeitsgemeinschaft für Datenverarbeitung und Lochkartentechnik |
| ADI | Automatic Data Input | | |

# A

| | | | |
|---|---|---|---|
| ADL | Armament Data Line | ADMS | Asynchronous Data Multiplexer Synchronizer |
| ADL | Artifical Delay Line | ADMS | Automatic Digital Message Switching |
| ADL | Authorized Data List | | |
| ADL | Automated Display Language | ADMSC | Automatic Digital Message Switching Center |
| ADL | Automated Drafting Language | | |
| ADL | Automatic Data Link | ADN | Analyseur Différentiel Numérique |
| ADL | Automatic Data Logger | | |
| ADL | Automatic Drafting Language | ADN | Array Declarator Name |
| | | ADO | Address Out |
| ADLATAD | Advise Latest Address | ADO | Avalanche Diode Oscillator |
| ADLM | Acoustic Digital Memory | | |
| ADLS | Airborne Data Link System | ADONIS | Automatic Digital On-line Instrumentation System |
| ADLT | Airborne Data Link Terminal | ADOPE | Automatic Decisions Optimizing Predicted Estimates |
| ADM | Acoustic Digital Memory | | |
| ADM | Activity Data Method | | |
| ADM | Add Magnitude | ADOT | Automatic Digital Optical Tracker |
| ADM | Add Memory | | |
| ADM | Add-on Module | ADP | Acceptance Data Package |
| ADM | Aide au Diagnostic Médical | ADP | Add Decimal Packed |
| | | ADP | Administrative Data Processing |
| ADM | Amplitude Demodulation | | |
| ADM | Amplitudendemodulation | ADP | Airborne Data Processor |
| ADM | Apollo Data Manager | ADP | Airport Development Program |
| ADM | Application Data Management | | |
| ADM | Application Description Manual | ADP | Alphabetic Duplicating Punch |
| | | ADP | Alphanumeric Data Printer |
| ADM | Asynchronous Disconnected Mode | | |
| ADM | Automated Data Management | ADP | Alphanumerischer Datenerfassungsplatz |
| | | ADP | American Data Processing |
| ADMA | Automatic Drafting Machine | ADP | Assembleur-Désassembleur de Paquets |
| ADMIN | Administration | ADP | Assumed Decimal Point |
| ADMIRE | Adaptive Decision-Maker in an Information Retrieval Environment | ADP | Automated Data Processing |
| | | ADP | Automatic Data Plotter |
| ADMIRE | Automatic Diagnostic Maintenance Information Retrieval | ADP | Automatic Data Processing |
| | | ADP | Automatic Data Processor |
| ADMIREL | Automatic and Dynamic Monitor with Immediate Relocation | ADP | Automatic Duplicator Printer |
| | | ADPACS | Automated Data Processing And Communications Service |
| ADMIRES | Advanced Management Information and Retrieval System | | |
| | | ADPC | Automatic Data Processing Center |
| ADMIRES | Automatic Diagnostic Maintenance Information Retrieval System | | |
| | | ADPCM | Adaptive Differential Pulse Code Modulator |
| ADMRL | Application Data Material Readiness List | ADPCM | Adaptive Differenz-Pulscodemodulation |

# A

| | | | |
|---|---|---|---|
| ADPCM | Adaptives Differenz-Pulscode-Modulationsverfahren | ADR | Automatic Data Recording |
| ADPE | Automatic Data Processing Equipment | ADR | Automatic Data Retrieval |
| ADPE | Auxiliary Data Processing Equipment | ADR | Automatic Digit Recognizer |
| ADPLL | All Digital Phase Locked Loop | ADR | Automatic Direct Reading |
| ADPLS | Automated Drawing Parts List System | ADR | Automatical Digital Relay |
| ADPM | Automatic Data Processing Machine | ADR CHK | Address Check |
| ADPP | Automatic Data Processing Program | ADRA | Automatic Dynamic Response Analyzer |
| ADPREP | Automatic Data Processing Resource Estimating Procedure | ADRAC | Automatic Digital Recording And Control |
| ADPS | Army Data Processing System | ADRB | Addessable |
| ADPS | Automated Data Processing System | ADRC | Automatic Data Rate Changer |
| ADPS | Automatic Data Processing System | ADRCHK | Address Check |
| ADPS | Automatic Display and Plotting Systems | ADRD | Automatic Data Rate Detection |
| ADPSO | Association of Data Processing Service Organizations | ADREP | Automatic Data processing Resource Estimating Procedure |
| ADPT | Adapter | ADRES | Aircraft Data Recording Evaluation System |
| ADPU | Airborne Digital Processing Unit | ADRES | Army Data Retrieval Engineering System |
| ADPU | Automatic Data Processing Unit | ADRG | Automatic Data Routing Group |
| ADQ | Almost Different Quasi-ternay code | ADRI | Add Delete Rework Instruction |
| ADR | Add Register | ADRI | Automatic Dead-Reckoning Instrument |
| ADR | Adder | ADRIS | Automatisierte Dokumenten-Recherche und Information über Standards |
| ADR | Address | | |
| ADR | Address Register | | |
| ADR | Adresse | ADRS | Address |
| ADR | Adressenregister | ADRS | A Departmental Reporting System |
| ADR | Adreßkonstante | ADRS | Airborne Digital Recording System |
| ADR | Airborne Digital Recorder | ADRS | Analog-to-digital Data Recording System |
| ADR | Alphanumeric Data Recording | ADRS-BG | A Departmental Reporting System-Business Graphics |
| ADR | Alternate Data Retry | ADRSA | Assistant Data Redording System Analyst |
| ADR | Analog Data Recorder | ADRT | Analog Data Recorder Transcriber |
| ADR | Analog-to-Digital Recorder | ADRU | Ausgabe Druckliste |
| ADR | Analytical Data Reflection | ADRV | Arbeitsgemeinschaft Deutscher Rechenzentrumsverbände |
| ADR | Angle Data Recorder | ADS | Accounting Data System |
| ADR | Applied Data Research | ADS | Accumulated Data Set |

# A

| | | | |
|---|---|---|---|
| ADS | Accurately Defined Systems | ADSOL | Analysis of Dynamical Systems On-Line |
| ADS | Activated Data Sheet | ADSS | Automatic Data Switching System |
| ADS | Address | | |
| ADS | Address Data Strobe | ADST | Anforderung an die Datensteuerung |
| ADS | Address Display Subsystem | ADST | AUTODIN Subscriber Terminal |
| ADS | Address Display System | | |
| ADS | Address Scan | ADSTAR | Automatic Document Storage And Retrieval |
| ADS | Administrations-Supervisor | ADSUM | Automatic Data Systems Uniform Practices |
| ADS | Adresse Spalte | | |
| ADS | Adressensteuerung | ADT | Active Disk Table |
| ADS | Adsorption | ADT | Adresse Table données |
| ADS | Advanced Data System | ADT | Airborne Digital Timer |
| ADS | Advanced Display System | ADT | Alphanumeric Display Tube |
| ADS | Air Data System | | |
| ADS | Airport Data System | ADT | Application Design Tool |
| ADS | American Data Systems | ADT | Application-Dedicated Terminal |
| ADS | Angle Data Subsystem | | |
| ADS | Application Development System | ADT | Asynchronous Data Transfer |
| ADS | Array Declarator Subscript | ADT | Automatic Data Translator |
| ADS | Auftragsdatenspeicher | ADT | Automatic Data Transmission |
| ADS | Auto Distribution System | ADT | Average Data Technique |
| ADS | Automated Data System | ADTAC | Automatic Digital Tracking Analyzer Computer |
| ADS | Automated Diagnostic System | | |
| ADS | Automatic Data Set | ADTD | Anticipated Data Transmission Data |
| ADS | Automatic Data Surveillance | ADTS | Amplitude Degradation Test System |
| ADS | Automatic Digital Switch | ADTU | Automatic Digital Test Unit |
| ADS | Automatisiertes Datenerfassungssystem | ADTU | Auxiliary Data Translator Unit |
| ADS/O | Application Development System/Online | ADU | Adapter Unit |
| ADS... | Anker Data System | ADU | Address Decoding Unit |
| ADSAS | Air-Derived Separation Assurance System | ADU | Analog Delay Unit |
| | | ADU | Analog Display Unit |
| ADSC | Automatic Data Service Center | ADU | Analog-Digital-Umschalter |
| ADSD | Addressed | ADU | Analog-Digital-Umsetzer |
| ADSEL | Address Selective | ADU | Analog-Digital-Umsetzung |
| ADSEP | Automatic Data Set Editing Program | ADU | Analog-Digital-Umwandler |
| ADSG | Alternative Delivery Schedule Generator | ADU | Analog-Digital-Umwandlung |
| ADSHIPDA | Advise Shipping Data | ADU | Automatic Data Unit |
| ADSHPDAT | Advise Shipping Data | ADU | Automatic Dialling Unit |
| ADSO | Automatic Display Switching Oscilloscope | ADU | Automatischer Datenumsetzer |

# A

| | | | |
|---|---|---|---|
| ADUCI | Association de Défense des Utilisateurs et Consommateurs d'Informatique | AE | Accidental Error |
| | | AE | Accumulated Error |
| | | AE | Added Entry |
| | | AE | Address Error |
| ADUKAM | Auswertprogramm für Durchlaufzeit/ -und Kapazitätauslastungs- Analysen und Hilfe von Momentaufnahmen | AE | Addressing Error |
| | | AE | Adresse Effective |
| | | AE | Adresseneingang |
| | | AE | Algebraic Equation |
| | | AE | Algebraische Eingabe |
| ADUM | Automated Data Unit Movement | AE | Algorithmic Element |
| | | AE | Alphanumeric Expression |
| ADUSA | Analog/Digital Umwandlung mit Statistischer Auswertung | AE | Analogeingabe |
| | | AE | Ancillary Equipment |
| | | AE | Anfangsergebnis |
| ADV | Advance | AE | Anschlußeinheit |
| ADV | Advice | AE | Anwendungsentwicklung |
| ADV | Allgemeine Datenverarbeitung | AE | Anzeigeeinheit |
| | | AE | Application Engineer |
| ADV | Arbeitsgemeinschaft für Datenverarbeitung | AE | Application Executive |
| | | AE | Arbeitseinheit |
| ADV | Automatische Datenverarbeitung | AE | Arithmetic Element |
| | | AE | Arithmetic Expression |
| ADV | Automatisierte Datenverarbeitung | AE | Attenuation Equalizer |
| | | AE | Auftragseingang |
| ADVA | Automatische Datenverarbeitungsanlage | AE | Auftragselement |
| | | AE | Automatic Electric |
| ADVE | Automatische Datenverarbeitungseinheit | AE | Automatic Equipment |
| | | AE | Automatikbefehl Ein |
| ADVG NW | Automatisierte Datenverarbeitung in Nordrhein-Westfalen | AE | Automatisierungseinrichtung |
| | | AEA | Active Element Array |
| ADVICE | Analytical Determination of the Values of Information to Combat Effectiveness | AEA | American Electronics Association |
| | | AEA | Automatic Error Analysis |
| | | AEB | Analyses Economiques Budget |
| ADVS | Automatisches Datenverarbeitungssystem | AEB | Automatic End of Block |
| ADW | Analog-Digital-Wandler | AEC | Advance Exit Common |
| ADW | Analog-Digital-Wandlung | AEC | Analog Electronic Computer |
| ADW | Arithmetic Data Word | | |
| ADW | Automated Data Wiring | AEC | Architectural, Engineering and Construction |
| ADWCP | Automated Digital Weather Communications Program | | |
| | | AEC | Arithmetic Element Controller |
| ADX | Automatic Data Exchange | AEC | Army Electronics Command |
| ADX | Add Index register | AEC | Atomic Energy Commission |
| ADZ | Adresse Zeile | | |
| AE | Abfrageeinheit | AEC | Automatic Error Correction |
| AE | Ablenkeinheit | | |
| AE | Abrechnungseinheit | AECOM | Army Electronics Command |
| AE | Absolute Error | | |
| AE | Absolute Expression | AED | ALGOL Extended for Design |
| AE | Abstimmeinheit | | |
| AE | Abtasteinschub | | |

# A

| | | | |
|---|---|---|---|
| AED | Advanced Engineering Data | AEN | Attenuation Equivalent Nettiness |
| AED | Arbeitsgemeinschaft für Entwicklungsplanung und Datenverarbeitung | AEOR | Arithmetic Element Output Register |
| AED | Association of Electronics Distributors | AEP | Administrative Exchange Protocol |
| AED | Automated Engineering Design | AEPEM | Association of Electronic Parts and Equipment Manufacturers |
| AED | Automated-systems Engineering Design | AER | Adressenerweiterungsregister |
| AEDCAP | Automated Engineering Design Circuit Analysis Program | AER | Analogeingabe mit Relaisdurchschaltung |
| AEDF | Advanced Engineering Data Form | AER | Asynchronous Exit Routine |
| AEDNET | Automated Engineering Design of Network | AERDL | Army Electronics Research and Development Laboratory |
| AEDP | Automatic Engineering Design Program | AERO | Automatic Earnings Recomputation Operation |
| AEDPS | Automated Engineering Documentation Preparation System | AES | Activ Electromagnetic System |
| AEDS | Advanced Engineering Data Set | AES | Anwendungs-Entwicklungssystem |
| AEDS | Association for Educational Data Systems | AES | Artificial Earth Satellite |
| AEDS | Association for Electronic Data Systems | AES | Auger Electron Spectroscopy |
| AEE | Analogeingabe, Elektronische | AESF | Array Element Successor Function |
| AEFC | Alkine Electrolyte Fuel Cell | AESKULAP | Auftragserfassungssystem mit Kommissionierung Und Lagerbestandsführung im Pharmagroßhandel |
| AEG | Active Element Group | | |
| AEGIS | An Existing Generalized Information System | AESOP | An Evolutionary System for Online Processing |
| AEI | Average Efficiency Index | | |
| AEL... | Associated Electrical Industries Ltd. | AESOP | An Experimental Structure for Online Planning |
| AEIMS | Administrative Engineering Information Management System | AESOP | Automated Engineering and Scientific Optimization Program |
| AEL | Acceptor Energy Level | AESU | Absolute Electrostatic Unit |
| AEL | Aerospace Electronics Laboratory | AET | Actual Exposure Time |
| AEL | American Electronic Laboratories | AET | All Events Trace |
| | | AETL | Armament and Electronics Test Laboratory |
| AEL | Average Effectiveness Level | AEUS | Absolute Electrical Unit Scale |
| AELP | Automatic Error Localization Program | AEVS | Automatic Electronic Voice Switch |
| AEM | Accelerated Evaluation Method | AEWIS | Army Electronic Warfare Information System |
| AEN | Adaption Error Note | | |

# A

| | | | |
|---|---|---|---|
| AF | Ablenkungsfaktor | AFC | Advanced Function of Communications |
| AF | Absolute Function | | |
| AF | Accounting Form | AFC | Analog-to-Frequency Converter |
| AF | Accuracy Factor | | |
| AF | Accuracy Figure | AFC | Audio Frequency Coder |
| AF | Activity File | AFC | Automated Filing Cabinets |
| AF | Addition Formula | | |
| AF | Address Field | AFC | Automatic Fare Collection |
| AF | Address File | | |
| AF | Address Format | AFC | Automatic Frequency Control |
| AF | Address Frame | | |
| AF | Addressing Format | AFCAL | Association Française de Calcul |
| AF | Administrative Function | | |
| AF | Advanced Functions | AFCALTI | Association Française de Calcul et de Traitement de l'Information |
| AF | Algebraic Function | | |
| AF | Alphabetic Field | | |
| AF | Alphabetic File | AFCAN | Association Française de Calcul Numérique |
| AF | Alternating Flow | | |
| AF | Amplification Factor | AFCAN | Analog Factor Calibration Network |
| AF | Analog Feedback | | |
| AF | Anlagenfaktor | AFCET | Association Française pour la Cybernétique Economique et Technique |
| AF | Arbitrary Function | | |
| AF | Arithmetical Function | | |
| AF | Attenuation Factor | AFCOM | Association For Computer Operations Managers |
| AF | Audio Frequency | | |
| AF | Ausführen | AFCPL | Air Force Computer Program Library |
| AF | Ausgangsfilter | | |
| AF | Autocorrelation Function | AFCRC | Air Force Cambridge Research Computer |
| AF | Automatic Following | | |
| AF | Availability Factor | AFCS | Automatic Fare Collection System |
| AF SIG GEN | Audio-Frequency-Signal Generator | | |
| | | AFCS | Automatic Flight Control System |
| AF/PC | Automatic Frequency/ Phase Controlled | | |
| | | AFD | Account Feed Device |
| AFA | Access File Attribute | AFD | Amplitude-Frequency Distortion |
| AFA | Air Force Association | | |
| AFA-SEF | Air Force Association-Space Education Foundation | AFD | Arithmetic Function Designator |
| | | AFD | Automatic Feeding Device |
| AFAC | Automatic Field Analog Computer | | |
| | | AFD | Avalanche-Forodiode |
| AFAFC | Air Force Accounting and Finance Center | AFDAP | Air Force Data Automation Planning |
| AFAI | Association Française d'Audit Informatique | AFDASTA | Air Force Data Station |
| | | AFDS | Amphibious Flagship Data System |
| AFAS | Association Française pour l'Avancement des Sciences | | |
| | | AFDSDC | Air Force Data System Design Center |
| AFAU | Administrator Für Anwendungen unter Unix | AFE | Auftragseingabe |
| | | AFE | Antiferroelectric |
| AFB | Active Feedback Block | AFEDPC | Air Force Electronic Data Processing Center |
| AFB | Air Force Base | | |
| AFB | Automatisierte Fernbedienung | AFELIS | Air Force Engineering and Logistics Information System |
| AFB | Auxiliary Function Bit | | |

# A

| | | | |
|---|---|---|---|
| AFF | A Flip-Flop | AFMI | Association Française |
| AFF | Automatic Feeding Form | | pour le développement |
| AFFS | Audio-Frequency | | de la Microinformatique |
| | Frequency Shift | AFMR | Antiferromagnetic |
| AFG | Analog Function | | Resonance |
| | Generator | AFN | Active Filter Network |
| AFG | Analytical Function | AFN | Automatische Frequenz- |
| | Generator | | nachstimmung |
| AFG | Arbitrary Function | AFNOR | Agence Française de |
| | Generator | | Normalization |
| AFG | Automatic Function | AFNOR | Association Française |
| | Generator | | de Normalisation |
| AFGI | Association Française | AFO | Arbeitsfolge |
| | de Gestion Industrielle | AFORSYS | Automatic industrial |
| AFH | Automatic Feed Hopper | | Forecasting System |
| AFI | Auftragsbearbeitung | AFOSR | Air Force Office of |
| | in der Fertigungs- | | Scientific Research |
| | industrie | AFP | Add Fixed Point |
| AFI | Aufträge in der | AFP | Advanced Flexible |
| | Fertigungsindustrie | | Processor |
| AFI | Automatische Fahrplan- | AFP | Automatic Feed Punch |
| | Information | AFP | Automatic Floating |
| AFIA | Association Française | | Point |
| | d'Intelligence | AFPA | Automatic Flow Process |
| | Artificielle | | Analysis |
| AFID | Arithmetic Function | AFPC | Automatic Frequency |
| | Identifier | | and Phase Control |
| AFIN | Association Française | AFPO | Arithmetical Fixed |
| | des Informaticiens | | Point Operation |
| AFIP | American Federation | AFR | Abfühlregister |
| | for Information | AFR | Acceptable Failure Rate |
| | Processing | AFR | Acceptance Failure Rate |
| AFIPS | American Federation | AFR | Application Function |
| | of Information | | Routine |
| | Processing Societies | AFR | Arithmetic Factor |
| AFIS | Automatisches Fahrplan- | | Register |
| | informationssystem | AFR | Automatic Format |
| AFIT | Automatic Fault Isolation | | Recognition |
| | Test | AFR | Automatische Frequenz- |
| AFIT | Automatic Fault Isolation | | regelung |
| | Tester | AFRA | Association Française |
| AFK | Amplituden/Frequenz- | | de Régulation et |
| | Kennlinie | | d'Automatisme |
| AFL | Abstract Family of | AFRC | Automatic Frequency |
| | Languages | | Ratio Control |
| AFL | Antisymmetric Filter | AFRD | Air Force Research |
| AFM | Amplitude-Frequency | | Division |
| | Modulation | AFRI | Association Française |
| AFM | Anschlußsteuerung | | de Robotique |
| | Fernschreibmaschine | | Industrielle |
| AFM | Associative Film Memory | AFS | Abonné Fictif de |
| AFM | Antifriction Metal | | Souscription |
| AFMDC | Air Force Machinability | AFS | Associative Film Store |
| | Data Center | AFS | Audio Frequency Shift |

# A

| | | | |
|---|---|---|---|
| AFS | Automatic Frequency Stabilization | AG DFV | Arbeitsgruppe Datenfernverarbeitung |
| AFS | Automatische Fertigungssteuerung | AGAA | Automatic Gain Adjusting Amplifier |
| AFS | Automatisierte Fertigungssteuerung | AGACS | Automatic Ground-to-Air Communications System |
| AFS | Automatisiertes Führungssystem | AGAMP | Automatic Gain adjusting Amplifier |
| AFSCC | Air Force Special Communications Center | AGC | Adaptive Gain Computer |
| | | AGC | Amplitude Gain Control |
| AFSK | Audio Frequency-Shift Keying | AGC | Apollo Guidance Computer |
| AFT | Acceptance Functional Test | AGC | Automatic Gauge Control |
| | | AGC | Automatic Gain Control |
| AFT | Active File Table | AGCC | Automatic Gain Control Calibration |
| AFT | Advance Feed Tape | | |
| AFT | Analog Facilities Terminal | AGCS | Automatic Ground Computer System |
| AFT | Audio Frequency Transformer | AGCSC | Automatic Ground Computer System Computer |
| AFT | Automatic Fine-Tuning | | |
| AFTAC | Air Force Technical Application Center | AGEC | Automatic Ground Environment Computer |
| AFTER | Automatic Functional Test and Evaluation Routine | AGED | Advisory Group on Electron Devices |
| | | AGENTEFO | Automatisches Generieren von Tests und Fehler-Ortungshilfen |
| AFTN | Aeronautical Fixed Telecommunications Network | AGEP | Advisory Group on Electronic Parts |
| AFU | Analog/Frequenz-Umsetzer | AGERD | Aerospace Ground Equipment Recommendation Data |
| AFUP | Association Française des Utilisateurs de Prime | | |
| AFUTT | Association Française des Utilisateurs du Téléphone et des Télécommunications | AGERD | Aerospace Ground Equipment Requirements Data |
| | | AGFR | Automatic Gain and Frequency Response |
| | | AGGR | Aggregate |
| AFUW | Association Française des Utilisateurs de Wang | AGILE | Automatic General Information Learning Equipment |
| AFW | Akademie für Führungskräfte der Wirtschaft | AGIPAC | Agie Interactive Programming And Calculation |
| AFZ | Aufzeichnung | | |
| AG | AND Gate | AGL | Applicon Graphic Language |
| AG | Acceptance Gage | | |
| AG | Acceptance Gauge | AGP | Automatic Gang Punch |
| AG | Adder Gate | AGPDC | Aeronutronic General Perturbations Differential Correction program |
| AG | Address Group | | |
| AG | Air Gap | | |
| AG | Air-to-Ground | | |
| AG | Arbeitsgang | | |
| AG | Arbeitsgruppe | AGPLAN | Arbeitsgemeinschaft für Planungsrechnung |
| AG | Arbeitsgrundlage | | |
| AG | Auftraggeber | | |
| AG | Ausgabegerät | | |
| AG | Automatisierungsgeräte | AGR | Alarmgruppenregister |

# A

| | | | |
|---|---|---|---|
| AGR | Alarm Group Register | AI | Adressage Indirect |
| AGREE | Advisory Group on Reliability of Electronic Equipment | AI | Alphabetic Information |
| | | AI | Alphabetic Interpreter |
| | | AI | Alphabetic Item |
| AGS | Abort Guidance System | AI | Alphanumeric Information |
| AGS | Advanced Guidance System | AI | Alphanumeric Instruction |
| | | AI | Alphanumeric Item |
| AGS | Applied Graphics Systems | AI | Alternate Instruction |
| AGS | Arbeitsgangstufe | AI | Amplifier Input |
| AGS | Automatic Gain Stabilization | AI | Analog Information |
| | | AI | Analog Input |
| AGS | Automatic Gain Stabilizer | AI | Apparent Impedance |
| | | AI | Arbeitsintensität |
| AGSP | Atlas General Survey Program | AI | Arithmetic Instruction |
| | | AI | Arithmetic Item |
| AGT | Anschlußgerät | AI | Array Identifier |
| AGU | Address Generation Unit | AI | Artificial Intelligence |
| AGV | Ausgabeverteiler | AI | Assembler Instruction |
| AGuC | Arbeitsgemeinschaft Mikrocomputer | AI | Assembly Instruction |
| | | AI | Attention Interruption |
| AH | Acceptor Handshake | AI | Ausgangsinformation |
| AH | Actual Hours | AI | Automated Index |
| AH | Add Halfword | AI | Automatic Input |
| AH | Ampere-Hour | AI | Automatic Interrupter |
| AH | Attention Handling | AI | Automatic Interruption |
| AHAC | Automated High Accuracy Comparator | AI | Automatisierter Index |
| | | AIA | Aerospace Industries Association |
| AHGC | Advanced Hardened Guidance Computer | AIA | Automatic Information Acquisition |
| AHL | A Hardware programming Language | AIAA | American Institute of Aeronautics and Astronautics |
| AHM | Ampere-Hour Meter | | |
| AHO | A harmonic Oscillator | | |
| AHPL | A Hardware Programming Language | AIAF | Absolutely Integral Algebraic Function |
| | | AIB | American Institute of Banking |
| AHR | Acceptable Hazard Rate | | |
| AHR | Adressenhilfsregister | | |
| AHR | Automatic Handwriting Reader | AIB | Analog Input Base |
| | | AIBT in | Active Item Balance Tape in |
| AHT | Average Holding Time | | |
| AHV | Accelerator High Voltage | AIBT out | Active Item Balance Tape out |
| AI | AND Inverter | | |
| AI | Access Instruction | AIC | Analytical Instruction Code |
| AI | Accounting Information | | |
| AI | Accrued Interest | AIC | Automatic Information Center |
| AI | Activité Individuelle | | |
| AI | Actual Instruction | AIC | Automatic Item Correction |
| AI | Add Impulse | | |
| AI | Add Instruction | AICA | Associazione Italiana per il Calcolo Automatico |
| AI | Additional Instruction | | |
| AI | Address Incomplete | AICE | American Institute of Consulting Engineers |
| AI | Address Index | | |
| AI | Address Information | AICPA | American Institute of Certified Public Accountants |
| AI | Address Instruction | | |
| AI | Adressage Immédiat | | |

- 25 -

# A

| | | | |
|---|---|---|---|
| AICT | Automatic Integrated Circuit Tester | AIDOS-FRS | Automatisiertes Informations-/und Dokumentationssystem - Faktenrecherchesystem |
| AIChE | American Institute of Chemical Engineers | | |
| AID | Abortion Information Data-bank | AIDR | Aerospace Internal Data Report |
| AID | Air Information Device | AIDS | Abort Inertial Digital System |
| AID | Algebraic Interpretive Dialog | AIDS | Abstracts Information Dissemination System |
| AID | Analog Input Description | | |
| AID | Analog Input Device | AIDS | Acceptor Idle State |
| AID | Analog Interface Device | AIDS | Acoustic Intelligence Data System |
| AID | Anmeldeidentifikation | | |
| AID | Area Identification | AIDS | Action Information Display System |
| AID | Attention Identification | | |
| AID | Attention Identifier | AIDS | Administrative Information Data System |
| AID | Auftragsabwicklung Im Dialog | | |
| AID | Auftragsbearbeitung Im Dialog | AIDS | Advanced Integrated Data System |
| | | AIDS | Advanced Interactive Display System |
| AID | Automatic Information Distribution | | |
| | | AIDS | Advanced Interconnection Development System |
| AID | Automatic Internal Diagnosis | AIDS | Aerospace Intelligence Data System |
| AID | Avalance Injection Diode | | |
| AIDA | Apparate zur Identifikation und Autorisierung | AIDS | Air Force Intelligence Data-handling System |
| AIDA | Automatic Inspection Data Accumulator | AIDS | Air Integrated Data System |
| AIDA | Automatic Inspection of Data | AIDS | Airborne Inertial Data System |
| AIDA | Automobile Information Data Advertising | AIDS | Airborne Integrated Data System |
| AIDAC | Assistance Information and Data Acquisition Center | AIDS | Airborne Integrated Display System |
| | | AIDS | Aircraft Integrated Data System |
| AIDAPS | Automatic Inspection, Diagnostic And Prognostic Systems | AIDS | All-purpose Interactive Debugging System |
| AIDATS | Army In-Flight Data Transmission System | AIDS | Architectural Interaction Design System |
| AIDE | Adapted Identification Decision Equipment | AIDS | Army Information and Data Systems |
| AIDE | Automated Integrated Design Engineering | AIDS | Automated Information Dissemination System |
| AIDE | Automatic Inline Device Evaluator | AIDS | Automated Information and Documentation System |
| AIDER | Analog Implemented Differential Equation-solving Routine | AIDS | Automated Integrated Data Systems |
| | | AIDS | Automatic In-flight Data System |
| AIDOS | Automatisiertes Informations-/und Dokumentationssystem | AIDS | Automatic Information Display System |

# A

| | | | |
|---|---|---|---|
| AIDS | Automatic Integrating Debugging System | AIM | Application Integrated Modules |
| AIDS | Automatic Inventory Dispatching System | AIM | Application Interface Module |
| AIDS | Automation Instrument Data Service | AIM | Associated Information Managers |
| AIDSCOM | Army Information and Data Systems Command | AIM | Assoziative Index-Methode |
| AIDTAC | Analog Integrator with Digital Tachometer | AIM | Automatic Invoicing Machine |
| AIDUS | Automated Information Directory Update System | AIM | Automatikimpulszeitmesser |
| AIDUS | Automated Input and Document Update System | AIM | Automatisches Informationsmanagement |
| AIE | Add Instruction Execution | AIM | Avalanche Induced Migration |
| AIE | Analog Input Expander | AIM/DL | AIM Description Language |
| AIE | Analytical Instruction Element | AIM/RDB | Advanced Information Manager/Relational Data Base |
| AIEE | American Institute of Electrical Engineers | AIMACO | Air Material Computer |
| AIENDF | Atomics International Evaluation Nuclear Data File | AIME | American Institute of Mechanical Engineers |
| AIF | Addressless Instruction Format | AIME | AUTODIN Interface in a Multiprogramming Environment |
| AIF | Arbeitsgemeinschaft Industrieller Forschungsvereinigungen | AIMES | Automated Inventory Management Evaluation System |
| AIF | Automated Intelligence File | AIMS | Advanced Information Memos |
| AIFTDS | Airborne Integrated Flight Test Data System | AIMS | Applied Information Management System |
| AIG | Address Indicating Group | AIMS | Auerbach Information Management System |
| AII | Automatic Imagery Interpretation | AIMS | Autoadaptive Inventory Management System |
| AIIE | American Institute of Industrial Engineers | AIMS | Automated Industrial Management System |
| AIK | Allgemeiner Immittanz-Konverter | AIMS | Automated Industry Management Services |
| AILS | Advanced Integrated Landing System | AIN | Analog Input |
| AILS | Automatisiertes Informationslenkungssystem der Standardisierung | AIO | Analog Input Operation |
| | | AIOD | Automatic Identification of Outward Dialling |
| AIM | Add, Initial, Multiprecision | AIOP | Analog Input/Output Package |
| AIM | Advance Information Memory | AIOS | Auxiliary Input/Output Software package |
| AIM | Advanced Information Manager | AIOS | Auxiliary Input/Output Statement |
| AIM | Air-Isolated Monolithic | AIP | Advanced Information Processing |
| AIM | American Institute of Management | AIP | American Institute of Physics |
| AIM | Analog Input Module | AIP | Amplifier Input |

- 27 -

# A

| | | | |
|---|---|---|---|
| AIP | Automatic Information Processing | AIS | Alphabetical Information Storage |
| AIP | Average Instructions per Second | AIS | Analog Instrumentation Subsystem |
| AIPE | American Institute of Plant Engineers | AIS | Arithmetic If Statement |
| AIPR | Average Input Pulse Rate | AIS | Atlas-Industrie-System |
| AIPS | Automated Information Processing System | AIS | Automated Instrumentation System |
| AIPS | Automatic Indexing and Proofreading System | AIS | Automatic Informational System |
| AIPU | Associative Information Processing Unit | AIS | Automatic Input of Subroutines |
| AIR | Active Index Register | AIS | Automatic Intercept Switch |
| AIR | Alphabetical Information Recording | AIS | Automatisiertes Informations-verarbeitungssystem |
| AIR | Association Interrogation Register | AISC | Association of Independent Software Companies |
| AIR | Attention Interrupt Request | AISD | Analog Information Storing Device |
| AIR | Automatic Indication of Range | AISS | Automatic Intercom Switching System |
| AIR | Automatic Information Reduction | AIT | Automatic Information Test |
| AIRCON | Automated Information and Reservation Computer Operated Network | AIV | Automatische Informationsverarbeitung |
| AIRIMP | Air Reservations Interline Message Procedure | AIVS | Automatisiertes Informations-verarbeitungssystem |
| AIRLORD | Airlines Load Optimization Recording and Display | AIW | Analytical Instruction Word |
| AIRLS | Advanced Interrogation, Recording, and Location System | AIZ | Arzneimittel-Informationszentrum |
| AIROF | Anodic Iridium Oxide Film | AJ | Absolute Judgement |
| | | AJ | Absolute Jump |
| | | AJ | Alloy Junction |
| AIRPAP | Air Pressure Analysis Program | AJ | Anderson Jacobson |
| | | AJ | Anti-Jamming |
| AIRS | Airport Information Retrieval System | AJ | Ausgabe Kopplung |
| AIRS | Automatic Image Retrieval System | AJAR | Automatic Junction Analyzer and Recorder |
| | | AJE | Autostart Job Entry |
| AIRS | Automatic Information Retrieval System | AJIS | Automated Jail Information System |
| AIRS | Automatisierte Informations-/und Rechensysteme | AJPO | ADA Joint Program Office |
| AIS | Advanced Information System | AJR | Automatic Job Recovery |
| | | AK | Adapter Kit |
| AIS | Advanced Instructional System | AK | Addition Key |
| | | AK | Address Kind |
| AIS | Alarm Inhibit Signal | AK | Adres-Kode |
| AIS | Alphabetical Indication Store | AK | Adressenkonstante |
| | | AK | Advancing Key |

# A

| | | | |
|---|---|---|---|
| AK | Akkumulator | AL | Address Language |
| AK | Allotment Key | AL | Address List |
| AK | Alphanumeric Keyboard | AL | Addressable Location |
| AK | Amount Keyboard | AL | Adressenleitung |
| AK | Amplitude Keyed | AL | Algorithmic Language |
| AK | Anschlußkosten | AL | Alphabetic |
| AK | Arbeitskarte | AL | Alphabetic Letters |
| AK | Arbeitskontakt | AL | Alphabetic Listing |
| AK | Arbeitskreis | AL | Anfangslader |
| AK | Armature Knockoff | AL | Anlage |
| AK | Aspektkatalog | AL | Array List |
| AK | Atkinson | AL | Artificial Language |
| AK | Attention Key | AL | Artificial Line |
| AK | Auswahlkippstufe | AL | Assembler Language |
| AK | Automatic Key | AL | Assembly List |
| AK | Automatic clock | AL | Assembly Listing |
| AK-SID | Aspektkatalog- | AL | Assets and Liabilities |
| | Sicherungsdatei | AL | Associative Law |
| AKA | Autokorrelationsanalyse | AL | Auftragsliste |
| AKD | Arbeitsgemeinschaft | AL | Ausgang löschen |
| | Kommunale Daten- | AL | Ausgangslogik |
| | verarbeitung | AL | Automatic Logging |
| AKDB | Anstalt für Kommunale | AL 1 B | Alphabetic 1 Bit |
| | Datenverarbeitung | AL/COM | Applied Logig's Com- |
| | in Bayern | | prehensive Computing |
| AKES | Arbeitskreis Experten- | ALA | American Library |
| | systeme | | Association |
| AKF | Autokorrelationsfunktion | ALA/BULA | Auftragserteilung für |
| AKIS | Alphabetisches Kunden- | | Leitungen und Anlagen/ |
| | informationssystem | | Buchung für Leitungen |
| AKK | Akkumulator | | und Anlagen |
| AKO | Automatisierte | ALABOL | Algorithmic and Business |
| | Korrespondenz | | Oriented Language |
| AKONA | Automatischer Konten- | ALAP | Associative Linear |
| | ausgleich | | Array Processor |
| AKOR | Arbeitskreis für | ALARM | Automatic Log And |
| | Operations-Research | | Restart Mechanism |
| AKS | Advanced Keyboarding | ALAS | Array Logic And Storage |
| | System | ALAS | Automated Literature |
| AKS | Ausgang für Kontrollsignal | | Alerting System |
| AKS | Autonomes Kassensystem | ALB | Alphabetic |
| AKT | Automatischer Kassen- | ALB | Assumed Leading Bit |
| | tresor | ALB | Automatisiertes |
| AKTIND | Aktienindex | | Liegenschafts-Buch |
| AKV | Automatische Kunden- | ALBIS | Australian Library Based |
| | wunschabhändige | | Information System |
| | Vorbereitung | ALBO | Automatic Line Build-Out |
| AKZ | Akkumulator- | ALBUM | Anwendungsvariables, |
| | Nahtstellenzusatz | | Literaturauswertendes, |
| AL | ALGOL | | Bibliographiengenerie- |
| AL | Absolute Limen | | rendes, Unitermakkumu- |
| AL | Absolute Loader | | lierendes Maschinen- |
| AL | Account Librarian | | programm |
| AL | Adaptive Logic | ALC | Adaptive Logic Circuit |
| AL | Add Logical | ALC | Allocate |

# A

| | | | |
|---|---|---|---|
| ALC | Assembly Language Coding | ALE | Address Latch Element |
| ALC | Automatic Level Control | ALE | Arithmetische Logische Einheit |
| ALC | Automatic Level Controller | ALEC | Algebraic Exponents and Coefficients |
| ALC | Automatic Load Control | ALERT | Architecture to Logic Equation Realization Technique |
| ALC | Automatic Locking Circuit | | |
| ALCAL | Algebraic Calculator Language | ALERT | Automated Law Enforcement Response Team |
| ALCAPP | Automatic List Classification And Profile Production | ALERT | Automatic Linguistic Extraction and Retrieval Technique |
| ALCO | ALGOL Compiler | ALF | Absorption Limiting Frequency |
| ALCOM | Algebraic Compiler | | |
| ALCOM | Algebraic Computer | ALF | Accuracy Limit Factor |
| ALCOR | ALGOL Compiler | ALF | Automatic Letter Facer |
| ALCOR | AlGOL Converter | ALF | Automatic Letter Facing |
| ALCORCode | ALGOL Converter Code | ALFA | A Language for Financial Analysis |
| ALCS | Analog Large Capacity Store | ALFA | Automatic Ledger Feed Attachment |
| ALCU | Algorithmierung von Lehrprogrammen für den Computergesteuerten Unterricht | ALFA | Automatic Line Fault Analysis |
| | | ALFA | Automated Loading of Features and Assemblies |
| ALD | Alarmeingabe, Dynamische | ALFA | Automatisiertes Luftfracht-Abwicklungsverfahren |
| ALD | Analog Line Driver | | |
| ALD | Automatic Logic Diagram | | |
| ALD | Automated Logic Design | | |
| ALDA | Apollo Launch Data System | ALFA | Automatisiertes Luftfrachtzollabwicklungssystem |
| ALDC | Army Logistics Data Center | | |
| | | ALFDT | Alpha Date |
| ALDC | Automatic Load and Drive Control | ALFRED | Associate Learning From Relative Environmental Data |
| ALDE | Alarmbildende Digitale Eingänge | | |
| | | ALFRTRAN | ALGOL to FORTRAN Translator |
| ALDE | Alarm-/Digital-Eingabe | | |
| ALDEP | Automated Layout Design Program | ALG | Algebra |
| | | ALG | Algebraic |
| ALDOS | Automatisches Lager-Dispositions- und Optimierungssystem | ALG | Asynchronous Line Group |
| | | ALGADDR | Algebraic Adder |
| | | ALGEC | Algorithmic Language for Economic Calculations |
| ALDP | Automatic Language Data Processing | | |
| | | ALGM | Algorithm |
| ALDPS | Automated Logistics Data Processing System | ALGN | Alignment |
| | | ALGOL | Algorithmic Oriented Language |
| ALDRI | Automatic Low Data Rate Input | | |
| | | ALI | Asociacion de Licenciados en Informatica |
| ALDS | Apollo Launch Data System | | |
| | | ALI | Autofahrer-Lenkungs-/ und Informationssystem |
| ALDS | Automatic Line Device Store | | |
| ALDS | Automatic Literature Distribution System | ALI | Automated Logic Implementation |

- 30 -

# A

| | | | |
|---|---|---|---|
| ALIAS | Algebraic Logic Investigation of Apollo Systems | ALNA | Algebraic Logic Network Analyzer |
| ALICS | Advanced Logistics Information and Control System | ALNI | Alloyed Nickel |
| | | ALNI | Aluminium-Nickel |
| | | ALNICO | Aluminium-Nickel-Cobalt |
| ALIDO | Amplitude and Latency Instrument with Digital Output | ALOB | Alphabetic O Bit |
| | | ALOC | Allocate |
| | | ALOC | Allocation |
| ALIGN | Alignment | ALOFT | A Language Oriented to Flight engineering and Testing |
| ALIN | Alignment | | |
| ALIR | Adder Left Input Register | | |
| ALIS | Advanced Life Information System | ALOR | Adder Left Output Register |
| ALIS | Arabic Latin Information System | ALOT | Allotment |
| | | ALOT | Allotted |
| ALIS | Automatic Link Set-up | ALOTM | Allotment |
| ALISS | Automatisiertes Leitungs- und Informations-System Standardwerk | ALP | Alternate Program |
| | | ALP | Arithmetic Logic Processor |
| ALK | Ausgabelochkarte | ALP | Assembly Language Program |
| ALK | Automatisierte Liegenschafts-Karte | ALP | Assistance Ligne de Produit |
| ALL | Accelerated Learning of Logic | | |
| | | ALP | Asynchronous Line Pairs |
| ALL | Address Locator Logic | ALP | Autocode List Processing |
| ALL | All-Logic Level | ALP | Automated Language Processing |
| ALL | Application Language Liberator | | |
| | | ALP | Automated Learning Process |
| ALL | Application Load List | | |
| ALLA | Allgemeine Anweisung | ALP | Automated Library Program |
| ALLC | Association of Literary and Linguistic Computing | | |
| | | ALP | Auxilary Language Processor |
| ALLDEPHI | Allgemeine Deutsche Philips Industrie GmbH | ALPAK | Algebra Package |
| | | ALPB | Alphabetic |
| ALLOC | Allocate | ALPH | Alphameric |
| ALLP | Audio-Lingual Language Programming | ALPHA | Alphabetical |
| | | ALPHA | Alphanumeric |
| ALM | Adding Listing Machine | ALPHA | Automatic Literature Processing, Handling and Analysis |
| ALM | Alarm | | |
| ALM | Alerting Message | | |
| ALMA | Alphanumeric Language for Music Analysis | ALPHAS | Automatic Literature Processing, Handling and Analysis System |
| ALMM | Algorithmus und Lösung für MM | | |
| | | ALPM | Alphanumeric |
| ALMS | Analytic Language Manipulation System | ALPS | Advanced Linear Programming System |
| ALMS | Automated Logic Mapping System | ALPS | Advanced Logic Processor System |
| ALMS | Automated Logic Matrix System | ALPS | Associated Logic Parallel System |
| ALMSA | Automated Logistics Management Systems Activity | ALPS | Automated Language Processing System |
| | | ALPS | Automated Library Processing Services |

# A

| | | | |
|---|---|---|---|
| ALPS | Automatic License Plate Scanning | ALTP | Automatic Linear Temperature Programmer |
| ALR | Alarm Reset | ALTPM | Algorithmus und Lösung für TPM |
| ALR | Automatische Lautstärkeregelung | ALTR | Alternate |
| ALRP | All Line Repeat Printing | ALTR | Alternator |
| ALS | Alphanumeric Logging System | ALTRAN | Algebraic Translator |
| ALS | Assembler Language Statement | ALTREC | Automatic Life Testing and Recording of Electronic Components |
| ALS | Associate List Selection | ALTRN | Alteration |
| ALS | Associate List Selector | ALU | Arithmetical and Logical Unit |
| ALS | Automated Library System | ALU | Arithmetic and Logic Unit |
| ALS | Automatic Landing System | ALUP | Automatische Lochstreifengesteuerte Universalprüfeinrichtung |
| ALS | Automatic Level Setting | | |
| ALS | Automatic Line Selection | | |
| ALS | Automatisches Leitungssystem | ALUP | Automatische Lochstreifengesteuerte Universelle Prüfeinrichtung |
| ALSS | Airline System Simulator | | |
| ALT | Accelerated Life Testing | ALUTROL | Arithmetic Logic Unit for Control |
| ALT | Algebraic Language Translator | ALWAC | Axel-Wennergren Automatic Computer |
| ALT | Alternate | | |
| ALT | Alternating | ALZ | Alarmzentrale |
| ALT | Alternation | ALZUDI | Algorithmische Zuordnungsdidaktik |
| ALT | Alternator | | |
| ALT | Altitude | AM | AND Module |
| ALT | Amber Light | AM | Abrechnungsmaschine |
| ALT | Application Load Table | AM | Abschnittsmarke |
| ALT | Automatic Language Translation | AM | Abstract Mathematics |
| | | AM | Access Matrix |
| ALTAC | Algebraic Translator And Compiler | AM | Access Mechanism |
| | | AM | Access Method |
| ALTAC | Algebraic Translator Assembler Compiler | AM | Account Manager |
| | | AM | Accounting Machine |
| ALTAIR | Automatic Logical Translation And Information Retrieval | AM | Accounting Method |
| | | AM | Accumulative Multiplication |
| ALTAPE | Automatic Line Tracing And Programming Equipment | AM | Acoustic Memory |
| | | AM | Active Memory |
| | | AM | Adding Machine |
| ALTARE | Automatic Logic Testing And Recording Equipment | AM | Adding Mechanism |
| | | AM | Addition Matrices |
| ALTDEV | Alternative Device | AM | Address Mark |
| ALTER | Alternate | AM | Address Match |
| ALTF | Alternate Field | AM | Address Modification |
| ALTIHP | Avionics Laboratory Technical Information Handling Profile | AM | Addressable Memory |
| | | AM | Addressed Memory |
| | | AM | Addressing Machine |
| ALTN | Alternate | AM | Addressing Matrix |
| ALTN | Alternation | AM | Addressing Method |
| ALTNTR | Alternator | AM | Addressograph Multigraph |

# A

| | | | |
|---|---|---|---|
| AM | Adjoint Matrix | AMANDA | Automatic Measurement and Analysis |
| AM | Alarm Message | | |
| AM | Alignment Mark | AMAP | Advanced Multiprogramming Analysis Procedure |
| AM | Alternate Mark | | |
| AM | Ammeter | | |
| AM | Amperemeter | AMAP | Advanced Multiprogramming Analysis Program |
| AM | Ampereminute | | |
| AM | Amplifier | | |
| AM | Amplitude | AMAR | Analog Multiplexer Address Register |
| AM | Amplitude Modulation | | |
| AM | Amplitudenmodulation | AMARS | Automatic Message Address Routing System |
| AM | Analog Memory | | |
| AM | Anfangsmarke | AMATA | Audible Manufacturing Training Aid |
| AM | Annular Magnet | | |
| AM | Anschlußmöglichkeit | AMB | Address Mark Bit |
| AM | Ante Meridium | AMB | Amber |
| AM | Anticipatory Modification | AMB | Ambient |
| AM | Arbeitsmittel | AMB | Auftrags-/und Maschinenbestand |
| AM | Arithmetic Mean | | |
| AM | Arithmetischer Mittelwert | AMB | Ausgabe Magnetband |
| AM | Arithmetisches Mittel | AMBA | Ausgabe Magnetbanddatei |
| AM | Assembly and Maintenance | AMBIT | Algebraic Manipulation By Identity Translation |
| AM | Associative Memory | AMC | Addressable Memory Clock |
| AM | Astabiler Multivibrator | AMC | Advanced Minuteman Computer |
| AM | Astable Multivibrator | | |
| AM | Asynchronous Modem | AMC | Alarm Monitor Computer |
| AM | Auslösemagnet | AMC | Automatic Message Counting |
| AM | Aussteuerungsmesser | | |
| AM | Automatic Memory | AMC | Automatic Mixture Control |
| AM | Auxiliary Memory | | |
| AM | Available Memory | AMC | Automatic Modulation Control |
| AM-DBS | Amplitude Modulation, Double-Sideband | AMCAP | Advanced Microwave Circuit Analysis Program |
| AM-SSB | Amplitude Modulation, Single-Sideband | | |
| AMA | American Management Association | AMCB | Access Method Control Block |
| AMA | American Medical Association | AMCC | American Medical Computer Center |
| AMA | Analog Major Alarm | AMCD | Addressograph Multigraph Copier Duplicator |
| AMA | Arbeitsgemeinschaft Meßwertaufnehmer | AMCOS | Aldermaston Mechanized Cataloguing and Order System |
| AMA | Automated Message Accounting | | |
| AMA | Automatic Malfunction Analysis | AMCR | Automatic Magnetic Card Reader |
| AMA | Automatic Message Accounting | AMCS | Adaptive Microprogrammed Control System |
| AMA-MTR | Automatic Message Accounting-Magnetic Tape Recording | AMCS | Advanced Manpower Control System |
| AMACUS | Automated Microfilm Aperture Car Updating System | AMD | Address Mark Detection |
| | | AMD | Advanced Memory Development |

# A

| | | | |
|---|---|---|---|
| AMD | Advanced Micro Devices | AMIF | Automated Map Information File |
| AMD | Air Movement Data | | |
| AMD | Arbeitskreis Mittlere Datentechnik | AMIGOS | Access Method for Indexed Data Generalised for Operating System |
| AMD | Associative Memory Device | AMII | Association Médicale d'Informatique Individuelle |
| AMD | Automatic Map Display | | |
| AMD | Auxiliary Memory Drum | | |
| AMDES | Automatic Masking-Data generation for electron -beam Exposure System | AMIL | A Microprogramming Language |
| | | AMIP | Analysis of Management Inventory Policy |
| AMDF | Army Master Data File | | |
| AMDF | Average Magnitude Difference Function | AMIP | Army Management Information Program |
| AMDFRMS | Army Master Data File Reader Microfilm System | AMIS | Advanced Management Information System |
| | | AMIS | Agribusiness Management Information System |
| AMDP | Arbeitsgemeinschaft für Methodik und Dokumentation in der Psychiatrie | AMIS | Airport Management Information System |
| AMDSB | Amplitude Modulation Double Side Band | AMIS | Automated Management Information System |
| AMDUE | Amount Due | AMIT | Ampex to IBM Tape |
| AME | Access Method Executor | AMK | Arbeitsmittelkarte |
| AME | Advanced Manufacturing Engineering | AML | Actual Measured Loss |
| | | AML | Algebraic Manipulation Language |
| AME | Associated Memory Equipment | AML | Amplitude Modulated Link |
| AME | Ausgabeeinheit Meldungen | AML | Amplitude Modulation with Limiter |
| AMECOS | Automatic Measuring Computing and Sorting | AML | Application Macro Library |
| AMES | Automatic Message Entry System | AML | Application Module Library |
| AMF | Analog Matched Filter | AML | Assembly Micro Library |
| AMFIS | American Microfilm Information Society | AML | Automatic Machine Loading |
| AMFIS | Automatic Microfilm Information System | AML | Automatic Magazine Loading |
| AMFM | Amplitude Modulation - Frequency Modulation | AML | Automatic Modulation Limiting |
| AMG | Address Mark Gate | AMLC | Asynchronous Multi Line Commercial processor |
| AMG | Automatic Model Generator | AMM | Auxiliary Magnetic Memory |
| AMH | Application Message Handler | AMME | Automated Multi-Media Exchange |
| AMH | Automated Medical History | AMMIC | Armament Maintenance Management Information Center |
| AMI | Address Modification Instructions | | |
| AMI | Alternate Mark Inversion code | AMMIP | Aviation Material Management Improvement Program |
| AMI | American Micro Systems | | |
| AMI | Association pour la Micro-Informatique | AMMP | Approved Modernization Maintenance Program |

# A

| | | | |
|---|---|---|---|
| AMMS | Automated Multi-Media Switch | AMPC | Area Mail Processing Center |
| AMMT | Automated Multi-Media Terminal | AMPC | Automatic Message Processing Center |
| AMNIP | Adaptive Man-machine Non-arithmetical Information Processing | AMPERES | Automated Maintenance Performance and Engineering Reliability Evaluation System |
| AMO | Adder for Multiple Operands | AMPEX | Automatic Programming-system Extended |
| AMO | Air-Mass-Zero | | |
| AMO | Alternate Molecular Orbit | AMPHR | Ampere-Hour |
| AMO | Analogeingabe für Momentanwerke | AMPL | Advanced Microprocessor Prototyping Laboratory |
| AMOE | Analogeingabe für Momentanwerke, Erweiterungsbaustein | AMPL | Amplifier |
| | | AMPL | Amplitude |
| | | AMPLFD | Amplified |
| AMOR | Associative Memory with Ordered Retrieval | AMPM | Auto-Manual Probe Multiplexer |
| AMOS | A Multi access On-line System | AMPPL | Associative Memory, Parallel Processing Language |
| AMOS | Adjustable Multi-class Organizing System | AMPR | Amplifier |
| AMOS | Associative Memory Organizing System | AMPR | Assembly Manufacturing Planning Record |
| AMOS | Automatic Meteorological Observation Station | AMPR | Assembly Manufacturing Process Record |
| | | AMPR | Application Module Processing Routine |
| AMOSS | Adaptive Mission-Oriented Software System | AMPS | Advanced Mobile Phone Service |
| AMP | Accounting Machine Program | AMPS | Amperes |
| | | AMPS | Assembly Manufacturing Payrolls System |
| AMP | Active Medium Propagation | AMPS | Automated Material Processing System |
| AMP | Adaptation Mathematical Processor | AMPS | Automatic Message Processing System |
| AMP | Add, Multi-Precision | | |
| AMP | Advanced Management Program | AMPS AC | Amperes Alternating Current |
| AMP | Amplifier | AMPS DC | Amperes Direct Current |
| AMP | Amplitude | AMPSIN | Adaptive Mode Planning System Input |
| AMP | Argonne Microprocessor | | |
| AMP | Associative Memory Processor | AMPT | Automatic Module Production Tester |
| AMP | Asymmetric Multi-processing System | AMPTD | Amplitude |
| | | AMQ | Analog Multiplexer Quantizer |
| AMP | Ausgabe Magnetplatte | | |
| AMP | Automated Maintenance Program | AMR | Address Modification Register |
| AMP | Automatic Multiprogram | AMR | Advanced Management Research |
| AMP | Automatic Multiplying Punch | AMR | Automated Management Reports |
| AMP AC | Ampere Alternating Current | AMR | Automatic Message Recording |
| AMP DC | Ampere Direct Current | | |

- 35 -

# A

| | | | | |
|---|---|---|---|---|
| AMR | Automatic Message Registering | | AMTU | Automatic Margin Test Unit |
| AMRS | Automatic Message Registering System | | AMU | Analog Multiplier Unit |
| | | | AMU | Antenna Matching Unit |
| AMRT | Accès Multiple à Répartition dans le Temps | | AMU | Atomic Mass Unit |
| | | | AMU | Auxiliary Memory Unit |
| AMS | Absatzmarktsystem | | AMV | Arithmetic Mean Value |
| AMS | Access Method Services | | AMV | Astabiler Multivibrator |
| AMS | Actual Minus Sign | | AMV | Astable Multivibrator |
| AMS | Administrative Management Society | | AMVF | Amplitude-Modulated Voice Frequency |
| AMS | Advanced Marksman Series | | AMVSB | Amplitude Modulation with Vestigial Side Band |
| AMS | Advanced Memory System | | AMWD | Address Mark Write Data |
| AMS | Altitude Measurement System | | AMX | Automatic Message Exchange |
| AMS | American Mathematical Society | | AMX | Ausgabematrix |
| | | | AMXT | Active Maximum Tasks |
| AMS | Analog Master Slice | | AMZ | Absorptionsmeßzange |
| AMS | Application Management System | | AN | Absolute Name |
| | | | AN | Abstract Number |
| AMS | Associative Memory System | | AN | Account Number |
| | | | AN | Add Normalized |
| AMS | Automatic Manual Station | | AN | Alphanumeric |
| AMSAT | American Satellite Corporation | | AN | Analizer |
| | | | AN | Analog Network |
| AMSCD | Amount Subject to Cash Discount | | AN | Analyse |
| | | | AN | AND |
| AMSEC | Analytical Method for System Evaluation and Control | | AN | AND NOT |
| | | | AN | Anlage |
| | | | AN | Anode |
| AMSR | Automated Microform Storage and Retrieval | | AN | Anpassungsnetzwerk |
| | | | AN | Anschaltung |
| AMSSB | Amplitude Modulation Single Sideband | | AN | Antenna |
| | | | AN | Arithmetic Notation |
| AMSTS | Automatic Multiparameter Semiconductor Test Set | | AN | Auftragnehmer |
| | | | ANA | Automatic Network Analyser |
| AMT | Amount | | ANA | Automatic Number Analysis |
| AMT | Analog Magnetic Tape | | | |
| AMT | Available Machine Time | | ANACOM | Analog Computer |
| AMT | Avalanche Memory Triode | | ANACONDA | Analytical Control and Data |
| AMT | Autodin Multimedia Terminal | | ANAFACT | Analyse Factorielle |
| AMTD | Automatic Magnetic Tape Dissemination | | ANAGOL | Analogrechner ALGOL |
| | | | ANAL | Analog |
| AMTI | Airborne Moving-Target Indicator | | ANAL | Analysis |
| | | | ANAL | Analytic |
| AMTRAN | Automatic Mathematical Translation | | ANAL | Analyzer |
| | | | ANALIT | Analysis of Automatic Line Insulation Test |
| AMTRAN | Automatic Mathematical Translator | | ANALOG | Analogrechner ALGOL |
| AMTRC | Amount Received | | ANAT | ANI Attendant number |
| AMTS | Analog Magnetic Tape Storage | | ANATRAN | Analog Translator |
| | | | ANAU | Analogausgabe |

# A

| | | | |
|---|---|---|---|
| ANAU | Analogausgabegerät | ANLAS | Anlagenabrechnungssystem |
| ANAVAR | Analyse de Variance | | |
| ANB-HP | Anschlußbaugruppe für Hochpegel | ANLG | Analog |
| | | ANLP | Alphanumeric Logic Package |
| ANBU | Anlagenbuchhaltung | | |
| ANCIR/TS | Analog Circuit-analysis by Time-share System | ANMT | Announcement |
| | | ANNET | Analyse von Netzwerken |
| ANCIRS | Automated News Clipping, Indexing, and Retrieval System | ANO. | AND NOT Operation |
| | | ANOCOVA | Analysis Of Covariance |
| | | ANOV | Analysis Of Variance |
| ANCLAV | Automatic Navigation Computer for Land and Amphibious Vehicles | ANR | Advisornummer |
| | | ANR | Alphanumeric Replacement |
| AND | All-Numeral Dial | ANR | Auftragsnummer |
| AND | Alphanumeric Display | ANRS | Automatic Noise Reduction System |
| AND | AND circuit | | |
| AND | Automatische Nachdisposition | ANRT | Association Nationale de la Recherche Technique |
| ANDAS | Automatic Navigation and Data Acquisition System | | |
| | | ANS | Active Network Synthesis |
| | | ANS | Actual Noise Silencer |
| ANDEP | Alphanumerischer Datenerfassungsplatz | ANS | Add Normalized Short |
| | | ANS | American National Standards |
| ANDS | Alphanumeric Displays | | |
| ANEBA | Alphanumeric Electronic Bit Analyzer | ANS | And to Storage |
| | | ANS | Ansatz |
| ANEC | Analysis Evaluation and Computation | ANS | Answer |
| | | ANS | Answering |
| ANEVAC | Analysis Evaluation And Computation | ANS | Area Navigation System |
| | | ANS | Automatic Navigation System |
| ANF | Anchored Filament | | |
| ANF | Anfang | ANSCII | American National Standard Code for Information Interchange |
| ANF | Anforderung | | |
| ANF | Audio Notch Filter | | |
| ANFADR | Anfangsadresse | ANSCOBOL | American National Standard Institute Common Business Oriented Language |
| ANG | Angular | | |
| ANG | Automatischer Nummerngeber | | |
| | | | |
| ANGLFN | Angle Function | ANSCR | Alphanumeric System for Classification on Recordings |
| ANI | Automatic Number Identification | | |
| | | ANSCSOCR | American National Standard Character Set for Optical Character Recognition |
| ANIEL | Asociacion Nacional de la Industria Electronica | | |
| ANIS | Allgemeines nicht Numerisches Informationssystem | | |
| | | ANSI | American National Standards Institute |
| ANITA | Analyse des Auftragsbestandes und Integration der Auftragsbearbeitung | ANSICOBOL | American National Standard Institute Common Business Oriented Language |
| | | | |
| ANK | Arbeitsgruppe Neue Kommunikationstechniken | | |
| | | ANSIM | Analog Simulator |
| | | ANSWER | Algorithm for Non-Synchronized Waveform Error Reduction |
| ANL | Add Normalized Long | | |
| ANL | Anlagen | | |
| ANL | Automatic Noise Limiter | | |

# A

| | | | |
|---|---|---|---|
| ANT | Antenna | AOC | All Ones Counter |
| ANTEX | Alphanumeric Terminal Executive | AOC | Automatic Operation Control |
| ANTILOG | Antilogarith | AOC | Automatic Output Control |
| ANTIOPE | Acquisition Numérique et Télévisualisation d'Images Organisées en Page d'Ecriture | AOC | Automatic Overload Circuit |
| | | AOC | Automatic Overload Control |
| ANTRAS | Analyse tragender Systeme | AOCL | Average Outgoing Count Limit |
| ANTS | Any Tape Search | | |
| ANTS | ARPA Network Terminal System | AOCR | Advanced Optical Character Recognition |
| ANTS | Automatic Nitrogen Transfer System | AOCT | Analog Output Conversion Time |
| ANUDS | Army Nuclear Data System | AOD | Acknowledgement Of Debt |
| ANUL | Annullation | AOD | Aktionsorientierte Datenverarbeitung |
| ANUM | Attendant Number | | |
| ANWDOK | Anwendungsdokumentation | AOD | Analog Output Device |
| ANWIHO | Anlauf, Wiederhochlauf | AOD | AND-OR Delay |
| AO | Abfrageoperation | AODA | Analog Output Driver Amplifier |
| AO | Access Opening | | |
| AO | Accumulator Overflow | AODS | Atlas Operational Data Summary |
| AO | Actual Operation | | |
| AO | Add-on | AOE | Add Order Execution |
| AO | Adder Output | AOI | AND/OR Invert |
| AO | Adding Operator | AOI | Automated Outgoing Interface |
| AO | Address Operation | | |
| AO | Address Order | AOIV | Automatically Created Inlet Valve |
| AO | Addressing Operation | | |
| AO | Alphabetic Order | AOL | Application-Oriented Language |
| AO | Alphanumeric Order | | |
| AO | Amplifier Output | AOLR | Amplifier Open Loop Response |
| AO | Analog Output | | |
| AO | AND OR | AOM | Add-On Memory |
| AO | AND Operation | AOM | Altos Office Manager |
| AO | AND Operator | AOMM | Add-On Main Memory |
| AO | Anwendungsorganisation | AOP | Advanced Onboard Processor |
| AO | Anwendungsorganisator | | |
| AO | Arithmetic Operation | AOPI | AND OR Power Inverter |
| AO | Arithmetic Operator | AOPSA | Advanced Optical Power Spectrum Analyzer |
| AO | Arithmetic Organ | | |
| AO | Assembly Order | AOQ | Average Outgoing Quality |
| AO | Asynchronous Operation | AOQ | Average Output Quality |
| AO | Atomic Orbital | AOQL | Average Outgoing Quality Level |
| AO | Automated Operator | | |
| AO | Automatic Operation | AOQL | Average Outgoing Quality Limit |
| AO | Auxiliary Operation | | |
| AO | Auxiliary Oscillator | AOR | Acknowledgement of Receipt |
| AOA | Accessible Operand Affiliation | | |
| | | AOR | Add One Right |
| AOB | Adder Output Buffer | AOR | Alphanumeric Optical Reader |
| AOBR | Analog Output Buffer Register | | |

# A

| | | | |
|---|---|---|---|
| AOR | Assembly Operations Record | AP | Adjustable Point |
| | | AP | Administrative Program |
| AOS | Add Or Substract | AP | Adreßpuffer |
| AOS | Advanced Operating System | AP | Advanced Programming |
| | | AP | After Peak |
| AOS | Algebraic Operation System | AP | After Perpendicular |
| | | AP | Algorithmic Procedure |
| AOS | Amplifier Output Stage | AP | Alphabetic Punch |
| AOS | Analog Output Submodule | AP | Alphanumeric Punching |
| AOS | Application-Oriented Subprogram | AP | Alteration Program |
| | | AP | Alternate Print |
| AOS/RT | Advanced Operating System/Real Time | AP | Alternate Program |
| | | AP | Alternative Program |
| AOSP | Active Optics Simulation Program | AP | Analytic Plotter |
| | | AP | Anpassungsschaltung |
| AOSP | Automatic Operating and Scheduling Program | AP | Anschlußplan |
| | | AP | Anschlußplatte |
| AOSS | Active Optics Simulation System | AP | Anschlußprozessor |
| | | AP | Anwenderprogramm |
| AOSS | Advanced Operations Support System | AP | Anwendungsprogramm |
| | | AP | Anwendungsprogrammierer |
| AOT | Analog Output Timer | | |
| AOT | AND-OR-Trigger | AP | Anwendungsprojekt |
| AOT | Average Operation Time | AP | Aperture |
| AOT | Auxiliary Output Tester | AP | Application Programming |
| AOV | Amplified Output Voltage | AP | Applications Processor |
| AOV | Analysis Of Variance | AP | Application Program |
| AOX | AND-OR Extender | AP | Applications Program |
| AP | A Pulse | AP | Applikationsprogramm |
| AP | Abonnentenpunkt | AP | Arbeitsplanung |
| AP | Abrufprogramm | AP | Arbeitsplatzdatei |
| AP | Absolute Program | AP | Arbeitsprogramm |
| AP | Absolute Programming | AP | Arbitrary Parameter |
| AP | Acceptable Program | AP | Arithmetic Problem |
| AP | Access Panel | AP | Arithmetic Progression |
| AP | Accidental Printing | AP | Assembled Program |
| AP | Accounting Period | AP | Assembler Program |
| AP | Accounting Process | AP | Assembly Program |
| AP | Accounts Payable | AP | Assignment Phase |
| AP | Accurate Programming | AP | Assignment Problem |
| AP | Action Potential | AP | Assignment Program |
| AP | Active Program | AP | Assistance Program |
| AP | Active Pull-up | AP | Attached Processor |
| AP | Acyclic Process | AP | Attenuator Pad |
| AP | Adapter Panel | AP | Auftragspuffer |
| AP | Adapter control Panel | AP | Ausgabeprogramm |
| AP | Add decimal Packed | AP | Automatic Program |
| AP | Adding Punch | AP | Automatic Programming |
| AP | Addition Position | AP | Automatic Punch |
| AP | Additive Process | AP | Automatic Punching |
| AP | Address Part | AP | Automatische Programmierung |
| AP | Address Portion | | |
| AP | Address Printing | AP | Automic Power |
| AP | Address Program | AP | Auxiliary Program |
| AP | Addressing Program | AP-CTL | Application Control |

# A

| | | | |
|---|---|---|---|
| AP-ESSQ | All-Pass Error Spectrum Shaping Quantizer | APC | Assembly Program Code |
| AP-INFO | Application Information | APC | Augmented Parity Check |
| AP/APC | Associate Processor/ Associative Processor Controller | APC | Automatic Peripheral Control |
| | | APC | Automatic Phase Control |
| APAC | Airsearch Parabolic Arc Computer | APC | Automatic Picture Control |
| APAC | Automatic Positioning And Control | APC | Automatic Potential Control |
| APACE | Aldermaston Project for the Application of Computers to Engineering | APC | Automatic Process Control |
| | | APC | Automatic Program Control |
| APACHE | Analog Programming And Checking | APC | Automatic Punching of Cards |
| APACS | Adaptive Planning And Control Sequence | APC | Automatically Prepunched Card |
| APADS | Automatic Programmer And Data System | APC | Average Power Control |
| | | APCA | Automatic Phono-Cardiac Analyzer |
| APAL | Array Processor Assembly Language | APCC | Apollo Program Control Center |
| APAM | Array Processor Access Method | APCG | Aperture Plate Character Generator |
| APAR | Apparatus | | |
| APAR | Authorized Program Analysis Report | APCHE | Automatic Programming Checkout Equipment |
| APAR | Automatic Programming And Recording | APCN | Active Pulse Compression Network |
| APAREL | A Parse Request Language | APCM | Adaptive Pulse Code Modulator |
| APAS | Automatic Performance Analysis System | APCM | Authorized Protective Connecting Module |
| APATS | Automatic Programming And Test System | APCON | Approach Control |
| APAVC | Almost Periodic Amplitude Variation Coding | APCP | Aquatic Plants Control Program |
| APB... | Adrema Pitney Bowes | APCR | Automatic Punched Card Recording |
| APBE | Arbeitsplatzbelegung | | |
| APC | Adaptive Processing Control | APCS | Associative Processor Computer System |
| APC | Additional Program Cycle | APD | Above Platen Device |
| | | APD | Acquisition Processor Display |
| APC | Address Plate Cabinet | | |
| APC | Address Punched Card | APD | Additional Program Drum |
| APC | Advanced Personal Computer | APD | Advanced Program Development |
| APC | Advanced Profession Computer | APD | Amplitude Probability Distribution |
| APC | Advanced Programming Course | APD | Analog-to-Pulse Duration |
| | | APD | Angular Position Digitizer |
| APC | All Purpose Computer | | |
| APC | Alphabetic Print Control | APD | Applications Program Division |
| APC | Analog-to-Pressure Converter | APD | Apprentissage Par Didacticiel |
| APC | Angular Position Counter | | |
| APC | Arbeitsplatzcomputer | APD | Approach Progress Display |

# A

| | | | |
|---|---|---|---|
| APD | Arbeitsplatzdatei | APG | Anregungspulsgenerator |
| APD | Auxiliary Power Distribution | APG | Application Program Generator |
| APD | Avalanche Photodiode | APG | Arbeitsplatzgruppe |
| APDL | Algorithmic Processor Description Language | APG | Auswerte-Programmgenerator |
| APDS | Advanced Personnel Data System | APG | Automated Process Generator |
| APDS | Advanced Planning Data Sheet | APG | Automatic Priority Group |
| APE | Automatische Prüfeinrichtung | APG | Automatic Program Generator |
| APE | Application Prototype Environment | APGES | Application Program Generating and Executive System |
| APE | Atomic Photoelectric Effect | API | AND Power Inverter |
| APE | Anpassungseinheit | API | Alignment Progress Indicator |
| APE | Application Prototyp Environment | API | All Purpose Interface |
| APE | Arbeitsplatzerfassungsbeleg | API | Anwendungsprogramm-Interface |
| APE | Automatic Positioning Equipment | API | Application Program Interface |
| APE | Automatische Programmladeeinrichtung | API | Application Programmer Interface |
| APEC | All Purpose Electronic Computer | API | Assembly Program Instruction |
| APEM | Association des Prestataires En Micrographie | API | Association des Professionels de l'Informatique |
| APEX | Amplitude Phase Extractor | API | Automatic Priority Interrupt |
| APEX | Amplitude and Phase Extraction | API | Automatic Program Interrupt |
| APEX | Analysis of Performance and Expense | APIC | Automatic Power Input Control |
| APEX | Assembler and Process Executive | APIC | Automatic Programming Information Centre |
| APEX | Assembler and Program Executive | APICON | Aircraft Position Information Converter |
| APEX | Automated Planning and Execution control system | APICS | Air Pollution Information and Computer System |
| APF | Advanced Program Feature | APICS | American Production and Inventory Control Society |
| APF | Area Protect Feature | | |
| APF | Authorized Program Facility | APIN | Atlas Propulsion Information Notice |
| APF | Automatic Program Finder | APK | Amplitude and Phase Keying |
| APF | Available Page Frame | APL | A Program Language |
| APFC | Automatic Phase and Frequency Control | APL | A Programming Language |
| APFM | All Purpose Fast Memory | APL | Ablaufplanungsverfahren |
| APFS | Auto Program Find System | APL | Absolute Program Loader |
| APG | Allgemeiner Programmgenerator | APL | Advanced Product Line |

- 41 -

# A

| | | | |
|---|---|---|---|
| APL | Advanced Programming Language | APMS | Automatic Pulse Measurement System |
| APL | Algorithmic Procedural Language | APN | All Pass Network |
| APL | Algorithmic Programming Language | APO | Advanced Program-Oriented language |
| APL | Applications Programming Language | APO | Advanced Programming Option |
| APL | Applied Physics Laboratory | APOS | Adaptive Problem-Oriented Software |
| APL | Assembly Program Language | APOSS | Automatic Point Of Sale System |
| APL | Associative Programming Language | APOTA | Automatic Positioning Telemetering Antenna |
| APL | Automatic Phase Lock | APP | Aerial Position Programmer |
| APL | Automatic Programming Language | APP | Alphabetic Printing Punch |
| APL | Average Picture Level | APP | Analyse Potentieller Probleme |
| APL | Average Picture-signal Level | APP | Antenna Position Programmer |
| APL-DI | APL Data Interface | APP | Anwenderprogrammpaket |
| APLA | Arbeitsplanausführung | APP | Apparatus |
| APLADA | Arbeitsplandatei | APP | Appendix |
| APLL | Automatic Phase-Locked Loop | APP | Application |
| APLM | Asynchronous Pulse-Length Modulation | APP | Applied |
| APLS | Automated Process Line System | APP | Approved |
| APLS | Automatic Printing Line Selection | APP | Approximate |
| APLSV | A Programming Language with Shared Variable | APP | Associative Parallel Processor |
| APLT | Automatic Programming Language Translation | APP | Automatic Power Protection |
| APLU | Automatic Program Loading Unit | APP | Automatic Prepunching |
| APM | Add Punch Machine | APP | Auxiliary Power Plant |
| APM | Advance Program Monitor | APPAR | Apparatus |
| APM | Alarm Panel Monitor | APPC | Advanced Program to Program Communication |
| APM | Aluminium Powder Material | APPD | Aviation Personnel Planning Data |
| APM | Analog Panel Meter | APPECS | Adaptive Pattern Perceiving Electronic Computer System |
| APM | Arbitrary Precision Multiplication | APPF | Additional Print Position Feature |
| APM | Associative Principle for Multiplication | APPI | Advanced Planning Procurement Information |
| APM | Automated Processing Method | APPL | Application |
| APM | Automatic Printing Machine | APPL | Applicable |
| APM | Auxiliary Processing Machine | APPL | Applied |
| APMMRI | Automatic Point Marking, Measuring and Recording Instrument | APPLIC | Application |
| | | APPLN | Application |
| | | APPN | Appropriation |
| | | APPON | Application |
| | | APPR | Approval |
| | | APPR | Approximately |

# A

| | |
|---|---|
| APPR | Approximation |
| APPS | Application Support system |
| APPX | Appendix |
| APQ | Arithmetic Processor Queue |
| APQ | Available Page Queue |
| APR | Alphanumeric Page Reader |
| APR | Alternate Path Retry |
| APR | Analog Parameter Record |
| APR | Annual Percentage Rate |
| APR | Assembly Program Run |
| APR | Ausgabe-Pufferregister |
| APR | Automated Punch Requisition |
| APR | Automatic Passbook Recording |
| APR | Automatic Pattern Recognition |
| APR | Automatic Production Recording |
| APR | Automatic Production Registering |
| APR | Automatic Programming and Recording |
| APR | Automatisches Produktions-Registriersystem |
| APRA | Auswahlprogrammrahmen |
| APRF | Automatic identification trunk Prefix |
| APRIL | Associative Processor with Integrated Logic |
| APRIL | Automatically Programmed Remote Indication Logged |
| APRM | Application Programmers Reference Manual |
| APROCH | Application pré-Programmée avec Choix |
| APRS | Automatic Position Reference System |
| APRS | Automatic Production Recording System |
| APRST | Automatic Progressive Register Sender Tester |
| APRXLY | Approximately |
| APS | Accessible Program Sequence |
| APS | Accessory Power Supply |
| APS | Actual Plus Sign |
| APS | Additional Program Step |
| APS | Alphanumeric Photocomposer System |
| APS | Amplifier Power Supply |
| APS | Analysis- und Prognosesystem |
| APS | Anlagen-Programm-System |
| APS | Anwenderprogrammsystem |
| APS | Application Programm Sampler |
| APS | Application Program Services |
| APS | Applied Peripheral Systems, Inc. |
| APS | Applikationsprogrammsystem |
| APS | Arbeitsplatzsystem |
| APS | Array Processing Subroutine |
| APS | Array Processor System |
| APS | Assembly Programming System |
| APS | Automatic Patching System |
| APS | Automatic Picture Setting |
| APS | Automatic Programming System |
| APS | Automatischer Probenspeicher |
| APS | Automatisierte Produktionssteuerung |
| APS | Auxiliary Power Supply |
| APS | Auxiliary Power System |
| APS | Auxiliary Program Storage |
| APSE | ADA Programming Support Environment |
| APSG | Area Program Support Group |
| APSI | Amperes Per Square Inch |
| APSK | Arbeitsplanstammkarte |
| APSP | Array Processing Subroutine Package |
| APSS | Analysis and Programming for Space Systems |
| APST | Association des Prestataires de Services Télétel |
| APSW | Altes Programmstatuswort |
| APT | Analog Program Tape |
| APT | Angular Position Transducer |
| APT | Automatic Parts Testing |
| APT | Automatic Picture Taking |
| APT | Automatic Picture Transmission |
| APT | Automatic Position Telemetering |

# A

| | | | |
|---|---|---|---|
| APT | Automatic Programming Technique | APX | Automatic Programming-system Extended |
| APT | Automatic Programming Tool | APY | Apply |
| APT | Automatic Programming for Tools | APZ | Anwendungs-Programm-Zentrum |
| APT | Automatically Programmed Tools | AQ | Any Quantity |
| | | AQ | Acquisition message |
| APT | Automatically Programmed Tooling | AQ | Analog Quantity |
| | | AQDHS | Air Quality Data Handling System |
| APT | Automatically Programming Tool | AQE | Allocated Queue Element |
| | | AQL | Acceptable Quality Level |
| APT | Automation Planning and Technology | AQL | Advanced Query Language |
| | | AQL | Average Quality Level |
| APT-AC | Automatically Programmed Tool-Advanced Contouring | AQL | Average Quality of the Lot |
| | | AQS | Automated Quotation Systems |
| APT-BP | Automatically Programmed Tool-Basic Positioning | AQT | Acceptabel Quality Test |
| | | AQUIS | Acquisition |
| APT-IC | Automatically Programmed Tool-Intermediate Contouring | AR | A Register |
| | | AR | Abfrageregister |
| | | AR | Abschreibungsrate |
| APT-IGS | Automatically Programmed Tool-Integrative Graphics System | AR | Abstimmanzeigeröhre |
| | | AR | Access Request |
| | | AR | Accounting Routine |
| APTE | Automatic Production Test Equipment | AR | Accounts Receivable |
| | | AR | Accumulating Reproducer |
| APTR | Automatic Picture Transmission Receiver | AR | Accumulative Register |
| | | AR | Accumulator Register |
| APTS | Application Program Test System | AR | Acid Resiting |
| | | AR | Active Routine |
| APTS | Automatic Picture Transmission System | AR | Activity Rate |
| | | AR | Actual Range |
| APTS | Automatic Programmer and Test System | AR | Add Register |
| | | AR | Addend Register |
| APTUS | Apparatus | AR | Addition Register |
| APU | Accessory Power Unit | AR | Address Range |
| APU | Additional Peripheral Unit | AR | Address Register |
| | | AR | Addressenregister |
| APU | Analytic Processing Unit | AR | Adreßregister |
| | | AR | Akkumulatives Register |
| APU | Arithmetic Processing Unit | AR | Allgemeines Register |
| | | AR | Allocation Register |
| APU | Assembler-Programmierungsumgebung | AR | Allocator Routine |
| | | AR | Alphabetic Register |
| APU | Audio Playback Unit | AR | Alphanumeric Representation |
| APU | Automatische Programmunterstützung | | |
| | | AR | Alphanumerical Reader |
| APU | Auxiliary Power Unit | AR | Amateur Radio |
| APUHS | Automatic Program Unit, High-Speed | AR | Amplifier |
| | | AR | Analog Representation |
| APULS | Automatic Program Unit, Low-Speed | AR | Analogrechner |
| | | AR | Antireflection |
| APW | Augmented Plane Wave | AR | Anzeigeröhre |

- 44 -

# A

| | | | |
|---|---|---|---|
| AR | Application Review | ARC | Automatic Relay Calculator |
| AR | Application Routine | | |
| AR | Arbeitsregister | ARC | Automatic Relay Computer |
| AR | Area | | |
| AR | Argon | ARC | Automatic Remote Control |
| AR | Arithmetic Register | | |
| AR | Arrière | ARC | Automatic Reset Counter |
| AR | Assembly Routine | | |
| AR | Assembly and Repair | ARC | Automatic Resolution Control |
| AR | Assignment Routine | | |
| AR | Asynchronous Repeater | ARC | Automatic Routing Character |
| AR | Attendance Record | | |
| AR | Attention Routine | ARC | Automatically Repaired Computer |
| AR | Ausgaberegister | | |
| AR | Ausgangsrechnung | ARC | Average Response Computer |
| AR | Ausgleichrechnung | | |
| AR | Automatic Radio | ARCADE | Automatic Radar Control And Data Equipment |
| AR | Automatic Reader | | |
| AR | Automatic Routine | ARCAS | Automatic Radar Chain Acquisition System |
| AR | Automatische Regelung | | |
| AR | Automatischer Regler | ARCB | A-Register C-Bit |
| AR | Auxiliary Register | ARCC | Askew Redundacy Check-Character |
| AR | Auxiliary Routine | | |
| ARA | Abbreviated Registered Address | ARCH | Archive |
| | | ARCH | Articulated Computer Hierarchy |
| ARA | Abnormal Return Address | | |
| ARA | Area | ARCH | Automated Reports Control Handling |
| ARAB | A-Register A-Bit | | |
| ARAL | Automatic Record Analysis Language | ARCHI | Archivierungsprogramm |
| | | ARCO | Automatic Reservations and Communications |
| ARAM | Analog Random Access Memory | | |
| | | ARCOM | Arctic Communication satellite |
| ARAPT | Atlantic Research Automatic Position Telemetering | | |
| | | ARCOS | Arzt-Computersystem |
| | | ARCS | Automatic Recognition of Continuous Speech |
| ARAT | Automatic Random Access Transport | | |
| | | ARCS | Automatisiertes Reproduktions-, Copier- und Sortiersystem |
| ARC | Add Row and Constant | | |
| ARC | Aiken Relay Calculator | | |
| ARC | Arcus | ARCT | Askew Redundacy Check-Track |
| ARC | Askew Redundancy Check | | |
| ARC | Atlantic Research Corporation | ARD | Address Register Decoding |
| ARC | Attached Resource Computer | ARD | Automatic Recorder of Deformation |
| ARC | Attendant Recall | ARDA | Analog Recording Dynamic Analyzer |
| ARC | Automatic Range Control | | |
| ARC | Automatic Ratio Control | ARDIS | Army Research and Development Information System |
| ARC | Automatic Reading of Characters | | |
| ARC | Automatic Reception Control | ARDME | Automatic Radar Data Measuring Equipment |
| ARC | Automatic Recovery Computer | ARDME | Automatic Range Detector and Measuring Equipment |

# A

| | | | |
|---|---|---|---|
| ARDS | Advanced Remote Display Station | ARL | Acceptable Reliability Level |
| ARDS | Advance Remote Display System | ARL | Automatic Record Level |
| | | ARM | ACRE/RETAIN Merge |
| ARDT | Automatic Remote Data Terminal | ARM | Address Register Modification |
| ARE | Algebraic Riccati Equation | ARM | Algorithmic Remote Manipulation |
| ARE | Ausgabeeinheit Rechneranschluß | ARM | Ampex Replacement Memories |
| ARE | Automatic Record Evaluation | ARM | Application Reference Manual |
| AREG | A Register | ARM | Armature |
| AREG | Accumulator Register | ARM | Asynchronous Response Mode |
| AREG | Address Register | | |
| ARELEM | Arithmetic Element | ARM | Automated Route Management |
| ARES | Automatic Record Evaluation System | ARM | Availibility, Reliability, Maintainability |
| ARFC | Average Rectified Forward Current | ARMA | Accumulator Reservoir Manifold Assembly |
| ARFPDS | Air Reserve Forces Personnel Data System | ARMA | American Records Management Association |
| ARG | Argument | | |
| ARGA | Appliance, Range, Adjust | ARMA | Auto-Regressive-Moving Average |
| ARGUS | Analytical Reports Gathering and Updating System | ARMACS | Aviation Resources Management And Control System |
| ARGUS | Automatic Routine Generating and Updating System | ARMC | Automatic-repeat Request Mode Counter |
| ARI | Automated Readability Index | ARMIP | Accounting and Reporting Management Improvement Program |
| ARIAS | Augmented Relational Intelligence Analysis System | ARMM | Analysis and Research of Methods for Management |
| ARIEL | Automated Real time Investment Exchange Ltd. | ARMMS | Automated Reconfigurable Modular Multiprocessor System |
| ARIES | Advanced Radar Information Evaluation System | ARMMS | Automated Reliability and Maintainability Measurement System |
| ARIS | Advanced Range Instrumentation Systems | | |
| | | ARMS | ADPE Resources Management System |
| ARIS | Advanced Remote Imaging Systems | ARMS | Airborne Ruggedized Memory System |
| ARIS | Aircraft Recording Instrumentation System | ARMS | Aircraft Resources Management System |
| ARISE | Appointment, Registration, Information System & Evaluation | ARMS | Automatic Radiation Monitoring System |
| ARITH | Arithmetic | ARMSPAN | Argonne Multi-channel Stored Program Analyzer |
| ARITH | Arithmetical | | |
| ARIÜ | Automatisches Registriergerät für Innere Überspannung | ARN | Address Reference Number |
| | | ARN | Arbeitsregister-Nummer |

# A

| | | | |
|---|---|---|---|
| ARND | Around | ARQP | Asset Record Quota Points |
| ARNR | Artikelnummer | ARR | Add Row and Row |
| ARO | After Receipt of Order | ARR | Address Reference Register |
| ARO | Analysis of Records Obtained | ARR | Amsterdamsche Relais Rekenmaschine |
| ARO | Applied Research Objective | ARR | Antenna Rotation Rate |
| ARO | Auxiliary Read-Out | ARR | Anti-Repeat Relay |
| AROM | Alterable Read-Only Memory | ARR | Arrange |
| AROM | Associative Read-Only Memory | ARR | Arrangement |
| ARP | Accept Response | ARR | Automatische Relais-rechenmaschine |
| ARP | Active Recordings Program | ARRAPS | Automatic Repetitive Reset And Program Start |
| ARP | Address Register Position | ARRE | Average Relative Representation Error |
| ARP | Analogous Random Process | ARRF | Automatic Recording and Reduction Facility |
| ARP | Analytical Rework Program | ARS | Accounts Receivable Statement |
| ARP | Arbeitsspeicher-residentes Programm | ARS | Advanced Record System |
| ARP | Automatic Receiver Program | ARS | Airline Reservations System |
| ARP | Automatic Recovery Program | ARS | Analog Recording System |
| ARP | Automatic Relative Plotter | ARS | Analog-Regelsystem |
| ARPA | Advanced Research Project Agency | ARS | Automatic Recording Spectrometer |
| ARPA | American Research Package | ARS | Automatic Route Selection |
| ARPAC | Argentine data Package network | ARS | Automatisiertes Reservierungssystem |
| ARPANET | Advanced Research Project Administration Network | ARS/E | Automatisiertes Reservierungssystem für Eisenbahnen |
| ARPANET | Advanced Research Projects Agency Network | ARSC | Analog Rotation Speed Control |
| ARPL | A Retrieval Process Language | ARSI | Anlageüberwachung Regelung, Steuerung, Informationsgewinnung |
| ARPQ | Asset Record Performance Quota | ARSM | Auswertung von Richtungs- und Streckenmessungen |
| ARPS | Approximate Relation-ship in Performances | ARSN | Automatische Regelung, Speisung, Netz |
| ARQ | Accept Request | ART | Accumulator Read Track |
| ARQ | Area Request | ART | Additional Reference Transmission |
| ARQ | Automatic repeat Request | ART | Additiver Referenzträger |
| ARQ | Automatic Request | ART | Advanced Receiver-Transmitter |
| ARQ | Automatic Request for repeat | ART | Advanced Research and Technology |
| ARQ | Automatic Retrans-mission Request | ART | Arithmetic Reading Test |
| | | ART | Article |
| | | ART | Artificial |

- 47 -

# A

| | | | |
|---|---|---|---|
| ART | Automatic Range Tracking | AS | Active Store |
| ART | Automatic Reporting Telephone | AS | Actual Sign |
| | | AS | Actuarial Science |
| ARTADS | Army Tactical Data System | AS | Actuarial Statistics |
| | | AS | Add-Substract |
| ARTL | Awaiting Results of Trial | AS | Adder Stage |
| ARTRAC | Advanced Range Testing Reporting And Control | AS | Addition Slip |
| | | AS | Additional Storage |
| ARTRAC | Advanced Real-Time Range Control | AS | Address Search |
| | | AS | Address Section |
| ARTS | Advanced Radar Traffic System | AS | Address Selection |
| | | AS | Address Selector |
| ARTS | Audio Response Time-shared System | AS | Address Start |
| | | AS | Address Statement |
| ARTS | Automatic Response Tape System | AS | Address Storage |
| | | AS | Address Store |
| ARTSS | Audio Response Time Shared System | AS | Address Substitution |
| | | AS | Address Switch |
| ARTTIS | Advanced Real Time Total Information System | AS | Address Syllable |
| | | AS | Address System |
| ARTU | Automatic Range Tracking Unit | AS | Addressable Storage |
| | | AS | Addressable Store |
| ARU | Acoustic Resistance Unit | AS | Addressing Scheme |
| ARU | Analog Remote Unit | AS | Addressing Signal |
| ARU | Audio Response Unit | AS | Addressing System |
| ARU | Automatic Range Unit | AS | Advance Selector |
| ARV | Alternate Record-Voice | AS | Aggregate Signal |
| ARWM | A-Register Word Mark | AS | Algebraic Sign |
| ARX | Automatic Retransmission Exchange | AS | Algebraical Sum |
| | | AS | Algorithmic System |
| ARZ | Apothekenrechenzentrum | AS | Alphabetic Sequence |
| ARZ | Ausbildungsrechenzentrum | AS | Alphabetic Sort |
| ARZ | Automatisierungs- und Rationalisierungszentrum | AS | Alphabetic Storage |
| | | AS | Alphabetic String |
| AS | Abfragesignal | AS | Alphanumeric Store |
| AS | Abnormal Statement | AS | Alter Statement |
| AS | Abrechnungssysteme | AS | Alternating Series |
| AS | Absatzsystem | AS | Ammeter Switch |
| AS | Absolute Symbol | AS | Ampere-Second |
| AS | Absolute System | AS | Analog Selection |
| AS | Acceptance Sampling | AS | Analog Signal |
| AS | Access Speed | AS | Analog Store |
| AS | Access Station | AS | Analog System |
| AS | Accessorial Service | AS | Anschlußsteuereinheit |
| AS | Accumulator Specification | AS | Anschlußstufe |
| AS | Account Sequence | AS | Anwendersystem |
| AS | Account Sheet | AS | Anwendungsschnittstelle |
| AS | Accounting Sequence | AS | Anwendungssimulation |
| AS | Accounting System | AS | Anwendungssystem |
| AS | Accumulating Speed | AS | Application Software |
| AS | Accumulator Shift | AS | Arbeitsspeicher |
| AS | Accumulator Sign | AS | Area Separator |
| AS | Acoustic Storage | AS | Arithmetic Section |
| AS | Acoustic Store | AS | Arithmetic Series |
| AS | Active Storage | AS | Arithmetic Shift |

# A

| | | | |
|---|---|---|---|
| AS | Arithmetic Statement | ASB | Additional Sense Byte |
| AS | Arithmetic Subroutine | ASB | Antreiben, Steuern, Bewegen |
| AS | Array Segment | | |
| AS | Assemble Subprogram | ASB | Arbeitssteuerblock |
| AS | Assembler | ASB | Asbestos |
| AS | Assemblersprache | ASB | Asymmetric Sideband |
| AS | Assembly Statement | ASBC | Advanced Standard Buried Collector |
| AS | Assignment Statement | | |
| AS | Assignment Symbol | ASBL | Assembler |
| AS | Associative Storage | ASBLY | Assembly |
| AS | Asymmetric | ASBU | Arab States Broadcasting Union |
| AS | Asymptotisch | | |
| AS | Aufzeichnungsspalt | ASC | Adaptive Signal Correction |
| AS | Ausführungsstruktur | | |
| AS | Ausgang Setzen | ASC | Add Substract Counter |
| AS | Ausgangssignal | ASC | Additive Source Current |
| AS | Ausschalter | ASC | Address Substitution Command |
| AS | Außendienststeuerung | | |
| AS | Automatic Stop | ASC | Advanced Scientific Computer |
| AS | Automation System | | |
| AS | Automatische Steuerung | ASC | Advanced Space Computer |
| AS | Auxiliary Storage | ASC | All-Steps Control |
| AS | Auxiliary Store | ASC | Amount Sign Code |
| AS | Availability Store | ASC | Ampere per Square Centimeter |
| AS | Available Store | | |
| AS... | Advanced Systems Ltd. | ASC | Analog Signal Converter |
| AS/IC | AS Information Center | ASC | Analog Signal Correlator |
| AS/RS | Automatic Storage and Retrieval System | ASC | Analog Strip Chart |
| | | ASC | Arbitrary Sequence Computer |
| ASA | Accelerated Storage Adapter | | |
| | | ASC | Associative Structure Computer |
| ASA | Access Store Address | | |
| ASA | American Standards Association | ASC | AUTODIN Switching Center |
| ASA | Amplifier and Switch Assembly | ASC | Automated System Character |
| ASA | Anti-Static-Agents | ASC | Automated System Charter |
| ASA | Automatic Spectrum Analyzer | ASC | Automatic Selectivity Control |
| ASA | Automatic Systems Analysis | ASC | Automatic Sensitivity Control |
| ASA | Auxiliary Store Area | | |
| ASAC | Automatic Selection of Any Channel | ASC | Automatic Switching Control |
| ASACS | Airborne Surveillance And Control System | ASC | Automatic Synchronized Control |
| ASAG | Auftragssteuer- und Arbeitsgangdaten | ASC | Automatic System Control |
| | | ASC | Auxiliary Store Capacity |
| ASAP | A Scientific Application Programmer | ASC | Auxiliary Switch normally Closed |
| ASAP | Analog System Assembly Pack | ASCA | Automatic Science Citation Alert |
| ASAP | As Soon As Possible | ASCAD | Aufgabe-Spezifischer-CAD-Systeme |
| ASAP | Automated Statistical Analysis Program | | |

# A

| | | | |
|---|---|---|---|
| ASCAT | Analog Self-Checking Automatic Tester | ASDC | Aeronomy and Space Data Center |
| ASCC | Advanced Systems Computer Center | ASDE | Antenna Slave Data Equipment |
| ASCC | Automatic Sequence Controlled Calculator | ASDEC | Automatic Selection of Digital Electronic Computers |
| ASCC | Automatic Sequence Controlled Computer | ASDI | Automatic Selective Dissemination of Information |
| ASCE | American Society of Civil Engineers | ASDIC | Armed Services Documents Intelligence Center |
| ASCII | American Standard Code for Information Interchange | ASDIRS | Army Study Documentation and Information Retrieval System |
| ASCO | Automatische Schnittplanoptimierung | ASDPSIM | Advanced System Data Processing Simulation |
| ASCO | Automatic Substainer Cut-Off | ASDR | Airborne Sample Data Reduction |
| ASCOM | Anti-Static Computer | ASDS | Automatisiertes System der Dispatchersteuerung |
| ASCORE | Automatic Shipboard Checkout and Readiness Equipment | ASDSRS | Automatic Spectrum Display and Signal Recognition System |
| ASCOT | Advanced Storage Control Test | ASDSVN | Army Switched Data and Secure Voice Network |
| ASCOT | Analog Simulation of Competitive Operational Tactics | ASDTIC | Analog Signal to Discrete Time Interval Converter |
| ASCP | Automatic System Checkout Program | ASE | Active Switching Element |
| ASCR | Analog Strip Chart Recorder | ASE | Adaptives Schwellenwertelement |
| ASCS | American Standard Character Set | ASE | Amplified Spontaneous Emission |
| ASCS | Automatic Scan Counter System | ASE | Anisotropic Stress Effect |
| ASCS | Automatic Stabilization and Control System | ASE | Anschlußsteuereinheit |
| | | ASE | Automatic Stabilization Equipment |
| ASCU | Automatic Scanning Control Unit | ASE | Automatic Support Equipment |
| ASD | Advanced Surface Design | | |
| ASD | Advanced Systems Development | ASEE | American Society for Engineering Education |
| ASD | Adverse State Detector | ASEP | Automatic Sequence Execution and Processor |
| ASD | Alphabetic Store Device | | |
| ASD | Assign Symbolic Device | ASER | Amplification by Stimulated Emission of Radiation |
| ASD | Auftragssteuerdaten | | |
| ASD | Automated Structural Design | ASETS | Automatic Storage Evaluator Test System |
| ASD | Automatic Synchronized Discriminator | ASF | Additional Storage Feature |
| ASDA | Advanced Saturn Data Adapter | ASF | Ampere per Square Foot |
| | | ASF | Amplitude Scale Factor |
| ASDACS | Acoustic Signal Data Analysis and Conversion System | ASF | Arithmetic Statement Function |

# A

| | | | |
|---|---|---|---|
| ASF | Assign Form | ASKS | Automatic Station Keeping System |
| ASF | Automatic Signal Filtration | ASL | Above Sea Level |
| ASF | Automatic Store and Forward | ASL | Advanced Simulation Language |
| ASF | Automatische Systemfunktion | ASL | Anschlußleitung |
| ASFW | Automatisiertes System des Finanzwesens | ASL | Association of Symbolic Logic |
| ASGBFR | Assign Buffer | ASL | Automatisiertes System der Leitung |
| ASGC | Advanced Saturn Guidance Computer | ASLIB | Association of Special Libraries and Information Bureaus |
| ASGN | Assign | | |
| ASGND | Assigned | ASLM | Asynchroner/Synchroner Leitungsmultiplexer |
| ASI | Advanced Systems Incorporated | ASLO | Assembly Lay-Out |
| ASI | Alphabetic Subject Index | ASLT | Advanced Solid Logic Technology |
| ASI | Amount of Semantic Information | ASM | Adaptive System |
| ASI | Ampere per Square Inch | ASM | Advanced System Management |
| ASI | Application Software, Incorporated | ASM | Allocation Strategy Module |
| ASI | Automated System Initialization | ASM | Ampex Semiconductor Memory |
| ASIC | AS Information Center | ASM | Analog Storage Module |
| ASID | Address Space Identification | ASM | Arbeitsspeicher-Multiplexer |
| ASID | Address Space Identifier | ASM | Assemble |
| ASID | Alarm Signal Input Device | ASM | Assembleur |
| ASII | American Science Information Institute | ASM | Assembly |
| ASIM | Analogsimulation | ASM | Association for Computing Machinery |
| ASIN | Agricultural Services Information Network | ASM | Association for Systems Management |
| ASINUS | Automatische Schaltungsinterpretation und -Untersuchung | ASM | Asynchronous State Machine |
| ASIRC | Aquatic Sciences Information Retrieval Center | ASM | Automated Space Management system |
| ASIS | Advanced Scientific Instruments | ASM | Autonomous Sequential Machine |
| ASIS | American Society for Information Science | ASM | Auxiliary Storage Manager |
| ASIST | Advanced Scientific Instruments Symbolic Translator | ASMBL | Assemble |
| | | ASMBLR | Assembler |
| ASK | Alphanumeric Standard Keyboard | ASMC | AUTODIN Station Maintenance Console |
| ASK | Amplitude-Shift Keying | ASMDDA | Air Surface Missile Digital Differential Analyzer |
| ASK | Analog Select Keyboard | | |
| ASK | Anschlußkabel | ASME | American Society of Mechanical Engineers |
| ASK | Arbeitsplan-Stammkarte | | |
| ASKA | Automatic System for Kinematic Analysis | ASMUS | Allgemeines Steuerprogramm für Multitask-Systeme |

# A

| | | | |
|---|---|---|---|
| ASN | Average Sample Number | ASPR | Alarm Signal Processing Routine |
| ASO | Alarm System Operation | | |
| ASO | Auxiliary Switch normally Open | ASPRIN | Application Systems and Programs Reference Information Network |
| ASOAP | Army Spectrometric Oil Analysis Program | ASPS | Acoustic Signal Processing System |
| ASOL | Automatisiertes System der Organisatorischen Leitung | ASPS | Automatic Specimen Positioning System |
| ASOP | Automatic Scheduling and Operating Program | ASQC | American Society of Quality Control |
| ASOP | Automated Structural Optimization Program | ASR | Ablaufsteuerrechner |
| | | ASR | Accumulator Shift Right |
| ASP | Ablaufsteuerprogramm | ASR | Address Start Register |
| ASP | Ablaufsteuerungs- programm | ASR | Address Switch Register |
| | | ASR | Amplitudensignalregelung |
| ASP | Activity Scheduling Program | ASR | Analog Shift Register |
| | | ASR | Aufbausystem für die Steuerungs- und Regelungstechnik |
| ASP | Addressable Storage Position | | |
| ASP | Adressenspeicher | ASR | Automatic Send/Receive |
| ASP | Advanced Study Program | ASR | Automatic Speech Recognition |
| ASP | Advanced Support Processor | ASR | Automatic Speech Recognizer |
| ASP | American Selling Price | | |
| ASP | Analyze Sample Pulse | ASR | Automatic Step Regulator |
| ASP | Anwendungssteuerungs- programm | ASR | Automatic Strength Regulation |
| ASP | Arbeitsspeicher | ASR | Available Supply Rate |
| ASP | Association Storage Processor | ASRC | Active Stock Record Card |
| | | ASRDI | Aerospace Safety Research and Data Institute |
| ASP | Associative-Data Structure Package | | |
| ASP | Attached Support Processor | ASRL | Average Sample Run Length |
| ASP | Automatic Sample Processor | ASRS | Automated Shareholder Record System |
| ASP | Automatic Schedule Procedure | ASRS | Automatic Seat Reservations System |
| ASP | Automatic Service Panel | ASRS | Automatic Send/Receive Set |
| ASP | Automatic Servo Plotter | | |
| ASP | Automatic Switching Panel | ASRS | Automatic Storage and Retrieval System |
| ASP | Automatic Synthesis Program | ASRU | Automatic Signal Recognition Unit |
| ASPA | Automated System Performance Analysis | ASS | Analog Simulation System |
| | | ASS | Analogue Switching Subsystem |
| ASPDE | Automatic Shaft Posi- tion Data Encoder | ASS | Anwender-System- Software |
| ASPER | Assembly System Pe- ripheral processors | | |
| | | ASS | Assembler |
| ASPLS | Any Special Symbol | ASS | Assemblersprache |
| ASPM | Automated System for Production Management | ASS | Assembly |
| | | ASS | Außendienst-Steuerungs- system |

# A

| | | | |
|---|---|---|---|
| ASS | Automatic Separation System | AST | Anfertigungsstapelware |
| ASS | Automatic Stabilization System | AST | Anti-Sidetone |
| | | AST | Arbeitsfeld-Steuerwerk |
| ASS | Automatic Start-up System | AST | Assembly and Structure Test |
| ASS | Automatic Station Selection | AST | Asterisk |
| | | AST | Asynchrones Steuergerät |
| ASS | Automatisiertes System der Statistik | AST | Asynchronsteuergerät |
| | | AST | Atlantic Standard Time |
| ASS | Auxiliary Store System | AST | Aufgabenstellung |
| ASSASSIN | Agricultural System for Storage And Subsequent Selection of Information | AST | Auftragssteuerung |
| | | AST | Außenstelle |
| | | ASTA | Automatic System Trouble Analysis |
| ASSB | Asynchronous Single Sideband | ASTABA | Auftragsstammband |
| | | ASTAP | Advanced Statistical Analysis Program |
| ASSB | Assembler | | |
| ASSB | Associative Buffer | ASTAP | Automatic Statistic Analysis Program |
| ASSBL | Assemble | | |
| ASSEM | Assemble | ASTC | Army Satellite Tracking Center |
| ASSEM | Assembly | | |
| ASSEMB | Assembler | ASTE | Association pour le développement des Sciences et Techniques de l'Environnement |
| ASSESS | Airborne Science Shuttle Experiment System Simulation | | |
| ASSET | Automated Spares Simulation Estimating Technique | ASTF | Automatisches System der Truppenführung |
| | | ASTIA | Armed Services Technical Information Agency |
| ASSGN | Assign | | |
| ASSKP | Automatisiertes System des Staatlichen Komitees für Preise | ASTL | Approved Supplier Tab List |
| | | ASTM | American Society for Testing and Materials |
| ASSM | Assembly | | |
| ASSMET | Assembler-Makros für Entscheidungstabellen | ASTME | American Society of Tool and Manufacturing Engineers |
| ASSORT | Automatic System for Selection Of Receiver and Transmitter | ASTOR | Address Storage Register |
| | | ASTP | Ageing and Surveillance Test Program |
| ASSR | Assembler | | |
| ASSRS | Adaptive Step-Size Random Search | ASTP | Automatisches System der Technologischen Produktionsvorbereitung |
| ASSVD | Automatisiertes System zur Sammlung und Verarbeitung von Daten | | |
| | | ASTR | Asynchronous/Synchronous Transmitter/Receiver |
| ASSVI | Automatisiertes System zur Sammlung und Verarbeitung von Informationen | ASTRA | Advanced Static Test Recording Apparatus |
| | | ASTRA | Advanced Structural Analyser |
| ASSY | Assembly | | |
| AST | AEG-Telefunken Software-Technik | ASTRA | Automatic Scheduling with Time integrated Resource Allocation |
| AST | Active Segment Table | ASTRA | Automatic Sorting, Testing, Recording Analysis |
| AST | Add Subtract Time | | |
| AST | Address Selection Track | | |

# A

| | | | |
|---|---|---|---|
| ASTRAC | Arizona Statistical Repetitive Analog Computer | AT | Address Track |
| | | AT | Address Transfer |
| | | AT | Address Translation |
| ASTRAL | Analog Schematic Translator to Algebraic Language | AT | Addressing Technique |
| | | AT | Adreßteil |
| | | AT | Advanced Technology |
| ASTRAL | Assurance and Stabilization Trends for Reliability by Analysis of Lots | AT | Air Temperature |
| | | AT | Aktionsteil |
| | | AT | Algorithm Theory |
| | | AT | Algorithm Translation |
| ASTU | Automatic Systems Test Unit | AT | Alphabetical Tabulator |
| | | AT | Alphanumerische Tastatur |
| ASU | Altitude Sensing Unit | AT | Ambient Temperature |
| ASU | Auxiliary Storage Unit | AT | Ampere-Turn |
| ASUT | Adapter Sub-Unit Tester | AT | Analog Transistor |
| ASV | Angle Stop Value | AT | Analysis Time |
| ASV | Arithmetic Simple Variable | AT | Anpaßteil |
| | | AT | Answer Table |
| ASV | Automatic Self-Verification | AT | Antenna |
| | | AT | Anzeigeteil |
| ASV | Automatische Sprecher-Verifikation | AT | Arithmetic Technique |
| | | AT | Astronomical Time |
| ASVO | Arbeitsschutzverordnung | AT | Atlantic Time |
| ASVOL | Assign Volume | AT | Atmosphere |
| ASW | Anwendersoftware | AT | Atom |
| ASW | Application Software | AT | Atomic Time |
| ASW | Arithmetic Series Weight | AT | Attenuator |
| ASW | Auswahl | AT | Audio Tape |
| ASW | Auxiliary Switch | AT | Audit Trail |
| ASW-A | Auswahl-Ausgabe | AT | Aural Transducer |
| ASWCR | Airborne Surveillance Warning and Control Radar | AT | Ausgangstext |
| | | AT | Auslösetaste |
| | | AT | Automatentabelle |
| ASWF | Arithmetic Series Weight Function | AT | Automatic Test |
| | | AT | Automatic Ticketing |
| ASWG | American Steel and Wire Gage | AT | Automatic Tracking |
| | | AT | Automatic Translation |
| ASWP 1 | Asymptotic Stability With Probability One | AT | Automatic Transmitter |
| | | AT | Autotransformer |
| ASWV | Arithmetic Series Weight Vector | AT | Availability Table |
| | | AT&T | American Telephone & Telegraph |
| ASYLT | Asynchronous Line Terminator | AT/WB | Ampere Turn per Weber |
| ASYMP | Asymptote | ATA | Asynchronous Terminal Adapter |
| AT | Abfragetaste | | |
| AT | Absolute Term | ATA | Additional Tape Attachment |
| AT | Access Technique | | |
| AT | Access Time | ATA | Anschlußsteuerung Tastatur |
| AT | Accounting Tabulating | ATA | Alternate Track Address |
| AT | Accounting Technique | ATA | Alternate Track Assignment |
| AT | Action Time | ATALA | Association pour l'étude et le développement de la Traduction Automatique et de la Linguistique Appliquée |
| AT | Add Time | | |
| AT | Addition Theorem | | |
| AT | Address Table | | |
| AT | Address Tape | | |

# A

| | | | |
|---|---|---|---|
| ATAP | Alternate Track Assignment Program | ATDS | Airborne Technical Data System |
| ATAR | Acquisition Tracking And Recognition | ATDS | Air Tactical Data System |
| ATAS | Automatic Test Analysis System | ATDS | Auxiliary Track Data Storage |
| ATB | Address Trace Block | ATDU | Alphanumeric Terminal Display Unit |
| ATBA | Absolute Time Base Accuracy | ATE | Automatic Test Equipment |
| ATBE | Absolute Time Base Error | ATE | Automatische Tasteinrichtung |
| ATBM | Average Time Between Maintenance | ATEC | Automated Test Equipment Complex |
| ATC | ASCII Terminal Controller | ATEC | Automatic Test Equipment Complex |
| ATC | Adaptive Transform Coding | ATEC | Automatic transmission of Telegrams by Computer |
| ATC | Adress Translation Chip | | |
| ATC | Aerial Tuning Capacitor | | |
| ATC | Air Traffic Control | | |
| ATC | Antenna Tuning Capacitor | ATECO | Automatic Telegram transmission with Computers |
| ATC | Asynchronous Terminal Controller | | |
| ATC | Autocoder To COBOL | ATECO | Automatisches Telegrammvermittlungssystem mit Computer |
| ATC | Automated Technical Control | | |
| ATC | Automatic Temperature Compensation | ATEMIS | Automatic Traffic Engineering and Management Information System |
| ATC | Automatic Threshold Control | | |
| ATC | Automatic Time Control | ATEPO | Auto Test in Elementary Programming and Operation |
| ATC | Automatic Tool Changing | | |
| ATC | Automatic Traffic Control | | |
| ATC | Automatic Tuning Control | ATER | Automatic Testing, Evaluation and Reporting |
| ATCA | Attitude and Translation Control Assembly | | |
| ATCAP | Army Telecommunications Automation Program | ATEV | Approximate Theoretical Error Variance |
| ATCAP | Automatic Thyristor Circuit Analysis Program | ATF | Accounting Tabulating Form |
| ATCC | Automatic Train Control Center | ATF | Actuating Transfer Function |
| ATCD | Attendant access Code | ATF | Algebraic Technological Function |
| ATCE | Automatic Test and Checkout Equipment | ATF | Automatic Target Finder |
| ATD | Alternate Tape Drive | ATFG | Analog Test Function Generator |
| ATD | Automatic Tape Degausser | | |
| ATD | Automatic Tape Delete | ATFM | Associative Thin-Film Memory |
| ATD | Automatic Tape Dispenser | | |
| ATD | Automatic Teaching Device | ATG | Adaptive Threshold Gate |
| | | ATG | Air-To-Ground |
| ATDM | Asynchronous Time-Division Multiplexer | ATG | Auftastgenerator |
| | | ATH | Automatic Tape Handler |
| ATDM | Asynchronous Time-Division Multiplexing | ATI | Action Tape In |
| | | ATI | Antenna Tuning Inductance |
| ATDPS | Airborne Tactical Data Processing System | ATI | Auxiliary Tape Input |

- 55 -

# A

| | | | |
|---|---|---|---|
| ATIP | Analog Tune In Progress | ATO | Automatic Train Operation |
| ATIS | Asahi Technical Information System | ATOLL | Acceptance Test Or Launch Language |
| ATK | Alphabetic Typewriter Keyboard | ATOLS | Automatic Testing On-Line System |
| ATL | Analog Threshold Logic | ATOM | Analog Tree-Organized Multiplexer |
| ATL | Automatic Telling | | |
| ATL | Automatic Test Line | ATOM | Automatic Testing Operating and Maintenance |
| ATLAS | Abbreviated Test Language for All Systems | | |
| ATLAS | Abbreviated Test Language for Avionics Systems | ATOMIC | Automatic Train Operation by Mini-Computer |
| ATLAS | Automated Tape Label Assignment System | ATOMICS | Advanced Traffic Observation and Management Information Collection System |
| ATLAS | Automated Telephone Line Address System | | |
| ATLAS | Automatic Tape Load Audit System | ATP | Acceptance Test Procedure |
| ATLAS | Automatic Translating Aiding System | ATP | Accumulated Total Punching |
| ATLC | Automatic Total Last Card | ATP | Alternative Term Plan |
| | | ATP | Arbeitsteiliger Prozeß |
| ATLE | Adaptive Threshold Logic Elements | ATP | Assembly Test Program |
| | | ATP | Asynchronous Transaction Processing facility |
| ATM | Address Translation Memory | | |
| | | ATP | Automated Test Plan |
| ATM | Ampere Turns per Moter | ATP | Automated Testing Procedure |
| ATM | Arbeitschutztechnische Mittel | | |
| | | ATP | Automatic Text Processing |
| ATM | Asynchronous Time Multiplexing | ATPC | Assistant for Telecommunications Program and Control |
| ATM | Atmosphere | | |
| ATM | Automated Telled Machines | ATPG | Automatic Test Pattern Generation |
| ATM | Auxiliary Tape Memory | | |
| ATMARS | Automatic Transmission Measuring And Recording System | ATPP | Aptitude Test for Programmer Personnel |
| | | ATR | Access Time of Reading |
| ATME | Automatic Test and Measurement Equipment | ATR | Accumulator Track Read |
| | | ATR | All Transistor |
| ATMOS | Adjustable Threshold MOS | ATR | Answer Time Recorder |
| ATMOS | Atmospheric | ATR | Antenna Transmit/Receive |
| ATMPR | Atmospheric Pressure | ATR | Assembly Test Recording |
| ATMS | Advanced Text Management System | ATR | Attribute |
| | | ATR | Automatic Transmitter |
| ATMS | Automatic Transmission Measuring System | ATRAC | Angle Tracking Computer |
| | | ATRID | Automatic Target Recognition Identification and Detection |
| ATN | Actual Test Number | | |
| ATN | Augmented Transition Network | | |
| | | ATRLS | Actual Time of Release |
| ATN | Attention | ATRO | Ausgabe Trommeldatei |
| ATO | Address Transfer Operation | ATRS | Advanced Technology Reader Sorter |
| ATO | Allocate To Order | ATRS | Assembly Test Recording System |
| ATO | Antimony Tin Oxide | | |

# A

| | | | |
|---|---|---|---|
| ATRS | Automatic Tape Response System | ATTD | Avalanche Transit Time Diode |
| ATS | Acquisition and Tracking System | ATTE | Automatic Transistor Test Equipment |
| ATS | Address Transfer Sequence | ATTEN | Attenuation |
| ATS | Advanced Text System | ATTEN | Attenuator |
| ATS | Administrative Terminal System | ATTENUAT | Attenuator |
| ATS | Advanced Teleprocessing System | ATTN | Attention |
| | | ATTN | Attenuation |
| | | ATTNINQ | Attention Inquiry |
| ATS | Advanced Terminal System | ATTO | Avalanche Transmit Time Oscillator |
| ATS | Ampere Turns | ATTR | Average Time To Repair |
| ATS | Applications Technology Satellite | ATTUN | Automatic Tuning |
| | | ATU | Antenna Tuning Unit |
| ATS | Arbitrating Test-and-Set | ATU | Arbeitstakt des Umsetzers |
| ATS | Astronomical Time Switch | ATUC | Average Total Unit Cost |
| ATS | Asymptotic Threshold Shift | ATURS | Automatic Traffic Usage Recording System |
| ATS | Audio-Test-Set | ATV | Allgemeine Technische Vorschriften |
| ATS | Automated Trading System | ATVM | Attenuator-Thermoelement Voltmeter |
| ATS | Automatic Telemetry System | | |
| ATS | Automatic Testing System | ATW | Access Time of Writing |
| | | ATW | Accumulator Track Write |
| | | ATW | Automatic Tape Winder |
| ATS | Automatic Text System | ATWS | Automatic Track While Scan |
| ATS | Automatisches Test-System | | |
| | | ATZ | Abtastzyklus |
| ATS-A | Automatisches Test-System für Analogtest | ATZ | Aufzeichnungstaktzähler |
| | | ATZ | Automatische Telefonzentrale |
| ATS-D | Automatisches Test-System für Digitale Schaltungen | AU | Adjunct Unit |
| | | AU | Angström Unit |
| ATS-D | Automatisches Test-System für Digitaltest | AU | Answer Unit |
| | | AU | Anwendungsunterstützung |
| ATSD | Airborne Traffic and Situation Display | AU | Arbeitsumschaltkontakt |
| | | AU | Arbeitsunterlage |
| ATSIT | Automatic Techniques for the Selection and Identification of Targets | AU | Arbeitsunterweisung |
| | | AU | Arbitrary Unit |
| | | AU | Arithmetic Unit |
| ATSP | Absolute Text and Storage Protect | AU | Assembler Unit |
| | | AU | Astronomical Unit |
| ATT | Adresse Table Travail | AU | Audion |
| ATT | Attenuated | AU | Aurum |
| ATT | Attenuation | AU | Autocoder |
| ATT | Attenuator | AU | Automatic |
| ATT | Audit Trail Tape | AUB | Automatikbetrieb |
| ATT | Avalanche Transmit Time | AUC | Additive Unit Codes |
| ATT... | American Telephone & Telegraph Company | AUC | Alternate Unit Codes |
| | | AUC | American Used Computer Corporation |
| ATTC | Automatic Transmission Test and Control | AUD | Asynchronous Unit Delay |
| | | AUD | Audible |

- 57 -

# A

| | | | |
|---|---|---|---|
| AUD | Auftragsdatei | AUSTIN | Automatic Substrate Tinner Inline |
| AUDAR | Autodyne Detection And Ranging | AUT | Administrative Utilities |
| AUDATEX | Auto-Daten-Expertise | AUT | Advanced User Terminals |
| AUDE | Aufbereitung der Deskriptoren-Konkordanzen | AUT | Amplifier Under Test |
| | | AUT | Authorized |
| AUDEV | Audio Devices | AUT | Automatic |
| AUDI | Auskunftsdienst | AUT MEAS | Automatic Measurement |
| AUDIO | Audiovisual | AUTD | Automated |
| AUDIOVIS | Audiovisual | AUTEVO | Automatisierung der Technologischen Produktionsvorbereitung |
| AUDIT | Aircraft Unitized Diagnostic Inspection and Test | | |
| | | AUTEVO | Automatisierte Technische Vorbereitung |
| AUDIT | Army Uniform Data Inquiry Technique | AUTIREM | Automatisiertes Informations- und Recherchesystem der Metallurgie |
| AUDIT | Automatic Unattended Detection Inspection Transmitter | | |
| | | AUTO | Automatic |
| AUDRE | Automatic Digit Recognizer | AUTO-TRIP | Automatic Transportation Research Investigation Programme |
| AUDREC | Automatic Digit Recognition | | |
| | | AUTOC | Autocorrelation |
| AUE | Allgemeine Überwachungseinrichtung | AUTOCON | Automatic Contour |
| | | AUTODIN | Automatic Digital Network |
| AUE | Amtsübertragung | | |
| AÜ | Additionsübertrag | AUTODIN | Automatic Digital Information Network |
| AÜ | Adressenübertrag | | |
| AÜ | Anpassungsübertrager | AUTODIN | Automatisches Digitales Netz |
| AUF | Auftragsabwicklung | | |
| AUFPRI | Auftragspriorität | AUTODOC | Automated Documentation |
| AUK | Alphanumeric Universal Keyboard | AUTOLIGN | Automatic Alignment |
| | | AUTOLING | Automated Linguistics |
| AUL | Add Unnormalized Long | AUTOMAD | Automatic Adaptation Data |
| AUL | Anrufumleitung | | |
| AUNT | Automatic Universal Translator | AUTOMAP | Automatical Map |
| | | AUTOMAP | Autocoder to Map translator |
| AUNTIE | Automatic Unit for National Taxation and Insurance | | |
| | | AUTOMAP | Automatic Machining Program |
| AUOB | Association des Utilisateurs d'Ordinateurs Burroughs | AUTOMAST | Automatic Mathematical Analysis and Symbolic Translation |
| | | | |
| AURS | Advanced Unit Record System | AUTOMEX | Automatic Message Exchange services |
| AURS | Alone Unit Record System | AUTONET | Automatic Network display |
| AURS | Automatic Unit Record Store | AUTONET | Automatisches Zeichnen von Netzplänen |
| AUS | Add Unnormalized Short | | |
| AUSB | Ausgabe Binär | AUTOPIC | Automatic Personnel Identification Code |
| AUSCOR | Automatic Scanning Correlator | | |
| | | AUTOPIT | Automatic Programming Including Technology |
| AUSI | Association des Utilisateurs de Systèmes Informatiques Cii HB | | |
| | | AUTOPLOT | Automatic Plotter |
| | | AUTOPOL | Automated Programming Of Latches |

# A

| | | | |
|---|---|---|---|
| AUTOPOL | Automatic Programming Of Lathes | AV | Aggregate Value |
| AUTOPROMPT | Automatic Programming of Machine Tools | AV | Algorithmic Variable |
| | | AV | Alphabetic Verifier |
| | | AV | Alternating Voltage |
| AUTOPROPS | Automatic Programming for Positioning System | AV | Analysis of Variance |
| | | AV | Angular Velocity |
| AUTOPSY | Automatic Operating System | AV | Arbeitsvorbereitung |
| | | AV | Arbitrary Value |
| AUTOSATE | Automated data Systems Analysis Technique | AV | Arithmetic Verb |
| | | AV | Array Variable |
| AUTOSCRIPT | Automated System for Composing, Revising, Illustrating and Phototypesetting | AV | Audio-Visual |
| | | AV | Audiovision |
| | | AV | Audiovisuell |
| | | AV | Avant |
| AUTOSPOT | Automatic System for Positioning Of Tools | AV | Average |
| | | AVA | Activity Vector Analysis |
| AUTOSTATIS | Automatic Statewide Auto Theft Inquiry System | AVA | Address-Value Attribute |
| | | AVA | Auftrags-Vergabe-Abrechnung |
| AUTOSTP | Automatic Stop | AVB | Analog Video Bandwidth |
| AUTOSTRAD | Automated System for Transportation Data | AVBL | Available |
| | | AVBS | Absolute Value Bit Synchronizer |
| AUTOSYN | Automatically Synchronous | AVC | Absolute Value Computer |
| AUTOTRAN | Automatic Translation | AVC | Alternate Voice Data |
| AUTOVON | Automatic Voice Network | AVC | Audio/Visual Center |
| AUTRA | Automatische Tragwerkberechnung | AVC | Automatic Voltage Control |
| | | AVC | Automatic Volume Control |
| AUTRA | Automatisierung und Rationalisierung | AVC | Average Variable Costs |
| | | AVD | Anode Voltage Drop |
| AUTRAN | Automatic Utility Translator | AVD | Alternate Voice Data |
| | | AVD | Alternate Voice and Data service |
| AUTRAX | Automatic Traffic Recording and Analysis complex | AVD | Automatic Voice Data |
| | | AVD | Automatic Voltage Digitizer |
| AUX | Auxiliary | | |
| AUX | Auxiliary Store | AVDA | Ausgabe Verarbeitungsdatei |
| AUXFUN | Auxiliary Function | | |
| AUXIL | Auxiliary | AVDS | Automated Vehicle Diagnostic System |
| AUXR | Auxiliary Register | | |
| AUXRC | Auxiliary Recording Circuit | AVDU | Audio-Visual Display Unit |
| | | AVE | Automatic Volume Expander |
| AUXRC | Auxiliary Recording Control | AVE | Automatic Volume Expansion |
| AUXY | Auxiliary | | |
| AV | Ablaufverfolger | AVEDAY | Average Day |
| AV | Absolute Value | AVERT | Automatic Verification Evaluation and Readiness Tester |
| AV | Absolute Vector | | |
| AV | Accumulated Value | | |
| AV | Accumulator Volume | AVF | Availability Factor |
| AV | Actual Value | AVG | Average |
| AV | Addierverstärker | AVGE | Average |
| AV | Address Validity | AVI | Adjustable Voltage Inverter |
| AV | Address Value | | |
| AV | Address Verification | | |

# A

| | | | |
|---|---|---|---|
| AVI | Automatic Vehicle Identification | AVR | Automatic Voltage Regulation |
| AVID | Advanced Visual Information Display | AVR | Automatic Volume Recognition |
| AVID | Airborne Vehicle Identification | AVR | Automatic Volume Regulation |
| AVIDAC | Argonne Version of Institute Digital Automatic Computer | AVR | Automatische Verstärkungsregelung |
| AVIP | Association of Viewdata Information Providers | AVRS | Audio/Video Recording System |
| AVIS | Advanced Visual Information System | AVS | Arbeitsvorbereitungs-System |
| AVIS | Audio-Visual Information System | AVSL | Available Space List |
| AVIS | Automatic Visual Inspection System | AVSS | Aided Visual Sensor System |
| AVL | Adelson-Velskii, Landis-Baum | AVST | Advanced Vehicle Simulation Technique |
| AVL | Available | AVST | Automated Visual Sensitivity Tester |
| AVLS | Automatisches Verkehrserfassungs- und Lenkungssystem | AVT | Audiovisual Tutorial |
| | | AVTA | Automatic Vocal Transaction Analysis |
| AVM | Advanced Virtual Machine | AVTA | Automatic Vocal Transaction Analyzer |
| AVM | Analysis Virtual Machine | AVVC | Altitude Vertical Velocity Computer |
| AVM | Audio-Visual Modulator | | |
| AVM | Automatic Vehicle Monitoring | AW | A Wire |
| | | AW | Abtastwert |
| AVNL | Automatic Video Noise Levelling | AW | Add Word |
| | | AW | Addierwerk |
| AVNL | Automatic Video Noise Limiter | AW | Adding Wheel |
| | | AW | Additional Word |
| AVNL | Automatic Video Noise Limiting | AW | Addressed Word |
| | | AW | Alphanumeric Word |
| AVO | Ampere, Volt, Ohm | AW | Amperewindungen |
| AVOID | Accelerated View Of Input Data | AW | Anfangswort |
| | | AW | Anpassungsnetzwerk |
| AVOLO | Automatic Voice Link Observation | AW | Anschaffungswert |
| | | AW | Anwendung |
| AVON | Amtliches Verzeichnis der Ortsnetzkennzahlen | AW | Anwendungsbereiche |
| | | AW | Anwendungs-Umfeld |
| AVOR | Arbeitsvorbereitung | AW | Apparent Watt |
| AVP | Address Verification Pulse | AW | Atomic Weight |
| | | AW | Ausgabewandler |
| AVP | Attached Virtual Processor | AW | Ausweisleser |
| | | AW Wire | Address Write Wire |
| AVP | Automatic Variable Perforating | AWACS | Airborne Warning And Control System |
| AVR | Absolute Value Representation | AWAG | Automatisches Wähl- und Ansagegerät |
| AVR | Ajustable Voltage Rectifier | AWBE | Automatic Weather Broadcast Equipment |
| AVR | Auto-Voltage Regulator | AWD | Automatische Wähleinrichtung für Datenverbindungen |
| AVR | Automatic Voltage Regulator | | |

# A

| | | | |
|---|---|---|---|
| AWD | Automatische Wähleinrichtung für Datenverkehr | AWSO | Assembly Work Schedule Order |
| AWD | Automatischer Wähldienst | AWT | Await |
| AWDATS | Artillery Weapons Data System | AWTAS | Automated Weapon Test Analysis System |
| AWDATS | Artillery Weapons Data Transmission System | AWU | Atomic Weight Unit |
| | | AWV | Arbeitsgemeinschaft für Wirtschaftliche Verwaltung e.V. |
| AWE | Automatische Wähleinrichtung | | |
| AWG | American Wire Gauge | AWWS | Automated Want and Warrent System |
| AWG | Art Work Generator | | |
| AWG | Auswertungs-Programmgenerator | AX | Axis |
| | | AX | AND Extender |
| AWGN | Additive White Gaussian Noise | AXS | Auxiliary Store |
| | | AYC | Accessory Change |
| AWIP | Automatic Wave Information Processor | AZ | Aktenzeichen |
| | | AZ | Anschlusszentrale |
| AWIS | Automatisches Wartungs-Informationssystem | AZ | Azimuth |
| | | AZA | Arbeitszeitaufwand |
| AWL | Aspektwert-Listen | AZA | Automatische Zeichenanlage |
| AWL | Atlas-Warten-Leitsystem | | |
| AWL | Average Word Load | AZAR | Adjustable Zero, Adjustable Range |
| AWL | Auswahllogik | | |
| AWN | Automaten-Werkzeug-Normen | AZC | Automatic Zero Check |
| | | AZM | Azimuth |
| AWO | Accounting Work Order | AZP | Ausbildungszentren-Platzbuchung |
| AWP | Arbeitswissenschaftliche Projektierung | | |
| | | AZR | Adressenzählregister |
| AWR | Absolutwertrechenmaschine | AZR | Ausgabezielregister |
| | | AZRE | Ausnutzung der Zentralrecheneinheit |
| AWR | Adaptive Waveform Recognition | | |
| | | AZS | Automatic Zero Set |
| AWR | Ausgabewortregister | AZSS | Allzweck-Schnellspeicher |
| AWS | Aktive Work Space | AZV | Abtastzeitrasterverschiebung |
| AWS | Automatic Weather Station | | |

# B

| | | | |
|---|---|---|---|
| B | Band | BA | Besuchsanregung |
| B | Bandbreite | BA | Betriebsart |
| B | Bandwidth | BA | Bildausgabe |
| B | Bar | BA | Bildaustastung |
| B | Barn | BA | Bildschirmanzeigegerät |
| B | Base | BA | Binary Add |
| B | Basis | BA | Binary Adder |
| B | Basiszahl | BA | Binary Addition |
| B | Battery | BA | Binary Arithmetic |
| B | Beam | BA | Bit Access |
| B | Bedienungsteil | BA | Bit Address |
| B | Befehlsregister | BA | Blank Address |
| B | Bell | BA | Block Address |
| B | Bestand | BA | Boolean Addition |
| B | Bias | BA | Boolean Algebra |
| B | Bit | BA | Boundary Alignment |
| B | Block | BA | Branch Address |
| B | Booster | BA | Bridging Amplifier |
| B | Boron | BA | Buchungsautomat |
| B | Branch | BA | Buffer Address |
| B | Break | BA | Buffer Amplifier |
| B | Breite | BA | Bus Available |
| B | Brightness | BA-SIS | Bibliographic Author or Subject Interactive Search |
| B | British Thermal Unit | | |
| B | Brückensymmetrie | | |
| B | Buch | BAA | Broadband Active Analyzer |
| B | Bus | | |
| B | Byte | BAA | Buffer Address Array |
| B & W | Black & White | BAAN | Budget Authorization Account Number |
| B-FMDCPSK | Binary-FM Differentially Coherent Phase-Shift-Keyed | BAAS | British Association for the Advancement of Science |
| B-H | Binary to Hexadecimal | | |
| B-LINE | Bell Laboratories Interpretative system | BAB | Betriebs-Abrechnungs-Bogen |
| B-O | Binary to Octal | BAB | Boundary Address Block |
| B... | Burroughs | BAB | Byte Address Buffer |
| B/C Net | Business Communications Network | BABEK | Basis-Software für dezentrale Berichts- und Kartier-Systeme |
| B/F | Buffer/Formatter | | |
| B/M | Bill of Materials | BABS | Bildausgabe über Bildschirm |
| BA | Barium | | |
| BA | Base | BAC | Basic Address Calculation |
| BA | Base Address | BAC | Binary-Analog Conversion |
| BA | Base Addressing | BAC | Binary Asymmetric Channel |
| BA | Basic | BAC | Biomedical Applications of Computers |
| BA | Basic Address | | |
| BA | Basic Assembler | BAC | Buffer Address Counter |
| BA | Basis Access | BAC | Baud Arbiter/Controller |
| BA | Batch Access | BACE | Basic Automatic Checkout Equipment |
| BA | Batch Assembly | | |
| BA | Battery | BACE | British Association of Consulting Engineers |
| BA | Befehlsaufruf | | |
| BA | Beginning Address | BACIS | Budget Accounting Information System |
| BA | Beschaffungsanweisung | | |

# B

| | | | |
|---|---|---|---|
| BACS | Banks Automated Clearing Services | BAM | Broadcasting Amplitude Modulation |
| BACUS | Booz, Allen and Hamilton Computer Utilization System | BAM | Buffered Access Method |
| | | BAM | Business Analysis Model |
| BAD | Bit Anomaly Detector | BAMBAM | Booklin Alert: Missing Books And Manuscripts |
| BADAS | Binary Automatic Data Annotation System | BAMOS | Batchprocessing Multi-language Operating System |
| BADC | Binary Asymmetric Dependent Channel | BAMS | Band Archiv Management Service |
| BAE | Beacon Antenna Equipment | BAN | Binäraspektname |
| BAE | Betriebswirtschaftliche Analysen, Einzelhandel | BAN | Bundeseinheitliche Artikel-Nummer |
| BAEQS | Bid-Asked Electronic Quotation System | BAN | Best Asymptotically Normal |
| BAG | Begin Area Group | BAN | Bionics Adaptive Network |
| BAG | Bildaufzeichnungsgerät | BANF | Blockanfangsadresse |
| BAH | Basic Adaptive Hardware | BAO | Basic Arithmetic Order |
| BAI | Buffer Alignment Information | BAO | Binary Arithmetical Operation |
| BAIC | Binary Asymmetric Independent Channel | BAP | Band Amplitude Product |
| | | BAP | Basic Assembly Program |
| BAID | Boolean Array Identifier | BAP | Bedingte Anforderung an die Programmsteuerung |
| BAIS | Bulletin Articles Information Subsystem | BAP | Branchenanwendungsprogramm |
| BAL | Balance | | |
| BAL | Balancing | BAPL | Base Assembly Parts List |
| BAL | Base Authorization List | BAPS | Bewegungs- und Ablauf-Programmiersprache |
| BAL | Basic Assembly Language | | |
| BAL | Boite A Lettres | BAPSI | Bildschirm-Arbeitsplatz-Simulation |
| BAL | Branch Linkage | | |
| BAL | Branch And Link | BAPT | Basic Applications Programmer Training |
| BAL | Business Application Language | | |
| | | BAR | Barometer |
| BAL V | Balance Voltage | BAR | Barrier gate |
| BALGOL | Burroughs ALGOL | BAR | Base Adder Register |
| BALITAC | Basic Literal Automatic Coding | BAR | Base Address Register |
| | | BAR | Base Register |
| BALLOTS | Bibliographic Automation of Large Library Operations using Time Sharing | BAR | Basic Address Register |
| | | BAR | Basisadreßregister |
| | | BAR | Battery Acquisition Radar |
| | | BAR | Bereitadressenregister |
| BALM | Block And List Manipulator | BAR | Bookkeeping Address Register |
| BALS | Balancing Set | BAR | Buffer Address Register |
| BALUN | Balanced-to-Unbalanced | BAR | Byte Address Register |
| BALUN | Balancing Unit | BARITT | Barrier Injection Transit Time |
| BAM | Basic Access Method | | |
| BAM | Belegartmerkmal | BARS | Beel Audit Relate System |
| BAM | Bit Access Memory | BARS | Budget Analysis Reporting System |
| BAM | Bitserieller Anschluß für Mehrfachsteuerungen | | |
| | | BARSA | Billing, Accounts Receivable Sales Analysis |
| BAM | Block Allocating Map | | |

# B

| | | | |
|---|---|---|---|
| BART | Bay Area Rapid Transit system | BASIS | Burroughs Advanced Statistical Inquiry System |
| BAS | Basic | | |
| BAS | Basic Activity Subset | BASO | Bandsortierprogramm |
| BAS | Berichts-/und Auskunftssystem | BASP | Backspace |
| | | BASP | Bild-Austast-Synchron-Pegel |
| BAS | Bildaustastsynchron-gemisch | BASP | Biomedical Analog Signal Processor |
| BAS | Bit Access Storage | | |
| BAS | Bit Access Store | BASR | Business Automation Specification Reports |
| BAS | Block Automation System | | |
| BAS | Blockorientiertes Automatisierungssystem | BASTEI | Bankspeicherung Technischer Informationen |
| BAS | Boolean Assignment Statement | BASYS | Basic System |
| | | BAT | Battery |
| BASE | Brokerage Accounting System Elements | BATCH | Block Allocated Transfer Channel |
| BASEX | Basic Experimental language | BATCHG | Battery Charging |
| | | BATE | Base Assembly and Test Equipment |
| BASF... | Badische Anilin und Sodafabrik AG | BATEX | Batch Executive |
| BASIC | Basic Algebraic Symbolic Interpretive Compiler | BATRY | Battery |
| | | BATS | Basic Additional Teleprocessing System |
| BASIC | Basic Appraisal System for Incoming Components | BATS | British Additional Teleprocessing Support |
| BASIC | Basic Automatic Stored Instruction Computer | BATT | Battery |
| BASIC | Beginner's Algebraic Symbolic Interpretive Compiler | BAU | Baseband Assembly Unit |
| | | BAUD | Baudot |
| | | BAV | Btx-Anwendervereinigung |
| BASIC | Beginners All purpose Symbolic Instruction Code | BAX | Beacon Airborne X-band |
| | | BAY | Bayonett |
| | | BAZ | Bandmarke Aufzeichnen |
| BASIC | Biological Abstracts Subjects In Context | BAZ | Batteriezusatz |
| | | BB | Back-to-Back |
| BASIC-X | BASIC-Extended | BB | Bandblock |
| BASIC ASS | BASIC Assembler | BB | Baseband |
| BASICPAC | Basic Package Computer | BB | Basic Block |
| BASICPAC | Basic Processor And Computer | BB | Begin Block |
| | | BB | Begin Bracket |
| BASICPAC | Battle Area Surveillance and Integrated Communications Processor And Computer | BB | Begin Bracket indicator |
| | | BB | Bereitschaftsbetrieb |
| | | BB | Best Best |
| | | BB | Besuchsbericht |
| BASIS | Banken-Service-Informations-System | BB | Betriebsbereich |
| | | BB | Binary Base |
| BASIS | Battelle Automated Search Information System | BB | Boole & Babbage Company |
| | | BB | Breakboard |
| BASIS | Bausteinsystem für Integrierte Steuerung | BB | Breitband |
| | | BB | Broadband |
| BASIS | Bibliothekarisches-Analytisches System zur Informationsspeicherung | BB | Buchungsbeleg |
| | | BB | Buchungsbescheinigung |
| | | BB | Busy Bit |
| BASIS | Budgetary And Scheduling Information System | BBA | Baseband Amplifier |
| | | BBB | Baseband Breadboard |

# B

| | | | |
|---|---|---|---|
| BBC | Binary Block Coding | BC | Basic Control |
| BBC | Broadband Conducted | BC | Batch Cancel |
| BBC | British Broadcasting Corporation | BC | Batched Compilation |
| | | BC | Battery Charger |
| BBC | Building Block Concept | BC | Bayonet Catch |
| BBD | Banques et Bases de Données | BC | Bedienungscode |
| | | BC | Befehlscode |
| BBD | Bucket Brigade Devices | BC | Before Computer |
| BBE | Binary Block Encoding | BC | Begin Column |
| BBK | Bread-Board Kit | BC | Beginning Character |
| BBK | Breitband-Kommunikation | BC | Bell Canada |
| BBK | Buchführung-Bilanz-Kostenrechnung | BC | Between Center |
| | | BC | Bidecimal Code |
| BBL | Basic Business Language | BC | Bidirectional Counter |
| BBL | Buried-Bit-Line | BC | Bin Card |
| BBM | Break Before Make | BC | Binärcode |
| BBN | Bolt Beranek and Newmann | BC | Binary Card |
| | | BC | Binary Cell |
| BBN | Bundeseinheitliche Betriebsnummer | BC | Binary Channel |
| | | BC | Binary Character |
| BBO | Binary Boolean Operation | BC | Binary Code |
| BBO | Booster Burn-Out | BC | Binary Coded |
| BBO | Gesamtverband Büromaschinen, Büromöbel, Organisationsmittel E.V. | BC | Binary Coding |
| | | BC | Binary Command |
| | | BC | Binary Conversion |
| BBOL | Building Block Oriented Language | BC | Binary Counter |
| | | BC | Biquinary Code |
| BBP | Batch Bulk Processing | BC | Bit Capacity |
| BBP | Building Block Principle | BC | Bit Chain |
| BBR | Bedarfs-/und Bestellrechnung | BC | Bit Check |
| | | BC | Bit Code |
| BBR | Broadband Radiated | BC | Bit Combination |
| BBS | Band-Betriebssystem | BC | Bit Configuration |
| BBS | Bang-Bang Servo | BC | Blank Card |
| BBS | Basis-Betriebssystem | BC | Blank Character |
| BBS | Bedienungsblattschreiber | BC | Blank Column |
| BBS | Betriebsblattschreiber | BC | Blank Command |
| BBT | Bundesverband Bürotechnik | BC | Blanking Circuit |
| | | BC | Blind Copy |
| BBUG | Bode & Babbage Uses Group | BC | Block Check |
| | | BC | Block Command |
| BBV | Breitbandvermittlung | BC | Block Count |
| BC | Back-Connected | BC | Boolean Coding |
| BC | Balance Card | BC | Boolean Complementation |
| BC | Balance Column | BC | Boundary Condition |
| BC | Balance Computer | BC | Branch Conditional |
| BC | Balance Control | BC | Branch on Condition |
| BC | Balance Counter | BC | Breaking Capacity |
| BC | Balanced Current | BC | Brightness Contrast |
| BC | Bare Copper | BC | Broadcast |
| BC | Base Collector | BC | Broadcast Control |
| BC | Base Connection | BC | Buffer Cell |
| BC | Base Count | BC | Buffer Cycle |
| BC | Basic Code | BC | Buffered Computer |
| BC | Basic Computer | BC | Büro-Computer |

# B

| | | | |
|---|---|---|---|
| BC | Burroughs Corporation | BCDIC | Binary Coded Decimal Information Code |
| BC | Bus Compatible | | |
| BC | Business Computer | BCDIC | Binary Coded Decimal Interchange Code |
| BC | Byte Counter | | |
| BCA | Basic Channel Adapter | BCDP | Battery Control Data Processor |
| BCA | Binary Coded Address | | |
| BCA | Buffered Communications Adapter | BCDP | Bubble Chamber Data Processing |
| BCAC | British Conference on Automation and Computation | BCDS | Board Command Data Sort |
| | | BCE | Beam Collimation Error |
| | | BCE | Boolean-Controlled Elements |
| BCAM | Basic Communication Access Method | | |
| | | BCE | Branch Command Execution |
| BCB | Binary Code Box | | |
| BCB | Bit Control Block | BCED | Bibliography of the Computer in Environmental Design |
| BCB | Block Control Byte | | |
| BCB | Broadcast Band | | |
| BCB | Buffer Control Block | BCF | Basic Concentration Facility |
| BCB | Button Cell Battery | | |
| BCC | Basis-Computer-Center | BCF | Basic Control Frequency |
| BCC | Binary Code Conversion | BCF | Bandpass Crystal Filter |
| BCC | Binary Coded Character | BCFSK | Binary Code Frequency Shift Keying |
| BCC | Binary Convolution Code | | |
| BCC | Block Character Check | BCG | Bidirectional Categorical Grammar |
| BCC | Block Check Character | | |
| BCC | Body-Centered Cubic | BCH | Binary Control Header |
| BCCC | Ballistic Compressor Computer Code | BCH | Binary Coded Hollerith |
| | | BCH | Bits per Circuit per Hour |
| BCCD | Bulk CCD | BCH | Block Control Header |
| BCCD | Buried CCD | BCH | Bose Chaudhuri |
| BCD | Base Commune de Données | BCHNR | Batch Number |
| BCD | Between Comfort and Discomfort | BCI | Balance Computer Index |
| | | BCI | Battery Condition Indicator |
| BCD | Binär Codiert Dezimal | | |
| BCD | Binär Codierte Dezimalform | BCI | Bell Canada International |
| | | BCI | Binary Coded Information |
| BCD | Binär Codierte Dezimalziffer | BCI | Box Car Integrator |
| | | BCI | Broadcast Interference |
| BCD | Binary Coded Data | BCK | Block |
| BCD | Binary Coded Decimal | BCL | Base-Coupled Logik |
| BCD | Binary Coded Digit | BCL | Basic Command Language |
| BCD | Binary Counted Decimal | BCL | Basic Counter Line |
| BCD | Blank Column Detection | BCL | Broadcast Listener |
| BCD | Business Conditions Digest | BCL... | Business Computer Ltd. |
| BCD/B | Binary-Coded Decimal/Binary | BCM | Basic Control Monitor |
| | | BCM | Battery Control and Monitor |
| BCD/Q | Binary-Coded Decimal/Quaternary | | |
| | | BCM | Binary Choice Model |
| BCDC | Binary Coded Decade Counter | BCM | Binary Code Memory |
| | | BCM | Binary Coded Matrix |
| BCDC | Binary Coded Decimal Counter | BCM | Binary Conversion Matrix |
| | | BCM | Bound Control Module |
| BCDD | Binary Coded Decimal Digit | BCM | Business Calculating Machine |

- 67 -

# B

| | | | |
|---|---|---|---|
| BCMOS | Bipolar CMOS | BCT | Bushing Current Transformer |
| BCN | Beacon | | |
| BCN | Binary Coded Notation | BCU | Basic Counter Unit |
| BCN | Binary Coded Number | BCU | Binary Counting Unit |
| BCNF | Boyce-Codd Normal Form | BCU | Block Control Unit |
| BCO | Basic Calculating Operation | BCU | Buffer Control Unit |
| | | BCU | Bus Control Unit |
| BCO | Battery Cut-Off | BCUG | Bilateral Closed User Group with outgoing |
| BCO | Binary Coded Octal | | |
| BCO | Bridge Cuttoff | BCUGO | Bilateral Closed User Group with Outgoing |
| BCOE | Bench Checkout Equipment | | |
| | | BCV | Brightness Contrast Value |
| BCOM | Burroughs Computer Output Microfilm | BCV | Bus Control Unit |
| | | BCW | Binary Code Word |
| BCP | Basic Control Program | BCW | Buffer Control Word |
| BCP | Bit Controlled Protocol | BCW | Buffing Control Word |
| BCP | Byte Control Protocol | BCWL | Binary Code Word Length |
| BCPL | Basic Combined Programming Language | BCWP | Budgeted Cost for Work Performed |
| BCPL | Bootstrap Combined Programming Language | BCWS | Budgeted Cost for Work Scheduled |
| BCR | Branch and Count Register | BD | Band |
| | | BD | Base Diameter |
| BCROS | Balanced Capacitor Read Only Storage | BD | Base de Données |
| | | BD | Basic Data |
| BCRS | Bar-Code Reader/Sorter | BD | Basis-Datenverarbeitung |
| BCRT | Binary Coded Range Time | BD | Baud |
| BCRT | Bright Cathode Ray Tube | BD | Begrenzer/Demodulator |
| BCRTS | Binary Coded Range Time Signal | BD | Belegdrucker |
| | | BD | Bezugsdämpfung |
| BCS | Basic Combined Subset | BD | Bibliographic Data |
| BCS | Basic Computer System | BD | Binärer Dekoder |
| BCS | Biocomputer Statistics | BD | Binary Decoder |
| BCS | Blip Counter System | BD | Binary Digit |
| BCS | Block Check Sequence | BD | Binary Display |
| BCS | Block Control Signal | BD | Binary Divide |
| BCS | Bombing Computer Set | BD | Binary-to-Decimal |
| BCS | Bridge Control System | BD | Bit Density |
| BCS | British Computer Society | BD | Bitdichte |
| BCS | Broadcast Communications System | BD | Blattdrucker |
| | | BD | Block Data |
| BCS | Buffer Cycle Select | BD | Block Diagram |
| BCS | Business Communications System | BD | Blockdiagramm |
| | | BD | Board |
| BCS | Business Communications Sciences, Inc. | BD | Booking Data |
| | | BD | Bouclage Distant |
| BCS | Business Control System | BD | Bus Driver |
| BCSOC | Binary Convolutional Self-Orthogonal Code | BD | Bus Duct |
| | | BD | Business Data |
| BCST | Broadcast | BD | Byte Device |
| BCSTN | Broadcasting Network | BDA | Binary Digit Adder |
| BCT | Bandwidth Compression Technique | BDA | Block Decoder Assembly |
| | | BDAM | Basic Direct Access Method |
| BCT | Binary Coded Tape | | |
| BCT | Branch on Count | BDC | Back-up Digital Computer |

# B

| | | | |
|---|---|---|---|
| BDC | Bin Data Cell | BDOS | BASIC Disk Operating System |
| BDC | Binary Decimal Counter | | |
| BDC | Binary Differential Counter | BDP | Basic Data Processing |
| | | BDP | Bulk Data Processing |
| BDC | Binary to Decimal Conversion | BDP | Business Data Processing |
| | | BDPI | Base Data Processing Installation |
| BDC | Binary-Decimal Converter | | |
| BDC | Bomb Data Center | BDPO | Business Data Processing Operation |
| BDCS | Basic Disk Operating System | | |
| | | BDPS | Brigade Data Processing System |
| BDCT | Broadcast | | |
| BDD | Binary Digital Data | BDPSC | Basic Data Processing Systems Center |
| BDD | Binary-to-Digital Decoder | | |
| BDDPI | Banque de Données du Droit de la Propriété Industrielle | BDPSK | Binary Differential Phase-Shift Keying |
| | | BDS | Base Data System |
| BDE | Batch Data Exchange | BDS | Base Divider Strip |
| BDE | Betriebsdatenerfassung | BDSG | Bundesdatenschutzgesetz |
| BDE | Bright Display Equipment | BDR | Base de Données Relationnelles |
| BDEAP | Bedienungs-Ein/Ausgabe-Programm | | |
| | | BDR | Base de Données Réparties |
| BDEC | Befehlsdecodierung | BDR | Basic Data Records |
| BDES | Batch Data Exchange Services | BDS | Baudatenservice |
| | | BDR | Bell Does not Ring |
| BDF | Base Detonating Fuse | BDS | Basis-Dialog-System |
| BDF | Boxcar Doppler Filter | BDS | Betriebsdaten-verarbeitungsstation |
| BDF | Bus Differential | | |
| BDG | Beacon Data Generation | BDS | Bias Discrete Spot |
| BDG | Bridge | BDS | Binary Decade Scaler |
| BDG | Bridging | BDS | Binary Digit System |
| BDH | Bearing, Distance and Heading | BDS | Block Data Statement |
| | | BDS | Block Data Subprogram |
| BDHI | Bearing, Distance, Heading Indicator | BDSG | Bundesdatenschutzgesetz |
| | | BDSP | Basic Data Set Project |
| BDI | Base-Diffusion Isolation | BDT | Base Deck to binary Tape |
| BDI | Bearing Deviation Indicator | BDT | Binary Deck to Tape |
| | | BDT | Binder Datentechnik |
| BDI | Betriebsdaten-Ist-Erfassungsgerät | BDT | Büro- und Datentechnik |
| | | BDT | Burst Delay Timer |
| BDI | Binary Discrete Input | BDTD | Balanced Digital Transmisson Device |
| BDI | Bombardier Data Indicator | | |
| BDI | Buffered Direct Injection | BDTR | Basic Data Transmission Routine |
| BDIA | Base Diameter | | |
| BDK | Bedienungselement, Kombiniert | BDU | Basic Device Unit |
| | | BDU | Basic Display Unit |
| BDL | Bad Data Lister | BDU | Biomedical Display Unit |
| BDL | Basic Design Language | BDV | Basis-Datenverarbeitung |
| BDL | Battery Data Link | BDV | Breakdown Voltage |
| BDLC | Burroughs Data Link Control | BDW | Betriebsgesellschaft Datenverarbeitung für Wertpapiergeschäfte |
| BDM | Binary Delta Modulation | | |
| BDM | Binary Digital Multiplier | BDW | Binary Data Word |
| BDMS | Burroughs Data Management System | BDW | Block Descriptor Word |
| | | BDWEK | Board Discrete Wire Equivalent List |
| BDO | Bus for Data Output | | |

- 69 -

# B

| | | | |
|---|---|---|---|
| BE | Back End | BED | Box External Data |
| BE | Band Elimination | BEDA | Bearbeitungsdauer |
| BE | Base Ejection | BEDAS | Betriebs-Daten-System |
| BE | Base Equation | BEE | Business Efficiency Exhibition |
| BE | Basic Equation | | |
| BE | Basiseinrichtung | BEEC | Binary Error Erasure Channel |
| BE | Batch End | | |
| BE | Bauelement | BEEF | Business and Engineering Enriched FORTRAN |
| BE | Bedienereingriff | | |
| BE | Beschaltungseinheit | BEER | Binary-Element Error Ratio |
| BE | Betriebseinheit | | |
| BE | Betriebselektronik | BEF | Band-Elimination Filter |
| BE | Betriebserde | BEF | Basic External Function |
| BE | Bezugselektrode | BEF | Buffered Emitter Follower |
| BE | Bildschirmeinheit | BEFA | Bildeingabe vom Fernsehabtaster |
| BE | Binding Energy | | |
| BE | Block End | BEFR | Betriebs-/Ersatz-Fixierregister |
| BE | Boolean Expression | | |
| BE | Bose-Einstein | BEG | Beginning |
| BE | Branch on Equal | BEGNR | Beginning Number |
| BE | Breaker End | BEGOREC | Beginning Of Record |
| BE ELIM | Band Elimination | BEGSR | Begin Subroutine |
| BE FAP | Bell laboratories FORTRAN Assembly Program | BEGUM | Belegverarbeitung für Girozentrale Unter Monitorsteuerung |
| BEA | Burroughs Extended ALGOL | BEH | Bulk Erase Head |
| | | BEIR | Biological Effects of Ionizing Radiation |
| BEAC | Boeing Engineering Analog Computer | | |
| | | BEJ | Base-Emitter Junction |
| BEACON | British European Airways Computer Network | BEK | Betriebsmitteleingabekarte |
| | | BEKR | Betriebs-/Ersatz-Kippstufenregister |
| BEAMA | British Electrical and Allied Manufacturers Association | | |
| | | BEL | Bell |
| | | BEL | Basic Equipment List |
| BEAMOS | Beam Accessed MOS | BELFAST | Bezugsregulierung, Lieferscheine, Fakturierung, Statistiken (Programmsystem für Zeitschriftengroßhandel) |
| BEAMOS | Beam Accessible MOS | | |
| BEAMOS | Beam Addressed MOS | | |
| BEAMS | Base Engineer Automated Management System | | |
| BEAP | Bedienungs-Ein-/Ausgabeprogramm | BELGFE | Beleglesefehlerprogramm für Datensichtgeräte |
| BEAR | Bulk Easy Access Readout | BELL | Bildeingabe vom Lochbandleser |
| BEAST | Brookings Economics And Statistical Translator | | |
| | | BEM | Biax Element Memory |
| | | BEMA | Business Equipment Manufacturers Association |
| BEB | Beam Entry Buffer | | |
| BEBS | Bestellblattschreiber | BEMF | Back Electromotive Force |
| BEBU | Betriebsbuchhaltung | BENDEX | Beneficiary Data Exchange |
| BEC | Binary Erasure Channel | | |
| BEC | British Engineers Club | BEP | Back-End-Processing |
| BEC | Burst-Error Channel | BEP | Bit Error Probability |
| BEC | Business Electronics Computer | BEP | Budget Execution Plan |
| | | BEPA | Binding Energy Per Atom |
| BECO | Booster Engine Cut-Off | BEPI | Budget Estimates Presentation Instruction |
| BED | Bridge-Element Delay | | |

# B

| | | | |
|---|---|---|---|
| BEPOC | Burrough's Electrographic Printer-plotter for Ordenance Computing | BF | Basic Format |
| | | BF | Basisfrequenz |
| | | BF | Batch Fabrication |
| BEPP | Binding Energy Per Particle | BF | Beat-Frequency |
| | | BF | Beauftragbare Funktion |
| BER | Binary Error Rate | BF | Beauftragte Funktion |
| BER | Bit Error Rate | BF | Befehlsfolgeregister |
| BER | Block Error Rate | BF | Best Fit |
| BERGE | Berichtegenerator | BF | Bewertungsfaktor |
| BERT | Basic Energy Reduction Technology | BF | Binary Function |
| | | BF | Block Factor |
| BERT | Bit Error Rate Tests | BF | Block Format |
| BES | Balanced Electrolyte Solution | BF | Blockungsfaktor |
| | | BF | Bold Face |
| BES | Besetzt | BF | Boolean Function |
| BES | Biax Element Store | BF | Bottom Face |
| BES | Block Error Status | BF | Branching Filter |
| BES | Bose-Einstein Statistics | BF | Breaker Failure |
| BES | Breitband-Einheitssystem | BF | Buffer |
| BESR | Betriebs-/Ersatz-Steuerregister | BF | Byte Field |
| | | BFA | Befehlsausgabe |
| BESS | Binary Electromagnetic Signal Signature | BFA | Buchungs-/und Fakturierautomat |
| BESSY | Betriebsdaten-Erfassungs- und Steuerungssystem | BFC | Budget and Forecast Calendarization |
| BEST | Basic Executive Scheduler and Timekeeper | BFCO | Band Filter Cutoff |
| | | BFD | Basic Field Descriptor |
| BEST | Business Electronic data processing Systems Technique | BFD | Beat-Frequency Detection |
| | | BFD | Begin Form Description |
| | | BFD | Bill Feed Device |
| BEST | Business Equipment Software Technique | BFD | Boolean Function Designator |
| BEST | Business Executive System for Time-sharing | BFE | Beam Forming Electrode |
| | | BFER | Base Field-Effect Resistor |
| BET | Balanced Emitter Technology | BFF | Buffered Flip-Flop |
| | | BFG | Binary Frequency Generator |
| BET | Balanced Emitter Transistor | BFID | Boolean Function Identifier |
| BET | Block Equivalence Tape | BFL | Back Focal Length |
| BETA | British Equipment Trade Association | BFL | Bandreduktion durch Frequenzverschachte- lung und mit Hilfe eines Laufzeitgliedes |
| BETA | Business Equipment Trade Association | | |
| BETINA | Bausteine für Ein Techni- sches Informations- system mit Netzanalyse | | |
| | | BFL | Beginning File Label |
| | | BFL | Buffered FET Logic |
| BEU | Basic Encoding Unit | BFMDS | Base Flight Management Data System |
| BEU | Binary Elementary Unit | | |
| BEX | Broadband Exchange | BFO | Beat-Frequency Oscillator |
| BEX | Broadside Exchange | BFORM | Budget Formulation |
| BEZNR | Bezirk-Nummer | BFP | Buffered Fast Printer |
| BF | Back-Feed | BFP | Built-in Functions Program |
| BF | Backface | BFPDDA | Binary Floating Point Digital Differential Analyzer |
| BF | Base Formula | | |
| BF | Base Fuse | | |

# B

| | | | |
|---|---|---|---|
| BFPHC | Basic Filter Power Handling Capacity | BH | Block Head |
| BFPR | Binary Floating Point Resistor | BH | Brake Horsepower |
| BFR | Barrier Film Rectifier | BH | Branch on High |
| BFR | Betriebsführungsrechner | BH | Brinell Hardness |
| BFR | Block Format Recording | BH | Buchhaltung |
| BFRD | Buffered | BHA | Base Helix Angle |
| BFRST | Buffer Start | BHC | Block Hardware Code |
| BFS | Band Filter Set | BHC | Blockhouse Computer |
| BFS | Bredth First Search | BHD | Binary Homing Device |
| BFS | Business File System | BHD | Bulkhead |
| BFTES | Business Function Translation and Execution System | BHG | Bauhauptgruppen |
| | | BHN | Brinell Hardness Number |
| | | BHOLD | Background Hold |
| | | BHP | Brake Horse-Power |
| | | BHR | Block Handling Routine |
| BG | Back Gear | BHS | Batteriehauptschalter |
| BG | Background | BHS | Binding Head Steel |
| BG | Bandgerät | BHSASSC | Block Handler Set Association |
| BG | Bandgeschwindigkeit | BHSL | Basic Hytran Simulation Language |
| BG | Basic Group | | |
| BG | Baugruppe | BI | Base Identifier |
| BG | Baugruppen und Geräte | BI | Base Injection |
| BG | Bearing | BI | Basic Information |
| BG | Bedienungsgröße | BI | Basic Instruction |
| BG | Bildschirmgerät | BI | Battery Inverter |
| BG | Bit Group | BI | Bezirksinspektor |
| BG | Bitgruppe | BI | Binary Information |
| BG | Block Gap | BI | Binary Input |
| BG | Bus Grant | BI | Binary Item |
| BG | Business Graphik | BI | Blank Instruction |
| BG-NR | Baugruppennummer | BI | Blanking Input |
| BGAM | Basic Graphic Access Method | BI | Block Instruction |
| | | BI | Branch Instruction |
| BGBL | Bundesgesetzblatt | BI | Branching Instruction |
| BGC | Binary Group Code | BI | Breakpoint Instruction |
| BGCOB | Background-compiler COBOL | BI | Buffer Index |
| | | BI-QUIN | Bi-quinary |
| BGD | Bloc de Gestion Directe | BIADI | Bureau Inter-Administration de Documentation Informatique |
| BGDD | Board Gardner Denver Data | | |
| BGE... | Bull General Electric | BIAM | Banque d'Information Automatisée sur les Médicaments |
| BGF | Basic Group Formation | | |
| BGP | Background Program | | |
| BGR | Begrenzungsregelung | BIAR | Base Interrupt Address Register |
| BGS | Beacon Ground S-band | | |
| BGS | Bildschirmgruppensteuergerät | BIAS | Bibliotheks-Ausleihesystem |
| BGT | Baugruppenträger | BIAT | Burn-In/Aging Tester |
| BGT | Basic Group Translator | BIB | Bildungszentrum für Informationsverarbeitende Berufe |
| BGU | Business Graphics Utility | | |
| BH | Basic Hardware | | |
| BH | Befehl Holen | | |
| BH | Binary-to-Hexadecimal | BIB | Biographical Information Blank |
| BH | Block Handler | | |

# B

| | | | |
|---|---|---|---|
| BIBD | Balanced Incomplete Block Designs | BIGENA | Bibliography and Index of Geology Exclusive of North America |
| BIBEAS | Bibliotheks-Eingabe-Ausgabe-System | BIGFET | Bipolar Insulated Gate FET |
| BIBLIO | Bibliotheksautomatisierung | BIGFON | Breitbandiges Integriertes Glasfaser-Fernmelde-ortsnetz |
| BIBO | Bounded Input Bounded Output | | |
| BIBOM | Binary Input-Binary Output Machine | BII | Background Illumination Intensity |
| BIBOMM | Binary Input-Binary Output Moore Machine | BIKOS | Büroinformations- und -Kommunikations-systeme |
| BIC | Bearer Identification Code | | |
| BIC | Biographical Inventory Creativity | BIL | Base Isolation Level |
| | | BIL | Block Input Length |
| BIC | Bureau of International Commerce | BIL | Blue Indicating Lamp |
| | | BIL | Buried Injector Logic |
| BICARSA | Billing, Inventory Control, Accounts Receivable, Sales Analysis | BILA | Battelle Institute Learning Automation |
| | | BILE | Balanced Inductor Logical Element |
| BICEPT | Book Indexing with Context and Entry Points from Text | BILI | Basic Issue List Items |
| | | BIM | Beginning of Information Mark |
| BICS | Burroughs Inventory Control System | BIM | Beginning of Information Marker |
| BIDAP | Bibliographic Data Processing program | BIM | Biographical Inventory for Medicine |
| BIDEC | Binary-to-Decimal | | |
| BIDEC | Binary-to-Decimal Converter | BIM | British Institute of Management |
| BIDS | Bendix Integrated Data System | BIM | Buslink-Interface-Moduln |
| | | BIMAC | Bistable Magnetic Core |
| BIDS | Burroughs Input and Display terminal | BIMACS | Blood bank Information and Management Control System |
| BIE | Branch Instruction Execution | | |
| | | BIMCAM | British Industrial Measuring and Control Apparatus Manufacturer's association |
| BIEE | British Institute of Electrical Engineers | | |
| BIFET | Bipolar Field Effect Transistor | | |
| | | BIMOS | Bipolar MOS |
| BIFID | Bifurcation Identification program | BIMS | Battlefield Integration Management System |
| BIFOA | Betriebswirtschaftliches Institut Für Organisation und Automation | BIN | Basic Information Network |
| | | BIN | Billion Instructions |
| | | BIN | Binary |
| BIFORE | Binary Fourier Representation | BIN | Binär |
| | | BINAC | Binary Automatic Computer |
| BIFS | Bell Information Flow System | BINET | Bicentennial Information Network |
| BIG | Base d'Information Généralisée | | |
| | | BINOM | Binominal |
| BIG | Bevan Information Generator | BINOMEXP | Binominal Expansion |
| | | BINPT | Binary Point |
| BIG | Business Investment Game | BINV | Binärsignalverarbeitung |

- 73 -

# B

| | | | |
|---|---|---|---|
| BIO | Basic Input/Output | BIS | Bereichs-Informations-Systeme |
| BIO | Basic Input/Output support program package | BIS | Betriebliches Informationssystem |
| BIO | Biological Information-processing Organization | BIS | Betriebswirtschaftliches Informationssystem |
| BIOM | Buffer Input-Output Memory | BIS | Bibliothekssatz |
| BIOMED | Biomedizinische Datenbank | BIS | Binary Information Signal |
| BIONICS | Biological electronics | BIS | Binary Input Signal |
| BIOR | Business Input/Output Rerun compiling system | BIS | Brain Information Service |
| | | BIS | Bureau d'Information Software |
| BIOS | BASIC Input/Output Supervisor | BIS | Business Information Service |
| BIOS | BASIC Input/Output System | BIS | Business Instruction Set |
| BIOS | Biological Satellite | BISAD | Business Information System Analysis and Design |
| BIOSIS | Bioscience Information Service | | |
| BIP | Binary Image Processor | BISAM | Basic Indexed Sequential Access Method |
| BIP | Books in Print | | |
| BIP | Bootstrap Input Program | BISDAM | Basic Index Sequential Data Access Method |
| BIP | Brutto-Inlandsprodukt | | |
| BIP | Bulk Information Processing | BISFA | British Industrial and Scientific Film Association |
| BIPA | Banque d'Information Politique et d'Actualité | BISMAC | Business Machine Computer |
| BIPAD | Binary Pattern Detector | BISMAPS | Business Informations System Modelling And Planning System |
| BIPCO | Built-In-Place Components | | |
| BIPE | Bureau d'Informations et de Prévisions Economiques | BISP | Business Information System Program |
| | | BIST | Built-In Self Test |
| BIPLEX | Binary Pattern Laser Extraction | BISY | Bildschirmtext-Informations-System |
| BIPLEX | Binary Pattern Logic Extraction | BISY | Bibliothekssystem |
| | | BISYNC | Bisynchronous transmission |
| BIPO | Bipolar | | |
| BIPS | Billion Instructions per Second | BISYNC | Binary Synchronous Communication |
| BIR | Break-In Relay | BIT | Basic indissoluble Information Unit |
| BIRDIE | Battery Integration and Radar Display Equipment | BIT | Binary Digit |
| | | BIT | Büro- und Informations-Technik |
| BIRE | British Institute of Radio Engineers | | |
| BIRS | Basic Indexing and Retrieval System | BIT | Built-In Test |
| | | BIT | Burroughs Integriertes Terminal |
| BIRS | Basic Information Retrieval System | BITE | Built-In Test Equipment |
| BIS | Basic Instruction Set | BITEL | Bildschirmtexttelefon |
| BIS | Bausteininterpretations-system | BITN | Bilateral Iterative Network |
| BIS | Beispiele Integrierter Schaltungen | BITOB | Bidirectional Transceiver with Optical Bypass |

- 74 -

# B

| | | | |
|---|---|---|---|
| BITS | Basis-IMS-Test-System | BKS | Basiskalkulationssystem |
| BITS | Binary Information Transfer System | BKS | Baukastensystem |
| | | BKSP | Backspace |
| BITS | Binary Intersystem Transmission Standard | BKU | Backup |
| | | BKUP | Backup |
| BITS | Boeing Intelligent Terminal System | BKWD | Backward |
| | | BKZ | Benutzerkennzeichen |
| BIU | Basic Information Unit | BL | Base Line |
| BIU | Bus Interface Unit | BL | Basic Linkage |
| BIVAR | Bivariant function generator | BL | Befehlslänge |
| | | BL | Belegleser |
| BIWA | Bibliotheks-Wartungs-programm | BL | Belegtlampe |
| | | BL | Beleuchtung |
| BIWAS | Bestell-Informations-Wareneingangs-Auszeichnungs-System | BL | Bell |
| | | BL | Binary Logic |
| | | BL | Bit Length |
| BIX | Binary Information Exchange | BL | Bit Location |
| | | BL | Black Letter |
| BJF | Batch Job Foreground | BL | Blanking |
| BJT | Bipolar Junction Transistor | BL | Blatt |
| | | BL | Blink Field |
| BJU | Beach Jumper Unit | BL | Block Label |
| BK | Basiskomponente | BL | Block Length |
| BK | Bereichskennung | BL | Block Loading |
| BK | Betriebskontrolle | BL | Blocklänge |
| BK | Betriebskontrollschaltung | BL | Blue Light |
| BK | Block | BL | Boolean Logic |
| BK | Block-Kennungsfeld | BL | Bottom Layer |
| BK | Block Keyboard | BL | Bouclage Local |
| BK | Break | BL | Branch on Low |
| BK | Break-in Keying | BL | Briggsian Logarithm |
| BK | Breitband-Kabelnetze | BL | Bus Link |
| BK | Breitwandkommunikation | BL&T | Blind Loaded and Traced |
| BK | Bürokommunikation | BLA | Befehlsausgang |
| BK-SDÜ | Benutzerkreis Schnelle Datenübertragung | BLA | Blocking Acknowledgement signal |
| BKB | Blockkontrolbyte | BLA | Bruttolohnabrechnung |
| BKB | Bus-Koppel-Baustein | BLADE | Basic Label Automation of Data through Electronics |
| BKD | Blackboard | | |
| BKDN | Breakdown | BLADES | Bell Laboratories Automatic Design System |
| BKDNDIO | Breakdown Diode | | |
| BKE | Bildkontrollempfänger | BLADS | Bell Laboratories Automatic Design System |
| BKER | Block Error Rate | | |
| BKF | Blocking Factor | BLC | Balance |
| BKG | Bürokopiergerät | BLC | Base Locator Cell |
| BKGD | Background | BLC | Befehlslängecode |
| BKI | Break-In | BLC | Boundary Layer Control |
| BKLR | Black Letter | BLC | Buffer Location Counter |
| BKO | Barkhausen-Kurz Oscillator | BLD | Beam-Lead Device |
| BKO | Betriebskosten | BLD | Below Limit of Detection |
| BKP | Breakpoint | BLE | Block Length Error |
| BKP | Baukostenplan | BLEACH | Babel Language Editing And Checking |
| BKPG | Bookkeeping | | |
| BKR | Baukontenrahmen | BLER | Block Error Rate |
| BKR | Breaker | BLERT | Block Error Rate Test |

# B

| | | | |
|---|---|---|---|
| BLESSED | Bell Little Electrodata Symbolic System for the Electrodata | BLO | Blower |
| | | BLO | Buffer Load point |
| | | BLOC | Blockade |
| BLEU | Bind Landing Experimental Unit | BLOC | Block Oriented Compiler |
| | | BLOC | Booth Library Online Circulation |
| BLF | Band-Limiting Filter | | |
| BLF | Blockungsfaktor | BLODI | Block Diagram |
| BLG | Blooming Gate | BLODI-G | Block Diagram Graphics |
| BLF | Bubble Lattice File | BLODIC | Block Diagram Compiler |
| BLF | Busy Lamp Field | BLOGIC | Block Logic Computer |
| BLI | Beiträge zur Linguistik und Informationsverarbeitung | BLP | Blue Line Print |
| | | BLP | Bypass Label Processing |
| | | BLPZZ | Bent Logarithmically Periodic Zig-Zags |
| BLIM | Buffer location-counter Limit | | |
| | | BLR | Bande Latérale Résiduelle |
| BLIMP | Boundary Layer Integral Matrix Procedure | BLS | Band Limited Signal |
| | | BLS | Belegtlampenschalter |
| BLIP | Background-Limited Infrared Photoconductor | BLS | Binary Light Switch |
| | | BLS | Bit Length Specification |
| BLIP | Block Diagram Interpreter Program | BLS | Buffered Line Selector |
| | | BLS | Bureau of Labor Statistics |
| BLIS | Bell Labs Interpretive System | BLSJICP | Beam Lead Sealed Junction Integrated Circuit Package |
| BLIS | Business Language Integrated System | | |
| | | BLT | Basic Language Translator |
| BLISS | Basic Language for Implementation of System Software | BLT | Blind Loaded with Tracer |
| | | BLU | Bande Latérale Unique |
| | | BLU | Basic Link Unit |
| BLISS | Basic List-oriented Information Structures System | BLU | Basic Logic Unit |
| | | BLU | Bipolar Line Unit |
| | | BLUE | Best Linear Unbiased Estimator |
| BLK | Belastungskapazität | | |
| BLK | Black | BLV | Beam-Lead-Verfahren |
| BLK | Blank | BLZ | Belegungszähler |
| BLK | Blink | BM | Backing Memory |
| BLK | Block | BM | Balancing Machine |
| BLKCNT | Block Count | BM | Bande Magnétique |
| BLKD | Blanked | BM | Basic Microprogram |
| BLKD | Blocked | BM | Beam Monitor |
| BLKG | Blocking | BM | Bearing Magnetic |
| BLKR | Block Rule | BM | Beginning Mark |
| BLKS | Blanking Signal | BM | Bench Mark |
| BLKS | Blocking Signal | BM | Betriebsmeßtechnik |
| BLL | Bedienungslochstreifenleser | BM | Billing Machine |
| | | BM | Binary Multiplication |
| BLL | Below Lower Limit | BM | Binary Multiply |
| BLLE | Balanced Line Logical Element | BM | Bistabiler Multivibrator |
| | | BM | Bistable Multivibrator |
| BLM | Ball Limiting Memory | BM | Block Mark |
| BLM | Basic Language Machine | BM | Block Marker |
| BLM | Bus and Lining Module | BM | Blockmarke |
| BLMPS | Base Level Military Personnel System | BM | Bookkeeping Machine |
| | | BM | Bootstrap Memory |
| BLMUX | Blockmultiplexkanal | BM | Braided Memory |
| BLNK | Blank | BM | Brightness Merit |

# B

| | | | |
|---|---|---|---|
| BM | Buffer Mark | BMKE | Betriebsmotor-kompensator-Einfach-Linienschreiber |
| BM | Buffer Memory | | |
| BM | Buffer Module | | |
| BM | Buffer/Multiplexer | BMKV | Betriebsmotor-kompensator-Vielfachpunktschreiber |
| BM | Bulk Memory | | |
| BM | Byte Machine | | |
| BM | Byte Mask | BML | Base-machine Microroutine Lenght |
| BM | Bytemaschine | | |
| BM | Bytemultiplex | BMM | Basic Modular Memory |
| BMA | Benutzermaschine | BMM | Bildschirmtext- |
| BMA | Betriebsmonitor-Alarm | | Mikrosoft-Meeting |
| BMAPS | Buckbee-Mears Automated Plotting System | BMMG | British Microcomputer Manufacturers Group |
| BMC | Base-machine Microinstruction Cycle | BMO | Base-machine Microroutine Overhead |
| BMC | Basic Machine Cycle | BMO | Basic Machine Operation |
| BMC | Basic Monthly Charge | BMP | Basic Mode Program |
| BMC | Biax Memory Core | BMP | Batch Message Processing |
| BMC | Binary Magnetic Core | BMPX | Block-Multiplexor |
| BMC | Binary Memory Cell | BMPX | Block-Multiplex-Kanal |
| BMC | Blind Mating Connector | BMR | Bibliography of Medical Reviews |
| BMC | Bubble Memory Controller | | |
| BMC | Bulk Media Conversion | BMS | Basic Mapping Support |
| BMC | Bulk-Modling Compound | BMS | Bit Mark Sequencing |
| BMC | Burst-Multiplexor-Channel | BMS | Biomedical Monitoring System |
| BMCS | Business Management Control System | BMS | Burroughs Management System |
| BMCSRP | Business Management Control System Research Project | BMSR | Betriebsmeß-, Steuer-/ und Regeltechnik |
| | | BMSR | Betriebsmessung, Steuerung und Regelung |
| BMD | Baseband Modulator-Demodulator | BMT | Basic Motion Time |
| BMD | Bubble Memory Device | BMT | Bibliography of Medical Translations |
| BMD | Buffer Memory Device | | |
| BME | Biax Memory Element | BMT | Bipolar Memory Technology |
| BME | Binary Memory Element | | |
| BMEP | Break Mean Effective Pressure | BMT | Block Marker Track |
| | | BMT | Büro, Mensch, Technik |
| BMEWS | Ballistic Missile Early Warning System | BMU | Backing Memory Unit |
| | | BMUX | Block Multiplex channel |
| BMF | Betriebsmittelfond | BMV | Bistable Multivibrator |
| BMFT | Bundesministerium für Forschung und Technologie | BMW | Beam Width |
| | | BMX | Base-machine Microroutine Execution |
| BMG | Business Management Game | BMXR | Block Multiplexer |
| | | BN | Base Notation |
| BMI | Batelle Memorial Institute | BN | Base Number |
| BMIS | Backgate MISFET | BN | Batch Numbering |
| BMISFET | Bulk MISFET | BN | Baumuster-Nummer |
| BMK | Bookkeeping Machine Keyboard | BN | Beacon |
| | | BN | Belastungsnetzwerk |
| BMKA | Bytemultiplexkanal-Anschluß | BN | Binary Notation |
| | | BN | Binary Number |

- 77 -

# B

| | | | |
|---|---|---|---|
| BN | Binary Number system | BO | Blocking Order |
| BN | Biquinary Notation | BO | Blocking Oscillator |
| BN | Biquinary Number | BO | Boolean |
| BN | Block Name | BO | Boolean Operation |
| BNA | Burrough's Network Architecture | BO | Boolean Operator |
| | | BO | Branch Office |
| BNC | Baby "N" Connector | BO | Branch on Overflow |
| BNC | Banking Network Computersysteme | BO | Branch Order |
| | | BO | Breakpoint Order |
| BNC | Bayonet Nut Connector | BO | Bus Out |
| BNC | Bulk Negative Conductance | BOA | Betriebliche Organisation und Abrechnung |
| BND | Band | BOA | Bipolar Operational Amplifier |
| BNDAFF | Best Null Detector And Flip Flop | | |
| | | BOA | Branch Office Administration |
| BNDC | Bulk Negative Differential Conductivity | BOA | Bürokommunikation, Organisation und Automatisierung |
| BNDDIS | Band Display | | |
| BNDO | Bureau National des Données Océaniques | BOA-MILS | Broad Ocean Area-Missile Impact Locating System |
| BNE | Branch on Not Equal | BOADICEA | British Overseas Airways Digital Information Computer for Electronic Automation |
| BNF | Backus Normal Form | | |
| BNF | Best Noise Figure | | |
| BNF | Boolean Normal Form | | |
| BNG | Branch No Group | | |
| BNG | Broadband Noise Generator | BOB | Bipolar Offset Binary |
| | | BOB | Bureau Of Budget |
| BNH | Branch on Not High | BOC | Basic Operating Company |
| BNI | Bureau d'orientation de la Normalisation en Informatique | BOC | Bell Operating Company |
| | | BOC | Best Output and Colour |
| | | BOC | Block Oriented Computer |
| BNIST | Bureau National de l'Information Scientifique et Technique | BOC | Bus Out Check |
| | | BOCOL | Basic Operating Consumer-Oriented Language |
| BNL | Branch on Not Low | BOD | Beneficial Occupancy Data |
| BNM | Branch on Not Minus | BOD | Beratungsgesellschaft für Organisation und Datenverarbeitung |
| BNN | Biquinary Number Notation | | |
| BNN | Boundary Network Node | BOE | Beginning of Extent |
| BNP | Background Noise Power | BOE | Belastungsorientierte Einplanung |
| BNP | Branch on Not Plus | | |
| BNR | Bell Northern Research | BOE | Branch Order Execution |
| BNR | Burner | BOF | Backout-on-the-Fly |
| BNRY | Binary | BOF | Beginning of File |
| BNS | Binary Number System | BOF | Binary Oxide Film |
| BNU | Basic Notch Unit | BOFADS | Business Office Forms Administration Data System |
| BNZ | Branch on Not Zero | | |
| BNZ | Byte Not Zero | | |
| BO | Beat Oscillator | BOFEEP | Boulder Optimized Field Engineering Estimating Procedure |
| BO | Binary-to-Octal | | |
| BO | Blackout | | |
| BO | Blanking Oscillator | BOG | Büro-Organisations-Gesellschaft |
| BO | Block Operation | | |
| BO | Block Order | BOI | Basis Of Issue |
| BO | Block Parity | BOI | Branch Output Interrupt |

# B

| | | | |
|---|---|---|---|
| BOIE | Bauorientierte Interaktive Entwicklung | BOS | Background Operating System |
| BOIMARS | Basis Of Issue Monitoring And Recording System | BOS | Basic Operating System |
| | | BOS | Batch Operating System |
| BOIS | Branch Office Information System | BOS | Bit Organized Store |
| | | BOS | Business Output and tailoring System |
| BOLD | Bibliographic On-Line Display | BOSIC | Bosch Symbolischer Instruktions-Code |
| BOLD | Bit Oriented Line Discipline | BOSS | Banken Online Service System |
| BOLIC | Branch Office Library Inventor Control | BOSS | Basic Operating System Software |
| BOLT | Basic Occupational Language Training | BOSS | Basis Of Standard System |
| BOM | Basic Operating Memory | BOSS | Bett's Open Shop System |
| BOM | Basic Operational Memory | BOSS | Biased Optimal Steering Selector |
| BOM | Basic Operating Monitor | | |
| BOM | Bill Of Material | BOT | Beginning Of Tape |
| BOM | Binary Order of Magnitude | BOT | Blackout Time |
| BOM | Bit Organized Memory | BOTM | Beginning Of Tape Marker |
| BOM | Break Offset Mapping | BOTMG | Bottoming |
| BOMAG | Bill Of Material Analyzer and Generator | BOUMAC | Boulder laboratory Macrosystem |
| BOMOS | Buried-Oxide MOS | BOUT | Bus Out |
| BOMP | Basis Organization and Maintenance Program | BP | B Pulse |
| | | BP | Back Projection |
| BOMP | Bill Of Material Processor | BP | Background Processing |
| BON | Betriebleitsystem für den Öffentlichen Nahverkehr | BP | Background Program |
| | | BP | Backspace Pawl |
| BONT | Benutzerorientiert | BP | Bad Parity |
| BONUS | Banken-Online-Universal-System | BP | Band-Pass |
| | | BP | Batch Processing |
| BOOK | Built-in Orderly Organized Knowledge | BP | Battery Package |
| | | BP | Bauprinzip |
| BOP | Balance Of Payments | BP | Bedienpult |
| BOP | Basic Operation Plan | BP | Bedienungsprozessor |
| BOP | Basic Operator Panel | BP | Bedienungspult |
| BOP | Binary Output Program | BP | Berechnungsprotokoll |
| BOP | Bit Oriented Protocol | BP | Betriebsabgabepreis |
| BOP | Bit-Orientierte Protokolle | BP | Between Perpendicular |
| BOP | Break Off Portion | BP | Bibliotheksprogramm |
| BOR | Beginning Of Record | BP | Bildpunkt |
| BORAM | Block Oriented Random Access Method | BP | Binary Place |
| | | BP | Binary Point |
| BORAM | Block Organized Random Access Method | BP | Binary Punch |
| | | BP | Binding Post |
| BORIS | Blackley Order Reception and Invoicing System | BP | Bioscience Program |
| | | BP | Bipolar |
| BORSA | Budget Orientiertes Rechnungswesen für Staatliche Aufgaben | BP | Bit Pair |
| | | BP | Bit Position |
| | | BP | Block Packaging |
| BORSA | Budgetorientiertes Rechungswesen für Staatliche Aufgaben | BP | Block Punch |
| | | BP | Boiling Point |
| | | BP | Boolean Part |

# B

| | | | |
|---|---|---|---|
| BP | Bootstrap Program | BPID | Book Physical Inventory Difference |
| BP | Bornier Programmable | | |
| BP | Branch on Plus | BPIT | Basic Parameter Input Tape |
| BP | Branch Program | | |
| BP | Branching Program | BPKFL | Block Packaging Flag |
| BP | Break Point | BPKT | Basic Program Knowledge Test |
| BP | Break Pointer | | |
| BP | Bubble Pulse | BPL | Band-Pass Limiter |
| BP | Bundespost | BPL | Basic Program Loader |
| BP | By-Pass | BPL | Burroughs Programming Language |
| BPA | Background Program Area | | |
| BPA | Break-Point Address-register | BPL | Business Planning Language |
| | | BPM | Bank Proof Machine |
| BPA | Broadband Power Amplifier | BPM | Batch Processing Monitor |
| | | BPM | Bi-Phase Modulation |
| BPA | Bureau Permanent des Actions | BPM | Breitbandpegelmesser |
| | | BPN | Bandpass Network |
| BPA-SDI | Bonneville Power Administration Selective Dissemination of Information | BPN | Breakdown Pulse Noise |
| | | BPN | Budget Project Number |
| | | BPO | British Post Office |
| | | BPOS | Batch Processing Operating System |
| BPAC | Budget Program Activity Code | | |
| | | BPOS | Block-print Position |
| BPAM | Basic Partitioned Access Method | BPP | Buffer Punch Program |
| | | BPPF | Basic Program Preparation Facility |
| BPAM | Basic Program Access Method | | |
| | | BPPF | Basic Program Preparation Facility program |
| BPB | Benutzerprogramm-bibliothek | | |
| | | BPR | Bar-Pattern Response |
| BPBS | Band/Platte Betriebssystem | BPR | Battery Powered Recorder |
| | | BPR | Bubble Position Register |
| BPC | Bandpass Crystal | BPRQ | Batch Partition Request Queue |
| BPC | Basic Programming for Computers | | |
| | | BPRS | Basic Parts Records Summary |
| BPC | Basic Punched Card | | |
| BPC | Batch Partition Controller | BPS | Basic Programming Suggest |
| BPC | Blank Punched Card | | |
| BPC | Block Priority Control | BPS | Basic Programming Support |
| BPC | Boston Programming Center | | |
| | | BPS | Basic Programming System |
| BPC | Buffer Punch Card | | |
| BPCF | Bandpass Crystal Filter | BPS | Batch Processing System |
| BPCM | Basic Punched Card Machine | BPS | Bill Processor System |
| | | BPS | Bits Per Second |
| BPDC | Berkeley Particle Data Center | BPS | Bytes Per Second |
| | | BPSK | Binary Phase Shift Keyed |
| BPDS | BASIC Programming Development System | BPSK | Binary Phase Shift Keying |
| BPE | Bit-Plane Encoding | BPSS | Basic Packet Switching Service |
| BPF | Band-Pass Filter | | |
| BPG | Break Pulse Generator | BPSS | Basic Production Scheduling System |
| BPI | Bits Per Inch | | |
| BPI | Break-Point Instruction | BPSS | Bell Packet Switching System |
| BPI | Byte Per Inch | | |

# B

| | | | |
|---|---|---|---|
| BPT | Bandpass Transformer | BRADS | Business Report Application Development System |
| BPT | Bipolar Transistor | | |
| BPT | Buffer Punch Transfer | | |
| BPU | Bande Passante Utile | BRAID | Bidirectional Reference Array, Internally Derived |
| BPU | Basic Processing Unit | | |
| BPU | Basisprogrammierunterstützung | | |
| | | BRAILLE | Balanced Resource Allocation Information for Logical Lucid Evaluation |
| BPZ | Blockweise Prioritätszuteilung | | |
| BQAP | Bilevel Quality Assurance Program | BRAINS | Behaviour Replication by Analog Instruction of the Nervous System |
| BQL | Basic Query Language | | |
| BQS | Basic Query System | | |
| BR | B-Register | BRASS | BEEF Reporting, Analysis, and Status System |
| BR | Badge Reader | | |
| BR | Band Rate | BRBB | B Register B Bit |
| BR | Band Reject | BRC | Base Register Contents |
| BR | Base Record | BRC | Basis Real Constant |
| BR | Base Register | BRC | Block Representation Code |
| BR | Basic Register | | |
| BR | Basic Routine | BRC | Branch Conditional |
| BR | Basisregister | BRC | Bunker Ramo Corporation |
| BR | Baureihe | BRC | Buffer Read Card |
| BR | Bedienrechner | BRCB | B-Register C Bit |
| BR | Bedienungsrechner | BRCD | Binary information with a Residue Check Digest |
| BR | Befehlsregister | | |
| BR | Belastungsregler | BRCDE | Branch Code |
| BR | Bend Radius | BRD | Balance Reading Device |
| BR | Betriebsrechner | BRD | Base Register Designator |
| BR | Betriebsrechnung | BRD | Binary Rate Divider |
| BR | Bibliotheksrechner | BRD | Blank Recording Disk |
| BR | Bimetallrelais | BRD | Bundesrepublik Deutschland |
| BR | Binary Record | | |
| BR | Binary Representation | BRDAT | Betriebsregisterdatei |
| BR | Bit Rate | BRDF | Basic Read Data Flow |
| BR | Bit Resolution | BRF | Band-Rejection Filter |
| BR | Blank Record | BRICS | Bureau of Research Information Control System |
| BR | Block Reading | | |
| BR | Block Reception | | |
| BR | Block Register | BRIGAPAD | British Rail Interactive Graphical Aid of Production And Design |
| BR | Boiling Range | | |
| BR | Booking Register | | |
| BR | Bootstrap Routine | BRIL | Brilliance |
| BR | Branch | BRITE | Basic Research in Industrial Technologies for Europe |
| BR | Branch Routine | | |
| BR | Break Relay | | |
| BR | Break Request | BRJE | BSC-Remote Job Entry |
| BR | Bromine | BRK | Break |
| BR | Bulk Resistance | BRK PT | Break Point |
| BR | Bunker Ramo | BRKG | Breaking |
| BR | Bus Request | BRKR | Breaker |
| BR | Byte Rate | BRKT | Bracket |
| BRA | Basic Record Audit | BRL | Beginning Reel Label |
| BRAD | Brookhaven Raster Display | BRL | Bit Rate Low |

# B

| | | | |
|---|---|---|---|
| BRL | Blockierringleitung | BS | Bildschirmeinheit |
| BRL | Branch and Link | BS | Bildschirmsteuereinheit |
| BRLESC | Ballistic Research Laboratory Electronic Scientific Computer | BS | Bildschirmsteuergerät |
| | | BS | Bildsender |
| | | BS | Binary Scale |
| BRM | Barometer | BS | Binary Scaler |
| BRM | Binary Rate Multiplier | BS | Binary Search |
| BRM | Binary Rate Multipler | BS | Binary Signal |
| BRO | Badge Readout | BS | Binary Substraction |
| BROM | Bipolar Read-Only Memory | BS | Binary Subtract |
| BROS | Basic Read Only Storage | BS | Binary Symbol |
| BROT-AS | Brotfabrik-Abrechnungs-System | BS | Binary System |
| | | BS | Biquinary System |
| BROV | Branch Overflow | BS | Bit Space |
| BRP | Buffer Read Program | BS | Bit String |
| BRS | Bibliographic Retrieval Services | BS | Blank Space |
| | | BS | Blattschreiber |
| BRS | Binary Ring Sequence | BS | Block Scheme |
| BRS | Block Rücksetzen | BS | Block Selection |
| BRS | Break Request Signal | BS | Block Size |
| BRST | Burst | BS | Block Sort |
| BRT | Bereit | BS | Block Storage |
| BRT | Binary Run Tape | BS | Block Structure |
| BRT | Bruttoregistertonne | BS | Blockstruktur |
| BRT | Buffer Read Transfer | BS | Booking Store |
| BRT | Byte Result Trigger | BS | Braided Store |
| BRU | Branch Unconditional | BS | Breakpoint Symbol |
| BRUCE | Buffer Register Under Computer Edict | BS | British Size |
| | | BS | British Standard |
| BRUIN | Brown University Interpreter | BS | Broadcast Station |
| | | BS | Bubble Storage |
| BRWM | B-Register Word Mark | BS | Buffer Store |
| BRZ | Bezirksrechenzentrum | BS | Bulk Storage |
| BRZFI | Branchenzentrum Fertigungsindustrie | BS | Bulk Store |
| | | BS | Bump Storage |
| BS | Backing Storage | BS | Bureau of Standards |
| BS | Backing Store | BS | Byte Size |
| BS | Backspace | BS | Bytes/Spur |
| BS | Balance Selection | BSA | Binary Switching Algebra |
| BS | Balance Selector | BSA | Binary Synchronous Adapter |
| BS | Balance Sheet | | |
| BS | Band Setting | BSA | Bit Sync Acquisition |
| BS | Band-Stop | BSA | Bulk-Semi-Array |
| BS | Bandsperre | BSAM | Basic Sequential Access Method |
| BS | Bandsystem | | |
| BS | Based Store | BSAM | Binary Sequential Access Method |
| BS | Basic Statement | | |
| BS | Basic Symbol | BSB | Backspace Block |
| BS | Batch Start | BSB | Baseband |
| BS | Baustein | BSB | Both Sideband |
| BS | Bearbeitungssystem | BSB | Buffer Store Block |
| BS | Bedingungsschlüssel | BSBG | Burst and Synchronous Bit Generator |
| BS | Betriebssystem | | |
| BS | Big System | BSC | Back Space Character |
| BS | Bildschirm | BSC | Back Spacing Control |

- 82 -

# B

| | | | |
|---|---|---|---|
| BSC | Backspace Contact | BSG | Bit Sync Generator |
| BSC | Basic | BSG | Bootstrap Gyro |
| BSC | Basic Synchronous Communication | BSG | British Standard Gauge |
| BSC | Basic message Switching Center | BSI | British Standards Institute |
| BSC | Binär Synchroner Code | BSI | British Standards Institution |
| BSC | Binary Store Circuit | BSI | Bitschiebeimpuls |
| BSC | Binary Symmetric Channel | BSI | Branch and Store Instruction |
| BSC | Binary Synchronous Communication | BSIC | Binary Symmetric Independent Channel |
| BSC | Binary Synchronous Control | BSIE | Bio-Sciences Information Exchange |
| BSC | Booking Search Control | | |
| BSC | Buffer Store Circuit | BSIL | Basic Switching Impulse insulation Level |
| BSC | Bus Service Center | | |
| BSC | Bus System Control | BSK | Back Space Key |
| BSC | Byte Size Control | BSK | Back Spacing Key |
| BSCA | Binary Synchronous Communications Adapter | BSL | Basic Switching-surge Level |
| BSCN | Bit Scan | BSL | Basic Systems Language |
| BSCS | Binary Synchronous Communication System | BSL | Bit Scanning Line |
| | | BSM | Back Space Mechanism |
| BSD | Berkeley Software Distribution | BSM | Basic Storage Module |
| | | BSM | Basic Systems Memory |
| BSD | Bipolarer Schalter und Decodierung | BSM | Betriebs-/und Steuer- meßplatz |
| BSD | Bit Storage Density | BSM | Betriebssystem München |
| BSD | Bit String Data | BSM | Bi-Stable Multivibrator |
| BSD | Btx Südwest Datenbank GmbH | BSMV | Bistable Multivibrator |
| | | BSN | Boundle Signal Name |
| BSD | Buffer Store Device | BSNEX | Bundle Signal Name Expanded |
| BSD | Bureau for System Development | BSO | Bildungsverwaltung und Schulorganisation |
| BSDA | Business and Defense Services Administration | BSO | Bit String Operator |
| BSDAM | Basic Sequential Data Access Method | BSO | Boston Systems Office |
| | | BSP | Back Space Pawl |
| BSDC | Binary Symmetric Dependent Channel | BSP | Basis-Software-Programm |
| | | BSP | Bedien-/und Service- Prozessor |
| BSDL | Boresight Datum Line | | |
| BSDP | Bell Systems Data Processing | BSP | Bruttosozialprodukt |
| | | BSPL | Behavioral Science Programming Language |
| BSE | Basic System Extensions | | |
| BSE | Betriebsschutzerde | BSR | Backspace Record |
| BSE | Betriebs-/und Schutzerdung | BSR | Backspace Register |
| | | BSR | Bank Sorter-Reader |
| BSE | Binary Store Element | BSR | Betriebssystem für Reale Adressierung |
| BSE | Bussteuereinheit | | |
| BSEP | Basic Skill Education Program | BSR | Binary Shift Register |
| | | BSR | Bit Shifting Register |
| BSF | Back Space File | BSR | Blip-Scan Radar |
| BSF | Bandwidth Shape Factor | BSR | Blip-Scan Ratio |
| BSF | Bedien-/und Schaltfeld | BSR | Buffered Sampler Reader |
| BSG | Betriebssteuergerät | BSS | Back Space Statement |

# B

| | | | |
|---|---|---|---|
| BSS | Backing Store System | BT | Bistable Trigger |
| BSS | Basis Synchronized Subset | BT | Bit Test |
| | | BT | Bittakt |
| BSS | Bausteinsystem | BT | Blinktaktgeber |
| BSS | Bibliothèque des Sous-programmes du Système | BT | Block Tag |
| | | BT | Block Transfer |
| BSS | Bildschirmsteuergerät | BT | Block Type |
| BSS | Bildschirmsystem | BT | Boolean Term |
| BSS | Bit Storage and Sense | BT | Bootstrap Technique |
| BSS | British Standard Specification | BT | British Telecom |
| | | BT | Busy Tone |
| BSSC | Bit Synchronizer - Signal Conditioner | BTA | Billable Time Authorization |
| BST | Back Spacing Time | BTA | Bürotechnik und Automation |
| BST | Beam-Switching Tube | | |
| BST | Befehlssteuerwerk | BTAM | Basic Tape Access Method |
| BST | Bildschirmtastatur | BTAM | Basic Telecommunications Access Method |
| BST | Binary Search Tree | | |
| BST | Binary Synchronous Transmission | BTAM | Basic Terminal Access Method |
| BST | Booster | BTAM-ES | BTAM Extended Support |
| BST | British Summer Time | BTAP | Bond Table Analysis Program |
| BST | Burst | | |
| BST | Business Systems Technology, Incorporated | BTAP | Bond Trade Analysis Program |
| BSTAT | Basic Status register | BTC | Batch Terminal Controller |
| BSTJ | Bell System Technical Journal | BTC | Bilateral Tape Card |
| | | BTC | Binary Two's Complement |
| BSTR | Befehlsstruktur | BTC | Bit Time Counter |
| BSTR | Booster | BTC | Block Terminating Character |
| BSTU | Basic Storage Unit | | |
| BSU | Backing Store Unit | BTC | Block Transfer Control |
| BSU | Bistable Storage Unit | BTC | Btx-Terminal-Controller |
| BSU | Bistable Store Unit | BTCU | Buffered Transmission Control Unit |
| BSV | Betriebssystem für virtuelle Adressierung | | |
| | | BTD | Balanced Tape Drive |
| BSV | Betriebssystem für Virtuelle Speicherung | BTD | Binary-To-Decimal |
| | | BTD | Bomb Testing Device |
| BSV | Boolean Simple Variable | BTD | Bulk Transmission of Data |
| BSWG | British Standard Wire Gauge | BTDAM | Basic Telecommunications Data Access Method |
| BSY | Busy | BTDC | Btx-Data-Collection |
| BSZ | Basisband-Symmetrierzusatz | BTDL | Basic Transient Diode Logic |
| BSZ | Benutzer-Service-Zentrum | BTE | Base de Temps Emission |
| BSZ | Bildschirmzeitung | BTE | Battery Terminal Equipment |
| BSZ | Block Store Zeros | | |
| BT | Back Transfer | BTE | Bidirectional Transceiver Element |
| BT | Basse Tension | | |
| BT | Bedarfsträger | BTE | Boltzmann Transport Equation |
| BT | Bedingungsteil | | |
| BT | Beginning of Tape | BTE | Bulk Tape Eraser |
| BT | Bias Temperature | BTF | Balanced Transformer |
| BT | Binary Translation | BTF | Basic Transaction Facility |
| BT | Binary Trigger | BTF | Binary Transversal Filter |

# B

| | | | |
|---|---|---|---|
| BTG | British Technology Group | BTSP | Bootstrap |
| BTHU | British Thermal Unit | BTSS | Basic Time-Sharing System |
| BTI | Basic Timesharing, Incorporated | BTST | Busy-Tone Start lead |
| | | BTT | Beginning to Tape Test |
| BTI | Bridged Tap Isolator | BTU | Basic Transmission Unit |
| BTI | British Telecom International | BTU | British Thermal Unit |
| | | BTV | Büro für Textverarbeitung |
| BTI | Byte Transfer In | BTX | Bildschirmtext |
| BTL | Beginning Tape Label | Btx-ASP | Bildschirmtext-Anwendungs-Steuerungs-Programm |
| BTL | Bell Telephone Laboratories | | |
| BTM | Back Transfer Mechanism | BTXIS | Btx-geschütztes betriebliches Informationssystem |
| BTM | Balance Totalizing Mechanism | | |
| BTM | Batch Time-sharing Monitor | BTXIS | Btx-Informationssystem |
| | | BTXIS | Btx-Informations- und Kommunikationssystem |
| BTM | Beginning of Tape Mark | | |
| BTM | Bell Telephone Manufacturing | BTYPE | Block Type |
| | | BTZ | Bildschirmtextzentrale |
| BTM | British Tabulating Machines Company | BU | Backup |
| | | BU | Bandumsetzer |
| BTM | Buffered Terminal Multiplexer | BU | Bandumsetzung |
| | | BU | Base Unit |
| BTMB | Btx-Mail-Box | BÜ | Befehlsübermittlung |
| BTN | Brutto-Tara-Netto-Rechner | BU | Binding Unit |
| | | BU | Bit Unit |
| BTN | Button | BU | Buchse |
| BTO | Block Transfer Order | BU | Buchstabenumschaltung |
| BTO | Blocking-Tube Oscillator | BU | Business Unit |
| BTO | Bürotechnik und Organisation | BUA | Built-Up Addressing |
| | | BUAB | Buchungsabschluß |
| BTO | Byte Transfer Out | BUBE | Buchungsbearbeitung |
| BTP | Batch Transfer Program | BUBI | Berufs- und Bildungsinformationssystem |
| BTP | Baukastensystem der Technologischen Projektierung | | |
| | | BUDC | Back-Up Digital Computer |
| | | BUDI | Buchdienst |
| BTPS | British Telecom Public System | BUDPLAN | Budget and Plans |
| | | BUDPLAN | Budget- und Planungsprogramm |
| BTR | Base de Temps Réception | | |
| BTR | Behind Tape Reader | BUE | Betriebsüberwachung |
| BTR | Behind-The Reader | BUEC | Back-Up Emergency Communication |
| BTR | Billable Time Report | | |
| BTR | Block Tape Recorder | BUF | Buffer |
| BTR | Bus Transfer | BUG | Basic Update Generator |
| BTRY | Battery | BUGRAF | Business-Grafic |
| BTS | Barrier Terminal Strip | BUGS | Brown University Graphics System |
| BTS | Basic Tape System | | |
| BTS | Batch Terminal Simulator | BUIC | Back-Up Interceptor Control |
| BTS | Bild-Text-System | | |
| BTS | Boolean Time Sequence | BUILD | Base for Uniform Language Definition |
| BTS | Bound Task Set | | |
| BTS | Branch Terminal System | BUIS | Barrier Up Indicator System |
| BTS | Brevet de Technicien Supérieur | | |
| | | BUISYS | Barrier Up Indicator System |
| BTS | Burst Trimmer Stacker | | |

# B

| | | | |
|---|---|---|---|
| BULKIO | Bulk Input/Output | BVS | Bibliotheks-Verbund-System |
| BULLCAT | Bull Calcul Automatique des Temps | BVS | Bildverarbeitungssystem |
| BULLRAC | Bull Random Access | BVS | Blockverteilersteuerung |
| BUMP | Back-Up Module Program | BVS | Block Vorsetzen |
| BUNCH | Burroughs/Univac/NCR/CDC/Honeywell | BVW | Binary Voltage Weigher |
| | | BW | Backward Wave |
| BUP | Back-Up Processor | BW | Band Width |
| BUPS | Beacon Ultra Portable S-band | BW | Beam Width |
| | | BW | Befehlswerk |
| BUPX | Beacon Ultra-Portable X-band | BW | Befehlswort |
| | | BW | Bezugswert |
| BUR | Basic Utility Routine | BW | Bit Word |
| BUR | Bureau | BWA | Betriebswirtschaftliche Auswertungen |
| BURS | Basic Unformatted Read System | BWAR | Budget Workload Analysis Report |
| BUS | Batterieumschalter | | |
| BUS | Bibliothèque Utilisateur Standard | BWC | Basic Weight Calculator |
| | | BWD | Backward |
| BÜS | Bedienerübungssystem | BWG | Birmingham Wire Gauge |
| BUSAC | Bureau of Ships Analog Computer | BWG | British Wire Gauge |
| | | BWI | Branch Workload Index |
| BUSEN | Bus Enable | BWM | Backward-Wave Magnetron |
| BUSS | Bus Unit Scan Station | BWO | Backward-Wave Oscillator |
| BUT | Button | BWOS | Backward-Wave Oscillator Synchronizer |
| BUZ | Buzzer | | |
| BUZZ | Buzzer | BWPA | Backward-Wave Parametric Amplifier |
| BV | Balanced Voltage | | |
| BV | Bandverstärker | BWPA | Backward-Wave Power Amplifier |
| BV | Baudot-Verdan | | |
| BV | Bedienungsvorschrift | BWR | Bandwidth Ratio |
| BV | Belegverarbeitung | BWR | Bremswegrechner |
| BV | Bildverstärker | BWS | Bewertungsschema |
| BV | Binary Value | BWS | Bildwiederholspeicher |
| BV | Boolean Variable | BWZ | Blank When Zero |
| BV | Breakdown Voltage | BX | Box |
| BVB | Besondere Vertragsbedingungen | BY | Budget Year |
| | | BY | Busy |
| BVB | Bundesverband der Büromaschinen-Importeure | BYDA | Busy/Don't Answer |
| | | BYMUX | Bytemultiplex |
| BVB | Bundesverband der Büromaschinen-Import- und Vertriebsunternehmen | BYP | By-Pass |
| | | BZ | Bearbeitungszentrum |
| | | BZ | Bedienungszeit |
| BVD | Beacon Video Digitizer | BZ | Befehlszähler |
| BVE | Befehlsvorbereitungseinheit | BZ | Befehlsregister |
| | | BZ | Betriebsstundenzähler |
| BVK | Bestands- und Verfügbarkeitskontrolle | BZ | Binärzähler |
| | | BZ | Branchenzentrum |
| BVLS | Battery-Voltage Limit System | BZ | Buzzer |
| | | BZB | Burghagens Zeitschrift für Bürotechnik und Informatik |
| BVP | Boundary Value Problem | | |
| BVRC | Banded Vector-to-Raster Converter | BZR | Befehlszählregister |
| | | BZR | Bytezähler |
| BVS | Bandverwaltungs-System | | |
| BVS | Belegverarbeitungssystem | | |

# C

| | | | |
|---|---|---|---|
| C | Cable | C/M | Communications Multiplexer |
| C | Call | | |
| C | Candella | C/M | Counts per Minute |
| C | Candle | C/N | Carrier-to-Noise |
| C | Capacitance | C/R | Command Response filed bit |
| C | Capacitor | | |
| C | Capacity | C/SPC | Cost/Schedule Planning and Control |
| C | Carbon | | |
| C | Carriage | C/SPCS | Cost/Schedule Planning and Control Specification |
| C | Catalog | | |
| C | Cathode | | |
| C | Cell | C/SPCS | Cost/Schedule Planning and Control System |
| C | Cellatron | | |
| C | Centigrade | C/SR | Counter/Shift Register |
| C | Centimeter | C/TDS | Count/Time Data System |
| C | Centre | CA | Cable |
| C | Character | CA | Call Address |
| C | Charakteristik | CA | Cancel |
| C | Charge | CA | Candle |
| C | Chromiance | CA | Capacitor |
| C | Circuit | CA | Card Alignment |
| C | Citation | CA | Card Application |
| C | Code | CA | Card Assembler |
| C | Coefficient | CA | Cascade Amplifier |
| C | Coil | CA | Cathode |
| C | Collector | CA | Cellular Automation |
| C | Column | CA | Chain Address |
| C | Common | CA | Chained Addressing |
| C | Compare | CA | Change Accumulation |
| C | Compteur | CA | Channel Adapter |
| C | Compute | CA | Channel Address |
| C | Computer | CA | Character Alignment |
| C | Computing | CA | Character Assignment |
| C | Conductor | CA | Check Addition |
| C | Contact | CA | Circuit Algebra |
| C | Control | CA | Circuit Analysis |
| C | Controller | CA | Circuity Adapter |
| C | Correct | CA | Clear Aperture |
| C | Count | CA | Clear and Add |
| C | Counter | CA | Clipping Amplifier |
| C | Cubic | CA | Coaxial |
| C | Current | CA | Coded Address |
| C | Current | CA | Collision Avoidance |
| C | Cycle | CA | Command Address |
| C & C | Command & Control | CA | Command Analyzer |
| C & C | Computers & Communications | CA | Command Attention |
| | | CA | Communications Adapter |
| $C^3$ | Communications, Command, Control | CA | Communications Attachments |
| C-MOS-RAM | Complementary MOS-RAM | CA | Complement Add |
| C-O | Coupled Oscillator | CA | Composants Acoustiques |
| C/E | Compile and Execute | CA | Computer Access |
| C/I | Carrier-to-Interference ratio | CA | Computer Amplifier |
| | | CA | Computer Analysis |

# C

| | | | |
|---|---|---|---|
| CA | Computer Application | CABS | Computerized Annotated Bibliography System |
| CA | Computer Assembly | | |
| CA | Computer Associates | CAC | Center for Advanced Computation |
| CA | Computer Associates International | CAC | Clear All Channels |
| CA | Computer Automation Limited | CAC | Command Address Change |
| | | CAC | Complete Address Constant |
| CA | Computers and Automation | CAC | Computer Acceleration Control |
| CA | Computing Automaton | | |
| CA | Conditional Addition | CAC | Computer-Assisted Counseling |
| CA | Conditional Assembly | | |
| CA | Constant Attenuation | CAC | Control And Coordination |
| CA | Contact Ammeter | CAC | Current Account Card |
| CA | Continuation Address | CAC | Cyclic Address Change |
| CA | Continued Addition | CACA | Computer-Aided Circuit Analysis |
| CA | Control Area | | |
| CA | Correct Algorithm | CACD | Compromise Approach to Compiler Design |
| CA | Count Attribute | | |
| CA | Coverage Analysis | CACD | Computer-Aided Circuit Design |
| CA | Current Address | | |
| CA | Cylinder Address | CACD | Computer-Automated Cargo Documentation |
| CA-SORT | Computer Associates GmbH Sortier-Programm | CACHE | Computer Aid for Chemical Engineering education |
| CAA | Civil Aeronautics Administration | | |
| CAA | Computer Amplifier Alarm | CACHE | Computer-controlled Automated Cargo Handling Envelope |
| CAA | Consecutive Access Addresses | | |
| CAAD | Computer-Aided Architectural Design | CACI | Consolidated Analysis Centers, Incorporated |
| CAAIS | Computer-Assisted Action Information System | CACT | Centre d'Assistance du Calcul Technique |
| CAAO | Conception Architecturale Assistée par Ordinateur | CACTIS | Computer Assistant to a Community Telephone Information Service |
| CAAS | Computer-Aided Approach Spacing | CACTOS | Computation And Communication Trade-Off Study |
| CAAS | Computer-Assisted Approach Sequencing | CAD | Cabling Diagram |
| | | CAD | Cadrage A Droite |
| CAAS | Computer-Assisted Approach System | CAD | Calculator-Aided Design |
| CAB | Cabinet | CAD | Cartridge Activated Device |
| CAB | Calculator Arithmetique Binaire | CAD | Character Assembler and Distributor |
| CAB | Channel Address Buffer | | |
| CAB | Channel Address Bus | CAD | Clear Add |
| CAB | Civil Aeronautics Board | CAD | Command Address |
| CAB | Computer Address Bus | CAD | Compensated Avalanche Diode |
| CAB | Computer-Aided Building | | |
| CABAS | Computerized Automated Blood Analysis System | CAD | Computer Access Device |
| | | CAD | Computer-Aided Design |
| CABLE | Computer-Assisted Bay-area Law Enforcement | CAD | Computer-Aided Drafting |
| | | CAD | Computer Analysis Department |
| CABR | Central Address Buffer Register | CAD | Computer-Aided Detection |

# C

| | | | |
|---|---|---|---|
| CAD | Computer-Aided Diagnosis | CADDAC | Central Analog Data Distributing And Controlling |
| CAD | Computer-Assisted Drafting | | |
| CAD | Computer-Automated Design | CADDE | Central Automatic Digital Data Encoder |
| CAD | Control And Display | CADDET | Computer-Aided Device Design in Two dimensions |
| CAD | Conversion Analogique-Digitale | CADDY | Carlsruhe Digital Design System |
| CAD | Counter And Decoder | | |
| CAD/CAM | Computer-Aided Design/Manufacturing | CADE | Computer-Aided Data Entry |
| CAD/CAM | Computer-Aided Design/Computer-Aided Manufacture | CADE | Computer-Aided Design |
| | | CADE | Computer-Aided Design and Engineering |
| CAD/CAM | Computer-Assisted Design/Computer-Assisted Manufacture | CADEM | Computer-Aided Design Engineering and Manufacturing |
| CADA | Computer-Aided Design or Analysis | CADEP | Computer-Aided Design of Electronic Products |
| CADA | Computer-Assisted Distribution and Assignment | CADEP | Computer-Assisted Description of Patterns |
| | | CADES | Computer-Assisted Data Entry System |
| CADAD | Computer-Aided Design and Application of Devices | CADET | Cant't Add - Doesn't Even Try |
| CADAM | Computer graphics Augmented Design And Manufacturing system | CADET | Computer-Aided Design and Electrical Test |
| | | CADET | Computer-Aided Design Engineering Technique |
| CADAM | Computer-Augmented Design And Manufacturing | CADET | Computer-Aided Design Experimental Translation |
| CADAPSO | Canadian Association of Data Processing Service Organizations | CADET | Computer-Aided Design Experimental Translator |
| CADAR | Computer-Aided Design, Analysis and Reliability | CADET | Covariance Analysis Describing-function Technique |
| CADAVRS | Computer-Assisted Dial Access Video Retrieval System | CADEX | Computer-Aided Design Exhibition |
| CADC | Central Air Data Computer | CADF | Commutated Antenna Direction Finder |
| CADC | Computer-Aided Design Center | CADF | Contract Administrative Data File |
| CADC | Corrective Action Data Center | CADFISS | Computation And Data Flow Integrated Subsystem |
| CADCOM | Computer-Aided Design for Communications | CADI | Computer Access Device Input |
| CADD | Computer-Aided Design and Drafting | CADI | Central Apollo Data Index |
| CADD | Computer-Assisted Design and Drafting | CADIAP | Comment And Data Integration And Printing |
| CADDA | Combined Analog-Digital Differential Analyzer | CADIC | Computer-Aided Design of Integrated Circuits |
| CADDAC | Central Analog Data Distributing And Computing system | CADICS | Computer-Aided Design of Industrial Cabling System |

# C

| | | | |
|---|---|---|---|
| CADIS | Computer-Aided Design Information System | CAE | Computer-Aided Engineering |
| CADISIM | Computer-Assisted Disposal Simulation | CAE | Computer-Assisted Education |
| CADL | Communications And Data Link | CAE | Computer-Assisted Engineering |
| CADLIC | Computer-Aided Design of Linear Integrated Circuits | CAE | Computer-Assisted Enrollment |
| CADM | Center Apollo Data Manager | CAE | Computer-Assisted Entry |
| CADMAC | Computer-Assisted Drawing Machine | CAE | Computer-Augmented Education |
| CADMINI | Computer Administrative Instruction | CAED | Computer-Aided Engineering Design |
| CADMOS | Computer Administrations und Organisationssysteme für Schulen | CAEDS | Computer-Aided Engineering Design System |
| | | CAEM | Computer-Aided Engineering and Manufacturing group |
| CADNIP | Cambridge Atmospheric Density Numerical Integration Program | CAEM | Cargo Airline Evaluation Model |
| CADOCR | Computer-Aided Design of Optical Character Recognition | CAESAR | Computerized Automation by Electronic System with Automated Reservations |
| CADOCS | Carrier Aircraft Data Operations Control System | CAF | Channel Address Field |
| | | CAF | Cleared As Filed |
| CADOPCART | Computer-Aided Design of Printed Circuit Artworks | CAF | Commande Automatique de Fréquence |
| | | CAF | Conjunctive Alterations File |
| CADPIN | Customs Automated Data Processing Intelligence Network | CAF | Conversion Assit Feature |
| | | CAF | Current Approved File |
| CADPO | Communicatons And Data Processing Operation | CAFC | Computed Automatic Frequency Control |
| CADRE | Common Applied Data Research Environment | CAFD | Contact Analog Flight Display |
| CADRE | Current Awareness and Document Retrieval for Engineers | CAFE | Computer-Aided Film Editor |
| | | CAFIT | Computer-Assisted Fault Isolation Test |
| CADS | Central Air Data Subsystem | CAFS | Content Addressable File Store |
| CADS | Conversational Analyzer and Drafting System | CAFS | Content Addressed File System |
| CADSS | Combined Analog-to-Digital System Simulator | CAG | Computer-Aided-Graphik |
| | | CAG | Computer-Assisted Graphics |
| CADSYS | Computer-Aided Design System | CAGC | Coded Automatic Gain Control |
| CAE | Calculatrice Arithmétique Electronique | CAGE | Compiler and Assembler by General Electric |
| CAE | Circular Average Error | CAHS | Comprehensive Automation of the Hydrometeorological Services |
| CAE | Compagnie d'Automatisme Européenne | | |
| CAE | Computer-Aided Education | | |

# C

| | | | |
|---|---|---|---|
| CAI | Channel Available Interruption | CAL | Calibrated |
| CAI | Code Acoustic Interrogator | CAL | Calibration |
| CAI | Computer Analog Input | CAL | Calorie |
| CAI | Computer Applications Inc. | CAL | Checking Automation Language |
| CAI | Computer-Administered Instruction | CAL | Common Assembler Language |
| CAI | Computer-Aided Instruction | CAL | Common Assembly Language |
| CAI | Computer-Aided-Industry | CAL | Computer Animation Language |
| CAI | Computer-Assisted Instruction | CAL | Computer-Assisted Learning |
| CAI | Conditional Assembler Instruction | CAL | Continuous Address List |
| CAI | Control and Acquisition Interface | CAL | Conversational Algebraic Language |
| CAL... | Computer Automation Inc. | CAL | Course Author Language |
| CAI/OP | Computer Analog Input/Output | CALAS | Computer-Aided Laboratory Automation System |
| CAIC | Computer-Assisted Indexing and Classification | CALAS | Computer-Assisted Language Analysis System |
| CAIMS | Conventional Ammunition Integrated Management System | CALBR | Calibration |
| | | CALC | Cargo Acceptance and Load Control |
| | | CALC | Calculate |
| | | CALC | Calculating |
| | | CALC | Calculation |
| CAIN | Calculation of Inertia | CALC | Calculator |
| CAIN | Cataloging & Indexing | CALCD | Calculated |
| CAINS | Computer-Aided Instruction System | CALCG | Calculating |
| | | CALCN | Calculation |
| CAINT | Computer-Assisted Interrogation | CALCOMP... | California Computer Products Inc. |
| CAIP | Computer-Assisted Index Program | CALD | Computer-Assisted Logic Design |
| CAIRA | Central Automated Inventory and Referral Activity | CALDIC | California Digital Computer |
| | | CALIB | Calibrate |
| CAIRS | Central Automated Inventory and Referral System | CALIB | Calibration |
| | | CALIBN | Calibration |
| | | CALIT | California Institute of Technology |
| CAIRS | Computer-Assisted Interactive Resources Scheduling System | CALL | Carat Assembled Logical Loader |
| CAIS | Canadian Association for Information Science | CALL | Computerized Ambulance Location Logic |
| CAISIM | Computer-Assisted Industrial Simulation | CALLAS | Computerangeschlossenes Lernleistungs-Analysesystem |
| CAKE | Computer-Assisted Keyboard Evaluator | CALM | Collected Algorithms for Learning Machines |
| CAKE | Computer-Assisted Key Entry | CALM | Computer-Aided Layout of Masks |
| CAL | Calculate | | |
| CAL | Calculated Average Life | CALM | Computer-Aided Learning Model |
| CAL | Calculator | | |

# C

| | | | |
|---|---|---|---|
| CALM | Computer-Assisted Libary Mechanization | CAM/RAM | Content Addressable Memory/Random Access Memory |
| CALMAT | Calcul Matriciel | | |
| CALOGSIM | Computer-Assisted Logistics Simulation | CAMA | Centralized Automatic Message Accounting |
| CALP | Computer Analysis of Library Postcards | CAMA | Computer-Aided Mathematical Analysis |
| CALR | Calculator | CAMA | Control and Automation Manufacturer Association |
| CALTEC | California Institute of Technology | CAMAC | Channel Allocation Monitor And Controller |
| CAM | Calculated Access Method | | |
| CAM | Call Accepted Message | CAMAC | Channel Allocation Monitoring And Control |
| CAM | Cartographic Automatic Mapping | CAMAC | Computer Application for Measurement And Control |
| CAM | Central Address Memory | | |
| CAM | Centre d'Automatisation pour le Management | CAMAC | Computer-Aided Measurement And Control |
| CAM | Checkout and Automatic Monitoring | CAMAC | Computer-Automated Measurement And Control |
| CAM | Checkout And Maintenance | | |
| CAM | Chinese Access Method | CAMAR | Common-Aperture Multi-function Array Radar |
| CAM | Clear and Add Magnitude | | |
| CAM | Communications Access Method | CAMCOS | Computer-Assisted Maintenance Planning and Control System |
| CAM | Comptage Automatique des Messages | CAMD | Computer-Aided Mechanical Design |
| CAM | Computer Address Matrix | | |
| CAM | Computer Applications to Manufacturing | CAMDS | Computer-Aided Medical Diagnostics System |
| CAM | Computer Assessment of Media | CAMERA | Cooperating Agency Method for Event Reporting and Analysis |
| CAM | Computer-Aided Management | CAMIC | Computer-Aided Microprocessing |
| CAM | Computer-Aided Manufacture | CAML | Computer-Accessed Microfiche Library |
| CAM | Computer-Aided Manufacturing | CAMMIS | Command Aircraft Maintenance Manpower Information System |
| CAM | Computer-Assisted Mailing | | |
| CAM | Computer-Assisted Manufacture | CAMP | Central Activity Monitoring Program |
| CAM | Computer-Assisted Manufacturing | CAMP | Communications Administrative Message Program |
| CAM | Computing Accounting Machine | | |
| CAM | Computing Attachment Machine | CAMP | Compiler for Automatic Machine Programming |
| CAM | Content Addressed Memory | CAMP | Computer Anwendungen für Management und Produktion |
| CAM | Contents Addressable Memory | CAMP | Computer Applications for Military Problems |
| CAM | Conventional Addressing Machine | CAMP | Computer-Aided Maintenance Project |
| CAM | Cybernetic Anthropomorphous Machine | CAMP | Computer-Aided Mask Preparation |

# C

| | |
|---|---|
| CAMP | Computer-Aided Mask Production |
| CAMP | Computer-Assisted Mathematics Program |
| CAMP | Computer-Assisted Menu Planning |
| CAMP | Computerized Aircraft Maintenance Program |
| CAMP | Controls And Monitoring Processor |
| CAMPRAD | Computer-Assisted Message Preparation Relay And Distribution |
| CAMPUS | Computerized Analytical Methods in Planning University System |
| CAMS | Computer Activity Monitor System |
| CAMS | Computer Automated Mailing System |
| CAMS | Cybernetic Anthropomorphous Machine System |
| CAMSAT | Camera Satellite |
| CAMSIM | Computer-Assisted Maintance Simulation |
| CAN | Calculator Analogique |
| CAN | Cancel |
| CAN | Cancellation |
| CAN | Configuration Accounting Number |
| CAN | Convertisseur Analogique Numérique |
| CAN | Cost Account Number |
| CAN | Customs Assigned Number |
| CAN/SDI | Canadian Selective Dissemination of Information |
| CANC | Cancel |
| CANC | Cancellation |
| CANC | Cancelled |
| CANCER | Computer Analysis of Nonlinear Circuits Excluding Radiation |
| CANCL | Cancellation |
| CANCL | Cancelling |
| CAND | Candelabra |
| CANDE | Command And Edit |
| CANO | Catalogue Number |
| CANOTT | Computer Analysis Of Troubles on Trunks |
| CANS | Computer-Assisted Network Scheduling system |
| CANTEC | Computer And Network Technology |
| CANTOT | Computer Analysis of Troubles On Trunk-circuits |
| CANTRAN | Cancel Transmission |
| CANTUS | Campusüberdeckendes Netz der Universität des Saarlandes |
| CAO | Collective Analysis Only |
| CAO | Conception Assistée par Ordinateur |
| CAO | Continuous Analog Output |
| CAORF | Computer-Aided Operations Research Facility |
| CAOS | Completely Automated Operational System |
| CAOS | Computer Applications Operating System |
| CAOS | Computer-Assisted Oscilloscope System |
| CAOS | Computer-Augmented Oscilloscope System |
| CAP | Capacitance |
| CAP | Capacitor |
| CAP | Capacity |
| CAP | Card Assembly Plant |
| CAP | Card Assembly Program |
| CAP | Centre d'Analyse et de Programmation |
| CAP | Classroom Assembly Program |
| CAP | Commercial Automatic Programming |
| CAP | Communications Analysis Package |
| CAP | Communications-pool Assembler Program |
| CAP | Component Acceptance Procedure |
| CAP | Computer-Aided-Publishing |
| CAP | Computer-Analyse und -Programmierung |
| CAP | Computer Analysis and Programmer Ltd. |
| CAP | Computer Analysis and Programming |
| CAP | Computer Analysts and Programmers |
| CAP | Computer-Aided Planning |
| CAP | Computer-Aided Presentation |
| CAP | Computer-Aided Production |
| CAP | Computer-Aided Programming |
| CAP | Computer-Aided Publishing |

# C

| | | | |
|---|---|---|---|
| CAP | Computer-Assisted Placement | CAPP | Computer-Aided Part Planning |
| CAP | Computer-Assisted Printing | CAPP | Computer-Aided Partitioning Program |
| CAP | Computer-Assisted Production | CAPP | Computer-Aided Process Planning |
| CAP | Computerized Assignment of Personnel | CAPRI | Coded Address Private Radio Intercommunications |
| CAP | Computers and Automation and People | CAPRI | Compact All-Purpose Range Instrument |
| CAP | Conflict Analysis Program | | |
| CAP | Conversion Aid Program | CAPRI | Computer-Aided Personal Reference Index |
| CAP | Cost Analysis Plan | | |
| CAP | Council on Advanced Programming | CAPRI | Computer-Automated Procurement-payment and Receipt of material Inclusive |
| CAP | Cryotron Associative Processor | | |
| CAP-RTL | Concurrent Algorithmic Programming language - Real Time Language | CAPRI | Computerized Advance Personnel Requirement and Inventory |
| CAP-SIM | Computer am Arbeitsplatz - Simulation | CAPPI | Constant Altitude Plan-Position Indicator |
| CAPA | Central Airborne Performance Analyzer | CAPS | Capital letters |
| | | CAPS | Cashier's Automatic Processing System |
| CAPAL | Computer And Photographic Assisted Learning | CAPS | Cassette Programming System |
| CAPARS | Computer-Aided Placement And Routing System | CAPS | Computer Application Service |
| CAPC | Computer-Aided Production Control | CAPS | Computer-Aided Packaging System |
| CAPCHE | Component Automatic Programmed Checkout Equipment | CAPS | Computer-Aided Pipe Sketching |
| CAPE | Communication Automatic Processing Equipment | CAPS | Computer-Aided Programming Software |
| CAPER | Core Analysis and Program Evaluation Recorder | CAPS | Computer-Assisted Placement Service |
| CAPICS | Computer-Aided Processing of Industrial Cabling Systems | CAPS | Computer-Assisted Problem Solving capacitors |
| | | CAPS | Computerized Agency Processing System |
| CAPITAL | Computer-Assisted Placing In The Areas of London | CAPS | Cost Account Performance Status report |
| CAPLIN | Computer-Assisted Physics Laboratory Instruction | CAPS | Courtauld's All-Purpose Simulator |
| CAPM | Computer-Aided Patient Management | CAPS | Customer Annual Progress Summary |
| CAPMEC | Computer Application for Planning Manufacturing Engineering Costs | CAPSS | Computer-Aided Pie Sketching System |
| | | CAPST | Capacitor Start |
| CAPO | Computer Aid in the Physicians Office | CAPTAIN | Character and Pattern Telephone Access Information Network system |
| CAPOSS | Capacity Planning and Operation Sequencing System | CAPTIN | Capacitance Pressure Transmitter Indicator |

# C

| | | | |
|---|---|---|---|
| CAPY | Capacity | CARDS | Computer-Aided Reliability Data Systems |
| CAQ | Computer-Aided Quality | | |
| CAQ | Computer-Assisted Quality | CARE | Computer-Aided Reliability Estimation |
| CAR | Card Adapter Register | | |
| CAR | Carriage | CARES | Computation And Research Evaluation System |
| CAR | Central Address Register | | |
| CAR | Channel Address Register | CARESIM | Computer-Assisted Repair Simulation |
| CAR | Check Authorization Record | CARHSPD | Carry, High Speed |
| CAR | Computer-Aided Robotics | CARIAC | Cardboard Illustrative Aid to Computation |
| CAR | Computer-Assisted Radiology | CARIS | Computerised Audio Report Information and Status |
| CAR | Computer-Assisted Research | | |
| CAR | Computer-Assisted Retrieval | CARIS | Computerized Agricultural Research Information System |
| CAR | Console Address Register | | |
| CAR | Control Unit Accumulator Register | CARL | Code Analysis Recording by Letters |
| CAR | Corrective Action Reply | | |
| CAR | Corrective Action Report | CARLA | Code Actuated Random Load Apparatus |
| CAR | Cylinder Address Register | | |
| CARAD | Computer-Aided Reliability And Design | CARMSIM | Computer-Assisted Reliability and Maintainability Simulation |
| CARAM | Content Addressable Random Access Memory | CARN | Conditional Analysis for Random Network |
| CARBINE | Computer Automated Realtime Betting Information Network | CARO | Clock Actuated Readout |
| | | CAROT | Centralized Automatic Recording On Trunks |
| CARD | Card Automated Reproduction and Distribution | CARP | Computed Air Release Point |
| CARD | Carrier Detector | | |
| CARD | Channel Allocation and Routing Data | CARPS | Calculus Rate Problem Solver |
| CARD | Coded Automatic Reading Device | CARR | Carriage |
| | | CARR | Carrier |
| CARD | Compact Automatic Retrieval Display | CARR | Combination Acknowledgement Reschedule Request |
| CARD | Compact Automatic Retrieval Device | CARR CUR | Carrier Current |
| | | CARR RET | Carriage Return |
| CARD | Computer-Aided Radar Design | CARR-FREQ | Carrier Frequency |
| | | CARRS | Close-in Automatic Route Restoral System |
| CARD | Computer-Assisted Route Development | CARS | Computer Audit Retrieval System |
| CARDA | Computer-Aided Reliability Data Analysis | CARS | Computer-Aided Ride Sharing |
| CARDAMAP | Cardiovascular Data Analysis by Machine Processing | CARS | Computer-Aided Routing System |
| CARDIAC | Cardboard Illustrative Aid to Computation | CARS | Computer-Augmented Resource System |
| CARDIS | Cargo Data Interchange System | CARS | Computerized Automotive Reporting Service |
| CARDS | Card Automated Reproduction and Distribution System | CARS | Continental Airlines Reservation System |
| | | CARSIMS | Carry, Simultaneous |

# C

| | | | |
|---|---|---|---|
| CART | Central Automatic Reliability Tester | CASA | Computer and Automated Systems Association |
| CART | Centralized Automatic Recorder and Tester | CASAPS | Computer Applied System Accounts Payable System |
| CART | Complete Automatic Reliability Testing | CASBL | Continuous Automated Single-Base Line |
| CART | Computer-Assisted Radiation Therapy | CASCADE | Colorado Automatic Single Crystal Analysis Diffraction Equipment |
| CART | Computerized Automatic Rating Technique | CASCAID | Careers Advisory Service Computerized Aid |
| CARTA | Computer-Aided Recorder Trap Analysis | CASD | Computer-Aided System Design |
| CARTA | Contour Analysis by Random Triangulation Algorithm | CASDAC | Computer-Aided Ship Design And Construction |
| CARTS | Computer-Automated Rapid Transit System | CASDOS | Computer-Aided Structural Detailing Of Ships |
| CAS | Cable Audit System | CASE | Common Access Switching Equipment |
| CAS | Calculated Air Speed | | |
| CAS | Calibrated Air Speed | CASE | Common-Application-Service-Elements |
| CAS | Cartidge Access System | | |
| CAS | Cell Address Set | CASE | Computer And System Engineering |
| CAS | Central Alarm System | | |
| CAS | Chain Acquisition System | CASE | Computer-Aided Software Engineering |
| CAS | Chemical Abstracts Service | | |
| CAS | Collision Avoidance System | CASE | Computer-Aided Structural Engineering |
| CAS | Column Address Select | | |
| CAS | Column Address Strobe | CASE | Computer-Aided System Evaluation |
| CAS | Communication Access System | CASE | Computer-Assisted System Evaluation |
| CAS | Communication Administration System | CASE | Computer-Automated Support Equipment |
| CAS | Compare Accumulator with Storage | CASE... | Computer and Systems Engineering Co. |
| CAS | Computer Accounting System | CASH | Call Accounting System for Hotels |
| CAS | Computer-Aided Systems | CASH | Computer-Aided System Hardware |
| CAS | Computer-Automated System | CASH | Computer-Automated System Hardware |
| CAS | Computerized Accounting System | CASIS | Computerunterstütztes Arbeitsschutz-Informationssystem |
| CAS | Content Addressable Storage | | |
| CAS | Content Addressed Storage | CASL | Control Automation System Logics |
| CAS | Control Automated System | | |
| CAS | Control Automation System | CASMIT | Control Automation System Manufacturing Interface Tape |
| CAS | Controlled Access System | | |
| CAS | Controller Access System | CASMOS | Computer Analysis and Simulation of MOS circuits |
| CAS | Controls Automation System | | |
| CAS | Cost Analysis System | CASO | Computer-Assisted System Operation |
| CAS | Customer Application Summary | | |

# C

| | | | |
|---|---|---|---|
| CASP | Crew Activities Scheduling Program | CAT | Computer-Aided Test |
| CASPAR | Cambridge Analogue Simulator for Predicting Atomic Reactions | CAT | Computer-Aided Testing |
| | | CAT | Computer-Aided Tool |
| | | CAT | Computer-Aided Topographie |
| CASPAR | Clarksons Automatic System for Passenger and Agents Reservations | CAT | Computer-Aided Tracking |
| | | CAT | Computer-Aided Translation |
| | | CAT | Computer-Assisted Testing |
| CASR | Cost And Schedule Reporting | CAT | Computer-Assisted Translation |
| CASS | Common Address Space Section | CAT | Computerized Axial Tomography |
| CASS | Computer Applications in Shipping and Shipbuilding | CAT | Computing Automation Technique |
| CASS | Computer Automatic Scheduling System | CAT | Continuous Automatic Test |
| | | CAT | Controlled Attenator Timer |
| CASS | Computerized Algorithmic Satellite Scheduler | CAT | Controlled Avalanche Transistor |
| CASSANDRA | Chromatogram Automatic Soaking, Scanning, And Digital Recording Apparatus | CAT | Cooled-Anode Transmitting tube |
| | | CAT | Current-Adjusting Type |
| CASSARS | Computer-Assisted Simulation of Supply And Related Systems | CATAL | Catalog |
| | | CATALYST | Computer-Assisted Teaching And Learning system |
| CAST | Computer Applications and Systems Technology | CATCH | Character Allocated Transfer Channel |
| CAST | Computerized Automatic System Tester | CATCH | Computer Analysis of Thermo-Chemical |
| CASTER | Computer-Assisted System for Total Effort Reduction | CATE | Comprehensive Automatic Test Equipment |
| | | CATE | Computer-Assisted Traffic Engineering |
| CASTER | Conversational And Service Terminal | CATE | Computer-controlled Automatic Test Equipment |
| CASTLE | Computer-Assisted System for Theatre Level Engineering | CATH | Cathode |
| | | CATH FOL | Cathode Follower |
| CAT | Cado-Aktions-Terminal | CATI | Centre d'Analyse et de Traitement de l'Information |
| CAT | Catalog | | |
| CAT | Centralized Automatic Testing | CATIA | Conception Assistée Tridimensionnelle Interactive |
| CAT | Character Assignment Table | | |
| CAT | Community Antenna Television | CATIA | Computer-Aided Three dimensional Interactive Application |
| CAT | Compile And Test | | |
| CAT | Component Acceptance Test | CATLG | Cataloguing |
| | | CATLINE | Catalog online |
| CAT | Computer Access Time | CATNIP | Computer-Assisted Technique for Numerical Index Preparation |
| CAT | Computer Analysis of Transistors | | |
| CAT | Computer of Average Transients | CATS | Category Switch |
| CAT | Computer-Aided Teaching | CATS | Centralized Automatic Test System |
| CAT | Computer-Aided Technology | | |

# C

| | | | |
|---|---|---|---|
| CATS | Comprehensive Analytical Test System | CB | Carry Byte |
| CATS | Computer Analysis of Tape Signals | CB | Central Battery |
| | | CB | Channel Byte |
| | | CB | Check Bit |
| CATS | Computer-Accessed Telemetry System | CB | Circuit Breaker |
| | | CB | Citizens Band |
| CATS | Computer-Aided Troubleshooting | CB | Clear Back |
| | | CB | Column Binary |
| CATS | Computer-Assisted Test Shop | CB | Command Byte |
| | | CB | Common Base |
| CATS | Computer-Assisted Trading System | CB | Common Battery |
| | | CB | Common Block |
| CATS | Computer-Automated Test System | CB | Computing Block |
| | | CB | Condition Bit |
| CATS | Computer-Automated Transit System | CB | Conditional Branch |
| | | CB | Conditional Breakpoint |
| CATS-A/P | Computerware Automated Total Systems - Accounts Payable | CB | Connecting Block |
| | | CB | Contact Breaker |
| | | CB | Continuous Breakdown |
| CATT | Centre for Advanced Technology Training | CB | Control Block |
| | | CB | Control Break |
| CATT | Controlled Avalanche Transmit Time | CB | Control Buffer |
| | | CB | Control Button |
| CATT | Cooled-Anode Transmitting Tube | CB | Control Byte |
| | | CB | Correction Bit |
| CATTS | Computer-Aided Training in Troubleshooting | CB | Count Bus |
| | | CB | Cubic |
| CATV | Community Antenna Television system | CB | Current Bit |
| | | CBA | C-Band transponder Antenna |
| CATV | Cable Antenna Television | | |
| CAU | Command Arithmetic Unit | CBA | Central Battery Apparatus |
| CAU | Calculatrice Arithmetique Universelle | CBA | Cost Benefit Analysis |
| | | CBA | Current Buffer Address |
| CAU | Complex Arithmetic Unit | CBAL | Counterbalance |
| CAU | Computer Advisory Unit | CBASIC | Commercial BASIC |
| CAUML | Computers and Automations's Universal Mailing List | CBATDS | Carrier-Based Airborne Tactical Data System |
| | | CBC | Chinese Binary Code |
| | | CBC | Circuit Board Card |
| CAUT | Caution | CBC | Code Binaire Cyclique |
| CAV | Constant Angular Velocity | CBC | Column Binary Code |
| CAVALCADE | Calibrating, Amplitude-Variation and Level-Correcting Analog-Digital Equipment | CBC | Computer Bar Code |
| | | CBC | Computer Based Concentrator |
| | | CBC | Consecutive Blank Column |
| CAVORT | Coherent Acceleration and Velocity Observations in Real Time | CBC | Cyclical Binary Code |
| | | CBCC | Common Bias, Common Control |
| CAW | Channel Address Word | CBCT | Circuit Board Card Tester |
| CAW | Common Antenna Working | CBCT | Customer Bank Communications Terminal |
| CAX | Community Automatic Exchange | | |
| | | CBD | Computer Block Diagram |
| CAZ | Commutating Auto-Zero | CBD | Constant Bit Density |
| CB | Capacitor Bank | CBDP | Communications Based Data Processing |
| CB | Card Batch | | |
| CB | Card Box | | |

# C

| | | | |
|---|---|---|---|
| CBDS | Circuit Board Design System | CBR | Circuit Board Rack |
| CBDT | Card Board Description Tape | CBR | Column Binary Read |
| | | CBS | Card Buffer Store |
| CBE | Central Battery Exchange | CBS | Central Battery Signalling |
| CBE | Computer Based Education | CBS | Central Battery Supply |
| CBEMA | Computer Business Equipment Manufacturers Association | CBS | Central Battery System |
| | | CBS | Central Bibliographic System |
| CBEMA | Canadian Business Equipment Manufacturers Association | CBS | Common Battery Signalling |
| | | CBS | Computer Backing Store |
| | | CBS | Computer Buffer Store |
| CBFS | Caesium Beam Frequency Standard | CBS | Consolidated Business Systems |
| | | CBSC | Common Bias, Single Control |
| CBH | Circuit Board Holder | | |
| CBI | Complementary Binary | CBT | Complementary Bipolar Transistor |
| CBI | Compound Batch Identification | | |
| | | CBT | Complex Before Transform |
| CBI | Computer Based Instruction | CBT | Computer Based Training |
| | | CBW | Constant-Bandwidth |
| CBI | Computer-Bildungs-Institut | CBX | Computerized Branch Exchange |
| CBI | Conditional Breakpoint Instruction | CC | Cable Connector |
| | | CC | Calculating Capacity |
| CBI | Control Break Item | CC | Calculator |
| CBIC | Complementary Bipolar Integrated Circuit | CC | Calibration Count |
| | | CC | Call Command |
| CBIS | Computer-Based Information System | CC | Call on Carry |
| | | CC | Carbon Copy |
| CBKCD | Customer Backorder Code | CC | Card Capacity |
| CBL | Cable | CC | Card Channel |
| CBL | Compressed Binary Loader | CC | Card Check |
| | | CC | Card Code |
| CBM | Compact Balancing Machine | CC | Card Collating |
| | | CC | Card Collator |
| CBM | Commodore Business Machine | CC | Card Column |
| | | CC | Card Control |
| CBM | Continental Ballistic Missile | CC | Card Controlled |
| | | CC | Card Count |
| CBM | Controlled Backmix | CC | Card Counter |
| CBMS | Computer-Based Management System | CC | Card Cycle |
| | | CC | Card-to-Card |
| CBMS | Computer-Based Message Systems | CC | Carriage Control |
| | | CC | Carrier Current |
| CBMS | Computer-Based Message Services | CC | Center-to-Center |
| | | CC | Central Computer |
| CBMU | Current Bit Monitor Unit | CC | Central Control |
| CBO | Computer Burst Order | CC | Ceramic Capacitor |
| CBP | Conditional Break-Point | CC | Chain Command |
| CBPI | Conditional Break-Point Instruction | CC | Channel Command |
| | | CC | Channel Controller |
| CBPU | Central Branch Processing Unit | CC | Character Change |
| | | CC | Character Code |
| CBR | Card Buffer Register | CC | Character Coded |
| CBR | Carry Byte Register | CC | Character Coding |

# C

| | | | |
|---|---|---|---|
| CC | Character Constant | CC | Computer Calculator |
| CC | Character Counter | CC | Computer Capacity |
| CC | Charge Coupled | CC | Computer Center |
| CC | Check Channel | CC | Computer Channel |
| CC | Check Character | CC | Computer Check |
| CC | Check Code | CC | Computer Code |
| CC | Check Computation | CC | Computer Consulting |
| CC | Circuit Card | CC | Computer Control |
| CC | Circuit Closing | CC | Computer Cycle |
| CC | Clipping Circuit | CC | Computing Centre |
| CC | Clock Card | CC | Concurrent Concession |
| CC | Clock Control | CC | Condition Code |
| CC | Close-Coupled | CC | Conditional Command |
| CC | Closed Circuit | CC | Conductive Channel |
| CC | Closing Coil | CC | Configuration Card |
| CC | Code Chain | CC | Connecting Circuit |
| CC | Code Character | CC | Consecutive Computer |
| CC | Code Chart | CC | Console Card |
| CC | Code Check | CC | Consolidated Computer Inc. |
| CC | Code Combination | | |
| CC | Code Control | CC | Constant Command |
| CC | Code Conversion | CC | Constant Current |
| CC | Code Converter | CC | Continuous Current |
| CC | Coded Character | CC | Continuation Cards |
| CC | Coded Command | CC | Control Card |
| CC | Coincidence Circuit | CC | Control Centre |
| CC | Coincident Current | CC | Control Change |
| CC | Colour Code | CC | Control Character |
| CC | Column Capacity | CC | Control Check |
| CC | Combinatory Code | CC | Control Circuit |
| CC | Command Card | CC | Control Clause |
| CC | Command Chaining | CC | Control Code |
| CC | Command Code | CC | Control Column |
| CC | Command Computer | CC | Control Command |
| CC | Command Control | CC | Control Computer |
| CC | Command Counter | CC | Control Connector |
| CC | Commande de Controle | CC | Control Console |
| CC | Comment Convention | CC | Control Counter |
| CC | Commercial Computer | CC | Control Cycle |
| CC | Common Carriers | CC | Conversion Code |
| CC | Common Channel | CC | Coordinates Computed |
| CC | Common Code | CC | Counting Code |
| CC | Common Collector | CC | Courant Continu |
| CC | Communication Code | CC | Cross Correlation |
| CC | Communication Control | CC | Cross Coupling |
| CC | Communication Controller | CC | Crystal Current |
| CC | Communications Centre | CC | Cubic Centimeter |
| CC | Communications Computer | CC | Cursor Control |
| CC | Compact Cassette | CC | Cycle Counter |
| CC | Comparator Circuit | CC | Cyclic Check |
| CC | Complete Carry | CC&S | Central Computer and Sequencer |
| CC | Complete Code | | |
| CC | Compound Condition | CC-AMDF | Cross Correlation-Average Magnitude Difference Function |
| CC | Compulsory Control | | |
| CC | Computation Center | | |

# C

| | | | |
|---|---|---|---|
| CC-CB | Common Collector-Common Base | CCB | Cyclic Check Byte |
| CC... | Consolidated Computer GmbH | CCBF | Computerbearbeitung Chemischer und Biologischer Forschungsergebnisse |
| CC/O | Composite Check-Out | | |
| CCA | Card Counting Attachment | CCBM | Card Controlled Billing Machine |
| CCA | Central Computer Accounting | CCBS | Center for Computerbased Behavioural Studies |
| CCA | Central Computer Agency | | |
| CCA | Centre de Calcul Analogique | CCBVP | Compound Correlated Bivariate Poisson |
| CCA | Channel-to-Channel Adapter | CCC | Card Controlled Calculator |
| CCA | Commerzielle Computer Applikation GmbH | CCC | Carrier Current Communication |
| CCA | Common Communications Adapter | CCC | Central Computer Complex |
| CCA | Communications Channel Adapter | CCC | Change and Configuration Control |
| CCA | Communications Control Area | CCC | Channel Command Call |
| | | CCC | Channel Control Check |
| CCA | Component Checkout Area | CCC | Chaos Computer Club |
| CCA | Computer & Control Abstracts | CCC | Classified Catalog Code |
| | | CCC | Common Control Circuit |
| CCA | Current Cost Accounting | CCC | Computer Communications Console |
| CCA | Customer Cost Analysis | CCC | Computer Communications Converter |
| CCA... | Computer Corporation of America | | |
| CCAA | Center for Computer Aided Analysis | CCC | Computer Control Company |
| | | CCC | Coordinate Conversion Computer |
| CCAM | Card Controlled Accounting Machine | CCC | Copy Control Character |
| CCAP | Communications Control Application Program | CCC | Cycle Control Counter |
| | | CCC | Cyclic Character Check |
| CCAP | Computer Controlled Applications Program | CCCB | Completion Code Control Block |
| CCATE | Computer-Controlled Automatic Test Equipment | CCCC | Consolidated Computer and Control Center |
| CCATS | Communications Command And Telemetry System | CCCE | Computer Communication Center Europe |
| CCB | Channel Command Block | CCCE | Computer Controlled Checkout Equipment |
| CCB | Channel Control Block | | |
| CCB | Character Control Block | CCCL | Complementary Constant Current Logic |
| CCB | Code Check Byte | | |
| CCB | Coded Current Block | CCCM | Coincident Current Core Memory |
| CCB | Command Control Block | | |
| CCB | Commercial Control Block | CCCM | Computer-Controlled Coordinate Measuring |
| CCB | Console-to-Computer Buffer | CCCRAM | Continuously Charge Coupled Random Access Memory |
| CCB | Contraband Control Base | | |
| CCB | Conventible Circuit Breaker | CCCS | Central Control Computer System |
| CCB | Conversational Control Block | CCCS | Coincident Current Core Storage |
| CCB | Cyclic Check Bit | | |

# C

| | | | |
|---|---|---|---|
| CCCS | Current Controlled Current Source | CCF | Continuous Card Feed |
| CCD | Card Code and Date | CCF | Controller Configuration Facility |
| CCD | Central Control Desk | CCF | Corporate Central File |
| CCD | Charge Complete Devices | CCF | Cross Correlation Function |
| CCD | Charge Coupled Device | CCF | Customer Calling Features |
| CCD | Collator Counting Device | | |
| CCD | Common Core of Data | CCFE | Corporate Central File - Engineering |
| CCD | Complementary Coded Decimal | CCFF | Critical Color Flicker Frequency |
| CCD | Computer Control Division | | |
| CCD | Computer-Controlled Display | CCFM | Cryogenic Continuous Film Memory |
| CCD | Core Current Driver | CCFP | Catalog Card Format Program |
| CCD... | Century Computer Deutschland GmbH | CCFT | Controlled Current Feedback Transformer |
| CCDA | Cable Cards Design Automation | CCG | Constant Current Generator |
| CCDA | Circuit Card Design Automation | CCH | Channel-Check Handler |
| CCDA | Computer-Compatible Data Acquisition | CCH | Computerized Criminal History |
| CCDC | Central Control and Display Console | CCHK | Continuity Check |
| CCDC | Computer Compatible Data Collection | CCHS | Cylinder-Cylinder-Head-Sector |
| CCDN | Corporate Consolidated Data Network | CCI | Card Computer Interface |
| | | CCI | Century Computer International |
| CCDP | Central Computer Development Program | CCI | Charge-Coupled Imager |
| CCDS | Computer Communications and Data Service | CCI | Circuit Condition Indicator |
| CCE | Channel Command Entry | CCI | Computer Communications Interface |
| CCE | Channel Control Error | | |
| CCE | Commission des Communautés Européennes | CCI | Computer Communications Inc. |
| CCE | Communications Control Equipment | CCI | Computer-Controlled Instruction |
| | | CCI | Condition Code Indicator |
| CCE | Complex Control Equipment | CCI | Continuous Card Input |
| | | CCI | Convert Clock Input |
| CCETT | Centre Commun d'Etudes de Télévision et Télécommunications | CCI | Current-Controlled Inductor |
| | | CCI... | Century Computer International Inc. |
| CCF | Central Computer Facility | | |
| CCF | Central Computing Facility | CCIA | Computer and Communications Industries Association |
| CCF | Central Control Facility | | |
| CCF | Chain Command Flag | CCIA | Console Computer Interface Adapter |
| CCF | Change Control Form | | |
| CCF | Circuit Characteristic Function | CCIC | Constant Cost Integer Code |
| CCF | COBOL Communications Facility | CCIC | Control Card Installation Card |
| CCF | Commutated Capacitor Filter | CCID | Control Channel Information Demodulator |

# C

| | | | |
|---|---|---|---|
| CCIM | Computer-to-Computer Interface Module | CCM | Constant Current Modulation |
| CCIM | Card Controlled Invoicing Machine | CCM | Copper Circuitized Module |
| CCIP | Continuously Computed Impact Point | CCM | Counter-Countermeasures |
| CCIR | Comité Consultatif International des Radiocommunications | CCMB | Centre de Communtation de Messages Bancaires |
| | | CCMD | Continuous Current Monitoring Device |
| CCIS | Command and Control Information System | CCMIS | Commodity Command Management Information System |
| CCIS | Common Channel Interoffice Signalling | CCMM | Complete Correlation Matrix Memory |
| CCIT | Comité Consultatif International Télégraphique | CCMP | Conversion Complete |
| | | CCMPTC | Central Computer Center |
| CCITT | Comité Consultatif International Télégraphique et Téléphonique | CCMS | Computer Centre Management System |
| | | CCMT | Computer Compatible Magnetic Tape |
| CCITT | Consultative Committee on International Telegraph and Telephone | CCMU | Computer Controller Multiplexer Unit |
| CCK | Channel Check | CCN | Channel Code Number |
| CCKW | Counterclockwise | CCN | Cluster-Controlled Node |
| CCL | Capacitor-Coupled Logic | CCN | Command Control Number |
| CCL | Channel Code Letter | CCNC | Common Channel Network Control |
| CCL | Coded Command Line | | |
| CCL | Command Control Language | CCNF | Canonical Conjunctive Normal Form |
| CCL | Common Command Language | CCNI | Current-Controlled Negative Inductance |
| CCL | Common Computer Language | CCNR | Current-Controlled Negative Resistance |
| CCL | Common Control Language | CCNT | Chief Controller |
| CCL | Composite Cell Logic | CCO | Complete Carry-Over |
| CCL | Computer Control Language | CCO | Constant Current Operation |
| CCL | Computer Control Loading | | |
| CCL | Contact Clock | CCO | Crystal-Controlled Oscillator |
| CCL | Customized Card List | | |
| CCL... | Consolidated Computer Ltd. | CCO | Current-Controlled Oscillator |
| CCLCD | Customized Card List Control Date | CCOCP | Corporate Customer Order Control Program |
| CCLKW | Counterclockwise | CCOP | Centralized Customer Order Processing |
| CCLKWS | Counterclockwise | | |
| CCLS | Computer-Controlled Launch Set | CCOP | Consolidated Customer Order Processing |
| CCM | Card Capacity Memory | CCOP | Consolidated Customer Order Program |
| CCM | Charge Coupled Memory | | |
| CCM | Combined Coding Machine | CCP | Calculatrice de Commande à Programme |
| CCM | Communications Controller Multichannel | | |
| | | CCP | Call Confirmation Protocol |
| CCM | Computer Control Mode | CCP | Central Control Position |
| CCM | Computer-Controlled Microscope | CCP | Certificate in Computer-Programming |

# C

| | | | |
|---|---|---|---|
| CCP | Channel Control Programme | CCR | Configuration Control Register |
| CCP | Character Controlled Protocol | CCR | Console Card Reader |
| | | CCR | Control Circuit Resistance |
| CCP | Character Count Protocol | CCR | Credit Card Register |
| CCP | Comand Processing Program | CCR | Critical Compression Ratio |
| CCP | Command Control Panel | CCR | Cyclic Correlation |
| CCP | Communication Control Package | CCRIA | Comité Consultatif de la Recherche en Informatique et Automatique |
| CCP | Communications Control Program | CCRO | Clock Controlled Readout |
| CCP | Computer Circuit Protector | CCROS | Card Capacitor Read-Only Store |
| CCP | Conditional Command Processor | CCROS | Card Capacitor Read-Only Storage |
| CCP | Connecting Card Perforator | CCRP | Continuously Computed Release Point |
| CCP | Console Command Processor | CCS | Capital Computer Suites Limited |
| CCP | Constant Card Processing | CCS | Card Capacity Store |
| CCP | Control Computer Program | CCS | Card Cornering Station |
| CCP | Critical Compression Pressure | CCS | Card Counting Sorter |
| | | CCS | Central Computer Station |
| CCP | Cross-Connection Point | CCS | Central Computing Site |
| CCP/M | Concurrent CP/M | CCS | Change Control System |
| CCPC | Communications Computer Programming Center | CCS | Cinema Computer System |
| | | CCS | Collector Coupled Structures |
| CCPMOP | Corporate Components Procurement Management Operating Procedures | CCS | Colour vision Constant Speed |
| CCPT | Controller Creation Parameter Table | CCS | Column Code Suppression |
| | | CCS | Command Control System |
| CCPT | Computer Controlled Positioning Table | CCS | Commercial Spooling System |
| CCR | Candle Computer Report | CCS | Common Command Set |
| CCR | Central Control Room | CCS | Common Channel Signal |
| CCR | Channel Check Record | CCS | Communication Collection System |
| CCR | Channel Command Register | CCS | Communications Control System |
| CCR | Channel Control Routine | | |
| CCR | Coaxial Cavity Resonator | CCS | Component Control Section |
| CCR | Command Chaining Retry | | |
| CCR | Command Control Receiver | CCS | Computer-Coded Search |
| CCR | Communications Change Request | CCS | Computer Control Station |
| | | CCS | Computer Control System |
| CCR | Compensated Character Recognition | CCS | Continuous Colour Sequence |
| CCR | Computer Character Recognition | CCS | Continuous Commercial Service |
| CCR | Computer Check Routine | CCS | Contour Control System |
| CCR | Computer-Controlled Retrieval | CCS | Control Card Statement |
| | | CCS | Control Command Store |
| CCR | Condition Code Register | CCS | Control Computer Subsystem |

# C

| | | | |
|---|---|---|---|
| CCS | Corporate Consolidation System | CCTI | Centre Commun de Traitement de l'Information |
| CCS | Custom Computer System | CCTI | Conditional Control Transfer Instruction |
| CCSA | Cascaded Carry Save Adder | CCTN | Correction |
| CCSA | Cascaded Carry Save Addition | CCTP | Card Controlled Tape Punch |
| CCSA | Common Control Switching Arrangement | CCTS | Configuration Control Test System |
| CCSC | Coordinating Committee on Satellite Communications | CCTV | Closed-Circuit Television |
| | | CCTVS | Closed-Circuit Television Subsystem |
| CCSD | Common Channel Signalling Device | CCU | Card Counting Unit |
| | | CCU | Central Calculator Unit |
| CCSDS | Consultative Committee for Space Data Systems | CCU | Central Computer Unit |
| | | CCU | Central Control Unit |
| CCSEM | Computer Controlled Scanning Electron Microscope | CCU | Channel Control Unit |
| | | CCU | Chart Comparison Unit |
| | | CCU | Cluster Control Unit |
| CCSI | Conditional Control Sequence Interruption | CCU | Combined Control Unit |
| | | CCU | Common Control Unit |
| CCSL | Communications and Control Systems Laboratory | CCU | Communication Control Unit |
| | | CCU | Computer Control Unit |
| CCSL | Compatible Current Sinking Logic | CCU | Console Control Unit |
| | | CCUAP | Computer Cable Upkeep Administrative Program |
| CCSPS | Central Computer Support Programming System | CCUF | Corporate Control Usage File |
| CCSR | Copper Cable Steal Reinforced | CCUP | Centralized Charging User Part |
| CCSS | Conversational Computer Statistical System | CCV | Code Converter |
| CCST | Center for Computer Sciences and Technology | CCV | Closed Circuit Voltage |
| | | CCVS | Current Controlled Voltage Source |
| CCSU | Computer Cross-Select Unit | CCVS | COBOL Compiler Validation System |
| CCT | Carriage Control Tape | | |
| CCT | Character Code Translation | CCW | Channel Command Word |
| CCT | Circuit Continuity Tester | CCW | Channel Control Word |
| CCT | Code Checking Time | CCW | Command Control Word |
| CCT | Communications Control Team | CCXD | Computer-Controlled X-ray Diffractometer |
| CCT | Computer Checking Time | CCY | Card Cycle |
| CCT | Computer Concepts Trainer | CD | Cable Duct |
| | | CD | Cadminum |
| CCT | Computer-Compatible Tape | CD | Calculating Device |
| | | CD | Calculation Diagram |
| CCT | Connecting Circuit | CD | Calendar Day |
| CCT | Constant Current Transformer | CD | Call Dispatch |
| | | CD | Candela |
| CCT | Crystal Controlled Transmitter | CD | Capacitive Discharge |
| | | CD | Capacitor Diode |
| CCTA | Central Computer and Telecommunications Agency | CD | Capacitor Discharge |
| | | CD | Card |
| | | CD | Card Desk |

# C

| | | | | |
|---|---|---|---|---|
| CD | Card Duplication | CD | Cycle Delay |
| CD | Card to Disk | CD RDR | Card Reader |
| CD | Carrier Detected | CD/NC | Computer-aided Design/ Numerical Control |
| CD | Catalogued Data | | |
| CD | Cathode of Diodes | CDA | Centralized Data Acquisition |
| CD | Cell Data | | |
| CD | Cellular Radio | CDA | Chain Data Address |
| CD | Center Distance | CDA | Chaining Data Address |
| CD | Chain Data | CDA | Command and Data Acquisition |
| CD | Chaining Data | | |
| CD | Channel Data | CDA | Convertisseur Digital/ Analogique |
| CD | Character Density | | |
| CD | Check Digit | CDAA | Central Data Analysis Area |
| CD | Checking Document | CDAO | Conception et Dessin Assistés par Ordinateur |
| CD | Circuit Discription | | |
| CD | Clock Driver | CDAS | Command and Data Acquisition Station |
| CD | Code | | |
| CD | Code Digit | CDB | Central Data Bank |
| CD | Coding Delay | CDB | Command Definition Block |
| CD | Collision Defect | CDB | Commercial Data Buffer |
| CD | Collision Detection | CDB | Common Data Bank |
| CD | Column Distributor | CDB | Common Data Base |
| CD | Command Decoder | CDB | Common Data Bus |
| CD | Command Definition | CDB | Component Data Bank |
| CD | Command Device | CDB | Corporate Data Base |
| CD | Commercial Data | CDB | Current Data Bit |
| CD | Common Denominator | CDB | Customer Data Block |
| CD | Common Digitizer | CDBN | Column Digit Binary Network |
| CD | Communication Data | | |
| CD | Compact-Disc | CDC | Call Direction Code |
| CD | Comparative Data | CDC | Card Design Center |
| CD | Compare Decimal | CDC | Central Data Control |
| CD | Compiling Duration | CDC | Central Digital Computer |
| CD | Component Demand | CDC | Channel Data Check |
| CD | Compressed Data | CDC | Characteristics Distortion Compensation |
| CD | Computer Data | | |
| CD | Computer Dependent | CDC | Code Directing Character |
| CD | Computer Design | CDC | Coder-Decoder Control |
| CD | Computer Diagram | CDC | Command Document Continue |
| CD | Computer Digest | | |
| CD | Computer Display | CDC | Command and Data-handling Console |
| CD | Computer Drum | | |
| CD | Computing Device | CDC | Common Data Carrier |
| CD | Confidential Data | CDC | Company Data Coordinator |
| CD | Continuous Duty | CDC | Computer Development Center |
| CD | Control Data | | |
| CD | Control Desk | CDC | Computer Display Channel |
| CD | Control Device | CDC | Configuration Data Control |
| CD | Core image Directory | | |
| CD | Count Data | CDC | Control Data Company |
| CD | Cross Domain | CDC | Control Data Computer |
| CD | Crystal Diode | CDC | Copper Data Center |
| CD | Crystal Driver | CDC | Countdown Clock |
| CD | Current Density | CDC | Course and Distance Calculator |
| CD | Current Discharge | | |

# C

| | | | |
|---|---|---|---|
| CDC | Course and Distance Computer | CDE | Controls and Display Equipment |
| CDC | Cryogenics Data Center | CDEBUG | Cobol symbolic Debugging package |
| CDC | Crystallographic Data Centre | CDED | Coded |
| CDC | Cyclic Decimal Code | CDEI | Control Data Education Institute |
| CDC... | Control Data Corporation | | |
| CDCE | Central Data-Conversion Equipment | CDEIS | Component Division Engineering Information System |
| CDCL | Command Document Capability List | CDEK | Computer Data Entry Keyboard |
| CDCN | Computer Decisions | | |
| CDCP | Command Display and Control Processor | CDES | Conversational Data Entry System |
| CDCR | Center for Documentation and Communication Research | CDEVC | Computer Development Center |
| | | CDEVC | Computer Development Centre |
| CDCS | Central Data Collection System | CDF | Chain Data Flag |
| CDCS | Cyber Data Control System | CDF | Change to Data Field |
| | | CDF | Chart Dynamic Flow |
| CDCT | Card Count | CDF | Combined Distributation Frame |
| CDCY | Card Cycle | | |
| CDD | Central Data Display | CDF | Command Decoder Film |
| CDD | Chart Distribution Data | CDF | Command Decoder Filter |
| CDD | Coded | CDF | Component Description File |
| CDD | Coded Decimal Digit | | |
| CDD | Colour Data Display | CDF | Components Data File |
| CDD | Combat Data Director | CDF | Continuous Document Feeding |
| CDD | Command Destruct Decoder | CDF | Control Data Field |
| CDD | Command Document Discard | CDF | Cumulative Density Function |
| CDD | Common Data Dictionary | CDF | Cumulative Distribution of Frequency |
| CDD | Compiler Directing Declarative | CDFCHB | Command Data Format Control Handbook |
| CDD | Computer Directed Drawing | CDG | Capacitor Diode Gate |
| CDDC | Center Data Descriptions Catalog | CDG | Coder-Decoder Group |
| | | CDG | Coding |
| CDDDS | Card Development Design Daily Status | CDH | Cable Distributation Head |
| CDDI | Computer-Directed Drawing Instrument | CDH | Command and Data-Handling |
| CDDP | Console Digital Display Programmer | CDHC | Command and Data Handling Console |
| CDDS | Central Data Distribution System | CDI | Called Line Identity |
| | | CDI | Capacitor Discharge Ignition |
| CDE | Channel Data Error | | |
| CDE | Code | CDI | Collector Diffusion Isolation |
| CDE | Command Document End | | |
| CDE | Complex Data Entry | CDI | Computer Direct Input |
| CDE | Consumption Data Exchange | CDI | Computer-Directed Instrument |
| CDE | Contents Directory Entry | CDI | Control Data Institute |

- 107 -

# C

| | | | |
|---|---|---|---|
| CDI | Course Deviation Indicator | CDOP | Component Description Operation Procedure |
| CDI-TTL | Collector-Diffusion-Isolated/Transistor-Transistor Logic | CDP | Call routine Display Panel |
| | | CDP | Celestial Data Processor |
| CDI... | Control Data Institute | CDP | Central Data Processing |
| CDIC | Components Division Inventory Control | CDP | Central Data Processor |
| | | CDP | Centralized Data Processing |
| CDICS | Centralized Dealer Inventory Control System | CDP | Centralized Data Processor |
| | | CDP | Certain Data Processing |
| CDIU | Central Digital Interface Unit | CDP | Certificate in Data Processing |
| CDK | Channel Data check | CDP | Certified Data Plan |
| CDL | Card Lever | CDP | Certified Data Processor |
| CDL | Command Definition Language | CDP | Check Digit Procedure |
| | | CDP | Checkout Data Processor |
| CDL | Common Display Logic | CDP | Command Data Processor |
| CDL | Compiler Description Language | CDP | Commercial Data Processing |
| CDL | Computer Design Language | CDP | Communication Data Processor |
| CDL | Condor Data Link | | |
| CDL | Contract Data List | CDP | Configuration Data Processor |
| CDL | Core Diode Logic | | |
| CDL | Current Discharge Line | CDP | Correlated Data Processor |
| CDL | Custom Dynamic Logic | CDP | Cost Data Plan |
| CDLA | Computer Dealers and Lessors Association | CDPB | Command Document Page Boundary |
| CDLS | Condor Data Link System | CDPB | Computation and Data Processing Branch |
| CDM | Card Document Machine | | |
| CDM | Carriage Drive Mechanism | CDPC | Central Data Processing Computer |
| CDM | Centre De Modulation | | |
| CDM | Code Division Multiplex | CDPC | Commercial Data Processing Center |
| CDM | Codiertes Digitales Meldesystem | | |
| | | CDPF | Composed Document Printing Facility |
| CDM | Computer Description Manual | CDPI | Command Data Processing and Instrumentation |
| CDM | Concentrateur Diffuseur de Messages | CDPIE | Command Data Processor Interface Equipment |
| CDM | Core Division Multiplexing | | |
| CDMA | Code Division Multiple Access | CDPIRS | Crash Data Position Indicator Recorder Subsystem |
| CDMM | Component Demand Maintenance Module | CDPP | Central Data Processing Program |
| CDMS | Central Data Management System | CDPSC | Computing and Data Processing Society of Canada |
| CDMS | Commercial Data Management System | | |
| CDMS | Communications Data Management System | CDPU | Central Data Processing Unit |
| CDN | Coded Decimal Notation | CDR | Call Data Recording |
| CDN | Coded Decimal Number | CDR | Call Detail Recording |
| CDN | Computer Decisions | CDR | Central Data Recording |
| CDNF | Canonical Disjunctive Normal Form | CDR | Channel Data Register |
| | | CDR | Command Document Resynchronisation |
| CDO | Community Dial Office | | |

# C

| | | | |
|---|---|---|---|
| CDR | Compare and Difference Right-half-words | CDSS | Contractual Data Status reporting System |
| CDR | Components Data Representative | CDSS | Customer Digital Switching System |
| CDR | Current Distribution Ratio | CDSU | Computer and Data Systems Unit |
| CDRL | Contract Data Requirements List | CDT | Cable Data Tape |
| CDRM | Cross-Domain Resource Manager | CDT | Command Definition Table |
| CDRS | Computer Data Recording System | CDT | Communications Display Terminal |
| CDS | Car Despatch System | CDT | Compressed-Data Tape |
| CDS | Case Data System | CDT | Computer Data Transmission |
| CDS | Catalogued Data Set | | |
| CDS | Century Data Systems | CDT | Control Data Terminal |
| CDS | Chip Design System | CDT | Control Digit Test |
| CDS | Circadian Data System | CDT | Controller Description Template |
| CDS | Command Document Start | | |
| CDS | Common Diagram System | CDT | Coordinate Data Transmission |
| CDS | Communications and Data Subsystem | CDT | Coordinate Data Transmitter |
| CDS | Compiler Declarative Statement | CDT | Countdown Time |
| CDS | Compiler Directing Statement | CDTCP | Communication and Data Transmission Control Program |
| CDS | Comprehensive Display System | CDTI | Centro para el Desarrollo Tecnologico e Industrial |
| CDS | Compressed Data Storage | | |
| CDS | Computer Data Switchboard | CDTIS | Components Division Technical Information System |
| CDS | Computer Duplex System | | |
| CDS | Computergesteuertes Datendrucksystem | CDTL | Complementary Diode Transistor Logic |
| CDS | Computerized Documentation Service | CDU | Calculatrice Digitale Universelle |
| CDS | Concentrated Data Set | CDU | Capacitor Discharge Unit |
| CDS | Configuration Data Service | CDU | Central Decode Unit |
| CDS | Configuration Data Set | CDU | Central Display Unit |
| CDS | Consumer Data Service | CDU | Classification Décimale Universelle |
| CDS | Consumer Dataservice System | CDU | Computer Deutschen Ursprungs |
| CDS | Container Dispositions System | CDU | Control Data Unit |
| CDSAM | Cash Discount Amount | CDU | Control Display Unit |
| CDSC | Communications Distribution and Switching Center | CDU | Coupling Data Unit |
| | | CDU | Coupling Display Unit |
| | | CDUI | Command Document User Information |
| CDSCD | Cash Discount Code | | |
| CDSE | Computer Driven Simulation Environment | CDV | Check Digit Verification |
| | | CDVSC | Current-Dependent Voltage Source Capacitor |
| CDSL | Connect Data Set to Line | | |
| CDSR | Contractual Data Status Reporting | CDW | Computer Data Word |
| | | CE | Cable Equalizer |
| CDSS | Compressed Data Storage System | CE | Calculateur Electronique |
| | | CE | Card Ejection |

- 109 -

# C

| | | | |
|---|---|---|---|
| CE | Card Error | CEC | Constant Electric Contact |
| CE | Chaining Error | CEC | Controlled Element Computer |
| CE | Channel End | | |
| CE | Chip-Enable | CECE | Comité pour l'Exploitation de Calculatrices Electroniques |
| CE | Circular Error | | |
| CE | Civil Engineering | | |
| CE | Clear Entry | CECL | Civil Engineering Computer Laboratory |
| CE | Code Equipment | | |
| CE | Coincidence Element | CECUA | Confederation of European Computer Users Association |
| CE | Common Ermitter | | |
| CE | Communications Electronics | CECUA | Conference of European Computer Users Association |
| CE | Commutator End | | |
| CE | Comparing Element | | |
| CE | Compensating Errors | CED | Computer Entry Device |
| CE | Compound Expression | CEDAC | Computerized Energy Distribution and Automated Control |
| CE | Compute Element | | |
| CE | Computer Engineer | | |
| CE | Computing Element | CEDAR | Computer aided Environmental Design Analysis and Realisation |
| CE | Computing Error | | |
| CE | Conditional Expression | | |
| CE | Constant Error | CEDDA | Center for Experiment Design and Data Analysis |
| CE | Constant Expression | | |
| CE | Consumer Electronics | CEDET | Computer-aided Design Experimental Translator |
| CE | Control Element | | |
| CE | Cost Effectiveness | CEDIJ | Centre d'Etudes et de Développement en Informatique Juridique |
| CE | Counducted Emission | | |
| CE | Customer Engineer | | |
| CE | Customer Engineering | CEDPA | Certificate in EDP Auditing |
| CE-CB | Common Emitter - Common Base | CEDPM | Central EDP Machine |
| CE/SD | Convolutional Encoding/ Sequential Decoding | CEE | Channel Equipment Error |
| | | CEF | Carrier Elimination Filter |
| CEA | Circular Error Average | | |
| CEA | Column Exit Address | CEF | Complementary Emitter Follower |
| CEA | Constant Extinction Angle | | |
| CEAC | Consulting Engineers Association of California | CEF | Computer Execute Function |
| | | CEF | Corporate Express File |
| CEARC | Computer Education and Applied Research Center | CEGL | Cause-Effect Graph Language |
| CEASE | Cost Engineering Automated System Estimate | CEI | Commission Electrotechnique Internationale |
| CEASRS | Civil Engineer Automated Specification Retrieval System | CEI | Communications Electronics Instruction |
| | | CEI | Computer Extended Instruction |
| CEATOMS | Control Engineering Approach To Management Systems | CEI | Contract End Item |
| | | CEI | Correct End Item |
| CEBIT | Centrum der Büro- und Informationstechnik | CEI | Cost Effectiveness Index |
| | | CEI... | Computing Efficiency Inc. |
| CEC | Card Extract Counter | CEIN | Contract End Item Number |
| CEC | Centralized Electronic Control | | |
| CEC | Chuo Electric Computer | CEIR | Corporation for Economic Industrial Research |

# C

| | | | |
|---|---|---|---|
| CEIR | Counsel for Economic and Industry Research | CEP | Complementary Even Parity |
| CEIS | Cost and Economic Information System | CEP | Computer Enhancement Process |
| CEL | Computer Economics Limited | CEP | Computer Entry Punch |
| CEL | Corporate Engineering List | CEP | Continuous Estimation Program |
| CEL | Crowding Effect Laser | CEPA | Civil Engineering Program Application |
| CELEX | Communitatis Europaeae Lex | CEPIA | Centre d'Etudes Pratiques d'Informatique et d'Automatique |
| CEM | Cost Evaluation Model | | |
| CEM | Customer Engineering Memorandum | CEPPA | Customer Engineering Product Performance Analysis |
| CEMA | Canadian Electrical Manufacturers Association | CEPT | Conférence Européenne des Postes et Télécommunications |
| CEMAC | Commitee of European associations of Manufacturers of Active electronic Components | CER | Ceramics |
| | | CER | Channel Error Record |
| CEMAC | Central Monitoring And Control | CER | Channel Error Routine |
| | | CER | Cost Estimating Relations |
| CEMAT | Centre d'Etudes Mécanographiques et d'Assistance Technique | CERC | Computer Entry and Readout Control |
| | | CERDIP | Ceramic Dual-In-line Package |
| CEMF | Counter Electromotive Force | CERE | Computer Entry and Readout Equipment |
| CEMIS | Client-Employee Management Information System | CERL | Computer based Education Research Laboratory |
| | | CERMET | Ceramic-to-Metal |
| CEMON | Customer Engineering Monitor | CERPACK | Ceramic Package |
| CEMS | Central Electronic Management System | CERR | Channel Error Recording Routine |
| CEN | Capacity Exceeding Number | CERRC | Complete Engine Repair Requirements Card |
| CENADEM | Centro Nacional de Desarrollo Micrografico | CERS | Communications Experimental Research Satellite |
| CENORI | Centre Normand de Recherche en Informatique | CES | Characteristic Equation System |
| CENOUT | Central Output | | |
| CENTACS | Center for Tactical Computer Sciences | CES | Common-Equipment System |
| | | CES | Computer Education System |
| CENTCON | Centralized Control | | |
| CENTY | Calculatrice Electronique Numérique Type | CES | Computer Education in Schools |
| CEO | Chief Executive Officer | CES | Computer Energy Storage |
| CEO | Comprehensive Electronic Office | CES | Computerunterstütztes Entwicklungssystem |
| CEOS... | Compania Espanola de Ordenadores y Systemas SA | CES | Consumer Electronic Show |
| | | CES | Corporate Engineering Standard |
| CEP | Circular Error Probability | CES | Cost Effectiveness Study |
| CEP | Civil Engineering Package | CESA | Canadian Engineering Standards Association |
| CEP | Column Exit Pulse | | |

- 111 -

# C

| | | | |
|---|---|---|---|
| CESD | Composite External Symbol Dictionary | CF | Characteristic Frequency |
| CESEMI | Computer Evaluation of Scanning Electron Microscope Image | CF | Characteristic Function |
| | | CF | Clock Frequency |
| | | CF | Code Figure |
| CESIA | Centre d'Etudes des Systèmes d'Information de l'Administration | CF | Coding Field |
| | | CF | Coding Form |
| | | CF | Coding Format |
| CESIL | Computer Education System Instructional Language | CF | Combined File |
| | | CF | Command Field |
| | | CF | Command Function |
| CESSL | Cell Space Simulation Language | CF | Communications Facility |
| | | CF | Compact Floppy |
| CET | Computerunterstütztes Entscheidungstraining | CF | Comparing Feature |
| | | CF | Complement Form |
| CET | Corrected Effective Temperature | CF | Completion Flag |
| | | CF | Condition Flag |
| CET | Cumulative Elapsed Time | CF | Consecutive Field |
| CET/OS | Corporate Express Transfer/Obsoletion System | CF | Console File |
| | | CF | Constant Frequency |
| | | CF | Context Free |
| CETAM | Centre d'Etudes et d'Applications Mécanographiques | CF | Continuous Feed |
| | | CF | Continuous Form |
| | | CF | Continuous Function |
| CETIS | Centre de Traitement de l'Information Scientifique | CF | Control Field |
| | | CF | Control Flag |
| | | CF | Conversion Factor |
| CETOS | Corporate Engineering Transfer and Obsoletion System | CF | Correction Factor |
| | | CF | Correlation Factor |
| | | CF | Count Field |
| CEU | Control Electronics Unit | CF | Count Forward |
| CEV | Cash Equivalent Value | CF | Crystal Filter |
| CEX | Carry Exit | CF | Cubic Foot |
| CEXP | Centre d'Exploitation | CF | Current Feedback |
| CF | Calculating Function | CFA | Colour Filtery Array |
| CF | Candle-Foot | CFA | Commodore-Fachausstellung |
| CF | Card Face | | |
| CF | Card Feed | CFA | Computer Family Architecture |
| CF | Card Field | | |
| CF | Card File | CFA | Cross-Fields Amplifier |
| CF | Carriage Free | CFAO | Conception et Fabrication Assistées par Ordinateur |
| CF | Carrier Frequency | | |
| CF | Carry Flag | CFAR | Constant False Alarm Rate |
| CF | Carry Forward | | |
| CF | Case File | CFB | Call Forward Busy |
| CF | Catalogued File | CFBS | Card Feed Barrier Strip |
| CF | Cathode Follower | CFC | Card Feed Compare |
| CF | Center Frequency | CFC | C-band Frequency Converter |
| CF | Central File | | |
| CF | Centrifugal Force | CFC | Control Feed Chart |
| CF | Chain Flag | CFCB | Card Feed Circuit Breaker |
| CF | Chaining Field | CFCB | Computer Format Control Buffer |
| CF | Chaining File | | |
| CF | Change Frequency | CFCFG | Context-Free Coded Fuzzy Grammar |
| CF | Character Fill | | |

# C

| | | | |
|---|---|---|---|
| CFCFL | Context-Free Coded Fuzzy Language | CFMS | Chain File Management System |
| CFCS | Cross Field Closing Switch | CFMS | Chained File Management System |
| CFCU | Common File Control Unit | CFMS | Compatibility Feature Mode Set |
| CFD | Card Feed Device | CFN | Chain Field Number |
| CFD | Computer Function Diagram | CFN | Check Following Numbers |
| CFE | Complement Field End | CFNA | Call Forward No Answer |
| CFE | Compteur Frappe Erronée | CFO | Carrier Frequency Oscillator |
| CFE | Contractor Furnished Equipment | CFO | Channel For Orders |
| CFER | Collector Field-Effect Resistor | CFOR | Conversational FORTRAN |
| | | CFP | Calculation Fices Points |
| CFF | Carry Flip-Flop | CFP | Carrier Frequency Pulse |
| CFF | Critical Flicker Frequency | CFP | Computer Forms Printer |
| | | CFP | Concept Formulation Package |
| CFF | Critical Fusion Frequency | CFP/TDP | Concept Formulation Package - Technical Development Plan |
| CFG | Context-Free Grammar | | |
| CFG | Configuration | | |
| CFGG | Context-Free Graph Grammar | CFPG | Context-Free Picture Grammar |
| CFH | Card Feed Hopper | CFR | Carbon-Film Resistor |
| CFH | COBOL File Handler | CFR | Catastrophic Failure Rate |
| CFI | Control Format Item | | |
| CFI | Crystal Frequency Indicator | CFR | Chance Failure Rate |
| | | CFR | Channel Failure Record |
| CFIA | Component Failure Impact Analysis | CFR | Cumulative Failure Rate |
| | | CFRD | Confidential, Formerly Restricted Data |
| CFIM | Compatibility Feature Initialize Mode | CFRO | Centre Français de Recherche Opérationnelle |
| CFK | Command Function Key | | |
| CFL | Coded Fuzzy Language | | |
| CFL | Context-Free Language | CFRS | Customer Float Reporting Service |
| CFLC | Compatibility Feature Load Constant | CFS | Card Feed Stop |
| CFLV | Compatibility Feature Load Variable | CFS | Carrier Frequency Shift |
| | | CFS | Centre Frequency Stabilisation |
| CFM | Card Feeding Mechanism | | |
| CFM | Cathode Follower Mixer | CFS | Circuit Failure Simulation |
| CFM | Central Facility Maintenance | | |
| | | CFS | Combined File Search |
| CFM | Circuit Feasibility Model | CFS | Common File System |
| CFM | Computer Feasibility Model | CFS | Component Failure Summary |
| CFM | Confirm | CFS | Computer Fast Storage |
| CFM | Confirmation | CFS | Computer File System |
| CFM | Continuous Film Memory | CFS | Computer Firmware Systems |
| CFM | Crystal Frequency Multiplier | CFS | Computer Function Symbol |
| CFM | Cubic Feet per Minute | | |
| CFM | Cylindrical Film Memory | CFS | Continuous Film Store |
| CFM... | Computer Field Maintenance Ltd. | CFS | Continuous Forms Stacker |

# C

| | | | |
|---|---|---|---|
| CFS | Cubic Feet per Second | CGL | Control Group Level |
| CFSC | Compatibility Feature Store Constant | CGLI | City and Guilds of London Institute |
| CFSDA | Cross-Frequency Statistical Deconvolution Algorithm | CGM | Compagnie Générale de Micromatique |
| CFSS | Combined File Search Strategy | CGM | Computer Graphics Meta-file |
| CFSV | Compatibility Feature Store Variable | CGMID | Character Generation Module Identifier |
| CFT | Charge-Flow Transistor | CGN | Computer Group News |
| CFT | Coated Foam Tape | CGO | Clear-and-Gate Operation |
| CFT | Continuous Fourier Transport | CGP | Capacitance Grid-Plate |
| CFTS | Computerized Flight Test System | CGPL | Conversational Graphical Programming Language |
| CFU | Control Functional Unit | CGR | Code Generating Routine |
| CFW | Call Forward | CGS | Centimeter-Gram-Second |
| CFY | Current Fiscal Year | CGS | Circuit Group congestion Signal |
| CG | Capacitance of Grid | CGS | Conditional Go-to-Statement |
| CG | Card Gripper | CGS | Cyclic Group Signal |
| CG | Card Guide | CGSE | Centimeter-Gram-Second-Electrostatic |
| CG | Cathode Grid | CGSE | Counter Group Selector Entry |
| CG | Center of Gravity | CGSM | Centimeter-Gram-Second Magnetic |
| CG | Centrigram | CGT | Current Gate Tube |
| CG | Channel Grant | CGU | Computergesteuerter Unterricht |
| CG | Character Generator | CGU | Code Generating Unit |
| CG | Clock Generator | CH | Candle Hour |
| CG | Code Generator | CH | Card Holder |
| CG | Code Group | CH | Card Hopper |
| CG | Coincidence Gate | CH | Chain |
| CG | Compiler Generator | CH | Chain Home |
| CG | Complement Gate | CH | Channel |
| CG | Computer Graphics | CH | Channel Hold |
| CG | Control Grid | CH | Character Sense |
| CG | Course Generator | CH | Charge |
| CGA | Contrast Gate Amplifier | CH | Check |
| CGA... | Compagnie Générale d'Automatisme | CH | Clock Hour |
| CGB | Convert Gray to Binary | CH | Code Holes |
| CGC | Cathode-Grid Capacitance | CH | Compare Halfword |
| CGE | Canadian General Electric | CH | Control Hole |
| CGF | Capacitance Grid-Filament | CH O | Character O |
| CGI | Computer-Generated Imagery | CHA | Cable-Harness Analyzer |
| CGI | Computer Graphics Interface | CHACOM | Chain of Command |
| CGI | Computer-Guided Instruction | CHAD | Code to Handle Angular Data |
| CGL... | Compagnie Générale d'Informatique | CHAL | Challenge |
| CGK | Computer Gesellschaft Konstanz | CHAMP | Character Manipulation Procedures |
| CGL | Colourgraphic programming Language | CHAMP | Cranfield Hybrid Automatic Maintenance Program |

# C

| | | | | |
|---|---|---|---|---|
| CHAMPION | Compatible Hardware And Milestone Program for Integrating Organizational Needs | | CHIC | Complex Hybrid Integrated Circuit |
| CHAN | Channel | | CHIC | Cermet Hybrid Integrated Circuit |
| CHAN ENT | Channel Entry | | CHICO | Coordination of Hybrid and Integrated Circuit Operations |
| CHAN SEL | Channel Selector | | | |
| CHAPS | Clearing House Automated Payment System | | CHICODER | Chinese language encoder |
| | | | CHIEF | Combined Helmboltz Integral Equation Formulation |
| CHAR | Character | | | |
| CHAR | Characteristics | | | |
| CHAR | Charge | | CHIF | Channel Interface |
| CHARAC | Characteristic | | CHIL | Current Hogging Injection Logic |
| CHARACT | Characteristic | | | |
| CHARM | Checking, Accounting and Reporting for Member firms | | CHIL | Current Hogging Integrated Logic |
| | | | CHILD | Cognitive Hybrid Intelligent Learing Device |
| CHARSET | Character Set | | | |
| CHART | Computerized Hierarchy And Relationship Table | | CHILD | Computer Having Intelligent Learning and Development |
| CHAS | Chassis | | | |
| CHAS PL | Chassis Plug | | CHILL | CCITT High Level Language |
| CHAS SKT | Chassis Socket | | | |
| CHASE | Cornell Hotel Administration Simulation Exercise | | CHIN | Characteristic Information |
| | | | CHIO | Channel Input/Output |
| | | | CHIO | Character-oriented Input/Output |
| CHB | Check Brushes | | | |
| CHB... | Compagnie Honeywell Bull | | CHIP | Chip Hermeticity In Plastic |
| CHC | Chaining Check | | CHIPS | Clearing Houses Interbank Payment System |
| CHCS | Computer Hardware Consultants and Services | | | |
| | | | CHIPS | Chemical engineering Information Processing System |
| CHCV | Channel Control Vector | | | |
| CHD... | Computer Haus Darmstadt | | | |
| CHDB | Compatible High-Density Bipolar | | CHK | Check |
| | | | CHKB | Check Bit |
| CHDL | Computer Hardware Description Language | | CHKD | Check Digit |
| | | | CHKDSK | Check Disk |
| CHE | Channel End | | CHKNO | Check Number |
| CHE | Channel Hot-Electron | | CHKP | Check Point |
| CHE | Check Entry | | CHKPROB | Check Problem |
| CHE | Component Handling Equipment | | CHKPT | Checkpoint |
| | | | CHKR | Checker |
| CHEAP | Committee for Handling European Automation Programmes | | CHL | Character Late |
| | | | CHL | Current Hogging Logic |
| | | | CHM | Compound Handling Machine |
| CHEC | Channel Evaluation and Call | | | |
| | | | CHN | Chain |
| CHEC | Checked | | CHN | Chaining |
| CHEOPS | Chemical Engineering Optimization System | | CHNG | Change |
| | | | CHNL | Channel |
| CHG | Change | | CHO | Character O |
| CHG | Charge | | CHP | Channel Pointer |
| CHGE | Charge | | CHP | Chopper |
| CHGOV | Change-Over | | CHPID | Channel Path Identifier |

# C

| | | | |
|---|---|---|---|
| CHPM | Change Priority Mask | CI | Conditional Instruction |
| CHPS | Characters Per Second | CI | Connective Instruction |
| CHR | Calculateur Hybride à Réseau | CI | Constant Instruction |
| CHR | Candle-Hour | CI | Continuous Input |
| CHR | Character Register | CI | Contract Item |
| CHR | Chrominance | CI | Control Information |
| CHR | Condenser Heat Rejection | CI | Control Instruction |
| CHRG | Charge | CI | Control Interval |
| CHRST | Characteristic | CI | Conversation Impossible |
| CHRTC | Characteristic | CI | Copy Instruction |
| CHT | Cable History Tape | CI | Corporate Instruction |
| CHT | Chart | CI | Crystal Impedance |
| CHU | Centigrade Heat Unit | CI | Current Interruption |
| CHUM | Computers and the Humanities | CI | Cut In |
| CI | Call Indicator | CIA | Centralized Information Acquisition |
| CI | Call Instruction | CIA | Channel Interface Adapter |
| CI | Calling Indicator | CIA | Comité Intersyndical d'Automatisation |
| CI | Calling Instruction | CIA | Communication Interrupt Analysis |
| CI | Card Index | | |
| CI | Card Input | CIA | Computer Industry Association |
| CI | Card Insertion | | |
| CI | Card Interpreter | CIA | Computer Interface Adapter |
| CI | Carriage Interlock | | |
| CI | Carrier-to-Interference | CIAME | Commission Inter-ministérielle des Appareils de Mesure |
| CI | Cartridge Image | | |
| CI | Chaining Instruction | | |
| CI | Channel Instruction | CIAPS | Customer-Integrated Automated Procurement System |
| CI | Characteristic Impedance | | |
| CI | Characteristic Independence | | |
| | | CIAT | Centres d'Informatique Appliquée aux Transports |
| CI | Check Indicator | | |
| CI | Check Information | CIB | Channel Interface Base |
| CI | Circuit Imprimé | CIB | COBOL Information Bulletin |
| CI | Circuit Intégré | | |
| CI | Circuit Interrupter | CIB | Command Input Buffer |
| CI | Code Information | CIB | Core Image Buffer |
| CI | Coded Identification | CIC | Card Inventory Control |
| CI | Coded Instruction | CIC | Centre International de Calcul |
| CI | Computing Instrument | | |
| CI | Column Indicator | CIC | Change Indicator Control |
| CI | Command Information | CIC | Chemistry Information Center |
| CI | Compare Instruction | | |
| CI | Complete Instruction | CIC | Circuit Identification Code |
| CI | Complex Instruction | | |
| CI | Computer Independent | CIC | Command Input Coupler |
| CI | Computer Indicator | CIC | Command Interface Control |
| CI | Computer Information | | |
| CI | Computer Input | CIC | Common Information Carrier |
| CI | Computer Instruction | | |
| CI | Computer Interconnect | CIC | Communications Intelligence Channel |
| CI | Computer Interconnection | | |
| CI | Computerized Instruction | CIC | Complex Integrated Circuit |
| CI | Concentrator-Identifier | | |

# C

| | | | |
|---|---|---|---|
| CIC | Computer Information Centre | CID NO | Component Identification Number |
| CIC | Conditional Information Content | CIDA | Channel Indirect Data Addressing |
| CIC | Content Indication Codes | CIDA | Current Input Differential Amplifier |
| CIC | Control Inquiry Card | | |
| CIC | Control Instruction Counter | CIDAS | Conversational Iterative Digital/Analog Simulator |
| CIC | CSNET Information Center | CIDB | Circuit Information Display Board |
| CIC | Custom Integrated Circuit | CIDF | Control Interval Definition Field |
| CIC | Customer Initiated Call | | |
| CICA | Configuration Identification Control and Accounting | CIDP | Computer Industry Development Potential |
| | | CIDPS | Continental Intelligence Data Processing System |
| CICAS | Computer Integrated Command and Attack System | CIDS | Chemical Information and Data System |
| CICE | Computer, Information, and Control Engineering | CIE | Coherent Infrared Energy |
| | | CIE | Computer Interrupt Equipment |
| CICI | Centre d'Information sur les Carrières liées à l'Informatique | CIED | Card Input Editor |
| | | CIEE | Computer Integrated Electronic Engineering |
| CICLOPS | Computers In Chemistry, Logic Oriented Planning of Syntheses | CIF | Capacitor Input Filter |
| | | CIF | Carriage, Insurance and Freight |
| CICP | Communications Interrupt Control Program | CIF | Cash in First |
| CICS | Customer Information Control System | CIF | Central Index File |
| | | CIF | Central Information Facility |
| CICS | Customer Inventory Control System | CIF | Central Information File |
| CICS/VS | Customer Inventory Control System/Virtual Storage | CIF | Central Instrumentation Facility |
| | | CIF | Central Integration Facility |
| CICS/VS | Customer Information Control System/Virtual Storage | CIF | Customer Information File |
| | | CIG | Collège d'Informatique et de Gestion |
| CID | Center for Information and Documentation | CIG | Computer Image Generation |
| CID | Charge Injection Device | CIG | Computer Investors Group |
| CID | Collection of Indexable Data | CIGFET | Complementary Isolated Gate Field Effect Transistor |
| CID | Column Indicating Device | | |
| CID | Communication Identifier | CIGREF | Club Informatique des Grandes Entreprises Françaises |
| CID | Compatibility Initialization Deck | | |
| CID | Component Identification | CIHE | Classified Intelligence Handling Environment |
| CID | Compositional Interdiffusion | CII | Current Indicator and Integrator |
| CID | Condensed Instruction Deck | CIL.. | Compagnie Internationale pour l'Informatique |
| CID | Connection Identifier | | |
| CID | Core Image Dump | CIK | Computer Institut Kollrich |

- 117 -

# C

| | | | |
|---|---|---|---|
| CIL | Call Information Line | CIMEF | Club Informatique des Moyennes Entreprises Françaises |
| CIL | Clear Indicating Lamp | | |
| CIL | Coded Instruction Line | | |
| CIL | Computer Independent Language | CIMMS | Civilian Information Manpower Management System |
| CIL | Condition Incident Logic | | |
| CIL | Core Image Library | CIMOS | Cincinnati Milacron Operating System |
| CIL | Current Inhibit Logic | | |
| CIL | Current Injection Logic | CIMPAC | Computer Integrated Manufacturing Process Analysis and Control |
| CIL... | Computer Instrumentation Ltd. | | |
| CILCA | Current Interest Late Charge Amount | CIMPLE | Card Image Manipulator for Large Entities |
| CILOMI | Compagnie Internationale pour la Location de Matériel Informatique | CIMS | Civilian Information Management System |
| | | CIMS | Computer Installation Management System |
| CILS | Computer Information Library Service | CIMS | Computer Integrated Measurement System |
| CILT | Centre for Information of Language Teaching | CIN | Carrier Input |
| CIM | Central Inventory Management | CIN | Change Identification Number |
| CIM | Cincinnati Milacron | CIN | Communication Identification Navigation |
| CIM | Code d'Identification de Message | CIN | Cooperative Information Network |
| CIM | Coded Impulse Modulation | | |
| CIM | Communications Interface Module | CINAP | Cincinnati Numerical Automatic Programming |
| CIM | Communications Interface Monitor | CIND | Computer Index of Neutron Data |
| CIM | Computer Input Microfilm | CINDA | Computer Index of Neutron Data |
| CIM | Computer Input Matrix | | |
| CIM | Computer Input Media | CINFAC | Cultural Information Analysis Center |
| CIM | Computer Input Microfilm | | |
| CIM | Computer Input Microfilming | CINS | Cryognetic Inertial Navigating System |
| CIM | Computer Input Multiplexer | CIO | Control Input/Output |
| | | CIO | Central Input/Output |
| CIM | Computer-Integrated Manufacture | CIOCS | Communication Input/Output Control System |
| CIM | Computer-Integrated Manufacturing | CIOE | Computer Input/Output Equipment |
| CIM | Continuous Image Microfilm | CIOS | Conseil International pour l'Organisation Scientifique |
| CIM | Critical Index Management | | |
| | | CIOU | Custom Input/Output Unit |
| CIM | Crystal Impedance Meter | CIP | Central Input Program |
| CIM | Cubic Inches per Minute | CIP | Centralized Information Processing |
| CIMAB | Centre d'Information des Matériels et Articles de Bureau | CIP | Certain Information Processing |
| CIMBA | Contractors Installation Make or Buy Authorization | CIP | Circuit Intégre Prédiffuse |
| | | CIP | Command Information Program |
| CIMCO | Card Image Correction | CIP | Common Input Processor |

# C

| | |
|---|---|
| CIP | Communications Interface Processor |
| CIP | Component Improvement Program |
| CIP | Composite Interface Program |
| CIP | Computer Information Processing |
| CIP | Computer Input Program |
| CIP | Computer Interchange Program |
| CIP | Computing Intensive Program |
| CIP | Console Interface Program |
| CIP | Consolidated Intelligence Program |
| CIP | Contract Information Processor |
| CIP | Conversion In Place |
| CIP | Count In Process |
| CIP | Crystallized Information Processing |
| CIP | Current Injection Probe |
| CIPER | Central Inventory of Production Equipment Records |
| CIPP | CTC Index Printing Program |
| CIPPP | Cooperative International Pupil-to-Pupil Program |
| CIPREC | Conversational and Interactive Project Evaluation and Control system |
| CIPS | Canadian Information Processing Society |
| CIPS | Centralized Information Processing System |
| CIQ | Computer Input Quantity |
| CIR | Center for Informatics Research |
| CIR | Characteristic Impedance Ratio |
| CIR | Circuit |
| CIR | Computerized Information Retrieval |
| CIR | Conditional Interrupt Request |
| CIR | Control Instruction Register |
| CIR | Control and Interrupt Register |
| CIR | Controlled Intact Reentry |
| CIR | Current Instruction Register |
| CIR BKR | Circuit Breaker |
| CIR CL | Circuit Closing |
| CIR OP | Circuit Opening |
| CIRC | Circulator |
| CIRC | Circumference |
| CIRC | Central Information Reference and Control |
| CIRCA | Computerized Information Retrieval and Current Awareness |
| CIRCAL | Circuit Analysis |
| CIRCLE | Combined Integrated Resource for Community Learning Experiment |
| CIRCOL | Central Information Reference and Control On-Line |
| CIRCUS | Circuit Simulator |
| CIRCUS | Calculation of Indirect Resources and Conversion to Unit Staff |
| CIRDP | Cost Information Reporting Data Plan |
| CIRE | Centre pour l'Innovation et la Recherche dans l'Enseignement |
| CIRK | CTC Information Retrieval from Keywords |
| CIRO | Card Inductor Read-Only |
| CIRO | Centre Interarmées de Recherche Opérationnelle |
| CIRS | Customer Information Record System |
| CIRS | Customer Information Reference System |
| CIRSY | Completely Integrated Reference System |
| CIRVIS | Communication Instructions for Reporting Vital Intelligence Sightings |
| CIS | Cambridge Interactive Sytems |
| CIS | Card Input Station |
| CIS | Cataloging In Source |
| CIS | Center for Information Sciences |
| CIS | Center for Information Services |
| CIS | Central Input System |
| CIS | Chip Identification System |
| CIS | Chip d'Identification-Sûreté |
| CIS | Common Input System |
| CIS | Communication Information System |

# C

| | | | |
|---|---|---|---|
| CIS | Communication and Instrumentation System | CISR | Corporate Interplant Status Record |
| CIS | Community Information System | CISRC | Computer and Information Science Research Center |
| CIS | Compact-Informations-System | CIT | Cable Interface Tape |
| CIS | Compatible Informations System | CIT | California Institute of Technology |
| CIS | Compiler Interpreter System | CIT | Call-In-Time |
| CIS | Composition Information Services | CIT | Card Image Tape |
| CIS | Computer Information Service | CIT | Carnegie Institute of Technology |
| CIS | Computer-Integrated System | CIT | Combinational Iterative Tree |
| CIS | Computer-In-Scheckkarte | CIT | Command Interface Test |
| CIS | Computer-oriented Information System | CIT | Command Interpretation Table |
| CIS | Computergestütztes Informationssystem | CITAB | Computer Instruction and Training Assistance for the Blind |
| CIS | Computerorientiertes Informationssystem | CITAP | Computerized Interactive Thermal Analysis Program |
| CIS | Conductor Insulator Semiconductor | CITE | Computer Integrated Test Equipment |
| CIS | Console Inquiry Station | CITE | Controller Input Test Equipment |
| CIS | Continental Information Systems Corporation | CITE | Council of Institute of Telecommunication Engineers |
| CIS | Control Indicator Set | | |
| CIS | Control Input Signal | CITE | Current Information Tapes for Engineers |
| CIS | Correction Information System | CITEC | Compagnie pour L'Informatique et Technique Electronique de Contrôle |
| CIS | Cost Information System | | |
| CIS | Cue Indexing System | CITEL | Compagnie Internationale de Téléinformatique |
| CIS | Current Information Selection | | |
| CIS | Custom Integrated System | CITEL | Conferencia Interaméricana de Telecomunicaciones |
| CIS | Customer Information System | | |
| CISC | Complex Instruction Set Computer | CITEMA | Centro de la Informatica, Técnica y Material Administrativos |
| CISCO | Compass Integrated System Compiler | CITI | Centre d'Information des Techniques Industrielles |
| CISED | Corporate Information Systems Education Department | | |
| | | CITIS | Centralized Integrated Technical Information System |
| CISI | Compagnie Internationale de Services en Informatique | | |
| | | CITS | Central Integrated Test Set |
| CISIL | Cost Information System Indirect Labour | CIU | Cable Interface Unit |
| CISNE | Computerized Informations System for Nursing Educators | CIU | Central Interpretation Unit |
| | | CIU | Computer Interface Unit |

# C

| | | | |
|---|---|---|---|
| CIU | Command Interface Unit | CL | Call Library |
| CIU | Communications Interface Unit | CL | Card Lever |
| | | CL | Card Lifter |
| CIU | Console Inquiry Unit | CL | Card Line |
| CIUP | Country Installed User Program | CL | Card Load |
| | | CL | Cartridge Loader |
| CIV | Code Inverter Verifier | CL | Cellular Logic |
| CIW | Computer Instruction Word | CL | Center Line |
| | | CL | Central Line |
| CIW | Current Instruction Word | CL | Change List |
| CJ | Card Jam | CL | Channel Loading |
| CJ | Clip Joint | CL | Chlorine |
| CJ | Cold Junction | CL | Circuit Layout |
| CJ | Conditional Jump | CL | Circuit Logic |
| CJC | Continuous Job Card | CL | Class |
| CJD | Card Jam Detector | CL | Clear |
| CJF | Conversational Job Facility | CL | Closed Loop |
| | | CL | Closing |
| CJI | Conditional Jump Instruction | CL | Cluster Definition |
| | | CL | Code Language |
| CJIS | Criminal Justice Information System | CL | Code Line |
| | | CL | Code List |
| CJL | Conversational Job Language | CL | Coding Language |
| | | CL | Coding Line |
| CJO | Conditional Jump Operation | CL | Command Language |
| | | CL | Command List |
| CJO | Conditional Jump Order | CL | Comment Line |
| CJTT | Computer Jobs Through Training | CL | Common Language |
| | | CL | Common Logarithm |
| CK | Check | CL | Compare Logical |
| CK | Circuit Check | CL | Compare Long |
| CK | Classification Keyboard | CL | Computational Linguistics |
| CK | Clearing Key | CL | Computer Laboratory |
| CK | Control Keyboard | CL | Computer Language |
| CK | Crystal Kit | CL | Computing Law |
| CKC | Check Character | CL | Confidence Limit |
| CKD | Checked | CL | Continuation Line |
| CKD | Completely Knocked Down | CL | Control Language |
| CKD | Count-Key-Data | CL | Control Leader |
| CKDIG | Check Digit | CL | Control Logic |
| CKDS | Cryptographic Key Data Set | CL | Conversion Loss |
| | | CL | Core image Library |
| CKIC | Chemical Kinetics Information Center | CL | Correction List |
| | | CL | Counter Logic |
| CKO | Checking Operator | CL | Cutter Location |
| CKR | Checker | CL | Cylinder |
| CKT | Circuit | CLA | Carry Look Ahead |
| CKT BKR | Circuit Breaker | CLA | Center Line Average |
| CKT CL | Circuit Closing | CLA | Clamp |
| CKT OP | Circuit Opening | CLA | Clear Accumulator |
| CKTBD | Circuit Board | CLA | Clear and Add |
| CKTSIM | Circuit Simulation | CLA | Communication Line Adapters |
| CKU | Computerkontrollierter Unterricht | | |
| | | CLA | Communication Link Analyzer |
| CKW | Clockwise | | |

- 121 -

# C

| | | | |
|---|---|---|---|
| CLA | Computer Law Association | CLC | Communications Link Controller |
| CLA | Computer Lessors' Association | CLC | Compare Logical |
| CLA | Control Logic Assembly | CLC | Compare Logical Characters |
| CLA | Custom Logic Array | CLC | Computer Leasing Company |
| CLAB | Computer Lösen Aufgaben des Bildungswesens | CLC | Computer Link Corporation |
| CLAD | Cover Layer Automated Design | CLC | Computerized Lubrication Control |
| CLAFIC | Class Featuring Information Compression | CLC | Control Language Compiler |
| CLAMP | Computer Listing and Analysis of Maintenance Program | CLCC | Closed-Loop Continuity Check |
| CLARA | Cornell Learning And Recognizing Automaton | CLCD | Clearinghouse and Laboratory for Census Data |
| CLAS | Communication Link Analyzer System | CLCS | Closed Loop Control System |
| CLASP | Circuit Layout, Automated Scheduling and Production | CLCS | Current Logic, Current Switching |
| CLASP | Clients Lifetime Advisory Service Program | CLD | Cleared |
| | | CLD | Closed |
| CLASP | Composite Launch And Spacecraft Program | CLD | Computer Logic Demonstrator |
| CLASP | Computer Laboratory System Project | CLD | Condensed Logic Diagram |
| | | CLD | Control Logic Diagram |
| CLASP | Computer Language for Aeronautics and Space Programming | CLD | Current-Limiting Device |
| | | CLDA | Control Logic and Drive Assembly |
| CLASP | Computer Liftof And Staging Program | CLDAS | Clinical Data Acquisition System |
| CLASS | Capacity Loading And Scheduling System | CLDAS | Clinical Laboratory Data Adquisition System |
| CLASS | Computer based Laboratory for Automated School Systems | CLDATA | Cutter Location Data |
| | | CLDG | Composite Language Development Group |
| CLASSIC | Classroom Interactive Computer | CLE | Counter List Entry |
| CLASSMATE | Computer Language to Aid and Stimulate Scientific, Mathematical And Technical Education | CLEAR | Closed Loop Evaluation And Reporting |
| | | CLEAR | Compiler, Loader, Executive Program, Assembler Routines |
| CLAT | Communication Line Adapter for Teletype | CLEAR | Controlled Library Environment And Resources |
| CLB | Communication Line Block | CLEM | Code Learning Machine |
| CLBA | Current Logical Byte Address | CLEN | Continuing Library Education Network |
| CLC | Card Lever Control | CLENE | Continuing Library Education Network Exchange |
| CLC | Central Logic Complex | | |
| CLC | Central Logic Control | | |
| CLC | Clear Carry | CLEO | Clear Language for Expressing Orders |

- 122 -

| | | | |
|---|---|---|---|
| CLF | Capacitive Loss Factor | CLIV | Core Logic Intervalometer |
| CLF | Check Label Field | CLK | Clock |
| CLF | Condensed Logic Flow | CLKW | Clockwise |
| CLFC | Condensed Logic Flow Chart | CLL | Circuit Load Logic |
| | | CLL | Clear Link |
| CLFM | Coherent Linear Frequency Modulated | CLLC | Corporate Low Level Code |
| | | CLM | Calling-Line Matrix |
| CLG | Compile Load and Go | CLM | Cancel Last Message |
| CLGNR | Catalog Number | CLM | Clamp |
| CLHU | Computation Laboratory of Harvard University | CLM | Clock Module |
| | | CLM | Column |
| CLI | Calling Line Identification | CLM | Configuration Load Manager |
| CLI | Calling Line Identity | CLMD | Clamped |
| CLI | Capacitor Leakage Indicator | CLML | Chicago Linear Music Language |
| CLI | Command Line Interpreter | CLMS | Clinical Laboratory Management System |
| CLI | Compare Logical Immediately | CLN | Clean |
| | | CLN | Colon |
| CLI | Computer Linguistics, Incorporated | CLO | Cellular Logic Operation |
| | | CLO | Complex Logical Operation |
| CLI | Core Logic Intervalometer | CLO | Computer Lock-On |
| CLIBOC | Chinese Linguistics Bibliography On Computer | CLOG | Complex Logarithm |
| | | CLP | Check Localization Program |
| CLIC | Communication Linear Integrated Circuit | CLP | Clamp |
| | | CLP | Clipper Positive |
| CLICS | Computer Linked Information for Container Shipping | CLP | Continuous Line Plotter |
| | | CLP | Current Line Pointer |
| | | CLPE | Counter List Printing Exit |
| CLID | Clustering Identification | CLR | Circuit Layout Record |
| CLIM | Calling Line Identity Message | CLR | Clear |
| | | CLR | Clearing |
| CLIM | Cellular Logic-In-Memory | CLR | Combined Line Recording |
| CLIP | Compiler Language for Information Processing system | CLR | Combined Line and Recording trunk |
| | | CLR | Combustible Limit Relay |
| CLIP | Cellular Logic Image Processor | CLR | Common Line Receiver |
| | | CLR | Computer Language Recorder |
| CLIP | Cellular Logic-array Image Processor | CLR | Computer Language Research |
| CLIP | Compiler and Language for Information Processing | CLR | Contact Load Resistor |
| | | CLR | Contrôle Longitudinal de Rédondance |
| CLIP | Coverage Line Inventory Profile | CLR | Council on Library Resources |
| CLIPR | Computer Laboratory for Instruction in Psychological Research | CLR | Current Limiting Resistor |
| | | CLRCH | Clear Channel |
| CLIS | Clearinghouse for Library and Information Sciences | CLRIO | Clear Input/Output |
| | | CLRU | Cambridge Language Research Unit |
| CLIST | Command List | | |

- 123 -

# C

| | | | |
|---|---|---|---|
| CLS | Class | CM | Chain Memory |
| CLS | Class of Service | CM | Charge Memory |
| CLS | Classification of Library Science | CM | Chess Master |
| | | CM | Circuit Merit |
| CLS | Clear and Subtract | CM | Circuit Module |
| CLS | Close | CM | Circulating Memory |
| CLS | Common Language System | CM | Classified Message |
| CLS | Computer Load Simulator | CM | Clear Memory |
| CLS | Constant Level Speech | CM | Code Modulation |
| CLS | Constraint Least Squares | CM | Coding Memory |
| CLS | Control Language Services | CM | Coincidence Memory |
| | | CM | Combined Multiplication |
| CLSIM | Clocked Logic Simulation | CM | Command |
| CLSNG | Closing | CM | Command Module |
| CLSS | Communication Link Subsystem | CM | Common Mode |
| | | CM | Communication Manager |
| CLT | Central Limit Theorem | CM | Communication Multiplexer |
| CLT | Channel Load Table | | |
| CLT | Clock Track | CM | Communications Monitor |
| CLT | Code Language Telegram | CM | Comparator |
| CLT | Communications Line Terminal | CM | Compile Processor |
| | | CM | Compiler Method |
| CLT | Communications Lines Terminator | CM | Complex Mode |
| | | CM | Compound Module |
| CLT | Component Library Tape | CM | Computer Memory |
| CLT | Computer Language Translator | CM | Computer Module |
| | | CM | Computermusik |
| CLT | Corporate Logic Tester | CM | Computing Machine |
| CLTG | Collecting | CM | Computing Machinery |
| CLTR | Collator | CM | Computing Media |
| CLU | Central Logic Unit | CM | Computing Medium |
| CLU | Circuit Line-Up | CM | Computing Memory |
| CLU | Clutch | CM | Configuration Management |
| CLU | Common Logic Unit | | |
| CLUE | Computer Learning Under Evaluation | CM | Connection Matrix |
| | | CM | Constant Memory |
| CLUMP | COMPOOL Lock-Up-Memory Print | CM | Continuous Monitor |
| | | CM | Control Mark |
| CLV | Constant Linear Velocity | CM | Control Memory |
| | | CM | Control Monitor |
| CLW | Correction Location Word | CM | Conversion Matrix |
| | | CM | Core Matrix |
| CLYDE | Computer-graphics Language for Your Design Equations | CM | Core Memory |
| | | CM | Corrective Maintenance |
| | | CM | Correlation Matrix |
| CM | Calculating Machine | CM | Countermeasure |
| CM | Calculating Memory | CM | Counting Machine |
| CM | Call on Minus | CM | Credit Memo |
| CM | Card Magazine | CM | Cross Modulation |
| CM | Card Matching | CM | Cryogenic Memory |
| CM | Card Memory | CM | Cryotron Memory |
| CM | Carrousel Memory | CM | Cubic Centimeter |
| CM | Carte Magnétique | CM | Cyclic Memory |
| CM | Cell Memory | CM-ECS | Central Memory - Extended Core Storage |
| CM | Central Memory | | |

# C

| | | | |
|---|---|---|---|
| CM... | Computer Microtechnology | CMC... | Computer Machinery Corporation |
| CM/M | Collector Module with Memory | CMC7 | Caractère Magnétique Codé à 7 bâtonnets |
| CM/T | Change Management Tracker | CMCC | Computer Monitor and Control Console |
| CMA | Colour Monitor Adapter | CMCCP | Cornell Medical Community Computer Project |
| CMA | Communications Managers Association | CMCT | Communicate |
| CMA | Complement Accumulator | CMCTL | Current Mode Complementary Transistor Logic |
| CMA | Complementary Marketing Agreement | CMD | Command |
| CMA | Composite Medium Amplifier | CMD | Computer Magnetic Drum |
| CMA | Computer-Marked Assignment | CMD | Computer Memory Devices Incorporated |
| CMA | Computer Monitor Adapter | CMD | Core Memory Driver |
| CMA | Contact-Making Ammeter | CMD | Courrier Mensuel Défauts |
| CMA | Credit Memorandum Authorization | CMDAC | Current Mode Digital-to-Analog Converter |
| CMAC | Computer Monitor And Control | CMDN | Catalog Management Data Notification |
| CMAL | Controlled Multiple Address Letter | CMDR | Command Message Detail Recorder |
| CMAP | Charge Materials Allocation Processor | CMDS | Card Manufacturing Daily Status |
| CMAP | Coordinate Measurement Analysis Program | CMDS | Centralized Message Data System |
| CMB | Code Matrix Block | CME | Computer Measurement and Evaluation |
| CMB | Core Memory Block | | |
| CMB | Core Memory Byte | CMEC | Convectron-Microsyn Erection Circuit |
| CMB | Compagnie des Machines Bull | CMES | Computer and Management Education Services |
| CMC | Caractère Magnétique Codé | CMF | Call Modification Feature |
| CMC | Code for Magnetic Characters | CMF | Capactiy Management Facilities |
| CMC | Coded Magnetic Character | CMF | Coherent Memory Filter |
| | | CMF | Command File |
| CMC | Command Module Computer | CMF | Command Message Formulator |
| CMC | Common Market Computer | | |
| CMC | Communicating Magnetic Card | CMF | Comprehensive Measurement Facility |
| CMC | Communications Mode Control | CMF | Condensed Master File |
| | | CMF | Cross Modulation Factor |
| CMC | Compact Machine Code | CMFI | Corporate Machine Features Index |
| CMC | Complement Carry | | |
| CMC | Concurrent Media Conversion | CMFLR | Cam Follower |
| | | CMG | Code Modulus Generator |
| CMC | Contact Making Clock | CMG | Computer Management Group |
| CMC | Core Memory Cycle | | |
| CMC | Cubitron Memory Cell | CMG | Computer Measurement Group, Incorporated |
| CMC | Customer Master Card | | |

# C

| | | | |
|---|---|---|---|
| CMG | Control Moment Gyroscope | CMO | Commercial Microsystems Operation |
| CMI | Call Macro-Instruction | CMO | Computer Microfilm Output |
| CMI | Computer Managed Instruction | CMO | Crystal Marker Oscillator |
| CMI... | Cambridge Memories Inc. | CMOD | Customer Module |
| CMIA | Command Management Inventory Accounting | CMOS | Complementary Metal-Oxide-Semiconductor |
| CMIC | Central Management Information Center | CMOS/SOS | Complementary-symmetry Metal Oxide Semiconductor/Silicon-On-Sapphire |
| CMIR | Common Mode Input Resistance | | |
| CMIS | Common Manufacturing Information System | CMP | Central Monitoring Position |
| CMIS | Computer Micro Image Systems | CMP | Compare |
| | | CMP | Computation |
| CMIS | Computer-oriented Management Information System | CMP | Computational |
| | | CMP | Computed Maximum Pressure |
| CMIS | Computerorientiertes Management-Informationssystem | CMP | Computer Master Program |
| | | CMP | Console Message Processor |
| CMIS | Controls Management Information System | CMP | Control and Maintenance Processor |
| CML | Common Machine Language | CMP | Control y Mantenimiento del Procesador |
| CML | Complement Link | | |
| CML | Complementary Micrologic | CMP | Corporate Manufacturing Practice |
| CML | Computer Managed Laboratory | CMPD | Computer Design |
| | | CMPJ | The Computer Journal |
| CML | Condensed Microprogram Logic | CMPL | Complete |
| | | CMPL | Complement |
| CML | Constrained Maximum Likelihood | CMPLM | Complément |
| | | CMPLX | Complex |
| CML | Current Mode Logic | CMPN | Compilation |
| CMLC | Corporate Machine Level Control | CMPNT | Component |
| | | CMPR | Compare |
| CMLT | Complete | CMPRD | Compared |
| CMM | CMOS Microcomputer Modules | CMPRG | Comparing |
| | | CMPRN | Comparison |
| CMM | Coherent Microwave Memory | CMPS | Command Module Procedures Simulator |
| CMM | Communications Multiplexer Module | CMPSN | Composition |
| | | CMPT | Component |
| CMM | Computer Main Memory | CMPT | Computer |
| CMMP | Computer Multi-Mini-Processor | CMR | Common Mode Rejection |
| | | CMR | Communications Moon Relay |
| CMMR | Confirmed and Made a Matter of Record | CMR | Continuous Maximum Rate |
| CMN | Column | CMRR | Common-Mode Rejection Ratio |
| CMN | Common Mode Noise | | |
| CMN | Communication | CMS | Cambridge Monitor System |
| CMND | Command | CMS | Computer base Message System |
| CMNT | Comment | | |

# C

| | | | |
|---|---|---|---|
| CMS | Computer Management System | CNI | Communication, Navigation and Identification |
| CMS | Conversational Monitor System | CNIL | Commission Nationale de l'Informatique et des Libertés |
| CMS | Conversation Monitor System | CNIPE | Centre National d'Information pour la Productivité des Entreprises |
| CMS | Current-Mode Switching | | |
| CMT | Circuit Master Tape | | |
| CMT | Core Measurement Table | | |
| CMT | Corrected Mean Temperature | CNIST | Centre National d'Informations Scientifiques et Techniques |
| CMU | Carnegie Mellon University | | |
| CMV | Computer-Mißbrauch-Versicherung | CNIT | Centre National des Industries et Techniques |
| CMV | Common Mode Voltage | CNJ | Copper-Nickel-Jacket |
| CMV | Contact Making Voltmeter | CNL | Cancel |
| CN | Carrier-to-Noise | CNL | Cancellation |
| CN | Commande Numérique | CNL | Circuit Net Loss |
| CN | Commutated Network | CNM | Communication Network Management |
| CN | Compensator | | |
| CN | Coordination Number | CNM | Communication Network Manager |
| CNA | Communications Network Architecture | CNMO | Commande Numérique de Machines-Outils |
| CNA | Convertisseur Numérique Analogique | CNN | Connection |
| CNA | Copper Nickel Alloy | CNO | Computer Not Operational |
| CNA | Cosmic Noise Absorption | CNP | Communications Network Processor |
| CNB | Communication Name Block | CNR | Carrier-to-Noise Ratio |
| CNC | Commande Numérique par Calculateur | CNR | Clutter-to-Noise Ratio |
| | | CNRS | Centre National de la Recherche Scientifique |
| CNC | Communications Network Controller | CNS | Communication Network System |
| CNC | Computer Numerical Control | CNS | Constant |
| CNC | Computerized Numerical Control | CNS | Control Network System |
| | | CNSL | Console |
| CNC | Consecutive Number Control | CNT | Count |
| | | CNT | Counter |
| CNCT | Connect | CNTL | Control |
| CND | Condition | CNTR | Center |
| CNDP | Communication Network Design Program | CNTR | Counter |
| | | CNTRL | Central |
| CNE | Compare Numerical Equal | CNTRL | Control |
| CNES | Centre National d'Etudes Spatiales | CNU | Compare Numeric Unequal |
| | | CNVT | Convert |
| CNET | Centre National d'Etudes des Télécommunications | CO | Cathode ray Oscilloscope |
| CNF | Confidence | CO | Central Office |
| CNI | Called Number Idenfication | CO | Changeover |
| CNI | Centre National de l'Informatique | CO | Checkout |
| | | CO | Classifier Overflow |
| CNI | Commissariat National à l'Informatique | CO | Close-Open |
| | | CO | COBOL |
| CNI | Communication | CO | Combined Operations |

# C

| | | | |
|---|---|---|---|
| CO | Communication | COBAS | Commerzielle Basis-Software |
| CO | Computer Operation | | |
| CO | Computer Output | COBERA | Cambridge Observation Error Analysis |
| CO | Computing Operation | | |
| CO | Conditional Order | COBESTCO | Computer Based Estimating Technique for Contractors |
| CO | Connective Operation | | |
| CO | Contact Operate | | |
| CO | Control Order | COBI | Coded Biphase |
| CO | Conversion Operation | COBILITY | COBOL Utility |
| CO | Counting Operation | COBINT | COBOL Interface |
| CO | Couple Output | COBIS | Computerunterstütztes Büro-Informationssystem |
| CO | Crossover | | |
| CO | Crystal Oscillator | | |
| CO | Customer Order | COBLOS | Computer Based Loan System |
| CO | Cut-Off | | |
| CO/NO | Current Operator/Next Operator | COBOL | Common Business Oriented Language |
| COA | Change Order Account | COBRA | Computerized Boolean Reliability Analysis |
| COA | Computer-Oriented Algorithm | COBRA | Computer Oriented Bearing Response Analysis |
| COA | Constant Output Amplifier | | |
| COAC | Clutter-Operated Anti-Clutter | COBRA | Consolidation Of Basic Records Audit |
| COACS | Common Office Automation Communication Structure | COBSTRU | COBOL-Struktur |
| | | COBU | The Computer Bulletin |
| COAD | Coordinate Adder | COC | Card Oriented Computer |
| COAD | Coordinate Adder Display | COC | Cardiology Office Computer |
| COADS | Command and Administrative Data System | COC | Coded Optical Character |
| COAM | Company-Owned And Maintained | COC | Command and Control |
| | | COC | Complete Operational Capability |
| COAM | Customer-Owned And Maintained | COC | Computer Operation Code |
| COAMP | Computer Analysis of Maintenance Policies | COC | Computer on the Chip |
| | | COC | Cross-Over Connector |
| COAP | Combat Optimization and Analysis Program | COCAS | Customer Order Control Automated System |
| COARIN | Commitee on Arabic in Informatics | COCO | Contractor Owned, Contractor Operated |
| COASP | Coordinated Aircraft/Stores Program | COCOS | Control Communications Software |
| COAT | Computer Operator Aptitude Test | COCR | Cylinder Overflow Control Record |
| COATS | Computer Operated Automatic Test System | COD | Carry-Over Data |
| | | COD | Cash On Delivery |
| COAU | Computers and Automation | COD | Coding |
| COAX | Coaxial | COD/DEC | Codierer/Decodierer |
| COAX | COBOL Abbreviation Expander | CODA | Computer Oriented Data Acquisition |
| COB | Card On Board | CODAC | Coordination of Operating Data by Automatic Computer |
| COB | Close Of Business | | |
| COB | COBOL | | |
| COB | Complementary Off-set Binary | CODACOP | COBOL Data Communication Philips |

# C

| | | | |
|---|---|---|---|
| CODAM | Contractor-Oriented Data Abstract Modules | CODOT | Classification of Occupations and Directory of Occupational Titles |
| CODAN | Carrier-Operated Device, Antinoise | | |
| CODAN | Coded Analysis | CODPS | Card Oriented Data Processing System |
| CODAP | Control Data Assembly Program | COE | Complete Operating Equipment |
| CODAR | Coherent Display Analyzing and Recording | COE | Computer Operations Europe |
| CODAR | Correlation Display Analyzing and Recording | COEBRA | Computerized Optimization of Elastic Booster Autopilot |
| CODAS | Customer-Oriented Data System | | |
| CODASYL | Conference on Data System Languages | COED | Composition and Editing Display |
| CODASYL | Committee on Data Systems Language | COED | Computer Operated Electronic Display |
| CODATA | Committee on Data for science and technology | COEF | Coefficient |
| | | COEI | Composition Of Ending Inventory |
| CODC | Canadian Oceanographic Data Centre | COF | Computer Operations Facility |
| CODEC | Coder-Decoder | | |
| CODED | Computer-Oriented Design of Electronic Devices | COF | Customer Order File |
| | | COF | Cut-Off Frequency |
| CODEIN | Computerized Drawing Electrical Information | COFEC | Cause Of Failure, Effect and Correction |
| CODEL | Computer Development Limited automatic coding system | COFIL | Core File |
| | | COFIRS | COBOL For IBM RPG Systems |
| CODEM | Coded modulator-Demodulator | COFIRS | COBOL From IBM RPG Specifications |
| CODEM | Computer-graphics-augmented Design and Manufacturing | COFRS | Computerized Freight Remittance System |
| | | COG | Centre Of Gravidity |
| CODES | Commutating Detection System | COG | Computer Operations Group |
| CODES | Computer Design and Evaluation System | COGAP | Computer Graphics Arrangement Program |
| CODIC | Colour Difference Computer | COGEB | Compatibilité Générale Et Budgetaire |
| CODIC | Computer Directed Communications | COGENT | Compiler and Generalized Translator |
| CODIL | Context Dependent Information Language | COGO | Coordinate Geometry |
| | | COGS | Continuous Orbital Guidance Sensor |
| CODILS | Commodity Oriented Digital Input Label System | COGS | Continuous Orbital Guidance System |
| CODINE | Conversational Design Information Network | COH OSC | Coherent Oscillator |
| | | COHO | Coherent Oscillator |
| CODIT | Computer Direct to Telegraph | COI | Computerorientierte Informationstechnik |
| CODN | Component Operational Data Notice | COIL | COMPAS Online Interactive Language |
| CODORACS | Coded Doppler Radar Command System | COIN | Complete Operating Information |

- 129 -

# C

| | | | |
|---|---|---|---|
| COINGRAD | Computer Oriented Interactive Graphical Analysis and Design | COLT | Computer Oriented Language Translator |
| COINS | Computerized Information System | COLT | Computer Oriented Logic Test |
| COINS | Control in Information Systems | COLT | Control Language Translator |
| COINS | Cooperative Intelligence Network System | COLTG | Completing |
| | | COLTN | Completion |
| COIS | Computer-Oriented Information System | COLTS | Communication On-Line Testing System |
| COL | Column | COM | Card Oriented Model |
| COL | Collation please/I collate | COM | Character Organized Memory |
| COL | Collector | COM | Command |
| COL | Computer Oriented Language | COM | Commercial |
| | | COM | Common |
| COL | Computerized Office Layout | COM | Communications |
| | | COM | Communications Operating Module |
| COLA | Constant Output Level Adapter | COM | Commutator |
| COLA | Cost Of Living Adjustment | COM | Compiler |
| COLAPS | Conversational Language Programming System | COM | Complement |
| | | COM | Computer Output Microfiche |
| COLASL | Compiler Los Alamos Scientific Laboratories | COM | Computer Output Microfilm |
| COLED | Combat Loss and Expenditure Data | COM | Computer Output Microfilmer |
| COLEQUAP | Consumer Level Quality Audit Program | COM | Computer Output Microfilming |
| COLEX | CIRC On-Line Experiment | COM | Computer Output Microform |
| COLI | Cost of Living Index | | |
| COLIDAR | Coherent Light Detection And Ranging | COM | Computer Output Mikrofilmkamera |
| COLIM | Collimator | | |
| COLINGO | Compile on Line and Go | COM | Curve Of Merit |
| COLL | Collect | COM-PASS | Complete Parallel Activity and Security System |
| COLL | Collection | | |
| COLL | Collector | | |
| COLLECT | Connectitut On-Line Law-Enforcement Communications and Teleprocessing | COM-STAT | Computer Stock Timing and Analysis Technique |
| | | COM-STEP | Computerized Spot Television Evaluation and Processing |
| COLLR | Collector | | |
| COLM | Collector Mesh | COMAC | Continuous Multiple-Access Collator |
| COLN | Column | | |
| COLOG | Cologarithm | COMAC | Continuous Multiple-Access Comparator |
| COLP | Collapse | | |
| COLQUAP | Consumer Level Quality Audit Program | COMACS | Common Manufacturing Accounting Control System |
| COLRAD | College on Research And Development | | |
| | | COMAD | Computer Methods for Automatic Diagnosis |
| COLT | Communication Line Terminator | | |
| | | COMANSEC | Computation and Analysis Section |
| COLT | Computerized On-Line Testing | | |

- 130 -

# C

| | | | |
|---|---|---|---|
| COMAP | Conversational Macro Package | COML | Commercial Language |
| COMAR | Computer, Areal Reconnaissance | COMLIP | Community Media Librarian Program |
| COMARS | Coordinate Measuring And Recording System | COMM | Communication |
| | | COMM | Commutator |
| COMAT | Computer-Assisted Training | COMMAND | Command Model for Analysis and Design |
| COMATS | Computer Operated Manufacturing And Test System | COMMANDS | Computer Operated Marketing, Mailing And News Distribution System |
| COMATS | Corporate Manufacturing Transfer System | COMMCEN | Communications Center |
| | | COMMEL | Communications Electronics |
| COMB | Cassetten-Orientiertes Modulares Buchungs-system | COMMEN | Compiler-Oriented for Multiprogramming and Multiprocessing Environments |
| COMB | Combination | | |
| COMBAT | Cost-Oriented Models Built to Analyze Tradeoffs | COMMEND | Computer-aided Mechanical Engineering Design |
| COMBO | Computation Of Miss-Between Orbits | COMMEND | Computer-assisted Mechanical Design |
| COMBRONET | Computerized Brockerage Network | COMMSWITCH | Communications failure detecting and Switching equipment |
| COMCAS | Computer-Oriented Model Control and Appraisal System | COMMZ | Communications Zone |
| | | COMN | Communication |
| COMCM | Communications Countermeasures | COMNET | Communications Network |
| | | COMNET | Computer Network |
| COMCODE | Commodity Code | COMO | Coherent Master Oscillator |
| COMDAC | Component Design Augmented by Computer | COMO | Computer Model |
| | | COMOL | Connection Model description Language |
| COMDET | Computer Mediated Drill and Educational Testing | COMP | Comparator |
| COMEF | Coherent Memory Filter | COMP | Compare |
| COMEINDORS | Composite Mechanized Information and Documentation Retrieval System | COMP | Comparison |
| | | COMP | Compensator |
| | | COMP | Compilation |
| | | COMP | Compiled |
| COMET | Chip On Module Evaluation Tester | COMP | Compiler |
| | | COMP | Component |
| COMET | Computer Operated Management Evaluation Technique | COMP | Composition |
| | | COMP | Computation |
| | | COMP | Computational |
| COMET | Computerized Message Transmission | COMP | Computer |
| | | COMP | Computer Oriented Microwaves Practices |
| COMFACTS | Communications Facilities Testing System | | |
| | | COMP | Computerization |
| COMIC | Colorant Mixer Computer | COMP | Computerize |
| COMIC | Customer Organized MOS Integrated Circuit | COMPAC | Computer Program for Automatic Control |
| COMIT | Computing system, Massachusetts Institute of Technology | COMPACS | Computer Oriented Manufacturing Production And Control System |
| COMJAM | Communications Jamming | COMPACT | Compatible Algebraic Compiler and Translator |
| COML | Commercial | | |

# C

| | | | |
|---|---|---|---|
| COMPACT | Computer Oriented Modular Planning And Control Technique | COMPCORP | Computer design Corporation |
| COMPACT | Computer Planning And Control Technique | COMPEL | Computer Parallel |
| COMPACT | Computer Predicting and Automatic Course Tracking | COMPENDEX | Computerized Engineering Index |
| | | COMPL | Complement |
| | | COMPO | Component |
| | | COMPOOL | Communication Pool |
| COMPANAL | Computer Analysis | COMPR | Compare |
| COMPANDER | Compressor-Expander | COMPROG | Computer Program |
| COMPAR | Comparative | COMPROSL | Compound Procedural Scientific Language |
| COMPAR | Comparator | | |
| COMPAR | Comparison | COMPSCAN | Computerized Scanner |
| COMPARE | Computerized Performance and Analysis Response Evaluation | COMPT | Chip On Module Parameter Tester |
| | | COMPT | Computer |
| COMPARE | Computer-Oriented Method of Program Analysis, Review and Evaluation | COMPTEXT | Computer Prepared Text |
| | | COMPTR | Comparator |
| | | COMPU | Computability |
| COMPARE | Console for Optical Measurement and Precise Analysis of Radiation from Electronics | COMPU | Computable |
| | | COMPU | Computation |
| | | COMPU | Computer |
| | | COMPU | Computerization |
| COMPAS | Computer-Oriented Method for Payroll Accounting and Statistics | COMPUT | Computing |
| | | COMPUTEST | Computer Testgeräte |
| | | COMSAP | Computerized Static Automatic-restoring-equipment for Power-system |
| COMPASS | Compiler-Assembler | | |
| COMPASS | Computer Optimal Media Planning And Selection System | | |
| | | COMSAT... | Communications Satellite Corp. |
| COMPASS | Computer Prüfungs-Analysesystem für Schulen | COMSEC | Communications Security |
| | | COMSEC | Computer Software Exchange Center |
| COMPASS | Computer for Advanced Spare Systems | COMSKEE | Computing and String Keeping language |
| COMPASS | Computer-Assisted | | |
| COMPASS | Computer-Oriented Management Planning And Scheduling System | COMSL | Communication System simulation Language |
| | | COMSOAL | Computer Method of Sequencing Operations for Assembly Lines |
| COMPASS | Computer-Oriented Method of Patterns Analysis for Switching Systems | | |
| | | COMSS | Compare String with String |
| COMPASS | Computer-Orientierte Methode für Planung und Ablauf-Steuerung in Seehäfen | COMSTAT | Competitive Statistical analysis |
| | | COMSTAT | Competitive Statistics |
| | | COMSTORE | Computer Storage |
| COMPASS | Computer-Prüfung/ Analyse-System für Schulen | COMSW | Compare String with Word |
| | | COMTECH | Computer Micrographics Technology |
| COMPASS | Controlled Overhead Management Performance And Standard System | COMTEST | Computertest |
| | | COMTRAN | Commercial Translator |
| | | COMTRAN | Commercial Translation |
| COMPAT | Compatibility | CON | Concentration |

# C

| | |
|---|---|
| CON | Connect |
| CON | Connecting |
| CON | Connection |
| CON | Connector |
| CON | Console |
| CON | Constant |
| CON | Continued |
| CON | Control |
| CON | Controller |
| CON | Converter |
| CON SKT | Connector Socket |
| CON SPEC | Construction Specification |
| CONALOG | Contact Analog |
| CONC | Concentration |
| CONC | Concentrated |
| CONCA | Continue Calling |
| CONCEPT | Computation On-line of Networks Chemical Engineering Process Technology |
| CONCOCON | Construction Cost Control |
| COND | Condenser |
| COND | Condition |
| COND | Conductivity |
| COND | Conductor |
| CONDOR | Communikation in Natürlicher Sprache mit Dialog-Orientiertem Retrieval-system |
| CONDR | Conductor |
| CONDTN | Condition |
| CONEDS | Conard Education Data System |
| CONELRAD | Control of Electromagnetic Radiation |
| CONEST | Construction Estimation |
| CONET | Concentrator Network |
| CONFESS | Conduction Fingerprint Electrooptic Search System |
| CONFIDAL | Conjugate Filter Data Link |
| CONGA | Concept Game |
| CONIN | Conselho Nacional de Informatica e Autonacao |
| CONIT | Connector for Networked Information Transfer |
| CONN | Connect |
| CONN | Connected |
| CONN | Connecting |
| CONN | Connection |
| CONN | Connector |
| CONPASP | Construction Project Alternative Selection Program |
| CONQUEST | Controlled Quality Established |
| CONRAD | Computerized National Range Documentation |
| CONS | Carrier Operated Noise Suppression |
| CONS | Console |
| CONS | Construction |
| CONSORT | Conservation Systems with Online Remote Terminals |
| CONSORT | Control Network System Of Receivers and Transmitters |
| CONST | Constant |
| CONST | Construction |
| CONSTN | Construction |
| CONSTR | Construction |
| CONSUL | Control Subroutine Language |
| CONT | Contact |
| CONT | Contents |
| CONT | Continue |
| CONT | Continued |
| CONT | Continuous |
| CONT | Control |
| CONT | Controller |
| CONT CKT | Control Circuit |
| CONT WD | Control Word |
| CONTA | Control Assembly |
| CONTACT | Control and Action |
| CONTH | Continue to Hold |
| CONTR | Control |
| CONTR | Controller |
| CONTRAN | Control Translator |
| CONTRANS | Conceptual Thought Random Net Simulation |
| CONTREAT | Continue Treatment |
| CONTRL | Control |
| CONUS | Continental United States complex |
| CONV | Convergence |
| CONV | Conversion |
| CONV | Converter |
| CONVR | Converter |
| COOL | Checkout Oriented Language |
| COOL | Control Oriented Language |
| COOLS | Community Office On-Line System |
| COP | Central Operator's Panel |
| COP | Central Ordering Point |
| COP | Character-Oriented Protocol |

# C

| | |
|---|---|
| COP | Checkout Of Program |
| COP | Coaxial Output Printer |
| COP | Coefficient Of Performance |
| COP | Communications Output Printer |
| COP | Computer Optimization Package |
| COP | Computer-Oriented Programming |
| COP | Control Optimization |
| COP | Control Optimizing Program |
| COP | Cost Performance |
| COP | Customer Order Processing |
| COPAC | Computer-Oriented Patient Accounting Control |
| COPAC | Continuous Operation Production Allocation and Control |
| COPAR | Computerized Operational Audit Routine |
| COPE | Centralized Online Processing Environment |
| COPE | Communications Oriented Peripheral Equipment |
| COPE | Communications Oriented Processing Equipment |
| COPE | Computer Operator Proficiency Examination |
| COPE | Console Operator Proficiency Examination |
| COPE | Currency Overprinting and Processing Equipment |
| COPES | Community-Oriented Program Environment Scale |
| COPES | Conceptually Oriented Program in Elementary Science |
| COPI | Computer Oriented Programmed Instruction |
| COPI | Customer Order Processing and Invoicing |
| COPIC | Computer Program Information Center |
| COPICS | Communications Oriented Production Information and Control System |
| COPICS | Copyright Office Publication and Interactive Cataloguing System |
| COPIS | Communication Oriented Production Information control System |
| COPP | Computerized Optical Prescription Processing |
| COPPR | Copy, Punch, Print |
| COPPS | Computer Oriented Police Planning System |
| COPRA | Computer für die Privat-Abrechnung |
| COPS | Calculator Oriented Processor System |
| COPS | Circuit Order Processing System |
| COPS | Computerized Optimization Procedure for Stabilizer |
| COPS | Control for Operations Programming and Systems |
| COPSAC | Computer Order Processing and Sales Accounting |
| COPTRAN | Communication Optimization Program Translator |
| COR | Carrier Operated Relay |
| COR | Carry-Over Register |
| COR | Command Register |
| COR | Correct |
| COR | Correction |
| COR | Corrective |
| COR | Correlation |
| CORA | Coherent Radar Array |
| CORA | Conditioned-Response Analog |
| CORAD | Correlation Radar |
| CORAL | Class-Oriented Ring Associated Language |
| CORAL | Comparison Of Recognition Algorithms |
| CORAL | Computer On-line Real-time Applications Language |
| CORANORD | Compagnie Régionale d'Applications mécanographiques du Nord |
| CORAS | Computer Rationalisierte Schulverwaltung |
| CORC | Conventional Ordnance Release Computer |
| CORC | Cornell Compiler |
| CORD | Computer Reinforced Design |
| CORD | Computer with Online Remote Devices |
| CORDAPS | Correlation Data Processing System |
| CORDAT | Coordinate Data |

# C

| | | | |
|---|---|---|---|
| CORDIC | Coordinate Rotation Digital Computer | COS | Cassette Operating System |
| CORDP | Correlated Radar Data Printout | COS | Character Organized Store |
| CORDS | Coherent On Receive Doppler System | COS | Class Of Service |
| CORE | Computer Oriented Reporting Efficiency | COS | Commercial Operating System |
| CORE | Core computer Related Equipment | COS | Communication Operating System |
| CORE... | Computer Related Equipment Ltd. | COS | Communication Operation Station |
| CORELAP | Computerized Relationship Layout Planning | COS | Compact Operating System |
| CORKS | Computer-Oriented Record Keeping System | COS | Compatibility Operating System |
| CORNAP | Computerized Network Analysis Program | COS | Complementary Symmetry |
| CORNET | Control switching arrangement Network | COS | Confusion Signal |
| COROS | Copper Oxide Read-Only Storage | COS | Cosinus |
| CORPIS | Corporate Planning Information System | COS | Cosmic |
| CORR | Correct | COS | Cray Operating System |
| CORR | Corrected | COS | Current Output Station |
| CORR | Correction | COS/MOS | Complementary-Symmetry MOS |
| CORR | Correlation | COSACS | Computer Operations Scheduling Accounting and Control System |
| CORR | Correspondence | COSACS | Computer-Oriented Scheduling And Control System |
| CORRECT | Customized Optical Reader Random Error Correction Technique | COSANOSTRA | Computer-Oriented System and Newly Organized Storage-to-Retrieval Apparatus |
| CORRN | Correction | COSATI | Committee On Scientific And Technical Information |
| CORS | Canadian Operational Research Society | COSBA | Computer Services and Bureaux Association |
| CORSAIR | Computer-Oriented Reference System for Automatic Information Retrieval | COSI | Committee On Science Information |
| | | COSI-CON | Crimp-On, Snap-In Contacts |
| CORSIA | Comité de Recherche pour la sécurité des Systèmes d'Information Automatisés | COSIMA | Computersysteme Im Arbeitsamt |
| | | COSINE | Computer Science In electrical Engineering |
| CORTET | COBOL-Orientierter Entscheidungstabellenvorübersetzer | COSINF | Convert Source Information |
| | | COSIP | Computer-System für Industrielle Prozeßsteuerung |
| CORTEX | Communications Oriented Real-Time Executive | COSMA | Computerselektion mit Matrizenmodellen |
| CORTS | Convert Range Telemetry System | COSMIC | Command Operations Simulation Model with Interrogation Control |
| COS | Calculator On Substrate | | |
| COS | Card Operating System | | |
| COS | Card-Oriented System | | |
| COS | Card Output Station | COSMIC | Computer-Operated Sequential Memory and Integrated Circuits |
| COS | Carry-Over Storage | | |

# C

| | | | |
|---|---|---|---|
| COSMIS | Computer Software Management and Information Services | COSYPLAN | Computergestützte System-Planung |
| COSMIS | Computer-System for Medical Information Services | COT | Card-Operated Typewriter |
| | | COT | Check-Out Time |
| | | COT | Class Of Traffic character |
| | | COT | Common Output Tape |
| COSMO | Computer-Stundenplan-Modell | COT | Computer-Output-Typesetting |
| COSMON | Component Open-Short Monitor | COTAR | Correlation Tracking And Ranging |
| COSMOS | Computer Optimization and Simulation Modelling for Operating Supermarkets | COTAR | Cosine-Trajectory Angle and Range |
| | | COTAR-AME | Correlation Tracking And Ranging-Angle Measuring Equipment |
| COSMOS | Computer-Oriented System for Manufacturing Order Synthesis | COTAR-DAS | Correlation Tracking And Ranging-Data Acquisition System |
| COSMOS | Console-Oriented Statistical Matrix Operator System | COTAR-DME | Correlation Tracking And Ranging-Data Measuring Equipment |
| COSMOS | Courtaulds' Own System for Matrix Operations and Statistics | COTC | Canadian Overseas Telecommunication Corporation |
| COSNOSTRA | Computer Oriented System New Organized Storage-To-Retrieval Apparatus | COTMS | Computer-Operated Transmission Measuring Set |
| COSOS | Conference On Self-Operating Systems | COTRANS | Coordinated Transfer Application System |
| COSOS | Combined Sorting System | COTS | Checkout Test Set |
| COSS | Com-share's Online Simulation System | COTT | Computer-Operated Thermal Tester |
| COSS | Computer-Optimized Storehouse System | COTTI | Commission de Traitement et de la Transmission de l'Information |
| COSSO | Computerservice und Software | COU | Computer Operating Unit |
| COST | Computer-Operated Sequential Tester | COU | Coupler |
| | | COUNT | Computer Operated Universal Test |
| COST | Coopération européenne Scientifique et Technique | COUP | Coupler |
| | | COUPL | Coupling |
| COSTAR | Computer-Stored Ambulatory Record | COURT | Cost Optimization Utilizing Reference Techniques |
| COSTAR | Conversational Online Storage And Retrieval | COUTS | Computer-Operated Universal Test System |
| COSTING | Cost accounting and Information system Guide | COV | Cut-Out Valve |
| | | COV | Counter-Operating Voltage |
| COSU | Computing Surveys | | |
| COSUMR | Column, Sum, Row | COV | Cut-Off Voltage |
| COSX | Control of Optimizing Series of Experiments | COWOCOR | Computer Wort Codierung und Recherche |
| COSY | Computergesteuertes Satzsystem | COZI | Communications Zone Indicator |
| COSY | Checkout Operating System | CP | Calculating Punch |
| | | CP | Calculator Printing |

# C

| | | | |
|---|---|---|---|
| CP | Call Program | CP | Component Part |
| CP | Call Progress | CP | Compteur de Programme |
| CP | Call on Positive | CP | Computed Point |
| CP | Called Program | CP | Computer |
| CP | Calling Program | CP | Computer Praxis |
| CP | Calorific Power | CP | Computer Printing |
| CP | Candle Power | CP | Computer Programming |
| CP | Card Perforator | CP | Computergesteuerte Programmierhilfe |
| CP | Card Printing | | |
| CP | Card Processing | CP | Computing Problem |
| CP | Card Program | CP | Computing Program |
| CP | Card Punch | CP | Conditional Probability |
| CP | Card to Printer | CP | Connection Point |
| CP | Card to Punch | CP | Connector Panel |
| CP | Catalogued Program | CP | Consecutive Processing |
| CP | Cathode Pulsed | CP | Consecutive Punching |
| CP | Central Processor | CP | Constant Potential |
| CP | Change Point | CP | Constant Pressure |
| CP | Change Program | CP | Constract and Purchase |
| CP | Channel Program | CP | Continuation Punch |
| CP | Character Printer | CP | Continuous Path |
| CP | Character Printing | CP | Continuous Punching |
| CP | Check Parity | CP | Control Panel |
| CP | Check Problem | CP | Control Part |
| CP | Check Program | CP | Control Point |
| CP | Checked Punching | CP | Control Print |
| CP | Checkpoint | CP | Control Procedures |
| CP | Circuit Package | CP | Control Processor |
| CP | Circular Pitch | CP | Control Program |
| CP | Circularly Polarized | CP | Control Programmer |
| CP | Clock Phase | CP | Control Punch |
| CP | Clock Program | CP | Controlling Program |
| CP | Clock Pulse | CP | Conversion Program |
| CP | Closed Program | CP | Converter Program |
| CP | Code Pattern | CP | Copy |
| CP | Code Position | CP | Corrected Program |
| CP | Code Program | CP | Coupling |
| CP | Code of Practice | CP | Cyclic Program |
| CP | Code of Procedure | CP V | Control Program Five |
| CP | Coded Program | CP-R | Control Program for Real-time |
| CP | Coding Printer | | |
| CP | Coefficient of Performance | CP/M | Control Program for Microprocessors |
| CP | Column Pitch | CPA | Channel Program Area |
| CP | Command Processor | CPA | Circuit Parameter Analysis |
| CP | Command Pulse | | |
| CP | Communications Processor | CPA | Closest Point of Approach |
| | | CPA | Colour Phase Alternation |
| CP | Compare | CPA | Commutative Principle for Addition |
| CP | Compare decimal Packed | | |
| CP | Compare Packed | CPA | Computer Power Australia |
| CP | Comparison | CPA | Controlled Pushdown Automaton |
| CP | Compiling Program | | |
| CP | Complementary Program | CPA | Critical Path Analysis |
| CP | Complex Programming | CPA | Cross-Program Auditor |

- 137 -

# C

| | | | |
|---|---|---|---|
| CPAB | Computer Programmer Aptitude Battery | CPCFC | Critical Parts Centralized Forecast Computation |
| CPAC | Computer Program Associate Contractor | CPCS | Check Processing Control System |
| CPAO | Conception de Programme Assistée par Ordinateur | CPCS | Check Processory Central System |
| CPAP | Control Parameter Assembly Program | CPD | Card Per Day |
| CPAU | Computers and Automation | CPD | Circuit Protection Device |
| CPAWS | Computer Planner and Aircraft Weighing Scales | CPD | Computer Produced Drawing |
| CPB | Channel Program Block | CPD | Cumulative Probabilitiy Distribution |
| CPB | Corporate Programming Bulletin | CPD | Connectez Poste de Données |
| CPBX | Control Private Branch Exchange | CPD | Consolidated Programming Document |
| CPC | Calculatrice à Programme par Cartes | CPD | Contact Potential Difference |
| CPC | Card-Programmed Calculator | CPDC | Computer Program Development Center |
| CPC | Card-Programmed Computer | CPDD | Command Post Digital Display |
| CPC | Central Processing Complex | CPDS | Command Processor Distributor Storage |
| CPC | Central Processor Chip | CPE | Call Parity Even |
| CPC | Ceramic-Printed Circuit | CPE | Central Processing Element |
| CPC | Ceramic-water Printed Circuit | CPE | Central Processor Element |
| CPC | Character Per Column | CPE | Central Programmer and Evaluator |
| CPC | Clock-Pulse Control | | |
| CPC | Coated Powder Cathode | CPE | Channel Processing Element |
| CPC | Column Position Counter | | |
| CPC | Commodity Punched Card | CPE | Charged Particle Equilibrum |
| CPC | Computer Planning Corporation | CPE | Circular Probable Error |
| CPC | Computer Process Control | CPE | COBOL Programming Environment |
| CPC | Computer Production Control | CPE | Computer Performance Evaluation |
| CPC | Computer Program Component | CPE | Computer Peripheral Equipment |
| CPC | Computer Program Counter | CPE | Computergestützte Planungs- und Entscheidungshilfen |
| CPC | Computerized Process Control | | |
| CPC | Construction Project Control | CPE | Counter Position Exit |
| CPC | Current Papers on Computer | CPE | Cross-Program Editor |
| | | CPE | Customer Premises |
| CPC | Current Papers on Computers and control | CPEP | Contractor Performance Evaluation Plan |
| CPC | Cycle Program Control | CPEQ | Corporation of Professional Engineers of Quebec |
| CPC | Cycle Program Counter | | |
| CPC | Cyclic Permutation Code | | |
| CPC | Cyclic Program Control | CPES | Contractor Performance Evaluation System |
| CPCEI | Computer Program Contract End Item | | |

# C

| | | | |
|---|---|---|---|
| CPEUG | Computer Performance Evaluation Users Group | CPIN | Change Package Identification Number |
| CPEX | Centre Principal d'Exploitation | CPIOCS | Communication Physical Input/Output Control System |
| CPF | Carbon Paper Feed | | |
| CPF | Central Processing Facility | CPIP | Computer Pneumatic Input Panel |
| CPF | Coded Print File | CPIP | Computer Program Implementation Process |
| CPF | Complete Power Failure | | |
| CPF | Control Program Facility | CPIT | Cost Price of the Items Terminated |
| CPFF | Cost Plus Fixed Fee | | |
| CPFR | Continuous Page Facsimile Recorder | CPJ | Conditional Program Jump |
| | | CPL | Canadian Program Library |
| CPG | Certified Program Generator | CPL | Central Program Library |
| | | CPL | Certified Parts List |
| CPG | CICS Program Generator | CPL | Certified Products List |
| CPG | Clock Pulse Generator | CPL | Charge Pumping Logic |
| CPG | COBOL Program Generator | CPL | Choice of Programming Languages |
| CPG | Communication Program Generator | CPL | Code Program Library |
| CPG | Current Pulse Generator | CPL | Coded Parts List |
| CPGS | Cross Program Generation System | CPL | Columns Per Line |
| | | CPL | Combined Programming Language |
| CPH | Cards Per Hour | | |
| CPH | Computergesteuerte Programmierhilfe | CPL | Commandeur Programmable à Logique |
| CPH | Copies Per Hour | CPL | Common Program Language |
| CPH | Cost Per Hour | CPL | Compiler |
| CPH | Counts Per Hour | CPL | Computer Program Library |
| CPH | Cycles Per Hours | | |
| CPI | Card Punch Interface | CPL | Conversational Planning Language |
| CPI | Center of Programmed Instruction | CPL | Corporate Programming List |
| CPI | Central Patents Index | | |
| CPI | Clock Pulse Interval | CPL | Couple |
| CPI | Commercial Performance Index | CPL | Current Product Line |
| | | CPLD | Compound Phase-Locked Demodulator |
| CPI | Computer Peripherals Inc. | | |
| CPI | Computer Prescribed Instruction | CPLD | Coupled |
| | | CPLG | Coupling |
| CPI | Computing Power Index | CPLMT | Complement |
| CPI | Conditional Program Interruption | CPLR | Coupler |
| | | CPLT | Complete |
| CPI | Control Position Indicator | CPM | COBOL Performance Monitor |
| CPI | Corporate Program Independent | | |
| | | CPM | Card Punch Memory |
| CPIAF | Cost Plus Incentive Award Fee | CPM | Cathode Pulse Method |
| | | CPM | Central Path Method |
| CPIC | Computer Program Integration Contractor | CPM | Characters Per Minute |
| | | CPM | Chip Placement Machine |
| CPIF | Cost Puls Incentive Fee | CPM | Communication Password Matrix |
| CPILS | Correlation Protected Integrated Landing System | | |
| | | CPM | Commutative Principle for Multiplication |

# C

| | | | |
|---|---|---|---|
| CPM | Computer Performance Monitor | CPR | Certification Print Routine |
| CPM | Connection Point Manager | CPR | Component to Part Record |
| CPM | Continuous Processing Machine | CPR | Computer |
| CPM | Control Program Monitor | CPR | Computer Personnel Research |
| CPM | Critical Path Method | CPR | Cost Performance Report |
| CPM-Cost | Critical Path Method with Cost | CPR | Current Page Register |
| | | CPR | Cursor Position Report |
| CPMA | Computer Peripheral Manufacturers Association | CPRV | Calculate Polynominal for Row Values |
| | | CPS | Capacity Planning System |
| CPMC | Computerized Planar Motion Carriage | CPS | Caractère Par Seconde |
| | | CPS | Card Processing System |
| CPMP | Control Program Management Package | CPS | Card Programming Support |
| | | CPS | Card Programming System |
| CPMS | Computer Performance Monitoring System | CPS | Card Punch Store |
| | | CPS | Cards Per Second |
| CPMS | Computer Plotting Matrix System | CPS | Central Processing System |
| | | CPS | Central Programming Service |
| CPN | Card Part Number | | |
| CPN | Code Program Name | CPS | Circuit Package Schematic |
| CPN | Code Program Number | CPS | Clock Pulse |
| CPN | Component Part Number | CPS | Combined Principles Simulator |
| CPO | Call on Parity Odd | | |
| CPO | Card Punch Operation | CPS | Computer Power Supply |
| CPO | Cartes Perforées Ordinateurs | CPS | Computer Program Specification |
| CPO | Changing Path of Operation | CPS | Computer Program System |
| | | CPS | Computer Programming System |
| CPO | Code Practice Oscillator | | |
| CPO | Computer Peripheral Operations | CPS | Console Programming System |
| CPO | Concurrent Peripheral Operations | CPS | Contingency Planning System |
| CPO | Controlled Precision Oscillator | CPS | Control Power Supply |
| | | CPS | Control Program Services |
| CPP | Card Print Processor | CPS | Conversational Programming System |
| CPP | Card Punching Printer | | |
| CPP | Command Processing Program | CPS | Cooley Programming System |
| CPP | Concurrent Peripheral Processing | CPS | Corporate Planning System |
| CPP | Corporate Programming Practice | CPS | Corporate Programming Standard |
| CPPC | Cost Plus a Percentage of Cost | CPS | Counts Per Second |
| | | CPS | Critical Path Scheduling |
| CPPM | Critical Path Programming Method | CPSAC | Cycles Per Second Alternating Current |
| CPPS | Critical Path Planning and Scheduling | CPSK | Coherent Phase Shift Keying |
| CPPS | Continuous Process Plant Scheduling | CPSK | Coherent Phase Shift Keyed |
| CPR | Cam Plate Readout | CPSR | Computer Professionals for Social Responsibility |
| CPR | Card Punching Rate | | |

# C

| | | | |
|---|---|---|---|
| CPSR | Cost and Performance Summary Report | CR | Call Register |
| CPSS | Central Processing Subsystem | CR | Call Request |
| | | CR | Cancel Request |
| CPSS | Common Program Support System | CR | Cancellation Request |
| | | CR | Capacity Record |
| CPST | Computer Programs in Science and Technology | CR | Card Reader |
| | | CR | Card Reading |
| | | CR | Card Recording |
| CPSU | Central Processor Sub-Unit | CR | Card Registration |
| | | CR | Card Reproducer |
| CPT | Capacitive Pressure Transducer | CR | Card Run |
| | | CR | Carriage Return |
| CPT | Chief Programmer Team | CR | Carry Register |
| CPT | Clock, Programming and Training | CR | Cathode-Ray |
| | | CR | Central Registry |
| CPT | Communication Password Table | CR | Chain Radar |
| | | CR | Change Release |
| CPT | Compatible Punched Tape | CR | Change Request |
| CPT | Computer Programming Training | CR | Character Reader |
| | | CR | Character Reading |
| CPT | Control Power Transformer | CR | Character Recognition |
| | | CR | Check Register |
| CPT | Critical Path Technique | CR | Check Routine |
| CPT | Customer Provided Terminal | CR | Check Run |
| | | CR | Circulating Register |
| CPTA | Computer Programming and Testing Activity | CR | Citizen Radio |
| | | CR | Classified Register |
| CPTC | Central Processor Test Console | CR | Closed Routine |
| | | CR | Code Reader |
| CPTO | Chefprogrammier-Team-organisation | CR | Code Receiver |
| | | CR | Coding Recorder |
| CPTR | Chief Pointer | CR | Coincidence Register |
| CPTY | Capacity | CR | Command Receiver |
| CPU | Card Punching Unit | CR | Command Register |
| CPU | Central Processing Unit | CR | Command Routine |
| CPU | Collective Protection Unit | CR | Common Return |
| CPU | Computer Peripheral Unit | CR | Compiling Routine |
| CPU | Cost Per Unit | CR | Computer Run |
| CPUID | Central Processing Unit Identification | CR | Computing Result |
| | | CR | Computing Reviews |
| CPW | Computations Per Word | CR | Computing Routine |
| CPWM | Clock Pulse Width Modulation | CR | Connector Register |
| | | CR | Contact Resistance |
| CPY | Copy | CR | Continuous Reading |
| CQ | Computer Queue | CR | Contract Report |
| CQA | Computer-aided Question Answering | CR | Contractor Report |
| | | CR | Control Receiver |
| CQAO | Contrôle de Qualité Assisté par Ordinateur | CR | Control Register |
| | | CR | Control Relay |
| CQM | Circuit Quality Monitor | CR | Control Routine |
| CQS | Common Queue Space | CR | Conversion Routine |
| CQTP | Capacitor Qualification Test Program | CR | Correct Routing |
| | | CR | Count Reverse |
| CR | C Register | CR | Counting Rate |
| CR | Calculating Register | CR | Credit |

- 141 -

# C

| | | | |
|---|---|---|---|
| CR | Creditable Record | CRC | Condition Reservation Code |
| CR | Crystal Rectifier | | |
| CR | Current Rate | CRC | Contract Requirement Card |
| CR | Current Relay | | |
| CR MT | Computer Readable Magnetic Tape | CRC | Control and Reporting Center |
| CR Tube | Cathode Ray Tube | CRC | Contrôle de Redondance Cyclique |
| CR/LF | Carriage Return/Line Feed | | |
| CRA | Carry Ripple Adder | CRC | Cross Reference Code |
| CRA | Catalog Recovery Area | CRC | Cyclic Redundancy Check |
| CRA | Catalogue Recovery Area | CRC | Cyclic Redundancy Checking |
| CRA | Computer Retailers' Area | | |
| CRA | Control Relay Automatic | CRCC | Cyclic Redundancy Check Character |
| CRA | Control Repeater Amplifier | CRCIS | Cybernetics Research Consultants Information Systems |
| CRAFT | Changing Radio Automatic Frequency Transmission | CRCRD | Credit Card Reader |
| CRAFT | Computerized Relative Allocation of Facilities Technique | CRCS | Code Restriction Class of Service |
| | | CRCT | Circuit |
| CRAM | Card Random Access Memory | CRCT | Correct |
| | | CRCTN | Correction |
| CRAM | Computerized Reliability Analysis Method | CRD | Capacitor-Resistor-Diode |
| | | CRD | Card |
| CRAM | Condensed Random Access Memory | CRD | Character Reading Device |
| | | CRD | Compte-Rendu de Défaut |
| CRAM | Conditional Relaxation Analysis Method | CRD | Computer Readout Device |
| | | CRDS | Card Release Daily Status |
| CRAMM | Coupon Reading And Marking Machine | CRDS | Component Repair Data Sheet |
| CRAS | Coder and Random Access Switch | CRDSD | Current Research and Development in Scientific Documentation |
| CRAZI | Count Routine Applied to Zero Input | | |
| | | CRE | Card Read Error |
| CRB | Code Restriction Block | CRE | Corrosion-Resistant |
| CRB | Computer Resale Broker | CREAM | Computer Realtime Access Method |
| CRB | Counter Read Back | | |
| CRB | Customer Record and Billing | CREAM | Computer Resource Allocation Model |
| CRBE | Conversational Remote Batch Entry | CREATE | Computational Resources for Engineering And Training and Education |
| CRC | Carriage Return Character | | |
| CRC | Carriage Return Code | CREDIT | Cost Reduction Early Decision Information Technique |
| CRC | Carriage Return Contact | | |
| CRC | Carrier Return Character | | |
| CRC | Central Read Control | CREE | Conversational Remote-batch Entry |
| CRC | Character Recognition Circuit | | |
| | | CREI | Centro Regional para la Ensenanza de la Informatica |
| CRC | Column Reference Centerline | | |
| CRC | Complete-Round Chart | CRES | Corrosion-Resistant |
| CRC | Computer Research Corporation | CRESS | Computerized Reader Enquiry Service System |

- 142 -

# C

| | | | |
|---|---|---|---|
| CREST | Computer-aided combat Reporting System | CRL | Character Recognition Logic |
| CREST | Computer Routine for Evaluation of Simulation Tactics | CRL | Corporate Records List |
| | | CRLB | Cosmic Ray Logic Box |
| | | CRLCD | Credit Limit Code |
| CREST | Consolidated Reporting and Evaluating System | CRLP | Current Loop |
| | | CRM | Cathode Ray Memory |
| CRESTS | Courtauld's Rapid Extract, Sort and Tabulate System | CRM | Change Request Material |
| | | CRM | Compte-Rendu de Mouvement |
| CRF | Capital Recovery Factor | | |
| CRF | Carrier Frequency | CRM | Computer Readable Medium |
| CRF | Central Retransmission Facility | | |
| | | CRM | Computer Resources Management |
| CRF | COMPOOL Request Form | | |
| CRF | Control Relay Forward | CRM | Control and Reproduce-ability Monitor |
| CRG | Carriage | | |
| CRG | Cross Reference Generator | CRM | Contrôle des Réponses Minutées |
| CRH | Control Relay, Hand | | |
| CRI | Carnegie Representation Language | CRM | Count Rate Meter |
| | | CRMR | Compte-Rendu de Mise en Route |
| CRI | Circuit Reliability Improvement | | |
| | | CRMR | Continuous-Reading Meter Relay |
| CRI | Comité de Recherche en Informatique | | |
| | | CRMS | Control and Reproducibility Monitor System |
| CRI | Computer Related Industries | | |
| CRIB | Computerized Resources Information Bank | CRMT | Circuit Rule Master Tape |
| | | CRN | Charge-Routing Network |
| CRIDON | Centre de Recherche d'Information et de Documentation Notariel | CRN | Correction |
| | | CRNO | Command Register Not Operable |
| CRIG | Capacitor Rate Integrating Gyroscope | CRO | Card Reader Operation |
| | | CRO | Carded for Record Only |
| CRIMP | Computer Report on Importance | CRO | Cathode Ray Oscillograph |
| | | CROC | Computer Review and Orientation Course |
| CRIMP | Customer Report on Importance | | |
| | | CROM | Capacitive Read-Only Memory |
| CRIS | Calibration Recall Information System | | |
| | | CROM | Control Read-Only Memory |
| CRIS | Command Retrieval Information System | | |
| | | CROP | Common Routing Output |
| CRIS | Counterintelligence Records Information System | CROS | Capacitor Read-Only Storage |
| | | CROSS | Computerized Rearrangement Of Special Subjects |
| CRIS | Current Research Information System | | |
| CRISP | Categories for Recursive Information Systems Postulation | CROSS | Computer Rearrangement Of Subject Specialities |
| | | CROSSBOW | Computerized Retrieval of Organic Structures Based On Wiswesser |
| CRJ | Command Reject | | |
| CRJE | Conversational Remote Job Entry | | |
| | | CROSSPATE | Coordinative Retrieval Of Selectively Sorted Permuted Analog-Title Entries |
| CRK | Carriage Release Key | | |
| CRK | Carriage Return Key | | |
| CRK | Cross Reference Keys | | |

# C

| | | | |
|---|---|---|---|
| CROWD | Continuous Read-Out of Work Dimensions | CRT | Control Relay Translator |
| CRP | Card Read Punch | CRT | Correct |
| CRP | Card Reader Program | CRT | Counter Recovery Time |
| CRP | Card Reader/Punch | CRT | Create |
| CRP | Channel Request Priority | CRTA | Cathode Ray Tube Addressing |
| CRP | Collimation and Registration Program | CRTF | Create Test File |
| CRP | Command Read Pulse | CRTG | Cartridge |
| CRP | Common Reference Point | CRTIS | Chicago Railroad Terminal Information System |
| CRP | Component Reliability Prediction | CRTL | Control |
| CRP | Computer Reset Pulse | CRTM | Cathode Ray Tube Memory |
| CRP | Computer Room People | CRTMBA | Criteria and Macrobudget Accounting |
| CRP | Controlled Reliability Program | CRTO | Cathode Ray Tube Oscilloscope |
| CRP | Corporate Record Practice | CRTOG | Cartography |
| CRPS | Common Release Processing System | CRTS | Cathode Ray Tube Storage |
| CRR | Conversion Result Register | CRTS | Controllable Radar Target Simulator |
| CRRA | Component Release Reliability Analysis | CRTT | Cathode Ray Tube Terminal |
| CRRS | Contribution Record Reporting System | CRTU | Combined Receiving and Transmitting Unit |
| CRS | Cathode Ray Store | CRU | Card Reader Unit |
| CRS | Centralized Referral System | CRU | Communication Register Unit |
| CRS | Chain Radar System | CRU | Computer Resource Unit |
| CRS | Character Recognition System | CRU | Customer Replaceable Unit |
| CRS | Checker Redundant Scheme | CRV | Constant Reflector Voltage |
| CRS | Citizens Radio Service | CRV | Contact-Resistance Variation |
| CRS | Command Retrieval System | CRV | Cryptography Verification Request |
| CRS | Computer Related Services | CRV DWG | Curve Drawing |
| CRS | Customized Routing Selector | CRWC | Complete Reading-Writing Cycle |
| CRS | Customized Routing System | CRYG | Carrying |
| CRSA | Current Routing Starting Address | CRYOSAR | Cryogenic Switching by Avalanche and Recombination |
| CRSG | Classification Research Study Group | CRYPTO | Cryptographic |
| CRSG | Corresponding | CRYPTONET | Crypto-communication Network |
| CRSN | Corporate Resource Sharing Network | CRYST | Crystal |
| CRST | Cathode Ray Storage Tube | CS | Calculating Speed |
| CRSVR | Crossover | CS | Calculating Store |
| CRT | Cathode Ray Tube | CS | Calculation Statement |
| CRT | Cathode Ray Typesetting | CS | Call Sequence |
| CRT | Channel Response Time | CS | Call Sign |
| CRT | Charactron Tube | CS | Call Signal |
| | | CS | Call Statement |
| | | CS | Call Store |

# C

| | | | |
|---|---|---|---|
| CS | Call System | CS | Combined Storage |
| CS | Capacitor Store | CS | Command Selection |
| CS | Caractère Spécial | CS | Command Statement |
| CS | Card Selection | CS | Command Structure |
| CS | Card Size | CS | Command System |
| CS | Card Socket | CS | Comment Statement |
| CS | Card Sorting | CS | Commercial Standard |
| CS | Card Stacker | CS | Commercial System |
| CS | Card Station | CS | Commit Stop |
| CS | Card Store | CS | Common Statement |
| CS | Card Support | CS | Communication System |
| CS | Casket Store | CS | Communications |
| CS | Cell Sequence | CS | Communications Services |
| CS | Cell Store | CS | Communications Subsystem |
| CS | Centistoke | | |
| CS | Centralized Scheduling | CS | Compact System |
| CS | Chain Store | CS | Compilation Stage |
| CS | Channel Search | CS | Complement Storage |
| CS | Channel Status | CS | Composite Score |
| CS | Character Selection | CS | Compound Statement |
| CS | Character Sense | CS | Compute Statement |
| CS | Character Sensing | CS | Computer Science |
| CS | Character Sequence | CS | Computer Store |
| CS | Character Set | CS | Computer Subprogram |
| CS | Character Speed | CS | Computer Subroutine |
| CS | Character String | CS | Computing Sequence |
| CS | Charge Storage | CS | Computing Speed |
| CS | Charge Store | CS | Computing Store |
| CS | Check Sorter | CS | Conditional Sentence |
| CS | Check Sum | CS | Conditional Statement |
| CS | Check Surface | CS | Conducted Susceptibility |
| CS | Checked Statement | CS | Connection Support |
| CS | Checking Sequence | CS | Context Sensitive |
| CS | Checking Subroutine | CS | Continuation Statement |
| CS | Checking System | CS | Continue Statement |
| CS | Chip-Select | CS | Continuous Scan |
| CS | Circuit Switching | CS | Control Scanner |
| CS | Circulating Store | CS | Control Section |
| CS | Clear and Substract | CS | Control Set |
| CS | Closed Subroutine | CS | Control Sharing |
| CS | Closed System | CS | Control Signal |
| CS | Code Selection | CS | Control Statement |
| CS | Code Sensor | CS | Control Station |
| CS | Code Signal | CS | Control Switch |
| CS | Code Symbol | CS | Control Symbol |
| CS | Code System | CS | Control System |
| CS | Coded Signal | CS | Controlled Storage |
| CS | Coding Section | CS | Controlled Store |
| CS | Coding Specification | CS | Controlled Switch |
| CS | Coding Store | CS | Core Shift |
| CS | Coincidence Store | CS | Core Storage |
| CS | Collation Sequence | CS | Core Store |
| CS | Column Separator | CS | Count Store |
| CS | Column Spacing | CS | Counting Switch |
| CS | Column Split | CS | Cross Section |

# C

| | | | |
|---|---|---|---|
| CS | Cryogenic Store | CSB | Complementary Straight Binary |
| CS | Currency Sign | | |
| CS | Current Strength | CSC | Care Store Control |
| CS | Current Switch | CSC | Central Switching-network Control |
| CS | Cycle Shift | | |
| CS | Cycles per Second | CSC | Change Schedule Chart |
| CS | Cyclic Store | CSC | Clock Start Command |
| CS-CB | Common Source - Common Base | CSC | Command Scheduling Chain |
| CS-CC | Common Source - Common Collector | CSC | Command Selector Control |
| CS-CE | Common Source - Common Emitter | CSC | Common Signalling Channel |
| CSA | Canadian Standards Association | CSC | Communications Simulator Console |
| CSA | Carry Save Adder | CSC | Communication Systems Center |
| CSA | Carry Save Addition | | |
| CSA | Certificate in Systems Analysis | CSC | Complete Store Cycle |
| | | CSC | Comprehensive Self-Check |
| CSA | Chopper Stabilized Amplifier | CSC | Computer Science Canada |
| | | CSC | Computer Science Center |
| CSA | Command Session Abort | CSC | Computer Sciences Corporation |
| CSA | Common System Area | | |
| CSA | Computer Sciences of Australia | CSC | Computer Search Center |
| | | CSC | Computer Service Center |
| CSA | Computer Services Association | CSC | Computer Society of Canada |
| CSA | Computer System Analyst | CSC | Computer Store Capacity |
| CSA | Computer Systems of America Inc. | CSC | Computer Subsystem Controller |
| CSA | Conditional Sum Adder | CSC | Computer-Selbst-erfahrungs-Center |
| CSA | Configuration Status Accounting | | |
| | | CSC | Consequence Counter |
| CSA | Cooperating Systems Architecture | CSC | Control Signalling Code |
| | | CSC | Control Systems Character |
| CSA | Core Store Allocation | CSC | Core Store Control |
| CSA | Current Source Amplifier | CSC | Course and Speed Calculator |
| CSAJTL | Current Switching Alloy Junction Transistor Logic | | |
| | | CSC | Course and Speed Computer |
| CSAP | Control System Analysis Program | CSC | Cylinder Seek Command |
| | | CSCB | Command Scheduling Control Block |
| CSAR | Communications Satellite Advanced Research | | |
| | | CSCC | Command Session Change Control |
| CSAR | Configuration Status Accounting Report | | |
| | | CSCF | Captive Spot Curve Follower |
| CSAR | Control Storage Address Register | | |
| | | CSCH | Clear Subchannel |
| CSAR | Control, Security, Auditing, Recovery | CSCS | Cost Schedule and Control System |
| CSB | Carrier and Sideband | CSCSC | Cost Schedule Cost System Criteria |
| CSB | Chained Segment Buffering | | |
| CSB | Channel Status Byte | CSD | Central Storage Device |
| CSB | Communications Scanner Base | CSD | Character String Data |
| | | CSD | Command Signal Decoder |

# C

| | | | |
|---|---|---|---|
| CSD | Command Systems Department | CSEIP | Center for the Study of the Evaluation of Instructional Programs |
| CSD | Communications System Development | CSF | Carrier Suppression Filter |
| CSD | Computer System Department | CSF | Communication Serviceability Facilities |
| CSD | Computer Systems Design | CSF | Completely Symmetric Function |
| CSD | Computer Systems Director | CSFI | Company Standard Form Instruction |
| CSD | Computergestützte Systementwicklung und Dokumentation | CSG | Context-Sensitive Grammar |
| CSD | Computerized Standard Data | CSG | Course Selection Guide |
| CSD | Constant Speed Drive | CSI | Code Sequence Introducer |
| CSD | Control System Dummy | CSI | Computer Sciences International |
| CSD | Controlled-Slip Differentials | CSI | Computer Systems International |
| CSD | Cord Store Dump | CSI | Conseils et Services en Informatique |
| CSD | Core Shift Driver | | |
| CSDBTL | Current Switching Diffused Base Transistor Logic | CSI | Control Sequence Introducer |
| CSDL | Current Switching Diode Logic | CSIC | Computer Stock Inventory Control |
| CSDN | Circuit Switched Data Network | CSIC | Computer System Interface Circuits |
| CSDP | Command Supply Discipline Program | CSIE | Council of Science and Industrial Education |
| CSDR | Control Storage Data Register | CSIRO | Commonwealth Scientific and Industrial Research Organisation |
| CSDR | Cross-Section Data Reduction | CSISRS | Cross Section Information, Storage and Retrieval System |
| CSDS | Command Ship Data System | CSK | Column Skipping Key |
| CSDS | Communication Signal Distribution System | CSK | Cyclic Shift Keying |
| | | CSL | Code Selection Language |
| CSE | Command Session End | CSL | Command Signal Limiter |
| CSE | Computer Science and Engineering | CSL | Commercial Source Language |
| CSE | Control System Engineering | CSL | Component Source List |
| CSE | Control and Switching Equipment | CSL | Computer Sensitive Language |
| CSE | Core Storage Element | CSL | Computer System Language |
| CSEA | California State Electronics Association | CSL | Computer Systems Laboratory |
| CSEA | Core Store Effective Address | CSL | Console |
| | | CSL | Context-Sensitive Language |
| CSECT | Control Section | CSL | Control and Simulation Language |
| CSEE | Compagnie de Signaux et d'Entreprises Electriques | CSL | Controlled Saturation Logic |
| CSEF | Current-Switch Emitter-Follower | CSL | Core Store Location |
| | | CSL | Corporate Source List |

# C

| | | | |
|---|---|---|---|
| CSL | Corporate Systems List | CSP | Commercial Subroutine Package |
| CSL | Current Sink Logic | CSP | Communications Satellite Program |
| CSL | Current Sourcing Logic | | |
| CSL | Current Switch Logic | CSP | Communications Symbiont Processor |
| CSM | Central Storage Module | | |
| CSM | Clock and Simulation tape Maintenance | CSP | Comparing Storage Position |
| CSM | Command and Service Module | CSP | Computer Simulation Program |
| CSM | Complete Sequential Machine | CSP | Control Setting Panel |
| CSM | Composite Signal Mixer | CSP | Control Signal Processor |
| CSM | Computer Schalt-Matrix | CSP | Control Switching Point |
| CSM | Computer Store Matrix | CSP | Control and Switching Point |
| CSM | Concurrent Service Monitor | CSP | Corporate Systems Practice |
| CSM | Continuous Sheet Memory | CSP | Cross System Product |
| CSM | Current Switching Mode | CSP | Current System Program |
| CSMA | Carrier-Sense Multiple-Access | CSP/AD | Cross System Product/ Application Development |
| CSMA | Communication Systems Management Association | CSP/AE | Cross System Product/ Application Execution |
| CSMA/CD | Carrier Sense Multiple Access/Collision Detection | CSP/Q | Cross System Product/ Query |
| CSML | Continuous Self-Mode Locking | CSPDN | Circuit Switched Public Data Network |
| CSMP | Continuous Simulation Modelling Program | CSPE | Control System for Plan Execution |
| CSMP | Continuous System Modelling Program | CSPG | Code Sequential Pulse Generator |
| CSMPS | Computerized Scientific Management Planning System | CSPM | Corporate Simulation and Planning Model |
| | | CSPO | Core Store Print-Out |
| CSMS | Computerized Specification Management System | CSPS | Coherent Signal Processing System |
| CSMT | CSM Message Type | CSR | Channel Service Register |
| CSN | Circuit Switching Network | CSR | Check Status Reply |
| CSN | Computer Service Network | CSR | Circulating Shift Register |
| | | CSR | Clamped Speed Regulator |
| CSN | Control Symbol Number | CSR | Complex Status Record |
| CSO | Chained Sequential Operation | CSR | Configuration Selection Register |
| CSO | Computer Service Office | CSR | Console Send-Receive |
| CSO | Consecutive Store Organization | CSR | Constant Stress Rate |
| | | CSR | Continuous Speech Recognition |
| CSO | Control System Operational | CSR | Contract Status Report |
| CSO | Core Store Operand | CSR | Control Shift Register |
| CSOP | Current Switch-circuit Optimization Program | CSR | Controlled Silicon Rectifier |
| CSP | Central Signal Processor | CSRL | Computer Science Research Laboratory |
| CSP | Channel Scheduling Process | CSRP | Cognitive Systems Research Program |
| CSP | Coder Sequential Pulse | | |

# C

| | | | |
|---|---|---|---|
| CSRP | Computer Systems Research Project | CSST | Computer System Science Training |
| CSRUIDR | Chemical Society Research Unit in Information Dissemination and Retrieval | CST | Carrier Supply, Transistorized |
| | | CST | Central Standard Time |
| | | CST | Channel Status Message |
| CSS | Character Sensing System | CST | Channel Status Table |
| CSS | Character String Scanner | CST | Code Segment Table |
| CSS | Clock Subsystem | CST | Computer Subtraction Time |
| CSS | Coded Switch System | | |
| CSS | Command Session Start | CST | Computer System Training |
| CSS | Communications Subsystem | CST | Console Terminal |
| | | CST | Control System Test |
| CSS | Computer Sales and Services | CST | Core Store Technique |
| | | CSTA | Combat Surveillance and Target Acquisition |
| CSS | Computer Scheduling System | CSTAB | Communications Subsystem Table |
| CSS | Computer Sharing Services | CSTAM | Cost Amount |
| CSS | Computer Subsystem | CSTD/GTD | Comité Spécial pour la transmission de Données/ Groupe Transmission |
| CSS | Computer System Simulator | | |
| CSS | Computerized Security System | CSTEX | Cost Extension |
| | | CSTP | Code Segment Table Pointer |
| CSS | Consecutive Sequential Storage | CSTPC | Cost Price |
| CSS | Control Statement Stream | CSTS | Computer Sciences Teleprocessing System |
| CSS | Control System Service | | |
| CSS | Conversational Software System | CSTS | Computer Sciences Time-Sharing system |
| CSS | Corporate Shareholder System | CSTU | Combined System Test Unit |
| CSS | Cryogenic Storage System | CSTUN | Cost per Unit |
| CSS | Customer Support Service | CSU | Central Switching Unit |
| CSSB | Compatible Single Sideband | CSU | Channel Service Unit |
| | | CSU | Circuit Switching Unit |
| CSSD | Communications System Status Display | CSU | Clear and Substract |
| | | CSU | Computer System Unit |
| CSSDA | Council of Social Science Data Archives | CSU | Computing Surveys |
| | | CSU | Constant Speed Unit |
| CSSEC | Computer Systems Support and Evaluation Command | CSU | Control System Utility |
| | | CSU | Core Storage Unit |
| CSSG | Computer Software and Services Group | CSU | Current Service Monitor |
| | | CSU | Customer Service Unit |
| CSSL | Continuous System Simulation Language | CSU | Customer Setup |
| | | CSUI | Command Session User Information |
| CSSL | Corporation Source System Listing | | |
| | | CSV | Characteristic Statistical Value |
| CSSN | Common Source Spot Noise | | |
| | | CSV | Corona Starting Voltage |
| CSSNF | Common Source Spot Noise Figure | CSV | Cycle-Stealing-Verfahren |
| | | CSW | Channel Status Word |
| CSSO | Control Sequential Storage Organization | CSW | Clear and Subtract Word |
| | | CSW | Continuous Seismic Wave |
| CSSP | Continuous System Simulation Program | CSW | Control Power Switch |

# C

| | | | |
|---|---|---|---|
| CSY | Codesynchronisier-einrichtung | CT | Current Transformer |
| | | CT/N | Counter, N stage |
| CT | Cable Transfer | CTA | Call Time Adjustor |
| CT | Calculating Time | CTA | Camp on Tone Allowed |
| CT | Card-to-Tape | CTA | Compteur Tabulation |
| CT | Carrier Telephone | CTA | Control Area |
| CT | Carrier Telephony | CTA | Controlled Airspace |
| CT | Casket Tape | CTA | Corporate Technological Assignment |
| CT | Central Time | | |
| CT | Centre Tap | CTA | Customer Technical Assistance |
| CT | Change Tracker | | |
| CT | Character Translator | CTAP | Circuit Transient Analysis Program |
| CT | Check Tape | | |
| CT | Checkout Tape | CTB | Communication Terminal Block |
| CT | Chronometer Time | | |
| CT | Cipher Telegram | CTB | Computer Time Brokers |
| CT | Circuit | CTB | Concentrator Terminal Buffer |
| CT | Circuit Theory | | |
| CT | Clock Time | CTC | Cam Timing Contact |
| CT | Clock Track | CTC | Cards-to-Tape Converter |
| CT | Code Table | CTC | Cassette/Tape Controller |
| CT | Code Telegram | CTC | Central Train Control |
| CT | Code Transcription | CTC | Centralized Traffic Control |
| CT | Code Transformation | | |
| CT | Code Translator | CTC | Channel Traffic Control |
| CT | Coded Tape | CTC | Channel-To-Channel |
| CT | Codetabelle | CTC | Cobol-To-Cobol |
| CT | Command Tape | CTC | Communications, Telemetry and Command |
| CT | Command Transmitter | | |
| CT | Commercial Translator | CTC | Complementary Two's Complement |
| CT | Compile Time | | |
| CT | Computer Tape | CTC | Computer Technology Center |
| CT | Computer Technology | | |
| CT | Computer Terminal | CTC | Computer Test Console |
| CT | Computer Test | CTC | Computer Test Corporation |
| CT | Computer Thermographer | CTC | Computer Transmission Corporation |
| CT | Computerized Tomographic | | |
| | | CTC | Contact |
| CT | Computing Time | CTC | Continuity Test Current |
| CT | Concentrateur de Terminaux | CTC | Counter Timer Circuit |
| | | CTC | Counter Timer Control |
| CT | Conditional Transfer | CTCA | Channel and Traffic Control Agency |
| CT | Conductivity Transmitter | | |
| CT | Conduit | CTCA | Channel-To-Channel Adapter |
| CT | Console Typewriter | | |
| CT | Control Tape | CTCC | Central Terminal Computer Controller |
| CT | Control Total | | |
| CT | Control Transformer | CTCDE | Commission Type Code |
| CT | Control Transmitter | CTCL | Count Clock |
| CT | Controller Type | CTCS | Chanel to Chanel Software |
| CT | Correct Time | | |
| CT | Count | CTCS | Consolidated Telemetry Checkout System |
| CT | Counter | | |
| CT | Counter/Timer | CTCU | Channel and Traffic Control Unit |
| CT | Current | | |

# C

| | | | |
|---|---|---|---|
| CTD | Camp on Tone Denied | CTL | Constructive Total Loss |
| CTD | Certified Test Data | CTL | Control |
| CTD | Charge Transfer Device | CTL | Control Line |
| CTD | Compile Time Diagnostic | CTL | Core Transistor Logic |
| CTDC | Chemical Thermodynamic Data Center | CTL | Core Transmission Logic |
| | | CTL PL | Control Panel |
| CTDC | Control Track Direction Computer | CTLBLKS | Control Blocks |
| | | CTLCD | Control Card |
| CTDL | Complementary Transistor Diode Logic | CTLCHAR | Control Character |
| | | CTLD | Controlled |
| CTDS | Code Translation Data System | CTLU | Control Unit |
| | | CTM | Communication Terminal Matrix |
| CTE | Cable Termination Equipment | CTM | Communications Terminal Module |
| CTE | Central Timing Equipment | | |
| CTE | Channel Translating Equipment | CTM... | Computertechnik Müller GmbH |
| CTE | Coefficient to Thermal Expansion | CTMC | Communications Terminal Module Controller |
| CTE | Compile Time Expression | CTMFU | Corporate Transfer Manufacturing File Update |
| CTE | Computer Telex Exchange | | |
| CTE | Counter Total Exit | CTN | Cable Termination Network |
| CTES | Computer Telex Exchange System | | |
| | | CTN | Clock Track Number |
| CTF | Closed Transaction File | CTNDS | Commercial Transport Navigation Display System |
| CTF | Common Test Facility | | |
| CTF | Continuous Tape Feed | | |
| CTF | Core Test Facility | CTNE | Compania Telefonica Nationale de Espana |
| CTFM | Continuous Transmission Frequency Modulated | | |
| | | CTP | Central Transfer Point |
| CTG | Cartridge | CTP | Charge Transforming Parameter |
| CTG | Counting | | |
| CTI | Centre de Traitement Informatique | CTP | Control Type |
| | | CTP | Cooperation Transaction Processing |
| CTI | Centre de Traitement de l'Information | | |
| | | CTR | Certified Test Record |
| CTI | Centro Tecnologico para Informatica | CTR | Complementary Transistor Register |
| CTI | Charge Transfer Inefficiency | CTR | Controlled Thermonuclear Reaction |
| CTI | Coax-Transceiver-Interface | CTR | Counter |
| | | CTR | Current Transfer Ratio |
| CTI | Conditional Transfer Instruction | CTRL | Complementary Transistor/Resistor Logic |
| CTI... | Cartridge Television Inc. | CTRL | Control |
| CTIN | Continue | CTS | Carriage Tape Simulator |
| CTINUS | Continuous | CTS | Carrier Test Switch |
| CTL | Cage Test Language | CTS | Central Timing System |
| CTL | Checkout Test Language | CTS | Centralized Title Services |
| CTL | Common Target Language | CTS | Charge Transfer Spectrum |
| CTL | Compiler Target Language | CTS | Clear To Send |
| CTL | Complementary Transistor Logic | CTS | Command and Telemetry System |
| CTL | Computer Technology Limited | CTS | Communication Terminal Synchronous |

# C

| | | | |
|---|---|---|---|
| CTS | Communication and Tracking Subsystem | CU | Crosstalk Unit |
| CTS | Communications Technology Satellite | CU | Crystal Unit |
| | | CU | Customer Use |
| | | CU-OFF | Control Unit offline |
| CTS | Compile Time Statement | CUA | Channel Unit Address |
| CTS | Component Test Set | CUA | Computer Users Association |
| CTS | Component Test System | | |
| CTS | Computer Test Stand | CUA | Computerunterstützte Ausbildung |
| CTS | Computized Type Setting | | |
| CTS | Conversational Terminal System | CUA | Control Unit Address |
| | | CUB | Central Unit Buffer |
| CTS | Conversational Time Sharing | CUB | Control Unit Busy |
| | | CUB | Cursor Backward |
| CTS | Corporate Terminal System | CUBE | Cooperative Users of Burroughs Equipment |
| CTSEL | Conversational Terminal System European Laboratories | CUC | Circuit Virtuel Commuté |
| | | CUC | Computer Users Committee |
| CTSS | Compatible Time-Sharing System | CUC | Computer Usage Company |
| | | CUCB | Control Unit Control Block |
| CTSS | Classroom Test Support System | CUCC | Computers in the Undergraduate Curriculum Conference |
| CTT | Central Trunk Terminals | | |
| CTT | Card-To-Tape | | |
| CTT | Carriage Tension Tape | CUCN | Communication Controller Nodes |
| CTT | Character Translate Table | | |
| CTT | Communication Terminal Table | CUCPAT | Computer Usage Company Programming Aptitude Test |
| CTT | Computerized Transverse Tomography | | |
| | | CUD | Control Unit Description |
| CTTAP | Card-to-Tape Program | CUD | Cursor Down |
| CTU | Centigrade Thermal Unit | CUDC | Computer Usage Development Corporation |
| CTU | Central Terminal Unit | | |
| CTU | Central Timing Unit | CUDN | Common User Data Network |
| CTU | Components Test Unit | | |
| CTUN | Commercial Telegrapher Union | CUDOS | Continuously Updated Dynamic Optimizing System |
| CTV | Closed-circuit Television | | |
| CTV | Colour Television | CUE | Computer Updating Equipment |
| CTV | Compile Time Variable | | |
| CTV | Computerisierte Textverarbeitung | CUE | Computer Utilization Efficiency |
| CTV | Computerunterstütze Textverarbeitung | CUE | Computer Utilizing English |
| | | CUE | Configuration Utilization Evaluator |
| CTVN | Call To Vacant Number | | |
| CTW | Console Typewriter | | |
| CTW | Control Typewriter | CUE | Control Unit End |
| CTX | Computer Telex Exchange | CUE | Cooperating Users Exchange |
| CU | Card Unit | | |
| CU | Central Unit | CUEING | Control Unit Error Insertion Generator |
| CU | Check Unit | | |
| CU | Clock Unit | CUEPEND | Control Unit End Pending |
| CU | Computer | CUES | Computer Utilities for Education Systems |
| CU | Computing Unit | | |
| CU | Control Unit | CUF | Cursor Forward |

- 152 -

# C

| | | | |
|---|---|---|---|
| CUG | Closed User Group | CUTE | COBOL Update and Test Environment |
| CUI | Control Unit Interface | | |
| CUJT | Complementary Unijunction Transistor | CUTS | Computer User Tape System |
| CULDATA | Comprehensive Unified Land Data | CUTS | Computer Utilized Turning System |
| CULP | Computer Usage List Processor | CUU | Channel-Unit-Unit |
| | | CUU | Computerunterstützter Unterricht |
| CULT | Chinese University Language Translator | CUU | Cursor Up |
| CUM | Computer Utilization Monitor | CUUL | Computerunterstützter Unterricht der Lufthansa |
| CUM LAUDE | Computerized Understanding of Morphology-Language Acquisition Under Development in Education | CUV | Computerunterstützte Verwaltung |
| | | CV | Caloritic Value |
| | | CV | Capacitance-Voltage |
| | | CV | Carte Vierge |
| CUMARC | Cumulated Machine-Readable Cataloguing | CV | Character Variable |
| | | CV | Common Version |
| CUN | Conditionally Unrestricted service | CV | Computer Variable |
| | | CV | Conditional Variable |
| CUODIC | Combinational, Unilateral, One-Dimensional, Iterative Circuits | CV | Constant Value |
| | | CV | Constant Voltage |
| | | CV | Constant Volume |
| CUP | Communication User Program | CV | Continuously Variable |
| | | CV | Control Volume |
| CUP | Computer Umwelt-Projekt | CV | Conversion |
| CUPID | Create, Update, Interrogate, and Display | CV | Converter |
| | | CV | Counter Voltage |
| CUPL | Cornell University Programming Language | CV | Create Volumes |
| | | CV-CC | Constant Voltage - Constant Current |
| CUPSEP | Computerunterstützte Planung und Steuerung der EDV-Produktion | CV/CL | Constant Voltage/ Current Limiting |
| | | CVAP | Cloud Velocity Analysis Program |
| CUR | Complex Utility Routine | | |
| CUR | Current | CVB | Communication Verb Block |
| CURAM | Current Amount | | |
| CURES | Computer Utilization Reporting System | CVB | Convert Binary |
| | | CVC | Circuit Virtuel Commuté |
| CURSR | Cursor | CVC | Current-Voltage Converter |
| CURT | Current | | |
| CURTS | Common User Radio Transmission System | CVC | Current Voltage Characteristic |
| | | CVD | Chemical Vapor Deposit |
| CUSA | Customer Address | CVD | Convert Decimal |
| CUSC | Channel Unit Signal Controller | CVD | Current-Voltage Diagram |
| | | CVIS | Computerized Vocational Information System |
| CUSCL | Customer Class | | |
| CUSNM | Customer Name | | |
| CUSNR | Customer Number | CVL | Continuous Velocity Log |
| CUSP | Customer-Programmierung | CVP | Circuit Virtuel Permanent |
| CUSPO | Customer Purchase Order | CVP | Codevergleich - Positiv |
| CUST | Customer | CVPDS | Command Video Prelaunch Distribution System |
| CUT | Circuit Under Test | | |
| CUT | Computer Under Test | | |
| | | CVR | Cine Video Recording |

# C

| | | | |
|---|---|---|---|
| CVR | Compact Vorrechner | CWAR | Continuous Wave Acquisition Radar |
| CVR | Constant Voltage Reference | CWBZ | Call Waiting-Buzz |
| CVR | Continuous Video Recorder | CWC | Command Word Chaining |
| | | CWD | Call Waiting Denied |
| CVR | Contrôle Vertical de Redondance | CWD | Computererwartungsdienst GmbH |
| CVR | Controlled Visual Rules | CWDBS | Colorado Water Data Bank System |
| CVR | Current-Voltage Regulator | CWF | Composite Wave Filter |
| CVS | Club de Vulgarisation Scientifique | CWF | Control Word Format |
| | | CWFF | Closed, Well-Formed Formula |
| CVS | Computer controlled Vehicle System | CWI | Clear Word Identifier |
| CVS | Computergesteuertes Verkehrssystem | CWIC | Compiler for Writing and Implementing Compilers |
| CVS | Constant Volume Sampler | CWIF | Continuous Wave Intermediate Frequency |
| CVS | Constant Volume Sampling | | |
| CVSG | Channel Verification Signal Generator | CWL | Constant Word Length |
| | | CWMOD | Control Word Modification |
| CVSN | Conversion | CWO | Carrier Wave Oscillator |
| CVT | Communication Vector Table | CWO | Continuous Wave Oscillator |
| CVT | Conditional Variable Test | CWP | Communicating Word Processors |
| CVT | Constant Voltage Transformer | CWP | Computer Word Processing |
| CVU | Constant Voltage Unit | CWPI | Configuration Word Package Item |
| CW | Call Word | | |
| CW | Calls Waiting | CWS | Caution and Warning System |
| CW | Carrier Wave | | |
| CW | Channel Word | CWS | Centre Wireless Station |
| CW | Clear and Write | CWS | Clockwise |
| CW | Clockwise | CWS | Command Word Sequence |
| CW | Code Word | CWSP | College Work-Study Program |
| CW | Codewandler | | |
| CW | Codewort | CWT | Call Waiting |
| CW | Command Word | CWT | Carrier-Wave Telegraphic |
| CW | Composite Wave | CWT | Carrier-Wave Transmission |
| CW | Computer Word | CWT | Command Word Trap |
| CW | Computerwoche | CWT | Computer World Trade |
| CW | Computerworld | CWTM | Call Waiting Time |
| CW | Continuous Wave | CWV | Continuous Wave Video |
| CW | Control Word | CX | Central Exchange |
| CW | Course Write | CX | Complex |
| CW SIG GEN | Continuous Wave Signal Generator | CX | Control Transmitter |
| | | CX | Convex |
| CW/FM | Continuous Wave Frequency Modulated | CX | Current Transformer |
| | | CXB | Communication Extension Block |
| CWA | Call Waiting Allowed | | |
| CWA | Common Work Area | CXP | Centre d'Expérimentation des Progiciels |
| CWA | Communications Workers of America | | |
| | | CY | Case copy |
| | | CY | Cybernetics |
| CWA | Contractor Work Authorization | CY | Cycle |

# C

| | | | |
|---|---|---|---|
| CYBORG | Cybermetic Organism | CZ | Computerzeitung |
| CYDAC | Cytophotometric Data Conversion | CZAM | Computer Zero Access Memory |
| CYDAC | Cytophotometric Data Converter | CZAS | Computer Zero Access Store |
| CYL | Cylinder | CZRT | Count Zero Refill Trigger |
| CZ | Call on Zero | CZT | Chip Z-Transform |
| CZ | Communications Zone | | |

# D

| | | | |
|---|---|---|---|
| D | Dämpfung | D/A | Decoder Abtastschaltung |
| D | Data | D/A | Digital/Analog |
| D | Data Mode | D/M | Demodulate-Modulate |
| D | Daten | D/M | Demodulator-Modulator |
| D | Datenfernsprecher | D/R | Direct or Reserve |
| D | Datentechnik | DA | Data Acceptance |
| D | Deci- | DA | Data Access |
| D | Decision | DA | Data Acquisition |
| D | Deka | DA | Data Address |
| D | Delay | DA | Data Administrator |
| D | Demodulator | DA | Data Analysis |
| D | Density | DA | Data Array |
| D | Design | DA | Data Automation |
| D | Deskripter | DA | Data Available |
| D | Destination | DA | Datenanalysator |
| D | Deterministic | DA | Datenaufbereitung |
| D | Deuterium | DA | Datenausgabe |
| D | Deviation | DA | Datenausgang |
| D | Dezimalpotenz | DA | Decimal Add |
| D | Diameter | DA | Decimal Adder |
| D | Dielectric | DA | Decimal Addition |
| D | Difference | DA | Decimal-to-Analog |
| D | Differential | DA | Decoded Address |
| D | Digit | DA | Deka- |
| D | Digital | DA | Demand Assignment |
| D | Diode | DA | Deposit Account |
| D | Direct | DA | Design Automation |
| D | Display | DA | Detector Amplifier |
| D | Disponiert | DA | Device Adapter |
| D | Dissipation | DA | Device Address |
| D | Distance | DA | Dicrete Address |
| D | Distortion | DA | Difference Amplifier |
| D | Divide | DA | Differential Address |
| D | Document | DA | Differential Amplifier |
| D | Doubled | DA | Differential Analyzer |
| D | Drain | DA | Differentialanalysator |
| D | Drawing | DA | Digit Absorption |
| D | Drive | DA | Digital-to-Analog |
| D | Driving | DA | Digitalausgabe |
| D | Drucker | DA | Dimensionsaufgabe |
| D | Drum | DA | Direct Access |
| D | Duty | DA | Direct Address |
| D-AE | Datenanschlußeinheit | DA | Discrete Address |
| D-An | Datenanschlußsatz | DA | Disk Access |
| D-F | Direct Flow | DA | Disk Address |
| D-GDG | Distributor-to-Group Display Generator | DA | Distribution Amplifier |
| | | DA | Documentation Aids |
| D-GDGE | Distributor-to-Group Display Generator Electronics | DA | Double Amplitude |
| | | DA | Double Armoured |
| | | DA | Drop Address |
| D-MESFET | Depletion-mode Metal Semiconductor FET | DA | Drum Address |
| | | DA | Dummy Address |
| D-O | Decimal-to-Octal | DA | Dummy Antenna |
| D-TSFF | Delay Transition Sensitive Flip Flop | DA | Dummy Argument |
| | | DAA | Data Access Arrangement |

# D

| | | | |
|---|---|---|---|
| DAA | Data Automation Activity | DAC | Digital Associates Corporation |
| DAA | Decimal Adjust Accumulator | DAC | Digital to Analog Circuit |
| DAA | Direct Access Arrangement | DAC | Digital to Analog Converter |
| DAA | Dual Address Adapter | DAC | Digital-Analogic Converter |
| DAAC | Data Acquisition and Analysis Complex | DAC | Digital-to-Analog Control |
| DAAC | Digital Adaptive Area Correlation | DAC | Digital-to-Analog Conversion |
| DAAD | Digital-Analog-Analog-Digital | DAC | Direct Access |
| DAAG | Diode AND-AND Gate | DAC | Direct Access Computing |
| DAAO | Dessin Animé Assisté par Ordinateur | DAC | Disk Access Control |
| DAB | Demand Adjustment Bucket | DAC | Disk Attachment Control |
| DAB | Display Assignment Bit | DAC | Display Analysis Console |
| DAB | Display Attention Bit | DAC | Duplicate Aperture Card |
| DAB | Distributeur Automatique de Billets | DAC-Q | Direct Access Queued |
| DAB | Divisional Administration Bulletin | DACA | Digital-to-Analog Control Apparatus |
| DAB | Dual Access Buffer | DACAC | Digital-to-Analog Converter, Alternating Current |
| DABA | Datenbank | | |
| DABA | Datenbasisauswertungssystem | DACAP | Discrete and Continuous Analysis Program |
| DABAL | Data Bank Language | DACAPS | Data Collection And Processing System |
| DABAS | Data Base System | | |
| DABES | Datenbestand | DACB | Device Address Control Block |
| DABS | Discrete Address Beacon System | DACB | Direct Algorithm Control Block |
| DABS | Discretely Addressed Beacon System | DACC | Data Acquisition and Checkout Computer |
| DAC | Data Accepted | DACC | Data And Computation Center |
| DAC | Data Acquisition Camera | | |
| DAC | Data Acquisition Card | DACC | Direct Access Communications Channel |
| DAC | Data Acquisition Chassis | | |
| DAC | Data Acquisition Computer | DACC | Display And Control Card |
| DAC | Data Acquisition Controller | DACDC | Digital-to-Analog Converter, Direct Current |
| DAC | Data Acquisition and Control | DACDIC | Digital-to-Analog Converter, Direct Current |
| DAC | Data Analysis Center | | |
| DAC | Data Analysis Console | DACE | Data Acquisition and Control Executive |
| DAC | Data Analysis Control | | |
| DAC | Data Analysis and Control | DACI | Direct Adjacent Channel Interference |
| DAC | Data-processing Center | | |
| DAC | Decimal Arithmetic Carry | DACM | Direct Addressable Core Memory |
| DAC | Decrement Accumulator | DACO | Data Consistency Orbit |
| DAC | Design Augmented by Computer | DACOM | Data and Configuration Management |
| DAC | Digital Arithmetic Center | | |

# D

| | | | |
|---|---|---|---|
| DACOM | Datascope Computer Output Microfilmer | DADC | Digital-Analog Data Conversion |
| DACOM | Double Average Comparison | DADC | Direct Access Data Channel |
| DACON | Data Controller | DADE | Data Acquisition and Decommutation Equipment |
| DACON | Digital-to-Analog Converter | | |
| DACOR | Data Correction | DADE | Digital Application and Documentation Equipment |
| DACOR | Data Correlation | | |
| DACOR | Data Correlator | | |
| DACPO | Data Count Printout | DADEC | Design And Demonstration Electronic Computer |
| DACQ | Data Acquisition | | |
| DACS | Data Access and Control System | DADEE | Dynamic Analog Differential Equation Equalizer |
| DACS | Data Acquisition Control System | | |
| | | DADIC | Data Dictionary |
| DACS | Data Acquisition and Computer System | DADIOS | Direct Analog/Discrete Input/Output System |
| DACS | Data Acquisition and Control System | DADIT | Daystrom Analog-to-Digital Integrating Translator |
| DACS | Data Acquisition and Correction System | | |
| | | DADR | Digital Angle Data Recorder |
| DACS | Dataset Control System | | |
| DACS | Design Aided by Computer System | DADS | Data Acquisition and Display System |
| DACS | Discrete Address Communications System | DADS | Digital Air Data-computer System |
| DACT | Direction des Affaires Commerciales et de la Télématique | DADS | Direct Access Data Set |
| | | DADS | Dosimetry Acquisition and Display System |
| DACU | Data Acquisition and Control Unit | DADS | Dynamic Allocation/Deallocation Subsystem |
| DACU | Data Acquisition Control Unit | DADSM | Direct Access Device Space Management |
| DACU | Device Attachment Control Unit | DAE | Datenanschlußeinheit |
| | | DAE | Data Acquisition Equipment |
| DAD | Data Acquisition Device | | |
| DAD | Data Automation Digest | DAEMON | Data Adaptive Evaluator and Monitor |
| DAD | Decimal Accumulating Device | | |
| | | DAER | Datenerfassung |
| DAD | Design Automation Division | DAF | Data Acquisition Facility |
| | | DAF | Data Analysis Facility |
| DAD | Device Address | DAF | Delay Amplification Factor |
| DAD | Digital Angle Data | | |
| DAD | Digital Arithmetic Centre | DAF | Delay Auditory Feedback |
| | | DAF | Destination Address Field |
| DAD | Digital Ausgabeblock, Dynamisch | | |
| | | DAF | Device Address Field |
| DAD | Digitalausgabe, Dynamisch | DAF | Direct Access File |
| | | DAFA | Data Accounting Flow Assessment |
| DAD | Direct Access Device | | |
| DAD | Doppler Analyzer Display | DAFC | Digital Automatic Frequency Control |
| DAD | Drums And Display | | |
| DADC | Digital Air Data Computer | DAFL | Digital Automatic Frequency Lock |

- 159 -

# D

| | | | |
|---|---|---|---|
| DAFM | Discard-At-Failure Maintenance | DAL | Document Address Lister |
| DAFT | Digital/Analog Function Table | DALC | Divided Access Line Circuit |
| DAFT | Digital-to-Analog Function Table | DALC | Dynamic Asynchronous Logic Circuit |
| DAFÜ | Datenfernübertragung | DALE | Digital Anemograph Logging Equipment |
| DAG | Datenanschaltgerät | DALS | Digital Approach and Landing System |
| DAG | Datenanschlußgerät | | |
| DAG | Diode AND Gate | DALS | Diver Auditory Localization System |
| DAGC | Delayed Automatic Gain Control | DALTS | Data Link Test Set |
| DAIR | Dial Access Information Retrieval | DAM | Data Addressed Memory |
| | | DAM | Data Association Message |
| DAIR | Direct Attitude and Identity Readout | DAM | Dateiauswertungen menügesteuert |
| DAIR | Driver Air, Information and Routing | DAM | Descriptor Attribute Matrix |
| DAIR | Dynamic Allocation Interface Routine | DAM | Digital Automatic Machine |
| DAIRE | Direct Altitude and Identification Readout Equipment | DAM | Digital-to-Analog Multiplier |
| | | DAM | Digitized Analog Magnetogram |
| DAIRS | Dial Access Information Retrieval System | DAM | Direct Access Memory |
| | | DAM | Direct Access Method |
| DAIS | Defense Automatic Integrated Switching system | DAM | Direct Addressable Memory |
| DAIS | Digital Avionics Information System | DAM | Dummy Average Memory |
| | | DAM | Duplex Adding Machine |
| DAISY | Data Acquisition and Interpretation System | DAMA | Demand-Assigned, Multiple-Access |
| DAISY | Data Analysis of the Interpreter System | DAMC | Digital Automatic Map Compilation |
| DAISY | Double precision Automatic Interpretive System | DAME | Data Acquisition and Monitoring Equipment |
| | | DAME | Digital Automatic Measuring Equipment |
| DAISY | Druckindustrie Abrechnungs- und Informationssystem | DAMIT | Data ACP by Massachusetts Institute of Technology |
| DAIU | Digital-to-Analog Interface Unit | DAMM | Datenschutz, Mittel und Maßnahmen |
| DAK | Dateienkatalog | | |
| DAK | Datenausgabekanal | DAMM | Direct Access Memory Management |
| DAK | Datenaustauschelement für kombinierten Betrieb | DAMOC | Director Autopilot Mode Organization Computer |
| DAKA | Datenkartei | | |
| DAKS | Dateikatalogsystem | DAMOD | Direct Access Module |
| DAL | Data Acquisition Language | DAMOS | Data Moving System |
| DAL | Data-Aided Loop | DAMPR | Digital Automatic Multiple Pressure Recorder |
| DAL | Datenanschlußleitung | | |
| DAL | Design Analysis Language | | |
| DAL | Digital Access Line | DAMPS | Data Acquisition Multiprogramming System |
| DAL | Divisional Administration List | | |

- 160 -

# D

| | | | |
|---|---|---|---|
| DAMPS | Data Acquisition Multi-processing System | DAPS | Direct Access Performance Software |
| DAN | Datenübertragungsanschluß | DAPS | Direct Access Programming System |
| DAN | Define Area Name | DAQ | Define Area Qualification |
| DAN | Deposit Account Number | DAR | Damage Assessment Routine |
| DAN | Document Accession Number | DAR | Datenausgaberegister |
| DANAC | Data Analysis And Classification | DAR | Defense Acquisition Radar |
| DANAC | Decca Area Navigation Computer | DAR | Device Address Ready |
| DANAS | Deposit Account Name and Address System | DAR | Differential Absorption Ratio |
| DANDR | Diagnostic and Repair | DAR | Dynamic Address Relocation |
| DANZKO | Datennetzkoordinator | DARE | Document Abstract Retrieval Equipment |
| DAO | Dessin Assisté par Ordinateur | DARE | Document Automated Reduction Equipment |
| DAO | Documentation Assistée par Ordinateur | DARE | Doppler Automatic Reduction Equipment |
| DAOB | Digital and Analog Output Basic | DARES | Data Analysis and Reduction System |
| DAOR | Discriminator Average Output Rate | DARLI | Digital Angular Readout Laser Interferometry |
| DAP | Data Access Protocol | DARPA | Defence Advanced Research Projects Agency |
| DAP | Data Acquisition Package | | |
| DAP | Data Acquisition Program | DARS | Digital Adaptible Recording System |
| DAP | Data Acquisition and Processing | DARS | Digital Attitude and Rate System |
| DAP | Data Automation Panel | | |
| DAP | Data Automation Proposal | DART | Data Analysis Recording Tape |
| DAP | Datenerfassungsplatz | | |
| DAP | Deformation Aufgerichteter Phasen | DART | Data Reduction Translator |
| DAP | Deformation of Aligned Phases | DART | Development Advanced Rate Techniques |
| DAP | Derived Attainable Performance | DART | Digital Automatic Rescheduling Technique |
| DAP | Diagnostic Assistance Program | DART | Diode Automatic Reliability Tester |
| DAP | Dial A Program | DART | Director And Response Tester |
| DAP | Diffused Alloy Power | | |
| DAP | Digital Assembly Program | DART | Dual Axis Rate Transducer |
| DAP | Digital Autopilot | DART | Dynamic Acoustic Response Trigger |
| DAP | Display-Arbeitsplatz | | |
| DAP | Direct Access Photomemory | DARTS | Design Aid for Real-Time Systems |
| DAP | Distributed Array Processor | DAS | Data Acquisition System |
| | | DAS | Data Automation System |
| DAP | Double Amplitude Peak value | DAS | Datatron Assembly System |
| DAPR | Digital Automatic Pattern Recognition | DAS | Datenausgabesteuerung |
| | | DAS | Datenstation |

# D

| | | | |
|---|---|---|---|
| DAS | Design Automation System | DASH | Dual Access Storage Handling |
| DAS | Device Analysis System | | |
| DAS | Digital Attenuator System | DASH | Dynamic ALGOL String Handling |
| DAS | Digital Attitude Simulation | DASI | Datensicherungsgerät |
| DAS | Digital-Analog Simulator | DASI | Datensiebprogramm |
| DAS | Digital-to-Analog Simulator | DASI | Dialog-Abrechnungssystem für Industriemakler |
| DAS | Digital-to-Analog Simulation | DASP | Director of Advanced Systems Planning |
| DAS | Digital/Analog System | DASPAN | Data-Spanning |
| DAS | Digitalausgabe, Statisch | DASR | Data Acquisition Statistical Recorder |
| DAS | Direct Access Store | | |
| DAS | Direct Access System | DASR | Design Audit Status Report |
| DAS | Directly Addressable Storage | DASS | Data Access Security System |
| DAS | Directory Assistance System | DASS | Datensammelsystem |
| DAS | Direkt-Abfrage-Sprache | DASS | Demand Assignment Signalling and Switching |
| DAS | Direktes Abfragesystem | | |
| DAS | Diskontinuierliches Analoges Signal | DASSA | Direct Access Storage Space Allocation |
| DAS | Document Aids System | DASSU | Demand-Assigned Signalling and Switching Unit |
| DAS | Documentation Aid System | DAST | Datenaustauschsteuerung |
| DAS | Durchschalteablauf- steuerung | DAST | Datenauswahlsteuerung |
| | | DAST | Datenstation |
| DAS/COTAR | Data Acquisition System/ Correlation Tracking And Ranging | DASTAR | Data Storage And Retrieval |
| | | DASY | Data Analysis System |
| DASCH | Datenschutz | DASY | Design Automation System |
| DASD | Data Acquisition Support Document | DASYS | Data System environment simulator |
| DASD | Direct Access Storage Device | DAT | Data Abstract Tape |
| DASDDR | Direct Access Storage Device Dump Restore | DAT | Data Acquisition Test |
| | | DAT | Disk Allocation Table |
| DASDI | Direct Access Storage Device Initialization program | DAT | Drum Access Time |
| | | DAT | Dynamic Address Translation |
| DASDI | Direct Access Store Device Initialization | DAT | Dynamic Address Translator |
| DASDI | Direct Access Store Disk Initialization | DATA | Datamation |
| | | DATA | Derivation And Tabulation Associates, Inc. |
| DASDL | Data And Structure Definition Language | DATA | Direct Access Terminal Application |
| DASDM | Direct Access Storage Data Management | DATA-STOR | Data Storage |
| DASDS | Direct Access Storage Devices | DATAC | Data Analog Computer |
| | | DATAC | Digital Automatic Tester And Classifier |
| DASF | Direct Access Storage Facility | DATACOL | Data Collection |
| DASH | Data Acquisition Sequential Histogram | DATACOM | Data Communications |
| | | DATACOR | Data Correction |

- 162 -

# D

| | |
|---|---|
| DATACOR | Data Correlator |
| DATAEND | Dezentrales Datenendverarbeitungssystem |
| DATAGEN | Data file Generator |
| DATAM | Data Attribute Modification |
| DATAMATION | Data Automation |
| DATAN | Data Analysis |
| DATAR | Digital Autotransducer And Recorder |
| DATAS | Data in Associative Storage |
| DATATELEX | Data processing Telecommunications Exchange |
| DATATERM | Data Terminal |
| DATCO | Data coordinating Committee |
| DATCOL | Data Collection |
| DATCOM | Data Compendium |
| DATDC | Data Analysis and Technique Development Center |
| DATE | Data Exchange |
| DATE | Data for Allotments Transmitted Electronically |
| DATEC | Differential and Alignment unit and Total Error Corrector |
| DATEC | Digital Adaptive Technique for Communications |
| DATEL | Data Telecommunications |
| DATEPLAN | Data Tabulation and Editing Programming Language |
| DATEX | Data Exchange |
| DATEX-L | Leitungsvermitteltes Datexnetz |
| DATEX-P | Data Exchange - Packet switching |
| DATEX-P | Paketvermitteltes Datexnetz |
| DATI | Drill Artwork Test Information |
| DATICO | Digital Automatic Tape Intelligence Checkout |
| DATIME | Date and Time |
| DATIN | Data Inserter |
| DATOM | Data Aids for Training, Operation and Maintenance |
| DATOR | Digital Auxiliary Track Output Radar |
| DATORG | Datenorganisation |
| DATRAN | Data Transmission |
| DATRAN... | Data Transmission Corporation |
| DATS | Data Accumulation and Transfer Sheet |
| DATS | Data Transmission System |
| DATS | Digital Avionics Transmission System |
| DATS | Dynamic Accuracy Test Set |
| DATTS | Data Acquisition Telecommand and Tracking Station |
| DAU | Data Acquisition Unit |
| DAU | Data Adapter Unit |
| DAU | Digital-Analog-Umsetzung |
| DAU | Digital-Analog-Umwandler |
| DAU | Digital-Analog-Umwandlung |
| DAU | Digital/Analog-Umsetzer |
| DAU | Display Adapter Unit |
| DAU | Dynamische Adreßumsetzung |
| DAV | Data Above Voice |
| DAV | Data Available |
| DAV | Data Valid |
| DAV | Delayed Automatic Volume |
| DAV | Direct Access Volume |
| DAVC | Delayed Automatic Volume Control |
| DAVFOS | Direkt Adressierbare Vertikale Formularsteuerungen |
| DAVFU | Direct Access Vertical Format Unit |
| DAVFU | Directly Addressable Vertical Format Unit |
| DAVI | Dynamic Antiresonant Vibration Isolator |
| DAVID | Daten-Verteil- und Informations-Dienst |
| DAVID | Dialogsystem zur Arzneimittel-Verordnungs-Information und Dokumentation |
| DAVIE | Digital Alphanumeric Video Insertion Equipment |
| DAVO | Dynamic Vocal |
| DAVOS | Datei-Verwaltungs- und Organisationssystem |
| DAVS | Datenverbindungssatz |
| DAW | Digital-Analog-Wandler |
| DAW | Digital-Analog-Wandlung |
| DAW | Disk Address Word |
| DAWID | Device for Automatic Word Identification and Discrimination |

# D

| | | | |
|---|---|---|---|
| DAWN | Digital Automatic Weather Network | DBBOR | Digital Building Block Oriented |
| DAWO | Datenspeicher für Wirtschaftsleitende Organe | DBBS | Datenbankbetriebssystem |
| | | DBC | Data Bank Coordinator |
| DAY | Dayton | DBC | Data Base Computer |
| DAZD | Double Anode Zenerdiode | DBC | Data Bibliography Card |
| DB | Data Bank | DBC | Data Bit Converter |
| DB | Data Base | DBC | Decimal-to-Binary Conversion |
| DB | Data Bit | | |
| DB | Data Block | DBC | Decomposed Block Code |
| DB | Data Booth | DBC | Digital Business Center |
| DB | Data Bus | DBC | Digital-Binary Converter |
| DB | Data Byte | DBCB | Data Base Control Block |
| DB | Database | DBCO | Digital Block Clock Oscillator |
| DB | Datenbank | | |
| DB | Datenbereitstellung | DBCP | Data Bank Control Project |
| DB | Datenbestand | DBCP | Data Bank Coordinator Procedure |
| DB | Datenbus | | |
| DB | Dead Band | DBCS | Database Control System |
| DB | Debit | DBD | Data Base Description |
| DB | Decimal Base | DBD | Double Base Diode |
| DB | Decimal-to-Binary | DBD | Data Base Definition |
| DB | Décodeur Binaire | DBD | Data Base Descriptor |
| DB | Detection Bit | DBD | Data Base Directory |
| DB | Device Busy | DBD | Distribution Board |
| DB | Diffused Base | DBDA | Data Base Design Aid |
| DB | Digital Block | DBDGEN | Data Base Description Generation |
| DB | Dimensioniertes Berechnen | | |
| DB | Direktionsbereich | DBDL | Data Base Definition Language |
| DB | Display Buffer | | |
| DB | Distributor Board | DBF | Data Base Facility |
| DB | Double Bayonet Base | DBF | Demodulator Band Filter |
| DB | Double Biased | DBF | Digital Beam Former |
| DB | Double Bottom | DBFF | Digital Block Flip-Flop |
| DB | Double Break | DBFU | Digital Beam Former Unit |
| DB | Dry Bulb | DBG | Datenbankgenerator |
| DB | Durchschnittsbestand | DBG | Debug |
| DB/DC | Data Base/Data Communications | DBH | Database-Handler |
| | | DBI | Data Based Interactive |
| DB/DC | Data Bank/Data Communication | DBI | Double Byte Interleaved |
| | | DBIA | Digital Block Inverting Amplifier |
| DBA | Data Base Administrator | | |
| DBA | Data Block Address | DBIL | Data Base Input Language |
| DBA | Datenbank Administrator | DBIS | Data Based Interactive System |
| DBA | Datenbus A | | |
| DBA | Diffused Base Alloy | DBK | Data Bank |
| DBAM | Data Base Access Method | DBL | Data Base Language |
| DBAO | Digital Block AND-OR gate | DBL | Data Base Load |
| | | DBL | Data Block Length |
| DBAWG | Database Administration Working Group | DBL | Data Bus Line |
| | | DBL | Doubler |
| DBB | Datenbus B | DBLPCH | Double Punch |
| DBB | Detector Back Bias | DBLTG | Database Language Task Group |
| DBB | Detector Balanced Bias | | |
| DBBL | Decimal Base Binary Logic | DBM | Data Base Manager |

# D

| | | | |
|---|---|---|---|
| DBM | Data Buffer Memory | DBRT | Direct Beam Refresh Tube |
| DBM | Data Buffer Mode | DBS | Data Base Software |
| DBM | Data Buffer Module | DBS | Data Base System |
| DBM | Data Bus Monitor | DBS | Datenbank-Software |
| DBM | Database Machine | DBS | Datenbankbetriebssystem |
| DBM | Decibel referred to one Milliwatt | DBS | Datenbanksystem |
| DBM | Double Balanced Mixer | DBS | Datenbankverwaltungssystem |
| DBMI | Data Base Management, Incorporated | DBS | Datenbearbeitungsstelle |
| DBMI | Data Base Management Intrinsic | DBS | Datenbereitstellungssystem |
| DBMS | Data Base Management Software | DBS | Direct Broadcast Satellite |
| DBMS | Data Base Management System | DBS | Distributor Buffer Storage |
| DBMS | Datenbank-Management-System | DBS | Dokumentenbereitstellungssystem |
| DBMS-OS | Data Based Management System/Operating System | DBS | Duplication Buffer Storage |
| DBMV | Digital Block Multivibrator | DBS/R | Datenbankbetriebssystem/Robotron |
| DBNA | Digital Block Non-inverting Amplifier | DBSC | Digital Block Slave Clock |
| DBO | Datenbank-Organisator | DBSP | Double Based Solid Propellant |
| DBO | Datenverarbeitung und Betriebswirtschaftliche Organisation | DBSS | Direct Broadcast Satellite Service |
| DBO | Design By Objective | DBST | Digital Block Schmitt Trigger |
| DBO | Dual Beam Oscilloscope | DBT | Data Bulk Transmission |
| DBOMP | Data Base Organization and Maintenance Processor | DBT | Datenbankbeschreibungstafel |
| DBOMP | Data Base Organization and Management Processor | DBT | Datenbanktechnologie |
| | | DBT | Depleted Base Transistor |
| | | DBT | Double Base Transistor |
| | | DBTG | Data Base Task Group |
| | | DBU | Data Base Utilities |
| DBON | Driver Block Output Node | DBUT | Data Base Update Time |
| DBORG | Datenbankorganisation | DBVS | Datenbankverwaltungssystem |
| DBOS | Disk Based Operating System | DBWC | Differential Ballistic Wind Computer |
| DBP | Data Base Processor | DC | Data Camera |
| DBP | Datenübertragungsbenutzerprogramm | DC | Data Capacity |
| | | DC | Data Card |
| DBP | Deutsche Bundespost | DC | Data Carrier |
| DBP | Dynamic transaction Backout Program | DC | Data Cartridge |
| | | DC | Data Cell |
| DBPS | Data Bank Program System | DC | Data Center |
| | | DC | Data Central |
| DBR | Data Base Relation | DC | Data Chain |
| DBR | Datenbankrechner | DC | Data Channel |
| DBR | Descriptor Base Register | DC | Data Check |
| DBRC | Data Base Recovery Control | DC | Data Classifier |
| | | DC | Data Code |
| | | DC | Data Coding |
| DBRT | Direct Beam Refresh Terminal | DC | Data Collection |
| | | DC | Data Communications |
| | | DC | Data Compatible |
| | | DC | Data Concentrator |

- 165 -

# D

| | | | |
|---|---|---|---|
| DC | Data Content | DC/AC | Direct Current/Alternating Current |
| DC | Data Control | | |
| DC | Data Controlled | DC/SR | Display Control/Storage and Retrieval |
| DC | Data Conversion | | |
| DC | Data Converter | DCA | Data Cell Array |
| DC | Data Counter | DCA | Data Corporation of America |
| DC | Data Cycle | | |
| DC | Decade Counter | DCA | Data Correction Amplifier |
| DC | Decimal Classification | DCA | Decade Counting Assembly |
| DC | Decimal Counter | DCA | Device Control Area |
| DC | Decode | DCA | Digital Command Assembly |
| DC | Define Constant | DCA | Digital Computers Association |
| DC | Definition Card | | |
| DC | Departmental Cluster | DCA | Direct Current Ampere |
| DC | Deposited Carbon | DCA | Direct Current Amplifier |
| DC | Design Change | DCA | Disassembly Compliance and Analysis |
| DC | Desk Calculator | | |
| DC | Destination Code | DCA | Dispatch Control Area |
| DC | Device Clear | DCA | Distributed Communications Architecture |
| DC | Device Code | | |
| DC | Device Configuration | DCA | Document Composition Architecture |
| DC | Device Control | | |
| DC | Differential Calculus | DCA | Document Content Architecture |
| DC | Digit Control | | |
| DC | Digital Card | DCA | Document Control and Approval |
| DC | Digital Clock | | |
| DC | Digital Code | DCA | Doppler Count Accumulator |
| DC | Digital Comparator | DCA | Drift Correction Angle |
| DC | Digital Computation | DCA-A | Disassembly Compliance and Analysis-Abbreviated |
| DC | Digital Computer | | |
| DC | Digital Computing | DCAM | Data Communication Access Method |
| DC | Digital Control | | |
| DC | Diode Cathode | DCAM | Discriminating Content Addressable Memory |
| DC | Direct Code | | |
| DC | Direct Control | DCAO | Digital Card AND-OR |
| DC | Direct Coupled | DCAP | Dynamic Checkout Assistance Program |
| DC | Direct Coupling | | |
| DC | Direct Current | DCAR | Disassembly Compliance and Analysis Report |
| DC | Direct Cycle | | |
| DC | Direction Center | DCAS | Data Collection and Analysis System |
| DC | Directional Coupler | | |
| DC | Discrete Command | DCAT | Device Class Access Type |
| DC | Discriminator | DCB | Data Control Block |
| DC | Disk Controller | DCB | Décimal Codé Binaire |
| DC | Disk to Card | DCB | Define Control Block |
| DC | Display Code | DCB | Device Code Byte |
| DC | Display Computer | DCB | Device Control Block |
| DC | Display Console | DCBD | Define Control Block Dummy |
| DC | Display Control | | |
| DC | Double Column | DCC | Data Carrier Conversion |
| DC | Double Contact | DCC | Data Circuit Concentrator |
| DC | Downward Compatible | DCC | Data Collecting Card |
| DC | Dump Core | DCC | Data Communication Channel |
| DC-DVM | Direct Current - Digital Voltmeter | DCC | Data Communications Controller |

# D

| | | | |
|---|---|---|---|
| DCC | Data Condition Code | DCCU | Data Communication Control Unit |
| DCC | Data Converter Check | | |
| DCC | Data Country Code | DCCU | Data Correlation Control Unit |
| DCC | Development Computer Center | | |
| | | DCD | Data Carrier Detector |
| DCC | Device Control Character | DCD | Data Cell Drive |
| DCC | Digital Communications Console | DCD | Data Collecting Device |
| | | DCD | Data Collection Device |
| DCC | Digital Computer Control | DCD | Decode |
| DCC | Digital Control Computer | DCD | Définition de Constantes Décimales |
| DCC | Direct Calculating Capability | | |
| | | DCD | Digital Correlation Detector |
| DCC | Direct Computer Control | | |
| DCC | Direct Current Clamp | DCD | Digital Countdown Display |
| DCC | Disburse Control Code | DCD | Diode-Capacitor-Diode |
| DCC | Disconnect Command Chaining | DCD | Double Channel Duplex |
| | | DCD | Dynamic Computer Display |
| DCC | Disconnected Command Chain | DCDG | Diode-Capacitor-Diode Gate |
| DCC | Discrimination and Control Computer | DCDL | Digital Control Design Language |
| DCC | Dispatch Center Console | DCDM | Digitally Controlled Delta Modulation |
| DCC | Display Channel Complex | | |
| DCC | Display Control Computer | DCDP | Defense Center Data Processing |
| DCC | Display Control Console | | |
| DCC | Document Control Center | DCDR | Decoder |
| DCC | Double Cotton Covered | DCDS | Data Correlation and Documentation System |
| DCCA | Design Change Cost Analysis | | |
| | | DCDS | Digital Control Design System |
| DCCB | Data Carrier Control Block | | |
| DCCC | Digital Command Communications Channel | DCDS | Digital Countdown Display System |
| DCCC | Double Current Cable Code | DCDS | Double-Cotton Double-Silk covered |
| DCCG | Digital Check Character Generator | | |
| | | DCDS | Dual Channel Dual Speed |
| DCCL | Digital Charge Coupled Logic | DCDT | Direct Current Displacement Transducer |
| DCCO | Digital Card Clock Oscillator | DCDU | Data Collection and Distribution Unit |
| DCCP | Digital Computer Control Panel | DCE | Data Carrier End |
| | | DCE | Data Circuit-terminating Equipment |
| DCCP | Digital Control Computer Program | | |
| | | DCE | Data Collecting Equipment |
| DCCR | Destination Control Chain Record | DCE | Data Communications Equipment |
| DCCS | Digital Command Communications System | DCE | Data Control Equipment |
| | | DCE | Data Conversion Equipment |
| DCCSA | Dictionary of Computer and Control Systems Abbreviations | DCE | Digital Computer Equipment |
| | | DCE | Discrete Control Equipment |
| DCCT | Direct Current Current Transformer | DCE | Displays Common Equipment |
| DCCU | Displays and Controls Control Unit | DCF | Data Channel Filter |
| | | DCF | Data Collection Form |

# D

| | | | |
|---|---|---|---|
| DCF | Data Communications Formatter | DCL | Data Capture Link |
| DCF | Data Communications Facility | DCL | Data Control List |
| | | DCL | Declare |
| DCF | Data Correlation Facility | DCL | Delete Character Line |
| DCF | Data Count Field | DCL | Design Choice Logic |
| DCF | Direct Control Feature | DCL | Designer's Choice Logic |
| DCF | Direct Current Feed | DCL | Die Card Lever |
| DCF | Discounted Cash Flow | DCL | Diebold Computer Leasing Inc. |
| DCF | Disk Control Field | DCL | Digital Computer Laboratory |
| DCF | Document Composition Facility | DCL | Diodeless Core Logic |
| DCFEM | Dynamic Crossed-Field Electron Multiplication | DCL | Direct Communications Link |
| DCFF | Direct Current Flip-Flop | DCL | Direct-Coupled Logic |
| DCFG | Digital Controlled Function Generator | DCLCS | Data Conversion and Limit Check Submodule |
| DCFL | Direct Coupled FET Logic | DCM | Data Communication Methods |
| DCFO | Direct Current Fan-Out | | |
| DCG | Diode Capacitor Gate | DCM | Data Communication Multiplexor |
| DCG | Direct Current Generator | | |
| DCG | Documentation Control Group | DCM | Diffused Current Mode |
| | | DCM | Digital Circuit Module |
| DCG | Doppler-Controlled Gain | DCM | Direct Current Mains |
| DCGFF | Diode-Coupled Gated Flip-Flop | DCM | Direction Cosine Matrix |
| | | DCM | Directory Control Module |
| DCI | Data Carrier Input | DCM | Distributed Control Module |
| DCI | Data Collection Interface | DCMA | Direct Current Milliamps |
| DCI | Data Communication Interlock | DCMA | Defense Contract Management Association |
| DCI | Data Communications Interrogate | DCMA | Duty Cycle Modulation Altenator |
| DCI | Decision Concepts Inc. | DCMH | Data Collection Module, Highspeed |
| DCI | Differential Current Integrator | DCML | Data Collection Module, Lowspeed |
| DCI | Digital Clock Indicator | | |
| DCI | Direct Carrier Injection | DCML | Decimal |
| DCI | Direct Coupled Inverter | DCMPTR | Degaussing Computer |
| DCIA | Digital Card Inverting Amplifier | DCMS | Data Capture and Management System |
| DCIB | Data Communication Input Buffer | DCMS | Data Communication Management Subsystem |
| DCIO | Direct Channel Interface Option | DCMS | Data Communication Management System |
| DCIP | Data Correction Indicator Panel | DCMS | Data Control Multiplex System |
| DCIP | Disk Cartridge Initialization Program | DCMT | Decrement |
| | | DCMT | Document |
| DCIS | Downrange Computer Input System | DCMV | Digital Card Multivibrator |
| | | DCN | Databases-in-Computer-Networks |
| DCIST | Directory of Computerized Information in Science and Technology | DCN | Digital Computer Newsletter |
| | | DCN | Document Control Number |
| DCK | Data Check | DCN | Dual-Coded Number |
| DCKP | Direct Current Key Pulsing | | |

- 168 -

# D

| | | | |
|---|---|---|---|
| DCNA | Data Communication Network Architecture | DCPG | Digital Clock Pulse Generator |
| DCNA | Digital Card Non-inverting Amplifier | DCPL | Distributed Control Programming Language |
| DCO | Data Carrier Output | DCPM | Decision Critical Path Method |
| DCO | Data Control Officer | | |
| DCO | Detailed Checkout | DCPS | Data Compression Processing System |
| DCO | Digitally Controlled Oscillator | DCPS | Data Control Panel Submodule |
| DCO | Dynamic Checkout | | |
| DCOA | Direct Current Operational Amplifier | DCPS | Digitally Controlled Power Source |
| DCOC | Drain Cut-Off Current | DCPS | Dynamic Crew Procedures Simulator |
| DCOL | Direct Control Oriented Language | DCPSK | Differentially Coherent Phase Shift Keyed |
| DCOS | Data Communication Output Selector | DCPSK | Differentially Coherent Phase Shift Keying |
| DCOS | Direct Couple Operating System | DCPSP | Direct Current Power Supply Panel |
| DCOS | Downrange Computer Output System | DCPV | Direct Current Peak Voltage |
| DCP | Data Carrier Production | | |
| DCP | Data Central Processor | DCQM | Digital Circuit Quality Monitor |
| DCP | Data Change Proposal | | |
| DCP | Data Check Program | DCR | Data Carrier Recognition |
| DCP | Data Collecting Platform | DCR | Data Conversion Receiver |
| DCP | Data Collecting Position | DCR | Data Coordinator and Retriever |
| DCP | Data Collection Platform | | |
| DCP | Data Communications Processor | DCR | Decision Circuit Reception |
| DCP | Data Control Processor | DCR | Decrease |
| DCP | Data Control Program | DCR | Decreasing |
| DCP | Data Conversion Program | DCR | Design Change Recommendation |
| DCP | Design Criteria Plan | | |
| DCP | Diagnostic Control Program | DCR | Destruct Command Receiver |
| DCP | Differential Computing Potentiometer | DCR | Detail Condition Register |
| | | DCR | Dielectric Card Reading |
| DCP | Digital Clock Pulse | DCR | Digital Communications Readout |
| DCP | Digital Communications Protocol | | |
| | | DCR | Digital Concentration Readout |
| DCP | Digital Computer Processor | DCR | Digital Conversion Receiver |
| DCP | Digital Computer Programming | | |
| | | DCR | Direct Current Resistance |
| DCP | Digital Cursor Positioner | DCR | Direct Current Restorer |
| DCP | Direct Current Panel | DCR | Directed Change Request |
| DCP | Display Control Panel | DCR | Disk Capture Restore |
| DCP | Distributed Communications Processor | DCRP | Deviation Change Request Proposal |
| DCP | Distributor Communication Processor | DCRS | Data Collection and Reduction System |
| | | DCRS | Document Control Remote Station |
| DCP | Dump Control Program | | |
| DCPC | Dual-Channel Port Controller | DCS | Data Carrier Store |
| | | DCS | Data Carrier System |

# D

| | | | |
|---|---|---|---|
| DCS | Data Cell Store | DCS | Document Control Station |
| DCS | Data Center Service | DCS | Document Control System |
| DCS | Data Channel Selection | DCS | Double Channel Simplex |
| DCS | Data Checking System | DCS | Double-Cotton Single-silk |
| DCS | Data Clarification System | DCS | Dummy Control Section |
| DCS | Data Classification System | DCS | Dynamic Computer System |
| DCS | Data Coding System | DCS/MIP | Dynamic Computer System/Multipurpose Information Processor |
| DCS | Data Collecting Station | | |
| DCS | Data Collecting System | | |
| DCS | Data Collection System | DCSA | Direct Current Servo Amplifier |
| DCS | Data Communication Subsystem | | |
| | | DCSB | Data Check Sense Bit |
| DCS | Data Communication System | DCSC | Digital Card Slave Clock |
| | | DCSG | Data Computation Subsystem Group |
| DCS | Data Conditioning System | | |
| DCS | Data Consolidation Simulation | DCSM | Deterministic Complete Sequential Machine |
| DCS | Data Control Service | DCSN | Data Carrier Sequence Number |
| DCS | Data Control System | | |
| DCS | Data Conversion System | DCST | Digital Card Schmitt Trigger |
| DCS | Data Correction System | | |
| DCS | Dedicated Computer System | DCT | Data Channel Transfer |
| DCS | Defense Communications System | DCT | Data Communication Terminal |
| DCS | Définition de Configuration Système | DCT | Data Conversion Transmitter |
| | | DCT | Decimal Code Translator |
| DCS | Design Control Specifications | DCT | Decoderteil |
| DCS | Destruct Command System | DCT | Destination Control Table |
| DCS | Diagnostic Compiler System | DCT | Device Characteristics Table |
| DCS | Dielectric Card Scanning | DCT | Digital Computer Trainer |
| DCS | Digit Selector Common | DCT | Digital Conversion Terminal |
| DCS | Digital Command System | | |
| DCS | Digital Communication System | DCT | Digital Curve Tracer |
| | | DCT | Direct Coupled Transistor |
| DCS | Digital Computer Speed | DCT | Discrete Cosine Transform |
| DCS | Digital Control Signal | DCT | Dispatcher Control Table |
| DCS | Digital Control System | DCT | Divide Check Test |
| DCS | Digital Countdown System | DCT | Document |
| DCS | Digitally Controlled System | DCTA | Documentation Control Testing Applications |
| DCS | Diode Capacitor Store | DCTC | Documentation Control Testing Center |
| DCS | Direct Current Sensor | | |
| DCS | Direct-Coupled System | DCTE | Data Circuit Terminating Equipment |
| DCS | Distributed Commercial System | | |
| | | DCTL | Data Control |
| DCS | Distributed Communications Software | DCTL | Diode Capacitor Transistor Logic |
| DCS | Distributed Computer System | DCTL | Direct Coupled Transistor Logic |
| DCS | Distributed Computing System | DCTS | Digital Coordinate Transformation System |
| DCS | Distributed Customer Service | DCTS | Document Control and Testing System |

- 170 -

# D

| | | | |
|---|---|---|---|
| DCTV | Digital Colour Television | DD | Decimal Data |
| DCU | Data Coding Unit | DD | Decimal Decode |
| DCU | Data Command Unit | DD | Decimal Devide |
| DCU | Data Communication Unit | DD | Decimal Digit |
| DCU | Data Control Unit | DD | Decimal Display |
| DCU | Decade Counting Unit | DD | Definition Direction |
| DCU | Decimal Counting Unit | DD | Deformation Dipole |
| DCU | Deskewing Control Unit | DD | Design Data |
| DCU | Device Control Unit | DD | Destination Determination |
| DCU | Diagnostic Control Unit | DD | Detailed Design |
| DCU | Digital Control Unit | DD | Device Data |
| DCU | Digital Counting Unit | DD | Digit Display |
| DCU | Disk Control Unit | DD | Digital Data |
| DCU | Display Control Unit | DD | Digital Display |
| DCU | Distribution Control Unit | DD | Direct Drive |
| DCU | Drum Control Unit | DD | Disagreement Detector |
| DCUTL | Direct Coupled Unipolar Transistor Logic | DD | Disconnecting Device |
| | | DD | Disjunctive Data |
| DCV | Data Converter | DD | Disk to Disk |
| DCV | Digital Coded Voice | DD | Display Description |
| DCV | Digitally Coded Voice | DD | Dividend |
| DCV | Direct Current Voltage | DD | Dot-and-Dash |
| DCV | Direct Current Volts | DD | Double Density |
| DCVG | Digital Control and Vector Generator | DD | Double Diffused |
| | | DD | Double Diode |
| DCVGLA | Digitally Controlled Variable-Gain Linear Amplifier | DD | Double Drift |
| | | DD | Drum Demand |
| | | DD | Dump Diode |
| DCVM | Direct Current Voltmeter | DD | Duplex Drive |
| DCVR | Direct Current Voltage Reference | DD/D | Data Dictionary/Directory |
| | | DDA | Demand Deposit Accounting |
| DCVR | Direct Durrent Voltage Regulator | DDA | Dezentralized Data Acquisition |
| DCW | Data Communication Write | | |
| DCW | Data Control Word | DDA | Digital Data Acquisition |
| DCW | Define Constant with Wordmark | DDA | Digital Differential Analyzer |
| DCW | Digital display Control and Warning light | DDA | Digital Display Alarm |
| | | DDA | Digitaler Differential-analysator |
| DCW | Display Call Waiting | | |
| DCWV | Direct Current Working Voltage | DDA | Direct Disk Attachment |
| | | DDA | Double-Displacement Amplitude |
| DCWV | Direct Current Working Volts | DDA | Dynamic Differential Analyzer |
| DCX | Data Communication Exchange | | |
| | | DDAM | Dynamic Design Analysis Method |
| DD | Data Decoding | | |
| DD | Data Definition | DDAS | Demand Deposit Accounting System |
| DD | Data Demand | | |
| DD | Data Density | DDAS | Design of Data Acquisition Subsystem |
| DD | Data Description | | |
| DD | Data Dictionary | DDAS | Digital Data Acquisition System |
| DD | Dateidefinition | | |
| DD | Datendarstellung | DDAS | Digital Data Archives System |
| DD | Datendefinition | | |

# D

| | | | |
|---|---|---|---|
| DDB | Data Display Board | DDDL | Data Dictionary Definition Language |
| DDB | Data Display Buffer | | |
| DDB | Decentralized Data Bank | DDDL | Dictionary Data Definition Language |
| DDB | Design Data Book | | |
| DDB | Device Descriptor Block | DDDL | Double Diffused Diode Logic |
| DDB | Digital Data Buffer | | |
| DDB | Document Data Base | DDDS | Digital Data Display System |
| DDB | Driller Down Buffer | | |
| DDBMS | Distributed Database Management System | DDDU | Display Data Distribution Unit |
| DDC | Data Description Committee | DDE | Dansk Data Elektronik |
| | | DDE | Differential Difference Equation |
| DDC | Data Display Central | | |
| DDC | Data Distribution Center | DDE | Digitaldatenerfassungseinheit |
| DDC | Decision, Design and the Computer | | |
| | | DDE | Direct Digital Encoder |
| DDC | Desk-type Digital Computer | DDE | Direction Départementale de l'Equipement |
| DDC | Digital Data Converter | DDE | Director Design Engineering |
| DDC | Digital Display Converter | | |
| DDC | Digital-to-Digital Converter | DDE | Double Diffused Epitaxial process |
| DDC | Digital-to-Digital Conversion | DDE/DDS | Direkte Dateneingabe/ Direkte Datensicherung |
| DDC | Direct Data Channel | DDF | Data Description Facility |
| DDC | Direct Data Collection | DDF | Dynamic Data Format |
| DDC | Direct Digital Computer | DDFF | Distributed Disk File Facility |
| DDC | Direct Digital Control | | |
| DDC | Direct Distance Dialling | DDG | Data Display Generator |
| DDC | Display Data Controller | DDG | Digital Data Group |
| DDC | Dual Data Collection | DDG | Digital Delay Generator |
| DDC | Dual Dielectric Charge | DDG | Digital Display Generator |
| DDC | Dual Directional Coupler | DDG... | Deutsche Datel Gesellschaft |
| DDCE | Digital Data Conversion Equipment | DDGE | Digital Display Generator Element |
| DDCMP | Digital Data Communications Message Protocol | DDH | Digital Data Handling |
| | | DDHA | Digital Data Handling Assembly |
| DDCS | Data Definition Control System | DDI | Data Dimensions Inc. |
| DDCS | Digital Data Calibration System | DDI | Data Display Indicator |
| | | DDI | Datenorganisation und Datenbanktechniken für Informationssystem |
| DDCS | Direct Digital Control System | | |
| DDD | Data Display Device | | |
| DDD | Detailed Data Display | DDI | Depth Deviation Indicator |
| DDD | Detailed-Design Document | DDI | Direct Data Input |
| DDD | Digital Display Detection | DDI | Direct Dialling In |
| DDD | Digital-Diagnostic-Diskette | DDI | Direct Digital Interface |
| | | DDIC | Digital Data Input Converter |
| DDD | Direct Distance Dialling | | |
| DDD | Double-Diode Detector | DDIE | Digital Display Indicator Element |
| DDD | Duplexed Display Distributor | | |
| | | DDIE | Direct Digital Interface Equipment |
| DDDA | Decimal-to-Digital Differential Analyzer | | |

# D

| | | | |
|---|---|---|---|
| DDIS | Digital Display Indicator Section | DDOCE | Digital Data Output Conversion Equipment |
| DDIS | Document Data Indexing Set | DDOL | Data Dictionary Online |
| DDIT | Diagnostic Data Interface Tape | DDP | Data Description Print |
| DDJ | Digital Differencing Junction | DDP | Data Display Panel |
| | | DDP | Data Distribution Panel |
| | | DDP | Database Definition Processor |
| DDK | Data Decimal Keyboard | DDP | Decentralized Data Processing |
| DDK | Deweys Dezimalklassifikation | | |
| | | DDP | Demand Data Processing |
| DDL | Data Definition Language | DDP | Design Data Package |
| DDL | Data Description Language | DDP | Design Data Printing |
| | | DDP | Design Drawing Program |
| DDL | Data Distribution List | DDP | Diagnostic Disk Pack |
| DDL | Descriptive Design Language | DDP | Differential Dynamic Programming |
| DDL | Digital Data Line | DDP | Digital Data Processor |
| DDL | Digital Data Link | DDP | Dipole Disk Pack |
| DDL | Digital Data Logger | DDP | Direct Data Processing |
| DDL | Digital Design Language | DDP | Distributed Data Path |
| DDL | Digital system Design Language | DDP | Distributed Data Processing |
| DDL | Dispersive Delay Line | DDP | Distributive Data Path |
| DDL | Dynamic Down-Loading | DDPE | Digital Data Processing Equipment |
| DDLC | Data Description Language Committee | | |
| | | DDPL | Data Drawing and Parts List |
| DDLC | Data Description Language Computer | DDPREP | Device Dependent Parameter conversion and Replacement |
| DDM | Data Demand Module | | |
| DDM | Data Description Modification | DDPS | Data Directed Programming System |
| DDM | Data Description Module | | |
| DDM | Derived Delta Modulation | DDPS | Digital Data Processing System |
| DDM | Design Drafting Manufacture | DDPS | Discrimination Data Processing System |
| DDM | Device Descriptor Module | | |
| DDM | Difference in Depth of Modulation | DDPU | Digital Data Processing Unit |
| DDM | Digital Dimmer Memory | DDQ | Dynmaic Data Queuing |
| DDM | Digital Display Machine | DDR | Data Dictionary Reporter |
| DDM | Digital Display Make-up | DDR | Dialectic Data Reader |
| DDM | Digital-Dehnmeßbrücke | DDR | Digital Data Receiver |
| DDM | Dynamic Depletion Mode | DDR | Digital Data Recorder |
| DDMS | Dictionary and Directory Management Subsystem | DDR | Digital Data Recording |
| | | DDR | Direct Drive |
| DDMS | Digital Data Measuring System | DDR | Downrange Data Report |
| | | DDR | Drawing Data Requirement |
| DDN | Data Definition Name | DDR | Dual Discrimination Ratio |
| DDN | Datei-Definitionsname | DDR | Dynamic Device Reallocation |
| DDN | Defense Data Network | | |
| DDN | Digital Data Network | DDR | Dynamic Device Reconfiguration |
| DDO | Direct Data Output | | |
| DDOCE | Digital Data Output Conversion Element | DDRA | Decimal Divide Restore Answer |

# D

| | | | |
|---|---|---|---|
| DDRC | Drawing Data Required for Change | DDSS | Diversified Data Services and Sciences |
| DDRD | Direct Data Recording Device | DDSU | Digital Data Storage Unit |
| DDRH | Digital Data Recording Head | DDT | Data Description Table |
| DDRI | Design Drafting Reference Information | DDT | Datei- und Datenbeschreibungstafel |
| DDRR | Directional Discontinuity Ring Radiator | DDT | Design and Debug Tool |
| DDRS | Digital Data Recording System | DDT | Device Descriptor Table |
| DDS | Darstellungsdatenstruktur | DDT | Digital Data Terminal |
| DDS | Data Definition Statement | DDT | Digital Data Transceiver |
| DDS | Data Description Specification | DDT | Digital Data Transmission |
| DDS | Data Dictionary System | DDT | Digital Data Transmitter |
| DDS | Data Display Subsystem | DDT | Digital Debugging Tape |
| DDS | Data Display System | DDT | Digital Debugging Technique |
| DDS | Data Distribution System | DDT | Digital Decoding Technique |
| DDS | Dataphone Digital Service | DDT | Digital Demodulation Technique |
| DDS | Dataption Digital Service | DDT | Display Date |
| DDS | Daten-Definitions-Spezifikationen | DDT | Doppler Data Translator |
| DDS | Datendialogsystem | DDT | Dynamic Debugging Tape |
| DDS | Deployable Defense System | DDT | Dynamic Debugging Technique |
| DDS | Device Dependent Section | DDTA | Deviations-Differentialthermoanalyse |
| DDS | Dienstleistungsdatenverarbeitungsstation | DDTE | Digital Data Terminal Equipment |
| DDS | Digital Data Service | DDTESM | Digital Data Terminal Equipment Service Module |
| DDS | Digital Data Servo | DDTESS | Digital Data Terminal Equipment Service Submodule |
| DDS | Digital Data System | DDTL | Diffused Diode Transistor Logic |
| DDS | Digital Display Scope | DDTL | Diode Diode Transistor Logic |
| DDS | Digital Dynamics Simulator | DDTL | Double Diffused Transistor Logic |
| DDS | Discarded Data Storage | DDTL | Double Diode Transistor Logic |
| DDS | Disk Data Storage | DDTS | Digital Data Transmission System |
| DDS | Diskontinuierliches Diskretes Signal | DDU | Digital Display Unit |
| DDS | Display Data Subsystem | DDU | Digital Distributing Unit |
| DDS | Distributed Database System | DDU | Disk Data Unit |
| DDS | Diversified Data System Inc. | DDU | Display and Debug Unit |
| DDS | Document Distribution Services | DDU | Dual Diversity Unit |
| DDS | Doppler Detection System | DDUMP | Disk Dump |
| DDS | Dummy Data Set | DDV | Direktdatenverbindung |
| DDS | Dynamic Dispatch System | DDV | Direkte Datenverarbeitung |
| DDSA | Digital Data Service Adapter | DDX | Digital Data Exchange |
| DDSM | Digital Data Switching Matrix | DE | Dämpfungsentzerrer |
| DDSMS | Digital Dispatch Security Monitoring System | DE | Data Element |
| | | DE | Data Encoder |

# D

| | | | |
|---|---|---|---|
| DE | Data Encoding | DEBAS | Debitorenbuchhaltung im Bausteinsystem |
| DE | Data Entry | | |
| DE | Data Error | DEBASS | Debug Assembler |
| DE | Data Evaluation | DEBS | Digital Electron Beam Scanner |
| DE | Data Exchange | | |
| DE | Dateneingabe | DEBUG | Debugging |
| DE | Datenelektronik | DEBUT | Delay-line Buffered Terminal |
| DE | Datenerfassung | | |
| DE | Decimal | DEBV | Direkteingabe-Buchungsverfahren |
| DE | Decimal Exponent | | |
| DE | Decision Element | DEC | Data Evaluation Centre |
| DE | Deemphasis | DEC | Data Exchange Control |
| DE | Deflection Error | DEC | Datenerfassungscentrale |
| DE | Description Entry | DEC | Decimal |
| DE | Design Engineering | DEC | Decimal Equivalent Chart |
| DE | Device End | DEC | Decision |
| DE | Dictating Equipment | DEC | Declination |
| DE | Differential Equation | DEC | Decodierer |
| DE | Digital Element | DEC | Decrease |
| DE | Digital Encoder | DEC | Detector |
| DE | Digital Equipment | DEC | Development Engineering Change |
| DE | Digitaleingabe | | |
| DE | Direct Entry | DEC | Digital Equipment Corp. |
| DE | Directory Element | DEC | Direct Energy Conversion |
| DE | Display Electronics | DEC | Document Effected Code |
| DE | Display Element | DEC | Document Evaluation Center |
| DE | Display Equipment | | |
| DE | Dispositionseinheit | DEC | Dry Electrolytic Capacitor |
| DE | Dokumentationseinheit | | |
| DE | Double Error | DEC... | Digital Equipment Corporation |
| DE | Double-Ended | | |
| DE | Durchschalteinheit | DECA | Display Electronic Control Assembly |
| DE/A | Direkt Ein/Ausgabe | | |
| DEA | Data Encryption Algorithm | DECACC | Decimal Accumulator |
| DEA | Data Exchange Agreement | DECACCN | Decimal Accumulation |
| DEA | Digital Electronic Automation | DECAL | DEC CAI Author Language |
| | | DECAL | Desk Calculator |
| DEA | Digitale Eingabe und Ausgabe | DECAL | Digital Equipment Corporations Adaptation to ALGOL |
| DEA | Display Electronic Assembly | | |
| | | DECAN | Dezentrale Computerleistungserfassung und Analyse |
| DEACON | Direct English Access and Control | | |
| DEACONS | Direct English Access and Control System | DECB | Data Event Control Block |
| | | DECFA | Distributed Emission Crossed-Field Amplifier |
| DEACTLH | Deactivate Line Halt | | |
| DEAL | Decision Evaluation And Logic | DECL | Diode-Emitter Coupled Logic |
| DEAS | Datenerfassungs- und Aufbereitungsstelle | DECLAB | DEC Laboratory |
| | | DECMOV | Decimal Move |
| DEAS | Dialogorientiertes Energie-Abrechnungs-System | DECN | Decision |
| | | DECNET | Digital Equipment Corporation Network |
| DEB | Data Extent Block | | |
| DEB | Debitoren | DECOMP | Decomposition Mathematical Programming |

# D

| | | | |
|---|---|---|---|
| DECOR | Digital Electronic Continuous Ranging | DEF | Datenerfassung und Fernverarbeitung |
| DECR | Decrement | DEF | Défaut |
| DECS | Dutch Exporters of Computer Service | DEF | Define |
| DECT | Distant-End Crosstalk | DEF | Definition |
| DECTAT | Decision Table Translator | DEF | Definitive |
| DECUS | Digital Equipment Computer Users Society | DEF | Déflection |
| DED | Data Element Descriptor | DEF | Destination Element Field |
| DED | Data Element Dictionary | DEFL | Deflection |
| DED | Data Element Directory | DEFL | Deflector |
| DED | Data End Device | DEFL | Diffusions/Emitterfolgelogik |
| DED | Digital Evaluation Device | DEFL | Diode Emitter Follower Logic |
| DED | Digitaleingabe, Dynamisch | DEFO | Datenerfassungsordnung |
| DED | Double Error Detection | DEFOG | Deterministic Factory Operation Game |
| DED-U | Digitaleingabe, dynamisch mit Unterbrechungssignalbildung | DEFT | Definite Time |
| | | DEFT | Driven Equilibrium Fourier Transform |
| DEDA | Data Entry and Display Assembly | DEFT | Dynamic Error Free Transmission |
| DEDAAS | Digital Electrophysiological Data Acquisition and Analysis System | DEFUNCT | Desirability Function |
| | | DEG | Datenendgerät |
| | | DEG | Datenerfassungsgerät |
| DEDAS | Direct Entry Dispatching Audio System | DEG | Degenerate |
| | | DEG | Degree |
| DEDB | Data Entry Data Base | DEG | Delay Error Generator |
| DEDM | Dedendum | DEG | Divisional Engineering Guide |
| DEDS | Data Entry and Display Subsystem | DEGEN | Degeneration |
| DEDS | Data Entry and Display System | DEGOR | Deutsche Gesellschaft für Operations-Research |
| DEDS | Digital Error Detection Subsystem | DEH | Digital Encoder Handbook |
| | | DEHB | Digital Encoder Handbook |
| DEDT | Data Set Definition Table | DEI | Digitalwerteingabe |
| DEDU | Data Encryption and Decryption Unit | DEI | Display Evaluation Index |
| | | DEK | Datenerhebungskatalog |
| DEDUCOM | Deductive Communicator | DEKO | Debitoren- und Kontokorrentrechnung |
| DEE | Dateneingabeeinheit | | |
| DEE | Dateneinrichtungseinheit | DEL | Delay |
| DEE | Datenendeinrichtung | DEL | Delete |
| DEE | Digital Evaluation Equipment | DEL | Delivery |
| | | DEL | Diode Electroluminescente |
| DEE | Digital Events Evaluator | DEL | Diode Emettrice de Lumière |
| DEE | Discrete Events Evaluator | | |
| DEEP | Data Exception Error Protection | DEL | Directly Executed Language |
| DEEP | Describe Each Element in the Procedure | DEL | Divisional Engineering List |
| DEEPDET | Double Exposure End-Point Detection Technique | DEL LN | Delay Line |
| | | DELE | Delete |
| DEER | Directional Explosive Echo Ranging | DELIMITER | Definite Limit Evaluator |
| | | DELNI | Digital Ethernet Local Network Interface |
| DEF | Datenerfassung | | |

# D

| | |
|---|---|
| DELPHI | Disposition- und Entscheidungslehrspiel zur Planung in Handel und Industrie |
| DELS | Diagnostics through Error and Logic Simulation |
| DELTA | Detailed Labor and Time Analysis |
| DELTIC | Delay Line Time Compressor |
| DELTIC | Delay Line Time Compression |
| DELTRAC | Delay Line Transmission Converter |
| DELY | Delivery |
| DEM | Demodulator |
| DEM | Development Engineering Memorandum |
| DEMATEL | Decision-Making And Trial Evaluation Laboratory |
| DEMATRON | Distributed Emission Magnetron amplifier |
| DEMED | Depletion Etch Method |
| DEMO | Demonstration |
| DEMOD | Demodulation |
| DEMOD | Demodulator |
| DEMON | Decision Mapping via Optimum Networks |
| DEMON | Demonstrate |
| DEMON | Demonstration |
| DEMON | Denkenkosha Multiaccess Online system |
| DEMS | Denomination System |
| DEMS | Development Engineering Management System |
| DEMUX | Demultiplexer |
| DEND | Dividend |
| DENS | Density |
| DEOS | Datenerfassungs-Organisationssystem |
| DEP | Data Exchange Program |
| DEP | Datenendplatz |
| DEP | Dependent |
| DEP | Derivative Evaluation Program |
| DEP | Display Executive Program |
| DEP | Document Evaluation Program |
| DEPART | Department |
| DEPENDS | Detail Part Engineering Drawing System |
| DEPI | Differential Equation Pseudo-code Interpreter |
| DEPICT | Defense Electronics Products Integrated Control Technique |
| DEPK | Datenendplatz-Kontrolldruck |
| DEPMIS | Depot Management Information System |
| DEPR | Depress |
| DEPT | Department |
| DEQ | Dequeue |
| DER | Darmstädter Elektronische Rechenanlage |
| DER | Dateneingaberegister |
| DER | Datumeingaberegister |
| DER | Declining Error Rate |
| DER | Design Error Rate |
| DER | Digital Event Recorder |
| DER | Document Error Report |
| DERD | Darstellung Extrahierter Radardaten |
| DERD | Display of Extracted Radar Data |
| DES | Data Encryption Standard |
| DES | Data Encryption System |
| DES | Data Entry Station |
| DES | Data Entry System |
| DES | Dateneingabesystem |
| DES | Dateneingebesteuerung |
| DES | Datenendstelle |
| DES | Datenerfassungsstelle |
| DES | Datenerfassungssystem |
| DES | Datumeingabesteuerung |
| DES | Demag EDV-Service |
| DES | Design |
| DES | Design and Evaluation System |
| DES | Designate |
| DES | Designation |
| DES | Destignator |
| DES | Differential Equation Solver |
| DES | Digital Expansion System |
| DES | Digitale Echosperre |
| DES | Digitaleingabe, Statisch |
| DES | Direct Entry System |
| DES | Division Engineering Standards |
| DES | Dual Exciter System |
| DES-U | Digitaleingabe, statisch mit Unterbrechungssignalbildung |
| DESC | Defense Electronics Supply Center |
| DESC | Dependency Selection Criterion |

# D

| | | | |
|---|---|---|---|
| DESC | Describe | DEV | Delay Equalizer, Variable |
| DESCF | Dependency Selection Criterion Flag | DEV | Development |
| | | DEV | Deviate |
| DESCG | Descending | DEV | Deviation |
| DESCNET | Data on Environmentally Significant Chemicals Network | DEV | Deviator |
| | | DEV | Device |
| | | DEV | Dioden-Erd-Verfahren |
| DESCR | Descrambler | DEV EQL | Deviation Equalizer |
| DESCR | Describe | DEVA | Develop Address |
| DESCR | Description | DEVAR | Device Address Register |
| DESCR | Descriptor | DEVD | Device Description |
| DESG | Designate | DEVIL | Direct Evaluation of Indexed Language |
| DESG | Designation | | |
| DESI | Defense Scientific Information and documentation center | DEVNAME | Device Name |
| | | DEVO | Datenerfassungsverordnung |
| | | DEVS | Datenerfassungs- und Verarbeitungsstation |
| DESIG | Designate | | |
| DESK FAX | Desk-top Facsimile | DEVSIS | Development of Sciences Information System |
| DESSIM | Design Simulator | | |
| DEST | Destination | DEVTYPE | Device Type |
| DEST | Digitaleingabe-Steuerung | DEXAN | Digital Experimental Airborne Navigator |
| DESTN | Destination | | |
| DET | Dateneingabetastatur | DEZ | Dezimal |
| DET | Design Evaluation Test | DF | Data Fetch |
| DET | Detection | DF | Data File |
| DET | Detector | DF | Data Flow |
| DET | Detektor | DF | Data Folder |
| DET | Device Error Tabulation | DF | Data Format |
| DET | Digital Event Timer | DF | Datenfeld |
| DET SYNC | Detector Synchronization | DF | Datenfernübertragung |
| DETAB | Decision Tables | DF | Datenfernverarbeitung |
| DETAB-GT | Decision Table/General Translator | DF | Datenfluß |
| | | DF | Datenfolge |
| DETAB-X | Decision Tables, Experimental | DF | Decimal Fraction |
| | | DF | Decision Feature |
| DETAP | Decision Table Processor | DF | Decision Function |
| DETAS | Dezentralisierte Textverarbeitung Am Sachbearbeiterplatz | DF | Deflection Factor |
| | | DF | Degree of Freedom |
| | | DF | Describing Function |
| DETD | Detected | DF | Device Function |
| DETEC | Detection | DF | Diagnostic Flag |
| DETERMIN | Determination | DF | Difference Frequency |
| DETG | Determining | DF | Differential Frequency |
| DETM | Determine | DF | Differenzfrequenz |
| DETN | Determination | DF | Digitaler Frequenzgeber |
| DETR | Detector | DF | Direct File |
| DETRAN | Decision table Translator | DF | Direction Finder |
| DETS | Digital Element Test Set | DF | Discrimination Factor |
| DEU | Data Entry Unit | DF | Discrimination Filter |
| DEU | Data Exchange Unit | DF | Discripteur de Fichier |
| DEU | Direct Entry Unit | DF | Disk File |
| DEUCE | Digital Electronic Universal Calculating Engine | DF | Dissipation Factor |
| | | DF | Distortion Factor |
| DEUCE | Digital Electronic Universal Computing Engine | DF | Distribution Frame |
| | | DF | Document Feeding |

# D

| | | | |
|---|---|---|---|
| DF | Double Feeder | DFG | Datenfernschaltegerät |
| DF | Draft Printer | DFG | Datenfreigabe |
| DF | Drum File | DFG | Deutsche Forschungsgemeinschaft |
| DF/DS | Data Facility/Device Support | DFG | Digital Function Generator |
| DFA | Describing Function Analyzer | DFG | Diode Function Generator |
| | | DFG | Discrete Frequency Generator |
| DFA | Digital Fault Analysis | | |
| DFA | Digital Frequency Analyzer | DFGA | Distributed Floating Gate Amplifier |
| DFA | Document Format Architecture | DFH | Dual Filter Hybrid |
| DFB | Distributed Feedback semiconductor | DFHSM | Data Facility Hierarchical Storage Manager |
| DFB | Distribution Fuse Board | DFIS | Digital Facsimile Interface System |
| DFC | Data Flow Chart | | |
| DFC | Data Flow Control | DFL | Display Formating Language |
| DFC | Defect | | |
| DFC | Disc File Controller | DFL | Divisional Facilities List |
| DFC | Disk File Check | DFL | Dynamic Function Language |
| DFC | Disk File Control | | |
| DFC | Display Formatting and Control | DFLD | Device Field |
| | | DFLD | Distribution-Free Logic Design |
| DFC | Document Flow Component | | |
| DFC | Double Frequency Changer | DFM | Digital Frequency Meter |
| DFC | Double Frequency Changing | DFM | Digital Frequency Monitor |
| DFC | Dual Feed Carriage | DFM | Digitaler Frequenzmesser |
| DFC | Dual Feed Channel | DFM | Digitaler Frequenzmonitor |
| DFCC | Dual Frame Cross Coupling | DFM | Distortion Factor Meter |
| | | DFMO | Doppler Filter Mixer-Oscillator |
| DFCHIP | Data Flow Chip | | |
| DFCLS | Digital Flight Control and Landing System | DFN | Defined |
| | | DFN | Deutsches Forschungs-Netz |
| DFCNV | Data File Conversion | | |
| DFCNVP | Data File Conversion Program | DFO | Decade Frequency Oscillator |
| DFCU | Disk File Control Unit | DFO | Dekadischer Frequenzoszillator |
| DFD | Data Field Description | | |
| DFD | Data Final Device | DFO | Direct Format Option |
| DFD | Dataflow-Diagramm | DFO | Disk File Organization |
| DFD | Datenflußdiagramm | DFOR | Disk File Organization Routine |
| DFD | Digital Flight Display | | |
| DFD | Digital Frequency Display | DFP | Data Facilities Program |
| DFDC | Disk File Descriptor Control | DFP | Data Facility Product |
| | | DFP | Data Fast Printer |
| DFDR | Digital Flight Data Recorder | DFP | Datenflußplan |
| | | DFP | Decimal Floating Point |
| DFE | Datenfernübertragungseinheit | DFP | Diode Flat Pack |
| | | DFP | Divisional Facilities Practice |
| DFE | Datenfernübertragunseinrichtung | DFP | Duns Financial Profile |
| DFE | Decision Feedbck Equalizer | DFPS | Digital Ferrite Phase Shifter |
| DFET | Drift FET | DFPT | Disk File Protection Table |
| DFF | Delay Flip-Flop | DFR | Data Flow Rate |
| DFF | Display Format Facility | DFR | Decreasing Failure Rate |

- 179 -

# D

| | | | |
|---|---|---|---|
| DFR | Disk File Read | DG | Data General Corporation |
| DFR | Double Frequency Recording | DG | Data Group |
| | | DG | Datagram |
| DFRL | Differential Relay | DG | Differential Gain |
| DFS | Depth First Search | DG | Differential Generator |
| DFS | Deutsche Fernmeldesatelliten | DG | Diode Gate |
| | | DG | Directional Gird |
| DFS | Deutsches Fernmelde-System | DG | Directional Gyro |
| | | DG | Display Gate |
| DFS | Deutsches Fernmeldesatelliten-System | DG | Doppelte Genauigkeit |
| | | DG | Double-Groove |
| DFS | Digital Frequency Synthesizer | DG | Durchschaltegruppe |
| | | DG/UX | Data General Unix |
| DFS | Digitaler Frequenzsynthesizer | DGBC | Digital Geoballistic Computer |
| DFS | Divisional Facilities Standard | DGBIT | Disagreement BIT |
| | | DGC | Data General Corporation |
| DFS | Dynamic Flight Simulator | DGC | Diagnostic |
| DFSK | Double Frequency Shift Keying | DGC | Digital Geoballistic Computer |
| DFSM | Deterministic Finite-State Machine | DGD | Deutsche Gesellschaft für Dokumentation |
| DFSP | Dünnschicht-Filmspeicher | DGDP | Double-Groove Double-Petticoat |
| DFSU | Disk File Storage Unit | | |
| DFT | Default value | DGE | Data Gathering Equipment |
| DFT | Destination Fetch Trigger | DGFB | Deutsche Gesellschaft Für Betriebswirtschaft |
| DFT | Diagnostic Fault Test | | |
| DFT | Diagnostic Function Test | DGFP | Deutsche Gesellschaft Für Personalführung |
| DFT | Digital Filtering Technique | DGK | Deutsche Gesellschaft für Kybernetik |
| DFT | Discrete Fourier Theorem | | |
| DFT | Discrete Fourier Transformation | DGL | Descriptive Geometry Language |
| DFT | Diskrete Fouriertransformation | DGL | Differentialgleichung |
| | | DGM | Data Gathering Monitoring |
| DFT | Distributed Transaction Facility | DGN | Distributed Graphics Network |
| DFT | Dünnfilmtechnik | DGNL | Diagonal |
| DFTG | Drafting | DGNS | Diagnose |
| DFTR | Deflector | DGO | Delay Generated Offset |
| DFU | Data File Utility | DGOR | Deutsche Gesellschaft für Operations Research |
| DFU | Disk File Unit | | |
| DFÜ | Datenfernübertragung | DGP | Data Generation Program |
| DFV | Datenfernverarbeitung | DGR | Daily Going Rate |
| DFV | Dialog-Datenfernverarbeitung | DGRST | Délégation Générale à la Recherche Scientifique et Technique |
| DFVM | Datenfernverarbeitungsmonitor | | |
| | | DGS | Data Ground Station |
| DFVS | Datenfernverarbeitungssystem | DGS | Datagram Service |
| | | DGS | Differentialgleichungssystem |
| DFW | Data Field Width | | |
| DFW | Disk File Write | DGS | Display Generation System |
| DG | Data Gathering | DGT | Deterministic Grammar Tree |
| DG | Data General | | |

# D

| | | | |
|---|---|---|---|
| DGT | Digit | DI/CMOS | Dielectrically Isolated CMOS |
| DGT | Direction Générale des Télécommunications | DI/DO | Data Input/Data Output |
| DGTL | Digital | DI/DO | Data Input/Data Output |
| DGWK | Deutsche Gesellschaft für Warenkennzeichnung GmbH | DI/DO | Digital Input/Digital Output |
| DGZ | Desired Ground Zero | DIA | Decentralized Information Acquisition |
| DH | Decimal to Hexadecimal | | |
| DH | Diensthabende | DIA | Device Interface Adaptor |
| DH | Directly Heated | DIA | Diagram |
| DH | Document Handling | DIA | Diameter |
| DH | Double Heterostructure | DIA | Digital Isolation Amplifier |
| DHCF | Distributed Host Command Facility | DIA | Document Interchange Architecture |
| DHD | Double Heat sink Diode | | |
| DHDS | Data Handling and Display Subsystem | DIA-LOGICS | Document Indexing And Listing Of Graphic Information Codes System |
| DHE | Data Handling Equipment | | |
| DHI | Disk Head Interference | | |
| DHLLP | Direct-High-Level Language Processor | DIA/DCA | Document Interchange Architecture/Document Content Architecture |
| DHP | Drum Head Plug | | |
| DHPE | Data Hardware Project Engineer | DIA/DCA | Document Interchange And Document Content Architecture |
| DHS | Data Handling System | | |
| DHSP | Data High Speed Printer | DIABUCH | Dialogbuchhaltung |
| DHT | Discrete Hilbert Transform | DIAC | Diode, Alternating Current |
| DHT | Drilled Hole Tester | DIACOS | Dialog-Computer-Satz |
| DI | Data In | DIAD | Drum Information Assembler and Dispatcher |
| DI | Data Information | | |
| DI | Data Input | DIADEM | Dialogorientierte Datenermittlungsmethode |
| DI | Data Interchange | | |
| DI | Data Item | DIADEM | Dialogorientiertes Auftragsabwicklungssystem für den Möbelhandel |
| DI | Datenverarbeitung und Informatik | | |
| DI | Decision Instruction | DIAG | Diagnose |
| DI | Declarative Instruction | DIAG | Diagnostic |
| DI | Demand Indicator | DIAG | Diagram |
| DI | Destroyed Information | DIAGN | Diagnostic |
| DI | Deviation Generator | DIAL | Data Interchange at the Application Level |
| DI | Diagnostician | | |
| DI | Diagnostic Instruction | DIAL | Databank Inquiry Answering Link |
| DI | Dielectric Isolation | | |
| DI | Digit Impulse | DIAL | Disk Interrogation Alternation and Loading |
| DI | Digital Input | | |
| DI | Direct Injection | DIAL | Drum Interrogation Alternation and Loading |
| DI | Disable Interrupt | | |
| DI | Discrete Input | DIALATOR | Diagnostic Logic simulator |
| DI | Display | DIALGOL | Dialect of ALGOL |
| DI | Display Instruction | DIAM | Data Independent Accessing Model |
| DI | Document Identifier | | |
| DI | Double Indexing | DIAM | Data Independent Architecture Model |
| DI | Double Injection | | |
| DI | Dummy Information | DIAM | Diameter |
| DI | Dummy Instruction | DIAN | Digital-Analog |

# D

| | | | |
|---|---|---|---|
| DIANA | Datentelefon mit Integrierter Analog-Netz-Anschaltung | DICANNE | Digital Interference Cancelling Adaptive Null Network Equipment |
| DIANA | Datenverarbeitungs-Informationausgabe Nach Anfrage | DICAP | Digital Circuit Analysis Program |
| DIANA | Diagnostic Analyzer | DICC | Digital Interface Code Converter |
| DIANA | Digital Analog | DICCS | Demurrage Inventory Control Card System |
| DIANE | Direct Information Access Network for Europe | DICE | Digital Integrated Circuit Element |
| DIAP | Digitally Implemented Analogue Processing | DICE | Digital Integrated Circuit Exerciser |
| DIAPASS | Dialogorientiertes Produktionsauftragssteuerungssystem | DICE | Digital Intercontinental Conversion Equipment |
| DIAS | Dynamic Inventory Analysis System | DICE | Digital Interface Countermeasures Equipment |
| DIAT | Do-it-yourself Investment Analysis Tables | DICE | Digitally Interfaced Countermeasures Equipment |
| DIB | Data Integrity Block | DICEF | Digital Communications Experimental Facility |
| DIB | Design Information Bulletin | DICN | Digital Computer Newsletter |
| DIB | Deutsches Institut für Betriebswirtschaft | DICON | Digital Communications and Orbiting Needles |
| DIB | Digital Input Basic | DICON | Digital Communication through Orbiting Needles |
| DIB | Disk Information Block | | |
| DIB | DL/I Interface Block | DICORTS | Digital Compare Recirculating Test System |
| DIBA | Dialog BASIC | | |
| DIBL | Drain Inducted Barrier Lowering | DICOST | Diagnostic Control System |
| DIBOL | Digital Business Oriented Language | DICS | Digital Channel Selection |
| DIBOL | Digital-equipment Business-Oriented Language | DID | Data Identification |
| | | DID | Data Input Device |
| DIBU | Dialogbuchhaltung | DID | Data Input Display |
| DIC | Data Input Check | DID | Data Item Description |
| DIC | Data Input Clerk | DID | Development Information Dissemination |
| DIC | Data Input Console | | |
| DIC | Data Insertion Converter | DID | Digital Information Detection |
| DIC | Data Interchange Code | | |
| DIC | Data Item Catalog | DID | Digital Information Display |
| DIC | Digital Input Channel | | |
| DIC | Digital Input Contact | DID | Direct Inward Dialing |
| DIC | Digital Input Control | DID | Drum Information Display |
| DIC | Digital Input group Contact | DIDA | Dispositionsdatei |
| | | DIDA | Dynamic Instrumentation Digital Analyzer |
| DIC | Digital Integrated Circuit | | |
| DIC | Digital Integrating Computer | DIDAC | Digital Data Computer |
| | | DIDACS | Digital Data Communications System |
| DIC | Discrete Integrated Circuit | | |
| | | DIDAD | Digital Data Display |
| DIC | Document Identifier Code | DIDAP | Digital Data Processor |
| DIC | Double Index Control | DIDAS | Dialog-Datenerfassung- und Steuersystem |
| DIC | Dual-In-line Case | | |

# D

| | | | |
|---|---|---|---|
| DIDAS | Digital Data Acquisition System | DIFFFT | Decimation-In-Frequency Fast Fourier Tranform |
| DIDAS | Digital Data System GmbH | DIFFOR | Differentiator |
| DIDAS | Dynamic Instrumentation Data Automobile System | DIFFTR | Differential Time Relay |
| DIDC | Digital Input Data Channel | DIFFTRAP | Digital Fast Fourier Transform Processor |
| DIDDF | Dual Input Discrete Describing Function | DIFR | Difference Register |
| DIDF | Dual Input Describing Function | DIFRACC | Digital Fractional Count Computer |
| DIDI | Digitales Diffusionsmodell | DIG | Digit |
| DIDI | Digitales Diffusionsprogramm | DIG | Digital |
| DIDO | Device Independent Disk Operation | DIGACC | Digital Guidance And Control Computer |
| DIDOCS | Devices Independent Display Operator Console Support | DIGCOM | Digital Computer |
| | | DIGEM | Digit Emitter |
| | | DIGEST | Diebold Generator for Statistical Tabulation |
| DIDOS | Distributed Data processing Operating System | DIGICOM | Digital Communications system |
| DIDS | Digital Display System | DIGICOM | Digital Computer |
| DIDS | Digital Information Display System | DIGIFON | Digitales Telefon |
| | | DIGILIN | Digital-Linear |
| DIECAST | Display Interaction Enhancing Computer Aided Shape Technique | DIGIMP | Digital Impulse |
| | | DIGIPLOT | Digital Plotter |
| | | DIGIPLOT | Digital Plotting |
| DIECP | Defense Item Entry Control Program | DIGITAC | Digital Tactical Airborne Computer |
| DIELI | Direction des Industries Electroniques et de l'Informatique | DIGM | Digitaler Meßwert |
| | | DIGOS | Digital-Geometrie-Orientiertes System |
| | | DIGPU | Digit Pickup |
| DIES | Data Interpretation and Evaluation System | DIGRM | Digit/Record Mark |
| | | DIGRMGM | Digit/Record Mark Group/Mark |
| DIF | Data Interchange Facility | | |
| DIF | Data Interchange Format | DIGRO | Digital Read-Out |
| DIF | Device Independent File | DIGSCOM | Digital Selective Communication |
| DIF | Device Input Format | | |
| DIF | Difference | DIGSEL | Digit Selector |
| DIF | Differential | DIGSELCOM | Digit Selector Common |
| DIF | Direction Finder | DIGTL | Digital |
| DIF | Document Interchange Facility | DIGYRAC | Digital Gyro Accelerometer |
| DIF AMP | Difference Amplifier | DIGZRTR | Digit Zero Trigger |
| DIFAD | Deutsches Institut Für Angewandte Datenverarbeitung | DIIC | Dielectrically Isolated Integrated Circuit |
| | | DIK | Direct Input Keyboard |
| DIFAR | Directional Frequency Analyzing and Recording | DIKOS | Digitales Kommunikationssystem |
| DIFF | Difference | DIL | Data-In-Line |
| DIFF | Different | DIL | Digital Integrated Logic |
| DIFF AMP | Difference Amplifier | DIL | Doppler Inertial LORAN |
| DIFF/FWR | Differentiator and Full Wave Rectifier | DIL | Dual-In-Line |
| | | DIL | Dual-In-Line socket |
| DIFFEQ | Differential Equations numerical integration | DIL | Dual-In-Line switch |

# D

| | | | |
|---|---|---|---|
| DILIC | Dual-In-Line Integrated Circuit | DINST | DIN Informationssystem Technik |
| DILOG | Distributed Logik Corporation | DIO | Data Input/Output |
| | | DIO | Diode |
| DILP | Dual-In-Line Package | DIOB | Digital Input/Output Buffer |
| DIM | Dimension | | |
| DIM | Display Image Manipulator | DIOCB | Device Input/Output Control Block |
| DIM | Display Image Manipulation | | |
| | | DIODE | Digital Input/Output Display Equipment |
| DIMA | Dialog- und Maskenverwaltungssystem | | |
| | | DIOI | Data Input/Output Interface |
| DIMA | Digitalisierung von Massen | | |
| DIMAS | Deutsches Integriertes Modulares Anwendungssystem | DIOM | Digital Input/Output Module |
| | | DIOM | Device I/O Manager |
| DIMAS | Deutsches Integriertes Modulares Abrechnungssystem | DIOP | Digital Input/Output Package |
| | | DIOS | Distributed Input/Output System |
| DIMATE | Depot-Installed Maintenance Automatic Test Equipment | DIOS | Distribution Information and Optimizing System |
| DIME | Dual Independent Map Encoding | DIP | Data Input Programming |
| | | DIP | Data Interchange Program |
| DIMES | Digital Image Manipulation and Enhancement Systems | DIP | Decentralized Information Processing |
| DIMOS | Doppelt Implantierter MOS | DIP | Demande d'Informations Prioritaires |
| DIMOS | Double Implanted MOS | | |
| DIMS | Distributed Intelligence Microprocessor System | DIP | Dial Pulse |
| | | DIP | Digital Incremental Plotter |
| DIMU | Digital-Multimeter | | |
| DIMUS | Digital Multibeam Steering | DIP | Digital Information Processing |
| DIN | Data Identification Number | | |
| | | DIP | Digital Interface Processor |
| DIN | Data-In-line | | |
| DIN | Deutsche Industrie Norm | DIP | Digitizer Input |
| DIN | Deutsches Institut für Normung e.V. | DIP | Disbursement In Process |
| | | DIP | Display Information Processor |
| DIN | Device Initialize | | |
| DIN | Digital Input | DIP | Display Information Processing |
| DIN | Discrete Input | | |
| DIN | Document Identification Number | DIP | Document Improvement Program |
| DINA | Digital Network Analyzer | DIP | Dual-In-line Package |
| DINA | Direct Noise Amplification | DIP | Dual-In-line Plastic |
| DINA | Direct Noise Amplifier | DIPAS | Dialog-Informations- und Personal-Abrechnungs-System |
| DINA | Distributed Information processing Network Architecture | | |
| | | DIPAS | Dialogorientiertes Personalabrechnungssystem |
| DINABOC | Digital Navigation And Bombing Computer | | |
| | | DIPE | Distributed Interactive Processing Environment |
| DINN | Dual Input Null Network | | |
| DINOS | Distributed Interactive Operating System | DIPH | Diaphragm |
| | | DIPLXR | Diplexer |
| DINS | Digital Inertial Navigation System | DIPS | Dendenkosha Information Processing Service |

# D

| | | | |
|---|---|---|---|
| DIPS | Denkenkosha Information Processing System | DIS | Dual Image System |
| | | DIS INT | Discrete Integrator |
| DIPS | Development Information Processing System | DISAC | Digital Simulated Analog Computer |
| DIPS | Digital Information Processing System | DISAC | Digital Simulator And Computer |
| DIPS | Digital Program Selection | DISAM | Direct Indexed Sequential Access Method |
| DIPS | Dual-In-line Packages | | |
| DIR | Data Input Rate | DISAN | Diskriminanzanalyse |
| DIR | Data Item Requirement | DISAP | Dialogsystem zur Arbeits-planerstellung |
| DIR | Data Terminal Ready | | |
| DIR | Dielectric Information Reading | DISAPPD | Disapproved |
| | | DISASM | Disassemble |
| DIR | Direct Information Recording | DISBL | Disable |
| | | DISC | Disconnect |
| DIR | Directory | DISC | Disconnected |
| DIR | Document Information Record | DISC | Discriminator |
| | | DISC | Dissemination Center |
| DIR COUP | Directional Coupler | DISC | Domestic International Sales Corporation |
| DIR FLT | Directional Filter | | |
| DIRAC | Direct Access | DISCH | Discharged |
| DIRAM | Digital Range Machine | DISCH | Discharging |
| DIRCOL | Direction Cosine Linkage | DISCHGE | Discharge |
| DIREC | Digital Rate Error Computer | DISCOLA | Digital Integrated Solid-state Controller for Low-cast Automation |
| DIRENT | Direct Entry | | |
| DIRS | DIM Data Input Information Retrieval System | DISCOM | Digital Selective Communications |
| DIS | Data Initialization Statement | DISCOMP | Diskette Compare |
| | | DISCOP | Digital Simulation of Continuous Processes |
| DIS | Data Input Station | | |
| DIS | Data Input Supervisor | | |
| DIS | Data Input System | DISCOS | Dialogisiertes Computer Satzsystem |
| DIS | Dedicated Information System | | |
| | | DISCR | Discriminate |
| DIS | Diagnose-Informations-system | DISCR | Discriminator |
| | | DISCRIM | Discriminator |
| DIS | Diagnostik-Informations-system | DISCRM | Discriminate |
| | | DISCRM | Discrimination |
| DIS | Dialog terminal System | DISCUS | Disposal and Collection User Simulation |
| DIS | Digital Instrumentation Subsystem | | |
| | | DISE | Digital Systems Education |
| DIS | Digital Instrumentation System | DISEGS | Diagnostic Segments |
| | | DISFP | Disc Indexed Sequential File Package |
| DIS | Direct Information Service | | |
| DIS | Disconnect | DISH | Discrete Identifiable Silicone Handler |
| DIS | Disconnection | | |
| DIS | Dispositionssystem | DISISS | Design of Information Systems In the Social Sciences |
| DIS | Distributed Intelligence System | | |
| | | DISLAN | Display Language |
| DIS | Divisional Information System | DISM | Delayed Impact Space Missile |
| DIS | Double Index Selection | | |
| DIS | Draft International Standard | DISM | Display Monitor |
| | | DISM | Dissimilar |

- 185 -

# D

| | |
|---|---|
| DISO DRUCK | Dialogorientiertes Informations-Steuerungs-Organisationssystem für die Druckindustrie |
| DISOSS | Distributed Office Support System |
| DISP | Dispatcher |
| DISP | Display |
| DISPDJC | Display Dependent Job Control tables |
| DISPL | Display |
| DISPN | Disposition |
| DISPOS | Dienstprogrammsystem |
| DISRP | Double Index Selection Register Party |
| DISS | Data Input Subsystem |
| DISSPLA | Display Integrated Software System and Plotting Language |
| DISSYS | Distribution System |
| DIST | Distance |
| DIST | Distortion |
| DIST | Distribution |
| DIST | Distributor |
| DISTAR | Direct Instructional System for Teaching Arithmetic and Reading |
| DISTR | Distributor |
| DISTRAN | Diagnostic FORTRAN |
| DISTRIX | Distributed UNIX |
| DISYNDA | Display of Synoptic Data |
| DIT | Data Input Tape |
| DIT | Data Input Technician |
| DIT | Data Inquiry Terminal |
| DIT | Digital Information Transmission |
| DIT | Dual Input Transponder |
| DITEC | Digital Television Communications |
| DITFFT | Decimation-In-Time Fast Fourier Transform |
| DITR | Deutsches Informationszentrum für Technische Regeln |
| DITRAN | Diagnostic FORTRAN |
| DITTO | Data Interfile Transfer, Testing and Operation utility |
| DITU | Digital Interface Test Unit |
| DIU | Data Input Unit |
| DIU | Data Interchange Utility |
| DIU | Data Interface Unit |
| DIU | Digital Input Unit |
| DIU | Digital Insertion Unit |
| DIU | Digital Interface Unit |
| DIU | Display Interface Unit |
| DIV | Data In Voice |
| DIV | Digital Input Voltage |
| DIV | Digital Input group Voltage |
| DIV | Digitale Vermittlung |
| DIV | Divergence |
| DIV | Divide |
| DIV | Dividend |
| DIV | Divider |
| DIV | Dividieren |
| DIV | Division |
| DIV | Dynamisch Integriertes Verbunddatenerfassungs- und Informationskommunikationssystem |
| DIVA | Data Input Voice Answerback |
| DIVA | Data Inquiry Voice Answer |
| DIVCHK | Divide Check |
| DIVD | Divided |
| DIVIC | Digital Variable Increment Computer |
| DIVN | Division |
| DIVOT | Digital to Voice Translator |
| DIVOT | Digital-to-Voice Transportation |
| DIVOTS | Data Input Voice Output Telephone System |
| DIX | Digital equipment, Intel and Xerox |
| DIXOS | DIETZ XOS-Betriebssystemerweiterung |
| DIY | Do It Yourself |
| DIZ | Dienstzentrale |
| DJC | Dependent Job Control |
| DJNET | Dependent Job control Network name |
| DJSU | Digital Junction Switching Unit |
| DK | Dezimalklassifikation |
| DK | Digit Keyboard |
| DK | Diskette |
| DK | Durchschaltekanalgruppe |
| DKAN | Datenkanal |
| DKB | Decimal Keyboard |
| DKB | Durchschaltekanalgruppe für Bitgruppen |
| DKM | DV-Strom-Kontrollmodul |
| DKO | Delay Key On |
| DKR | Datenkoordinierungsrechner |
| DKS | Data Key Signal |

# D

| | | | |
|---|---|---|---|
| DKS | Digital Kodierte Sprache | DLCN | Distiributed-Loop Computer Network |
| DKT | Digitalkonzentrator | | |
| DKT | Diskette | DLCO | Decade LC Oscillator |
| DKU | Display Keyboard Unit | DLCS | Data Line Concentration System |
| DKWIC | Double Key Word In Context | DLD | Delay Line Driver |
| DL | Data Language | DLDR | Differential Line Driver/ Receiver |
| DL | Data Length | | |
| DL | Data Limit | DLE | Data Link Escape |
| DL | Data Line | DLEN | Display Entry |
| DL | Data Link | DLET | Delete |
| DL | Data List | DLF | Document Library Facility |
| DL | Data Logger | DLFDU | Data Line Flight Direction Unit |
| DL | Data Logging | | |
| DL | Data Logic | DLFET | Depletion-mode Load Field Effect Transistor |
| DL | Datenfeld-Länge | | |
| DL | Datenlänge | DLG | Datenlesegerät |
| DL | Datenleitung | DLH | Data Link Hardware |
| DL | Datenleser | DLH | Data Lower Half byte |
| DL | Dead Load | DLIMP | Descriptive Language for Implementing Macro-Processors |
| DL | Dedicated Line | | |
| DL | Delay | | |
| DL | Delay Line | DLK | Data Link |
| DL | Design Language | DLL | Delay Locked Loop |
| DL | Dielectric Loading | DLL | Dynamic Linkage Loader |
| DL | Difference Limen | DLM | Data Line Monitor |
| DL | Difference Limit | DLM | Data Link Monitor |
| DL | Digit Line | DLM | Datenleitungsmeßgerät |
| DL | Diode Limiter | DLM | Delay Line Memory |
| DL | Diode Logic | DLM | Digital Logic Module |
| DL | Disarm Line | DLM | Distributed Logic Memory |
| DL | Disjunctively Linear | DLN | Digital Ladder Network |
| DL | Distributed Lab | DLO | Delayed Output |
| DL | Double Ledger | DLO | Dense Linear Ordering |
| DL | Dynamic Load | DLO | Double Local Oscillator |
| DL... | Data Laboratories Ltd. | DLO | Dual Loop Oscillator |
| DL/I | Data Language/I | DLOS | Dynamic Logic Simulation |
| DL/I CHKP | DL/I Checkpoint | DLP | Data Link Processor |
| DLA | Data Link Adapter | DLP | Data Listing Programs |
| DLA | Data Link Address | DLP | Dienstleistungsprozedur |
| DLA | Dateileitadresse | DLP | Double Layer Polysilicon |
| DLA | Define user Label Area | DLPG | DIM Data Input Listenprogrammgenerator |
| DLAB | Disk Label | | |
| DLABI | Disk Label Information | DLR | Delay Line Register |
| DLAT | Directory Look-Aside Table | DLRP | Data Link Reference Point |
| DLB | Discrete Linear Basis | DLS | Data Librarian System |
| DLBL | Disk Label | DLS | Data Link Set |
| DLC | Data Line Card | DLS | Data Link Simulator |
| DLC | Data Link Control | DLS | Data Link Software |
| DLC | Decision Logic Control | DLS | Data Logging System |
| DLC | Digital Logic Circuit | DLS | Datenleitstelle |
| DLC | Direct Lift Control | DLS | Delay Line Store |
| DLC | Duplex Line Control | DLS | Dialogsystem |
| DLCC | Data Link Control Chip | DLS | Digital Ladder Structure |

# D

| | | | |
|---|---|---|---|
| DLS | Digital Logic System | DM | Disconnected Mode |
| DLS | Discrete Least Squares | DM | Disk Monitor |
| DLS | Distributed Logic Store | DM | District Manager |
| DLS | Document Library Services | DM | Double-Make |
| DLT | Data Line Terminal | DM | Drum |
| DLT | Data Line Translator | DM | Drum Module |
| DLT | Data Link Terminal | DM | Dynamic Memory |
| DLT | Data Link Transceiver | DMA | Data Management Analysis |
| DLT | Data Link Translator | DMA | Decimal Matrix Adder |
| DLT | Data Loop Transceiver | DMA | Direct Memory Access |
| DLT | Decision Logic Table | DMA | Direct Memory Address |
| DLT | Decision Logic Translator | DMA | Drum Memory Adapter |
| DLT | Delete | DMA | Drum Memory Assembly |
| DLT | Depletion Layer Transistor | DMAC | Direct Memory Access Channel |
| DLTM | Data Link Test Message | | |
| DLTPM | Date of Last Payment | DMAC | Direct Memory Access Control |
| DLTS | Deep Level Transient Spectroscopy | | |
| | | DMAC | Direct Memory Access Controller |
| DLU | Data Line Unit | | |
| DLU | Digitizer Logic Unit | DMACS | Descriptive Macro Code generation System |
| DLU | Display Logic Unit | | |
| DLU | Dual Logical Units | DMAD | Diagnostic Machine Aids/Digital |
| DLVD | Delivered | | |
| DLVRY | Delivery | DMAP | Direct Matrix Abstraction Process |
| DLY | Delay | | |
| DLY | Diffusion Linted Yield | DMAT | Digital Module Automatic Tester |
| DLYD | Delayed | | |
| DLZ | Dämpfungs- und Laufzeitentzerrer | DMB | Data Management Block |
| | | DMB | Dynamic Memory Block |
| DLZ | Durchlaufzeit | DMBDIR | Data Management Block Directory |
| DM | Data Management | | |
| DM | Data Manager | DMC | DSIF Monitor and Control subsystem |
| DM | Data Memory | | |
| DM | Datenmultiplexer | DMC | Data Management Channel |
| DM | Debit Memo | DMC | Data Management Control |
| DM | Debugging Mode | DMC | Design Manufacturing Change |
| DM | Decimal Multiply | | |
| DM | Decision Maker | DMC | Digital Microcircuit |
| DM | Decision Mate | DMC | Digital Multiplex Control |
| DM | Decoder Matrix | DMC | Direct Multiplex Control |
| DM | Delta Modulation | DMC | Disk Memory Controller |
| DM | Delta Modulator | DMCC | Dual Multiple Column Control |
| DM | Demand Meter | | |
| DM | Dezimeter | DMCL | Device Media Control Language |
| DM | Diagnostic Message | | |
| DM | Diagnostic Monitor | DMCU | Disk Memory Control Unit |
| DM | Different Microprogram | DMD | Data Measuring Device |
| DM | Differential MOde | DMD | Digital Map Display |
| DM | Digital Memory | DMD | Digital Message Device |
| DM | Digital Modulation | DMD | Digital-Mehrkanal-Drucker |
| DM | Digital Modulator | | |
| DM | Digital Multimeter | DMD | Disk Memory Drive |
| DM | Digital-Multiplexgerät | DMD | Dual Mode Display |
| DM | Diode Matrix | DMDC | Dual Module Display and Control |
| DM | Diode Memory | | |

# D

| | | | |
|---|---|---|---|
| DMDP | Data Maintenance Diagnostic Program | DMO | Decimal Multiply Operation |
| DME | Distance Measuring Equipment | DMO | Diode Microwave Oscillator |
| DME | Dynamic Mission Equivalent | DMOS | Diffused MOS |
| | | DMOS | Discrete MOS |
| DMED | Digital Message Entrance Device | DMOS | Doppeldiffusions-Metall-Oxyd-Silizium |
| DMED | Digital Message Entry Device | DMOS | Double-diffused Metal Oxide Semiconductor |
| DMF | Data Manipulating Function | DMOST | Double-diffused Metal Oxide Semiconductor Technology |
| DMF | Development Master File | | |
| DMF | Digital Matched Filter | DMOST | Double-diffused Metal Oxide Semiconductor Transistor |
| DMF | Disc Management Facility | | |
| DMF | Distributed Management Facility | | |
| | | DMP | Data Management Plan |
| DMGEN | Diffusion Mask Generator | DMP | Demultiplexer |
| DMGZ | Demagnetize | DMP | Digital Mass Programmer |
| DMH | Device Message Handler | DMP | Disk Management Program |
| DMI | Declarative Macro-Instruction | DMP | Dump |
| | | DMR | Data Management Routine |
| DMI | Digital Measuring Instrument | DMR | Defective Material Report |
| | | DMR | Digital Meter Reader |
| DMI | Digital Multiplex Interface | DMR | Dynamic Modular Replacement |
| DMI | Digital Multiplexed Interface | DMS | Data Management System |
| | | DMS | Data Measuring System |
| DMI | Digital Multiplexing Interface | DMS | Data Monitoring System |
| | | DMS | Data Multiplex System |
| DMI | Disable Manual Input | DMS | Data-base Management System |
| DMIC | Defense Metals Information Center | | |
| | | DMS | Datenmanagementsystem |
| DML | Data Macro Language | DMS | Decision Making System |
| DML | Data Management Language | DMS | Development Management System |
| DML | Data Manipulation Language | DMS | Digital MUMPS Standard |
| | | DMS | Digital Measuring System |
| DML | Database Manipulation Language | DMS | Digital Multiplex Switching system |
| DML | Device Media Language | DMS | Digital Multiplexing Synchronizer |
| DML | Digitized Message Link | | |
| DML | Direct Memory Line | DMS | Disk Monitor System |
| DMLTG | Data Manipulation Language Task Group | DMS | Display Management System |
| | | DMS | Distributed Maintenance Service |
| DMM | Digital Mass Memory | | |
| DMM | Digital Multimeter | DMS | Document Management System |
| DMM | Digitaler Matrix-multiplizierer | | |
| | | DMS | Drum Memory System |
| DMM | Dynamic Magnetic Memory | DMS | Dynamic Magnetic Store |
| DMMC | Digital Multi-Meter Control | DMS/CS | Data Management System/Computer Subsystem |
| DMN | Differential Mode Noise | | |
| DMNSC | Digital Main Network Switching Center | DMSP | Data Meteorological Satellite Program |

- 189 -

# D

| | | | |
|---|---|---|---|
| DMSPSM | Data Management System Problem Specification Model | DNA | Distributed Network Architecture |
| DMSS | Data Multiplex Subsystem | DNB | Distribution Number Bank |
| DMST | Dynamic Magnetic Storage Technique | DNC | Data Name Card |
| | | DNC | Direct Numerical Control |
| DMT | Device Mask Table | DNCG | Digital Null Command Generator |
| DMT | Digital Magnetic Tape | DNCS | Distribution Network Communication System |
| DMT | Digital Message Terminal | | |
| DMT | Dimensional Motion Time | DND | Dividend |
| DMT | Disk operating system Module Tester | DND | Do Not Disturb |
| | | DNDG | Dynamic Network Data Generator |
| DMTI | Doppler Moving Target Indicator | DNE | Datennetz-Diagnoseeinrichtung |
| DMTPS | Digital Magnetic Tape Plotting System | DNF | Decimal Number Format |
| DMTS | Digital Module Test Set | DNF | Disjunctive Normal Form |
| DMTS | Dynamic Multi-Tasking System | DNF | Disjunktive Normalform |
| | | DNF | Do Not Fill |
| DMU | Data Management Unit | DNIC | Data Network Identification Code |
| DMU | Data Management Utilities | | |
| DMU | Data Measurement Unit | DNKZ | Datennetzkontrollzentrum |
| DMU | Digital Message Unit | DNL | Do Not List |
| DMUS | Data Management Utilities System | DNL | Do Not Load |
| | | DNL | Dynamic Noise Limiter |
| DMUX | Demultiplexer | DNOS | Distributed Network Operating System |
| DMUX | Digital-Multiplexgerät | | |
| DMV | Deutsche Mathematische Vereinigung | DNRZ | Delayed Non-Return-to-Zero |
| DMW | Decimeter Wave | DNS | Decimal Number System |
| DMX | Data Multiplex | DNS | Discrete Network Simulation |
| DMX | Demultiplexer | | |
| DMY | Day Month Year | DNS | Distributed Network Software |
| DN | Data Name | | |
| DN | Data Number | DNSP | Datenübertragungs- und Netzsteuerprogramm |
| DN | Datanet | | |
| DN | Dateiname | DNST | Datennebenstelle |
| DN | Datenname | DNT | Detent |
| DN | Decanewton | DNT | Device Name Table |
| DN | Deci-Nepper | DNU | Do Not Use |
| DN | Decimal Notation | DNWS | Discrete Network Simulation |
| DN | Decimal Number | | |
| DN | Decoder Network | DO | Data Operation |
| DN | Develop Number | DO | Data Organization |
| DN | Diagnostic | DO | Data Output |
| DN | Dienstnummer | DO | Defense Order |
| DN | Digital Notation | DO | Deviating Oscillator |
| DN | Directory Number | DO | Digital Output |
| DN | Double Negation | DO | Diode Outline |
| DN | Down | DO | Direct Operand |
| DNA | Data Not Available | DO | Direct Order |
| DNA | Deutscher Normenausschuß | DO | Direkte Organisation |
| | | DO | Discrete Output |
| DNA | Digital Network Architecture | DO | Doppler |
| | | DO | Draw Out |

# D

| | | | |
|---|---|---|---|
| DO | Drop Out | DOF | Degree Of Freedom |
| DO/IT | Digital Output/Input Translator | DOF | Device Output Format |
| DOARS | Donnelly Official Airline Reservation System | DOFIC | Domain Originated Functional Integrated Circuit |
| DOB | Dynamically Obtained Buffer | DOFLT | Date Of Last issue |
| DOBIS | Dortmunder Online Bibliothekssystem | DOG | Drop Out Generator |
| | | DOI | Decision Oriented Information |
| DOC | Data Optimizing Computer | DOI | Descent Orbit Insertion |
| DOC | Data Output Clock | DOI | Digital Operation Interpreter |
| DOC | Data and Operations Center | DOKAUS | Dokumentations- und Auskunftssystem |
| DOC | Data, Operation and Control | DOKIS | Dokumentations-Informations-System |
| DOC | Decimal-to-Octal Conversion | DOKON | Dokumentationsformate-Konverter |
| DOC | Digital Output Control | DOKRET | Dokumenten-Retrieval |
| DOC | Direct Operating Cost | DOKSYS | Dokumentationssystem |
| DOC | Display Operator Console | DOKZENT | Dokumentationszentrum |
| DOC | Document | DOL | Daily Operating Log |
| DOC | Documentation | DOL | Data Optimizing Language |
| DOC | Dynamic Overload Control | DOL | Design Oriented Language |
| DOCA | Documentation Automatique | DOL | Direct On-Line |
| DOCDEL | Documents Delivered Electronically | DOL | Display Oriented Language |
| | | DOL | Dynamic Octal Load |
| DOCPROC | Document Processing | DOLARS | Digital Off-Line Automatic Recording System |
| DOCS | Documents | | |
| DOCS | Dynamic Operations Control System | DOLARS | Disk On-Line Accounts Receivable System |
| DOCTOR | Display-Oriented Communication Tool for Online Retrieval | DOLIN | Design On-Line |
| | | DOLLS | Delayed Opening Leaflet System |
| DOCU | Document | DOLOG | Do Logic |
| DOCUM | Document | DOLPRO | Design Oriented Language Program |
| DOCUS | Display-Oriented Compiler Usage System | DOLT | Delay Oriented Logic Tester |
| DOD | Direct Outward Dialling | DOM | Data Output Mixer |
| DODAS | Digital Oceanographic Data Acquisition System | DOM | Digit Organized Memory |
| | | DOM | Digital Ohmmeter |
| DODIK | Dialogorientierte Datenverarbeitung Im Krankenhaus | DOMA | Dokumentation Maschinenbau |
| | | DOMD | Digital Oxygen Metering Device |
| DODP | Disk Oriented Data Processing | DOMINA | Distribution-Oriented Management Information Analyzer |
| DOE | Data Origination Event | | |
| DOE | Department Of Energy | DOMINIG | Datenverarbeitung für Organisations- und Managementaufgaben zur Integration des Normierten Informationsflusses im Gesundheitswesen |
| DOE | Device Oriented Electronic | | |
| DOES | Direct Order Entry System | | |
| DOES | Disk-Oriented Engineering System | | |
| DOES | Distribution Order Entry System | | |

# D

| | | | |
|---|---|---|---|
| DON | Disque Optique Numérique | DOS/ES | Disk Operating System/ESER |
| DONA | Dynamic Organizational Network Analysis | DOS/ES | Diskovaja Operacionnaja Sistema/Edinaja Sistema |
| DONUT | Digitally Operated Network Using Threshold | DOS/P | Disk Operating System/Prime |
| DOP | Display Output Processor | DOS/PT | Disk Operating System/Performance Tool |
| DOPA | Dynamic Output Printer Analyser | DOS/RS | Disk Operating System/Real Storage |
| DOPI | Delay-On-Pull-IN | DOS/S | Disk Operating System/Standard |
| DOPIC | Documentation Of Program In Core | DOS/VS | Disk Operating System/Virtual Storage |
| DOPLOC | Doppler Phase Lock | DOS/VSE | Disk Operating System/Virtual Storage Extended |
| DOPOS | Doped Poly-Silicon | DOSE | Distributed Office Support Executive |
| DOPOS | Doped Poly-Silicon diffusion source | DOSF | Distributed Office Support Facility |
| DOPS | Digital Optical Protection System | DOSY | Digiset-Orientiertes Satzsystem |
| DOPS | Display Observer Performance Study | DOT | Data Organizing Translator |
| DOR | Digital Optical Recorder | DOT | Data Output Tape |
| DOR | Digital Optical Recording | DOT | Digital Output Timer |
| DOR | Divisor | DOT | Direction Opérationnelle des Télécommunications |
| DORACE | Design Organization, Record, Analyze, Charge, Estimate | DOT | Domain Tip |
| DORAN | Doppler Range And Navigation | DOT | Duplex One-Tape |
| DORCA | Dynamic Operational Requirements and Cost Analysis | DOT | Dynamic Operation Test |
| DORI | Displace on Order - Replace Installed | DOTAN | Digitales Optisches Teilnehmer-Anschlußnetz |
| DORIN | Darstellungsmethoden für Organisations- und Informationssysteme | DOTC | Data Observing Testing Console |
| DORIS | Designer's On-line Real-time Interactive Secretary | DOTIPOS | Deep Ocean Test Instrument Placement and Observation System |
| DORIS | Direct Order Recording and Invoicing System | DOTRAM | Domain-Tip Random Access Memory |
| DORIS | Dornier Recycling Informationssystem | DOUSER | Doppler Unbeamed Search Radar |
| DORO | Displace on Order - Replace on Order | DOUT | Data Out |
| DORS | Dialog-Overlay-Recovery-Steuerung | DOUT | Data-Out-line |
| DOS | Data Organization Service | DOV | Data Over Voice |
| DOS | Day Of Sale | DOVACK | Differential, Oral, Visual, Aural, Computerized Kinestetic |
| DOS | Digital Operation System | DOVAP | Doppler Velocity And Position |
| DOS | Discrete, Open-loop and Selfplaced | DP | Data Path |
| DOS | Disk Operating System | DP | Data Phone |
| DOS | Disk Oriented System | DP | Data Plotter |
| DOS | Dokumentensatz | DP | Data Port |
| | | DP | Data Preparation |
| | | DP | Data Presentation |

# D

| | | | |
|---|---|---|---|
| DP | Data Print | DP | Dual Printing |
| DP | Data Printer | DP | Dummy Procedure |
| DP | Data Processing | DP | Dynamic Programmer |
| DP | Data Processor | DP | Dynamic Programming |
| DP | Data Program | DP | Dynamische Programmierung |
| DP | Data Protection | | |
| DP | Data Pulse | DPA | Data Processing Accounting |
| DP | Datenpuffer | | |
| DP | Datenübertragungsprogramm | DPA | Data Processing Activities |
| DP | Decimal Point | DPA | Data Processing Algorithm |
| DP | Dedicated Peripherie | DPA | Data Processing Area |
| DP | Deep Penetration | DPA | Decimal Point Alignment |
| DP | Definitive Program | DPA | Delay Path Analysis |
| DP | Deflection Plate | DPA | Dial Pulse Acceptor |
| DP | Description Pattern | DPA | Digital Pulse Analyzer |
| DP | Design Program | DPA | Direct Processor Adaptor |
| DP | Designation Punching | DPA | Display/Printer Adapter |
| DP | Destination Punching | DPACD | Data Processing Agreement and Customer Documents |
| DP | Detail Printing | | |
| DP | Détection de Porteuse | DPAGE | Device Page |
| DP | Device Pool | DPAIS | Data Processing Advance Information System |
| DP | Dew Point | | |
| DP | Diagnostic Program | DPAS | Dezentrales Prozeßautomatisierungs-System |
| DP | Dial Pulse | | |
| DP | Dial Pulsing | DPAT | Drum-Programmed Automatic Tester |
| DP | Diametral Pinch | | |
| DP | Dienstprogramm | DPB | Data Plotting Board |
| DP | Differential Phase | DPB | Data Processing Branch |
| DP | Digit Position | DPB | Deposit Pass Book |
| DP | Digit Present | DPB | Dynamic Pool Block |
| DP | Digit Pulse | DPBC | Double Punch and Blank Column |
| DP | Digit Punching | | |
| DP | Digital Plotter | DPC | Data Processing Capacity |
| DP | Digital Position | DPC | Data Processing Center |
| DP | Digital Processing | DPC | Data Processing Central |
| DP | Digital Product | DPC | Data Processing Circuit |
| DP | Direct Program | DPC | Data Processing Computer |
| DP | Direct Programming | DPC | Data Processing Control |
| DP | Discriminator Program | DPC | Destination Point Code |
| DP | Disk to Printer | DPC | Digital Phase Comparator |
| DP | Distribution Point | DPC | Digital Pressure Converter |
| DP | Distribution Programmer | DPC | Digital Printing Computer |
| DP | Disturb Pulse | DPC | Digital Process Controller |
| DP | Divide decimal Packed | DPC | Digital Pulse Converter |
| DP | Document-Publishing | DPC | Direct Program Control |
| DP | Documentation Program | DPC | Disc Pack Controller |
| DP | Double Precision | DPC | Display Power Control |
| DP | Double Program | DPC | Double Paper Covered |
| DP | Double Punch | DPC | Dual Punch Card |
| DP | Double Pole | DPC | Dual Purpose Card |
| DP | Draft Proposal | DPCA | Data Processing Control Area |
| DP | Drawing Program | | |
| DP | Drive Pulse | DPCC | Data Processing Control Center |
| DP | Driving Power | | |

# D

| | | | |
|---|---|---|---|
| DPCE | Data Processing Customer Engineering | DPI | Data Processing Installation |
| DPCM | Delta Pulse Code Modulation | DPI | Digital Pseudo-random Inspection |
| DPCM | Differential Pulse Code Modulation | DPL.. | Data Pathing Inc. |
| DPCM | Differenz Pulse Code Modulation | DPI/O | Data Processing Input/Output |
| DPCM | Differenz-Pulscode-modulation | DPIF | Driving-Point Impedance Function |
| DPCS | Data Processing and Communications System | DPL | Data Programming Language |
| DPCTE | Data Processor and Computer Test Equipment | DPL | Design and Programming Language |
| DPCU | Digital Processing and Control Unit | DPL | Display and Panel |
| DPCX | Distributed Processing Control Executive | DPL | Divisional Programming List |
| DPD | Data Processing Department | DPL | Document Processing Language |
| DPD | Data Processsing Division | DPLF | Data Phone Line Formatter |
| DPD | Data Products Division | DPLF | Digital Phone Line Formatter |
| DPD | Data Project Directive | DPLIS | Development Pilot Line Information System |
| DPD | Define the Page Data set | DPLL | Digital PLL |
| DPD | Digit Plane Driver | DPLXR | Duplexer |
| DPD | Digital Phase Difference | DPLY | Display |
| DPD | Disk Pack Data | DPM | Data Plant Management |
| DPD | Double-Plug Diode | DPM | Data Processing Machine |
| DPDA | Deterministic Push-Down Automation | DPM | Data Processing Magazine |
| | | DPM | Data Processing Manager |
| DPDT | Double-Pole Double-Throw | DPM | Data Processing Model |
| DPE | Data Processing Equipment | DPM | Decimal Point Mechanism |
| DPE | Demande Pour Emettre | DPM | Digital Panel Meter |
| DPE | Distributor-to-Printer Electronics | DPM | Digital Power Meter |
| | | DPM | Digitalpegelmesser |
| DPE | Dynamic Phase Error | DPM | Distributed Presentation Management |
| DPEM | Data Processing Equipment Manufacturer | DPM | Documents Per Minute |
| DPESE | Densely Packaged Encased Standard Element | DPM | Dynamic Programming Method |
| DPF | Data Processing Facility | DPMA | Data Processing Management Association |
| DPFM | Discrete time Pulse Frequency Modulation | DPMIS | Data Processing Management Information System |
| DPFM | Dual-Polarization Frequency Modulation | DPMO | Data Processing Machine Order |
| DPG | Data Processing Group | DPMOAP | Data Processing Machine Operators And Programmers |
| DPG | Data of Permanent Grade | | |
| DPG | Diagnostic Programming Group | DPN | Data Processing Network |
| | | DPN | Diamond Pyramid hardness Number |
| DPG | Digital Pattern Generator | | |
| DPH | Disc Pack Handler | DPNL | Distribution Panel |
| DPHQ | Data Processing Headquarters | DPO | Data Processing Operation |
| DPI | Data Processing Industry | | |

# D

| | | | |
|---|---|---|---|
| DPO | Delayed Pulse Oscillator | DPS | Data Processing Station |
| DPO | Digital Processing Oscilloscope | DPS | Data Processing Subsystem |
| | | DPS | Data Processing System |
| DPO | Double-Pulse Operation | DPS | Dateiparametersatz |
| DPO | Drop-Out | DPS | Decimal Point Setting |
| DPODP | Double Precision Orbit Determination Program | DPS | Delayed Printer Simulator |
| | | DPS | DEMAG Programmier-System |
| DPOM | Data Processing Orders and Movements | DPS | Departmental Processing System |
| DPOP | Data Printout Program | | |
| DPOW | Data Processing Order Worksheet | DPS | Descent Power System |
| | | DPS | Design Problem Solver |
| DPP | Data Processing Program | DPS | Dial Pulse Sender |
| DPP | Decentralized Printing Program | DPS | Dialectic Problem Solver |
| | | DPS | Differential Phase Shift |
| DPP | Divisional Programming Practice | DPS | Differential Phase Shifting |
| DPP | Dynamic Programming Procedure | DPS | Digital Phase Shifter |
| | | DPS | Digital Plotter System |
| DPPA | Double-Pumped Parametric Amplifier | DPS | Digital Processing System |
| | | DPS | Diode Phase Shifter |
| DPPC | Data Processing Products Contract | DPS | Disk Programming System |
| | | DPS | Display Power Supply |
| DPPE | Data Processing Project Engineer | DPS | Distibuted Presentation Services |
| DPPM | Differential Pulse Position Modulation | DPS | Distributed Processing System |
| DPPROG | Data Processing Programming | DPS | Distributed Programming System |
| DPPX | Distributed Processing Programming Executive | DPS | Divisional Programming Standard |
| DPPX/BASE | Distributed Processing Programming Executive Base | DPS | Document Processing System |
| | | DPS | Documentation and Programming System |
| DPPX/DTMS | DPPX/Data base and Transaction Management System | DPS | Dokumentations- und Programmier-System |
| | | DPS | Druckpufferspeicher |
| DPPX/SP | Distributed Processing Programming Executive/System Product | DPS | Dynamic Program Structure |
| | | DPSA | Data Processing Sales Administration |
| DPR | Data Plotting Routine | | |
| DPR | Data Processing Request | DPSA | Data Processing Supplies Association |
| DPR | Design and Partitioning for Restability | DPSC | Data Processing Service Center |
| DPR | Dial Pulse Receiver | | |
| DPR | Dial Pulse Repeater | DPSK | Differential Phase Shift Keying |
| DPR | Dual Pen Recorder | | |
| DPREP | Disk Prepping | DPSM | Diode Phase Shifter Module |
| DPS | Data Polling Signal | | |
| DPS | Data Present Signal | DPSMM | Dynamically Partitioned Second Moment Model |
| DPS | Data Presentation System | | |
| DPS | Data Process Service GmbH | DPSS | Data Processing Subsystem |
| DPS | Data Processing Service | DPSS | Data Processing Switching System |
| DPS | Data Processing Standards | | |

# D

| | | | |
|---|---|---|---|
| DPSS | Data Processing System Simulator | DQM | Dormant Queue Manager |
| DPSS | Diagnostic Program Subsystem | DQV | Differenzquotientenverfahren |
| DPSS | Display Presentation Subsystem | DR | Daily Relay |
| | | DR | Damping Ratio |
| DPSS | Domain Professional Support Service | DR | Data Rate |
| | | DR | Data Re-organizer |
| DPSS | Double-Pole Snap Switch | DR | Data Reader |
| DPST | Double-Pole Single-Throw | DR | Data Reading |
| DPST SW | Double-Pole Single-Throw Switch | DR | Data Receiver |
| | | DR | Data Recognition |
| DPST-NC | Double-Pole Single-Throw Normally Closed | DR | Data Record |
| | | DR | Data Recorder |
| DPST-NO | Double-Pole Single-Throw Normally Open | DR | Data Recording |
| | | DR | Data Reduction |
| DPSW | Double-Pole Switch | DR | Data Register |
| DPT | Data Processing Technique | DR | Data Report |
| DPT | Data Processing Theory | DR | Data Requirements |
| DPT | Data Processing Time | DR | Data Research |
| DPT | Data Punched Tape | DR | Debugging Routine |
| DPT | Department | DR | Destructive Reading |
| DPT | Description Price Transmittal | DR | Diagnostic Routine |
| | | DR | Dielectric Reader |
| DPTE | Data Processing Terminal Equipment | DR | Dielectric Reading |
| | | DR | Dienst-Rechner |
| DPTS | Digital Programming Test Set | DR | Digit Reading |
| | | DR | Digital Recording |
| DPTT | Double-Pole Triple-Throw | DR | Digital Representation |
| DPTW | Double-Pedestal Typewriter | DR | Digital Resolver |
| | | DR | Digitalrechner |
| DPU | Data Processing Unit | DR | Digitalregenerator |
| DPU | Digit Pickup | DR | Diode Rectifier |
| DPU | Display Processing Unit | DR | Direct Recording |
| DPU | Display Processor Unit | DR | Disk Recorder |
| DPU | Document Processing Unit | DR | Distributor |
| DPU | Dynamic Pulse Unit | DR | Divisionsregister |
| DPVS | Digitally Programmed Voltage Source | DR | Document Reader |
| | | DR | Double Reading |
| DPWR | Data Process Work Request | DR | Draw |
| DQ | Data Quantity | DR | Drawer |
| DQ | Datenquelle | DR | Drawing |
| DQ | Decode Queue | DR | Drill Rod |
| DQ | Definite Quantity | DR | Drive |
| DQ | Dienstqualität | DR | Driver |
| DQ | Dormant Queue | DR | Drucker |
| DQ/DS | Datenquelle/-senke | DR | Dummy Record |
| DQC | Data Quality Control | DRA | Data Reproducing Apparatus |
| DQCB | Disk Queue Control Block | DRA | Dead Reckoning Analyser |
| DQCM | Data Quality Control Monitor | DRA | Digital Record Analyzer |
| | | DRA | Doppler Radar |
| DQE | Descriptor Queue Element | DRA | Double Register Arithmetic |
| DQM | Data Quality Monitors | | |
| DQM | Digital Queue Meter | DRA | Druckausgabe |
| DQM | Digital Quality Monitor | DRA | Drum Read Amplifier |

- 196 -

# D

| | | | |
|---|---|---|---|
| DRAC | Distributed Read Address Counter | DRD | Data Requirement Description |
| DRADS | Degradation of Radar Defense System | DRD | Drum Read Driver |
| DRAFT | Document Read And Format Translator | DRDE | Data Record Description Entry |
| DRAI | Dead Reckoning Analog Indicator | DRDP | Director of Radar Data Processing |
| DRAI | Dead Reckoning Analyzer Indicator | DRDS | Dynamic Reconfiguration Data Set |
| DRAM | Dynamischer RAM | DRDTO | Detection Radar Data Take-Off |
| DRAM | Dynamic Random Access Memory | DRE | Data Record Extension |
| | | DRE | Data Reduction Equipment |
| DRAMI | Digital Range Measuring Instrument | DRE | Dead Reckoning Equipment |
| | | DRE | Direct Reading Encoder |
| DRAMS | Digital Recording And Measuring System | DREAC | Drum Experimental Automatic Computer |
| DRANS | Data Reduction and Analysis Subsystem | DREBIT | Dresdner Bank - Bildschirmtext |
| DRAPE | Data Recording And Processing Equipment | DRECAM | Dresdner Bank - Cash-Management-System |
| DRAPF | Data Reduction And Processing Facility | DRED | Data Routing and Error Detector |
| DRAT | Data Reduction and Analysis Tape | DRED | Data Routing and Error Detecting |
| DRAW | Digital Read After Write disc | DREG | D Register |
| | | DREG | Data Regulation |
| | | DRELOBA | Dresdner Logik-Bausteine |
| DRAW | Direct Read After Write | DRF | Data Reporting Form |
| | | DRF | Data Requirement Form |
| DRAW | Drawing | DRG | Digital Rangeing Generator |
| DRB | Decimal Register Binary | DRGE | Druckgenerator |
| DRC | Damage Risk Criterion | DRH | Data Reading Head |
| DRC | Data Rate Changer | DRH | Digital Readout Head |
| DRC | Data Record Clause | DRI | Data Reduction Interpreter |
| DRC | Data Recording Camera | DRI | Dead Reckoning Indicator |
| DRC | Data Recording Code | DRI | Decision Relevant Information |
| DRC | Data Recording Control | | |
| DRC | Data Recovery Center | DRI | Digit Record Identification |
| DRC | Data Reduction Centre | | |
| DRC | Data Reduction Compiler | DRI... | Data Recording Instrument Co. Ltd. |
| DRC | Data Reduction Complex | | |
| DRC | Data Reduction Computer | DRID | Direct Readout Image Dissector |
| DRC | Data Regeneration Code | | |
| DRC | Data Return Capsule | DRIFT | Diagnostic Retrievable Information For Teachers |
| DRC | Data Return Code | | |
| DRC | Device Release Command | DRIFT | Diversity Receiving Instrumentation of Telemetry |
| DRC | Direct-Reaction Calculation | | |
| DRC | Document Record Card | DRILL | Direct Routing Investigation of Line Layouts |
| DRCC | Document Records Control Committee | | |
| DRCS | Dynamically Redifinable Character Set | DRIP | Data Reduction Input Program |
| DRD | Data Recording Device | DRIP | Data Reduction for Interception Program |
| DRD | Data Reduction Division | | |

# D

| | | | |
|---|---|---|---|
| DRIP | Dead Reckoning Information Processor | DRQ | Data Ready Queue |
| DRIR | Direct Readout Infrared | DRR | Data Read Register |
| DRISS | Digital Read-In Subsystem | DRR | Data Ready Reset |
| DRIT | DDR Retrieval and Indexing Terminology | DRR | Data Redundancy Reduction |
| DRJ | Data Requirements Justification | DRR | Digital Radar Relay |
| DRK | Data Record Key | DRR | Direct Reading Ratio |
| DRK | Data Request Keyboard | DRR | Direct Reading Receiver |
| DRL | Data Record Language | DRRS | Direct Reading Ratio Set |
| DRL | Data Requirement List | DRS | Data Reaction System |
| DRL | Data Requirements Language | DRS | Data Receiving Station |
| DRL | Data Retrieval Language | DRS | Data Record Skip |
| DRL | Divisional Records List | DRS | Data Recording Set |
| DRM | Data Recording Medium | DRS | Data Recording System |
| DRM | Decimal Rate Multiplier | DRS | Data Recovery System |
| DRM | Digital Range Machine | DRS | Data Reduction Software |
| DRM | Digital Ratiometer | DRS | Data Reduction System |
| DRM | Distributed Real time Multiprocessor | DRS | Data Relay Satellite |
| DRN | Data Record Name | DRS | Data Requirements Specification |
| DRN | Data Reference Number | DRS | Data Retrieval System |
| DRO | Data Re-Organizer | DRS | Datenreduktionssystem |
| DRO | Data Read-Out | DRS | Diagnostic Rework Sheet |
| DRO | Destructive Read-Only | DRS | Digital Radar Simulator |
| DRO | Destructive Read-Out | DRS | Digital Readout System |
| DRO | Digital Readout | DRS | Digital Recording System |
| DRO | Digital Readout Oscilloscope | DRS | Direct Release System |
| DRO | Doubly Resonant Oscillator | DRS | Disk Resident System |
| DROD | Delayed Readout Detector | DRS | Distributed Resource System |
| DRON | Data Reduction | DRS | Divisional Records Standard |
| DROO | Digital Read-Out Oscilloscope | DRS | Document Retrieval System |
| DROS | Data Returned from Overseas | DRS | Dry Reed Switch |
| DROS | Disk Remote Operating System | DRSA | Data Recording System Analyst |
| DROS | Disk Resident Operating System | DRSG | Digital Recorder Signal Generator |
| DRP | Data Rapid Printer | DRSR | Dresser |
| DRP | Data Reduction Procedure | DRSS | Data Relay Satellite System |
| DRP | Data Reduction Program | DRT | Data Remote Transfer |
| DRP | Dead Reckoning Plotter | DRT | Decade Ratio Transformer |
| DRP | Diebold Research Program | DRT | Device Reference Table |
| DRP | Digital Recording Process | DRT | Digital Readout Timer |
| DRP | Divisional Records Practice | DRT | Diode Recovery Tester |
| DRP | Documentation Research Project | DRT | Direct Reading Telemetering |
| DRPR | Drawing Practice | DRT | Distant Remote Transceiver |
| DRPS | Dry Reed Pushbutton Switch | DRTC | Documentation Research and Training Centre |
| | | DRTL | Diode Resistor Transistor Logic |

# D

| | | | |
|---|---|---|---|
| DRTS | Data Remote Transfer System | DS | Delimiter Statement |
| DRU | Digital Range Unit | DS | Demand Scanner |
| DRU | Drucker | DS | Descent Stage |
| DRUB | Digital Remote Unit Buffer | DS | Descriptive Statement |
| | | DS | Design Specification |
| DRUCKSY | Druckerei-System | DS | Design Standards |
| DRV | Data Recovery Vehicle | DS | Device Selector |
| DRV | Drive | DS | Dial System |
| DRVR | Driver | DS | Digit Select |
| DRW | Data Return Word | DS | Digit Selection |
| DRX | Distributed Resource Executive | DS | Digit Selector |
| | | DS | Digit Sorting |
| DRZ | Deutsches Rechenzentrum | DS | Digit Switch |
| DRZ | Direktionsrechenzentrum | DS | Digital Section |
| DRZ | Distriktrechenzentrum | DS | Digital Selection |
| DS | Danish Standard | DS | Digital Signal |
| DS | Data Sample | DS | Digital Store |
| DS | Data Scanning | DS | Digitale Schnittstelle |
| DS | Data Security | DS | Dimension Statement |
| DS | Data Segments | DS | Diode Store |
| DS | Data Selection | DS | Diode Switch |
| DS | Data Sender | DS | Diodenstufe |
| DS | Data Sequence | DS | Directing Station |
| DS | Data Series | DS | Disconnecting Switch |
| DS | Data Services | DS | Disk Station |
| DS | Data Set | DS | Disk Storage |
| DS | Data Sheet | DS | Disk Store |
| DS | Data Signal | DS | Diskretes Signal |
| DS | Data Sorter | DS | Display Statement |
| DS | Data Source | DS | Display Station |
| DS | Data Specification | DS | Display and Storage |
| DS | Data Storage | DS | Distinguishing Sequence |
| DS | Data Store | DS | Distributed Systems |
| DS | Data Stream | DS | Distribution Services |
| DS | Data Strobe | DS | Divide Statement |
| DS | Data Structure | DS | Document Spacing |
| DS | Data Symbol | DS | Dokumentation Schweiß-technik |
| DS | Data Synchronization | DS | Double Storage |
| DS | Data System | DS | Double Silk |
| DS | Datensatz | DS | Drive Scanner |
| DS | Datensenke | DS | Drive Surface |
| DS | Datenservice | DS | Drive System |
| DS | Datensichtgerät | DS | Driving Signal |
| DS | Datensichtstation | DS | Druckseite |
| DS | Datenströme | DS | Drum Storage |
| DS | Datensystem | DS | Drum Store |
| DS | Decimal Substract | DS | Dummy Statement |
| DS | Decision Symbol | DS | Durchschaltesteuerung |
| DS | Decoder Simulator | DS | Dynamic Store |
| DS | Deep Screw | DS | Dynamic Subroutine |
| DS | Define Storage | DS-SS | Direct Sequence Spread Spectrum |
| DS | Define Symbol | | |
| DS | Definition of Symbol | DS/MCP | Data Switch/Message Control Program |
| DS | Dekadenschalter | | |

# D

| | | | |
|---|---|---|---|
| DS/VSE | Decision Support/VSE | DSBDC | Double Sideband, Decreased Carrier |
| DSA | Data Systems Automation | | |
| DSA | Datenstrukturanalyse | DSBDC | Double Sideband, Diminished Carrier |
| DSA | Define Symbol Address | | |
| DSA | Demand Statement Analysis | DSBDC | Double Sideband, Discrete Carrier |
| DSA | Design Schedule Analysis | DSBEC | Double Sideband, Emitted Carrier |
| DSA | Desired Start Address | | |
| DSA | Device-Specific-Adapter | DSBK | Data Set by Key |
| DSA | Dezentrale System-architektur | DSBL | Disable |
| | | DSBLD | Disabled |
| DSA | Diffusion Self-Aligned | DSBSC | Double Sideband Suppressed Carrier |
| DSA | Digital Signal Analyzer | | |
| DSA | Direct Storage Access | DSBTC | Double Sideband Transmitted Carrier |
| DSA | Disc-Space-Accounting | | |
| DSA | Discrete Sample Analyzer | DSBWC | Double Sideband with Carrier |
| DSA | Distributed Systems Architecture | | |
| | | DSC | Data Selection Circuit |
| DSA | Drum Store Adapter | DSC | Data Set Control |
| DSA | Dynamic Signal Analyzer | DSC | Data Store Cell |
| DSA | Dynamic Storage Allocation | DSC | Data Stream Compatibility |
| | | DSC | Data Sub-Central |
| DSA | Dynamic Storage Area | DSC | Data Synchronizer Channel |
| DSA MOS | Diffusion Self-Aligned Metal-Oxide Semi-conductor | DSC | Data Synchronizing Channel |
| | | DSC | Decimal Classification System |
| DSA MOST | Diffusion Self Aligned MOS Transistor | | |
| | | DSC | Design Stability Code |
| DSABL | Disable | DSC | Differential Signal Control |
| DSAC | Data Set Authory Credential | | |
| | | DSC | Digital Setpoint Control |
| DSAF | Destination Subarea Field | DSC | Digital Signal Converter |
| | | DSC | Direct Synchronized Control |
| DSAI | Digital Solar-Aspect Indicator | | |
| | | DSC | Disk Storage Controller |
| DSAM | Direct Sequential Access Method | DSC | Disk Store Control |
| | | DSC | Double-Silk Covered |
| DSAP | Data Systems Automation Program | DSC | Drain Saturation Current |
| | | DSC | Dynamic Sequential Control |
| DSAR | Data Sampling Automatic Receiver | | |
| | | DSC | Dynamic Standby Computer |
| DSB | Data Services Bureau | DSCA | Default System Control Area |
| DSB | Data Set Block | | |
| DSB | Datensammelband | DSCAT | Data Set Catalog |
| DSB | Datenschutzbeauftragter | DSCB | Data Set Control Block |
| DSB | Datensteuerblock | DSCC | Deep Space Communications Complex |
| DSB | Decade Synchro Bridge | | |
| DSB | Device Status Byte | DSCC | Double-Silk Cotton Covered |
| DSB | Digital Storage Buffer | | |
| DSB | Distribution Switchboard | DSCCD | Discount Code |
| DSB | Double Sideband | DSCN | Discontinue |
| DSB | Dünnschichtbrücke | DSCP | Data Service Command Processor |
| DSBAMRC | Double Sideband Amplitude Modulation Reduced Carrier | | |
| | | DSCP | Disk System Control Programming |

# D

| | | | |
|---|---|---|---|
| DSCRM | Discriminator | DSEA | Data Storage Electronics Assembly |
| DSCS | Desk Side Computer System | DSECT | Dummy Control Section |
| DSCS | Digital Simulator Computer System | DSEL | Deselect |
| DSCT | Defective Sectors Table | DSELCY | Deselect Cycle |
| DSCT | Double Secondary Current Transformer | DSEMIT | Digit Selector Emitter |
| | | DSENQ | Data Set Enqueue |
| DSCU | Disk Store Control Unit | DSF | Data Scanning and Formating |
| DSD | Data Scanner Distributor | | |
| DSD | Data Set Definition | DSF | Digital Simulation Facility |
| DSD | Data Set Deletion | | |
| DSD | Data Status Display | DSF | Drum Store Function |
| DSD | Data Storage Device | DSG | Data Set Group |
| DSD | Data Systems Designator | DSG | Data Standards Group |
| DSD | Data Systems Division | DSG | Datenschutzgesetz |
| DSD | Digital System Design | DSG | Datensichtgerät |
| DSD | Disk Storage Device | DSG | Digital Signal Generator |
| DSD | Disk Store Drive | DSG | Drehstromgenerator |
| DSD | Dual Speed Drive | DSGN | Design |
| DSD | Dynamic System Display | DSGN | Designation |
| DSDD | Double Sided Double Density | DSGN | Designer |
| | | DSGs | Data-Set-Groups |
| DSDL | Distributed System Definition Language | DSI | Data Set Identifier |
| | | DSI | Data Stream Interface |
| DSDP | Data System Development Plan | DSI | Data Submitted Information |
| DSDS | Dataphone Switched Digital Service | DSI | Data System Integration |
| | | DSI | Diffusion Sélective de l'Information |
| DSDS | Document Survey Data Sheet | DSI | Digital Signal Interpolation |
| DSDT | Deformographic Storage Display Tube | DSI | Digital Speech Interpolation |
| DSDT | Discrete Space and Discrete Time | DSI | Dynamic System Interchange |
| DSE | Data Security Erase | DSIC | Demand Statement Index and Control |
| DSE | Data Set Extension | | |
| DSE | Data Set Extent | DSID | Data Set Identification |
| DSE | Data Server Element | DSIF | Deep-Space Instrumentation Facility |
| DSE | Data Storage Equipment | | |
| DSE | Data Switching Exchange | DSIR | Department of Scientific Industrial Research |
| DSE | Data Systems Engineering | | |
| DSE | Datensicherungs- einrichtung | DSK | Delay Shift Keying |
| | | DSK | Direkter Speicherkanal |
| DSE | Datensystementwicklung | DSK | Diskette |
| DSE | Détection Séquentielle d'Evènements | DSKY | Display System Keyboard |
| | | DSKY | Display and Keyboard |
| DSE | Digit Selector Emitter | DSL | Data Services Laboratory |
| DSE | Digital Shaft Encoder | DSL | Data Set Label |
| DSE | Distributed Systems Environment | DSL | Data Simulation Language |
| DSE | Document Spacing Error | DSL | Data Specifications Library |
| DSE | Domain Software Environment | | |
| | | DSL | Deep Scattering Layer |
| DSE | Drucksteuereinheit | DSL | Design-Language |

# D

| | | | |
|---|---|---|---|
| DSL | Development Support Library | DSNX | Distributed System Node Executive |
| DSL | Digital Simulation Language | DSO | Data Set Optimizer |
| | | DSO | Data Store Organization |
| DSL | Direct Swift Link | DSO | Digital Storage Oscilloscope |
| DSL | Divisional Systems List | | |
| DSLO | Distributed Systems License Option | DSO | Digitale Speicher-Oszilloskope |
| DSM | Data Service Manager | DSO | Direct System Output |
| DSM | Data Specification Methodology | DSO | Display Switching Oscilloscope |
| DSM | Data Storage Memory | DSORG | Data Set Organization |
| DSM | Data Structure Manipulator | DSP | Data Service Partition |
| DSM | Delta-Sigma Modulator | DSP | Data Store Position |
| DSM | Demand Statement Manipulation | DSP | Dateispiegel |
| | | DSP | Datenspeicher |
| DSM | Deterministic State Machine | DSP | Datensystemplanung |
| | | DSP | Device Stop |
| DSM | Digital Simulation Model | DSP | Digital Schnell-Programmierbar |
| DSM | Direction of Systems Management | | |
| | | DSP | Digital Signal Processing |
| DSM | Disk Sort/Merge | DSP | Digital Signal Processor |
| DSM | Disk Space Management | DSP | Digital Strip Printer |
| DSM | Disk Space Manager | DSP | Disassemble Sequence Parameter |
| DSM | Dynamic Scattering Mode | | |
| DSM | Dynamic Storage Mechanism | DSP | Display |
| | | DSP | Distributed System Program |
| DSMG | Designated Systems Management Group | DSP | Distribution System Program |
| DSMT | Dual-Speed Magnetic Transducer | DSP | Documentation Standards Package |
| DSN | Data Set Name | DSP | Double-Silver Plated |
| DSN | Data Set Number | DSP | Drain-Source Protected |
| DSN | Data Systems News | DSP | Drive Sample Pulse |
| DSN | Data-Smoothing Network | DSP | Dynamic Serial Program |
| DSN | Datensatzname | DSP | Dynamic Support Program |
| DSN | Deep Space Network | DSPAR | Distributed System Partition |
| DSN | Descriptive Supplement Number | | |
| | | DSPE | Data Set Pointer Entry |
| DSN | Distributed Network System | DSPL | Datensichtplatz |
| | | DSPLY | Display |
| DSN | Distributed Systems Network | DSPM | Displacement |
| | | DSPMT | Displacement |
| DSN/DS | DSN/Distributed Systems | DSPN | Disposition |
| DSN/IMF | DSN/Interactive Mainframe Facility | DSPNAME | Dynamic Support Program Name |
| DSN/INP | DSN/Intelligent Network Processor | DSPS | Digital Signal Processing System |
| DSN/MRJE | DSN/Multi-leaving Remote Job Entry | DSPS | Dynamic Serial Program Structure |
| DSN/MTS | DSN/Multipoint Terminal Software | DSQD | Double Sided Quad Density |
| | | DSR | Data Scanning and Routing |
| DSN/RJE | DSN/Remote Job Entry | DSR | Data Set Ready |
| DSNT | Data Set Name Table | DSR | Data Set Register |

# D

| | | | |
|---|---|---|---|
| DSR | Data Specification Request | DSS | Digital Storage System |
| DSR | Data Survey Report | DSS | Digital Subset |
| DSR | Data Word Register | DSS | Digital Subsystem |
| DSR | Datensammelrechner | DSS | Digital Switching Subsystem |
| DSR | Datensammelregister | | |
| DSR | Datenstationsrechner | DSS | Direct Station Selection |
| DSR | Device Status Report | DSS | Disc Storage Subsystem |
| DSR | Diagnostic Shift Register | DSS | Disc Subsystem |
| DSR | Digit Storage Relay | DSS | Disk Storage System |
| DSR | Digital Stepping Recorder | DSS | Disk Support System |
| DSR | Direct Stage Recorder | DSS | Display Subsystem |
| DSR | Discriminating Selector Repeater | DSS | Distributed Satellite Software |
| DSR | Dispositionssteuerrechner | DSS | Distributed System Satellite |
| DSR | Distributed State Response | DSS | Distribution System Simulator |
| DSR | Druckstreifenregistrierbaustein | DSS | Drum Storage System |
| | | DSS | Drum Store System |
| DSR | Dual Shift Right | DSS | Dynamic Steady State |
| DSR | Dynamic Status Recording | DSS | Dynamic Support System |
| DSR | Dynamic Storage Relocation | DSS | Dynamic Systems Synthesizer |
| DSR | Dynamic Storage Report | DSSB | Data Selection and Storage Buffer |
| DSRB | Data Services Request Block | DSSB | Double-Single Sideband |
| DSRC | Double-Sideband Reduced Carrier | DSSC | Double Sideband Suppressed Carrier |
| DSRI | Data Set to Record Interface | DSSC | Double-Silk Single-Cotton |
| DSRN | Data Set Reference Number | DSSM | Digital Signal Sinusodial Modulation |
| DSRS | Data Signalling Rate Select | DSSM | Dynamic Sequencing and Segmentation Model |
| DSRS | Direct Scope Recording System | DSSN | Data Set Serial Number |
| DSS | Data Sampling System | DST | Data Segment Table |
| DSS | Data Selection System | DST | Data Service Task |
| DSS | Data Set Security | DST | Data Summary Tape |
| DSS | Data Specification System | DST | Data Systems Test |
| | | DST | Datenstation |
| DSS | Data Storage Subsystem | DST | Destination |
| DSS | Data Storage System | DST | Device Service Task |
| DSS | Data Systems Specification | DST | Digital Subscriber Terminal |
| DSS | Daten-Sofortauskunftssystem | DST | Direct Satellite Terminal |
| DSS | Datensammelsystem | DST | Discrete Slant Transform |
| DSS | Datensichtstation | DST | Dünnschichttransistor |
| DSS | Datenspeicher Statistik | DSTB | Datastrobe |
| DSS | Decision Support System | DSTC | Distance |
| DSS | Development Support System | DSTC | Double Sideband Transmitted Carrier |
| DSS | Digital Signal Synchronizer | DSTCD | District Code |
| | | DSTE | Data Subscriber Terminal Equipment |
| DSS | Digital Simulator System | DSTL | Digital Summation Threshold Logic |

# D

| | | | |
|---|---|---|---|
| DSTN | Destination | DT | Demande de Transfer |
| DSTP | Data Self Test Program | DT | Depletiontransistor |
| DSTPR | Dezentrales Steuer- programm | DT | Device Trigger |
| | | DT | Device Triggering |
| DSTR | Distort | DT | Dialling Tone |
| DSTR | Distribution | DT | Difference Threshold |
| DSTR | Distributor | DT | Differential Time |
| DSTS | Desk Side Time Shared | DT | Digit Track |
| DSU | Data Sequentializer Unit | DT | Digital Technique |
| DSU | Data Service Unit | DT | Digital Transmitter |
| DSU | Data Storage Unit | DT | Diode-Transistor |
| DSU | Data Synchronization Unit | DT | Disk Tape |
| DSU | Data Synchronizer Unit | DT | Disk to Tape |
| DSU | Daten-Service und Unter- nehmensberatungen GmbH | DT | Display Terminal |
| | | DT | Document Terminator |
| DSU | Decoder Switching Unit | DT | Documentation Terminology |
| DSU | Deskewing Synchronizer Unit | DT | Dokumentations- Terminologie |
| DSU | Device Switching Unit | | |
| DSU | Digital Service Unit | DT | Double-Throw switch |
| DSU | Digital-Stochastik- Umsetzer | DT | Double Track |
| | | DT | Double-Throw |
| DSU | Disk Storage Unit | DT/RSS | Data Transmission/ Recording Subsystem |
| DSU | Disk Store Unit | | |
| DSU | Disk Synchronizer Unit | DTA | Data |
| DSU | Drum Storage Unit | DTA | Datenträgeraustausch |
| DSV | Datensofortverarbeitung | DTA | Diagnosetestablauf |
| DSW | Data Status Word | DTA | Differenz-Thermoanalyse |
| DSW | Device Status Word | DTAARA | Data Area |
| DSW | Drum Switch | DTARS | Digital Transmission And Routing System |
| DSWR | Datenverarbeitung im Steuerwesen, in der Wirtschaft und im Rechtswesen | DTAS | Data Transmission And Switching |
| | | DTAS | Digital Transmission And Switching |
| DSX | Distributed Systems Executive | DTASI | Digital Time Assignment Speech Interpolation |
| DT | Data | | |
| DT | Data Tape | DTB | Decimal-To-Binary |
| DT | Data Technique | DTC | Data Transmission Channel |
| DT | Data Telecommunication | DTC | Decision Threshold Computer |
| DT | Data Terminal | | |
| DT | Data Text | DTC | Desk Top Computer |
| DT | Data Track | DTC | Digital Tape Conversion |
| DT | Data Transducer | DTC | Digital to Tone Converter |
| DT | Data Transfer | DTC | Document Transformation Component |
| DT | Data Translator | | |
| DT | Data Transmission | DTCP | Diode-Transistor Compound Pair |
| DT | Data Transmitter | | |
| DT | Datentechnik | DTCR | Data Transfer and Certification Record |
| DT | Datenteil | | |
| DT | Datenträger | DTCS | Data Transmission and Control System |
| DT | Decay Time | | |
| DT | Decision Table | DTCS | Digital-Tests Command System |
| DT | Decision Time | | |
| DT | Dedicated Terminal | DTD | Data Transfer Device |

# D

| | | | |
|---|---|---|---|
| DTDS | Digital Television Display System | DTL | Diode Transistor Logic |
| DTE | Data Ten to Eleven | DTL | Dioden-Transistor-Logik |
| DTE | Data Terminal Equipment | DTL | Direct-To-Line |
| DTE | Data Transmission Equipment | DTL | Disburse To Location |
| DTE | Data Transmission Exchange | DTL | Double Transistor Logic |
| | | DTL-DTL | Detail-to-Detail |
| DTE | Data Transmitting Equipment | DTL-HDG | Detail-to-Heading |
| | | DTLS | Digital Television Lightware System |
| DTE | Datenträger-Erzeuger | DTLZ | Diode Transistor Logic Z |
| DTE | Digital Television Encoder | DTLZ | Diode Transistor Logic with Z-effect |
| DTE | Digital Tune Enable | | |
| DTE | Display Tester Element | DTLZ | Dioden-Transistor-Logik mit Z Diode |
| DTE... | Deutsche Télémécanique GmbH | DTLZD | Diode Transistor Logic with Zener Diodes |
| DTENT | Date of Entry | DTM | Delay Timer Multiplier |
| DTES | Datenträger-Eingabestation | DTM | Digital Talk-out Module |
| DTF | Data Transmission Factor | DTM | Digital Television Monitor |
| DTF | Data Transmission Feature | DTM | Display Time |
| DTF | Data Transmission Function | DTM | Duration Time Modulation |
| | | DTM | Dynamic Transient Master control block |
| DTF | Dateidefinition | | |
| DTF | Define The File | DTMF | Dual-Tone Multifrequency |
| DTF | Deterministic Transfer Function | DTMN | Datamation |
| | | DTMS | Data base and Transaction Management System |
| DTFA | Digital Transfer Function Analyzer | DTMS | Digital Test Measurement System |
| DTFCD | Define The File for Card Device | DTMS | Digital Test Monitor System |
| DTFDA | Define The File for Direct Access | DTMS | Digital Test Monitoring System |
| DTFDI | Define The File for Device Independent | DTO | Data Take-Off |
| | | DTO | Disburse-To-Order |
| DTFIS | Define The File for Indexed Sequential | DTO | Dollar Trade-Off |
| | | DTOL | Digital Test Oriented Language |
| DTFMT | Define The File for Magnetic Tape | DTP | Data Tape Punch |
| DTFPR | Define The File for Printer | DTP | Directory Tape Processor |
| | | DTP | Discrete Transient Protection |
| DTFSD | Define The File for Sequential DASD | DTP | Dolph Tchebyscheff Pattern |
| DTG | Data Time Group | DTP | Drum Timing Pulse |
| DTG | Display Transmission Generator | DTPA | Dynamic Transient Pool Area |
| DTH | Dialogtesthilfe | DTPD | Divider Time Pulse Distributor |
| DTI | Data Team International | | |
| DTI | Digital Test Indicator | DTPL | Domain Tip Propagation Logic |
| DTI | Display Terminal Interchange | DTPM | Dynamic Transient Pool Management |
| DTI | Distortion Transmission Impairment | DTPMT | Date of Payment |
| DTIP | Digital Tune In Progress | DTR | Daily Transaction Reporting |
| DTL | Data Transistor Logic | | |
| DTL | Detail | | |

# D

| | | | | |
|---|---|---|---|---|
| DTR | Data Tape Reader | | DTU | Data Transmission Unit |
| DTR | Data Tape Recorder | | DTU | Digital Tape Unit |
| DTR | Data Telemetering Register | | DTU | Digital Telemetry Unit |
| | | | DTU | Digital Time Unit |
| DTR | Data Telemetry Register | | DTU | Digital Transmission Unit |
| DTR | Data Terminal Ready | | DTU | Digital Tuning Unit |
| DTR | Data Transfer Rate | | DTU | Display Terminal Unit |
| DTR | Definite Time Relay | | DTUA | Data Transmission Unit Außenstelle |
| DTR | Demand Totalyzing Relay | | | |
| DTR | Dielectric Tape Reading | | DTUOC | Digital Tire Uniformity Optimizer Computer |
| DTR | Digital Tape Recorder | | | |
| DTR | Digital Telemetering Register | | DTUTF | Digital Tape Unit Test Facility |
| DTR | Disposable Tape Reel | | DTUZ | Data Transmission Unit Zentrale |
| DTR | Distribution Tape Real | | | |
| DTRCT | Date of Receipt | | DTV | Datenträger-Verarbeitung |
| DTRM | Determine | | DTV | Digital Television |
| DTRN | Direction des Télécommunications du Résau National | | DTV | Durchschnittlicher Täglicher Verkehr |
| | | | DTVC | Digital Transmission and Verification Converter |
| DTS | Data Terminal Screen | | | |
| DTS | Data Terminal Systems | | | |
| DTS | Data Test Station | | DTVM | Differential Thermocouple Voltmeter |
| DTS | Data Transfer Sequence | | | |
| DTS | Data Transfer System | | DTVM | Digital Time and Voltage Module |
| DTS | Data Transmission Service | | | |
| DTS | Data Transmission Subsystem | | DTY CY | Duty Cycle |
| | | | DU | Data Unit |
| DTS | Data Transmission System | | DU | Datenumsetzer |
| DTS | Diagnostic and Test System | | DU | Digital Unit |
| | | | DU | Disk Unit |
| DTS | Dielectric Tape Scanning | | DU | Dump |
| DTS | Digital Telemetering System | | DÜ | Datenübertrager |
| | | | DÜ | Datenübertragung |
| DTS | Double-Throw Switch | | DÜ | Datenfernübertragung |
| DTS | Dynamic Transient Segment register save | | DÜ | Differentialübertrager |
| | | | DÜ | Differenzübertrager |
| DTSC | Drum Test Self Check | | DÜ | Direktübertragung |
| DTSG | Data Transmission Study Group | | DÜ-AL | Datenübertragung-Anschlußleitung |
| DTSS | Dartmouth Time-Sharing System | | DÜ-Netz | Datenübermittlungsnetz |
| | | | DUA | Device Unit Address |
| DTT | Data Transmission Technique | | DUA | Digitronics Users Association |
| DTT | Data Transmission Terminal | | DUAL | Data Use and Access Laboratories |
| DTT | Defective Tracks Table | | | |
| DTT | Domain Tip Technology | | DUAL | Dynamic Universal Assembly Language |
| DTTL | Data Transition Tracking Loop | | | |
| | | | DUART | Dual Universal Asynchronous Receiver/Transmitter |
| DTTU | Data Transmission Terminal Unit | | | |
| DTU | Data Telecommunication Unit | | DUBA | Durchlaufzeit- Und Bestandsanalyse |
| | | | DUC | Data Utilization Console |
| DTU | Data Transfer Unit | | DUC | Defined User Command |
| DTU | Data Transformation Unit | | | |

# D

| | | | |
|---|---|---|---|
| DUCE | Denied-Usage Channel Evaluator | DUS | Diagnostic Utility System |
| DUCO | Duplex-Controller | DÜS | Datenübermittlungssystem |
| DUCS | Display Unit Control System | DÜS | Datenübertragungssystem |
| DUCY | Duty Cycle | DUSP | Datenerfassungs- Und Speicherprogramm |
| DUE | Datenübertragung | | |
| DUE | Datenübertragungseinrichtung | DÜST | Datenübertragungssteuereinheit |
| DÜE | Datenübertragungseinheit | DUST | Datenübertragungssteuerung |
| DÜE | Datenübertragungseinrichtung | DÜST | Datenübertragungssteuerung |
| DUET | Datenübertragungsterminal | | |
| DUET | Dual Emitter Transistor | DUST | Datenumsetzerstelle |
| DUF | Diffusion Under Field | DÜSTA | Datenübertragungssteuerung für Außenstationen |
| DUF | Diffusion Under Film | | |
| DUFLE | Digital Universal Fault Locating Equipment | DUSTA | Datenübertragungssteuerung für Außenstationen |
| DUG | Digitales Umschaltgerät | | |
| DÜGO | Datenübertragungsgebührenordnung | DUSTA | Duty Station |
| DUH | Data Upper Half-byte | DUT | Device Under Test |
| DUI | Duration of Unscheduled Interruptions | DUT | Diplôme Universitaire de Technologie |
| DUL | Design Ultimate Load | DUTAP | Decodier- und Textausgabeprogramm |
| DUMPGEN | Dump Generation | | |
| DUN | Data Users Note | DUV | Data Under Voice |
| DÜN | Datenübermittlungsnetz | DÜV | Datenübertragungs- und Vermittlungssystem |
| DUNMIRE | Dundee University Numerical Methods Information Retrieval Experiment | DÜV | Datenübertragungs- und Verteiler-System |
| | | DÜV | Datenüberwachung und -Verteilung |
| DUNS | Data Universal Numbering System | DÜVO | Datenübermittlungsverordnung |
| DUO | Datatron Users Organization | DÜVO | Datenübertragungsverordnung |
| DÜO | Datenübertragungsordnung | | |
| DUP | Data User Part | DUX | Data Utility complex |
| DUP | Datenübertragungsprozessor | DV | Data Volume |
| | | DV | Datenverarbeitung |
| DUP | Disk Utility Program | DV | Decimal Value |
| DUP | Dump Utility Program | DV | Device |
| DUP | Duplex | DV | Differential Voltage |
| DUP | Duplicate | DV | Digital Video |
| DUP | Duplicating | DV | Direct Voltage |
| DUP | Duplication | DV | Divisor |
| DUPC | Displayed Under Program Control | DV | Double Vibration |
| | | DV | Druckvermerk |
| DUPL | Duplicate | DV | Druckvorschrift |
| DUPL | Duplication | DV | Dummy Variable |
| DUPLI | Duplicate | DV-AH | Datenverarbeitung Außer Haus |
| DUR | Duration | | |
| DURA | Duration | DV-FK | DV-Führungskraft |
| DUS | Data User Station | DV-OLFU | Datenverarbeitung On-Line Feldunterstützung |
| DUS | Data Utilization Station | | |

# D

| | | | |
|---|---|---|---|
| DVA | Data Valid | DVP | Data Validation Program |
| DVA | Datenverarbeitungsanlage | DVP | Datenverarbeitungsperipherie |
| DVA | Donnée Validée | | |
| DVB | Datenvertriebsbüro | DVP | Divide or Proceed |
| DVB | Device Base control block | DVR | Daten Vertriebsrechenzentrum |
| DVB | Digital Video Bandwidth | | |
| DVBST | Direct-View Bistable Storage Tube | DVR | Datenverarbeitung im Recht |
| DVC | Device | DVR | Datenverarbeitungsvorrechner |
| DVC | Digital Voice Communication | DVR | Divisor |
| DVCDN | Device down | DVS | Daten-Verbundsystem |
| DVCND | Device down Command | DVS | Datenverarbeitung Sindelfingen |
| DVCO | Dual Voltage Controlled Oscillator | DVS | Datenverarbeitungsstation |
| DVCUP | Device up | DVS | Datenverarbeitungsstelle |
| DVD | Datenverarbeitung Distrikt | DVS | Datenverarbeitungssystem |
| | | DVS | Datenvermittlungssystem |
| DVD | Datenverarbeitungsdienst | DVS | Datev-Verbundsystem |
| | | DVS | Digital Voltage Source |
| DVD | Detail Velocity Display | DVS | Digitales Vermittlungssystem |
| DVD | Direct-View Device | | |
| DVD | Dividend | DVS | Durchschalteverbindungsspeicher |
| DVDS | Digital Video Display System | | |
| | | DVS | Dynamic Vertical Sensor |
| DVE | Datenverarbeitungseinrichtung | DVS-NW | Datenvermittlungssystem Nordrhein-Westfalen |
| DVE | Device End | DVSINIT | Device Session Initialization |
| DVET | Data Vetting program | | |
| DVFO | Digital Variable Frequency Oscillator | DVST | Datenvermittlungsstelle |
| | | DVST | Daylight Viewing Storage Tube |
| DVG | Datenverarbeitungsgesellschaft | | |
| | | DVST | Direct View bistable Storage Tube |
| DVH | Divide or Halt | | |
| DVI | Datenverarbeitungsinstitut | DVST | Direct-View Storage Tube |
| DVIA | Dual Video Adapter | DVST-L | Datenvermittlungsstelle - Leitung |
| DVK | Datenverarbeitungskomplex | | |
| | | DVST-L | Datenvermittlungsstelle mit Leitungsvermittlung |
| DVK ETW | Datenverarbeitungskomplex Ersatzteilwirtschaft | | |
| | | DVST-P | Datenvermittlungsstelle mit Paketvermittlung |
| DVL | Datenverbundleitung | DVT | Datenverteiler |
| DVLP | Develop | DVT | Device Vector Table |
| DVM | Digital Voltmeter | DVT | Dynamic Velocity Taper |
| DVM | Digitalvoltmeter | DVTK | Datenverarbeitungsteilkomplex |
| DVM | Discrete Variational Method | | |
| | | DVTL | Dovetail |
| DVMD | Digital Voltmeter Display | DVTP | Divide Time Pulse |
| DVMS | Digital Voice Messaging System | DVTVM | Digital Vacuum Tube Voltmeter |
| DVN | Division | DVV | Datenverarbeitung in Versicherungsunternehmen |
| DVO | Decimal Voltage Output | | |
| DVOM | Digital Volt-Ohmmeter | DVW | Datenverarbeitungs-Wirtschaftlichkeitsberechnungen |
| DVOR | Doppler VHF Omnidirectional Radio range | | |

# D

| | | | | |
|---|---|---|---|---|
| DVX | Digital Voice Exchange | | DXT | Data Extract |
| DVZ | Datenverarbeitungs- zentrum | | DY | Day |
| | | | DY | Dynode |
| DW | Data Word | | DYCMOS | Dynamic CMOS |
| DW | Device Wait | | DYDAT | Dynamische Daten |
| DW | Doppelwort | | DYDE | Dynamische Debugger |
| DW | Double Word | | DYN | Dynamic |
| DW | Drop Wire | | DYN | Dyne |
| DW | Druckwerk | | DYNA | Dynamics Analyzer- programmer |
| DW | Drum Write | | | |
| DW | Durchwahl | | DYNAM | Dynamic |
| DW SU Cy | Data Word Set-Up Cycle | | DYNAMO | Dynamic Allocation Model |
| DWA | Double Word Address | | DYNAMO | Dynamic Modeller |
| DWAC | Distributed Write Address Counter | | DYNAMO-S | Dynamic Modeller- Simulator |
| DWASUCY | Data Word A Setup Cycle | | DYNASAR | Dynamic Systems Analyzer |
| DWC | Data Word Cycle | | DYNATERM | Dynamische Auftrags- Terminierung |
| DWCS | Data Word Cycles | | | |
| DWD | Data Word | | DYNDADIS | Dynamic Data Display System |
| DWD | Drum Write Drive | | | |
| DWDCTR | Drum Word Counter | | DYNSYS | Dynamics Systems Simulator |
| DWE | Digitale Wahleinheit | | | |
| DWE | Dokumentation, Werbung, Edukation | | DYPOL | Dynamic Planning Of Liquidity |
| DWEL | Discrete Wire Equivalence List | | DYPS | Dynamisches Programmier- system |
| DWF | Data Word Format | | DYSAC | Digitally Simulated Analog Computer |
| DWF | Disk Work File | | | |
| DWG | Drawing | | DYSAC | Dynamic Storage Analog Computer |
| DWI | Descriptive Word Index | | | |
| DWI | Descriptor Word Index | | DYSTAC | Dynamic Storage Analog Computer |
| DWL | Data Word Length | | | |
| DWL | Dominant Wavelength | | DYSTAC | Dynamic-memory and Storage Analog Computer |
| DWM | Dioden-Widerstands-Matrix | | | |
| DWN | Down | | DYSTAL | Dynamic Storage Allocation |
| DWN | Durchwahlnummer | | | |
| DWR | Data Write Register | | DYSTAL | Dynamic Storage Allocation Language |
| DWR | Digital Wired Recorder | | | |
| DWS | Dynamic Work Storage | | DYSYS | Digital Dynamic System Simulator |
| DWSS | Double Wiper Slide Switch | | | |
| DWT | Discrete Walsh Transform | | DZ | Datenzentrale |
| DWTRFCY | Data Word Transfer Cycle | | DZ | Decimal Zoned |
| DX | Differential Crosstalk | | DZ | Dezimalzähler |
| DX | Distant | | DZ | Direkte Zugriffsmethode |
| DX | Duplex | | DZA | Dezentrale Abfrageeinheit |
| DX-L | Datexnetz mit Leitungs- vermittlung | | DZB | Datenzwischenbänder |
| | | | DZK | Durchlaufzeitkarten |
| DX-P | Datexnetz mit Paket- vermittlung | | DZR | Digitales Zeitrelais |
| | | | DZT | Digit Zero Trigger |
| DXAM | Distributed indexed Access Method | | DZTL | Diode Z Transistor Logic |
| | | | DZTL | Dioden-Z-Dioden- Transistor-Logik |
| DXC | Data Exchange Control | | | |
| DXP | Dynamic Extended Pathing | | DZW | Dokumentationszentrale Wasser |
| DXS | Data Exchange System | | | |

# E

| | | | |
|---|---|---|---|
| E | Echo | EAL | Expected Average Life |
| E | Eingabe | EAL... | Electronic Associates Ltd. |
| E | Emitter | EALM | Electronically Addressed Light Modulator |
| E | Energy | | |
| E | Entry | EAM | Einseitenband-Amplitudenmodulation |
| E-B | Emitter-Basis | | |
| E-IGFET | Enhancement Insulated Gate Field-Effect Transistor | EAM | Electric Adding Machine |
| | | EAM | Electric Addition Mechanism |
| E-IGFET | Equivalent Insulated Gate Field-Effect Transistor | EAM | Electrical Accounting Machine |
| E-JFET | Enhancement Mode Junction FET | EAM | Electrically Alterable Memory |
| E-O | Even-Odd | EAM | Electromechanic Accounting Machine |
| E-PROM | Erasable PROM | | |
| E/A | Eingabe/Ausgabe | EAM | Electronic Accounting Machine |
| E/A SVC | E/A Supervisor Call | | |
| E/A-T | Ein-/Ausgabeterminal | EAM | Electronic Automatic Machine |
| E/D MOSFET | Enhancement/Depletion MOSFET | EAM | Elementary Access Method |
| E/S | Entrée/Sortie | EAM | Evanescent Access Method |
| E/S TIEP | Engineering/Service Test and Independent Evaluation Program | EAN | Europäische Artikel Numerierung |
| | | EAN | Europäische Artikel-nummer |
| E/S3 | Engineering/Scientific Support System | EAN | European Article Number |
| E/Z | Equal Zero | | |
| EA | Effective Address | EAN | European Article Numbering |
| EA | Ein-/Ausgabe | | |
| EA | Einzelanschluss | EANDC | European-American Nuclear Data Center |
| EA | Entrée Accumulateur | | |
| EA | Entscheidungsanalyse | EANDRO | Electrically Alterable Non-Destructive Read-Out |
| EA | Equalizing line Amplifier | | |
| EA | Extended Address | | |
| EAA | Engineer and Architecture Association | EANS | European Article Numbering System |
| EAC | End Around Carry | EAO | Eingabe-Ausgabe-Operation |
| EACC | Error Adaptive Control Computer | EAO | Eingabe-Ausgabe-Organisation |
| EACD | Ein-Ausgabecodierer | | |
| EACW | Ein-Ausgabecodewandler | EAO | Enseignement Assisté par Ordinateur |
| EAE | Ein-/Ausgabeeinheit | | |
| EAE | Extended Arithmetic Element | EAO | Ensenanza Asistida por Ordenator |
| EAF | Electron Arc Furnance | EAP | Ein-/Ausgabeprogramm |
| EAG | End of Area Group | EAP | Ein-/Ausgabeprozessor |
| EAG | Equipment Advisory Group | EAP | Ein-/Ausgabepuffer |
| EAI | Electronic-Aided Instruction | EAP | Emulatoranschluß-programm |
| EAI... | Electronic Associates Inc. | EAP | Etude Analyse Programmation |
| EAK | Eingabe-Ausgabe-Kanal | | |
| EAKS | Ein/Ausgabe Kontroll-System | EAPG | Eingangsarbeitsplatzgruppe |
| | | EAR | Effective Address Register |
| EAL | Electromagnetic Amplifying Lens | EAR | Ein-/Ausgaberegister |
| | | EAR | Electronic Analog Resolver |

# E

| | | | |
|---|---|---|---|
| EAR | Electronic Audio Recognition | EASE | Engineering Automatic System for Solving Equations |
| EAR | Electronic Aural Responder | | |
| EAR | Elektronischer Analogrechner | EASIAC | Easy Instruction Automatic Computer |
| EAR | Elementauswahlregister | EASL | Engineering Analysis and Simulation Language |
| EAR | Error Analysis Routine | | |
| EARL | Easy Access Report Language | EASP | Einfache Anweisungssprache |
| EARL | Electronically Accessible Russian Lexicon | EAST | Eingabe-Ausgabe-Steuerung |
| EARL | Extended Algorithmic "R" Language | EASY | Early Acquisition System |
| | | EASY | Efficient Assembly System |
| EARN | European Academic and Research Network | EASY | Engine Analyzer System |
| | | EASY | Engineering Analysis System |
| EAROM | Electrically Alterable Read Only Memory | EASY | Exchange Assembly System |
| EAROM | Electronically Alterable Read Only Memory | EASYPERS | Erfassungs- und Auswertungssystem von Personaldaten |
| EAROS | Electrically Alterable Read Only Store | EAT | Ein-/Ausgabeeinheit-Tester |
| EARP | Equipment Allowance Revision Program | EAT | Elektronisches Arbeitstagebuch |
| EARRVI | Exchange in Array Rows Row Values according to Indices | EAT | Encoder Address Translator |
| | | EAT | Environmental Acceptance Test |
| EARS | Environmental Analog Recording System | EAT | Expected Approach Time |
| EAS | Educational Analog Simulator | EATZ | Elektronische, Automatische Telefonzentrale |
| EAS | Eingabe-Ausgabe-Steuersystem | EAU | Erase All Unprotected |
| | | EAU | Extended Arithmetic Unit |
| EAS | Eingabe-Ausgabe-Steuerung | EAW | Eingabe-Ausgabe-Werk |
| | | EAW | Eingabeauswahl |
| EAS | Eingabe/Ausgabesystem | EAW | Equivalent Average Word |
| EAS | Electron Accelerator System | EAWKR | Eingabeauswahlknotenregister |
| EAS | Electronic Accounting System | EAWR | Eingabeauswahlregister |
| | | EAX | Electronic Automatic Exchange |
| EAS | Electronic Automatic Switch | EAZ | EDV-Ausbildungszentrum |
| EAS | End-Around Shift | EAZ | Elektronische Abrechnungszentrale |
| EAS | Error Analysis Study | | |
| EAS | Extended Area Service | EB | Eingangsblock |
| EASAMS | Elliot Automation Space and Advanced Military System | EB | Einseitenband |
| | | EB | Electron Beam |
| | | EB | Elément Binaire |
| EASE | Electrical Automatic Support Equipment | EB | Elementary Block |
| | | EB | Emitter-Base |
| EASE | Electronic Airborne Systems Evaluator | EB | Encoder Buffer |
| | | EB | End Bracket |
| EASE | Electronic Analog and Simulation Equipment | EB | Erase Bit |
| | | EB | Erasing Bit |
| EASE | Encoder for Algorithmic Syntactic English | EB | Eröffnungsbilanz |
| | | EB | Event Block |

# E

| | | | |
|---|---|---|---|
| EB | Externes Befehlssignal | EBMF | Electron Beam Micro-fabricator |
| EB-ROM | Extended Bit ROM | | |
| EBA | Einzelblattablage | EBP | Etch-Back Process |
| EBAM | Electron Beam Accessed Memory | EBPA | Electron Beam Parametric Amplifier |
| EBAM | Electron Beam Addressed Memory | EBQ | Economic Batch Quantity |
| | | EBR | Electron Beam Readout |
| EBB | Extra Best Best | EBR | Electron Beam Recorder |
| EBC | Electronic Batch Control | EBR | Electron Beam Recording |
| EBC | Externer Bildschirmtext-Computer | EBR | Electron Beam Remelting |
| | | EBR | Epoxy Bridge Rectifier |
| EBCD | Extended Binary Coded Decimal | EBR | Experimental Breeder Reactor |
| EBCDI | Extended Binary Coded Decimal Interchange | EBS | Echtzeitbetriebssystem |
| | | EBS | Eingabebaugruppe Steuerung |
| EBCDIC | Extended Binary Coded Decimal Interchange Code | EBS | Electric Backing Store |
| | | EBS | Electron Beam Scanlaser |
| EBCDS | Extended Binary Coded Decimals | EBS | Electron Beam System |
| | | EBS | Elektronische Blockstelle |
| EBCM | Extended Boundary Condition Method | EBS | Energy Band Structure |
| | | EBS | External Bulk Store |
| EBD | Empfangsbezugsdämpfung | EBT | Electron Beam Technique |
| EBD | Equivalent Binary Digit | EBT | Emitter Ballast Transistor |
| EBDA | Eingabe Bewegungsdatei | EBU | European Broadcasting Union |
| EBDNS | Empfangsbezugsdämpfung des Nationalen Systems | | |
| | | EBW | Electron Beam Welding |
| EBE | Einheitliches Betriebsereignis | EBW | Exploding Bridge Wire |
| | | EC | Earth Current |
| EBES | Electron Beam Exposure System | EC | Edge Connector |
| | | EC | Editing Character |
| EBG | Electronics Buyer's Guide | EC | Editor Compiler |
| EBI | Elektronisches Besucher-Informationssystem | EC | Electric Calculator |
| | | EC | Electric Control |
| EBI | Equivalent Background Input | EC | Electric Current |
| | | EC | Electrical Conductivity |
| EBIC | Electron Beam Induced Current | EC | Electrical Conductor |
| | | EC | Electromechanical Computer |
| EBICON | Electron Bombardmend Induced Conductivity | EC | Electron Coupled |
| EBIS | Encyclopedia of Business Information Sources | EC | Electron Coupling |
| | | EC | Electronic Calculator |
| EBIT | Electron Beam Injection Transistor | EC | Electronic Computer |
| | | EC | Electronic Conductivity |
| EBK | Eröffnungsbilanzkonto | EC | Electronic Counter |
| EBL | Electron Beam Lithography | EC | Emulator Control |
| EBM | Early-Break-Make | EC | Enamel Covered |
| EBM | Einseitenbandmodulation | EC | Encode |
| EBM | Electric Backing Memory | EC | End Carry |
| EBM | Electric Billing Machine | EC | Ending Character |
| EBM | Electric Buffer Memory | EC | Engineering Change |
| EBM | Electron Beam Melting | EC | Engineering Construction |
| EBM | Electron Beam Multiplier | EC | Engineering Corps |
| EBMD | Electron Beam Mode Discharger | EC | Environment Condition |
| | | EC | Equipment Check |

# E

| | | | |
|---|---|---|---|
| EC | Error Code | ECC | Executive Computer Concepts |
| EC | Error Correcting | ECC | Executive Computer Course |
| EC | Error Correction | ECC | Experimental Computer Complex |
| EC | Evaluation Center | | |
| EC | Executable Code | ECCAI | European Coordinating Committee for Artificial Intelligence |
| EC | Execution Cycle | | |
| EC | Executive Control | | |
| EC | Extended Control | | |
| EC/LS | Environmental Control and Life Support | ECCCS | Emergency Command Control Communications System |
| ECA | Echo suppression Allowed | | |
| ECA | Electronic Control Amplifier | ECCL | Error Checking and Correction Logic |
| ECA | Electronic Control Assembly | ECCM | Electronic Counter-Counter-Measures |
| ECA | Engineering Change Announcement | ECCS | Electronically Changeable Control Store |
| ECA | Engineering Cost Analysis | ECCSL | Emitter Coupled Current Steering Logic |
| ECA | Enter Control Area | | |
| ECAC | Electromagnetic Compatibility Analysis Center | ECD | Echo suppression Denied |
| | | ECD | Electric Chart Drive |
| | | ECD | Electrochronic Display |
| ECAD | Error Check Analysis Diagram | ECD | Electronic Calculator Device |
| ECAP | Electronic Circuit Analysis Program | ECD | Energy Conversion Device |
| | | ECD | Environnement de Controle et de Décision |
| ECARS | Electronic Coordinator graph And Readout System | | |
| | | ECD | Error Control Device |
| ECASS | Experimental Computer Aided Shop Scheduling | ECDB | Engineering Change Data Base |
| | | ECDC | Electrochemical Diffused Collector |
| ECB | Edit Control Block | | |
| ECB | Event Control Block | ECDC | Engineering Configuration Data Control |
| ECC | Eighty Column Card | | |
| ECC | Electrocardiocorder | ECDIN | Environmental Chemical Data and Information Network |
| ECC | Electron Coupled Control | | |
| ECC | Electron Coupling Control | | |
| ECC | Electronic Card Chips | ECDIN | European Chemical Data and Information Network |
| ECC | Electronic Computer Center | | |
| ECC | Electronic Counting Circuit | ECDR | Encoder |
| | | ECE | Engineering Capacity Exchange |
| ECC | Emitter Coupled Circuits | | |
| ECC | Engineering Change Control | ECES | Education and Career Exploration System |
| ECC | Engineering Change Correction | ECF | Electro-Conductive Film |
| | | ECF | Error Correction Feature |
| ECC | Engineering Control Code | ECF | Expanded Code File |
| | | ECG | Electro-Cardiogram |
| ECC | Error Checking and Correction | ECG | Electrochemical Ginding |
| ECC | Error Controlled Code | ECH | Erase Character |
| ECC | Error Correction Circuitry | ECHO | Electronic Components Harmonization Organization |
| ECC | Error Correction Code | | |
| ECC | European Competence Center | | |
| ECC | Execute Control Cycle | ECHO | Electronic Computing Hospital Oriented |

# E

| | | | |
|---|---|---|---|
| ECHO | Evolution of Competing Hierarchical Organizations | ECMR | Effective Common Mode Rejection |
| ECI | Electronic Control Instrumentation | ECN | Engineering Change Notice |
| | | ECNL | Equivalent Continuous Noise Level |
| ECI | European Cooperation in Informatics | ECNO | Engineering Change Notice One |
| ECI... | Electronic Communications Inc. | ECNOS | Engineering Change Notice System |
| ECIP | European Co-operation in Information Processing | ECNRT | Emitter-Controlled Negative Resistance Triode |
| ECK | Elektronisch Codierbare Kundenspeicher | ECO | Electron-Coupled Oscillator |
| ECK | Equipment Check | | |
| ECL | Eddy Current Loss | ECO | Electronic Central Office |
| ECL | Emitter Coupled Logic | ECO | Electronic Contact Operate |
| ECL | Endicott Computation Laboratory | ECO | Engineering Changes Order |
| ECL | Equipment Component List | ECOC | European Conference on Optical Communication |
| ECL | Exchange Control Logic | | |
| ECL | Executive Control Language | ECOM | Electronic Computer Originated Mail |
| ECL | Extended Control Language | ECOMA | European Computer Measurement Association |
| ECLAT | European Computer Leasing And Trading Association | ECOR | Economic Order |
| | | ECOR | Error Control Register |
| | | ECORQ | Economic Order Quantity |
| ECLG | Edit-Compile-Link-and-Go-Zyklus | ECP | Electromagnetic Compatibility Program |
| ECLO | Emitter-Coupled Logic Operator | ECP | Electronic Calculating Punch |
| ECM | Electric Calculating Machine | ECP | Electronic Circuit Protector |
| ECM | Electric Cipher Machine | ECP | Electronic Coding Pad |
| ECM | Electric Coding Machine | ECP | Electrostatic Card Printer |
| ECM | Electrochemical Machining | ECP | Emitter-Coupled Pair |
| ECM | Electronic Counter Measures | ECP | Emulator Control Program |
| | | ECP | Engineering Change Proposal |
| ECM | Error Correcting Memory | | |
| ECM | Extended Capacity Memory | ECP | Engineering Change Proposed |
| ECM | Extended Core Memory | ECP | Error Correcting Program |
| ECM | Extended Core Module | ECPI | Electronic Computer Programming Institute |
| ECM | External Core Memory | | |
| ECMA | European Computer Manufacturers | ECPM | Environmental Control and Processing Module |
| ECMA | European Computer Manufacturers Association | ECPNL | Equivalent Continuous Perceived Noise Level |
| ECMALGOL | European Computer Manufacturer Association Algorithmic Language | ECPS | Extended Control Program Support |
| | | ECR | Edit, Count, Recode |
| ECME | Electronic Counter Measures Equipment | ECR | Electronic Cash Register |
| | | ECR | Electronic Character Recognition |
| ECMP | Electronic Counter Measures Program | ECR | Electronic Control Relay |

# E

| | | | |
|---|---|---|---|
| ECR | Engineering Change Request | ECSIL | Experimental Cross-Section Information Library |
| ECR | Error Cause Removal | | |
| ECR | Error Control Receiver | ECSL | Extended Control and Simulation Language |
| ECR | Error Correcting Routine | | |
| ECR | Excess Carrier Ratio | ECSS | Extendable Computer System Simulator |
| ECR | Executive Communication Region | ECSS | Extended Computer System Simulator |
| ECR | Executive Control Routine | | |
| ECR | Extended Coverage Range | ECSTASY | Economical Storage and Access System |
| ECRC | Electronic Component Reliability Center | ECSTASY | Electronic Control for Switching and Tele-metering Automobile Systems |
| ECRC | European Computer-industry Research Centre | | |
| ECRDC | Electronic Component Research and Development Center | ECT | Eddy Current Testing |
| | | ECT | Edit Control Table |
| | | ECT | Electric Checking Tabulator |
| ECRV | Extended Curve | | |
| ECS | Electronic Circulating Store | ECT | Environment Control Table |
| | | ECT | Error Control Translator |
| ECS | Electronic Communication System | ECT | Error Control Transmitter |
| | | ECTA | Electronics Component Test Area |
| ECS | Electronic Control and Surveillance | ECTA | Everyman's Contingency Table Analyzer |
| ECS | Electronic Control Switch | | |
| ECS | Electronics Control System | ECTF | Engineering Change Tracking File |
| ECS | Embedded Computer System | | |
| | | ECTL | Emitter-Coupled Transistor Logic |
| ECS | Enable Control System | | |
| ECS | End Cell Switch | ECU | Electronic Computing Unit |
| ECS | Engine Control System | ECU | Electronic Control Unit |
| ECS | Engineering Change Summary | ECU | Electronic Conversion Unit |
| | | ECU | Environmental Control Unit |
| ECS | Engineering Control System | | |
| | | ECW | Eingabecodewandler |
| ECS | Enterprise Communications System | ECWD | Error Channel Word |
| | | ECX | Electronically Controlled telephone Exchange |
| ECS | Environmental Control System | | |
| | | ED | Edit |
| ECS | Equipment Control System | ED | Edited |
| ECS | Error Correction Servo | ED | Edition |
| ECS | Error Correction Signal | ED | Editor |
| ECS | European Communications Satellite | ED | Editorial |
| | | ED | Einschaltdauer |
| ECS | Executive Control System | ED | Electrical Differential |
| ECS | Expanded Character Set | ED | Electrochemical Diffused |
| ECS | Extended Core Storage | ED | Electrodynamics |
| ECS-CM | Extended Core Storage-Central Memory | ED | Electron Device |
| | | ED | Electron Diffraction |
| ECSA | European Computing Services Association | ED | Electronic Device |
| | | ED | Electronic Differential analyzer |
| ECSEC | European Center for Scientific/Engineering Computing | | |
| | | ED | Electronic Digital analyzer |
| | | ED | Electronic Display |

# E

| | | | |
|---|---|---|---|
| ED | Emission des Données | EDC | Emergency Digital Computer |
| ED | Encoded Data | EDC | Energy Discharge Capacitor |
| ED | End of Data | | |
| ED | Engine Drive | EDC | Engineering Data Control |
| ED | Engineering Data | EDC | Error Detecting Code |
| ED | Enhancement/Depletion | EDC | Error Detection and Correction |
| ED | Erase in Display | | |
| ED | Ergebnisdruck | EDC | European Documentation Centre |
| ED | Error Detecting | | |
| ED | Error Detection | EDC | External Data Carrier |
| ED | Esaki Diode | EDCG | Error Detection Code Generator |
| ED | Evalution and Development | | |
| ED | Existence Doubtful | EDCOM | Editor and Compiler |
| ED | Expanded Display | EDCPF | Environmental Data Collection and Processing Facility |
| ED | External Declaration | | |
| ED | External Delay | | |
| ED | External Device | EDCU | Eight Digit Calculator Unit |
| EDA | Effective Doubleword Address | | |
| EDA | Electronic Differential Analyzer | EDCV | Enamel Double-Cotton Varnish |
| EDA | Electronic Data Acquisition | EDCW | External Devise Control Word |
| EDA | Electronic Design Automation | EDD | Electronic Data Display |
| | | EDD | Electronic Document Distribution |
| EDA | Electronic Digital Analyzer | EDD | Engineering Design Data |
| EDA | Elektronische Diagrammauswertung und Datenaufbereitung | EDD | Envelope Delay Distortion |
| | | EDDA | Electronic Demand Deposit Accounting |
| EDA | Entwicklung Dialogorientiertes Anwendersystem | EDDF | Error Detection and Decision Feedback |
| EDA | Error Detector Assembly | EDDP | Engineering Design Data Package |
| EDAB | Energiedaten Berlin | | |
| EDAC | Error Detection And Correction | EDE | Electronic Design Engineering |
| EDACT | Engineering Drawings to Automatic Control Tapes | EDE | Emergency Decelerating |
| | | EDE | Emitter Dip Effect |
| EDAPS | Electronic Data Processing System | EDE | Ende Der Eingabe |
| | | EDED | Error Detection Encoder/Decoder |
| EDASS | Environmental Data Acquisition Sub-System | EDES | Einfach-Daten-Erfassungs-System |
| EDAX | Energy Dispersion Analyzer X-ray | EDF | Engineering Data File |
| EDB | Educational Data Bank | EDF | Engineering Data Form |
| EDB | Einheitsdurchschreibebuchhaltung | EDF | Experiment Data Frame |
| | | EDG | Exploratory Development Goals |
| EDB | Electronic Data Bank | | |
| EDB | Elektronische Datenbearbeitung | EDGE | Electronic Data Gathering Equipment |
| EDB | Engineering Data Base | EDGE | Experimental Display Generation |
| EDC | Electronic Data Collection | | |
| EDC | Electronic Desk Calculator | EDGE | Experimental Display Generator |
| EDC | Electronic Digital Computer | EDGECON | Edge Connector |

- 217 -

# E

| | | | |
|---|---|---|---|
| EDHE | Experimental Data Handling Equipment | EDM | Electrical Discharge Machining |
| EDI | Echo Doppler Indicator | EDM | Electro-Discharge Machine |
| EDI | Electron Diffraction Instrument | EDM | Electronic Data Memory |
| EDI | Epitaxy Diffusion Isolation | EDM | Electronic Design and Manufacture |
| EDI | Error Detection Instrument | EDM | Electronic Design Management system |
| EDIAC | Electronic Display of Indexing Association and Content | EDM | Electronic Drafting Machine |
| EDIAC | Engineering Decision Integrator And Communicator | EDM | Error Detection Mechanism |
| EDICS | European Dealer Information and Communication System | EDM | Error Diagnostic Message |
| | | EDMF | Extended Data Management Facility |
| EDICT | Engineering Document Information Collection Task | EDMICS | Engineering Data Management Information Control System |
| EDICT | Engineering Document Information Collection Technique | EDMK | Edit and Mark |
| | | EDMS | Engineering Data Management Service |
| EDIS | Engineering Data Information System | EDMS | Engineering Data Management System |
| EDIT | Edited | EDMS | Engineering Data Microreproduction System |
| EDIT | Editing | | |
| EDIT | Edition | EDMS | Evolutionary Data Management System |
| EDIT | Editor | | |
| EDIT | Editorial | EDMS | Extended Data Management System |
| EDIT | Engineering Design Intelligent Terminal | EDN | Edition |
| EDIT | Error Deletion by Interactive Transmission | EDN | Emetteur de Données Numériques |
| EDITAR | Electronic Digital Tracking And Ranging | EDO | Effective Diameter of Objective |
| EDITEX | Editeur de Textes | EDO | Einheitliche Dateiorganisation |
| EDITOR | Electronic Data Input Through Optical Recognition | EDO | Electric Data Output |
| | | EDO | Engineering Duties Only |
| | | EDO | Error Demodulator Output |
| EDITP | Engineering Development Integration Test Program | EDOS | Extended Disk Operating System |
| EDITS | Electronic Data Information Technical Service | EDOS/RJE | Extended Disk Operating System with Remote Job Entry facilities |
| EDK | Einheitsdifferentialkosten | | |
| EDK | Elektronische Datenkommunikation | EDP | Economical Data Processing |
| EDL | Electric Delay Line | | |
| EDL | Engineering Data Library | EDP | Electric Data Printing |
| EDLCC | Electronic Data Local Communication Complex | EDP | Electric Dot Printer |
| | | EDP | Electronic Data Processing |
| EDLCC | Electronic Data Local Control Center | EDP | Electronic Document Processing |
| EDLS | Ethernet Data Link Service | EDP | Electrophoretic Display |
| EDM | Electric Dipole Moment | EDP | Experimental Data Processor |
| EDM | Electric Discharge Machine | EDP | External Data Processing |

# E

| | | | |
|---|---|---|---|
| EDP/OR | Electronic Data Processing/Operations Research | EDRS | Engineering Data Retrieval System |
| EDP/PR | Electronic Data Processing/Performance Review | EDRS | Expanded Data Reporting System |
| | | EDS | Educational Data Systems |
| | | EDS | Electric Data Scanning |
| EDPA | Environmental Data Planning Associates | EDS | Electric Data Storage |
| | | EDS | Electromagnetic Data Storage |
| EDPACS | Electronic Data Processing Audit, Control and Security | EDS | Electronic Data Station |
| | | EDS | Electronic Data Storage |
| EDPC | Electronic Data Processing Center | EDS | Electronic Data Switching |
| | | EDS | Electronic Data Switching system |
| EDPD | Electronic Data Processing Device | EDS | Electronic Data System |
| EDPE | Electronic Data Processing Equipment | EDS | Electronic Data Systems Corporation |
| EDPIS | Electronic Data Processing and Information System | EDS | Electronic Document Storage |
| | | EDS | Elektronische Datenverarbeitungsstation |
| EDPLOT | Engineering Data Plotting | | |
| EDPM | Electric Data Processing Machine | EDS | Elektronisches Datenverarbeitungssystem |
| EDPM | Electronic Data Processing Machine | EDS | Elektronisches Datenvermittlungssystem |
| EDPO | Electronic Data Processing Operation | EDS | Elektronisches Datenwählsystem |
| EDPO | Electronic Data Processing Organization | EDS | Emamel Double-Silk |
| | | EDS | Emergency Detection System |
| EDPRD... | EDP Resources Deutschland AG | EDS | Engineering Data Sheet |
| EDPS | Electronic Data Processing System | EDS | Engineering Data Systems |
| | | EDS | Engineering Design System |
| EDPS | Electronic Distributor Parts Show | EDS | Entry Data Subsystem |
| | | EDS | Environmental Data Service |
| EDPS | Exploratory Development Program Summary | EDS | Error Diagnostic Signal |
| EDPT | Electronic Data Processing Test | EDS | Erweiterter Datenstrom |
| | | EDS | European Distribution System |
| EDR | Electric Digital Reading | | |
| EDR | Electronic Data Reading | EDS | Exchangeable Disc Store |
| EDR | Electronic Data Recording | EDS | External Drum Store |
| EDR | Electronic Digit Reading | EDSA | Electronic Data Storage Automatic computer |
| EDR | Electronic Document Reader | | |
| | | EDSAC | Electronic Delay Storage Automatic Calculator |
| EDR | Engineering Data Representative | EDSAC | Electronic Delay Storage Automatic Computer |
| EDR | Equivalent Direct Radiation | EDSAC | Electronic Discrete Sequential Automatic Computer |
| EDR | Error Detection Routine | | |
| EDR | Experiment Data Records | | |
| EDRCC | Electronic Data Remote Communications Complex | EDSDM | Electronic Document Storage Datamanagement |
| EDRI | Electronic Distributors' Research Institute | EDSP | Erzeugnisdatenspeicher |

# E

| | | | |
|---|---|---|---|
| EDSR | Electronic Digital Slide Rule | EDVM | Elektronische Datenverarbeitungsmaschine |
| EDSS | Electronic Data Switching System | EDVS | Elektronisches Datenverarbeitungssystem |
| EDST | Elastic Diaphragm Switch Technology | EDVS | Elektronisches Datenverteilungssystem |
| EDST | Elastische Diaphragma-Schalt-Technologie | EDVSZ | Elektronisches Datenverarbeitungs- und Speicherzentrum |
| EDSTM | Environmental Data Service Technical Memoranda | EDW | Elementary Data Word |
| | | EDX | Event Driven Executive |
| EDSV | Enamel Double-Silk Varnish | EE | Echo Equalizer |
| | | EE | Electrical Engineer |
| EDT | Edit | EE | Electrical Engineering |
| EDT | Editor | EE | Electrical Equipment |
| EDT | Einfache Datentechnik | EE | Electronic Engineering |
| EDT | Electric Data Transmission | EE | Electronics Engineer |
| | | EE | Elektroenergie |
| EDT | Electronic Data Transmission | EE | Endeinrichtung |
| | | EE | Error Excepted |
| EDT | End Data Transmission | EE | Error Expected |
| EDT | End of Data Transfer | EE | External Environment |
| EDT | Engineering Description Tape | EEA | Electronics Engineering Association |
| EDTC | Electronic Desk Top Computer | EEA | Error Exit Address |
| | | EECA | Engineering Economic Cost Analysis |
| EDTCC | Electronic Data Traffic Control Center | EECA | European Electronic Components manufacturers Association |
| EDTCC | Electronic Data Traffic Control Complex | | |
| EDTCC | Electronic Data Transmission Communications Center | EECL | Emitter Emitter Coupled Logic |
| | | EECMA | European Electronic Components Manufacturers Association |
| EDTD | Edit Description | | |
| EDU | Electronic Display Unit | | |
| EDU | Exponential Decay Unit | EED | Electroexplosive Device |
| EDUF | Einsatz für Datenverarbeitung und Unternehmerisches Führungsverhalten | EED | Erase to End of Display |
| | | EEG | Ensemble Electronique de Gestion |
| | | EEG | Ersatzendabnehmergruppe |
| EDV | Elektronische Datenverarbeitung | EEI | Essential Elements of Information |
| EDVA | Elektronische Datenverarbeitungsanlage | EEIC | Elevated Electrode IC |
| | | EEL | Emitter-to-Emitter coupled Logic |
| EDVAC | Electronic Digital-Vernier Analog Computer | EEL | Erase to End of Line |
| EDVAC | Electronic Discrete Variable Automatic Calculator | EEM | Electronic Equipment Monitoring |
| | | EEM | Emission Electron Microscope |
| EDVAC | Electronic Discrete Variable Automatic Computer | EEM | Engineer Electrical and Mechanical |
| EDVAP | Electronic Digital-Vernier Analog Plotter | EEMIS | Energy Emergency Management Information System |
| EDVE | EDV-Englisch | | |

# E

| | | | |
|---|---|---|---|
| EEMTIC | Electrical and Electronic Measurement and Test Instrument Conference | EFF | Effektiv |
| | | EFFECT | Effectivity |
| | | EFI | Eingabe Für Inkrement |
| EEN | Equipment Engineering Notice | EFI | Electronic Fuel Injection |
| | | EFI | Error Function Integral |
| EEO | Equal Employment Opportunity | EFIV | Erfolgs- und Finanzvorschau |
| EEP | Electronic Event Programmer | EFL | Effective Focal Length |
| | | EFL | Emitter Function Logic |
| EEPROM | Electrically Erasable Programmable Read-Only Memory | EFL | Emitter-Folger Logik |
| | | EFL | Emitter-Follower Logic |
| | | EFL | Emitterfunktionslogik |
| EER | Etch Epitaxial Refill | EFL | Ending File Label |
| EER | Explosive Echo Ranging | EFL | Error Frequency Limit |
| EEROM | Electrically Erasable Read-Only Memory | EFL | Equivalent Focal Length |
| | | EFP | Economical File Processing |
| EETF | Electronic Environmental Test Facility | EFP | Error-Free Performance |
| | | EFP | Expanded Function operator Panel |
| EEV | English Electric Valve | | |
| EF | Eingabefolge | EFPH | Equivalent Full Power Hour |
| EF | Eingangsfilter | | |
| EF | Elektronisches Filter | EFR | Eingabefolgeregister |
| EF | Elevation Finder | EFR | Electronic Failure Report |
| EF | Emitter Follower | EFRAP | Exchange Feeder Route Analysis Program |
| EF | Empfangsfilter | | |
| EF | Endfile | EFS | Electronic Frequency Selection |
| EF | Endfolge | | |
| EF | Entire Function | EFS | End File Statement |
| EF | Executive Function | EFS | Error-Free Seconds |
| EFAS | Electronic Flash Approach System | EFT | Earliest Finish Time |
| | | EFT | Efficient File Treatment |
| EFC | Electronic Frequency Control | EFT | Electronic Funds Transfer |
| | | EFTS | Electronic Funds Transfer System |
| EFC | Emitter Follower Cascade | | |
| EFCL | Error-Free Communication Link | EFY | End of Fiscal Year |
| | | EG | Eingabegerät |
| EFCOM | Electricity Flow Computer | EG | Environment Generator |
| EFCS | Emitter Follower Current Switch | EGA | EDV-Gestützter Arbeitsplatz |
| EFD | End of Form Description | EGAO | Expression Graphique Assistée par Ordinateur |
| EFDA | European Federation of Data processing Associations | EGIU | Error Generator Injection Unit |
| EFDARS | Expandable Flight Data Acquisition and Recording System | EGP | Erzeugnisgruppenart |
| | | EGPA | Erlangen General Purpose Array |
| EFDAS | Epsilon Flight Data Acquisition System | EGPS | Electric Ground Power System |
| EFDPMA | Education Foundation of the Data Processing Management Association | EGRS | Electronic and Geodetic Ranging Satellite |
| | | EGS | Engineering Graphics System |
| EFE | External Field Emission | | |
| EFET | Enhancement mode FET | EGS | Extended Graphic Subsystem |
| EFET | Epoxy Field Effect Transistor | | |
| | | EGT | Equipment Group Tester |

# E

| | | | | |
|---|---|---|---|---|
| EH | Electric Heater | | EIC | Equipment Identification Code |
| EH | Engineering Hardware | | EID | End Item Description |
| EH | Erase Head | | EID | End Item Designator |
| EH | Erasing Head | | EID | Erdöl-Informationsdienst |
| EHA | Effective Halfword Address | | EID | Exposure Intensity Distribution |
| EHC | Einzelhandelscomputer | | EIDAP | Emitter Isolated Difference Amplifier Paralleling |
| EHC | Electrical Height Calculator | | EIDN | Einheitliches Integriertes Digitales Netz |
| EHD | Electrohydrodynamic | | EIES | ESPRIT Information Exchange System |
| EHF | End Half | | EIF | External Information Flow |
| EHF | Extremely High Frequency | | EIFED | Einführung in die Elektronische Daten- verarbeitung |
| EHKP | Einheitlich Höheres Kommunikationsprotokoll | | EIG | Electronic Image Generator |
| EHP | Effective Horse Power | | EIGE | Einlesegenerator |
| EHP | Electrical Horse Power | | EIII | European Independent Information Industry |
| EHP | Electron-Hole Pair | | EIII | Electrical Industry Information Institute |
| EHR | Error Handling Routine | | EIK | Elektronische Informa- tionsverarbeitung und Kybernetik |
| EHT | Extremely High Tension | | | |
| EHV | Extra High Voltage | | EIK | Extended Interaction Klystron |
| EHV | Extremely High Voltage | | | |
| EHW | Equivalent Hours Worked | | EIL | Electron Injection Laser |
| EI | Eingangsinformation | | EIL | Event Index Log |
| EI | Electromagnetic Interference | | EIM | Electric Invoicing Machine |
| EI | Electronic Installation | | EIM | End-of-Information Marker |
| EI | Electronic Interface | | EIM | Excitability Inducing Material |
| EI | Enable Interrupt | | EIMF | End Item Maintenance Form |
| EI | End Injection | | | |
| EI | End Item | | EIMS | End Item Maintenance Sheet |
| EI | Execution Interrupt | | | |
| EI | Exit Instruction | | EIMTS | End Item Maintenance Transmittal Sheet |
| EI | External Interrupt | | | |
| EI/NI | Electron Irradiation and Neutron Irradiation | | EIN | Education Information Network |
| EIA | Electrical Industries Association | | EIN | Erase Input |
| EIA | Electronic Industries Association | | EIN | Eulerian Iterative Nonsteady |
| EIA | Electronic Invoicing Automaton | | EIN | European Informatics Network |
| EIAC | Electronic Industries Association of Canada | | EINAS | Einzelanschaltung |
| | | | EINAUF | Einzelauftrag |
| EIAC | Ergonomics Information Analysis Centre | | EINB | Eingabe, Binär |
| | | | EINB | Eingabebereich |
| EIB | Error Information Block | | EING | Eingabegerät |
| EIB | Error Interrupt Buffer | | EIO | Execute Input/Output |
| EIC | Electromagnetic Interference Control | | | |
| EIC | Electron Induced Conduction | | | |
| EIC | Energy Information Center | | | |
| EIC | Engineer In Charge | | | |
| EIC | Engineering Information Center | | | |

# E

| | | | |
|---|---|---|---|
| EIOC | Equivalent Input Offset Current | EIS | Ericsson Information Systems |
| EIOP | External Input/Output Processor | EIS | Extended Instruction Set |
| EIOS | Extended Input/Output System | EIT | Electric Information Technique |
| EIOV | Equivalent Input Offset Voltage | EIT | Engineer In Training |
| EIP | Emulator Interface Program | EIU | Executive Independent Utilities |
| EIP | EXEC Interchange Program | EIUP | Executive Independent Utilities Program |
| EIPC | European Institute of Printed Circuits | EIVM | Elektronische Informationsverarbeitungsmaschine |
| EIPC | Extended Interprocess Communication | EIZ | Endbenutzer-Informations-Zentrum |
| EIR | Einschaltroutine | EJ | Eccles-Jordan circuit |
| EIR | Emergency Information Readiness | EJ | Eject |
| EIR | End Item Requirement | EJC | Electrical Joint Compound |
| EIR | Error Interrupt Request | EJC | Engineer's Joint Council |
| EIRD | Experiment Integration Requirements Document | EJCC | Eastern Joint Computer Conference |
| EIRP | Equivalent Isotropically Radiated Power | EJN | Ejection |
| | | EJS | Engineering Job Sheet |
| EIRV | Error Interrupt Request Vector | EJT | Eccles-Jordan Trigger |
| | | EK | Einheitsklassifikation |
| EIS | Economic Information System | EK | Einkauf |
| | | EK | Elektronik |
| EIS | Einkaufsinformationssystem | EK | Endkontrolle |
| | | EK | Erase Key |
| EIS | Electric Information Storage | EK | Erkenner |
| | | EKB | Electronic Key Board |
| EIS | Electrolyte Insulator Semiconductor | EKB | Electronic Knowledge Bank |
| | | EKBS | Electronics Keyboard System |
| EIS | Electromagnetic Intelligence System | EKDV | Elektronische Kombinierte Datenverarbeitung |
| EIS | End Interruption Sequence | EKE | Eingabekontrolleinrichtung |
| EIS | End Item Specification | EKF | Erweitertes Kalmanfilter |
| EIS | Engineering Information Series | EKG | Electrocardiogram |
| | | EKIS | Elektronisches Informations- und Kommunikationssystem |
| EIS | Entwurf Integrierter Schaltkreise | EKN | Ereignisknoten-Netzplan |
| EIS | Entwurf integrierter Schaltungen | EKO | Eingabeeinheit Kommando |
| | | EKO | Energie-Kosten-Optimierung |
| EIS | Environmental Impact Statement | EKONS | Einheitliches Kontonummern-System |
| EIS | Environmental Information System | EKOS | Energie-Kosten-Optimierungs-System |
| EIS | Epson Informations System | EKR | Eingabekopplungsregister |
| EIS | Equipment Information Series | EKR | Erzeugniskostenrechnung |
| EIS | Equipment Information System | EKS | Electrocardiogram Simulator |

# E

| | | | |
|---|---|---|---|
| EKS | Electronic Keyboard System | ELECOM | Electronic Computer |
| EKS | Energiekreis | ELECOM | Electronic Computing |
| EKS | Erkenntnisspeicher | ELECT | Electric |
| EKW | Electrical Kilowatt | ELECT | Electrolyte |
| EL | Eichleitung | ELECTC | Electronic Control |
| EL | Eingangslogik | ELECTL | Electrical |
| EL | Electrical | ELECTR | Electricity |
| EL | Electricity | ELECTRON | Electronic |
| EL | Electroluminescence | ELECTY | Electricity |
| EL | Electroluminiszenz | ELEM | Element |
| EL | Elektrizität | ELEP | Electronic converter of Electric Power |
| EL | Elektron | ELF | Electroluminiscent Ferroelectric |
| EL | Elektronik | | |
| EL | End Line | ELF | Electronic Location Finder |
| EL | Energy Loss | ELF | Extensible Language Facility |
| EL | Entry Local | | |
| EL | Erase Line | ELF | Extremely-Low Frequency |
| EL | Etched Lead | ELFC | Electroluminiscent Ferroelectric Cell |
| EL | External Logic | | |
| EL... | N/V/ Electrologica | ELG | Electrolytic Grinding |
| ELA | Electron Linear Accelerator | ELG | Even Linear Grammars |
| | | ELI | English Language Interface |
| ELAC | Electroacoustic | ELI | Equitable Life Interpreter |
| ELAN | Elementary Language | ELIAS-I | Entry Level Interactive Application System-One |
| ELARD | Elektrischer Analogrechner Darmstadt | | |
| | | ELIM | Eliminate |
| ELCA | Earth Landing Control Area | ELIM | Elimination |
| | | ELINT | Electromagnetic Intelligence |
| ELCO | Electrolytic Capacitor | | |
| ELCO | Eliminate and Count | ELINT | Electronic Intelligence |
| ELCT | Electricity | ELIP | Electrostatic Latent Image Photography |
| ELCT | Electronic | | |
| ELCTD | Electrode | ELIRT | Environmental Laboratories Information Retrieval Technique |
| ELCTRN | Electron | | |
| ELCU | Electrical Control Unit | | |
| ELD | Edge-Lighted Display | ELK | Eingabe-Lochkarte |
| ELD | Electroluminescent Diode | ELLIAS | Expandable Level Interactive Application System |
| ELD | Electrolytic Liquid Display | | |
| | | ELM | Electrical Length Measurement |
| ELD | Encapsulated Light Diffusion | | |
| | | ELM | Element Load Model |
| ELD | Error Logging Device | ELM | Error Latency Model |
| ELD | Extra Long Distance | ELM | Error Log Manager |
| ELDA | Elektronische Digitalausgabe | ELMAP | Exchange Line Multiplexer Analysis Program |
| ELDAS | Elektronisches Direktanwahl-System | | |
| | | ELMAS | Elektronisches Mitteilungs- und Archivsystem |
| ELDC | Economic Load Dispatching Computer | | |
| | | ELMS | Equipment Library Management System |
| ELDE | Elektronische Digitaleingabe | | |
| | | ELMS | Experimental Library Management System |
| ELE | Element | | |
| ELECD | Electrode | ELONG | Elongate |
| ELECN | Electronic | ELONG | Elongation |

# E

| | | | |
|---|---|---|---|
| ELP | Eigenleistungsprüfung | EM | Electronic countermeasure Malfunction |
| ELP | Eingabelogikprüfprogramm | | |
| ELP | Error Localization Program | EM | Electrostatic Memory |
| ELPC | Electroluminescent Photoconductive | EM | Elektromotor |
| | | EM | Emergency Maintenance |
| | | EM | Encoder Matrix |
| ELPE | Electroluminescent Photoelectric | EM | End Mark |
| | | EM | End of Media |
| ELPH | Elliptical Head | EM | End of Medium |
| ELPR | Electroluminescent-Photoresponsive | EM | End of Message |
| | | EM | Endmonitor |
| ELR | Electronic Label Reader | EM | Erasable Memory |
| ELR | Exchange Line Relay | EM | Error Message |
| ELRAC | Electronic Reconnaissance Accessory | EM | Error Multiplier |
| | | EM | Exact Match |
| ELS | Economic Lot Size | EM | External Memory |
| ELS | Eingabelochstreifen | EM | External Microprogram |
| ELS | Electrical System | EM | Externer Modus |
| ELS | Elektronischer Lochstreifenstanzer | EM | External Monitoring |
| | | EMA | Electronic Measuring Apparatus |
| ELSA | Elektronisches Lichtschaltzeilen-Ausgabegerät | EMA | Elektromagnetischer Antrieb |
| ELSB | Edge Lighted Status Board | | |
| ELSEC | Electronic Security | EMA | Extended Mercury Autocode |
| ELSI | Extra Large Scale Integrated | | |
| | | EMA | Extended Mercury Autocoder |
| ELSI | Extra Large Scale Integration | EMAD | Engine Modification And Disassembly |
| ELSIE | Electronic Letter Sorting Indicator Equipment | | |
| | | EMAGO | Elektromagnetische Orientierung |
| ELSIE | Electronic Signaling and Indicating Equipment | EMAR | Experimental Memory Address Register |
| ELT | Electrometer | | |
| ELT | Emergency Locator Transmitter | EMAS | Edinburgh Multi-Access System |
| ELTC | Electric | EMATS | Emergency Mission Automatic Transmission Service |
| ELV | Electrically operated Valve | | |
| ELV | Extra Low Voltage | | |
| ELVIS | Electroluminescent Vertical Indication System | EMATS | Experimental Message Automatic Transmission System |
| ELVIS | Esco-Laser-Vision und Videotex-Informations-System | EMB | Early-Make-Break |
| | | EMB | Eingabemagnetband |
| | | EMBA | Eingabe Magnetbanddatei |
| EM | Einbaumodem | EMC | Electromagnetic Compatibility |
| EM | Einseitenbandmodulation | | |
| EM | Electric Memory | EMC | Electronic Material Change |
| EM | Electromagnet | | |
| EM | Electromagnetic | EMC | Electronic Mode Control |
| EM | Electromagnetic Memory | EMC | Engineering Military Circuits |
| EM | Electromechanical | | |
| EM | Electromicroscopic | EMC | Excess Minority Carries |
| EM | Electron Microscope | EMCDAS | Electro-Magnetic Compatibility Data Acquisition System |
| EM | Electronic Memory | | |
| EM | Electronic Multiplier | | |

# E

| | | | |
|---|---|---|---|
| EMCON | Emery Control | EMIRTEL | Emirate Telecommunication Corporation |
| EMCON | Emission Control | EMIS | Ecosystem of Machines Information System |
| EMCOPS | Electromagnetic Compatibility Operational System | EMIS | Effluent Management Information System |
| EMCP | Electromagnetic Compatibility Program | EMIS | Engineering Maintenance Information System |
| EMCS | Excerpta Medica Computer System | EMIS | Extension Management Information System |
| EMCTP | Electromagnetic Compatibility Test Plan | EMIT | Emitter |
| EMD | Electric Motor Driven | EMIT | Engineering Management Information Technique |
| EMD | Entry Monitor Display | EMK | Elektromotorische Kraft |
| EMDB | Engineering Master Data Base | EMK | Elektronische Kraft |
| EMDR | Emulated Machine Description Record | EMK | Europäischer Mikrofilm-Kongreß |
| EME | Eingabeeinheit Meldungen | EML | Emulator |
| EME | Electromagnetic Energy | EML | Equal Matrix Language |
| EME | Extension Memory | EML | Equipment Modification List |
| EMERGCON | Emergency Condition | EML | Expected Measured Loss |
| EMETF | Electromagnetic Environmental Test Facility | EMM | Electric Matrix Memory |
| EMF | Electromotive Force | EMM | Electromagnetic Measurement |
| EMF | Electronic Manufacturing Facility | EMM | Electron Mirror Microscope |
| EMF | Engineering Master File | EMM | Electronic Magnetic Memory |
| EMFIS | Experimentelles Führungs- und Informationssystem | EMM | Electronic Memories and Magnetic Corporation |
| EMFT | Extended Multiprogramming with a Fixed number of Tasks | EMM | Error Matrix Method |
| EMG | Electromyography | EMMA | Electronic Mask Making Apparatus |
| EMH | Expedited Message Handling | EMMA | Electronic Mathematic Model-Analog |
| EMI | Electrical Measuring Instrument | EMMA | Electron Microscopy and Microanalysis |
| EMI | Electromagnetic Impulse | EMMS | Electronic Mail and Message System |
| EMI | Electromagnetic Interference | EMO | Electromechanical Optical |
| EMI | Enable Manual Input | EMP | Eingabemagnetplatte |
| EMIC | Electronic Materials Information Center | EMP | Electromagnetic Power |
| EMIC | Engineering Management Inquiry Console | EMP | Electromagnetic Pulse |
| EMICE | Electromagnetic Interference Control Engineer | EMP | Electromechanical Power |
| | | EMP | Electron Micro-Probe |
| | | EMP | Erasable Memory Program |
| EMIDEC | Electrical & Musical Industries Data Electronic Computer | EMPF | Entscheidungsempfehlung |
| | | EMPHASIS | Evaluation Management using Past History Analysis for Scientific Inventory Simulation |
| EMIL | Elektronisches Messe-Informations-Leitsystem | EMPIRE | Electro-Magnetic Performance Information Research |
| EMINT | Electromagnetic Intelligence | | |

# E

| | | | |
|---|---|---|---|
| EMPIS | Engineering Materials and Process Information Service | EMT | Express Master Tape |
| EMPS | Einheitliche Modulare Programmstruktur | EMTECH | Electromagnetic Technology |
| EMR | Electromagnetic Radiation | EMTF | Equivalent Mean Time to Failure |
| EMR | Electromechanical Research | EMTF | Estimated Mean Time to Failure |
| EMR | Electromechanical Research Inc. | EMTR | Emitter |
| EMR | Equipment Maintenance Report | EMTR | Enlisted Master Tape Record |
| EMR | Error Monitor Register | EMTTF | Equivalent Mean Time To Failure |
| EMR | Executive Management Responsibility | EMU | Electrical Multiple Unit |
| | | EMU | Electro-Magnetic Unit |
| EMRIC | Educational Media Research Information Center | EMU | Electromotive Unit |
| | | EMU | Expanded Memory Unit |
| | | EMU | Extravehicular Mobility Unit |
| EMS | Early MARC Search | EMUX | Electrical Multiplex |
| EMS | Einheitliches Mikrofilmsystem | EMV | Elektromagnetischer Verschluß |
| EMS | Electric Matrix Store | EMV | Elektromagnetische Verträglichkeit |
| EMS | Electromagnetic Susceptibility | EMW | Electromagnetic Wave |
| EMS | Electromotive Surface | EMW | Elektromagnetische Welle |
| EMS | Electronic Mail System | EMW | Elektromechanisches Werk |
| EMS | Electronic Management System | EN | End |
| EMS | Electronic Medical System | EN | Engineering Note |
| EMS | Electronic Message Service | EN | Entkopplungsnetzwerk |
| EMS | Electronic Message System | EN | Entry Name |
| EMS | Electronic Micro System | EN | Europa-Norm |
| EMS | Elektronisch-Mikroprozessorgesteuertes Speicherprogramm | EN | European Norm |
| | | EN | External Name |
| | | ENA | Extended Network Addressing |
| EMS | Emission Spectrograph | ENABL | Enable |
| EMS | Emulator Monitor System | ENABLD | Enabled |
| EMS | Entwicklungs-Modul-System | ENAP | Economic Network Analysis Program |
| EMS | Extended Main Storage | ENBL | Enable |
| EMS | Extended Maintenance Service | ENBLD | Enabled |
| | | ENC | Encoder |
| EMS | Extended Memory Store | ENCD | Encode |
| EMS | Extended Monitor System | ENCON | Energy Conservation |
| EMSA | Electron Microscope Society of America | ENCORE | Enlarged Compact by Response |
| EMSC | Electronic Message Service Center | ENCR | Encoder |
| | | END | End of Data |
| EMSIDE | Electromagnetic Signature Identification and Data Evaluation | END | Endicott |
| | | END | Endimpuls |
| | | ENDADR | Endadresse |
| EMT | Early Memory Test | ENDEX | Environmental Data index |
| EMT | Electrical Metal Tubing | ENDF | Evaluated Nuclear Data File |
| EMT | Electrostatic Memory Tube | | |
| EMT | Elektromeßtechnik | | |

# E

| | | | |
|---|---|---|---|
| ENDS | Euratom Nuclear Documentation System | EO | Engineering Order |
| ENDSR | End Subroutine | EO | Executive Order |
| ENG | Electronic News Gathering | EO | Exklusive ODER-Schaltung |
| | | EO | Exponent Overflow |
| ENG | Engineer | EO | Extend and Offset |
| ENGR | Engineer | EO | Extended Operation |
| ENGRG | Engineering | EOA | End Of Address |
| ENGY | Energy | EOAP | Event Oriented Application Program |
| ENI | Ecole Nationale d'Informatique | EOAU | Electrooptical Alignment Unit |
| ENI | Equivalent Noise Input | EOB | End Of Block |
| ENIAC | Electronic Numerical Integrator And Calculator | EOBM | End of Block Mark |
| | | EOC | Elementary Operated Control |
| ENIAC | Electronic Numerical Integrator And Computer | EOC | End Of Card |
| | | EOC | End Of Chain |
| ENIS | Energiesektor | EOC | End Of Communication |
| ENIS | Energiesektorales Informationssystem | EOC | End Of Conversion |
| | | EOC | End Of Convert |
| ENK | Enter Key | EOC | Even-Odd Check |
| ENP | Enable Presentation | EOCY | End Of Calendar Year |
| ENQ | Enquiry | EOD | End Of Data |
| ENR | Equivalent Noise Ratio | EODAP | Earth and Ocean Dynamic Applications Program |
| ENR | Equivalent Noise Resistance | EODARS | Electrooptical Direction And Ranging System |
| ENR | Excess Noise Ratio | | |
| ENRZ | Enhanced Non-Return-to-Zero | EODC | End Of Data Carrier |
| | | EODD | Electrooptical Digital Deflector |
| ENS | Extended Network Service | | |
| ENSAD | Einheitliches Nachrichtensystem für Analoge und Digitale Vermittlung | EOE | Electronic-Optic-Electronic |
| | | EOE | End Of Extent |
| | | EOE | Errors and Omissions Expected |
| ENSAD | Elektronisches Nachrichtensystem für Analoge und Digitale Vermittlung | EOF | End Of Field |
| | | EOF | End Of File |
| | | EOF | End Of Form |
| ENSI | Equivalent Noise-Sideband Input | EOFL | End Of File Label |
| | | EOFO | End Of File Option |
| ENSPTT | Ecole Nationale Supérieure des PTT | EOFR | End Of File Record |
| | | EOFS | End Of File Statement |
| ENST | Ecole Nationale Supérieure des Télécommunications | EOG | Electrooculography |
| | | EOI | End Of Identity |
| ENT | Effective Noise Temperature | EOI | End Of Idle |
| | | EOI | End Of Inquiry |
| ENT | Enter | EOI | End Of Item |
| ENT | Entry | EOIU | End Of Interaction Unit |
| ENT | Entry equivalent Noise Temperature | EOJ | End Of Job |
| | | EOJS | End Of Job Statement |
| ENTC | Engine Negative Torque Control | EOL | End Of Life |
| | | EOL | End Of Line |
| EO | Elementaroperation | EOL | End Of List |
| EO | Elementary Operation | EOL | Expression Oriented Language |
| EO | Emergency Order | | |
| EO | End Order | | |
| EO | End of Operation | | |

# E

| | | | |
|---|---|---|---|
| EOLM | Electrooptical Light Modulator | EOTP | End Of Tape Pulse |
| EOLT | End Of Logic Tape | EOTR | End Of Transmission Record |
| EOM | End Of Message | EOTS | Electronical Optical Tracking System |
| EOM | End Of Month | | |
| EOMG | End of Message Group | EOV | Electrically Operated Valve |
| EOMI | End Of Message Incomplete | | |
| EOMRU | End of Message Recovery Unit | EOV | End Of Volume |
| | | EOVM | End Of Valid Message |
| EON | End Of Number | EOY | End Of Year |
| EOOC | Exchange Oriented Operator Control | EP | Eingabeprogramm |
| | | EP | Electric Power |
| EOP | Electrical/Optical | EP | Electrically Polarized |
| EOP | End Of Part | EP | Electrolytic Printing |
| EOP | End Of Program | EP | Electronic Package |
| EOP | End Operation | EP | Electronic Printer |
| EOP | End Output | EP | Electronic Printing |
| EOP | Engineering Operating Procedure | EP | Electronic Processing |
| | | EP | Electroplate |
| EOQ | Economic Order Quantity | EP | Element Processor |
| EOR | End Of Record | EP | Emulation Processing |
| EOR | End Of Reel | EP | Emulation Program |
| EOR | End Of Report | EP | Emulation System |
| EOR | End Of Run | EP | Emulator Program |
| EOR | Error Of Reading | EP | End Paper |
| EOR | Exclusive OR | EP | End Printing |
| EOR | Explosive Ordnance Reconnaissance | EP | End of Program |
| | | EP | Entry Point |
| EORC | End Of Record Character | EP | Epitaxial-Planar |
| EOS | Echtzeitoperationssystem | EP | Error Print |
| EOS | Economic Order Splitting | EP | Error Program |
| EOS | Electro-Optical System | EP | Erzeugnisplanung |
| EOS | End Of Segment | EP | Etched Plate |
| EOS | End Of Selection signal | EP | Evaluation Program |
| EOS | End Of String | EP | Executable Program |
| EOS | End Operation Suppress | EP | Executive Program |
| EOS | End Of Session | EP | Extended Play |
| EOS | Extended Operating System | EP | Extended Port |
| | | EP | External Program |
| EOSC | Extended Operating System Card | EP | Extreme Pressure |
| | | EP/AB | Erfassungsprotokoll/ Auftragsbestägigung |
| EOSEQ | End Order Sequence | | |
| EOSF | Electro-Optical Simulation Facility | EPA | Electron Probe Analyzer |
| | | EPA | Elektronische Platzbuchungsanlage |
| EOSMD | Extended Operating System Magnetic Drum | | |
| | | EPA | Environmental Protection Agency |
| EOSRU | End Of Session Recovery Unit | | |
| | | EPABX | Electronic Private Automatic Business Exchange |
| EOT | End Of Tape | | |
| EOT | End Of Task | EPAI | Exchange of Publicity Available Information |
| EOT | End Of Test | | |
| EOT | End Of Text | EPAM | Elementary Perceiver And Memorizer |
| EOT | End Of Track | | |
| EOT | End Of Transmission | EPBX | Electronic Private Branch Exchange |
| EOTL | End Of Tape Label | | |

# E

| | | | |
|---|---|---|---|
| EPC | Easy Processing Channel | EPIC | Epitaxial Passivated Integrated Circuit |
| EPC | Edge Perforated Card | | |
| EPC | Edge Punched Card | EPIC | Evaluator Programmer Integrated Circuit |
| EPC | Electronic Program Control | EPIC | Executive Planning Information and Communication system |
| EPC | Engine Performance Computer | | |
| EPC | Engineering Part Card | EPICS | Extended Purpose Inline Console System |
| EPC | Engineering Parts Counter | | |
| EPC | Extended Plotter Code | EPID | Electrophoretic Image Display |
| EPC | Extended Plotter Commands | | |
| EPCO | Emergency Power Cut-Off | EPIDIS | Ensemble de Programmes Intégrés pour la Distribution |
| EPCOT | Experimental Prototype Community Of Tomorrow | | |
| | | EPIS | Electronic Program Identification System |
| EPCU | Electrical Power Control Unit | EPL | Early Programming Language |
| EPD | Earth Potential Difference | | |
| EPD | Electric Power Distribution | EPL | Einheitliche Prozessrechner-Linie |
| EPD | Electronic Programming Device | EPL | European Program Library |
| | | EPL | Extensible Programming Language |
| EPD | Engineering Planning Document | EPLAN | Econometric Planning Language |
| EPDC | Economic Power Dispatch Computer | EPLO | Electronic Plotting |
| EPDCC | Elementary Potential Digital Computing Component | EPM | Eichpegelmesser |
| | | EPM | Electric Printing Machine |
| EPDCE | Elementary Potential Digital Computing Element | EPM | Electric Printing Mechanism |
| | | EPM | Electric Pulse Motor |
| EPDS | Electric Power Distribution System | EPM | Electronic Permanent Memory |
| EPEC | Emerson Programmer Evaluator Controller | EPM | Enhanced Pulse Modulation |
| | | EPM | External Polarization Modulation |
| EPEX | Einzelpostennachweis-Export | EPMA | Electronic Parts Manufacturers Association |
| EPF | Easy Programming Facility | EPMA | Electronic Printing Machine |
| EPF | Erase Preceding Field | | |
| EPF | Executive Program Function | EPMAU | Expected Present Multi-Attribute Utility |
| EPG | Edit Program Generator | EPMS | Enlisted Personal Management System |
| EPI | Evaluation Position Indicator | | |
| | | EPN | Effective Perceived Noise |
| EPI | External Program Interruption | EPNL | Effective Perceived Noise Level |
| EPI... | Electronic Process Inc. | EPNS | Electroplated Nickel Silber |
| EPIC | Electronic Properties Information Center | | |
| | | EPNdB | Effective Perceived Noise level dB |
| EPIC | Employment of Personnel In Computing | EPO | Emergency Power-Off |
| EPIC | Engineering Planning Information Coordination | EPO | Enseignement Programmé par Ordinateur |

# E

| | | | |
|---|---|---|---|
| EPO | Experimental Processing Operation | EPT | Engineering Programming and Technology |
| EPOC | Early Parts On Change | EPT | Environmental Proof Test |
| EPOCH | Early Parts On Change Hold | EPTE | Existed Prior To Entry |
| EPOCS | Effectual Planning for Operation of Container System | EPU | Electrical Power Unit |
| | | EPU | Expandable Processor Unit |
| | | EPU | External Programmer Unit |
| EPOS | EDV-Postauszeichnungs- und Abrechnungssystem | EPUT | Events Per Unit Time |
| | | EPX | Eurotech Packet Exchange |
| EPOS | Elektro-Installations- Programm- und Organi- sations-System | EQ | Equal |
| | | EQ | Equalizer |
| | | EQ | Equate |
| EPOS | Epson Praxis-Orientiertes Text-System | EQ | Equation |
| | | EQ | Equipment |
| EPP | Executive Peachpack | EQ | Equivalent |
| EPPI | Electronic Plan Position Indicator | EQC | Equipment Check |
| | | EQCC | Entry Querry Control Console |
| EPPI | Electronic Programmed Procurement Information | EQDD | Equipment Density Data |
| | | EQG | Equalizing |
| EPR | Echtzeit-Prozessrechner | EQL | Equal |
| EPR | Eingabe-Pufferregister | EQL | Equalizer |
| EPR | Electron Paramagnetic Resonance | EQL | Expected Quality Level |
| | | EQN | Equation |
| EPR | Entry Point Register | EQP | Equip |
| EPR | Equivalent Parallel Resistance | EQP | Equipment |
| | | EQPCHK | Equipment Check |
| EPR | Error Pattern Register | EQPMT | Equipment |
| EPR | Excess Parts Request | EQPT | Equipment |
| EPRD | Electrical Power Requirements Data | EQU | Equate |
| | | EQUAL | Equalizer |
| EPROM | Electrically Programmable Read-Only Memory | EQUIP | Equation Input Processor |
| | | EQUIP | Equipment |
| EPROM | Erasable Programmable Read-Only Memory | EQUIP | Equipment Usage Information Program |
| EPS | Econometric Program System | EQUIPT | Equipment |
| | | EQUIV | Equivalent |
| EPS | Electric Power Storage | ER | Echo Ranging |
| EPS | Electrical Power Supply | ER | Editor Routine |
| EPS | Electronic Permanent Store | ER | Effectivness Report |
| | | ER | Eingaberegister |
| EPS | Elektronischer Programm- speicher | ER | Eingangsrechnung |
| | | ER | Eingangsregler |
| EPS | Engineering Process Specification | ER | Electric Reader |
| | | ER | Electrical Resistance |
| EPS | Engineering Product Description | ER | Electro-Refined |
| | | ER | Electronic Reader |
| EPS | Executive Picture Show | ER | Electronic Reconnaissance |
| EPS | External Page Storage | ER | Elektronenrechner |
| EPSS | Experimental Packet Switching Service | ER | End Routine |
| | | ER | End of Run |
| EPST | Extended Partition Specification Table | ER | Entry Remote |
| | | ER | Entscheidungsregel |
| EPT | Edge Point Threshold | ER | Ergänzungsrechner |
| EPT | Electricstatic Printing Tube | ER | Error Relay |

# E

| | | | |
|---|---|---|---|
| ER | Ersatzrechner | ERF | Error Function |
| ER | Evaluation Routine | ERFC | Error Function Complement |
| ER | Exchange Register | | |
| ER | Executive Routine | ERFDP | Earth Resources Flight Data Processor |
| ER | Expected Result | | |
| ER | Explicit Route | ERFI | Error Function, Integral |
| ER | External Register | ERFOLG | Ermittlungssysteme Für Optimale Lukrative Geldanlage |
| ER | External Resistance | | |
| ER | Externer Rechner | | |
| ERA | Electrical Research Association | ERFPI | Extended Range Floating Point Interpretive System |
| ERA | Electronic Reading Automation | | |
| | | ERG | Electron Radiography |
| ERA | Elektronische Rechen-anlage | ERG | Electroretinography |
| | | ERG | Erase Gap |
| ERA | Elektronische Reisezug-Auskunft | ERGDAT | Ergebnisdatei |
| | | ERGS | Electronic Route-Guidance System |
| ERA | Engineering Record Automation | | |
| | | ERH | Electric Reading Head |
| ERAN | Examine and Repair As Necessary | ERIA | Estudios y Realizaciones en Informatica Aplicada |
| ERAS | Erase | ERIC | Education Resources Information Center |
| ERAU | Emetteur-Récepteur Asynchrone Universel | | |
| | | ERIC | Educational Research Information Center |
| ERB | Execution Request Block | | |
| ERC | Edge Reading Controller | ERIC | Energy Rate Input Controller |
| ERC | Equatorial Ring Current | | |
| ERC | Error Retry Count | ERIC | European Road Information Centre |
| ERCC | Error Checking and Correcting | | |
| | | ERIC-AE | Educational Resources Information Center - Adult Education |
| ERCC | Error Checking and Correction | | |
| ERCCC | Error checking and Correcting Code | ERIC-CEA | ERIC - Clearinghouse on Educational Administration |
| ERCMAP | Entity Relationship to Codasyl Mapping | | |
| | | ERIC-CIR | ERIC - Clearinghouse on Information Resources |
| ERCR | Electronic Retina Computing Reader | | |
| | | ERIC-CLIS | ERIC - Clearinghouse on Library and Information Sciences |
| ERCR | Error Cause Register | | |
| ERD | Electronic Reading Device | | |
| ERD | Electronic Recording Device | ERIC-IR | ERIC - Information Resources |
| ERD | Exponentially Retrograded Diode | ERIC-IRCD | ERIC - Information Retrieval Center on the Disadvantaged |
| ERDDA | Extended Resolution Digital Differential Analyzer | | |
| | | ERISA | Employee Retirement Income Security Act. |
| ERDET | Error Detection | ERISTAR | Earth Resources Informa-tion Storage, Trans-formation, Analysis, and Retrieval |
| ERE | Eingabeeinheit Rechner-anschluß | | |
| ERE | Event Recorder Evaluator | | |
| EREP | Environment Record Edit and Print | ERL | Echo Return Loss |
| | | ERL | Ending Reel Label |
| EREP | Environmental Recording, Editing and Printing | ERL | Equipment Revision Level |
| | | ERL | Event Record Log |

# E

| | | | |
|---|---|---|---|
| ERM | Edge Reading Meter | ERS | External Random Storage |
| ERM | Elektronische Rechen-maschine | ERS | External Regulation System |
| ERM | Error Recovery Manager | ERSER | Expanded Reactance Series Resonator |
| ERM | Error Recovery Module | | |
| ERMA | Electrical Reproduction Method of Accounting | ERSO | Electronics Research and Service Organization |
| ERMA | Electronic Recording Machine | ERSR | Equipment Reliability Status Report |
| ERMA | Electronic Recording Method of Accounting | ERT | Elektronische Rechentechnik |
| ERNA | Elektronische Rechner-gesteuerte Nachrichten-vermittlungsanlage | ERT | Environmental Research Technology |
| | | ERT | Equipment Repair Time |
| ERNIE | Electronic Random Numbering and Indicating Equipment | ERT | Estimated Removal Time |
| | | ERT | Estimated Repair Time |
| | | ERTBP | Emergency Restart Transaction Backout Program |
| EROCP | Extended Remote Operator Control Panel | ERV | Externer Rechnerverbund |
| EROM | Erasable Read-Only Memory | ERW | Electronic Resistance Welding |
| EROS | Eleminate Range zero System | ERZ | Elektronisches Rechenzentrum |
| ERP | Earth Reference Pulse | | |
| ERP | Effective Radiated Power | ES | Echo Sounding |
| ERP | Emitted Radio Power | ES | Editing Symbol |
| ERP | End Response | ES | Eingangsschalter |
| ERP | Error Recovery Procedures | ES | Eingangsschaltung |
| ERP | External Research Program | ES | Electric Scanner |
| ERP | Externspeicherresidentes Programm | ES | Electric Storage |
| | | ES | Electric Store |
| ERPLD | Extended Range Phased Locked Demodulator | ES | Electrochemical Society |
| | | ES | Electrolytic Storage |
| ERQ | End Request | ES | Electromagnetic Storage |
| ERR | Error | ES | Electromagnetic Store |
| ERR | Error description | ES | Electromagnetic Switching |
| ERRAN | Error Analysis | ES | Electronic Store |
| ERRC | Error Character | ES | Electronic Switch |
| ERRDF | Earth Resources Research Data Facilities | ES | Electrostatic Store |
| | | ES | Electrostatis |
| ERRDF | Earth Resources Research Data Facility | ES | Elektromagnetische Speicherung |
| ERRSYS | Errata System | ES | Elektromagnetischer Speicher |
| ERS | Early Reporting System | | |
| ERS | Einzelrechnersystem | ES | Elektronenrechnersystem |
| ERS | Electronic Remote Switching | ES | Elektronenstrahlschalter |
| | | ES | Elektronische Steuerung |
| ERS | Elektronisch Rechnende Schreibmaschine | ES | Empfänger-Sender |
| | | ES | Empfangssatz |
| ERS | Equipment Record System | ES | Endbenutzer-Service |
| ERS | Ereignisfolge-Registriersystem | ES | Endstelle |
| | | ES | Energiesystem |
| ERS | Exception Reporting System | ES | Engineering Specification |
| | | ES | Enter Statement |
| ERS | Experimental Retrieval System | ES | Entfernte Station |
| | | ES | Equivalence Statement |

# E

| | | | |
|---|---|---|---|
| ES | Erasable Storage | ESD | Element Status Display |
| ES | Erasable Store | ESD | Energy Storage Device |
| ES | Erase Signal | ESD | External Symbol Dictionary |
| ES | Erkennungssignal | | |
| ES | Exclusive Segment | ESD | External Symbol Directory |
| ES | Executable Statement | ESDA | Europäisches Datenzentrum |
| ES | Execute Statement | | |
| ES | Exit Statement | ESDAC | European Space Data Centre |
| ES | Experimental Station | | |
| ES | Expertensystem | ESDL | Electro-technical-laboratory System Description Language |
| ES | Explicit Storage | | |
| ES | Extended Support | | |
| ES | External Statement | ESDM | Erzeugnis-System "Digitale Messung und Meßwertausgabe" |
| ES | External Store | | |
| ESA | End of Storage Area | | |
| ESA | Engineers and Scientists of America | ESDP | Evolutionary System for Data Processing |
| ESA | European Space Research Organisation | ESDS | Elemental Standard Data System |
| ESA | Extra Shift Authorization | ESDS | Entry Sequenced Data Set |
| ESAIRA | Electronically Scanned Airborne Intercept Radar | ESDT | Electrostatic Storage Display Tube |
| ESAR | Electronically Scanned Array Radar | ESDTR | Electronic Selector Dropout Tape Read |
| ESAR | Electronically Steerable Array Radar | ESDU | Engineering Science Data Unit |
| ESAV | Einheitssystem der Automatisierten Verfahrenstechnik | ESE | Eigene Speichereinheit |
| | | ESE | Electrical Support Equipment |
| ESB | Einseitenband | ESEG | Einheitssystem der Elektronik und des Gerätebaus |
| ESB | Electric Storage Battery | | |
| ESB | Electrical Simulation of Brain | | |
| | | ESEM | Elastostatik-Elementmethode |
| ESBAR | Epitaxial Schottky Barrier | | |
| ESC | Educational Scientific Computer | ESEN | Einheitliches System der Elektronischen Nachrichtentechnik |
| ESC | Electron Shop Computer | | |
| ESC | Electrostatic Compatibility | ESER | Einheitliche Systeme der Elektronischen Rechentechnik |
| ESC | Emulation Sub-Channel | | |
| ESC | Entrée/Sortie Compteur | ESFI | Epitaxial Silicon Film on Isolators |
| ESC | Error Status Code | | |
| ESC | Escape | ESFK | Electrostatically Focused Klystron |
| ESC | Escapement | | |
| ESCA | Electron Spectroscopy for Chemical Analysis | ESG | Electrically Suspended Gyroscope |
| ESCA | European Computer Service Association | ESG | Electronic Sweep Generator |
| ESCAPE | Expansion Symbolic Compiling Assembly Program for Engineering | ESG | English Standard Gauge |
| | | ESG | European Software Company GmbH |
| ESD | Echo Sounding Device | ESG | Expanded Sweep Generator |
| ESD | Electrostatic Discharge | ESH | Equivalent Standard Hours |
| ESD | Electrostatic Storage Deflection | ESI | Engineering and Scientific Interpreter |

# E

| | | | |
|---|---|---|---|
| ESI | Experiment Information System | ESP | Execution Scheduling Processor |
| ESI | Externally Specified Index | ESP | Executive and Scheduling Program |
| ESI | Extremely Sensitive Information | ESP | Expandable Stored Program |
| ESIA | Externally Specified Index Address | ESP | Externspeicher |
| | | ESP | Extrasensory Perception |
| ESIAC | ESI Analog Computer | ESPAR | Electronically Steerable Phased Array Radar |
| ESID | External Symbol Identification | ESPO | Echtzeitsteuerprogramm, Plattenspeicherorientiert |
| ESIOA | Extended Serial Input/ Output Adapter | ESPOL | Executive System Programming Oriented Language |
| ESIS | Electronic Store Information System | | |
| ESIS | Elektronisches Supermarkt-Informationssystem | ESPRIT | European Starter Project for the Research in Information Technology |
| ESIS | Executive Selection Inventory System | ESPRIT | European Strategic Program for Research and development in Information Technology |
| ESK | Externer Speicherkanal | | |
| ESKK | Einheitssystem der Klassifizierung und Kodierung | | |
| ESKO | Echtzeitsteuerprogrammsystem, Kernspeicherorientiert | ESPRIT | European Strategic Program of Research in Information Technology |
| ESL | Elbit Symbolic Language | ESR | Effective Series Resistance |
| ESL | Electronic Systems Laboratory | ESR | Effective Shunt Resistance |
| ESL | Erstellung von Schnittlisten | ESR | Effective Signal Radiated |
| | | ESR | Einheitliches System der Rechnertechnik |
| ESL | European Systems Language | ESR | Electric Store Register |
| ESM | Elastomeric Shield Material | ESR | Electron Spin Resonance |
| | | ESR | Electronic Scanning Radar |
| ESM | Electronic Switch Module | ESR | Equivalent Series Resistance |
| ESM | Energie-Sparmaßnahmen | | |
| ESMA | Electronic Sales and Marketing Association | ESR | Error Search Routine |
| | | ESR | Event Storage Record |
| ESN | Effective Segment Number | ESRO | European Space Research Organization |
| ESN | Extended Systems Networking | ESRS | Electronic Scanning Radar System |
| ESO | Engineering Salle d'Ordinateur | ESRUS | Einheitliches System von Rechnungsführung Und Statistik |
| ESONE | European Standard Of Nuclear Electronics | | |
| ESP | Early Shipment Programm | ESS | Electron Spin Spectra |
| ESP | Echeloned Series Processor | ESS | Electronic Speech Synthesis |
| ESP | Economic Software Package | | |
| ESP | Editable Stored Program | ESS | Electronic Switching System |
| ESP | Efficiency Speed Power | | |
| ESP | Eingangsspeicher | ESS | Emplaced Scientific Station |
| ESP | Electrosensitive Programming | ESS | Engineering Scheduling System |
| ESP | Error Search Program | | |
| ESP | Erstwertspeicher | ESS | Erzeugnisstruktursätze |
| ESP | Erstwertsperre | ESS | Establishment Subsystem |

- 235 -

# E

| | | | |
|---|---|---|---|
| ESS | External Serial Storage | ET | Ending Tape |
| ESSA | Electronic Scanning and Stabilizing Antenna | ET | Energy Transfer |
| | | ET | Entscheidungstabelle |
| ESSADF | Electronic Switching System Arranged with Data Features | ET | Evaluation Test |
| | | ETA | Equipment Transfer Authorization |
| ESSDERC | European Solid State Devices Research Conference | ETA | Estimated Time of Arrival |
| | | ETAADS | Engine Technical And Administrative Data System |
| ESSFL | Electron Steady State Fermi Level | | |
| | | ETAB | Entscheidungstabelle |
| ESSS | Engineering/Scientific Support System | ETAM | Entry Telecommunication Access Method |
| ESSU | Electronic Selective Switching Unit | | |
| | | ETB | Electrical Time Base |
| EST | Earliest Start Time | ETB | End of Text Block |
| EST | Eingangssteuerung | ETB | End-of-Transmission Block |
| EST | Electrostatic Storage Tube | ETC | Electronic Table Calculator |
| EST | Electrostatic Store Tube | | |
| EST | Elément Simulation Technique | ETC | Electronic Temperature Control |
| EST | Estimate | ETC | Electronic Tuning Control |
| EST | Estimation | ETC | Electronic Typing Calculator |
| EST | Estimator | | |
| ESTC | Eastern Tape Center | ETC | Eleven Thirty Conversion |
| ESTD | Einheitssystem der Technologischen Dokumentation | ETC | Europäisches Technik-Centrum |
| | | ETC | Excess-Three Code |
| ESTG | Estimating | ETC | Extended Text Compositor |
| ESTI | Estimation | ETCD | Equipement de Terminaison de Circuit de Données |
| ESTMR | Estimator | | |
| ESTPV | Einheitliches System der Technischen Produktionsvorbereitung | ETCD | Equipement de Terminaux de Circuit de Données |
| | | ETCG | Elapsed Time Code Generator |
| ESTV | Error Statistics by Tape Volume | ETD | Electric Typewriter Division |
| ESU | Electrostatic Units | | |
| ESU | External Store Unit | ETD | Equipement Terminal de Données |
| ESV | Electrostatic Voltmeter | | |
| ESV | Enamel Single-silk Varnish | ETD | Ersatzteildienst |
| ESV | Error Statistics by Volume | ETD | Estimated Time of Departure |
| ESW | Error Status Word | | |
| ESX | Extended Systems Executive | ETD | Event Time Digitizer |
| | | ETDL | Electronics Technology and Device Laboratory |
| ET | Edge Triggered | | |
| ET | Einlagerungstelegraphie | ETE | External Test Equipment |
| ET | Einschaltetaste | ETEDS | Electromagnetic Test Environment Data System |
| ET | Einzelakt | | |
| ET | Electric Typewriter | ETEX | Eingabe Textdatei |
| ET | Electrical Time | ETF | Environmental Test Facility |
| ET | Electrical Typewriter | | |
| ET | Electronic Teleprinter | ETI | Elapsed Time Indicator |
| ET | Elektronik | ETIM | Elapsed Time |
| ET | Elektrotechnik | ETL | Emitter follower Transistor Logic |
| ET | Empfangstakt | | |
| ET | End of Transaction | | |

# E

| | | | |
|---|---|---|---|
| ETL | Emitterfolger-Transistor-Logik | ETSAL | Electronic Terms for Space Age Language |
| ETL | Ending Tape Label | ETSK | Entscheidungstabellen-Strukturkalkül |
| ETL | Epitaxial Transistor Logic | ETSO | Extended Time-Sharing Option |
| ETL | Equipement Terminal de Lignes | ETSQ | Electrical Time, Superquick |
| ETL | Etching by Transmitted Light | ETSS | Electronic Tandem Switching System |
| ETM | Elapsed Time Meter | ETT | End of Tape Test |
| ETM | Electronic Test and Maintenance | ETT | Entscheidungstabellentechnik |
| ETM | End of Tape Marker | ETTD | Equipment Terminal de Traitement de Données |
| ETM | Ending Tape Maker | ETTI | End Translation Time Indicator |
| ETMD | Essential Technical Medical Data | ETV | Epitaxial Tuning Vector |
| ETMF | Execution Time Multiplication Factor | ETVM | Electrostatic Transistorized Voltmeter |
| ETMF | Extended Telecommunications Modules Feature | ETVÜ | Entscheidungstabellenvorübersetzer |
| ETN | Equipment Table Nomenclature | ETX | End of Text |
| ETOS | Extended Tape Operating System | ETX | Ende des Textes |
| ETP | Electrical Tough Pitch | ETXR | End of Text Exit Routine |
| ETP | Experimental Test Procedure | ETZ | Elektronische Zeitung |
| ETP | Extended Tape Processing | EU | Electronics Unit |
| ETP | Extended Term Plan | EU | Emulator Program |
| ETPR | Execution Time Print Routine | EU | End User |
| ETR | Elapsed Time Recorder | EU | Exponent Underflow |
| ETR | Elektronischer Tischrechner | EUA | Erase Unprotected to Address |
| ETR | Engineering Test Reactor | EUCLID | Easily Used Computer Language for Illustrations and Drawings |
| ETR | Estimated Time of Return | EUCLID | Experimental Use Computer, London Integrated Display |
| ETR | Extended Temperature Range | EUDISED | European Documentation and Information System for Education |
| ETRO | Eingabe Trommeldatei | | |
| ETS | Electronic Teleaccounting System | EULTG | End User Language Task Group |
| ETS | Electronic Telegraph System | EUR | Executive Utility Routine |
| ETS | Electronic Test Set | EURIM | European conference on Research of Information services and libraries Management |
| ETS | Electronic Timing Set | | |
| ETS | Electronic Translator System | | |
| ETS | Entry Terminal System | EUROCOMP | The European Computing Congress |
| ETS | Entscheidungstabellensystem | EUROCRA | European OCR Association |
| ETS | European Telecommunications Systems | EUROMICRO | European association for Microprocessing and Microprogramming |
| ETS | European Teleprocessing System | | |
| ETS | External Time Sharing | EURONET | European Network |

# E

| | | | |
|---|---|---|---|
| EUSIDIC | European associations of Scientific Information Dissemination Centers | EWG | Environmental Working Group |
| EUT | Equipment Under Test | EWH | Expected Working Hours |
| EUT | Express Update Tape | EWICS | European Workshop on Industrial Computer Systems |
| EUUG | European Unix systems Users Group | EWIS | Einwohner-Informationssystem |
| EUV | Externe UV | | |
| EV | Electron Volt | EWK | Endwertkarte |
| EV | Empfangsverstärker | EWM | End of Warning Marker |
| EV | Error Voltage | EWR | Early Warning Radar |
| EV | Erzeugnisvertrieb | EWR | Eingabewortregister |
| EV | Exposure Value | EWR | Electronic Word Recognizer |
| EVA | Electronic Velocity Analyzer | EWS | Early Warning Signal |
| | | EWS | Elektronisches Wählsystem |
| EVA | Elektronisch Verwaltete Akten | EWS | Empfangswartespeicher |
| | | EWS | Ergonomic Work Stations |
| EVA | Error Volume Analysis | EWSD | Elektronisches Wählsystem Digital |
| EVAT | Electrical Verifying Assembly Tool | EX | Eject X |
| EVC | Error Vector Computer | EX | Examination |
| EVDA | Eingabe Verarbeitungsdatei | EX | Examine |
| EVDE | External Visual Display Equipment | EX | Example |
| | | EX | Exclusive OR |
| EVDL | Electrically Variable Delay Line | EX | Execute |
| | | EX | Executor |
| EVDL | Electronically Variable Delay Line | EX | Exit |
| | | EX | Experimental |
| EVI | Energieversorgungs-Informationssystem | EX | Exponent |
| | | EX | Extract |
| EVIC | Evaluation Integrated Circuit | EX | Extraction |
| | | EX-OR | Exclusive OR |
| EVM | Electronic Voltmeter | EXAM | Examine |
| EVM | Electrostatic Voltmeter | EXAM | Examinate |
| EVOM | Electronic Volt-Ohmmeter | EXAM | Examination |
| EVOP | Evolutionary Operations | EXAM | Experimental Aerospace Multiprocessor |
| EVPREP | Event Preparation | | |
| EVR | Electronic Video Recorder | EXAMD | Examined |
| EVR | Electronic Video Recording | EXAMG | Examining |
| EVS | Elektronisches Vertriebssystem | EXAMN | Examination |
| | | EXAPT | Exact Automatic Programming of Tools |
| EVS | Electrooptical Viewing System | EXAPT | Extented Subset of APT |
| EVT | Eignungs- und Verwendungstest | EXC | Excess |
| | | EXC | Execution |
| EVT | Extreme Value Theory | EXCD | Exceed |
| EVU | Elektrizitätsversorgungs-Unternehmen | EXCDG | Exceeding |
| | | EXCH | Exchange |
| EW | Early Warning | EXCLU | Exclusive |
| EW | Edit Word | EXCP | Except |
| EW | Electrically Welded | EXCP | Execute Channel Program |
| EWA | Effective Word Address | EXCPAM | Execute Channel Program Access Method |
| EWA | Electronic Writing Automaton | EXCV | Excessive |
| EWB | Einheitswertbogen | EXD | Examined |

# E

| | | | |
|---|---|---|---|
| EXD | External Device | EXPTL | Exponential |
| EXDAMS | Extendable Debugging And Monitoring System | EXR | Exception Request |
| | | EXREDCON | Exercise Readiness Condition |
| EXDAMS | Extended Debugging And Monitoring System | EXSR | Executive Subroutine |
| EXDC | External Data Controller | EXSR | Exit Subroutine |
| EXDKZ | Externes Datenträgerkennzeichen | EXST | Execute Stack |
| | | EXSTA | Experimental Station |
| EXE | Execute | EXT | Extend |
| EXE | Externes Element | EXT | Extension |
| EXEC | Execute | EXT | External |
| EXEC | Executive | EXT | Extra |
| EXEC | Executive control system | EXT | Extreme |
| EXECN | Execution | EXTEL... | Exchange Telegraph Co. Ltd. |
| EXECV | Executive | | |
| EXERPS | Extended Error Recovery Procedures | EXTM | Extended Telecommunication |
| EXET | Execute Time | EXTM | Extended Telecommunications Module |
| EXLIST | Exit List | | |
| EXLST | Exit List | EXTRA | Exponentially Tapered Reactive Antenna |
| EXMETNET | Experimental Meteorological sounding rocket research Network | | |
| | | EXTRN | External Reference |
| | | EXTSN | Extension |
| EXP | Expand | EZ | Electrical zero |
| EXP | Expansion | EZ | Erfassungszeit |
| EXP | Exponential | EZ | Erinnerungszeiger |
| EXP | Exposure | EZGM | Erweiterte Zugriffmethode |
| EXPERT | Executive Program Exploiting Real-Time | EZM | Elektronikzentrum München |
| | | EZR | Eingabezielregister |
| EXPERT | Expanded PERT | EZÜ | Elektronische Zahlungsüberweisung |
| EXPL | Explanation | | |
| EXPR | Expression | EZV | Elektronischer Zahlungsverkehr |
| EXPRESS | Expandable Parts Records and Structure System | | |

# F

| | | | |
|---|---|---|---|
| F | Fahrenheit | FAAS | Fixed Assets Accounting System |
| F | Farad | | |
| F | Feedback | FAATE | Fault Analyzing Automatic Test Equipment |
| F | Fernmeldewesen | | |
| F | Festspeicher | FAB | Frequenzaufbereitung |
| F | Field | FAC | Factor |
| F | Filament | FAC | Fakturierungscomputer |
| F | File | FAC | Field Accelerator |
| F | Filter | FAC | File Access Channel |
| F | Fixed | FAC | Film Aperture Card |
| F | Flag | FAC | Filter Address Correction |
| F | Force | FAC | Final Assembly Control |
| F | Foreground | FAC | First Alarm Code |
| F | Formulate | FAC | Forward Air Controller |
| F | Fraktion | FAC | Four-Address Code |
| F | Frequency | FAC | Four-Address Computer |
| F | Frequenz | FAC | Fuse Arming Computer |
| F | Fühler | FACCE | Family Concept of Computing Elements |
| F | Function | | |
| F | Fuse | FACCM | Fast Access Charge-Coupled Memory |
| F&A | Finance and Administration | | |
| | | FACD | Foreign Area Customer Dialling |
| F&D | Facilities and Design | | |
| F-ADU | Frequenz-Analog/ Digital-Umsetzer | FACE | Factory Automatic Checkout Equipment |
| F-Bit | Final Bit | FACE | Field Alterable Control Element |
| F/D | Focal to Diameter ratio | | |
| F/L | Fetch/Load | FACE | Field Artillery Computer Equipment |
| F/V | Frequency to Voltage converter | | |
| | | FACE | Field Artillery Computing Equipment |
| FA | Factory Automation | | |
| FA | Fehleranzeige | FACE | Functional Automatic Circuit Evaluator |
| FA | Fernmeldeamt | | |
| FA | Field Address | FACES | FORTRAN Automatic Code Evaluation System |
| FA | File Addressing | | |
| FA | File Attribute | FACI | First Article Configuration Inspection |
| FA | Final Address | | |
| FA | Flat-gain Amplifier | FACP | Fully Automated Computer Program |
| FA | Flexible Addressing | | |
| FA | Floating Add | FACR | Fourier Analysis Cyclic Reduction |
| FA | Floating Address | | |
| FA | Forced-Air-cooled | FACRS | FORTRAN Analytical Cross Reference System |
| FA | Fourier Analysis | | |
| FA | Frame Antenna | FACS | Facsimile |
| FA | Frequency Adjustment | FACS | Factory Assembly Control System |
| FA | Frequency Agility | | |
| FA | Frequenzaufbereitung | FACS | Fine Attitude Control System |
| FA | Full Adder | | |
| FA | Fully Automatic | FACS | Floating decimal Abstract Coding System |
| FA | Further Assemblies | | |
| FA&T | Final Assembly and Test | FACS | Fully Automatic Compiling System |
| FAAP | Fixed Assets Accounting Package | | |
| | | FACT | Factual Compiler |
| FAAR | Forward Area Alerting Radar | FACT | Flexible Automatic Circuit Tester |

# F

| | | | |
|---|---|---|---|
| FACT | Flight Acceptance Composite Test | FAIRS | Failure Analysis Information Retrieval System |
| FACT | Fully Automated Cataloguing Technique | FAIRS | Federal Aviation Information Retrieval System |
| FACT | Fully Automatic Compiler-Translator | FAK | Freigabe der Ablaufkette |
| | | FAKT | Feldaktivitätenbericht |
| FACT | Fully Automatic Compiling Technique | FAKTA | Faktorenanalyse |
| | | FAKTYR | Fachbereich-Kybernetik-Retrievalsystem |
| FACT | Functional Alternating Current Tester | FAL | Financial Analysis Language |
| FACTOR | Fourteen-O-one Automatically Controlled Test Optimizing Routine | FAL | Finite Automation Language |
| | | FAL | Frequency Allocation List |
| FACTS | Facilities Administration Consolidated Tape System | FALCON | Frequenzanaloger Converter |
| FAD | Failure Activity Determination | FALGEN | Fachabteilungslistengenerator |
| FAD | Floating Add | FALT | FADAC Automatic Logic Tester |
| FAD | Floating Add Double | | |
| FADAC | Field Army Digital Automatic Computer | FALT | Field Artillery Logic Tester |
| FADAC | Field Artillery Digital Automatic Computer | FALTRAN | FORTRAN-to-ALGOL Translator |
| FADAC | Field Artillery Digital Atomic Computer | FAM | Fast Access Memory |
| | | FAM | Fast Auxiliary Memory |
| FADAC | Field Atomic Digital Automatic Computer | FAM | File Access Method |
| | | FAM | Floating Add Magnitude |
| FADAP | Fleet Antisubmarine Data Analysis Program | FAM | Frequency Allocation Multiplex |
| FADM | Forced Attribute Display Mode | FAM | Frequency Amplitude Modulation |
| FADR | Funktioneller Aufbau Digitaler Rechensysteme | FAMA | Fachausschuß für Moderne Abrechnungssysteme |
| FADSN | Floating Add Double Suppress Normal | FAMA | Fachausschuß für Moderne Abrechnungssysteme beim Institut der Wirtschaftsprüfer |
| FAE | Final Approach Equipment | | |
| FAGC | Fast Automatic Gain Control | | |
| FAHQMT | Fully Automatic High Quality Machine Translation | FAMAS | Financial Analysis and Management System |
| | | FAMAS | Financial And Management Accounting System |
| FAHQT | Fully Automatic, High Quality Translation | FAME | Ferro-Acoustic Memory |
| FAI | Five-Address Instruction | FAMIS | Financial And Management Information System |
| FAI | Four-Address Instruction | | |
| FAI | Frequency Azimuth Intensity | FAMOS | Floating-gate-Avalanche-injection-Metal-Oxide-Semiconductor |
| FAIB | Fédération des Associations d'Informaticiens de Belgique | FAMOUS | File Access Maintenance Output Universal System |
| FAIR | Fast Access Information Retrieval | FAMP | Ferrite Aperture Memory Plate |
| FAIR | File Access Interface Routines | FAMPR | Feature Assembly Manufacturing Process Record |

# F

| | | | |
|---|---|---|---|
| FAMS | Forecasting And Modelling System | FAST | Field Automated Systems Test |
| FAND-FOR | Fan-in Determined-Fan-Out Registered | FAST | Field data Applications Systems and Techniques |
| FANUC | Fujitsu Automatic Numerical Control | FAST | Final Automated Systems Test |
| FAO | Fabrication Assistée par Ordinateur | FAST | Financial Analysis System |
| FAO | Four-Address Operation | FAST | Fingerprint Access and Searching Technique |
| FAP | FORTRAN Assembly Program | FAST | Flexible Algebraic Scientific Translator |
| FAP | Financial Analysis Program | FAST | Flexible Automatic Systems Tester |
| FAP | Floating point Arithmetic Package | FAST | Formal Autoindexing of Scientific Texts |
| FAP | Fully Automatic Program | FAST | Formula And Statements Translator |
| FAP | Functional Assignment Panel | FAST | Formula Automatic Scaler Translator |
| FAPS | Financial Analysis and Planning System | FAST | Four Address to Soap Translator |
| FAQ | Fair Average Quality | FAST | Fully Automatic Sorting and Testing |
| FAR | Failure Analysis Report | | |
| FAR | Field Altering and Reconditioning | FAST | Functional Analysis Specification Tree |
| FAR | Forward Acquisition Radar | FASTAR | Frequency Angle Scanning, Tracking And Ranging |
| FARADA | Failure Rate Data | | |
| FARGO | Fourteen-O-One Automatic Report Generating Operation | FASTFOR | Fast FORTRAN |
| | | FASTI | Fast Access to Systems Technical Information |
| FARS | File Analysis for Random access Storage | FASTI | Fast Access to System Test Information |
| FAS | Fast Access Storage | FAT | Fast Automatic Transfer |
| FAS | Fast Access Store | FAT | Ferngesteuerter Adressierbarer Teilnehmer-Konverter |
| FAS | Fertigungsabschnitt | | |
| FAS | Filtered Air Supply | | |
| FAS | Fragen-Auswertungs-System | FAT | Final Assembly Test |
| | | FAT | Formula Assembler Translator |
| FAS | Free Alongside | | |
| FAS | Full Automatic Search | FAT | Frappe A Tort |
| FASB | Fetch-And-Set Bit | FATAL | Fully Automatic Test Algebraic Language |
| FASB | Financial Accounting Standards Board | | |
| FASDCC | Field Army Switched Digital Communications Center | FATCAT | Frequency And Time Circuit Analysis Technique |
| | | FATDL | Frequency And Time-division Data Link |
| FASDER | Filing And Source-Data for Easier Retrieval | | |
| FASP | Frequency Analysis of System Program | FATE | Fusing and Arming Test Experiments |
| | | FATR | Fixed Autotransformer |
| FAST | FORTRAN Automatic Symbol Translator | FATS | Fernsteuerbares, Adressierbares Teilnehmerkonvertsystem |
| FAST | Facility for Automatic Sorting and Testing | | |
| FAST | Fast Automatic Shuttle Transfer | FATS | FORTRAN Automatic Timing System |

# F

| | | | |
|---|---|---|---|
| FAU | Frequenzaufbereitung | FBS | Finanzbuchhaltungssystem |
| FAUST | Fehleranalyse Und -statistik | FBS | Finish Build Schedule |
| | | FBSB | Forward Biased Second Breakdown |
| FAV | Full Analog Video | | |
| FAX | Facsimile | FBT | Facility Block Table |
| FAXDIN | Facsimile Transmission over AUTODIN | FBT | Fast BIFORE Transform |
| | | FBT | Flyback Transformer |
| FAXE | Facsimile Equipment | FBV | Funkbetriebsvorschrift |
| FB | Feedback | FC | Failure Count |
| FB | Fehlerbedingung | FC | Family Code |
| FB | Fehlerbyte | FC | Ferrite Core |
| FB | Flag Bit | FC | Field Code |
| FB | Flag Byte | FC | Field Compare |
| FB | Full Back | FC | File Chain |
| FB | Function Bit | FC | File Code |
| FB | Funktionsblock | FC | File Command |
| FB | Fuse Block | FC | File Connector |
| FB | Fuse Box | FC | File Control |
| FBA | Fixed-Block-Architektur | FC | File Conversion |
| FBA | Forward Branching Algorithm | FC | Fill Code |
| | | FC | Fire Control |
| FBC | Feed Back Control | FC | Flight Computer |
| FBC | Feedback Balanced Code | FC | Font Change Character |
| FBC | Finish Build Claims | FC | Footcandle |
| FBC | Fully Buffered Channel | FC | Format Code |
| FBC | Functional Bit Coding | FC | Format Control |
| FBD | Fachnormenausschluß Bibliotheks- und Dokumentationswesen | FC | Freiburger Code |
| | | FC | Frequency Changer |
| | | FC | Frequency Conversion |
| FBD | Feststehendes Blockdruckwerk | FC | Frequency Converter |
| | | FC | Fuel Cell |
| FBD | Flow Block Diagram | FC | Function Call |
| FBE | Fernbetriebseinheit | FC | Function Code |
| FBF | Feedback Filter | FC | Functional Checkout |
| FBG | Fernbediengerät | FC | Functional Code |
| FBG | Flachbaugruppe | FCA | Fault Correction Array |
| FBI | Fortlaufende Bestellpositionsidentifikation | FCA | Fixed Coaxial Attenuator |
| | | FCA | Floating Channel Addressing |
| FBI | Forum de la Bureautique et de l'Informatique | | |
| | | FCA | Frequency Control Analysis |
| FBK | Fast Back | | |
| FBL | Form Block Line | FCA | Frequency Control and Analysis |
| FBLK | Functional Block | | |
| FBM | Field Bill of Material | FCAF | Frequency Control Analysis Facility |
| FBM | Fix Block Modus | | |
| FBM | Fleet Ballistic Missile | FCAR | Forms Control Address Register |
| FBN | Feed Back Network | | |
| FBOE | Frequency Band Of Emission | FCAT | Floating Si-gate Channel corner Avalanche Transition |
| FBP | Final Boiling Point | | |
| FBP | Formularbeschreibungsprogramm | | |
| | | FCB | File Control Block |
| FBQE | Free Block Queue Element | FCB | Format Control Buffer |
| FBR | Feedback Resistance | FCB | Forms Control Buffer |
| FBR | Fixed Base Representation | FCB | Function Control Block |
| FBS | Fernbetriebssystem | FCB | Function Control Byte |

# F

| | | | |
|---|---|---|---|
| FCC | Faced-centred Cubic Crystal | FCIN | Fast Carry Iterative Network |
| FCC | Federal Communications Commission | FCL | Feedback Control Loop |
| | | FCL | Feeder Control Logic |
| FCC | Federal Communications Committee | FCM | Feature Code Master |
| | | FCM | Ferrite Core Matrix |
| FCC | Fire Control Computer | FCM | Ferrite Core Memory |
| FCC | Flat Conductor Cable | FCNI | Flux Control Negative Inductance |
| FCC | Font Change Character | | |
| FCC | Forbidden Combination Check | FCO | Field Change Order |
| | | FCO | Field Checkout |
| FCC | Frequency-to-Current Converter | FCO | Fixed Cycle Operation |
| | | FCO | Functional Checkout |
| FCCA | Forestry, Conservation, and Communications Association | FCP | Facility Control Program |
| | | FCP | Fast Card Punch |
| | | FCP | Feed Control Panel |
| FCCC | Forbidden Code Combination Check | FCP | File Control Processor |
| | | FCP | File Control Program |
| FCCR | Feature Customization Control Record | FCP | Function Control Package |
| | | FCP | Function Control Program |
| FCCTS | Federal COBOL Compiler Testing Service | FCPC | Fleet Computer Programming Center |
| FCD | Failure Correction Decoding | FCPCP | Fleet Computer Programming Center Pacific |
| FCD | Frequency Compression Demodulator | FCR | File Component Rules |
| | | FCR | File Control Routine |
| FCDR | Failure and Consumption Data Report | FCR | Final Configuration Review |
| FCDR | Failure Cause Data Report | FCR | Fire Control Radar |
| FCDT | Four Coil Differential Transformer | FCR | Fuse Current Rating |
| | | FCS | Failure Consumption Sheet |
| FCE | Field Checkout Equipment | FCS | Feedback Control System |
| FCE | Final Control Element | FCS | Ferrite Core Store |
| FCEI | Facility Contract End Item | FCS | File Control System |
| FCF | Flow Control Function | FCS | Fire Control System |
| FCF | Fourier Coefficient Filter | FCS | Frame Check Sequence |
| FCF | Frequency Compression Feedback | FCS | Frame Checking Sequence |
| | | FCS | Function Control Sequence |
| FCFS | First Come, First Served | FCS | Functional Checkout Set |
| FCFT | Fixed Code, Fixed Time | FCT | Field Controlled Thyristor |
| FCGU | Fernseh- und Computer-gesteuerter Unterricht | FCT | Filament Center Tap |
| | | FCT | File Control Table |
| FCGU | Fernseh- und Computer-unterstützter Gruppen-unterricht | FCT | Frequency Clock Trigger |
| | | FCT | Function |
| | | FCTN | Function |
| FCGU | Film- und Computer-unterstützter Gruppen-unterricht | FCU | Feed Control Unit |
| | | FCU | File Control Unit |
| | | FCU | Frequency Converter Unit |
| FCH | Fächer | FCUR | Field Change Uninstalled Report |
| FCH | Fetch | | |
| FCI | Flux Changes per Inch | FCV | Flip-Chip-Verfahren |
| FCI | Functional Configuration Identification | FCW | Fast Cyclotron Wave |
| | | FCW | Format Control Word |
| FCIG | Field Change Identification Guide | FD | Feedback Decoding |
| | | FD | Fehlerdetektor |

- 245 -

# F

| | | | |
|---|---|---|---|
| FD | Field Definition | FDC | Frame Dependent Control |
| FD | Field Description | FDC | Frequency Domain Coding |
| FD | Field Descriptor | FDC | Full Digital Correlator |
| FD | Field time waveform Distortion | FDC | Function Digits Code |
| | | FDCMPT | Fire Direction Computer |
| FD | File Description | FDD | Field Data Department |
| FD | File Directory | FDD | Floating Digital Drive |
| FD | Flächendiode | FDD | Frequency Difference Detector |
| FD | Flange local Distance | | |
| FD | Floating Decimal | FDD | Frequency Divider and Distributor |
| FD | Floating Divide | | |
| FD | Floating Dollar | FDDL | Frequency Division Data Link |
| FD | Floppy Disk | | |
| FD | Flußdiagramm | FDDLP | Frequency Division Data Link Printout |
| FD | Formulardrucker | | |
| FD | Fotodiode | FDDLPO | Frequency Division Data Link Printout |
| FD | Frame Difference | | |
| FD | Freier Deskriptor | FDE | Field Decelerator |
| FD | Frequency Distribution | FDE | File Description Entry |
| FD | Frequency Diversity | FDEBUG | FORTRAN Debugging |
| FD | Frequency Divider | FDEBUG | FORTRAN symbolic Debugging package |
| FD | Frequency Division | | |
| FD | Frequency Doubler | FDEDIT | Floppy Disc Editor |
| FD | Frequenzdekade | FDF | File Description Files |
| FD | Full Duplex | FDF | Foreign Disc Facility |
| FD | Function Designator | FDG | Fractional Doppler Gate |
| FD | Functional Description | FDGS | Factory Data Gathering System |
| FDA | Fast Data Acquisition | | |
| FDA | File Description Attribute | FDH | Floating Divide or Halt |
| FDA | File Descriptor Area | FDI | Field Discharge |
| FDA | Floating Decimal Arithmetic | FDIS | Freeway Driver Information System |
| FDA | Frequency Distortion Analyzer | FDL | Ferrit Diode Limiter |
| | | FDL | Fixed Delay Line |
| FDAD | Freie-Deskriptoren-Addressensatz | FDL | Forms Description Language |
| | | FDM | Fehlerdämpfungsmesser |
| FDAD | Full Disk Address | FDM | File Definition Macro-instruction |
| FDAS | Floppy Disk Anschaltung | | |
| FDAS | Frequency Distribution Analysis Sheet | FDM | Finit-Differenzen-Methode |
| | | FDM | Finite Differential Method |
| FDASM | Floppy Disk Assembler | FDM | Five Digit Multiplier |
| FDAU | Flight Data Acquisition Unit | FDM | Frequency Deviation Meter |
| | | FDM | Frequency Diversity Multiplex |
| FDB | Field Descriptor Block | | |
| FDB | Field Dynamic Braking | FDM | Frequency Division Modulation |
| FDBK | Feedback | | |
| FDC | Fast Data Collecting | FDM | Frequency Division Multiplexing |
| FDC | Field Data Computer | | |
| FDC | File Definition Control | FDM | Frequency Division Multiplex |
| FDC | Firing Data Computer | | |
| FDC | Flight Director Computer | FDM | Frequency Division Multiplexor |
| FDC | Floppy Disk Controller | | |
| FDC | Fluid Digital Computer | FDM | Frequenzdemodulation |
| FDC | Form Definition Component | FDMA | Frequency Division Multiplex Access |

- 246 -

# F

| | | | |
|---|---|---|---|
| FDMS | Frequency Division Multiplexing System | FDS | Function Defining Statement |
| FDMVC | Frequency Division Multi-plex Voice Communication | FDSU | Flight Data Storage Unit |
| | | FDT | Fast Data Transmission |
| | | FDT | Field Definition Tables |
| FDN | Field Designator Number | FDT | Full Duplex Teletype |
| FDN | File Definition Name | FDT | Function Data Table |
| FDNR | Frequency Dependent Negative Resistance | FDTK | Floating Drift Tube Klystron |
| FDOS | Floppy Disk Operating System | FDU | Frequency Determining Unit |
| FDP | Factory Data Processing | FDU | Frequency Divider Unit |
| FDP | Fast Digital Processor | FDUP | Full Duplex |
| FDP | Field Development Program | FDV | Full Duplex Vocoder |
| | | FDW | Flat Data Wing |
| FDP | Flight Data Processing | FDX | Full Duplex |
| FDP | Flow Diagram Processor | FE | Ferroelectric |
| FDP | Form Description Program | FE | Field Engineer |
| FDPO | Floating Decimal Point Operation | FE | Field Engineering |
| | | FE | Field Erase |
| FDPSK | Frequency Differential PSK | FE | Field Error |
| | | FE | Field Exit |
| FDR | Fast Dump Restore | FE | File Editor |
| FDR | Feeder | FE | File Extent |
| FDR | Field Definition Record | FE | Filtereinsatz |
| FDR | File Data Register | FE | Filtereinschub |
| FDR | Final Data Report | FE | Finite Element |
| FDR | Fixkostendeckungsrechnung | FE | Finites Element |
| FDR | Flight Data Recoder | FE | Format Effector |
| FDR | Floating Divide Remainder | FE | Framing Error |
| FDR | Format Description Record | FE | Frühestes Ende |
| FDR | Frequency Diversity Radar | FE | Funktionelement |
| FDR | Frequency Domain Reflectometry | FE | Funktiongrundelement |
| | | FE | Funktionseinheit |
| FDRF | Financial Data Records Folder | FEA | Failure Effect Analysis |
| | | FEA | Field Effect Amplifier |
| FDRT | Flexible Digital Receiving Terminal | FEA | Finite Element Analysis |
| | | FEABL | Finite Element Analysis Basic Library |
| FDS | Fast Data Store | | |
| FDS | Fast Diode Switch | FEALD | Field Engineering Automated Logic Diagram |
| FDS | Fast Drive Scanner | | |
| FDS | Ferrite Disk Store | FEAP | FORTRAN Executive Assembly Program |
| FDS | Fighter Data Storage | | |
| FDS | File Definition Statement | FEAR | Failure Effect Analysis Report |
| FDS | File Description System | | |
| FDS | Financial Data Sciences, Incorporated | FEARS | Fourth Element Application and Rates System |
| FDS | Financial management Display System | FEASIBLE | Finite Element Analysis Sensibly Implemented By Least Effort |
| FDS | Flexible Display System | | |
| FDS | Flight Data Subsystem | FEAT | Feature |
| FDS | Float Dollar Sign | FEAT | Financial Evaluation and Analysis Technique |
| FDS | Fluid Distribution System | | |
| FDS | FORTRAN Deductive System | FEAT | Frequency of Every Allowable Term |

- 247 -

# F

| | | | |
|---|---|---|---|
| FEB | Functional Electronic Block | FEIM | Federation Européenne des Importeurs de Machines de bureau |
| FEBOS | Fensterbau-Organisations-System | FEIM | Field Engineering Installation Manual |
| FEBS | Function Electronic Blocks | FEIS | Funktionseinheitensystem |
| FEC | File End Closing | FEISM | Field Engineering Instructional Systems Manual |
| FEC | Format Effector Character | | |
| FEC | Forward Error Correcting | | |
| FEC | Forward Error Correction | FEK | Funktionseinheitenklasse |
| FEC | Forward Error Corrective | FEL | File End Label |
| FEC | Frankfurter Elektronik Center | FELDAT | Feldbeschreibungsdatei |
| | | FEM | Ferroelectric Memory |
| FEC | Front End Computer | FEM | Field Effect Modified transistor |
| FEC | Front End Control | | |
| FECB | File Extend Control Block | FEM | Field Emission Microscope |
| FECES | Forward Error Control Electronics System | FEM | Finite Element Method |
| | | FEM | Finiter Elemente |
| FED | Field Effect Device | FEM | Five-level End of Message |
| FED | Field Effect Diode | FEMC | Finite Element Modelling Optimization |
| FED | Field Engineering Department | | |
| | | FEMDM | Field Engineering Maintenance Diagram Manual |
| FED | Form Editor | | |
| FED | Format Element Descriptor | FEMECA | Failure/Error Mode, Effect and Critically Analysis |
| FED | Front-End-Processor | | |
| FEDAC | Forward Error Detection And Correction | FEMI | Field Engineering Manual of Instruction |
| FEDAM | Finite Element Data Management | FEMIS | Field Engineering Management Information System |
| FEDAP | Feeder Data Assembly Program | FEMM | Field Engineering Maintenance Manual |
| FEDGE | Finite Element Data Generation | FEMPX | Front End Multiplexer |
| | | FEOLL | Forschungs- und Entwicklungszentrum für Objektivierte Lehr- und Lernverfahren |
| FEDIS | Front End Design Information System | | |
| FEDM | Field Engineering Diagram Manual | | |
| | | FEOV | Forced End Of Volume |
| FEE | Fill Exit Entry | FEP | FORTRAN Enhancement Package |
| FEE | Final End Entry | | |
| FEEATT | Ferro-Electric Education Audio Tuning Tape | FEP | Front End Processing |
| | | FEP | Front End Processor |
| FEEDBAC | Foreign Exchange Eurodollars and Branch Accounting | FEP | Front-End-Prozessoren |
| | | FEPAM | Ferngesteuertes Prüfen, Alarmieren und Messen |
| FEEL | Ferro-Electric Electro-Luminescence | FEPLUS | Fertigungsplanung- und Steuerungssystem |
| FEF | Factory Express File | FER | Fehlerregister |
| FEF | Film End File | FER | Field-Effect Resistor |
| FEFET | Ferro-Electric Field Effect Transistor | FER | Field Engineering Responsible |
| FEFO | First-Ended, First-Out | FER | Forward Error Reporting |
| FEGH | Field Engineering General Handbook | FERIC | False Entries in Records of Interstate Carriers |
| FEI | Funktionseinheit | FERPIC | Ferroelectric ceramic Picture device |
| FEIK | Funktionseinheitenkomplex | | |

# F

| | | | |
|---|---|---|---|
| FERS | Financial Engineering Reporting System | FF | Full Field |
| FERST | Freight and Equipment Reporting System for Transportation | FFA | Fast Fourier Analysis |
| | | FFA | Fast Fourier Analyzer |
| | | FFA | Function-to Function Architecture |
| FERTIS | Fertigungs-Informations-System | FFAG | Fixed Field Alternating Gradient |
| FERUT | Ferranti-computer at the University of Toronto | FFB | Functional Flow Block |
| | | FFBD | Functional Flow Block Diagram |
| FES | Far End Suppressor | | |
| FES | Ferroelectric Storage | FFBM | Field Feature Bill of Material |
| FES | File Extension Specification | FFC | Fault and Facilities Control |
| FES | Fundamental Electrical Standards | FFC | Flat Field Conjugate |
| FESR | Finite Energy Sum Rule | FFC | Flip-Flop Circuit |
| FESRR | Field Engineering System Reference Report | FFC | Flip-Flop Complementary |
| | | FFC | Form Feed Character |
| FESS | Finite Element Solution System | FFD | Free Flight Data |
| | | FFD | Functional Flow Diagram |
| FET | Feldeffekttransistor | FFE | Formatfreie Eingabe |
| FET | Field Effect Transistor | FFEC | Field-Free Emission Current |
| FET | Frühester Endtermin | | |
| FET | Full Electric Typewriter | FFF | Feed Forward Filter |
| FET | Full Electronic Typewriter | FFF | Ferro-resonant Flip Flop |
| FETE | FORTRAN Execution Time Estimator | FFG | Freie Funktionsgruppe |
| | | FFHT | Fast Fourier-Hadamard Transform |
| FETH | Field Effect Thyristor | | |
| FETMM | Field Engineering Theory Maintenance Manual | FFI | Field Feature Index |
| | | FFII | Fédération Française des Informaticiens Indépendants |
| FETOM | Field Engineering Theory of Operation Manual | | |
| FETS | Field Effect Transistors | FFL | Field Failure |
| FETT | Feldeffekt Transistor Technologie | FFL | Flip-Flop Latch |
| | | FFL | Front Focal Length |
| FETT | Field Effect Tetrode Transistor | FFLSC | Feedforward Linear Sequential Circuit |
| FETVM | Field-Effect Transistorized Voltmeter | FFM | Festfrequenz-Modems |
| | | FFM | Fixed Freqency Mode |
| FEUS | File Enquiry and Update System | FFM | Flat Field Program |
| | | FFP | Fast Field Program |
| FEVAC | Ferroelectric Variable Capacitor | FFP | Fast FORTRAN Processor |
| | | FFP | Firm-Fixed Price |
| FEZ | Frühester Endzeitpunkt | FFPI | Flip-Flop Position Indicator |
| FF | Fan Fold | | |
| FF | File Feed | FFR | Flip-Flop Register |
| FF | File Field | FFRD | Flip-Flop Relay Driver |
| FF | File Finish | FFRR | Full Frequency Range Recording |
| FF | File Format | | |
| FF | First Fit | FFS | Flexibles Fertigungs-System |
| FF | Fixed Focus | | |
| FF | Flat Film | FFS | Flip-Flop Storage |
| FF | Flip Flop | FFS | Formatted File System |
| FF | Form Factor | FFSA | Field Functional System Assembly and checkout |
| FF | Form Feed | | |

# F

| | | | |
|---|---|---|---|
| FFT | Fast Fourier Transform | FHSRB | File History Selection Request Block |
| FFT | Fast Fourier Transformation | FHT | Fast Hadamard Transform |
| FFTF | Fast Flux Test Facility | FHT | Finite Hilbert Transform |
| FFTP | Fast Fourier Transform Processor | FHT | Fully Heat Treated |
| | | FI | Factory Invoice |
| FFTP | Fast Fourier Transform Pruning | FI | Fan In |
| | | FI | Fernmeldetechnisches Institut |
| FFVUR | Front Feed Visual Unit Record | FI | Fertigungsinsel |
| FFZ | Flexibles Fertigungszentrum | FI | Field Intensity |
| | | FI | File Identification |
| FG | Field Gain | FI | File Identifier |
| FG | Filament Ground | FI | File Initialization |
| FG | Final Grid | FI | File Interlock |
| FG | Fisher Graphics | FI | Fixed Interval |
| FG | Formantglied | FI | Flow Indicator |
| FG | Function Generator | FI | Format Identifier |
| FG | Funktionsgeber | FI | Format Item |
| FG | Funktionsgenerator | FI | Free In |
| FG | Funktionsglied | FI | Function Instruction |
| FG | Funktionsgruppe | FI/O | Frame Input/Output |
| FGCS | Fifth Generation Computer-Systems | FIAD | Flame Ionization Analyzer and Detector |
| FGD | Fine Grain Data | FIAT | Floating Interpretive Automatic Translator |
| FGDAC | Function Generating Digital-to-Analog Converter | FIB | Fachinformationsbank |
| | | FIBAS | Finanzbuchhaltung im Bausteinsystem |
| FGI | Finish Goods Inventory | | |
| FGL | Fourth-Generation-Languages | FIBEL | Formen Integrierter Bestimmung von Lernfolgen |
| FGP | Foreground Program | | |
| FGPSS | FORTRAN General Purpose System Simulator | FIBU | Finanzbuchhaltung |
| | | FIBU | Finanzbuchhaltungssystem |
| FGR | Floating Gate Reset | FIC | Field Information Centre |
| FGRAL | FORTRAN Graph Algorithmic Language | FIC | Field Installation Charge |
| | | FIC | Film Integrated Circuit |
| FGS | Farbgrafik-System | FIC | First-In-Chain |
| FGT | Fernschaltgerät | FIC | Frequency Interference Control |
| FGT | Floating Gate Transistor | | |
| FH | Feed Hopper | FICA | Federal Insurance Contribution Act |
| FHA | French Holden Algorithm | | |
| FHB | Flat Head Brass | FICA | Fédération Internationale de Contrôle Automatique |
| FHD | Ferrohydrodynamic | | |
| FHD | First Harmonic Distortion | FICB | File Identification Control Block |
| FHD | Fixed Head Disk | | |
| FHF | Fixed Head File | FICC | Freaon Isopropyl Circuit Cleaner |
| FHL | File Header Label | | |
| FHMA | Frequency Hopping Multiple Access | FICO | File under Control |
| | | FICOB | Fédération de l'Informatique, de la Communication et l'Organisation de Bureau |
| FHP | Fixed Header Prefix | | |
| FHP | Friction Horsepower | | |
| FHS | File Handling System | | |
| FHS | Flat Head Steel | FICR | Financial Inventory Control Report |
| FHS | Forward Heat Shield | | |

# F

| | | | |
|---|---|---|---|
| FICS | Factory Information Control System | FIMIS | Financial Management Information System |
| FID | Fédération Internationale de Documentation | FIML | Full-Information Maximum Likelihood |
| FID | Flame Ionization Detector | FIMM | Finite Input Memory Machine |
| FID | Format Identification | | |
| FIDAC | Film Input to Digital Automatic Computer | FIMS | Financial Information Management System |
| FIDACSYS | Film Input to Digital Automatic Computer System | FIN | Final |
| | | FIN | Finish |
| | | FINA | Following Items Not Available |
| FIDAS | Formularorientiertes Interaktives Datenbanksystem | FINAC | Fast Interline Nonactivate Automatic Control |
| FIDO | Function Input Diagnostic Output | FINAL | Financial Analysis Language |
| FIDT | Forced Incident Destiny Testing | FINAS | Finanzbuchhaltungs- und Abrechnungssystem |
| FIF | Financial Information File | FIND | Facsimile Information Network Development |
| FIFF | First-In, First-Fit | | |
| FIFO | First-In, First-Out | FIND | File Interrogation of Nineteenhundred Data |
| FIFO | Floating Input-Floating Output | FINK | Finanzbuchhaltung im Krankenhaus |
| FIG | Figure | | |
| FIG | Floated Integration Gyro | FINQ | Final Queue |
| FIGS | Figure Shift upper case | FINREP | Final Reply |
| FIGS | Figures | FINST | Final Station |
| FIGS | Figures Shift | FINSystem | Finance System |
| FII | Field Installation Instruction | FINTR | Financial Transaction |
| | | FIOA | File Input/Output Area |
| FIIIV | Full Information Iterated Instrumental Variable | FIOP | FORTRAN Input Output Package |
| FIIT | Fault Isolation Interface Test | FIOU | Film Input/Output Unit |
| | | FIP | Fault Isolation Program |
| FIL | Filament | FIP | Finance Image Processor |
| FIL | Filter | FIP | Fixed Interconnection Pattern |
| FIL-HB | Fillister Head Brass | | |
| FIL-HS | Fillister Head Steel | FIPS | Federal Information Processing Standards |
| FILAKS | Fiat-Lancia-Kommunikations-System | FIPS | Festkommainterpretationssystem |
| FILAS | Filialbetriebe-Abrechnungssystem | | |
| | | FIPS | Floating-point Interpretation System |
| FILER | File Information Language Executive Routine | FIPS-PUB | Federal Information Processing Standards-Publication |
| FILO | First In Last Out | | |
| FIM | Fetch Immediate | | |
| FIM | Field Intensity Meter | FIPS-PUBS | Federal Information Processing Standards-Publications |
| FIM | Field Ion Microscope | | |
| FIM | Forschungsinstitut für Mikroprozessortechnik | FIPSR | Federal Information Processing Standards Register |
| FIM | Frequenz-Intermodulationsverzerrung | | |
| | | FIR | Far Infrared |
| FIMATE | Factory Installed Maintenance Automatic Test | FIR | Fast Information Retrieval |
| | | FIR | Fault Interrupt Routine |

# F

| | | | |
|---|---|---|---|
| FIR | Finite Impulse Response | FISAR | Fleet Information Storage And Retrieval |
| FIR | First | | |
| FIR | Forschungsinstitut für Rationalisierung | FISHROD | Fiche Information Selectively Held and Retrieved On Demand |
| FIR | Functional Item Replacement | FIST | Fault Isolation by Semi-automatic Techniques |
| FIRAV | First Available | | |
| FIRETRAC | Firing Error Trajectory Recorder And Computer | FISU | Filling Signal Units |
| | | FIT | Field Installation Time |
| FIRM | Financial Information for Resources Management | FIT | Floating Input Transistor |
| | | FITAL | Financial Terminal Application Language |
| FIRM | Flowcharting Is Realistic Management | FITGO | Floating Input To Ground Output |
| FIRM | Führungsdaten durch Inte-griertes Rechnungswesen mit Modularprogrammen | FITS | Flexible Integrated Tool System |
| FIRMS | Forcasting Information Retrieval of Management System | FITS | Fourteen-O-one Input-output Tape System |
| | | FIVS | Faktographisches Informa-tionsverarbeitungssystem |
| FIRQ | Fast Interrupt Request | | |
| FIRS | Faktographisches Infor-mationsrecherchesystem | FIX | Fixture |
| | | FIZ | Fachinformationszentrum |
| FIRS | File Interrogation and Reporting System | FIZIT | Französisches Informa-tionszentrum für Industrie und Technik |
| FIRS | Full Input Record Storage | | |
| FIRST | Fast Information Retrieval for Surface Transportation | FJ | Fixed Jack |
| | | FJ | Fused Junction |
| | | FJCA | Federal Japan Communica-tion Association |
| FIRST | Financial Information Reporting System | FJCC | Fall Joint Computer Conference |
| FIRTI | Far Infrared Target Indicator | FJIC | Federal Job Information Center |
| FIS | Fachinformationssystem | | |
| FIS | Fehlertolerantes Informationssystem | FK | Fehlerklasse |
| | | FK | Festkomma |
| FIS | Field Information System | FK | Führungskraft |
| FIS | Field Instruction System | FKA | Flüssigkristall-Anzeige |
| FIS | File Identification Statement | FKB | Fernsehkompatibles Bild-schirmgerät |
| FIS | Financial Information System | FKB | Function Key Button |
| | | FKC | Function Key Calling |
| FIS | Fixed Instruction System | FKD | Fernmeldekreisdirektion |
| FIS | Flexible Instruction System | FKG | Fehlerkorrekturgerät |
| | | FKP | Funktions-Kontroll-Programm |
| FIS | Flughafen-Informations-system | | |
| | | FKS | Festkörperschaltkreis |
| FIS | Forschungsplanungs-Informationssystem | FKZ | Fernkennzahl |
| | | FKZ | Freies Kennzeichen |
| FIS | Fuhrpark-Informations-system | FL | Field Length |
| | | FL | Field Loss |
| FIS | Führungs-Informations-System | FL | File |
| | | FL | File Label |
| FIS | Funktionales Informations-System | FL | File Limit |
| | | FL | Filler |

# F

| | | | |
|---|---|---|---|
| FL | Filter | FLD | Field |
| FL | Focal Length | FLDEC | Floating point Decimal |
| FL | Footlambert | FLDL | Field Length |
| FL | Formal Language | FLDOL | Floating Dollar |
| FL | Formal Logic | FLDOP | Field Operation |
| FL | Format List | FLDS | Fault Locating Diagnostics |
| FL | Formula Language | FLDS | Fixed-Length Distinguishing Sequence |
| FL | Fotoleiter | | |
| FLA | First Level Address | FLE | Free List Exhausted |
| FLA | Full Load Ampere | FLEA | Flux Logic Element Array |
| FLAC | Florida Automatic Computer | FLEA | Flux Logic Evaluation Assembly |
| FLAD | Fluorescence-Activated Display | FLECC | Federal Libraries Experiment in Co-operative Cataloguing |
| FLAD | Fluoreszenzaktives Display | | |
| FLAD | Fluoreszenzaktiviertes Display | FLEXER | Fundamental Loop Exerciser |
| FLAG | FORTRAN Load And Go | | |
| FLAIR | Fleet Location And Information Reporting | FLEXIMIS | Flexible Management Information System |
| FLAM | Fault Location And Monitoring | FLF | Fault Location Facility |
| | | FLF | Final Limit Forward |
| FLAME | Fault Location Automated by Monitored Emulation | FLF | Fixed Length Field |
| | | FLF | Flip-Flop |
| FLANG | Flowchart Language | FLF | Follow-the-Leader Feedback |
| FLAP | File Layout and Allocation Program | | |
| | | FLG | Flag |
| FLAP | First Level Adaptive Program | FLHP | Filter, Highpass |
| | | FLI | Fault Location Indicator |
| FLAP | Flexibles Automatisches Printprogramm | FLI | Full Length Instruction |
| | | FLIC | Fault Location Indicating Console |
| FLAP | FORTRAN List Array Processor | FLIDAP | Flight Data Position |
| FLARE | Fault Locating And Reporting Equipment | FLIDEN | Flight Data Entry |
| | | FLINT | Facilities Loading Investigation New Technique |
| FLAT | Flight-Aided Tracking | | |
| FLB | Fixed-Length Block | FLINT | Floating Interpretive language |
| FLBE | Filter Band Elimination | | |
| FLBE | Filter Band Eliminator | FLIP | Film Library Instantaneous Presentation |
| FLBE | Filter for Band Elimination | | |
| FLBH | Filter, Band High | FLIP | Floating Indexed Point |
| FLBIN | Floating-point Binary | FLIP | Floating Instrument Platform |
| FLBP | Filter Bandpass | | |
| FLC | File Label Card | FLIP | Floating Point Interpretive Program |
| FLC | Five Level Code | | |
| FLC | Fixed Length Computer | FLIP | Format-directed List Processor |
| FLCDG | Flow Control Data Generator | | |
| FLCO | Flight information and Control of Operation | FLIP | Free-form Language for Image Processing |
| | | FLIRT | FORTRAN Logical Information Retrieval Technique |
| FLCR | Fixed Length Cavity Resonance | | |
| FLCS | Fiber optics Low Cost System | FLITE | Flight Information Test Element |
| FLCT | Flow Control | FLK | Flächenlochkarte |

- 253 -

# F

| | | | |
|---|---|---|---|
| FLL | Field Length for Large core memory | FM | Ferrite Memory |
| FLL | Final Limit, Lower | FM | Ferritenmental |
| FLL | Frequency Locked Loop | FM | Ferromagnetic Memory |
| FLLS | Frequency-Locked Loops | FM | Fichier Membre |
| FLN | Flourescence Line Narrowing | FM | Field Manager |
| | | FM | Field Manual |
| FLO | Fault-Location Oscillator | FM | Field Mark |
| FLOCON | Floor Control | FM | Figure of Merit |
| FLODAC | Fluid-Operated Digital Automatic Computer | FM | File Maintenance |
| | | FM | File Management |
| FLOOD | Fleet Observation of Oceanographic Data | FM | File Mark |
| | | FM | File Merge |
| FLOP | Floating Octal Point | FM | Film Microelectronics |
| FLOPS | Floating point Operations Per Second | FM | Finder Matrix |
| | | FM | Fixed Memory |
| FLP | Facility Location Planner | FM | Floating Multiply |
| FLP | Faulty Location Panel | FM | Fonction Manuelle |
| FLP | Floating Point | FM | Format Management |
| FLPL | FORTRAN List Processing Language | FM | Frequency Meter |
| | | FM | Frequency Modulation |
| FLR | File Label Record | FM | Frequency Multiplex |
| FLR | Filter | FM | Frequenzmodulation |
| FLR | Final Limit, Reverse | FM | Function Management |
| FLR | Fixed-Length Record | FM | Function Multiplier |
| FLR | Floating-point Register | FM | Functional Module |
| FLR | Forward Looking Radar | FM... | Ferranti Ltd. |
| FLS | Fault Locator System | FM/AM | Frequency Modulation/ Amplitude Modulation |
| FLS | Field Length for Small core memory | FMA | Failure Mode Analysis |
| | | FMA | Fundamental Mode Asynchronous |
| FLS | Field Logistic System | | |
| FLSH | Flash timing | FMAIN | File Maintenance |
| FLT | Fault Locating Test | FMB | File Mask Bit |
| FLT | Fault Location Technology | FMC | Ferrite Memory Core |
| FLT | Fault Location Test | FMC | File Mask Command |
| FLT | Fault Locative Test | FMC | Finite Memory Channel |
| FLT | Filter | FMC | Fuel Management Computer |
| FLT | Floating | | |
| FLT | Functional Logic Trend | FMCW | Frequency Modulated Continuous Wave |
| FLTG | Floating | | |
| FLTR | Filter | FMD | Frequency of Minimum Delay |
| FLUC | Fluctuate | | |
| FLUC | Fluctuating | FMD | Function Management Data |
| FLUC | Fluctuation | | |
| FLUID | Facility for Listing, Updating and Interpreting Deck | FME | Fehlermeldung, Extern |
| | | FME | Frequency Measuring Equipment |
| FLW | Fault Location Word | FMEA | Failure Mode and Effect Analysis |
| FLW | Fixed-Length Word | | |
| FM | Facilities Management | FMEVA | Floating point Mean and Variance |
| FM | Fast Memory | | |
| FM | Feedback Mechanism | FMF | Flexible Manufacturing Factory |
| FM | Fehlermenge | | |
| FM | Fermium | FMFB | Frequency Modulation with Feedback |
| FM | Fernmelde-.... | | |

- 254 -

# F

| | | | |
|---|---|---|---|
| FMH | Function Management Header | FMSS | Financial and Merchandising Service System |
| FMI | Field Maintenance Instructions | FMT | Feature Machine Type |
| | | FMT | Format |
| FMIC | Frequency Monitoring and Interference Control | FMT | Free Memory Table |
| | | FMTS | Field Maintenance Test Station |
| FMICS | Financial Management Information and Control System | FMWT | Field Merge by World Trade |
| FMISC | Field Measurement Information System Center | FN | Fernnetz |
| | | FN | File Name |
| FML | File Manipulation Language | FN | File Number |
| | | FN | Function |
| FMLS | Full Matrix Least Squares | FN | Function Name |
| FMMA | Finite-Memory Moving-Average | FNA | Fachnormenausschuss |
| | | FNA | Fédération Nationale de l'Automation |
| FMO | Frequency Multiplier Oscillator | | |
| | | FNA | Free Network Addresses |
| FMO | Functional Microoperation | FNA | Frequency Network Analyzer |
| FMP | Fast-access Memory Parity Error | FNAP | FORTRAN Network Analysis Program |
| FMP | Fernschreibmultiplexer | | |
| FMP | Ferrite Memory Plane | FNI | Fachnormenausschuss Informations-Verarbeitung |
| FMP | Field Maintenance Prozessor | FNI | Fachnormenausschuß Informationsverarbeitung i. Normenausschuß |
| FMP | File Merge Phase | | |
| FMPE | Fast Memory Parity error | | |
| FMPM | Frequency Modulation/ Phase Modulation | FNIE | Fédération Nationale des Industries Electroniques |
| FMPS | Functional Mathematical Programming System | FNIM | Fachnormenausschuß Identifikationsmerkmale |
| FMQ | Frequency Modulated Quartz | FNP | Front-end Network Processor |
| FMR | Fehlermusterregister | FNP | Front Network Processor |
| FMR | File Mask Register | FNP | Fusion Point |
| FMR | Frequency Modulated Radar | FNS | Functional Signal |
| | | FO | Fan Out |
| FMRM | Field Management Reference Manual | FO | Fast Operate |
| | | FO | Fast Operating |
| FMS | FORTRAN Monitor System | FO | Fernmeldeordnung |
| FMS | File Maintenance System | FO | File Organization |
| FMS | File Management Supervisor | FO | Filter Output |
| | | FO | Follow-On |
| FMS | File Management System | FO | FORTRAN |
| FMS | Financial Management System | FO | Free Out |
| | | FO | Full Out |
| FMS | Flexible Manufacturing System | FOB | Function Operation Block |
| | | FOC | First Of Chain |
| FMS | Flexible Maschinensysteme | FOC | Folding Operation Code |
| FMS | Food Management System | FOC | Follow-On Contract |
| FMS | Fuel Management System | FOCAL | Formula Calculator |
| FMS | Fuhrpark-Management-System | FOCAL | Formulating On-line Calculations in Algebraic Language |
| FMSK | Form Skip | | |

# F

| | | | | |
|---|---|---|---|---|
| FOCAS | Ford Operating Cost Analysis System | | FORAST | Formula Assembler Translator |
| FOCI | First Operational Computer Installation | | FORBLOC | FORTRAN-compiled Block-oriented |
| FOCIS | Financial Online Central Information System | | FORC | Formula Coder |
| | | | FORCK | Format Checking |
| FOCOHANA | Fourier Coefficient Harmonic Analyzer | | FORCOL | Fourteen Column |
| | | | FORDAC | FORTRAN Data Acquisition and Control |
| FOCOS | FORDAC Conversational System | | FORDAC | FORTRAN Data Application and Control |
| FOCP | Fluid-Operated Card Processor | | FORDAP | FORTRAN Dynamic Analyzer Program |
| FOCUS | Financially Oriented Computer Updating Service | | FOREMAN | Form Retrieval and Manipulation Language |
| FOCUS | Form Of Control Users System | | FORESDAT | Formerly Restricted Data |
| | | | FORM | Format |
| FOCUS | FORTRAN Oriented Control and Universal Simulator | | FORM | Formula |
| | | | FORMA | FORTRAN Matrix Analysis |
| | | | FORMAC | Formula Assembler Compiler |
| FOCUS | Forum Of Control data Users | | FORMAC | Formula Manipulation Compiler |
| FOD | Fluidic Output Device | | |
| FODAAP | Fleet Operational Data Acquisition and Analysis Program | | FORMAL | Formula Manipulation Language |
| | | | FORMAT | FORTRAN Matrix Abstraction Techniques |
| FODAAS | Field Online Data Acquisition and Analysis System | | FORMEX | Formal Executor |
| | | | FORMKZ | Formularkennzeichen |
| FOG | Frequency Offset Generator | | FORMS | File Organization Modelling System |
| FOI | Faulty Operator Intervention | | FORMS | Form Matrix from Scalar |
| | | | FORMTL | Form Tool |
| FOI | First Order Interpolator | | FORSYS | Forschungsinformationssystem |
| FOIL | File Oriented Interpretive Language | | |
| | | | FORT | FORTRAN |
| FOM | Figure Of Merit | | FORTE | File Organisation Technique |
| FOMM | Finite Output-Memory Machine | | |
| | | | FORTET | FORTRAN-orientierte Entscheidungstabellen |
| FOMOT | Four Mode Ternary | | |
| FOODAP | Food Distributors Application | | FORTOCOM | FORTRAN One Compiler |
| | | | FORTRAN | Formula Translation |
| FOOS | Function-Oriented Organizational Structure | | FORTRAN | Formula Translator |
| | | | FORTSIM | FORTRAN Simulation |
| FOOSP | Fourteen-O-One Statistical Program | | FORWARD | Feedback Of Repair, Workshop And Reliability Data |
| FOP | First Order Predictor | | |
| FOPI | First Order Polynomial Interpolator | | FOS | FORTRAN Operating System |
| FOPLIS | Forschungsplanungs-Informationssystem | | FOS | Field Oriented Support |
| | | | FOS | File Operating System |
| FOPP | First Order Polynomial Predictor | | FOS | First Order Subroutine |
| | | | FOS | Floppy Operating System |
| FOPT | Fiber Optic Photo Transfer | | FOS | Fundamental Operating System |
| FOR | Fan-Out Registered | | |

- 256 -

# F

| | | | |
|---|---|---|---|
| FOSDIC | Film Optical Scanning Device for Input to Computers | FPC | Fixed Program Computer |
| | | FPC | Flexible Program Computer |
| FOSDIC | Film Optical Sensing Device for Input to Computers | FPC | Floating Point Calculation |
| | | FPC | Floating Point Computation |
| FOSIL | Focal Simulator Language | FPC | Floating Point Constant |
| FOSPLAN | Formal Space Planning language | FPC | Frequency Plane Correlator |
| FOU | Field Operating Unit | FPD | Flame Photometric Detector |
| FOV | Field Of View | | |
| FOX | Fiber Optic Extension | FPD | Flat Pack Diode |
| FOX... | Foxboro | FPD | Floating Point Device |
| FP | Faceplate | FPD | Floating Point Division |
| FP | Facility Program | FPD | Floating Point Data |
| FP | Feedback Positive | FPDP | Flight Path Design Program |
| FP | Festpunkt | | |
| FP | Field Printing | FPDS | Fleet Problem Data System |
| FP | File Packing | | |
| FP | File Parameter | FPE | FORTRAN Programming Environment |
| FP | File Processing | | |
| FP | File Processor | FPE | Functional Program Elements |
| FP | File Protect | | |
| FP | Fixed Point | FPF | Feed Per Foot |
| FP | Flat Pack | FPF | File Protection Function |
| FP | Flexible Programming | FPG | Festprogrammgeber |
| FP | Flight Programmer | FPG | Festprogrammgenerator |
| FP | Floating Point | FPG | Firing Pulse Generator |
| FP | Foot Pounds | FPG | Fixed Program Generator |
| FP | Foreground Program | FPGA | Field Programmable Gate Array |
| FP | Formal Parameter | | |
| FP | Format Primary | FPH | Floating Point Hardware |
| FP | Forward Perpendicular | FPI | Financement du Plan Informatique |
| FP | Freezing Point | | |
| FP | Freie Pufferzeit | FPI | Floating Point Instruction |
| FP | Full Period | FPIS | Forward Propagation by Ionospheric Scatter |
| FP | Function Part | | |
| FP | Function Procedure | FPL | Field Processing Language |
| FP | Funktionsprinzip | FPL | File Parameter List |
| FPA | Failure Print Address | FPL | Final Protective Line |
| FPA | Fixed Point Addition | FPL | Formal Parameter List |
| FPA | Fixed Point Arithmetic | FPL | Foxboro Process Language |
| FPA | Floating Point Addition | FPL | Foxboro Programming Language |
| FPA | Floating Point Arithmetic | | |
| FPA | Focal Plane Array | FPL | Frequency Phase Lock |
| FPA | Formation Professionnelle des Adultes | FPL... | Freelance Programmers Ltd. |
| FPBG | Final Program and Budget Guidance | FPLA | Field Programmable Logic Array |
| FPC | Facility Power Control | FPLS | Field Programmable Logic Sequencer |
| FPC | Fast Positive Complex | | |
| FPC | File Parameter Card | FPM | Facsimile Posting Machine |
| FPC | Fixed Point Calculation | FPM | Feet Per Minute |
| FPC | Fixed Point Computation | FPM | Ferrite Plate Memory |
| FPC | Fixed Point Computer | FPM | Financial Planning Model |

# F

| | | | |
|---|---|---|---|
| FPM | Floating Point Method | FPS | Future Programming System |
| FPM | Floating Point Multiplication | FPT | Female Pipe Thread |
| FPM | Frequency Position Modulation | FPT | File Parameter Table |
| | | FPT | First Pass Trigger |
| FPM | Functional Planning Matrices | FPT | Floating Point Trap |
| | | FPT | Full Power Trial |
| FPMI | Frequency Position Modulation with phase Increments | FPTS | Forward Propagation Tropospheric Scatter |
| | | FPU | Fixed Point Unit |
| FPN | Fixed Pattern Noise | FPU | Floating Point Underflow |
| FPN | Fixed Point Number | | |
| FPN | Floating Point Number | FPV | Fixed Point Value |
| FPO | Fixed Path of Operation | FPV | Fixed Point Variable |
| FPO | Fixed Point Operation | FPW | Fixed Point Word |
| FPP | Facility Power Panel | FQA | Field Quality Audit |
| FPP | Floating Point Processor | FQE | Free Queue Element |
| FPP | Floating Point Programming | FQK | Fully Qualified Key |
| | | FQPR | Frequency Programmer |
| FPP | Formal Parameter Part | FQS | Friendly Query System |
| FPR | Fixed Point Representation | FR | Failure Rate |
| FPR | Fixed Program Receive | FR | Fast Register |
| FPR | Floating Point Register | FR | Fast Release |
| FPR | Floating Point Representation | FR | Feed Reel |
| | | FR | Field Reporting |
| FPR | Floating Point Routine | FR | Field Requisition |
| FPR | Forms Printing Requisition | FR | Field Resistance |
| FPROM | Field Programmable Read Only Memory | FR | Field Reversing |
| | | FR | File Revision |
| FPS | Federated Programming System | FR | Finanz- und Rechnungswesen |
| FPS | Feet Per Second | FR | Flash Ranging |
| FPS | Ferrite Plate Store | FR | Floating Register |
| FPS | Festplattenspeicher | FR | Fourierreihe |
| FPS | Field Power Supply | FR | Frame |
| FPS | Field Programming System | FR | Frame Rate |
| FPS | Financial Planning Simulator | FR | Frame Reprint |
| | | FR | Frequency |
| FPS | Financial Planning System | FR | Frequency Range |
| FPS | Fixed Point Subtraction | FR | Frequency Response |
| FPS | Fixed Point System | FR | Front |
| FPS | Fixed Program Send | FR | Full Rate |
| FPS | Floating Point Subroutine | FR | Function Reference |
| FPS | Floating Point System | FRA | Floating Reset Add |
| FPS | Floating Point Systems, Incorporated | FRAC | Fraction |
| | | FRAC | Fractionator Reflux Analog Computer |
| FPS | Focus Projection and Scanning | FRACI | Form Row from Array Components with given Index |
| FPS | Foot-Pound-Second | | |
| FPS | Foreground Program Start | | |
| FPS | Forschungs- und Prüfgemeinschaft Software | FRAN | Framed structure Analysis |
| | | FRAPO | Frage-Antwort-Processing-Operator |
| FPS | Frames Per Second | | |
| FPS | Freiprogrammierbare Steuerung | FRAPS | Frage-Antwort-Processing-System |

# F

| | | | |
|---|---|---|---|
| FRAS | Feature Ratio Analysis System | FRN | Feedrate Number |
| FRC | Failure Recurrence Control | FRN | File Reference Number |
| FRC | Functional Residue Capacity | FRO | Force Routine Order |
| | | FRO | Free Running Operations |
| FRCS | Feature Ration Control System | FROLIC | Formal Retrieval Oriented Language for Indexing Content |
| FRD | Failure Rate Data | FROM | Factory programmable Read-Only Memory |
| FRD | Floating Round | | |
| FRD | Formerly Restricted Data | FROM | Fusible Read-Only Memory |
| FRD | Functional Referenced Device | FROSS | Fast Read Only Storage Simulation |
| FRED | Fast Random Enquiry Display | FRP | Fast Rise Pulse |
| | | FRP | Fiberglass Reinforced Plastic |
| FRED | Fast Reading Electronic Digitizer | FRP | File Retention Period |
| | | FRP | File Rules Pointer |
| FRED | Figure Reading Electronic Device | FRP | Flag Register Processing |
| | | FRP | Freie Rückwärtspufferzeit |
| FRED | FORTRAN Routines for the Elliott Display | FRR | Fast Recovery Rectifier |
| | | FRR | Functional Recovery Routine |
| FREDA | Fully Remote Data Acquisition | FRS | Failure Reporting System |
| FREDI | Flight Range and Endurance Data Indicator | FRS | Faktenrecherchesystem |
| | | FRS | Fashion Reporter System |
| FREQ | Frequency | FRS | Fast Retrieval Storage |
| FREQ CH | Frequency Changer | FRS | Feature Recognition System |
| FREQ IND | Frequency Indicator | | |
| FREQCONV | Frequency Converter | FRS | File Rücksetzen |
| FREQM | Frequency Meter | FRS | First Remove Subroutine |
| FREQMULT | Frequency Multiplier | FRS | Floating Report Sign |
| FRESCAN | Frequency Scanning | FRS | Formatted Read Statement |
| FRET | Functional Reliability End Test | FRS | Fragility Response System |
| | | FRS | Frequency Response Survey |
| FRET | Functional Reliability Evaluation Technique | FRSPC | Free Space |
| FRIEDA | Friedrichshainer Datenbank | FRT | Flow Recording Transmitter |
| FRIEND | Fast Running Interpreter Enabling Natural Diagnosis | FRU | Failing-field Replaceable Unit |
| | | FRU | Field Replaceable Unit |
| FRINGE | File and Report Information processing Generator | FRUGAL | FORTRAN Rules Used as a General Applications Language |
| FRJ | File Return Jump | FRV | Formant Restoring Vocoder |
| FRK | Flach-Reedkontakt | | |
| FRL | Fixed Record Length | FRXD | Fully-automatic Re-perforator Transmitter Distributor |
| FRM | Film Reading Machine | | |
| FRM | Fixed Range Mark | | |
| FRM | Frame | FRZ | Fachrechenzentrum |
| FRM | Free Running Multivibrator | FS | Facility Status |
| FRM | Frequency Meter | FS | Factor Storage |
| FRMG | Framing | FS | Fail Safe |
| FRMR | Frame Reject | FS | Fairchild Semiconductor |
| FRMV | Free Running Multivibrator | FS | Fast Store |

# F

| | | | |
|---|---|---|---|
| FS | Feedback, Stabilized | FSA | Fine Structure Analysis |
| FS | Female Soldered | FSA | Fixed Starting Address |
| FS | Femtosekunden | FSA | Floating Storage Addressing |
| FS | Fernschreiben | | |
| FS | Fernschreiber | FSA | Formatter/Sense Amplifier |
| FS | Ferrite Store | FSA | Frequency Selective Amplifier |
| FS | Ferromagnetic Storage | | |
| FS | Fertigungssystem | FSA | Full Scale Accuracy |
| FS | Festspeicher | FSAB | Floating Subtract Absolute |
| FS | Festwertspeicher | FSADR | Fortsetzungsadresse |
| FS | Field Selection | FSAF | Frequency Shift Audio Frequency |
| FS | Field Separator | | |
| FS | Field Service | FSB | Formularsteuerband |
| FS | Field Specification | FSB | Forward Space Block |
| FS | Figure Shift | FSB | Fractional Sampling Bit |
| FS | Figure Switching | FSB | Free Storage Block |
| FS | File Scan | FSBSEM | Free Storage Block Semaphore |
| FS | File Search | | |
| FS | File Section | FSBW | Frame-Space-Bandwidth product |
| FS | File Separator | | |
| FS | File Server | FSC | Fault Simulation Comparator |
| FS | File Store | | |
| FS | File Structure | FSC | Federal Systems Center |
| FS | Final Selector | FSC | Field Separator Character |
| FS | First Stage | FSC | Field Support Center |
| FS | Fixed Sequence | FSC | Final Systems Check |
| FS | Fixed Storage | FSC | Finite State Channel |
| FS | Floating Sign | FSC | Fixed Self-Contacting |
| FS | Floating Subtract | FSC | Frequency Shift Converter |
| FS | Foot-Second | FSC | Full Scale range |
| FS | Format Secondary | FSCB | File System Control Block |
| FS | Format Selector | FSCW | Fast Space Charge Wave |
| FS | Format Specification | FSD | Federal Systems Division |
| FS | Format Statement | FSD | Field Support Diagram |
| FS | Fortschrittszahlensystem | FSD | File Search Device |
| | | FSD | Flying Spot Digitizer |
| FS | Fourier Series | FSD | Foster-Seeley Discriminator |
| FS | Frequency Shift | | |
| FS | Frequency Synthesizer | FSD | Full Scale Deflection |
| FS | Frequenzsyntheser | FSE | Fernschalteinheit |
| FS | Full Scale | FSE | Fernschalteinrichtung |
| FS | Full Size | FSE | File Scan Equipment |
| FS | Full Subtractor | FSE | Fill Start Entry |
| FS | Function Set | FSE | Full Screen Editor |
| FS | Function Specification | FSF | File Scan Function |
| FS | Function Statement | FSF | Fixed Sequence Format |
| FS | Function Subprogram | FSF | Forward Space File |
| FS | Functional Symbol | FSG | Finite State Grammar |
| FS | Funktionssymbol | FSG | Frequency of Signal Generator |
| FS | Future Series | | |
| FS | Future System | FSH | Final Shift |
| FSA | Failing Storage Address | FSIT | Flat-Screen Image Tube |
| FSA | Festkörper-Symbol-Anzeige | FSK | Fernschreibkoppelelement, kombiniert |
| FSA | Field Search Argument | FSK | Figure Shift Key |

# F

| | | | |
|---|---|---|---|
| FSK | Folgeschlußkarte | FSTD | Flight Simulation Test Data |
| FSK | Frequency-Shift Keying | FSTV | Fast Scan Television |
| FSL | Finite State Language | FSU | Ferrite Store Unit |
| FSL | Formal Semantic Language | FSU | Field Storage Unit |
| FSL | Frequency Selective Limiter | FSU | File Support Utility |
| FSM | Field Strength Meter | FSU | Full Scale Unit |
| FSM | Finite State Machine | FSURAM | Functional Storage Unit Random Access Method |
| FSM | Folded Sideband Modulation | FSUROS | Functional Storage Unit Read Only Storage |
| FSM | Formatted Screen Manager | FSV | Floating point Status Vector |
| FSM | Frequency Shift Modulation | FSVM | Frequency Selective Voltmeter |
| FSMWI | Free Space Microwave Interferometer | FSW | Final Status Word |
| FSN | Federal Stock Number | FSW | Fork Status Word |
| FSN | File Sequence Number | FT | Field Test |
| FSN | File Serial Number | FT | Field Transfer |
| FSNR | Freie Satznummern | FT | File Transfer |
| FSO | Fast Shift Operation | FT | Filing Time |
| FSO | Full Scale Output | FT | Float Time |
| FSO | Full Screen Output | FT | Flow Time |
| FSO | Full Space Output | FT | Flush Threshold |
| FSP | Festspeicher | FT | Folgetext |
| FSP | Filter Simulation Program | FT | Format Tape |
| FSP | Fixed Store Procedure | FT | Formula Translation |
| FSP | Fixed Stored Program | FT | Formula Translator |
| FSP | Fleet Scheduling Program | FT | Formulartrenngerät |
| FSP | Full Screen Processing | FT | Fototransistor |
| FSP | Full Screen Product | FT | Fourier Transform |
| FSPRO | Fehlersuchprogramm | FT | Fouriertransformation |
| FSR | Feedback Shift Register | FT | Frame Transfer |
| FSR | Fernschreiber | FT | Frequency Tracker |
| FSR | Field Strength Ratio | FT | Frequency and Time |
| FSR | File Space Rules | FT | Frequenzteiler |
| FSR | Final Shift Register | FT | Frühester Termin |
| FSR | Forward Space Record | FT | Full Time |
| FSR | Frequency Shift Receiver | FT | Function Translator |
| FSR | Full Scale Range | FT | Functional Test |
| FSS | Federal Supply Schedule | FTA | Fast Turnaround |
| FSS | Field System Support | FTA | File Transfer Agent |
| FSS | Formatiertes Speichersystem | FTAB | Field Tab |
| FSSM | Flying Spot Scanner Memory | FTAS | Fast Time Analyzer System |
| FST | Factory Service Tape | FTB | Frequency Time Base |
| FST | Fertigungssteuerung | FTC | Fast Time Constant |
| FST | File Status Table | FTC | Fast Time Control |
| FST | Finite Sampling Time | FTC | Fault Tolerant Computing |
| FST | Frequency Shift Transmission | FTC | Fault Tolerant Controller |
| FST | Functional Simulator and Translator | FTC | Frequency Time Control |
| FSTC | Federal Software Testing Center | FTD | Field Terminated Diode |
| | | FTD | Frequency Translation Distortion |
| | | FTD | Functional Test Data |

# F

| | | | |
|---|---|---|---|
| FTDAS | Flight Test Data Acquisition System | FTS | Financial Transaction System |
| FTE | Factory Test Equipment | FTS | Flight Telemetry System |
| FTE | Frame Table Entry | FTS | Fourier Transform Spectrometer |
| FTE | Functional Test Equipment | | |
| FTF | File Transfer Facility | FTS | Fourier Transform Spectrophotometer |
| FTF | Flare Tube Fitting | | |
| FTFET | Four-Terminal Field-Effect Transistor | FTS | Frequency Time Standard |
| | | FTS | Frequency and Timing Subsystem |
| FTG | Function Timing Generator | | |
| FTH | Fourier Transform Hologram | FTSPS | Field Technical Support Programming System |
| FTI | File Trailer Identifier | FTT | Fault Test |
| FTI | Frequency Time Indicator | FTU | Frequency Transfer Unit |
| FTI | Frequency Time Intensity | FTU | Functional Test Unit |
| FTL | Fast Trailer Label | FTX | Fault Tolerance Extension |
| FTL | Fast Transient Loader | FTZ | Fernmeldetechnisches Zentralamt |
| FTL | Fast Transit Link | | |
| FTL | Faster Than Light | FU | Fehlerunterbrechung |
| FTL | Format Tape Loop | FU | Feldunterstützung |
| FTLO | Fast Tuned Local Oscillator | FÜ | Fernübertragungssystem |
| | | FU | Frequenzumformer |
| FTLP | Fixed Term Lease Plan | FU | Frequenzumsetzer |
| FTM | Failed To Make | FU | Function Unit |
| FTM | Frequency Time Modulation | FU | Functional Unit |
| | | FU | Fuse |
| FTN | Field Transfer Notice | FUD | Fear, Uncertainty, Doubt |
| FTO | Fourier Transform Operator | FUD | Field Use Date |
| | | FUD | Fire Up Decoder |
| FTP | Fast Tape Perforator | FUDR | Failure and Usage Data Report |
| FTP | Fast Tape Punch | | |
| FTP | Field Test Program | FUIF | Fire Unit Integration Facility |
| FTP | File Transfer Paket | | |
| FTP | File Transfer Program | FUN | Function |
| FTP | File Transfer Protocol | FUNC | Function |
| FTP | Fixed Term Plan | FUND | Fundamental |
| FTP | Fourier Transform Processor | FUO | Final Used On |
| | | FUP | File Utility Program |
| FTP | Function Table Program | FUPL | Field Use Parts List |
| FTP | Functional Test Procedure | FUR | Fehlerunterbrechungs-routine |
| FTR | Factor | | |
| FTR | Fixed Target Rejection filter | FURST | FORTRAN Utility System |
| | | FUS | Fusible |
| FTR | Floating Time Recording | FUSED | Field Unit System Engineering Document |
| FTR | Functional Test Report | | |
| FTR | Functional Test Request | FV | Fehlverhalten |
| FTR | Functional Test Requipment | FV | Frequency-to-Voltage |
| | | FV | Frequenzverstellung |
| FTS | Federal Telecommunication System | FV | Frequenzvervielfacher |
| | | FV | Front View |
| FTS | Field Transfer System | FV | Full Voltage |
| FTS | File Transfer Service | FVC | Frequency-to-Voltage Converter |
| FTS | File Transfer Spooler | | |
| FTS | File Transfer System | FVD | Front Vertex back focal Distance |
| FTS | Financial Terminal System | | |

# F

| | | | |
|---|---|---|---|
| FVE | Fernverkehrseinheit | FWHM | Full Width a Half Maximum |
| FVS | File Vorsetzen | | |
| FW | Face Width | FWHT | Fast Walsh-Hadamard Transform |
| FW | Failure Warning | | |
| FW | Festwertspeicher | FWKT | Fast Walsh-Kaczmarz Transform |
| FW | Festwort | | |
| FW | Festwörter | FWL | Finite World Length |
| FW | Field Width | FWL | Fixed Word Length |
| FW | Filament Wound | FWN | Fernwirknetz |
| FW | Finanzwesen | FWP | Full Write Pulse |
| FW | Firmware | FWPT | Fast Walsh-Paley Transform |
| FW | Fiscal Week | | |
| FW | Fixed-Length Word | FWR | Fehlerwortregister |
| FW | Forward Wave | FWR | Full Wave Rectifier |
| FW | Full Weight | FWS | Filter Wedge Spectrometer |
| FW | Full Word | FWS | Fixed Wireless Station |
| FW | Full Wave | FWS | Formatted Write Statement |
| FW | Function Word | | |
| FWA | Festwortadresse | FWT | Fast Walsh Transform |
| FWA | File Work Application | FWT | Fernwirktechnik |
| FWA | File Work Area | FWWMR | Fire-, Water-, Weather-, Mildew-Resistant |
| FWA | Final Writing Amplifier | | |
| FWA | First Word Address | FX | Foreign Exchange |
| FWA | Fixed Word Address | FXP | Fixed Point |
| FWA | Forward Wave Amplifier | FXPU | Fixed Point Unit |
| FWAC | Full Wave Alternating Current | FY | Fiscal Year |
| | | FYDS | Fiscal Year Data Summary |
| FWAS | Failure Warning and Analysis System | FZ | Festzeichen |
| | | FZ | Float Zone |
| FWB | Full Word Boundary | FZ | Frühester Zeitpunkt |
| FWD | Forward | FZE | Fernschreibzeichen-erkenner |
| FWDC | Full Wave Direct Current | | |
| FWE | Fernwirkempfänger | FZR | Funktionszustandsregister |
| FWG | Fernwirkgeber | FZSTO | Frozen Storage |
| FWH | Flexible Working Hours | | |

# G

| | | | |
|---|---|---|---|
| G | Gap | GADAM | Gesellschaft für Angewandte Datenverarbeitung und Automation in der Medizin |
| G | Gate | | |
| G | Gauss | | |
| G | Geber | | |
| G | Generator | GADDR | Group Address |
| G | Giga | GADL | Ground-to-Air Data Link |
| G | Gleichstom | GADSAR | General Aniline & Film Corporation Document Storage And Retrieval |
| G | Gravity | | |
| G | Grid | | |
| G | Ground | GAETAN | Gestion Automatique de l'Enregistrement à Traitement Alphanumérique |
| G... | General Electric | | |
| G-G | Ground-to-Ground | | |
| G-M | Geiger-Müller | | |
| G/M | Groups per Message | GAG | Ground-to-Air-to-Ground |
| G/XMTR | Guidance Transmitter | GAGDT | Ground-to-Air-to-Ground Data Terminal |
| GA | Gain of Antenna | | |
| GA | Gauge | GAI | Gate Alarm Indicator |
| GA | Gemeinschaftsanlage | GAIS | Gebäudereiniger - Abrechnungs- und Informationssystem |
| GA | Gemeinschaftsanschluss | | |
| GA | General Accounting | | |
| GA | General Assembly | GAL | Gallon |
| GA | Generated Address | GALPAT | Galloping Pattern |
| GA | Generator-Amplifier | GALS | Generalized Assembly Line Simulator |
| GA | Glide Angle | | |
| GA | Go Ahead | GALS | Gravity Anomaly Location System |
| GA | Go Around | | |
| GA | Graphic Acquisition | GAM | Graphic Access Method |
| GA | Graphic Addition | GAM | Graphic Arts Machine |
| GA | Graphic Ammeter | GAMA | Graphics Assisted Management Applications |
| GA | Ground-to-Air | | |
| GA | Group Addressing | GAMBIT | Gas Markets Balanced with Investment in Transmission |
| GA | Group Advance | | |
| GA | Guidance Amplifier | | |
| GA... | General Automation | GAMBIT | Gate Modulated Bipolar Transistor |
| GAA | Geldausgabeautomaten | | |
| GAAR | Graphic Attention Analysis Routine | GAME | Gaming Analysis of Management Effectiveness |
| GAARD | General Automation Automatic Recovery Device | GAMIC | Gamma Incomplet |
| | | GAMLOGS | Gamma ray Logs |
| GAB | Guichet Automatique de Banque | GAMM | German Association for applied Mathematics and Mechanics |
| GABS | Gewerkschaftliches Abrechnungs- und Buchungssystem | GAMM | Gesellschaft für Angewandte Mathematik und Mechanik |
| GACB | Graphic Attention Control Block | | |
| GACT | Greenwich Apparent Civil Time | GAMM | Gestion Administrative et Médicale du Malade |
| GAD | Gate Anomaly Detector | GAMMA | Generalized Automatic Method of Matrix Assembly |
| GAD | Germanium Alloy Diffused | | |
| GAD | Gesellschaft für Automatische Datenverarbeitung eG | GAMMA | Graphically Aided Mathematical Machine |
| GAD | Graphic Active Device | GAMSI | Groupe d'Application des Méthodes et des Systèmes d'Information |

# G

| | | | |
|---|---|---|---|
| GAN | Generalized Activity Network | GAS | Graphics Attachment Support |
| GAN | Generating and Analyzing Networks | GASL | General Activity Simulation Language |
| GAN | Gleitpunkt-Addition Normalisiert | GASP | General Academic Simulation Program |
| GANDALF | General Alpha Numeric Direct Access Library Facility | GASP | General Activity Simulation Program |
| GAO | General Accounting Office | GASP | General Analysis of System Performance |
| GAO | Gesellschaft für Angewandte Organisation in der Datenverarbeitung | GASP | GEVIC Arithmetic Simulation Program |
| GAP | General Accounting Package | GASP | Global Air Sampling Program |
| GAP | General Assembly Program | GASP | Graph Algorithm Software Package |
| GAP | Générateur Automatique de Programmes | GASP | Graphic Applications Subroutine Package |
| GAP | Goodyear Associative Processor | GASP | GRATIS And Simulator Production system |
| GAP | Graphical Automatic Programming | GASR | Graphic Attention Service Routine |
| GAP | Graphics Application Program | GASS | Generalized Assembly System |
| GAP | Grundlagen für Anwendungsprogrammierung | GAT | Generalized Algebraic Translator |
| GAP | Guide for Application Programming | GAT | Georgetown Automatic Translation |
| GAPA | Guichet d'Affranchissement Postal Automatique | GAT | Georgetown Automatic Translator |
| GAPL | Group Assembly Parts List | GAT | Greenwich Apparent Time |
| GAPSS | Graphical Analysis Procedures for System Simulation | GAT | Ground-to-Air Transmitter |
| | | GATAC | General Accessment Tridimensional Analog Computer |
| GAPT | Graphical Automatically Programmed Tools | GATAM | General Automation Telecommunications Access Method |
| GAR | Geräteadreßregister | | |
| GAR | Growth Analysis and Review | GATAP | Generelles Aggregierungs-, Tabellierungs- und Auswertungsprogramm |
| GAR | Guided Aircraft Rocket | | |
| GARD | Gamma Atomic Radiation Detector | GATB | General Aptitude Test Battery |
| GARD | General Address Reading Device | GATD | Graphic Analysis of Threedimensional Data |
| GARDAE | Gathers Alarms, Reports, Displays And Evaluates | GATE | Generalized Algebraic Translator Extended |
| GARF | Ground Approach Radio Fuse | GATNIP | Graphic Approach To Numerical Information Processing |
| GARLIC | General Analysis Regardless of Logical Interconnection of Circuits | | |
| | | GATO | Gate Assisted Turnoff thyristor |
| GARMAC | Garment Mechanization And Control | GATR | Ground-to-Air Transmitting Receiving |
| GARP | Global Atmospheric Research Program | | |

- 266 -

# G

| | | | |
|---|---|---|---|
| GATT | General Agreement on Tariffs and Trade | GCAP | Graphic Curve Analysis Program |
| GATT | Ground-to-Air Transmitter Terminal | GCAP | Ground Capability |
| GAVE | Groupe de l'édition Audio-visuelle et Electronique | GCB | Graphic Control Byte |
| | | GCB | Great Circle Bearing |
| GB | Gain Bandwidth | GCC | Ground Control Center |
| GB | Geschäftsbereich | GCC | Guidance Checkout Computer |
| GB | Gigabyte | GCCA | Graphic Communications Computer Association |
| GB | Gold Bonded | | |
| GB | Grid Bias | GCD | Gain Control Driver |
| GB | Grounded Base | GCD | Gate Controlled Diode |
| GBA | Give Better Address | GCD | Global Console Director |
| GBC | Ground-Based Computer | GCD | Graphic Codepoint Definition |
| GBG | Geschlossene Benutzergruppe | GCD | Greatest Common Divisor |
| GBGB | Graded Band Gap Base | GCE | Group Control Entry |
| GBI | Ground Back-up Instrument | GCE | Group Control Exit |
| GBK | Großbaukasten | GCF | Greatest Common Factor |
| GBM | General Bookkeeping Machine | GCFA | Gridded Crossed Field Amplifier |
| GBM | Group Band Modem | GCFR | Gas Cooled Fast Reactor |
| GBP | Gain Bandwidth Product | GCI | Graphics-Command-Interpreter |
| GBP | Generalized Bridge Program | GCI | Ground Controlled Interception |
| GBS | Grundbetriebssystem | | |
| GBS | Group Busy Signal | GCI | Group Control Interruption |
| GBSAS | Ground Based Scanning Antenna System | GCL | Gate Circuit Logic |
| | | GCL | Ground Controlled Landing |
| GBT | Gassenbesetzton | GCLPF | Ground Capacitor LPF |
| GBT | Graded-Base Transistor | GCM | Greatest Common Multiple |
| GBTG | Generalized data Base Task Group | GCMA | Government Contact Management Association of America, Inc. |
| GBW | Gain Bandwidth | | |
| GBWA | Grundmittel-Bruttowert der Ausrüstungen | GCMS | Gas Chromatography and Mass Spectroscopy |
| GC | Gain Control | GCN | Gauge Code Number |
| GC | Gaschromatographic | GCN | Greenwich Civil Noon |
| GC | Gate Circuit | GCOS | General Comprehensive Operation Supervisor |
| GC | Geiger Counter | | |
| GC | General Computer | GCOS | Generalized Comprehensive Operating System |
| GC | Graphic Console | | |
| GC | Great Circle | GCP | Gain Control Pulse |
| GC | Ground Control | GCP | Generalized Computer Program |
| GC | Grounded Collector | | |
| GC | Guidance Computer | GCP | Guidance Computer |
| GCA | Gain Control Amplifier | GCR | General Component Reference |
| GCA | Global Communication Area | | |
| | | GCR | Ground Control Radar |
| GCA | Ground Controlled Approach | GCR | Group Coded Record |
| | | GCR | Group Coded Recording |
| GCA | Group Capacity Analysis | GCS | Gate Controlled Switch |
| GCAP | General Circuit Analysis Program | GCS | General Computer Systems Incorporated |

# G

| | |
|---|---|
| GCS | Group Control System |
| GCSC | Guidance Control and Sequencing Computer |
| GCSMP | Graphic Continuous System Modelling Program |
| GCT | General Classification Test |
| GCT | Greenwich Civil Time |
| GCU | Graphic Control Unit |
| GCU | Gyroscope Coupling Unit |
| GCW | General Continuous Wave |
| GD | Gap Digit |
| GD | Gate Driver |
| GD | Gegenstandsdatei |
| GD | Germanium Diode |
| GD | Given Data |
| GD | Graphic Data |
| GD | Graphic Display |
| GD | Große Datentechnik |
| GD | Ground Detector |
| GD | Grown Diffused |
| GD | Guard Digit |
| GD | Guide |
| GDA | Global Data Area |
| GDA | Good Data Area |
| GDA | Graphic Data Acquisition |
| GDAD | Gebundene-Deskriptoren-Adressensatz |
| GDAM | General Data Access Method |
| GDAP | GEOS Data Adjustment Program |
| GDAS | Ground Data Acquisition System |
| GDB | Graphic Data Byte |
| GDBMS | Generalized Data Base Management System |
| GDBS | Geo facilities Data Base Support |
| GDC | Gated Digital Correlator |
| GDC | General-purpose Digital Computer |
| GDC | German Data Centre |
| GDC | Graphik-Display-Controller |
| GDC | Guidance Data Converter |
| GDC | Gun Direction Computer |
| GDC... | Gesellschaft für Datensysteme und Computer mbH |
| GDD | Gas Discharge Display |
| GDD | Gesellschaft für Datenschutz und Datensicherung |
| GDDM | Graphical Data Display Manager |
| GDDM | Graphische Daten-Darstellung und Management |
| GDE | Ground Data Equipment |
| GDF | Graphical Display File |
| GDF | Group Distribution Frame |
| GDG | Generation Data Gap |
| GDG | Generation Data Group |
| GDG | Group Display Generator |
| GDH | Ground Data Handling |
| GDHS | Ground Data Handling System |
| GDI | Graphic Data Input |
| GDJB | Guidance Computer Junction Box |
| GDL | Glas Development Laser system |
| GDL | Gleichrichterdioden für Leistungselektronik |
| GDL | Global Data Link |
| GDLZ | Gesamtdurchlaufzeit |
| GDM | Glass Disk Memory |
| GDMS | Generalized Data Management System |
| GDN | Gleichstrom-Datenübertragungsgerät für Niederpegel |
| GDN | Gleichstrom-Datenübertragungseinrichtung für Niedrige Sendespannung |
| GDN | Gleichstrom-Datenübertragung mit Niedrigpegel |
| GDO | Gesellschaft Deutscher Organisation e.V. |
| GDO | Gesellschaft für Datenverarbeitung und Organisation |
| GDO | Graphic Data Output |
| GDO | Grid-Dip Oscillator |
| GDOA | Graphic Data Output Area |
| GDP | Generalized Data Processor |
| GDP | Geometric Data Processing |
| GDP | Graphic Data Processing |
| GDP | Graphic Data Products |
| GDPS | Generalized Disk Programming System |
| GDPS | Global Data Processing System |
| GDQF | Graphical Display and Query Facility |
| GDR | Geodetic Data Reduction |
| GDR | Group Delay Response |
| GDRCT | Gardner Denver Rework Command Tape |
| GDS | Gemeinschaftsdatenstation |

# G

| | | | |
|---|---|---|---|
| GDS | Gemeinschaftsdaten-verarbeitungsstation | GECOS | General Electric Comprehensive Operating System |
| GDS | Geodetic Data Site | GED | Gesprächsdauer |
| GDS | Glass Disk Store | GEDAN | General Data Analyzer |
| GDS | Global Data-processing System | GEDD | Gun-Effect Digital Device |
| | | GEDL | General Electric Data Link |
| GDS | Graphic Data System | GEE | General Evaluation Equipment |
| GDS | Graphic Design System | | |
| GDT | Ground Delay Time | GEEP | General Electric Electronic Processor |
| GDU | Graphic Display Unit | | |
| GDU | Graphical Display Unit | GEESE | General Electric Electronic System Evaluator |
| GDV | Geometrische Datenverarbeitung | | |
| GDV | Gesellschaft für Datenverarbeitung | GEF | Ground Equipment Failure |
| | | GEFIV | Gesellschaftliche Folgen von Staatlichen Informationsverbundsystemen |
| GDV | Grafische Datenverarbeitung | | |
| GDV | Grafische Datenverarbeitungsanlage | GEG | Generalized Euclidean Geometry |
| GDVA | Grafische Datenverarbeitungsanlage | GEI | Gesellschaft für Elektronische Informationsverarbeitung |
| GE | Gas Ejection | | |
| GE | Gaussian Elemination | GEIMS | General Electric Inventory Management System |
| GE | General Electric | | |
| GE | Geräteanschluß | GEISHA | Geodetic Inertial Survey and Horizontal Alignment |
| GE | Geräteanschlußeinheit | | |
| GE | Germanium | GEISI | General Electric Information Systems Italy |
| GE | Graphic Escape | | |
| GE | Greater than or Equal | GEK | Geomagnetic Electrokinetograph |
| GE | Grounded Emitter | | |
| GE-TSS | General Electric-Time-Sharing System | GELMAT | Gelöschte Materialsätze |
| | | GEM | General Environment Managers |
| GEA | Gesellschaft für Elektronik & Automation | | |
| | | GEM | General Epitaxial Monolith |
| GEA | Graph Extended ALCOL | GEM | General Evaluation Model |
| GEAK | Grafische Eingabe/Ausgabe-Kontrolle | GEM | General Event Monitor |
| | | GEM | General Experimental Monitor |
| GECAP | General Electric Computer Analysis Program | | |
| | | GEM | Generalized Effectiveness Method |
| GECECS | General Electric Chemical Engineering Calculation System | | |
| | | GEM | Graphic Environment Managers |
| GECEP | General Civil Engineering Package | | |
| | | GEM | Graphic Expression Machine |
| GECI | Gestion et Exploitation des Centres Informatiques | GEM | Ground Effect Machine |
| | | GEMCS | General Engineering and Management Computation System |
| GECIS | General Electric Co. Information Systems | | |
| GECOM | General Compiler | GEMMA | Guide d'Études des Modes de Marches et d'Arrêts |
| GECOM | General Electric Compiler | | |
| GECOM | Generalized Computer | GEMS | General Electrical and Mechanical Systems |
| GECOR | General Communication Routine | | |
| | | GEMS/PAC | Global Environmental Monitoring Service/Program Activity Centre |
| GECOS | General Comprehensive Operating Supervisor | | |
| | | GEN | General |

# G

| | | | |
|---|---|---|---|
| GEN | Generate | GEPURS | General Electric general Purpose |
| GEN | Generation | GERM DIO | Germanium Diode |
| GEN | Generator | GEROS | General Routing Optimization System |
| GENA | Gepufferte Nachrichtensteuerung | GERSIS | General Electric Range Safety Instrumentation System |
| GENA | Gepufferte Nachrichtenverarbeitung | GERT | Graphical Evaluation and Review Technique |
| GENA | German Extended Network Access | GERTIE | GEORGE Remote Terminal Interrogative Environment |
| GENCOD | Groupement d'Etudes de Normalisation et de Codification | GERTS | General Electric Remote Terminal Supervisor |
| GENDA | General Data Analysis | GERTS | General Remote Terminal Supervisor |
| GENDARE | Generalized Data Reduction, Evaluation | GERTS | General Remote Transmission Supervisor |
| GENDAS | General Data Analysis and Simulation | GES | GAMMA European Systems |
| GENDRA | Generalized Data Reduction and Analysis | GES | Generalised Edit System |
| GENESYS | General Engineering System | GES | Gesellschaft für Elektronische Systemforschung |
| GENIRAS | General Information Retrieval and Application System | GES | Globales Externes Schema |
| GENISYS | Generalized Information System | GES | Ground Electronics System |
| GENN | Generation | GESAL | General Electric Symbolic Assembly Language |
| GENOP | Generator für Normierte Programme | GESAL | General Symbolic Assembly Language |
| GENSTOR | General Storage | GESAT | Gesellschaft für die Vermarktung von Fernmeldesatelliten-Systemen mbH |
| GENTEX | General Telegraph Exchange | GESCOM | General Electric Scientific Colour Matching |
| GENU | Generated Nonelementary Unit | GESMA | Gesellschaft für Software und Marketing |
| GENUS | Generatorunterstützte Softwareproduktion | GESPL | Generalised Edit System Programming Language |
| GEOPS | Geodesy Program System | GEST | General System Theory |
| GEORGE | General Organisational Environment | GEST | Graphic Evaluation Systems Technique |
| GEOS | Geodetic Earth Orbiting Satellite | GESTI | General System Theory Implementer |
| GEP | Gebührenerfassungsplatz | GESTRU | Gegenstandsstrukturdatei |
| GEP | General Extraction Program | GET | Germanium Transistor |
| GEP | Generalisiertes Extraktionsprogramm | GET | Graphic Editing of Text |
| GEPAC | General Electric Programmable Automatic Computer | GET | Ground Elapsed Time |
| GEPAC | General Purpose Automatic Checkout | GETEL | General Test Engineer Language |
| GEPL | Guide Européen des Produits Logiciels | GETOL | Ground Effect Take-Off and Landing |
| GEPS | Global Engineering Product Specification | GETS | Generalized Electronic Trouble Shooting |
| | | GETWS | Get Word from String |

# G

| | | | |
|---|---|---|---|
| GEUEP | General Electric Utility Engineering Program | GGE | General Graphical Editing |
| GEVIC | General Electric Variable Increment Computer | GGG | Gadolinium-Gallium-Granat |
| GF | Gauge Factor | GGRZ | Gemeinsames Gebietsrechenzentrum |
| GF | Generator Field | GGS | Graphic Generator System |
| GF | Gestaffelte Fehlerabschaltung | GHN | Get Hold Next |
| GFA | Gegenstandsspezialisierter Fertigungsabschnitt | GHNP | Get Hold Next within Parent |
| GFA | Groupe Fermé d'Abonné | GHOST | Global Horizontal Sounding Technique |
| GFC | Gas Filled Counter | GHU | Get Hold Unique |
| GFCS | Gun Fired Control System | GHVSNAME | Group Home Volume Set Name |
| GFD | Gap Filler Data | GHz | Gigahertz |
| GFE | Generalized Front-End interface | GI | General Index |
| GFI | Gap Filler Input | GI | General Information |
| GFI | Groupement Français d'Informatique | GI | General Input |
| GFIML | Gap Filler Input Message Label | GI | General Instrument |
| GFIPNTR | Group File Index Pointer | GI | Gesellschaft für Informatik |
| GFLD | Generator Field | GI | Grid Interval |
| GFMS | Generalized File Management System | GI | Ground Interception |
| GFO | Gesellschaft Für Organisation e.V. | GI | Group Indicate |
| GFPBBD | Groupement Français des Producteurs de Banques et Bases de Données | GI | Group Item |
| | | GIA | Gestion Informatique de l'Apprentissage |
| | | GIA | Graphic Information Acquisition |
| GFPM | Gated Frequency Position Modulation | GIAM | Graphischer Interaktiver Anwendungs-Monitor |
| GFQ | Grundfondsquote | GIAM | Graphisches Interaktives Anwendungs-Modul |
| GFR | German Federal Republic | GIANT | Geological Information And Name Tabulating system |
| GFRC | General File and Record Control | | |
| GFRC | General File and Recording Control | GIANT | General Information and Analysis Tool |
| GFRP | Glas Fibre Reinforced Plastic | GIAP | Graphisch Interaktiver Arbeits-Platz |
| GFT | Generalized Fast Transform | GIBUS | Groupe Informatiste de Bibliothèque Universitaire et Spécialisée |
| GFT | Germaniumflächentransistor | GIC | Group Indicate Clause |
| GFU | Gesellschaft für Unternehmens- und Projektmanagement | GIC | Group Indicate Cycle |
| | | GICI | Groupement Interministériel pour les Circuits Intégrés |
| GFV | Guided Flight Vehicle | GICS | General Information and Control System |
| GFW | Glas Filament Wound | | |
| GFW | Ground Fault Warning | GID | Gesellschaft für Information und Dokumentation |
| GG | Gleichstromgenerator | | |
| GG | Grundgerät | GID... | Gesellschaft für Industrielle Datenverarbeitung mbH |
| GGC | Ground Guidance Computer | | |
| GGD | Gategesteuerte Diode | | |

# G

| | | | |
|---|---|---|---|
| GID-IZ | Gesellschaft für Information und Dokumentation - Informationszentrum | GIP | General Interpretative Program |
| GIDDAT | Gegenstandsidentdatei | GIP | Gestion Integrée du Personnel |
| GIDEX | Government Industry Data Exchange | GIP | Graphic Input Program |
| GIE | Group Indication Elimination | GIP | Graphic Interactive Processing |
| GIEA | General Industrial Electric Automation | GIP | Großkunden-Intensivplanung |
| GIEL | Groupement des Industries Electroniques | GIPS | Gleitkomma-Interpretiersystem |
| GIF | General Information File | GIPS | Ground Information Processing System |
| GIF | Gulf It to FORTRAN | GIPSSY | Generalized Interactive Program for the Simulation of System |
| GIFI | General Information File Interrogation | | |
| GIFS | Generalized Interrelated Flow Simulation | GIPSY | Generalized Information Processing System |
| GIFT | General Information File Tester | GIR | Generalized Information Retrieval |
| GIFT | General Internal FORTRAN Translator | GIRL | General Information Report Language |
| GIGI | General Imaging Generator and Interpreter | GIRL | General Information Retrieval Language |
| GIGO | Garbage In Garbage Out | GIRL | Graph Information Retrieval Language |
| GIGS | Gemini Inertial Guidance System | GIRLS | General Information Retrieval and Listing System |
| GIHS | Generalized Information Handling System | | |
| GIL | General Instruction Logic | GIRMA | Groupement Intersyndical des Robots et des Machines Automatisées |
| GIL | Gesellschaft für Informationsverarbeitung | | |
| GILT | General Inertial Logic Test | GIRSS | General Information Retrieval System Simulation |
| GILT | Get Interconnected Local Textsystems | GIS | General Information System |
| GIM | General Information Manual | GIS | General Inquiry System |
| GIM | Generalized Information Management | GIS | Generalised Information System |
| GIM | Graphic Integrated Manual | GIS | Generalized Initialization Sequencer |
| GIMIC | Guard ring Isolated Molitic IC | GIS | Government Information System |
| GIMS | Generalized Information Management System | | |
| GIN | General Information Notice | GIS | Graphic Input System |
| GINA | Graphical Input for Network Analysis | GIS/VS | Generalized Information System/Virtual Storage |
| GINFIS | Gemeinschaftliches Integriertes Finanz-Informations-System | GISMO | General Interpretative System for Matrix Operations |
| GINO | Graphical Input/Output | GISP | General Information System for Planning |
| GIOC | Generalized Input/Output Controller | GIT | Graph Isomorphism Tester |
| GIP | General Internal Process | GIU | Guidance Interface Unit |

# G

| | | | |
|---|---|---|---|
| GIZ | Genossenschaftliche Informationszentrale | GLD | Generalized Logic Diagram |
| GJ | Geschäftsjahr | GLDS | Gemini Launch Data System |
| GJ | Grown Junction | GLEAM | Graphic Layout and Engineering Aid Method |
| GJC | Gang Job Card | | |
| GJE | Gauss-Jordan Elimination | GLEAN | Graphic Layout and Engineering Aid Method |
| GJP | Graphic Job Processor | | |
| GK | Gleitkomma | GLEEP | Graphite Low Energy Experimental Pile |
| GK | Großkunde | | |
| GK | Gruppenkennzeichen | GLEX | General Ledger and Expense system |
| GKA | Gebrauchswert-Kosten-Analyse | | |
| | | GLH | Gehalts- und Lohnabrechnung für den Handel |
| GKD | Gemeinsame Kommunale Datenzentralen | | |
| | | GLIC | General Ledger Identification Code |
| GKR | Gemeinschaftskontenrahmen | | |
| | | GLINT | Global Intelligence |
| GKR | Gleitkommaregister | GLK | Gleitkomma |
| GKS | Gebrauchswert-Kosten-Synthese | GLN | Group Level Number |
| | | GLOAD | General Loader |
| GKS | Gerätekanalsteuerung | GLOCOM | Global Communications system |
| GKS | Globales Konzeptuelles Schema | | |
| | | GLODIS | General Language Operated Decision Implementation System |
| GKS | Graphic Kernel System | | |
| GKS | Graphical Kernel System | | |
| GKS | Graphisches Kern-System | GLODISL | General Language Operated Decision Implementation System Language |
| GKSS | Graphics Kernel Systems Standard | | |
| GKT | Gültigkeit | GLOL | Goday Logic Language |
| GKTP | Grundklassifikator für Technologische Prozesse | GLOP | GEVIC Logic Operation Program |
| GL | Gate Leads | GLOPAC | Gyroscopic Lower Power Attitude Control |
| GL | General Ledger | | |
| GL | Gleichrichter | GLOPR | Goday Logic Processor |
| GL | Graphic Language | GLP | Graphic Language Processor |
| GL | Greatest Length | | |
| GL | Grid Leak | GLPPS | Graphical Lathe Part Programming System |
| GL | Ground Level | | |
| GL | Group Librarian | GLR | Graphic Level Recorder |
| GLACT | General Ledger Account | GLS | General Ledger System |
| GLANCE | Global Lightweight Air Navigation Computing Equipment | GLS | Generalized Logic Simulator |
| | | GLSA | General Ledger Subsidiary Account |
| GLAP | Generalized Life Analysis Program | | |
| | | GLSE | Generalized Least Squares Estimation |
| GLAS | General Logic Analysis Simulator | | |
| | | GLUE | Graphics Library User Extension |
| GLAS | General Logic Analysis System | | |
| | | GM | Gaseous Mixture |
| GLAZ | Zeiterfassung für Mitarbeiter mit gleicher Arbeitszeit | GM | Gated Memory |
| | | GM | General Memory |
| | | GM | General Motors |
| GLC | Gas Liquid Chromatography | GM | Geometric Mean |
| | | GM | Greenwich Meridian |
| GLC | Ground Level Concentration | GM | Grid Modulation |
| | | GM | Group Multiplication |

# G

| | | | |
|---|---|---|---|
| GM | Group Mark | GMV | Guaranteed Minimum Value |
| GM | Gruppenmarke | GMWM | Group Mark with Word Mark |
| GM | Guided Missile | GMX | Generalized Monitor Experimental |
| GMAP | General Macro Assembler Processor | GN | Gaussian Noise |
| GMAP | Generelles Makro-Assemblierungsprogramm | GN | General Network |
| | | GN | Generator |
| GMAT | Greenwich Mean Astronomical Time | GN | Gerätenummer |
| | | GN | Get Next |
| GMCM | Guided Missile Countermeasures | GNA | Graphics Network Architecture |
| GMCR | General Monitor Checking Routine | GNAT | General Numerical Analysis of Transport |
| GMD | Geometric Mean Distance | GNATS | Generalized Numerical Analysis of Thermal System |
| GMD... | Gesellschaft für Mathematik und Datenverarbeitung mbH | GNB | Gesellschaft für Neue Berufe mbH |
| GMD-APM | Gesellschaft für Mathematik und Datenverarbeitung, Abt. Projekt-Management | GNC | Graphical Numerical Control |
| | | GNC | Guidance and Navigation Computer |
| GMDEP | Guided Missile Data Exchange Program | GND | Ground |
| GMDH | Group Method of Data Handling | GNE | Guidance and Navigation Electronics |
| GMDS | Gesellschaft für Medizinische Dokumentation und Statistik | GNG | Gaussian Noise Generator |
| | | GNL | General |
| | | GNOM | Graphic and Numeric Operation Method |
| GME | General Micro-Electronics | | |
| GME | Group Modulation Equipment | GNOM | Graphische und Numerische Organisationsmethode |
| GMF | Generated Message Format | | |
| GMFCS | Guided Missile Fire Control System | GNP | Get Next within Parent |
| | | GNP | Gross National Product |
| GMI | General Memory Interface | GNR | Guest Name Record |
| GMIS | Government Management Information System | GNS | Globale Netz-Subebene |
| | | GNTR | Generator |
| GML | Generalized Mark-up Language | GO | General Output |
| | | GO | Generator für Onlineanwendungen |
| GMM | Galvanomagnetic Method | | |
| GMM | Glass-Metal Module | GO | Geometrical Optic |
| GMMRIT | Glass-Metal Module Release Interface Tape | GO | Geräteoberteil |
| | | GO | Graphic Output |
| GMO | Gesellschaft für Moderne Organisationsverfahren | GO | Großsichtoszillograf |
| | | GO-E | GO TO Executive |
| GMÖOR | Gesellschaft für Mathematik, Ökonomie und Operations-Research | GO-I | GO TO Instruction |
| | | GO-L | GO TO Logic |
| | | GOAL | General Organization Analysis Language |
| GMOS | GPSS Modelled Operating System | | |
| | | GOAL | Generator for Optimized Application Languages |
| GMP | General Machine Program | | |
| GMR | Ground Mapping Radar | GOAL | Ground Operations Aerospace Language |
| GMS | Generalized Main Scheduling | | |
| | | GOAT | Gerber Oscillogram Amplitude Translator |
| GMT | Greenwich Mean Time | | |

# G

| | | | |
|---|---|---|---|
| GOCAP | Graphic Output Circuit Analysis Program | GOV | Governor |
| GOCI | General Operator Computer Interaction | GP | Gang Punch |
| | | GP | General Products |
| | | GP | General Program |
| GOCR | Gated-Off Controlled Rectifier | GP | General Purpose |
| | | GP | Generalized Programming |
| GODAS | Graphically Oriented Design and Analysis System | GP | Generator Potential |
| | | GP | Generator Program |
| | | GP | Gesamte Pufferzeit |
| GODV | Grundsätze Ordnungsmäßiger Datenverarbeitung | GP | Gesamter Puffer |
| | | GP | Glide Path |
| GODVA | Grundsätze Ordnungsmäßiger DV-Arbeitsabwicklung | GP | Graph Plotter |
| | | GP | Grid Pulse |
| GODVD | Grundsätze Ordnungsmäßiger DV-Dokumentation | GP | Großplattenspeicher |
| | | GP | Ground Protective |
| GOE | Ground Operating Equipment | GP | Group Printing |
| | | GPA | Gate Pulse Amplifier |
| GOL | General Operating Language | GPA | General Purpose Amplifier |
| | | GPA | General Purpose Analysis |
| GOLD | Geometric On-Line Definition | GPA | Gesellschaft für Produkt- und Anwendungstechnik |
| GOLD | Graphic On-Line Display | GPA | Graphical PERT Analog |
| GOLEM | Großplattenspeicher Listenorientierte Ermittlungsmethode | GPAC | General-Purpose Analog Computer |
| | | GPAO | Gestion de Production Assistée par Ordinateur |
| GOLS | General On-Line Stack | GPAR | Generalized Performance Analysis and Reporting system |
| GOP | General Operational Plot | | |
| GOP | Gesellschaft für Organisations- und Programmiersysteme | | |
| | | GPASS | Group Password |
| | | GPAT | General-Purpose Automatic Test |
| GOR | Gained Output Ratio | | |
| GOR | General Operational Requirement | GPATS | General Purpose Automatic Test System |
| GORID | Ground Optical Recorder for Intercept Determination | GPC | General Peripheral Controller |
| | | GPC | General Precision Connector |
| GORS | General Online Retrieval System | | |
| | | GPC | General Purpose Computer |
| GOS | Global Observational System | GPC | General Purpose Controller |
| | | GPC/P | General Purpose Controller/Processor |
| GOS | Grundsätze ordnungsgemäßer Speicherbuchführung | | |
| | | GPCH | Gang Punch |
| | | GPCP | General Purpose Contouring Program |
| GOS | Graphical Output Scheme | | |
| GOS | Graphic Operating System | | |
| GOSS | Ground Operational Support System | GPCP | Generalized Process Control Programming |
| GOSSIP | Generalized Organizational System Summarizer and Information Processor | GPCS | General Purpose Control System |
| | | GPD | General Purpose Data |
| | | GPD | General Purpose Discipline |
| GOSY | Graphic Output System | GPDC | General Purpose Digital Computer |
| GOTRAN | GO FORTRAN | | |
| GOTS | Graphically Oriented Time-sharing System | GPDL | Graphical Picture Drawing Language |
| GOV | Generator Output Voltage | | |

- 275 -

# G

| | | | |
|---|---|---|---|
| GPDS | General Purpose Display System | GPO | Government Printing Office |
| GPE | Générateur de Programmes d'Edition | GPOS | General Purpose Operating System |
| GPEXS | General Parts Explosion System | GPP | Graphic Part Programmer |
| GPGL | General Purpose Graphic Language | GPR | General Purpose Radar |
| | | GPR | General Purpose Register |
| GPI | General Process Interface | GPR | Graphic Problem Representation |
| GPI | General Purpose Interface | GPRSS | General Purpose Remote Sensor System |
| GPI | Generalized Package Interface | GPS | General Problem Solver |
| GPI | Generalized Packaging Interface | GPS | General Problem Solving |
| | | GPS | General Purpose Simulator |
| GPI | Ground Position Indicator | GPS | Gesellschaft zur Prüfung von Software |
| GPI/O | General-Purpose Input/Ouput | GPS | Gestellpufferspeicher |
| GPIA | General Purpose Interface Adapter | GPS | Graphic Programming Service |
| GPIB | General Purpose Interface Bus | GPSDIC | General Purpose Scientific Document Image Code |
| GPIOP | General Purpose Input Output Prozessor | GPSL | General Purpose Simulation Language |
| GPKD | General-Purpose Keyboard and Display | GPSP | General Purpose Software Program |
| GPL | Gemini Programming Language | GPSS | General Purpose Simulation System |
| GPL | General Purpose Language | GPSS | General Purpose System Simulator |
| GPL | Generalized Parameter List | GPSU | Ground Power Supply Unit |
| GPL | Generalized Programming Language | GPT | General Purpose Terminal |
| | | GPTI | General Purpose Terminal Interchange |
| GPL | Graphics Programming Language | GPU | Graphic Processing Unit |
| | | GPU | Graphics Processor Unit |
| GPLP | General Purpose Linear Programming | GPUCP | General Purpose User Control Program |
| GPM | General Purpose Macrogenerator | GPX | Generalized Programming Extended |
| GPM | General Purpose Microprocessor | GQ | Grundfondsquote |
| GPMS | General Purpose Microprogram Simulator | GR | General Reconnaissance |
| | | GR | General Register |
| GPMS | General Purpose Multiplex System | GR | General Reserve |
| | | GR | General Routine |
| GPN | General Performance Number | GR | Generating Routine |
| | | GR | Generator Running |
| GPNI | Groupement Professionnel National de l'Informatique | GR | Germanium Rectifier |
| | | GR | Gesamtregister |
| | | GR | Gleichrichter |
| GPNNC | General Purpose Non Numeric Computer | GR | Graph Reader |
| | | GR | Greater |
| GPO | General Post Office | GR | Grid Resistor |
| GPO | General Purpose Oscilloscope | GR | Großrechenanlage |
| | | GR | Großrechner |
| GPO | General Purpose Output | GR | Group |

- 276 -

# G

| | | | |
|---|---|---|---|
| GR | Gruppe Rücksetzen | GRASP | Generalized Reentry Application Simulation Program |
| GRA | Großrechenanlage | | |
| GRA... | Gesellschaft für Rechnergesteuerte Anlagen mbH | GRASP | Generalized Retrieval And Storage Program |
| GRACE | Graphic Arts Composing Equipment | GRASP | Graphic Service Program |
| GRACE | Group Routing And Charging Equipment | GRASPIN | Graphical Specification and formal Implementation of Nonsequential system |
| GRAD | General Recursive Algebra and Differentiation | | |
| GRAD | Graduate Resume Accumulation and Distribution | GRATIS | Generation, Reduction And Training Input System |
| GRADB | Generalized Remote Access Data Base | GRC | Group Repeat Count |
| | | GRD | Greatest Response Data |
| GRADPET | Graphic Data Presentation and Edit | GRDP | Graphic Data Processing |
| | | GRDSR | Geographically Referenced Data Storage and Retrieval |
| GRADS | Generalized Remote Access Data-base System | | |
| GRAF | Graphic Addition to FORTRAN | GRE | Going Rate Estimates |
| | | GRE | Ground Radar Equipment |
| GRAFCET | Graphe de Commande Étap-Transition | GRED | Generalized Random Extract Device |
| GRAFLAN | Graphic Language | GREMAS | Genealogical Retrieval by Magnetic tape Storage |
| GRAIL | Graphic Input Language | | |
| GRAL | Graph Algorithm | GREMAS | Genealogische Recherche durch Magnetbandspeicherung |
| GRAMPA | General Analytic Model for Process Analysis | | |
| GRAMS | Ground Recording And Monitoring System | GREMAS | Genealogisches Recherchieren durch Magnetbandspeicher |
| GRAPD | Greated Response Amplitude Probabilility Data | | |
| | | GRETA | Gestion Rationnelle et Elaborée pour le Traitement de l'Adresse |
| GRAPDEN | Graphic Data Entry | | |
| GRAPE | Graphical Analysis of Program Execution | GREXIT | Greatest Extreme in an Interval of Time |
| GRAPH | Graphics | GRIBS | Grafisches Interaktives Basissystem |
| GRAPHDEN | Graphic Data Entry | | |
| GRAPHIDI | Graphical Interpretive Display | GRID | Graphic Interactive Display |
| GRAPHOR | Graphes d'Ordonnancement | GRID | Graphic Remote Integrated Display |
| GRAPHPAK | Graphisches Anwendungspaket | GRIN | Graphical Input |
| | | GRIND | Graphical Interpretive Display |
| GRAPPA | Grafisches Projektplanungs-Analysesystem | | |
| | | GRIND | Group Indicate |
| GRARD | Goddard Range And Range Data | GRINS | General Retrieval Inquiry Negotiation Structure |
| GRARR | Goddard Range And Range Rate | GRIPHOS | General Retrieval and Information Processor for Humanities Oriented Studies |
| GRASP | General Read And Simulate Program | | |
| GRASP | General Resource Allocation and Scheduling Program | GRIPS | Gaming, Random Interfacing and Problem Structuring |
| GRASP | General Risk Analysis Simulation Program | | |

- 277 -

# G

| | |
|---|---|
| GRIPS | General Relation based Information Processing System |
| GRIPS | Gesellschaft für Rechnersysteme und Integrierte Prozeßsteuerungen m.b.H |
| GRIPS | Gift Reporting and Information Processing System |
| GRIS | Graphisch-Interaktives System |
| GRIT | Graduated Reduction In Tensions |
| GRM | Generalized Reed-Muller |
| GRNC | Group Number no Count |
| GRODE | Große Digitaleingabe |
| GROM | Graphics Read-Only Memory |
| GROOVE | Generated Realtime Output Operations on Voltage-controlled Equipment |
| GROS | Goods Receiving Online System |
| GRP | Gaussian Random Process |
| GRP | Glass Reinforced Plastic |
| GRP | Group |
| GRR | Guidance Reference Release |
| GRS | General Retrieval System |
| GRS | Generalized Retrieval System |
| GRS | Global Resource Serialisation |
| GRST | Großspeichersteurung |
| GRSUP | Group Suppression |
| GRT | General Recomplement Trigger |
| GRT | Grant |
| GRTS | Goddard Real-Time System |
| GRUNA | Gruppennachweis |
| GRV | Graphic Recording Voltmeter |
| GRVA | Graphic Varmeter |
| GRW | Graphic Recording Wattmeter |
| GRWT | Gross Weight |
| GRZ | Genossenschafts-Rechenzentrale |
| GRZ | Großrechenzentrum |
| GS | Galvanized Steel |
| GS | Gebersignal |
| GS | General Search |
| GS | General Statement |
| GS | General Storage |
| GS | General Store |
| GS | Generalized Sign |
| GS | Generate Statement |
| GS | Geschäftsstelle |
| GS | Gestreute Speicherungsform |
| GS | Glide Slope |
| GS | Großraumspeicher |
| GS | Großspeicher |
| GS | Ground Speed |
| GS | Group Selector |
| GS | Group Separator |
| GS | Grundsektor |
| GS | Gruppe Setzen |
| GS | Gruppensignal |
| GS | Gyroscope |
| GSA | General Services Administration |
| GSA | General Storage Assignment |
| GSAM | General Sequential Access Method |
| GSAM | Generalized Sequential Access Method |
| GSC | Group Switching Centre |
| GSCU | Ground Support Cooling Unit |
| GSD | General Situation Display |
| GSD | General System Division |
| GSD | General Systems Development Corporation |
| GSDB | Geophysics & Space Data Bulletin |
| GSDC | Geodetic Satellites Data Center |
| GSDSP | Generalized Statistical Document Search Pattern |
| GSDT | Generalized Syntax Directed Translation |
| GSE | Gemeinsam benützte Speichereinheit |
| GSE | Gerätesteuereinheit |
| GSE | Ground Support Equipment |
| GSEC | Group Security |
| GSF | General Source File |
| GSI | Général de Service Informatique |
| GSI | Giant Scale Integration |
| GSI | Grand Scale Integration |
| GSI | Ground Speed Indicator |
| GSI | Groupement de Services Informatiques |
| GSL | Generalized Simulation Language |
| GSL | Generation Strategy Language |

# G

| | | | |
|---|---|---|---|
| GSM | Generalized Sequential Machine | GT | Gas Tube |
| GSP | Gang Summary Punch | GT | Generatorteil |
| GSP | General Simulation Program | GT | Glass Tube |
| GSP | Geodetic Satellite Program | GT | Greater Than |
| GSP | Graphic Subroutine Package | GT | Ground Transmit |
| GSP | Großraumspeicher | GT | Group Transformation |
| GSP | Großspeicher | GT | Grundtext |
| GSP | Group Step Pulse | GTB | Grafiken und Tabellen |
| GSP | Guidance Signal Processor | GTC | Gain Time Constant |
| GSPAN | Graphic S Plane Analysis | GTC | Gain Time Control |
| GSPC | Graphic Standard Planning Committee | GTCR | Gate Turn-off Controlled Rectifier |
| GSPG | Graphics System Program Group | GTD | Gear Test Data |
| GSPR | Guidance Signal Processor Repeater | GTD | Geometrical Theory of Diffraction |
| GSPST | Großspeichersteuerung | GTD | Graphic Tablet Display |
| GSR | Galvanic Skin Resistance | GTDI | Guideline Transportation Data Interchange |
| GSR | Galvanic Skin Response | GTE | General Telephone and Electric |
| GSR | Gap Spacing Routine | GTE | General Television and Electronic |
| GSR | Global Shared Resources | GTE | Ground Transport Equipment |
| GSR | Group Selection Register | GTEIS | General Telephone and Electronic Information Systems |
| GSR | Group Selective Register | GTF | Gaussian-Type Function |
| GSS | Gesteuertes Stapelfernübertragungssystem | GTF | Gauß-Typ-Funktion |
| GSS | Global Surveillance System | GTF | General Trace Facility |
| GSS | Großspeicher-Steuergerät | GTF | Generalized Trace Facility |
| GSSC | Ground Support Simulation Computer | GTF | Generalized Transformation Function |
| GSSC | Group Support Simulation Computer | GTF PARS | Generalized Trace Facility Performance Analysis and Reporting System |
| GST | General Systems Theory | GTG | Gating |
| GST | Global Storage Table | GTL | Geometrical and Technological Language |
| GST | Grundeinheit Steuerung | GTL | Georgia Tech Language |
| GSTN | General Switched Telephone Network | GTM | Grand Total Memory |
| GSTP | Ground System Test Procedure | GTMS | Graphic Text Management System |
| GSU | General Service Unit | GTN | Global Transaction Network |
| GSUM | Grundsprachedaten Umsetzprogramm | GTO | Gate Turn-Off |
| GSV | Ground-to-Surface Vessel radar | GTOL | Graphic Take-Off Language |
| GSVC | Generalized Supervisor Call | GTP | Gap Time Pulse |
| GSW | Grundsoftware | GTP | General Test Plan |
| GSWR | Galvanized Steel Wire Rope | GTP | General Tracking Program |
| GSX | Graphics Systems Extension | GTPI | General Teleprocessing Interface |
| GT | Game Theory | GTS | General Technical Services |
| GT | Gap Time | | |

# G

| | | | |
|---|---|---|---|
| GTS | Gesellschaft für Computer-Terminal-Systeme | GUN | Groupement des Utilisateurs NCR |
| GTS | Global Telecommunication System | GURS | General Update and Retrieval System |
| GTS | Go To Statement | GUS | General User System |
| GTS | Graphics Terminal System | GUSIT | General Usage Shorts and Impedance Tests |
| GTT | Gate Terminal | | |
| GTV | Gate Valve | GUSTO | Guidance Using Stable Tuning Oscillations |
| GTW | Gesellschaft für Technik und Wirtschaft | GUUG | German Unix Users Group |
| GTXT | Generate character Text | GV | Gruppenverbinder |
| GTXT | Generate Text | GV | Gruppenverstärker |
| GÜ | Geräteübersicht | GV/RV | Gruppen- und Richtungsverbinder |
| GU | Geräteunterteil | | |
| GU | Get Unique | GVV | Gewählte Virtuelle Verbindung |
| GU | Group User | | |
| GU | Gruppenumsetzer | GW | Ganzwort |
| GU | Gruppenumsetzung | GW | General Warning |
| GUB | Generalized Upper Bounding | GW | Gigawatt |
| GUD | Gesellschaft für Unternehmensberatung und Datenverarbeitung | GW | Gleichspannung/ Wechselspannung |
| | | GW | Gleichstrom/Wechselstrom |
| | | GW | Gleichstromwandler |
| GUERAP | General Unwanted Energy Rejection Analysis Program | GWDRS | Ground Winds Data Reduction System |
| | | GWPM | Gross Words Per Minute |
| GUI | Groupement des Utilisateurs ICL | GXA | Gun-diode X-band Amplifier |
| GUIDE | Guidance for Users of Integrated Data processing Equipment | GZ | Ground Zero |
| | | GZPS | Gestellzeilenpufferspeicher |
| GULP | General Utility Language Processor | GZR | Gerätezustandsregister |
| | | GZTPRD | Ground Zero Tape Read |
| GULP | General Utility Library Program | GZS | Gesellschaft für Zahlungssysteme |
| GUN | Generic Unit Name | | |

# H

| | | | |
|---|---|---|---|
| H | Haben | HAD | Home Address Data |
| H | Halb | HAD | Horizontal Array of Dipoles |
| H | Halbaddierer | | |
| H | Halbwort | HADES | Halbautomatisches Datenerfassungssystem |
| H | Halt | | |
| H | Hardness | HADES | Hypersonic Air Data Entry System |
| H | Hardware | | |
| H | Head | HADIOS | Honeywell Analog Digital I/O Subsystem |
| H | Heat | | |
| H | Height | HADIS | Huddersfield And District Information Service |
| H | Hekto | | |
| H | Hersteller | HADR | Hilfsadreßregister |
| H | High | HADS | Hypersonic Air Data Sensor |
| H | Horizontal | | |
| H | Hour | HADTS | High Accuracy Data Transmission System |
| H | Hundert | | |
| H | Hundred | HAEB | Header Analysis Error Byte |
| H... | Honeywell | HAF | High Abrasion Furnace |
| H-B | Hexadecimal-to-Binary | HAF | High Altitude Fluorescence |
| H-D | Hexadecimal to Decimal | HAFO | Institut für Halbleiterforschung |
| H-PD | Hough-Powell Device | | |
| H-PD | Hough-Powell Digitizer | HAI | Holland Automation International |
| H/B | Handbook | | |
| H/C | Hand Carry | HAISAM | Hashed Index Sequential Access Method |
| H/DS | Head-to-Drum Separation | | |
| H/P | High Position | HAIST | Human Abilities In Software Technology |
| HA | Half Add | | |
| HA | Half Adder | HAL | Hard Array Logic |
| HA | Half Adjust | HAL | Heuristically-programmed Algorithmic |
| HA | Halt | | |
| HA | Hardware | HAL | Highly Automated Logic |
| HA | Hauptabschnitt | HAL | Honeywell Author Language |
| HA | Hauptadresse | | |
| HA | Hauptamt | HALDIS | Halifax and District Information Service |
| HA | Hauptanschluß | | |
| HA | Hauptaufgabe | HALPAS | Halberg Programm-Ablauf-Steuerung |
| HA | Head Address | | |
| HA | Home Address | HALSIM | Hardware Logic Simulator |
| HA | Hour Angle | HAM | Hand Adding Machine |
| HAA | Human Action Analysis | HAM | Hand Addressing Machine |
| HAAS | Honeywell Automotive Accounting System | HAM | Hardware Associative Memory |
| HAB | Hauptbuch | HAM | High Activity Mode |
| HABS | Human relations area files Automated Bibliographic System | HAM | High-Availability Manager |
| | | HAMA | Hardware-Machine |
| | | HAN | Hauptauftragnehmer |
| HAC | Hydraulic Analog Computer | HAO | Home Address Operation |
| | | HAP | Harvest Assembly Program |
| HACS | Hazard Assessment Computer System | HAP | High-Altitude Platform |
| | | HAPDAR | Hard Point Demonstration Array Radar |
| HACU | Handling And Conditioning Unit | | |
| | | HAPRO | Hauptprogramm |
| HAD | Half-Amplitude pulse Duration | HAR | Harmonic |
| | | HAR | Home Address Record |
| HAD | High Accuracy Data | HAR | Host-Anpassungsrechner |

# H

| | | | |
|---|---|---|---|
| HAR/TAR | Host- und Terminal-anpassungsrechner | HAU | Horizontal Arithmetic Unit |
| HARAC | High Altitude Resonance Absorption Calculation | HAYSTAQ | Have You Stored Answers to Questions? |
| HARCO | Hyperbolic Area Covering navigation system | HAZ | Heat Affected Zone |
| | | HB | High Band |
| HARD | Hardware | HB | Homing Beacon |
| HARDTS | High-Accuracy Radar Data Transmission System | HB... | Honeywell Bull |
| | | HBC | High Breaking Capacity |
| HARE | High Altitude Recombination Energy | HBC | Honeywell Business Compiler |
| HARM | Harmonic | HBC | Honeywell Business Computer |
| HARP | High Altitude Relay Point | HBC | Hydrogen Bubble Chamber |
| HARP | High Altitude Research Project | HBD | Half Byte Decimal |
| | | HBDT | High Bit Density Tape |
| HARS | Heading and Attitude Reference System | HBFR | Hilfsbefehlsregister |
| | | HBG | Hauptbaugruppe |
| HARTRAN | Harwell Atlas FORTRAN | HBR | High Bit Rate |
| HAS | Hauptanschluß | HBT | Halbleiterblocktechnik |
| HAS | Head Address Set | HBW | Hot Bridge Wire |
| HAS | Heading and Attitude Sensor | HC | Half Command |
| | | HC | Half Cycle |
| HAS | Hubschrauber-Anflugsystem | HC | Hand Compute |
| HASP | High-Altitude Sampling Program | HC | Handling Capacity |
| | | HC | Hard Copy |
| HASP | High-Altitude Sounding Project | HC | Hardware Check |
| | | HC | Head Card |
| HASP | Houston Atomic Spooling Priority | HC | Head Control |
| | | HC | Header Card |
| HASP | Houston Attached Support Processor | HC | Header Check |
| | | HC | Heading Card |
| HASP | Houston Automatic Spool Process | HC | Heat Coil |
| | | HC | Heavy Current |
| HASP | Houston Automatic Spooling and Printing system | HC | Held Code |
| | | HC | Heuristic Concepts |
| | | HC | High Capacitance |
| HASP | Houston Automatic Spooling Priority system | HC | High Capacity |
| | | HC | High Carbon |
| HASP | Houston Automatic Spooling Program | HC | High Conductivity |
| | | HC | High Current |
| HASP/RJE | Houston Automatic Spooling Priority with Remote Job Entry | HC | Holding Coil |
| | | HC | Hollerith Card |
| | | HC | Hollerith Code |
| HASS | High Availability Subsystem | HC | Horizontal Check |
| | | HC | Hybrid Circuit |
| HASSS | High Accuracy Spacecraft Separation System | HC | Hybrid Computer |
| | | HCA | Hand Copy Adapter |
| HASTP | Hauptsteuerprogramm | HCBS | Host Computer Basic Software |
| HASVR | High Altitude Space Velocity Radar | | |
| | | HCC | Hole Count Check |
| HAT | Handover Transmitter | HCD | High Current Diode |
| HAT | Head Address Transfer | HCD | Hoffman Core Driver |
| HAT | High Altitude Testing | HCD | Hot-Carrier Diode |
| HATRAC | Handover Transfer and Receiver Accept Change | HCE | Hollow-Cathode Effect |
| | | HCF | High Capacity File |

# H

| | | | |
|---|---|---|---|
| HCF | Highest Common Factor | HDAC | Hybrid Digital-Analog Circuit |
| HCF | Host Command Facility | HDAM | Hierarchical Direct Access Method |
| HCG | Horizontal location of Center of Gravity | HDAS | Hydrographic Data Acquisition System |
| HCJ | Honeywell Computer Journal | HDB | High Density Bipolar |
| HCL | High, Common, Low relay | HDB | High Density Buffer |
| HCL | Hopper Card Lever | HDBC | High Density Bipolar Code |
| HCM | Hard-Core Monitor | HDBK | Handbook |
| HCO | Hard Copy Output | HDC | Half Duplex Circuit |
| HCP | Hard Copy Printer | HDC | Hexadecimal Code |
| HCP | Hemispherical Candle Power | HDC | High Duty Cycle |
| HCP | Hexagonal Closed Packed | HDC | Home Data Channel |
| HCP | Horizontal Candle Power | HDCD | Head Card |
| HCP | Host Command Processor | HDD | High Density Data |
| HCP | Host Communication Processor | HDDB | High Dummy Descriptor Block |
| HCP | Host Command Processor | HDDI | Host Displaywriter Document Interchange |
| HCR | Human Computing Resources | HDDR | High Density Digital magnetic Recording |
| HCS | Helicopter Computer System | HDDR | High Density Digital Recording |
| HCS | High Capacity Storage | HDDS | High-Density Data System |
| HCS | Homogeneous Computer System | HDDT | High Density Digital Tape |
| HCSS | Hospital Computer Sharing System | HDED | Hard Decision Error Detector |
| HCT | Hard Copy Task | HDEP | High Density Electronic Packaging |
| HCT | Hybrid Computer Technique | HDF | High-frequency Direction-Finder |
| HCU | Hypertape Control Unit | HDF | Horizontal Data Flow |
| HCUA | Honeywell Computer User's Association | HDF | Horizontal Distributing Frame |
| HD | Half Duplex | HDG | Heading |
| HD | Hardware Description languages | HDG-DTL | Heading to Detail |
| | | HDG-HDG | Heading to Heading |
| HD | Harmonic Distortion | HDI | Head Disk Interference |
| HD | Head | HDI | Horizon Direction Indicator |
| HD | Head Diameter | | |
| HD | Head Driver | | |
| HD | Heading | HDI | Horizontal Display Indicator |
| HD | Heading to Detail | | |
| HD | Heavy Duty | HDL | Hardware Description Language |
| HD | Hexadecimal | | |
| HD | Hierarchical Direct | HDL | Hydrologic Data Laboratory |
| HD | High Density | | |
| HD | Hinweisdaten | HDLC | High-level Data Laboratory |
| HD | Hochleistungsdrucker | | |
| HD | Hold | HDLC | High-level Data Link Control procedure |
| HDA | Head Disc Assembly | | |
| HDA | Heavy Duty Amplifier | HDLC | High-level Data Link Control |
| HDA | High Density Acid | | |
| HDA | Highway-to-group Demultiplexer Address-generator | HDLC | High-level Data Link Controller |

# H

| | |
|---|---|
| HDLG | Handling |
| HDLS | Hardware Description Language System |
| HDM | High Data Mode |
| HDMR | High Density Moderated Reactor |
| HDMS | High Density Memory System |
| HDOC | Handy Dandy Orbital Computer |
| HDOS | Heath Disk Operating System |
| HDP | High-Density-Package |
| HDP | Horizontal Data Processing |
| HDR | Header |
| HDR | Health Data Recorder |
| HDR | High Data Rate |
| HDR | High Data Register |
| HDR | High Density Recorder |
| HDRSS | High Data Rate Storage System |
| HDRT | High Density Recording Tape |
| HDS | Half Duplex System |
| HDS | Hardware Development System |
| HDS | Hundreds |
| HDSG | Hessisches Datenschutzgesetz |
| HDST | High Density Shock Tube |
| HDT | Half Duplex Teletype |
| HDT | Heat Deflection Temperature |
| HDTV | High Definition TV |
| HDUP | Half Duplex |
| HDV | Halt Device |
| HDVS | High-Definition-Video-System |
| HDW | Hardware |
| HDW | Hydrodynamics Welding |
| HDWA | Hardware |
| HDWCON | Hardware Confidence |
| HDWE | Hardware |
| HDX | Half Duplex |
| HDY | Heavy Duty |
| HE | Hardware Evaluator |
| HE | Hardware Executive |
| HE | Heat Exchange |
| HE | Heavy Enamelled |
| HE | Help |
| HE | High Efficiency |
| HE | High Energy |
| HE | High Explosive |
| HE | Hydroelectric |
| HEALS | Honeywell Error Analysis and Logging System |
| HEAP | High Explosive Armour Piercing |
| HEAT | Heating |
| HEC | Hollerith Electronic Computer |
| HECAD | Human Engineering Computer Aided Design |
| HECATE | Heat Exchanger Computerised Aid for Technical Engineering |
| HECLINET | Health Care Literature Information Network |
| HED | Horizontal Electrical Dipole |
| HED | Human Engineering Data |
| HEDC | Hasselblad Electric Data Camera |
| HEDGE | Human factor Evaluation Data for General Equipment |
| HEED | High Energy Electron Diffraction |
| HEGIS | Higher Education General Information Survey |
| HEIAC | Hydraulic Engineering Information Analysis Center |
| HEIAS | Human Engineering Information and Analysis Service |
| HELD | Harrison/Endicott Liaison Program |
| HELP | Harris Enhanced Language for Programmable Logik |
| HELP | Header List Printing |
| HELP | Header Listing Program |
| HELP | Health Evaluation through Logical Processing |
| HELP | Heckman's Electronic Library Program |
| HELP | Heuristic Etching-pattern Layout Program |
| HELP | Highly Extendable Language Processor |
| HELP | Hitachi Effective Library for Programming |
| HELP | Hybrid Electronic Layout Program |
| HELPIS | Higher Education Learning Program Information Service |
| HELPR | Handbook of Electronic Parts Reliability |

# H

| | | | |
|---|---|---|---|
| HEM | Hybrid Electromagnet wave | HF BD | High-Frequency Band |
| HEM | Hybrid Electromagnetic Mode | HF/SSB | High Frequency/Single Sideband |
| HEMIS | Health Education Materials Information Service | HFA | High Frequency Amplifier |
| | | HFA | High Frequency Antenna |
| | | HFC | High Frequency Current |
| HEMT | High Electron Mobility Transfer | HFDF | High Frequency Direction Finder |
| HEMT | High Electron Mobility Transistor | HFDF | High Frequency Distribution Frame |
| HEMT | High Electron Movement Transistor | HFI | High Frequency Input |
| | | HFM | Held For Manufacturing |
| HEO | Higher Executive Order | HFM | Held For Material |
| HEP | Heterogene-Element-Processor | HFM | High Frequency Mode |
| | | HFO | High Frequency Oscillator |
| HEP | Hierarchisches Entscheidungsprinzip | HFP | Hand Feed Punch |
| | | HFR | Hold For Release |
| HEP | High Energy Physics | HFRDF | High Frequency Radio Direction Finding |
| HEPAS | Hessisches Planungs-informations- und Analysesystem | HFRDF | High Frequency Repeater Distribution Frame |
| HEPOLIS | Hessisches Polizei-Informationssystem | HFT | Held For Tooling |
| | | HFV | Hochfrequenzverstärker |
| HEPP | Hoffman Evaluation Program and Procedure | HFWD | Halfword |
| | | HG | Harmonic Generator |
| HERALD | Harbour Echo Ranging And Listening Device | HG | Head Group |
| | | HGA | High Gain Antenna |
| HERAP | Human Error Research and Analysis Program | HGD | Highway-to-Group Demultiplexer |
| HERMAN | Hierarchical Environmental Retrieval for Management Access and Networking | HGL | Hierarchical Graph Language |
| | | HGR | Head Gear Receiver |
| HERO | Heath-Roboter | HGT | High Group Transmitting |
| HERS | Hardware Error Recovery System | HH | Heading to Heading |
| | | HHC | Hand Held Computer |
| HERTIS | Hertfordshire Technical Information Service | HHF | Hyper High Frequency |
| | | HHMMSS | Hour-Hour/Minute-Minute/Second-Second |
| HES | Handeingabestelle | | |
| HES | Handendstelle | HI | Halt Instruction |
| HETP | Height Equivalent to a Theoretical Plate | HI | High |
| | | HI | High Intensity |
| HETS | High Environmental Test System | HI | Holding Instruction |
| | | HI | Housekeeping Instruction |
| HETS | High Equivalent to a Theoretical Stage | HI... | Houston Instrument Corp. |
| | | HI-PASS | High Pass |
| HEU | Hydroelectric Unit | HI-STEP | High-speed integrated Space Transportation Evaluation Program |
| HEW | Department of Health, Education and Welfare | | |
| | | HI/LO | High-Low |
| HEX | Hexadecimal | HIAC | High Accuracy |
| HEX | Hexadezimal | HIAS | Human Intellect Augmentation System |
| HEX | Hexagonal | | |
| HfD | Hauptanschluß für Direktruf | HIBS | Health Information Base System |
| HF | High Frequency | HIC | Hybrid Integrated Circuit |
| HF | Hochfrequenz | | |

- 285 -

# H

| | | | |
|---|---|---|---|
| HICAPCOM | High Capacity Communication system | HIQ | High Quality |
| HIDAM | Hierarchical Indexed Direct Access Method | HIR | Hardware Instruction Retry |
| HIDAN | High Density Air Navigation | HIRAC | High Random Access |
| HIDES | Highway Design System | HIRAN | High precision short Range Navigation |
| HIDF | Horizontal Intermediate Distribution Frame | HIRD | High Information Rate Display |
| HIDM | High-Information Delta Modulation | HIRS | Holographic Information Retrieval System |
| HIDRESS | High Data Rate Storage Subsystem | HIS | Hardware Interrupt System |
| HIESIM | Hierarchische Simulation | HIS | Headquarters Information System |
| HIF | High Impedance Follower | HIS | Hochschul-Informations-System GmbH |
| HIFAM | High-Fidelity Amplitude Modulation | HIS | Holt Information System |
| HIFAX-NET | Hitachi Facsimile-Network | HIS | Honeywell Information System |
| HIFI | High Fidelity | HIS | Hospital Information System |
| HIFIT | High Frequency Input Transistor | HISAM | Hierarchical Indexed Sequential Access Method |
| HII | High Input Impedance | HISARS | Hydrologic Information Storage And Retrieval System |
| HIIS | Honeywell Institute of Information Sciences | HISI... | Honeywell Information System Italia |
| HIL | Horizontale Informationsleitung | HISID | Harris Information Systems International Division |
| HILAS | Hierarchisches System für Lagersteuerung | HISP | Health Information Sharing Project |
| HIN | Hybrid Integrated Network | HISP | Hilfsspeicher |
| HINIL | High Noise Immunity Logic | HISS | High Intensity Sound Simulator |
| HIO | Halt I/O | HISSG | Hospital Information Systems Sharing Group |
| HIP | Hierarchical Information Processor | HISTORIC | Hursley Information System Terminal Oriented Retrieval Information Center |
| HIP | Host Interface Processor | HISTORIC | Hursley Information System Terminal Originated Reference and Information Control |
| HIP | Hyperbolic Integer Programming | HIT | Hypersonic Interference Technology |
| HIPAC | Heavy Ion Plasma Accelerator | HITAC | Hitachi Computer |
| HIPAC | Hitachi Parametron Automatic Computer | HIVIP | Hitachi Visual Image Processing |
| HIPAR | High Power Acquisition Radar | HJFET | Heterojunction JFET |
| HIPO | Hierarchical Input Process Output | HJFET | Hetero-Junction-gate Field Effect Transistor |
| HIPO | Hierarchy Input Process Output | HKR | Haushaltskassenrechnungswesen |
| HIPO | Hierarchy Input Processing Output | | |
| HIPO | Hierarchy plus Input, Process, Output | | |
| HIPO | Hospital Indicator for Physicians' Orders | | |
| HIPS | Hyperintense Proximal Scanning | | |

# H

| | | | |
|---|---|---|---|
| HL | Halbleiter | HMDF | Horizontal Main Distributing Frame |
| HL | Half Life | | |
| HL | Hauptleitung | HMIS | Headquarters Manufacturing Information System |
| HL | Header Label | | |
| HL | Heavy Loading | | |
| HL | High Level | HML | Harvest Maintenance Language |
| HL | High Low | | |
| HLBT | Halbleiterblocktechnik | HMLI | High Memory Load Indicator |
| HLC | Head Label Check | | |
| HLC | High Level Center | HMN | Hamburger Methode der Netzplantechnik |
| HLC | High Level Compiler | | |
| HLD | Hold | HMM | Hybrider Matrizenmultiplizierer |
| HLDB | Hot-Line, Dead-Bus | | |
| HLDG | Holding | HMOS | High density MOS |
| HLEP | High Level End-to-end Protocol | HMOS | High performance MOS |
| | | HMOS | High speed MOS |
| HLFT | Holographic Lensless Fourier Transform | HMP | High Melting Point |
| | | HMS | Hardened Memory System |
| HLI | Hard Limited Integrator | HMS | Hierarchical Memory Storage |
| HLK | Handlochkarte | | |
| HLL | High Level Language | HMS | Honeywell Manufacturing System |
| HLL | High Level Logic | | |
| HLM | High Level Mixer | HMSDC | Hybrid Multiplexed Synchro Digital Converter |
| HLOV | High Level Output Voltage | | |
| HLRM | High Level Radio Modulator | | |
| | | HMT | Hand Mircotelephone |
| HLS | High Level Scheduler | HN | Hauptnenner |
| HLSE | High Level, Single Ended | HN | Horn |
| HLSI | Hybrid Large Scale Integrated | HN | Host Node |
| | | HNA | Hydraulic Network Analysis |
| HLSI | Hybrid Large Scale Integration | HNC | Hand Numerical Control |
| | | HNC | Higher National Certificate |
| HLSUA | Honeywell Large Systems Users Association | | |
| | | HND | Higher National Diploma |
| HLT | Halt | HNDS | Handset |
| HLTL | High Level Test Language | HNDST | Handset |
| HLTL | High Level Transistor Logic | HNIL | High Noise Immunity Logic |
| | | HNR | Handwritten Numeral Recognition |
| HLTTL | High Level Transistor Transistor Logic | | |
| | | HNT | Hunt |
| HM | Hardware Malfunction | HO | Hardware Operation |
| HM | Hardware Monitoring | HO | Heading |
| HM | Hausmodul | HO | High Order |
| HM | Heater Middle | HO | Horizontal Output |
| HM | Hold Mode | HO | Housekeeping Operation |
| HM | Hollerith Machine | HO | Human Operator |
| HM | Hologram Memory | HO | Hunting Oscillator |
| HM | Hysteresis Moter | HOALM | Holographic Optically Addressed Light Modulation |
| HMA | Highway Memory Address | | |
| HMB | Hochohm-Meßbrücke | | |
| HMC | Heading Marker Correction | HOAM | Hand Operated Adding Machine |
| HMD | Handbuch der Maschinellen Datenverarbeitung | | |
| | | HOB | High Order Bit |
| HMD | Hot Metal Detector | HOBOT | House-cleaning robot |
| HMD | Hydraulic Mean Depth | | |

# H

| | | | |
|---|---|---|---|
| HOC | Heterodyne Optical Correlation | HOST | Harmonically Optimized Stabilization Technique |
| HOC | High Output Current | HOST | Houston Operations Simulation Technique |
| HOC | Hokushin Computer | HOT | Handover Transmitter |
| HOCEM | Hierarchically Organized Cybernetic Electric Machine | HOT | Holographic One-Two |
| HOCUS | Hand Or Computer Universal Simulation | HOT | Horizontal Output Transformer |
| HOCUS | Hand Or Computer Universal Simulator | HOVSA | Horizontale Oder Vertikale Struktur-Auflösung |
| HOD | Higher Order Digit | HP | Hand Punch |
| HODRAL | Hokushin Data Reduction Algorithm Language | HP | Hauptprogramm |
| | | HP | Hewlett Packard |
| HODS | Hydrographic Oceanographic Data Sheets | HP | High Performance |
| | | HP | High Power |
| HOE | Holographic Optical Element | HP | High Pressure |
| | | HP | Hilfsprogramm |
| HOF | Head Of Form | HP | Hochpaß |
| HOFCO | Horizontal Function Checkout | HP | Horizontal Polarization |
| | | HP | Horse Power |
| HOI | HYTRAN Operator Interpreter | HP... | Hewlett Packard |
| | | HP DS | HP Distributed Systems |
| HOK | Hauptordnungskriterium | HP-DSN | Hewlett Packard Distributed Systems Network |
| HOL | High-Order Language | | |
| HOLDCP | Hold, Computed | HP-ESSQ | High-Pass Error Spectrum Shaping Quantizer |
| HOLDPB | Hold Pushbutton | | |
| HOM | High Order Multiplier | HP-GL | Hewlett Packard Graphics Language |
| HOM | Higher Order Mismatch | | |
| HON | Hold Off Normal | HP-IB | Hewlett Packard Interface Bus |
| HOPS | Harvest Operating System | | |
| HOPS | Highway Optimization Program System | HP-IL | Hewlett Packard Interface Loop |
| HOPSTOP | Hopper Stop | HP-UX | Hewlett Packard - Unix |
| HOQ | High Order Quotient | HP/PCS | Hewlett Packard/Process Computer Systems |
| HOR | Horizontal | | |
| HORAB | Honorarabrechnung | HP/h | Horse Power/hour |
| HORAD | Horizontal Radar Display | HPA | High Power Amplifier |
| HORAS | Hotelreservierungs- und Abrechnungssystem | HPAG | High Performance Air-to-Ground |
| HOREST | Handelsorientierte Einkaufsdisposition mit Saison- und Trendberücksichtigung | HPBW | Half-Power Bandwidth |
| | | HPC | Hand Punched Card |
| | | HPC | Hardware Program Counter |
| HOREST | Handelsorientiertes Einkaufsdispositionssystem mit Trendberücksichtigung | HPC | Helicopter Performance Computer |
| | | HPC | Hollerith Punched Card |
| | | HPC | Horizonted Parity Check |
| HOS | Hardwired Operating System | HPCB | Hundreds Position C Bit |
| HOSP | High Order Storage Position | HPCM | High speed Pulse Code Modulation |
| HOSPACT | Hospital Patient Accounting | HPCM | Hybrid Pulse Code Modulation |
| | | HPD | High Power Drive |

# H

| | | | |
|---|---|---|---|
| HPDSN | Hewlett Packard Distributed Systems Network | HR | High Resistance |
| HPEX | High Priority Exit | HR | High Resistor |
| HPF | High Pass Filter | HR | High Resolution |
| HPF | High Performance File | HR | High Resolving |
| HPF | High Power Field | HR | Hilfsrechner |
| HPF | Highest Possible Frequency | HR | Hilfsregister |
| HPF | Highest Probable Frequency | HR | Hintergrundrechner |
| HPF | Horizontal Position Finder | HR | Hour |
| HPL | High-level Programming Language | HR | Hybridrechner |
| HPLL | Hybrid Phase Locked Loop | HR-LED | High Radiation Light Emitting Device |
| HPMA | High-Power Microwave Assembly | HRA | Hybridrechneranlage |
| HPMS | High Performance Main Storage | HRB | High-Reliability Baustein |
| HPN | High Pass Network | HRC | Harmonic Response Characteristic |
| HPN | High Pass Notch | HRC | High Redundant Code |
| HPO | High Performance Option | HRC | High Rupturing Capacity |
| HPP | Half Page Printer | HRC | Hybrid Receiver Circuit |
| HPP | High Performance Processor | HRC | Hypothetical Reference Circuit |
| HPPF | Host Program Preparation Facility | HRD | Hertzsprung-Russel Diagram |
| HPPS | Hewlett Packard Printer Submodule | HRD | High Resolution Display |
| HPR | Halt and Proceed | HRDP | Hypothetical Reference Digital Path |
| HPR | Hauptspeicherresidente Programme | HRES | High Resolution Electronic System |
| HPRO | Hauptprogramm | HRF | Height Range Finder |
| HPROM | Harris Programmable Read-Only Memory | HRF | High Resolution Facsimile |
| HPS | High Primary Sequence | HRI | Height Range Indicator |
| HPS | Highest Possible Score | HRI | Horizon Reference Indicator |
| HPS | Höhere Programmiersprache | HRIM | High Resolution Infrared Measurement |
| HPSD | High Power Switching Device | HRIR | High Resolution Infrared Radiometer |
| HPT | High Point | HRIR | High Resolution Infrared Receiver |
| HPT | High Profile Terminal | HRIS | Highway Research Information Service |
| HPT | Horizontal Plot Table | HRL | Hochregallager der M.A.N. |
| HPTR | Hilfsprogramm auf Trommel | HRM | High Reliability Module |
| HQ | High Quality | HRMR | Human Readable/Machine Readable |
| HQS | High Quality Sound | HRP | Hauptspeicherresidentes Programm |
| HR | Hand Radar | HRRTC | High Resolution Real Time Clock |
| HR | Hand Reset | HRS | High Resolution System |
| HR | Hardware Representation | HRS | Hybridenrechensystem |
| HR | Hauptrechner | HRS | Hybrides Rechensystem |
| HR | Heading Record | HRT | High Rate Telemetry |
| HR | Heat Resistance | HRT | High Resolution Timer |
| HR | Heavy Duty Relay | HRT | Home Record Tape |
| HR | Height Range | | |
| HR | High Reflector | | |

# H

| | | | |
|---|---|---|---|
| HRTM | Hardware Real-Time Monitor | HSC | High Speed Counter |
| HRTS | High-Rate Telemetry System | HSCA | Horizontal Sweep Circuit Analyzer |
| HRZ | Hochschul-Rechenzentrum | HSCF | Health Sciences Computing Facility |
| HRZN | Horizon | HSCF | High Speed Card Feed |
| HS | Haftspeicher | HSCH | Halt Subchannel |
| HS | Half Subtractor | HSCM | High Speed Computing Machine |
| HS | Hand Switch | | |
| HS | Handset | HSCP | High Speed Card Perforator |
| HS | Hauptsatz | | |
| HS | Hauptschalter | HSCP | High Speed Card Punch |
| HS | Hauptspeicher | HSCR | High Speed Card Reader |
| HS | Header Statement | HSCS | High Speed Contact Sense |
| HS | Heading Statement | HSD | Hierarchically Structured Data |
| HS | Hermetically Sealed | | |
| HS | Hierarchical Sequential | HSD | Horizontal Situation Display |
| HS | Hierarchically Structural | | |
| HS | Hierarchisch-Sequentiell | HSDA | High Speed Data Acquisition |
| HS | Hierarchiv Sequential | | |
| HS | High Shock resistant | HSDA | High Speed Data Assembly |
| HS | High Speed | HSDA | Homomorphic Statistical Deconvolution Algorithm |
| HS | Hilfsspeicher | | |
| HS | Hollerith System | HSDAS | High Speed Data Acquisition System |
| HS | Horizontal Synchronization | | |
| HS | Hypersonic | HSDC | High Speed Data Channel |
| HS-DARS | High Speed Data Acquisition and Reduction System | HSDCA | High Speed Data Channel Adapter |
| | | HSDF | High Speed Digital Filter |
| HS/MS | Hochspannung/Mittelspannung | HSDI | High Speed Digital Interface |
| HSA | High Speed Adapter | HSDL | High Speed Data Line |
| HSA | High Speed Adder | HSDL | High Speed Data Link |
| HSA | High Speed Arithmetic | HSDP | Hardsite Data Processor |
| HSA | Highway Switch Address | HSDRS | High Speed Digital Recording System |
| HSA | Hören-Sprechen-Aufnehmen | | |
| | | HSDS | High Speed Drum System |
| HSAC | High-Speed Analog Computer | HSDT | High Speed Data Transmission |
| HSAD | Hauptspeicheradapter | HSE | High Speed Encoder |
| HSADC | High Speed Analog-to-Digital Converter | HSE | High Speed Exchange |
| | | HSE | Hole Storage Effect |
| HSAI | High Speed Analog Input | HSEP | High Speed Electrostatic Printer |
| HSALU | High Speed Arithmetic Logic Unit | | |
| | | HSF | High Speed Feed |
| HSAM | Hierarchical Sequential Access Method | HSG | Housing |
| | | HSGR | High Speed General Register |
| HSAM | High Speed Accounting Machine | | |
| | | HSI | Hardware-Software Interface |
| HSB | Hauptsteuerblock | | |
| HSB | Heat Shield Boost | HSI | Hardwired Serial Interface |
| HSBR | High Speed Bombing Radar | HSIC | High Speed Integrated Circuit |
| HSC | Half Select Current | | |
| HSC | Head Select Circuit | HSIC | High Speed Interface Controller |
| HSC | High Speed Carry | | |

# H

| | | | |
|---|---|---|---|
| HSIMP | High Speed Interface Message Processor | HSS | High Speed Skip |
| HSIR | High Speed Information Retrieval | HSS | High Speed Stop |
| | | HSS | High Speed Storage |
| HSIS | Human Services Information System | HSS | High Speed Store |
| | | HSS | High Speed System |
| HSKAS | Hauptsatz-Kategoriensatz | HSS | Host Support Services |
| HSL | High Speed Logic | HSSCT | High Speed Shorts and Continuity Tester |
| HSL | Hytran Simulation Language | HSSG | High Speed Symbol Generator |
| HSLM | High Speed Line Manager | HST | Harmonic and Spurious Totalizer |
| HSLP | High Speed Line Printer | | |
| HSM | Hierarchical Storage Manager | HST | Hawaiian Standard Time |
| | | HST | High Speed Telemetry |
| HSM | High Speed Memory | HST | High Speed Teleprinting |
| HSM | High Speed Modular | HST | High Speed Terminal |
| HSM | High Speed Multiplication | HST | High Speed Test |
| HSMB | High Speed Memory Block | HST | High Speed Typewriter |
| HSMIMP | High Speed Modular Interface Message Processor | HSTP | Hauptsteuerprogramm |
| | | HSTP | High Speed Tape Punch |
| HSML | High Speed Modular Logic | HSTPR | Hilfssteuerprogramm |
| HSMS | High Speed Microwave Switch | HSTR | Hauptsteuerprogramm |
| | | HSTT | High Speed Tape Transmitter |
| HSO | Head Selection Operation | | |
| HSO | High Speed Operation | HSTTL | High Speed Transistor-Transistor Logic |
| HSP | Hauptspeicher | | |
| HSP | High Speed Printer | HSV | Hauptspeicher-vermittlungseinheit |
| HSP | High Speed Processor | | |
| HSP | High Speed Punch | HSVMA | High Speed Video Motion Analyzer |
| HSP | Hilfsspeicher | | |
| HSP | Hilfsspeicherplatz | HSW | Hilfssystem Werkzeugmaschine |
| HSP | Hintergrundspeicher | | |
| HSPA | High Speed Parallel Adder | HSXP | High Speed Xerographic Printer |
| HSPC | High Speed Printer Control | | |
| HSPD | High Speed | HSZD | Hermetically Sealed Z Diode |
| HSPDEXCH | High Speed Exchange | | |
| HSPM | High Speed Print Mechanism | HT | Hadamard Transform |
| | | HT | Halt and Transfer |
| HSPTP | High Speed Paper Tape Punch | HT | Handling Time |
| | | HT | Hauptteil |
| HSPTR | High Speed Paper Tape Reader | HT | Height |
| | | HT | High Temperature |
| HSR | Harbour Surveillance Radar | HT | High Tension |
| | | HT | High Torque |
| HSR | High Speed Reader | HT | Hilbert Transform |
| HSR | High Speed Relay | HT | Holding Time |
| HSRA | High Speed data Regeneration Assembly | HT | Horizontal Tab |
| | | HT | Horizontal Tabulation |
| HSRJE | High Speed Remote Job Entry | HT | Horizontal Tabulator |
| | | HT | Hors-Tension |
| HSRO | High Speed Repetitive Operation | HT | Hors-Texte |
| | | HTA | Hunting Allowed |
| HSS | Hardware Specification Sheet | HTC | Height-to-Time Converter |
| | | HTC | Hybrid Tape Circuit |
| HSS | Head Select Signal | HTD | Hunting Denied |

# H

| | | | |
|---|---|---|---|
| HTDC | High Tension Direct Current | HVD | Half Value Depth |
| HTDE | Half Time Digit Emitter | HVDC | High Voltage Direct Converter |
| HTE | Half Time Emitter | HVDC | High Voltage Direct Current |
| HTF | Host Transaction Facility | HVDF | High frequency and Very high frequency Direction Finder |
| HTJ | Hardware Trade Journal | | |
| HTL | High Threshold Logic | | |
| HTL | High-noise Threshold Logic | HVHF | High Very High Frequency |
| HTMOS | High Threshold MOS | HVIRS | Hull Vibration Information Retrieval System |
| HTO | Horizontal Take-Off | | |
| HTPV | High Temperature Power and Voltage | HVL | High Value Layer |
| HTR | Halt and Transfer | HVM | High Voltage Module |
| HTRAP | Height Reply Analysis Processor | HVP | High Voltage Potential |
| | | HVP | High Volume Program |
| HTRB | High Temperature Reverse Bias | HVP | Horizontal/Vertical Position control |
| HTS | High Tensile Steel | HVPS | High Voltage Power Supply |
| HTS | Horizontal Tabulation Set | HVR | High Voltage Relay |
| HTS | Humble Timesharing Company | HVS | Home Volume Set |
| | | HVST | Hauptverkehrsstunde |
| HTTL | High-Power Transistor-Transistor Logic | HVST | Hauptvermittlungsstelle |
| | | HVT | Half-Value Thickness |
| HTTL | High-speed Transistor-Transistor Logic | HVT | High Voltage Threshold |
| | | HVTR | Home Video Tape Recorder |
| HTU | Hasler Telex-Unit | HVY | Heavy |
| HTU | Height of Transfer Unit | HW | Halbwort |
| HTZ | Haustelefonzentrale | HW | Half Wave |
| HU-PCM | Hybrid Unidigit Pulse Code Modulation | HW | Half Word |
| | | HW | Hardware |
| HUCR | Harvard University Character Recognizer | HW | Hauptwort |
| | | HW | Hot Wire |
| HUD | Head-Up Display | HWB | Half Word Boundary |
| HUDWAC | Head-Up Display Weapon Aiming Computer | HWB | Handwörterbuch |
| | | HWC | Half Word Constant |
| HUGO | High Usable Geophysical Observation | HWD | Hight, Width, Depth |
| | | HWFPB | Half Word Fixed Point Binary |
| HULA | High-density Unit Logic Array | HWM | Highway Memory |
| HULA | Highly-integrated Unit Logic Assembly | HWP | Half Write Pulse |
| | | HWP | Hardware Work Package |
| HUMARIS | Human Materials Resources Information System | HWR | Half Wave Rectifier |
| | | HWY | Highway |
| | | HX | Halbduplex |
| HV | Half Value | HX | Hardware-Exchange |
| HV | Hauptverteiler | HX | Heat Exchanger |
| HV | Hauptverwaltung | HX | High index |
| HV | Hidden Variable | HXDP | Honeywell Experimental Distributed Processor |
| HV | High Vacuum | | |
| HV | High Velocity | HYB | Hybrid |
| HV | High Voltage | HYBALL | Hybrid Analog Logic Language |
| HV | Hypervelocity | | |
| HVAC | High Voltage Alternating Current | HYBLOC | Hybrid Computer Block-Oriented Compiler |
| HVC | Hardened Voice Channel | HYCOL | Hybrid Computer Link |

# H

| | | | |
|---|---|---|---|
| HYCOTRAN | Hybrid Computer Translator | HYDRAPAD | Hydraulic Positioning And Drilling |
| HYDAC | Hybrid Digital-Analog Computing | HYLA | Hybrid Language Assembler |
| | | HYPERDOP | Hyperbolic Doppler |
| HYDAC | Hybrid Digital-to-Analog Computer | HYPTP | Hypertape |
| | | HYSCAN | Hybrid Scanning |
| HYDAPT | Hybrid Digital-Analog Pulse Time | HYTRAN | Hybrid Translator |
| | | HZ | Hauptzentrale |
| HYDAS | Hydrographic Data Acquisition System | HZD | Hessische Zentrale für Datenverarbeitung |

# I

| | | | |
|---|---|---|---|
| I | Identifizierer | IA | Information Acquisition |
| I | Illumination | IA | Information Adressée |
| I | Index | IA | Information Approximation |
| I | Indexregister | IA | Informationsausgabe |
| I | Indicating | IA | Informationsausgang |
| I | Indicator | IA | Infra-Audible |
| I | Indikator | IA | Ingenious Addressing |
| I | Industrial | IA | Initial Address |
| I | Inertia | IA | Initial Appearance |
| I | Information | IA | Inkrementalausgabe |
| I | Informationsentropie | IA | Inkrementausgabe |
| I | Informationsgehalt | IA | Instruction Address |
| I | Infra- | IA | Instruction Alignment |
| I | Input | IA | Instruction Area |
| I | Instruction | IA | Instruction Array |
| I | Instructor | IA | Instrumentation Amplifier |
| I | Integer | IA | Interactive Access |
| I | Integral | IA | Interface Adapter |
| I | Integrator | IA | Interface Amplifier |
| I | Intensity | IA | International Angström |
| I | Interactive | IA | Internationales Alphabet |
| I | Interference | IA | Interval Arithmetic |
| I | Interphone | IA | Invalid Address |
| I | Inverter | IA | Inverter Assembly |
| I | Iodine | IA | Iteration Algorithm |
| I&C | Installation and Checkout | IA/SR | Intelligence Analysis/ Storage and Retrieval |
| I&R | Intelligence and Reconnaissance | IA5 | International Alphabet No. 5 |
| I&SE | Installation and Service Engineering | IAA | Informationsaustauschader |
| I-R | Interrogator-Responder | IAAC | International Association for Analog Computation |
| I-REG | Indexregister | IAB | Informationsaufbereitung |
| I-REG | Instruktionsregister | IABG | Industrieanlagen-Betriebsgesellschaft mbH |
| I.A. | Imprimante Administrative | | |
| I/D | Instruction/Data | IABS | Integration of Algebraic Boolean Simulation |
| I/E | Insert/Extract | | |
| I/E | Instruction/Execution | IAC | Immediate Access |
| I/EX | Instruction/Execution | IAC | Increment Accumulator |
| I/F | Interface | IAC | Information Analysis Center |
| I/O | Input/Output | | |
| I/P | Identification of Position | IAC | Information And Communication |
| IA | Immediate Access | | |
| IA | Immediate Addressing | IAC | Installation-Alteration-Cancellation |
| IA | Implicit Addressing | | |
| IA | Implied Address | IAC | Instruction Address Change |
| IA | Implied Association | IAC | Integration Assembly Checkout |
| IA | Impulsanzahl | | |
| IA | Index Accumulator | IAC | Intelligenter Asynchroner Controller |
| IA | Index Analyzer | | |
| IA | Indexed Address | IAC | International Algebraic Compiler |
| IA | Index Array | | |
| IA | Indicateur d'Appel | | |
| IA | Indirect Address | IAC | International Analysis Code |
| IA | Indirect Addressing | IAC | International Association of Cybernetics |
| IA | Industrial Accounting | | |

# I

| | | | |
|---|---|---|---|
| IAC | Iterative Analog Computer | IAIE | Integral Absolute Ideal Error |
| IACS | Inertial Attitude Control System | IAIS | Industrial Aerodynamics Information Service |
| IACS | Integrated Armament Control System | IAK | Informationsaustauschkanal |
| IACS | International Annealed Copperstandard | IAL | Interdivisional Administration List |
| IACSS | International Association for Computer Systems Security | IAL | International Algebraic Language |
| IAD | Information Acquisition and Dissemination | IAL | International Algorithmic Language |
| IAD | Initiation Area Discriminator | IAL | Investment Analysis Language |
| IAD | Integrated Automatic Documentation | IALE | Integral Absolute Linear Error |
| IAD | Integriertes Automatisiertes Dokumentationssystem | IAM | Impuls-Amplituden-Modulation |
| | | IAM | Impulse Amplitude Modulation |
| IAD | International Astrophysical Decade | IAM | Initial Address Message |
| IADE | Integral Absolute Delay Error | IAM | Institut für Angewandte Mikroelektronik |
| IADIC | Integrating Analog-to-Digital Converter | IAM | Interactive Algebraic Manipulation |
| IADIC | Integration Analog-to-Digital Converter | IAN | International Area Network |
| IADPC | Inter-Agency Data Processing Committee | IAO | Ingénierie Assistée par Ordinateur |
| IAE | Integral Absolute Error | IAO | International Automation Operation |
| IAE | Integrated Absolute Error | | |
| IAE | Interface Adapter Element | IAOR | International Abstracts in Operations Research |
| IAEA | International Atomic Energy Agency | IAP | Immediate Access Processing |
| IAEI | Institut d'Automatique et d'Electronique Industrielle | IAP | Industry Applications Programs |
| IAF | Information And Forwarding | IAP | Initial Approach |
| | | IAP | Industry Application Program |
| IAGC | Instantaneous Automatic Gain Control | IAP | Informationsarbeitsplatz |
| IAI | Informational Acquisition and Interpretation | IAPS | Interactive Programming System |
| IAI | Initial Address Information | IAPS | Interaktives Programmier-System |
| IAI | Institut Africain d'Informatique | IAQ | International Association for Quality |
| IAI | Institut für Angewandte Informatik | IAR | Instruction Address Register |
| IAI | International Acquisition and Interpretation | IARD | Information Analysis and Retrieval Division |
| IAID | Integrating Analog Input Device | IARU | International Amateur Radio Union |
| IAID | Integriertes, Automatisierbares Information- und Dokumentationssystem | IAS | Immediate Access Storage |
| | | IAS | Immediate Access Store |

| | | | |
|---|---|---|---|
| IAS | Institute of Advanced Studies | IB | Information Bulletin |
| IAS | Instrument Approach System | IB | Information Bus |
| | | IB | Informationsbank |
| IAS | Integrated Analytical System | IB | Input Block |
| | | IB | Input Buffer |
| IAS | Integrated Autodin System | IB | Instruction Block |
| IAS | Interactive Application System | IB | Instruction Buffer |
| | | IB | Interface Bus |
| IAS | Interactive Application Supervisor | IB | International Broadcasting |
| | | IB | Interne Bereitschaft |
| IAS | Intermediate Access Store | IBA | Independent Broadcasting Authority |
| IASA | Insurance Accounting and Statistical Association | IBA | Information Block Address |
| | | IBA | Ion-Backscattering Analysis |
| IASC | Indexing and Abstracting Society of Canada | IBAC | Instantaneous Broadcast Audience Counting |
| IASSIST | International Association for Social Science Information Service and Technology | IBC | Information Bit Content |
| | | IBC | Input Block Count |
| | | IBCFA | Injected Beam Cross-Field Amplifier |
| IAT | Index Address Table | IBD | Impulsbreitendiskriminator |
| IAT | Indexable Address Tag | IBD | Intermediate Block Diagram |
| IAT | Individual Acceptance Test | | |
| IAT | Interrupt Address Table | IBFN | Integriertes Breitband-Fernmelde-Netz |
| IATA | International Air Transport Association | | |
| IATAE | International Accounting and Traffic Analysis Equipment | IBG | Inter-Block Gap |
| | | IBI | Intergovernmental Bureau for Informatics |
| IATCS | International Air Traffic Communications System | IBI | International Bureau for Informatics · |
| IAU | Interface Adapter Unit | IBI-ICC | IBI International Computation Centre |
| IAUF | Institut für Automation und Unternehmens-forschung | | |
| | | IBID | International Bibliography, Information, and Documentation |
| IAVC | Instantaneous Automatic Video Control | IBIS | Integriertes Bord-Informationssystem |
| IAVC | Instantaneous Automatic Volume Control | IBIS | Integriertes Büro-Informations-System |
| IAVD | Internationale Arbeitsge-meinschaft der Verbände für Dienstleistungen aus Datenverarbeitung und Informationstechnik | IBIS | Intense Bunched Ion Source |
| | | IBIS | Intranet Business Information System |
| | | IBIS | Issue Based Information System |
| IAW | In Accordance With | | |
| IAW | Informationssystem Außenwirtschaft | IBISL | Integriertes Bestands-bearbeitungs- und Informationssystem für Lebensversicherungen |
| IB | Identification Beacon | | |
| IB | Identification Block | | |
| IB | Incentive Base | IBKS | Informations-Betriebs-daten-Kontroll-System |
| IB | Index Bit | | |
| IB | Index Block | IBL | Intermediate Behavioural Language |
| IB | Indicator Board | | |
| IB | Information Bit | IBM | International Business Machine |
| IB | Information Block | | |

- 297 -

# I

| | | | |
|---|---|---|---|
| IBM | Internationale Büromaschinen GmbH | IC | Idle Character |
| | | IC | Idling Cycle |
| IBM FSS | IBM Federal Supply Schedule | IC | If Clause |
| | | IC | Ignore Character |
| IBM... | International Business Machines Corp. | IC | Illegal Character |
| | | IC | ILLIAC Chamber |
| IBMCE | IBM Customer Engineer | IC | Imparity Check |
| IBMJ | IBM Journal of research and development | IC | Increase |
| | | IC | Incremental Computer |
| IBMSJ | IBM Systems Journal | IC | Incrémentation mémoire |
| IBN | Identification Beacon | IC | Index Correction |
| IBN | Indexed By Name | IC | Indication Cycle |
| IBOC | Internal Binary Operation Code | IC | Indicator Card |
| | | IC | Inductive Coupling |
| IBOLS | Integrated Business Oriented Language Support | IC | Inductive-Capacitive |
| | | IC | Information Carrier |
| | | IC | Information Center |
| IBP | Incremental Bar Printer | IC | Information Collection |
| IBP | Initial Boiling Point | IC | Information Company of America |
| IBP | International Banking Package | IC | Information Configuration |
| IBR | Index-Barrikaden-Register | IC | Information Content |
| IBR | Integrated Bridge Rectifier | IC | Ingénieur Commercial |
| IBS | Informations-Bereitstellungs-System | IC | Inhibiting Circuit |
| | | IC | Initial Card |
| IBS | Informationsbankensystem | IC | Initial Command |
| IBS | Input Buffer Storage | IC | Initial Condition |
| IBS | Input Buffer Store | IC | Inlet Contact |
| IBS | Integriertes Buchhaltungssystem | IC | Input Card |
| | | IC | Input Channel |
| IBS | Integriertes Büroverwaltungs-System | IC | Input Circuit |
| | | IC | Input Code |
| IBS | International Business System | IC | Inquiry Control |
| | | IC | Insert Character |
| IBSAT | Indexing By Statistical Analysis Techniques | IC | Insert Cursor |
| | | IC | Insertion Character |
| IBSR | Interactive Bibliographic Search and Retrieval | IC | Instruction Card |
| | | IC | Instruction Code |
| IBSYS | IBM Batchprocessing System | IC | Instruction Coding |
| | | IC | Instruction Complement |
| IBSYS | Initial Basic System | IC | Instruction Counter |
| IBT | Instrumented Bend Test | IC | Instruction Cycle |
| IBT | Interrupt Bit Table | IC | Integrated Circuit |
| IBT | Inverse BIFORE Transform | IC | Integrator Card |
| IBT | Ion-implanted Base Transistor | IC | Interceptor Computer |
| | | IC | Interchange Center |
| IBU | Independant Business Unit | IC | Intercommunication |
| IBV | Integrierte Benutzerverwaltung | IC | Interconnection |
| | | IC | Interface Control |
| IBW | Impulse Bandwidth | IC | Interior Communications |
| IBW | Information Bandwidth | IC | Intermediate Circuit |
| IBW | Institut für Bürowirtschaft | IC | Internal Clock |
| IBW | Intelligence Bandwidth | IC | Internal Code |
| IC | Identification Character | IC | Internal Connection |
| IC | Identifying Code | IC | Internal Control |

# I

| | | | |
|---|---|---|---|
| IC | Internal Conversion | ICAP | Intermediate Course Applications Programming |
| IC | International Code | ICAR | Integrated Command Accounting and Reporting |
| IC | International Control | | |
| IC | Interpreter Code | ICARUS | Intercontinental Aerospacecraft Range Unlimited System |
| IC | Interrogation Coding | | |
| IC | Interruption Code | | |
| IC | Invalid Character | ICAS | Intermittent Commercial and Amateur Service |
| IC | Invalid Code | | |
| IC | Inventory Control | ICAS | International Computer Access Service |
| IC | Inventory Count | | |
| IC | Iteration Count | ICB | Incoming Calls Barred |
| IC OPAMP | Integrated Circuit Operational Amplifier | ICB | Integrated Circuits Breadboard |
| IC/T | Integrated Computer/ Telemetry | ICB | Intermediate Control Break |
| ICA | Ignition Control Additive | ICB | International Computer Bibliography |
| ICA | Industrial Communication Association | ICB | Interrupt Control Block |
| ICA | Input Communications Adapter | ICB | Interruption Control Block |
| | | ICBP | Intercompany Billing Price |
| ICA | Integrated Communication Attachment | ICBR | Input Channel Buffer Register |
| ICA | Integrated Communications Adapter | ICBS | Interconnected Business System |
| ICA | Intercompany Agreement | ICC | Illegal Code Combination |
| ICA | Intergovernment Council for Automatic data processing | ICC | Information Control Center |
| | | ICC | Input Code Converter |
| ICA | International Communication Association | ICC | Installation Calibration and Checkout |
| ICA | International Computer Association | ICC | Integrated Circuit Computer |
| ICAD | Integrated Control And Display | ICC | Integrated Communications Controller |
| ICADE | Interactive Computer Aided Design Evaluation | ICC | Inter-Computer Coupler |
| | | ICC | Intercomputer Coupler |
| ICADI | Interamerican Center for Agricultural Documentation and Information | ICC | Interface Control Check |
| | | ICC | Intermediate Control Change |
| ICADS | Interdata Computer Aided Drafting System | ICC | International Chamber of Commerce |
| ICAE | Integrated Communications Adapter Extension | ICC | International Communications Corporation |
| ICAI | Institute for Computer-Assisted Information | ICC | International Computation Centre |
| ICAM | Integrated Communications Access Method | ICC | International Computer Center |
| ICAM | Integrated Computer-Aided Manufacturing | ICC | International Computing Center |
| ICAN | Integrated Circuit Analysis | ICC | International Conference on Communication |
| ICAN | Interactive Computer Aided of Norway | ICC | Invalid Character Check |
| ICAO | International Civil Aviation Organization | ICC | Invitational Computer Conference |

- 299 -

# I

| | | | |
|---|---|---|---|
| ICCA | International Computer Chess Association | ICE | Integrated Circuit Engineering |
| ICCA | International Conference on Computer Applications | ICE | Integrated Circuit Engineering Corporation |
| ICCAD | International Center for Computer Aided Design | ICE | Integrated Cooling for Electronics |
| ICCC | IEEE Conference on Computer Communications | ICE | Inter-Computer Electronics, Incorporated |
| ICCC | International Council for Computer Communication | ICE | Interconnection Equipment |
| ICCDP | Integrated Circuit Communications Data Processor | ICE | Intermediate Cable Equalizers |
| ICCE | International Council for Computers in Education | ICELA | International Computer Exposition for Latin America |
| ICCF | Interactive Computer Controlling Facility | ICEM | Integrated Computer aided Engineering and Manufacturing packet |
| ICCF | Interactive Computing Control Facility | ICEMS | Intra-Company Electronic Mail System |
| ICCH | International Conference on Computers and the Humanities | ICER | Infrared Cell, Electronically Refrigerated |
| ICCP | Information, Computers, and Communications Policy | ICES | Integrated Civil Engineering System |
| ICCP | Institute for Certification of Computer Professionals | ICES | International Civil Engineering System |
| | | ICF | Insert Character in Field |
| | | ICF | Interactive Command Facility |
| ICCS | Intersite Control and Communications System | ICF | Interactive Communications Feature |
| ICCU | Inter-Computer Communication Unit | ICF | Intercommunication Flip-flop |
| ICD | Index to Class Directory | ICF | Intermediate Control Field |
| ICD | Input Control Device | ICF | Item Control File |
| ICD | Insert Character in Display | ICF | Société des Ingénieurs Civils de France |
| ICD | Interface Control Dimension | ICFE | Intra-Collisional Field Effect |
| ICD | Ion-Controlled Diode | ICFET | Inhomogeneous Channel Field Effect Transistor |
| ICDB | Integrated Corporated Data Base | ICG | Interactive Computer Graphics |
| ICDCP | Interface Control Drawing Change Proposal | ICG | Interaktive Computergrafik |
| ICDES | Item Class Description | | |
| ICDS | Input Command Data Set | ICI | Incoming Call Indicator |
| ICDU | Inertial Coupling Data Unit | ICI | Instruction Check Indicator |
| ICE | In-Circuit Emulation | ICI | Interchannel Interference |
| ICE | In-Circuit Emulator | ICI | International Commission on Illumination |
| ICE | Industrial Computer Enclosure | ICIA | International Centre of Information on Antibiotics |
| ICE | Information Collecting Equipment | | |
| ICE | Input Checking Equipment | ICIM | International Computers Indian Manufacture |
| ICE | Input Control Electronics | | |

- 300 -

| | | | |
|---|---|---|---|
| ICIP | International Conference on Information Processing | ICN | Instrumentation and Calibration Network |
| ICIREPAT | International Commitee in Information Retrieval among Examining Patent offices | ICN | Interne Codenummer |
| | | ICNF | Irredundant Conjunctive Normal Formula |
| | | ICNI | Integrated Communications, Navigation, and Identification |
| ICIST | Institut Canadien de l'Information Scientifique et Technique | ICON | Image Converter |
| | | ICON | Integrated Control |
| ICL | Incoming Line | ICOS | Integrated Checkout System |
| ICL | Inrush Current Limiter | | |
| ICL | Insert Character in Line | ICOT | Institute for new generation Computer Technology |
| ICL | Instrument Controlled Landing | | |
| ICL | Integrated Circuit Logic | ICP | Ignition Control Programmer |
| ICL | International Computers Limited | ICP | Independent Card Punch |
| | | ICP | Information Controlled Printer |
| ICL | Interrupt Class List | | |
| ICL... | International Computer Ltd. | ICP | Input Control Program |
| | | ICP | Integral Circuit Packet |
| ICLCES | International Computers Limited Computer Education for Schools | ICP | Integrated Circuit Package |
| | | ICP | Integrated Circuit Program |
| | | ICP | International Candle Power |
| ICLCUA | International Computers Limited Computer Users Association | ICP | International Computer Programs |
| | | ICP | International Computer Programs, Incorporated |
| ICLM | Induced Course Load Matrix | | |
| | | ICP | Interpreting Card Punch |
| ICM | Improved Capability Missile | ICP | Interval Control Program |
| | | ICP | Inventory Control Point |
| ICM | Information Center Menue | ICP | Inventory Control Program |
| | | ICPAC | Instantaneous Compressor Performance Analysis Computer |
| ICM | Initial Condition Mode | | |
| ICM | Institute of Computer Management | | |
| | | ICPCI | International Conference on the Performance of Computer Installations |
| ICM | Integrated Circuit Mask | | |
| ICM | International Commission for Mathematical instruction | | |
| | | ICPFF | Incentive Cost Plus Fixed Fee |
| ICM | Inverted Coaxial Magnetron | ICPL | Initial Control Program Load |
| ICMIS | Integrated Computerized Management Information System | ICPP | Interactive Computer Presentation Panel |
| | | ICPR | Incoming Capital Property Record |
| ICMM | Incomplete Correlation Matrix Memory | ICPS | Interim Critical Parts planning System |
| ICMP | Interchannel Master Pulse | | |
| ICMS | Integrated Circuit and Message Switch | ICR | Impulse Checking Routine |
| | | ICR | Impulse Check Routine |
| ICN | Idle Channel Noise | ICR | Independent Component Release |
| ICN | Indicator Coupling Network | | |
| | | ICR | Input Card Reader |
| ICN | Information Communication System | ICR | Input and Compare Register |

# I

| | | | |
|---|---|---|---|
| ICR | Instruction Counting Register | ICS | International Computer System |
| ICR | Intelligent Character Recognition | ICS | International Computing Symposium |
| ICR | Interface Control Register | ICS | Interphone Control Station |
| ICR | Interrupt Code Register | ICS | Interpretive Computer Simulator |
| ICR | Interrupt Control Register | | |
| ICR | Ironcore Reactor | ICS | Interrupt Control Stack |
| ICR | Item Control Record | ICS | Inventory Change Sheet |
| ICRB | Inscribe | ICS | Inventory Control System |
| ICRD | Index of Codes for Research Drugs | ICS... | Information Computer Systems Ltd. |
| ICRH | Institute for Computer Research in the Humanities | ICSE | Intermediate Current Stability Experiment |
| | | ICSECT | Identify Control Section |
| ICRMS | Integrated Computer Reactor Monitoring System | ICSID | International Council of Societies of Industrial Design |
| ICRP | International Commission on Radiological Protection | ICSL | Interactive Continuous Simulation Language |
| | | ICSL | International Computing Services Limited |
| ICRT | Incorrect | | |
| ICRU | International Commission on Radiological Units | ICST | Institute for Computer Sciences and Technology |
| ICS | Identify Control Section | ICSTI | International Centre for Scientific and Technical Information |
| ICS | Industry and Custom Systems | | |
| ICS | Informatica, Calculo y Sistemas | ICSU | International Council of Scientific Unions |
| ICS | Information Carrier System | ICT | Igniter Circuit Tester |
| | | ICT | Image Converter Tube |
| ICS | Information Centre Software | ICT | Incoming Trunk |
| | | ICT | Incremental Change Type |
| ICS | Information Control System | ICT | Initiation Control and Termination |
| ICS | Inland Computer Service | ICT | Inspection Control Test |
| ICS | Insert Card Section | ICT | Institute of Computer Technology |
| ICS | Institute of Computer Science | | |
| ICS | Institution of Computer Sciences | ICT | Insulating Core Transformer |
| | | ICT | International Circuit Technology |
| ICS | Instrumentation and Control Subsystem | | |
| | | ICT... | International Computers and Tabulators Ltd. |
| ICS | Integrated Checkout System | | |
| | | ICTL | Input Control |
| ICS | Integrated Communication System | ICU | Indicator Control Unit |
| | | ICU | Instruction Control Unit |
| ICS | Integrated Control Storage | ICU | Instructors Computer Utility |
| ICS | Inter Computer Synchronizer | | |
| | | ICU | Integrated Control Unit |
| ICS | Interactive Communication Software | ICU | Interactive Chart Utility |
| | | ICU | Interactive Charting Utility |
| ICS | Interactive Control System | | |
| ICS | Interactive Counting System | ICU | Interface Control Unit |
| | | ICU | Interrupt Controlling Unit |

# I

| | | | |
|---|---|---|---|
| ICU/PLANIT | Instructors Computer Utility/Programming Language for Interactive Teaching | ID | Intermediate Description |
| | | ID | Intermodulation Distortion |
| | | ID | Internal Diameter |
| | | ID | Interrupt Decoder |
| ICV | Initial Chaining Value | ID | Interrupt Decoding |
| ICV | Internal Correction Voltage | ID | Inventory Data |
| | | ID | Inverted |
| ICW | Interblock Communication Word | ID | Item Description |
| | | ID NO | Identification Number |
| ICW | Interface Control Word | ID NUMB | Identification Number |
| ICW | Interrupt Continuous Wave | IDA | Indirect Data Addressing |
| ICW | Interrupted Continuous Wave | IDA | Indirekte Datenadressierung |
| ICWT | Interrupt Continuous Wave Telegraphy | IDA | Industrial Development Authority |
| ICX | International Computer Exchange | IDA | Information Distributed Architecture |
| ICX | International Customer Executive | IDA | Informations-Daten-Anlage |
| | | IDA | Inpatient Data Administration |
| ICXP | International Customer Executive Program | IDA | Input Data Assembler |
| ICY | Instruction Cycle | IDA | Integrated Debugging Aid |
| ICYCLE | Instruction Cycle | IDA | Integrated Digital Access |
| ID | Idem | IDA | Integrated Disc Adapter |
| ID | Identification | IDA | Integrated Differential Analyzer |
| ID | Identification Data | | |
| ID | Identification Device | IDA | Interactive Debugging Aid |
| ID | Identifier | IDA | Interconnect Device Arrangement |
| ID | Identifikation | | |
| ID | Identifizierer | IDA | Intermediate Dialect of ATLAS |
| ID | Implicit Declaration | | |
| ID | Incorporation Data | IDA | Ionospheric Dispersion Analysis |
| ID | Indicating Device | | |
| ID | Indicator | IDA | Iterative Differential Analyzer |
| ID | Indicator Driver | | |
| ID | Inductance | IDAC | Integrated Data Acquisition and Control |
| ID | Industrial Diamond | | |
| ID | Industrial Digital | IDAC | Interconnecting Digital-Analog Converter |
| ID | Informal Document | | |
| ID | Information Density | IDAC | Interim Data Acquisition |
| ID | Information Distribution | IDADS | Information Displays Automatic-Drafting System |
| ID | Information Distributor | | |
| ID | Informationsdarstellung | | |
| ID | Initial Data | IDAK | Integriertes Datenverarbeitungs- und Auskunftssystem |
| ID | Inline Dictionaries | | |
| ID | Inner Diameter | | |
| ID | Input Diode | IDAK | Integriertes Datenverarbeitungs- und Auskunftssystem für die Krankenkassen |
| ID | Input Division | | |
| ID | Inside Diameter | | |
| ID | Instruction Decoding | | |
| ID | Integrated Display | IDAL | Indirect Data Address List |
| ID | Integrating Device | IDAM | Index Direct Access Method |
| ID | Interconnection Diagram | | |
| ID | Interferometer and Doppler | IDAMS | Image Display And Manipulation System |

# I

| | | | |
|---|---|---|---|
| IDAP | Intelligence Data Acquisition and Processing | IDC | Interceptor Distance Computer |
| IDAP | Iterative Differential Analyzer Pinboard | IDC | Internal Document Control |
| IDAPS | Image Data Processing System | IDC | International Documentation in Chemistry |
| IDAS | Industrial Data Acquisition System | IDC | Internationale Dokumentationsgesellschaft für Chemie |
| IDAS | Information Displays Automatic drafting System | IDC... | International Data Corporation |
| IDAS | Informations- und Datensysteme, GmbH | IDCB | Immediate Device Control Block |
| IDAS | Integrated Dual Accounting System | IDCC | International Data Coordinating Center |
| IDAS | Interaktives Datenbank-Abfrage-System | IDCCC | Interim Data Communication Collection Center |
| IDAS | International Database Access Service | IDCMA | Independent Data Communications Manufacturers Association |
| IDAS | Iterative Differential Analyzer Slave | IDCN | Interchangeability Document Change Notice |
| IDAST | Interpolated Data And Speech Transmission | IDCN | International Diplomatic Computer Network |
| IDATE | Institut pour le Développement et l'Aménagement des Télécommunications et de l'Economie | IDCP | International Data Collecting Platform |
| | | IDCS | Integrated Data Coding System |
| IDAW | Indirect Data Address Word | IDCSS | Intermediate Defence Communications Satellite System |
| IDB | Inertial Data Box | | |
| IDB | Information Database | IDCTR | Inductor |
| IDB | Informationsdatenbank | IDCU | Improved Digital Computer Unit |
| IDB | Informationsdienst Bibliothekswesen | IDD | Identifizierungsdatei |
| IDB | Initial Dummy Block | IDD | Imaging and Display Device |
| IDB | Inspection Data Bulletin | | |
| IDB | Integrated Data Base | IDD | Inline Data Dictionary |
| IDBP | Intel Data Base Processor | IDD | Integrated Data Dictionary |
| IDBPF | Interdigital Band Pass Filter | IDDC | International Demographic Data Center |
| IDBRST | ID Burst check | IDDS | Improved Data Display System |
| IDC | Identification Card | | |
| IDC | Image Dissector Camera | IDDS | Instrumentation Data Distribution System |
| IDC | Information Dissemination Committee | IDDS | Integrated Data Display System |
| IDC | Input Data Carrier | | |
| IDC | Input Display Console | IDDS | International Digital Data Service |
| IDC | Installation Data Confirmation | IDE | Interactive Display Emulator |
| IDC | Instantaneous Derivation Control | | |
| | | IDE | Interim Data Element |
| IDC | Instruction Distribution Channel | IDEA | Inductive Data Exploration and Analyses |
| IDC | Insulation Displacement Connector | IDEA | Industrial Design Exploiting Automation |

# I

| | | | |
|---|---|---|---|
| IDEA | Integrated Digital Electronic Automatic | IDEP | Interservice Data Exchange Programming |
| IDEA | Interactive Data Entry and Access | IDES | Information and Data Exchange System |
| IDEA | Interactive Differential Equation Algorithm | IDEX | Initial Defense Experiment |
| IDEA | Interaktive Daten-Eingabe und -Abfrage | IDF | Identifier |
| IDEA | Interface and Display Electronics Assembly | IDF | Indicating Direction Finder |
| IDEAL | Interactive Development Environment for an Application's Life-cycle | IDF | Input Data Flow |
| | | IDF | Instructional Dialogue Facility |
| IDEAL/PDF | IDEAL/Panel Definition Facility | IDF | Integrated Data File |
| IDEAL/PDL | IDEAL/Procedure Definition Language | IDF | Interactive Diagnostic Facility |
| IDEAL/RDF | IDEAL/Report Definition Facility | IDF | Intermediate Distributing Frame |
| IDEALS | Ideal Design of Effective And Logical Systems | IDF | Intermediate Distribution Frame |
| IDEAS | Inquiry Data Entry Access System | IDF | Internal Distribution Frame |
| IDEAS | Integrated Design Analysis System | IDF | International Distress Frequency |
| IDEAS | Integrated Design and Engineering Automated System | IDFC | Identification Field Checking |
| | | IDFR | Identified Friendly |
| | | IDFT | Inverse Discrete Fourier Transform |
| IDEB | Interessenvereinigung Der EDV Benutzer | IDG | International Data Group |
| IDECS | Image Discrimination, Enhancement, and Combination System | IDGIT | Integrated Data Generation Implementation Technique |
| | | IDH... | International Data Highways Ltd. |
| IDECS | Image Discrimination, Enhancement, Combination and Sampling | IDHS | Integrated Data Handling System |
| | | IDHS | Intelligence Data Handling System |
| IDEEA | Information and Data Exchange Experimental Activities | IDI | Improved Data Interchange |
| | | IDI | Institut de Développement Industriel |
| IDEM | Interactive Data Exchange Module | IDI | Intelligent Dual Interface |
| IDEN | Identification | IDIAL | Interaktives Dialogsystem |
| IDEN | Interactive Data Entry Network | IDIIOM | Information Displays, Incorporated's Input/ Output Machine |
| IDENT | Identification | | |
| IDENT | Identifikation | IDIK | Integrierte Datenverarbeitung Im Krankenhaus |
| IDENT | Identify | | |
| IDEP | Industry Data Exchange Program | IDIOT | Instrumentation Digital On-line Transcriber |
| | | IDIR | Indirect |
| IDEP | Inter-department Data Exchange Program | IDIS | Institut für Dokumentation und Information über Sozialmedizin |
| IDEP | Interagency Data Exchange Program | | |
| | | IDIS | Intrusion Detection and Identification System |
| IDEP | Interservice Data Exchange Program | | |
| | | IDITEM | Identifier Item |

# I

| | | | |
|---|---|---|---|
| IDK | Informations-, Datenverwaltungs- und Kommunikationssystem | IDNF | Irredundant Disjunctive Normal Formula |
| IDK | Installation Durch Kunden | IDO | Immediate Data Output |
| IDK | Integrierte Datenverarbeitung für Kommunalverwaltungen | IDO | Institut für Datentechnik und Organisation |
| IDL | Idle | IDOC | Inner Diameter Of Counter conductor |
| IDL | Instruction Definition List | IDOL | Improved Disk-time Overlap |
| IDL | Intelligent Database Language | IDOS | Integrated Disk-Operating System |
| IDL | International Data Line | IDP | Industrial Data Processing |
| IDLC | Integrated Digital Logic Circuit | IDP | Input Data Processor |
| IDLIB | Item Description Library | IDP | Institute of Data Processing |
| IDLOD | Idle waiting to Load | IDP | Instructor Display Panel |
| IDM | Impuls-Dauer-Modulation | IDP | Integrated Data Presentation |
| IDM | Instant Dimmer Memory | IDP | Integrated Data Processing |
| IDM | Instructional Diagram Manual | IDP | Intermodulation Distortion Percentage |
| IDM | Integrated Delta Modulation | IDPC | Integrated Data Processing Center |
| IDM | Integrating Delta Modulation | IDPG | Impact Data Pulse Generator |
| IDM | Intelligent Database Machine | IDPM | Institute of Data Processing Management |
| IDM | Intelligente Datenbankmaschine | IDPS | Integrated Data Processing System |
| IDM | Interpolating Delta Modulator | IDQA | Individual Document Quality Assurance |
| IDMH | Input Destination Message Handler | IDR | Identification Record |
| IDML | Interactive Data Manipulation Language | IDR | Incremental Digital Recorder |
| IDML | Internal Data Manipulation Language | IDR | Industrial Data Reduction |
| | | IDR | Input Date Request |
| IDMS | Integrated Data base Management System | IDRV | Ionic Drive |
| IDMS | Integrated Data Management System | IDS | Image Display System |
| | | IDS | Image Distribution System |
| IDMS | Interaktives Daten Management System | IDS | Impulse Duplexer Study |
| | | IDS | Industrie-Dialog-System |
| IDMSCV | IDMS Central Version | IDS | Inertial Data System |
| IDN | Integrated Data Network | IDS | Information Distribution System |
| IDN | Integrated Digital Network | | |
| IDN | Integrierte Digitale Netze | IDS | Input Data Strobe |
| IDN | Integriertes Datennetz | IDS | Instrument Data System |
| IDN | Integriertes Digitales Nachrichtensystem | IDS | Integrated Data Storage |
| | | IDS | Integrated Data Store |
| IDN | Integriertes Digitales Netz | IDS | Integrated Data System |
| IDN | Integriertes Fernschreib- und Datennetz | IDS | Integrierte Datenspeicherung |
| | | IDS | Interactive Data System |
| IDN | Integriertes Text- und Datennetz | IDS | Intercept Data Storage |
| | | IDS | Interim Decay Storage |

# I

| | | | |
|---|---|---|---|
| IDS | International Dealer Systems | IDVM | Integrating Digital Voltmeter |
| IDSB | Independent Double Side Band | IDVS | Informations- und Datenverarbeitungssystem |
| IDSC | International Distributed Systems Centre | IDVS | Integriertes Datenverarbeitungssystem |
| IDSM | Inertial Damped Servomotor | IDW | Informations- und Dokumentationswissenschaft |
| IDSM | Informations- und Dokumentationssystem der Massenmedien | IDW | Input Data Word |
| | | IDW | Institut für Dokumentationswesen |
| IDSP | Intercept Data Storage Position | IDW | Interdigitaler Wandler |
| | | IDX | Index |
| IDSS | Integral Direct Station Selection | IDZ | Informations- und Dokumentationszentrum |
| IDSTO | Idle used for Storage | IDZGW | Informations- und Dokumentationszentrum für Gewerbliche Wirtschaft |
| IDT | Identification Table | | |
| IDT | Image Dissector Tube | | |
| IDT | Input Data Translator | IE | Index Error |
| IDT | Integriertes Daten- und Testverarbeitungssystem | IE | Indicator Equipment |
| | | IE | Industrial Engineer |
| IDT | Integriertes, Dialogorientiertes Testsystem | IE | Information Exchange |
| | | IE | Informationseingabe |
| IDT | Interdigital Transducer | IE | Informationseingang |
| IDTP | Integrated Data Transmittal Package | IE | Informationseinheit |
| | | IE | Infrared Emission |
| IDTS | Instrumentation Data Test Station | IE | Initial Equipment |
| | | IE | Instruction Element |
| IDTS | Instrumentation Data Transmission System | IE | Integral Electronics |
| | | IE | Interface Equipment |
| IDTSC | Instrumentation Data Transmission System Controller | IE | Internal Environment |
| | | IE | Interrogation Entryregister |
| IDU | Interactive Data base Utility | IEA | International Instruments, Electronics and Automation Exhibition |
| IDU | Indicator Drive Unit | | |
| IDU | Industrial Development Unit | IEAP | Integrierter Ein-Ausgabe-Prozessor |
| IDV | Individuelle Datenverarbeitung | IEB | Integrierte Elektronische Baugruppe |
| IDV | Institut für Datenverarbeitung | IEB | Interdivisional Engineering Bulletin |
| IDV | Institut für Datenverwaltung | IEC | Incremental Engineering Change |
| IDV | Institut für elektronische Datenverarbeitung Zürich | IEC | Infused Emitter Coupling |
| | | IEC | Integrated Electronic Circuit |
| IDV | Integrating Digital Voltmeter | IEC | Integrated Electronic Component |
| IDV | Integrierte Datenverarbeitung | IEC | Integrated Environmental Control |
| IDVF | Integrierte Datenverarbeitung im Fernmeldebereich | IEC | Integrated Equipment Components |
| IDVID | Immersed Deflection Vidicon Device | IEC | Intermittend Electrical Contact |

# I

| | | | |
|---|---|---|---|
| IEC | International Electronic Committee | IERE | Institution of Electronic and Radio Engineers |
| IEC | International Electronical Commission | IERFC | Integrated Error Function Complement |
| IEC | International Electrotechnical Committee | IES | Identify External Symbol |
| | | IES | Integral Error Squared |
| IEC | International Electrotechnical Commission | IES | Integrated Electronic System |
| IEC | Internationale Elektrotechnische Organisation | IES | Intrinsic Electric Strength |
| | | IES | Inventory Equipment Sheet |
| IEC | Item Entry Control | | |
| IED | Individual Effective Dose | IESP | Integrated Electronic Signal Processor |
| IED | Initial Effective Data | | |
| IED | Integrated Environmental Design | IET | Initial Engine Test |
| | | IETF | Initial Engine Test Facility |
| IEE | Induced Electron Emission | | |
| IEE | Institution of Electrical Engineers | IETF | Initial Engine Test Firing |
| | | IETN | Institut Européen des Techniques Nouvelles |
| IEEC | IEEE Electronic Computers | | |
| IEED | IEEE Electronic Devices | IEU | Instruction Execution Unit |
| IEEE | Institute of Electrical and Electronics Engineering | IEU | Interface Electronics Unit |
| | | IEV | International Electrotechnical Vocabulary |
| IEEE | Institute of Electrical and Electronics Engineers | | |
| | | IEXEC | Instruction Execution |
| IEEETC | IEEE Transactions on Computer | IEZ | Internationales Elektronikzentrum |
| IEEETEC | IEEE Transactions on Electronic Computer | IF | Identification Field |
| | | IF | Identifier Field |
| IEF | Interactive Entry Facility | IF | Image Frequency |
| IEG | Information Exchange Group | IF | Impulsformer |
| | | IF | Indexing Feature |
| IEG | Interdivisional Engineering Guide | IF | Information |
| | | IF | Information Feedback |
| IEIA | Integrated Educational Information Agency | IF | Information Flow |
| | | IF | Information Format |
| IEL | Information Exchange List | IF | Information Function |
| IEL | Interdivisional Engineering List | IF | Infrared |
| | | IF | Instruction Fetch |
| IEL | International Electrotechnical Commission | IF | Instruction Folder |
| | | IF | Instruction Format |
| IEO | Integrated Electronic Office | IF | Instruktionsfluß |
| | | IF | Instrument Flight |
| IEOS | Integrated Electronical Office System | IF | Interactive FORTRAN |
| | | IF | Intermediate Frequency |
| IEP | Information Exchange Program | IF | Intermediate Function |
| | | IF | Interrupt Flag |
| IEP | Interdivisional Engineering Practices | IF | Inventory File |
| | | IF | Inverter and cathode Follower |
| IER | Impression/Enregistrement de Résultats | | |
| | | IFA | Institut Für Automation |
| IER | Instruction Execution Rate | IFA | Integrated File Adapter |
| IER | Internal Execution Rate | IFA | Interface Adapter |
| IERA | Institut d'Etudes et de Recherches pour l'Arabisation | IFA | Intermediate Frequency Amplifier |
| | | IFA | Inverse-Function Amplifier |

# I

| | | | |
|---|---|---|---|
| IFABO | Internationale Fachmesse für Büroorganisation | IFES | International Field Engineering Service |
| IFAC | Inter-Firm Accounting project | IFESI | Institut Français des Experts en Systèmes d'Information |
| IFAC | International Federation of Automatic Control | IFF | Impulsfolgefrequenz |
| IFACI | Institut Français des Auditeurs et Contrôleurs Internes | IFF | Interrogation Friend of Foe |
| | | IFFT | Inverse Fast Fourier Transform |
| IFAM | Information Systems for Associative Memories | IFI | Internationales Fernlehrinstitut |
| IFATCA | International Federation of Air Traffic Control Associations | IFIP | International Federation for Information Processing |
| IFB | Information for Business | IFIP | International Federation of Information Processing |
| IFB | Integrierte Finanzbuchhaltung | | |
| IFB | Interdivisional Facilities Bulletin | IFIPS | International Federation of Information Processing Societies |
| IFB | Interrupt Feedback Line | | |
| IFB | Invitation For Bid | IFIS | Infrared Flights Inspection System |
| IFC | In Flight Calibrator | | |
| IFC | Incremental Frequency Control | IFIS | Integrated Flight Instrumentation System |
| IFC | Instantaneous Frequency Correlation | IFIS | International Food Information Service |
| IFC | Instruction Flow Chart | IFL | Induction Field Locator |
| IFC | Integrated Fire Control | IFL | Integer Function Language |
| IFC | Interface Clear | IFL | Interdivisional Facilities List |
| IFCB | Interrupt Fan Control Block | | |
| IFCC | Interface Control Check | IFLA | International Federation of Library Associations |
| IFCEB | International Foundation for Computerbased Education in Banking | IFMIS | Integrated Facilities Management Information System |
| IFCN | Interfacility Communication Network | IFN | Information |
| | | IFO | Information |
| IFCR | Interface Control Register | IFO | Integriertes Finanzbuchhaltungs-Online-System |
| IFCS | In-Flight Checkout System | | |
| IFCS | International Federation of Computer Sciences | IFOR | Interactive FORTRAN |
| | | IFORS | International Federation of Operational Research Science |
| IFCU | Interface Control Unit | | |
| IFD | Instantaneous Frequency Discriminator | | |
| | | IFORS | International Federation of Operations Research Societies |
| IFD | Institut Für Dokumentation | | |
| IFDC | Integrated Facilities Design Criteria | | |
| | | IFP | Instruction Fetch Phase |
| IFDO | International Federation of Data Organizations | IFP | Interplant Finished Parts |
| | | IFPEC | Improved Floating Point Engineering Change |
| IFDR | Interface Data Register | | |
| IFDS | Inertial Flight Data System | IFPG | Intermediate Frequency Pulse Generator |
| IFDS | Integrated Flagship Data System | IFPM | In-Flight Performance Monitor |
| IFE | Internal Field Emission | | |

# I

| | | | |
|---|---|---|---|
| IFPO | Interplant Finished Parts Order | IFTM | In-Flight Test and Maintenance |
| IFPS | Interactive Financial Planning System | IFTS | In-Flight Test System |
| | | IFU | Interface Unit |
| IFR | Impulsform-Regenerator | IG | Impulse Generator |
| IFR | Increasing Failure Rate | IG | Impulsgeber |
| IFR | Information Flow Rate | IG | Impulsgenerator |
| IFR | Infrared | IG | Information Group |
| IFR | Instantaneous Frequency Receivers | IG | Informationsgewinnung |
| | | IG | Interblock Gap |
| IFR | Instrument Flight Rules | IG | International Gateway |
| IFR | Intermediate Frequency Range | IG | Inverse Gate |
| | | IGA | Integrierter Geräteanschluß |
| IFR | Internal Function Register | | |
| IFR | Interrupt Flag Register | IGCS | Integrated Guidance and Control System |
| IFR | Intrinsic Failure rate | | |
| IFRAS | IBM Feature Ratio Analysis System | IGD | Informationsgesellschaft für Datenverarbeitung |
| IFRC | Instantaneous Frequency Correlation | IGD | Interaction Graphics Display |
| IFRO | Internal Feed Rate Override | IGES | Initial Graphic Exchange Specifics |
| IFRU | Interference Rejection Unit | IGES | Initial Graphic Exchange Specification |
| IFS | Impuls-Fernwirk-System | IGES | Initial Graphics Exchange Standard |
| IFS | Independent Front Suspension | | |
| | | IGFA | Integrierter Gegenstandsspezialisierter Fertigungsabschnitt |
| IFS | Information Flow Standards | | |
| IFS | Information Flow System | | |
| IFS | Input Factor Storage | IGFET | Insulated Gate Field Effect Transistor |
| IFS | Integrated Flight System | | |
| IFS | Integriertes Fernmeldesystem | IGFET | Isolated Gate Field Effect Transistor |
| IFS | Interactive File Sharing | IGG | Inhibit Gate Generator |
| IFS | Interactive Financial System | IGGS | Interactive Geo-facilities Graphic Support |
| IFS | Interaktives Finanzsystem | IGI | Information General Incorporated |
| IFS | Interchange Field Separator | IGI | Inner Grid Injection |
| IFS | Interdivisional Facilities Standard | IGL | Information Grouping Logic |
| IFS | Intermediate Frequency Strip | IGL | Interactive Graphics Library |
| IFS | Interrelated Flow Simulation | IGM | Intelligentes Grafikmodul |
| | | IGM | Interactive Guidance Mode |
| IFSN | Iterative Full-Switch Network | IGMOS | Insulated-Gate Metal Oxide Semiconductor |
| IFT | Input Frequency Tolerance | IGMOSFET | Insulated-Gate Metal Oxide Semiconductor FET |
| IFT | Institut für Textverarbeitung | | |
| | | IGN | Ignition |
| IFT | Intermediate Frequency Transformer | IGN | Ignore |
| | | IGO | Impulse-Governed Oscillator |
| IFT | Internal Function Test | | |
| IFT | International Frequency Table | IGOR | Instrument Ground Optical Recording |

# I

| | | | |
|---|---|---|---|
| IGOR | Intercept Ground Optical Recorder | II | Initial Issue |
| IGRAD | IBM Government Research And Development program | II | Input Impedance |
| | | II | Input Information |
| IGS | Identify Graphic Subrepertoire | II | Input Instruction |
| | | II | Inventory and Inspection |
| IGS | Improved Gray Scale | II | Inverse Integrator |
| IGS | Integrated Graphics System | II-MOS | Ion-Implantated MOS |
| | | IIA | ILA Interrupt Address |
| IGS | Interactive Graphics System | IIA | Institute of Internal Auditors |
| IGS | Interchange Group Separator | IIA | Invert Indicators from Accumulator |
| IGSL | Interactive Gaming Simulation Language | IIASA | International Institute for Advanced Systems Applications |
| IGT | Insulated-Gate Tetrode | IIASA | International Institute for Applied Systems Analysis |
| IGT | Interactive Graphic Terminal | | |
| IGT | Internally Generated Transaction | IIASA | Internationales Institut für Angewandte Systemanalyse |
| IGTDS | Interactive Graphic Transit Design System | IIC | Integrated Interface Circuit |
| IGTP | Interactive Graphic Terminal Package | IIC | International Import Certificate |
| IGTS | Interactive Graphic Transit Simulator | IIC | Isotopes Information Center |
| IGV | Inlet Guide Vane | | |
| IH | Indirect Heating | IID | Insurgent Incident Data |
| IH | Interrupt Handler | IID | International Institute of Documentation |
| IHD | Impulshöhendiskriminator | | |
| IHF | Independent High Frequency | IID | Internationales Institut für Dokumentation |
| IHF | Inhibit Halt Flip-flop | IIF | Information Item File |
| IHO | In-House Operation | IIG | Institut für Informationsverarbeitung |
| IHP | Indicated Horsepower | | |
| IHP | Inner Helmholtz Plane | IIL | Integrated Injection Logic |
| IHP | Interrupt Handling Process | IIL | Integrierte Injektionslogik |
| IHPF | Ideal High-Pass Filter | IIN | Item Identification Number |
| IHS | Information Handling Services | IIO | Information Item Only |
| | | IIPACS | Integrated Information Presentation And Control System |
| IHSBR | Improved High-Speed Bombing Radar | | |
| IHSS | Inhouse-Schnittstelle | IIPBM | Index of Individually Planned Bills of Material |
| IHTS | Integrated Hybrid Transistor Switch | IIPM | Input Image Processing Method |
| II | Identifying Information | | |
| II | Ignore Instruction | IIR | Infinite Impulse Response |
| II | Illegal Instruction | IIR | Invert Indicators of the Right-half |
| II | Image Intensifier | | |
| II | Image Interpretation | IIRMS | Industrial Information's Record Management System |
| II | Imperative Instruction | | |
| II | Indexing Instruction | IIRS | Integriertes Informationsrecherchesystem |
| II | Indicator Instruction | | |
| II | Information Input | IIS | Immediate Image System |
| II | Initial Instruction | IIS | Increasing Index Sequency |

- 311 -

# I

| | | | |
|---|---|---|---|
| IIS | Individual Information System | IL | Including Loading |
| IIS | Information Input Signal | IL | Indicating Lamp |
| IIS | Installation Information System | IL | Indicator Location |
| | | IL | Individual Line |
| IIS | Institut für Informations- systeme | IL | Information Language |
| | | IL | Information Loss |
| IIS | Institute of Information Scientists | IL | Inhibit Line |
| | | IL | Instruction Label |
| IIS | Integral Information System | IL | Insulator |
| | | IL | Intensity Level |
| IIS | Integrated Instrument System | IL | Intercommunication Link |
| | | IL | Intermediate Language |
| IIS | Interactive Instructional System | IL | Internal Logic |
| | | IL | Interpretive Language |
| IIS | Intrinsic Instruction Set | IL | Interrupt Level |
| IIT | Information Input Terminal | IL | Interrupt List |
| IIT | Institute of Information Technology | IL/I | Implementation Language/I |
| | | ILA | Initial Load Address |
| IITRAN | Illinois Institute of Technology Translator | ILA | Iterative Logic Array |
| | | ILAN | Industrial Local Area Network |
| IIU | Input Interface Unit | | |
| IIUP | International Installed User Program | ILAN | Input Language |
| | | ILAR | Interrupt List Address Register |
| IJC | Individual Job Card | | |
| IJCAI | International Joint Council on Artificial Intelligence | ILAS | Interrelated Logic Accumulating Scanner |
| | | ILB | Independant Lateral Band |
| | | ILB | Inner Lead Bonding |
| IJJU | International Jitter- Jammer Unit | ILBT | Interrupt Level Branch Table |
| IJP | Internal Job Process | ILC | In-Line Code |
| IJP | Internal Job Processing | ILC | Initiate Logical Connection |
| IJP | International Job Processing | ILC | Input Language Conversion |
| | | ILC | Input Language Converter |
| IKC | Inquiry Keyboard Control | ILC | Instruction Length Code |
| IKD | Internationaler Kongreß für Datenverarbeitung | ILC | Instruction Length Coding |
| | | ILC | Instruction Length Counter |
| IKK | Informationen zur Kernforschung und Kerntechnik | ILC | Instruction Location Counter |
| | | ILC | Integrated Logic Circuit |
| IKOS | Interaktives Kostenrech- nungs- und Erfolgs- steuerungssystem | ILCC | Integrated Launch Control and Checkout |
| | | ILCCD | Interest/Late Charge Code |
| IKR | Industrie-Konten-Rahmen | ILD | Injection Laser Diode |
| IKS | Informationskreis | ILD | Instructional Logic Diagram |
| IKS | Informationskreisschaltung | | |
| IKS | Integriertes Kassen- und Wirtschaftssystem | ILD | Intermediate Level Diagram |
| IKS | Internes Kontrollsystem | ILD | Intermediate Level Diagramming |
| IKZ | Impulskennzeichen | | |
| IKZ | Impulswahlkennzeichen | ILD | Intermediate Logic Diagram |
| IL | Identification Letter | | |
| IL | Identifying Label | ILDA | Inter-Laboratory Data Acceptance |
| IL | Illogical Logic | | |
| IL | Imaging Language | ILDP | In-Line Data Processing |

# I

| | | | |
|---|---|---|---|
| ILDS | Integrated Logistics Data System | ILS | Instrumenten-Landesystem |
| ILE | Integral Linear Error | ILSAM | International Language for Servicing And Maintenance |
| ILE | Interface Latch Element | | |
| ILF | Inductive Loss Factor | ILSE | Integriertes Laborsystem für Sicherheitsprüfungen an Elektrogeräten |
| ILF | Infralow Frequency | | |
| ILIC | In-Line Integrated Circuit | | |
| ILIC | International Library Information Center | ILSE | Integrierte Leitungssteuereinheit |
| ILID | Institut für Landwirtschaftliche Information und Dokumentation | ILSW | Interrupt Level Status Word |
| | | ILT | Inter-Line Transfer |
| ILINET | Interlibrary Loan and Information Network | ILW | Intermediate-Level Wastes |
| ILIXCO... | International Liquid Xtal Corp. | IM | Ideal Modulation |
| | | IM | Image copy |
| ILL | Input Logic Level | IM | Image Memory |
| ILLIAC | Illinois Automatic Computer | IM | Impuls Modulation |
| | | IM | Index Marker |
| ILLIAC | Illinois Integrator and Automatic Computer | IM | Informal Memo |
| | | IM | Information Memory |
| ILLIAD | Illinois Algorithmic Decoder | IM | Initialization Mode |
| | | IM | Input Machine |
| ILLINET | Illinois Library and Information Network | IM | Input Memory |
| | | IM | Input Message |
| ILLINET | Interlibrary Loan und Information Network | IM | Installation Manual |
| | | IM | Installation and Maintenance |
| ILLIP | Illinois Integer Programming | IM | Instrumentation |
| ILLUM | Illumination | IM | Instrumentation of Measurement |
| ILM | Impulslängenmodulation | | |
| ILM | Information Logic Machine | IM | Interactive Mode |
| ILM | Informationsübertragung Lochkarte-Magnetband | IM | Interface Module |
| | | IM | Intermodulation |
| ILN | Instruction List Name | IM | Internal Memory |
| ILN | Internal Line Number | IM | Inverse Matrix |
| ILN | Interne Leitungsnummer | IMA | Image Mémoire Absolue |
| ILO | Injection Locked Oscillator | IMA | Information Médicale Automatisée |
| ILOS | Integrierte Logistik-Software | IMA | Intermodulationsabstand |
| | | IMA | Invalid Memory Address |
| ILOS | Integriertes Logistik-System | IMA | Ion-Microspectroscope Analysis |
| ILP | Initial Load Program | IMAC | Integrated Microwave Amplifier Converter |
| ILP | In-Line Printer | | |
| ILP | In-Line Processing | IMACS | International Association for Mathematics And Computer Simulation |
| ILP | Intermediate Language Processor | | |
| ILPF | Ideal Low-Pass Filter | IMAG | Image |
| ILS | Ideal Liquids Structures | IMAG | Institut de Mathématiques Appliquées de Grenoble |
| ILS | In-Line Subroutine | | |
| ILS | Informations-Leitstelle | IMAGE | Information Management by Application Generation |
| ILS | Instruktionslängenschlüssel | | |
| ILS | Instrument Landing System | IMANCO | Image Analysing Computer |

# I

| | |
|---|---|
| IMAUS | Integriertes Marketing-Analyse- und Überwachungssystem |
| IMB | Input Memory Buffer |
| IMBAU | Integrierte Modulare Bausoftware |
| IMBT | Inverse Modifier BIFORE Transform |
| IMC | Image Motion Compensation |
| IMC | Information Memory Cell |
| IMC | Institute of Measurement and Control |
| IMC | Instrument Meteorological Conditions |
| IMC | Integrated Microelectronic Circuit |
| IMC | Integrated Monolithic Circuit |
| IMC | Integrated Multiplexer Channel |
| IMC | International Maintenance Centre |
| IMC | Item Management Coding |
| IMC | Item Master Card |
| IMCAS | Interactive Man/Computer Augmentation System |
| IMCP | Item Management Coding Program |
| IMCV | Input Media Conversion |
| IMD | Immediate |
| IMD | Independent Marketing Division |
| IMD | Information Marketing Development |
| IMD | Information Marketing Division |
| IMD | Institute für Medizinische Datenverarbeitung |
| IMD | Interactive Map Definition |
| IMD | Intermodulation Distortion |
| IMD | Introduction Manuelle des Données |
| IMDES | Item Management Data Element Standardization |
| IMDT | Interaktives MAP Design und Test |
| IME | Intégration à Moyenne Echelle |
| IMEP | Indicated Mean Effective Pressure |
| IMF | Image Matched Filter |
| IMF | Information management system Management Facilities |
| IMF | Interactive Macro Facility |
| IMF | Interactive Mainframe Facility |
| IMF | Internal Magnetic Focus tube |
| IMF | Independent Macro Facility |
| IMG | Image |
| IMG | Impulsmustergenerator |
| IMG | Integrated Matching Gate |
| IMH | Individual Machine History |
| IMH | Intermodal Message Handler |
| IMHU | Incoming Message Holding Unit |
| IMI | Imperative Macro-Instruction |
| IMI | Information Management Inc. |
| IMI | International Marketing Institute |
| IMIC | Internal Modulation Information Coding |
| IMIR | Interceptor Missile Interrogation Radar |
| IMIS | Integrated Management Information System |
| IMIS | Integrated Municipal Information System |
| IMIS | Integriertes Management - Informationssystem |
| IMIS | International Marketing Information Service |
| IMITAC | Image Input To Automatic Computers |
| IML | Initial Microcode Load |
| IML | Initial Microprogram Load |
| IML | Interdivisional Manufacturing List |
| IML | Intermediate Machine Language |
| IMM | Integrated Magnetic Memory |
| IMM PU | Immediate Pickup |
| IMMAC | Inventory Management and Material Control |
| IMMIRS | Integrated Maintenance Management Information Retrieval System |
| IMO | Improper Order |
| IMOS | Interactive Multi-programming Operating System |
| IMOS | Ion implanted MOS |
| IMP | Impedance |
| IMP | Impression |

# I

| | |
|---|---|
| IMP | Imprimante |
| IMP | Improved Manufacturing Procedure |
| IMP | Improved Multiprocessor |
| IMP | Impuls |
| IMP | Indicator Maintenance Panel |
| IMP | Input Message Processor |
| IMP | Integrated Maintenance Package |
| IMP | Integrated Manufacturing Planning |
| IMP | Integrated Memory Processor |
| IMP | Integrated Microprocessors |
| IMP | Integrated Microprocessors Network |
| IMP | Integrated Microwave Products |
| IMP | Inter-Message Processor |
| IMP | Inter-industry Management Program |
| IMP | Interactive Machine-language Programming |
| IMP | Interactive Minicomputer Programming |
| IMP | Interdivisional Manufacturing Practice |
| IMP | Interface Message Processor |
| IMP | Interplanetary Monitoring Platform |
| IMP | Interpretive Master Program |
| IMP | Intrinsic Multiprocessing |
| IMP.GEN | Impulse Generator |
| IMPAC | Industrial Multilevel Process Analysis and Control |
| IMPAC | Information for Management Planning Analysis and Coordination |
| IMPAC | Inventory Management Program And Control |
| IMPACT | Improved Manufacturing Planning and Assembly Control Technique |
| IMPACT | Instructional Model Prototypes Attainable in Computerized Graining |
| IMPACT | Integrated Management Planning And Control Techniques |
| IMPACT | Integrated Managerial Programming Analysis Control Technique |
| IMPACT | Integrated Manufacturing Planning And Control Technique |
| IMPACT | Integrated Module Packaging Technology |
| IMPACT | Inventory Management Product And Control Techniques |
| IMPACT | Inventory Management Program And Control Techniques |
| IMPACTS | Instant Media Planning and Analysis by Computer Time Sharing |
| IMPATT | Impact-Avalanche-Transit-Time |
| IMPI | Internal Microprogramming Interface |
| IMPICS | Integrated Management Planning, Information and Control System |
| IMPICS | Integrated Manufacturing Program Information and Control System |
| IMPICS | Integriertes Management-Planungs-Informations- und Kontrollsystem |
| IMPL | Initial Microprogram Load |
| IMPOS | Interactive Multi-Programming Operating System |
| IMPRESS | Interdisciplinary Machine Processing for Research and Education in Social Sciences |
| IMPS | Integrated Master Programming and Scheduling |
| IMPS | Interpersonal Messaging Process System |
| IMPS | Interplanetary Measurement Probes |
| IMPTS | Improved Programmer Test Station |
| IMR | Interrupt Mask Register |
| IMR | Inventory Management Record |
| IMR | Inventory Measurement Report |
| IMRA | Infrared Monochromatic Radiation |
| IMRADS | Information Management, Retrieval, And Dissemination System |
| IMRAN | International Marine Radio Aids to Navigation |

- 315 -

# I

| | | | |
|---|---|---|---|
| IMS | Index Management System | IN | Installation |
| IMS | Indirect Measuring System | IN | Insulator |
| IMS | Industrial Management Society | IN | Integrating Network |
| IMS | Industry Marketing Segment | IN | Interference-to-Noise ratio |
| IMS | Information Maintenance System | INA | IBM Nachrichten |
| | | INA | Informationssystem für den Niedergelassenen Arzt |
| IMS | Information Management System | INA | International Normal Atmosphere |
| IMS | Information Marketing Segment | INAKOH | Integriertes Abrechnungs- und Informationskonzept für Handelsunternehmen |
| IMS | Informationsmeßsystem | | |
| IMS | Installation Measurement System | INAP | Inverse Nyquist Analysis Program |
| IMS | Institue of Management Sciences | INAS | Inertial Navigation and Attack Systems |
| IMS | Institute of Mathematical Statistics | INAV | Informationsverarbeitung für die Angebots- verfolgung |
| IMS | Instruction Management System | INC | Improved Navigation Computer |
| IMS | Intelligenter Matrix- Schalter | INC | Inclinable |
| | | INC | Include |
| IMS | Interdivisional Manu- facturing Standard | INC | Incoming |
| | | INC | Inertial Navigation Computer |
| IMS | Intermediate Multi- processing System | | |
| IMS | International Management System Corporation | INC | Input Control |
| | | INC | Item Name Code |
| IMS | Inventory Management and Simulator | INCA | Inventory Control and Analysis |
| IMS ADF | IMS Application Development Facility | INCH | Independent Channel |
| | | INCH | Independent Channel Handler |
| IMS/VS | Information Management System/Virtual Storage | | |
| | | INCH | Integrated Chopper |
| IMSAC | Institut Mécanographique de Statistique et d'Application Comptable | INCIRS | International Communi- cation Information Retrieval System |
| IMSDALOC | IMS Dynamic Allocation | INCITE | Instructional Notation for Computer-controlled Inspection and Test Equipment |
| IMSE | Integrated Mean Square Error | | |
| IMSIM | Image Simulator | | |
| IMSL | International Mathe- matical and Statistical Libraries | INCL | Include |
| | | INCL | Inclusive |
| | | INCLD | Included |
| IMSR | Immissionsschutzrechner | INCO | Information and Control |
| IMT | Impulse Modulated Telemetry | INCOM | Indikator Compiler |
| | | INCOS | Inspections and Control System |
| IMU | Inertial Measuring Unit | | |
| IMX | Inquiry Message Exchange | INCOS | Integrated Control System |
| IN | Identification Number | INCPLT | Incomplete |
| IN | Inch | INCR | Increase |
| IN | Information Network | INCR | Increment |
| IN | Informationsnutzung | INCR | Increment Register |
| IN | Input | INCR | Interrupt Control Register |

| | | | |
|---|---|---|---|
| INCRB | Inscribe | INFARVGL | Informationsausgabe-registervergleicher |
| INCST | Invoice Cost | | |
| INCUM | Indiana Computer Users Meeting | INFE | Informationseingabe |
| | | INFER | Informationseingabe-register |
| IND | Index | | |
| IND | Indicate | INFERFGL | Informationseingabe-registervergleicher |
| IND | Indication | | |
| IND | Indicator | INFIRS | Inverted File Information Retrieval System |
| IND | Indikator | | |
| IND | Inductance | INFN | Infinite |
| IND | Induction | INFN | Information |
| IND | Institut für Nachrichtengeräte und Datenverarbeitung | INFO | Information |
| | | INFO | Information Network and File Organization |
| IND A | Indexible Address | INFO | Information Network For Operations |
| INDAC | Industrial Data Acquisition and Control | | |
| | | INFO-COM | Information Communications |
| INDC | International Nuclear Data Committee | INFO-TERM | Informationszentrum für Terminologie |
| INDCD | Industry Code | | |
| INDCTR | Indicator | INFOCEN | Information Center |
| INDEX | Inter-NASA Data Exchange | INFOKOM | Gesellschaft für Informations- und Kommunikationstechnik |
| INDIC | Indicate | | |
| INDIC | Indication | | |
| INDIC | Indicator | INFOL | Information Oriented Language |
| INDICAT | Indices Directory Catalog | | |
| INDIRS | Indiana Information Retrieval System | INFONET | Information Network |
| | | INFOR | Information Network and File Organization |
| INDIS | Industrial Information System | | |
| | | INFOR | Interactive FORTRAN |
| INDN | Indication | INFORCHIN | Internationales Zweiginformationssystem für Chemie und Chemische Industrie |
| INDN CY | Indication Cycle | | |
| INDOC | Indian National Documentation Centre | | |
| INDOC | Information Documentation and Communication | INFOREP | Informatique Répartie |
| | | INFOREQ | Information Requested |
| INDOGEN | Integriertes Dokumentations- und Generatorsystem | INFORM | Information Network for Information Retrieval Management |
| INDR | Indicator | INFORM | Information Network For Online Retrieval Maintenance |
| INDREG | Inductance Regulator | | |
| INDTR | Indicator-Transmitter | | |
| INEFIP | Integriertes Erfolgs- und Finanzplanungsmodell | INFORM | Institute For Operations Research and Management |
| INEL | Internationale Fachmesse für industrielle Elektronik | INFORMS | Information Organization Reporting and Management System |
| INELG | Ineligible | INFOS | Informatik-Organisationssysteme |
| INF | Interface | | |
| INF | Irredundant Normal Form | INFOS | Informationssystem |
| INFA | Informationsausgabe | INFOSWITCH | Information Switching |
| INFAD | Institut Für Automatisierte Datenverarbeitung | INFOTERM | International Information centre for Terminology |
| INFAR | Informationsausgaberegister | INFRAL | Information Retrieval Automatic Language |

# I

| | | | |
|---|---|---|---|
| INFROSS | Information Requirements Of the Social Sciences | INP | Intelligent Network Processor |
| ING | Inertial Navigation Gyro | INPACON | Input Audit and Control |
| ING | Intense Neutron Generator | INPADOC | International Patent Documentation Centre |
| INGA | Interactive Graphic Analysis | INPBM | Information Not Provided By Manufacturer |
| INGA | Interaktive Graphische Analyse | INPC | Impulse Noise Performance Curve |
| INGAS | Integriertes Großhandels-Abrechnungssystem | INPI | Institut National de la Propriété Industrielle |
| INGROS | Integriertes Großhandelssystem | INPOL | Informationssystem der Polizei |
| INGROS | Integriertes Großhandelsinformationssystem | INPR | Initialisierungsprogramm |
| INH | Inhibit | INPRINT | Integrated Program for Information Transfer |
| INHB | Inhibit | INPROCNS | Information Processing in the Central Nervous System |
| INHBD | Inhibited | | |
| INHIB | Inhibition | | |
| INI | Instituto Nacional de Industria | INQ | Inquiry |
| INIB | Internationale Normeninformationsbank | INR | Increment Register |
| | | INR | Interference-to-Noise Ratio |
| INIC | Inverse Negative Impedance Converter | INREQ | Information on Request |
| INIS | Internationales Nuklear-Informationssystem | INREQ | Information Requested |
| | | INREQS | Information Requests |
| INIT | Initial | INRIA | Institut National de Recherche en Informatique et Automatique |
| INIT | Initiate | | |
| INIT | Inititator | | |
| INKA | Informationssystem Karlsruhe | INS | Inertial Navigation Sensor |
| | | INS | Information Network System |
| INKAS | Integriertes Konstruktions- und Arbeitsplanungssystem | | |
| | | INS | Information System |
| | | INS | Insulation |
| INL | Initial | INS | Inter-Nation Simulation |
| INL | Internal Noise Level | INS | International Navigation System |
| INLAN | Instant Language | | |
| INLC | Initial Launch Capability | INS | Interstation Noise Suppression |
| INLETS | Inline Execution Tests | | |
| INLK | Interlock | INS | Ion Neutralization Spectroscopy |
| INLP | Integer Non-Linear Programming | | |
| | | INS CHAR | Insert Character |
| INN | Intermediate Network Node | INSATRAC | Interception by Satellite Tracking |
| INO | Iterative Nichtlineare Optimierung | INSCRB | Inscribe |
| | | INSDOC | Indian National Scientific Documentation Centre |
| INOHYC | Integrated Optical Hybrid Circuit | | |
| | | INSEE | Institut National de la Statistique et des Etudes Economiques |
| INOPBL | Inoperable | | |
| INP | In Process | | |
| INP | Indium Phosphide | INSIGHT | Interactive System for Investigation by Graphic of Hydrological Trends |
| INP | Inert Nitrogen Protection | | |
| INP | Inhibit Presentation | | |
| INP | Input | INSITE | Integral Sensor Interpretation Techniques |

# I

| | | | |
|---|---|---|---|
| INSN | Instruction | INTCR | Input Tape Cartridge Reader |
| INSP | Inspect | INTEC | Interference |
| INSP | Inspection | INTEL | Intelligence |
| INSPEC | Information Service in Physics, Electrotechnology and Control | INTELSAT | International Telecommunications Satellite |
| INSPECC | Information Service for Physics, Electrotechnology, Computers and Control | INTERALIS | International Advanced File Information System |
| | | INTERCOM | Intercommunications Monitor |
| INSPECT | Integrated Nationwide System for Processing Entries from Customers Terminals | INTERCOM | Interlanguage Communications |
| | | INTERESTP | Integrated Retrieval and Statistic Program |
| INST | Instantaneous | INTERFACE | Internationally Recognized Format for Automatic Commercial Exchange |
| INST | Instruction | | |
| INST | Instrument | | |
| INSTAR | Inertialess Scanning, Tracking And Ranging | INTERKAMA | Internationaler Kongreß mit Ausstellung für Meßtechnik und Automation |
| INSTARS | Information Storage And Retrieval Systems | | |
| | | INTERMEC | Interface Mechanism |
| INSTL | Installation | INTERNALIS | International Advanced Life Information System |
| INSTLN | Installation | | |
| INSTM | Instrument | INTERNET | Interactive Network |
| INSTN | Instruction | INTERPERS | Interactive Personnel System |
| INSTNS | Instructions | | |
| INSTR | Instruction | INTERPERS | Interaktives Personalsystem |
| INSTR | Instruktion | | |
| INSTR | Instrument | INTET | Informationstechnik und Theoretische Elektrotechnik |
| INSTRMT | Instrument | | |
| INSTRU | Instrument | | |
| INSTRUCT | Instruction | INTFER | Interference |
| INT | Initial | INTG | Integrated |
| INT | Institut für Nachrichtentechnik | INTG | Interpreting |
| | | INTG | Interrogate |
| INT | Integer | INTG | Interrogator |
| INT | Integral | INTGR | Integrate |
| INT | Integrating | INTGR | Integrating |
| INT | Integration | INTGR | Integrator |
| INT | Integrator | INTGT | Integrate |
| INT | Intercept | INTGTR | Integrator |
| INT | Internal | INTIME | Interactive Textual Information Management Experiment |
| INT | Interphone | | |
| INT | Interpreter | | |
| INT | Interrogate | INTIP | Integrated Information Processing |
| INT | Interrupt | | |
| INT | Interruption | INTIPS | Integrated Information Processing System |
| INT | Intersection | | |
| INT CON | Internal Connection | INTIPS | Intelligence Information Processing System |
| INTCH | Interchange | | |
| INTCO | International Code of signals | INTLK | Interlock |
| | | INTMT | Intermittent |
| INTCON | Interconnection | INTOP | International Operations simulation |
| INTCON | International Connection | | |
| INTCP | Intercept | INTP | Interpreter |

# I

| | | | |
|---|---|---|---|
| INTPHTR | Interphase Transformer | IO | Iterative Operation |
| INTR | Intercept Treatment | IOA | Input/Output Adapter |
| INTR | Interrupt | IOA | Input Output Address |
| INTRALAB | Information Transfer Laboratory | IOA | Input/Output Area |
| | | IOA | Input/Output Attachment |
| INTRAN | Input Transformer | IOAU | Input/Output Access Unit |
| INTRAN | Input Translator | IOAU | Input/Output Arithmetic Unit |
| INTRDR | Internal Reader | | |
| INTREX | Information Transfer Experiments | IOB | Input/Output Block |
| | | IOB | Input/Output Buffer |
| INTRG | Interrogate | IOBS | Input/Output Buffer Store |
| INTRG | Interrogation | IOC | Illegal Operation Code |
| INTROG | Interrogate | IOC | Inclusive Or Circuit |
| INTRPT | Interrupt | IOC | Initial Operational Capability |
| INTUG | International communications User Group | | |
| | | IOC | Input/Output Channel |
| INTUG | International Telecommunications Users' Group | IOC | Input/Output Control |
| | | IOC | Input/Output Controller |
| INTV | Interval | IOC | Input/Output Converter |
| INV | Invalid | IOC | Integrated Operating Capability |
| INV | Inventories | | |
| INV | Inventory | IOC | Item On Change |
| INV | Inverse | IOCC | Input/Output Code Converter |
| INV | Invert | | |
| INV | Inverter | IOCC | Input/Output Command Control |
| INV | Invocation | | |
| INVAL | Invalid | IOCC | Input/Output Control Center |
| INVAM | Invoice Amount | | |
| INVAS | Integriertes Verfahren zur Aufwandsschätzung | IOCC | Input/Output Control Command |
| INVES | Integriertes Verkaufsabrechnungs-System | IOCC | International Optical Computer Conference |
| INVLV | Inventory Level Evaluation | IOCD | Input/Output under Countcontrol and Disconnect |
| INVNR | Invoice Number | | |
| INVNÜ | Institut für Nachrichtenverarbeitung und Nachrichtenübertragung | IOCDS | Input/Output Configuration Data Set |
| | | IOCON | Input/Output Converter |
| INVSTGN | Investigation | IOCP | Input/Output Configuration Program |
| INVT | Invert | | |
| INX | Index character | IOCP | Input/Output Control Program |
| INZ | Initialize | | |
| INZEA | Integrierte Zeit-Erfassung und Auswertung | IOCP | Input/Output under Countcontrol and Proceed |
| INZIDENZ | Informationssystem Zur Integrierten Dialogverarbeitung Energieabrechnung, -beratung und Zählerverwaltung | IOCR | Input Output Control Routine |
| | | IOCS | Input/Output Control Service |
| | | IOCS | Input/Output Control System |
| IO | Illegal Operation | IOCU | Input/Output Control Unit |
| IO | Image Orthicon | IOD | Input/Output Device |
| IO | Index Operator | IOD | Input/Output Dump |
| IO | Indexing Operation | IOD | Insertion Of Data |
| IO | Initial Order | IODAS | Industrial Online Data Acquisition System |
| IO | Input/Output | | |
| IO | Interpretive Operation | | |

| | | | |
|---|---|---|---|
| IODB | Input/Output Data Buffer | IOREG | Input/Output Register |
| IODC | Input/Output Data Channel | IOREQ | Input/Output Request Queue |
| IODC | Input/Output Data Control | | |
| IODC | Input/Output Define Card | IORQ | Input/Output Request |
| IODC | Input/Output Delay Counter | IORT | Input/Output of a Record and Transfer |
| IODD | Ideal One-Dimensional Device | IOS | Inbound Operation Signal |
| | | IOS | Input Output Supervisor |
| IODE | International Oceanographic Data Exchange | IOS | Input/Output Selector |
| | | IOS | Input/Output Sense |
| IODT | Input/Output Data Transfer | IOS | Input/Output Skip |
| IOE | Input/Output Error | IOS | Input/Output Statement |
| IOE | Intake Opposite Exhaust | IOS | Input/Output Switch |
| IOF | Input/Output Function | IOS | Input/Output Synchronizer |
| IOF | Interactive Operator Facility | IOS | Input/Output System |
| | | IOS | Interplant Order Status |
| IOG | Input/Output Gate | IOSAP | Input/Output Subordinate Application Program |
| IOGS | Input/Output Group Switch | | |
| IOH | Input/Output Handler | IOSIM | Input/Output Simulator |
| IOI | Input/Output Interrupt | IOSP | Input/Output under Signal and Proceed |
| IOIM | Input/Output Interrupt Message | | |
| | | IOSR | Input/Output Service Routine |
| IOL | Input/Output Line | | |
| IOL | Input/Output List | IOSR | Input/Output Support Routine |
| IOL | Input/Output Logic | | |
| IOL | Instantaneous Overload | IOST | Input/Output under Signal and Transfer |
| IOLC | Integrated Optical Logic Circuit | | |
| | | IOSYS | Input/Output System |
| IOM | Input/Output Manager | IOT | In-Orbit-Test |
| IOM | Input/Output Multiplexer | IOT | Initial Orbit Time |
| IOMP | Input/Output Message Processor | IOT | Input/Output Termination |
| | | IOT | Input/Output Test |
| IOMQ | Input/Output Manager Queue | IOT | Input/Output Transfer |
| | | IOT | Input/Output Typewriter |
| IOMS | Input/Output Management System | IOT | Institut für Organisationsforschung und Technologieanwendung |
| IOMSG | Input/Output Message | | |
| IOO | Input/Output Operation | IOTA | Incremental Operational Tape Adapter |
| IOP | Input/Output Package | | |
| IOP | Input/Output Pool | IOTA | Information Overload Testing Apparatus |
| IOP | Input/Output Processor | | |
| IOP | Input/Output Program | IOTA | Input/Output Transaction Area |
| IOP | Input/Output Pulse | | |
| IOPE | Input/Output Parity Error | IOTA | Instant Oxide Thickness Analyzer |
| IOPKG | Input/Output Package | | |
| IOPL | Intermittent Operating Life | IOTA | Integrated Online Text Arrangement |
| IOPS | Input/Output Programming System | IOU | Immediate Operation Use |
| | | IOU | Input/Output Unit |
| IOQ | Input Output Queue | IOX | Input/Output Executive |
| IOR | Input/Output Register | IP | Identification Point |
| IOR | Input/Output Request | IP | Identification of Position |
| IOR | Input/Output Routine | IP | Identifying Perforation |
| IORB | Input/Output Request Block | IP | Identifying Punch |
| | | IP | Idle Period |

# I

| | | | |
|---|---|---|---|
| IP | Image Processing | IPA | Integrated Photodetection Assemblies |
| IP | Image Processor | | |
| IP | Impulse Program | IPA | Intermediate Power Amplifier |
| IP | Inactive Program | | |
| IP | Incorrect Program | IPAC | Information Processing And Control |
| IP | Independent Program | | |
| IP | Index Point | IPAC | Interaktive Planung, Auswertung und Controlling |
| IP | Index of Performance | | |
| IP | Index of Preprogramming | IPACS | Interactive Pattern Analysis and Classification System |
| IP | Index of Programming | | |
| IP | Indicator Panel | | |
| IP | Induced Polarization | IPAD | Integrated Program for Aerospace-vehicle Design |
| IP | Industrial Production | | |
| IP | Information Parameter | IPAG | Information, Planning, and Analysis Group |
| IP | Information Pool | | |
| IP | Information Processing | IPAM | Inter Partition Access Method |
| IP | Information Processor | | |
| IP | Information Provider | IPAP | Interactive Parameter Analysis Program |
| IP | Information Pulse | | |
| IP | Informationsparameter | IPARS | International Passenger Airline Reservation System |
| IP | Inhibit Pulse | | |
| IP | Initial Parameter | | |
| IP | Initial Phase | IPARS | International Programmed Airline Reservations System |
| IP | Initial Point | | |
| IP | Initialization Phase | | |
| IP | Input | IPAS | Informatives Personalabrechnungssystem |
| IP | Input Parameter | | |
| IP | Input Procedure | IPAS | Interactive Process Applications System |
| IP | Input Processor | | |
| IP | Input Program | IPB | Illustrated Parts Book |
| IP | Instruction Pulse | IPB | Illustrated Parts Breakdown |
| IP | Instructional Program | | |
| IP | Instrument Panel | IPB | Inter Processor Bus |
| IP | Integer Part | IPB | Interconnection and Programming Bay |
| IP | Integer Programming | | |
| IP | Interactive Processing | IPB | Interdivisional Programming Bulletin |
| IP | Interface Process | | |
| IP | Interface Programmable | IPBM | Integrated Planning Bill of Material |
| IP | Intermediate Pressure | | |
| IP | International Programming Limited | IPC | Illustrated Parts Catalog |
| | | IPC | Independently Programmed Computer |
| IP | Internet Protocol | | |
| IP | Interpolationsrechner | IPC | Industrial Process Control |
| IP | Interpretive Program | IPC | Information Processing Center |
| IP | Interrogation Program | | |
| IP | Isoelectric Point | IPC | Information Processing Code |
| IP | Item Processing | | |
| IPA | Image Power Amplifier | IPC | Institute of Printed Circuits |
| IPA | Information Processing Architecture | | |
| | | IPC | Integrated Peripheral Channel |
| IPA | Information Processing Association | | |
| | | IPC | Integrated Process Control |
| IPA | Institut für Produktionstechnik und Automatisierung | IPC | Inter-Process Communication module |
| | | IPC | Internal Product Code |

# I

| | | | |
|---|---|---|---|
| IPC | Interprocess Communication | IPI | Industrial Product Information |
| IPC | Interprocess Control | IPI | Intelligent Peripheral Interface |
| IPC | Interprocessor Channel | | |
| IPCC | Information Processing in Command and Control | IPI | Internal Product Identifier |
| IPCCS | Information Processing in Command and Control System | IPI | Inventory, Print, and Index |
| | | IPI/MIS | Individually Planned Instruction/Management and Information System |
| IPCS | Interactive Problem Control System | | |
| IPCS | International Personal Computing Service | IPIC | In Process Inventory Control |
| | | IPICS | Initial Production and Information Control System |
| IPD | Impact Prediction Data | | |
| IPD | Initial Patient Data | | |
| IPD | Insertion Phase Delay | IPIP | Information Processing Improvement Program |
| IPD | Integrated Pin Diode | | |
| IPD | Inversion Phase Delay | IPIS | Integriertes Personal-informations-System |
| IPDF | Input Data Funnel | | |
| IPDP | Intervals of Pulsations of Diminishing Period | IPK | Institut für Produktionsanlagen und Konstruktionstechnik |
| IPDS | Instrument Pool Data System | | |
| | | IPK | Integrierte Prozeßkontrolle |
| IPDS | Integrated Personnel Data System | | |
| | | IPL | Inactive Program List |
| IPDT | Integrationsprogramm für Daten und Text | IPL | Industrial Programming Language |
| IPE | Incentive PERT Events | IPL | Information Processing Language |
| IPE | Information Processing Equipment | | |
| | | IPL | Initial Program Load |
| IPE | Installation Performance Evaluation | IPL | Initial Program Loader |
| | | IPL | Initial Program Loading |
| IPE | Institution of Production Engineers | IPL | Input Parameter List |
| | | IPL | Interdivisional Programming List |
| IPE | Internationale Programm-Entwicklung | | |
| | | IPL | Internal Product Label |
| IPE | Interpret Parity Error | IPL-V | Information Processing Language-V |
| IPE | Inverted Print Edit | | |
| IPF | Input Filter | | |
| IPF | Interactive Processing Facility | IPLP | Initial Program Load Procedure |
| | | IPM | Impulses Per Minute |
| IPF | Interactive Productivity Facility | IPM | Impulsmodulation |
| | | IPM | Inches Per Minute |
| IPFM | Integral Pulse Frequency Modulation | IPM | Incidental Phase Modulation |
| IPG | In-circuit Program Generator | IPM | Information Processing Machine |
| IPG | Internal Problem Generator | IPM | Institut für Praktische Mathematik |
| IPH | Inches Per Hour | IPM | Interference Prediction Model |
| IPI | In Process Inventory | | |
| IPI | Individual Progress Instructional | IPM | Internal Polarization Modulation |
| IPI | Individually Prescribed Instruction | IPM | Interrupt Per Minute |
| | | IPM | Interruptions Per Minute |

# I

| | | | |
|---|---|---|---|
| IPMB | Integriertes Programm-system für Mittelbetrie-be der Bauwirtschaft | IPS | Impulse Pro Sekunde |
| IPMF | In Process Material File | IPS | Inches Per Second |
| IPMS | Integrated Program Management System | IPS | Increased Processing Speed |
| IPMS | Interpersonal Messaging System | IPS | Information Processing Standards |
| IPN | Inspection Progress Notifications | IPS | Information Processing System |
| IPO | Incoming Parts Order Control | IPS | Informations- und Planungssystem |
| IPO | Inquiry Programmed Operations | IPS | Installation Performance Specification |
| IPO | Installation Planning Organization | IPS | Instruction Per Second |
| IPO | Installation Productivity Option | IPS | Instruction Prescription System |
| IPO/E | Installation Productivity Option/Extended | IPS | Instrument Power Supply |
| IPOM | Installation Planning Operation Manual | IPS | Integriertes Planungs-System |
| IPOT | Inductive Potential divider | IPS | Interactive Processing System |
| IPOT | Inductive Potentiometer | IPS | Interactive Programming System |
| IPP | Imaging Photopolarimeter | IPS | Interceptor Pilot Simulator |
| IPP | Impact Predictor Computer | IPS | Interdivisional Pro-gramming Standard |
| IPP | Input Processor Program | IPS | Interpretive Programming System |
| IPP | Interdivisional Pro-gramming Practice | IPS | Interrupt Per Second |
| IPP | Interplant Parts Planning | IPS | Item Processing System |
| IPP | Interplant Purchase | IPSB | Interface zum Parallel System Bus |
| IPPF | Instruction Preprocessing Function | IPSC | Information Processing Standards for Computers |
| IPPI | Instructional Procedures Preference Inventory | IPSJ | Information Processing Society of Japan |
| IPPN | Interplant Part Number | IPSN | International Packet Switching Network |
| IPPS | Integrierte Produktions-planung und -steuerung | IPSS | International Packet Switched Service |
| IPQ | Inactive Program Queue | IPSSB | Information Processing Systems Standards Board |
| IPQC | In-Process Quality Control | IPT | Improved Programming Technologies |
| IPR | In-Process Review | IPT | Information Processing Theory |
| IPR | Initial Program Reset | IPT | Input Punched Tape |
| IPR | Interplant Parts Requirements | IPT | Internal Pipe Thread |
| IPR | Isolated Pacing Response | IPT | Interphase Transformer |
| IPRO | International Patent Research Office | IPT | Inverse Path Table |
| IPROS | Interaktives Prognose-system | IPTC | International Press Tele-communication Center |
| IPS | Image Processing System | IPTP | Inplant Test Program |
| IPS | Implicit Program Section | IPTS | Inplant Terminal System |
| IPS | Improved Processing System | IPTS | International Practical Temperature Scale |

# I

| | | | |
|---|---|---|---|
| IPTS | Interplant Transmission System | IR | Information Retrieval |
| IPU | Immediate Pickup | IR | Information and Retrieval |
| IPU | Instruction Processing Unit | IR | Informationsreproduktion |
| IPU | Instruction Processor Unit | IR | Informationsringtausch |
| IPU | Integrating Processor Unit | IR | Infra-Red |
| IPU | Internal Processing Unit | IR | Infrared Radiation |
| IPWT | Interprocessor Wait Timer | IR | Initialized Routine |
| IPZ | Integrata Programmierzentrum | IR | Initializer Routine |
| IQ | Information Quantity | IR | Input Reader |
| IQ | Information Quick | IR | Input Register |
| IQ | Informationsquelle | IR | Input Request |
| IQ | Input Queue | IR | Input Routine |
| IQ | Instrument Quality | IR | Inside Radius |
| IQ | Intelligence Quotient | IR | Insoluble Residue |
| IQ | Interne Quittung | IR | Instantaneous Relay |
| IQE | Interruption Queue Element | IR | Instruction Register |
| IQF | Interactive Query Facility | IR | Instruction Ring |
| IQI | Image Quality Indicator | IR | Instrument Reading |
| IQIS | Internationales Quellenorientiertes Informationssystem | IR | Instrumention Register |
| | | IR | Insulation Resistance |
| | | IR | Intermediate Register |
| | | IR | Internal Register |
| | | IR | Internal Resistance |
| IQL | Incoming Quality Level | IR | Interpolationsrechner |
| IQL | Interactive Query Language | IR | Interpreting Routine |
| IQL | Intermediate Query Language | IR | Interpretive Routine |
| | | IR | Interrogator-Responder |
| | | IR | Interrupt Register |
| IQMH | Input Queue Message Handler | IR | Interrupt Routine |
| | | IR | Inventory Record |
| IQR | Instruction Queue Register | IR | Irradiance |
| IQRP | Interactive Query and Report Processor | IR-LED | Infrared Light Emitting Diode |
| IQS | Interactive Query System | IR/M | Industrieroboter und Manipulatoren |
| IR | In-dial Register | IRA | Individual Retrievement Account |
| IR | Incident Report | | |
| IR | Independent Release | IRA | Information Retrieval using APL |
| IR | Index Record | | |
| IR | Index Register | IRA | Institut für Realzeitdatenverarbeitung und Automation |
| IR | Indexing Register | | |
| IR | Indexregister | | |
| IR | Indicator Reading | IRAC | Integrated Random Access Channel |
| IR | Indicator Register | | |
| IR | Industrial Relations | IRAN | Inspection and Repair As Necessary |
| IR | Industrial Robot | | |
| IR | Industrie-Roboter | IRANDOC | Iranian Documentation Centre |
| IR | Information Rate | | |
| IR | Information Reading | IRAR | Impulse Response Area Ratio |
| IR | Information Record | | |
| IR | Information Recording | IRAR | Integrator Register Address Register |
| IR | Information Representation | | |
| IR | Information Request | IRASER | Infrared Amplification by Stimulated Emission of Radiation |
| IR | Information Restoring | | |

# I

| | | | |
|---|---|---|---|
| IRATE | Interactive Retrieval And Text Editor | IRHD | International Rubber Hardness Degrees |
| IRB | Interrupt Request Block | IRI | Input Reader Interpreter |
| IRB | Interdivisonal Records Bulletin | IRI | Institut für Rationalisierung und Informatik GmbH |
| IRBT | Intelligent Remote Batch Terminal | IRI | Integrated Range Instrumentation |
| IRC | Improper Routing Character | IRIA | Infrared Information and Analysis |
| IRC | Information Research Center | IRIA | Institut de Recherche d'Informatique et d'Automatique |
| IRC | Infrared Countermeasure | | |
| IRC | Integrator Register Counter | IRIG | Inertial Rate Integrating Gyroscope |
| IRC | International Record Carriers | IRIS | IBM Recruitment Information System |
| IRC | Inter-Region Communication | IRIS | Industrial Relations Information System |
| IRCG | Incident Report Code Guide | IRIS | Information Resources Information System |
| IRCM | Infrared Countermeasures | IRIS | Infrared Information System |
| IRCR | Integrator Register Control Register | IRIS | Infrared Interferometer Spectrometer |
| IRCS | Intercomplex Radio Communications System | IRIS | Instant response information Reconnaissance Intelligence System |
| IRD | Information Records Division | | |
| IRD | International Resource Development | IRIS | Instantaneous Retrieval Information System |
| IRDATA | Industrial Robot Data | IRIS | Institute's Retrieval of Information Study |
| IRDL | Information Retrieval and Display Language | IRIS | Integrated Reservation and Information System |
| IRDS | Integrated Reliability Data System | IRIS | Integriertes Rechnerverbund- und Inhouse-System |
| IRE | Institute of Radio Engineers | | |
| IRED | Infra-Red-Emitting Diode | IRIS | Integriertes Reservierungs- und Informationssystem |
| IREST | Institut de Recherches Economiques et Sociales sur les Télécommunications | | |
| | | IRIS | Interactive Realtime Information System |
| IRETIJ | Institut de Recherche pour le Traitement de l'Information Juridique | IRISA | Institut de Recherche en Informatique et Systèmes Aléatoires |
| IRF | Impedance Reduction Factor | IRL | Index Retrieval Language |
| | | IRL | Information Retrieval Language |
| IRF | Interrogation Recurrence Frequency | IRLS | Interrogation, Recording and Locating System |
| IRFIS | International Research Forum in Information Science | IRLS | Interrogation, Recording of Location Subsystem |
| IRG | Inertial Rate Gyro | IRM | Interactive Request Modification |
| IRG | Interrecord Gap | | |
| IRGAR | Infrared Gas Radiation | IRM | Information Resource Management |
| IRH | Inductive Recording Head | | |

# I

| | | | |
|---|---|---|---|
| IRM | Infrared Measurement | IRS | Inquiry and Reporting System |
| IRM | Intermediate Range Monitor | IRS | Integrated Retrieval System |
| IRMA | Information Recension and Manuscript Assembly | IRS | Interchange Record Separator |
| IRMFET | Infrared-sensing MOSFET | IRS | Interdivisional Records Standard |
| IRMS | Information Retrieval and Management System | IRS | Internal Revenue Service |
| IROAN | Inspect and Repair Only As Needed | IRS | International Referral System |
| IROD | Instantaneous Readout Detector | IRS | Interrecord Separator |
| IROM | Ion-implanted Read Only Memory | IRSET | Institut de Recherches Sociales et Economiques sur les Télécommunications |
| IROS | Increased Reliability Of System | | |
| IROT | Information Read-Out Time | IRSP | Infrared Spectrometer |
| IRP | Individualized Reading Program | IRSS | Intelligent Remote Station Support |
| IRP | Informationsrecherche-prozeß | IRT | Index Return Character |
| IRP | Initial Receiving Point | IRT | Informationsrecherche-technologie |
| IRP | Integrated Reference Package | IRT | Information Retrieval Technique |
| IRP | Interdivisional Records Practice | IRT | Informationsrecherche-thesaurus |
| IRP | Intermediate Representation of Program | IRT | Infrared Tracker |
| IRP | Interrupt Processor | IRT | Interrogator-Responder-Transponder |
| IRP | Inventory and Requirements Planning | IRU | Inertial Reference Unit |
| | | IRUC | Information and Research Utilization Center |
| IRPG | Interactive Report Generator | IRV | International Reference Version |
| IRPL | Industrial Robot Programming Language | IRX | Interactive Resource Executive |
| IRPT | Interrupt | IS | If Statement |
| IRQ | Interrupt Request | IS | Impact Switch |
| IRQC | Infrared Quantum Counter | IS | Imperative Sentence |
| | | IS | Imperative Statement |
| IRR | Internal Rate of Return | IS | Include Statement |
| IRR | Irrung | IS | Incomplete Sequence |
| IRRL | Information Retrieval Research Laboratory | IS | Index Sequential |
| | | IS | Indexing in Source |
| IRS | Information Receiving Station | IS | Indexsequentielle Speicherungsform |
| IRS | Information Referral Service | IS | Information Science |
| | | IS | Information Selection |
| IRS | Information Retrieval Service | IS | Information Separator |
| | | IS | Information Signal |
| IRS | Information Retrieval System | IS | Information Source |
| | | IS | Information Storage |
| IRS | Informationsrecherche-system | IS | Information Stream |
| | | IS | Information Supply |
| IRS | Input Read Submodule | IS | Information System |

# I

| | | | |
|---|---|---|---|
| IS | Informationssystem | ISA | Interrupt Storage Area |
| IS | Infrared Spectroscopy | ISA | Invalid Storage Address |
| IS | Inhibiting Signal | ISABEL | Integriertes System für Automatische Belegverarbeitung |
| IS | Initial State | | |
| IS | Initiate Session | | |
| IS | Initiate Statement | ISAC | Informationsfluß-Symbolik für Angewandte Computertechnik |
| IS | Input Section | | |
| IS | Input Simulator | | |
| IS | Input Source | ISAD | Information Science and Automation Division |
| IS | Input Storage | | |
| IS | Input Store | ISADAC | Interim Standard Airborne Digital Computer |
| IS | Input Stream | | |
| IS | Insertion Sequence | ISADC | Interim Standard Airborne Digital Computer |
| IS | Instruction Sequence | | |
| IS | Instruction Set | ISADPM | International Society for the Abolition of Data Processing Machines |
| IS | Instruction Sheet | | |
| IS | Instruction Stream | | |
| IS | Instruction System | ISAIV | Integriertes System der Automatisierten Informationsverarbeitung |
| IS | Instructional System | | |
| IS | Instrument | | |
| IS | Integrated Software | ISAIV | Integriertes System der Automatischen Informationsverarbeitung |
| IS | Integrierte Schaltung | | |
| IS | Integrierte Software | | |
| IS | Integrierter Schalterkreis | ISAL | Information Service Access Line |
| IS | Integrierter Schaltkreis | | |
| IS | Intelligence Signal | ISAL | Information System Access Line |
| IS | Interactive Systems | | |
| IS | Interblock Space | ISAM | Indexed Sequential Access Method |
| IS | Interface Summary | | |
| IS | Interference Suppressor | ISAM | Integrated Switching And Multiplexing |
| IS | Intermediate Store | | |
| IS | Internal Shield | ISAM-VLR | Indexed Sequential Access Method Variable Length Record |
| IS | Internal Storage | | |
| IS | Internal Store | | |
| IS | Interpolationsspeicher | ISAP | Information Sort And Predict |
| IS | Interpretationsschlüssel | | |
| IS | Interpretive System | ISAP | Interactive Survey Analysis Package |
| IS | Interrupt State | | |
| IS | Interval Signal | ISAP | International Sourcing Analysis Program |
| IS | Inventory System | | |
| IS&D | Integrate Sample and Dump | ISAR | Information Storage And Retrieval |
| IS-VT | Integrierter Software-Vertrieb | ISAS | Information Science and Automation Section |
| ISA | Information Science Abstracts | ISAS | Informationssystem zur Administrativen Steuerung |
| ISA | Initial Storage Area | | |
| ISA | Inspection Summary Analysis | ISB | Independent-Sideband |
| | | ISB | Informationssystem für das Bauwesen |
| ISA | Instrument Society of America | ISB | Initial Status Byte |
| ISA | Interlaced Storage Assignment | ISB | Interdivisional System Bulletin |
| ISA | International Standard Atmosphere | ISBB | Inhibit Switch B Bit |

| | | | |
|---|---|---|---|
| ISBD | Information Services Business Division | ISDS | Indexed Sequential Data Set |
| ISBD | International Standard Bibliographic Description | ISDS | Integrated Ship Design System |
| ISBN | International Standard Book Number | ISDS | International Serials Data System |
| ISC | Implicit Subroutine Call | ISDS/IC | International Serials Data System/International Centre |
| ISC | Implied Subroutine Call | | |
| ISC | Information Store Cell | | |
| ISC | Inhibit Switch C bit | ISE | Institute for Software Engineering |
| ISC | Integrated Storage Control | | |
| ISC | Interactive Sciences Corporation | ISE | Integral Square Error |
| | | ISE | Integrated System Environment |
| ISC | International Signal Code | | |
| ISC | Interstellar Communications | ISE | International Software Enterprise |
| ISC | Intersystems Communication | ISE | International Standard Electric Corporation |
| ISCAN | Inertialess Steerable Communication Antenna | ISEP | Institut Supérieur d'Electronique de Paris |
| ISCBL | Interrupt System Control Block List | ISEP | International Standard Equipment Practice |
| ISCC | International Service Coordination Centre | ISEPS | International Sun-Earth Physics Satellites programme |
| ISCO | Institut d'études Sémantiques et Cognitives | | |
| | | ISF | Identification Sequence Field |
| ISCP | Inventory Stock Cataloguing Program | ISF | Integrated Subject File |
| ISCS | Information Services Computer System | ISF | Interrecord Sequence Field |
| | | ISFET | Ion-Sensitive FET |
| ISD | IBM Standard Data | ISFMS | Indexed Sequential File Management System |
| ISD | IBM Standard-Daten | | |
| ISD | Impulse Storing Device | ISG | Integrated Source Graphics |
| ISD | Induction System Deposit | ISGE | Interactive Screen Generator and Editor |
| ISD | Information Services Division | | |
| ISD | Information Storage Density | ISGI | Internationales System der Gesellschaftswissenschaftlichen Information |
| ISD | Informations Systems Division | ISH | Inventory Shortage |
| | | ISHM | International Society for Hybrid Microelectronics |
| ISD | Interactive Screen Definition | | |
| | | ISI | Industrielles Steuerungs- und Informationssystem |
| ISD | Internal Symbol Dictionary | | |
| ISD | Internal Symbolic Dictionary | ISI | Information Science Institute and society |
| ISDF | Indexed Sequential Data File | ISI | Informationssystem INTERKAMA |
| ISDG | Information Science Discussion Group | ISI | Institut de la Sécurité Informatique |
| ISDN | Integrated Service Data Network | ISI | Institute for Scientific Information |
| ISDN | Integrated Services Digital Network | ISI | Integral Systems Incorporated |
| ISDOS | Information System Design and Optimisation System | ISI | Intelligent Standard Interface |

# I

| | | | | |
|---|---|---|---|---|
| ISI | Intelligent System Interface | | ISM | Industrial Scientific and Medical |
| ISI | Internal Specified Index | | ISM | Industrial, Scientific, Medicus apparatus |
| ISI | Intersymbol Interference | | ISM | Industrial, Scientific, and Medical equipment |
| ISIC | Inter-Symbol Interference Corrector | | ISM | Information System for Management |
| ISIE | Integral Square Ideal Error | | ISM | Information Systems Manual |
| ISIM | Inhibit Simultaneity | | ISM | Informationssystem Materialwirtschaft |
| ISIS | Index-Sequentielles Informationssystem | | ISM | Informationssystem Mode |
| ISIS | Infratest Software Information Service | | ISMAP | Instrumentation System Margin Analysis Program |
| ISIS | Infratest Software Informationssystem | | ISMEA | Institut Supérieur de Micro-Electronique Appliquée |
| ISIS | Integral Service Information System | | ISMH | Input Source Message Handler |
| ISIS | Integrated Scientific Information System | | ISMI | Impoved Space-Manned Interceptor |
| ISIS | Integrated Set of Information Systems | | ISMMP | International Standard Methods for Measuring Performances |
| ISIS | Integrated Strike and Interceptor System | | ISMOD | Indexed Sequential Module |
| ISIS | Intel System Implementation Supervisor | | ISMS | Integrity and Schedule Management Subsystem |
| ISIS | Internal Systems Information System | | ISMUS | Iowa State computerized Music System |
| ISIS | Internally Switched Interface System | | ISN | Input Sequence Number |
| ISK | Informationssystem Krankenkasse | | ISN | Internal Statement Number |
| ISK | Insert Storage Key | | ISN | Internal Sequence Number |
| ISL | Information Search Language | | ISO | Independent Sales Organization |
| ISL | Information System Language | | ISO | Individual System Operation |
| ISL | Information Systems Laboratory | | ISO | Information Systems Office |
| ISL | Initial Spare parts List | | ISO | Information-Structure-Oriented |
| ISL | Initial System Load | | ISO | Intermediate Station Operation |
| ISL | Initial System Loading | | ISO | International Organization for Standardization |
| ISL | Injection-coupled Synchronous Logic | | ISO | International Science Organization |
| ISL | Instructional Systems Language | | ISO | International Standardization Organization |
| ISL | Integrated Schottky Logic | | ISO | International Standards Organization |
| ISL | Interactive Simulation Language | | ISO | Isometric |
| ISL | Interdivisional Systems List | | ISO | Isotropic |
| ISL | Interface Socket Listing | | | |
| ISLE | Intergral Square Linear Error | | | |
| ISLS | Interrogation-path Sidelobe Suppression | | | |

# I

| | | | |
|---|---|---|---|
| ISO OCR | International Standards Organization standards on Optical Character Recognition | ISPICE | Interactive Simulated Program with Integrated Circuit Emphasis |
| ISO/DIS | ISO Draft International Standard | ISPL | Incremental System Programming Language |
| ISOCRAF-A | International Standard Optical Character Recognition, Alphanumeric Font type A | ISPL | Initial Spare Parts List |
| | | ISPOS | Integrierendes System für die Projektierung Optimaler Schiffe |
| ISODATA | Iterative Self-Organizing Data Analysis Technique A | ISPT | Inquiry Station Program Tape |
| | | ISR | Image Storage Retrieval |
| ISONE | International Standard Of Nuclear Electronics | ISR | Information Storage and Retrieval |
| ISOPAR | Improved Symbolic Optimizing Assembly Routine | ISR | Initial Selection Routine |
| | | ISR | Input Select and Reset |
| ISORID | Information System On Research In Documentation | ISR | Input Status Register |
| | | ISR | Interrupt Service Routine |
| ISOTEC | Integrierte Software-Technologie | ISR | Interrupt Status Register |
| | | ISR | Intersecting Storage Ring |
| ISP | Image Storage Panel | ISR | Intersection Stockage Ring |
| ISP | Information Systems Partner Unternehmensberatung GmbH | ISRD | Information Storage, Retrieval and Dissemination |
| ISP | Information Systems Program | ISRS | Information Search and Recording System |
| | | ISRT | Insert |
| ISP | Information Sur Produit | ISS | Ideal Solidus Structures |
| ISP | Initial Status Presentation | ISS | Impulseingang für Schrittsteuern |
| ISP | Instruction Set Processor | ISS | Index Sequential Storage |
| ISP | Integrated Scientific Processor | ISS | Information Sampling System |
| ISP | Interception System Processor | ISS | Information Storage System |
| ISP | Interdivisional Systems Practice | ISS | Informationsspeichersystem |
| ISP | Internally Stored Program | ISS | Initial Selection Sequence |
| ISP | Interstage Punching | ISS | Input Subsystem |
| ISP | Italian Society of Physics | ISS | Integrated Switch Stick |
| ISPA | International Software Products Association | ISS | Interdivisional Systems Standard |
| ISPC | Industry Standard Plotting Commands | ISS | Interrupt Service Subroutines |
| ISPC | International Storage Product Center | ISS | Intrinsic Instruction Set |
| | | ISS | Ion Silicon System |
| ISPEC | Insulation Specification | ISS KEP | Informationsspeichersystem für den Konstruktiven Entwicklungsprozeß |
| ISPF | Interactive System Product Facility | | |
| ISPF | Interactive System Productivity Facility | ISSCC | International Solid State Circuits Conference |
| ISPF/PSD | Interactive System Productivity/Program System Development | ISSEM | Information System Security Evaluation Methodology |

# I

| | | | |
|---|---|---|---|
| ISSKON | Informationsspeicher-system Konstruktion | ISX | Information Switching Exchange |
| ISSM | Incompletely Specified Sequential Machine | ISYB | Inhibit Switch Y Bit |
| ISSN | International Standard Serial Number | ISZM | Indizierte Sequentielle Zugriffsmethode |
| ISSR | Information Storage Selection and Retrieval | IT | Idle Time |
| | | IT | Indent Tab character |
| ISSS | Information Selection and Sampling System | IT | Index Table |
| | | IT | Information Technique |
| ISSS | Installation Service Supply Support | IT | Information Technology |
| | | IT | Information Theory |
| IST | Incompatible Simultaneous Transfer | IT | Information Track |
| | | IT | Informationstechnik |
| IST | Incredibly Small Transistor | IT | Informationstheorie |
| IST | Information Science and Technology | IT | Informationsträger |
| | | IT | Input Tape |
| IST | Informationssystem Technik | IT | Input Time |
| IST | Input Stack Tape | IT | Input Translator |
| IST | Institut für Software-technik | IT | Instant Transactions |
| | | IT | Instruction Termination |
| IST | Integrated Switching and Transmission | IT | Instruction Type |
| | | IT | Instrument Transformer |
| IST | Integrated System Transformer | IT | Instrumentation Tape |
| | | IT | Insulating Transformer |
| IST | Integrated Systems Test | IT | Interface Tape |
| IST | Internal Symbol Table | IT | Interfering Transmitter |
| IST | Interrupt Service Task | IT | Internal Translator |
| ISTAR | Image Storage Translation And Reproduction | IT | Interrogating Typewriter |
| | | IT | Interrogator Transponder |
| ISTAR | Information Storage Translation And Reproduction | IT | Interrupt |
| | | IT | Interval Timer |
| | | IT | Inventory Transfer |
| ISTIM | Interchange of Scientific and Technical Informa-tion in Machine language | IT | Irradiation Time |
| | | IT | Item Transfer |
| | | ITA | Intelligenter Tastatur-Adapter |
| ISTP | Information System Theory Project | ITA | International Telegraphy Alphabet |
| ISU | Instruction-Stream-Units | ITA | Internationales Tele-grafenalphabet |
| ISU | Interface Switching Unit | | |
| ISU | Interference Suppression Unit | ITAC | Interprocessor Tasking And Communications |
| ISUDS | Iterative Scheme Using a Direct Solution | ITAE | Integral of Time multi-plied Absolute Error |
| ISV | Independent Software Vendor | ITAE | Integral of Time-multiplied Absolute value of Error |
| ISW | Informatonssystem für Werkstoffkennwerte | | |
| | | ITAE | Integrated Time and Absolute Error |
| ISW | Initial Status Word | | |
| ISW | Instruction Word Stack | ITAS | Integrated Transport Accounting System |
| ISW | Internal Status Word | | |
| ISWM | Inhibit Switch Word Mark | ITB | Integral Terminal Block |
| ISWTI | Internationales System für Wissenschaftliche und Technische Informationen | ITB | Integrated Test Block |
| | | ITB | Intermediate Text Block |

# I

| | | | |
|---|---|---|---|
| ITB | Intermediate Transmission Block | ITIRC | IBM Technical Information Retrieval Center |
| ITBE | Interchannel Time Base Error | ITIRC | International Technical Information and Retrieval Center |
| ITC | Individual Table of Contents | ITIS | Interactive Terminal Interface System |
| ITC | Ingénieur Technico-Commercial | ITIS | Internal Translation Information Subsystem |
| ITC | Input Transaction Card | ITIU | Inventory Temporarily In Use |
| ITC | Integral Tube Components | | |
| ITC | Intelligent Telecommunications Controller | ITL | IBM Technical Liaison |
| ITC | International Teletype Code | ITL | Ignition Transmission Line |
| | | ITL | Integrated-Transfer-Launch |
| ITC | Intertropical Convergence | | |
| ITC | Investment Tax Credit | ITL | Inverse Time Limit |
| ITC | Ionic Thermoconductivity | ITM | Inch Trim Moment |
| ITCIS | Integrated Telephone Customer Information System | ITM | Ingénieur Technique de Maintenance |
| | | ITM | Instruction Trace Monitor |
| ITCLC | Item Class Code | ITM | Intercommunication Teleprocessing Monitor |
| ITCP | Integrated Test and Checkout Procedures | ITMAS | IBM Traffic Management System |
| ITDD | Integrated Tunnel Diode Device | ITMI | Institut Technique de la Machine Intelligente |
| ITDS | Integrated Technical Data System | ITMIS | Integrated Transportation Management Information System |
| ITDSC | Item Description | | |
| ITE | Institute of Telecommunication Engineers | ITN | Interamerican Telecommunication Network |
| ITE | Interaktiver Terminal Emulator | ITNBR | Item Number |
| | | ITNL | Internal |
| ITEM | Internationale Technische Messe | ITNSA | Item Net Sales Amount |
| | | ITO | Indium-Tin-Oxide |
| ITEWS | Integrated Tactical Electronic Warfare System | ITP | Input Translator Program |
| | | ITP | Integrated Test Program |
| ITF | Integrated Test Facility | ITP | Interpretive Trace Program |
| ITF | Interactive Terminal Facility | | |
| ITFS | Instructional Television Fixed Services | ITPI | Integrated Transactional Processing Interface |
| ITG | Iterative Test Generator | ITPS | IBM Teleprocessing System |
| ITGEN | Input Tape Generator program | ITPS | Integrated Teleprocessing System |
| ITI | Initial Task Index | ITPS | Intel Transaction Processing System |
| ITI | Integrated Task Index | | |
| ITI | Integrated Task Indices | ITPS | Internal Teleprocessing System |
| ITI | Interactive Terminal Interface | ITPS | Interplant-file Processing System |
| ITI | Interface de Terminal Interactif | ITR | Incore Thermionic Reactor |
| ITIPI | Interim Tactical Information Processing and Interpretation | ITR | Instrumentation Tape Recorder |
| | | ITR | Integrated Thyristor Rectifier |

# I

| | | | |
|---|---|---|---|
| ITR | Inventory Transfer Receipt | ITV | Industrial Television |
| ITR | Inverse Time Relay | ITV | Instructional Television |
| ITR | Isolation Test Routine | ITVAC | Industrial Transistor Value Automatic Computer |
| ITRI | Industrial Technology Research Institute | ITVB | International Television Broadcasting |
| ITS | Import Tabulation System | ITWT | Intertask message Wait Timer |
| ITS | Industrial Translator System | ITX | Information Transfer Exchange |
| ITS | Industrielles Translator System | ITX | Interactive Transaction Executive |
| ITS | Inertial Timing Switch | IU | Indicating Unit |
| ITS | Informatics Teaching System | IU | Information Unit |
| ITS | Information Transfer State | IU | Information Unlimited |
| ITS | Information Transmission System | IÜ | Informationsübertragung |
| ITS | Insertion Test Signal | IU | Input Unit |
| ITS | Institute for Telecommunication Sciences | IU | Instrument Unit |
| ITS | Instrument and Telemetry System | IU | Instrumentation Unit |
| ITS | Instrumentation and Telemetry System | IU | Interference Unit |
| | | IUA | Iomec Users Association |
| ITS | Insulation Test Specification | IUE | Instruction Unit Execution |
| | | IUF | Inquiry Unit File |
| ITS | Integrierte Transportsteuerung | IUP | Independent Utility Program |
| ITS | Integriertes Transportsteuerungs-System | IUP | Installed User Procedure |
| | | IUP | Installed User Program |
| ITS | Intelligent Terminal Service | IUR | Internes Unterbrechungsregister |
| ITS | Interactive Training System | IUS | Information Unit Set |
| ITS | Interactive Terminal Service | IUS | Information Unlimites Software |
| ITS | Internal Time Sharing | IUS | Installed User System |
| ITS | International Telecommunications Service | IV | Inaccessible Value |
| | | IV | Incremented Value |
| ITS | International Temperature Scale | IV | Independent Variable |
| | | IV | Index Value |
| ITS | International Time Sharing Corporation | IV | Information Volume |
| | | IV | Informationsverarbeitung |
| ITS | Interval Test System | IV | Informationsversorgung |
| ITS | Invitation To Send | IV | Initial Velocity |
| ITSS | Interim Time Sharing System | IV | Input Voltage |
| | | IV | Inspecteur de Ville |
| ITT | International Telephone and Telegraph | IV | Integrierverstärker |
| | | IV | Intermediate Voltage |
| ITT... | International Telephone and Telegraph Corporation | IV | Interval |
| | | IV | Inverter |
| ITTWC | ITT World Communications, Incorporated | IVALA | Integrated Visual Approach and Landing Aid |
| | | IVAR | Internal Variable |
| ITU | International Telecommunication Union | IVD | Inductive Voltage Divider |
| | | IVD | Information Viewing Device |
| | | IVD | Interpolated Voice Data |
| | | IVD | Invalid Decimal |

# I

| | | | |
|---|---|---|---|
| IVD | Ion Vapor Deposition | IWE | Instantaneous Word Encoder |
| IVDS | Independent Variable Depth SONAR | IWF | Information Word Format |
| IVDS | Integrated Voice & Data Switching | IWG | Implementation Working Group |
| IVF | Image View Facility | IWG | Iron Wire Gauge |
| IVF | Image View Function | IWI | International Workload Index |
| IVF | Interactive View Facility | | |
| IVI | Instant Visual Index | IWIM | Institut für Wissenschaftsinformation in der Medizin |
| IVIP | Integriertes Verarbeitungs- und Informationssystem für Personaldaten | IWISE | Internal Wang Intersystem Exchange |
| IVIS | Interaktives Video-Informationssystem | IWLS | Iterative Weighted Least Squares |
| IVM | Improved Visible Marker | IWP | International information/Word Processing Association |
| IVM | Informationsverarbeitungsmaschine | | |
| IVMU | Inertial Velocity Measurement Unit | IWPA | International Word Processing Association |
| IVP | Initial Value Problem | | |
| IVP | Installation Verification Procedure | IWQ | Input Work Queue |
| | | IWS | Information Word Structure |
| IVR | Instrumented Visual Range | IWS | Integrated Workstation |
| IVR | Integrated Voltage Regulator | IWS | Internal Work Station |
| | | IWT | Informationssystem Wissenschaft und Technik |
| IVR | Integrierter Vorrechner | | |
| IVS | IBM Verantwortlicher Service | IWT | Inhibit Word Trigger |
| | | IWTS | Integrated Wire Termination System |
| IVS | Informationsverarbeitendes System | IWU | Interworking Unit |
| IVS | Informationsverarbeitungssystem | IWV | Impulswählverfahren |
| | | IX | Index |
| IVS | Informationsvermittlungsstelle | IX | Ion Exchange |
| | | IX | Interface Executive |
| IVS | Integrated Versaplot Software | IXCU | Integrated Transmission Control Unit |
| IVS | Interactive Videotex System | IXF | Information Exchange Facility |
| IVSI | Inertial lead Vertical Speed Indicator | IXR | Intelligent Transparent Restore |
| IVV | Instantaneous Vertical Velocity | IYB | Inhibit Y Bit |
| | | IZ | Informationszentrum |
| IW | Impulswähler | IZ | Internationale Zentrale |
| IW | Index Word | IZA | Integriertes Zeiterfassungs- und Auswertungssystem |
| IW | Indicator Word | | |
| IW | Information Word | | |
| IW | Informationswandlung | IZDV | Internationale Zusammenarbeit zur Dokumentation über Verkehrswirtschaft |
| IW | Inside Width | | |
| IW | Instruction Word | | |
| IW | Isotopic Weight | IZIS | Internationales Zweiginformationssystem |
| IWA | Interpreter Work Area | | |
| IWA | Interrupt Work Area | IZIZ | Internationale Zeit Impuls Zahlung |
| IWCS | Integrated Wideband Communications System | | |

**IZWTI** Internationales Zentrum
für Wissenschaftliche
und Technische
Information

# J

| | | | |
|---|---|---|---|
| J | Jack | JCC | Job Control Card |
| J | Job | JCC | Joint Computer Conference |
| J | Joule | JCCD | Junction Charge-Coupled Device |
| J | Jumper | | |
| J | Junction | JCCE | Joint Committee on Communications and Electronics |
| J/S | Jam to Signal | | |
| J/S | Justified | | |
| JA | Job Analysis | JCEC | Joint Communications Electronics Committee |
| JA | Jump Address | | |
| JACC | Joint Automatic Control Conference | JCFI | Job Control File Internal |
| | | JCFS | Job Control File Source |
| JACM | Journal of the ACM | JCIT | Jerusalem Conference on Information Technology |
| JAD | Juristische Automatische Dokumentation | | |
| | | JCL | Job Control Language |
| JADPU | Joint Automatic Data Processing Unit | JCLOT | Joint Closed Loop Operations Test |
| JAICI | Japan Association for International Chemical Information | JCP | Job Control Parameter |
| | | JCP | Job Control Program |
| | | JCP | Journal Control Program |
| JAKIS | Japanese Keyword Indexing Simulation | JCP | JOVIAL Control Program |
| | | JCS | Job Control Statement |
| JAKIS | Japanese Keyword Indexing Simulator | JCS | Job Control System |
| | | JCS | Job Creation Subsidiary |
| JAL | Job Account Log | JCT | Job Control Table |
| JAM | Joint Analyzed Make-up | JCT | Journal Control Table |
| JAMASS | Japanese Medical Abstract Scanning System | JCT | Junction |
| | | JCTN | Junction |
| JAN | Joint Army Navy | JCUDI | Japan Computer Usage Development Institute |
| JAPIC | Japan Pharmaceutical Information Center | JCVS | JOVIAL Compiler Validation System |
| JARS | Job Accounting Report System | | |
| | | JCW | Job Control Word |
| JAS | Job Accounting System | JD | Junction Diode |
| JAS | Job Analysis System | JD | Journal of Documentation |
| JASDA | Julie Automatic Sonic Data Analyzer | JDAB | Job Description Accounting Block |
| JASIS | Journal of the American Society for Information Science | JDC | Job Description Card |
| | | JDC | Junction Diode Circuit |
| | | JDR | Job Distribution Register |
| JATO | Jet Assisted Take-Off | JDS | Job Diagnosis Survey |
| JAVS | JOVIAL Automated Verification System | JDS | Job Data Sheet |
| | | JE | Journal d'Erreurs |
| JB | Junction Box | JE | Journal Exploitation |
| JBCNTRL | Job Control | JECC | Japan Electronic Computer Centre |
| JBCOUNT | Job account | | |
| JC | Jack Connection | JECL | Job Entry Control Language |
| JC | Jam Contact | | |
| JC | Job Control | JECNS | Joint Electronic Communications Nomenclature System |
| JC | JOVIAL Compiler | | |
| JC | Jump Command | | |
| JC | Jump on Carry | JECS | Job Entry Central Service |
| JC | Junction | | |
| JCA | JCL Conversion Aid | JED | Job Entry Definition |
| JCA | Journal Control Area | JEDEC | Joint Electron Device Engineering Council |
| JCB | Job Control Block | | |

# J

| | | | |
|---|---|---|---|
| JEIDA | Japan Electronic Industry Development Association | JIS | Job Information Station |
| JEIPAC | JICST Electronic Information Processing Automatic Computer | JIS | Job Input Stream |
| | | JIT | Job Instruction Training |
| | | JIT | Just-In-Time |
| | | JJ | Josephson Junction |
| JEPIA | Japan Electronic Part Industry Association | JJL | Josephson Junction Logic |
| | | JK | Jack |
| JEPS | Job Entry Peripheral Service | JL | Job Library |
| | | JL | Jump Last |
| JES | Job Entry Subsystem | JM | Job Management |
| JES | Job Entry System | JM | Jump on Minus |
| JES | Job-Eingabe-System | JM | Junction Module |
| JESA | Japanese Engineering Standards Association | JMCOL | Jumps Monthly Compute Output Listing |
| JETS | Job Executive and Transfer Satellite | JMED | Jungle Message Encoder-Decoder |
| JF | Jump Function | JMM | Joint Man-Machine system |
| JF | Junction Frequency | JMOS | Joint MOS |
| JFCB | Job File Control Block | JMPR | Jumper |
| JFE | Justified Field Entry | JMR | Job Management Record |
| JFED | Junction Field Effect Device | JMS | Jump to Subroutine |
| | | JNC | Jump on No Carry |
| JFER | Junction Field-Effect Resistor | JND | Just Noticeable Difference |
| | | JNL | Jump Not Last |
| JFET | Junction Field Effect Transistor | JNLNO | Journal Number |
| | | JNODC | Japanese National Oceanographic Data Centre |
| JFET T | Junction Field-Effect Transistor Tetrode | JNZ | Jump on No Zero |
| | | JO | Jump Order |
| JGFET | Junction Gate Field Effect Transistor | JOBD | Job Description |
| | | JOBLIB | Job Library |
| JGN | Junction Gate Number | JOBMAN | Job Management |
| JI | Job Information | JOBNO | Job Number |
| JI | Job Instruction | JOBOL | Job Organization Language |
| JI | Josephson Interferometer | JOBQ | Job Queue |
| JI | Jump Instruction | JOBTICS | Job and Time Control System |
| JI | Junction Isolation | | |
| JIB | Job Information Block | JOC | Joint Operations Center |
| JIC | Job Information Card | JOCIT | JOVIAL Compiler Implementation Tool |
| JIC | Joint Industry Conference | | |
| JICST | Japan Information Centre of Science and Technology | JOD | Joint Occupancy Data |
| | | JOD | Journal Of Development |
| | | JOHNNIAC | Johns von Neumann Integrator and Automatic Computer |
| JIFDATS | Joint In-Flight Data Acquisition and Transmission System | | |
| | | JOL | Job Organization Language |
| JIFDATS | Joint In-Flight Data Transmission System | JOL | Job Orientation Language |
| | | JOLA | Journal Of Library Automation |
| JIFTS | Joint In-Flight Transmission System | | |
| | | JONSDAP | Joint North Sea Data Acquisition Program |
| JIIA | Journées Internationales de l'Informatique et de l'Automatique | | |
| | | JONSDAP | Joint North Sea Data Acquisition Project |
| JIP | Joint Input Processing | JONSIS | Joint North Sea Information Systems |
| JIS | Japanese Industrial Standard | | |

# J

| | | | |
|---|---|---|---|
| JOP | Jonction Omnibus Parallèle | JSS | Job Shop Simulation |
| JOP | Jonction Parallèle | JSSPG | Job Shop Simulation Program Generator |
| JOS | Job Order Sheet | | |
| JOSS | JOHNNIAC Open Shop System | JST | Job Step Task |
| JOT | Job-Oriented Terminal | JSTCB | Job Step Task Control Block |
| JOT | Jump-Oriented Terminal | | |
| JOVIAL | Jules' Own Version of International Algebraic Language | JT | Job Table |
| | | JT | Job Time |
| | | JT | Job Timing |
| JP | Jet Propellant | JT | Joint |
| JP | Job Processing | JT | Journal Tape |
| JP | Jones Plug | JT | Journal Teleprinter |
| JP | Jumper | JT | Junction Transistor |
| JP | Junction Panel | JTC | Joint Transform Correlator |
| JP | Junction Point | JTCP | JOVIAL Test Control Program |
| JP | Jute Protected | | |
| JPA | Job Pack Area | JTDS | Joint Track Data Storage |
| JPACQ | Job Pack Area Control Queue | JTE | Junction Tandem Exchange |
| | | JTIDS | Joint Tactical Information Distribution System |
| JPE | Jump on Parity Even | | |
| JPO | Jump on Parity Odd | JTM | Josephson Tunneling Memory |
| JPW | Job Processing Word | | |
| JQ | Job Queue | JTP | Job Transfer Program |
| JR | Jouet Rationnel | JTR | Journal Tape Reader |
| JRS | Job Release Scheme | JTRA | Job Task Requirements Analysis |
| JRS | Junction Relay Set | | |
| JS | Jam Strobe | JUB | Job Unit Block |
| JS | Job Scheduler | JUDGE | Judged Utility Decision Generator |
| JS | Job Specification | | |
| JS | Job Statement | JUDY | Just a Useful Device for You |
| JS | Job Stream | | |
| JSB | Job to Subroutine | JUG | Joint Users Group |
| JSD | Jackson-System Development | JUG | Junction Gate |
| | | JUGFET | Junction Gate Field Effect Transistor |
| JSD | Justification Service Digit | | |
| JSI | Job Step Index | JUN | Jump Unconditionally |
| JSIA | Japan Software Industry Association | JURIS | Juristisches Informationssystem |
| JSIA | Joint Service Induction Area | JURIS | Justice Retrieval Inquiry System |
| JSM | Job Stream Manager | JV | Jobvariable |
| JSP | Jackson Structured Programm | JZ | Jump on Zero |

# K

| | | | |
|---|---|---|---|
| K | Kathode | KATERM | Kapazitätsplanungs- und Terminierungssystem |
| K | Kelvin | | |
| K | Kernel | KATP | Keyboard-Actuated Tape Punch |
| K | Key | | |
| K | Kilo | KAU | Keyboard Adapter Unit |
| K | Klystron | KAUB | Kundenauftragsbearbeitung |
| K | Kolonne | KB | Keybank |
| K | Kommunikationstechnik | KB | Keyboard |
| K | Kontakt | KB | Keyboard Button |
| K | Kontrolle | KB | Kilobaud |
| K | Konzentrator | KB | Kilobyte |
| K | Korrektur | KB | Kleinbuchungsautomat |
| K... | Kent Ltd. | KBD | Keyboard |
| KA | Kanalanschluß | KBE | Keyboard Encoder |
| KA | Kanalausgangsschaltung | KBE | Keyboard Entry |
| KA | Kartenart | KBL | Keyboard Lock |
| KA | Kernspeicher-Adreßregister | KBL | Kleinbuchungsautomat mit Lochbandausgabe |
| KA | Key Address | KBM | Knowleage Base Machine |
| KA | Keyed Address | KBP | Keyboard Process |
| KA | Künstliche Anforderung | KBP | Keyboard Punch |
| KAB | Kundenauftragsbestand | KBPS | Kilobits Per Second |
| KAD | Kanaladressendecoder | KBS | Kilobit per Second |
| KADR | Konstruktiver Aufbau Digitaler Rechenanlagen | KBS | Kilobytes per Second |
| | | KBS | Kommunikationsbaustein |
| KADS | Kompatible Anwendungs- und Dialog-Sprache | KBSR | Keyboard B Scale Reset |
| | | KBT | Keyword Branch Table |
| KAG | Kassettengerät | KBU | Keyboard Unlock |
| KAGT | Kassettengerät-Treiber | KBZ | Kreisbetriebszentrum |
| KAL | Klinger Analysis Language | KC | Key Command |
| KALDAS | Kidsgrove ALGOL Digital-Analog Simulation | KC | Key Controlled |
| | | KC | Keyboard Computer |
| KAMAT | Kostenart Material | KC | Keyboard Control |
| KAN | Kanal | KC | Kilocycle |
| KAN | Koppelanordnung | KCB | Keyboard Change Button |
| KANDIDATS | Kansas Digital Image Data System | KCC | Keyboard Common Contact |
| | | KCM | Keyboard Calculating Machine |
| KANOS | Kanzlei-Organisation | | |
| KANU | Kontinuierliche Anlagen-überwachung | KCP | Key Card Punch |
| | | KCP | Keyboard Controlled Printer |
| KAP | Kapazität | | |
| KAP | Kunden-Anwendungs-Programm | KCPS | Kilocycles Per Second |
| | | KCRT | Keyboard Cathode Ray Tube |
| KAPSTA | Kapazitätsstammdatei | | |
| KAR | Kleinanalogrechner | KCS | Kilo Characters per Second |
| KAS | Kontinuierliches Analoges Signal | KCSC | Kidde Computer Services Company |
| KASCHA | Kastriertes Schach | KD | Kartendoppler |
| KASS | Keyboard A Scale Start | KD | Kette von Daten |
| KAT | Key-to-Address Transformation | KD | Key Data |
| | | KD | Key to Disk |
| KAT | Koordinierungsausschuß Terminologie der Information und Dokumentation | KD | Keyboard, Display |
| | | KDB | Koordinaten-Datenbanksystem |

# K

| | | | |
|---|---|---|---|
| KDBS | Kompatible Datenbank-schnittstellen | KEV | Kabelendverteiler |
| KDBS | Kompatible Schnittstelle für Datenbanksysteme | KEWIS | Kommunales Einwohner-Informationssystem |
| KDC | Keyed Display Console | KEYBD | Keyboard |
| KDCS | Kompatible Datenkommu-nikationsschnittstellen | KEYWD | Keyword |
| KDD... | Kokusai Denshin Denwa Corporation | KF | Key Field |
| | | KF | Key Function |
| | | KF | Kompensationsfilter |
| | | KF | Kontrollfeld |
| KDE | Keyboard Data Entry | KF | Koppelfeld |
| KDEC | Kanaldecodierung | KF | Korrelationsfunktion |
| KDH | Key Depressions per Hour | KFA | Koppelfeldanschluß |
| KDKS | Kompatible Datenkommu-nikations-Schnittstelle | KFAM | Keyed File Access Method |
| | | KFS | Kontrollfernschreiber |
| KDN | Kommunale Datenverarbei-tung Nordrhein-Westfalen | KFZ | Kraftfahrzeug |
| | | KFZ-AS | KFZ-Abrechnungs-System |
| KDO | Kommunale Datenverarbei-tung Oldenburg | KG | Kennungsgeber |
| | | KG | Kennzeichengruppe |
| KDOS | Key Display Operating System | KG | Koppelgruppe |
| | | KGE | Key Greater or Equal |
| KDP | Known Datum Point | KGRZ | Kommunale Gebiets-rechenzentren |
| KDR | Keyboard Data Recorder | | |
| KDS | Key Display System | KGS | Known Good System |
| KDS | Kommerzielle Dialog Software | KGS | Kommando-Geräte-Steuerung |
| KDS | Kommunale Datenzentrale Südniedersachsen | KGS | Kommerzielles Gesamt-system |
| KDT | Keyboard Display Terminal | KGST | Kommunale Gemein-schaftsstelle für Ver-waltungsvereinfachung |
| KDVA | Klein-Datenverarbeitungs-anlage | | |
| KDVZ | Kommunale Daten-verarbeitungszentrale | KHS | Krankenhaus-System |
| | | KHz | Kilohertz |
| KE | Kanaleingangsschaltung | KI | Kernspeicher-Informations-register |
| KE | Kanalende | | |
| KE | Karteneinheit | KI | Key Instruction |
| KE | Kern | KI | Keyboard Input |
| KE | Keyboard Entry | KI | Keyboard Inquiry |
| KE | Kinetic Energy | KI | Keyboard Interface |
| KEAS | Knot Equivalent Air Speed | KI | Künstliche Intelligenz |
| KEE | Knowledge Engineering Environment | KIA | Kobus-Interface-Adapter |
| | | KIDES | Kienzle Datenerfassung- und -sammelsystem |
| KEG | Kommission der Euro-päischen Gemeinschaft | | |
| | | KIDES | Kienzle Datenerfassungs-system |
| KEP | Key Entry Processing | | |
| KEP | Konstruktiver Entwick-lungsprozeß | KIE | Kosten pro Informations-einheit |
| KEPROM | Keyed-access EPROM | KIGST | Kirchliche Gemeinschafts-stelle für elektronische Datenverarbeitung |
| KEQ | Key Equal | | |
| KER | Kurzfristige Erfolgs-rechnung | | |
| | | KIK | Kunden- und Interessenten-Kartei |
| KES | Kanaleingangschaltung | | |
| KES | Karteneinschub | KIM | Keyboard Input Matrix |
| KESB | Kompatibles Einseiten-bandsystem | KIM | Kölner Integrationsmodell |
| | | KIN | Keyboard Input |

# K

| | | | |
|---|---|---|---|
| KINET | Kienzle Netzwerksystem | KM | Keyboard Machine |
| KINFIS | Kommunales Integriertes Finanz-Informations-system | KM | Keying Machine |
| | | KM | Klirrfaktormesser |
| | | KM | Knowledge Multiplier |
| KIPO | Keyboard Input Printout | KM | Kommunikationsmanager |
| KIPS | Knowledge Information Processing System | KM | Kritisches Muster |
| | | KM | Kundenmarketing |
| KIS | Keyboard Input Simulation | KMC | Kilomegacycles |
| KIS | Kommunales Informations-system | KMD | Keyword Macro-Definition |
| | | KMDR | Key Marketing Data Report |
| KIS | Krankenhaus-Informations-system | KME | Komplexe Micromodul-einheit |
| KIS | Kriminalpolizeiliches Informations-System | KMER | Kodak Metal Etch Resist |
| KIS | Kunden-Informations-System | KMI | Keyword Macro Instruction |
| | | KMR | Kommandoregister |
| KIS | Kundenintegrierte Schaltung | KMR | Kommunikations-Mikro-rechner |
| KISS | Keep It Short, Stupid! | KMS | Keysort Multiple Selectors |
| KISS | Keep It Simple Sir | KMSD | Konzentrator für Mittel-schnelle Datennetze |
| KISS | Keep It Simple, Stupid! | | |
| KISS | Kennedy Integrated Simulation System | KMU | Kleine und Mittlere Unternehmen |
| KISS | Keyed Indexed Sequential Search | KN | Kommerzieller Nach-richtensender |
| KITEXT | Kienzle Textsystem | KNA | Koppelnetz-Abtaster |
| KIU | Keyboard Interface Unit | KNR | Kursnummer |
| KJS | Kodak Job Sheet | KO | Key Order |
| KK | Karteikarte | KO | Keyword Operand |
| KK | Kartenkennzeichen | KO | Kick-Off |
| KK | Kartenkennzeichnung | KO | Kilo Octet |
| KK | Kugelkopf | KOA | Kostenart |
| KKA | Kreuzkorrelationsanalyse | KOB | Korrekturbereich |
| KKDS | Kompatible Schnittstelle für Komplexe Datenbank-systeme | KÖBES | Kölner Besucher-Informations-System |
| | | KOBUS | Koaxial-Bus |
| KKF | Kostenkontrolle Fremd-leistungen | KOC | Keyboard Oriented Computer |
| KKK | Kundenkontaktkartei | KODAS | Kommunales Datenanalyse-System |
| KL | Kartenleser | | |
| KL | Kartenlocher | KOK | Kontrollkarte |
| KL | Key Length | KOKIS | Kommunales Kraftfahr-zeug-Zulassungs-Informationssystem |
| KL | Key Lever | | |
| KL | Klartext | | |
| KL | Kommalampe | KOLK | Kosten- und Leistungs-rechnung in Kranken-häusern |
| KL | Kontrollampe | | |
| KLA | Klystron Amplifier | | |
| KLDS | Kompatible Schnittstelle für Lineare Datenbank-systeme | KÖLN | Kooperative Ökonomische Lern-Nachhilfen |
| | | KOMPAKS | Kompaktes Anwendungs-paket für Kredit-institute |
| KLE | Kassettenleser | | |
| KLIC | Key Letter In Context | | |
| KLM | Kopf-Lademagneten | KOMPASS | Komplexe Planung Als Sachgebietorientiertes System |
| KLO | Klystron Oscillator | | |
| KLP | Kosten-Leistungsplatz | | |

# K

| | | | |
|---|---|---|---|
| KOMSTAT | Konkurrenz-Machinen-Statistik | KPT | Keyboard Printing Telegraph |
| KOMSTAT | Konkurrenz-Maschinen-Status | KPV | Kurzprüfverfahren |
| KON | Konsole | KR | Keying Relay |
| KONKORD | Kundenorientiertes System für Kreditinstitute mit Online Datenerfassung und Realtime-Disposition | KR | Kleinrechner |
| | | KR | Koinzidenzregister |
| | | KR | Kommunikationsrechner |
| | | KR | Koppelreihe |
| | | KR | Korrekturregler |
| KONST | Konstante | KRA | Kleinabrechnungsautomat |
| KOP | Kaufmännisch Orientierte Programmiersprache | KRA | Kleinrechenanlage |
| | | KRA | Korrelations- und Regressionsanalyse |
| KOPIAS | Kommunikationsorientiertes Produktions-, Informations- und Abrechnungssystem | KRE | Kreditoren |
| | | KRED | Kreditwesen |
| | | KRP | Kombinierte Routine-Prüfeinrichtung |
| KOPS | Kilo Operationen Pro Sekunde | | |
| | | KRS | Kleinrechnersystem |
| KOPS | Kilo Opérations Par Seconde | KRSB | Kompatibles Restseitenbandsystem |
| KOR | Kommandoregister | KRU | Kilo Ressources Unit |
| KOR | Kostenrechnung | KRZN | Kommunales Rechenzentrum Niederrhein |
| KORSTIC | Korea Scientific and Technological Information Centre | | |
| | | KS | Kartenstanzer |
| | | KS | Kellerspeicher |
| KOS | Kent On-Line System | KS | Kernspeicher |
| KOS | Konstantenspeicher | KS | Key Sender |
| KOSIMA | Kontrollen, Signale und Maschinelle Analysen | KS | Keying Sequence |
| | | KS | Keying Speed |
| KOZ | Kürzeste-Operationszeit | KS | Kontrollsignal |
| KP | Key Pulsing | KS | Kontrollstreifen |
| KP | Key Punch | KSAD | Körperschaftssätze-Adressensatz |
| KP | Keyboard Perforator | | |
| KP | Keyboard Punch | KSAM | Keyed Sequential Access Method |
| KP | Keyword Parameter | | |
| KP | Kickplate | KSD | Kontrollstreifenausdruck |
| KP | Koppelpunkt | KSD | Kontrollstreifendruck |
| KP | Kurzwahlprogrammspeicher | KSDS | Key Sequenced Data Set |
| | | KSDS | Kompatible Systemdatei-Schnittstelle |
| KPC | Key Punch Cabinet | | |
| KPC | Keyboard Priority Controller | KSE | Kanalsteuereinheit |
| | | KSE | Kernspeicher, Extern |
| KPE | Key-Point Error | KSE | Keyboard Source Entry |
| KPIC | Key Phrase In Context | KSG | Kartensteuergerät |
| KPO | Key Performance Objectives | KSOC | Key Symbol Out of Context |
| | | KSP | Kernspeicher |
| KPO | Key-Punch Operator | KSP | Keyset Panel |
| KPP | Keyboard Page Printer | KSPA | Krupp Standardsystem Personalabrechnung |
| KPP | Keypoint Program | | |
| KPR | Kodak Photoresist | KSPA | Krupp Standardsystem Personalverwaltung und -Abrechnung |
| KPS | Keypunch Performance System | | |
| | | KSPS | Konzentratorsteuerprogrammsystem |
| KPSM | Klystron Power Supply Modulator | | |

# K

| | | | |
|---|---|---|---|
| KSR | Keyboard Send/Receive | KVL | Konzentratorverbindungsleitung |
| KSR | Kleinsteuerrechner | | |
| KSST | Kernspeichersteuerung | KVM | Koppelvielfachmarkierung |
| KST | Kanalsteuerung | KVP | Kilovolt Peak |
| KST | Kartenstanzer | KVS | Kundenverantwortlicher Service |
| KST | Known Segment Table | | |
| KST | Kostenstelle | KVST | Knotenvermittlungsstelle |
| KSU | Key Service Unit | KW | Keyword |
| KSU | Key Storage Unit | KW | Kilowatt |
| KT | Kennzeichentaste | KW | Kilo-Wort |
| KT | Keyboard Transmitter | KWA | Kommunikations-Wertanalyse |
| KT | Kommataste | | |
| KTFR | Kodak Thin Film Resist | KWAC | Key Word And Context |
| KTK | Kolonnen-Treiber-Karte | KWAC | Key Word Augmented in Context |
| KTN | Kontrollnummer | | |
| KTR | Keyboard Typing Reperforator | KWD | Keyword |
| | | KWE | Kennwertermittlung |
| KTS | Key Telephone System | KWEST | Key Word Extracted as a String of Terms |
| KTS | Komitee für Terminologie und Sprachfragen | KWI | Kreditinstitute auf dem Weg zum Informationssystem |
| KTU | Key Telephone Unit | | |
| KTV | Kongreß für Textverarbeitung | | |
| | | KWIC | Keyword In Context |
| KTZ | Konzentratorzentrale | KWIP | Key Word In Permutation |
| KU | Kanalumschalter | KWIT | Keyword In Title |
| KU | Kanalumsetzer | KWO | Keyword Ordered |
| KU | Kurzunterbrechung | KWOC | Keyword Out of Context |
| KU | Kurzzeitunterbrechung | KWOT | Keyword Out of Title |
| KUA | Kartenunterart | KWS | Kurzwellensender |
| KUB | Kurztest-Band | KWUDC | Keyword and Universal Decimal Classification |
| KUDIS | Kurzfristige Disposition | | |
| KUED | Kodak Unitized Engineering Data | KWY | Keyway |
| | | KY | Keying |
| KUIPNET | Kyoto University Information Processing Network | KY | Keying device |
| | | KYBD | Keyboard |
| KUMA | Kurzfristige Maschinenbelastung | KZ | Kennziffer |
| | | KZ | Knotenzentrale |
| KUP | Kanalumschalteplatte | KZB | Kennzeichen Bearbeitung |
| KUT | Keyboard Under Test | KZE | Kanalzustandserkenner |
| KV | Kanalverstärker | KZE | Koppelnetz-Zugriffseinrichtung |
| KV | Kilovolt | | |
| KV | Koppelvielfach | KZL | Kennzeichenliste |
| KVA | Kilovolt Ampere | KZR | Kanalzustandsregister |
| KVAC | Kilovolt Alternating Current | KZU | Kennzeichen für Umschlüsselung |
| KVCP | Kilovolt Constant Potential | KZU | Kennzeichenumsetzer |
| | | KZW | Kurzzeitwecker |

# L

| | | | |
|---|---|---|---|
| L | Label | LA | Light wire Armoured |
| L | Lamp | LA | Lightning Arrester |
| L | Large | LA | Line Adapter |
| L | Latitude | LA | Line Addressing |
| L | Launch | LA | Link Address |
| L | Left | LA | Link Allotter |
| L | Leistung | LA | Linker Akkumulator |
| L | Length | LA | Linking Address |
| L | Lengthwise | LA | Load Address |
| L | Leseleitung | LA | Location Address |
| L | Level | LA | Logarithmic Amplifier |
| L | Lichtgriffel | LA | Logic Automation |
| L | Lichtstift | LA | Look Ahead |
| L | Lift | LA | Low Angle |
| L | Line | LAA | Load Area Address |
| L | List | LAAS | Laboratoire d'Automatique et d'Analyse des Systèmes |
| L | Liste | | |
| L | Listening | | |
| L | Load | LAB | Label |
| L | Lochen | LAB | Leitungsanschlußbaugruppe |
| L | Locher | LAB | Line Adapter Base |
| L | Lochkarte | LABIS | Laboratory Information System |
| L | Logarithm | | |
| L | Logarithmic | LABTYP | Label Type |
| L | Logik | LAC | Load Accumulator |
| L | Long | LAC | Logic AND Circuit |
| L | Looper | LACE | Local Automatic Circuit Exchange |
| L | Low | | |
| L | Lumen | LACES | London Airport Cargo EDP Scheme |
| L | Luminance | | |
| L-EDV/PRT | Leiteinrichtung für Elektronische Datenverarbeitung und Prozeßrechentechnik | LACES | Los Angeles Council for Engineering Societies |
| | | LACIRS | Latin American Communication Information Retrieval System |
| L-I-W | Loss-In-Weight | | |
| L-R DSB | Left minus Right Double Sideband | LACONIQ | Laboratory Computer Online Inquiry |
| L/H | Low-to-High | LACR | Low Altitude Coverage Radar |
| L/M | Lines per Minute | | |
| L/MF | Low and Medium Frequency | LAD | Laufende Adresse |
| | | LAD | Load Address |
| L/R | Locus of Radius | LAD | Location Aid Device |
| L/W | Lumen/Watt | LAD | Logarithmic Analog to Digital |
| LØ | Level Zero | | |
| LA | Label | LAD | Logic and Adder |
| LA | Laboratory Automation | LAD | Logical Aptitude Device |
| LA | Laden Adresse | LAD | Low Accuracy Data |
| LA | Lag Angle | LADAPT | Lookup dictionary Adapter program |
| LA | Lead Angle | | |
| LA | Leading Address | LADB | Laboratory Animal Data Bank |
| LA | Learning Automaton | | |
| LA | Left Address | LADER | Life Assurance Direct Entry and Retrieval |
| LA | Lehrautomat | | |
| LA | Leistungsausrüstung | LADIES | Los Alamos Digital Image Enhancement Software |
| LA | Level Amplifier | | |

# L

| | | | |
|---|---|---|---|
| LADS | Linear Analysis and Design of Structures | LAMP | Labour And Materials Planning |
| LADS | Listener Addressed State | LAMP | Library Additions and Maintenance Program |
| LADS | Logic Automation Documentation System | LAMP | Logic Analyzer for Maintenance Planner |
| LADT | Local Area Data Transport | | |
| LAE | Left Arithmetic Element | LAMP | Logic Analyzer for Maintenance Planning |
| LAE | Leitungsanpassungseinheit | | |
| LAE | Leitungsanschlußeinsatz | LAMSAC | Local Authorities Management Services And Computer committee |
| LAE | Linear Algebraic Equation | | |
| LAEC | Los Angeles Electronic Club | LAN | Landing aid |
| LAF | Long Address Format | LAN | Local Area Network |
| LAFIS | Local Authority Financial Information System | LANAC | Laminar Navigation and Anti-Collision system |
| LAG | Load And Go assembler | LANCE | Local Aera Network Controller for Ethernet |
| LAGER | Layout Generating Routine | | |
| LAGER | Light-table Artwork Generation | LANDS | Language Development System |
| LAH | Logical Analyzer of Hypothesis | LANG | Language |
| | | LANKO | Lebensmittel-Anwendungs-Konzept |
| LAHA | Linear Array Hybrid Assembly | LANKO | Lebensmittelhandel-Anwendungskonzept |
| LAIICS | Latin American Institute for Information and Computer Sciences | LANNET | Large Artificial Nerve Net |
| | | LANNET | Large Artificial Neuron Network |
| LAIRS | Labor Agreement Information Retrieval System | LAP | Lattice Assessment Program |
| LAL | Local Adjunct Language | | |
| LAL | Location Administration List | LAP | Lenslett Array Processor |
| | | LAP | Lesson Assembly Program |
| LAL | Lower Acceptance Level | LAP | Linear Arithmetic Processor |
| LALR | Left After Left-Right | | |
| LALS | Logic Automation Layout System | LAP | Link Access Procedure |
| | | LAP | Link Access Protocol |
| LALSD | Language for Automated Logic and System Design | LAP | List Assembly Program |
| | | LAP | List Assembly Programming |
| LAM | Laminated | | |
| LAM | Line Adapter Module | LAP | Load, Assemble Pack |
| LAM | Load Accumulator with Magnitude | LAP | Location Administration Practice |
| LAM | Loop Adder and Modifier | LAP A | Line Access Protocol Asynchronous mode |
| LAM | Loop Addition and Modification | LAP B | Line Access Protocol Balanced mode |
| LAMA | Langfristige Maschinenbelastung | LAP-B | Link Access Procedure Balanced |
| LAMA | Local Automatic Message Accounting | LAPADS | Lightweight Acoustic Processing and Display System |
| LAMBDA | Language for Manufacturing Business and Distribution Activities | | |
| | | LAPDOG | Low-Altitude Pursuit Drive On Ground |
| LAMIS | Local Authority Management Information System | LAPUT | Light Activated Programmable Unijunction Transistor |
| LAMIS | Los Angeles Municipal Information System | | |

# L

| | | | |
|---|---|---|---|
| LAPX | Link Access Protocol half-duplex | LASER | Light Amplification by Stimulated Emission of Radiation |
| LAR | Local Acquisition Radar | | |
| LAR | Low Angle Reentry | LASIE | Library Automated Systems Information Exchange |
| LARAM | Line Addressable RAM | | |
| LARC | Large Automatic Research Computer | LASL | Los Alamos Scientific Laboratory |
| LARC | Leukocyte Automatic Recognition Computer | LASOS | Laser Annealed Silicon On Sapphire |
| LARC | Library Automation and Research Communications | LASP | Local Attached Support Processor |
| LARC | Life Assurance Rates Calculation | LASPR | Lastprognose-Programm |
| LARC | Livermore Automatic Research Calculator | LASR | Letter writing with Automatic Send-Receive |
| LARC | Livermore Automatic Research Computer | LASS | Laser Activated Semiconductor Switch |
| LARCT | Last Radio Contact | LASS | Library Automated Service System |
| LARDS | Low Accuracy Radar Data transmission System | LASS | Light Activated Silicon Switch |
| LARDTS | Low Accuracy Radar Data Transmission System | LASS | Line Analog Speech Synthesizer |
| LARIAT | Laser Radar Intelligence Acquisition Technology | LASSO | Laser Search and Secure Observer |
| LARS | Logisches Arbeitsrechnersystem | LAST | Logic Analysis and Simulation Technique |
| LARSIS | Library Association Reference and Special Information Section | LAT | Lateral |
| | | LAT | Latitude |
| | | LAT | Leitungsanpassungsteil |
| LAS | Large Astronomical Satellite | LAT | Local Apparent Time |
| LAS | Leitungsanschlußsteuerung | LATAR | Laser Augmented Target Acquisition and Recognition |
| LAS | Light Activated Switch | | |
| LAS | Line Adapter Set | LATPK | Latch Pick |
| LAS | Location Administration Standard | LATRIX | Light Accessible Transistor matrix |
| LAS | Logic Analysis System | LATS | Litton Automated Test Set |
| LAS | Logical Assignment Statement | LATS | Long-Acting Thyroid Stimulator |
| LAS | Logische Algorithmenschemata | LATV | Logic and Array Test Vehicle |
| LAS | Low-Altitude Satellite | LAU | Line Adapter Unit |
| LAS | Luftfracht-Abwicklungs-System | LAU | Lower Arithmetic Unit |
| | | LAUF | Lochstreifenaufbereitung |
| LASA | Large Aperture Seismic Array | LAVA | Linear Amplifier for Various Applications |
| LASCR | Light-Activated Silicon-Controlled Rectifier | LAW | Local Air Warning |
| | | LAYDET | Layer Detection |
| LASAR | Logic Analysis Stimulus And Response | LAZ | Lampenanzeige |
| | | LB | Lecteur de Bande |
| LASAR | Logic Automated Stimulus And Response | LB | Letter Blank |
| | | LB | Library |
| LASEORS | London And South Eastern Operational Research Society | LB | Line Buffer |
| | | LB | Load Block |

# L

| | | | |
|---|---|---|---|
| LB | Local Battery | LC | Line Circuit |
| LB | Lochband | LC | Line Code |
| LBA | Lochbandausgabegerät | LC | Line Connector |
| LBB | Logical Building Block | LC | Line Construction |
| LBBB | Left Bundle Branch Block | LC | Line Counter |
| LBD | Logic Block Diagram | LC | Line of Communication |
| LBE | Leit- und Bedieneinrichtung | LC | Line of Contact |
| | | LC | Link Circuit |
| LBE | Lochbandeingabe | LC | Link Connection |
| LBE | Lochbandeingabegerät | LC | Liquid Crystal |
| LBE | Lochbandeinlesen | LC | Load Card |
| LBF | Lagerbestandsführung für den Handel | LC | Load Carrier |
| | | LC | Load Cell |
| LBF | Load Bit Field | LC | Load Center |
| LBG | Load Balancing Group | LC | Load Compensating |
| LBJCC | London Borough Joint Computer Committee | LC | Location Counter |
| | | LC | Logic Cell |
| LBK | Lochbandkarte | LC | Logic Corporation |
| LBKZ | Lochbandkennzeichen | LC | Logical Channel |
| LBL | Label | LC | Logical Circuit |
| LBL | Lochbandleser | LC | Lokalisierungscode |
| LBLTYP | Label Type | LC | Loss of Contract |
| LBM | Load Buffer Memory | LC | Lower Case |
| LBN | Logical Block Number | LC | Lower Characters |
| LBO | Logical Base Operator | LC | Lower Control |
| LBP | Lenght Between Perpendiculars | LC | Luminosity Class |
| | | LC/SLT | Low Cost/Solid Logic Technology |
| LBP | Line Binder Post | | |
| LBP | Lochbandpuffer | LCA | Library Communication Area |
| LBR | Laser Beam Recording | | |
| LBRC | Left Bomb Release Computer | LCA | Local Communication Adapter |
| LBRET | Label Return | LCAP | Loop Carrier Analysis Program |
| LBRT | Lochbandroutine | | |
| LBS | Line Buffer System | LCARRC | Linear Combine Array Rows according to Row Components |
| LBS | Local Buffer Store | | |
| LBS | Lochbandstanzer | | |
| LBS | Lochbandstation | LCB | Line Control Block |
| LBS | Lochstreifenbetriebssystem | LCB | Line to Computer Buffer |
| | | LCB | Load Descriptor Block |
| LBST | Lochbandstanzer | LCB | Low Cost Bipolar |
| LBT | Listen-Before-Talk | LCC | Language for Conversational Computing |
| LBT | Low Bit Test | | |
| LBU | Launcher Booster Unit | LCC | Last Column Contact |
| LBX | Lexar Business Exchange | LCC | Launch Control Center |
| LC | Label Checking | LCC | Leadless-Chip Carrier |
| LC | Large Card | LCC | Liquid Crystal Cell |
| LC | Last Card | LCC | Local Communications Complex |
| LC | Late Commitment | | |
| LC | Layout Character | LCC | Low-Cost-Communication |
| LC | Lead Covered | LCCA | Low Cost Calculating Attachment |
| LC | Leading Card | | |
| LC | Length Code | LCCA | Low Cost Calculator Attachment |
| LC | Level Control | | |
| LC | Line Carrying | | |

# L

| | | | |
|---|---|---|---|
| LCCA | Low Cost Computer Attachment | LCK | Lock |
| LCCC | Launch Control Center Computer | LCL | Limited Channel Logout |
| | | LCL | Linkage Control Language |
| | | LCL | Local |
| LCCC | Leadless Ceramic Chip Carrier | LCL | Lower Card Lever |
| | | LCL | Lower Control Limit |
| LCCN | Library of Congress Card Number | LCL MOD | Local Mode |
| | | LCL TMOUT | Local Timeout |
| LCCP | Life Cycle Computer Program | LCLS-SLT | Low Cost Low Speed Solid Logic Technology |
| LCD | Least Common Denominator | LCLU | Landing Control and Logic Unit |
| LCD | Line Control Definer | LCLV | Liquid Crystal Light Valve |
| LCD | Liquid Crystal Display | | |
| LCD | Local Climatological Data | LCM | Large Capacity Memory |
| LCD | Lowest Common Denominator | LCM | Large Core Memory |
| | | LCM | Least Common Multiple |
| LCDDS | Leased Circuit Digital Data Service | LCM | Low Cost Memory |
| | | LCM | Low Cost Module |
| LCDPRGSTR | Last Card Program Start | LCM | Lowest Common Multiple |
| LCDTE | Last Cut Date | LCN | Load Classification Number |
| LCDTL | Load-Compensated Diode Transitor Logic | LCN | Local Computer Networks |
| LCDTL | Low Current Diode Transistor Logic | LCO | Langage de Commande des Opérations |
| LCE | Launch Complex Equipment | LCO | Langage de Contrôle des Opérations |
| LCER | Library Computer Equipment Review | LCO | Latching Contact Operate |
| | | LCO | Logical Circuit Operator |
| LCES | Least Cost Estimating and Scheduling | LCOM | Line of Communication |
| | | LCOSS | Lead Computing Optical Sighting System |
| LCF | Local Cycle Fatigue | | |
| LCF | Low Cost File | LCP | Language Conversion Processor |
| LCFS | Last Come First Served | | |
| LCFSPR | Last Come First Served Pre-emptive Resumé | LCP | Language Conversion Program |
| LCG | Look-ahead Carry Generator | LCP | Large Computer Project |
| | | LCP | Last Card Program start |
| LCGS | Lead Computing Gun Sight | LCP | Left handed Circular Polarization |
| LCGT/IGS | Low Cost Graphics Terminal/Interactive Graphics System | | |
| | | LCP | Link Control Procedure |
| | | LCP | Loading Control Program |
| LCH | Load Channel | LCP | Logique de Construction des Programmes |
| LCH | Logical Channel queue | | |
| LCHT | Logical Channel Table | LCP | Loi de Construction des Programmes |
| LCI | Last Card Indication | | |
| LCI | Learner Centred Instruction | LCPRD | Low Cost Page Reader |
| | | LCPS | Last Card, Program Start |
| LCI | Learner Controlled Instruction | LCQ | Logical Channel Queue |
| | | LCR | Label Checking Routine |
| LCI | Listing Control Instruction | LCR | Laboratoire Central de Recherches |
| LCI | Logarithmic Computing Instrument | | |
| | | LCR | Level Counter Register |
| LCIE | Laboratoire Central des Industries Electriques | LCR | Level Crossing Rate |
| | | LCR | Load Complement Register |

# L

| | | | |
|---|---|---|---|
| LCROS | Large Capacity Read Only Storage | LDA | Lost Data |
| | | LDAD | Lokaldaten-Adressensatz |
| LCS | Label Control Statement | LDAS | Logic Design Automation System |
| LCS | Laboratory of Computer Science | LDB | Large Data Base |
| LCS | Large Capacity Storage | LDB | Load B-register |
| LCS | Large Capacity Store | LDB | Local Data Buffer |
| LCS | Large Computer System | LDC | Laboratory Data Control |
| LCS | Large Core Storage | LDC | Laser Discharge Capacitor |
| LCS | Large Core Store | LDC | Latitude Data Computer |
| LCS | Lateral Channel Stop | LDC | Line Data Channel |
| LCS | Least Cost Scheduling | LDC | Line Drop Compensator |
| LCS | Line Coding Storage | LDC | Liquidated Damage Clause |
| LCS | Logique de Conception des Systèmes | LDC | Listing Desk Calculator |
| | | LDC | Location Dependent Code |
| LCT | Last Card Total | LDC | Lower Dead Centre |
| LCT | Linkage Control Table | LDD | Langage de Définition des Données |
| LCTDL | Load Compensated Transistor Diode Logic | LDD | Low Density Data |
| LCU | Local Control Unit | LDDI | Local Distributed Data Interface |
| LCU | Logical Control Unit | | |
| LCVD | Least Coincidence Voltage Detector | LDDL | Logical Data Definition Language |
| LCW | Lock Control Word | LDDS | Low Density Data System |
| LCW | Logical Channel Word | LDE | Linear Differential Equation |
| LCZR | Localizer | | |
| LD | Label Definition | LDE | Long-Delay Echo |
| LD | Lamp Driver | LDG | Leading |
| LD | Laserdiode | LDG | Loading |
| LD | Lecteur de Documents | LDI | Langage de Définition des Informations |
| LD | Ledger Device | | |
| LD | Leitung Datenverarbeitung | LDI | Lark-Device-Interface |
| LD | Leitungsdurchschalter | LDI | Lossless Digital Integrator |
| LD | Lethal Dosis | | |
| LD | Line Drawing | LDL | Language Description Language |
| LD | Line Driver | | |
| LD | Linear Decision | LDL | Logic Design Language |
| LD | Load | LDL | Logical Data Language |
| LD | Load Data | LDM | Limited Distance Modem |
| LD | Load Descriptor | LDM | Linear Delta Modulation |
| LD | Loader | LDM | List Data Memory |
| LD | Loading Data | LDM | Load Data from Memory |
| LD | Locate Data | LDM | Load Distribution Matrix |
| LD | Logarithmus Dualis | LDM | Long-Delay Monostable |
| LD | Logic Diagram | LDMOS | Lateral-planar Double-diffused Metal Oxide Semiconductor |
| LD | Logic Driver | | |
| LD | Logical Decision | | |
| LD | Logical Device | LDMOST | Lateral Double-diffused MOST |
| LD | Long Distance | | |
| LD | Loss and Damage | LDMX | Local Digital Message Exchange |
| LD | Lumineszenzdiode | | |
| LDA | Line Data Area | LDN | Logical Device Number |
| LDA | Line Driving Amplifier | LDN | Listed Directory Number |
| LDA | Locate Drum Address | LDO | Logical Device Order |
| LDA | Logical Device Address | LDP | Laboratory Data Processor |

# L

| | | | |
|---|---|---|---|
| LDP | Laboratory Data Products | LE | Light Equipment |
| LDP | Language Data Processing | LE | Linkage Editor |
| LDP | Logical Data Processing | LE | Loading Error |
| LDPC | Logistic Data Processing Centre | LE | Logic Element |
| | | LE-BSS | Leistungselektronik-Bausteinsystem |
| LDPE | Low Density Polyethylene | | |
| LDPT | Load Point | LEA | Light Emitting Array |
| LDR | Light Dependent Resistor | LEA | Line Equalizing Amplifier |
| LDR | Linear Decision Rules | LEA | Linear Embedding Algorithm |
| LDR | Loader | | |
| LDR | Loop Dial Repeating | LEACOS | Leasing Computer System |
| LDR | Low Data Rate | LEADER | Lehigh Automatic Device for Efficient Retrieval |
| LDR | Low Data Register | | |
| LDRA | Low Data Rate Auxiliary | LEADS | Law Enforcement Automated Data System |
| LDRI | Low Data Rate Input | | |
| LDRS | Language Design for Reliable Software | LEADS | Library Experimental Automated Demonstration System |
| LDRT | Low Data Rate | | |
| LDS | Landesamt für Datenverarbeitung und Statistik | LEAF | LISP Extended Algebraic Facility |
| LDS | Large Disk Storage | LEAF | Low Energy Accelerator Facility |
| LDS | Last Data Sample | | |
| LDS | Local Data Processor | LEANS | Lehigh Analog Simulator |
| LDS | Logistics Data Sheet | LEAP | Laboratory Evaluation and Accreditation Program |
| LDS/NW | Landesamt für Datenverarbeitung und Statistik in Nordrhein-Westfalen | LEAP | Lambda Efficiency Analysis Program |
| LDSYS | Load System | LEAP | Language for Expression for Associative Procedures |
| LDT | Level Detector | | |
| LDT | Linear Differential Transformer | LEAP | Leading Edge Account Program |
| LDT | Load Terminate | | |
| LDT | Loader Definition Table | LEAP | Leading Edge Applications Program |
| LDT | Logic Design Translator | | |
| LDT | Logical Device Table | LEAP | Lifetime Element Advancing Program |
| LDT | Long Distance Transmission | LEAP | Lift-off Elevation and Azimuth Programmer |
| LDTX | Logical Device Table Extension | LEAP | Lockheed Electronic Assembly Program |
| LDU | Lamp Display Unit | | |
| LDU | Light Display Unit | LEAP | Logistics Evaluation and Analysis Program |
| LDV | Linguistische Datenverarbeitung | | |
| | | LEAPS | Law Enforcement Agencies Processing System |
| LDVZ | Landesdatenverarbeitungszentrale | | |
| | | LEAR | Logistics Evaluation And Review technique |
| LDWD | Load Word | | |
| LDX | Long Distance Xerography | LEAS | Logisches Eingabe/Ausgabe System |
| LE | Large Enhanced | | |
| LE | Leading Edge | LEAS | Lower Echelon Automatic Switchboard |
| LE | Left End | | |
| LE | Lehreinheit | LEASY | Lineares Ein/Ausgabesystem |
| LE | Leitungsanschlußeinheit | | |
| LE | Leitungsendgerät | LEBIS | Lebensmittel-orientiertes on-line-Informations-System |
| LE | Less than or Equal | | |
| LE | Less than or Equal to | | |

- 353 -

# L

| | | | |
|---|---|---|---|
| LEC | Laboratoire d'Essais des Calculateurs | LES | Local Engineering Standards |
| LEC | Langage Exploitation Condense | LES | Location Engineering Standards |
| LEC | Latest Engineering Change | LES | Lokales Externes Schema |
| LEC | List Execution Condition | LESA | Leitungssatz-Abtaster |
| LECC | Linear Error Correcting Code | LESS | Least cost Estimating and Scheduling System |
| LED | Landesamt für Elektronische Datenverarbeitung | LET | Life Environmental Testing |
| | | LET | Linear Energy Transfer |
| LED | Licht-Emittierende Diode | LET | Location Equivalence Table |
| LED | Lichtemissionsdiode | LET | Logical Equipment Table |
| LED | Light Emitting Diode | LETAM | Low End Telecommunications Access Method |
| LEDAS | Lebensmittel-Dispositions- und Abrechnungssystem | LETI | Laboratoire d'Electronique et de Technologie de l'Informatique |
| LEDD | Light-Emitting Diode Display | | |
| LEDP | Large Electronic Display Panel | LETIS | Leicestershire Technical Information Service |
| LEDS | Law Enforcement Data System | LEVTAB | Level Table |
| | | LEWIS | Low Entry Wholesale Information System |
| LEDT | Limited Entry Decision Table | LEXIS | Lexikographik-Informationssystem |
| LEED | Low-Energy Electron Diffraction | LF | Label Field |
| | | LF | Line Feed |
| LEEDS | Library Exemplary Elementary Demonstration of Springfield | LF | Line Field |
| | | LF | Loadable Format |
| LEF | Light Emitting Film | LF | Logic Function |
| LEFA | Leistungserfassung und -abrechnung | LF | Logical File |
| | | LF | Low Frequencies |
| LEFC | L-band Electronic Frequency Converter | LF | Low Frequency |
| | | LF-VLF | Low Frequency - Very Low Frequency |
| LEGIS | Lerngesteuertes Informationssystem | LFA | Last Field Address |
| LEIN | Law Enforcement Information Network | LFA | Last File Address |
| | | LFA | Logical File Area |
| LEL | Location Engineering List | LFA | Low-Frequency Amplifier |
| LELU | Launch Enable Logic Unit | LFAR | Last Frame Address Register |
| LEMRAS | Law Enforcement Manpower Resource Allocation System | LFB | Location Facilities Bulletin |
| LEN | Length | LFC | L-band Frequency Converter |
| LEN | Light-Emitting Numerics | | |
| LEP | Laboratoire d'Electronique et de Physique appliquée | LFC | Laminar Flow Control |
| | | LFC | Leader First Character |
| | | LFC | Line Feed Code |
| LEP | Location Engineering Practices | LFC | Low Frequency Correction |
| | | LFC | Low Frequency Current |
| LEP | Lowest Effective Power | LFCB | Load FCB |
| LERB | Line Error Block | LFCP | Logic File Control Processor |
| LERMISTOR | Learning Materials Information Store | | |
| | | LFD | Langfristige Datenhaltung |
| LES | Launch Escape System | LFD | Least Fatal Dose |
| LES | Light Emitting Source | LFD | Line Feed |

- 354 -

# L

| | | | |
|---|---|---|---|
| LFDF | Low Frequency Direction Finder | LH | Latent Heat |
| LFE | Logarithmic Feedback Element | LH | Left Hand |
| | | LH | Link Header |
| | | LH | Load Halfword |
| LFG | Low Frequency Generator | LH | Low noise High output |
| LFL | Location Facilities List | LH | Low-High |
| LFM | Line Feed Mechanism | LH | Lower Halt |
| LFM | Linear Frequency Modulator | LH | Lower Hold |
| | | LH/RH | Left Hand/Right Hand |
| LFM | Logic Feasibility Model | LHASA | Logic and Heuristic Applied to Synthetic Analysis |
| LFM | Logical File Member | | |
| LFO | Low-Frequency Oscillator | | |
| LFP | Location Facilities Practice | LHC | Left Hand Components |
| | | LHCOMPO | Left Hand Components |
| LFQ | Light Foot Quantizer | LHCP | Left Hand Circular Polarization |
| LFR | Line-Frequency Rejection | | |
| LFRD | Lot Fraction Reliability Deviation | LHD | Left Hand Drive |
| | | LHE | Left Hand End |
| LFS | Location Facilities Standard | LHK | Last Hunt Key |
| | | LHM | Left Hand circulary polarized Mode |
| LFS | Logical File System | | |
| LFS | Loop Feedback Signal | LHR | Lower Hybrid Resonance |
| LFSA | Low Frequency Spectrum Analyzer | LHTR | Lighthouse Transmitter-Receiver |
| LFSR | Linear Feedback Shift Register | LI | Label Identification |
| | | LI | Label Identifier |
| LFT | Leap-Frog Test | LI | Label Information |
| LFT | Left | LI | Language Interpretation |
| LFT | Lensless Fourier Transformation | LI | Level Indicator |
| | | LI | Librarian |
| LFT | Logical File Transfer | LI | Link Interface |
| LFU | Least Frequently Used | LI | Linking Instruction |
| LG | Landing Gear | LI | List Instruction |
| LG | Leg | LI | Load Instruction |
| LG | Length | LI | Location Identifier |
| LG | Line Generator | LI | Logic Instruction |
| LG | Logging | LI | Low Intensity |
| LG | Logik | LI/ON | Logical Input/Output Network |
| LG | Loop Gain | | |
| LGA | Light-Gun Amplifier | LIA | Label Information Area |
| LGA | Logical Add | LIASS | Logistik-Informations-Auswertungs-Steuerungs-System |
| LGE | Logic Gate Expander | | |
| LGG | Light-Gun pulse Generator | | |
| LGI | Lohn- und Gehaltsabrechnung für die Industrie | LIB | Library |
| | | LIB | Line Interface Base |
| LGL | Logical Left | LIB/AM | Librarian/Access Method |
| LGM | Logical Multiply | LIBAUDIT | Librarian Auditing facility |
| LGN | Line Gate Number | | |
| LGN | Logical Group Number | LIBGIS | Library General Information Survey |
| LGN | Logical Negation | | |
| LGP | Language Generator and Processor | LIBGIS | Library General Information System |
| LGR | Leitungsgruppe | LIBNAT | Library Network Analysis Theory |
| LGR | Logical Right | | |
| LGTH | Length | | |

# L

| | | | |
|---|---|---|---|
| LIBOL | Litton Business Oriented Language | LIMS | Laboratory Information Management System |
| LIBR | Library | LIMSI | Laboratoire d'Informatique pour la Mécanique et les Sciences de l'Ingénieur |
| LIBSY | Licht-Bus-System | | |
| LIC | Langage Intermédiaire Condensé | | |
| LIC | Last-In-Chain | LIN | Line |
| LIC | Last-Instruction-Cycle | LIN | Line Item Number |
| LIC | Line Integrated Circuit | LINAC | Linear Accelerator |
| LIC | Linear Integrated Circuit | LINC | Laboratory Instrument Computer |
| LICOF | Land lines Communications Facilities | LINC | Langage Interactif Naturel de Création de Programme |
| LID | Leadless Inverted Device | | |
| LID | Lehrer-Individual-Datei | LINC | Lincoln Computer |
| LID | Lehrinstitut für Dokumentation | LINC | Logischer Informations-Netz-Computer |
| LID | Leitstelle für Information und Dokumentation | LINCOTT | Liaison, Interface, Coupling, Technology Transfer |
| LID | Locked-In Device | | |
| LIDAR | Light Detection And Ranging | LINCS | Language Information Network and Clearinghouse System |
| LIDIA | Learning In Dialog | | |
| LIDIA | Lernen Im Dialog | LINCS | Large scale Information Control System |
| LIDS | Logistics Integrated Data System | LIND | Line Description |
| LIEF | Launch Information Exchange Facility | LINGO | Linear Network-analysis by General Operations |
| LIFA | Linzer Interaktiver FORTRAN Analyzer | LINK | Lambeth Information Network |
| LIFMOP | Linearly Frequency-Modulated Pulse | LINKLIB | Linked Library |
| | | LINS | LORAN Inertial System |
| LIFO | Last-In, First-Out | LIO | Leiten, Informieren, Organisieren |
| LIFT | Logically Integrated FORTRAN Translator | LIO | Local Interconnect Option |
| LII | Lease Installed Inventory | LIOC | Lighted Independent Of Computer |
| LIIIV | Limited Information Iterated Instrumental Variable | LIOCS | Logical Input Output Control System |
| LIKOM | Lichtbus-Koppelmodul | LIOM | Line Input/Output Manager |
| LIL | Law of the Iterated Logarithm | LIP | Local Initiatives Program |
| | | LIPL | Linear Information Processing Language |
| LILO | Last In Last Out | | |
| LIM | Limit | LIPS | Laboratory Information Processing System |
| LIM | Line Interface Module | | |
| LIM | Logic In Memory | LIPS | Laboratory Interconnection Programming System |
| LIMAC | Large Integrated Monolithic Array Computer | | |
| | | LIPS | Laser Image Processing Scanner |
| LIMES | Litton-Management-Erfolgssystem | LIR | Line Integral Refractometer |
| LIMFAC | Limiting Factor | | |
| LIML | Limited Information Maximum Likelihood | LIR | Load-Indicating Resistor |
| | | LIRES | Literature Retrieval System |
| LIMP | Language-Independent Macro-Processor | LIRF | Low Intensity Reciprocity Failure |

# L

| | | | |
|---|---|---|---|
| LIRG | Library and Information Research Group | LISTIO | List current Input/Output assignments |
| LIROC | Last Instruction Read Out Cycle | LISTS | Library Information System Time-Sharing |
| LIRS | Lance Information Retrieval System | LISY | Library Information System |
| LIRS | Library Information Retrieval System | LIT | Load Initial Table |
| LIS | Label Information Statement | LIT | Liquid Injection Technique |
| LIS | Laboratory Information System | LIT | Logical Interface Tape |
| LIS | Landesinformationssystem | LIT FILE | Lesson Information Table File |
| LIS | Leistungsinformationssystem | LITA/ISAS | Library and Information Technology Association/ Information Science and Automation Section |
| LIS | Library and Information Science | LITASTOR | Light Tapping Storage |
| LIS | Lineare Integrierte Schaltung | LITE | Legal Information Through Electronics |
| LIS | Lockheed Information System | LITS | Laboratory for Information Transmission Systems |
| LIS | Logical IF Statement | LIU | Logic Input and Update |
| LIS | Lokales Internes Schema | LIU | Logical Installable Unit |
| LIS | Loop Input Signal | LIU | Logical Installation Unit |
| LIS | Lot Inspection Summary | LIU | Logical Installment Unit |
| LIS | Low-Inductance Stripline | LIV | Legislative Indexing Vocabulary |
| LISA | LARC Instruction Assembly | LIV | Low Input Voltage |
| LISA | Library Systems Analysis | LIVC | Low Input Voltage Converter |
| LISA | Linear System Analysis | LIVCR | Low Input Voltage Conversion Regulation |
| LISA | Local Integrated Software Architecture | LJE | Local Job Entry |
| LISARDS | Library Information Search And Retrieval Data System | LJP | Local Job Processing |
| | | LK | Leitungskonzentrator |
| | | LK | Letzte Karte |
| | | LK | Link |
| LISMEX | Library and Information Science Meeting Exchange | LK | Lochkarte |
| | | LKA | Lochkartenanlage |
| LISP | List Processing | LKA | Lochkartenausgabe |
| LISP | List Processor | LKB | Lochkartenbeschrifter |
| LISP | List Programming | LKE | Lochkarteneingabe |
| LISP | Listensprache | LKED | Linkage Editor |
| LIST | Language for Input Simulation | LKG | Leakage |
| | | LKG | Lochkartengerät |
| LIST | Library and Information Science Today | LKK | Lochkartenkennzeichen |
| | | LKK | Lochkennkarte |
| LIST | Logisch-Integrative Strukturierung von Texten | LKL | Lochkartenleser |
| | | LKL | Lochkartenlocher |
| | | LKLS | Lochkartenleser/-stanzer |
| LISTAR | Lincoln Information Storage and Associative Retrieval | LKM | Lochkartenmaschine |
| | | LKP | Lochkartenprüfer |
| | | LKR | Lochkartenrechner |
| LISTEN | Library and Information Science Training and Education Network | LKS | Lochkartenstanzer |
| | | LKS | Lokales Konzeptuelles Schema |

# L

| | | | |
|---|---|---|---|
| LKSAA | Lokales Kommunikationssystem im Auswärtigen Amt | LLRM | Low-Level Radio Modulator |
| LKV | Lochkartenverarbeitung | LLS | Low Level Subroutine |
| LKV | Lochkartenverfahren | LLT | Load Library Tape |
| LKZ | Landeskennzahl | LM | Large Memory |
| LL | Light Line | LM | Laser Memory |
| LL | Limited Liability | LM | Latch Magnet |
| LL | Linking Loader | LM | Learning Machine |
| LL | Liquid Limit | LM | Learning Matrix |
| LL | Live Load | LM | Library Material |
| LL | Load Long | LM | Line Mark |
| LL | Loader Library | LM | Linear Memory |
| LL | Local Loop | LM | Load Mode |
| LL | Lochstreifenleser | LM | Load Module |
| LL | Logical Line | LM | Load Multiple |
| LL | Loudness Level | LM | Logical Multiplication |
| LL | Low Level | LM | Logical Multiply |
| LL | Lower Limit | LM | Lumen |
| LL | Lücke Löschen | LMAD | Logic Machine Aids Digital |
| LL-BAM | Lincoln Laboratory - Boolean Algebra Minimizer | LMARS | Library Management And Retrieval System |
| LLA | Load List Area | LMB | Location Manufacturing Bulletin |
| LLC | Logic Level Control | LMCP | Laboratory Module Computer |
| LLC | Logical Link Control | | |
| LLC | Low Level Code | LMCSS | Letter Mail Code Sort System |
| LLCTL | Last Line Control | | |
| LLE | Load List Element | LMD | Logarithmic Mean Difference |
| LLF | Lichtleitfaser | | |
| LLF | Link Line Frame | LMF | Linear Matched Filter |
| LLFET | Linear Load Field Effect Transistor | LMGEN | Load Module Generator |
| | | LMI | Linear Matrix Inequality |
| LLFM | Landline Frequency Modulation | LMI | Logistics Management Information |
| LLG | Line-to-Line-to-Ground | LMIC | Liquid Metals Information Center |
| LLG | Logical Line Group | | |
| LLGL | Low Level Graphical Language | LMICS | Logistics Management Information and Control System |
| LLIV | Low Level Input Voltage | | |
| LLL | Local-Local Link | LMIS | Labour Market Information System |
| LLL | Loose Leaf Ledger | | |
| LLL | Low Level Language | LMIS | Logistics Management Information System |
| LLL | Low Level Logic | | |
| LLLTV | Low-Light-Level Television | LML | Lagemaschinenlogik |
| | | LML | Location Manufacturing List |
| LLO | Local Lock Out | | |
| LLPI | Logical Low Power Inverter | LMLR | Load Memory Lockout Register |
| LLPN | Lumped, Linear, Parametric Network | LMN | Load Matching Network |
| | | LMO | Lens-Modulated Oscillator |
| LLR | Load Limiting Resistor | LMO | Linear Master Oscillator |
| LLR | Long Length Record | LMP | Light Metal Products |
| LLRD | Long Life Recording Data | LMP | Location Manufacturing Practice |
| LLRES | Load-Limiting Resistor | | |

# L

| | | | |
|---|---|---|---|
| LMR | Library Maintenance Routine | LO | Lieferorder |
| LMR | Lineare Mehrfach-regression | LO | Lift-Off |
| | | LO | Load |
| | | LO | Local Oscillator |
| LMRS | Lockheed Maintenance Recording System | LO | Lochung |
| | | LO | Lock-On |
| LMS | Least Mean Square | LO | Lock-Out |
| LMS | Level Measuring Set | LO | Log |
| LMS | Library Maintenance System | LO | Logic Operand |
| | | LO | Logic Operator |
| LMS | Library Management System | LO | Logical Operation |
| | | LO | Low |
| LMS | Location Manufacturing Standard | LO | Low Order |
| | | LO... | Lorenz |
| LMS | Lochkartenmaschinen-station | LO-PASS | Low Pass |
| | | LO-QG | Locked Oscillator-Quadrature Grid |
| LMS | Logic Metadata System | | |
| LMS | London Mathematical Society | LOA | Length of Output Area |
| | | LOA | Length Overall |
| LMT | Length, Mass, Time | LOAC | Low Accuracy |
| LMT | Limit | LOAMP | Logarithmic Amplifier |
| LMT | Local Mean Time | LOAS | Lift-Off Acquisiston System |
| LMT | Logic Master Tape | | |
| LMTD | Logarithmic Mean Temperature Difference | LOB | Line Of Balance |
| | | LOB | Line Of Bearing |
| LMVE | Linear, Minimum Variance Estimation | LOB | Loop Operation Block |
| | | LOBAR | Long-Baseline Radar |
| LN | Label Name | LOC | Laboratory Office Computer |
| LN | Lagenummer | | |
| LN | Language Name | LOC | Language Oriented Computer |
| LN | Leeds and Northrup | | |
| LN | Line | LOC | Large Optical Cavity |
| LN | Load Name | LOC | Last Of Chain |
| LN | Load Negative | LOC | Line Of Communication |
| LNA | Low Noise Amplifier | LOC | Lines Of Code |
| LNADR | Line Address | LOC | Local |
| LNAME | Line Name | LOC | Localizer |
| LNB | Längste Nichtbenutzung | LOC | Locate |
| LNC | Line Number Clause | LOC | Location |
| LNCHR | Launcher | LOC | Logic OR Circuit |
| LNG | Length | LOCA | Low cost Computer Attachment |
| LNKEDT | Linkage Editor | | |
| LNL | Load Negative Long | LOCAL | Laboratory program for Computer Assisted Learning |
| LNR | Low-Noise Receiver | | |
| LNS | Lesen Nach Schreiben | | |
| LNS | Load Negative Short | LOCAL | Load On Call |
| LNS | Lokale Netz-Subebene | LOCATE | Library Of Congress Automation Techniques Exchange |
| LNT | Liquid-Nitrogen Temperature | | |
| LNTWA | Low Noise Travelling-Wave Amplifier | LOCATS | Low-cost Card Test System |
| LNTWTA | Low-Noise Travelling-Wave Tube Amplifier | LOCCK | Location Check |
| | | LOCEP | Local Epitaxy |
| LO | Language Output | LOCI | Logarithmic Computing Instrument |
| LO | Layout | | |

# L

| | | | |
|---|---|---|---|
| LOCMOS | Local Oxidation CMOS | LOGI | Log In |
| LOCMOS | Local Oxidation Complementary MOS | LOGIPAC | Logical Processor And Computer |
| LOCMOS | Locally Oxidized CMOS | LOGIT | Logical Inference Tester |
| LOCO | Local Copy | LOGL | Logical |
| LOCOS | Local Oxidation of Silicon | LOGLAN | Logical Language |
| LOCS | Logic and Control Simulator | LOGMIS | Logistics Management Information System |
| LOD | Launch Order Decoder | LOGO | Log Out |
| LOD | Length Of Day | LOGOS | Language Of Generalized Operational Simulation |
| LOD | Letter Of Disposition | | |
| LOD | Load | LOGR | Logistical Ratio |
| LOD | Loaded | LOGRAM | Logical program |
| LOD | Lockout Denied | LOGTAB | Logic Tables |
| LOD | Low Density | LOI | Loss On Ignition |
| LODCS | Lunar Orbiter Data Conversion System | LOIS | Library Order Information System |
| LODESTAR | Logically Organized Data Entry, Storage And Recording | LOKI | A Logic-Oriented approach to Knowledge and data bases supporting natural user Interaction |
| LODUS | Low Data-rate UHF Satellite | LOKOVO | Lohn- und Gehalts- korrektur der Vormonate |
| LOF | Local Oscillator Frequency | | |
| LOF | Lowest Operating Frequency | LOL | Length Of Lead |
| | | LOL | Limited Operating Life |
| LOF | List Overflow | LOLA | Layman Oriented Language |
| LOFAR | Low Frequency Analysis and Recording | LOLA | Library On-Line Acquisition |
| LOFT | Loss Of Fluid Test | LOLITA | Language for the On-Line Investigation and Transformation of Abstractions |
| LOG | Lage Optimal Gestalten | | |
| LOG | Logarithm | | |
| LOG | Logarithmus | | |
| LOG | Logging | LOLITA | Library On-Line Informa- tion and Text Access |
| LOG | Logic | | |
| LOG | Logical | LOMA | Life Office Management Association |
| LOG | Logisch | | |
| LOG | Lohn und Gehalt | LOMAC... | Logical Machine Corp. |
| LOG AMP | Logarithmic Amplifier | LOMAT | Language Oriented Machine Analysis Table |
| LOG COMP | Logistics Computer | | |
| LOG FTC | Logarithmic Fast Time Constant | LOMIS | Locator-Map In Source |
| | | LOMOS | Long-channel Metal Oxide Semiconductor |
| LOG IF AMP | Logarithmic Intermediate- Frequency Amplifier | | |
| | | LOMOST | Long-channel MOST |
| LOGA | Lohn-/Gehaltsabrech- nungssystem | LOMUSS | Lockheed Multipurpose Simulation System |
| LOGAL | Logical Algorithmic Language | LOOM | Line of Operator Oriented Machines |
| LOGALGOL | Logical Algorithmic Language | LOP | Level Of Programming |
| | | LOP | Life Of Program |
| LOGANDS | Logical commands | LOP | Line Of Position |
| LOGE | Logarithm to the base E | LOP | Logic Processor |
| LOGE | Lohn-/Gehaltsabrechnung | LOPAC | Load Optimisation and Passenger Acceptance Control |
| LOGEL | Logic Generating Language | | |
| LOGEL | Logical Generating Language | | |

# L

| | | | |
|---|---|---|---|
| LOPAD | Logarithmic Online data Processing system for Analog Data | LP | Leiterplatte |
| | | LP | Leitungsprogramm |
| | | LP | Leitungspuffer |
| LOPAD | Logarithmic Outline Processing for Analog Data | LP | Lesepuffer |
| | | LP | Licence Program |
| LOPAIR | Long Path Infrared | LP | Lift Platen |
| LOPAR | Low Power Acquisition Radar | LP | Lighting Panel |
| | | LP | Line Printer |
| LOPT | Line Output Transformer | LP | Line Printing |
| LOQ | Low Order Quotient | LP | Line Program |
| LOR | Line Oriented Routine | LP | Linear Printer |
| LOR | Low-frequency Omni-Range | LP | Linear Program |
| | | LP | Linear Programming |
| LORAC | Long-Range Accuracy | LP | Lineare Planungsrechnung |
| LORAN | Long Range Navigation | LP | Lineare Programmierung |
| LORDS | Logic and Register-transfer Design System | LP | List Printer |
| | | LP | List Procedure |
| LOREC | Long Range Earth Current | LP | List Processing |
| LORPGAC | Long Range Proving Ground Automatic Computer | LP | Lizenzprogramm |
| | | LP | Load Point |
| LOS | Lager- und Organisations-system | LP | Load Positive |
| | | LP | Load Program |
| LOS | Line Of Sight | LP | Loading Procedure |
| LOS | Loop Output Signal | LP | Lochen/Prüfen |
| LOS | Loss Of Signal | LP | Logarithmic Program |
| LOS | Loss Of Station | LP | Logic Program |
| LÖS | Lösung | LP | Longitudinal Parity |
| LOSARP | Line-Of Sight And Repeater Placement program | LP | Loop |
| | | LP | Low Pass |
| | | LP | Low Point |
| LOSAT | Language Oriented System Analysis Table | LP | Low Power |
| | | LP | Low Pressure |
| LOSAT | Language Oriented Systems Audit Table | LP | Low Primary |
| | | LP/MOSS | Linear Programming/Mathematical Optimization Subroutine System |
| LOSOS | Local Oxidation of Silicon-On-Sapphire | | |
| LOSR | Limit Of Stack Register | LPA | Level Parameter Address |
| LOSS | Landing Observer Signal System | LPA | Link Pack Area |
| | | LPA | Load Point Address |
| LOT | Laminate Overlay Transistor | LPA | Long-Periodic Antenna |
| | | LPACQ | Link Pack Area Control Queue |
| LOT | List On Tape | | |
| LOTIS | Logic, Timing, Sequencing | LPARNT | Logical Parent pointer |
| LOTP | Logical Operation Time Projection | LPB | Load Program Block |
| | | LPBM | Logic Parts Bill Master |
| LOTSE | Logistik-Tele-Service | LPC | Laboratory Precision Connector |
| LP | Label Parameter | | |
| LP | Label Processing | LPC | Lateral Parity Check |
| LP | Ladeprogramm | LPC | Linear Power Control |
| LP | Language Processor | LPC | Linear Power Controller |
| LP | Latch Pick | LPC | Linear Predictive Coder |
| LP | Layout Procedure | LPC | Linear Predictive Coding |
| LP | Learning Program | LPC | Longitudinal Parity Check |
| LP | Left Platen | LPC | Loop-Control relay |
| LP | Lehrprogramm | LPC | Low Power Channel |

# L

| | | | |
|---|---|---|---|
| LPC | Low Power Counter | LPP | Location Programming Practice |
| LPCM | Linear Predictive Coding Microprocessor | LPPC | Load-Point Photocell |
| LPCOMP | Logical Physical Comparator | LPR | Line Position Register |
| | | LPR | Line Printer |
| LPD | Language Processing and Debugging | LPRB | Loaded Program Block |
| | | LPRD | Latch Program Register D |
| LPDC | Least Positive Down Count | LPREPORT | Linear Programming Report |
| LPDTL | Low-Power Diode-Transistor Logic | LPRTL | Low Power Resistor Transistor Logic |
| LPE | Liquid Phase Epitaxy | | |
| LPE | Local Peripheral Equipment | LPS | Laboratory Peripheral System |
| LPF | Low-Pass Filter | LPS | Langage de Programmation de Système |
| LPFGEN | Linear Programming File Generator | LPS | Line Procedure Specification |
| LPFPRINT | Linear Programming File Print | LPS | Line Program Selector |
| LPG | Langage de Programmation de Gestion | LPS | Linear Programming System |
| LPG | List Program Generator | LPS | Lines Per Second |
| LPG | List Programming Generator | LPS | Load Positive Short |
| | | LPS | Location Programming Standard |
| LPG | Listenprogrammgenerator | | |
| LPH | Line Protocol Handler | LPS | Low Power Schottky |
| LPI | Learner Paced Instruction | LPS | Low Primary Sequence |
| LPI | Line Program Impulse | LPSD | Latest Possible Start Date |
| LPI | Lines Per Inch | LPSOL | Linear Programming Solution |
| LPI | Logic Parts Indicator | | |
| LPK | Loop Key | LPSTTL | Low Power Schottky Transistor-Transistor Logic |
| LPL | Linear Programming Language | | |
| LPL | List Processing Language | LPSW | Load Program Status Word |
| LPL | Load Positive Long | LPT | Load Point |
| LPL | Loaded Program List | LPT | Longest Processing Time |
| LPL | Location Programming List | LPT | Low Power Test |
| LPL | Low Power Logic | LPTF | Low Power Test Facility |
| LPM | Laser Precision Microfabrication | LPTTL | Low-Power Transistor-Transistor Logic |
| LPM | Leitungsprozedurmodul | LPTTL | Low Power TTL |
| LPM | Line Per Minute | LPU | Line Printer Unit |
| LPM | Linear Programming Method | LPUL | Least Positive Up Level |
| | | LPUU | Linear Programming Under Uncertainly |
| LPM | Local Processor Memory | | |
| LPMATGEN | Linear Programming Matrix Generation | LQ | Limiting Quality |
| | | LQP | Letter Quality Printer |
| LPMOSS | Linear Programming Mathematical Optimization Subroutine System | LR | Label Reference |
| | | LR | Labelling Reader |
| | | LR | Labelling Reading |
| LPN | Logical Page Number | LR | Lagerechner |
| LPO | Logical-Physical Output | LR | Last Record |
| LPO | Low Power Output | LR | Lecteur Reproducteur |
| LPP | Linear Program Part | LR | Left/Right |
| LPP | Linear Programming Problem | LR | Leseregister |
| | | LR | Level Recorder |

# L

| | | | |
|---|---|---|---|
| LR | Library Routine | LRL | Location Records List |
| LR | Line Register | LRLTRAN | Lawrence Radiation Laboratory Translator |
| LR | Line Relay | | |
| LR | Linear Routine | LRM | Latching Relay Matrix |
| LR | Link Register | LRM | Letter Reading Machine |
| LR | Load Ratio | LRN | Long Range Navigation |
| LR | Load Register | LRP | Location Records Practice |
| LR | Load Resistor | LRP | Logical Record Processor |
| LR | Loading Routine | LRP | Long Range Plan |
| LR | Local Register | LRP | Low Range Path |
| LR | Lock Range | LRR | Long Range Radar |
| LR | Logarithmic Register | LRRP | Lowest Required Radiated Power |
| LR | Logical Record | | |
| LR | Logical Routine | LRS | Location Records Standard |
| LR | Long Range | LRS | Long Range Search |
| LR | Low Register | LRS | Long Right Shift |
| LR | Low Resistance | LRS | Longitudinal Redundancy Shift |
| LRA | Load Real Address | | |
| LRASV | Long-Range Air-to-Surface Vessel radar | LRSS | Long Range Survey System |
| | | LRT | Load Ratio Transformer |
| LRB | Load Request Block | LRTF | Long Range Technical Forecast |
| LRB | Location Records Bulletin | | |
| LRC | Level-Recording Controller | LRU | Least Recently Used |
| | | LRU | Line-Replaceable Unit |
| LRC | Load Ratio Control | LRY | Latching Relay |
| LRC | Longitudinal Redundancy Check | LRZ | Leibnitz-Rechenzentrum |
| | | LS | Label Sector |
| LRC | Longitudinal Redundancy Character | LS | Label Statement |
| | | LS | Laboratory System |
| LRCC | Longitudinal Redundancy Check Character | LS | Language Specification |
| | | LS | Language Statement |
| LRCO | Limited Radiocommunication Outlet | LS | Laser System |
| | | LS | Late Scramble |
| LRCO | Limited Remote Communication Outlet | LS | Leased |
| | | LS | Least Significant |
| LRCR | Longitudinal Redundancy Check Register | LS | Left Shift |
| | | LS | Left Sign |
| LRD | Long Range Data | LS | Leistungsschalter |
| LRE | Longitudinal Redundancy Error | LS | Leitungsschnittstelle |
| | | LS | Letter Shift |
| LRECL | Logical Record Length | LS | Level Switch |
| LRF | Lawrence Radiation Facility | LS | Library Subroutine |
| | | LS | Lieferschein |
| LRF | Logical Record Facility | LS | Light Source |
| LRFG | Language Regular Fuzzy Grammar | LS | Limit Stop switch |
| | | LS | Limit Switch |
| LRG | Long Range | LS | Line Selector |
| LRI | Last Record Indicator | LS | Line Skipping |
| LRI | Long-range Radar Input | LS | Line Spacing |
| LRIM | Long Range Input Monitor | LS | Linear Store |
| LRIP | Language Research In Progress | LS | Linked Subroutine |
| | | LS | Load Short |
| LRIR | Low Resolution Infrared Radiometer | LS | Load Storage |
| | | LS | Lobe Switching |
| LRL | Loading Routine Library | LS | Local Storage |

# L

| | | | |
|---|---|---|---|
| LS | Location Starting | LSD | Limites Space charge Drift |
| LS | Location Storage | LSD | Linkage System Diagnostics |
| LS | Lochstreifen | | |
| LS | Lochstreifensender | LSD | Low Speed Data |
| LS | Lochstreifenstanzer | LSDI | Large Scale Display Integration |
| LS | Locking Shift | | |
| LS | Logic Shift | LSDS | Large Screen Display System |
| LS | Logic Symbol | | |
| LS | Logical Segment | LSE | Langage Symbolique d'Enseignement |
| LS | Logistisches System | | |
| LS | Long Short | LSE | Lenguaje Simbolico de Ensenanza |
| LS | Loudspeaker | | |
| LS | Low Secondary | LSE | Lese-Stanzeinheit |
| LS | Low Speed | LSE | Lineares Schnellwertelement |
| LSA | Limited Space-charge Accumulator | | |
| | | LSE | Lochstreifeneingabe |
| LSA | Line Sensing Amplifier | LSE | Lochstreifeneingabegerät |
| LSA | Lochstreifenausgabe | LSE | Locical Switching Element |
| LSA | Lochstreifenausgabegerät | LSF | Local Supply France |
| LSA | Logarithmic Sense Amplifier | LSF | Loss Factor |
| | | LSFM | Linear Stepped Frequency Modulation |
| LSA | Logic State Analyzer | | |
| LSA | Low Speed Adapter | LSG | Local Supply Germany |
| LSA | Low-cost Solar Array | LSHER | Load Sheet Reference |
| LSAC | Low Speed Access to Computer | LSHI | Large-Scale Hybrid Integration |
| LSAG | Lochstreifenaufspulgerät | LSI | Large Scale Integration |
| LSAR | Local Storage Address Register | LSI | Largest Single Item |
| | | LSI | Linear Sequence of Instructions |
| LSB | Last Significant Bit | | |
| LSB | Least Significant Bit | LSIC | Large Scale Integrated Circuit |
| LSB | Least Significant Byte | | |
| LSB | Line Speed Buffer | LSIC | Large Scale Integrated Circuitry |
| LSB | Location Systems Bulletin | | |
| LSB | Lower Sideband | LSIC | Low Speed Integrated Circuit |
| LSC | Large Scale Computer | | |
| LSC | Least Significant Character | LSID | Local Session Identification |
| LSC | Linear Sequential Circuit | LSIG | Least Significant |
| LSC | Loehmer Schulcomputer | LSIG | Least Significant |
| LSC | Logic Shift Command | LSIS | Lloyds Shipping Information Services |
| LSC | Loop Station Connector | | |
| LSCB | Load System Control Block | LSIT | Large Scale Integration Technology |
| LSCL | Limit Switch Closed | | |
| LSCP | Low Speed Card Punch | LSK | Lochstreifeneingabe und -ausgabe, Kombiniert |
| LSD | Langage Simple pour Débutants | | |
| | | LSK | Lochstreifenkarte |
| LSD | Language for Systems Development | LSL | Ladder Static Logic |
| | | LSL | Langsame Störsichere Logik |
| LSD | Large Screen Display | LSL | Location Systems List |
| LSD | Least Significant Decade | LSL | Lochstreifenleser |
| LSD | Least Significant Difference | LSL | Lochstreifenlocher |
| | | LSL | Low-Speed Logic |
| LSD | Least Significant Digit | LSLI | Large Scale Linear Integration |
| LSD | Light Sensing Device | | |

# L

| | | | | |
|---|---|---|---|---|
| LSLM | Low Speed Line Manager | LST | Line Schedule Terminal |
| LSM | Logic Selection Module | LST | Line-to-Store Transfer |
| LSM | Logicel, Spécifique, Mesure | LST | List |
| | | LST | Local Standard Time |
| LSM | Low Speed Modem | LST | Local Summer Time |
| LSN | Line Stabilization Network | LST | Lochstreifenstanzer |
| LSN | Linear Sequential Network | LST | Lochstreifensteuerung |
| LSN | Load Sharing Network | LST | Logic Service Terminal |
| LSNLIS | Lunar Science Natural Language Information System | LST | Low Speed Tape |
| | | LSTOR | Local Storage |
| | | LSTOR | Local Store |
| LSP | Language for Special Purposes | LSTTL | Low-power Schottky Transistor-Transistor-Logic |
| LSP | Leitsätze für die Preisermittlung | | |
| | | LSU | Local Storage Unit |
| LSP | Leitungssteuerungsprozessor | LSU | Local Store Unit |
| | | LSÜ | Lochschriftübersetzer |
| | | LSU | Logic Storage Unit |
| LSP | Load Scratch Pad | LSUC | Lower Sideband Up-Converter |
| LSP | Location Systems Practice | | |
| LSP | Lochspalte | | |
| LSP | Logical Signal Processor | LSW | Least Significant Word |
| LSP | Loop Splice Plate | LSW | Limit Switch |
| LSP | Low Speed Printer | LSWD | Linear System With Delay |
| LSPD | Low Speed | LSYD | Language for Systems Development |
| LSPTP | Low-Speed Paper Tape Punch | | |
| | | LT | Label Track |
| LSQA | Local System Queue Area | LT | Laboratory Test |
| LSQM | Large Systems Qualification Monitor | LT | Ladetakt |
| | | LT | Language Translation |
| LSR | Lese/Schreibregister | LT | Language Translator |
| LSR | Load Shifting Register | LT | Latch Trip |
| LSR | Load Shifting Resistor | LT | Lead Time |
| LSR | Load Storage Register | LT | Leistungstransistor |
| LSR | Local Shared Resources | LT | Less Than |
| LSR | Location Standards Representative | LT | Level Transmitter |
| | | LT | Level Trigger |
| LSS | Language Support System | LT | Light Test |
| LSS | Large Scale Standard | LT | Limit |
| LSS | Large Scale System | LT | Line Telecommunications |
| LSS | Line Sequential System | LT | Line Telegraphy |
| LSS | Linear Selection System | LT | Line Terminator |
| LSS | Location Systems Standard | LT | Linie Terminal |
| LSS | Lochstreifenstanzer | LT | Link Trailer |
| LSS | Loop Surge Suppressor | LT | Load and Test |
| LSSD | Level Sensitive Scan Design | LT | Local Time |
| | | LT | Logic Term |
| LSSM | Local Scientific Survey Module | LT | Logic Theory |
| | | LT | Logical Theory |
| LSSPC | Large Systems and Storage Product Center | LT | Low Temperature |
| | | LT | Low Tension |
| LSST | Lochstreifenstanzer | LTA | Lighter Than Air |
| LSSU | Link Status Signal Units | LTA | Logic Time Analyzer |
| LST | Large-capacity Storage | LTAS | Load Transit And Set |
| LST | Late Start Time | LTB | Line Time Base |
| LST | Left Store | LTB | Low Tension Battery |

# L

| | | | |
|---|---|---|---|
| LTBO | Linear Time Base Oscillator | LTS | Language Translation System |
| LTC | Language Translation Computer | LTS | Laser-Triggered Switch |
| LTC | Language and Time-sharing Center | LTS | Lateral Test Simulator |
| | | LTS | Launch Telemetry Station |
| LTC | Linear Transmission Channel | LTS | Line Test |
| | | LTS | Logisches Terminalsystem |
| LTC | Long Time Constant | LTS | Long Term Storage |
| LTDS | Logic Test Data System | LTS | Long Term Stability |
| LTE | Linear Threshold Element | LTT | Language Translation Table |
| LTEIL | Leistungsteil | LTTL | Low-power Transistor-Transistor Logic |
| LTERM | Logical Terminal | | |
| LTF | Life Time Function | LTTR | Long Term Tape Recorder |
| LTFRD | Lot Tolerance Fraction Reliability Deviation | LTÜ | Lampentaste, Übergabe |
| | | LTU | Line Termination Unit |
| LTG | Line Trunk Group | LTWA | Log Tape Write Ahead |
| LTH | Latch | LU | Level Unit |
| LTH | Logical Track Header | LU | Line Unit |
| LTHA | Long-Term Heat Ageing | LU | Load Unit |
| LTHD | Latched | LU | Logic Unit |
| LTHG | Latching | LU | Logical Unit |
| LTI | Linear Time-Invariant | LUB | Logic Unit Block |
| LTI | Local-Terminal-Interfaces | LUB | Logical Unit Block |
| LTIS | Linear Time-Invariant System | LUB | Lubricant |
| | | LUCB | Load UCB |
| LTL | Lincoln Terminal Language | LUCID | Language Used to Communicate Information system Design |
| LTL | Line-To-Line | | |
| LTM | Load Ton Miles | | |
| LTMPS | Logischer Test-Mikroprogrammspeicher | LUCID | Language for Utility Checkout and Instrumentation Development |
| LTN | Line Terminating Network | LUCID | Loughborough University Computerized Information and Drawings |
| LTP | Leapfrog Test Program | | |
| LTP | Library Technology Program | | |
| | | LUCIS | London University Central Information Services |
| LTP | Line Type Processor | | |
| LTP | Lower Trip Point | LUCOM | Lunar Communication system |
| LTPC | Local Time Pseudo Clock | | |
| LTPCB | Logical Terminal Program Control Block | LUCS | London University Computer Services |
| LTPD | Lot Tolerance Percent Defective | LUCS | London University Computing Services |
| LTPL | Long Term Procedural Language | LUCUS | London University Computer Services |
| LTR | Langue Temps Réel | LUD | Logical Unit Description |
| LTR | Left Test Register | LUE | Leitungsübertragungseinsatz |
| LTR | Letter | | |
| LTR | List Test Register | LUF | Lowest Usable Frequency |
| LTR | Locale Transmesso Ricevuto | LUG | Lohn Und Gehalt |
| | | LUHF | Lowest Usable High Frequency |
| LTROM | Linear Transformer Read-Only Memory | | |
| | | LUI | Logical Unit of Information |
| LTRS | Letters Shift | | |
| LTRS | Letter Shift lower case | LÜK | Logischer Übertragungskanal |

# L

| | | | |
|---|---|---|---|
| LUMB | Langsame Umbuchung | LVTR | Low power Very high frequency Transmitter-Receiver |
| LUMUS | Lang- Und Mittelfristige Unternehmensplanung mit Netzplantechnik-Systemen | | |
| | | LW | Laden Wort |
| LUN | Logical Unit Number | LW | Lange Welle |
| LUNAME | Logical Unit Name | LW | Last Word |
| LUST | List Update Sort and Total | LW | Laufwerk |
| LUT | Launch Umbilical Tower | LW | Leave Word |
| LUV | Logical User View | LW | Leitwerk |
| LUW | Local Unit of Work | LW | Light Weight |
| LV | Laser Vision | LW | Lime Wash |
| LV | Leitungsvermittlung | LW | Load Word |
| LV | Leitungsverstärker | LW | Long Wave |
| LV | Level | LW/D | Laser Welder/Driller |
| LV | Logic Variable | LWA | Logical Work Area |
| LV | Low Voltage | LWB | Long Wheel Base |
| LV | Luncheon Voucher | LWC | Liquid Water Content |
| LVA | Logarithmic Video Amplifier | LWC | Loop Wiring Concentrator |
| | | LWD | Label Writing Device |
| LVA | Low Voltage Avalanche | LWD | Larger Word |
| LVCD | Least Voltage Coincidence Detection | LWD | Limit Word |
| | | LWI | Laden Wort Indirekt |
| LVCD | Least Voltage Coincidence Detector | LWL | Lichtwellenleiter |
| | | LWL | Lichtwellenleitung |
| LVD | Linguistische Datenverarbeitung | LWL | Load Water Line |
| | | LWR | Lower |
| LVD | Low Voltage Drop | LWRU | Light-Weight Radar Unit |
| LVDA | Launch Vehicle Data Adapter | LWS | Library Work Space |
| | | LWS | Light Warning Set |
| LVDC | Launch Vehicle Digital Computer | LWSR | Light-Weight Search Radar |
| | | LWSS | Letter Writing Support System |
| LVDT | Linear Variable Differential Transducer | | |
| | | LWT | Listen-While-Talk |
| LVDT | Linear Variable Differential Transformer | LWT | Local Winter Time |
| | | LX | Logical Exchange |
| LVHF | Low Very High Frequency | LX | Low Index |
| LVHV | Low Volume High Velocity | LX | Lux |
| LVI | Low Viscosity Index | LX... | Logabox |
| LVIEW | Local View | LXI | Load Index Immediate |
| LVL | Level | LXMAR | Load External Memory Address Register |
| LVM | Limit Value Monitor | | |
| LVMOST | Lateral V-groove depletion MOST | LYR | Layer |
| | | LYRIC | Language for Your Remote Instruction by Computer |
| LVOR | Low-power Very high frequency Omnidirectional Range | | |
| | | LZ | Leading Zero |
| | | LZ | Leerzeichen |
| LVP | Low Voltage Protection | LZ | Left Zero |
| LVPS | Low Voltage Power Supply | LZ | Left-hand Zero |
| LVR | Lagerverwaltungsrechner | LZ | Leistungszeit |
| LVR | Longitudinal Video Recorder | LZ | Leiterzahl |
| | | LZ | Live Zero |
| LVR | Low Voltage Relay | LZE | Lichtzeicheneinrichtung |
| LVRCN | Lehigh Valley Regional Computing Network | LZI | Level Zero Indicator |
| | | LZK | Laufzeitkette |
| LVT | Linear Velocity Transducer | LZP | Langzeitprogramm |

# L

| | | | |
|---|---|---|---|
| LZP | Left Zero Print | LZS | Laufzeitsystem |
| LZPR | Left Zero Print | LZT | Local Zone Time |
| LZS | Langzeitspeicher | LZZ | Lesezwangszyklus |

# M

| | | | |
|---|---|---|---|
| M | Mach number | M-ULE | Multiplexer als Universelle Logische Einheit |
| M | Machine | M/PL | Miniature Plug |
| M | Magnetic | M.I.T. | Massachusetts Institute of Technology |
| M | Magnetic moment | | |
| M | Magnetic vector | | |
| M | Magnetization | MA | Machine Account |
| M | Magnetron | MA | Machine Accounting |
| M | Main channel | MA | Machine Address |
| M | Maintenance | MA | Magnetic Amplifier |
| M | Manual | MA | Main Alarm |
| M | Marker | MA | Maintenance Agreement |
| M | Markierer | MA | Manual Access |
| M | Maschine | MA | Maschinenaufarbeitung |
| M | Mass | MA | Maschinenauftrag |
| M | Maxwell | MA | Mast Aerial |
| M | Mechanical | MA | Master Station |
| M | Medium | MA | Matrix Algebra |
| M | Medium power | MA | Mechanical Advantage |
| M | Mega | MA | Mechano-acoustic |
| M | Megohm | MA | Mega Ampere |
| M | Member | MA | Mémoire Associative |
| M | Mémoire | MA | Mémoire Auxiliaire |
| M | Memory | MA | Memory Address |
| M | Menge | MA | Memory Available |
| M | Merge | MA | Message Assembler |
| M | Metallic | MA | Meßausgang |
| M | Micro ... | MA | Micro-Alloy |
| M | Microphone | MA | Milliammeter |
| M | Middle | MA | Milliampere |
| M | Million | MA | Mode d'Adressage |
| M | Minute | MA | Modify Address |
| M | Mired | MA | Multiple Address |
| M | Mobile | MA | Myria |
| M | Mode | MAA | Mathematical Association of America |
| M | Model | | |
| M | Modem | MAAC | Milliampere Alternating Current |
| M | Modifier function bit | | |
| M | Modulator | MAARC | Magnetic Annular Arc |
| M | Modulus | MAARM | Memory-Aided Anti-Radiation Missile |
| M | Molecular weight | | |
| M | Moment | MAARS | Multi-Access Agent Reservation System |
| M | Moment of force | | |
| M | Monitor | MAB | Maschinelles Austauschformat für Bibliotheken |
| M | More data bit | | |
| M | Multiplexer | MAB | Maschinenauftragsbeleg |
| M | Multiply | MAB | Maschinenauftragsblätter |
| M | Mutual | MABI | Mathematische Bibliothek |
| M&S | Maintenance and Supply | MABILA | Maschinelle Bilanzanalyse |
| M-B | Make-Break | MABIS | Maschinelle Bilanz-Simulation |
| M-Bit | More data Bit | | |
| M-D | Modulation-Demodulation | MABU | Maschinenbuchhaltung |
| M-DAS | Multispectral Data Analysis System | MAC | Machine Aided Cognition |
| | | MAC | Magnetic Account Card |
| M-RTOS | Miniature-Real Time Operating System | MAC | Magnetic Account Computer |

# M

| | | | |
|---|---|---|---|
| MAC | Man And Computer | MACH | Multi-user Airport Control & Handling |
| MAC | Management And Computer | MACHAN | Machine Analysis |
| MAC | Manufacturing Analysis Code | MACMIS | Maintenance And Construction Management Information System |
| MAC | Master Accounting Card | | |
| MAC | Master Air Data | MACOM | Multi-Applications Computer |
| MAC | Maximum Admissible Concentration | MACP | Macro Control Processor |
| MAC | Maximum Allowable Concentration | MACP | Macroprocesseur |
| MAC | Maximumcoder | MACP | Mission Analysis Computer Program |
| MAC | Mean Aerodynamic Chord | | |
| MAC | Measurement And Control | MACRO | Macroinstruction |
| MAC | Media Access Control | MACS | Management and Computer Services Incorporated |
| MAC | Mémoire Adressable par son Contenu | MACS | Media Account Control System |
| MAC | Memory Access Command | | |
| MAC | Memory Access Controller | MACS | Medium Altitude Communications Satellite |
| MAC | Memory Address Counter | | |
| MAC | Memory Assisted Cognition | MACS | Modular Application Customizing System |
| MAC | Men And Computer | | |
| MAC | Minimum Access Coding | MACS | Monitoring And Control System |
| MAC | Monitor And Control | | |
| MAC | Monthly Average Charge | MACS | Multi-purpose Acquisition and Control System |
| MAC | Multi Access Computing | | |
| MAC | Multi-Action Computer | MACSS | Medium Altitude Communication Satellite System |
| MAC | Multi-Address Circuit | | |
| MAC | Multi-Application Computer | | |
| MAC | Multiple Access Computer | MAD | Machine Analysis Display |
| MAC | Multiple Access Computing | MAD | Magnetic Airborne Detector |
| MAC | Multiple Access Control | MAD | Magnetic Anomaly Detection |
| MAC | Multiple Address Computer | | |
| MAC | Multiple Analog Components | MAD | Maintenance Analysis Diagram |
| MAC Unit | Magnetic Account Card Unit | MAD | Maintenance Assembly and Disassembly |
| MACARS | Microfilm Aperture Card Automated Retrieval System | MAD | Mean Absolute Deviation |
| | | MAD | Memory Access Director |
| | | MAD | Memory And Display |
| MACC | Madison Area Computing Center | MAD | Message Assembler and Distributor |
| MACDAC | Man Communication and Display for an Automatic Computer | MAD | Michigan Algorithm Decoder |
| | | MAD | Michigan Algorithmic Decoder |
| MACE | Machine-Aided Composition and Editing | MAD | Mittlere Absolute Abweichung |
| MACE | Management Applications in a Computer Environment | MAD | Modular Advanced Design |
| | | MAD | Multi Aperture Device |
| | | MAD | Multiple Access Device |
| MACE | Master Control Executive | MAD | Multiple and Add |
| MACH | Machine | MADA | Maschinelle Analyse Der Anwendung |
| MACH | Manual Assist Chip Handler | | |
| | | MADA | Maschinelle Datenanalyse |

# M

| | | | |
|---|---|---|---|
| MADA | Multiple Access Discrete Address | MADM | Maintenance Automated Data Management |
| MADAM | Manchester Automatic Digital Machine | MADM | Manchester Automatic Digital Machine |
| MADAM | Moderately Advanced Data Management | MADO | Merkur-Adressen-Datenorganisation |
| MADAM | Multi-purpose Automatic Data Analysis Machine | MADOK | Magnetband-Austauschformat für Dokumentationszwecke |
| MADAP | Maastricht Automatic Data Processing | MADOK | Maschinelle Austauschformate für die Dokumentation |
| MADAR | Malfunction Analysis Detection And Recording | MADOS | Magnetic Domain Storage |
| MADAR | Malfunction And Data Recorder | MADP | Mémoire à Accès Direct Programmable |
| MADBLOC | Mad-language Block Oriented Computer | MADPL | Mémoire à Accès Direct de Programme Localisable |
| MADC | Milliampere Direct Current | MADRE | Magnetic Drum Receiving Equipment |
| MADCAR | Management Data Charting And Review | MADRE | Martin Automatic Data Reduction Equipment |
| MADDAM | Macro module And Digital Differential Analyzer Machine | MADREC | Malfunction And Detection Recording |
| MADDAM | Macromodule and Digital Differential Analyzer Machine | MADREC | Malfunction Detection and Recording |
| MADDAM | Multiplexed Analog-to-Digital-Digital-to-Analog Multiplexed | MADRID | Merkur-Adressen-identifiziersystem |
| | | MADS | Machine-Aided Drafting System |
| MADDIDA | Magnetic Drum Digital Differential Analyzer | MADS | Mechanical Analysis and Design System |
| MADE | Microalloy Diffused Electrode | MADS | Meteorological Airborne Data System |
| MADE | Minimum Airborne Digital Equipment | MADS | Multi-Access Data Service |
| MADE | Mobile Automatic Data Experiment | MADS | Multiple Access Data Systems |
| MADE | Multichannel Analog-to-digital Data Encoder | MADS | Multiple Access Digital System |
| MADGE | Microwave Aircraft Digital Guidance Equipment | MADS | Multiply and Adds |
| | | MADT | Magnetband-Dienstprogramm für Testprogramme |
| MADI | Master Data Index | | |
| MADIC | Machinery Acoustic Data Information Center | MADT | Micro-Alloy Diffusion Technique |
| MADICT | Modular Advanced Development Integrated Circuit Tester | MADT | Micro-Alloy Diffused Transistor |
| | | MADU | Medium Access Data Unit |
| MADIS | Manual Aircraft Data Input System | MAE | Machine à Ecrire |
| | | MAE | Mean Absolute Error |
| MADIS | Maskenorientiertes Dialogsystem | MAECON | Mid-America Electronics Convention |
| MADIS | Millivolt Analog-to-Digital Instrumentation System | MAESTRO | Machine-Assisted Education System for Teaching by Remote Operation |

# M

| | | | |
|---|---|---|---|
| MAF | Magnetic Account Feeding | MAGIC | Motorola Automatically Generated Integrated Circuit |
| MAF | Major Academic Field | | |
| MAF | Minimum Audible Field | | |
| MAF | Multiple Access Facility | MAGIC | Multipurpose And Generalized Interface to COBOL |
| MAF | Multiple Access Facility | | |
| MAF | Multiple Attachment Feature | | |
| MAFAS | Maschinelle Auftragsbearbeitung mit Fabrikate-Stückliste | MAGLATCH | Magnetic Latch |
| | | MAGLOC | Magnetic Logic Computer |
| | | MAGMOD | Magnetic Modulator |
| | | MAGN | Magnetic |
| MAFCO | Magnetic Field Code | MAGPI | Manufacturing Automatic General Packaging Interface |
| MAFL | Multi-Aperture Ferrite Logic | | |
| MAG | Magazine | MAGPI | Manufacturing Automation Generalized Package Interface |
| MAG | Magnet | | |
| MAG | Magnetic | | |
| MAG | Magnetism | MAGPIE | Machine Automatically Generating Production Inventory Evaluation |
| MAG | Magnetron | | |
| MAG | Marker-Adder Generator | | |
| MAG | Maximum Available Gain | MAGTAPE | Magnetic Tape |
| MAG-FET | Metal-Aluminium-Germanium Field-Effect Transistor | MAH | Microinstruction Address Holder |
| | | MAI | Machine-Aided Index |
| MAGAMP | Magnetic Amplifier | MAI | Machine-Aided Indexing |
| MAGCARD | Magnetic Card | MAI | Memory Access Interface |
| MAGEIN | Magnetband-Eingabe | MAI | Multiple Access Interface |
| MAGEN | Matrix Generating | MAI | Multiple Address Instruction |
| MAGFET | Magnetic Field Effect Transistor | | |
| | | MAL... | Management Assistance Inc. |
| MAGI | Master Group Information system | | |
| | | MAID | Monrobot Automatic Internal Diagnosis |
| MAGI | Mathematical Applications Group, Incorporated | | |
| | | MAIDS | Machine-Aided Information and Dissemination System |
| MAGIC | Machine Aided Graphics for Illustration and Composition | | |
| | | MAIDS | Multipurpose Automatic Inspection and Diagnostic System |
| MAGIC | Machine for Automated Graphics Interface to a Computer | | |
| | | MAIK | Maschinelle Anlagenbuchhaltung Im Krankenhaus |
| MAGIC | Manchester Guardian Index Computerization | | |
| | | MAINSITE | Modular Automated Integrated Systems Interoperability Test and Evaluation |
| MAGIC | Matrix Algebra General Interpretive Coding | | |
| MAGIC | Matrix Analysis via Generative and Interpretive Computations | | |
| | | MAINSTAR | Main Storage Address Register |
| | | MAINT | Maintenance |
| MAGIC | Method for Asynchronous Graphics Integral Control | MAIR | Molecular Airborne Intercept Radar |
| MAGIC | Midac Automatic General Integrated Computation | MAIS | Marktanalysen-Informationssystem |
| MAGIC | Modern Analytical Generator of Improved Circuits | MAIS | Microfilm Alpha Index System |
| MAGIC | Modified Action Generated Input Control | MAJAC | Maintenance Anti-Jam Console |

- 372 -

# M

| | | | |
|---|---|---|---|
| MAK | Materialanforderungskarte | MANIAC | Mathematical Analyzer Numerical Integrator And Computer |
| MAKO | Magnetbandeingabe und -kontrolleinrichtung | | |
| MAL | Macro-Assembly Language | MANIAC | Mechanical And Numerical Integrator And Calculator |
| MAL | Malfunction | | |
| MAL | Monolithic Array Logic | | |
| MALE | Multiaperture Logic Element | MANIAC | Mechanical And Numerical Integrator And Computer |
| MALF | Malfunction | MANIP | Manual Input |
| MALIMIT | Master List of Medical Indexing Terms | MANIX | Machine Aids to Nike-X |
| | | MANO | Manually Operated |
| MALT | Mnemonic Assembly Language Translator | MANOP | Manual of Operation |
| | | MANOVA | Multivariate Analysis Of Variance |
| MALU | Mode Annunciator and Logic Unit | MANTIS | Manchester Technical Information Service |
| MAM | Medium Access Memory | | |
| MAM | Memory Array Module | MANTRAP | Machine And Network Transient Program |
| MAM | Missing Address Marker | | |
| MAM | Monolithic Array Memory | MAO | Maintenance Assistée par Ordinateur |
| MAM | Multiple Access to Memory | | |
| MAM | Multiple Address Machine | MAO | Management And Organization |
| MAM | Multiple Address Message | | |
| MAM | Multiuser Access Method | MAO | Mechanization of Algebraic Operations |
| MAMA | Manual-Automatic Multi-point Apparatus | | |
| | | MAOP | Matrix Operation Program |
| MAMBO | Maschinelle Auftrags- und Maschinenbestandsorganisation | MAOP | Matrizenoperationsprogramm |
| | | MAOS | Metal Aluminium Oxide Semiconductor |
| MAMI | Machine-Aided Manufacturing Information | | |
| | | MAP | Machine Analyzer Package |
| MAMIE | Magnetic Amplification of Microwave Integrated Emissions | MAP | Machine-Aided Programming |
| | | MAP | Macro Arithmetic Processor |
| MAMIE | Minimum Automatic Machine for Interpolation and Extrapolation | MAP | Macro-Assembly Program |
| | | MAP | Magnetic Account Processing |
| MAMMAX | Machine Made and Machine Aided Index | MAP | Magnetic Amount Printer |
| | | MAP | Main Arithmetic Processor |
| MAMO | Matrixmodul | MAP | Maintenance Analysis Procedure |
| MAMS | Memory And Memory Sequencer | | |
| | | MAP | Management Analysis Program |
| MAN | Mantisse | | |
| MAN | Manual | MAP | Management And Programming |
| MAN | Materialaufwandsnormativ | | |
| MAN | Microwave Aerospace Navigation | MAP | Manifold Absolute Pressure |
| | | MAP | Manpower Analysis Procedure |
| MAN OP | Manually Operated | | |
| MANAV | Manoeuvring And Navigation system | MAP | Manufacture Automation Protocol |
| MAND | Multiplikand | MAP | Manufacturing Automation Protocol |
| MANDRO | Mechanically Alterable Non-Destructive Read-Out | | |
| | | MAP | Map Analyzer Program |
| MANFEP | Manitoba Finite Element Program | MAP | Marketing Assistance Program |

# M

| | | | |
|---|---|---|---|
| MAP | Master Activity Programming | MAPS | Machine Automated Parts System |
| MAP | Mathematical Analysis without Programming | MAPS | Makro-Programmspeichereinheit |
| MAP | Measurement Analysis Program | MAPS | Management Aids Program Suite |
| MAP | Mechanized Assignment Processing | MAPS | Management Analysis and Planning System |
| MAP | Memory Allocation and Protection | MAPS | Marketing Analysis and Planning System |
| MAP | Message Acceptable Pulse | MAPS | Maximum Available Path Selection |
| MAP | Message Acceptance Pulse | | |
| MAP | Method of Approximating Programming | MAPS | Microprogrammable Arithmetic-Processor System |
| MAP | Minimal Access Programming | MAPS | Modern Accounts Payable System |
| MAP | Mise Au Point | | |
| MAP | Model And Program | MAPS | Multiple Address Processing System |
| MAP | Modelling and Analysis Package | MAPS | Multiple Application Partition Supervision |
| MAP | Modular Acoustic Processor | MAPS | Multivariate Analysis, Participation, and Structure |
| MAP | Modular Applications Program | | |
| MAP | Module Analysis Processor | MAPT | Modular Automatic Panel Test |
| MAP | Module Assembly Plant | | |
| MAP | MORT Assembly Program | MAPU | Multiple Address Processing Unit |
| MAP | Multibus Accounting Package | MAR | Machine-Aided Retrieval |
| MAP | Multiple Address Processing system | MAR | Malfunction Array Radar |
| MAP | Multiple Aim Point | MAR | Manufacturing Analysis Report |
| MAP | Multiple Allocation Procedure | MAR | Manufacturing Assembly Report |
| MAP | Multiple Array Processor | MAR | Materialabrechnung |
| MAPCHE | Mobile Automatic Programmed Checkout Equipment | MAR | Memory Address Register |
| | | MAR | Microanalytical Reagent |
| | | MAR | Microprogram Address Register |
| MAPD | Maximum Allowable Percent Defective | MAR | Minimum Access Routine |
| MAPID | Machine-Aided program for Preparation for Instruction Data | MAR | Miscellaneous Apparatus Rack |
| | | MAR | Multifunction Array Radar |
| MAPLE | Manpower Planning and Evaluation | MARBAS | Marketing im Bank- und Sparkassenbetrieb |
| MAPMIS | Manpower And Personnel Management Information System | MARBI | Machine-Readable form of Bibliographic Information |
| | | MARC | Machine Readable Catalog |
| MAPPLE | Macro-Associative Processor Programming Language | MARC | Machine Readable Cataloguing |
| | | MARC | Machine Readable Code |
| MAPR | Manual Action Prerequisite | MARC | Magnetic Abrasion Resistant Coating |
| MAPR | Matched Processor | | |
| MAPRES | Miniair Passenger Reservations System | MARC | Manufacturing Activity Release and Control |

# M

| | | | |
|---|---|---|---|
| MARC | Monitor And Results Computer | MARS | Machine Assisted Reference Section |
| MARC | Mortgage Account Report Compiler | MARS | Maschinelle Rechnungsschreibung |
| MARC | Multi-Axial Radial Circuit | MARS | Memory-Address Register Storage |
| MARC | Multiple Access Remote Computing | MARS | Military Amateur Radio System |
| MARCCO | Master Real-time Circulation Controller | MARS | Millimeter-wave Amplification by Resonance Saturation |
| MARCIA | Mathematical Analysis of Requirement for Career Information Appraisal | MARS | Modular Access Random Storage |
| MARCIS | Machine Readable Cataloguing Israel | MARS | Monitoring, Accounting, Reporting, and Statistical |
| MARCOM | Microwave Airborne Communications relay | MARS | Motorola Automatic Routing System |
| MARCS | Marine Computer System | | |
| MARDAN | Marine Digital Analyzer | MARS | Multi-Access Retrieval System |
| MAREX | Maschinelle Rechnungsschreibung Export | MARS | Multi-Aperture Reluctance Switch |
| MARGA | Market Game | | |
| MARGEN | Management Report Generator | MARS | Multiple Access Retrieval System |
| MARGIE | Memory, Analysis, Response, Generation, and Interference on English | MARS | Multiple Accounts Reports System |
| | | MARS | Multiple Apertured Reluctance Switch |
| MARIDAS | Maritime Data System | MARS/SIP | Mohawk Access and Retrieval System/Self-Interpreting Program |
| MARIS | Material Readiness Index System | | |
| MARIS | Multiple Access Reservation and Information System | MART | Maintenance Analysis Review Technique |
| MARKI | Marketing in Kreditinstituten | MART | Maintenance via Remote-Telecommunication |
| MARL | Memory Address Register, Lower | MART | Mean Active Repair Time |
| | | MARTAC | Martin Automatic Computer |
| MARLIN | Mid-Atlantic Research Libraries Information Network | MARTEC | Martin Thin-film Electronic Circuit |
| MARLIS | Multiple Aspect Relevance Linkage Information System | MARTI | Maneuverable Reentry Technology Investigation |
| | | MARTOS | Multi Access Real Time Operating System |
| MARO | Magnetbandroutine | | |
| MARS | Machine Retrieval System | MARU | Memory Address Register, Upper |
| MARS | Magnetostatic Rate Sensor | MARV | Maneuverable Anti-Radar Vehicle |
| MARS | Manufacturing Automated Records System | MAS | Makrosprache |
| MARS | Marconi Automatic Relay System | MAS | Material Application Service |
| MARS | Marketing Activities Reporting System | MAS | Meßwerterfassungs- und Auswertungssystem |
| MARS | Martin Automatic Reporting System | MAS | Metal Aluminium Semiconductor |

# M

| | | | |
|---|---|---|---|
| MAS | Metal-Alumina Semiconductor | MASR | Memory Address Select Register |
| MAS | Micro-Assembly System | MASROM | Metal-Aluminium-Silicon Read-Only Memory |
| MAS | Microprogram Automation System | MASS | Machine And System Scheduling |
| MAS | Microprogramming Automation System | MASS | Magnetstreifenschreiber |
| MAS | Modular Accounting System | MASS | MARC Automated Serials System |
| MAS | Modulares Anwendungssystem | MASS | Master Administrative Software System |
| MAS | Multi-Access Spool | MASS | Monitor and Assembly System |
| MAS | Multi-Access System | | |
| MAS | Multiple Access System | MASS | Multiple Access Sequential System |
| MAS | Network Administration Station | MASSDAR | Modular Analysis, Speed-up, Sampling and Data Reduction |
| MAS-FET | Metal-Aluminium-Silicon Field-Effect Transistor | MASSES | Multiple Application Shared System for Elementary and Secondary schools |
| MASA | Mechanized And Standards Automation | | |
| MASA | Methods Analysis Standards Automation | MASSOP | Multi-Automatic System for Simulation and Operational Planning |
| MASA | Methods and Standards Automation | | |
| MASC | Master Cost | MAST | Merchandise Analysis Study |
| MASC | Multilayer Aluminium oxide Silicon dioxide Combination | MAST | Multiple Application Storage Tube |
| MASC | Multiplicative and Additive Signature Correction | MAST | Multivalued Advanced Simulation Technique |
| MASCOT | Management Advisory System using Computerized Optimization Techniques | MASTAP | Master System Tape |
| | | MASTER | Multiple Access Shared Time Executive Routine |
| | | MASTIF | Multiple Access Space Test Inertia Facility |
| MASCOT | Modular Approach to Software Construction Operation and Test | MASW | Master Switch |
| | | MAT | Machine Aided Translation |
| MASCOT | Motorola Automatic Sequential Computer Operated Tester | MAT | Machine Analysis Table |
| | | MAT | Machine Audit Table |
| | | MAT | Machine Available Time |
| MASER | Microwave Amplification by Stimulated Emission of Radiation | MAT | Machine-Aided Translation |
| | | MAT | Mathematical Automata Theory |
| MASFET | Metal Alumina Silicon FET | MAT | Mechanical Assembly Technique |
| MASIS | Management And Scientific Information System | MAT | Micro-Alloy Transistor |
| | | MAT | Minimum Access Time |
| MASK | Maneuvering And Sea-Keeping masking | MAT | Mobile Aerial Target |
| | | MAT | Monolithic Array Tester |
| MASP | Mémoire à Accès Sélectif Programmable | MAT | Monolithic Automatic Tester |
| | | MAT | MORT Address Table |
| MASPL | Mémoire à Accès Sélectif de Programme Localisable | MATA | Multiple Answering Teaching Aid |

# M

| | | | |
|---|---|---|---|
| MATB | Materialbedarfsermittlung | MAVIS | Medical Audio-Visual-aids Information Service |
| MATE | Machine-Aided Translation Editing | MAW | Management Aid Workstations |
| MATE | Memory Assisted Terminal Equipment | MAW | Marine Aircraft Wing |
| MATE | Multiple Access Time-division Experiment | MAWI | Materialwirtschaft |
| | | MAX | Maximum |
| MATE | Multisystem Automatic Test Equipment | MAX | Maxwell |
| | | MAXA | Maximum Available |
| MATH | Mathematical | MAXBL | Maximum Balance |
| MATH | Mathematics | MAXUPO | Maximum Undistorted Power Output |
| MATHEM OPT | Mathematische Optimierung | MAZ | Magnetaufzeichnung |
| MATHN | Mathematician | MAZ | Magnetische Aufzeichnung |
| MATHPAC | Mathematical Package | MAZ | Meldeanrufzeichen |
| MATIC | Multiple Area Technical Information Center | MB | Magnetband |
| | | MB | Magnetbandgerät |
| MATICO | Machine Application to Technical Information Center Operations | MB | Magnetbandschreiber |
| | | MB | Magnetbandspeicher |
| | | MB | Magnetic Belt |
| MATICO | Material-Informations-system mit Computern | MB | Mailbox |
| | | MB | Main Battery |
| MATL | Material | MB | Maschinenblätter |
| MATLAN | Matrix Language | MB | Mask Bit |
| MATPS | Machine Aided Technical Processing System | MB | Master Block |
| | | MB | Mechanische Bauelemente |
| MATRS | Miniature Airborne Telemetry Receiving Station | MB | Megabit |
| | | MB | Megabyte |
| MATS | Multi-Application Teleprocessing System | MB | Memory Bank |
| | | MB | Memory Bit |
| MATS | Multiple Access Time Sharing | MB | Memory Buffer |
| | | MB | Message Buffer |
| MATSYS | Matrix System | MB | Methodenbank |
| MATV | Master-Antenna Television | MB | Mikrobefehl |
| MATVER | Materialverbrauch | MB | Milliarden Bytes |
| MAU | Maintenance Analysis Unit | MB | Million Byte |
| MAU | Media Access Unit | MB | Millionen Bytes |
| MAU | Multiplexed Arithmetic Unit | MB/S | Megabit per Second |
| | | MB/S | Megabyte per Second |
| MAUD | Memory Address Utilization Display | MBA | Magnetbandausgabe |
| | | MBAP | Marketingbüro-Anwendungsprojekte |
| MAUDE | Morse Automatic Decoder | | |
| MAUS | Markt-Analyse- und Überwachungssystem | MBB | Make-Before-Break |
| | | MBC | Magnetband-Cassette |
| MAUS | Meß-Auswerte-Sprache | MBC | Memory Buffer Capacity |
| MAVA | Modular Audio-Visual Aid | MBC | Message Beginning Character |
| MAVAR | Microwave Amplification by Variable Reactance | | |
| | | MBC | Miniature Bayonet Cap |
| MAVAR | Modulating Amplifier using Variable Resistance | MBC | Miniaturized Ballistic Computer |
| | | MBC | Modified Binary Code |
| MAVIN | Machine-Assisted Vendor Information Network | MBC | Multiple Board Computer |
| | | MBCS | Member of the British Computer Society |
| MAVIS | Maize Virus Information Service | | |
| | | MBD | Magnetic Bubble Device |

# M

| | | | |
|---|---|---|---|
| MBDD | Machine Base De Données | MBSE | Magnetbandsteuereinheit |
| MBDR | Make-or-Buy Data Record | MBST | Magnetbandsteuerung |
| MBE | Magnetbandeingabe | MBT | Metal Base Transistor |
| MBE | Magnetbandeinheit | MBT | Metallbasistransistor |
| MBE | Molecular Beam Epitaxy | MBT | Memory Block Table |
| MBF | Modulator Band Filter | MBT | Modified BIFORE Transform |
| MBG | Magnetbandgerät | | |
| MBG | Magnetbandsteuergerät | MBTWK | Multiple-Beam Travelling-Wave Klystron |
| MBI | Magnetbandtechnik für Informationsverarbeitung | MBV | Minimum Breakdown Voltage |
| MBI | Mitbewerberinformation | | |
| MBK | Magnetbandkassette | MBWO | Microwave Backward-Wave Oscillator |
| MBK | Multiple-Beam Klystron | | |
| MBKG | Magnetbandkassettengerät | MBX | Mailbox |
| MBL | Miniature Button Light | MBX | Management By Exception |
| MBM | Magnetic Bubble Memory | MBY | Make Busy |
| MBM | Main Bulk Memory | MBZ | Must Be Zero |
| MBM | Monolithic Buffer Memory | MC | Machine Card |
| MBO | Management By Objectives | MC | Machine Check |
| MBO | Marktindex für Büroorganisation | MC | Machine Code |
| | | MC | Machine Command |
| MBO | Monostable Blocking Oscillator | MC | Machine Cycle |
| | | MC | Magnetic Card |
| MBP | Mathematischer Beratungs- und Programmierungsdienst | MC | Magnetic Clutch |
| | | MC | Magnetic Core |
| | | MC | Make Contact |
| MBPR | Magnetbandprüfsystem | MC | Management Committee |
| MBPS | Million of Bits Per Second | MC | Manual Control |
| MBR | Manufacturing Basic Record | MC | Manufacturing Change |
| | | MC | Manufacturing Control |
| MBR | Material Basic Record | MC | Marginal Check |
| MBR | Member | MC | Maschinencode |
| MBR | Memory Buffer Register | MC | Master Card |
| MBR | Mikrobefehlsregister | MC | Master Clock |
| MBR | Mini Badge Reader | MC | Master Control |
| MBR-E | Memory Buffer Register, Even | MC | Mathematical Centre |
| | | MC | Maximum Count output |
| MBR-O | Memory Buffer Register, Odd | MC | Mechanical Computer |
| | | MC | Media Copy |
| MBS | Magnetbandspeicher | MC | Megacycle |
| MBS | Magnetbandsteuergerät | MC | Mémoire Centrale |
| MBS | Magnetron Beam Switching | MC | Memory Capacity |
| MBS | Main Buffer Storage | MC | Memory Circuit |
| MBS | Management By System | MC | Memory Clear |
| MBS | Master Build Schedule | MC | Memory Control |
| MBS | Maximum Batch Size | MC | Memory Core |
| MBS | Mechanischer Binärspeicher | MC | Mercury Contact |
| | | MC | Message Code |
| MBS | Modellbanksystem | MC | Metercandle |
| MBS | Multibit Shifter | MC | Metric Carat |
| MBS | Multiple Business Systems | MC | Micro Computer |
| MBS | Mutual Broadcasting System | MC | Microminiature Circuit |
| | | MC | Mikrocomputer |
| MBSA | Model-Based System Analysis | MC | Military Computer |
| | | MC | Million Characters |

# M

| | | | |
|---|---|---|---|
| MC | Mission Computer | MCBF | Mean Cycles Between Failures |
| MC | Mnemonic Code | | |
| MC | Mode Control | MCBP | Mini-Computer Byte Counter |
| MC | Model Computer | | |
| MC | Modem Controller | MCC | Machine Control Character |
| MC | Modular Computer | MCC | Magnetic Card Code |
| MC | Monitor Call | MCC | Magnetic Card Computer |
| MC | Mot-Clé | MCC | Magnetic Core Calculator |
| MC | Moving Coil | MCC | Magnetic Core Computer |
| MC | Multichip | MCC | Main Communications Center |
| MC | Multicomputing | | |
| MC | Multiple Contact | MCC | Management Controls Corporation, Inc. |
| MC | Multiple Copy | | |
| MC | Multiplex Channel | MCC | Manufacturing Control Centre |
| MC | Mutual Coupling | | |
| MC/S | Megacycles per Second | MCC | Master Control Code |
| MCA | Massachusetts Computer Associates | MCC | Memory Control Circuit |
| | | MCC | Micro Computer Control |
| MCA | Material Control Area | MCC | Miniature Center Cap |
| MCA | Modified Clenshaw Algorithm | MCC | Modulation with Constant Coefficient |
| MCA | Monte Carlo Analysis | MCC | Monitor Control Console |
| MCA | Multichannel Analyzer | MCC | Multi-Chip-Carrier |
| MCA | Multiplexing Channel Adapter | MCC | Multichannel Communications Control |
| MCA | Multiprocessor Communications Adapter | MCC | Multicomponent Circuit |
| | | MCC | Multiple Column Control |
| MCAD | Monte Carlo Design | MCC | Multiple Computer Complex |
| MCALS | Minnesota Computer-Aided Library System | | |
| | | MCCA | Media Conversion Computer Assembly |
| MCAP | Microwave Circuit Analysis Package | | |
| | | MCCB | Moulded-Case Circuit Breaker |
| MCAP | Multiple Channel Analysis Program | | |
| | | MCCC | Machine Code Control Character |
| MCAR | Machine Check Analysis and Recording | | |
| | | MCCCT | Manufacturing Computer Controlled Circuit Tester |
| MCAR | Machine Check Analysis Recording | | |
| MCAUTO | McDonnell Douglas Automation | MCCCT | Modular Computer Controlled Continuity Tester |
| MCB | Master Circuit Breaker | | |
| MCB | Memory Check Bit | MCCD | Meander channel CCD |
| MCB | Miniature Circuit Breaker | MCCD | Meander Charge Coupled Device |
| MCB | Modular Computer Breadboard | | |
| | | MCCD | Multiplexed CCD |
| MCB | Multi-Chip-Baustein | MCCP | Mission Control Computer Program |
| MCB | Multi-Chip-Bauteile system | | |
| | | MCCU | Multichannel Communication Control Unit |
| MCBC | Main Channel Byte Counter | | |
| | | MCD | Marginal Check and Distribution |
| MCBETH | Military Computer Basic Environment for Test Handling | | |
| | | MCD | Monitor Criteria Data |
| | | MCDP | Micro-programmed Communication Data Processor |
| MCBF | Mean Characters Between Failures | | |

- 379 -

# M

| | | | |
|---|---|---|---|
| MCDS | Management Control Data System | MCL | Multi-Collector Logic |
| MCDS | Multi-Channel Data System | MCM | Magnetic Card Magazine |
| | | MCM | Magnetic Card Memory |
| MCDS-AC | MCDS-Asynchronous Card | MCM | Magnetic Computer Memory |
| MCE | Magnetic Card Executive | MCM | Magnetic Core Memory |
| MCF | Magnetic Card Feeding | MCM | Management Control Model |
| MCF | Master Circuit File | | |
| MCF | Master Copy Flag | MCM | Mechanical Calculating Machine |
| MCF | Mean Carrier Frequency | | |
| MCF | Military Computer Family | MCM | Merged Charge Memory |
| MCF | Monolithic Crystal Filter | MCM | Micro Circuit Module |
| MCF | Monthly Control Figure | MCM | Micro Computer Machines |
| MCFF | Master Clear Flip-Flop | MCM | Monte Carlo Method |
| MCG | Man-Computer Graphics | MCM | Multi-Chip Module |
| MCG | Memory Character Generator | MCM | Multilayer Ceramic Module |
| | | MCM | Must Complete Mode |
| MCG | Microwave Command Guidance | MCMM | Magnetic Core Memory Matrix |
| MCGS | Microwave Command Guidance System | MCMOS | Motorola Complementary MOS |
| MCH | Machine | MCMS | Multi-Channel Memory System |
| MCH | Machine Check Handler | MCN | Multiple Call Non-ringing |
| MCH | Machine Check interruption | MCND | Machine Condition |
| MCHN | Machine | MCO | Master Card Operation |
| MCI | Machine Check Indicator | MCO | Multiple Channel Oscilloscope |
| MCI | Machine Check Interrupt | | |
| MCI | Magnetic Card Information | MCOM | Mathematics of Computation |
| MCI | Microwave Communications Inc. | | |
| | | MCP | Magnetic Character Printer |
| MCI | Multichip Integration | | |
| MCIC | Metals and Ceramics Information Center | MCP | Management Control Program |
| MCID | Multipurpose Concealed Intrusion Detector | MCP | Manual Card Punching |
| | | MCP | Master Control Program |
| MCIS | Maintenance Control Information System | MCP | Memory Centered Processor |
| MCIS | Management Controlled Information System | MCP | Memory Centered Processing |
| MCIS | Materials Control Information System | MCP | Message Control Program |
| | | MCP | Micro-Channel Plate |
| MCIT | Management Controls and Information Technology | MCP | Module de Calcul automatique de Passes |
| MCL | Macro Creation Language | MCP | Multichannel Communication Program |
| MCL | Master Clear Line | | |
| MCL | Mémoire Controle ou Local | MCP | Multiple Chip Package |
| MCL | Memory Control and Logging | MCPA | Memory Clock Pulse Amplifier |
| MCL | Memory Core Loader | MCPDP | Meander Channels Plasma Display Panel |
| MCL | Microcomputer Compiler Language | | |
| | | MCPP | Mikrocomputer-Programmierplatz |
| MCL | Mini Circuits Laboratory | | |
| MCL | Minimal Computer Load | MCPS | Megacycles Per Second |
| MCL | Minority Carrier Lifetime | MCPYF | Master Copy Flag |
| MCL | Monitor Control Language | | |

# M

| | | | |
|---|---|---|---|
| MCQ | Memory Call Queue | MCS | Motor Control System |
| MCR | Magnetic Card Reader | MCS | Multi-channel Communication System |
| MCR | Magnetic Card Recording | | |
| MCR | Magnetic Character Reader | MCS | Multi-Channel Switch |
| | | MCS | Multi-Channel System |
| MCR | Magnetic Chararcter Recognition | MCS | Multi-Computer System |
| | | MCS | Multi-purpose Communications and Signalling |
| MCR | Magnetic Core Register | | |
| MCR | Manufacturing Change Request | MCS | Multichannel Communication System |
| MCR | Master Control Routine | MCS | Multicomputer Communication System |
| MCR | Maximum Continuous Rating | | |
| | | MCS | Multiple Column Select |
| MCR | Micro-Computer Report | MCS | Multiple Column Selector |
| MCR | Multi-Contact Relay | MCS | Multiple Computer System |
| MCR | Multiple Call Ringing | MCS | Multiple Console Support |
| MCRR | Machine Check Recording and Recovery | MCS | Multiprogrammed Computer System |
| MCRS | Maintenance Computing and Recording System | MCST | Magnetic Card Selectric Typewriter |
| MCRS | Micrographic Catalog Retrieval System | MCT | Machine Computing Technique |
| MCRWV | Microwave | MCT | Magnetic Card and Tape unit |
| MCS | Magnetic Card Storage | | |
| MCS | Magnetic Card Store | MCT | Magnetic Character Typewriter |
| MCS | Magnetic Card System | | |
| MCS | Magnetic Character Sensing | MCT | Magnetically Coupled Transformer |
| MCS | Magnetic Core Storage | MCT | Master Configuration Table |
| MCS | Magnetic Core Store | | |
| MCS | Main Control Station | MCT | Memory Cycle Time |
| MCS | Maintenance Control System | MCTR | Message Center |
| | | MCU | Machine Control Unit |
| MCS | Management Control System | MCU | Magnet Control Unit |
| | | MCU | Magnetic Card Unit |
| MCS | Mass Core Store | MCU | Main Computational Unit |
| MCS | Master Control System | MCU | Master Control Unit |
| MCS | Medical Coding System | MCU | Measurement Control Unit |
| MCS | Megacycles per Second | MCU | Microprocessor Control Unit |
| MCS | Menzies Communications Systems GmbH | | |
| | | MCU | Microprogram Control Unit |
| MCS | Message Control System | MCU | Microprogrammed Control Unit |
| MCS | Micro-Computer System | | |
| MCS | Microwave Carrier Supply | MCU | Mikrocomputer-Universalkarte |
| MCS | Mikrofilm Computer Service | | |
| | | MCU | Mini-Computer Unit |
| MCS | Mobile Calibration Station | MCU | Multiprocessor Communication Unit |
| MCS | Modernes Cassetten-System | | |
| | | MCUG | Military Computer Users Group |
| MCS | Modular Computer System | | |
| MCS | Modulare Computer und Software Systeme AG | MCUIS | Master Control and User Interface Software |
| MCS | Modulation Controlled Synchronization | MCVG | Memory Character Vector Generator |
| MCS | Monitor Converter System | MCW | Modulated Carrier Wave |

# M

| | | | |
|---|---|---|---|
| MCW | Modulated Continuous Wave | MDAS | Miniature Data Acquisition System |
| MCW | Maintenance Control Word | MDAU | Multiplizierender Digital-Analog-Umsetzer |
| MCX | Minimum Cost Expediting | | |
| MCX | Minimum Cost Estimating | MDB | Material Data Bank |
| MD | Machine Description | MDB | Memory Data Bank |
| MD | Macro Directory | MDBS | Micro Data Base System |
| MD | Macro-Data | MDBS | Mikro-Datenbank-managementsystem |
| MD | Magnet Driver | | |
| MD | Magnetdrahtspeicher | MDBUPD | Master Data Base Update |
| MD | Magnetic Disk | MDC | Machinability Data Center |
| MD | Magnetic Drum | MDC | Magnetic Drum Calculator |
| MD | Maintenance Documentation | MDC | Main Digital Computer |
| | | MDC | Maintenance Data Collection |
| MD | Management Data | | |
| MD | Management Domain | MDC | Material Disposition Control |
| MD | Manual Data | | |
| MD | Manufacturing and Distribution | MDC | Meteorological Data Collection |
| MD | Master Data | MDC | Mini-Desk Calculator |
| MD | Matrix-Decoder | MDC | Minimum Delay Coding |
| MD | Maximum Demand | MDC | Multiple Device Controller |
| MD | Mean Deviation | MDC | Multistage Depressed Collectors |
| MD | Measuring Data | | |
| MD | Medium Duty | | |
| MD | Memory Device | MDCC | Master Data Control Console |
| MD | Memory Dump | MDCS | Maintenance Data Collection System |
| MD | Message Data | | |
| MD | Message per Day | MDCS | Material Data Collection System |
| MD | Micro Diagnostics | | |
| MD | Modulation-Demodulation | MDCU | Mobile Dynamic Checkout Unit |
| MD | Modulator | | |
| MD | Monitor Displays | MDD | Machine Dependent Data |
| MD | Motor Drive | MDD | Mission Data Display |
| MD | Multiple Data | MDD | Multiple Disk Drive |
| MD | Multiple Divide | MDDPM | Magnetic Drum Data Processing Machine |
| MD | Multiply/Divide | | |
| MD... | Macrodata | MDDR | Minimum-Distance Decoding Rule |
| MDA | Mechanical Data Acquisition | | |
| MDA | Mechanical Design Automation | MDDS | Microcomputer Disk Development System |
| | | MDDT | Master Digital Data Tape |
| MDA | Monolithic Design Automation | MDDU | Manual Data Display Unit |
| | | MDE | Magnetic Decision Element |
| MDA | Multi-Docking Adapter | MDE | Measuring Data Evaluation |
| MDA | Multidimensional Access | MDE | Mobile Data Entry |
| MDA | Multidimensional Analysis | MDE | Mobile Dateneingabe |
| MDAC | Multiplying Digital-to-Analog Converter | MDE | Mobile Datenerfassung |
| | | MDE | Modular Design of Electronics |
| MDAP | Machining and Display Application | | |
| | | MDE-RES | Mauvaises Données à l'Entrée - Résultats Erronés à la Sortie |
| MDAS | Medical Data Acquisition System | | |
| | | MDF | Magnetic Drum Function |
| MDAS | Meteorological Data Acquisition System | MDF | Main Distributing Frame |

# M

| | | | |
|---|---|---|---|
| MDF | Main Distribution Frame | MDM | Multiprocessing Diagnostic Monitor |
| MDF | Master Card File | | |
| MDF | Master Data File | MDMA | Magnetic Drum Memory Address |
| MDF | Material Disbursement File | | |
| MDF | Medium frequency Direction Finder | MDMFM | Miniature Digital Matched Filter Module |
| MDF | Mild Detonating Fuse | MDMP | Magnetic Drum Memory Program |
| MDF | Multiple Domain Feature | | |
| MDFM | Magnetic Drum File Memory | MDNS | Modified Decimal Number System |
| MDFS | Magnetdünnschicht-Filmspeicher | MDO | Maximum Data Organization |
| MDFT | Monolithische Dünnfilm-technik | MDOS | Magnetic Disk Operating System |
| MDG | Multiplier Decoder Gate | MDOS | Multiprocessor Disk Operating System |
| MDH | Macro Definition Header | | |
| MDH | Magnetic Drum Head | MDOT | Modular Digital Output Timer |
| MDI | Magnetic Data Inscriber | | |
| MDI | Magnetic Direction Indicator | MDP | Machine Development Program |
| MDI | Manual Data Input | MDP | Magnetic Drum Program |
| MDI | Multiple Display Indicator | MDP | Maintenance Diagnostic Program |
| MDIE | Mother-Daughter Ionosphere Experiment | MDP | Manual Data Processing |
| MDIF | Manual Data Input Function | MDP | Master Display Panel |
| MDIS | Manual Data Input Section | MDP | Mechanized Data Processing |
| MDIS | Manual Data Input System | | |
| MDIU | Manual Data Input Unit | MDP | Microprocessor Debugging Procedures |
| MDIU | Manual Data Insertion Unit | | |
| MDK | Memory Dump Key | MDP | Microprocessor Debugging Program |
| MDKU | Manual Data Keyboard Unit | MDP | Minimum Delay Programming |
| MDL | Management Data List | | |
| MDL | Master Data Library | MDP | Modell-, Daten- und Programmspeicher |
| MDL | Mechanial Design Language | MDP | Modifizierte Dynamische Programmierung |
| MDL | Miniature Display Light | | |
| MDL | Modular Design Language | MDP | Motor Driven Punch |
| MDL | Module | MDP | Motorola Data Processor |
| MDL | Mohawk Data Language | MDP | Mountain Data Processor |
| MDLS | Marine Data Logger System | MDPG | Magnetic Digital-Pulse Generator |
| MDM | Magnetic Disk Memory | MDPM | Mechanical Data Processing Method |
| MDM | Magnetic Drum Memory | | |
| MDM | Magneto-optical Display Memory | MDPMA | Member of the Data Processing Managers Association |
| MDM | Manufacturing Data Management | | |
| MDM | Maximum Design Meter | MDQS | Management Data Query System |
| MDM | Menüunterstützter Diskmonitor | MDR | Machine Design Rate |
| | | MDR | Magnet Drum Recorder |
| MDM | Metal-Dielectric-Metal | MDR | Magnetic Disk Recorder |
| MDM | Modem | MDR | Magnetic Disk Recording |
| MDM | Modified Dependency Matrix | MDR | Magnetic Document Reader |

# M

| | | | |
|---|---|---|---|
| MDR | Magnetic field-Dependent Resistor | MDS | Minimum Detectable Signal |
| MDR | Maintenance Data Report | MDS | Minimum Discernible Signal |
| MDR | Manual Data Room | | |
| MDR | Mark Document Reader | MDS | Modern Data System |
| MDR | Market Data Retrieval | MDS | Mohawk Data Sciences Corporation |
| MDR | Master Data Records | | |
| MDR | Memory Data Register | MDS | Multidimensional System |
| MDR | Mission Data Reduction | MDS | Multiple Data Set |
| MDR | Multichannel Data Recorder | MDS/JCC | Medical Data System/ Joint Camera Computer |
| MDRFILE | Material Disbursement Requirement File | MDSA | Magnetic Drum Store Address |
| MDRS | Manpower Data Relay Station | MDSA | Multiple Disc Sampling Apparatus |
| MDRU | Manual Data Readout Unit | MDSD | Magnetic Data Storage Device |
| MDS | Magnetband-Digital- speicher | MDSG | Magnetic Disk Storage Device |
| MDS | Magnetdrahtspeicher | | |
| MDS | Magnetic Data Storage | MDSIC | Metal-Dielectric Semi- conductor Integrated Circuit |
| MDS | Magnetic Disk Storage | | |
| MDS | Magnetic Disk Store | | |
| MDS | Magnetic Drum Storage | MDSP | Magnetdrahtspeicher |
| MDS | Magnetic Drum Store | MDSP | Magnetic Drum Store Program |
| MDS | Magnetic Drum System | | |
| MDS | Main Data Store | MDSS | Magnetic Drum Storage System |
| MDS | Main Device Scheduler | | |
| MDS | Maintenance Data System | MDSS | Magnetic Drum Sub- System |
| MDS | Malfunction Detection Subsystem | MDSS | Mass Digital Storage System |
| MDS | Malfunction Detection System | MDSS | Meteorological Data Sounding System |
| MDS | Management Decision System | MDSS | Mission Data Support System |
| MDS | Management Display System | MDSU | Magnetic Drum Storage Unit |
| MDS | Manual Data Supervisor | | |
| MDS | Manufacturing Data Series | MDT | Manual Data Technician |
| MDS | Market Data System | MDT | Massendatentransporter |
| MDS | Mass Digital Storage | MDT | Mean Down Time |
| MDS | Master Data Set | MDT | Medium Data Technique |
| MDS | Master Data Structure | MDT | Mittlere Datentechnik |
| MDS | Master Drum Sender | MDT | Modified Data Tag |
| MDS | Medical Data System | MDTL | Modified Diode- Transistor-Logic |
| MDS | Memory Disk System | | |
| MDS | Metal Dielectric Semiconductor | MDTS | Megabit Digital-to- Troposcatter Subsystem |
| MDS | Microcomputer Develop- ment System | MDTS | Modular Data Transaction System |
| MDS | Microprocessor Develop- ment System | MDTS | Modular Data Transfer System |
| MDS | Microprogram Design System | MDTS | Modular Data Transmission System |
| MDS | Microprogram Develop- ment System | MDU | Magnetic Disk Unit |
| | | MDU | Message Decoder Unit |

# M

| | | | |
|---|---|---|---|
| MDUL | Module | MECTL | Multi-Emitter Coupled Transistor Logic |
| MDUS | Medium Data Utilization Station | MED | Medium |
| MDV | Mannesmann Datenverarbeitung | MED | Microelectronic Device |
| MDV | Map and Data Viewer | MED | Multiformat Electroluminescent Display |
| MDV | Mittlere Datenverarbeitung | MED REC | Media Record |
| MDVC | Miniature Digital Voltmeter and Counter | MEDAC | Military Electronic Data Advisory Committee |
| MDY | Month Day Year | MEDACS | Medical Administrative Control System |
| MDZ | Middle Zero | MEDAL | Micro-mechanized Engineering Data for Automated Logistics |
| ME | Machine Error | | |
| ME | Magnetband-Eingabeelement | MEDALS | Modular Engineering Drafting And Library System |
| ME | Manufacturing Engineering | | |
| ME | Measurement Engine | MEDALS | Modular Engineering Draughting And Library System |
| ME | Measuring Element | | |
| ME | Mechanical Efficiency | | |
| ME | Mechanical Engineer | MEDAS | Microfilm Enhanced Data System |
| ME | Mengeneinheit | | |
| ME | Meßwerterfasser | MEDHOC | Macro-Economic Databank House Of Commons |
| ME | Micro-Electronic | | |
| ME | Millitary Engineer | MEDI | Marine Environmental Data Information |
| ME | Mining Engineer | | |
| ME | Modular Electronics | MEDI | Mössbauer Effect Data Index |
| ME | Molecular Electronics | | |
| MEA | Multimode Error Analysis | MEDIA | Magnavox Electronic Data Image Apparatus |
| MEACON | Masking beacon | | |
| MEAP | Mikroprogrammierter Ein-/Ausgabeprozessor | MEDIA | Missile Error Data Integration Analysis |
| MEAR | Maintenance Engineering Analysis Report | MEDIA | Modular Electronic Digital Instrumentation Assemblies |
| MEB | Methodenbank | | |
| MEBES | Manufacturing Electron-Beam Exposure System | MEDIATOR | Media Time Ordering and Reporting |
| MEC | Mengencoder | MEDIC | Medical Electronic Data Interpretation and Correlation |
| MEC | Miniature Electronic Components | | |
| MEC | Minimum Energy Curve | MEDICO | Model Experiment in Drug Indexing by Computer |
| MECA | Maintainable Electronic Component Assembly | | |
| MECA | Missiles Electronics and Computer Assembly | MEDINFO | Medical Informatics |
| | | MEDIS | Medical Information System |
| MECA | Multi-valued Electronic Circuit Analysis | MEDISTARS | Medical Information Storage And Retrieval System |
| MECCA | Mechanized Catalog | | |
| MECES | Multi-Experimental Controlled Entry System | MEDIUM | Missile Era Data Integration, Ultimate Method |
| MECFOCS | Machine Error Correction First Order Card Status | MEDLARS | Medical Literature Analysis and Retrieval System |
| MECL | Motorola Emitter Coupled Logic | | |
| MECL | Multi-Emitter Coupled Logic | MEDLINE | MEDLARS online |

# M

| | | | |
|---|---|---|---|
| MEDMIS | Medical Management Information System | MELSA | Mitsubishi Extensive Large Scale Array |
| MEDOL | Medically Oriented Language | MEM | Mars Excursion Module |
| | | MEM | Member |
| MEDS | Marine Embarkation Data System | MEM | Mémoire Morte |
| | | MEM | Memory |
| MEDSARS | Maintenance Engineering Data Storage And Retrieval System | MEM-MDLE | Memory Module |
| | | MEMA | Microelectronics Modular Assembly |
| MEDUSA | Multiple-Element Directional Universally Steerable Antenna | MEMB | Membran |
| | | MEMBERS | Microprogrammed Experimental Machine with a Basic Executive for Realtime Systems |
| MEE | Machine à Ecrire Electrique | | |
| MEE | Ministerium für Elektrotechnik und Elektronik | MEMBRAIN | Micro-Electronic Memories and Brains |
| MEECN | Minimum Essential Emergency Communications Network | MEMCARD | Memory Card |
| | | MEMISTOR | Memory resistor |
| | | MEMISTOR | Memory resistor storage device |
| MEETAT | Maximum improvement in Electronics Effectiveness Through Advanced Techniques | MEMO | Maximizing the Efficiency of Machine Operations |
| | | MEMO | Memorandum |
| MEG | Megohm | MEMOCS | Mitsubishi Electric Corporation Multiterm Out-of Context System |
| MEG | Miniature Electronic Gyro | | |
| MEGA | Megaampere | | |
| MEGAFLOP | Mega Floating Point | MEMPE | Memory Parity Error |
| MEGC | Megacycle per second | MEMPT | Memory Point |
| MEGV | Megavolt | MEMTEST | Membrane Test Language |
| MEGW | Megawatt | MEN | Multiple Earthed Neutral |
| MEGWH | Megawatt-Hour | MEN | Multiple Event Networks |
| MEIS | Manufacturing Engineering Information System | MENS | Message Entry System |
| | | MEOS | Meßsystem für Echtzeitoperationssysteme |
| MEIU | Management Education Information Unit | | |
| | | MEP | Mean Effective Pressure |
| MEK | Mehrfacheinzelkanal | MEP | Mise En Page |
| MEK | Meßwerterfassungskomplex | MEPDP | Meander Electrodes Plasma Display Panel |
| MEKTS | Modular Electronic Key Telephone System | | |
| | | MER | Minimum Energy Requirement |
| MEL | Many-Element Laser | | |
| MEL | Micro-Electronics | MER | Multiple Ejector Rack |
| MEL | Micro-Energy Logic | MERA | Molecular Electronics for Radar Applications |
| MEL | Multi-Emitter-Logic | | |
| MELCOM | Mitsubishi Electronic Computer | MERANDA | Multiple Events Recorder And Data Analysis |
| MELEC | Microelectronics | MERGE | Mechanized Retrieval for Greater Efficiency |
| MELEM | Microelement | | |
| MELF | Metal Electrode Facebonding | MERLIN | Machine Readable Library Information |
| MELISS | Mitsubishi Electric Corporation Literature and Information Search Service | MERT | Manufacturing Engineering Report Technique |
| | | MERT | Multi-Environment Real Time |
| MELISSA | Metal Linguistic Syntax Specification Analyzer | MES | Management-Entscheidungssystem |

# M

| | | | |
|---|---|---|---|
| MES | Mapping and Earth Science | MEVA | Maschinelle Erstellung Von Arbeitsmethodenanalysen |
| MES | Maschineneingabestelle | | |
| MES | Maschinenendstelle | MEVA | Mechanisierte Erstellung Von Analysen |
| MES | Materialeinsatzschlüssel | | |
| MES | Materialentnahmeschein | MEW | Microwave Early Warning |
| MES | Menü-Entwicklungssystem | MEX | Memory Exchange |
| MES | Messung | MEX | Military Exchange |
| MES | Metal Semiconductor | MEXIT | Macro-definition Exit |
| MES | Mikrocomputer-Entwicklungssystem | MF | Machine Failure |
| | | MF | Machine Fault |
| MES | Miscellaneous Equipment Specification | MF | Machine Format |
| | | MF | Machine-Finished |
| MES | Multiple Enquiry System | MF | Magnetic Field |
| MES FET | Metal-Semiconductor Field-Effect Transistor | MF | Mandatory File |
| | | MF | Maschinenfehler |
| MESCO | Message Electronic Switching Computer | MF | Master File |
| | | MF | Measurement Facility |
| MESFET | Metal-Schottky FET | MF | Medium Frequency |
| MESFET | Metal Semiconductor Field Effect Transistor | MF | Memory Field |
| | | MF | Microfarad |
| MESFET | Metall-Semikonduktor-Feldeffekt-Transistor | MF | Microfiche |
| | | MF | Microfilm |
| MESG | Maximum Experimental Safe Gap | MF | Mikrofilm |
| | | MF | Modify Field |
| MESP | Meldespeicher | MF | Mono-Flop |
| MESS | Misalignment Estimation Software System | MF | Multi-Frequency |
| | | MF | Multiplying Factor |
| MESUCORA | Measurement, Control, Regulation, Automation | MF | Multiprogrammfaktor |
| | | MF-ADR | Mikrofilmausgabegerät |
| MET | Meteorological broadcasts | MF-N | Microfiche, Negative |
| MET | Modified Expansion Tube | MFA | Mehrfachanschluss |
| MET | Multi-Emitter Transistor | MFA | Mikrocomputertechnik in der Facharbeiter-Ausbildung |
| META | Methods of Extraction Text Automatically | | |
| METAL | Metal Language | MFAG | Mikrofilmausgabegerät |
| METALS | Mechanical Translation and Analysis of Language System | MFAR | Mehrfachanschlussrichtung |
| | | MFAR | Multi-Function Array Radar |
| METAP | Meldungs- und Tastatur-Alarme von Prozessen | MFASP | Mikrofichearbeitsspeicher |
| | | MFB | Master File Block |
| METAPLAN | Methods of Extracting Text Automatically Programming Language | MFB | Mehrfunktionenbaustein |
| | | MFB | Mixed Functional Block |
| | | MFB | Motional Feedback |
| METHAPLAN | Methodenbank Ablaufsystem für Planung und Analyse | MFC | Magnetic Film Counter |
| | | MFC | Magnetic tape Field Scan |
| | | MFC | Manual Frequency Control |
| METHODOS | Methodisches Organisationssystem | MFC | Mehrfrequenz-Codewahl |
| | | MFC | Mehrfrequenzcode |
| METRG | Metering | MFC | Memory Field Contents |
| METS | Multi-Executive Time-Sharing | MFC | Micro-Functional Circuit |
| | | MFC | Microfilm Frame Card |
| METSAT | Meteorological Satellite | MFC | Multi-Fit-Coder |
| MEU | Message Encoder Unit | MFC | Multi-Frequency Code |
| MEU | Multiplexer Encoder Unit | MFC | Multi-Function Circuit |
| MEV | Mémoire Vive | MFC | Multifunction Converter |

# M

| | | | |
|---|---|---|---|
| MFC | Multiple Folding Characteristics | MFP | Mean Free Path |
| MFCM | Multi-Function Card Machine | MFP | Mémoire Fixe Programmable |
| MFCS | Mathematical Foundations of Computer Science | MFP | Microfiche, Positive |
| | | MFP | Minimum Flight Path |
| MFCU | Multi-Function Card Unit | MFP | Mitarbeiterförderungsprogramm |
| MFD | Magnetic Frequency Detector | MFP | Multi Functions Printer |
| MFD | Magnetofluid Dynamics | MFPA | Monolithic FPA |
| MFD | Manufactured | MFPU | Mémoire Fixe Programmable en Usine |
| MFD | Master File Directory | MFR | Manufacture |
| MFDC | Multi-File Data Carrier | MFR | Multi-Frequency Receiver |
| MFDF | Medium-Frequency Direction Finder | MFR | Multifunction Receiver |
| | | MFRS | Multifunction Receiver System |
| MFDSUL | Multi-Function Data Set Utility Language | MFS | Magnetic Film Storage |
| MFE | Multi-Function Executive | MFS | Magnetic Film Store |
| MFF | Magnetic Flip-Flop | MFS | Magnetic tape Field Search |
| MFF | Monostabiles Flip-Flop | MFS | Maximum File Size |
| MFFC | Master Function Flow Chart | MFS | Message Format Service |
| | | MFS | Message Formatting Service |
| MFG | Manufacturing | | |
| MFG | Mehrfrequenzgenerator | MFS | Metall-Ferroelektrikum-Halbleiter-Speicher |
| MFG | Multi-purpose Function Generator | MFS | Multi-Frequency System |
| MFGC | Manufacturing Code | MFS | Multi-Function System |
| MFH | Magnetic Film Handler | MFS | Multiple Frequency Synthesizer |
| MFI | Machine Feature Index | | |
| MFKE | Mehrfunktions-Karteneinheit | MFSK | Multiple Frequency Shift Keying |
| MFKP | Multi-Frequency Key Pulsing | MFSP | Magnetfilmspeicher |
| | | MFSP | Material Flow Simulation Program |
| MFLD | Message Field | | |
| MFM | Magnetic Film Memory | MFSP | Materialfluß-Simulationsprogramm |
| MFM | Magnetic Foil Memory | | |
| MFM | Memory Feasibility Model | MFSR | Magnetic Film Strip Recorder |
| MFM | Modified Frequency Modulation | MFST | Metal-Ferroelectric-Semiconductor Transistor |
| MFM | Modifiziertes Frequenzmodulationsverfahren | | |
| | | MFT | Machine Function Test |
| MFM | Modulation de Fréquence Modifiée | MFT | Mikrofilmtechnik |
| | | MFT | Multiprocessing with a Fixed Number of Tasks |
| MFM | Multifunctional Memory | | |
| MFMA | Monolithic Ferrite Memory Array | MFT | Multiprogramming Fixed Task |
| MFMU | Multi-Function Memory Unit | MFT | Multiprogramming with a Fixed number of Tasks |
| MFN | Multiple-Function Network | MFT | Multitasking with a Fixed number of Tasks |
| MFO | Master Frequency Oscillator | | |
| | | MFTD | Maximally Flat Time Delay |
| MFO | Mehrfachfeldoperator | MFTU | Multi-Function Tape Unit |
| MFO | Multiple File Option | MFTU | Multiple Function Tape Unit |
| MFP | Magnetic Field Potential | | |
| MFP | Master File Program | MFU | Magnetic Film Unit |

# M

| | | | |
|---|---|---|---|
| MFUSYS | Microfiche File Update System | MGT | Metal Gate Technology |
| MFV | Mehrfrequenzcode-Verfahren | MH | Magnetic Head |
| | | MH | Medium Hard |
| MFV | Mehrfrequenzverfahren | MH | Message Handler |
| MFV | Mehrfrequenz-Wähl-verfahren | MH | Millihenry |
| | | MH | Multiply Halfword |
| MFV | Microfilm Viewer | MHC | Mechanical Height Computer |
| MG | Machine Glazed | | |
| MG | Machine Group | MHD | Magnetohydrodynamics |
| MG | Magnetbandgerät | MHD | Minimale Hamming-Distanz |
| MG | Marginal relay | | |
| MG | Markengeber | MHD | Moving Head Disc |
| MG | Master Gauge | MHDF | Medium- and High-frequency Direction Finder |
| MG | Mehrfachgruppe | | |
| MG | Mehrfachgruppensystem | MHF | Medium High Frequency |
| MG | Message Generator | MHF | Message Handling Facility |
| MG | Metal-Glass combination | MHF | Multi-Host Facility |
| MG | Motor-Generator | MHG | Message Header Generator |
| MG | Multigage | MHHZO | Move-High-to-High Zone |
| MGC | Manual Gain Control | MHLZO | Move-High-to-Low Zone |
| MGC | Missile Guidance Computer | MHI | Montage/Handhabung/Industrieroboter |
| MGCC | Missile Guidance and Control Computer | MHI | Montage/Handhabung/Industrieroboter-Forschung |
| MGCR | Maritime Gas-Cooled Reactor | | |
| MGD | Magnetogasdynamics | MHIC | Microwave Hybrid Integrated Circuit |
| MGEN | Module Generation | | |
| MGF | Memory Gate First | MHL | Medium Heavy Loaded |
| MGG | Memory Gate Generator | MHL | Microprocessor Host Loader |
| MGK | Magnetkarte | | |
| MGK | Materialgemeinkosten | MHLZO | Move-High-to-Low Zone |
| MGL | Machine Group Listing | MHM | Minimum Hardware Modification |
| MGL | Matrix Generator Language | | |
| | | MHOS | Multi-Hospital Operating System |
| MGM | Master Group Multiplexer | | |
| MGP | Magnetic and Graphic Products | MHP | Monitorhilfsprogramm |
| | | MHS | Message Handling System |
| MGP | Memory Graphics Program | MHS | Magnetic Head Scanner |
| MGP-PP | Memory Graphics Program - Post-Processing | MHT | Message-Handling-Terminal |
| MGPR | Multiple General Purpose Register | MHTL | Motorola High Threshold Logic |
| MGPS | Memory Graphics Processing System | MHVDF | Medium-, High- and Very high-frequency Direction Finder |
| MGR | Manual Gate Register | | |
| MGR | Maschinengruppe | MHZ | Megahertz |
| MGR | Micro-Graphic Reporting | MI | Machine Instruction |
| MGRL | MIND Grammar Rule Language | MI | Machine Interface |
| | | MI | Macro Instruction |
| MGRW | Matrix Generator and Report Writer | MI | Main Interface |
| | | MI | Mandatory Instruction |
| MGS | Microcomputer Graphic System | MI | Manual Inlet |
| | | MI | Manual Input |
| MGT | Mean Greenwich Time | MI | Marketing Identifier |

# M

| | | | |
|---|---|---|---|
| MI | Maschineninventarnummer | MIC | Memory Interface Connection |
| MI | Mask Instruction | MIC | Message Identification Code |
| MI | Master Index | | |
| MI | Memory Information | | |
| MI | Metal Interface | MIC | Message-Interrupt Controller |
| MI | Mica | MIC | Microcomputer |
| MI | Micro Instruction | MIC | Microelectronic Integrated Circuit |
| MI | Miller Integrator | | |
| MI | Miscellaneous Input | MIC | Micrometer |
| MI | Mischer | MIC | Microphone |
| MI | Multiple Instructions | MIC | Microprogrammed micro-computer |
| MI | Multiply Instruction | | |
| MI | Mutual Inductance | MIC | Microwave |
| MI | Mutual Information | MIC | Microwave Integrated Circuit |
| MI/DAC | Management Information for Design And Control | | |
| | | MIC | Middle-In-Chain |
| MIA | Maschinelle Informations-fluß-Analyse | MIC | Mikrocomputer |
| | | MIC | Minimum Ignition Current |
| MIA | Maschinelle Inventur-Auswertung | MIC | Minimum Issue Control |
| | | MIC | Missing Interrupt Character |
| MIA | Metal Interface Amplifier | | |
| MIA | Multiplexer Interface Adapter | MIC | Missing Interruption Checker |
| MIAC | Minimum Automatic Computer | MIC | Mittelwertcoder |
| | | MIC | Modulation d'Impulsions Codées |
| MIACS | Manufacturing Information And Control System | | |
| | | MIC | Modulation par Impulsion et Codage |
| MIACS-TD | Manufacturing Information And Control System-Transaction Driven | | |
| | | MIC | Modulation par Impulsions Codées |
| MIADS | Map Information Assembly and Display System | MIC | Monolithic Integrated Circuit |
| MIAGE | Méthodes Informatiques Appliquées à la Gestion | MIC | Monolithic Interface Circuit |
| MIARS | Maintenance Information Automated Retrieval System | MIC | Multilayer Integrated Circuit |
| | | MIC | Multiple Input Change |
| MIAS | Management Information and Accounting System | MICA | Macro Instruction Compiler Assembler |
| MIB | Manual Input Buffer | MICA | Man-computer Inter-action in Commercial Applications |
| MIB | Member Information Bank | | |
| MIB | Miniaturbaustein | | |
| MIB | Multilayer Interconnection Board | MICADO | Mission pour la Conception Assistée et le Dessin par Ordinateur |
| MIBA | Multiple Input Binary Adder | | |
| | | MICAM | Microammeter |
| MIC | Machine Index Card | MICC | Miniature Integrated Circuit Computer |
| MIC | Machine Instruction Code | | |
| MIC | Management Inventory Classification | MICCS | Minuteman Integrated Command and Control System |
| MIC | Management Inventory Code | | |
| MIC | Management Inventory Control | MICM | Magnetic Ink Character Method |
| MIC | Mathematics Information Center | | |

# M

| | | | |
|---|---|---|---|
| MICM | Monolithic Integrated Circuit Mask | MIDAC | Management Information for Decision And Control |
| MICON | Microprocessor Control | MIDAC | Michigan Digital Automatic Computer |
| MICOS | Medical Information and Communication System | MIDAR | Microwave Detection And Ranging |
| MICOS | Modular Industrial Control Oriented System | MIDAS | Management Information Dataflow System |
| MICPAK | Modular Integrated Circuit Package | MIDAS | Management Information Decision and Accounting Simulator |
| MICR | Magnetic Ink Character Reader | MIDAS | Market Information Data System |
| MICR | Magnetic Ink Character Recognition | MIDAS | Marktinformations-Datensystem |
| MICRAM | Microminiature Indivicual Component Reliably Assembled Module | MIDAS | Materials for Industry Data and Applications Service |
| MICRO | Multiple Indexing and Console Retrieval Options | MIDAS | Measurement Information Data And System |
| MICRO-PAC | Micromodule data Processor And Computer | MIDAS | Measurement Information Data Analytic System |
| MICROACE | Microminiature Automatic Checkout Equipment | MIDAS | Meterological Information and Data Acquisition System |
| MICROSIM | Microinstruction Simulator | | |
| MICRS | Magnetic Ink Character Recognition System | MIDAS | MICOM Digital Analysis code |
| MICS | Machine Inventory Control System | MIDAS | Micro-Image Data Addition System |
| MICS | Magnetic Ink Character Set | MIDAS | Microprogrammable Integrated Data Acquisition System |
| MICS | Manufacturing Information Control System | | |
| MICS | Management Information Control System | MIDAS | Miniature Data Acquisition System |
| MICS | Management Information and Control System | MIDAS | Missile Defense Alarm System |
| MICS | Manufacturing Information and Control System | MIDAS | Missile Intercept Data Acquisition System |
| MICS | Manufacturing Information Control System | MIDAS | Mixed Data Structure |
| | | MIDAS | Modified Integration Digital to Analog Simulation |
| MICS | Material Information and Control System | | |
| MICS | Microfiche Interface Controller System | MIDAS | Modified Integration Digital to Analog Simulator |
| MICS | Microwave Integrated Circuits | MIDAS | Modular Integrated Direct Access System |
| MICS | MVS Integrated Control System | MIDAS | Modular Interactive Data Acquisition System |
| MICSIM | Microsimulator | | |
| MID | Message Input Descriptor | MIDAS | Modulator Isolation Diagnostic Analysis System |
| MID | Message Input Device | | |
| MID | Multiplier-Inverted Divider | MIDAS | Monte Carlo Investigation Data System |
| MIDA | Miniature-Integrated-Diode Assembly | | |

# M

| | | | |
|---|---|---|---|
| MIDAS | Multiple Index Direct Access System | MIL | Micro Implementation Language |
| MIDAS | Multiple Input Data Acquisition System | MIL | Micro Instruction Language |
| MIDAS | Myriad Interactive Data Analysis System | MIL | Microsystem International Limited |
| MIDGETROL | Midget control | MIL | Microsystem Limited |
| MIDI | Musical Instrument Digital Interface | MIL | Military |
| MIDIS | Management Information for Distribution | MIL | Military Standard |
| | | MIL | Millinch |
| MIDIST | Mission Interministérielle De l'Information Scientifique et Technique | MILDD | Military-Industry Logistic Data Development |
| | | MILDDU | Military-Industry Logistics Data Development Unit |
| MIDMS | Machine Independent Data Management System | MILDIP | Military Industry Logistics Data Interchange Procedure |
| MIDORI | Modern Information and Documentation Organizing and Rearrangement, Inc. | MILE | Matrix Inversion and Linear Equations |
| | | MILP | Mices Integer Linear Programming |
| MIDOS | Mikrocomputer Disk Operating System | MILPAS | Miscellaneous Information Listing Program Apollo Spacecraft |
| MIDS | Management Information and Decision System | MILSIMDS | Military Standard Item Management Data System |
| MIDS | Management Information Display System | MILSTD | Military Standards |
| MIDU | Malfunction Insertion and Display Unit | MIM | Management Information Marketing |
| MIF | Machine Installed File | MIM | Management Informatique Marketing |
| MIF | Manual Intervention Facility | MIM | Metal-Insulator-Metal |
| MIF | Master Index File | MIM | Microinstruction Memory |
| MIFE | Minimum Independent Failure Element | MIM | Modem Interface Module |
| | | MIM | Modified Index Method |
| MIFR | Master Informational Frequency | MIM | Montreal International software Market |
| MIG | Message Identification Group | MIMA | Mittelfristige Maschinenbelastung |
| MIG | Multi-Informations-Generator | MIMD | Multiple Instruction Multiple Data |
| MIH | Missing Interruption Handler | MIMD | Multiple-Instruction-Multiple-Data-machine |
| MIIS | Metal Insulation Insulation Semiconductor | MIMD | Multiple Instruction-Multiple-Data-stream |
| MIIS | Miscellaneous Inputs Information Subsystem | MIMIC | Microfilm Information Master Image Converter |
| MIJID | Marché International des Jeux vidéo de l'Informatique individuelle et Domestique | MIMO | Man In, Machine Out |
| | | MIMO | Miniature Image Orthicon |
| | | MIMOS-FET | Metal-Insulator-Metal Oxide Semiconductor-Field-Effect Transistor |
| MIK | Mikroelektronik | | |
| MIKE | Multiple Inverted Key Environment | MIMS | Medical Information Management System |
| MIKSAM | Multiple Indexed Keyed Sequential Access Method | MIMS | Metal-Insulator-Metal Semiconductor |

# M

| | | | |
|---|---|---|---|
| MIMS | Micromation Subroutine | MINS | Miniature Inertial Navigation System |
| MIMS | Multi-Item Multi-Source | | |
| MIMT | Micromation Translator | MINT | Material Identification and New item control Technique |
| MIN | Manual Incoming operation | | |
| MIN | Minimum | | |
| MIN MC | Minimum Material Condition | MIO | Million |
| | | MIOP | Multiplex Input Output Processor |
| MIN-LED | Metal Insulating N-type LED | MIOP | Multiplexed I/O Processor |
| MINAC | Miniature Navigation Airborne Computer | MIOP | Multiplexor Input/Output Processor |
| MINCAL | Miniature Calculator | MIOS | Modular Input-Output System |
| MINCOS | Modular Inventory Control System | MIP | Manual Input Processing |
| MIND | Multifunctional Integrated Design | MIP | Manual Input Program |
| | | MIP | Matrix Inversion Program |
| | | MIP | Memory In Pulse |
| MINDAC | Marine Inertial Navigation Data Assimilation Computer | MIP | Method Improvement Program |
| MINDAC | Miniature Inertial Navigation Digital Automatic Computer | MIP | Microwave Interference Protection |
| | | MIP | Mikroprozessor |
| MINE | Montana Information Network and Exchange | MIP | Minimum Impulse Pulse |
| | | MIP | Mixed Integer Programming |
| MINELCO | Miniature Electronic Component | MIP | Modular Information Processor |
| MINERVA | Multiple Input Network for Evaluating Reactions, Votes and Attitudes | MIPAS | Management Information Planning and Accountancy System |
| MINI | Miniature | | |
| MINI | Minicomputer Industry National Interchange | MIPE | Modular Information Processing Equipment |
| MINI-DADS | Minimum Digital Air Data System | MIPL | Machine Independent Program Language |
| MINIAC | Minimal Automatic Computer | MIPS | Megainstructions Per Second |
| MINIAPS | Miniature Accessory Power Supply | MIPS | Metal Insulator Piezo-electric Semiconductor |
| MINIC | Minicomputer | MIPS | Military Information Processing System |
| MINICOM | Minimum Communications | | |
| MINING | Machine Independent Numerical Interactive Graphics | MIPS | Million Instruction Per Second |
| | | MIPS | Millionen Instruktionen Pro Sekunde |
| MINIPERT | Minimum Program Evaluation and Review Technique | MIPS | Millions of Instructions Per Second |
| MINIT | Minimum Interference Threshold | MIPS | Missile Information Processing System |
| MINITEX | Minnesota Interlibrary Teletype Experiment | MIPSU | Micro Program Storage Unit |
| MINITROL | Miniature Control | MIR | Magnetic Ink Read |
| MINITS | Miniature Time Sharing | MIR | Memory Information Register |
| MINPRT | Miniature Processing Time | | |
| MINS | Management Information Network System | MIR | Memory Input Register |
| | | MIR | Microinstruction Register |

# M

| | |
|---|---|
| MIR | Multiple Internal Reflection |
| MIR | Music Information Retrieval |
| MIRA | Multifunction Inertial Reference Assembly |
| MIRAC | Microfilmed Reports and Accounts |
| MIRACL | Macro-Implemented Realtime Analytical Chemistry Language |
| MIRACLE | Mokum Industrial Research Automatic Calculator for Laboratory and Engineering |
| MIRACODE | Microfilm Information Retrieval Access Code |
| MIRAGE | Microprogrammable Interactive Raster Graphics Equipment |
| MIRAID | Maintenance Information Retrieval Aid |
| MIRFAC | Mathematics In Recognizable Form Automatically Compiled |
| MIRPS | Multiple Information Retrieval by Parallel Selection |
| MIRROS | Modulation Inducing Reactive Retrodirective Optical System |
| MIRS | Marketing Information Retrieval System |
| MIRS | Micro Interactive Retrieval System |
| MIS | Management Information Services |
| MIS | Management Information System |
| MIS | Management Inquiry System |
| MIS | Management-Informations-system |
| MIS | Managment Information Science |
| MIS | Manufacturing Information System |
| MIS | Marketing Information System |
| MIS | Master Integrated Schedule |
| MIS | Matrix Interpretative Scheme |
| MIS | Medical Information System |
| MIS | Metal Insulator Semiconductor |
| MIS | Metal-thin film Insulator-Semiconductor |
| MIS | Mikrofilm-Informations-System |
| MIS | Mission Information System |
| MIS | Monats-Informations-System |
| MIS | Multistate Information System |
| MISAR | Microprocessed Sensing and Automatic Regulation |
| MISAR | Miniature Information Storage And Retrieval |
| MISC | Miscellaneous |
| MISD | Multiple Instruction Single Data stream |
| MISD | Multiple Instruction Single Data |
| MISDAS | Multiple Input Scanning Data Acquisition System |
| MISER | Management Information System for Expenditure Reporting |
| MISFET | Metal Insulator Semi-conductor Field Effect Transistor |
| MISI | Micro Information Systems, Incorporated |
| MISI... | Micro Information Systems Inc. |
| MISIAS | Management Information Systems Inventory and Analysis System |
| MISIC | Metal-Insulator-Semi-conductor Integrated Circuit |
| MISL | Military Intelligence Service Language |
| MISM | Metal-Insulator-Semi-conductor-Metal |
| MISO | Multi-Input, Single Output |
| MISP | Medical Information System Program |
| MISPL | Management Informations-system für die Planung |
| MISRC | Management Information System Research Center |
| MISS | Multi-Item Single Source |
| MISS LESS | Management Information Scheduling - a Segment of LESS |

# M

| | | | |
|---|---|---|---|
| MISSD | Minuteman Integrated Schedules, Status and Data | MIXWARE | Mixed hardware |
| | | MIXWARE | Mixed software |
| MISSIL | Management Information System Symbolic Interpretive Language | MIZ | Management-Informationszentrum |
| | | MIZ | Materialinformationszentrum |
| MIST | Metal Insulator Semiconductor Transistor | MJ | Major alarm |
| | | MJS | Multi-Job Scheduling |
| MIST | Modular Intermittent Sort and Test device | MK | Magnetkarte |
| | | MK | Magnetkontensystem |
| MIST | Multi-Input Standard Tape | MK | Magnetkonto |
| MISTER | Management Information System for Time, Expenses, and Resources | MK | Magnetkontokarte |
| | | MK | Magnetkopf |
| | | MK | Mikrophone |
| MISTER | Mobile Integrated System Trainer, Evaluator, and Recorder | MK | Morsekode |
| | | MKA | Magnetbandkassetten-Aufnahmegerät |
| MISTIC | Michigan State Integral Computer | MKA | Multikonferenzanlage |
| | | MKC | Magnetkontencomputer |
| MISTRAM | Missile Trajectory Measurement system | MKE | Magnetkonteneinheit |
| | | MKG | Marketing |
| MISTRIS | Microfiche Information Storage and Retrieval for Intelligence Support | MKG | Magnetkontokartengerät |
| | | MKK | Magnetkontokarte |
| | | MKR | Magnetbandkassetten-Registrierbaustein |
| MIT | Massachusetts Institute of Technology | MKS | Magnetband-Kassettenspeicher |
| MIT | Master Instruction Tape | | |
| MIT | Master Interface Tape | MKS | Magnetkartenspeicher |
| MIT | Military Intelligence Translator | MKS | Magnetkernspeicher |
| | | MKS | Management-Kommunikationssystem |
| MIT | Modular Intermediate Termination | MKS | Metre-Kilogram-Second system |
| MITATT | Mixed Tunneling and Avalanche Transit-Time | MKSA | Meter-Kilogram-Second-Ampere system |
| MITE | Microelectronic Integrated Test and Evaluation | MKSP | Magnetkartenspeicher |
| | | MKTG | Marketing |
| MITE | Microelectronic Test and Evaluation | MKV | Magnetkontenverarbeitung |
| | | MKV | Multikommunikationsverbund |
| MITE | Mikroelektronische Integrierte Testeinrichtung | MKVE | Magnetkontenverarbeitungseinheit |
| MITE | Multiple Input Terminal Equipment | ML | Machine Language |
| | | ML | Macro Language |
| MITI | Ministry of International Trade and Industry | ML | Macro Library |
| | | ML | Maintenance Level |
| MITILAC | Massachusetts Institute of Technology Information Laboratory Automatic Coding | ML | Management-Leistung |
| | | ML | Markierungsleser |
| | | ML | Mathematical Logic |
| MITS | Multiplex Information Transfer System | ML | Maximum Likelihood |
| | | ML | Mehrfachlochung |
| MIU | Message Injection Unit | ML | Mehrlogikschaltung |
| MIU | Multiple Interface Unit | ML | Memory Location |
| MIX | Metropolitan Information Exchange | ML | Memory Logic |
| | | ML | Methods of Limits |
| MIX | Mixer | | |

# M

| | |
|---|---|
| ML | Microline |
| ML | Mission Life |
| MLA | Mehrfachleitungsanschluß |
| MLA | Microprocessor Language Assembler |
| MLA | Multi-Line Adapter |
| MLA | Multileaving Adapter |
| MLB | Multi-purpose Logic Block |
| MLB | Multilayer Board |
| MLC | Machine Language Code |
| MLC | Machine Language Coding |
| MLC | Machine Level Control |
| MLC | Machine Location Card |
| MLC | Magnetic Ledger Card |
| MLC | Medium-Level Center |
| MLC | Microelectronic Logic Circuit |
| MLC | Minimum Latency Coding |
| MLC | Motor Landing Craft |
| MLC | Multi-Layer Ceramic |
| MLC | Multi-Layer Circuit |
| MLC | Multi-Line Controller |
| MLC | Multilayer Laminated Ceramic |
| MLC | Multilink Control |
| MLC | Multilink Control Field |
| MLC | Multiple Line Card |
| MLC | Multiplex Logic Circuit |
| MLCA | Machine Level Control Address |
| MLCA | Multi-Line-Communications Adapter |
| MLCB | Multi-Layer Circuit Board |
| MLCP | Machine Language Control Program |
| MLCP | Multiline Communications Processor |
| MLD | Medium Lethal Dose |
| MLD | Minimum Lethal Dose |
| MLD | Minimum Line of Detection |
| MLD | Multi-Loop Digital controller |
| MLDL | Mooring Line Data Line |
| MLDSP | Multi-Level Continuous Sampling Plan |
| MLE | Maximum Likelihood Estimate |
| MLE | Microprocessor Language Editor |
| MLED | Motorola Light Emitting Diode |
| MLI | Marker Light Indicator |
| MLI | Multileaving Interface |
| MLIS | Metal Liquid Insulator Semiconductor |
| MLK | Maschinenlochkarte |
| MLL | Master Logic List |
| MLL | Mode-Locked Laser |
| MLLV | Mehrlagenleiterplatten-Vormaterial |
| MLM | Mixed Level Matrix |
| MLMIS | Minnesota Land Management Information System |
| MLMS | Modified Least Mean Square |
| MLO | Marxistisch-Leninistische Organisationswissenschaft |
| MLO | Memory Lock Out |
| MLP | Machine Language Program |
| MLP | Mechanical Line Printer |
| MLP | Mikrofilm Laser Plotter |
| MLP | Minimum Latency Programming |
| MLP | Multi-Level Programmer |
| MLP | Multilink Procedure |
| MLP | Multiparametric Linear Programming |
| MLP | Multiple Language Page |
| MLP | Multiple Line Print |
| MLP | Multiple Line Printing |
| MLPC | Multi-Layer Printed Circuit |
| MLPCB | Multi-Layer Printed Circuit Board |
| MLPW | Multi-Layer Printed Wiring |
| MLPWB | Multi-Layer Printed Wiring Board |
| MLR | Main Line of Resistance |
| MLR | Memory Location Register |
| MLR | Memory Lockout Register |
| MLR | Multiple Line Read |
| MLR | Multiple Line Reading |
| MLR | Multiplier Left Register |
| MLR | Multiply and Round |
| MLREG | Multiple Linear Regression |
| MLS | Machine Literature Searching |
| MLS | Machine Literature Search |
| MLS | Machine Loading Schedule |
| MLS | Microprogram List System |
| MLS | Microwave Landing System |
| MLS | Mixed Language System |
| MLS | Multi-Language System |
| MLS | Multiple Ledger System |

# M

| | | | |
|---|---|---|---|
| MLSDS | Missile Launch Site Data Sheet | MM | Multimode |
| MLSI | Multilevel Large Scale Integration | MMA | Main Memory Address |
| | | MMA | Maximum Mean Accuracy |
| | | MMA | Message Mode Adapter |
| MLSR | Maximal Language Shift Register | MMA | Multiple Memory Adapter |
| | | MMA | Multiple Module Access |
| MLSR | Maximal Length Shift Register | MMA | Multiplexed Matrix Array |
| | | MMAC | Micro-Miniature Analog Circuit |
| MLSS | Mixed Liquor Suspended Solids | MMB | Modell- und Methodenbank |
| MLT | Mean Length of Turn | MMBS | Magnetomotorischer Binärspeicher |
| MLT | Median Lethal Time | | |
| MLT | Micro Layer Transistor | MMC | Micro-Miniature Connector |
| MLT | Module Logic Technology | MMC | Missile Motion Computer |
| MLT | Monolithic Logic Technology | MMC | Monthly Maintenance Charge |
| MLT | Monolithtechnik | MMC | Multi-Mikrocomputer |
| MLT | Multi-Level Technology | MMCD | Master Monitor Criteria Data |
| MLT | Multiplikation | | |
| MLTY | Military | MMD | Moving Map Display |
| MLU | Memory Loading Unit | MMD | Multimode Display |
| MLU | Memory Logic Unit | MMDC | Mount Misalignment Data Collection |
| MLU | Multiple Logical Unit | | |
| MLV | Muster-Leistungs-Verzeichnis | MMDS | Martin Marietta Data Systems |
| MLY | Mask Limited Yield | MMDS | Merchant Marine Data Sheet |
| MLY | Multiply | | |
| MM | Macromodule | MMF | Magnetomotive Force |
| MM | Magnetic Memory | MMF | Message Management Feature |
| MM | Magnetic Moment | | |
| MM | Main Memory | MMF | Micro Main Frame |
| MM | Maintenance Manual | MMF | Micromicrofarad |
| MM | Marketing Manager | MMG | Meßmarkengeber |
| MM | Mass Memory | MMH | Methode der Multimoment-Häufigkeitszählung |
| MM | Master Machine | | |
| MM | Master Monitor | | |
| MM | Mathematisches Modell | MMI | Man Machine Interface |
| MM | Matrix Memory | MMI/O | Memory Mapped Input/Output |
| MM | Megamega | | |
| MM | Mémoire Morte | MMIC | Millimeter-Wave Integrated Circuit |
| MM | Memory Management | | |
| MM | Memory Module | MMICS | Maintenance Management Information and Control System |
| MM | Memory Multiplexer | | |
| MM | Message Management | | |
| MM | Meßmarke | MMIPS | Man-Machine Interactive Processing System |
| MM | Micro-Module | | |
| MM | Microfilm Memory | MMIS | Maintenance Management Information System |
| MM | Middle Management | | |
| MM | Middle Marker | MMIS | Material-Management-Informationssystem |
| MM | Mikrocomputermodus | | |
| MM | Mission Module | MMIS | Medical Management Information System |
| MM | Mittleres Management | | |
| MM | Moduliertes Merkmal | MMIS | Municipal Management Information System |
| MM | Monostabiler Multivibrator | | |
| MM | Monostable Multivibrator | | |

# M

| | | | |
|---|---|---|---|
| MMK | Mensch-Maschine-Kommunikation | MMSI | Multi-Medium-Scale Integration |
| MML | Man-Machine Language | MMST | Multi-Mode Storage Tube |
| MML | Microprogrammed MOSFET Logic | MMT | Milling Machine Taper |
| | | MMU | Mass Memory Unit |
| MML | Micro-Mainframe-Link | MMU | Memory Management Unit |
| MML | Monitor Meta Language | MMU | Memory Management Utilities |
| MMM | Magnetic Memory Matrix | | |
| MMM | Minnesota Mining and Manufacturing Co. | MMU | Message Mapping Utility |
| | | MMV | Monostabiler Multivibrator |
| MMM | Monolithic Main Memory | MMV | Monostable Multivibrator |
| MMM | Multi-Media Message | MMZ | Multimoment-Zeitmessung |
| MMM | Multi-Mode-Matrix display | MN | Magnetic North |
| MMMC | Minimum Monthly Maintenance Charge | MN | Manual |
| | | MN | Menue |
| MMMIS | Maintenance & Material Management Information System | MN | Minor alarm |
| | | MN | Minus |
| | | MNA | Modified Nodal Admittance |
| MMO | Main Machine Operation | MNC | Multinational Company |
| MMO | Multi-Mode Operation | MNCS | Multiprint Network Control System |
| MMOD | Micromodule | | |
| MMOST | Memory Metal-Oxide Semiconductor Transistor | MNDP | Multi-National Data Processing |
| MMP | Main Memory Print | MNF | Minimum Normal Form |
| MMP | Mémoire Morte Programmable | MNL OPR | Manually Operated |
| | | MNLS | Modified New Least Squares |
| MMP | Microprogrammable Multi-Processor | MNO | Metal-Nitride-Oxide |
| | | MNOS | Metal Nitride Oxide Semiconductor |
| MMP | Molecule Model Program | | |
| MMP | Multiplex Message Processor | MNOS | Metal Nitride Oxide Silicon |
| MMPT | Man-Machine Partnership Translation | MNOS | Metall-Nitrid-Oxide-Substrat |
| MMPU | Mémoire Morte Programmable en Usine | MNOS-LAD | MNOS-Lawinendiode |
| | | MNOS-OT | MNOS-Oberflächengesteuerter Transistor |
| MMR | Main Memory Register | | |
| MMR | Message Metering Recall | | |
| MMRI | Multi Media Reviews Index | MNOSFET | Metal-Nitride-Oxide-Silicon Field-Effect Transistor |
| MMS | Man-Machine System | | |
| MMS | Manufacturing Monitoring System | MNOST | Metal-Nitride-Oxide-Silicon Transistor |
| MMS | Mask-Management-System | MNPD | Missile and Nuclear Programming Data |
| MMS | Mass Memory Store | | |
| MMS | Mass Memory Subsystem | MNS | Metal-Nitride-Semiconductor |
| MMS | Mass Memory System | | |
| MMS | Microfiche Management Software | MNS | Metal-Nitride-Silicon |
| | | MNS | Metal-thermal-Nitride-Silicon |
| MMS | Microfiche Management System | | |
| | | MNS | Minutes |
| MMS | Multi-Modular Storage | MNSFET | Metal-Nitride-Semiconductor Field-Effect Transistor |
| MMS | Multiprogramming for Medium Systems | | |
| MMSE | Minimum-Mean-Squared Error | MNTR | Monitor |

- 398 -

# M

| | | | |
|---|---|---|---|
| MO | Machine Operation | MOC | Monolithic integrated Circuit |
| MO | Machine Operator | | |
| MO | Machine-Outil | MOC-LAMP | Method Of Characteristic Laser And Mixing Program |
| MO | Mailbox Owner | | |
| MO | Manual Operation | | |
| MO | Master Oscillator | MOCN | Machine-Outil à Commande Numérique |
| MO | Memory Operation | | |
| MO | Memory Organization | MOCROSECS | Microfilm Sequential Coding System |
| MO | Molecular Orbital | | |
| MO | Monitor | MOCSW | Monitor and Operations Control Software |
| MO | Monitor Oscilloscope | | |
| MO | Monitor Output | MOD | Magnetic-Optical Display |
| MO | Motor | MOD | Message Output Desciption |
| MO | Multiple Operation | MOD | Message Output Descriptor |
| MO | Multiplying Operator | MOD | Microfilm Output Device |
| MOA | Matrix Output Amplifier | MOD | Microwave Oscillating Diode |
| MOB | Maschinenorientierte Bibliotheksorganisation | MOD | Model |
| MOB | Message Operation Block | MOD | Modell |
| MOBDIC | Mobile Digital Computer | MOD | Modification |
| MOBIDA | Mobile Datenerfassung | MOD | Modifier |
| MOBIDA | Mobiles Datenerfassungs- und Verarbeitungsgerät | MOD | Modify |
| | | MOD | Modulation |
| MOBIDAC | Mobile Data Acquisition system | MOD | Modulator |
| | | MOD | Module |
| MOBIDIC | Mobile Digital Computer | MOD/DEMOD | Modulator/Demodulator |
| MOBIL-AC | Mobile Accounting and Control | MOD/DEMOD | Modulation/Demodulation |
| MOBIS | Management-Oriented Budget Information System | MODA | Motion Detector and Alarm |
| | | MODAC | Mountain Digital Automatic Computer |
| MOBL | Macro-Oriented Business Language | MODAC | Mountain system Digital Automatic Computer |
| MOBOL | Mohawk Business Oriented Language | MODAP | Multiple Operational Data Acquisition Program |
| MOBULA | Model Building Language | MODAPS | Maintenance and Operational Data Presentation Study |
| MOC | Magnetic Optic Converter | | |
| MOC | Mask Order Control | | |
| MOC | Master Operation Card | MODAPS | Model Data Acquisition and Processing System |
| MOC | Master Operational Controller | | |
| | | MODAS | Modell-Datenbanksystem |
| MOC | Mathematical Operations Computer | MODB | Military Occupational Data Bank |
| MOC | Mathematics Of Computation | MODCOMP | Modular Computer |
| | | MODE | Monitor Data Equipment |
| MOC | Memory Operating Characteristic | MODEFA | Mode Forecasting system |
| | | MODEM | Modulate-Demodulate |
| MOC | Memory Operation Control | MODEM | Modulator-Demodulator |
| MOC | Microfilm Output Computer | MODLE | Meteorological Office Data-Logging Equipment |
| MOC | Minimum Operating Characteristics | MODM | Magnet-Optical Display Memory |
| MOC | Mission Operation Computer | MODOK | Modulare Dokumentation |

- 399 -

# M

| | | | |
|---|---|---|---|
| MODP | Modern Programming Practices | MONIC | Moniteur Inter-Compilations |
| MODS | Major Operation Data System | MONOS | Metal-Oxide Nitride-Oxide Semiconductor |
| MODS | Manned Orbital Development System | MONOS | Monitor Out of Service |
| MODS | Manpower Operation Data System | MONS | Monitoring System |
| MODS | Medically Orientated Data System | MONTIS | Monteur-Informationssystem |
| MODUS | Modular One Dynamic User System | MONTREAL | Monitor für Realzeit-System |
| MOE | Measure Of Effectiveness | MOP | Matrix Operations Programming |
| MOERO | Medium Orbiting Earth Resources Observatory | MOP | Memory Out Pulse |
| MOF | Master Order File | MOP | Modelloperation |
| MOF | Maximum Observed Frequency | MOP | Modelloperator |
| MOF | Maximum Operating Frequency | MOP | MORT Plotter |
| MOG | Micro-Ordinateur de Guichet | MOP | Multi access On-line Programming |
| MOGA | Microwave and Optical Generation and Amplification | MOP | Multiple Online Programming |
| MOH | Music On Hold | MOP | Multiple Operation |
| MOIV | Mechanically Operated Inlet Value | MOP | Multiple Output Program |
| MOL | Machine Oriented Language | MOPA | Master-Oscillator Power-Amplifier |
| MOL | Manned Orbiting Laboratory | MOPAFD | Master Oscillator Power Amplifier Frequency Doubler |
| MOL | Maximum Output Level | MOPAR | Master Oscillator Power Amplifier Radar |
| MOLAB | Mobil lunar Laboratory | MOPB | Manually Operated Plotting Board |
| MOLDS | Management On-Line Data System | MOPL | Machine Oriented Program Language |
| MOLDS | Multiple On-Line Debugging System | MOPS | Machine Oriented Programming System |
| MOLECOM | Molecularized Computer | MOPS | Magneto-Optic Photoconductor Sandwich |
| MOLECOM | Molecularized digital Computer | MOPS | Maschinenorientierte Programmiersprache |
| MOLP | Multiple Objective Linear Programming | MOPS | Maschinenorientiertes Programmsystem |
| MOLS | Modified On-Line Sequential | MOPS | Megaoperations Per Second |
| MOM | Magneto-Optic Method | MOPS | Million Operationen Pro Sekunde |
| MOM | Metal Oxide Metal | MOPSY | Multi-programming Operating System |
| MOM | Moment | MOQUISS | Modulares Qualitätsinformations- und Steuerungs-System |
| MOMS | Multimegabit Operation Multiplexer System | MOR | Master Operational Record |
| MON | Monitor | MOR | Medium frequency Omnirange |
| MONA | Multitape One-way Non-writing Automaton | MOR | Memory Operand |
| MONES | Moniteur d'Entrées/Sorties | MOR | Memory Output Register |

# M

| | | | |
|---|---|---|---|
| MOR | Meteorological Optical Range | MOS-IC | Metal-Oxide Semiconductor Integrated Circuit |
| MOR | MORT Recording | MOS-MSI | Metal-Oxide Semiconductor Medium Scale Integration |
| MOR | Multiplikator | | |
| MORIF | Microprogram Optimization technique considering Resource occupancy and Instruction Formats | MOS-VLSI | Metal-Oxide Semiconductor/Very Large Scale Integration |
| MORL | Manned Orbital Research Laboratory | MOS/SOS | Metal-Oxide Semiconductor/Silicon-On-Sapphire |
| MORT | Master Operational Recording Tape | MOSAIC | Macro-Operating Symbolic Assembler and Information Compiler |
| MORT | Morse Tape | | |
| MOS | Magnetic tape Operating System | MOSAIC | Macro Operation Symbolic Assembler and Information Compiler |
| MOS | Management Operation System | | |
| MOS | Maschinenorientierte Sprache | MOSAIC | Metal-Oxide Semiconductor Advanced Integrated Circuit |
| MOS | Maschinenorientierte Systemunterlagen | | |
| MOS | Maschinenorientiertes System | MOSAIC | Metal-Oxide Silicon Advanced Integrated Circuit |
| MOS | Master Operation System | | |
| MOS | Métal Oxyde Semiconducteur | MOSAICS | Melcom Optical Software Applications for Integrated Commercial Systems |
| MOS | Metal-Oxide Semiconductor | | |
| MOS | Metal-Oxide Silicon | MOSAR | Modulation Scan Array Radar |
| MOS | Metal-Oxide Substrate | | |
| MOS | Microcomputer-Operating-System | MOSASR | Metal-Oxide Semiconductor Analog Shift Register |
| MOS | Modular Operating System | | |
| MOS | Mulituser Operating System | MOSCOR | Modular System for Computation Of Requirements |
| MOS | Multicomputer Operating System | MOSCOS | Molins Operational Shop Control System |
| MOS | Multifunctional Operating System | MOSE | Multi-Operating System Environment |
| MOS RAM | Metal-Oxide Semiconductor Random Access Memory | MOSFET | Metal-Oxide Semiconductor Field Effect Transistor |
| MOS ROM | Metal-Oxide Semiconductor Read Only Memory | MOSFET-IC | MOSFET Integrated Circuit |
| MOS-C | MOS Capacitor | MOSIM | Modulares Simulationssystem |
| MOS-C | MOS Capacitor of requirements | MOSL | Manned Orbital Space Laboratory |
| MOS-DIP | Metal-Oxide Semiconductor-Dual Inline Package | MOSLSI | Metal-Oxide Semiconductor Large Scale Integration |
| MOS-FET-IC | Metal-Oxide Semiconductor Field Effect Transistor Integrated Circuit | MOSM | Metal-Oxide Semimetal |
| | | MOSROM | MOS Read Only Memory |

# M

| | | | |
|---|---|---|---|
| MOSS | Manned Orbital Space Station | MP | Mathematical Programming |
| MOST | Macro-Oriented System Technique | MP | Matrix Printer |
| | | MP | Mechanical Part |
| MOST | Metal-Oxide Semi-conductor Transistor | MP | Mechanical Punch |
| | | MP | Megapond |
| MOST | Metal-Oxide Surface Transistor | MP | Mehrprozessor |
| | | MP | Meldungspuffer |
| MOST | Metal-Oxide-Silicon Transistor | MP | Melting Point |
| | | MP | Memory Pointer |
| MOST | Metall-Oxid-Silizium-Transistor | MP | Memory Protection |
| | | MP | Merge Program |
| MOST | Micromation Output Software Translator | MP | Message Processor |
| | | MP | Meßpunkt |
| MOST | Modular Operating System Tool | MP | Metallized Paper |
| | | MP | Micro-Program |
| MOSTL | MOS Transmission Line | MP | Micro-Programming |
| MOT | Motor | MP | Microfilm, Positive |
| MOT | Mean Outage Time | MP | Mikroprozessor |
| MOTAM | Mohawk Terminal Access Method | MP | Minimum Phase |
| | | MP | Modular Program |
| MOTARDES | Moving Target Detection System | MP | Monitor Printer |
| | | MP | Monitor Program |
| MOTU | Mobile Optical Tracking Unit | MP | Motor Punch |
| | | MP | Mounting Panel |
| MOV | Metal Oxide Varistor | MP | Multi-Point |
| MOV | Move | MP | Multi-Pulse |
| MOVL | Move Left | MP | Multi-Purpose |
| MOVR | Move Right | MP | Multiple Programming |
| MOVRI | Manually Operated Visual Response Indicator | MP | Multiple Punch |
| | | MP | Multiplex |
| MOW | Mechanized Order Writing | MP | Multiplexer |
| MOXET | Metal-Oxide Enhancement Transistor | MP | Multiplication |
| | | MP | Multiplier |
| MP | Machine Processing | MP | Multiplikation |
| MP | Machine Program | MP | Multiplizieren |
| MP | Machine Programming | MP | Multipole |
| MP | Magnetic Print | MP | Multiprocessing |
| MP | Magnetplatte | MP | Multiprocessor |
| MP | Magnetplattenspeicher | MP | Multiprogramming |
| MP | Main Phase | MP/AOS | Micro Processor/Advanced Operating System |
| MP | Main Processor | | |
| MP | Main Program | MP/M | Monitor Program for Microcomputers |
| MP | Maintenance Point | | |
| MP | Maintenance Programming | MPA | Maximum Permissible Amount |
| MP | Manual Perforator | | |
| MP | Manual Program | MPA | Modulated Pulse Amplifier |
| MP | Manual Punch | MPA | Motion Picture Amplifier |
| MP | Manufacturing Process | MPA | Multi-Precision Arithmetic |
| MP | Manufacturing Procedure | MPA | Multiple-Period Average |
| MP | Marketing Program | MPAA | Mechanization of Printed-circuit Amplifier Assembly |
| MP | Master Program | | |
| MP | Matched Pair | | |
| MP | Material Planning | MPAD | Multiple Adaptor |

# M

| | | | |
|---|---|---|---|
| MPB | Momentary Pushbutton switch | MPDS | Microtek-Personal-Development-System |
| MPB | Multilayer Printed Board | MPDW | Multipair Distribution Wire |
| MPB | Multiprogrammbetrieb | MPE | Mathematical and Physical science and Engineering |
| MPC | Machine Punch Card | | |
| MPC | Main Processor Control | MPE | Maximum Permissible Exposure |
| MPC | Marginal Punched Card | | |
| MPC | Master Parts Card | MPE | Multi Programming Executive |
| MPC | Master Program Chart | | |
| MPC | Material Program Code | MPECC | Multi-Processor Experimental Computer Complex |
| MPC | Maximum Permissible Concentration | | |
| MPC | Message Parity Character | MPF | Master Program File |
| MPC | Microfilm Punched Card | MPG | Mathematic Products Group |
| MPC | Microprogram Control | | |
| MPC | Microprogrammed Controller | MPG | Microwave Pulse Generator |
| MPC | MORT Processor Control | MPG | Miniature Precision Gyrocompass |
| MPC | Multi-Process Controller | | |
| MPC | Multi-Processor Computer | MPGS | Micro Program Generating System |
| MPC | Multi-Programming Computer | MPI | Main Program Input |
| MPC | Multi-Punch Control | MPI | Manpower and Personnel Information system |
| MPC | Multiprocessing | | |
| MPC | Multiprogram Control | MPI | Manual Program Input |
| MPCB | Multilayer Printed Circuit Board | MPI | Mean Point of Impact |
| | | MPI | Message Processing Interrupt count |
| MPCC | Multi-Processor Computer Complex | | |
| | | MPI | Moyennes et Petites Industries |
| MPCC | Multi Protocol Communications Circuit | | |
| | | MPK | Memory Protect Key |
| MPCC | Multi Protocol Communications Controller | MPK | Multiple Page Keyboard |
| | | MPKE | Meß-, Prüf- und Kontrolleinrichtung |
| MPCD | Minimum Perceptable Colour Difference | | |
| | | MPL | Macro-Programming Language |
| MPCD | Minimum Perceptable Difference | | |
| | | MPL | Magnetplatte |
| MPCR | Maximum Performance-to-Cost Ratio | MPL | Master Parts List |
| | | MPL | Materialbereitstellungsplanungsverfahren |
| MPCS | Manufacturing Planning and Control System | | |
| | | MPL | Mathematical Programming Language |
| MPD | Magnetoplasmadynamics | | |
| MPD | Maximum Permissible Dose | MPL | Maximum Permissible Level |
| MPD | Maximum Phase Deviation | | |
| MPD | Missing Pulse Detector | MPL | Message Processing Language |
| MPDC | Mechanical Properties Data Center | | |
| | | MPL | Microdata Programming Language |
| MPDM | Maintenance Planning Data Manual | | |
| | | MPL | Microprogramming Language |
| MPDR | Microprogram Data Register | | |
| | | MPL | Mnemonic Programming Language |
| MPDS | Mechanical Provisioning Data System | | |
| | | MPL | Modified Programmers Language |
| MPDS | Message Processing and Distribution System | | |
| | | MPL | Multiple |

# M

| | | | |
|---|---|---|---|
| MPM | Magnetic Phase Modulator | MPR | Mehr-Prozessor-Rechner |
| MPM | Magnetic Plate Memory | MPR | Memory Protection Register |
| MPM | Message-Processing Module | MPR | Message Parameter Record |
| MPM | Metra-Potential-Methode | MPR | Mikroprozessor-Regler |
| MPM | Microprogrammed Microcomputer | MPR | Minimum Performance Recommendation |
| MPM | Monitor Program for Microcomputers | MPR | Multiply and Round |
| MPM | Multiprocessing Mode | MPRG | Microprogram |
| MPM | Multiprocessing Module | MPROG | Microprogram |
| MPM | Multiprogramming Mode | MPS | Machine Program System |
| MPN | Manufacturing Productivity Network | MPS | Machine Programming System |
| MPN | Modell- und Programmiernachweis | MPS | Magnetplatten-System |
| MPN | Most Probable Number | MPS | Magnetplattenspeicher |
| MPO | Main Program Output | MPS | Magnetplattenstapel |
| MPO | Materialposition | MPS | Maintenance Processor Subsystem |
| MPO | Maximum Power Output | MPS | Manual Processing Station |
| MPO | Memory Print-Out | MPS | Maschinenprogrammsystem |
| MPO | Model Parts Only | MPS | Master Program System |
| MPO | Multi-Programming Operation | MPS | Material Processing System |
| MPOI | Master Program Of Instruction | MPS | Mathematical Programming System |
| MPOS | Multi-Programming Operating System | MPS | Mean Piston Speed |
| MPP | Manual Printing Package | MPS | Measurement Processor Subsystem |
| MPP | Mémoire Permanente Programmable | MPS | Medium Power Standard |
| MPP | Message Processing Program | MPS | Memory Processor Switch |
| MPP | Microfilm Printer/Plotter | MPS | Memory Protect Switch |
| MPPC | Master Program Phasing Chart | MPS | Meß- und Prüfsystem |
| MPPE | Memory Protect Parity Error | MPS | Meter Per Second |
| MPPH | Motion Picture Phonograph | MPS | Meter Pulse Sender |
| MPPL | Multi-Purpose Programming Language | MPS | Micro-Processor System |
| MPPM | Multi-carrier Pulse Position Modulation | MPS | Micro-Processor-Series |
| MPPS | Message Processing Procedures | MPS | Microprocessor System |
| MPPS | Message Processing Procedure Specification | MPS | Mikro-Prozessor-Serie |
| MPPS | Multipunch Print Suppression | MPS | Mikroprogrammspeicher |
| MPPU | Mémoire Permanente Programmable en Usine | MPS | Mikroprogrammsystem |
| MPR | Manufacturing Parts Record | MPS | Mikroprozessor-System |
| MPR | Mark Page Reader | MPS | Minimum Performance Standard |
| MPR | Medium Power Radar | MPS | Modem Pair Simulator |
| | | MPS | Multi-Prozessor-System |
| | | MPS | Multiple Partition Support |
| | | MPS | Multiplication Per Second |
| | | MPS | Multiplikation Pro Sekunde |
| | | MPS | Multiport Modulator-Demodulator Sharing |
| | | MPS | Multiport MODEM Sharing |
| | | MPS | Multiprocessing System |
| | | MPS | Multiprocessor Series |
| | | MPS | Multiprocessor System |
| | | MPS | Multiprogramming Support |

# M

| | | | |
|---|---|---|---|
| MPS | Multiprogramming System | MPWB | Multilayer Printed Wiring Board |
| MPS | Multipunch Print Suppression | MPX | Multi-Programming Executive |
| MPSC | Multi Protocol Serial Controller | MPX | Multiplex |
| MPSCC | Multi-Protocol Serial Communication Controller | MPX | Multiplexer |
| | | MPX | Multiplexor |
| | | MPX | Multiprogramming Executive system |
| MPSCL | Mathematical Programming System Control Language | MPX STOR | Multiplex Storage |
| | | MPXG | Multiplexing |
| MPSE | Magnetplattensteuer-einheit | MPXR | Multiplexer |
| | | MPY | Multiply |
| MPSE | Matrixprogrammierbare Steuereinrichtung | MQ | Message Queue |
| | | MQ | Multiple Quotient |
| MPSP | Magnetplattenspeicher | MQ | Multiplier Quotient |
| MPSP | Mikroprogrammspeicher | MQB | Multiplier-Quotient Buffer |
| MPSRG | Mathematical Programming System Report Generator | MQL | Mini Query Language |
| | | MQR | Multiplier Quotient Register |
| MPSST | Microprocessor Series Software Tools | MQU | Multiplier Quotient Unit |
| | | MR | Machine Record |
| MPST | Mehrprozessor-Steuerung | MR | Machine Routine |
| MPSX | Machine Programming System Extended | MR | Magnetic Reading |
| | | MR | Magnetic Recorder |
| MPSX | Mathematical Programming System Extended | MR | Magnetic Recording |
| | | MR | Magnetic Relay |
| | | MR | Magnetoresistor |
| MPSX-MIP | Mathematical Programming System Extended - Methods Improvement Program | MR | Main Register |
| | | MR | Main Routine |
| | | MR | Map Reference |
| | | MR | Mark Recognition |
| MPSX/MIP | MPS Extended Methods Improvement Program | MR | Maschinelles Rechnen |
| | | MR | Maschinenrichtung |
| MPT | Master Punched Tape | MR | Mask Recording |
| MPT | Medium Profile Terminal | MR | Mask Register |
| MPT | Micro-Probe Tester | MR | Master Relay |
| MPT | Micro-Programming Technique | MR | Master Routine |
| | | MR | Matching Range |
| MPT | Micropotentiometer | MR | Matching Record |
| MPT | Multipoint Tester | MR | Mehrrechner |
| MPTE | Multi-Purpose Test Equipment | MR | Mehrrechnersystem |
| | | MR | Memory Recall |
| MPTF | Micro-Program Temporary Fix | MR | Memory Register |
| | | MR | Memory Relay |
| MPTR | Message Pointer | MR | Memory Requirement |
| MPU | Measurement Processing Unit | MR | Message Register |
| | | MR | Message Registration |
| MPU | Micro-Processing Unit | MR | Microfilm Reader |
| MPU | Micro-Processor Unit | MR | Microminiature Relay |
| MPU | Miniature Power Unit | MR | Mikrorechner |
| MPU | Moyens et Petits Utilisateurs | MR | Mittelrechner |
| | | MR | Moisture Resistant |
| MPUL | Most Positive Up Level | MR | Monitor Recorder |
| MPW | Modified Plane Wave | MR | Monitor Routine |

# M

| | | | |
|---|---|---|---|
| MR | Multi-Register | MRF | Multipath Reduction Factor |
| MR | Multiple Requesting | | |
| MR | Multiplier Register | MRFL | Master Radio Frequency List |
| MR | Multiplikatorregister | | |
| MR.ATOMIC | Multiple Rapid Automatic Test Of Monolithic Integrated Circuits | MRG | Medium Range |
| | | MRH | Magnetic Reading Head |
| | | MRH | Magnetic Recording Head |
| MR/W | Multiple Read/Write | MRI | Medium Range Interceptor |
| MRA | Matrix Reducibility Algorithm | MRI | Miscellaneous Radar Input |
| | | MRI | Multiply Row by Itself |
| MRA | Minimum Reception Altitude | MRIR | Medium Resolution Infrared Radiometer |
| MRA | Multiple Regression Analysis | MRIS | Maritime Research Information Service |
| MRAD | Mass Random Access Disk | MRIS | Market Research Information Service |
| MRADS | Mass Random Access Data Storage | MRIS | Medical Record Information Service |
| MRAP | Management Review and Analysis Program | MRK | Message Registration Key |
| MRB | Minor Request Block | MRKD | Marked |
| MRB | Modified Reflected Binary | MRL | Matrix-Reporting-Language |
| MRBM | Medium Range Ballistic Missible | MRM | Machine Readable Material |
| MRC | Machine Readable Character | MRM | Magnetic Ring Modulator |
| | | MRM | Magnetic Rod Memory |
| MRC | Magnetic Rectifier Control | MRN | Minimum Reject Number |
| MRC | Manufacturing Records Control | MRN | Modell-Rechnernetzwerk |
| | | MRO | Maintenance, Repair and Operating |
| MRC | Master Resident Core | | |
| MRC | Mathematics Research Center | MRO | Multi-Region Operation |
| | | MROM | Microprogram Read-Only Memory |
| MRC | Maximum Reverse Current | | |
| MRC | Mini-Remote Concentrator | MRP | Machine Readable Passport |
| MRC | Minimum Redundancy Code | MRP | Manufacturing Record Processor |
| MRD | Machine Readable Data | MRP | Manufacturing Resource Planning |
| MRD | Matrix Read Data | | |
| MRD | Memory Raster Display | MRP | Material Record Processor |
| MRD | Military Reference Data | MRP | Material Requirements Planning |
| MRDC | Machine Readable Data Carrier | | |
| | | MRP | Microfiche Reader/Printer |
| MRDF | Machine-Readable Data File | MRP | Microfilm Reader/Printer |
| | | MRP | Microprocessor ROM Programmer |
| MRDF | Maritime Radio Direction Finding | | |
| | | MRP | Multiple Request Program |
| MRDIS | Message Reproduction Distribution System | MRP | Multiple Requestor Program |
| MRDOS | Mapped Realtime Disk Operating System | MRPE | Memory Register Parity Error |
| MRDR | Morning Report Data Record | MRPS | Management Resources Planning System |
| MRE | Mean Radial Error | MRQ | Memory Return Queue |
| MRE | Multiple-Response Enable | MRQ | Message Request Queue |
| MRF | Master Reference File | MRR | Mode Request Register |
| MRF | Multi-Reading Feature | MRR | Mains Restoration Relay |

# M

| | | | |
|---|---|---|---|
| MRR | Microfilm Reader Recorder | MRX... | Memorex |
| MRR | Mode Request Register | MS | Machine Selection |
| MRR | Multiplier Right Register | MS | Machinery Steel |
| MRR | Multiply Row by Row | MS | Macromodulator System |
| MRRE | Maximum Relative Representation Error | MS | Magnetic South |
| | | MS | Magnetic Storage |
| MRS | Magnetic Reader/Sorter | MS | Magnetic Store |
| MRS | Magnetic Rod Storage | MS | Magnetostriction |
| MRS | Magnetic Rod Store | MS | Magnetstreifen |
| MRS | Malfunction Reporting System | MS | Main Storage |
| | | MS | Main Store |
| MRS | Manned Reconnaissance Satellite | MS | Main Switch |
| | | MS | Makrosprache |
| MRS | Mark Reading Station | MS | Mark Sense |
| MRS | Master Release Sequence | MS | Mark Sensing |
| MRS | Mehrrechnersystem | MS | Marketing Support |
| MRS | Modular Retrieval System | MS | Maschinensprache |
| MRS | Multiply Row by Scalar | MS | Maschinensteuerung |
| MRS | Multiregion Support facility | MS | Mass Spectrometry |
| | | MS | Mass Storage |
| MRSAR | Multiply Row by Scalar and Add Row | MS | Master Scheduler |
| | | MS | Master Slice |
| MRSARX | Multiply Row by Scalar and Add Row from index X | MS | Master Switch |
| | | MS | Master-Slave |
| MRSD | Maximum Rated Standard Deviation | MS | Match Station |
| | | MS | Material Specification |
| MRT | Master Reply Table | MS | Matrix Storage |
| MRT | Maximum Repair Time | MS | Matrix Store |
| MRT | Mean Repair Time | MS | Maximum Stress |
| MRT | Message Register Terminal | MS | Mean Square |
| MRT | Multiple Reference Table | MS | Measuring Set |
| MRTC | Military Real Time Computer | MS | Measuring System |
| | | MS | Medium Soft |
| MRTL | Milliwatt RTL | MS | Memory Size |
| MRTL | Milliwatt Resistor Transistor Logic | MS | Memory Stack |
| | | MS | Memory System |
| MRTL | Motorola Resistor Transistor Logic | MS | Message Stack |
| | | MS | Message Switching |
| MRTR | Maximum Readout Transfer Ratio | MS | Messinstrument |
| | | MS | Metal Semiconductor |
| MRU | Machine Records Unit | MS | Metric Size |
| MRU | Material Recovery Unit | MS | Microsoft |
| MRU | Message Retransmission Unit | MS | Mikrosekunde |
| | | MS | Mild Steel |
| MRU | Microwave Relay Unit | MS | Military Standard |
| MRU | Mobile Radio Unit | MS | Millisekunde |
| MRV | Multiple Reentry Vehicle | MS | Mitbewerberprogramm von Softwarefirmen |
| MRVC | Monthly Requirement Value Code | MS | Mode Statement |
| | | MS | Monostable |
| MRWC | Multiple Read-Write Computer | MS | Most Severe |
| | | MS | Multi-Stage |
| MRWC | Multiple Reading and Writing with Computing | MS | Multiple Signal |
| | | MS | Multiplexer Storage |
| MRX | Memorex Corporation | MS | Multiply Statement |

# M

| | | | |
|---|---|---|---|
| MS/S | Megasamples per Second | MSCP | Mass Storage Control Protokoll |
| MS/s | Million Samples per second | MSCP | Master Shielding Computer Program |
| MSA | Magazine Storage A | | |
| MSA | Main Store Address | | |
| MSA | Management Science America, Incorporated | MSCP | Mean Spherical Candle Power |
| MSA | Mark-Space-Amplituden-multiplikationsprinzip | MSCP | Microcomputer Synchronous Control Package |
| MSA | Matrix Scheme for Algorithms | MSCS | Mass Storage Control System |
| MSA | Matrizenschema des Algorithmus | MSCU | Multi Stations Control Unit |
| MSA | Multivariate Statistical Analyzer | MSD | Magazine Storage D |
| | | MSD | Magnetic Storage Drum |
| MSAC | Moore School Automatic Computer | MSD | Mark Sensed Data |
| | | MSD | Mass Storage Device |
| MSAR | Mikroprogrammspeicher-Adreßregister | MSD | Master Standard Data |
| | | MSD | Mean Solar Day |
| MSAS | Medium Speed Access Store | MSD | Mean Square Difference |
| | | MSD | Mechanischer Schnelldrucker |
| MSB | Magazine Storage B | | |
| MSB | Main Switchboard | MSD | Mission Systems Data |
| MSB | Make Set Busy | MSD | Most Significant Decade |
| MSB | More Significant Bit | MSD | Most Significant Digit |
| MSB | Most Significant Bit | MSD | Multifrequency Signal Detector |
| MSB | Most Significant Byte | | |
| MSC | Magnetically Settable Counter | MSDB | Main Storage Data Base |
| | | MSDC | Mass Spectrometry Data Centre |
| MSC | Main Storage Controller | | |
| MSC | Mark Sensing Card | MSDP | Missile Site Data Processor |
| MSC | Mass Storage Control | | |
| MSC | Mass Storage Controller | MSDPS | Missile Site Data Processing System |
| MSC | Master Slave Circuit | | |
| MSC | Medium Scale Computer | MSDPSS | Missile Site Data Processing Subsystem |
| MSC | Memory Selection Circuit | | |
| MSC | Memory Storage Control | MSDR | Main Storage Data Register |
| MSC | Micro-Software-Catalog | | |
| MSC | Mile of Standard Cable | MSDR | Multiplexer Storage Data Register |
| MSC | Most Significant Character | | |
| MSC | Multiple Scan Correlator | MSDS | Magnetic Storage Drum System |
| MSC | Multiple Systems Coupling | | |
| MSCC | Magnetic-Strip Credit Card | MSDS | Message Switching Data Service |
| MSCDR | Mohawk Synchronous Communication Data Recorder | MSDS | Multispectral Data System |
| | | MSDS | Multispectral Scanner and Data System |
| MSCE | Main Storage Control Element | MSDS | Multispectral Scanner and Data Subsystem |
| MSCE | Main Store Control Element | MSE | Mask Superposition Error |
| | | MSE | Mean Square Error |
| MSCF | Multi System Control Facility | MSE | Mehrfachschwellenwertelement |
| MSCH | Modify Subchannel | MSE | Mikrosteuereinrichtung |
| MSCLE | Maximum Space Charge Limited Emission | MSE | Minimum-Size Effect |
| | | MSE | Multi Screen Editor |

- 408 -

# M

| | | | |
|---|---|---|---|
| MSEC | Millisecond | MSK | Mask |
| MSF | Manned Space Flight | MSK | Micro-floppy Standard Komitee |
| MSF | Mass Storage Facility | | |
| MSF | Medium Standard Frequency | MSK | Minimum-frequency Shift Keying |
| MSF | Monolithische Speicherfertigung | MSK | Minimum Shift Keying |
| | | MSKE | Mehrrechnersystem-Koordinatorelement |
| MSFDPS | Manned Space Flight Data Processing System | MSL | Maximum Service Life |
| MSFET | Metal-on-Silicon Field-Effect Transistor | MSL | Mean Sea Level |
| | | MSLP | Marketing Service Lizenzprogramm |
| MSFET | Metal-Semiconductor FET | | |
| MSFET | Metal-Silicon Field Effect Transistor | MSLT | Military Solid Logic Technology |
| MSFF | Master-Slave Flip-Flop | MSM | Metal-Semiconductor-Metal |
| MSG | Maximum Stable Gain | | |
| MSG | Message | MSM | Moore Sequential Machine |
| MSG | Message miscellaneous Simulation Generator | MSM | Multiple Systems Manager |
| | | MSMP | Multiple Source Moiré Patterns |
| MSG | Model System Generator | | |
| MSG | Miscellaneous Simulation Generator | MSMV | Monostable Multivibrator |
| | | MSNF | Multi-System Networking Facility |
| MSG | Multiplicand Select Gate | | |
| MSG/WTG | Message Waiting | MSNF | Multiple Systems Network Facility |
| MSGCL | Message Class | | |
| MSGDFT | Message Default reply | MSO | Multiple System Operator |
| MSGF | Message File | MSOP | Minimum Sum-Of-Product |
| MSGQ | Message Queue | MSOR | Management Seminar Operation Research |
| MSHER | Master Sheet Reference | | |
| MSHI | Medium Scale Hybrid Integration | MSOS | Mass Storage Operating System |
| MSHP | Maintain System History Program | MSP | Manual Switching Position |
| | | MSP | Mark-Sensed Punching |
| MSI | Machine Sensible Information | MSP | Medium Speed Printer |
| | | MSP | Mode Select Panel |
| MSI | Manned Satellite Inspector | MSP | Modular System Program |
| MSI | Marketing Systems, Incorporated | MSP | Most Significant Position |
| | | MSPFE | Multi Sensor Programmable Feature Extractor |
| MSI | Medium-Scale Integrated | | |
| MSI | Medium-Scale Integrator | MSPG | Magnetic Shock Pulse Generator |
| MSI | Medium-Scale Integration | | |
| MSI | Medium Size Integration | MSPR | Maschinensprache |
| MSI | Middle-Scale Integration | MSPS | Media Selection and Program Schedule |
| MSI | Moderate Scale Integration | | |
| MSI | Multiple Systems Integrity | MSR | Magnetic Shift Register |
| MSI... | Marketing Systems Inc. | MSR | Magnetic Storage Ring |
| MSIG | Most Significant | MSR | Magnetic Stripe Reader |
| MSIR | Management Seminar Information Retrieval | MSR | Mark Sheet Reader |
| | | MSR | Mass Storage Resident |
| MSIS | Mask Shop Information System | MSR | Material Status Report |
| | | MSR | Mean Square Root |
| MSIS | Multi-State Information System | MSR | Mechanized Storage and Retrieval |
| MSISL | Moore School Information System Laboratory | MSR | Memory Search Register |
| | | MSR | Messen-Steuern-Regeln |

# M

| | | | |
|---|---|---|---|
| MSR | Meß-, Steuerungs- und Regelungstechnik | MST | Monolithic System Technology |
| MSR | Missile Sight Radar | MST | Monolithische Schaltungstechnik |
| MSR | Mode Status Register | | |
| MSR | Multijunction Semiconductor Rectifier | MST | Monolithische Systemtechnologie |
| MSR | Multiplex Share Routine | MSTA | Master Tape |
| MSRJE | Multiple Session Remote Job Entry | MSTOR | Main Storage |
| | | MSTS | Multi-Subscriber Time-Shared |
| MSS | Machine Switching System | | |
| MSS | Magnetic Slot Scanner | MSTS | Multi-Subscriber Time Sharing |
| MSS | Magnetic Strip Store | | |
| MSS | Management Science Systems | MSTU | Meßstellenumschalter |
| | | MSU | Main Storage Unit |
| MSS | Management-Steuerungssystem | MSU | Memory Service Unit |
| | | MSU | Message Signal Units |
| MSS | Manager's Systems Summary | MSU | Modem Sharing Unit |
| | | MSVC | Mass Storage Volume Control |
| MSS | Manual Safety Switch | | |
| MSS | Mass Storage Subsystem | MSVI | Mass Storage Volume Inventory |
| MSS | Mass Storage System | | |
| MSS | Massenspeichersystem | MSW | Master Switch |
| MSS | Mean Solar Second | MSW | Micro Switch |
| MSS | Message Switching System | MSX | Microsoft Standard Extended |
| MSS | Metastable Stated | | |
| MSS | Mobile Subscriber Station | MT | Machine Time |
| MSS | Monthly Sales Summary | MT | Machine Translation |
| MSS | Multiple Secondary and Selection | MT | Machine Type |
| | | MT | Magnetic Tape |
| MSS | Multispectral Scanner | MT | Magnettrommel |
| MSSC | Main Storage Stock Control | MT | Magnettrommelspeicher |
| | | MT | Maintask |
| MSSC | Mass Storage System Communicator | MT | Mannesmann Terminal |
| | | MT | Maschinentisch |
| MSSF | Monitoring and System Support Facility | MT | Maximum Torque |
| | | MT | Mean Time |
| MSSN | Mean-Square Signal-to-Noise | MT | Measurement |
| | | MT | Measuring Transformer |
| MSSP | Magnetstreifenspeicher | MT | Mechanical Translation |
| MSSS | Maintenance and Service Sub-System | MT | Mechanical Transport |
| | | MT | Memory Technique |
| MSSS | Multisatellit-Support-System | MT | Message Transfer |
| | | MT | Meßtaste |
| MST | MAMO Status Test | MT | Meßtrigger |
| MST | Mathematical Systems Theory | MT | Mikrotelegramm |
| | | MT | Mode Transducer |
| MST | Mean Solar Time | MT | Morse Tape |
| MST | Measurement monolithic Systems Technology | MT | Motor Terminal |
| | | MT | Multi-Tasking |
| MST | Memory System Tester | MT | Multiple Transfer |
| MST | Memotron Storage Tube | MT... | Mannesmann Tally |
| MST | Meßstelle | MT/MF | Magnetic Tape to Microfilm |
| MST | Mise Sous-Tension | | |
| MST | Modular Solid Technology | MTA | Magnetic Tape Addressing |

# M

| | | | |
|---|---|---|---|
| MTA | Maintenance set Allowed | MTBS | Mean Time Between Stops |
| MTA | Message Transfer Agent | MTBSF | Mean Time Between Significant Failure |
| MTA | Modified Tape-Armoured cable | MTBSF | Mean Time Between System Failure |
| MTA | Motion Time Analysis | MTBUM | Mean Time Between Unscheduled Maintenance |
| MTA | Multiple Terminal Access | | |
| MTA | Multiterminal Adapter | MTBUR | Mean Time Between Unscheduled Removal |
| MTAC | Mathematical Tables and other Aids to Computation | MTC | Magnetic Tape Cartridge |
| MTAE | Message Transfer Agent Entity | MTC | Magnetic Tape Cassette |
| | | MTC | Magnetic Tape Check |
| MTAM | Magnetic Tape Analog Memory | MTC | Magnetic Tape Code |
| | | MTC | Magnetic Tape Command |
| MTAM | Magnetic Tape Auxiliary Memory | MTC | Magnetic Tape Control |
| | | MTC | Magnetic Tape Controller |
| MTAR | Mean Time Awaiting Repairs | MTC | Magnetic Tape Converter |
| | | MTC | Maintenance Time Constraint |
| MTB | Magnetic Tape Block | | |
| MTB | Maintenance of True Bearing | MTC | Master Table of Contents |
| | | MTC | Master Tape Control |
| MTB | Maschinentagebuch | MTC | Material Transfer Card |
| MTBC | Mean Time Between Component failures | MTC | Memory Test Computer |
| | | MTC | Micrographic Technology Corporation |
| MTBCD | Mean Time Between Confirmed Defects | | |
| | | MTC | Mission and Test Computer |
| MTBCF | Mean Time Between Component Failures | MTC | Mobile Tactical Computer |
| | | MTC... | Micrographic Technology Corporation |
| MTBD | Mean Time Between Defects | | |
| | | MTCA | Multiple Terminal Communication Adapter |
| MTBDR | Mean Time Between Depot Repair | | |
| | | MTCF | Mean Time to Catastrophic Failure |
| MTBF | Maximal Time Between Faults | | |
| | | MTCM | Magnetic Tape Controlled Machine |
| MTBF | Mean Time Before Failure | | |
| MTBF | Mean Time Between Failure | MTCS | Minimum core Teleprocessing Control System |
| MTBFF | Mean Time Between First Failure | | |
| | | MTCU | Magnetic Tape Control Unit |
| MTBFL | Mean Time Between Function Loss | | |
| | | MTD | Magnetic Tape Drive |
| MTBM | Mean Time Between Maintenance | MTD | Maintenance set Denied |
| | | MTD | Master Tape Data |
| MTBM | Mean Time Between Malfunctions | MTD | Mean Temperature Difference |
| | | | |
| MTBMA | Mean Time Between Maintenance Action | MTD | Mean Time Down |
| | | MTD | Microprocessor Tape Duplicator |
| MTBO | Mean Time Between Overhauls | | |
| | | MTD | Minimal Toxic Dose |
| MTBR | Mean Time Between Repair | MTD | Mounted |
| | | MTDA | Marine Tactical Data |
| MTBR | Mean Time Between Removal | MTDB | Magnetic Tape Data Block |
| | | MTDC | Magnetic Tape Data Collecting |
| MTBR | Mean Time Between Replacement | | |

# M

| | | | |
|---|---|---|---|
| MTDM | Magnetic Tape Data Memory | MTNS | Metal-Thick-Nitride-Semiconductor |
| MTDS | Magnetic Tape Data Store | MTNS | Metal-Thick-Nitride-Silicon |
| MTDS | Marine Tactical Data Store | MTNS | Metal-Thick oxide-Nitride-Silicon |
| MTDS | Missile Trajectory Data System | MTO | Magnetic Tape Output |
| MTE | Magnetic Tape Encoder | MTO | Master-Terminal-Operator |
| MTE | Magnetic Tape Equipment | MTO | Multi-Task Operation |
| MTE | Maximum Tracking Error | MTOS | Magnetic Tape Operating System |
| MTE | Multi-Terminal Emulator | MTOS | Metal-Thick-Oxide Semiconductor |
| MTF | Mean Time to Failure | MTOS | Metal-Thick-Oxide-Silicon |
| MTF | Mechanical Time Fuse | MTOS | Metal-Thin-Oxide-Silicon |
| MTF | Modulation Transfer Function | MTP | Magnetic Tape Processing |
| MTFF | Mean Time to First Failure | MTP | Magnetic Tape Program |
| MTFM | Magnetic Thin-Film Memory | MTP | Manufacturing Training Program |
| MTG | Macroblock Test Generator | MTP | Master Terminal Program |
| MTG | Magnetongerät | MTP | Matrix Transform Processor |
| MTG | Meldetextgeber | MTP | Mechanical Thermal Pulse |
| MTG | Mounting | MTP | Message Transfer Part |
| MTG | Multiple Trigger Generator | MTP | Miniature Trimmer Potentiometer |
| MTH | Magnetic Tape Handler | MTPL | Magnetic Tape Program Library |
| MTI | Magnetic Tape Information | MTPS | Magnetic Tape Programming System |
| MTI | Magnetic Tape Input | MTR | Magnetic Tape Reader |
| MTI | Maintenance Task Information system | MTR | Magnetic Tape Recorder |
| MTI | Modified Ternary Inverter | MTR | Magnetic Tape Routine |
| MTI | Moving Target Indicator | MTR | Magnetic-core Transistor Relay |
| MTL | Machine Translation of Language | MTR | Magnettrommel |
| MTL | Marged Transistor Logic | MTR | Magnettrommelspeicher |
| MTL | Material | MTR | Material Transaction Register |
| MTL | Merged Transistor Logic | MTR | Material Transfer Recorder |
| MTL | Message Transfer Layer | MTR | Materials Testing Reactor |
| MTL | Microelectronic Testing Laboratory | MTR | Maximum Time to Replace |
| MTL | Multi-Turn Loop | MTR | Mean Time to Removal |
| MTLP | Master Tape Loading Program | MTR | Mean Time to Repair |
| MTM | Magnetic Tape Mark | MTR | Mean Time to Replace |
| MTM | Magnetic Tape Memory | MTR | Mean Time to Restore |
| MTM | Method of Time Measurement | MTR | Meter |
| MTM | Multi Terminal Manager | MTR | Missile Tracking Radar |
| MTM | Multiple Time Measurement | MTR | Motor |
| MTMF | Multiple Task Management Feature | MTR | Moving Target Reactor |
| MTMGPD | Methods Time Measurement and General Purpose Data | MTR | Multiple-Track Radar range |
| MTMOD | Magnetic Tape Module | MTRE | Magnetic Tape Recorder End |
| MTMS | Memory Tape Management System | | |

# M

| | | | |
|---|---|---|---|
| MTRS | Magnetic Tape Record Start | MTTL | Motorola Transistor Transistor Logic |
| MTS | Magnetic Tape Sorting | MTTR | Maximum Time To Repair |
| MTS | Magnetic Tape Station | MTTR | Maximum Time To Replace |
| MTS | Magnetic Tape Storage | MTTR | Mean Time To Repair |
| MTS | Magnetic Tape Store | MTTR | Mean Time To Replace |
| MTS | Magnetic Tape Subsystem | MTTR | Mean Time To Restore |
| MTS | Magnetic Tape System | MTTSF | Mean Time To System Failure |
| MTS | Magnettrommelspeicher | MTU | Magnetic Tape Unit |
| MTS | Manufacturing Tracking System | MTU | Master Trigger Unit |
| MTS | Marketing-Transaktions-system | MTU | Multiplexer and Terminal Unit |
| MTS | Memory Test System | MTUR | Mean Time to Unscheduled Repair |
| MTS | Message Transfer System | | |
| MTS | Michigan Terminal System | MTV | Mensch-Technik-Verbund |
| MTS | Michigan Time Sharing | MTVAL | Master Tape Validation |
| MTS | Missile Tracking System | MTWP | Multiplier Travelling-Wave Phototube |
| MTS | Module Testing System | | |
| MTS | Money Transfer System | MTX | Matrix |
| MTS | Multi-Terminal-System | MU | Machine Unit |
| MTS | Multi-Tool-System | MU | Machine Utilization |
| MTSC | Magnetic Tape Selectric Composer | MU | Mailbox User |
| | | MU | Marketing Unit |
| MTSE | Magnetic Tape Splicing Equipment | MU | Maschinelle Übersetzung |
| | | MU | Memory Unit |
| MTSF | Mean Time to System Failure | MU | Message Unit |
| | | MU | Multiple Unit |
| MTSO | Mean Time to Switch Over | MUART | Microprocessor Universal Asynchronous Receiver Transmitter |
| MTSP | Magnettrommelspeicher | | |
| MTSR | Mean Time to System Restoration | | |
| | | MUC | MAMO Using Control |
| MTSS | Magnetic Tape Storage System | MUC | Multiple-Use Counter |
| | | MUCAP | Microcapacitor |
| MTST | Magnetic Tape Selectric Typewriter | MUCH-FET | Multi-Channel Field Effect Transistor |
| MTT | Magnetic Tape Terminal | MUD | Memory Unit Drum |
| MTT | Magnetic Tape Track | MUDAID | Multivariate, Univariate, and Discriminant Analysis of Irregular Data |
| MTT | Magnetic Tape Transport | | |
| MTT | Microprogram Trace Tape | | |
| MTT | Multi-Terminal pro Task | | |
| MTT | Multi-Terminal Task | MUDAP | Makrosprache zur Unter-stützung der Daten-prüfung |
| MTTA | Mean Time To Arrive | | |
| MTTD | Mean Time To Diagnosis | | |
| MTTE | Multi-Threshold Threshold Element | MUDAS | Multiprogramming Datenservice GmbH |
| MTTF | Mean Time To Failure | MUDCAP | Multi-Dimensional Contin-gency Analysis Program |
| MTTFF | Mean Time To First Failure | | |
| | | MUDD | Multisource Unified Data Distribution |
| MTTFSF | Mean Time To First System Failure | MUDDC | Multi-Unit Direct Digital Control |
| MTTFSR | Mean Time to First System Repair | | |
| | | MUDPIE | Museum and University Data Processing Information Exchange |
| MTTL | Modified Transistor Transistor Logic | | |

# M

| | | | |
|---|---|---|---|
| MUF | Maximum Usable Frequency | MUS | Magnetic Unloading System |
| MUG | Maximum Usable Gain | MUS | Manual Update Service |
| MUGOLIS | Manchester User Group for On-Line Information Systems | MÜS | Maschinenüberwachungssystem |
| MUI | Mode Unnumbered and Independent | MUS | Meßstellenumschalter |
| MUL | Material Und Lager | MUSA | Multiple-Unit Steerable Antenna |
| MUL | Multiply | MUSC | Multi-Unit Supervisory Control |
| MULDEM | Multiplexer/Demultiplexer | | |
| MULM | Multiplexer Universal Logic Module | MUSE | Machine User Symbolic Environment |
| MULT | Multiple | MUSE | Minicomputer Users in Secondary Education |
| MULT | Multiplication | | |
| MULT | Multiplier | MUSE | Modcom Users Exchange |
| MULT | Multiplizieren | MUSE | Modular Utilities for Systems Education |
| MULTICS | Multiplexed Information and Computing Service | MUSIC | Machine Utilisation Statistical Information Collection |
| MULTICS | Multiplexed Information and Computing System | | |
| MULTIPAC | Multiple Pool Processor And Computer | MUSIC | McGill University System for Interactive Computing |
| MULTIPLE | Multipurpose Program that Learns | MUSIC | Multi-User System for Integrated Control |
| MULTITRAN | Multiple Translation | | |
| MULTIV | Multivibrator | MUSR | Multiple Use Selective Routing |
| MULTR | Multimeter | | |
| MULTR | Multiplier | MUST | Message User Service Transcriber |
| MUM | Multi-Use Manuscript | | |
| MUM | Multi-Use Mnemonics | MUSTANG | Mumps Software Tools And Generator |
| MUM | Multi-User Micro | | |
| MUMPS | Massachusetts general hospital Multi-Programming System | MUT | Modular Universal Terminal |
| | | MUT | Module Under Test |
| MUMPS | Massachusetts Utility Multi-Programming System | MUT | Mutilated |
| | | MUX | Multiplex |
| | | MUX | Multiplexer |
| MUMS | Modular Unified Microprocessor System | MUX | Multiplexeur |
| | | MUX | Multiplexing |
| MUMS | Multiple Use MARC System | MUX | Multiplexkanal |
| | | MUX | Multiplexor |
| MUO | Machine Used On | MUX ARC | Multiplexing Automatic Error Correction |
| MUPF | Modified Ultraspherical Polynomial Filter | | |
| | | MUXE | Multiplexing Equipment |
| MUPID | Mehrzweck Universell vorprogrammierbarer Intelligenter Decoder | MV | Magnetischer Verstärker |
| | | MV | Maintenance Version |
| | | MV | Mean Value |
| MUPO | Maximum Undistorted Power Output | MV | Mean Variation |
| | | MV | Mean Voltage |
| MUPS | Multiple Utility Peripheral System | MV | Measured Value |
| | | MV | Medium Voltage |
| MURG | Machine Utilization Report Generator | MV | Megavoltage |
| | | MV | Mémoire Vive |
| MURS | Machine Utilization Reporting System | MV | Mercury Vapor |
| | | MV | Millivolt |

# M

| | | | |
|---|---|---|---|
| MV | Millivoltmeter | MVT | Multiprocessing with a Variable number of Tasks |
| MV | Minimalvariante | MVT | Multiprogramming with a Variable number of Tasks |
| MV | Mischverstärker | | |
| MV | Multiconverter Vector | | |
| MV | Multivibrator | MVT | Multitasking with a Variable number of Tasks |
| MV(R) | Multilink Variable (Receive State) | MVTR | Moisture Vapour Transmission Rate |
| MV(S) | Multilink Variable (Send State) | MVZ | Meßwertverarbeitungszentrale |
| MVA | Megavoltampere | | |
| MVAR | Megavar | MVZ | Move Zones |
| MVAR | Megavolt-Ampere Reactive | MW | Machine Word |
| | | MW | Manual Word |
| MVB | Multivibrator | MW | Maschinenwort |
| MVC | Manual Volume Control | MW | Medium Wave |
| MVC | Medium Value Computer | MW | Megawatt |
| MVC | Move Characters | MW | Memory Word |
| MVC | Multi-Variant Counter | MW | Memory Write |
| MVC | Multiple Variate Counter | MW | Message Wait |
| MVDF | Medium- and Very high-frequency Direction Finder | MW | Meßwandler |
| | | MW | Microwave |
| | | MW | Modulated Wave |
| MVE | Mikroverarbeitungseinheit | MW | Multi-Wire |
| MVI | Move Immediate | MW | Multilink Window size |
| MVL | Multiple-Valued Logic | MW | Multiply Word |
| MVL-IR | Multiple-Variable-Length-Iterative-Realization | MW | Multiwiring |
| | | MW | Music Wire |
| MVL-SRR | Multiple-Variable-Length-Shift-Register-Realization | MWAE | Meßwertabtrageeinheit |
| | | MWB | Multilayer Wiring Board |
| | | MWE | Megawatt Electric |
| MVM | Multiple Virtual Memory | MWE | Meßwerterfassung |
| MVN | Move Numeric | MWI | Message-Waiting Indicator |
| MVO | Move with Offset | MWL | Machine Word Length |
| MVP | Multi-Variable Programming | MWL | Master Warning Light |
| | | MWL | Memory Word Length |
| MVPS | Medium-Voltage Power Supply | MWM | Mindestweitergabemenge |
| | | MWMSE | Minimum-Weighted Mean-Square-Error |
| MVR | Monolithic Voltage Regulator | MWP | Maximum Working Pressure |
| MVR | Multivalenzrecherche | | |
| MVRO | Minimum-Variance Reduced-Order | MWR | Mean Width Ratio |
| | | MWS | Magnetic Wire Storage |
| MVRS | Multivalenzrecherchesystem | MWS | Magnetic Wire Store |
| | | MWS | Material-Wirtschafts-System |
| MVS | Mehrfache Virtuelle Speicher | MWS | Medical Work Station |
| MVS | Minimum Visible Signal | MWS | Microwave Station |
| MVS | Multiple Virtual Storage | MWSR | Magnetic Wire Shift Register |
| MVS | Multiple Virtual Systems | | |
| MVS-SE | MVS-System Extensions | MWV | Maximum Working Voltage |
| MVS/BDT | MVS/Bulk Data Transfer | MX | Matrix |
| MVS/SP | Multiple Virtual Storage/System Produkt | MX | Multiplex |
| | | MXD | Mixed |
| MVS/XA | Multiple Virtual Storage/Extended Architecture | MXM | Matrix Memory |
| | | MXR | Mask Index Register |

# M

| | | | |
|---|---|---|---|
| MXS | Message Exchange System | MZ | Minus Zero |
| MXT | Maximum Tasks | MZA | Maschinenzeitaufwand |
| MY | Man-Year | MZA | Maschinenzusatzauftrag |
| MYAP | Mask-limited Yield Analysis Program | MZL | Magnetischer Zeichenleser |
| | | MZS | Mehrfachzugriffssystem |
| MZ | Maschinenzeit | MZT | Mehrzweck-Terminal |
| MZ | Mathematische Zeitschrift | MZZA | Mittlere Zeit zwischen Zwei Ausfällen |
| MZ | Memory Zone | | |
| MZ | Mikrobefehlszähler | | |

# N

| | | | |
|---|---|---|---|
| N | Nachricht | NAL | National Agricultural Library |
| N | Neper | | |
| N | Neutral | NAL | Native Assembly Language |
| N | Neutron | NAM | National Association of Manufacturers |
| N | Newton | | |
| N | Nitrogen | NAMIS | Nitride-barrier Avalanche-injection Metal-Insulator-Semiconductor |
| N | No | | |
| N | Normal | | |
| N | Number of turns | NAND | Negative AND |
| N | Number of bits | NAND | Not AND |
| N | Number of revolutions | NAP | National Account Program |
| N(R) | Transmitter Receive sequence number | NAP | Network Access Point |
| | | NAP | Network Analysis Program |
| N(S) | Transmitter Send sequence number | NAP | Not Applicable |
| | | NAP | Numerical Analysis Problem |
| N/A | Numérique/Analogique | NAPA | National Association of Purchasing Agents |
| NA | Neutral Axis | | |
| NA | Not Applicable | NAPAC | National Program for Acquisitions and Cataloguing |
| NA | Not Assigned | | |
| NA | Numerical Aperture | | |
| NAA | National Association of Accountants | NAPALM | National ADP Program for AMC Logistics Management |
| NAA | Neutron Activation Analysis | | |
| | | NAPC | NCR's Applied COBOL |
| NAB | National Association of Broadcasting | NAPLPS | North American Presentation Level Protocol Syntax |
| NABET | National Association of Broadcast Employees and Technicians | NAPTIS | National Air Pollution Technical Information System |
| NABUG | National Association of Broadcast Unions and Guilds | NAR | Net Assimilation Rate |
| | | NAR | Netzwerkadreßregister |
| NAC | Neutral-Aufbereitungs-Code | NAR | Non-Addressable Register |
| | | NAR | Normanschlußregister |
| NACC | National Automatic Controls Conference | NAR | Numerical Analysis Research |
| NACOM | National Communications | NARAD | Naval Air Research And Development |
| NACP | Node Abnormal Condition Program | NARDA | National Appliance and Radio TV Dealers Association |
| NAD | Network Administration | | |
| NAD | Noise Amplitude Distribution | NARDIC | Navy Research and Development Information Center |
| NADC | Naval Air Development Center | | |
| NAE | Netzabschlußeinrichtung | NARDIS | Navy Automated Research and Development Information System |
| NAECON | National Aerospace Electrical Convention | | |
| NAED | National Association of Electrical Distributors | NAREC | Naval Research Electronic Computer |
| NAI | Network Applications Interface | NARM | National Association of Relay Manufacturers |
| NAIR | Narrow Absorption Infrared | NARTB | National Association of Radio and TV Broadcasters |
| NAK | Negative Acknowledge | | |

- 417 -

# N

| | | | |
|---|---|---|---|
| NARUC | National Association of Regulatory Utility Commissioners | NAV | Navigation |
| | | NAVA | National Audio-Visual Association |
| NAS | National Academy of Sciences | NAVCM | Navigation Countermeasure |
| NAS | National Advanced Systems | NAVCOMMSTA | Naval Communications Station |
| NAS | National Airspace System | NAVDAC | Navigation Data Assimilation Computer |
| NAS | Network Administrative Station | NAVIS | Nachrichtenverbindung mit integrierter Speicherung |
| NASA | National Aeronautics and Space Administration | NAVIC | Navy Information Center |
| NASAP | Network Analysis for Systems Applications Program | NAVLIS | Navy Logistics Information System |
| | | NAVRA | Navigation Radar |
| NASARR | North American Search And Ranging Radar | NAVSAT | Navigational Satellite |
| | | NAW | National Association of Wholesalers |
| NASCOM | NASA Communications | | |
| NASD | National Association of Securities Dealers | NB | Narrow Band |
| | | NB | Negative Balance |
| NASDAQ | National Association of Securities Dealers Automated Quotation system | NB | Netzbetrieb |
| | | NB | No Bias |
| | | NB | Number of Bytes |
| NASF | Network Administration Storage Facility | NBA | Narrow Band Allocation |
| | | NBAC | Negative Balance All Cycles |
| NASIC | Northeast Academic Science Information Center | NBBL | N-Base Binary Logic |
| | | NBC | Narrow Band Conducted |
| NASOPT | Netzwerk-Analyse-System mit Optimierung | NBC | National Broadcasting Company |
| NASPA | National Society of Public Accountants | NBC | Noise Balancing Circuit |
| | | NBC | Noise Balancing Control |
| NASU | National Association of IBM System/3 Users | NBCV | Narrow Band Coherent Video |
| NAT | Natural Unit | NBDC | National Bomb Data Center |
| NAT | Network Analysis Technique | NBDL | Narrow Band Data Line |
| NAT | Normal Allowed Time | NBDL | Narrow Band Data Link |
| NATA | Numerical Analysis Thermal Application | NBF | Niederfrequenzbandfilter |
| | | NBFM | Narrow Band Frequency Modulation |
| NATCS | National Air Traffic Control Service | NBN | Nixdorf-Breitband-Netz |
| NATE | Neutral Atmosphere Temperature Experiment | NBR | Narrow Band Radiated |
| | | NBR | Number |
| NATESA | National Alliance of TV and Electronic Service Association | NBS | National Bureau of Standards |
| | | NBS | New British Standard |
| NATIP | Navy Technical Information Program | NBS | Numeric Backspace character |
| NATTS | National Association for Trade and Technical Schools | NBSFS | NBS Frequency Standard |
| | | NBT | Negative Balance Test |
| | | NBVM | Narrow Band Voice Modulation |
| NAU | Network Addressable Unit | NC | Name Card |
| NAU | Network Administration Utility | NC | Navigation Computer |

# N

| | | | |
|---|---|---|---|
| NC | Network Calculator | NCDS | Naval Combat Data System |
| NC | Network Control | | |
| NC | Network Controller | NCECS | North Carolina Educational Computing System |
| NC | Nixdorf Computer AG | | |
| NC | No Card | NCF | Naval Communications Facility |
| NC | No Change | | |
| NC | No Circuits | NCF | Network Configuration Facility |
| NC | No Code | | |
| NC | No Coil | NCFSK | Non-Coherent Frequency Shift Keying |
| NC | No Connection | | |
| NC | Noise Criterion | NCG | Null Command Generator |
| NC | Non Conversational | NCG | Numerical Control Graphics |
| NC | Nonlinear Capacitance | | |
| NC | Normally Closed | NCGA | National Computer Graphics Association |
| NC | Numeric Coding | | |
| NC | Numerical Code | NCH | Number has been Changed |
| NC | Numerical Coding | NCI | Nichtcodierte Information |
| NC | Numerical Control | NCI | Non-Coded Information |
| NC | Numerically Controlled | NCI | Numerical Coded Instruction |
| NCA | Northwest Computing Association | | |
| | | NCIC | National Crime Information Center |
| NCADS | Numerical Control Advisory and Demonstration Service | NCILT | National Center for Industrial Language Training |
| NCAG | Nixdorf Computer AG | | |
| NCAP | Nonlinear Circuit Analysis Program | NCIS | Navy Cost Information System |
| | | NCL | Network Control Language |
| NCAVAE | National Committee for Audio-Visual Aids in Education | NCL | Normal Card Listing |
| | | NCL | Numerically Controlled Lathe |
| NCBS | National Data Buoy System | | |
| NCC | National Computer Center | NCLP | Numerically Controlled Line Plotter |
| NCC | National Computer Conference | NCM | Numerically Controlled Machine |
| NCC | National Computing Center | | |
| | | NCMC | Numerical Control Machining Center |
| NCC | Navigation Computer Control | NCME | Numerically Controlled Machine Equipment |
| NCC | Network Control Centre | | |
| NCC | Network Control Centrum | NCMI | National Country Maintenance Index |
| NCC | Network Control Computer | | |
| | | NCMT | Numerically Controlled Machine Tool |
| NCC | Nixdorf Computer Corporation | NCN | Nixdorf Communication Network |
| NCC | Normally Closed Contact | | |
| NCCF | Network Communication Control Facility | NCNB | National Computer Network of Britain |
| | | NCO | Number-Controlled Oscillator |
| NCCN | National Committee on Computer Networks | | |
| | | NCO | Numerically Controlled Oscillator |
| NCCOP | North Carolina Computer Orientation Project | | |
| | | NCOCT | Net Checking and Ordering Category Table |
| NCDCF | National Civil Defense Computer Facility | | |
| | | NCP | Network Control Process |
| NCDM | Numerical Control Drafting Machine | NCP | Network Control Processor |

# N

| | | | |
|---|---|---|---|
| NCP | Network Control Program | NDB | Network Debugger |
| NCP | Node Communications Controller | NDB | Non-Directional Beacon |
| | | NDBC | National Data Buoy Center |
| NCP/VS | Network Control Program Virtual Storage | NDBDP | National Data Buoy Development Project |
| NCPAS | National Computer Program Abstract Service | NDBP | National Data Buoy Project |
| | | NDC | National Data Center |
| NCPI | National Computer Program Index | NDC | National Documentation Center |
| NCPL | National Centre for Programmed Learning | NDC | Navigational Digital Computer |
| NCPM | Non-Critical Phase Matching | NDC | Non-Destructive Cursor |
| | | NDC | Normalized Device Coordinates |
| NCPPL | Numerical Control Parts Programming Language | NDD | No Digit Display |
| NCPS | National Commission on Product Safety | NDDP | NATO Defense Data Program |
| NCR | No Carbon Required | NDE | Non-Destructive Examination |
| NCR... | National Cash Register Company | NDE | Nonlinear Differential Equation |
| NCS | National Communications System | NDF | Neutral Data File |
| NCS | Network Communication System | NDF | No Defect Found |
| | | NDF | Nonrecursive Digital Filter |
| NCS | Network Control Station | | |
| NCS | Numerical Control Society | NDHS | Nimbus Data Handling System |
| NCS | Numerical Control System | | |
| NCTA | National Cable Television Association | NDI | Numerical Designation Index |
| NCTS | Non-Contacting Test System | NDIC | Nuclear Data Information Center |
| NCU | Navigation Computer Unit | NDL | Network Definition Language |
| NCU | Network Control Unit | | |
| NCU | Numerical Control Unit | NDL | Nonconductive Data Link |
| NCV | No Commercial Value | NDM | Negative Differential Mobility |
| NCW | Non-Code Word | | |
| ND | Network Description | NDM | Normal Data Mode |
| ND | Netzwerk-Dienst | NDM | Normal Disconnect Mode |
| ND | Nicht-Deskriptor | NDN | New Data Network |
| ND | No Delay | NDN | Non-Delivery Notification |
| ND | No Detect | NDOS | Network Disk Operating System |
| ND | Non-Delay | | |
| ND | Non-Directional | NDP | Normal Diametral Pitch |
| ND | Non-Director | NDP | Numeric Data Processing |
| ND | Non-sharable Devices | NDPCAL | National Development Program in Computer Assisted Learning |
| ND | Nondeterministic | | |
| ND | Norsk Data | | |
| ND | Number Detector | NDPF | NASA Data Processing Facility |
| ND | Numeric Data | | |
| ND | Numerical Display | NDPIC | Navy Department Program Information Center |
| NDA | Non-Destructive Addition | | |
| NDAC | No Data Accepted | NDPS | National Data Processing Service |
| NDB | Nautical Directional Beacon | | |
| | | NDR | Net Difference Report |

# N

| | | | |
|---|---|---|---|
| NDR | Network Data Reduction | NEBULA | Natural Electronic Business Users Language |
| NDR | Non-Destructive Read | NEC | National Electric Code |
| NDR | Normaldrucker | NEC | No Error Check |
| NDRC | Nutrient Data Research Center | NEC... | Nippon Electric Co. |
| NDRM | Non-Destructive Readout Memory | NECHI | Northeast Consortium for Health Information |
| NDRO | Non-Destructive Read-Only | NECI | Noise Exposure Computer Integrator |
| NDRO | Non-Destructive Readout | NED | Navigation Error Data |
| NDROS | Non-Destructive Read-Only Storage | NED | New Editor |
| | | NEDA | National Electronics Distributors Association |
| NDRW | Non-Destructive Read and Write | NEDC | National Economic Development Council |
| NDRW | Non-Destructive Read-Write | NEDELA | Network Definition Language |
| NDS | Network Development System | NEDLAN | Network Defining Language |
| NDS | Neutron Doped Silicon | | |
| NDSM | Nondeterministic State Machine | NEDN | Naval Environmental Data Network |
| NDT | Network Description Template | NEDN | Navy's Environmental Data Network |
| NDT | Non-Destructive Testing | NEDS | National Emission Data System |
| NDTP | Nuclear Data Tape Program | NEDSA | Non-Erasing Deterministic Stack Automation |
| NDU | Nuclear Data Unit | | |
| NDUC | Nimbus Data Utilization Center | NEEDS | New England Educational Data Systems |
| NDZ | Nicht Druckbares Zeichen | NEF | Noise Equivalent Flux |
| NE | Nachrichteneinheit | NEFO | National Electronics Facilities Organization |
| NE | Network Expansion | | |
| NE | Netzeinsatz | NEG | Negative |
| NE | Noise-Equivalent | NEGAS | Netzplangesteuertes Auftragsabwicklungs-System |
| NE | Non Equal to | | |
| NE | North-East | | |
| NE | Not Editable | NEGIT | Negative Impedance Transistor |
| NE | Not Equal to | | |
| NE | Numeric Editing | NEGPR | Negative Print |
| NEA | Negative Electron Affinity | NEGT | Negate |
| NEA | Netzersatzanlage | NEI | Noise Equivalent Input |
| NEA | Numérotation Européenne des Articles | NEI | Noise Equivalent Intensity |
| | | NEI | Not Elsewhere Included |
| NEAC | Nippon Electric Automatic Computer | NEI | Not Elsewhere Indicated |
| | | NEIC | National Energy Information Center |
| NEADS | Network Engineering Administrative Data System | NEISS | National Electronic Injury Surveillance System |
| NEAR | Network-Interface-Adapter | NEL | Neon Light |
| | | NELAPT | National Engineering Laboratory Automatically Programmed Tools |
| NEAT | NCR Electronic Auto-coding Technique | | |
| NEB | National Enterprise Board | NELDIC | Nippon Electric Layout Design system for Integrated Circuits |
| NEB | Noise Equivalent Bandwidth | | |

# N

| | | | |
|---|---|---|---|
| NELIAC | Naval Electronics Laboratory International Algebraic Compiler | NEWS | Network Error Warning System |
| NELIAC | Navy Electronic Laboratory International ALGOL Compiler | NEXUS | Numerical Examination of Urban Smog |
| NEM | Non-Erasable Memory | NF | Name Field |
| NEM | Not Elsewhere Mentioned | NF | Niederfrequenz |
| NEM | Numbered Error Message | NF | Noise Factor |
| NEMA | National Electrical Manufacturer's Association | NF | Noise Figure |
| NEMAG | Negative Effective Mass Amplifiers and Generation | NF | Noise Frequency |
| | | NF | Normal Form |
| | | NF | Normal Frequency |
| | | NF | Normalform |
| NEMIS | Network Management Information System | NF | Normalformat |
| | | NF | Norme Française |
| NEMP | Nuclear Electromagnetic Pulse | NF | Number Format |
| | | NFB | Negative Feedback |
| NEP | Never-Ending Program | NFC | Name Formula Card |
| NEP | Node Error Program | NFCR | New Flexible Code Restriction |
| NEP | Noise Equivalent Power | NFDC | National Fire Data Center |
| NEP/CON | National Electronic Packing and production Conference | NFDC | National Flight Data Center |
| | | NFDS | National Fire Data System |
| NEPD | Noise Equivalent Power Density | NFE | Nearly Free Electron |
| | | NFE | No First Error |
| NEPDB | Navy Environmental Protection Data Base | NFF | No Fault Found |
| | | NFG | Niederfrequenzgenerator |
| NERIS | National Energy Referral and Information System | NFLDS | National Fire Loss Data System |
| NEROS | Neue Rationelle Organisationssysteme | NFM | Narrow-band Frequency Modulation |
| NES | Near-End Suppressor | NFP | Network Facilities Package |
| NES | Noise Equivalent Signal | NFP | Niederfrequenz-Pegelmesser |
| NES | Non-Erasable Storage | | |
| NES | Non-Erasable Store | NFP | Not File Protect |
| NES | Not Elsewhere Specified | NFPA | National Fire Protection Association |
| NESC | National Electrical Safety Code | | |
| | | NFQ | Night Frequency |
| NET | Network | NFR | No Further Requirement |
| NET | Noise Equivalent Temperature | NFS | Narrow band Frequency Shift |
| NET | Noise Evaluation Test | NFS | New Financial System |
| NET | Nummernendetaste | NFS | Non-Functional Status |
| NETDS | Near-Earth Tracking and Data System | NFSAIS | National Federation of Science Abstracting and Indexing Services |
| NETGEN | Netzgenerierungsprogramm | | |
| | | NFT | Network File Transfer |
| NETS | Network Electrical Technique System | NFT | No Filing Time |
| | | NFTV | Niederfrequenz Television |
| NETSET | Network Synthesis and Evaluation Technique | NFTW | National Federation of Telephone Workers |
| NEUCC | Northern Europe University Computing Complex | NFV | Niederfrequenzverstärker |
| | | NG | Nachrichtengröße |
| NEUT | Neutral | NG | National Guard |

# N

| | | | |
|---|---|---|---|
| NG | Netzgruppe | NIAT | Non-Indexable Address Tag |
| NG | New Generation | NIB | National Information Bureau |
| NG | Nitroglycerine | | |
| NG | Noise Generator | NIB | Node Initialization Block |
| NG | Normalgenerator | NIB | Noninterference Basis |
| NG | Not Greater than | NIBL | National Industrial Basic Language |
| NGC | Next Group Clause | | |
| NGCC | National Guard Computer Center | NIBS | National Inventory Billing System |
| NGDA | New Generation Design Automation | NIC | National Invention Council |
| | | NIC | Natural Image Computer |
| NGDC | National Geophysical Data Center | NIC | Negative Immittance Converter |
| NGHZ | Netzgruppenhauptzentrale | NIC | Negative Impedance Converter |
| NGI | Nichtgrafische Information | | |
| NGIS | Next Generation Information System | NIC | Net Information Content |
| | | NIC | Network Information Center |
| NGL | Network Generation Language | NIC | Network Interchange Computer |
| NGLC | Next Generation Level Control | NIC | Network Interface Cards |
| | | NIC | Network Interface Controller |
| NGP | Next Generation Processing | | |
| NGSP | National Geodetic Satellite Program | NIC | Netzwerk-Interface-Controller |
| | | NIC | Nineteenhundred Indexing and Cataloguing |
| NGT | New Generation Technology | | |
| NGT | Next Generation Technology | NIC | Not In Contact |
| | | NICB | National Industrial Conference Board |
| NGT | Noise Generator Tube | | |
| NHI | National Health Insurance | NICE | National Information Conference and Exposition |
| NHPIC | National Health Planning Information Center | | |
| | | NICOL | New Integrated Computer Language |
| NHR | Non-Harmonic Rejection | | |
| NHS | National Health Service | NICOL | New International Commercial Language |
| NHS | Netz-Hauptschrank | | |
| NI | No line Identification available | NICOL | Nineteenhundred Commercial Language |
| | | NID | Network In-Dialling |
| NI | Noise Index | NIDA | Numerically Integrating Differential Analyzer |
| NI | Non-Indicate | | |
| NI | Non-inverting Input | | |
| NI | Normenausschuß Informationsverarbeitung | NIDAS | Nixdorf Integrated Data Accounting System |
| | | NIDE | Numerical Integration of Differential Equations |
| NI | Numeric Item | | |
| NI | Numerical Index | NIDOC | National Information and Documentation Centre |
| NIA | Network Interface Adapter | | |
| NIA | No Input Acknowledge | NIF | Noise Improvement Factor |
| NIA-F | Network Interface Adapter - Front side | NIFTY | Nixdorf File utility |
| | | NIH | National Institute of Health |
| NIA-R | Network Interface Adapter - Remote/terminal side | | |
| | | NIH | Not Invented Here |
| NIAM | Nijssen's Informations-Analyse-Methode | NII | Negative Immittance Inverter |
| NIAP | Non-Inverting Amplifier Pair | | |

# N

| | | | |
|---|---|---|---|
| NII | Negative Impedance Inverter | NIR | Near Infrared |
| NIK | Negativ-Immittanz-Konverter | NIR | Next Instruction Register |
| | | NIRC | National Information Retrieval Colloquium |
| NIK | Netz aus Instanzen und Kanälen | NIRI | National Information Research Institute |
| NIL | Noise Immission Level | NIS | National Information System |
| NIL | Nothing | | |
| NIM | Netzwerk-Interface-Modul | NIS | Nächster Indexsatz |
| NIM | Non-Interrupt Mode | NIS | Network Information Services |
| NIM | Nuclear Instruments Module | NIS | Network Information System |
| NIMMS | Nineteenhundred Integrated Modular Management System | NIS | Netz-Informations-System |
| NIMO | Numerical Indicator Multiple Oscilloscope | NIS | Not In Stock |
| | | NIS | Number Indicating System |
| NIMPA | Newly Installed Machine Performance Analysis | NIS | Numerical Information Storage |
| NIMROD | National Institute for Medical Research On-line Data-base | NISARC | National Information Storage And Retrieval Center |
| NIMROD | Nineteenhundred Management and Recovery Of Documentation | NISC | National Information System for Chemistry |
| | | NISC | Not-in-Synchronization Counter |
| NIMS | Nineteenhundred Information for Management Systems | NISE | Normalized Integral Squared Error |
| NIN | National Information Network | NISM | National Information System for Mathematics |
| NIN | Not In | NISM | Non-deterministic Incomplete Sequential Machine |
| NIN | Not Initialized | | |
| NINO | Nothing In Nothing Out | | |
| NIOBE | Numerical Integration Of the Boltzmann-transport Equation | NISP | National Information System for Psychology |
| | | NISPA | National Information System for Physics and Astronomy |
| NIOS | Network Input/Output System | | |
| NIOS | Nixdorf Integrated Office Software | NISSAT | National Information System for Science And Technology |
| NIOSH | National Institute for Occupational Safety and Health | NIST | National Information system for Science & Technology |
| NIP | Non Impact Printer | | |
| NIP | Non-Indexing Part | NIT | Napierian Digit |
| NIPO | Negative Input/Positive Output | NIT | Native Interface Tester |
| | | NIT | Nearly Intelligent Terminal |
| NIPP | Non-Impact Printing Process | NIT | Niveau d'Interruption |
| NIPP | Non-Impact Printing Project | NIT | Notice d'Information Technique |
| NIPS | National Information Processing System | NIT | Numerical Indicator Tube |
| | | NITC | National Information Transfer Centre |
| NIPTS | Noise Induced Permanent Threshold Shift | | |

# N

| | | | |
|---|---|---|---|
| NITTS | Noise Induced Temporary Threshold Shift | NLS | New Least Squares |
| NIU | Network Interface Unit | NLS | No-Load-Speed |
| NJCC | National Joint Computers Committee | NLS | Non-Linear System |
| NJE | Network-Job-Entry | NLS | Non-Linear Systems Corporation System |
| NJE | Netz-Jobeingabe | NLS | Non-Linear Systems, Incorporated |
| NJI | Network Job Interface | NLS | Nonlinear Smoothing |
| NJP | Network Job Processing | NLSDAP | Nonlinear System Data Presentation |
| NK | Netzknoten | | |
| NKA | Nutzen-Kosten-Analyse | NLSSTUF | Nonlinear System Statistical Utility Feature |
| NKE | Netzkontrolleinrichtung | | |
| NKF | Nonlinear Kalmar Filter | | |
| NKU | Nutzen-Kostenuntersuchung | NLT | Negative Leitung durch Transistoren |
| NKZ | Netzkontrollzentrum | | |
| NL | Natural Logarithm | NLT | Negative Line Transmission |
| NL | New Line | | |
| NL | Niederlassung | NLT | Negative Line with Transistors |
| NL | Noise Limiter | | |
| NL | Non-Linear | NLT | New Logic Technology |
| NL | Not Less than | NLT | Nucleus Load Table |
| NL | Number Language | NM | Nanomemory |
| NLC | Non-Linear Capacitor | NM | Nautical Mile |
| NLD | Non-Linear Distortion | NM | Negative Matrix |
| NLDB | Natural Language Data Base | NM | Network Manager |
| | | NM | No Message |
| NLDM | Network Logical Data Manager | NM | Noise Margin |
| | | NM | Noise Meter |
| NLE | Non-Linear Element | NM | Not Measured |
| NLF | No-Load Field | NM | Null Matrix |
| NLG | Noise Landing Gear | NM | Number Module |
| NLI | Non-Linear Interpolating | NM | Numbering Machine |
| NLIS | Navy Logistics Information System | NM | Numeric Move |
| | | NM | Numerical Machining |
| NLKF | Non-Linear Kalman Filter | NM | Numérique Médical |
| NLL | Negative Logic Level | NMA | National Management Association |
| NLM | National Library of Medicine | | |
| | | NMA | National Microfilm Association |
| NLM | Noise Level Monitor | | |
| NLO | Non-Linear Optics | NMAA | National Machine Accountants Association |
| NLO | Non-Linear Optimizer | | |
| NLP | Natural Language Processing | NMAC | National/Medical Audio-visual Center |
| NLP | Non-Linear Programming | NMC | Navigation Map Computer |
| NLP | Nonlinear Program | NMC | Non-Marginal Check |
| NLPS | N-Large energy gap, P-Small energy gap | NMDL | Navy Management Data List |
| NLQ | Near Letter Quality | NME | National Military Establishment |
| NLR | Noise Load Ratio | | |
| NLR | Non-Linear Resistance | NME | Noise-Measuring Equipment |
| NLR | Non-Linear Resistor | | |
| NLRB | National Labour Relations Board | NMG | Numerical Master Geometry |
| NLREG | Nichtlineare Regression | NMI | National Maintenance Index |
| NLREG | Non-Linear Regression | | |

# N

| | | | | |
|---|---|---|---|---|
| NMI | Nautical Miles | | NOD | Navigation Orientation Display |
| NMI | Nonmaskable Interrupt | | NOD | Network-Out-Dialling |
| NMM | Network Measurement Machine | | NOD | Night Observation Device |
| NMO | Normal Mode Operation | | NODAC | Naval Ordnance Data Automation Center |
| NMOS | N-channel MOS | | NODC | National Oceanographic Data Center |
| NMOS | N-type MOS | | | |
| NMP | Numeric Machine Program | | NOF | National Optical Fond |
| NMPS | Nautical Miles Per Second | | NOFIN | No Further Information |
| NMR | N-Modular Redundancy | | NOG... | Neue Organisations-maschinengesellschaft |
| NMR | Normal Mode Rejection | | | |
| NMS | Network Management Services | | NOHP | Not Otherwise Herein Provided |
| NMS | Network Management System | | NOI | Network Operator Interface |
| NMS | Netzwerk Management System | | NOI | No-Operation Instruction |
| | | | NOI | Not Otherwise Identified |
| NMSFT | Network Management System File-Transfer | | NOI | Not Otherwise Indexed |
| | | | NOIBN | Not Otherwise Indexed By Name |
| NMSRO | Network Management System Remote-Operating | | NOLAP | Non-Linear Analysis Program |
| NMT | Nordic Mobile Telephone | | NOLOG | No Logging |
| NMTBA | National Machine Tool Builders Association | | NOM | Nominal |
| | | | NOMA | National Office Management Association |
| NN | National Number | | | |
| NN | Nearest Neighbour | | NOMC | Network Operation and Management Center |
| NN | Network Node | | | |
| NN | Normativnutzungsdauer | | NOMDA | National Office Machine Dealers Association |
| NNA | New Network Architecture | | | |
| NNB | Netznachbildung | | NOMEN | Nomenclature |
| NNC | Non-Numeric Character | | NOMIS | Naval Ordnance Management Information System |
| NND | Normativ der Nutzungsdauer | | | |
| | | | NON-DB | Non Data Base |
| NND | Normative Nutzungsdauer | | NONCOHO | Noncoherent Oscillator |
| NND | Normativnutzungsdauer | | NONRTNZ | Nonreturn to Zero |
| NNI | Noise and Number Index | | NOP | No Operation |
| NNR | New Nonofficial Remedies | | NOP | Nulloperation |
| NNSP | Nachrichtennetz-Steuerungsprogramm | | NOP | Normierte Programmierung |
| | | | NOP | Not Otherwise Provided |
| NNSS | Navy Navigation Satellite System | | NOPA | National Office Products Association |
| NNW | North-North-West | | NOR | Negative OR |
| NO | Nomenklatur | | NOR | Network-Oriented Routine |
| NO | Normally Open | | NOR | No Record |
| NO | Not Obtainable | | NOR | Normal |
| NO | Not Operational | | NOR | Not OR |
| NO | Number | | NOR | Not Operationally Ready |
| NO | Numerische Ortsdatei | | NOR | Not Otherwise Rated |
| NOC | Network Operation Control | | NORAC | No Radio Contacts |
| NOC | Normally Open Contact | | NORC | Naval Ordnance Research Calculator |
| NOC | Notation Of Content | | | |
| NOCIG | Night-Only Computer Image Generation | | NORC | Naval Ordnance Research Computer |

# N

| | | | |
|---|---|---|---|
| NORCOM | Nonrecurring Cost Model | NPC | Non-Printing Character |
| NORD | Non-destructive Readout | NPC | Numerical Positioning Control |
| NORDO | No Radio | NPC | Numerical Print Control |
| NORLUCS | Norther software consultants Library Updating and Compiling System | NPD | Network Protective Device |
| | | NPDA | Network Problem Determination Aid |
| NORM | Normal | NPDA | Network Problem Determination Application |
| NORM | Normalizing | | |
| NORMAL | Nova Realtime Macro Language | NPDN | Nordic Public Data Network |
| NORMARC | Norwegian Machine Readable Cataloguing | NPEF | New Product Evaluation Form |
| NORMZ | Normalize | NPEX | Normal Priority Exit |
| NORMZ | Normalizing | NPG | Nonprocessor Grant |
| NORPAK | Norway Packet network | NPG | Normierte Programmierung |
| NOS | Network Operating System | NPG | Normalized Programming Generator |
| NOS | Not Otherwise Specified | | |
| NOS | Not Otherwise Stated | NPII | Net Point Installed Increase |
| NOS | Nought Output Signal | | |
| NOS | Number of Stops | NPIRI | Net Product Installed Record Increase |
| NOSP | Network Operation Support Program | NPIS | National Physics Information System |
| NOSS | Nimbus Operational Satellite System | NPK | Non-Printing Key |
| NOTIS | Northwestern Online Totally Integrated System | NPK | Normpositionskatalog |
| | | NPL | N-series Plug |
| | | NPL | National Physical Laboratory |
| NOTRDY | Not Ready | | |
| NOVCAM | Non-Volatile Charge-Addressed Memory | NPL | Natural Programming Language |
| NOVRAM | Non-Volatile Random Access Memory | NPL | Networked Product Line |
| | | NPL | New Process Line |
| NP | Net Proceeds | NPL | New Processor Line |
| NP | Network Program | NPL | New Product Line |
| NP | Non Print | NPL | New Programming Language |
| NP | Non Procurable | | |
| NP | Normierte Programmierung | NPL | No Programming Language |
| NP | Null Parameter | NPLA | New Product Line Audit |
| NP | Numeric Punch | NPLAS | New Programming Language Adapter Simulation |
| NPA | Network Performance Analyzer | | |
| NPA | Normal Pressure Angle | NPLCS | New Programming Language Channel Simulation |
| NPA | Numerical Production Analysis | | |
| NPAAS | National Passenger Accounting and Analysis Scheme | NPM | Navy Programming Manual |
| | | NPM | Network Performance Monitor |
| NPAC | National Program for Acquisition and Cataloguing | NPN | Negative/Positive/Negative |
| | | NPO | Negative-Positive-zero |
| NPAS | New Products Analysis System | NPP | New Product Planning |
| | | NPP | Netzplanprogramm |
| NPC | Network Program Control | NPR | Noise Power Ratio |

# N

| | | | |
|---|---|---|---|
| NPR | Nonprocessor Request | NRDR | Non-Resetting Data Reconstructor |
| NPR | Numerical Position Readout | NRE | Negative Resistance Elements |
| NPR... | National Property Register Ltd. | NRF | No Record Found |
| NPRDRCV | Nonproductive Receive | NRFD | Not Ready For Data |
| NPRI | Net Product Record Increase | NRFI | Not Ready For Issue |
| NPRO | Non-Process Run-Out | NRIC | Non-Reciprocal Impedance Converter |
| NPS | Network Processing Supervisor | NRIS | Natural Resource Information System |
| NPS | Normiertes Programmiersystem | NRM | Next to Reading Matter |
| | | NRM | Normal Response Mode |
| NPSI | National Product Satisfaction Index | NRM | Normalize |
| | | NRM | Numeral Reading Machine |
| NPSI | NCP Packet Switching Interface | NRMA | National Retail Merchant Association |
| NPSI | Network Packet Switching Interface | NRMEC... | North American Rockwell Micro Electronics Co. |
| NPSW | Neues Programmstatuswort | NRMS | Nominal Root Mean Square |
| | | NRP | Narrow-band Random Process |
| NPT | Network Planning Technique | NRP | Non-Relocatable Program |
| NPT | Netzplantechnik | NRP | Normal Rated Power |
| NPT | Non Programmable Terminal | NRP | Null Reading Position |
| | | NRT | Near Real Time |
| NPT | Normal Pressure and Temperature | NRT | Net Registered Tonnage |
| | | NRT | Non Real Time |
| NPTR | Net Process Throughput Rate | NRT | Non Requestor Terminal |
| | | NRTC | Normalized Re-instrumented Terrain Computer |
| NQA | Niveau de Qualité Acceptable | | |
| NR | N-Operanden Register | NRTL | Nonlinear Resistor Transistor Logic |
| NR | New Range | | |
| NR | Noise Ratio | NRU | Non Replaceable Unit |
| NR | Noise Reduction | NRW | Non-Reversed Word |
| NR | Nonreactive | NRZ | Non Return to Zero |
| NR | Nonrecoverables | NRZ/C | Non Return to Zero Change |
| NR | Number | | |
| NR | Number is ... | NRZ/M | Non Return to Zero Mark |
| NR | Number/my call | NRZI | No Return to Zero Invert |
| NR | Nummer | NRZI | Non Return to Zero Indiscrete |
| NRA | Naval Ratio Activity | | |
| NRA | Negative Resistance Amplifier | NRZL | Non Return to Zero Level |
| | | NRZM | Non Return to Zero Mark recording |
| NRC | National Research Council | | |
| NRCD | National Reprographic Centre for Documentation | NRZM | Non Retrun to Zero with Mark |
| NRDC | National Research and Development Council | NRZR | Non Return to Zero Recording |
| NRDC... | National Research Development Corp. | NRZS | Non Return to Zero Space |
| NRDF | Nonrecursive Digital Filter | NS | Nanosecond |
| NRDR | Non-Resetting Data Reconstruction | NS | Nanoseconde |
| | | NS | Nanosekunde |

# N

| | | | |
|---|---|---|---|
| NS | National Semiconductor | NSP | Network Services Protocol |
| NS | National Standard | NSP | Non-Series/Parallel |
| NS | Nebenspeicher | NSP | Nonstandard Part approval |
| NS | Network Services | NSP | Normal Stage Punching |
| NS | New Style | NSP | Numeric Space character |
| NS | New System | NSPE | National Society of Professional Engineers |
| NS | No Stock | | |
| NS | Noise Sensitivity | NSPE | Network Service Procedure Error |
| NS | Non-Sequenced | | |
| NS | Normalanschlußsperre | NSPI | National Society for Performance and Instruction |
| NS | Not Specified | | |
| NS | Note Statement | NSPRDS | New Systems Personnel Requirements Data System |
| NS | Nought State | | |
| NS | Null Statement | | |
| NS | Number Series | NSPT | Normsprechtext |
| NS | Number System | NSR | Noise-to-Signal Ratio |
| NS | Numerical Signal | NSRDC | National Standards Reference Data Center |
| NS | Numerische Steuerung | | |
| NS | Nummernschalter | NSRDS | National Standard Reference Data System |
| NSA | National Security Agency | | |
| NSA | Network-unit Switch Addressgenerator | NSRI | Net Sales Revenue Increase |
| NSA | Non-Sequenced Acknowledgement | NSS | National Space Station |
| | | NSS | New Simulation System |
| NSAG | N-channel Self-Aligned-Gate | NSSDC | National Space Science Data Center |
| NSB | Nachrichtensteuerblock | NSTA | National Swedish Telephone Agency |
| NSC | Native Sub-Channel | | |
| NSC | Network Switching Centre | NSTA | Nebenstellenanlage |
| NSC | Noise Suppression Circuit | NSTIC | Naval Science Technical Information Centre |
| NSC | Numerical Sequence Code | | |
| NSD | Nonlinear Sampled Data | NSUI | Net Sales Unit Increase |
| NSDC | National Serials Data Centre | NSV | Nonautomatic Self-Verification |
| NSDRC | National Standard Data Reference Center | NSWTI | Nationale Systeme für die Wissenschaftliche und Technische Information |
| NSDU | Network Service Data Unit | | |
| NSE | Niederspannungseinschub | NT | Nachrichtentechnik |
| NSEC | Nanosecond | NT | Network Termination Unit |
| NSF | National Science Foundation | NT | Netztakt |
| | | NT | Netzteil |
| NSF | Negotiated Search Facility | NT | New Technology |
| NSFL | New Strip File | NT | No Transmission |
| NSG | Noise Signal Generator | NT | Normaltakt |
| NSI | Next Sequential Instruction | NT | Northern Telecom |
| NSI | Non-Sequenced Information | NT | Not Tested |
| | | NT | Numbering Transmitter |
| NSI | Nonstandard Item | NT | Numerical Table |
| NSIL | Non Saturating Inverter Logic | NT | Nutzungszeitabhängige Tarifierung |
| NSL | New Simulation Language | NTA | National Telecommunications Agency |
| NSM | Negative Sample Mode | | |
| NSM | Network Storage Module | NTB | Neue Technik im Büro |
| NSM | Nondeterministic Sequential Machine | NTC | Negative Temperature Coefficient |

# N

| | | | | |
|---|---|---|---|---|
| NTC | Non Transmission Compensated | | NTVA | Non-deterministic Time-Variant Automation |
| NTDS | Naval Tactical Data System | | NÜ | Nachrichtenübertrager |
| NTDS | Naval Technical Data System | | NÜ | Nachrichtenübertragung |
| | | | NU | Number Unobtainable |
| NTDSC | Nondestructive Testing Data Support Center | | NU | Numeric |
| NTE | Netztakteinheit | | NUA | Network User's Association |
| NTE | Non-orthogonal Timing Error | | NUC | Not Under Control |
| | | | NUC | Nucleus |
| NTF | No Trouble Found | | NUCOL | Numerical Control Language |
| NTG | Nachrichtentechnische Gesellschaft | | NUDAC | Nuclear Data Center |
| | | | NUDOR | Numerical Data processor |
| NTI | Noeud de Transit International | | NÜE | Nachrichtenübertragungs-Steuereinheit |
| NTI | Noise Transmission Impairment | | NUI | Network User Identification |
| NTIA | National Telecommunication and Information Administration | | NUL | No Upper Limit |
| | | | NUL | Null |
| | | | NUM | Numeral |
| NTIAC | Nondestructive Testing Information and Analysis Center | | NUM | Numeric |
| | | | NUMIS | Navy Uniform Management Information System |
| NTIS | National Technical Information Service | | NUPD | Non Uniform Punched Document |
| NTL | Non-uniform Transmission Line | | NÜS | Nachrichtenübertragungssystem |
| NTL | Nonthreshold Logic | | NUS | Nominal Ultimate Strength |
| NTL | Note Technique de Lancement | | NUSUM | Numerical Summary Message |
| NTN | National Terminal Number | | NUTIS | Numerical and Textile Information System |
| NTO | Network Terminal Option | | NUTL | Non Uniform Transmission Line |
| NTOMA | National Tool and die Manufacturers | | | |
| | | | NV | Nachrichtenverarbeitung |
| NTP | Near Time Processing | | NV | Netzverteiler |
| NTP | Network Terminating Point | | NV | Neutralization Value |
| NTP | Netzteilprüfgerät | | NV | No Volatile |
| NTP | Normal Temperature and Pressure | | NVA | No Voltage Amplification |
| | | | NVAS | Nachrichtenverarbeitendes Anwender-System |
| NTP | Northern Telecom Practices | | NVG | Null Voltage Generator |
| NTR | Nine Thousand Remote | | NVM | Non Volatile Matter |
| NTR | Noise Temperature Ratio | | NVM | Non Volatile Memory |
| NTR | Nothing To Report | | NVR | No Voltage Release |
| NTS | Negative Torque Signal | | NVRAM | Non Volatile Random Access Memory |
| NTS | Not To Scale | | | |
| NTT | Nippon Telegraph and Telephone | | NVSM | Non Volatile Semiconductor Memory |
| NTT | Nippon Telegraph and Telephone Public Corporation | | NVSMD | Non Volatile Semiconductor Memory Device |
| NTT | Number Theoretic Transform | | NWDC | Navigation Weapon Delivery Computer |
| NTU | Network Terminating Unit | | NWDS | Number of Words |
| NTU | Number to Transfer Units | | | |

# N

| | | | |
|---|---|---|---|
| NWDSEN | Number of Words per Entry | NYPC | New York Programming Center |
| NWE | Narrow-Width Effect | | |
| NWG | National Wire Gauge | NYR | Not Yet Required |
| NWH | Normal Working Hours | NYSIIS | New York State Identification and Intelligence System |
| NWI | National Workload Index | | |
| NWP | Numerical Weather Prediction | | |
| | | NYSPIN | New York State Police Intelligence Network |
| NWS | Nachrichten-Warteschlange | | |
| | | NZAPS | Nike Zeus Automatic Programming System |
| NXMIS | Mike-X Management Information System | | |
| | | NZE | North-Zenith-East system |
| NXT | Next | NZR | Non Zero Result |
| NYAP | New York Assembly Program | NZT | Non Zero Test |

# O

| | | | |
|---|---|---|---|
| O | Ohm | OAIDE | Operational Assistance and Instructive Data Equipment |
| O | Operation | | |
| O | Operator | | |
| O | Oscillator | OAK | Ordnungsaspektwert-Katalog |
| O | Output | | |
| O | Overall readability | OAL | Object Authorization List |
| O | Oxygen | OALS | Oregon total information system Automated Library Services |
| O | Oxzillator | | |
| O & M | Organization & Methods | | |
| O&C | Operations and Checkout | OAME | Orbital Altitude and Maneuvering Electronics |
| O-B | Octal-to-Binary | | |
| O-H | Octal-to-Hexadecimal | OAMP | Optical Analog Matrix Processing |
| O/D | On Demand | | |
| O/F | Orbital Flight | OAMS | Orbit Attitude and Manoeuver System |
| O/L | Operations/Logistics | | |
| O/R | On Request | OAN | ODER-Ausgang negiert |
| O/R | Originator/Recipient | OAP | Office Analyse- und Planungsdienst |
| O/S | Operating System | | |
| OA | Odd Address | OAPM | Optimal Amplitude and Phase Modulation |
| OA | ODER-Ausgang | | |
| OA | Office Automation | OAR | Object Address Register |
| OA | Omnirange Antenna | OAR | Operand Address Register |
| OA | Operand Address | OAR | Operandenadreßregister |
| OA | Operating Assembly | OAR | Operational Address Register |
| OA | Operational Amplifier | | |
| OA | Operational Analysis | OAR | Operations Activity Recorder |
| OA | Operator Access | | |
| OA | Operator Availability | OAR | Operationsadressregister |
| OA | Order Address | OAR | Operator Autorization Record |
| OA | Organisationsanweisung | | |
| OA | Organisationsautomat | OAR | Optical Automatic Ranging |
| OA | Original Address | OARAC | Office of Air Research Automatic Computer |
| OA | Outgoing Access | | |
| OA | Output Axis | OAS | One-Address System |
| OABETA | Office Appliance and Business Equipment Trades Association | OAS | Operational Announcing System |
| | | OAS | Organizational Accounting Structure |
| OAC | Office Automation Conference | OASE | Office Automation Services |
| OAC | One-Address Code | | |
| OAC | One-Address Computer | OASF | Orbital Astronomy Support Facility |
| OAC | Optimal Automatic Control | OASI | Old Age and Survivors' Insurance |
| OACP | Operational Analysis Code Package | OASIS | Ocean Atmospheric Surveillance and Information System |
| OAD | Operational Active Data | | |
| OAD | Operational Availability Data | OASIS | Oceanic and Atmospheric Scientific Information System |
| OAF | Option opérateur Afficheur | | |
| OAF | Origin Address Field | OASIS | On-line Administrative Information System |
| OAF | Original Address Field | | |
| OAI | One-Address Instruction | OASIS | Operational Automated Ship's Information System |
| OAI | OR Accumulators to Indicators | | |

# O

| | | | |
|---|---|---|---|
| OASIS | Operational Automatic Scheduling Information System | OC | Operational Command |
| | | OC | Operational Computer |
| | | OC | Operations Control |
| OASIS | Orders, Accounting, Stock, Invoicing and Statistics | OC | Operationscharakteristik |
| | | OC | Operationscode |
| | | OC | Operator Call |
| OASIS | Outpatient Appointment Schedule Information System | OC | Operator Command |
| | | OC | Order Cancel |
| | | OC | Order Code |
| OAT | Operating Ambient Temperature | OC | Order Confirmation |
| | | OC | Outlet Contact |
| OAT | Ordnungsaspektwert-Tabelle | OC | Output Card |
| | | OC | Output Code |
| OAT | Outside Air Temperature | OC | Output Computer |
| OAT | Oxide-Aligned Transistor | OCAL | Online Cryptanalytic Aid Language |
| OAV | Organisations-Arbeitsvorbereitung | |  |
| | | OCASP | Olivetti Complete Accounting and Stock Package |
| OAV | Output Available | | |
| OB | Operation Block | | |
| OB | Ordnungsbegriff | OCB | Outgoing Calls Barred |
| OB | Outboard Buffer | OCB | Override Control Bit |
| OB | Output Block | OCBP | Output Control Block Pointer |
| OB | Output Buffer | | |
| OBAC | One Bit Adder Computer | OCBR | Output Channel Buffer Register |
| OBC | On-Board Computer | | |
| OBD | Omnibearing Distance | OCC | Occupée |
| OBF | Output-Buffer-Fall | OCC | Occupied |
| OBI | Omnibearing Indicator | OCC | Offset Course Computer |
| OBJ | Object | OCC | Open-Circuit Characteristic |
| OBK | Open Breaker Keying | | |
| OBL | Optischer Belegleser | OCC | Operational Computer Complex |
| OBLS | Optischer Beleglesesortierer | | |
| | | OCC | Operational Control Center |
| OBN | Out-of-Band Noise | | |
| OBP | On-Board Processor | OCC | Operator Control Command |
| OBR | Org-Ware-Benutzerring | | |
| OBR | Outboard Recorder | OCC | Order Control Card |
| OBR | Outboard Recording | OCC | Output Code Converter |
| OBS | Observation | OCCF | Operator Communication Control Facility |
| OBS | Omnibearing Selector | | |
| OBS | Output Buffer Storage | OCCS | Office of Computer and Communications System |
| OBS | Output Buffer Store | | |
| OBTN | Obtain | OCD | Off Chip Driver |
| OC | Object Computer | OCD | Output-only Console Device |
| OC | Occurs | | |
| OC | On Cards | OCDF | Operations Control and Display Facility |
| OC | Open Circuit | | |
| OC | Open Collector | OCDMS | On-board Check-out and Data Management System |
| OC | Open-Closed | | |
| OC | Operand Channel | OCDS | Output Command Data Set |
| OC | Operating Characteristics | OCF | Operation Code Field |
| OC | Operating Coil | OCF | Operator Console Facility |
| OC | Operation Check | OCF | Operator Control Facility |
| OC | Operation Code | ÖCG | Österreichische Computer Gesellschaft |
| OC | Operation Control | | |

# O

| | | | |
|---|---|---|---|
| OCHRE | Optical Character Recognition Engine | OCS | Order Control System |
| OCI | Office of Computer Information | OCT | Octal |
| | | OCT | Online Configuration Tool |
| OCI | Open-Circuit Inductance | OCT | Operator Control Table |
| OCI | Optical-Coupled Isolator | OCT | Output Clock Trigger |
| OCK | Operation Control Key | OCTL | Open-Circuited Transmission Line |
| OCL | Operating Control Language | OCU | Office Channel Unit |
| OCL | Operation Control Language | OCU | Operational Control Unit |
| | | OCU | Oscillator Clock Unit |
| OCL | Operational Check List | OCVD | Open-Circuit-Voltage-Decay |
| OCL | Operational Control Level | OCW | Orange-Cyan-Wideband |
| OCL | Operator Control Language | OD | Object Data |
| OCM | One Chip Module | OD | Oceanographic Data |
| OCO | Open-Close-Open | OD | Omnidirection |
| OCO | Operational Checkout | OD | Operational Data |
| OCP | Operating Control Procedure | OD | Operational Decoder |
| | | OD | Optical Density |
| OCP | Operational Checkout Procedure | OD | Ordnance Data |
| | | OD | Ordnungsdaten |
| OCP | Operational Control Program | OD | Organisation und Datenverarbeitung |
| OCP | Operator's Control Panel | OD | Oragnisation/Datenverarbeitung |
| OCP | Optimally Coded Program | | |
| OCP | Order Code Processor | OD | Original Data |
| OCP | Output Control Program | OD | Original Design |
| OCP | Output Control Pulse | OD | Output Data |
| OCR | Optical Card Reader | OD | Outside Diameter |
| OCR | Optical Character Reading | ODA | Office Document Architecture |
| OCR | Optical Character Recognition | ODA | One-Digit Adder |
| OCR | Order Change Record | ODA | Operational Data Analysis |
| OCR | Overcurrent Relay | ODA | Optischer Dokumentenabtaster |
| OCR-A | Optical Character Recognition-font A | | |
| | | ODAP | Operation Data Analysis Program |
| OCR-B | Optical Character Recognition-font B | ODAS | Ocean Data Acquisition System |
| OCRD | Office of Chief of Research and Development | ODB | Ordinateur De Bureau |
| | | ODB | Output Data Bulk |
| OCRIT | Optical Character Recognizing Intelligent Terminal | ODB | Output-to-Display Buffer |
| | | ODC | Optical Data Collecting |
| | | ODC | Orbital Data Collector |
| OCRS | Optical Character Recognition System | ODC | Output Data Carrier |
| | | ODCC | Onboard Digital Computer Control |
| OCRUA | OCR Users Association | | |
| OCRUA | Optical Character Recognition Users Association | ODCS | Online Data Compression System |
| OCS | Office Computer System | ODD | Operator Distance Dialling |
| OCS | Office Computing System | ODD | Optical Data Digitizer |
| OCS | Operation Control System | ODDH | On-board Digital Data Handling |
| OCS | Optical Character Scanner | | |
| OCS | Optical Computer System | ODDS | Oceanographic Digital Data System |
| OCS | Optimizing Control System | | |

- 435 -

# O

| | | | |
|---|---|---|---|
| ODE | Ordinary Differential Equation | ODT | Ocean Data Transmitter |
| ODESSA | Ocean Data Environmental Science Service Acquisition | ODT | Octal Debugging Technique |
| | | ODT | On-line Debugging Technique |
| ODG | Orbit Data Generator | ODT | Outside Diameter Tube |
| ODI | Office pour le Development Industriel | ODU | Output Display Unit |
| | | ODV | ODT Directory Vector |
| ODIN | On-line Dokumentations- und Informationsnetz | OE | Open End |
| | | OE | Organe Externe |
| ODM | On-line Display and Maintenance | OEA | Office Executives Association |
| ODM | Orbital Determination Module | OEC | Odd-Even Check |
| | | OECD | Organization for Economic Cooperation and Development |
| ODN | Own Doppler Nullifier | | |
| ODNA | Operational Data and Notices to Airmen | OED | Opto-Electronic Display |
| | | OEDV | Organisationseinheit Datenverarbeitung |
| ODOP | Orbital Doppler | | |
| ODP | Open Data Path | OEE | Odd-Even Effect |
| ODP | Operational Development Program | OEF | Origin Element Field |
| | | OEI | Overall Efficiency Index |
| ODP | Optical Data Processing | OEIMC | Oklahoma Environmental Information and Media Center |
| ODP | Original Document Processing | | |
| ODP | Output-to-Display Parity error | OEM | Original Equipment Manufacturer |
| ODPCS | Oceanographic Data Processing and Control Systems | OEM | Original Equipment Market |
| | | OEM | Other Equipment Manufacturer |
| ODR | Omnidirectional Range | OEMI | Office Equipment Manufacturer's Institute |
| ODR | Original Data Record | | |
| ODRN | Orbiting Data Relay Network | OEMI | Original Equipment Manufacturer's Information |
| ODRS | Orbiting Data Relay System | OEMI | Other Equipment Manufacturer's Information |
| ODS | Ocean Data Station | OEP | Open End Program |
| ODS | Office Dialog System | OEPS | Office of Educational Programs and Services |
| ODS | One Digit Subtractor | | |
| ODS | Operational Data Summary | OER | Odd-Even Rule |
| ODS | Operational Display System | OER | Operational Equipment Requirement |
| ODS | Optical Discrimination System | OER | Oxygen Enhancement Ratio |
| ODS | Optical Display System | OES | ODT Entry String |
| ODS | Optischer Dokumentensortierer | OES | Order Entry System |
| | | OF | Operand Field |
| ODS | Organisation - Datenverarbeitung - Software | OF | Operational Fixed |
| | | OF | Optional Feature |
| ODS | Organisations- und Datenverarbeitungsstation | OF | Optional File |
| | | OF | Oscillator Frequency |
| | | OF | Output File |
| ODS | Output Data Set | OFA | Oil-immersed Forced-Air-cooled |
| ODS | Output Data Strobe | | |
| ODSB | Ocean Data Station Buoy | OFC | One-Flow Cascade cycle |
| ODT | Object Definition Table | OFC | Operational Flight Control |

# O

| | | | |
|---|---|---|---|
| OFC | Orthonormal Function Coding | OI | Object Instruction |
| OFC | Overflow Card | OI | Oil-Immersed |
| OFC | Overflow Control | OI | Oil-Insulated |
| OFD | Overflow Data | OI | Operating Instructions |
| OFG | Optical Frequency Generator | OI | Operator Instruction |
| | | OI | Organizational Instruction |
| OFI | Overflow Indicator | OI | Output Impedance |
| OFL | Off-Line | OI | Output Instruction |
| OFLD | Off-Load | OIAS | Occupational Information Access System |
| OFR | On-Frequency Repeater | OIC | Officer In Charge |
| OFR | Operational Failure Report | OIC | Only-In-Chain |
| OFR | Optical Film Reader | OIC | Optical Integrated Circuit |
| OFR | Ordering Function Register | OID | Operator Identification |
| OFR | Over Frequency Relay | OIDPS | Oversea Intelligence Data Processing System |
| OFR | Overflow Register | | |
| OFS | Offset | OIFC | Oil-Insulated Fan-Cooled |
| OFS | Output Format Specification | OIL | Orange Indicating Lamp |
| | | OIM | Operator Interface Manager |
| OFT | Oberflächenfeldeffekt-transistor | | |
| | | OIP | Optical Image Processing |
| OFTA | Observatoire Français des Techniques Avancées | OIP | Optical Image Processor |
| | | OIPS | Optical Image Processing System |
| OFTMS | Output Format Table Modification Submodule | | |
| | | OIR | Object Information Repository |
| OG | Ogee | | |
| OG | Operationsgruppe | OIS | Office Information System |
| OG | OR Gate | OIS | Operating Information System |
| OG | Outgoing | | |
| OG | Output Gate | OIS | Optical Information Storage |
| ÖGI | Österreichische Gesellschaft für Informatik | | |
| | | OIS | Ounce Inches per Second |
| OGI | Outer Grid Injection | OIS | Output Information Signal |
| OGL | Outgoing Line | OISC | Oil-Insulated Self-Cooled |
| OGR | Outgoing Repeater | OIT | Optical Image Terminal |
| OGRS | Outgoing Relay Set | OIU | Optical Image Unit |
| OGT | Outgoing Trunk | OIWC | Oil-Insulated Water-Cooled |
| OGU | Outgoing Unit | OJT | On the Job Training |
| OH | Ohmic Heating | OK | Optokoppler |
| OH | Oil Hardened | OK | Ordnungskriterium |
| OH | On Hand | OKI-TRAC | Oki Transistorized Computer |
| OH | Operational Hardware | | |
| OH | Oval Head screw | OKIS | Offenbacher Kunden-informationssystem |
| OH | Overhead | | |
| OHC | Overhead Camshaft | OL | Object Language |
| OHD | Over-the-Horizon Detection | OL | Off-Line |
| | | OL | Offering Line |
| OHDMS | Operational Hydromet Data Management System | OL | On-Line |
| | | OL | Open Loop |
| | | OL | Oscillating Limiter |
| OHM | Ohmmeter | OL | Output List |
| OHP | Outer Helmholtz Plane | OL | Output Logic |
| OHP | Oxygen at High Pressure | OL | Overhead Line |
| OHS | Open Hearth Steel | OL | Overlap |
| OHV | Overhead Valve | OL | Overload |

# O

| | | | |
|---|---|---|---|
| OLAC | Off-Line Adaptive Computers | OLPARS | On-Line Pattern Analysis and Recognition System |
| OLAF | Operand Lattice File | OLPS | On-Line Programming System |
| OLB | Outer Lead Bonding | | |
| OLC | On-Line Computer | OLQ | On-Line Query |
| OLC | One Level Code | OLRT | On-Line Real Time |
| OLC | Open Loop Control | OLS | Off-Line Storage |
| OLC | Operational Logical Circuit | OLS | On-Line System |
| | | OLS | Optical Landing System |
| OLC | Outgoing Line Circuit | OLSA | Off-Line Selectric Analyser |
| OLCA | On-Line Circuit Analysis | | |
| OLCS | On-Line Computer System | OLSASS | On-Line System Availability and Service Simulation |
| OLD | On-Line Debug | | |
| OLD | Open Loop Damping | | |
| OLDAP | On-Line Data Processor | OLSC | On-Line Scientific Computer |
| OLDAS | On-Line Digital Analog Simulator | | |
| | | OLSS | On-Line Software System |
| OLDC | Off-Line Data Collecting | OLT | Off-Line Transmission |
| OLDC | On-Line Data Collecting | OLT | On-Line Teller |
| OLDE | On-Line Data Entry | OLT | On-Line Testing |
| OLDI | On-Line Data Input | OLT | On-Line Transmission |
| OLDO | On-Line Data Output | OLTEC | Online Test Control Program |
| OLDP | Off-Line Data Processing | | |
| OLDP | On-Line Data Processing | OLTEP | On-Line Test Executive Program |
| OLDR | On-Line Data Reduction | | |
| OLDS | On-Line Display System | OLTS | On-Line Test Section |
| OLE | On-Line Edit | OLTS | On-Line Test System |
| OLE | On-Line English | OLTS | On-Line Transaction System |
| OLE | On-Line Equipment | | |
| OLERT | On-Line Executive for Real-Time | OLTSEP | On-Line Test Standalone Executive Program |
| OLF | On-Line Filing | OLTT | On-Line Teller Terminal |
| OLFU | On-Line Feldunterstützung | OLTT | On-Line Terminal Test |
| OLG | Open Level Generation | OLU | On-Line Unit |
| OLGA | Organisationslehrgang für Assistenten | OLZ | Online-Zusatz |
| | | OM | Oberes Management |
| OLHMIS | On-Line Hospital Management Information System | OM | Object Machine |
| | | OM | Object Mapping |
| OLI | On-Line Input | OM | Object Module |
| OLI | Out-of-Lock Indicator | OM | Objektmodul |
| OLID | On-Line Identification | OM | Operand Manipulation |
| OLIVER | On-Line Interactive Variable Editing Reporter | OM | Operational Maintenance |
| | | OM | Operational Management |
| | | OM | Operational Monitor |
| OLL | Optischer Lochstreifenleser | OM | Operations and Maintenance |
| OLM | On-Line Monitor | OM | Operations Manual |
| OLMC | On-Line Machine Control | OM | Operator's Manual |
| OLO | Off-Line Operation | OM | Ordre de Modification |
| OLO | On-Line Output | OM | Organic Matter |
| OLP | Object Language Program | OM | Orthogonal Memory |
| OLP | Off-Line Processing | OM | Outer Marker |
| OLP | On-Line Processing | OM | Output Machine |
| OLP | Order Load Print | OM | Output Memory |
| OLP | Oxygen-Lance Power | OM | Overturning Moment |

# O

| | | | |
|---|---|---|---|
| OMA | Optical Multi-channel Analyzer | OMS | Ovonic Memory Switch |
| OMACS | Online Manufacturing And Control System | OMT | Orthogonal Mode Transducer |
| OMAR | Optical Mark Reader | OMTI | Omnium de Traitement de l'Information |
| OMAR | Order Maintenance Analysis Report | OMU | Optical Measuring Unit |
| OMAT | Office of Manpower and Automation Training | OMU | Optical Memory Unit |
| OMB | Office of Management and Budget | OMUP | Operations and Maintenance User Part |
| OMB | Outer Marker Beacon | OMV | Optimaler Medienverbund |
| OMC | Operations Monitoring Computer | ON | Octane Number |
| OMDE | On-line Maskendefinition | ÖN | Öffentliches Netz |
| OMDM | Opto-Mechanical Display Module | ON | Oil-immersed Natural cooled |
| OME | Optische Merkmalerkennung | ON-OFF | Oscillatory, Non-Oscillatory Flip-Flop |
| OMEC | Optimized Microminature Electronic Circuit | ONAL | Off-Net Access Line |
| OMF | Object Module File | ONB | Ortsnetzbereich |
| OMI | Operating Memorandum-Information | ONCT | On-line COBOL Trace |
| OMI | Optical Measurement Instrument | ONDA | On-line Dauerprogramm für den Sparkassenbetrieb |
| OMIBAC | Ordinal Memory Inspecting Binary Automatic Computer | ONDA | Online Datenverarbeitung |
| OMIS | Operational Management Information System | ONDA | Online Dauerprogramm |
| OML | Object Module Library | ONE | Open Network Environment |
| OMMIC | Ordnance Maintenance Management Information Center | ONFD | On-line-File-Display |
| | | ONKZ | Ortsnetzkennzahl |
| | | ONL | On-Line |
| OMNI | Optimum Management with Necessary Information | ONMAT | Online Materialabrechnung |
| | | ONP | On-Premise extension |
| OMP | Operating Maintenance Panel | ONSTAT | Ortsnetzstationsdatei |
| | | OOE | Odd-Odd Effect |
| OMP | Operating Maintenance Procedures | OOF | Office Of the Future |
| | | OOK | On-Off Keying |
| OMP | Operation Mode Program | OOL | Operator-Oriented Language |
| OMP | Operational Micro-Program | OOM | Original Online Module |
| | | OOO | Out Of Order |
| OMPR | Optical Mark Page Reader | OOP | Offline Orthophoto Printer |
| OMR | Optical Mark Read | OOPS | Off-line Operating Simulator |
| OMR | Optical Mark Reader | | |
| OMR | Optical Mark Reading | OOPS | On-line Object Patching System |
| OMR | Optical Mark Recognition | | |
| OMS | Office Management System | OOQ | Original Order Quantity |
| | | OP | Objektprogramm |
| OMS | Operational Monitoring System | OP | Observation Post |
| | | OP | Office Printer |
| OMS | Output Multiplex Synchronizer | OP | Office Products |
| | | OP | Open Program |
| | | OP | Operand |
| | | OP | Operate |
| | | OP | Operating |
| | | OP | Operating Point |
| | | OP | Operating Procedure |

# O

| | | | |
|---|---|---|---|
| OP | Operating Program | OPDD | Operational Plan Data Document |
| OP | Operating System | OPDESC | Operation Description |
| OP | Operation | OPDF | Output Data Funnel |
| OP | Operation Part | OPE | Operations Project Engineer |
| OP | Operational Priority | | |
| OP | Operationscode | OPER | Operational Rights |
| OP | Operationsregister | OPERA | Operational Analysis |
| OP | Operationsteil | OPERG | Operating |
| OP | Operationsverstärker | OPF | Output Filter |
| OP | Operator | OPFET | Optical Field Effect Transistor |
| OP | Operator Performance | | |
| OP | Optimum Program | OPI | Object Program Instruction |
| OP | Optimum Programming | OPI | Office of Public Information |
| OP | Ordinateur Personnel | | |
| OP | Organization Problem | OPICT | Operator Interface Control Block |
| OP | Out of Print | | |
| OP | Outport | OPIM | Order Processing and Inventory Monitoring |
| OP | Output | | |
| OP | Output Processor | OPINS | Oakland Planning Information System |
| OP | Output Program | | |
| OP | Output Puncher | OPL | Old Product Line |
| OP | Overproof | OPLE | Omega Position Location Experiment |
| OPA | Operational Amplifier | | |
| OPA | Optoelectronic Pulse Amplifier | OPM | Operations Per Minute |
| | | OPM | Operator Programming Method |
| OPADEC | Optical Particle Decoy | | |
| OPAL | Operational Performance Analysis Language | OPMS | On-the-machine Probe Measuring System |
| OPAL | Optical Platform Alignment Linkage | OPN | Open |
| | | OPN | Operation |
| OPAMP | Operational Amplifier | OPND | Operand |
| OPC | Object Program Card | OPNG | Opening |
| OPC | Odd Parity Check | OPO | Optical Parametric Oscillator |
| OPC | Open Printed Circuit | | |
| OPC | Operations Control | OPO | Other Programmed Operations |
| OPC | Operations Planning and Control | | |
| | | OPORD | Operations Order |
| OPC | Operationscode | OPORDER | Operations Order |
| OPC | Originating Point Code | OPOS | Offene Posten |
| OPC | Output Punched Card | OPOS | Oxygen-dopped Polysilicon |
| OPCE | Operator Control Element | OPP | Octal Print Punch |
| OPCODE | Operations Code | OPP | Operator Preparation Program |
| OPCOM | Operations Communications | | |
| | | OPP | Opposite |
| OPCON | Operation and Control | OPP | Optical Printer Projector |
| OPCON | Operational Control | OPP | Oriented Polypropylene |
| OPCON | Operations Control | OPPE | Office of Programming, Planning, and Evaluation |
| OPCON | Optimizing Control | | |
| OPCTR | Operator Counter | OPPOSIT | Optimization of a Production Process by an Ordered Simulation and Iteration Technique |
| OPD | Object Program Deck | | |
| OPD | Observed Position Data | | |
| OPD | Office Products Division | | |
| OPDAC | Optical Data Converter | | |
| OPDAR | Optical Detection And Ranging | OPPR | Operating Program |
| | | OPR | Operate |

# O

| | |
|---|---|
| OPR | Operating |
| OPR | Operation Register |
| OPR | Operator |
| OPR | Operator calls |
| OPR | Optical Page Reader |
| OPR | Optical Page Reading |
| OPRAD | Operations Research And Development |
| OPREG | Operation Register |
| OPREG | Operationsregister |
| OPREMA | Optik-Rechenmaschine |
| OPREMA | Optische Rechenmaschine |
| OPRFLT | Operator Fault |
| OPRNL | Operational |
| OPRO | Operations Order |
| OPS | On-line Process Synthesizer |
| OPS | Online Process Synthesis |
| OPS | Operational Paging System |
| OPS | Operations Per Second |
| OPS | Operations Planning System |
| OPS | Operativspeicher |
| OPS | Optical Power Spectrum |
| OPSADT | Optically Programmable Semi-Automatic DC Tester |
| OPSAM | Optical Storage Access Method |
| OPSCON | Operations Control |
| OPSCOP | Operations Control Program |
| OPSIM | Operational Simulator |
| OPSUM | Operation Summary |
| OPT | Optical |
| OPT | Optics |
| OPT | Optimized Production Technology |
| OPT | Optimum |
| OPT | Option |
| OPT | Output Punched Tape |
| OPT | Output Transformer |
| OPTA | Optimal Performance Theoretical Attainable |
| OPTG | Operating |
| OPTIC | Optical Procedural Task Instruction Compiler |
| OPTIM | Order Point Technique for Inventory Management |
| OPTIMAL | Office Products Total Integrierte Maschinelle Auftrags- und Lagerabrechnung |
| OPTIMOS | Optimized Metal Oxide Semiconductor |
| OPTINUTZ | Optimale Nutzung von Laderäumen |
| OPTO | Optical-To-Optical |
| OPTOEL | Optoelectronics |
| OPTOL | Optimized Test Oriented Language |
| OPTR | Optical Punched Tape Reader |
| OPTRONICS | Optical electronics |
| OPTRONIK | Optische Elektronik |
| OPTS | On-line Peripheral Test System |
| OPTS | On-line Program Testing System |
| OPTS | Operations |
| OPTUL | Optical Pulse Transmitter Using Laser |
| OPU | Operator Processing Unit |
| OPUP | Operator Position User Part |
| OPUR | Object Program Utility Routines |
| OPUS | Octal Program Updating System |
| OPUS | Online Projektunterstützungssystem |
| OPUS | Optimization Program for Unstable Secondaries |
| OPV | Ohms Per Volt |
| OPV | Operationsverstärker |
| OPW | Operating Weight |
| OPW | Operationswerk |
| OPW | Orthogonalized Plane Wave |
| OPZ | Operationszentrale |
| OQ | Output Quantity |
| OQ | Output Queue |
| OQL | Observed Quality Level |
| OQL | Online Query Language |
| OQL | Outgoing Quality Level |
| OR | Object Routine |
| OR | Omnidirectional Range |
| OR | Open Routine |
| OR | Operand Register |
| OR | Operandenregister |
| OR | Operation Rate |
| OR | Operation Register |
| OR | Operational Readiness |
| OR | Operational Research |
| OR | Operations Requirement |
| OR | Operations Research |
| OR | Operationsregister |
| OR | Operator |
| OR | Operator Routine |
| OR | Optical Reader |
| OR | Order Register |

# O

| | | | |
|---|---|---|---|
| OR | Order Release | ORDEAL | Oak Ridge Data Evaluation and Analysis Language |
| OR | Ordering Register | | |
| OR | Out of Range | ORDER | Organization and Retrieval of Data for Efficient Research |
| OR | Output Record | | |
| OR | Output Register | | |
| OR | Output Routine | ORDIR | Omnirange Digital Radar |
| OR | Outside Radius | ORDIS | Optical Reading Direct Input System |
| OR | Overall Resistance | | |
| OR | Overflow Register | ORDS | Observation Requirement Data Sheet |
| OR | Overhaul and Repair | | |
| OR | Overload Relay | ORDVAC | Ordnance Variable Automatic Computer |
| ORA | OR Accumulator | | |
| ORA | Output Register Address | ORE | Operation Request Element |
| ORACLE | Oak Ridge Automatic Computer and Logical Engine | | |
| | | ORESA | Operations Research/ Systems Analysis |
| ORACLE | Optimum Record Automation for Court and Law Enforcement | ORG | Organisation |
| | | ORG | Organisationsdaten |
| | | ORG | Origin |
| ORACLE | Optional Reception of Announcements by Coded Line Electronics | ORGWARE | Organisationsware |
| | | ORI | Octane Requirement Increase |
| ORAN | Orbital Analysis | ORI | Operational Readiness Inspection |
| ORB | Omnidirectional Radio Beacon | | |
| | | ORINT | Oriented Integrator |
| ORB | Operations Request Block | ORION | Online Retrieval of Information over a Network |
| ORBA | Organisationsberatung | | |
| ORBIS | Orbiting Radio Beacon Ionospheric Satellite | | |
| | | ORLY | Overload Relay |
| ORBIT | Oak Ridge Binary Internal Translator | ORM | Operators Reference Manual |
| ORBIT | On-line, Real-time Branch Information Transmission | ORMAC | Oral Response Machine |
| | | OROM | Optical Read Only Memory |
| ORBIT | On-line Reduced Bandwidth Information Transfer | OROS | Optical Read-Only Storage |
| | | ORP | Optional Response Poll |
| ORBIT | On-line Retrieval of Bibliographic Information-Timeshared | ORR | Omnidirectional Radar Range |
| | | ORR | Omnidirectional Radio Range |
| ORBIT | ORACLE Binary Internal Translator | | |
| | | ORR | Orbital Rendez-vous Radar |
| ORBIT | Order Billing Inventory Technique | ORRAS | Optical Research Radiometrical Analysis Systems |
| ORC | Operation Research Center | | |
| ORCHIS | Oak Ridge Computerized Hierarchical Information System | ORRAS | Optical Research Radiometrical System |
| | | ORS | Operations Research Society |
| ORCP | Optical Reader Card Punch | ORS | Optimal Real Storage |
| ORD | Operation Readiness Demonstration | ORS | OR to Storage |
| | | ORSA | Operations Research Society of America |
| ORD | Optical Rotary Dispersion | | |
| ORD | Order | ORSI | Operations Research Society of India |
| ORDA | Gesellschaft für Organisation und Datenverarbeitung | | |
| | | ORSJ | Operations Research Society of Japan |

# O

| | | | |
|---|---|---|---|
| ORT | Operational Readiness Test | OSCAR | Online System for Controlling Activities and Resources |
| ORT | Organisation und Rechentechnik | | |
| ORT | Overhand Radar Technology | OSCAR | Oxygen Steelmaking Computer And Recorder |
| ORTAI | Orbit-To-Air Intercept | | |
| ORTI | Optimisation des Réseaux de Télé-Informatique | OSCP | Oscilloscope |
| | | OSD | Office of the Secretary of Defense |
| ORU | Optimal Replaceable Unit | | |
| ORV | Orbital Rescue Vehicle | OSD | Operational Sequence Diagram |
| ORVID | Online Röntgenbefunde über Videodisplay | | |
| | | OSD | Operational Systems Development |
| ORZ | Omnirange Zero | | |
| ORZ | Organisations- und Rechenzentrum | OSDP | On-Site Data Processing |
| | | OSDP | On-Site Data Processor |
| OS | Oberes Seitenband | OSE | Operational Support Equipment |
| OS | Odd Symmetric | | |
| OS | Off-Scale | OSE | Output Service Element |
| OS | Old Style | OSEAS | Ocean Sampling and Environmental Analysis System |
| OS | One Side | | |
| OS | One-Shot multivibrator | | |
| OS | Open Shop | OSF | Open System Facilities |
| OS | Open Statement | OSFET | Oxide Semiconductor Field Effect Transistor |
| OS | Open Subroutine | | |
| OS | Operating System | OSHA | Occupational Safety and Health Administration |
| OS | Operation Sheet | | |
| OS | Operation System | OSI | ONLINE Software International Inc. |
| OS | Operational Sequence | | |
| OS | Operationssystem | OSI | Open System Interface |
| OS | Optical Scanning | OSI | Open Systems Interconnect |
| OS | Ordnance Surveying | OSI | Open Systems Interconnection |
| OS | Oscilloscope | | |
| OS | Oszillograf | OSI | Optimum Scale Integration |
| OS | Oszillogramm | OSI | Optional Stop Instruction |
| OS | Output Signal | OSI | OR Storage to Indicators |
| OS | Output Source | OSIA | Open System Interconnection Architecture |
| OS | Output Store | | |
| OS-KOCO | Organisations-System Kosten- und Leistungsrechnung in COBOL | OSIE | Open System Environment |
| | | OSIRIS | Online Search Information Retrieval and Information Storage |
| OS Q | Operating System Q | | |
| OS/VS | Operating System/Virtual Storage | OSIS | Ocean Surveillance Information System |
| OSA | Open Systems Architecture | OSIS | Office of Scientific Information Service |
| OSAF | Origin Subarea Field | | |
| OSAM | Overflow Sequential Access Method | OSIS | Organization Structure Information System |
| OSB | Oberes Seitenband | OSKO | Organisationssystem, Kernspeicherorientiert |
| OSB | Organisations- und Systemberatung GmbH | | |
| | | OSM | Operating System Monitor |
| OSC | Oscillate | OSMV | One-Shot Multivibrator |
| OSC | Oscillation | OSNS | Open Systems Network Support |
| OSC | Oscillator | | |
| OSC | Oscillograph | OSO | One-Shot Operation |
| OSC | Oscilloscope | OSOS | Oxide Silicon Oxide Semiconductor |
| OSC | Own Ship's Course | | |

# O

| | | | |
|---|---|---|---|
| OSP | Operations- und Serviceprozessor | OTA | Office of Technology Assessment |
| OSPS | Open Systems Presentation Support | OTA | Open Test Assembly |
| | | OTA | Operational Transconductance Amplifier |
| OSR | Offener Status Register | OTANZ | Output Tape Analyzer |
| OSR | Optical Scanning Recognition | OTB | Off-Track Betting |
| OSR | OR with Switch Register | OTB... | Off-Track Betting Corp. |
| OSR | Output Shift Register | OTC | Over The Counter |
| OSR | Output Status Register | OTC | Overseas Telecommunications Commission |
| OSRD | Office of Scientific Research and Development | OTE | Operational Test Equipment |
| OSRD | Office of Standard Reference Data | OTF | Optical Transfer Function |
| | | OTF | Optimum Traffic Frequency |
| OSRMD | Office of Scientific Research, Mechanics Division | OTH | Over The Horizon |
| | | OTHR | Over-The-Horizon Radar |
| OSS | Office of Space Sciences | OTI | Office Technology Interface |
| OSS | Optical Surveillance System | OTI | Optimum Time Invariant |
| OSS | Orbital Space Station | OTIS | Order Trend Information System |
| OSSF | Operating System Storage Facility | OTIS | Oregon Total Information System |
| OSSL | Operating System Simulation Language | OTIU | Overseas Technical Information Unit |
| OSST | Operating System Symbol Table | OTL | Output Transformer Less |
| OSSY | On-line Steuerungssystem | OTLN | Outline |
| OST | Office of Science and Technology | OTLP | Zero Transmission Level Point |
| OST | On Site Test | OTM | Office of Telecommunications Management |
| OST | Operational System Test | | |
| OST | Operationssteuerung | OTM | Old Transversal Magnetic |
| OST | Operative Steuerung | OTP | Office of Telecommunications Policy |
| OST | Operator Station Task | | |
| OSTI | Office for Scientific and Technical Information | OTP | One-Time Process |
| | | OTP | Operational Test Procedure |
| OSTRUMPE | Operating System Trump Extended | OTPS | One-Time Process System |
| OSTS | Open Systems Transport Support | OTR | Optical Tracking |
| | | OTR | Overload Time Relay |
| OSV | Orbital Support Vehicle | OTRAC | Oscillogram Trace reader |
| OT | Office of Telecommunications | OTS | Office of Technical Services |
| OT | Oiltight | OTS | Operational Time Synchronization |
| OT | On Truck | | |
| OT | Onward Transfer | OTS | Optical Technology Satellite |
| OT | Operating Time | | |
| OT | Operation Time | OTS | Orbital Test Satellite |
| OT | Operational Test | OTS | Out-of-house Time Sharing |
| OT | Output Tape | OTT | One Terminal per Task |
| OT | Outside Test | OTT | One-Time Tape |
| OT | Overall Test | OTU | Operational Test Unit |
| OT | Overtime | OTU | Operational Training Unit |

- 444 -

# O

| | | | |
|---|---|---|---|
| OTV | Operational Television | OVLD | Overload |
| OU | Operational Unit | OVLP | Overlap |
| OU | Output Unit | OVLY | Overlay |
| OUD | Operational Use Data | OVR | Override |
| OUF | Optimum Usual Frequency | OVR | Overrun |
| OUL | Optical Universal Link | OVRD | Override |
| OUN | Operational Unit Number | OVRFLW | Overflow |
| OUQ | Operational Unit Queue | OVRN | Overrun |
| OUT | Outgoing | OVST | Ortsvermittlungsstelle |
| OUT | Output | OW | One-Way |
| OUTLIM | Output Limiting | OW | Open Wire |
| OUTLIM | Output Limiting facility | OW | Operand Word |
| OUTQ | Output Queue | OW | Optional Word |
| OUTRAN | Output Translator | OW | Order Wire |
| OUTREG | Output Register | OWC | Order Wire Circuit |
| OV | Operationsverstärker | OWF | Optimum Working Frequency |
| OV | Orbiting Vehicle | | |
| OV | Ortsverkehr | OWN | Owner |
| OV | Overflow | OWQ | Output Work Queue |
| OV | Overvoltage | OWS | Ocean Weather Station |
| OV | Overwrite | OWS | Orbital Workshop |
| OVAC | Zero Volt Alternating Current | OWSP | One Word Storage Programmer |
| OVD | Outer Vapour Deposition | OXIL | Oxide Insulation Logic |
| OVDC | Zero Volt Direct Current | OXIS | Oxide Isolation |
| OVF | Overvoltage Factor | OXY | Oxygen |
| OVFLO | Overflow | OZ | Organisationszentrum |
| OVID | Optische Beleglesung Video Image Digitalisierung | OZ | Ortszentrale |
| | | OZ | Ozone |
| OVL | Overlap | OZL | Optischer Zeilenleser |

# P

| | | | |
|---|---|---|---|
| P | Page | PA | Packet Adapter |
| P | Parität | PA | Paging Algorithm |
| P | Parity | PA | Parallel Access |
| P | Peg | PA | Parallel Adder |
| P | Perforate | PA | Parametric Amplifier |
| P | Perforating | PA | Performance Analysis |
| P | Perforation | PA | Phase Angle |
| P | Period | PA | Physical Address |
| P | Peta | PA | Polar-to-Analog |
| P | Phone | PA | Power Amplifier |
| P | Phosphorous | PA | Pre-Amplifier |
| P | Physical | PA | Pre-Assembler |
| P | Pick | PA | Precision Angle |
| P | Plate | PA | Preliminary Amplifier |
| P | Plug | PA | Pressure Angle |
| P | Polar | PA | Presumptive Address |
| P | Polarization | PA | Probability of Acceptance |
| P | Pole | PA | Problemanalyse |
| P | Positive | PA | Process Automation |
| P | Potentiometer | PA | Product Analyst |
| P | Power | PA | Product Assurance |
| P | Pressure | PA | Program Access |
| P | Primary | PA | Program Account |
| P | Prismatic joint | PA | Program Address |
| P | Probe | PA | Program Amplifier |
| P | Processor | PA | Program Analysis |
| P | Programm | PA | Program Attention |
| P | Proportionnel | PA | Programmablauf |
| P | Proton | PA | Programmausnahme |
| P | Prozessor | PA | Programmed Addressing |
| P | Puls | PA | Programmed Algorithm |
| P | Pulse | PA | Programmed Arithmetic |
| P | Punch | PA | Programmgesteuerte Anforderung |
| P... | Perforateur Honeywell Bull | | |
| P... | Philips Electrologica | PA | Programming Address |
| P&VR | Pure and Vulcanized Rubber insulation | PA | Programming Aid |
| | | PA | Prüfadapter |
| P(R) | Packet Receive sequence number | PA | Pseudo Address |
| | | PA | Public Address |
| P(S) | Packet Send sequence number | PA | Pulse Amplifier |
| | | PAAR | Precision Approach Airfield Radar |
| P-C | Processor Controller | | |
| P-C | Pulse Counter | PAAR | Product Assurance Analysis Report |
| P-S | Pressure-Sensitive | | |
| P-TAPE | Paper Tape | PAB | Primary Application Block |
| P-Z | Peak to Zero | PABLA | Problem Analysis By Logical Approach |
| P-pulse | Position Pulse | | |
| P/F | Poll bit/Final bit | PABLOS | Program to Analyze the Block System |
| P/N | Part Number | | |
| P/NÜE | Programmierbare Nachrichtenübertragungseinheit | PABX | Private Automatic Branch Exchange |
| | | PAC | Personal Analog Computer |
| P/P | Point to Point | PAC | Pneumatic Analog Computer |
| P/S | Point of Shipment | | |
| PA | Package Application | PAC | Primary Address Code |

# P

| | | | |
|---|---|---|---|
| PAC | Printing Automatic Calculator | PACIFIC | Planning, Accounting, and Control Information For use In Construction |
| PAC | Production Activity | | |
| PAC | Program Action Code | PACIR | Practical Approach to Chemical Information Retrieval |
| PAC | Program Address Counter | | |
| PAC | Program Addressable Clock | PACIT | Process Automation for Cable Interface Tape |
| PAC | Program Authorized Credentials | PACM | Pulse Amplitude Code Modulation |
| PAC | Programmable Automatic Comparator | PACOR | Passive Correlation and Ranging station |
| PAC | Programmable Automotive Controller | PACOS | Process Automation Control Operating System |
| PAC | Programme d'Application Courante | PACS | Picture Archiving and Communications System |
| PAC | Project Analysis and Control | | |
| PACC | PERT Associated Cost Control | PACT | Pay Actual Computer Time |
| PACC | Product Administration and Contract Control | PACT | Plessey Automated COBOL Test |
| PACCT | PERT And Cost Correlation Technique | PACT | Print Active Computer Tables |
| PACE | Package for Architectural Computer Evaluation | PACT | Production Analysis Control Technique |
| PACE | Packaged CRAM Executive | PACT | Program for Automatic Coding Techniques |
| PACE | Performance Assessments through Communications Emulation | PACT | Programmable Asynchronous Clustered Teleprocessing |
| PACE | Phased Array Control Electronics | PACT | Programmable Automatic Continuity Tester |
| PACE | Precision Analog Computing Equipment | PACT | Programmed Analysis Computer Transfer |
| PACE | Process and Assembly Computerized Environment | PACT | Programmed Automatic Circuit Tester |
| PACE | Processing And Control Element | PACT | Project for the Advancement of Coding Techniques |
| PACE | Professional Application Creation Environment | PACTS | Programmer Aptitude Competence Test System |
| PACE | Program Action Code Extension | PACUIT | Packet Circuit |
| PACE | Program Analysis Control and Evaluation | PACX | Private Automatic Computer Exchange |
| PACE | Programmed Automatic Communications Equipment | PAD | Packet Assembler/Disassembler |
| | | PAD | Packet Assembly/Disassembly |
| PACER | Process Assembly Case Evaluator Routine | PAD | Post-Alloy-Diffused |
| | | PAD | Power Amplifier Driver |
| PACER | Program Assisted Console Evaluation and Review | PAD | Program Analysis for Documentation |
| PACER | Programmed Automatic Circuit Evaluator and Recorder | PAD | Programmable Algorithm for Drafting |
| | | PAD | Programme Assembleur-Désassembleur |

- 448 -

# P

| | | | |
|---|---|---|---|
| PAD | Programmierbares Analog- und Digitalprüfsystem | PAI | Planung und Analyse von Investitionen |
| PADA | Payroll Automation for the Department of Agriculture | PAI | Precise Angle Indicator |
| | | PAI | Process Automation Interface |
| PADAR | Passive Detection And Ranging | PAI | Production Acceptance Inspection |
| PADAT | Psychological Abstracts Direct Access Terminal | PAI | Programmer Appraisal Instrument |
| PADE | Pad Automatic Data Equipment | PAID | Personnel and Accounting Integrated Data |
| PADEL | Pattern Description Language | PAID | Programmers Aid In Debugging |
| PADRE | Patient Automatic Data Recording Equipment | PAINS | Patient Information System |
| PADRE | Portable Automatic Data Recording Equipment | PAIR | Performance And Integration Retrofit |
| PADS | Passive-Active Data Simulation | PAIR | Product Analysis Incident Report |
| PADS | Personnel Automated Data System | PAIR | Product Analysis Information Report |
| PADS | Precision Antenna Display System | PAIRS | Product Assurance Information Retrieval System |
| PADS | Program Allocator to Drum Storage | PAIS | Project Analysis Information System |
| PADT | Post-Ally Diffused Transistor | PAIS | Public Affaires Information Service |
| PAE | Prêt A Emettre | PAISY | Personal-Abrechnungs- und administratives Informations-System |
| PAE | Programmausgabeeinrichtung | | |
| PAE | Prozeßausgabeeinrichtung | PAISY | Personal-Abrechnungs- und Informations-System |
| PAEM | Program Analysis and Evaluation Model | PAL | Paßwort-Aspektliste |
| PAF | Plasma-Anzeigefeld | PAL | Patent Associated Literature |
| PAF | Peripheral Address Field | | |
| PAF | Printed And Fired | PAL | Pedagogic Algoritnmic Language |
| PAFE | Plan d'Action en faceur de la Filière Electronique | PAL | Performance Assessment Logic |
| PAFEC | Program for Automatic Finite Element Calculation | PAL | Permanent Artificial Lighting |
| PAG | Page | PAL | Phase-Alternation Line |
| PAG | Programmablaufgraph | PAL | Philips Assembler Language |
| PAGE | Page Generation | | |
| PAGE | Page Generator | PAL | Precision Artwork Language |
| PAGE | PERT Automated Graphical Extension | PAL | Process Assembler Language |
| PAGEN | Pattern Generation | PAL | Process Assembly Language |
| PAGEN | Pattern Generator | | |
| PAGEOS | Passive Geodetic Earth Orbiting Satellite | PAL | Program Abstract Library |
| | | PAL | Program Assembler Language |
| PAGOS | Program for the Analysis of General Optical Systems | PAL | Programmable Array Logic |

# P

| | | | |
|---|---|---|---|
| PAL | Programmed Application Library | PAM/FM | Pulse Amplitude Modulation/Frequency Modulation |
| PAL | Psychoacoustic Laboratory | | |
| PALAAS | Property And Liability Agency Accounting System | PAM/PDM | Pulse Amplitude Modulation/Pulse Duration Modulation |
| PALAS | Personal Advanced Logic Analysis System | PAMA | Pulse Address Multiple Access |
| PALASM | PAL-Assembler | PAMAK | Puls-Amplituden-Modulierter Ansage-Koppler |
| PALC | Passenger Acceptance and Load Control | | |
| PALD | Phase Alternation Line Delay | PAMD | Parallel Access Multiple Distribution |
| PALIS | Property And Liability Information System | PAMD | Price And Management Data |
| PALOG | Prüfautomaten für Logikbaugruppen | PAMELA | Patient Automatic Monitoring Endless Loop Attachment |
| PALS | Pre-Announcement Level System | PAMF | Programmable Analog Matched Filter |
| PALS | Precision Approach and Landing System | PAMI | Personnel Accounting Machine Installation |
| PALU | Pixel Arithmetic-Logic Unit | PAMM | Precision Automatic Measuring Machine |
| PAM | Page Allocation Map | | |
| PAM | Partitioned Access Method | PAMPER | Product And Machine Performance |
| PAM | Peripheral Adapter Module | | |
| PAM | Persönlicher Anwendungs-Monitor | PAMS | Pad Abort Measuring System |
| PAM | Persönlicher Applikations-Monitor | PAMS | Paging Area Memory Space |
| | | PAMUX | Parallel Addressable Multiplexer |
| PAM | Pole Amplitude Modulation | | |
| PAM | Primary Access Method | PANAR | Panoramic radar |
| PAM | Prioritätsausgabemeldung | PANDA | Portable Atmospheric Noise Data Acquisition |
| PAM | Process Automation Monitor | PANDA | Prestel Advanced Network Design Architecture |
| PAM | Programmable Addressing Machine | PANDIT | Produce an Adjusted Nuclear Data Input Tape |
| PAM | Programmed Accounting Machine | PANE | Performance Analysis of electrical Networks |
| PAM | Programmed Associative Memory | PANES | Part-program Nesting |
| PAM | Puls-Amplituden Modulationsverfahren | PANIC | Parameter Analysis of Integrated Circuits |
| PAM | Pulsamplitudenmodulation | PANSY | Program Analysis System |
| | | PANTES | Panel Tester |
| PAM | Pulse Address Modem | PAO | Production Assistée par Ordinateur |
| PAM | Pulse Amplitude Modulation | | |
| PAM-PDM | Pulse Amplitude Modulation - Pulse Duration Modulation | PAO | Programmation Assistée par Ordinateur |
| | | PAP | Papierende |
| PAM/FM | Pulse Amplitude Modulated - Frequency Modulated | PAP | Performance Analysis Program |
| | | PAP | Port A Punch |
| | | PAP | Programmablaufplan |

# P

| | | | |
|---|---|---|---|
| PAPA | Package de Paie | PARD | Precision Annotated Retrieval Display |
| PAPA | Pilotanwendungen des öffentlichen Datenpaketvermittlungsdienstes | PARDOP | Passive Ranging Doppler |
| | | PARDP | Perimeter Acquisition Radar Data Processor |
| PAPA | Probabilistic Automatic Pattern Analyzer | PARE | Program for Analytical Reliability Estimation |
| PAPA | Programmer And Probability Analyzer | PARE | Programmed Analysis and Resources Evaluation |
| PAPM | Pulse Amplitude and Phase Modulated | PARIS | Postal Address Reader Indexer System |
| PAPM | Pulse Amplitude and Phase Modulation | PARIS | Pulse Analysis-Recording Information System |
| PAPS | Performance Analysis and Prediction Study | PARM | Parameter |
| PAPS | Program Analysis Procedure System | PARM | Program Analysis for Resource Management |
| PAQ | Production, Accounting, Quality | PARMA | Program for Analysis, Reporting and Maintenance |
| PAR | Page Address Register | PAROS | Passive Ranging On Submarines |
| PAR | Paragraph | | |
| PAR | Parameter | PAROS | Programmed Automated Replenishment Ordering System |
| PAR | Parameter Request | | |
| PAR | Performance Analysis and Review | PARR | Procurement Authorization and Receiving Report |
| PAR | Perimeter Array Radar | | |
| PAR | Point Address Register | PARRS | Psychological Abstracts Reference Retrieval System |
| PAR | Precision Approach Radar | | |
| PAR | Problem Analysis and Response | PARS | Passenger Airline Reservation System |
| PAR | Program Access Request | | |
| PAR | Program Activity Recording | PARS | Performance Analysis and Reporting System |
| PAR | Program Address Register | PARS | Produktions-Automations-Rationalisierungs-System |
| PAR | Program Adjustment Request | | |
| PAR | Program Appraisal and Review | PARS | Programmed Airline Reservations System |
| PAR | Proposal Analysis Report | PARSAC | Particle Size Analog Computer |
| PAR | Pulse Acquisition Radar | | |
| PAR | Pulse Address Register | PARSIM | Plant Appropriation Request Simulation |
| PAR | Punch Address Register | | |
| PARA | Paragraph | PARSYN | Parametric Synthesis part partial |
| PARABOL | Parabolic | | |
| PARADE | Passive-Active Ranging And Determination | PARTEI | Purchasing Agents of the Radio, TV, and Electronics Industries |
| PARALOST | Parametrisch gesteuertes Programm zur Generierung von Speziellen Lochstreifen-Programmen | PARTIS | Partielles Informations-System |
| | | PARTNER | Proof of Analog Results Through Numerically Equivalent Routine |
| PARAMP | Parametric Amplifier | | |
| PARASYN | Parametric Synthesis | | |
| PARC | Progressive Aircraft Reconditioning Cycle | PAS | Personalabrechnungs- und Auskunftssystem |
| PARD | Parts Application Reliability Data | PAS | Personalabrechnungssystem |

# P

| | |
|---|---|
| PAS | Personnel Accounting System |
| PAS | Phase Address System |
| PAS | Planning And Scheduling |
| PAS | Primary Alert System |
| PAS | Process Automation System |
| PAS | Program Alternative Simulation |
| PAS | Programm Address Storage |
| PAS | Programmablauf-Steuerung |
| PAS | Prozess-Automatisierungssprache |
| PAS | Public Address System |
| PASAR | Psychological Abstracts Search And Retrieval |
| PASCAL | Philips Automatic Sequence Calculator |
| PASCAL | Programme Appliqué à la Sélection et à la Compilation Automatique de la Litérature |
| PASE | Power Assisted Storage Equipment |
| PASG | Pulse Amplifier Symbol Generator |
| PASG | Pulse Analyzer Signal Generator |
| PASOMAF | Planung, Abrechnung, Stammdatenarchivierung, Optimierung, Materialrechnung, Abrechnung, Finanzen |
| PASRO | PASCAL for Robots |
| PASS | Passive Acquisition Surveillance System |
| PASS | Position And Surveyance System |
| PASS | Program Aid Software System |
| PASS | Program Alternative Simulation System |
| PASS | Programmed Access Security System |
| PASSAT | Programm zur Automatischen Selektion von Stichworten Aus Texten |
| PASSION | Program for Algebraic Sequences Specifically of Input-Output Nature |
| PASSWD | Password |
| PASTIC | Pakistan Scientific and Technological Information Centre |
| PASY | Personalabrechnungssystem |
| PAT | Parametric Artificial Talker |
| PAT | Patent |
| PAT | Pattern |
| PAT | Pattern Analysis Test |
| PAT | Performance Acceptance Test |
| PAT | Peripheral Allocation Table |
| PAT | Personalized Array Translator |
| PAT | Procedure for Automatic Testing |
| PAT | Production Acceptance Test |
| PAT | Produktionsdatenerfassung, Auftragsüberwachung und Terminplanung |
| PAT | Program Altitude Test |
| PAT | Program Analyzer Tool |
| PAT | Programm-Ablauf Täglich |
| PAT | Programmable Automatic Tester |
| PAT | Programmer Aptitude Test |
| PAT | Programmer Aptitude Tester |
| PAT | Prompt-/Answer-Table |
| PAT | Proportional to Absolute Temperature |
| PAT | Prüfautomat für Teilnehmereinrichtungen |
| PAT | Pseudo-Adder Tree |
| PATA | Pneumatic All-Terrain Amphibian |
| PATE | Programmed Automatic Telemetry Evaluator |
| PATELL | Psychological Abstracts Tape Edition Lease or Licensing |
| PATH | Performance Analysis and Test Histories |
| PATI | Passive Airborne Time-difference Intercept |
| PATIO | Program Addressable Table Index Operation |
| PATN | Pattern |
| PATRIC | Pattern Recognition and Information Correlation |
| PATRIC | Pattern Recognition, Interpretation and Correlation |
| PATRICIA | Practical Algorithm To Retrieve Information Coded In Alphanumeric |

# P

| | | | |
|---|---|---|---|
| PATROL | Program for Administrative Traffic Reports On-Line | PB | Primary Buffer |
| | | PB | Program Block |
| | | PB | Program Breakdown |
| PATS | Precision Altimeter Techniques | PB | Programm Base |
| | | PB | Programmbank |
| PATS | Programmable Automatic Testing System | PB | Programmbibliothek |
| | | PB | Programmblatt |
| PATSY | Programmed Automatic Testing System | PB | Programmblätter |
| | | PB | Programmblock |
| PATT | Partial Automatic Translation Technique | PB | Programming Block |
| | | PB | Prüfen auf Bereich |
| PATT | Programmable Automatic Transistor Tester | PB | Punch Block |
| | | PB | Punch Buffer |
| PATT | Programmierbarer Automatischer Transistorentester | PB | Push Button |
| | | PB... | Packard Bell |
| | | PBA | Printed Board Assembly |
| PATT | Project for the Analysis of Technology Transfer | PBAR | Print Buffer Address Register |
| PATTERN | Planning Assistance Through Technical Evaluation of Relevance Numbers | PBAR | Programming, Budgeting, Accounting, and Reporting |
| | | PBB | Parallel By Bit |
| PAU | Parallel Arithmetic Unit | PBBS | Programmbankbetriebssystem |
| PAU | Pattern Articulation Unit | | |
| PAU | Pilotless Aircraft Unit | PBC | Periodic Binary Convolutional |
| PAU | Program Analysis Unit | | |
| PAV | Phase Angle Voltmeter | PBC | Peripheral Board Controller |
| PAV | Position And Velocity | | |
| PAV | Program Activation Vector | PBC | Peripheral Bus Computer |
| PAV | Protocole d'Appareil Virtuel | PBC | Prefix Block Code |
| | | PBC | Program Booking Centre |
| PAVE | Programmed Analysis for Value Engineering | PBC | Pure Binary Code |
| | | PBCC | Palm Beach Computer Consultants |
| PAW | Powered All the Way | | |
| PAW | Programmed Automatic Welding | PBCS | Plugboard Circuit Breaker System |
| PAWOS | Portable Automatic Weather Observable Station | PBDG | Push Button Data Generator |
| | | PBF | Pseudo-Binary Format |
| PAWS | Programmed Automatic Welding System | PBI | Process Branch Indicator |
| | | PBIB | Partially Balanced Incomplete Block |
| PAX | Place Address in Index | | |
| PAX | Private Automatic Exchange | PBIT | Parity Bit |
| | | PBL | Planetary Boundary Layer |
| PAYE | Pay As You Earn | PBM | Prozeß-Betriebssystem |
| PB | Parameterblock | PBM | Pulsbreitenmodulation |
| PB | Paritätsbit | PBM | Pulsbreitenmodulator |
| PB | Parity Bit | PBM | Pulsbreitenmoduliert |
| PB | Perforateur de Bande | PBM | Pulse Burst Modulation |
| PB | Peripheral Buffer | PBMI | Purchase Base Machine Inventory |
| PB | Phonetically Balanced | | |
| PB | Playback | PBOS | Programmband-organisationssystem |
| PB | Plot Board | | |
| PB | Plugboard | PBP | Payrole, Budgeting, Personnel-system |
| PB | Power Box | | |

# P

| | | | |
|---|---|---|---|
| PBP | Push-Button Panel | PC | Prediction Computer |
| PBPS | Post Boost Propulsion System | PC | Prepunched Card |
| | | PC | Print Check |
| PBR | Procedure Base Register | PC | Print Command |
| PBR | Programm-Basis-Register | PC | Print Complement |
| PBS | Paritätsbitsteuerung | PC | Print Control |
| PBS | Plattenbetriebssystem | PC | Print Cycle |
| PBS | Procedure Branching Statement | PC | Print of Curve |
| | | PC | Printed Card |
| PBS | Process Batch Size | PC | Printed Character |
| PBS | Program Breakdown Structure | PC | Printed Circuit |
| | | PC | Printer Control |
| PBS | Program Buffer Storage | PC | Priority Code |
| PBS | Programmbaustein | PC | Private Code |
| PBS | Protokollblattschreiber | PC | Priveleged Character |
| PBS | Punch Barrier Strip | PC | Procedure Coordinator |
| PBS | Push-Button Switch | PC | Process Change |
| PBSW | Pull-Button Switch | PC | Process Control |
| PBT | Parity Bit Test | PC | Process Controller pseudocode |
| PBT | Programmierbares Bildschirmterminal | | |
| | | PC | Processor Code |
| PBV | Post Boost Vehicle | PC | Processor Controller |
| PBX | Private Branch Exchange | PC | Product Code |
| PC | Page Copy | PC | Production Control |
| PC | Paper Copy | PC | Professional Computer |
| PC | Parallel Computer | PC | Program Card |
| PC | Parameter Card | PC | Program Change |
| PC | Parameter Checkout | PC | Program Check |
| PC | Parity Check | PC | Program Code |
| PC | Part Card | PC | Program Command |
| PC | Patch Card | PC | Program Control |
| PC | Patch Conversion | PC | Program Counter |
| PC | Path Control | PC | Program Cycle |
| PC | Performance Check | PC | Programmable Control |
| PC | Personal Computer | PC | Programmable Controller |
| PC | Personal Computing | PC | Programmed Check |
| PC | Petty Cash | PC | Programmed Computation |
| PC | Phase Control | PC | Programmed Console |
| PC | Philco Corporation | PC | Programmed Control |
| PC | Photo Cell | PC | Programmer-Comparator |
| PC | Photoconductive | PC | Programming Cost |
| PC | Photoconductor | PC | Programming Course |
| PC | Picture | PC | Protokoll-Converter |
| PC | Pilot Card | PC | Provisional Costs |
| PC | Pitch Circle | PC | Pulsating Current |
| PC | Pitch Control | PC | Pulse Code |
| PC | Plotting Chart | PC | Pulse Comparator |
| PC | Plug Card | PC | Pulse Controller |
| PC | Plug Compatible | PC | Pulse Counter |
| PC | Point Clause | PC | Punch Code |
| PC | Polar-to-Cartesian | PC | Punch Column |
| PC | Position Cursor | PC | Punch Control |
| PC | Positive Column | PC | Punched Card |
| PC | Power Circuit | PC | Punched Code |
| PC | Precharge-Eingang | PC | Pyrocarbon |

# P

| | | | |
|---|---|---|---|
| PC AT | Personal Computer Advanced Technology | PCC | Program Controlled Computer |
| PCA | Personal Computer Attachment | PCC | Program Cycle Controller |
| PCA | Polar-Cap Absorption | PCC | Protocol Communications Controller |
| PCA | Primary Communication Attachment | PCC | Protocol Converter Concentrator |
| PCA | Program Change Analysis | PCC | Pulse Counter Chain |
| PCA | Program Controlled Accounting | PCC | Punched Card Code |
| | | PCC | Punched Card Control |
| PCA | Program Coupler Assembly | PCC | Punched Card Counting |
| PCA | Punched Card Accounting | PCCAF | Procedure Change Control Action Form |
| PCAC | Partially Conserved Axial Current | PCCD | Peristaltic Charge Coupled Device |
| PCAD | Personal Computer Aided Design | PCCL | Pulse Coupled Complementary Logic |
| PCAM | Punched-Card Accounting Machine | PCCN | Part Card Change Notice |
| PCAT | Product Category | PCCP | Product Cost Curve Picture |
| PCAT | Punched Card Accounting Technique | PCCR | Procurement Code Change Request |
| PCB | Page Control Block | | |
| PCB | Polychlorinated Biphenylene | PCCS | Photographic Camera Control System |
| PCB | Power Circuit Breaker | PCCS | Program Change Control System |
| PCB | Printed Circuit Board | | |
| PCB | Process Control Block | PCCT | Punched Card Controlled Typewrite |
| PCB | Processor Control Block | | |
| PCB | Program Communication Block | PCCU | Punched Card Control Unit |
| PCB | Program Control Block | PCD | Partition Control Descriptor |
| PCB | Punch Circuit Breaker | | |
| PCBB | Programme de Calcul de Bilan Brut | PCD | Plasma-Coupled Devices |
| | | PCD | Preconfigured Definition |
| PCBC | Partially Conserved Baryon Current | PCD | Production Common Digitizer |
| PCBC | Punched Card Blank Column | PCD | Program Change Decision |
| | | PCD | Programmed Cutting Director |
| PCBGEN | PCB Generation | | |
| PCC | Parity Check Circuit | PCD | Punched Card Data |
| PCC | Partial Crystal Control | PCDC | Program Controlled Digital Computer |
| PCC | Point of Compound Curve | | |
| PCC | Posting Control Code | PCDDS | Private Circuit Digital Data Service |
| PCC | Print Character Counter | | |
| PCC | Printer Carriage Control | PCDP | Punched Card Data Processing equipment |
| PCC | Process Change Control | | |
| PCC | Process Control Computer | PCDR | Procedure |
| | | PCDS | Power Conversation and Distribution System |
| PCC | Processor Control Card | | |
| PCC | Program Card Control | PCDS | Project Control Drawing System |
| PCC | Program Compatible Computer | | |
| | | PCDU | Power and Coolant Distribution Unit |
| PCC | Program Control Card | | |
| PCC | Program Controlled Calculator | PCE | Peripheral Control Element |

# P

| | | | | |
|---|---|---|---|---|
| PCE | Personal Computer Emulator | | PCI | Product Configuration Identification |
| PCE | Photocell Emitter | | PCI | Product Cost Index |
| PCE | Pool Control Error | | PCI | Program Check Interrupt |
| PCE | Print Cycle Exit | | PCI | Program Check Interruption |
| PCE | Process Control Element | | | |
| PCE | Processing and Control Element | | PCI | Program Control Instruction |
| PCE | Processor Control Element | | PCI | Program Controlled Interruption |
| PCE | Processor de Contrôle et d'Echange | | PCI | Programmable Communication Interface |
| PCE | Program Cost Estimate | | PCI | Programmed Control Interrupt |
| PCE | Punched Card Equipment | | | |
| PCEM | Process Chain Evaluation Model | | PCI | Project Control Information |
| PCEOS | Process Control Extension to Operating System | | PCI | Pseudo-Code Instruction |
| PCES | Production Control Experimental System | | PCI | Punched Card Input |
| | | | PCIC | Program Control Information Card |
| PCEU | Pulse Compression/ Expansion Unit | | PCIL | Private Core Image Library |
| PCF | Primary Checkpoint File | | | |
| PCF | Primary Control Field | | PCIM | Parallel Character Input Module |
| PCF | Processed Citation File | | | |
| PCF | Pulse Compression Filter | | PCIU | Parts Controlled by Identifiable Unit |
| PCF | Pulse-to-Cycle Fraction | | | |
| PCF | Punched Card Feed | | PCK | Printed Circuit Keyboard |
| PCFM | Production Control File Manager | | PCK | Processor Controlled Keying |
| PCG | Planning and Control Guide | | PCKB | Printed Circuit Keyboard |
| | | | PCL | PL1 Control Language |
| PCG | Printed Circuit Generator | | PCL | Phase Correction Loop |
| PCGL | Printed Circuit Generated Level | | PCL | Positive Control Line |
| | | | PCL | Preliminary Change Letter |
| PCH | Patch | | PCL | Printed Circuit Lamp |
| PCH | Prepare Chassis | | PCL | Process Control Language |
| PCH | Punch | | PCL | Punch Card Lever |
| PCHG | Punching | | PCM | Parallel Calculating Mechanism |
| PCHN | Programmed Course, Home Nursing | | PCM | Parity Check Matrix |
| PCI | Packet Communication, Incorporated | | PCM | Peripheral Computer Manufacturer |
| PCI | Panel Call Indicator | | PCM | Pitch Control Motor |
| PCI | Pattern Correspondence Index | | PCM | Plug Compatible Machines |
| | | | PCM | Plug Compatible Mainframer |
| PCI | Pattern of Cockpit Indication | | PCM | Plug Compatible Maker |
| PCI | Peripheral Command Indicator | | PCM | Plug Compatible Manufacturer |
| PCI | Peripheral Control Instruction | | PCM | Plug Compatible Memory |
| | | | PCM | Plug Compatible Module |
| PCI | Photon Coupled Isolator | | PCM | Primary Code Modulation |
| PCI | Pilot Controller Integration | | PCM | Process Communication Monitor |
| PCI | Planning Card Index | | PCM | Production Control Master |

- 456 -

# P

| | | | |
|---|---|---|---|
| PCM | Pulscodemodulation | PCO | Punched Card Order |
| PCM | Pulse Code Modulation | PCO | Punched Card Output |
| PCM | Pulse Code Modulator | PCOM | Parallel Character Output Module |
| PCM | Pulse Count Modulation | | |
| PCM | Punch Card Machine | PCOS | Personal Computer Operating System |
| PCM | Punched Card Method | | |
| PCM/DHS | Pulse Code Modulation/ Data Handling System | PCOS | Process Control Operating System |
| PCM/FM | Pulse Code Modulation/ Frequence Modulation | PCOS | Punched Card Oriented System |
| PCM/FSK/AM | Pulse Code Modulation/ Frequency Shift Keying/ Amplitude Modulation | PCP | Parallel Cascade Processor |
| | | PCP | Parallel Circular Plate |
| | | PCP | Peripheral Control Program |
| PCM/PM | Pulse Code Modulation/ Phase Modulation | PCP | Peripheral Control Pulse |
| | | PCP | Picture Check Print |
| PCM/PN | Pulse Code Modulation/ Pseudo-Noise | PCP | Primary Control Program |
| | | PCP | Printed Circuit Patchboard |
| PCM/PS | Pulse Code Modulation/ Phase-Shift | PCP | Printed Circuit Program |
| | | PCP | Printing Card Punch |
| PCMD | Pulse Code Modulation Digital | PCP | Process Control Program |
| | | PCP | Processor Control Program |
| PCME | Pulse Code Modulation Event | PCP | Program Change Procedure |
| | | PCP | Program Change Proposal |
| PCMI | Photochromic Micro Image | PCP | Program Control Plan |
| PCMK | Pulscode-Multiplexkanal | PCP | Program Control Program |
| PCMR | Patient Computer Medical Record | PCP | Programmable Circuit Processor |
| PCMS | Punched Card Machine System | PCP | Project Change Proposal |
| | | PCP | Project Control Plan |
| PCMTE | Pulse Code Modulation and Timing Equipment | PCP | Pseudo-Code Program |
| | | PCP | Punch Card Programming |
| PCMTEA | Pulse Code Modulation and Timing Electronics Assembly | PCP | Punch Control Panel |
| | | PCP | Punched Card Perforator |
| | | PCP | Punched Card Processing |
| PCMTS | Pulse Code Modulation Telemetry System | PCP | Punched Card Programming |
| PCN | Part Control Number | | |
| PCN | Process Change Notice | PCP | Punched Card Punch |
| PCN | Procurement Control Number | PCPCN | Part Card Procurement Change Notice |
| PCN | Product Control Number | PCPG | Primary Clock Pulse Generator |
| PCN | Production Change Number | | |
| PCN | Program Control Number | PCPI | Program Controlled Program Interruption |
| PCN | Project Control Number | | |
| PCN | Proposal Control Number | PCPM | PERT Cost Performance Measurement |
| PCN | Pulse Compression Network | | |
| | | PCPM | Program Controlled Printing Machine |
| PCNE | Protocol Converter for Native Equipment | | |
| | | PCPP | Printing Card Proof Punch |
| PCNR | Part Control Number Request | PCPS | Program Change Packages |
| | | PCPS | Pulse-Coded Processing System |
| PCO | Picture Control Oscilloscope | | |
| | | PCQ | Production Control Quantometer |
| PCO | Procuring Contrast Offer | | |
| PCO | Program Change Order | PCR | Partial Carriage Return |

# P

| | | | |
|---|---|---|---|
| PCR | Per Call Rate | PCS | Process Communication System |
| PCR | Peripheral Control Routine | PCS | Process Computer System |
| PCR | Photoconductive Relay | PCS | Process Control Specification |
| PCR | Planning Change Request | | |
| PCR | Planning Check Request | PCS | Process Control System |
| PCR | Print Contrast Ratio | PCS | Production Control System |
| PCR | Procedure Change Request | PCS | Program Checkout System |
| PCR | Process Control Rack | PCS | Program Control System |
| PCR | Production Control Record | PCS | Program Counter Store |
| PCR | Program Change Request | PCS | Programme de Contrôle du Système |
| PCR | Program Check Routine | | |
| PCR | Program Control Register | PCS | Programmed Control Sequencer |
| PCR | Program Control Report | | |
| PCR | Program Controlled Reading | PCS | Project Control System |
| | | PCS | Pseudo-Code System |
| PCR | Program Counter | PCS | Punch Column Skip |
| PCR | Programmer in Charge of Records | PCS | Punched Card Selector |
| | | PCS | Punched Card System |
| PCR | Pulse Compression Radar | PCSC | Power Conditioning, Switching and Control |
| PCR | Punch Card Reader | | |
| PCR | Punch Card Register | PCSDS | Pump Controls and Data System |
| PCR | Punched Card Reader | | |
| PCR | Punched Card Reading | PCSL | Procurement Component Supplier List |
| PCR | Put Control Read | | |
| PCRS | Punched Card Reading System | PCSP | Program Communications Support Program |
| PCS | Package Checking System | | |
| PCS | Packaging Checking System | PCT | Page Copy Teleprinter |
| | | PCT | Partition Control Table |
| PCS | Packaging and Checkup System | PCT | Percent |
| | | PCT | Photon Coupled Transistor |
| PCS | Perforated Card System | PCT | Picture |
| PCS | Periodical Control System | PCT | Planning and Control Technique |
| PCS | Peripheral Computer System | | |
| | | PCT | Point-Contact Transistor |
| PCS | Peripheral Control System | PCT | Portable Camera-Transmitter |
| PCS | Periphere Computer Systeme | | |
| | | PCT | Potential Current Transformer |
| PCS | Personal Computing System | | |
| | | PCT | Printed Circuit Tester |
| PCS | Phase Compensator System | PCT | Printer Carriage Tape |
| PCS | Philips Chefzahlen-System | PCT | Program Call Table |
| PCS | Planning Control Sheet | PCT | Program Concept Trainer |
| PCS | Pointing Control System | PCT | Program Control Table |
| PCS | Position Control System | PCT | Program Controlled Transfer |
| PCS | Power Conversion System | | |
| PCS | Precedence Charting System | PCT | Program Counter Timer |
| | | PCT | Punched Card Technique |
| PCS | Preferred Character Set | PCTE | Portable Common Tool Environment |
| PCS | Prime Compatible Set | | |
| PCS | Print Contrast Scale | PCTM | Pulse Count Modulation |
| PCS | Print Contrast Signal | PCTR | Program Control Test Routine |
| PCS | Process Communication Supervisor | | |
| | | PCTR | Program Counter |

# P

| | | | |
|---|---|---|---|
| PCTV | Printed Circuit Test Vehicle | PD | Priority Directive |
| PCU | Packet Communication Unit | PD | Probability Density |
| | | PD | Process Descriptor |
| | | PD | Processing Data |
| PCU | Page Clean-Up | PD | Procurement Division |
| PCU | Pegel-Code-Umsetzer | PD | Profession Digital |
| PCU | Peripheral Control Unit | PD | Program Debugging |
| PCU | Photocopy Unit | PD | Program Directive |
| PCU | Power Control Unit | PD | Program Director |
| PCU | Power Conversion Unit | PD | Program Disk |
| PCU | Primary Control Unit | PD | Program Display |
| PCU | Print Control Unit | PD | Program Distributor |
| PCU | Program Control Unit | PD | Program Drum |
| PCU | Progress Control Unit | PD | Programming Device |
| PCU | Punched Card Utility | PD | Projected Display |
| PCV | Percevoir | PD | Propellant Dispersion |
| PCV | Pollution Control Value | PD | Proportional plus Derivative |
| PCV | Pressure Control Value | | |
| PCV | Printed Circuit Vehicle | PD | Proportionnel et Derivé |
| PCVZ | Pulscode-Vermittlungs-zentrale | PD | Pulsdauer |
| | | PD | Pulse Doppler |
| PCW | Program Control Word | PD | Pulse Driver |
| PCW | Pulsed Continuous Wave | PD | Pulse Duration |
| PCW | Put Control Write | PD | Punch Delay |
| PD | Packed Data | PD | Punch Device |
| PD | Packing Density | PD | Punch Die |
| PD | Paid | PD | Punch Driver |
| PD | Paralleldrucker | PD | Punched Data |
| PD | Parity Digit | PD-O | Program Directive-Operations |
| PD | Passive Detection | | |
| PD | Pattern Detection | PDA | Parallel Data Adapter |
| PD | Per Diem | PDA | Patient Data Automation |
| PD | Performance Data | PDA | Peak Distribution Analyzer |
| PD | Period | PDA | Peripheral Data Acquisition |
| PD | Periodic Duty | | |
| PD | Peripheral Device | PDA | Physical Device Address |
| PD | Personal Designer | PDA | Post Diffused Alloyed |
| PD | Pessimistische Dauer | PDA | Post-Deflection Acceleration |
| PD | Phase Discriminator | | |
| PD | Phasendiskriminator | PDA | Primary Data Acquisition |
| PD | Physical Development | PDA | Probability Discret Automata |
| PD | Piece Détachée | | |
| PD | Pitch Diameter | PDA | Probability Distribution Analyzer |
| PD | Plasma-Deposited | | |
| PD | Plotting Display | PDA | Property Disposal Authorization |
| PD | Polar Distance | | |
| PD | Position Description | PDA | Proposed Development Approach |
| PD | Positive Displacement | | |
| PD | Potential Difference | PDA | Pulse Demodulation Analysis |
| PD | Potentialdifferenz | | |
| PD | Power Distribution | PDA | Pulse Distribution Amplifier |
| PD | Power Divider | | |
| PD | Preliminary Design | PDA | Punch Die Assembly |
| PD | Pressure Difference | PDA | Push-Down Acceptor |
| PD | Printer Driver | PDA | Push-Down Automaton |

# P

| | | | | |
|---|---|---|---|---|
| PDAID | Problem Determination Aid | | PDF | Probability Density Function |
| PDAIDS | Problem Determination Aids | | PDF | Probability Distribution Function |
| PDAP | Program Data Analysis Plan | | PDF | Problem Data Field |
| PDB | Patentdatenbank | | PDFC | Power Dissipation Factor per Column |
| PDB | Planungsdatenbasis | | PDFG | Planar Distributed Function Generators |
| PDBM | Pulse Delay Binary Modulation | | PDFRR | Program Directors Flight Readiness Review |
| PDC | Parallel Data Communicator | | PDG | Peak Detector Gated |
| PDC | Parallel Data Controller | | PDI | Panel Data Interface |
| PDC | Parallel Digital Computer | | PDI | Periodic |
| PDC | Parts Distribution Center | | PDI | Pictorial Deviation Indicator |
| PDC | Photo-Data Card | | PDI | Picture Discription Instructions |
| PDC | Photonuclear Data Center | | | |
| PDC | Power Distribution Control | | PDI | Pilot Direction Indicator |
| PDC | Premission Documentation Change | | PDI | Power Dissipation Index |
| PDC | Printing Desk Calculator | | PDI | Process Data Input |
| PDC | Professional Development Committee | | PDI | Project Data Index |
| | | | PDIO | Photodiode |
| PDC | Proficiency Data Card | | PDL | Partial Differential-equations Language |
| PDC | Programmable Desk Calculator | | PDL | Picture Description Language |
| PDC | Programmable Digital Clock | | PDL | Positive Diode Logic |
| | | | PDL | Precision Delay Line |
| PDC | Programmable Digital Controller | | PDL | Procedure Definition Language |
| PDC | Pulse Duration Commutator | | PDL | Program Design Language |
| | | | PDL | Programmable Digital Logic |
| PDC | Punched Data Carrier | | | |
| PDCL | Provisioning Data Check List | | PDL | Programmed Digital Logic |
| | | | PDL | Protocol Description Language |
| PDCS | Performance Data Computer System | | PDLT | P-channel Depletion Load in Triode |
| PDCS | Processing Distribution and Control System | | PDM | Pegel- und Dämpfungs-meßplatz |
| PDD | Packed Decimal Data | | | |
| PDD | Precision Depth Digitizer | | PDM | Permanent Data Memory |
| PDD | Program Design Data | | PDM | Phase-Displacement |
| PDD | Projected Data Display | | PDM | Photographic Data Memory |
| PDDC | Progressive Die Design by Computer | | PDM | Precedence Diagramming Method |
| PDE | Partial Differential Equation | | PDM | Primärdatenmenge |
| PDE | Prospective Data Element | | PDM | Primary Data Management |
| PDEL | Partial Differential Equation Language | | PDM | Print Down Module |
| | | | PDM | Program Decision Memo |
| PDF | Parallel Data Field | | PDM | Programmable Data Mover |
| PDF | Parallel Disk File | | PDM | Puls- und Dämpfungs-meßplatz |
| PDF | Point Detonating Fuse | | | |
| PDF | Private Database Facility | | PDM | Puls-Dauer-Modulation |
| | | | PDM | Pulse Delta Modulation |

# P

| | | | |
|---|---|---|---|
| PDM | Pulse Duration Modulation | PDPS | Program Data Processing Section |
| PDM | Push Down Memory | | |
| PDM MODEM | Pulse Duration Modulation MODEM | PDPS | Program Data Processing System |
| PDM/FM | Pulse Duration Modulation/Frequency Modulation | PDQ | Passed Data-set Queue |
| | | PDQ | Photo Data Quantizer |
| PDME | Precision Distance Measuring Equipment | PDQ | Program for Descriptive Query |
| PDMM | Pulse Duration Modulation Modem | PDQ | Programmed Data Quantizer |
| PDMM | Push Down Memory MODEM | PDR | Page Data Register |
| PDMS | Physiological Data Monitoring System | PDR | Periscope Depth Range |
| | | PDR | Phase Data Recorder |
| PDMS | Plant Design Management System | PDR | Power Directional Relay |
| | | PDR | Precision Depth Recorder |
| PDMU | Passive Data Memory Unit | PDR | Predetection Recording |
| PDN | Problem Documentation Number | PDR | Preliminary Data Report |
| | | PDR | Preliminary Design Review |
| PDN | Processeur de Données Numériques | PDR | Primary Data Recording |
| | | PDR | Priority Data Reduction |
| PDN | Programmsystem für Datenübertragung und Netzsteuerung | PDR | Process Dynamics Recorder |
| | | PDR | Processed Data Recorder |
| PDN | Public Data Network | PDR | Procurement Data Reference |
| PDO | Process Data Output | | |
| PDO | Program Directive-Operations | PDR | Program Discrepancy Report |
| PDP | Partial Drive Pulse | PDR | Program Drum Recording |
| PDP | Plasma Display Panel | PDR | Publication Data Request |
| PDP | Polysilicon-Dielectric-Polysilicon | PDR | Pulse Duty Ratio |
| | | PDRF | Parts Data Record File |
| PDP | Poste de Données Prêt | PDS | Parameterdatenstruktur |
| PDP | Problem Determination Procedure | PDS | Partitioned Data Set |
| | | PDS | Permissible Data Symbol |
| PDP | Procurement Data Package | PDS | Personal Data System |
| PDP | Product Documentation Procedures | PDS | Personnel Data Summary |
| | | PDS | Photo Document Sensor |
| PDP | Program Definition Phase | PDS | Photographic Display System |
| PDP | Program Development Plan | | |
| PDP | Programmable Data Processor | PDS | Photometric Data System |
| | | PDS | Planification des Systèmes |
| PDP | Programmed Data Processing | | |
| | | PDS | Planning Data Sheet |
| PDP | Programmed Data Processor | PDS | Power Density Spectra |
| | | PDS | Power Distribution System |
| PDP | Programmed Digital Processor | PDS | Primary Data Set |
| | | PDS | Primary Data Store |
| PDPC | Position Display Parallax Corrected | PDS | Problem Descriptor System |
| | | PDS | Procurement Data Sheet |
| PDPM | Programmable Data Processing Machine | PDS | Product Data Sheet |
| | | PDS | Product Demand Structure |
| PDPS | Parts Data Processing System | PDS | Production Data Sheet |
| | | PDS | Program Data Source |
| PDPS | Program Definition Phase Studies | PDS | Program Distribution System |

# P

| | | | | |
|---|---|---|---|---|
| PDS | Programmable Data System | | PE | Permissible Error |
| PDS | Programming Documentation Standard | | PE | Personalentwicklung |
| | | | PE | Phase Encoded |
| PDS | Projektdatenspeicher | | PE | Phase Encoding |
| PDS | Propellant Dispersion System | | PE | Photoelectric |
| | | | PE | Plattenantriebseinheit |
| PDS | Punch Driver Selectric | | PE | Platteneinheit |
| PDS... | Pacific Data Systems Inc. | | PE | Pointeur d'Effacement |
| PDSMAN | Partitioned Dataset Managements | | PE | Polyethylene potential Energy |
| PDSP | Personnel Data System Planning | | PE | Position Error |
| | | | PE | Post Edit |
| PDSP | Projektierungsprozeß-bezogener Datenspeicher | | PE | Power Equipment |
| | | | PE | Primitive Equation |
| PDT | Parallel Data Transmission | | PE | Print End |
| PDT | Parameter Descriptor Table | | PE | Probable Error |
| | | | PE | Process Engineering |
| PDT | Personendatenterminal | | PE | Processing Element |
| PDT | Post alloy Diffused Transistor | | PE | Professional Engineer |
| | | | PE | Program Element |
| PDT | Posting Data Transfer | | PE | Program End |
| PDT | Program Distribution Transmitter | | PE | Programmed Exciter |
| | | | PE | Programmeinheit |
| PDT | Prozeßdatentechnik | | PE | Programmende |
| PDT | Pulse Delay Time | | PE | Programmentwicklung |
| PDTA | Production Tape | | PE | Programming Error |
| PDTE | Packet-mode Data Terminal Equipment | | PE | Programmsteuereinheit |
| | | | PE | Protective Earth |
| PDÜ | Peripherer Daten-übertragungsteil | | PE | Prozeßeinheit |
| | | | PE | Prozeßelement |
| PDU | Phase Demodulation Unit | | PE | Prüfeinheit |
| PDU | Pilot Display Unit | | PE | Prüfelektronik |
| PDU | Pressure Distribution Unit | | PE | Pulse Encoding |
| PDU | Protocol Data Unit | | PE | Punch Emitter |
| PDV | Prozeßdatenverarbeitung | | PE CARD | Production-Estimate Card |
| PDV | Prozeßlenkung mit Daten-verarbeitungsanlagen | | PEA | Pattern Error Analysis |
| | | | PEA | Program Element Administrator |
| PDV | Prozeßsteuerung mit Datenverarbeitung | | PEA | Prozeß-Eingabe-Ausgabe |
| | | | PEA | Prozeß-Eingabe-Ausgabe-einheit |
| PDVS | Patentdatenverarbeitungs-system | | | |
| PDVS | Primärdatenverarbeitungs-system | | PEA | Prozeß-Eingabe-Ausgabe-peripherie |
| | | | PEA | Prozeßeingabe und -ausgabe |
| PDX | Private Digital Exchange | | | |
| PDX | Processor-controlled Digital Exchange | | PEA | Prozeßeingabe- und Ausgabeeinrichtung |
| PE | Paper Empty | | PEAC | Program Establishment And Control |
| PE | Parity Error | | | |
| PE | Peripheral Equipment | | PEAR | Production Error Analysis Report |
| PE | Periphere Einheit | | | |
| PE | Periphere Einrichtung | | PEAR | Program Error Analysis Report |
| PE | Perkin-Elmer | | | |
| PE | Permanent Echo | | PEARL | Parts Explosion And Retrieval Language |
| PE | Permanent Error | | | |

# P

| | | | |
|---|---|---|---|
| PEARL | Periodicals Automation Rand Library | PED | Phosphorus Enhanced Diffusion |
| PEARL | Process and Experiment Automation Real-time Language | PED | Photoemission Diode |
| | | PED | Program Element Directive |
| PEAS | Physikalisches Eingabe/ Ausgabesystem | PED | Program Execution Directive |
| PEAT | Programmer Exercised Autopilot Test | PED | Proton-Excited Diffusion |
| | | PEDA | Personnel/Equipment Data Analysis |
| PEATMOS | Primitive Equation And Trajectory Model Output Statistics | PEDANT | Preprogrammable Evaluations based on a Data Normalizing Technique |
| PEB | Program Element Breakdown | | |
| PEBL | Programmable Electron Beam Lithography | PEDATIS | Personaldaten-informationssystem |
| PEC | Packaged Electronic Circuit | PEDMS | Portable and Extensible Data Management System |
| PEC | Page End Character | PEDRO | Perkins Engineering Data Retrieval Organization |
| PEC | Photo-Electric Cell | | |
| PEC | Previous Element Coding | PEDRO | Pneumatic Energy Detector with Optics |
| PEC | Print Error Check | | |
| PEC | Program Element Code | PEDS | Philips Engineering and Development System |
| PEC | Program Environment Control | | |
| | | PEE | Program Estimation Equation |
| PEC | Program Event Counter | | |
| PEC | Program Exception Code | PEE | Programm-Entwicklungs-Ebene |
| PEC | Projected Effective Coverage | | |
| | | PEEP | Pilot's Electronic Eye-level Presentation |
| PEC... | Peripheral Equipment Corp. | | |
| | | PEF | Physical Electronics Facility |
| PECA | Pre-Engineering Change Action | | |
| | | PEF | Program Estimating Factor |
| PECA | Proposed Engineering Change Assessment | PEF | Pulse Eliminating Filter |
| | | PEG | Prime Event Generation |
| PECL | Plessey Electron Coupled Logic | PEGS | Parametric Evaluation Geometric System |
| PECN | Process Equipment Change Notification | PEGS | Parametric Evaluation of Generalized Systems |
| PECOS | Program Environment Checkout System | PEI | Preliminary Engineering Inspection |
| PECOS | Project Evaluation and Cost Optimisation System | PEIC | Periodic Error Integrating Controller |
| | | PEIR | Process Evaluation and Information Reduction |
| PECR | Photo-Electric Card Reader | | |
| | | PEL | Picture Element |
| PECR | Program Error Correction Report | PEL | Plant Engineer's Language |
| | | PEM | Photoelectromagnetic |
| PECS | Portable Environmental Control System | PEM | Processing Element Module |
| | | PEM | Processor Element Memory |
| PECS | Programmable Electronic Call Simulator | PEM | Product Engineering Measure |
| PECU | Print Edit Control Unit | PEM | Product Engineering Memo |
| PED | Personnel Equipment Data | PEM | Production Engineering Measure |

# P

| | | | |
|---|---|---|---|
| PEM | Program Element Monitor | PEPR | Precision Encoding and Pattern Recognition |
| PEM | Program Execution Monitor | PEPR | Precision Encoding and Pattern Recognizer |
| PEN | Pentode | PEPSS | Programmable Equipment for Personnel Subsystem Simulation |
| PEN | Program Element Number | | |
| PEN | Program Error Note | | |
| PENA | Primary Emission Neuron Activation | PEPSY | Programmentwicklungs- und -pflegesystem |
| PENCIL | Pictorial Encoding Language | PER | Performance Evaluation Routine |
| PENNSTAC | Penn State Automatic Computer | PER | PERT Event Report |
| PENT | Penetration | PER | Phase Encoding Recording |
| PENT | Pentode | PER | Photo-Electric Reader |
| PENULT | Penultimate | PER | Photo-Electric Reading |
| PEOS | Propulsion and Electrical Operating System | PER | Preliminary Engineering Report |
| PEP | Partitioned Emulation Programming | PER | Product Engineering Release |
| PEP | Partitioned Emulator Program | PER | Program Event Recording |
| PEP | Peak Envelope Power | PER | Programmereignis- registrierung |
| PEP | Performance Effectiveness Program | PER | Programmgesteuerte Elektronische Rechen- anlage |
| PEP | Performance Evaluation Program | | |
| PEP | Personal Exercise Programmer | PERC | Peace on Earth, Research Center |
| PEP | Personalized Engineering Program | PERCON | Peripheral Converter |
| | | PERCOS | Performance Coding System |
| PEP | Planar-Epitaxial | PERCY | Photoelectric Recognition Cybernetics |
| PEP | Process Evaluation Program | | |
| PEP | Program Error Program | PERF | Perforate |
| PEP | Program Evaluation Procedure | PERF | Perforator |
| | | PERGO | Project Evaluation and Review with Graphic Output |
| PEP | Programmable Extention Package | | |
| PEP | Programmed End Point | PERL | Perception-Enhanced Resolution Logic |
| PEP | Programmierbares Erweiterungspaket | PERLT | Planen, Entwickeln, Realisieren komplexer Lager- und Transport- systeme |
| PEP | Pulse Echo Pattern | | |
| PEP | Pulse Effective Power | | |
| PEPE | Parallel Element Processing Element | PERM | Permanent |
| | | PERM | Permeability |
| PEPE | Parallel Element Processing Ensemble | PERM | Programmed Evaluation for Repetitive Manufacture |
| PEPP | Planetary Entry Parachute Program | PERM | Programmgesteuerte Elektronische Rechen- maschine |
| PEPPER | Photo Electric Portable Probe Reader | | |
| PEPPI | Projected Elevation of Product Performance Indices | PERM | Programmgesteuerte, Elektronische Rechen- anlage München |

# P

| | | | | |
|---|---|---|---|---|
| PERMACAP | Personnel Management and Accounting Card Processing | | PESA | Program Executive Storage Area |
| PERMACAP | Personnel Management and Accounting Card Processor | | PESAF | Programmsystem zum Erzeugen, Speichern und Abrufen von Formatbildern mit eingabegesteuerter Bildfolge |
| PERMACAPS | Personnel Management and Accounting Card Processor System | | PESD | Power Electronics Semiconductor Department |
| PERP | Personnel Processing | | PESD | Program Element Summary Data |
| PERS | Personalinformations-System | | | |
| PERS | Program for Evaluation of Rejects and Substitutions | | PESD | Program Execution Sub-Directive |
| | | | PESDS | Program Element Summary Data Sheet |
| PERSEUS | Personalentlohnungs- Und Informationssystem | | PEST | Parameter Estimation by Sequential Testing |
| PERSINS | Personnel Information System | | PEST | Project Engineer Scheduling Technique |
| PERSINSCOM | Personnel Information Systems Command | | PESY | Peripheral Exchange Synchronization |
| PERSIR | Personnel Inventory Report | | PET | Patterned Epitaxial Technology |
| PERSIS | Personalinformations-system | | PET | Performance Evaluation Test |
| PERSIS | Personnel Information System | | PET | Peripheral Equipment Tester |
| PERSON | Personnel Simulation Online | | PET | Personal Electronic Transaction computer |
| PERSPROC | Personnel Processing | | PET | Philco Epoxy Transistor |
| PERSTATREP | Personnel Status Report | | PET | Physical Equipment Table |
| PERSY | Peripheral exchange Synchronization | | PET | Plausibilitätskontrolle mit Entscheidungstabellen |
| PERT | Program Estimation Revaluation Technique | | PET | Position Event Time |
| PERT | Program Evaluation Research Task | | PET | Postes et Télécommunications |
| PERT | Program Evaluation Research Test | | PET | Production Environmental Testing |
| PERT | Program Evaluation and Review Technique | | PET | Production Experimental Test |
| PERT | Project Evaluation and Review Technique | | PET | Program Evaluation Technique |
| PERT-NAP | Program Evaluation Review Technique-Network Automatic Plotting | | PETA | Portable Electronic Traffic Analyzer |
| | | | PETE | Pneumatic End To End |
| PERTICO | Program Evaluation Review Technique with Cost | | PETR | Photo-Electric Tape Reader |
| PERTSIM | Program Evaluation Review Technique Simulation | | PETRUS | Protokoll-Entwicklungs- und Testrechner-Universal-System |
| | | | PETS | Pacific Electronic Trade Show |
| PERU | Production Equipment Records Unit | | PETS | Posting and Enquiry Terminal System |
| PES | Photoelectric Scanner | | | |

# P

| | | | |
|---|---|---|---|
| PETS | Programmed Extended Time Sharing | PFD | Primary Flash Distillate |
| PETV | Planar Epitaxial Tuning Vector | PFD | Primary Flight Display |
| | | PFD | Program Flow Diagram |
| PEU | Programm-Ende Unterprogramm | PFDA | Post Flight Data Analysis |
| | | PFE | Primary Feedback Element |
| PEV | Peak Envelope Voltage | PFFT | Parallel Fast Fourier Transform |
| PEWS | Parts Early Warning System | PFG | Primary Frequency Generator |
| PEXRAD | Programmed Electronic X-Ray Automatic Diffractometer | PFG | Programmable Frequency Generator |
| | | PFI | Product Features Index |
| PF | Page Fault | PFILE | Physical File |
| PF | Page Formatter | PFK | Phasenfrequenzkennlinie |
| PF | Paper Feed | PFK | Program Function Key |
| PF | Physical File | PFK | Programm Function Keyboard |
| PF | Power Factor | | |
| PF | Primary File | PFK | Programmfunktionstaste |
| PF | Private File | PFLL | Phase and Frequency Locked Loop |
| PF | Probability of Failure | | |
| PF | Program Fetch | PFM | Package Feasibility Model |
| PF | Program Flow | PFM | Physical File Member |
| PF | Program Function | PFM | Power Factor Meter |
| PF | Programmable Format | PFM | Production File Manager |
| PF | Programmed Function | PFM | Pulse Frequency Modulation |
| PF | Programming Fault | | |
| PF | Protection Factor | PFM | Pulsfrequenzmodulation |
| PF | Puffer | PFMS | Plant Facilities Management System |
| PF | Pulse Feedback | | |
| PF | Pulse Frequency | PFN | Pulse Forming Network |
| PF | Punch Feed | PFN | Pulsformungsnetzwerk |
| PFA | Parallel Full Adder | PFORM | Print Format |
| PFA | Parametric Ferrite Amplifier | PFR | Parts Failure Rate |
| | | PFR | Polarized Field frequency Relay |
| PFA | Product and Field Activity | | |
| PFA | Pulverized Fuel Ash | PFR | Power Fail Recovery |
| PFA | Pure Fluid Amplifier | PFR | Power Fail Restart |
| PFAM | Programmed Frequency Amplitude Modulation | PFR | Programmable Film Reader |
| PFAM | Programmed Frequency Amplitude Modulator | PFR | Programmed Film Reader |
| | | PFR | Prototype Fast Reactor |
| PFB | Pre-Formed Beams | PFR | Pulse Frequency |
| PFC | Paper Format Control | PFR | Punch Feed Read |
| PFC | Positive Feedback Circuit | PFRS | Portable Field Recording System |
| PFC | Power Factor Capacitor | | |
| PFC | Program Flow Chart | PFRS | Programmed Film Reader System |
| PFCB | Page Frame Control Block | | |
| PFCC | Power Factor Corrector Capacitor | PFS | Pacific Data Systems Incorporated |
| PFCE | Performance | PFS | Page Format Selection |
| PFCS | Primary Flight Control System | PFS | Physical File System |
| | | PFS | Precision Frequency Source |
| PFCU | Parallel File Control Unit | | |
| PFD | Phase-Frequency Distortion | PFS | Programmable Frequency Standard |

# P

| | | | |
|---|---|---|---|
| PFS | Programmierbarer Festwertspeicher | PGEM | Professional Group Engineering Management |
| PFSR | Program Financial Status Report | PGF | Präsentation Graphische Funktionen |
| PFT | Page Frame Table | PGF | Presentation Graphic Facility |
| PFT | Paper, Flat Tape | | |
| PFT | Prime Factor Transform | PGF | Presentation Graphics Feature |
| PFV | Peak Forward Voltage | | |
| PFW | Punch Feed Write | PGF | Programme de Gestion des Fichiers |
| PG | Page | | |
| PG | Parity Generate | PGHFE | Professional Group Human Factors in Electronics |
| PG | Pegelgenerator | | |
| PG | Peripheres Gerät | PGI | Paris district Gestion Informatique |
| PG | Picture Generator | | |
| PG | Pilotgenerator | PGI | Professional Group Instrumentation |
| PG | Power Gain | | |
| PG | Pressure Gauge | PGI | Programme de Gestion des Interruptions |
| PG | Primärgruppe | | |
| PG | Program Generator | PGIE | Professional Group Industrial Electronics |
| PG | Program Group | | |
| PG | Programmgenerator | PGIS | Project Grant Information System |
| PG | Programmiergerät | | |
| PG | Protective Ground | PGIT | Professional Group Information Theory |
| PG | Pulse Generator | | |
| PGA | Programmable Gate Array | PGLIN | Page and Line |
| | | PGM | Program |
| PGAC | Professional Group Automatic Control | PGM FLGS | Program Flags |
| | | PGME | Professional Group Medical Electronics |
| PGAPL | Preliminary Group Assembly Parts List | PGMITT | Professional Group Microwave Theory and Techniques |
| PGBL | Pluggable | | |
| PGBM | Pulse Gated Binary Modulation | PGNC | Payload Guidance Navigation and Control |
| PGBTS | Professional Group Broadcast Transmission Systems | PGNCS | Primary Guidance and Navigation Control System |
| PGC | Polynomial Generator Checker | PGNS | Primary Guidance and Navigation System |
| PGC | Programmed Gain Control | PGP | Pulse Glide Path |
| PGCS | Professional Group Communications Systems | PGR | Precision Graphic Recorder |
| PGCT | Professional Group Circuit Theory | PGR | Presentation Graphics Routines |
| PGD | Pulse Generator Display | PGR | Psychogalvanic Response |
| PGDS | Pioneer Ground Data System | PGRF | Pulse Group Repetition Frequency |
| PGDS | Pulse Generator Display System | PGS | Plan Graphics Support |
| | | PGS | Power Generation System |
| PGE | Page | PGS | Power Generator Section |
| PGE | Professional Group Education | PGS | Process Guiding System |
| | | PGS | Program Generation System |
| PGEC | Professional Group on Electronic Computers | | |
| | | PGS | Program Generator System |
| PGED | Professional Group Electronic Devices | PGS | Programmgeneratorsystem |

# P

| | | | |
|---|---|---|---|
| PGT | Page Table | PI | Pausenimpuls |
| PGU | Power Generator Unit | PI | Penetration Index |
| PGU | Primärgruppenumsetzer | PI | Performance Index |
| PH | Page Heading | PI | Periphere Initiative |
| PH | Phase | PI | Perpetual Inventory |
| PH | Power House | PI | Photo Interpretation |
| PH | Process Handling | PI | Pilotless Interceptor |
| PHA | Parallel Half Adder | PI | Planning Index |
| PHA | Programmable Host Access | PI | Plug-In |
| PHA | Pulse Height Analysis | PI | Point Initiating |
| PHA | Pulse Height Analyzer | PI | Point Insulating |
| PHA | Pulse Height Analyzing | PI | Point of Intersection |
| PHA | Pulshöhenanalyse | PI | Polling Interrupt |
| PHABIA | Pharmazeutische Bildschirmanwendung | PI | Position Indication |
| | | PI | Power Indicator |
| PHAM | Phase Amplitude Monopulse | PI | Power Input |
| | | PI | Power Interlock |
| PHB | Personalhandbuch | PI | Preliminary Input |
| PHB | Program Header Block | PI | Presentation Image |
| PHD | Phase Detector | PI | Presumptive Instruction |
| PHD | Phase shift Driver | PI | Primary Input |
| PHD | Programmhilfsdatei | PI | Print Image |
| PHD | Pulse Height Discrimination | PI | Priority Interrupt |
| | | PI | Privileged Instruction |
| PHD | Pulse Height Discriminator | PI | Process Interrupt |
| PHENO | Precise Hybrid Elements for Nonlinear Operation | PI | Processor Interface |
| | | PI | Productivity Index |
| PHFET | Photosensitive Field Effect Transistor | PI | Program Identification |
| | | PI | Program Identifier |
| PHI | Position and Homing Indicator | PI | Program Indicator |
| | | PI | Program Information |
| PHICT | Philips Inventory Control Technique | PI | Program Input |
| | | PI | Program Instruction |
| PHINTS | Phase locked Interferometric Tracking System | PI | Program Interrupt |
| | | PI | Program Interrupter |
| PHLAG | Philips petroleum Load And Go system | PI | Program Interruption |
| | | PI | Program Introduction |
| PHM | Phase Meter | PI | Program Isolation |
| PHM | Phase Modulation | PI | Program Item |
| PHOLAS | Philips Host Language System | PI | Programmed Information |
| | | PI | Programmed Instruction |
| PHOSIAC | Photographically Stored Information Analog Comparator | PI | Programmed Interrupt |
| | | PI | Programmierte Instruktion |
| | | PI | Proportional Integral |
| PHP | Pound per Horsepower | PI | Proportional plus Integral |
| PHR | Pulse-Height Resolution | PI | Pseudo-Instruction |
| PHS | Pan Head Steel | PI | Pulse Input |
| PHS | Parallel Half Subtracter | PI-FET | Piezoelectric Field-Effect Transistor |
| PHT | Phototube | | |
| PHTC | Pulse Height-to-Time Converter | PI/SO | Parallel Input with Serial Output |
| PHV | Phase Velocity | PIA | Parallel Interface Adapter |
| PI | Paper Insulated | | |
| PI | Parallel Input | PIA | Peripheral Interface Adapter |
| PI | Parity Insert | | |

# P

| | | | |
|---|---|---|---|
| PIA | Personnel Inventory Analysis | PICE | Program Instruction Control Element |
| PIA | Plug-In Amplifier | PICE | Programmable Integrated Control Equipment |
| PIA | Pres-Installation Acceptance | PICC | Provisional International Computation Center |
| PIACS | Pacific Integrated Automatic Communications Systems | PICLS | Purdue University Instructional and Computational Learning System |
| PIAPACS | Psychophysical Information Acquisition, Processing And Control System | PICM | Production and Inventory Cost Minimizer |
| PIB | Program Information Block | PICOE | Programmed Initiations, Commitments, Obligations and Expenditures |
| PIB | Programm-Informationsblock | | |
| PIB | Pulse Interference Blanker | PICOLO | Peripheres Interaktives Computersystem von Logotec |
| PIC | Particle In Cell | | |
| PIC | Periodic Inspection Control | | |
| PIC | Pheripherie-Controller | PICOS | Production Information and Control System |
| PIC | Photographic Interpretation Center | PICS | Part Inventory Control System |
| PIC | Physics Information Center | | |
| PIC | Picture | PICS | Personnel Information Communication System |
| PIC | Picture Interactive Computer system | PICS | Phone-In Consulting Service |
| PIC | Plastic-Insulated Cable | | |
| PIC | Polyethlene Insulated Conductor | PICS | Physical Inventory Control System |
| PIC | Position-Independent Code | PICS | Plug-in Inventory Control System |
| PIC | Positive Impedance Converter | PICS | Procurement Information Control System |
| PIC | Power Information Center | PICS | Production Information and Control Subsystem |
| PIC | Priority Interrupt Controller | PICS | Production Information and Control System |
| PIC | Production Information and Control | | |
| PIC | Professional Image Computer | PICS | Production Inventory Control System |
| PIC | Program Information Code | PICT | Philips Inventory Control Technique |
| PIC | Program Interrupt Control | | |
| PIC | Programmed Information Center | PID | Personnel Identification Device |
| PIC | Programmed Instruction Centre | PID | Pictorial Information Digitizer |
| PIC | Pulse Ionisation Chamber | PID | Picture Input Device |
| PICA | Power Industry Computer Applications | PID | Pilotdetektor |
| | | PID | Program Information Department |
| PICA | Program Interruption Control Area | PID | Proportional Integral Derivation |
| PICA | Project Integrated Cataloguing Automation | PID | Proportional Integral Differential |
| PICASSO | Pen Input to Computer And Scanned Screen Output | PID | Proportional plus Integral plus Derivative |
| PICC | Partial Inventory Consumption Claim | PID | Proportional-Integral-Derivative |

# P

| | | | |
|---|---|---|---|
| PID | Proportionnel Intégral et Derivé | PII | Positive Immittance Inverter |
| PID | Prüfen auf Identität | PIIN | Procurement Instrument Identification Numbering |
| PID | Publications and Information Directorate | PIK | Positiv-Immittanz-Konverter |
| PIDAM | Plug-In Digital and Analog Module | PIL | Pitt Interpretive Language |
| PIDC | Photo-Induced Discharge Characteristic | PIL | Pittsburgh Interpretive Language |
| PIDEP | Pre-Interservice Data Exchange Program | PIL | Precision In-Line |
| PIDP | Programmable Indicator Data Processor | PIL | Priority Interrupt Level |
| | | PIL | Processing Information List |
| PIDS | Public Investment Data System | PIL | Program Interrupt Level |
| PIE | Parallel Instruction Execution | PILC | Paper-Insulated Lead-Covered cable |
| PIE | Parallel Interface Element | PILE | Product Inventory Level Estimator |
| PIE | Plug-In Electronics | PILL | Programmed Instruction Language Learning |
| PIE | Program Input Equipment | | |
| PIE | Program Interrupt Element | PILOT | Permutation Indexed Literature Of Technology |
| PIE | Program Interrupt Entry | | |
| PIE | Program Investment Evaluation | PILOT | Philips-Interaktives Lernsystem für Operator-Training |
| PIE | Pulse Interference Elimination | PILOT | Piloted Low-speed Test |
| PIE | Pulse Interference Eliminator | PILOT | Printing Industry Language for Operations of Typesetting |
| PIE | Pulse Interference Emitting | PILOT | Programmed Inquiry, Learning Or Teaching |
| PIER | Product Inventory Electronically Recorded | PILOT | Programmed Inquiry, Learning Or Technology |
| PIES | Packaged Interchangeable Electronic System | PILOT | Programmed Inquiry, Learning Or Testing |
| PIES | Procurement Information Exchange System | PIM | Parallel Inference Machine |
| PIES | Program Information and Evaluation System | PIM | Permanent Information Memory |
| PIF | Page Image Format | PIM | Personality-Interfacemodul |
| PIF | Perpetual Inventory File | PIM | Plated Interconnecting Matrix |
| PIF | Playload Integration Facility | PIM | Precision Indicator of the Meridian |
| PIF | Proportional-Integral Filter | PIM | Process Interface Module |
| PIFAL | Program Instruction Frequency Analyzer | PIM | Product Information Memoranda |
| PIFR | Program Interrupt Flag Register | PIM | Program Integration Manual |
| PIGA | Pendulous Integrating Gyroscope Accelerometer | PIM | Pulse Intensity Modulation |
| PIGFET | P-channel Insulated-Gate Field-Effect Transistor | PIM | Pulse Interval Modulation |
| | | PIMS | Parts Inventory Management System |
| PIGME | Programmed Inert Gas Multi-Electrode | PIN | Parallel Input |

- 470 -

# P

| | | | |
|---|---|---|---|
| PIN | Personal Identification Number | PIP | Probabilistic Information Processor |
| PIN | Personenidentifikationsnummern | PIP | Professional Information Processor |
| PIN | Persönliche Identifikations-Nummer | PIP | Program Integration Plan |
| PIN | Piece Identification Number | PIP | Program in Progress |
| PIN | Police Information Network | PIP | Programa de Intercambio Perifericos |
| PIN | Position Indicator | PIP | Programm Im Programm |
| PIN | Positive-Intrinsic-Negative | PIP | Programmable Integrated Processor |
| PIN | Process Identification Number | PIP | Programmed Individual Presentation |
| PIN | Program Identification Number | PIP | Programmed Interconnection Patterns |
| PIN | Programming Information | PIP | Programmer Incentive Plan |
| PING | Pulsed Inertial Navigation and Guidance | PIP | Pulse Input Proportional |
| PINO | Positive Input/Negative Output | PIP | Pulsed Integrating Pendulum |
| PINS | Portable Inertial Navigation System | PIPA | Pulse Integration Pendulum Accelerometer |
| PINT | Power Integrated Transistors | PIPER | Pulsed Intense Plasma for Exploratory Research |
| PIO | Parallel Input/Output | PIPIT | Peripheral Interface and Program Interrupt Translator |
| PIO | Peripheral Input/Output | PIPS | Paperless Item Processing System |
| PIO | Physical Input/Output | PIPS | Pattern Information Processing System |
| PIO | Positive Iterative Operation | PIPS | Production Information Processing System |
| PIO | Processor Input/Output | PIPS | Pulsed Integrating Pendulums |
| PIO | Programmable Input-Output chip | PIR | Packaging Information Record |
| PIO | Programmed Input/Output | PIR | Parallel-Injection Readout |
| PIOC | Program Input/Ouput Cassette | PIR | Polling Interrupt Routine |
| PIOCS | Physical Input/Output Control System | PIR | Program Instruction Register |
| PIOM | Physical Input/Output Manager | PIR | Program Interrupt Register |
| PIOU | Parallel Input/Output Unit | PIR | Program-Index-Register |
| PIP | Parts Inventory Program | PIR | Pulse Input Register |
| PIP | Peripheral Interchange Program | PIRETS | Pittsburgh Information Retrieval System |
| PIP | Perpetual Inventory Program | PIRL | PRISM Information Retrieval Language |
| PIP | Photo Interpretive Program | PIRN | Preliminary Interface Revision Notice |
| PIP | Pollution Information Project | PIRP | Prison Information Reform Project |
| PIP | Predicted Impact Point | PIRR | Problem Investigation and Repair Record |
| PIP | Probabilistic Information Processing | PIRS | Personal Information Retrieval System |

# P

| | | | |
|---|---|---|---|
| PIRS | Project Information Retrieval System | PK | Personalkennzeichen |
| | | PK | Persönliches Kennwort |
| PIRSY | Piesteritzer Informations-recherchesystem | PK | Printing Key |
| | | PK | Programmed Keyboard |
| PIRT | Placement by an Interchange and Rate Technique | PK | Programmierter Kanal |
| | | PK | Programmkapazität |
| | | PK | Programmkarte |
| PIRT | Precision Infrared Triangulation | PK | Programmkomplex |
| | | PK | Protection Key |
| PIRV | Programmed Interrupt Request Vector | PK | Protokollkonverter |
| | | PK | Prüf- und Kontroll-einrichtung |
| PIS | Patienten-Informations-system | | |
| | | PKB | Portable Keyboard |
| PIS | Personalinformations-system | PKC | Position Keeping Computer |
| | | PKD | Packed |
| PIS | Personnel Information System | PKG | Package |
| | | PKG | Packing |
| PIS | Polling Interrupt Sequence | PKG SPEC | Packaging Specifications |
| PIS | Program Indicators | PKI... | Philips Kommunikations Industrie AG |
| PIS | Program Interrupt System | | |
| PIS | Pulse Integration System | PKLA | Produktionskontroll- und -lenkungsanlage |
| PISA | Programmable Interactive Screen Application | | |
| | | PKP | Preknock Pulse |
| PISCES | Production Information Stocks and Cot Enquiry System | PKS | Programmgesellschaft für Kabel- und Satelliten-rundfunk GmbH |
| PISH | Program Instrumentation Summary Handbook | PKS | Projekt-Kontrollsystem |
| | | PKS | Protokollkonverter-System |
| PISW | Process Interrupt Status Word | | |
| | | PKS | Prozeßkontrollsatz |
| PIT | Parameter Input Tape | PKT | Phase Keying Technique |
| PIT | Peripheral Input Tape | PKZ | Personenkennzeichen |
| PIT | Print Illegal and Trace | PL | Packaging List |
| PIT | Processing Index Terms | PL | Parts List |
| PIT | Program Instruction Tape | PL | Patch Loader |
| PIT | Programmable Interval Timer | PL | Peak Loss |
| | | PL | Personnel Letters |
| PIT | Programmed Instruction Text | PL | Phase Line |
| | | PL | Phase Locking |
| PIT | Progressive Inspection Tag | PL | Photoluminescence |
| PITTC | Philips International Telecommunications Training Centre | PL | Pilot Line |
| | | PL | Plain Language |
| | | PL | Plate |
| PIU | Path Information Unit | PL | Plotter |
| PIU | Peripheral Interface Unit | PL | Plug |
| PIU | Plug-In Unit | PL | Pluggable |
| PIV | Peak Inverse Voltage | PL | Power Line |
| PIV | Positive Infinitely Variable | PL | Präsentationslogik |
| PIX | Parallel Interface Extender | PL | Probabilistic Logic |
| PJ | Patching Jackfield | PL | Procedure Library |
| PJ | Program Jump | PL | Product Line |
| PJPC | Plug/Jack Patch Cord | PL | Production Language |
| PK | Pack | PL | Produktive Laufzeit |
| PK | Paßwort-Katalog | PL | Profit and Loss |
| PK | Peak | PL | Progam Length |

# P

| | | | |
|---|---|---|---|
| PL | Program Language | PLANIT | Programming Language for Interactive Teaching |
| PL | Program Level | | |
| PL | Program Library | PLANS | Program Logistics And Network Scheduling |
| PL | Program Limit | | |
| PL | Program Line | PLAT | Pilot Landing Aid Television |
| PL | Program List | | |
| PL | Program Loader | PLATMOS | Platinum-diffused Metal Oxide Semiconductor |
| PL | Program Logic | | |
| PL | Programmed Learning | PLATO | Programmed Logic for Automated Teaching Operations |
| PL | Programmiertes Lernen | | |
| PL | Programming Language | | |
| PL | Proportional Limit | PLATON | Programme de Logistique pour l'Apprentissage à l'aide de la Technologie de l'Ordinateur Numérique |
| PL | Prüfen auf Leer | | |
| PL | Pulse Length | | |
| PL | Pulslage | | |
| PL/I | Programming Language I | | |
| PL/M | Programming Language for Microcomputers | PLAVO | Planungsvorbereitung |
| | | PLB | Print Line Buffer |
| | | PLB | Prozeßleitblock |
| PL/M | Programming Language for Microprocessor | PLC | Power-Line Carrier |
| | | PLC | Prime Level Code |
| PL/MATH | Procedure Library Mathematics | PLC | Print Line Complete |
| | | PLC | Process Line Control |
| PLA | Programmable Logic Array | PLC | Product Level Control |
| PLA | Programmed Logic Array | PLC | Program Level Change |
| PLA | Programmierbare Logische Arrays | PLC | Program Linking Code |
| | | PLC | Programmable Logic Controller |
| PLA | Proton Linear Accelerator | | |
| PLACE | Positioner Layout And Cell Evaluator | PLC | Programming Language Committee |
| PLACE | Programming Language for Automatic Checkout Equipment | PLCB | Program List Control Block |
| | | PLCB | Pseudo-Line Control Block |
| | | PLCL | Phase-Locked Control Loop |
| PLAD | Plasma Diode | | |
| PLAID | Programmed Learning Aid | PLD | Partial Line Down |
| PLAKON | Platten-Konzentrator | PLD | Phase Linked Demodulator |
| PLAN | Problem Language Analyzer | PLD | Phase Locked Demodulator |
| | | PLD | Program Load Device |
| PLAN | Program for Learning in Accordance with Needs | PLD | Pulse Length Discriminator |
| | | PLDF | Piecewise Linear Discriminant Function |
| PLANCODE | Planning, Control and Decision Evaluation system | PLDL | Phase Locked Control Loop |
| | | PLDTS | Propellant Loading Data Transmission System |
| PLANES | Programmed Language-based Enquiry System | | |
| | | PLE | Phase Loading Entry |
| PLANET | Planned Logistics Analysis and Evaluation Technique | PLE | Programmable Logic Elements |
| PLANET | Private Local Area Network | PLE | Programming Language Evaluation |
| PLANIS | Planungsinformations-system | | |
| | | PLE | Prudent Limit of Endurance |
| PLANIT | Programmed Language for Interaction and Testing | PLEA | PL/I Extraction Analysis |
| | | PLEA | Psychologistical Learning for Efficiency and Assurance |
| PLANIT | Programming Language for Interaction and Teaching | | |

# P

| | | | |
|---|---|---|---|
| PLEX | PL/1 List Extension | PLOT | Program Logic Table |
| PLF | Phase Lock Frequency | PLP | Passive Low Pass |
| PLFD | Private Leitung Für Direktruf | PLP | Pattern Learning Parser |
| | | PLP | Photolithographic Process |
| PLG | Plug | PLP | Product Line Planning |
| PLG | Problemlösungsgraphik | PLP | Programming Language Processing |
| PLG | Process Line Generator | | |
| PLI | Power Level Indicator | PLPL | Programmable Logic Programming Language |
| PLIANT | Procedural Language Implementing Analog Technique | PLPO | Phase-Locked Pulsed Oscillator |
| PLIDOS | Persönliches Literatur-Informations- und Dokumentations-System | PLPS | Presentation Level Protocol Standard |
| | | PLR | Pressure Level Recorder |
| PLIM | Post Launch Information Message | PLR | Program Library Release |
| | | PLR | Program Life Requirement |
| PLIN | Power Line Impedance Network | PLR | Program Line Recording |
| | | PLR | Program Lock-in Register |
| PLIP | Preamplifier-Limited Infrared Photoconductor | PLRAM | Program Locatable Random-Access Memory |
| PLIS | Planungs-Inquiry-System | PLRS | Position Location Reporting System |
| PLK | Parameterlochkarte | | |
| PLK | Plastik-Lochkarte | PLS | Philips Logik System |
| PLK | Plattenkassette | PLS | Produktionslenkungssystem |
| PLL | Phase-Locked Logic | | |
| PLL | Phase-Locked Loop | PLS | Programmable Logic Sequence |
| PLL | Positive Logic Level | | |
| PLL | Program Load Library | PLS | Prozeß-Leit-System |
| PLL | Program Load Limit | PLSI | Planar Least Squares Inverse |
| PLLDF | Phase-Locked Loop with Decision Feedback | | |
| | | PLT | Phase-Locked Time |
| PLLR | Phase-Locked Loop Receiver | PLT | Plotting |
| | | PLT | Program Library Tape |
| PLLT | Program Load Library Tape | PLT | Program List Table |
| | | PLT | Program Load Tape |
| PLM | Planetary rotation Machine | PLT | Programmed Learning Textbook |
| PLM | Planned Maintenace | | |
| PLM | Program Logic Manual | PLT | Programmed Light Table |
| PLM | Programmable Logic Matrix | PLTT | Private Line Teletypewriter Service |
| PLM | Pulse Length Modulation | PLU | Partial Line Up |
| PLM | Pulse Length Monitor | PLU | Pluggable Unit |
| PLM | Pulslängemodulation | PLU | Price Look Up |
| PLMATH | Procedure Library Mathematics | PLU | Program Library Unit |
| | | PLUM | Programming Language for Users of MAVIS |
| PLNRCODE | Planner Code | | |
| PLO | Phase-Locked Oscillator | PLUS | PERT Lifecycle Unified System |
| PLO | Program Line Organization | | |
| PLO | Programmed Local Oscillator | PLUS | Program Library Update System |
| PLO | Pulsed Locked Oscillator | PLV | Publicité sur le Lieu de Vente |
| PLOD | Periodic List Of Data | | |
| PLOP | Pilot Line Operating Procedure | PLY | Photo Limited Yield |
| | | PLZ | Postleitzahl |
| PLOP | Pressure Line Of Position | PM | Parallel Memory |

# P

| | | | |
|---|---|---|---|
| PM | Pegelmesser | PMBX | Private Manual Branch Exchange |
| PM | Peripheral Memory | PMC | Plaster Moulded Cornice |
| PM | Permanent Magnet | PMC | Printing Memory Computer |
| PM | Permanent Memory | PMC | Priority Maintenance Contract |
| PM | Phase Modulated | PMC | Process, Monitoring, Control |
| PM | Phase Modulation | PMC | Program Marginal Checking |
| PM | Phase Modulator | PMC | Programmable Machine Control |
| PM | Phasenmodulation | PMC | Programmable Matrix Controller |
| PM | Photomultiplier | PMC | Pseudo-Machine Code |
| PM | Polatization Modulation | PMCS | Pulse-Modulated Communication System |
| PM | Polling Method | PMCT | Program Management Control Table |
| PM | Polling Mode | PMCV | Programmed Multichannel Valve |
| PM | Port Mask | PMD | Positional Macro-Definition |
| PM | Post Meridian | PMD | Post Mortem Dumps |
| PM | Praxis der Mathematik | PMD | Program Management Directive |
| PM | Premium Memory | PMD | Program Module Directory |
| PM | Premixer | PMD | Program Monitoring and Diagnosis |
| PM | Preventive Maintenance | PMD | Programmed Multiple Development |
| PM | Principle of Multiplying | PMD | Projected Map Display |
| PM | Print Matrix | PMDS | Projected Map Display Set |
| PM | Printing Mechanism | PME | Passive Microelectronic Element |
| PM | Priority Message | PME | Petites et Moyennes Entreprises |
| PM | Privileged Mode | PME | Photomagnetoelectric |
| PM | Problemmaschine | PME | Photomagnetoelectric Effect |
| PM | Procedures Manual | PME | Planning Market Estimate |
| PM | Process Manual | PME | Preventive Maintenance Effectiveness |
| PM | Processor Module | PME | Primärmultiplexeinrichtung |
| PM | Product Marketing | PME | Product Market Estimate |
| PM | Program | PME | Protective Multiple Earthing |
| PM | Program Management | PMEE | Prime Mission Electronic Equipment |
| PM | Program Memory | PMEV | Panel Mounting Electronic Voltmeter |
| PM | Program Mode | PMF | Page Management Facility |
| PM | Program Module | PMF | Parts Master File |
| PM | Program Monitor | | |
| PM | Programmed Machine | | |
| PM | Programming Manual | | |
| PM | Programming Matrix | | |
| PM | Programming Method | | |
| PM | Programming Module | | |
| PM | Projektmanagement | | |
| PM | Protected Memory | | |
| PM | Pseudo Memory | | |
| PM | Pulse Modulation | | |
| PM | Pulse code Modulation | | |
| PM | Pulsmodulation | | |
| PM | Purpose-Made | | |
| PMA | Preamplifier Module Assembly | | |
| PMA | Prime Macro-Assembler | | |
| PMAC | Parallel Memory Address Counter | | |
| PMAR | Program Memory Address Register | | |
| PMB | Program Memory Block | | |
| PMB | Prozessor-Memory-Bus | | |

# P

| | | | |
|---|---|---|---|
| PMF | Performance Measurement Facility | PMP | Planar Metallization with Polymer |
| PMF | Personnel Master File | PMP | Post Mortem Program |
| PMF | Print Management Facility | PMP | Premodulation Processor |
| PMF | Product Measurement Facility | PMP | Preventive Maintenance Plan |
| PMF | Programmable Matched Filter | PMP | Product and Marketing Planning |
| PMG | Phase Modulation Generator | PMP | Program Monitor Panel |
| PMG | Prediction Marker Generator | PMPE | Punch Memory Parity Error |
| PMI | Personnel Management Information | PMR | Patient Master Record |
| PMI | Petites et Moyennes Industries | PMR | Post Mortem Routine |
| | | PMR | Programmed Mixture Ratio |
| PMI | Positional Macro Instruction | PMS | Performance Management Software |
| PMI | Preventive Maintenance Inspection | PMS | Performance Measurement System |
| | | PMS | Peripheral Monitor System |
| PMI | Program Management Instruction | PMS | Personnel Management System |
| PMI | Programming Methods Incorporated | PMS | Processor Memory Switch |
| | | PMS | Processor, Memories and Switches |
| PMI | Pseudo Matrix Isolation | PMS | Program Management Support |
| PMIC | Personnel Management Information Center | PMS | Program Management System |
| PMIN | Processor Memory Interconnection Network | PMS | Programmed Mode Switch |
| PMIS | Personnel Management Information System | PMS | Project Management System |
| PMIS | Printing Management Information System | PMS | Projektmanagement-Steuersystem |
| PMIS | Program Measurement Information System | PMS | Public Message Service |
| | | PMSDP | Prefabricated Multilayer Section Design Program |
| PML | Power Minimized Logic | PMSM | Product Marketing Strategy Model |
| PMM | Pulse-Mode Multiplex | | |
| PMMA | Polymethylmethacrylate | PMSP | Plant Modelling System Program |
| PMMC | Permanent-Magnet Movable Coil | PMT | Page Map Table |
| PMMP | Post Mortem Memory Print | PMT | Phase Modulated Transmission |
| PMMP | Preventive Maintenance Management Program | PMT | Photomultiplier Tube |
| PMMT | Processeur Multiprotocole Multiligne des Transmission | PMT | Physical Master Tape |
| | | PMT | Portable Magnetic Tape |
| | | PMT | Precious Metal Tip |
| PMN | Program Management Network | PMT | Prepare Master Tape |
| | | PMT | Programmed Math Tutorial |
| PMNT | Permanent | PMT | Prompt |
| PMOS | P-Channel MOS | PMTE | Page Map Table Entry |
| PMOSFET | P-channel MOSFET | PMTS | Predetermined Motion Time System |
| PMOST | P-channel MOST | | |
| PMP | Passive Measurement Program | PMU | Performance Monitor Unit |
| | | PMU | Portable Memory Unit |

# P

| | | | |
|---|---|---|---|
| PMW | Pulse Modulated Wave | PNMT | Positive-Negative Metal Transistor |
| PMX | Private Manual Exchange | PNP | Positiv, Negativ, Positiv |
| PN | Part Number | PNP | Positive-Negative-Positive |
| PN | Perceived Noise | PNP | Precision Navigation Processor |
| PN | Perforation Number | | |
| PN | Performance Number | PNP | Programmed Numerical Path-controller |
| PN | Personalnummer | | |
| PN | Phon | PNPN | Positive-Negative-Positive-Negative |
| PN | Polnische Notation | | |
| PN | Positiv-Negativ | PNR | Page Number Register |
| PN | Positive-Negative | PNR | Passenger Name Record |
| PN | Printer | PNR | Purchase Notice and Release |
| PN | Procedure Name | | |
| PN | Program Name | PNT | Point |
| PN | Program Notice | PNTG | Printing |
| PN | Program Number | PNW | Prioritäten-Netzwerk |
| PN | Proportional Navigation | PNX | Private Network Exchange |
| PN | Prüfen auf Numerisch | PO | Page Overflow |
| PN | Pseudo-Noise | PO | Parallel Output |
| PN-FET | Positive-Negative-Field-Effect Transistor | PO | Partitioned Organisation |
| | | PO | Polarity |
| PN-TDMA | Pseudo-Noise Time Division Multiple Access | PO | Post Office |
| | | PO | Power Oscillator |
| PNA | Programmes Nationaux d'Applications | PO | Power Output |
| | | PO | Pressure Oscillation |
| PNA | Project Network Analysis | PO | Primary Outlet |
| PNC | Police National Computer | PO | Primary Output |
| PNC | Programmed Numerical Control | PO | Print-Out |
| | | PO | Privileged Operation |
| PNCH | Punch | PO | Produktionsorder |
| PNCL | Percent Non-Conforming Lots | PO | Program Objection |
| | | PO | Program Objective |
| PNCU | Police National Computer Unit | PO | Program Organization |
| | | PO | Program Oriented |
| PND | Present Next Digit | PO | Program Originator |
| PNDC | Parallel Network Digital Computer | PO | Program Output |
| | | PO | Programmed Operation |
| PNEC | Part Number Engineering Change | PO | Programmed Oscillator |
| | | PO | Projekt-Organisation |
| PNEUC | Physical Non-Eliminated Unit Check | PO | Pulse Oscillator |
| | | PO | Punch Off |
| PNG | Pseudo Noise Generator | PO | Punch Operation |
| PNG | Pseudorandom Number Generator | PO | Punch Operator |
| | | PO | Punch-Out |
| PNK | Personalnummernkarte | PO | Purchase Option |
| PNK | Programmierbarer Netzknoten | PO | Purchase Order |
| | | POA | Power Amplifier |
| PNK | Programmierter Netzknoten | POA | Probability Of Acceptance |
| | | POA | Problem Oriented Assembler |
| PNL | Panel | | |
| PNL | Passenger Name List | POASP | Plans and Operations Automated Storage Program |
| PNL | Perceived-Noise Level | | |
| PNM | Pulse-Number Modulation | POB | Principles of Operation Bulletin |
| PNMF | Pseudo-Noise-Matched Filter | | |

# P

| | | | |
|---|---|---|---|
| POB | Problemorientierter Baustein | POKE | Processor Oriented Key Entry |
| POB | Proceeding push Out Base | POL | Philips Optical Language |
| POB | Program Operation Block | POL | Polarization |
| POB | Push-Out Base | POL | Polling |
| POC | Parallel Optical Computer | POL | Power Optimized Logic |
| POC | Parts On Change | POL | Problem-Oriented Language |
| POC | Patch Output Converter | | |
| POC | Process Operators Console | POL | Procedure-Oriented Language |
| POCO | Position Computer | | |
| POCP | Program Objection Change Proposal | POL | Process-Oriented Language |
| | | POL | Program-Oriented Language |
| POCR | Processor Oriented Character Recognition | POLAC | Problem-Oriented Language for Analytical Chemistry |
| POD | Point of Origin Device | | |
| POD | Pulse Omission Detector | | |
| PODAF | Post Operation Data Analysis Facility | POLARS | Pathology Online Logging And Reporting System |
| PODAS | Portable Data Acquisition System | POLAS | Polizei-Auskunftssystem |
| | | POLDPS | Pioneer Off-Line Data-Processing System |
| PODS | Portable Data Store | | |
| PODS | Post-Operative Destruct System | POLE | Point-Of-Last-Environment restart |
| POE | Ponta Override Entry | POLIS | Polizei-Informations-system |
| POE | Print Out Effect | | |
| POEM | Program Oriented External Monitor | POLIS | Polynomial Interpreting System |
| POET | Portable Orders Entry Terminal | POLO | Problem-Oriented Language Organizer |
| POF | Point-Of-Failure restart | POLREG | Polynomiale Regression |
| POF | Program Order Form | POLRG | Polynormregressions-generator |
| POGO | Problem-Oriented Graphics Operation | POLY | Polyethylene |
| POGO | Programmer-Oriented Graphics Operation | POLYTRAN | Polytranslation analysis and programming |
| POH | Power-On Hours | POM | Pay-Off Matrix |
| POI | Program Operator Interface | POM | Photo-Optical Memory |
| | | POM | Printer Output Microfilm |
| POI | Program Of Instruction | POM | Prise des Origines Machine |
| POINT | Performance Oriented Integrated Technology | POM | Production Order Master |
| | | POM | Program Operation Mode |
| POINTER | Particle Orientation Interferometer | POM | Programmierbares Ordnungs- und Magaziniersystem |
| POIS | Procurement Operations and Information System | POM | Purchase Order Management |
| POISE | Panel On In-flight Scientific Experiments | POMD | Program Operation Mode |
| | | POMI | Photochromic Microimage |
| POISE | Practice-Oriented Information System Experiment | POMIL | Problem Oriented Machine Independent Language |
| POKAL | Produktionsprogramm-herstellung mit Kapazitätsausgleich und Liefertermin-ermittlung | POMP | Precoded Originating Mail Processor |
| | | POMP | Problem-Oriented Management of Patients |

# P

| | | | |
|---|---|---|---|
| POMR | Problem-Oriented Medical Records | POS | Programming Optimizing System |
| PON | Production Order Notification | POS | Purchase Order Status |
| PON | Purchase Order Notice | POSD | Program for Optical System Design |
| POOF | Peripheral Online Oriented Function | POSFET | Piezoelectric Oxide Semiconductor Field-Effect Transistor |
| POOP | Principles Of Operation | POSH | Permuted On Subject Headings |
| POP | Power On/off Protection | | |
| POP | Predicted Order Program | POSS | Photooptical Surveillance System |
| POP | Printing Out Paper | | |
| POP | Program Obligation Plan | POST | Posting |
| POP | Program Operating Plan | POSTER | Post-Strike Emergency Reporting |
| POP | Project Optimisation Procedure | POT | Partial Operating Time |
| POPL | Pinciples Of Programming Language | POT | Potential |
| | | POT | Potentiometer |
| POPL | Problem-Oriented Programming Language | POTC | PERT Orientation and Training Center |
| POPS | Pantograph Optical Projection System | POTP | Physical Operation Time Projection |
| POPSI | Postulate-based Permuted Subject Indexing | POTS | Plain Old Telephone Service |
| POR | Power-On Reset | POTS | Photo-Optical Terrain Simulator |
| POR | Problem Oriented Routine | | |
| POR | Problem-Oriented Record | POV | Peak Operating Voltage |
| POR | Problemorientierte Routine | POW | Peripheral Output Writer |
| POR | Program-Oriented Routine | POWER | PERT Oriented Work-scheduling and Evaluation Routine |
| PORC | Purchase Order Requisition Control | | |
| PORNO | Purchase Order Number | POWER | Priority Output Writers, Execution processors and input Readers |
| PORT | Photo-Optical Recorder Tracker | | |
| PORT | Photo-Optical Recording Tracker | POWER | Programmed Offline Waste Reduction |
| PORT | Portable | POWS | Pyrotechnic Outside Warning System |
| POS | Partial Output Signal | | |
| POS | Pascal Operating System | PP | Page Printer |
| POS | Point Of Sale | PP | Panel Point |
| POS | Position | PP | Parallel Printer |
| POS | Positive | PP | Parallel Processing |
| POS | Pressure Operated Switch | PP | Parallel Programming |
| POS | Primary Operating System | PP | Parametric Programming |
| POS | Probability Of Survival | PP | Partial Product |
| POS | Problem-Oriented Software | PP | Partial Program |
| | | PP | Password Protection |
| POS | Problem-Oriented System | PP | Patch Panel |
| POS | Problemorientierte Systemunterlagen | PP | Patchboard Programming |
| | | PP | Pattern Processing |
| POS | Processor Operating System | PP | Peak Power |
| | | PP | Peak to Peak |
| POS | Program Order Sequence | PP | Perforation Pitch |
| POS | Programmier-Optimierungssystem | PP | Peripheral Processor |
| | | PP | Pipeline Processor |

# P

| | | | |
|---|---|---|---|
| PP | Polynominal Programming | PPBES | Program Planning-Budgeting-Evaluation System |
| PP | Postprocessor | | |
| PP | Preliminary Program | | |
| PP | Preparatory Program | PPBG | Preliminary Program and Budget Guidance |
| PP | Preprocessor | | |
| PP | Pressure Proof | PPBS | Planning Programming and Budgeting System |
| PP | Primary Processor | | |
| PP | Print Position | PPBS | Program Performance Budgetary Systems |
| PP | Print Program | | |
| PP | Print/Punch | PPC | Partial Pay Card |
| PP | Printer Perforator | PPC | Personal Programmers Club |
| PP | Priority Processing | | |
| PP | Problem Program | PPC | Phased Program Construction |
| PP | Processing Program | | |
| PP | Product Publication | PPC | Planar Positive Column |
| PP | Produktionsprozeß | PPC | Process Problem Chart |
| PP | Program Paper | PPC | Production and Planning Control |
| PP | Program Parameter | | |
| PP | Program Part | PPC | Program Planning and Control |
| PP | Program Plan | | |
| PP | Program Position | PPC | Program Product Center |
| PP | Program Processing | PPC | Pulsed Power Circuit |
| PP | Program Product | PPCC | Pan Pacific Computer Conference |
| PP | Program Pulse | | |
| PP | Programming Problem | PPCE | Print Position Control Exit |
| PP | Programming Program | | |
| PP | Programmpaket | PPCM | Predictive Pulse Code Modulation |
| PP | Programmprodukt | | |
| PP | Pseudo Program | PPCO | Periodically Phase-Controlled Oscillator |
| PP | Pseudoprogramm | | |
| PP | Pulse Pair | PPD | Payload Position Data |
| PP | Push-Pull | PPD | Personnel Planning Data |
| PPA | Parallel Processing Automata | PPD | Product and Process Description |
| PPA | Photo Peak Analysis | PPD | Program Planning Document |
| PPA | Pre-Planned Application | | |
| PPA | Product Performance Analysis | PPD | Provisioning Procurement Data |
| PPA | Program Product Announcement | PPD | Punch Program Drum |
| PPA | Protected Partition Area | PPDB | Personnel Planning Data Book |
| PPA | Prozeß-Peripherie-Ansteuerung | PPDB | Point-Positioning Data Base |
| PPA | Purchasing Programs Administrator | PPDD | Plan Position Data Display |
| PPA | Push-Pull Amplifier | PPDS | Primary Processor and Data Storage |
| PPAM | Privileged Primary Access Method | | |
| | | PPE | Peripheral Processor Element |
| PPB | Planning, Programming, Budgeting | PPE | Premodulation Processor Equipment |
| PPB | Provisioning Parts Breakdown | PPE | Print-Punch Editor |
| PPBAS | Planning, Programming, Budgeting, Accounting System | PPE | Problem Program Efficiency |

# P

| | | | |
|---|---|---|---|
| PPE | Problem Program Evaluator | PPM | Perodic Permanent Magnet |
| PPEP | Pen Plotter Emulation Plotsoftware | PPM | Planned Preventive Maintenance |
| PPF | Program Protect Flag | PPM | Product Program Manager |
| PPFUN | Post-Processor Function | PPM | Pulse Period Modulation |
| PPG | Primary Pattern Generator | PPM | Pulse Position Modulation |
| PPG | Print Pattern Generator | PPM | Pulse-Phase Modulation |
| PPG | Program Pulse Generator | PPM | Pulses Per Minute |
| PPG | Programmable Pattern Generator | PPM | Pulsphasenmodulation |
| PPG | Propulsion and Power Generator | PPM | Pulspositions-Modulationsverfahren |
| PPGM | Planning-Programming Guidance Memo | PPM | Pulspositionsmodulation |
| PPHA | Peak Pulse Height Analysis | PPMS | Product Procedure Maintenance System |
| PPI | Parts Parameter Information | PPMS | Program Performance Measurement System |
| PPI | Personalpolitische Information | PPN | Procurement Program Number |
| PPI | Personnel Planning Information | PPO | Performance Prediction Overview |
| PPI | Plan-Position Indicator | PPO | Push-Pull Output |
| PPI | Print Position Indicator | PPP | Peak Pulse Power |
| PPI | Programmable Parallel Interface | PPP | Phase Program Planning |
| PPI | Programmable Peripheral Interface | PPP | Phased Project Planning |
| PPI | Pulses Per Inch | PPP | Produktionsprogrammplanung |
| PPID | Product IBM Program Information Department | PPP | Programmed Production Planning |
| PPIU | Programmable Peripheral Interface Unit | PPP | Push-Pull Power |
| PPL | Passed Parameter List | PPPA | Push-Pull Power Amplifier |
| PPL | Photogrammetric Programming Language | PPPI | Precision Plan Position Indicator |
| PPL | Polymorphic Programming Language | PPPL | Program Preferred Parts List |
| PPL | Preferred Parts List | PPPS | Pulse Pairs Per Second |
| PPL | Preliminary Parts List | PPR | Page Printing Receiver |
| PPL | Process Peripherals Limited | PPR | Paper |
| PPL | Production Process Level | PPR | Partial Product Read |
| PPL | Provisioning Parts List | PPR | Parts Planning Record |
| PPL | Purchased Parts List | PPR | Photoplastic Recording |
| PPLOT | Post-processor Plot | PPR | Post-Punch Read |
| PPLOT | Post-processor Plotter | PPR | Primary Program Routine |
| PPLS | Preferred Parts List System | PPR | Product Performance Report |
| PPM | Parallel Processing Machine | PPR | Production Parts Record |
| PPM | Parts Per Million | PPR | Program Planning Report |
| PPM | Periode Principale de Maintenance | PPR | Purchasing Programs Representative |
| PPM | Periodic Pulse Metering | PPRF | Pulse Pair Repetition Frequency |
| | | PPS | Parallel Processing System |
| | | PPS | Partitioned Priority System |
| | | PPS | Patchboard Programming System |

# P

| | | | |
|---|---|---|---|
| PPS | Peripheral Processor System | PPT | Programmer Productivity Techniques |
| PPS | Peripheres Prozessorsystem | PPT | Punched Paper Tape |
| PPS | Phosphorous Propellant System | PPTP | Power Proportioning Temperature Programmer |
| PPS | Picture Per Second | PPTR | Punched Paper Tape Reader |
| PPS | Potentialplanungssystem | PPTR | Punched Paper Tape Reading |
| PPS | Primary Propulsion System | PPTS | Punched Paper Tape Speed |
| PPS | Priority Processing System | PPU | Peripheral Processing Unit |
| PPS | Problemorientierte Programmiersprache | PPU | Peripheral Processor Unit |
| PPS | Product Performance Specification | PPW | Partial Product Write |
| | | PQA | Protected Queue Area |
| PPS | Produktionsplanung und -steuerung | PQC | Production Quality Control |
| | | PQE | Partition Queue Element |
| PPS | Produktionsplanungs- und Produktionssteuerungssystem | PQEL | Partition Queue Element |
| | | PQEP | Product Quality Evaluation Plan |
| PPS | Program Planning System | PQGS | Propellant Quantity Gauging Systems |
| PPS | Program Product Specification | PQS | Picolo-Quadranten-Suchsystem |
| PPS | Program Production Supervisor | PQS | Product Quotient Storage |
| PPS | Programmable Patch System | PQVS | Platten-Quellenprogramm-Verwaltungssystem |
| PPS | Programmable Power Supply | PR | Page Reader |
| | | PR | Pattern Recognition |
| PPS | Programming Program Strela | PR | Pattern Recognizer |
| | | PR | Pegelregler |
| PPS | Project Profile System | PR | Perforation Rate |
| PPS | Project Proposal Summary | PR | Photographic Reconnaissance |
| PPS | Projekt-Planungs- und Steuerungssystem | PR | Physical Record |
| PPS | Pulses Per Second | PR | Plyrating-prismary Radar |
| PPSC | Parallel Processing System Compiler | PR | Position Register |
| | | PR | Postal Rate commission |
| PPSN | Present Position | PR | Prefix Resolution |
| PPSN | Public Packet-Switched Network | PR | Primary Rate |
| | | PR | Primary Runout |
| PPSS | Product and Process Status System | PR | Principal Register |
| | | PR | Print |
| PPSS | Produktionsplanung und Steuerungssystem | PR | Print Restore |
| | | PR | Printer |
| PPSS | Project Planning and Scheduling System | PR | Printing |
| | | PR | Printing Reperforator |
| PPST | Prefix Partition Specification Table | PR | Priority Routine |
| | | PR | Proceedings |
| PPT | Parts Procurement Time | PR | Processor |
| PPT | Periodic Program Termination | PR | Product Register |
| | | PR | Program Register |
| PPT | Primary Program operator interface Task | PR | Program Repeat |
| | | PR | Program Requirements |
| PPT | Processing Program Table | PR | Program Resolution monitor |
| PPT | Program Punched Tape | PR | Program Routine |

# P

| | | | |
|---|---|---|---|
| PR | Programmierer | PRAM | Processing Rate Analytic Model |
| PR | Programmierung | | |
| PR | Protect | PRAM | Program Requirements Analysis Method |
| PR | Prozessor | | |
| PR | Prozessrechner | PRAM | Programmable Random Access Memory |
| PR | Prozeß | | |
| PR | Prozeßroutine | PRAM | Programme für Angewandte Mathematik |
| PR | Pseudorandum | | |
| PR | Pseudoregister | PRAN | Production Analyser |
| PR | Public Relations | PRAP | Prozeßablaufplan |
| PR | Pulse Rate | PRAS | Prozeßrechneranwendersystem |
| PR | Pulse Ratio | | |
| PR | Pulse Regeneration | PRAS | Prozeßrechneranwendungssystem |
| PR | Punch Routine | | |
| PR | Punching Rate | PRAUT | Prozeß-Automatisierungssystem |
| PR-1 | Print Register 1 | | |
| PRA | Precision Axis | PRAVDA | Programmsystem für die Ablauforganisation des Vertriebes von Datenverarbeitungsanlagen |
| PRA | Prime Responsable Authority | | |
| PRA | Print Alphamerically | | |
| PRA | Production Reader Assembly | PRB | Program Request Block |
| | | PRB | Program Request Buffer |
| PRA | Program Reader Assembly | PRB | Programmaufrufblock |
| PRA | Prozeßrechneranlage | PRB | Pseudo Random Binary |
| PRAAD | Photo-Resist Apply And Dry | PRBS | Pseudo Random Binary Sequence |
| PRACE | Photo-Resist Align, Contact and Expose | PRC | Part Requirement Card |
| | | PRC | Partial Read Current |
| PRACL | Page Replacement Algorithm and Control Logic | PRC | Parts Release Card |
| | | PRC | Periodic Reverse Current |
| | | PRC | Point of Reverse Curve |
| PRACOS | Praxis-Computer-System | PRC | Postal Rate Commision |
| PRADAB | Produktionsauftragsdatenbank | PRC | Primary Return Code |
| | | PRC | Production Control |
| PRADO | Projektabwicklungs- und Dokumentationssystem | PRC | Program Range Change |
| | | PRC | Program Request Control |
| PRADOR | Pulse repetition frequency Ranging Doppler Radar | PRC | Program Required Credentials |
| PRADOS | Projektabwicklungs- und Dokumentationssystem | PRCC | Parts Request Card Code |
| | | PRCC | Peripheriespeicherresidenter Common Code |
| PRAG | Programmsystem zur Auswertung von Gaschromatografie | PRCCS | Parts Return Control Card System |
| | | PRCS SPEC | Process Specification |
| PRAG | Programmsystem zur Auswertung von Gaschromatogrammen | PRD | Period |
| | | PRD | Personnel Requirements Data |
| PRAGMA | Processing Routines Aided by Graphics for Manipulation of Arrays | PRD | Personnel Resources Data |
| | | PRD | Power Requirement Data |
| | | PRD | Prime Radar Digitizer |
| PRAIS | Pesticide Residue Analysis Information Service | PRD | Printer Driver |
| | | PRD | Printer Dump |
| PRAKOS | Prozeß-, Ablauf- und Kontrollsteuerung | PRD | Productive |
| | | PRD | Program Requirements Data |
| PRAM | Page Replacement Analysis Models | | |

# P

| | | | |
|---|---|---|---|
| PRD | Program Requirements Document | PRFCS | Pattern Recognition Feedback Control System |
| PRDR | Procedure | PRG | Program |
| PRDS | Processed Radar Display System | PRG | Program control mode |
| | | PRGM | Program |
| PRDV | Peak Reading Digital Voltmeter | PRGM RGTR | Program Register |
| | | PRGMR | Programmer |
| PRE | Preliminary amplifier | PRI | Plan Repeater Indicator |
| PREAMP | Preamplifier | PRI | Primary |
| PREC | Precision | PRI | Program Interrupt |
| PRECIS | Preserved Context Indexing System | PRI | Pulse Rate Indicator |
| | | PRI | Pulse Repetition Interval |
| PREDICT | PERT Resource Expenditure Determination of ICT | PRIC | Parts Reliability Information Center |
| | | PRID | Planning Record Identifier |
| PREDICT | Prediction of Radiation Effects by Digital Computer Techniques | PRIDE | Programmed Reliability In Design |
| | | PRIG | Printing |
| | | PRIM | Primary |
| PREDICT | Process Reliability, Evaluation and Determination of Integrated Circuit Techniques | PRIMAS | Programm zum Recherchieren und Indexieren mit Maschinenhilfe |
| | | PRIMAS | Programm zur Indexierung mit Maschinenhilfe |
| PREF | Prefix | PRIMAS | Projekt-, Informations- und Management-System |
| PREP | Product Reliability Evaluation Program | | |
| PREP | Programmed Electronics Pattern | PRIME | Plannig through Retrieval of Information for Management Extrapolation |
| PREP | Project Return Evaluation Program | | |
| PREPARE | Project for Retraining of Employable Persons As Relates to EDP | PRIME | Precision Integrator for Meteorological Echoes |
| | | PRIME | Precision Recovery Including Manoeuverable Entry |
| PRES | Pressure | | |
| PRESS | Pressure | | |
| PRESS | Product Records Engineering Support System | PRIME | Primate Information Management Experiment |
| PRESS | Project Review, Evaluation and Scheduling System | PRIME | Prime Computer, Incorporated |
| PRESSAR | Presentation Equipment for Show Scan Radar | PRIME | Programmed Instruction for Management Education |
| PRESTO | Program for Rapid Earth-to-Space Trajectory Optimization | PRIMER | Patient Record Information for Education Requirements |
| PRESTO | Program Reporting and Evaluation System for Total Operations | PRIN | Principle |
| | | PRIN-CIR | Printed Circuit |
| | | PRINC | Principle |
| PREV | Previous | PRINC-APIC | Princeton Reliability Information Center-Apollo Parts Information Center |
| PREVAN | Precompiler for Vector Analysis | | |
| PRF | Profile | | |
| PRF | Prozeßrechnerfunktion | PRINCE | Programmed International Computer Environment |
| PRF | Pulse Rate Frequency | | |
| PRF | Pulse Recurrence Frequency | PRINCE | Programmed Reinforced Instruction Necessary to Continuing Education |
| PRF | Pulse Repetition Frequency | | |

# P

| | | | |
|---|---|---|---|
| PRINFOD | Printed Information Distribution | PRM | Program Resolution Monitor |
| PRINSYS | Product Information System | PRM | Programming and Resources Management |
| PRINT | Pre-edited Interpretive system | PRM | Pulse Rate Modulation |
| PRINT | Preedited Interpreter | PRM | Pulse Ratio Modulator |
| PRINT | Preedited Interpretive | PRMOD | Printer Module |
| PRINT | Print Recognition Input Terminal | PRMR | Primer |
| | | PRN | Previous Result Negative |
| PRINT | Printed | PRN | Print Numerically |
| PRIO | Prioritätsberechnung | PRN | Pseudo-Random Noise |
| PRIP | Pattern Recognition and Image Processing | PRN | Pseudo-Random Number |
| | | PRN | Pulse Ranging Navigation |
| PRISE | Pennsylvania's Regional Instruction System for Education | PRNTG | Printing |
| | | PRO | Print Octal |
| | | PROB | Problem |
| PRISE | Program for Integrated Shipboard Electronics | PROBARE | Programmbaustein für ein integriertes Rechnungswesen |
| PRISM | Personnel Record Information System for Management | PROBE | Pro-Recognition Of Baleful Errors |
| | | PROC | Procedure |
| PRISM | Personnel Requirements Information System Methodology | PROC | Proceedings |
| | | PROC | Process |
| | | PROC | Processor |
| PRISM | Powerful Resource for Information and System Management | PROC | Programming Computer |
| | | PROC CHECK | Process Check |
| | | PROCAL | Programmable Calculator |
| PRISM | Program Integrated System Maintenance | PROCAS | Process Calculation System |
| PRISM | Program Reliability Information System for Management | PROCD | Procedure |
| | | PROCD | Proceed |
| | | PROCO | Programmed Combustion |
| PRISM | Program Reporting and Information System for Management | PROCOL | Process Control Oriented Language |
| | | PROCOM | Prognose Compiler |
| PRISM | Pulse Repetition Interval Sorting Matrix | PROCOMP | Process Computer |
| | | PROCOMP | Program Compiler |
| PRISMA | Permanent Reorganisierendes Informationssystem Merkmalrorientierter Anwenderdaten | PROCOPT | Processing Option |
| | | PROCSIM | Processor Simulation |
| | | PROCSY | Purdue Remote Online Console System |
| PRISMA | Prognose- und Informations-System für das Materialwesen | PROCTOR | Priority Routing Organizer for Computer Transfers and Operations of Registers |
| PRK | Phase Reversal Keying | | |
| PRK | Prozeßrechnerkomplex | PROCTOT | Priority Routine Organizer for Computer Transfers and Operation Transfers |
| PRL | Periodical requirements | | |
| PRL | Private Line | | |
| PRL | Pulldown Resistor Logic | PROCU | Processing Unit |
| PRL | Pulse-Reflection Logic | PROCUP | Paper Roll Cutting Programm |
| PRLM | Preliminary | | |
| PRM | Parameter | PROD | Product |
| PRM | Power Range Monitor | PROD | Production |
| PRM | Program Reference Manual | PROD | Produkt |

# P

| | | | |
|---|---|---|---|
| PRODAC | Programmed Digital Automatic Control | PROMESA | Programme zur Kontrolle des Medizinischen Sachbedarfs im Krankenhaus |
| PRODASTE | Programm für die Datenanalyse Statistischer Erhebungen | PROMIDA | Programmiersprache für die Mittlere Datentechnik |
| PRODIA | Produktionsdiagramm | | |
| PRODIP | Programm Distribution Program | PROMIS | Problem-Oriented Medical Information System |
| PRODOK | Programmpaket für projektbegleitende Dokumentation | PROMIS | Project Oriented Management Information System |
| PROF | Parameter Profile | PROMIS | Prosecutors Management Information System |
| PROF | Profile | | |
| PROF | Programmable Operator Facility | PROMISE | Programming Managers Information System |
| PROFAC | Propulsive Fluid Accumulator | PROMO | Programmation autmatisée des Machines-Outils |
| PROFAN | Programmsystem Für Aufbauunterlagen | PROMOCM | Project Monitor and Control Method |
| PROFI | Programmiersystem für Profilträger-Bohrmaschinen | PROMOF | Programmierte Modulare Finanzbuchhaltung |
| | | PROMPT | Production Reviewing Organizing and Monitoring of Performance Techniques |
| PROFILE | Programmed Functional Indices for Laboratory Evaluation | | |
| PROFIT | Programmed Reviewing Ordering and Forecasting Inventory Technique | PROMPT | Program Monitoring and Planning Techniques |
| | | PROMPT | Program Reporting, Organization, and Management Planning Technique |
| PROFS | Professional Office System | PROMS | Program Modelling and Simulation |
| PROG | Program | | |
| PROG | Programmed | PROMS | Program Modelling System |
| PROG | Programming | PRONTO | Program for Numerical Tool Operation |
| PROGDEV | Program Device | | |
| PROGR | Programmer | PROP | Performance Review for Operating Programs |
| PROGRES | Programmiersprache für Realzeit Systeme | PROP | Produktionsplanung |
| PROJACS | Project Analysis and Control System | PROP | Programm-Optimierte Projektarbeit |
| PROKON | Prozeß-Kontroll-System | PROP | Proposal online reparation |
| PROKOS | Programmsystem Kostenrechnung | PROPG | Propagate |
| | | PROPLAN | Produktionsplanung |
| PROLAMAT | Programming Language for numerically controlled Machine Tools | PROPSIM | Propagation Simulator |
| | | PROSA | Programmierungssystem mit Symbolischen Adressen |
| PROLAN | Processed Language | | |
| PROLOG | Program Logistics | PROSA | Programming system with Symbolic Addresses |
| PROLOG | Programmsystem Lohn und Gehalt | PROSE | Production Scheduler |
| PROM | Pockels-Readout-Optical Modulator | PROSEL | Process control and Sequencing Language |
| PROM | Programmable Read-Only Memory | PROSEL | Process Sequencing Language |
| PROMCOM | Project Monitoring and Control Method | PROSI | Prozeß-Simulation |
| | | PROSIG | Procedure Signal |

# P

| | | | |
|---|---|---|---|
| PROSIM | Production system Simulator | PRSG | Pseudo-Random Signal Generator |
| PROSIS | Programmpaket Statistisches Informationssystem | PRST | Probability Ratio Sequential Test |
| PROSPER | Procedure for Personalizing an envelope program | PRT | Pattern Recognition Technique |
| | | PRT | Portable Remote Terminal |
| PROSPER | Profit Simulation Planning and Evaluation of Risk | PRT | Print |
| | | PRT | Printed Receive Tape |
| PROSPRO | Process Supervisory Program | PRT | Printer |
| | | PRT | Production Run Tape |
| PROSYT | Programmsystem zur Tabellenbearbeitung | PRT | Program Reference Table |
| | | PRT | Protocol |
| PROTEC | Produktionstechnik | PRT | Prozessrechentechnik |
| PROWA | Programm für die Warenwirtschaft im Textilfachhandel | PRT | Pulse Recurrence Time |
| | | PRT | Pulse Repetition Time |
| | | PRTB | Pursue Real-Time BASIC |
| PROWORD | Procedure Word | PRTD | Printed |
| PROXI | Projection by Reflection Optics of Xerographic Images | PRTG | Printing |
| | | PRTIMG | Print Image |
| | | PRTY | Priority |
| PRP | Partial Read Pulse | PRU | Program Research Unit |
| PRP | Peripherspeicherresidentes Programm | PRUNCATS | Program Relay Universal Card Analysis Test System |
| PRP | Prepare | | |
| PRP | Programmed Random Process | PRV | Peak Reserve Voltage |
| | | PRV | Pressure-Reducing Valve |
| PRP | Pseudo-Random Pulse | PRV | Pseudo Register Vector |
| PRP | Pulse Repetition Period | PRVA | Programmable Rotary Vane Attenuator |
| PRPQ | Program Request for Price Quotation | | |
| | | PRVD | Purchase Request for Vendor Data |
| PRPQ | Programming Request for Price Quotation | PRVD | Procurement Request for Vendor Data |
| PRPS | Program Requirement Process Specification | PRW | Per cent Rated Wattage |
| | | PS | Parallel Storage |
| PRPT | Proportion | PS | Parallel Store |
| PRQ | Partition Request Queue | PS | Parallel-to-Serial |
| PRR | Program Request Register | PS | Parity Switch |
| PRR | Program Revision Report | PS | Part Surface |
| PRR | Pulse Repetition Rate | PS | Pause Statement |
| PRRM | Program Review and Resources Management | PS | Pegelsender |
| | | PS | Perform Statement |
| PRS | Pattern Recognition System | PS | Peripheral Storage |
| | | PS | Peripheral Store |
| PRS | Personal Recording System | PS | Permanent Storage |
| | | PS | Permanent Store |
| PRS | Polynomial Remainder Sequence | PS | Phase Shift |
| | | PS | Phase Shifter |
| PRS | Printed Record Storage | PS | Phasensynchronisierung |
| PRS | Program Request System | PS | Physical Sequential |
| PRS | Programmed Radar Simulator | PS | Picosekunde |
| | | PS | Picture Storage |
| PRS | Prozeßrechnersystem | PS | Planning and Scheduling |
| PRS | Pseudo-Random Sequence | PS | Planung und Steuerung |
| PRS | Pseudo-Random-Signal | | |

# P

| | | | |
|---|---|---|---|
| PS | Plattenspeicher | PS | Pull Switch |
| PS | Plotter System | PS | Pulse Shape |
| PS | Point Shifting | PS | Pulse Shaper |
| PS | Polling Signal | PS | Punch Storage |
| PS | Potentiometer Synchron | PS | Punch Store |
| PS | Power Source | PSA | Peripherals Suppliers Association |
| PS | Power Supply | | |
| PS | Presentation Services | PSA | Permanent Storage Area |
| PS | Pressure Switch | PSA | Planning Simulation Accounting |
| PS | Primary Storage | | |
| PS | Print Scan | PSA | Polysilicon Self-Aligned |
| PS | Print Storage | PSA | Power Servo Amplifier |
| PS | Printer Start | PSA | Prefix Save Area |
| PS | Printing Speed | PSA | Primary Store Address |
| PS | Problem Statement | PSA | Problem Statement Analyzer |
| PS | Procedure Signal | | |
| PS | Procedure Statement | PSA | Process Service Area |
| PS | Procedure Subprogram | PSA | Program Study Authorization |
| PS | Process Specification | | |
| PS | Process Storage | PSA | Protected Storage Address |
| PS | Processing State | PSAL | Programming Systems Activity Log |
| PS | Processing Station | | |
| PS | Processor Storage | PSAR | Parts and Supplies Adjustment Request |
| PS | Product Service | | |
| PS | Produktionsplanung und -steuerung | PSAR | Process Storage Address Register |
| PS | Program Scheduling | PSAR | Programmable Synchronous/Asynchronous Receiver |
| PS | Program Section | | |
| PS | Program Segment | | |
| PS | Program Selector | PSARP | Programmable Signal And Response Processor |
| PS | Program Shaft | | |
| PS | Program Shift | PSAS | Programming System Announcement Summary |
| PS | Program Source | | |
| PS | Program Specification | PSAT | Programmable Synchronous/Asynchronous Transmitter |
| PS | Program Start | | |
| PS | Program Stateword | | |
| PS | Program Status | PSB | Process Specification Block |
| PS | Program Storage | | |
| PS | Program Store | PSB | Program Specification Block |
| PS | Program Structure | | |
| PS | Program Summary | PSB | Programmspezifikationsblock |
| PS | Program System | | |
| PS | Programmable Switch | PSBDIR | Program Specification Block Directory |
| PS | Programmiersystem | | |
| PS | Programmierungssprache | PSBGEN | PSG Generation |
| PS | Programming System | PSC | Permanent Split Capacitor |
| PS | Programmschlüssel | PSC | Phase-Sensitive Converter |
| PS | Programmstatus | PSC | Primary Store Capacity |
| PS | Programmsteuerung | PSC | Problem Specification Card |
| PS | Programmsystem | | |
| PS | Projektsteuerungssystem | PSC | Process Schedule Control |
| PS | Proof Stress | PSC | Production Schedule Confirmation |
| PS | Protected Storage | | |
| PS | Protected Store | PSC | Production Scheduling and Control |
| PS | Proton Synchrotron | | |

- 488 -

# P

| | | | |
|---|---|---|---|
| PSC | Program Sequence Control | PSE | Programmierbare Steuereinheit |
| PSC | Program Status Chart | | |
| PSC | Program Structure Code | PSE | Prozedursteuereinheit |
| PSC | Program Support Coordinator | PSF | Pounds per Square Foot |
| | | PSF | Power Separation Filter |
| PSC | Program Switching Center | PSF | Problemspezifische Sprache für diskrete Förderprozesse |
| PSC | Programming Sciences Corporation | | |
| PSC | Pseudo-Store Cell | PSF | Process Signal Former |
| PSC | Public Service Commission | PSF | Prozeßsignalformer |
| PSC | Pulse Shape Control | PSG | Pagelschreibgerät |
| PSCB | Presentation Services Command Processor | PSG | Phosphosilicate Glass |
| | | PSG | Phrase Structure Grammar |
| PSCC | Power System Computation Conference | PSG | Planning System Generator |
| | | PSG | Prask-Structive Grammar |
| PSCE | Peripheral Store Control Element | PSG | Program Systems Guide |
| | | PSG | Programmsteuergerät |
| PSCE | Program Support Customer Engineer | PSG | Pulse Signal Generator |
| | | PSG | Pulse Sweep Generator |
| PSCF | Primary System Control Facility | PSG | Pulsed Strain Gauge |
| | | PSHRPQ | Program Support for Hardware RPQ |
| PSCF | Processor Storage Control Function | PSI | Packet Switching Interface |
| PSD | Phase-Sensitive Demodulator | PSI | Parameter Setting Instruction |
| PSD | Phase-Sensitive Detector | PSI | Parameter Signature Identification |
| PSD | Polysilicon Diode | | |
| PSD | Position Sensitive light Detector | PSI | Peripheral Subsystem Interface |
| PSD | Power Spectral Density | PSI | Permuted Subject Index |
| PSD | Primary Standard Data | PSI | Petit Système Informatique |
| PSD | Procedural Support Data | | |
| PSD | Processing Status Display | PSI | Plan-Speed Indicator |
| PSD | Program Status Document | PSI | Pounds per Square Inch |
| PSD | Programmstatusdoppelwort | PSI | Preprogrammed Self-Instruction |
| PSD | Pulse Shape Discrimination | | |
| PSDB | Physical Segment Descriptor Block | PSI | Problem Solving Information |
| | | PSI | Process System Index |
| PSDN | Packet Switched Data Network | PSI... | Prozess-Steuerungs- und Informationssystem GmbH |
| PSDN | Public Switched Data Network | | |
| | | PSICP | Program Support Inventory Control Point |
| PSDP | Phase Structure and Dependency Parser | | |
| | | PSIEP | Project on Scientific Information Exchange in Psychology |
| PSDR | Process Storage Data Register | | |
| PSE | Packet Switching Exchange | PSIL | Preferred-frequency Speech Interference Level |
| PSE | Please | | |
| PSE | Print Scan Emitter | | |
| PSE | Product Support Engineering | PSIP | Project on Scientific Information in Psychology |
| PSE | Programmierbare Steuereinrichtung | PSIS | Programming Systems Information System |
| PSE | Programm- und Systementwicklung | PSK | Phase-Shift Keyed |

# P

| | | | |
|---|---|---|---|
| PSK | Phase-Shift Keying | PSP | Programmiersprache |
| PSK | Plattenspeicher, Kombiniert | PSPP | Program System Package Plan |
| PSK | Programmsystemkomplex | PSPR | Programmiersprache |
| PSKM | Phase Shift Keying MODEM | PSPS | Program Support Plan Summary |
| PSL | Phase Sequency Logic | PSR | Parts and Supply Requisition |
| PSL | Problem Statement Language | PSR | Prioritäts-Statusregister |
| PSL | Prozessor-Steuer-Liste | PSR | Processor State Register |
| PSLAP | Power Supply Load Analysis Program | PSR | Program Study Request |
| PSM | Peak Selector Memory | PSR | Program Support Requirements |
| PSM | Photo Sensing Mark | PSR | Programm-Silben-Register |
| PSM | Production Systems Management | PSR | Programming Status Report |
| PSM | Program Sensitive Malfunction | PSR | Programming Support Representative |
| PSM | Program Support Management | PSR | Protected Service Routine |
| PSM | Program Support Material | PSRD | Program Support Requirements Documents |
| PSM | Programming System Memorandum | PSRR | Power Supply Rejection Ratio |
| PSM | Programming Systems Manual | PSRR | Product and Support Requirement Request |
| PSM | Proportional Spacing Machine | PSS | Packet Switch Service |
| PSM | Pulse Slope Modulation | PSS | Packet Switch Stream |
| PSM | Pultschreibmaschine | PSS | Packet Switching Service |
| PSMT | Paced Sequential Memory Task | PSS | Packet Switching System |
| | | PSS | Parallel Search Storage |
| PSN | Position | PSS | Passenger Service System |
| PSN | Print Sequence Number | PSS | Patent Search System |
| PSN | Public Switched Network | PSS | Patentsuchsystem |
| PSNR | Power Signal-to-Noise Ratio | PSS | Personal Signalling System |
| PSO | Pilot Systems Operator | PSS | Planungs- und Steuersystem |
| PSOS | P-channel SOS | PSS | Plattenspeichersteuerung |
| PSP | Packet Satellite Program terminal | PSS | Power Supply System |
| PSP | Packet Switching Processor | PSS | Priority Scheduling System |
| | | PSS | Problem Solving State |
| PSP | Peak Sideband Power | PSS | Process Switching Services |
| PSP | Planet Scan Platform | PSS | Produktionssteuerungssystem |
| PSP | Planned Standard Programming | PSS | Programmable Store System |
| PSP | Plattenspeicher | PSS | Programming Systems Support |
| PSP | Power System Planning | PSS | Propulsion Support System |
| PSP | Printing Summary Punch | PSSC | Programmer and Star-tracker Signal Controller |
| PSP | Problem-Solving Program | | |
| PSP | Program Support Plan | PST | Pacific Standard Time |
| PSP | Programm-Struktur-Prozessor | PST | Partition Specification Table |
| PSP | Programmable Signal Processor | PST | Polished Surface Technique |

# P

| | | | |
|---|---|---|---|
| PST | Positive Sign Trigger | PT | Prepunched Tape |
| PST | Priority Selection Table | PT | Primary Timer |
| PST | Program Status Table | PT | Printer Terminal |
| PST | Program Synchronization Table | PT | Printing Tape |
| | | PT | Process Time |
| PST | Programmsteuerung | PT | Product Test |
| PST | Programmstruktur | PT | Program Tab |
| PSTN | Public Service Telephone Network | PT | Program Table |
| | | PT | Program Tape |
| PSTN | Public Switched Telephone Network | PT | Program Termination |
| | | PT | Program Test |
| PSTP | Programmable Strategy Theorem Prover | PT | Program Text |
| | | PT | Program Time |
| PSTP | Programmsystem Teileplanung | PT | Program Track |
| | | PT | Program Transfer |
| PSU | Parallel-Serien-Umsetzer | PT | Program Translation |
| PSU | Port Sharing Unit | PT | Program Transmitter |
| PSU | Power Supply Unit | PT | Programmed Testing |
| PSU | Program Storage Unit | PT | Programmed Timing |
| PSV | Platzscheckverfahren | PT | Programmer Training |
| PSV | Program Status Vector | PT | Programmer and Timer |
| PSVM | Phase Sensitive Voltmeter | PT | Programmierbarer Terminal |
| PSW | Potentiometer Slide Wire | | |
| PSW | Processor Status Word | PT | Programming Theory |
| PSW | Program Status Word | PT | Programming Time |
| PSW | Programmierbares Schaltwerk | PT | Programmtechnik |
| | | PT | Promptor |
| PSW | Programming Status Word | PT | Prüftafel |
| PSW | Programmstatuswort | PT | Prüftaste |
| PSW | Prozessorstatuswort | PT | Pseudotetrade |
| PSWR | Power Standing Wave Ratio | PT | Pulse Time |
| | | PT | Pulse Timer |
| PSY | Programmiersystem | PT | Pulse Train |
| PSYCHE | Programming Systems Yearly Cost Headcount Estimate | PT | Pulse Tranformer |
| | | PT | Punch Transfer |
| | | PT | Punched Tape |
| PSYCO | Peripheral System Checkout | PT CT | Path Count |
| | | PTA | Page Table Address |
| PT | Page Table | PTA | Photo Transistor Amplifier |
| PT | Page Terminator | PTA | Planar Turbulence Amplifier |
| PT | Paper Tape | | |
| PT | Partition Table | PTA | Program Time Analyzer |
| PT | Pencil Tube | PTA | Programmed Translation Array |
| PT | Perforated Tape | | |
| PT | Period Tapering | PTA | Pulse Torquing Assembly |
| PT | Peripheral Transfer | PTAB | Programmzustandstabelle |
| PT | Pilot Tape | PTAT | Proportional To Absolute Temperature |
| PT | Pilot Test | | |
| PT | Pipe Thread | PTB | Page Table Base |
| PT | Point | PTB | Physikalische Technische Bundesanstalt |
| PT | Point courrant | | |
| PT | Point location | PTC | Paper Tape Code |
| PT | Portable | PTC | Paper Tape Control |
| PT | Positional Tolerancing | PTC | Paper Tape-to-card Converter |
| PT | Potential Transformer | | |

# P

| | | | |
|---|---|---|---|
| PTC | Positive Temperature Coefficient | PTI | Plant Transfer In |
| PTC | Power Testing Code | PTI | Punched Tape Information |
| PTC | Process and Test Control | PTIB | Program Testing Information Bulletin |
| PTC | Program Test Controller | PTIL | Parts Test Information List |
| PTC | Programmed Transmission Control | PTIM | Punched Tape Invoicing Machine |
| PTC | Programmer Training Center | PTIOS | Plant Transfer In Operating System |
| PTC | Pulse Time Code | PTJ | Pulse Train Jitter |
| PTC | Punched Tape Card | PTL | Process and Test Language |
| PTC | Punched Tape Check | PTL | Pulse Transmission Logic |
| PTC | Punched Tape Code | PTLS | Program-controlled Train Leading System |
| PTCR | Pad Terminal Connection Room | PTM | Pass Through Mode |
| PTCR | Positive Temperature Co-efficient or Resistance | PTM | Phase-Time Modulation |
| PTCS | Propellant Tanking Computer System | PTM | Photo Tracing Machine |
| | | PTM | Photo-Multiplier |
| PTCU | Punched Tape Control Unit | PTM | Pre-Tuned Module |
| PTD | Paper Tape Date | PTM | Product Test Monitor |
| PTD | Printed | PTM | Program Time Multiplex |
| PTD | Programmable Thermal Desorber | PTM | Program Timing and Maintenance |
| PTDI | Punched Tape Data Input | PTM | Program Timing and Miscellaneous |
| PTDL | Programmable Tapped Delay Line | PTM | Program Trouble Memoranda |
| PTDTL | Pumped Tunnel Diode Transistor Logic | PTM | Program Trouble Memorandum |
| PTE | Page Table Entry | PTM | Programmable Terminal Multiplexor |
| PTE | Peculiar Test Equipment | | |
| PTE | Perforated Tape Exchange | | |
| PTE | Personal Terminal Environment | PTM | Proof Test Model |
| | | PTM | Pulse Time Modulation |
| PTE | Plant Transaction Entry | PTM | Pulse Time Multiplex |
| PTE | Process and Test Equipment | PTM | Punch-Through Modulation |
| | | PTM | Punched Tape Memory |
| PTE | Punched Tape Equipment | PTML | PNPN Transistor Magnetic Logic |
| PTERM | Physical Terminal | | |
| PTERM | Platterminal | PTMOD | Paper Tape Module |
| PTEX | Programmierte Textverarbeitung | PTMS | Pattern Transformation Memory System |
| PTF | Program Temporary Fix | PTO | Permeability Tuned Oscillator |
| PTF | Programmable Transversal Filter | PTO | Plant Transfer Out |
| PTF | Programming Temporary Fixed | PTO | Power Take-Off |
| | | PTO | Punched Tape Output |
| PTF | Punched Tape Feed | PTOP | Program Test and Operations Plan |
| PTFD | Punched Tape Feed Device | | |
| PTG | Personal Training Guide | PTOPC | Program-To-Program Communications |
| PTG | Place To Go | | |
| PTG | Printing | PTOS | Punched Tape Oriented System |
| PTGC | Programmed Temperature Gas Chromatography | | |
| | | PTP | Paper Tape Perforator |
| PTH | Path | PTP | Paper Tape Printer |

- 492 -

# P

| | | | |
|---|---|---|---|
| PTP | Paper Tape Punch | PTS | Pure Time Sharing |
| PTP | Parameter Test Program | PTSP | Proceed-To-Select Protocol |
| PTP | Peak-To-Peak | | |
| PTP | Point To Point | PTT | Paper Tape Transmission |
| PTP | Preferred Target Point | PTT | Paper Tape Typewriter |
| PTP | Print-To-Point | PTT | Parity Test Track |
| PTP | Printing Tape Puncher | PTT | Perforated Tape Transmitter |
| PTP | Program Tape Punch | | |
| PTP | Programmed Text Processing | PTT | Post..... |
| | | PTT | Post, Telegraph and Telephone |
| PTP | Punched Tape Perforator | | |
| PTP | Punched Tape Programming | PTT | Post, Telephone and Telegraph Administration |
| PTP | Punched Tape Punch | PTT | Postes, Télécommunications, Télédiffusion |
| PTPS | Parallel-Tuned/ Parallel-Stabilized | PTT | Postes, Télégraphe et Téléphone |
| PTPU | Program Tape Preparation Unit | PTT | Processing Program Table |
| PTR | Paper Tape Reader | PTT | Program Technical Training |
| PTR | Paper Tape Reading | | |
| PTR | Perforated Tape Reader | PTT | Program Test Tape |
| PTR | Permanent Traffic Recording | PTT | Punched Tape Technique |
| | | PTT | Push To Talk |
| PTR | Photoelectric Tape Reader | PTTC | Paper Tape Transmission Code |
| PTR | Pointer | | |
| PTR | Polar-To-Rectangular | PTTC | Perforated Tape and Transmission Code |
| PTR | Pool Test Reactor | | |
| PTR | Portable Tape Recorder | PTTC | Perforated Tape and Transmission Control |
| PTR | Position Track Radar | | |
| PTR | Printer | PTTC | Public Telephone and Telegraph Codes |
| PTR | Processor Tape Read | | |
| PTR | Program Test Routine | PTU | Paper Tape Unit |
| PTR | Program Trouble Report | PTU | Parallel Transmission Unit |
| PTR | Punch Tape Reader | PTU | PICE Terminal Unit |
| PTR | Punched Tape Recorder | PTU | Programmable Test Unit |
| PTRA | Paper Tape Reader Adapter | PTU | Punched Tape Unit |
| | | PTV | Predetermined Time Value |
| PTRC | Paper Tape Reader Control | PTV | Programmierte Textverarbeitung |
| PTRH | Punched Tape Reading Head | | |
| | | PTV | Punch-Through Varactor |
| PTRP | Paper Tape Reader Punch | PTW | Page Table Word |
| PTS | Paper Tape System | PTW | Programmable Typewriter |
| PTS | Perforated Tape Subsystem | PTWAM | Page Table Word Associative Memory |
| PTS | Permanent Threshold Shift | | |
| PTS | Pneumatic Test Set | PTY | Parity |
| PTS | Power Transient Suppressor | PTY | Priority |
| | | PU | Pegelumsetzer |
| PTS | Proceed To Select | PU | Peripheral Unit |
| PTS | Program Test System | PU | Physical Unit |
| PTS | Programmable Terminal System | PU | Pick-Up |
| | | PU | Pluggable Unit |
| PTS | Programmer Test Station | PU | Port-Unit |
| PTS | Propellant Transfer System | PU | Power Unit |
| PTS | Puffertaktsteuerung | PU | Prefix Update |
| PTS | Punched Tape Speed | PU | Print Unit |

# P

| | |
|---|---|
| PU | Processing Unit |
| PU | Processor Unit |
| PU | Program Unit |
| PU | Programmierte Unterweisung |
| PU | Programmierter Unterricht |
| PU | Programmunterbrechung |
| PU | Propulsion Unit |
| PU | Punch |
| PUA | Physical Unit Address |
| PUB | Physical Unit Block |
| PUB | Public |
| PUBL | Publication |
| PUC | Permanent Unit Code |
| PUC | Plant of Unit Control |
| PUC | Punctured Uniform Code |
| PUCK | Propellant Utilization Checkout Kit |
| PUCP | Physical Unit Control Point |
| PUCP | Process Unit Control Panel |
| PUCR | Plant Unit Cost Report |
| PUCS | Propellant Utilization Control System |
| PUDT | Propellant Utilization Data Translator |
| PUE | Programme d'Unité d'Echange |
| PUF | Physical Update File |
| PUF | Pufferfeld |
| PUFFT | Purdue University Fast FORTRAN Translator |
| PUG | Pascal Users' Group |
| PUI | Physical Unit of Information |
| PUIMP | Pickup Impulse |
| PUJT | Programmable Unijunction Transistor |
| PULL-B-SW | Pull-Button Switch |
| PULM | Programmable Universal Logic Module |
| PULSE | Program of Universal Logic Simulation for Electronics |
| PULSE | Public Urban Locator Service |
| PUMP | Parts Usage Maintenance Program |
| PUMT | Programmable Universal Module Tester |
| PUN | Punch |
| PUNC | Practical, Unpretentious, Nomographic Computer |
| PUNC | Program Unit Counter |
| PUNDIT | Portable Ultrasonic Non-destructive Digital Indicating Tester |
| PUP | Peripheral Unit Processor |
| PUP | Program Unit Punch |
| PUR | Peripheres Unterbrechungsregister |
| PUR | Program Utility Routine |
| PUR | Programm-Umsetzer-Routine |
| PUR | Purge |
| PURDAX | Public Utility Revenue Data Acquisition |
| PURS | Program Usage Replenishment System |
| PUS | Programmunterbrechungssignal |
| PUSI | Peripheral Unit Selection Instruction |
| PUSR | Peripheral Unit Selection Register |
| PUT | Programmable Unijunction Transistor |
| PUT | Programmierbarer Unijunction-Transistor |
| PUTI | Peripheral Unit Test Instruction |
| PUTWS | Put Word in String |
| PUV | Pufferverwaltung |
| PV | Papiervorschub |
| PV | Peak-to-Valley |
| PV | Photovoltaic |
| PV | Positive Volume |
| PV | Precision Visuals |
| PV | Produkt-Vertrieb |
| PVA | Procedure Value Analysis |
| PVAC | Present Value of Annual Charges |
| PVAD | Position Velocity and Attitude Display |
| PVB | Potentiometric Voltmeter Bridge |
| PVC | Permanent Virtual Channel |
| PVC | Permanent Virtual Circuit |
| PVC | Photo Voltaic Cell |
| PVC | Position and Velocity Computer |
| PVC | Potential Volume Change |
| PVC | Punch Validity Check |
| PVD | Plan View Display |
| PVDL | Precision Variable Delay Line |
| PVI | Precision Visuals International |

# P

| | | | |
|---|---|---|---|
| PVM | Paketvermittlungs-prozedurmodul | PWK | Paßwortkatalog |
| PVMS | Paged Virtual Memory System | PWL | Piecewise Linear |
| | | PWL | Power Level |
| PVOR | Precision VHF Omni-directional Range | PWM | Plated Wire Memory |
| | | PWM | Pulse-Width Modulation |
| | | PWM | Pulse-Width Modulator |
| PVP | Program Verification Package | PWM | Pulse-Width Multiplier |
| | | PWM-AF | Pulse-Width Modulated Audio Frequency |
| PVR | Precision Voltage Reference | PWM-FM | Pulse-Width Modulation Frequency Modulation |
| PVS | Performance Verification System | PWMI | Pulse Width-Modulated Inverter |
| PVS | Personal Value System | | |
| PVS | Personen-Verkehrs-System | PWP | Partial Write Pulse |
| PVS | Program Validation Services | PWP | Plain Writing Printer |
| | | PWR | Power |
| PVS | Prozeßvideosystem | PWR | Pressurized Water Reactor |
| PVSt | Paketvermittlungsstelle | PWR | Program Work Requirement |
| PVT | Page View Terminal | | |
| PVT | Pressure-Volume-Temperature | PWR | Programmschaltwerk mit Regelantrieb |
| PVTR | Portable Video Tape Recorder | PWR SPLY | Power Supply |
| | | PWR-AMPL | Power Amplifier |
| PVX | Phosphorous-doped Vapor-deposited oxide | PWR-SUP | Power Supply |
| | | PWR/U | Power Unit |
| PW | Parameter Word | PWS | Plasma Waveguide Switch |
| PW | Pilot Wire | PWS | Private Wire Service |
| PW | Polaritätswechsel | PWS | Professional Workstation |
| PW | Printed Wiring | PWS | Programmer's Workstation |
| PW | Procedure Word | PWS | Programmschaltwerk mit Schrittantrieb |
| PW | Program Word | | |
| PW | Programmwechsel | PWS | Programmwarteschlange |
| PW | Pulse Width | PWS/VSE | Programmer's Work Station/Virtual Storage Extended |
| PWB | Printed Wire Board | | |
| PWB | Printed Wiring Board | | |
| PWB | Programmer's Workbench | PWT | Programmschaltwerk mit Tandemantrieb |
| PWC | Printed Wiring Card | | |
| PWC | Pulse-Width Coded | PWT | Propulsion Wind Tunnel |
| PWC | Pulse-Width Coder | PX | Private Exchange |
| PWC | Pulse-Width Coding | PX | Pulse Stretcher |
| PWD | Power Distributor | PX | Pulse Transformer |
| PWD | Process Word | PXA | Pulsed Xenon Arc |
| PWD | Pulse-Width Detection | PZ | Pegellinienzusatz |
| PWD | Pulse-Width Detector | PZ | Phase Zero |
| PWD | Pulse-Width Discriminator | PZ | Prüfzustand |
| PWE | Pulse-Width Encoder | PZ | Puls Zero |
| PWE | Pulse-Width Encoding | PZBS | Pseudozufällige Binärsignale |
| PWF | Power Warning Feature | | |
| PWF | Present Worth Factor | PZE | Personalzeitermittlung |
| PWI | Pilot Warning Indicator | PZR | Programmzustandsregister |
| PWI | Proximity Warning Indicator | PZR | Prüfzustandssimulationsregister |
| PWIN | Prototype WWMCCS Intercomputer Network | PZT | Piezo-electric Transducer |
| | | PZU | Peripheriezugriff |
| PWIP | Physical Work In Process | | |

# Q

| | | | |
|---|---|---|---|
| Q | Qualifier bit | QCI | Quality Control Information |
| Q | Quality | | |
| Q | Quality factor | QCM | Quantitative Computer Management |
| Q | Quantity of electicity | | |
| Q | Query | QCM | Quartz Crystal Monitor |
| Q | Queue | QCM | Questionnaire à Choix Multiples |
| Q | Queued | | |
| Q | Quotient | QCN | Quibinary Coded Notation |
| Q/A | Question/Answer | QCPLL | Quadrature Channel Phase-Locked-Loop |
| Q/O | Q Zero compiler | | |
| QA | Quality Assurance | QCR | Quality Control Reliability |
| QA | Query Analyzer | QCR | Queue Control Record |
| QA | Quick Acting | QCS | Quality Control Standard |
| QAAS | Quality Assurance Acceptance Standard | QCT | Queue Control Table |
| | | QCT | Quiescent Carrier Telephony |
| QAD | Quality Assurance Data | | |
| QADS | Quality Assurance Data System | QCU | Quick Change Unit |
| | | QCW | Quadrature Continuous Wave |
| QAGC | Quiet Automatic Gain Control | | |
| | | QD | Queue Discipline |
| QAM | Quadrature Amplitude Modulation | QD | Quick Disconnection |
| | | QD | Quick Disk |
| QAM | Question Answering System | QD | Quota Slip |
| | | QDC | Quick Dependable Communications |
| QAM | Queued Access Method | | |
| QAM | Quick Access Memory | QDC | Quick Disconnect Coupling |
| QAP | Quality Assurance Program | QDF | Quartz Crystal Filter |
| | | QDLM | Quartz Delay Line Memory |
| QAR | Quick Access Recording | QDLS | Quartz Delay Line Store |
| QAS | Quick Access Storage | QDM | Quick Disconnect, Miniature |
| QAS | Quick Access Store | | |
| QAVC | Quiet Automatic Volume Control | QDM | Quick Disconnector, Miniature |
| QB | Quick Break | QE | Quantum Efficiency |
| QBE | Query By Example | QE | Quiescence Communication |
| QBG | Qualified Binary Grouping | QEA | Queue Element Area |
| QBIB | Quellbibliothek-Verwaltungsprogramm | QEBR | Quasi Equilibrium Boltzmann Relations |
| QC | Quality Control | QEC | Quick Engine Change |
| QC | Quantum Count | QECB | Queue Element Control Block |
| QC | Quartz Crystal | | |
| QC | Quibinary Code | QED | Quick Editor |
| QC | Quick Connect | QED | Quick-text Editor |
| QC | Quickchange | QEL | Queue Element |
| QC | Quiescence-completed | QEP | Quality Evaluation Program |
| QCAM | Queued Communications Access Method | | |
| | | QEP | Quality Examination Program |
| QCB | Queue Control Block | | |
| QCC | Quality Control Chain | QEW | Quittierter Erstwert |
| QCCARS | Quality Control Collection Analysis and Reporting System | QF | Quality Factor |
| | | QF | Quick Firing |
| | | QFE | Query Formulation and Encoding |
| QCD | Quality Control Data | | |
| QCE | Quality Control Engineering | QFM | Quantized Frequency Modulation |

# Q

| | | | |
|---|---|---|---|
| QFMR | Quantized Frequency Modulation Repeater | QMF | Query Management Facility |
| QFT | Quadriga Fourier Transform | QMI | Quadratic Matrix Inequality |
| QG | Quadrature Grid | QMI | Qualification Maintainability Inspection |
| QGU | Quartärgruppenumsetzer | | |
| QGU | Quartärgruppenumsetzung | QMP | Quarterly Machine Performance |
| QGV | Quantized Gate Video | | |
| QHC | Quarter Half Circle | QMPA | Queue Manager Parameter Area |
| QI | Quarterly Index | | |
| QI | Quiet Ionosphere | QMQB | Quick-Make, Quick-Break |
| QIAC | Quantime Image Analyzing Computer | QMR | Qualitative Material Requirement |
| QIAM | Queued Indexed Access Memory | QMX | Quarternary Matrix |
| | | QNT | Quantizer |
| QIC | Quality Information Center | QO | Quarzoszillator |
| QIC | Quality Insurance Chain | QOD | Quantitative Oceanographic Data |
| QIC | Quantel Interactive Code | | |
| QIC | Quarter Inch Committee | QOD | Quick-Opening Device |
| QIC | Quarter Inch Compatibility | QOH | Quantity On Hand |
| QIC | Quarter-Inch Cartridge drive compatibility | QP | Quadratic Programming |
| | | QP | Quality Product |
| QIL | Quad-In-Line | QP | Quantization Problem |
| QIP | Quad In-line Package | QP | Quartered Partition |
| QIP | Query Interpretation Program | QP | Queue Processor |
| | | QP | Quick Processing |
| QIS | Qualitätsinformationssystem | QPA | Quality Performance Analysis |
| QIS | Quality Insurance System | QPAC | Qualified Productivity Aid for Computing |
| QIS | Quellenorientiertes Informationssystem | QPAM | Quantized Pulsed Amplitude Modulation |
| QISAM | Queued Indexed Sequential Access Method | QPD | Quadrature Phase Detector |
| QIT | Quality Information and Test | QPL | Qualified Products List |
| | | QPM | Quantized Pulse Modulation |
| QL | Quantum Leap | | |
| QL | Query Language | QPP | Quantized Pulse Position |
| QL/I | Query Language One | QPP | Quiescent Push Pull |
| QLAP | Quick Look Analysis Program | QPPM | Quantized Pulse Position Modulation |
| QLDS | Quick Look Data Station | QPRI | Qualitative Personnel Requirements Information |
| QLP | Query Language Processor | | |
| QLP | Quick-Look-Processor | QPSK | Quadrature Phase-Shift Keying |
| QLSM | Quasi-Linear Sequential Machine | QPSK | Quadruple Phase Shift Keying |
| QM | Quadrature Modulation | | |
| QM | Quartz Memory | QPSK | Quaternary Phase Shift Keying |
| QM | Queue Management | | |
| QM | Queue Manager | QQP | Quick Query Program |
| QMB | Quick Make-and-Break | QQS | Quick Query System |
| QMDPC | Quartermaster Data Processing Center | QR | Quality and Reliability |
| | | QR | Quality Requirement |
| QME | Queueing Matrix Evaluation | QR | Quick Reaction |
| | | QR | Quick Response |

# Q

| | | | |
|---|---|---|---|
| QR | Quotient Register | QTP | Qualification Test Procedure |
| QRA | Quality and Reliability Assurance | QTY | Quantity |
| QRA | Quasi-Random Access | QTYOH | Quantity On Hand |
| QRBM | Quasi-Random Band Model | QTYOO | Quantity On Order |
| QRC | Quick Reaction Capability | QTYOR | Quantity Ordered |
| QRCD | Qualitative Reliability Consumption Data | QU | Quartiärgruppen-Umsetzer |
| | | QUAC | Quadratic Arc Computer |
| QRI | Qualitative Requirements Information | QUAD | Quadrant |
| | | QUAL | Qualification |
| QRI | Quick-Reaction Interceptor | QUAL | Qualifier |
| | | QUAL | Quality |
| QRMS | Quasi Root Mean Square | QUAM | Quadrature Amplitude Modulation |
| QRS | Query/Reporting-System | | |
| QRTZ | Quartz | QUAP | Questionnaire Analysis Program |
| QS | Quadratisches Sieb | | |
| QS | Qualification Symbol | QUARK | Question And Response Kit |
| QS | Qualifizierte Software | QUASER | Quantum Amplification by Stimulated Emission of Radiation |
| QS | Qualitätssicherung | | |
| QS | Qualitätssteuerung | | |
| QS | Quality of Service | QUBAL | Queen's University Belfast Algorithmic Language |
| QS | Quartz Store | | |
| QS | Quellensprache | QUDAMP | Queen's University Databank on Atomic and Molecular Physics |
| QS | Queueing System | | |
| QS | Quick Sweep | | |
| QS | Quittieren Sichtmelder | QED | Quick Editor |
| QSA | Quantified System Analysis | QUERY | Question and Enquiry |
| QSAM | Queued Sequential Access Method | QUEST | Quality Electrical Systems Test |
| QSAMOS | Quadruple Self-Aligned Metal Oxide Semiconductor | QUICKTRAN | Quick Translation |
| | | QUIDS | Quick Interactive Documentation System |
| QSC | Quartz Store Capacity | QUIL | Quad-In-Line |
| QSDAM | Queued Sequential Data Access Method | QUIP | Quad-In-line Package |
| | | QUIP | Query Interactive Processor |
| QSM | Quarter-Squares Multiplier | | |
| QSRS | Quasi Stellar Radio Source | QUIP | Questionnaire Interpreter Program |
| QSYSOPR | Q-System-Operator | | |
| QT | Qualification Test | QUIP | Quick Inquiry Processor |
| QT | Quart | QUISAM | Queued Indexed Sequential Access Method |
| QT | Quasi-Transverse | | |
| QT | Queueing Theory | QUOT | Quotient |
| QT | Quittungstaste | QUOTA | Quadrant Online Testing Aid |
| QTAM | Queued Telecommunication Access Method | | |
| | | QUP | Quellenprogramm |
| QTAM | Queued Teleprocessing Access Method | QUPR | Quellenprogramm |
| | | QVL | Querverbindungsleitung |
| QTAM | Queued Transmission Access Method | QVT | Quality Verification Testing |
| QTD | Quadruple Terminal Digits | QWA | Quarter-Wave Antenna |
| QTDAM | Queued Telecommunication Data Access Method | QZ | Quantisiertes Zeichen |
| | | QZF | Quasizufallsfolge |

# R

| | | | |
|---|---|---|---|
| R | Radical | RA | Rapport d'Activité |
| R | Radio | RA | Rational number |
| R | Radius | RA | Read Amplifier |
| R | Random addressing | RA | Receiver Auxiliary relay |
| R | Range | RA | Rechenanlage |
| R | Rasterdruck | RA | Record Address |
| R | Read | RA | Record Automation |
| R | Réaumur | RA | Recording Amplifier |
| R | Received | RA | Register Address |
| R | Receiver | RA | Register Allotter |
| R | Reception | RA | Relative Address |
| R | Rechenwerk | RA | Remote Access |
| R | Rechnung | RA | Repair Action |
| R | Rechter Akkumulator | RA | Repeat to Address |
| R | Record | RA | Restart Address |
| R | Record Automation | RA | Resultatausgabe |
| R | Recording Amplifier | RA | Return Address |
| R | Rectifier | RA | Return Authorization |
| R | Red primary | RA | Right Accumulator |
| R | Redundancy | RA | Right Address |
| R | Redundanz | RA | Running Accumulator |
| R | Regelung | RAA | Radar Aircraft Altitude calculator |
| R | Register | | |
| R | Regulator | RAA | Random Access Addressing |
| R | Relation | RAAP | Residue Arithmetic Associative Processor |
| R | Relay | | |
| R | Reluctance | RAB | Rechnungsausgangsbuch |
| R | Render | RAC | Random Access Controller |
| R | Repeater | RAC | Read Address Counter |
| R | Reprint | RAC | Rectified Alternating Current |
| R | Resistance | | |
| R | Resistor | RAC | Redesigned Altitude Computer |
| R | Rest | | |
| R | Right | RAC | Relative Address Coding |
| R | Roentgen | RACC | Radiation And Contamination Control |
| R | Roger | | |
| R | Routine | RACE | Random Access Computer Equipment |
| R | Rückmeldung | | |
| R | Ruhekontakt | RACE | Random Access Control Equipment |
| R | Rydberg constant | | |
| R & D | Research & Development | RACE | Rapid Automatic Checkout Equipment |
| R&E | Research and Engineering | | |
| R&QA | Reliability and Quality Assurance | RACE | Regional Automatic Circuit Exchange |
| R&S | Research and Statistics | RACE | Remote Automatic Computing Equipment |
| R/C | Radio Command | | |
| R/C | Radio Control | RACE | Research on Automatic Computation Electronics |
| R/C | Range Clearance | | |
| R/Q | Resolver/Quantizer | RACE | Response Analysis for Call Evaluation |
| R/R | Readout and Relay | | |
| R/R | Record/Retransit | RACE | Routine And Cost Estimate |
| R/S | Run/Stop | RACEP | Random Access and Correlation for Extented Performance |
| R/W | Read/Write | | |
| RA | Radar Altimeter | | |
| RA | Random Access | | |

# R

| | | | |
|---|---|---|---|
| RACER | Rapid Card Embedding and Routing | RADACS | Rapid Digital Automatic Computing System |
| RACF | Resource Access Control Facility | RADAL | Radio Detection And Location |
| RACIS | Radar Computer Interaction Simulator | RADANT | Radom Antenna |
| | | RADAR | Radio Detection And Ranging |
| RACKET | Routines for Arithmetic Computation of Key set Evaluation Tables | RADAS | Random Access Discrete Address System |
| RACMAP | Research Analysis Corporation Macro Assembly Program | RADAR | Random Access Dump And Reload |
| | | RADAR | Receivable Accounts Data-entry And Retrieval |
| RACMD | Radio Countermeasures and Deception | RADAT | Radar Data Transmission |
| RACO | Rapid Automatic Checkout | RADAT | Radio Direction And Track |
| RACOM | Random Communication | RADAT | Radiosonde-observation Data |
| RACS | Random Access Control System | RADATA | Radar Automatic Data Transmission Assembly |
| RACS | Remote Access Computing System | RADATA | Radar Data Transmission and Assembly |
| RACS | Remote Automatic Calibration System | RADATAC | Radiation Data Acquisition Chart |
| RACS | Remote Automatic Control System | RADC | Reliability Analysis Data Center |
| RACT | Remote Access Computer Technique | RADC | Rome Air Development Center |
| RACU | Remote Acquisition and Checkout Unit | RADCM | Radar Countermeasures |
| | | RADCON | Radar Data Converter |
| RACUU | Rahmenprogramm für Computerunterstützten Unterricht | RADDAC | Radar Analog Digital Data And Control |
| RAD | Radian | RADDS | Raytheon Automated Digital Design System |
| RAD | Radiation Absorbed Dose | | |
| RAD | Radiation Detector | RADEM | Random Access Delta Modulation |
| RAD | Radiation Dosage | | |
| RAD | Radio | RADEX | Radar Data Extractor |
| RAD | Random Access Data | RADFAC | Radiating Facility |
| RAD | Random Access Disc | RADIAC | Radioactivity Detection, Identification And Computation |
| RAD | Rapid Access Data | | |
| RAD | Rapid Access Disc | | |
| RAD | Rapid Access Drum | RADIAC | Radioactivity Detection, Indication, And Computation |
| RAD | Relative Air Density | | |
| RADA | Random Access Discrete Address | RADIALS | Research And Development Information And Library Science |
| RADAC | Radar Analog Digital data And Control | | |
| RADAC | Rapid Data Collection | RADIC | Redifon Analogue-Digital Computer |
| RADAC | Rapid Digital Automatic Computing | RADIC | Redifon Analogue-Digital Computing |
| RADAC | Raytheon Automatic Drafting Artwork Compiler | RADIC | Research And Development Information Center |
| RADACS | Random Access Discrete Address Communications System | RADICORD | Radar Digitzer and recorder |

# R

| | | | |
|---|---|---|---|
| RADICS... | Research And Development In Computer Systems Ltd | RAID | Random Access Image Device |
| RADIICAL | Retrieval and Automatic Dissemination of Information from Index Chemicus And Line-notation | RAID | Rapid Automatic Inscribing Device |
| | | RAID | Remote Access Interactive Debugger |
| RADINT | Radar Intelligence | RAIDS | Rapid Availability of Information and Data for Safety |
| RADIQUAD | Radio Quadrangle | | |
| RADIR | Random Access Document Indexing and Retrieval | | |
| | | RAIE | Random Access Index Edit |
| RADIST | Radar Distance | RAILS | Remote Area Instrument Landing Sensor |
| RADLE | Responsive Automatic Dial-out and Line-transfer Equipment | | |
| | | RAINDX | Random Access Index edit |
| | | RAINIT | Random Access Initializer |
| RADNOTE | Radio Note | RAIP | Rewe Abrechnungs- und Informationsprogramm |
| RADOME | Radar Dome | | |
| RADOP | Radar Doppler | RAIR | Remote Access Immediate Response |
| RADOP | Radar Operator | | |
| RADOPWEAP | Radar Optical Weapons | RAIR | Random Access Information Retrieval |
| RADOT | Real-time Automatic Digital Optical Tracker | | |
| | | RAK | Relaisausgabe, Kurz-schließbaugruppe |
| RADPLANBD | Radio Planning Board | | |
| RADREL | Radio Relay | RAL | Rapid Access Loop |
| RADRON | Radar squadron | RAL | Regional Adjunct Language |
| RADRU | Rapid Access Data Retrieval Unit | RAL | Register-Ausweis-Leser |
| | | RALF | Rapid Access to Literature via Fragmentation-codes |
| RADS | Random Access Data Store | | |
| RADSIM | Random Access Discrete address system Simulator | RALLOC | Random access Allocation |
| | | RALU | Register and Arithmetic and Logic Unit |
| RADTT | Radio Teletype | | |
| RADVS | Radar Altimeter and Doppler Velocity Sensor | RALU | Register Arithemic Logic Unit |
| RAE | Radio Astronomy Explorer satellite | RALW | Radioactive Liquid Waste |
| | | RAM | Radar Absorbing Material |
| RAE | Random Access Edit | RAM | Radio Attenuation Measurement |
| RAE | Range Azimuth Elevation | | |
| RAE | Right Arithmetic Element | RAM | Random Access Memory |
| RAE | Right Ascension Encoder | RAM | Random Access Method |
| RAEN | Radio Amateur Emergency Network | RAM | Random Adaptive Module |
| | | RAM | Rapid Access Memory |
| RAES | Remote Access Editing System | RAM | Reduced Automaton Matrix |
| RAF | Recoded Address File | RAM | Relaxing Avalanche Mode |
| RAF | Robotique et Automatisation Flexible | RAM | Representative Average Machine |
| RAFT | Radially Adjustable Facility Tube | RAM | Resident Access Method |
| | | RAM | Return Address Memory |
| RAFT | Recomp Algebraic Formula Translator | RAMA | Random Access Memory Accounting |
| RAGS | Routine Analysis, Generation and Simulation | RAMAC | Random Access |
| | | RAMAC | Random Access Memory Accounting |
| RAHM | Random Access Hybrid Memory | | |
| | | RAMAC | Random Access Method of Accounting and Control |
| RAI | Random Access and Inquiry | | |

# R

| | | | |
|---|---|---|---|
| RAMAC | Random Access or Memory Accounting | RANDID | Rapid Alpha Numeric Digital Indicating Device |
| RAMAG | Reliability And Maintainability Action Groups | RANDIS | Random Disc file |
| RAMARK | Radar Marker | RANDIS | Random Disk |
| RAMB | Random Access Memory Buffer | RANDO | Radiotherapy Analog Dosimetry |
| RAMCL | Representative Average Machine Card List | RANR | Recorded Announcement trunk Route |
| RAMD | Random Access Memory Device | RANSAD | Random Access Noise-like Signal Address |
| RAMIS | Rapid Access Management Information System | RAO | Recherche Assistée par Ordinateur |
| RAMM | Random Access Memory Module | RAP | Random Access Program |
| RAMM | Random Access MOS Memory | RAP | Random Access Programming |
| RAMMS | Responsive Automated Material Management System | RAP | Rechner-Anpassungs-Prozessor |
| | | RAP | Rechner-Anschluß-Prozessor |
| RAMP | Radar Masking Parameter | RAP | Redundancy Adjustment of Probability |
| RAMP | Random Access Memory Program | RAP | Reset After Punch |
| RAMP | Reliability, Availability, Maintainability Program | RAP | Resident Assembler Program |
| RAMP | Revenue Analysis of Marketing and Production | RAP | Response Analysis Program |
| | | RAP | Resource Allocation Processor |
| RAMPAC | Random Access Memory Package | RAP | Rocket-Assisted Projectile |
| RAMPART | Radar Advanced Measurements Program for Analysis of Reentry Techniques | RAPAS | Rechnergestütztes Anordnungs-Planungs-System |
| | | RAPCOE | Random Access Programming and Checkout Equipment |
| RAMPS | Resources Allocation and Multi-Project Scheduling | RAPCON | Radar Approach Control center |
| RAMS | Random Access Measurement System | RAPD | Reach through Avalanche Photodiode |
| RAMS | Random Access Memories | | |
| RAMS | Random Access Memory Storage | RAPD | Response Amplitude Probabilitity Data |
| RAMUS | Remote Access Multi-User System | RAPE | Radar Arithmetic Processing Element |
| RAN | Read-Around Numbers | RAPID | Random Access Personnel Information Disseminator |
| RAN | Recorded Announcement | | |
| RAN | Relaisausgabe, Naß | RAPID | Random Access Photographic Index and Display |
| RANCID | Real And Not Corrected Input Data | | |
| RANCOM | Random Communication | RAPID | Rapid Accurate Polynomial Interpolation Device |
| RANDAM | Random Access Non-Destructive Advanced Memory | RAPID | Reactor And Plant Integrated Dynamics |
| RANDANAL | Randomization Analyser | RAPID | Relative Address Programming Implementation Device |
| RANDEP | Rechnender Alphanumerischer Datenerfassungsplatz | | |

# R

| | | | |
|---|---|---|---|
| RAPID | Remote Automatic Parts Input for Dealers | RARI | Reporting, And Routing Instructions |
| RAPID | Research in Automatic Photocomposition and Information Dissemination | RARS | Register Access Ready Set |
| | | RAS | Radio Astronomy Satellite |
| | | RAS | Random Access Storage |
| | | RAS | Random Access Store |
| RAPID | Retrieval of Automatically Processed Information on Drugs | RAS | Rapid Access Storage |
| | | RAS | Rapid Access Store |
| | | RAS | Rectified Air Speed |
| RAPID | Retrieval through Automated Publication and Information Digest | RAS | Reference Address for Small-core-memory |
| | | RAS | Relaisausgabe, Sicherungsbaugruppe |
| RAPID | Rocketdyne Automatic Processing of Integrated Data | RAS | Reliability, Availability, Security |
| RAPID | Rotating Associative Processor for Information Dissemination | RAS | Reliability-Availability-Serviceability |
| | | RAS | Rien A Signaler |
| RAPID | Ryan Automatic Plot Indicator Device | RAS | Row Address Select |
| | | RAS | Rückkehradressenspeicher |
| RAPIDS | Random Access Personnel Information Dissemination System | RASB | Rapid Access to Sequential Blocks |
| | | RASCAL | Rudimentary Adaptive System for Computer-Aided Learning |
| RAPIDS | Rapid Automated Problem Identification System | | |
| RAPIDTRAC | Real-time Automatic Programmed Intersection Digital Traffic Control | RASCH | Rationelle Auftragsschreibung |
| | | RASE | Rapid Automatic Sweep Equipment |
| RAPIT | Record and Process Input Tables | RASER | Radio frequency Amplification by Stimulated Emission of Radiation |
| RAPLOT | Radar Plotting | | |
| RAPPI | Random Access Plan Position Indicator | RASP | Random Access Stored Program |
| RAPPORT | Rapid Alert Programmed, Power-management Of Radar Targets | RASS | Register, Address, Skip and Special chip |
| | | RASSR | Reliable Advanced Solid-State Radar |
| RAPS | Radar Automatic Plotting System | RASTA | Radiation Special Test Apparatus |
| RAPS | Remote Access Power Support system | RASTAC | Random Access Storage And Control |
| RAPS | Retrieval Analysis and Presentation System | RASTAD | Random Access Storage And Display |
| RAPTAP | Random Access Parallel Tape | RASTES | Reliable, Available, Serviceable, Transformable and Efficient Systems |
| RAPTAP | Rapid Access Parallel Tape | | |
| RAR | Rapid Access Recording | | |
| RAR | Reader Address Register | | |
| RAR | Record And Report | | |
| RAR | Return Address Register | RAT | Reading Access Time |
| RAR | ROM Address Register | RAT | Relaisausgabe, Trocken |
| RARA | Random Access to Random Access | RAT | Reliability Assurance Test |
| | | RAT | Routing Automation Technique |
| RARAD | Radar Advisory | | |
| RAREP | Radar weather Report | RATAC | Radar Analog Target Acquisition Computer |

# R

| | | | |
|---|---|---|---|
| RATAC | Radar Target Acquisition | RB | Return to Bias |
| RATAN | Radar And Television Aid to Navigation | RBA | Radar Beacon Antenna |
| | | RBA | Recovery Beacon Antenna |
| RATC | Radar-Aided Tracking Computer | RBA | Rekursiver Binominaler Algorithmus |
| RATC | Rate Aided Tracking Computer | RBA | Relative Block Address |
| | | RBA | Relative Byte Address |
| RATCC | Radar Air-Traffic Control Center | RBA | Remote Batch Address method |
| RATE | Remote Automatic Telemetry Equipment | RBAM | Remote Batch Access Method |
| RATEL | Radiotelephone | RBB | Reset Busy Bit |
| RATEL | Raytheon Automatic Test Equipment Language | RBBP | Remote Batch Business Package |
| RATER | Response Analysis Tester | RBC | Reflected Binary Code |
| RATFOR | Rational FORTRAN | RBDE | Radar Bright Display Equipment |
| RATG | Radiotelegraph | | |
| RATIO | Ratiometer | RBDT | Reverse Blocking Diode Thyristor |
| RATLE | Road Accident Tabulation Language | | |
| | | RBE | Relative Biological Effectiveness |
| RATP | Régie Autonome des Transports Parisiens | RBE | Relative Biological Efficiency |
| RATR | Reliability Abstracts and Technical Review | RBE | Remote Batch Entry |
| | | RBF | Ready Bit Feedback |
| RATRAN | Radar Triangle Navigation | RBI | Request Better Information |
| RATS | Random Access Tape Store | | |
| RATSCAT | Radar Target Scatter | RBI | Require Better Information |
| RATT | Radio-Teletype | RBI | Ripple Blanking Input |
| RAVE | Radar Acquisition Visual-tracking Equipment | RBL | Residual Byte Length |
| | | RBM | Real-time Batch Monitor |
| RAVE | Random Access Viewing Equipment | RBO | Ripple Blanking Output |
| | | RBOD | Required Beneficial Occupance Data |
| RAVE | Rapid Automatic Variable Evaluator | | |
| | | RBP | Registered Business Programmer |
| RAVIR | Radar Video Recording | | |
| RAW | Read After Write | RBP | Remote Batch Processing |
| RAWIN | Radar Wind sounding | RBQ | Request Block Queue |
| RAWRAM | Read And Write Random Access Memory | RBR | Radar Boresight Range |
| | | RBS | Radar Beacon Station |
| RAX | Remote Access Execution | RBS | Random Barrage System |
| RAX | Rural Automatic Exchange | RBS | Read Buffer Storage |
| RAYCOM | Raytheon Computer | RBS | Read-Back Signal |
| RAYDAC | Raytheon Digital Automatic Computer | RBS | Recoverable Booster System |
| RAZ | Remise A Zéro | RBS | Recovered Batch Storage |
| RAZ | Retour A Zéro | RBS | Remote Batch System |
| RAZP | Resettable Automatic Zero Point | RBS | Roboter-Betriebssystem |
| | | RBT | Remote Batch Terminal |
| RB | Radar Beacon | RBT | Resistance Bulb Thermometer |
| RB | Read Back | | |
| RB | Read Buffer | RBU | Remote Buffer Unit |
| RB | Record Block | RBWO | Resonant Backward Wave Oscillator |
| RB | Remote Batch | | |
| RB | Request Block | RC | Radar Control |
| RB | Reset Bit | | |

- 506 -

# R

| | | | |
|---|---|---|---|
| RC | Range Computer | RCB | Record Control Block |
| RC | Range Control | RCB | Record Control Byte |
| RC | Raw Card | RCB | Request Control Block |
| RC | Ray-Control electrode | RCB | Resource Control Block |
| RC | Read Clock | RCBC | Rapid Cycling Bubble Chamber |
| RC | Read and Compute | | |
| RC | Readable Character | RCC | Radio Common Channel |
| RC | Reader Code | RCC | Read Channel Continue |
| RC | Record Carriers | RCC | Read Control Channel |
| RC | Record Code | RCC | Read Control Circuit |
| RC | Record Count | RCC | Reader Common Contact |
| RC | Recording Carrier | RCC | Real-time Computer Complex |
| RC | Redundancy Check | | |
| RC | Redundant Code | RCC | Recovery Control Center |
| RC | Reference Code | RCC | Refinery Computer Control |
| RC | Regional Center | | |
| RC | Register Card | RCC | Regional Computer Center |
| RC | Reinforced Concrete | RCC | Remote Communications Central |
| RC | Relative Coding | | |
| RC | Relay Computer | RCC | Remote Communications Complex |
| RC | Remote Computing | | |
| RC | Remote Control | RCC | Remote Computing Capability |
| RC | Reparaturcode | | |
| RC | Repeat Count | RCC | Resistance-Capacitance Coupling |
| RC | Repetitive Command | | |
| RC | Request Cancel | RCC | Ring Closed Circuit |
| RC | Requirement Computation | RCC | Rod Cluster Control |
| RC | Research Center | RCC | Routing Control Center |
| RC | Reserve Counter | RCCTL | Resistor Capacitor Coupled Transistor Logic |
| RC | Reset Command | | |
| RC | Reset Control | RCD | Record |
| RC | Resistance Capacitance | RCDC | Radar Course Directing Central |
| RC | Resistance-Coupled | | |
| RC | Résistance/Capacité | RCDC | Radiation Chemistry Data Center |
| RC | Resistor Capacitor circuit | | |
| RC | Retrieval Center | RCDCD | Record Code |
| RC | Return Code | RCDCD | Recorded Code |
| RC | Return Command | RCDD | Recorded |
| RC | Reverse Current | RCDG | Recording |
| RC | Reversible Counter | RCDM | Request for Credit or Debit Memorandum |
| RC | Rollback Counter | | |
| RC | Rubber Covered | RCDMS | Reliability Central Data Management System |
| RC... | Regnecentralen | | |
| RCA... | Radio Corporation of America | RCDR | Recorder |
| | | RCE | Rapid Circuit Etch |
| RCAF | Returned Customer Assignment Form | RCE | Remote Control Equipment |
| | | RCEEA | Radio Communications and Electric Engineering Association |
| RCAG | Remote-Controlled Air-Ground communication site | | |
| | | RCEI | Range Communications Electronics Instructions |
| RCAR | Return Code Analysis Routine | | |
| | | RCF | Reader's Comment Form |
| RCAT | Radio-Code Aptitude Test | RCF | Recall Finder |
| RCB | Rationalisation des Choix Budgétaires | RCF | Remote Cluster Facility |
| | | RCHP | Reset Channel Path |

# R

| | | | |
|---|---|---|---|
| RCI | Radar Coverage Indicator | RCS | Reentry Control System |
| RCI | Read Channel Initialize | RCS | Reloadable Control Storage |
| RCI | Referenced Card Index | | |
| RCIA | Remote Control Interface Adapter | RCS | Reloadable Control Store |
| | | RCS | Reloadable Core Storage |
| RCL | Read Clock | RCS | Remote Computing Service |
| RCL | Recalculate | RCS | Remote Computing System |
| RCL | Receive Clock | RCS | Remote Control System |
| RCL | Reclaim | RCS | Reversing Colour Sequence |
| RCM | Radar Countermeasures | RCSG | Restarting Computer and Symbol Generator |
| RCM | Radio Countermeasures | | |
| RCM | Read Clutch Magnet | RCT | Reference Clock Trigger |
| RCM | Reconfiguration Monitor | RCT | Region Control Task |
| RCM | Relay Calculating Machine | RCT | Representative Calculating Time |
| RCM | Revenue Cost Model | | |
| RCM | Rod Cell Memory | RCT | Resistor-Capacitor-Transistor |
| RCN | Record Control Number | | |
| RCO | Reactor Core | RCT | Resolve Control Transformer |
| RCO | Remote Control Office | | |
| RCO | Remote Control Oscillator | RCT | Return Control Transfer |
| RCO | Representative Calculating Operation | RCT | Reverse-Conducting Thyristor |
| RCOM | Remote Communication Message | RCTL | Resistance Coupled Transistor Logic |
| RCOND | Reset Conditional | RCTL | Resistor Capacitor Transistor Logic |
| RCP | Raw Card Plant | | |
| RCP | Recognition and Control Processor | RCTSR | Radio Code Test Speed on Response |
| RCP | Remote Communication Processor | RCU | Relay Control Unit |
| | | RCU | Remote Control Unit |
| RCP | Request for Capital Property | RCU | Resistor Capacitor Unit |
| | | RCUP | Remote Control User Part |
| RCP | Réseau à Commutation de Paquets | RCV | Receive |
| | | RCV | Receiving |
| RCP | Réseau expérimental à Commutation par Paquet | RCV TMOUT | Receive Timeout |
| | | RCVD | Received |
| RCPN | Raw Card Part Number | RCVG | Receiving |
| RCPT | Receipt | RCVR | Receiver |
| RCPT | Reception | RCVY | Recovery |
| RCQ | Record Correction and Quality | RCW | Read, Compute, Write |
| | | RCW | Register Containing Word |
| RCR | Reader Control Relay | RCWP | Rubber-Covered, Weather-Proof |
| RCR | Removal Card Request | | |
| RCR | Required Carrier Return character | RCWV | Rated Continuous Working Voltage |
| RCR | Reverse Current Relay | RCX | Remote Cluster Executive |
| RCS | Radar Cross Section | RD | Radar Data |
| RCS | Radio Command System | RD | Radar Display |
| RCS | Range Corrector Setting | RD | Radiation Detection |
| RCS | Reaction Control Subsystem | RD | Random Data |
| | | RD | Range Data |
| RCS | Reaction Control System | RD | Ratio Detector |
| RCS | Real Core Supervisor | RD | Rauschdiode |
| RCS | Rearward Communications System | RD | Raw Data |
| | | RD | Read |

# R

| | | | |
|---|---|---|---|
| RD | Read Data | RDDP | Response Document Discard Positive |
| RD | Read Delay | | |
| RD | Received Data | RDE | Radar Display Equipment |
| RD | Réception des Données | RDE | Radial Defect Examination |
| RD | Recognition Differential | RDE | Reliable Data Extractor |
| RD | Rectifier Diode | RDEC | Request for Documents for an Engineering Change |
| RD | Reduce | | |
| RD | Reference Data | RDEP | Response Document End Positive |
| RD | Register Drive | | |
| RD | Register Driver | RDEVQ | Reset Device Queue |
| RD | Relay Driver | RDF | Radar Direction Finder |
| RD | Relocatable Directory | RDF | Radio Direction Finder |
| RD | Request Descriptor | RDF | Radio Direction Finding |
| RD | Research and Development | RDF | Read Data Flow |
| RD | Restricted Data | RDF | Record Definition Field |
| RD | Retrieval Device | RDF | Recursive Digital Filter |
| RD | Rewind Device | RDF | Relational Data File |
| RD | Routine Definition | RDF | Repeater Distribution Frame |
| RD CHK | Read Check | | |
| RDA | Reliability Design Analysis | RDG | Reading |
| | | RDG | Reducing |
| RDA | Rufdatenaufzeichnung | RDG | Resolver Differential Generator |
| RDA | Run-time Debugging Aid | | |
| RDAA | Range Doppler Angle/Angle | RDGR | Response Document General Reject |
| RDAS | Reflectivity Data Acquisition System | RDH | Remote Device Handler |
| RDAU | Remote Data Acquisition Unit | RDHS | Realzeit-Datenhaltungs-System |
| RDB | Radar Decoy Balloon | RDI | Released Data Index |
| RDB | Reference Data and Bias | RDI | Remote Data Input |
| RDB | Route Data Block | RDI | Remote Display Interface |
| RDBA | Remote Data Base Access | RDI | Retrieval of Digital Information |
| RDBK | Read Back | | |
| RDBL | Readable | RDL | Report Definition Language |
| RDBMS | Relational Data Base Management System | RDL | Resistance Diode Logic |
| RDC | Read Data Channel | RDM | Read from Memory |
| RDC | Receive Data Condition | RDM | Recording Demand Meter |
| RDC | Reduce | RDM | Remote Digital Multiplexer |
| RDC | Redundant Digit Check | | |
| RDC | Reliability Data Central | RDMS | Relational Data Model System |
| RDC | Reliability Data Control | | |
| RDC | Remote Data Collection | RDMU | Range Drift Measuring Unit |
| RDC | Remote Data Concentrator | | |
| RDC | Rufdecodierer | RDN | Redundancy |
| RDCD | Read Card | RDNG | Reading |
| RDCF | Restricted Data Cover Folder | RDO | Radio Readout |
| | | RDO | Readout |
| RDCLP | Response Document Capability List Positive | RDO | Rechnungswesen Daten-technik Organisation |
| RDCN | Reduction | RDOS | Real-Time Disc Operating System |
| RDCR | Reducer | | |
| RDD | Read Direct | RDOUT | Readout |
| RDD | Read Disconnect Delay | RDP | Radar Data Processing |
| | | RDP | Radiosonde Data Processor |

# R

| | | | |
|---|---|---|---|
| RDP | Remote Data Processing | RE | Rate Effect |
| RDP | Remote Data Processor | RE | Read Emitter |
| RDP | Research Data Publication | RE | Read End |
| RDPB | Radar Data Plotting Board | RE | Read Error |
| RDPBN | Response Document Page Boundary Negative | RE | Reading Error |
| | | RE | Real number |
| RDPBP | Response Document Page Boundary Positive | RE | Rechner |
| | | RE | Rechnungseingang |
| RDPC | Radar Data Processing Center | RE | Recording Error |
| | | RE | Recursively Enumerable |
| RDPE | Radar Data Processing Equipment | RE | Reentry |
| | | RE | Regelelement |
| RDPM | Random Data Processing Machine | RE | Regular Expression |
| | | RE | Reset |
| RDPS | Radar Data Processing System | RE | Royal Engineers |
| | | REA | Redundant Error Amplifier |
| RDR | Radar | REA | Request for Engineering Action |
| RDR | Read form ROM | | |
| RDR | Reader | REAC | Reeves Electronic Analog Computer |
| RDR | Reliability Diagnostic Report | | |
| | | REACT | Record Evaluate And Control Time system |
| RDR | Ruf-Daten-Rechner | | |
| RDRF | Receive Data Register Full | REACT | Register Enforced Automated Control Technique |
| RDRINT | Radar Intermittent | | |
| RDRP | Response Document Resynchronisation Positive | REACT | Report Evaluation And Calculation Tool |
| RDRXMTR | Radar Transmitter | READ | Real-time Electronic Access and Display |
| RDS | Radio-Daten-System | | |
| RDS | Raytheon Data Systems | READ | Remote Electronic Alphanumeric Display |
| RDS | Remote Disk Station | | |
| RDS | Requirements Data System | READCOMM | Read Communication |
| RDT | Remote Data Transmitter | READI | Rocket Engine Analyzer and Decision Instrumentation |
| RDT | Research, Development and Test | | |
| RDT | Resource Definition Table | REAL | Resource Allocation |
| RDT | Rework Data Tape | REAM | Retrieval of Engineering Aperture Masters |
| RDT&E | Research, Development, Test and Evaluation | | |
| | | REB | Radar Evaluation Branch |
| RDTL | Resistor Diode Transistor Logic | REBI | Rechenbetrieb Binnenhandel |
| RDTS | Remote Data Transmission Subsystem | REC | Receipt |
| | | REC | Receive |
| RDTSR | Rapid Data Transmission System for Requisitioning | REC | Receiver |
| | | REC | Record |
| | | REC | Recorder |
| RDU | Remote Display Unit | REC | Recording |
| RDVP | Radar Video-data Processor | REC | Rectifier |
| | | REC | Request for Engineering Change |
| RDW | Record Descriptor Word | | |
| RDY | Ready | REC MARK | Record Mark |
| RE | Radiated Emission | RECA | Repetitive Element Column Analysis |
| RE | Radiation Effects | | |
| RE | Radio Exposure | RECD | Received |
| RE | Randeinheit | RECD | Record |
| RE | Rare Earths | RECG | Radioelectrocardiograph |

# R

| | |
|---|---|
| RECIPE | Recomp Computer Interpretive Program Expediter |
| RECMD | Reset at End of Command |
| RECMF | Radio and Electronic Component Manufacturer's Federation |
| RECO | Receive Only |
| RECOMP | Recomplement |
| RECOMP | Redstone Computer |
| RECOVER | Realize Effective Continuous Operation Via Error Response |
| RECR | Receiver |
| RECP | Receptacle |
| RECRAS | Retrieval-system for Current Research of Agricultural Science |
| RECSTA | Receiving Station |
| RECVD | Received |
| RECVE | Receive |
| RED | Read Error Diagnostics |
| RED | Reducing |
| REDA | Relais-Digital-Ausgabe |
| REDA | Relaisausgänge und Elektronische Digital-Ausgänge |
| REDAC | Racal Electronics Design and Analysis by Computer |
| REDAP | Reentrant Data Processing |
| REDCAP | Reliability Evaluation and Dynamic Checkout Assistance Program |
| REDE | Receiver-Decoder |
| REDE | Receiver-decoder-Demultiplexer |
| REDI | Real Estate Data, Incorporated |
| REDIT | Random access Edit |
| REDLARS | Reading Literature Analysis and Retrieval Service |
| REDN | Reduction |
| REEG | Radioelektron-encephalograph |
| REENG | Remote Engineering |
| REEP | Regression Estimation of Event Probabilities |
| REEP | Range Estimating and Evaluation Procedure |
| REF | Range Error Function |
| REF | Reference |
| REF | Referenzdaten |
| REFE | Rechenfeld |
| REFLECS | Retrieval From the Literature on Electronics and Computer Sciences |
| REFORS | Replacement Forecasting System |
| REFSMMAT | Reference Stable Member Matrix |
| REFSYS | Reference System |
| REFÜ | Rechnungsführung |
| REG | Register |
| REG | Registration |
| REG | Registry |
| REG | Regression analysis |
| REG | Regulator |
| REGAL | Range and Evaluation Guidance for Approach and Landing |
| REGAL | Remote Generalized Application Language |
| REGIS | Register |
| REGIS | Remote Graphic Instruction Set |
| REGRA | Regressionsanalyse |
| REI | Recognition Equipment, Incorporated |
| REI | Request for Engineering Investigation |
| REIC | Radiation Effects Information Center |
| REINS | Requirements Electronic Input System |
| REIS | Readiness Information System |
| REJ | Reject |
| REKOAN | Rechnergestützte Konstruktion von Antrieben |
| REKONE | Rechnergestützte Konstruktion Elektrischer Antriebe |
| REL | Rapidly Extensible Language |
| REL | Rate of Energy Loss |
| REL | Relais |
| REL | Relation |
| REL | Relay |
| REL | Release |
| RELCODE | Relative Code |
| RELCOMP | Reliability Computation |
| RELOG | Relais und Logik |
| REM | Rapid Eye Movement |
| REM | Recognition Memory |
| REM | Reliability Engineering Model |
| REMAD | Remote Magnetic Anomaly Detection |

# R

| | | | |
|---|---|---|---|
| REMAS | Regie Makler-Software | RES | Resistor |
| REMC | Resin Encapsulated Mica Capacitor | RES | Restore |
| | | RESB | Reverse Erased Second Breakdown |
| REMCAM | Repairable Multilayer Circuit Assembly Method | RESCAN | Reflecting Satellite Communications Antenna |
| REMG | Radioelectro-myocardiograph | RESDAT | Restricted Data |
| REMIS | Real Estate Management Information System | RESER | Reentry System Evaluation Radar |
| REMIT | Research Effort Management Information Tabulation | RESET | Resetting |
| | | RESEX | Resource Executive |
| | | RESFLD | Residual Field |
| REMSTAR | Remote Electronic Microfilm Storage Transmission And Retrieval | RESI | Reaktionssicherheit |
| | | RESI | Reservierungssystem Interflug |
| REN | Remote Enable | RESOLN | Resolution |
| RENDIS | Rechnergestützter Entwurf Digitaler Steuerungen | RESOLUT | Resolution |
| | | RESP | Remote-batch Station Program |
| RENM | Ready for Next Message | | |
| REO | Regenerated Electrical Output | RESPOND | Retrieval, Entry, Storage, and Processing of Online Network Data |
| REOT | Right-End-Of-Tape | | |
| REP | Range Error Probable | RESRVN | Reservation |
| REP | Repeat | RESS | Radar Echo Simulation Subsystem |
| REP | Request for Proposal | | |
| REP-OP | Repetitive Operation | REST | Reentry Environment and Systems Technology |
| REPERF | Reperforator | | |
| REPIS | Reserve Personnel management Information System | REST | Restricted radar Electronic Scan Technique |
| REPL | Replace | REST | Restore |
| REPPAC | Repetitive Pulses Plasma Accelerator | RESTR | Restorer |
| | | RET | Relative Excess Time |
| REPROM | Reprogrammable Memory | RET | Return |
| REPROM | Reprogrammable Read-Only Memory | RETA | Retrieval of Enriched Textual Abstracts |
| REPT | Repeat | RETAIN | Remote Technical Assistance and Information Network |
| REPTD | Repeated | | |
| REQ | Request | | |
| REQ | Require | RETIF | Réseau Téléinformatique Ferroviaire |
| REQD | Required | | |
| REQEX | Request Execute | RETN | Retain |
| REQP | Recursive Equality Quadratic Programming | RETOP | Real-Time Optimizing Program |
| RER | Residual Error Rate | RETP | Retape |
| RER | Reverse Error Reporting | RETSA | Real Time Spectral Analysis |
| REREX | Remote Readout Experiment | RETSPL | Reference Equivalent Threshold Sound Pressure Level |
| RERL | Residual Equivalent Return Loss | | |
| RES | Remote Entry Services | REU | Remote Entry Unit |
| RES | Remote Entry Subsystem | REV | Reentry Vehicle |
| RES | Remote Entry System | REV | Reverse |
| RES | Reserve | REV | Review |
| RES | Reset | REV | Revolution |
| RES | Resistance | REV CUR | Reverse Current |

# R

| | | | |
|---|---|---|---|
| REV/MIN | Revolutions per Minute | RFI | Radio Frequency Interference |
| REVOCON | Remote Volume Control | | |
| REVOP | Random Evolutionary Operation | RFI | Ready For Issue |
| | | RFI | Remote File Inquiry |
| REVS | Rotor Entry Vehicle System | RFI | Request For Information |
| | | RFL | Rotating Field Logic |
| REW | Read, Execute, Write | RFM | Reactive Factor Meter |
| REW | Rechenwerk | RFNA | Radio Frequency Noise Analyzer |
| REW | Rewind | | |
| REWDAC | Retrieval by title Words, Discriptors And Classification | RFNM | Ready For Next Message |
| | | RFO | Radio Frequency Oscillator |
| | | RFP | Request For Parts |
| REX | Real-time Executive | RFP | Request For Price |
| REX | Route Extension | RFP | Request For Proposal |
| RF | Radio Frequency | RFQ | Request For Quotation |
| RF | Range Finder | RFR | Reject Failure Rate |
| RF | Rating Factor | RFS | Radio-Frequency Shift |
| RF | Reactive Factor | RFS | Ready For Sending |
| RF | Read Forward | RFS | Ready For Service |
| RF | Reading Function | RFS | Rendering Floating and Set |
| RF | Rechnerfamilie | RFSP | Rigid Frame Selection Program |
| RF | Record Format | | |
| RF | Recorder File | RFST | Rapid Frequency Settling Time |
| RF | Report File | | |
| RF | Reserve Free | RFT | Radio Frequency Transformer |
| RF | Resistance Factor | | |
| RF | Result Field | RFT | Recursive Function Theory |
| RF SAT | Radio Frequency Saturation | RFT | Request For Test |
| | | RFW | Read Full Word |
| RFA | Radio Frequency Amplifier | RFW | Reversible Full-Wave |
| RFA | Register Field Address | RFWAC | Reversible Full-Wave Alternating Current |
| RFA | Remote File Access | | |
| RFB | Reliability Functional Block | RFWDC | Reversible Full-Wave Direct Current |
| RFC | Radio Frequency Charts | RG | Radar Guidance |
| RFC | Radio Frequency Choke | RG | Radio Guide |
| RFC | Radio Frequency Coil | RG | Range |
| RFC | Report Format Control | RG | Rangierbaugruppe |
| RFCP | Radio-Frequency Compatibility Program | RG | Rate Gyroscope |
| | | RG | Record Gap |
| RFD | Ready For Data | RG | Recording |
| RFD | Reentry Flight Demonstration | RG | Register |
| | | RG | Report Generator |
| RFE | Rechnergesteuerte Fahrausweiserstellung | RG | Reset Gate |
| | | RG | Residue Generator |
| RFEI | Request For Engineering Information | RG | Reverse Gate |
| | | RG(N) | Register (N) stages |
| RFFD | Radio Frequency Fault Detection | RGA | Rate Gyro Assembly |
| | | RGA | Remote Gain Amplifier |
| RFG | Radar Field Gradient | RGA | Ring Again |
| RFG | Ramp Function Generator | RGB | Red, Green, Blue |
| RFG | Receive Format Generator | RGB | Rot/Grün/Blau |
| RFI | Radio Frequency Interchange | RGE | Range |
| | | RGEN | Regenerate |

# R

| | | | |
|---|---|---|---|
| RGL | Report Generator Language | RHU | Reserved for Hardware Use |
| RGLR | Regulator | RHW | Right Half Word |
| RGM | Recorder Group Monitor | RHWAC | Reversible Half Wave Alternating Current |
| RGNCD | Region Code | | |
| RGP | Radar Glider Positioning | RI | Radar Input |
| RGP | Rate Gyro Package | RI | Radar Intercept |
| RGR | Rechnergeführte Regelung | RI | Radio Influence |
| RGR | Routing Register | RI | Radio Interference |
| RGS | Radio Guidance System | RI | Rapport d'Intervention |
| RGS | Rate Gyro System | RI | Read Instruction |
| RGT | Resonant Gate Transistor | RI | Read-In |
| RGT | Right | RI | Record Input |
| RGTR | Register | RI | Reflective Insulation |
| RGU | Rechnergestützter Unterricht | RI | Register Immediate |
| | | RI | Reliability Index |
| RGZ | Recommended Ground Zero | RI | Repetitive Instruction |
| | | RI | Resistance Inductance |
| RGZ | Reorganize | RI | Return Instruction |
| RH | Radiological Health | RI | Reverse Image |
| RH | Read Head | RI | Richtungskennzeichen |
| RH | Receiver Hopping mode | RI | Ring Indicator |
| RH | Relative Humidity | RI | Rotating Inventory |
| RH | Report Heading | RI | Routing Identifier |
| RH | Request Header | RIA | Research Institute of America |
| RH | Response Header | | |
| RH | Right Hand | RIA | Reset Indicators from Accumulator |
| RH | Running Hour | | |
| RHAW | Radar Homing And Warning | RIA | Robot Institute of America |
| | | RIACT | Retrieval of Information About Census Tapes |
| RHC | Right Hand Components | | |
| RHCP | Righthand Circular Polarization | RIB | Read Interrupt Buffer |
| | | RIB | Recheninstitut für das Bauwesen |
| RHD | Radar Horizon Distance | | |
| RHD | Radioactive Health Data | RIB | Relevé d'Identité Bancaire |
| RHE | Radiation Hazard Effects | RIC | Radar Input Control |
| RHEED | Reflected High Energy Electron Diffraction | RIC | Reciprocal Impedance Converter |
| RHEO | Rheostat | RIC | Record Identification Code |
| RHI | Radar Height Indicator | RIC | Registered IBM Confidential |
| RHI | Rang Height Indicator | | |
| RHIN | Réseaux Hétérogènes Informatiques Normalisés | RIC | Request for Interplant Commitment |
| RHM | Right-Hand polarized Mode | RIC | Resistor Inductor Capacitor |
| RHO | Remote Host Option | | |
| RHOGI | Radar Homing Guidance | RIC | Revolving Inventory Count |
| RHP | Reduced Hard Pressure | RIC | Rotating Inventory Control |
| RHR | Rejectable Hazard Rate | RICASIP | Research Information Center and Advisory Service on Information Processing |
| RHRZ | Regionales Hochschulrechenzentrum | | |
| RHS | Right Hand Side | | |
| RHSO | Rechenzentren der Hessischen Sparkassenorganisation | RICE | Regional Information and Communication Exchange |
| | | RICS | Range Instumentation and Control System |
| RHT | Release Hardware Test | | |

# R

| | | | |
|---|---|---|---|
| RID | Rechnerinterne Darstellung | RIO | Reconfiguration of Input/Output |
| RID | Report-Identifikationsnummer | RIO | Reporting In and Out |
| RIDL | Referential Idea Language | RIO | Resume Input/Output |
| RIDS | Reset Information Data Set | RIOS | Remote Input/Output System |
| RIE | Radio Interference Elimination | RIOT | Real-time Input/Output Transducer |
| RIE | Radio Interference Eliminator | RIOT | Real-time Input/Output Translator |
| RIE | Reactive Ion Etching | RIOT | Remote Input/Output Terminal |
| RIE | Réseau Informatique Européen | RIOT | Retrieval of Information by On-line Terminal |
| RIE | Royal Institute of Engineers | RIP | Random Inspection Program |
| RIF | Radio Influence Field | RIP | Real-time Integrated-control Processor |
| RIF | Reliability Improvement Factor | RIP | Receipt In Process |
| RIFI | Radio Interference Field Intensity | RIP | Register Indicator Panel |
| RIGFET | Resistive Insulated-Gate Field Effect Transistor | RIPFCOMTF | Rapid Item Processor to Facilitate Complex Operations on Magnetic Tape Files |
| RII | Record Identifying Indicator | | |
| RIIM | Reset Individual Interrupt Mask | RIPS | Range Instrumentation Planning Study |
| RIL | Radio Interference Level | RIQS | Remote Information Query System |
| RIL | Red Indicator Lamp | | |
| RIM | Radar Input Mapper | RIR | Read-only memory Instruction Register |
| RIM | Read In Mode | | |
| RIM | Rechnerinternes Modellabbild | RIR | Relative Indexregister |
| RIM | Referenz-Informations-Management | RIR | Reporting Interface Record |
| RIM | Request Initialization Mode | RIR | Ribbon-to-Ribbon |
| | | RIRMS | Remote Information Retrieval and Management System |
| RIM | Resource Interface Module | | |
| RIMM | Reset Immediate | RIRS | Reliability Information Retrieval System |
| RIMP | Remote Input Message Processor | | |
| | | RIS | Range Instrumentation Ship |
| RIMS | Record Information Movement Study | RIS | Rechnergestütztes Informationssystem |
| RIMS | Regional Information Management System | RIS | Record Input Subroutine |
| | | RIS | Relationales Index-System |
| RIMS | Remote Information Management System | RIS | Requirements planning and inventory control System |
| RIN | Register In | | |
| RIN | Register Instruction | | |
| RIN | Regular Inertial Navigator | RIS | Research Information Service |
| RIN | Resource Identification Number | RIS | Reset Indicators from Storage |
| RINAL | Radar Inertial Altimeter | | |
| RIND | Research Institute of National Defense | RIS | Resistor Insulator Semiconductor |
| RINT | Radar Intermittent | RIS | Rest to Initial State |

- 515 -

# R

| | | | |
|---|---|---|---|
| RIS | Revolution Indicating System | RKW | Rationalisierungs-kuratorium der Deutschen Wirtschaft |
| RISC | Reduced Instruction Set Computer | RKZ | Registerkennzeichnung |
| RISC | Remote Information Systems Center | RL | Radiation Laboratory |
| | | RL | Reactive Loss |
| RIST | Radar Installed System Tester | RL | Reading List |
| | | RL | Rechenlocher |
| RIT | Radio Information Test | RL | Rechnerlogik |
| RIT | Receiving and Inspection Test | RL | Record Length |
| | | RL | Reference Language |
| RIT | Release Information Tape | RL | Reference Line |
| RITA | Rand Intelligent Terminal Agent | RL | Relay Logic |
| | | RL | Relocatable Library |
| RITA | Réseau Intégré de Transmission Automatique | RL | Relocation |
| | | RL | Remote Location |
| RITA | Road Information Transmitted Aurally | RL | Remote Loop |
| | | RL | Research Laboratory |
| RITD | Réseau Intégrant la Téléphonie et les Données | RL | Resistor Logic |
| | | RL | Return Loss |
| RITE | Rapid Information Technique for Evaluation | RL | Routine Library |
| | | RL | Rückwärtslesen |
| RITS | Remote Input Terminal System | RLA | Remote Loop Adapter |
| | | RLC | Radio Launch Control system |
| RIU | Remote Inquiry Unit | | |
| RIV | Retrospective Informationsvermittlung | RLC | Receive Logic Chassis |
| | | RLD | Relocation Dictionary |
| RIVAL | Rapid Insurance Valuation Language | RLD | Relocation List Dictionary |
| | | RLE | Rate of Loss of Energy |
| RJE | Remote Job Entry | RLE | Réseau Local d'Entreprise |
| RJIS | Regional Justice Information System | RLE | Réseau Local d'Etablissement |
| RJP | Remote Job Processing | RLF | Record Length Field |
| RJS | Return Jump Statement | RLF | Release Form |
| RK | Randlochkarte | RLF | Release Line Feed |
| RK | Rauschklirrmeßplatz | RLIS | Rechnergestütztes Leitungs-Informationssystem |
| RK | Rechnerkern | | |
| RK | Rechnerkopplung | | |
| RK | Regelkreis | RLK | Randlochkarte |
| RK | Remote-Konzentrator | RLL | Real Logic List |
| RK | Reset Key | RLL | Recall |
| RKA | Regressions- und Korrelationsanalyse | RLL | Run Length Limited |
| | | RLM | Resident Load Module |
| RKD | Read Key Data | RLP | Requirements Language Processor |
| RKG | Radioelectrokardiograph | | |
| RKINFSYS | Rock Information System | RLS | Release |
| RKL | Rufkontrollampe | RLS DEST | Release Destination |
| RKO | Range Keeper Operator | RLS SRC | Release Source |
| RKP | Relative Key Position | RLSD | Receive Line Signal Detection |
| RKR SW | Rocker Switch | | |
| RKS | Rückspulen | RLTS | Radio Linked Telemetry System |
| RKSE | Rückspulen/Entladen | | |
| RKTS | Robot Keyboard Testing System | RLU | Recovery Log Unit |
| | | RLU | Relay Logic Unit |
| | | RLY | Relay |

# R

| | | | |
|---|---|---|---|
| RM | Radio Monitoring | RML | Read Major Line |
| RM | Range Market | RML | Research Machines Limited |
| RM | Rapid Memory | | |
| RM | Reading Machine | RMM | Read-Mostly Memory |
| RM | Readout Matrix | RMOS | Real Memory Operating System |
| RM | Real Matrix | | |
| RM | Really Memory | RMOS | Realtime Multitasking Operation System |
| RM | Rechenmaschine | | |
| RM | Recognition Matrix | RMOS | Refractory Metal Oxide Semiconductor |
| RM | Record Mark | | |
| RM | Recording Medium | RMR | Remote Meter Reading |
| RM | Rectangular Module | RMR | Request Mode Register |
| RM | Reference Manual | RMS | Random Mass Storage |
| RM | Reference Mark | RMS | Raster Memory system |
| RM | Referenz-Modell | RMS | Recovery Management Support |
| RM | Regular Matrix | | |
| RM | Remote | RMS | Remote Maintenance Service |
| RM | Remote Multiplexer | | |
| RM | Response Message | RMS | Remote Multiplexer System |
| RM | Return on Minus | | |
| RM | Rhein-Main-Rechenzentrum | RMS | Resource Manager System |
| | | RMS | Root Mean Square |
| RM | Rod Memory | RMS | Rückmeldesystem |
| RM | Routing Matrix | RMSE | Root-Mean-Square Error |
| RM | Rückmeldesignal | RMSR | Recovery Management Support and Recording |
| RMA | Rapid Memory Address | | |
| RMA | Remote Maintenance Analysis | RMSR | Recovery Management Support Recorder |
| RMA | Remote Management Agent | RMTBF | Reciprocal Mean Time Between Failure |
| RMA | Rental Machine Asset | RMU | Remote Maneuvering Unit |
| RMA | Request for Manufacturing Action | RMU | Remote Measuring Unit |
| | | RMV | Remove |
| RMAR | Returned Material Activity Report | RN | Radio Noise |
| | | RN | Random Number |
| RMC | Record Mark Control | RN | Rechnernetz |
| RMC | Relay Mode Control | RN | Record Name |
| RMC | Remote Manual Control | RN | Reference Noise |
| RMC | Remote Message Concentrator | RN | Report Name |
| | | RN | Rufnummer |
| RMC | Rod Memory Computer | RNAW | Rufnummernauswerter |
| RMD | Rangier-Moduln Digital | RNC | Return on No Carry |
| RMDR | Remainder | RNF | Radio Noise Figure |
| RMER | Return Material and Equipment Report | RNF | Receiver Noise Figure |
| | | RNG | Radio Range |
| RMF | Resource Measurement Facility | RNG COMP | Range Computer |
| | | RNIS | Réseau Numérique à Integration de Services |
| RMF | Routing Master File | | |
| RMI | Radio-Magnetic Indicator | RNIS | Réseau Numérique avec Intégration des Services |
| RMI | Registre de Mémoire Intermédiaire | | |
| | | RNIT | Radio Noise Interference Test |
| RMI | Roll Mode Interrogation | | |
| RMIS | Resource Management Information System | RNM | Rename |
| | | RNP | Random Number Processing |
| RML | Radar Microwave Link | | |

- 517 -

# R

| | | | |
|---|---|---|---|
| RNP | Remote Network Processor | ROCKET | Rand's Omnibus Calculator of the Kinetics of Earth Trajectories |
| RNP | Ringing Number Pick-up | | |
| RNPG | Ringing Number Pick-up Group | ROCOMP | Read Out Complete |
| RNR | Receive Not Ready | ROCP | Radar Out of Commission for Parts |
| RNR | Ring Number Read | | |
| RNS | Recherche du Numéro de Séquence | ROCP | Remote Operator Control Panel |
| RNS | Residue Number System | ROCR | Remote Optical Character Recognition |
| RNV | Radio Noise Voltage | | |
| RNW | Rechnernetzwerk | ROCS | Remote Online Communication System |
| RNW | Ring Number Write | | |
| RNX | Restricted Numeric Exchange | ROD | Record On Demand |
| | | ROD | Regional Operational Data |
| RO | Radar Operator | ROD | Required Operational Data |
| RO | Range Operation | RODATA | Registered Organization Data |
| RO | Read Only | | |
| RO | Read-Out | RODIAC | Rotary Dual Input for Analog Computation |
| RO | Receive Only | | |
| RO | Rechenoperation | RODS | Realtime Operations, Dispatching and Scheduling |
| RO | Recherche Opérationnelle | | |
| RO | Record Output | | |
| RO | Record Overflow | ROE | Read-Out Exit |
| RO | Round Off | ROHSC | Read Out High Speed Count |
| RO | Routine Order | | |
| ROA | Realistic Operational Amplifier | ROI | Range Operations Instructions |
| ROA | Recorded Overflow Announcement | ROI | Read-Only Instruction |
| | | ROI | Recessed Oxide Isolation |
| ROAR | ROS Address Register | ROI | Resources Objectives, Incorporated |
| ROAR | Royal Optimizing Assembly Routine | ROI | Return On Investment |
| ROB | Radar Order of Battle | ROJ | Range On Jamming |
| ROBINS | Roberts Information Services | ROL | Request On-Line |
| | | ROL | Request Online Status |
| ROBOT | Record Organization Based On Transposition | ROL | Roll |
| | | ROLF | Remotely Operated Longwall Face |
| ROC | Read-Out Circuit | | |
| ROC | Read-Out Clock | ROLL | Rollback |
| ROC | Receiver Operating Characteristics | ROLTS | Remote On-Line Testing System |
| ROC | Reconnaissance Optique des Caractères | ROM | Read-Only Memory |
| | | ROM | Readout Memory |
| ROC | Recoverable Overlay Candidate | ROM | Rough Order of Magnitude |
| | | ROMM | Read-Only Memory Module |
| ROC | Required Operation Capability | ROMON | Receiving-Only Monitor |
| | | ROMP | Read-Only Memory, Programmable |
| ROCAPPI | Research On Computer Applications for the Printing and Publishing Industries | ROMR | Read-Only Memory Register |
| | | ROMS | Read-Only Memories |
| ROCF | Remote Operator Control Facility | ROMS | Read-Only Memory Storage |
| ROCH | Routed Chain | RON | Research Octance Number |
| | | RON | Run Occurence Number |

- 518 -

# R

| | | | |
|---|---|---|---|
| RONTR | Receive-Only Non-Typing Reperforator | RP | Reference Point |
| | | RP | Register Printer |
| ROP | Receive-Only Printer | RP | Relative Pressure |
| ROPP | Receive-Only Paper Printer | RP | Relative Program |
| | | RP | Relative Programming |
| ROR | Range-Only Radar | RP | Reliability Program |
| RORDIS | Real-time Oriented Dealer Invoicing System | RP | Relocatable Program |
| | | RP | Repeater |
| ROS | Read-Only Storage | RP | Reply Paid |
| ROS | Read-Only Store | RP | Report Writer |
| ROS | Remote Operating System | RP | Reproducing Punch |
| ROS | Resident Operating System | RP | Rerun Program |
| ROS | Ridge Operating System | RP | Return on Positive |
| ROS DR | Read-Only Storage Driver | RP | Routine Program |
| ROSA | Recording Optical Spectrum Analyzer | RP | Running Program |
| | | RPA | Release Process Automation |
| ROSCOE | Remote Operating System Conventional Operating Environment | RPA | Remote Peripheral Access |
| | | RPB | Regional Processor Bus |
| | | RPBX | Remote Private Branch Exchange |
| ROSE | Remotely Operated Special Equipment | | |
| | | RPC | Remote Position Control |
| ROSE | Retrieval by On-line Search | RPC | Remote Procedure Call |
| | | RPC | Row Parity Check |
| ROT | Radar On Target | RPCU | Rochester Processor Control Unit |
| ROT | Rate Of Turn | | |
| ROT | Rotor | RPD | Radar Planning Device |
| ROTAM | Request-Oriented Telecommunication Access Method | RPD | Renewal Parts Data |
| | | RPD | Resistance Pressure Detector |
| ROTR | Receive Only Tape Reperforator | RPD | Retarding Potential Difference |
| ROTR | Receive Only Typing Reperforator | RPDS | Retired Personnel Data System |
| ROTR S/P | Receiving-Only Typing Reperforator Series to Parallel | RPDT | Radar Prediction Data Table |
| | | RPE | Radial Probable Error |
| ROUT | Register Out | RPE | Remote Peripheral Equipment |
| ROUT | Retrieval Of Unformatted Text | | |
| | | RPE | Remote Procedure Error |
| ROVD | Relay Operated Voltage Divider | RPE | Required Page End character |
| ROW | Rest Of the World | | |
| ROX | Recessed Oxide | RPE | Return on Parity Even |
| RP | Random Process | RPF | ROSCOE Programming Facility |
| RP | Rapid Processing | | |
| RP | Read Pulse | RPFC | Recurrent Peak Forward Current |
| RP | Reading Program | | |
| RP | Real Processor | RPG | Report Process Generator |
| RP | Reception Poor | RPG | Report Program Generator |
| RP | Rechenprozessor | RPGPS | Report Program Generator Programming System |
| RP | Rechnerzeit-Preis | | |
| RP | Recommended Practice | RPH | Revolutions Per Hour |
| RP | Record Processor | RPI | Radar Precipitation Integrator |
| RP | Recorded Program | | |
| RP | Recovery Phase | | |

- 519 -

# R

| | | | |
|---|---|---|---|
| RPI | RAMIS Programmer Interface | RPRS | Random Pulse Radar System |
| RPI | Relay Position Indicator | RPRT | Report |
| RPI | Réseau de Production Industrielle | RPS | Random Pulse Sequence |
| RPI | Reversals Per Inch | RPS | Realtime Programming System |
| RPI | Rework Pictorial Instruction | RPS | Recovered Parts Storage |
| RPI | Rework Print Image | RPS | Regulated Power Supply |
| RPL | Radar Processing Language | RPS | Remote Processing Service |
| RPL | Rechenplan | RPS | Remote Processing System |
| RPL | Relocatable Program Library | RPS | Revolutions Per Second |
| RPL | Replace | RPS | Rhône Poulenc Systèmes |
| RPL | Request Parameter List | RPS | Rotational Position Sensing |
| RPL | Research Programming Language | RPT | Repeat |
| RPL | Running Progam Language | RPT | Report |
| RPM | Random Phase Modulator | RPTR | Repeater |
| RPM | Rate Per Minute | RPU | Radio Phone Unit |
| RPM | Regulated Power Module | RPU | Radio Propagation Unit |
| RPM | Reliability Performance Measure | RPV | Remotely Piloted Vehicle |
| RPM | Remote Performance Monitoring | RPW | Running Process Word |
| RPM | Repeat Mode | RPY | Reply |
| RPM | Resupply Provisions Module | RQ | Ready Queue |
| RPM | Revolutions Per Minute | RQ | Result-store Queue |
| RPM | Rotations Per Minute | RQA | Recursive Queue Analyzer |
| RPM | Runs Per Minute | RQC | Radar Quality Control |
| RPMC | Remote Performance Monitoring and Control | RQE | Reply Queue Element |
| RPMI | Revolutions-Per-Minute Indicator | RQE | Request Queue Element |
| RPN | Reverse Polish Notation | RQI | Request for Initialization |
| RPO | Return on Parity Odd | RQIO | Request Input/Output |
| RPOA | Recognized Private Operating Agency | RQL | Reference Quality Level |
| RPP | Radar Power Programmer | RQS | Rate Quoting System |
| RPP | Rasterpunktprüfung | RQS | Request |
| RPP | Relative Processing Power | RR | Radio Relay |
| RPPI | Remote Plan Position Indicator | RR | Rapid Recording |
| RPQ | Release Product Qualification | RR | Re-Read |
| RPQ | Request for Price Quotation | RR | Read Records |
| RPQFI | Request for Price Quotation Feature Index | RR | Readout and Relay |
| RPR | Read Printer | RR | Receive Ready |
| RPR | Reverse Phase Relay | RR | Rechenregister |
| RPR | Reverse Power Relay | RR | Record Removal |
| RPROM | Reprogrammable Read-Only Memory | RR | Recorder |
| | | RR | Recurrence Rate |
| | | RR | Reference Record |
| | | RR | Register Reset |
| | | RR | Register to Register operation |
| | | RR | Register-Register |
| | | RR | Register-to-Register |
| | | RR | Registre de Réception |
| | | RR | Repetition Rate |
| | | RR | Rerun Routine |
| | | RR | Restart Routine |
| | | RR | Result Register |
| | | RR | Resultatregister |

# R

| | | | |
|---|---|---|---|
| RR | Return Rate | RRZ | Regionales Rechenzentrum |
| RR | Reverse Reading | RRZ | Rheinisches Genossen- |
| RR | Rollback Routine | | schafts-Rechen- |
| RR | Running Reverse | | zentrum eG |
| RR... | Remington Rand | RRZN | Regionales Rechenzentrum |
| RRC | Rate Radio Computer | | Niedersachsen |
| RRC | Remote Readable Counter | RS | Radar Simulator |
| RRCS | Rate and Route Computer System | RS | Random Sequence |
| | | RS | Rapid Storage |
| RRD | Re-Read | RS | Rapid Store |
| RRD | Resonant Reed Decoder | RS | Read Statement |
| RRDC | Railroad Data Center | RS | Reader Stop |
| RRDR | Raw Radar Data Recorder | RS | Reading Speed |
| RRDS | Relative Record Data Set | RS | Rechnersystem |
| RRDTL | Resistor-Resistor Diode-Transistor Logic | RS | Rechnungsführung und Statistik |
| RREAC | Royal Radar Establishment Automatic Computer | RS | Recommended Standard |
| | | RS | Record Separator |
| RREG | R Register | RS | Record Storage |
| RRF | Release Remote File | RS | Referenzsignal |
| RRF | Resonant Ring Filter | RS | Register Speicherbefehl |
| RRF | Routing Reference File | RS | Register Storage |
| RRH | Regionales Rechenzentrum Heidelberg | RS | Register-Speicher |
| | | RS | Registersucher |
| RRHICMD | Remote Reading High-Intensity Constant Monitoring Device | RS | Relay Store |
| | | RS | Remote Station |
| | | RS | Request Signal |
| RRI | Range-Rate Indicator | RS | Reset key |
| RRIP | Report Reduction Improvement Program | RS | Resetting |
| | | RS | Resident Software |
| RRIS | Railroad Research Information Service | RS | Results Sign |
| | | RS | Retrospective Search |
| RRM | Range Rate Memory | RS | Return Statement |
| RRN | Relative Record Number | RS | Rewind Speed |
| RRNS | Redundant Residue Number System | RS | Rewind Statement |
| | | RS | Routing Selector |
| RRP | Reader and Reader-Printer | RS | Rücksetz-Signal |
| RRP | Recovery/Restart-Procedure | RS&I | Rules, Standards and Instructions |
| RRPG | Regular Right Part Grammar | RSA | Register Save Area |
| | | RSA | Remote Station Alarm |
| RRPTN | Receiving Report Number | RSA | Remote Storage Activities |
| RRRV | Rate of Rise of Restriking Voltage | RSA | Requirements Statement Analyser |
| RRS | Radio Research Station | RSAC | Radiological Safety Analysis Computer |
| RRS | Required Response Spectrum | RSAC | Radiological Safety Computer |
| RRS | Restraint Release System | | |
| RRT | Reroute | RSAM | Relative Sequential Access Method |
| RRTTL | Resistor-Resistor Transistor-Transistor Logic | RSAP | Response Session Abort Positive |
| RRU | Radiobiological Research Unit | RSB | Reel Storage Bin |
| | | RSBA | Retransmission Still Being Attempted |
| RRU | Remote Readout Unit | | |

# R

| | | | |
|---|---|---|---|
| RSC | Remote Scientific Computing | RSL | Requirement Statement Language |
| RSC | Resource | RSLS | Reply-path Side-Lobe Suppression |
| RSCCP | Response Session Change Control Positive | RSLT | Result |
| RSCH | Resume Subchannel | RSM | Rapid Search Machine |
| RSCIE | Remote Station Communication Interface Equipment | RSM | Real Storage Management |
| | | RSM | Reed Switching Matrix |
| | | RSM | Resident Sector Management |
| RSCS | Remote Spooling Communication Subsystem | RSM | Resource Management System |
| RSD | Relative Standard Deviation | RSM | Resume |
| | | RSM | Rücksetzen, Manuell |
| RSDC | Range Safety Data Coordinator | RSN | Radiation Surveillance Network |
| RSDP | Remote Site Data Processing | RSN | Record Sequence Number |
| RSDP | Remote Site Data Processor | RSOU | Read Sign Over Units |
| | | RSP | Record Select Program |
| RSDP | Request for Special Devices and Products | RSP | Reentry Systems Program |
| | | RSP | Required Space character |
| RSDS | Relative Sequential Data Set | RSP | Resource-Sharing Protocol |
| | | RSPT | Real Storage Page Table |
| RSDT | Remote Station Data Terminal | RSR | Reinforcement Status Register |
| RSE | Rechner-Statuseinheit | RSR | Restore |
| RSE | Request Select Entry | RSR | Reverse Switching Rectifier |
| RSE | Requests for Self Enhancement | RSRC | Request for Special Review and Comment |
| RSEP | Response Session End Positive | RSRS | Radio and Space Research Station |
| RSERV | Relocatable library Service function | RSS | Range Safety Switch |
| RSET | Receiver Signal Element Timing | RSS | Range Safety System |
| | | RSS | Redundant Switch Selector |
| RSEU | Remote Scanner-Encoder Unit | RSS | Remote Systems Scanner |
| | | RSS | Residual Sum of Squares |
| RSF | Remote Service Facility | RSS | Resources Security System |
| RSF | Remote Support Facility | RSS | Rework Support System |
| RSFF | Reset-Set Flipflop | RSS | Root Sum Square |
| RSH | Right Shift | RSSDA | Regional Social Science Data Archive |
| RSI | Request for Shipping Instructions | RSSL | Raytheon Scientific Simulation Language |
| RSI | Retrieval of Stored Information | RSSN | Response Session Start Negative |
| RSI | Ring State Indicator | RSSP | Response Session Start Positive |
| RSIC | Redstone Scientific Information Center | RST | Read Symbol Table |
| RSID | Resource Identification table | RST | Readability, Strength, Tone |
| RSIL | Rechnergestützte Systeme zur Information der Leitung | RST | Rechenstanzer |
| | | RST | Register and Self-Test |
| RSJ | Rolled Steel Joist | RST | Remotely Submitted Transaction |

# R

| | | | |
|---|---|---|---|
| RST | Reset | RTA | Response Time Analyzer |
| RST | Reset-Set Trigger | RTACF | Real-Time Auxiliary Computing Facility |
| RST | Restore | | |
| RSTD | Restricted | RTAM | Remote Telecommunication Access Method |
| RSTR | Restore Row | | |
| RSTS | Resource Time-Sharing system | RTAM | Remote Terminal Access Method |
| RSU | Record Storage Unit | RTAM | Resident Terminal Access Method |
| RSU | Reserved for Software Use | | |
| RSU | Rot/Schwarz-Umschaltung | RTAS | Rapid Telephone Access System |
| RSUI | Response Session User Information | RTB | Radial Time Base |
| RSV | Reserve | RTB | Read Tape Binary |
| RSVD | Reserved | RTB | Read Time Binary |
| RSVP | Remote System Verification Program | RTB | Resistance Temperature Bridge |
| RSVR | Random Sample Vocabulary Recognition | RTB | Response/Throughput Bias |
| | | RTB | Return To Base |
| RSW | Retarded Surface Wave | RTC | Radio Transmission Control |
| RT | Radar Tracking radiotelegraphy | RTC | Reader Tape Contact |
| RT | Radiotelephony | RTC | Real-Time Channel |
| RT | Rangement du Tampon | RTC | Real-Time Clock |
| RT | Rated Time | RTC | Real-Time Command |
| RT | Ratio Transformer unit | RTC | Real-Time Computation |
| RT | Read Transfer | RTC | Real-Time Computer |
| RT | Reading Time | RTC | Register Test Circuit |
| RT | Readout Technique | RTC | Relative Time Clock |
| RT | Real-Time | RTC | Remote Terminal Controller |
| RT | Received Text | | |
| RT | Receiver Transmitter | RTCC | Real-Time Computer Complex |
| RT | Receiving Terminal | | |
| RT | Recovery Time | RTCF | Real-Time Computer Facility |
| RT | Reduction Table | | |
| RT | Register Transfer | RTCIP | Real-Time Cell Identification Processor |
| RT | Registered Transmitter | | |
| RT | Registre de Transmission | RTCM | Real-Time Control Memory |
| RT | Related Term | | |
| RT | Relational Technology | RTCP | Real-Time Control Program |
| RT | Remote Terminal | | |
| RT | Reperforator Transmitter | RTCS | Real-Time Computer System |
| RT | Research and Technology | | |
| RT | Reset Trigger | RTCS | Remote Tape Control System |
| RT | Resistance Thermometer | | |
| RT | Resistor Transistor | RTCU | Real-Time Control Unit |
| RT | Resolver Transformer of receiver | RTD | Read Tape Decimal |
| | | RTD | Real-Time Display |
| RT | Resolving Transmitter | RTD | Resistance Temperature Detector |
| RT | Ringing Tone | | |
| RT | Room Temperature | RTDAS | Real-Time Data Automation System |
| RT/IOC | Real-Time Input/Output Control | RTDC | Real-Time Data Channel |
| RTA | Real Time Analyzer | RTDD | Real-Time Data Distribution |
| RTA | Reliability Test Assembly | | |
| RTA | Resident Transient Area | | |

# R

| | | | |
|---|---|---|---|
| RTDD | Remote Timing and Data Distribution | RTL | Resistor Trimming Language |
| RTDDC | Real-Time Digital Data Correction | RTL | Resistor-Transistor-Logik |
| | | RTLOC | Root Locus |
| RTDE | Range Time Data Editor | RTM | Rapid Tuning Magnetron |
| RTDHS | Real-Time Data Handling System | RTM | Raster-Tunnel-Mikroscope |
| | | RTM | Real-Time Management |
| RTDM | Réseau de Transmission de Données de la Marine | RTM | Real-Time Mode |
| | | RTM | Real-Time Monitor |
| RTDP | Real-Time Data Processing | RTM | Real-Time Multi-programming |
| RTDR | Reliability Test Data Report | | |
| | | RTM | Receiver-Transmitter Modulator |
| RTDS | Real-Time Data System | | |
| RTDT | Real-Time Data Translator | RTM | Recording Tachometer |
| RTDTL | Resistor Tunnel Diode Transistor Logic | RTM | Register Transfer Module |
| | | RTM | Registered Trade Mark |
| RTE | Real-Time Executive | RTM | Response Time Monitor |
| RTE | Route | RTMB | Route and Member number |
| RTED | Return-To-Earth Digital | RTMD | Real-Time Multiplexer Display |
| RTER | Real-Time Executive Routine | | |
| | | RTMOS | Real-Time Multi-programming Operating System |
| RTES | Real-Time Executive System | | |
| | | RTN | Réseau de Télétraitement Nixdorf |
| RTEX | Real-Time Executive | | |
| RTEX | Real-time Telecommunications Executive | RTN | Return |
| | | RTN | Routine |
| RTF | Real-Time FORTRAN | RTNE | Routine |
| RTG | Radioisotope Thermoelectric Generator | RTO | Real-Time Operation |
| | | RTO | Real-Time Output |
| RTG | Routing | RTO | Referred To Output |
| RTGV | Real-Time Generation of Video | RTO | Response Time Option |
| | | RTOS | Real-Time Operating System |
| RTHCR | Real-Time Hand print Character Recognition | | |
| | | RTP | Real-Time Peripheral |
| RTI | Real-Time Input | RTP | Real-Time Processing |
| RTI | Real-Time Interface | RTP | Real-Time Program |
| RTI | Real-Time Interference | RTP | Real-Time Programming |
| RTI | Referred To Input | RTP | Référence Téléphonique |
| RTIG | Random Time Interval Generator | RTP | Remote Transfer Point |
| | | RTP | Requirement and Test Procedure |
| RTIM | Recall Time | | |
| RTIO | Real-Time Input-Output | RTPH | Round Trips Per Hour |
| RTIO | Remote Terminal Input/Output | RTPL | Real-Time Procedural Language |
| RTIOIS | Real-Time Input-Output Interface Subsystem | RTPM | Real-Time Program Management |
| RTIRS | Real-Time Information Retrieval System | RTPS | Real-Time Telemetry Processing System |
| RTK | Range Tracker | | |
| RTL | Real-Time Language | RTQC | Real-Time Quality Control |
| RTL | Recovery and Transaction Logging system | RTR | Ready To Receive |
| | | RTR | Real-Time Readout |
| RTL | Register Transfer Language | RTR | Repeater Test Rack |
| | | RTRCDS | Real-Time Reconnaissance Cockpit Display System |

# R

| | | | |
|---|---|---|---|
| RTRL | Real-Time Requirements Language | RU | Roentgen Unit |
| RTRO | Real-Time Readout | RUBIN | Rechnerunterstützung Bei Nachrichten |
| RTRP | Remote Terminal Routine Package | RUC | Reporting Unit Code |
| RTS | Radar Tracking Station | RUCAPS | Really Universal Computer Aided Production System |
| RTS | Reactive Terminal Service | RUDI | Rapid Universal Digital Instrumentation |
| RTS | Real-Time Simulation | | |
| RTS | Real-Time Simulator | RUG | Recomp Users Group |
| RTS | Real-Time System | RUG | Report and Update program Generator |
| RTS | Rechnergesteuertes Text-System | RUIN | Regional and Urban Information Network |
| RTS | Reliable Transfer Server | | |
| RTS | Remote Terminal Scanning | RUL | Refractoriness Under Load |
| RTS | Remote Terminal Supervisor | RUM | Remote Underwater Manipulator |
| RTS | Remote Terminal System | RUN | Rewind and Unload |
| RTS | Remote Test System | RUNIT | Route Unit |
| RTS | Request To Send | RUSDIC | Russian Dictionary |
| RTS | Response Time System | RUSH | Remote Use of Shared Hardware |
| RTS | Return To Sender | | |
| RTSDS | Real-Time Scheduling Display System | RUSH | Remote Use of Standard Hardware |
| RTSRS | Real-Time Simulation Research System | RUST | Rechnungsführung Und Statistik |
| RTSS | Real-Time Scientific System | RUU | Rechnerunterstützter Unterricht |
| RTT | Radioteletype | RV | Rated Voltage |
| RTT | Real-Time Telemetry | RV | Rechnerverbund |
| RTT | Régie des Téléphones et Télégraphes | RV | Reduced Voltage |
| | | RV | Reserved |
| RTTD | Real-Time Telemetry Data | RVA | Reactive Volt-Ampere meter |
| RTTDS | Real-Time Telemetry Data System | RVA | Recorded Voice Announcement |
| RTTS | Real-Time Telemetry System | RVA | Reliability Variation Analysis |
| RTTV | Real-Time Television | | |
| RTTY | Radio Teletypewriter | RVD | Radar Video Digitizer |
| RTU | Real-Time Unit | RVDP | Radar Video Data Processor |
| RTU | Remote Terminal Unit | | |
| RTUS | Real-Time Units | RVE | Radar Video Extractor |
| RTV | Retrieve | RVG | Read Voltage Generator |
| RTVP | Real-Time Video Processing | RVG | Reference Voltage Generator |
| RTW | Real-Time Working | RVI | Reverse Interrupt |
| RTX | Real-Time Executive | RVK | Rechner-Verbindungskanal |
| RTXE | Real-Time Executive Extended | RVK | Revoke |
| | | RVL | VEB Robotron-Vertrieb Leipzig |
| RTY | Retry | | |
| RU | Rechnergestützter Unterricht | RVM | Reactive Voltmeter |
| | | RVMF | Real Virtual Machine hardware assist Features |
| RU | Reproducing Unit | | |
| RU | Request Unit | RVP | Radar Video Preprocessor |
| RU | Response Unit | RVR | Radar Video Recorder |
| RU | Restricted Usage | RVR | Runway Visual Range |

# R

| | | | |
|---|---|---|---|
| RVRS | Reverse | RWST | Rechenwerksteuerung |
| RVS | Rechnerverbundsystem | RWT | Read-Write-Tape |
| RVS | Reverse Video Space | RWV | Read-Write-Verify |
| RVT | Reading and Vocabulary Test | RWVRC | Read/Write Vertical Redundancy Check |
| RVT | Resource Vector Table | RWW | Read-While-Write |
| RW | Random Word | RX | Receive |
| RW | Read Word | RX | Receiver |
| RW | Rechenwert | RX | Register Index |
| RW | Rechnungswesen | RX | Register to Indexed memory |
| RW | Report-Writer | | |
| RW | Reserved Word | RX | Register-to-Index storage operation |
| RW | Resistance Welding | | |
| RW | Rücklaufwert | RX | Resolver-Transmitter |
| RWA | Read-Write Amplifier | RXDS | Rank Xerox Data Systems |
| RWAI | Rechnungswesen Ausland Interface | RXOS | Rank Xerox Operating System |
| RWB | Richtlinien für Wirtschaftlichkeitsberechnungen | RY | Relay |
| | | RZ | Rechenzentrum |
| RWC | Read, Write, Compute | RZ | Retour Zéro |
| RWC | Read, Write, and Compare | RZ | Return to Zero |
| RWC | Read, Write, and Continue | RZ-P | Return-to-Zero-Polarized |
| RWC | Read-Write Cycle | RZB | Rechenzentrum Buchhandel |
| RWC | Receive With Code | | |
| RWCS | Report Writer Control System | RZC | Return-to-Zero Code |
| | | RZDR | Rechenzentrum der Deutschen Reichsbahn |
| RWD | Rewind | | |
| RWE | Rechenwerkserweiterung | RZG | Rechenzentrum Graz |
| RWG | Rechenzentrale Württemberger Genossenschaften | RZKN | Rechenzentrum der Kollektiven Nutzung |
| RWH | Read-Write Head | RZM | Réservation de Zones en Mémoire |
| RWI | Read, Write, and Initialize | | |
| | | RZM | Return to Zero Mark |
| RWKB | Regular Wentzel-Kramer-Brillourin | RZM | Return-to-Zero Method |
| | | RZO | Rechenzentrum der Ortskrankenkassen |
| RWM | Random Work Method | | |
| RWM | Read/Write Memory | RZO-WL | Rechenzentrum der Ortskrankenkassen in Westfalen-Lippe |
| RWM | Rectangular-Wave Modulation | | |
| RWO | Right/Wrong Omits | RZR | Return-to-Zero Recording |
| RWP | Rain Water Pipe | RZS | VEB Rechenzentrum Statistik |
| RWR | Read-Write Register | | |

# S

| | | | |
|---|---|---|---|
| S | Saldo | SA | Sales Analysis |
| S | Satz | SA | Satzadresse |
| S | Schriftart | SA | Schreibautomat |
| S | Secondary | SA | Scratch Area |
| S | Secret | SA | Search Algorithm |
| S | Sector | SA | Search Argument |
| S | Selector | SA | Secondary Address |
| S | Separate | SA | Sector Address |
| S | Sequential | SA | Seek Address |
| S | Set | SA | Select Address |
| S | Setzen | SA | Selection Addressing |
| S | Share | SA | Semi-Adder |
| S | Siemens AG | SA | Send Ahead |
| S | Signed | SA | Sense Address |
| S | Small | SA | Sense Amplifier |
| S | Solid | SA | Sequence Access |
| S | Sortierung | SA | Sequential Access |
| S | Source | SA | Sequential Addressing |
| S | Speech | SA | Serial Adder |
| S | Speicher | SA | Service Aids |
| S | Speicherung | SA | Set Arithmetic |
| S | Spherical joint | SA | Set Attribute |
| S | Spool | SA | Simultaneous Access |
| S | Start | SA | Single-Armoured |
| S | Statement | SA | Situationsanalyse |
| S | Stop | SA | Slow Acting relay |
| S | Storage | SA | Sortie Accumulateur |
| S | Streumatrix | SA | Sortierautomatik |
| S | Subtract | SA | Specific Address |
| S | Sulphur | SA | Spectrum Analyzer |
| S | Summe | SA | Staging Adapter |
| S | Supervisor | SA | Start Address |
| S | Switch | SA | Storage Address |
| S | Switcher | SA | Storage Area |
| S | Symbol | SA | Store Accumulator |
| S | Synchronisierimpuls | SA | Store Address |
| S... | Siemens | SA | Stress Anneal |
| S & L | Savings & Loan | SA | String Analysis |
| S and S | Speech and Simplex | SA | Successive Approximation |
| S frame | Supervisory frame | SA | Summing Amplifier |
| S+D | Speech plus Duplex | SA | Symbolic Address |
| S-Bus | Speicher-Bus | SA | Symbolic Assembler |
| S-P | Systems and Procedures | SA | Systemanschluß |
| S/F | Store and Forward | SA | Systems Analysis |
| S/H | Sample and Hold | SA-BO | Sense Amplifier-Blocking Oscillator |
| S/I | Signal-to-Intermodulation ratio | SAA | Storage Accounting Area |
| S/N | Signal to Noise ratio | SAAFARI | South African Airways Fully Automatic Reservations Installation |
| S/N | Stress Number | | |
| S/O | Select/Omit | | |
| S/O | Send Only | SAAGS | Semi-Automatic Artwork Generator System |
| S/OFF | Sign Off | | |
| S/ON | Sign On | SAAM | Simulation, Analysis And Modelling |
| S/R | Subroutine | | |
| SA | Sales Aid | | |

# S

| | | | |
|---|---|---|---|
| SAAOC | System of Analysis and Assignment of Operations according to Capacities | SACCHS | Scottish Advisory Committee on the Computers in the Health Service |
| SAB | Secondary Application Block | SACCM | Slow Access Charge-Coupled Memory |
| SAB | Session Awareness Block | SACCS | SAC Automated Command and Control System |
| SAB | Signalaufbereitung | | |
| SAB | Storage Address Bus | SACCS | Semi-Automatic Computer Conversion System |
| SAB | Sync Address Bus | | |
| SAB | System Advisory Board | SACE | Semiautomatic Checkout Equipment |
| SABE | Society for Automation in Business Education | SACE | Systems Acceptance Checkout Equipment |
| SABER | Semi-Automatic Business Environment Research | SACMAP | Selective Automatic Computational Matching And Positioning |
| SABIR | Semi-Automatic Bibliographic Information Retrieval | SACMOS | Self Aligned CMOS |
| SABIRS | Semi-Automatic Bibliographic Information Retrieval System | SACNET | Secure Automatic Communications Network |
| | | SACO | Select Address and Contract Operate |
| SABM | Set Asynchronous Balanced Mode | SACS | Scientific and Administrative Computing System |
| SABME | Set Asynchronous Balanced Mode Extended | SACT | Semi-Automatic Core Tester |
| SABRAC | Sabra Computer | | |
| SABRE | Sales And Business Reservations done Electronically | SAD | Sentence Appraiser and Diagrammer |
| | | SAD | Serial Analog Delay |
| SABRE | Semi-Automatic Business-Related Environment | SAD | Silicon Alloy Diffused |
| | | SAD | Situation Attention Display |
| SABRE | Singer Accounting and Business Reporting | SAD | Special Adapter Device |
| SABU | Semi-Automatic Back-Up | SAD | Sprache zur Auswertung von Dateien |
| SAC | Semiautomatic Coding | | |
| SAC | Semiautomatic Core | SAD | System Activity Display |
| SAC | Signature Authorization Card | SAD | Système d'Acquisition de Données |
| SAC | Signature Authorization Chart | SAD | Système d'Aide à la Décision |
| SAC | Single Access Computer | SADA | Seismic Array Data Analyzer |
| SAC | Single Address Code | | |
| SAC | Single Address Computer | SADA | Sortie Accés Direct Aléatoire |
| SAC | Storage Access Channel | | |
| SAC | Storage Address Character | SADAP | Simplified Automatic Data Plotter |
| SAC | Storage Address Counter | | |
| SAC | Store Access Control | SADAR | Satellite Data Reduction |
| SAC | Store And Clear | SADAS | Semi-Automatic Data Acquisition System |
| SAC | Strategic Air Command | | |
| SACAC | South African Council for Automation and Computation | SADAS | Sperry Airborne Data Acquisition System |
| | | SADC | Sequential Analog-to-Digital Computer |
| SACAD | Stress Analysis and Computer Aided-Design | SADF | Statistical Analysis of Documentation Files |
| SACC | System Accessibility | | |

# S

| | | | |
|---|---|---|---|
| SADG | System Application Design Guide | SAFARI | Système Automatisé pour les Fichiers Administratifs et de Répertoire des Individus |
| SADI | Sanders Associates Direct Indexing | | |
| SADI | Secretarial Automated Document Index | SAFE | Secure Automated Facility Environment |
| SADIC | Solid state Analog to Digital Computer | SAFE | Security Audit and Field Evaluation |
| SADIE | Scanning Analog-to-Digital Input Equipment | SAFEORD | Safety of Explosive Ordnance Databank |
| SADIE | Secure Automatic Data Information Exchange | SAFIR | Standardisiertes Anwenderprogrammsystem Finanzbuchhaltung Im Realzeitbetrieb |
| SADIE | Sterling And Decimal Invoicing Electronically | | |
| SADL | Spares Application Data List | SAFO | Système Automatique du Frêt Orly |
| SADP | Synthetic Array Data Processor | SAFR | Speicherausgabe-Anforderungsregister |
| SADPO | Systems Analysis and Data Processing Office | SAG | Self-Aligned Gate |
| SADS | Single Application Data Sheet | SAG | Standard Address Generator |
| SADSAC | Sample Data Simulator And Computer | SAG | Syntax Analyzer Generator |
| | | SAG | Systemanschlußgruppe |
| SADSAC | Seiler ALGOL Digitally Simulated Analog Computer | SAGA | System for Automatic Generation and Analysis |
| | | SAGE | Semi-Automatic Ground Environment |
| SADSACT | Self-Aligned Descriptors from Self And Cited Titles | SAGE | Simulateur d'Apprentissage de la Gestion des Entreprises |
| SADSAM | Sentence Appraiser and Diagrammer, Semantic Analyzer Machine | SAGECE | Système Automatique pour la Gestion et l'Echange des Comptes Economiques |
| SADT | Structured Analysis and Design Technique | SAGEM | Société d'Applications Générales d'Electricité et de Mécanique |
| SADT | Surface Alloy Diffused base Transistor | SAGFET | Self Aligned Gate Field Effect Transistor |
| SAE | Schneller Abtaster und Einsteller | SAGMOS | Self-Aligning Gate MOS |
| SAE | Self Aligned Emitter | SAHC | Sleep Analyzing Hybrid Computer |
| SAE | Semi-Automatic Encoding | | |
| SAE | Shaft Angle Encoder | SAHF | Semi Automatic Height Finder |
| SAE | Signal-Abfrage-Einrichtung | | |
| SAE | Simple Arithmetic Expression | SAHYB | Simulation of Analog and Hybrid computers |
| SAERIS | South Australia Education Resource Information System | SAI | Sense Amplifier Inhibit |
| | | SAI | Single Address Instruction |
| | | SAIC | Société d'Applications de l'Informatique et du Calcul |
| SAES | Sputter Auger Electron Spectroscopy | | |
| SAF | Speicher-Ausgabe-Anforderung | SAID | Semi-Automatic Integrated Documentation |
| SAF | Staging Adapter Failure | SAID | Speech Analog Input to Digitizer |
| SAF | Symmetry Adapter Function | | |

# S

| | | | |
|---|---|---|---|
| SAID | Speech Autoinstruction Device | SAM | Sales Achievement Measurement |
| SAID | System Analysis Index for Diagnosis | SAM | Scanning Auger-Microprobe |
| SAIL | Structural Analysis Input Language | SAM | Search Address Mark |
| | | SAM | Selective Access Memory |
| SAILIS | South African Institute for Librarianship and Information Science | SAM | Selective Addressable Memory |
| | | SAM | Selective Auto-Monitoring tracing routine |
| SAILLE | Système de génération Automatique d'Instructions Logiques en Langages Evolués | SAM | Selective Automatic Monitoring |
| | | SAM | Selective Automonitoring |
| SAILS | Software Adaptable Integrated Logic System | SAM | Self-Addressing Memory |
| | | SAM | Semantic Analyzing Machine |
| SAIM | Systems Analysis and Integration Model | SAM | Semi-Automatic Mathematics |
| SAIMS | Selected Acquisitions Information Management System | SAM | Semiconductor Advanced Memory |
| SAINT | Satellite Interceptor | SAM | Sensor-system for Automation and Measurement |
| SAINT | Symbolic Automatic Integration | SAM | Sequential Access Memory |
| SAINT | Systems Analysis of Integrated Network of Tasks | SAM | Sequential Access Method |
| | | SAM | Sequentially Addressed Memory |
| SAK | Stammauftragskarte | SAM | Serial Access Memory |
| SAKI | Selektive Aktiv-Informationsverteilung | SAM | Serial Analog Memory |
| | | SAM | Service Attitude Measurement |
| SAKI | Solatron Automatic Keyboard Instructor | SAM | Signal Analyzing Monitor |
| SAL | Set Address Limit | SAM | Simulation of Analog Methods |
| SAL | Simple Author Language | | |
| SAL | South American program Library | SAM | Sindelfinger Arbeitsmethodenplanung |
| SAL | Symbolic Assembly Language | SAM | Slow Access Memory |
| | | SAM | Social Accounting Matrix |
| SAL | System Automatisierter Leitungshilfen | SAM | Society for Advancement of Management |
| SAL | Systems Activity Log | SAM | Software Associative Memory |
| SAL | Systems Assembly Language | | |
| | | SAM | Sort And Merge |
| SALDRI | Semi-Automatic Low Data Rate Input | SAM | Speicherausgabe-Anforderungsregister-Meldung |
| SALE | Simple Algebraic Language for Engineers | SAM | Speicherausgabemeldung |
| | | SAM | Sprachausgabegerät in Multiplextechnik |
| SALINET | Satellite Library Information Network | SAM | Subsequent Address Message |
| SALS | Solid state Acoustoelectric Light Scanner | SAM | Surface-to-Air Missile |
| SALT | Sequential Automated Logic Test | SAM | Symbolic and Algebraic Manipulation |
| SALT | Stand Alone Terminal | SAM | Synchronous Amplitude Modulation |
| SALT | Symbolic Algebraic Language Translator | SAM | System Activity Monitor |

# S

| | | | |
|---|---|---|---|
| SAM | System Analysis Machine | SAMS | Satellite Automonitor System |
| SAM | System Applications Microcomputer | SAMSON | Sample-Mitarbeiter-Steuerung-Online |
| SAM | System for Accumulating Measurements | SAMSON | Strategic Automatic Message Switching Operational Network |
| SAM | Systems Analysis Module | | |
| SAMA | Scientific Apparatus Makers Association | SAMSY | Standard Abwasser Meß-wertverarbeitungssystem |
| SAMANTHA | System for the Automated Management of Text from a Hierarchical Arrangement | SAMUX | Serial Addressable Multiplexer |
| | | SAN | Symbolischer Aspektname |
| SAMECS | Structural Analysis Method for Evaluation of Complex Structures | SAND | Sorting and Assembly of New Data |
| | | SANDS | Sequentially Addressable Numeric Display System |
| SAMFOR | Sequential Access Method in FORTRAN | SANFO | Systemanwendungsprogramm für Fordhändler |
| SAMI | Systems Activity Measurement Instrument | SANMIS | Sanitation Management Information System |
| SAMI | Systems Activity Measuring Instruction | SANOVA | Simultaneous Analysis Of Variance |
| SAMIS | Structural Analysis and Matrix Interpretation System | SANPER | Système d'Analyse de Performances |
| SAMIS | Structural Analysis and Matrix Interpretative System | SANS | Simplified Account-Numbering System |
| | | SANTA | Systematic Analog Network Testing Approach |
| SAMNOS | Self-Aligning-gate Metal Nitride Oxide Semiconductor | SAO | Select Address and Operate |
| SAMO | Statische ALGOL-Modellbeschreibung | SAO | Stücklisten- und Arbeitsplanorganisation |
| SAMOA | Sortier- und Auswahlprogramm mit Mehrfachausgabe zur Organisation von Abläufen | SAP | Satellitenprogramm |
| | | SAP | Schweizer Automatik Pool |
| | | SAP | Select Application Protocol |
| SAMOS | Satellite And Missile Observation System | SAP | Share Assembly Program |
| | | SAP | Simulation Analyzer Program |
| SAMOS | Satellite Monitoring System | SAP | Spezielles Anwendungsprogramm |
| SAMOS | Self-Aligning-gate Metal Oxide Semiconductor | | |
| | | SAP | Sprachausgabepuffer |
| SAMOS | Silicon and Aluminium Metal Oxide Semiconductor | SAP | Subordinate Application Program |
| | | SAP | Survey Analysis Program |
| SAMOS | Stacked gate Avalanche injection - type MOS | SAP | Symbolic Address Program |
| | | SAP | Symbolic Assembly Program |
| SAMPD | Sampled | | |
| SAMPLE | Survey Analysis Macro Programming Language | SAP | Systems Assurance Program |
| SAMPS | Semi-Automated Message Processing System | SAPCH | Semi-Automatic Program Checkout |
| SAMS | Sampling Analog Memory System | SAPCONS | Self Adaptive Program Control System |

# S

| | | | |
|---|---|---|---|
| SAPE | Society for Automation in Professional Education | SAROAD | Storage And Retrieval Of Airquality Data |
| SAPHO | SABENA Automated Passenger Handling Operations | SARP | Schedule And Report Procedure |
| SAPI | Service Access Point Identifier | SARP | Sophisticated Automatic Radar Processing |
| SAPIR | System for Automatic Processing and Indexing of Reports | SARPS | Standards And Recommended Practices |
| | | SARS | Sensor Analog Relay System |
| SAPL | Semi-Automatic Program Library | SARS | Single-Axis Reference System |
| SAPOAD | Systèmes Applications Projet Opération Action Détail | SART | Système d'Assistance aux Renseignements Téléphoniques |
| SAPOAD | Systems Applications Project Operation Action Detail | SARTS | Switched Access Remote Test System |
| SAPOS | Select Address and Provide Output Signal | SARU | Systems Analysis Research Unit |
| SAR | Save Address Register | SARUM | Systems Analysis Research Unit Model |
| SAR | Special Apparatus Rack | SAS | Semi-Automatic Search |
| SAR | Speicheradressenregister | SAS | Sendeablaufsteuerung |
| SAR | Speicherauswahlregister | SAS | Serial Address Sequence |
| SAR | Stack Address Register | SAS | Single Address System |
| SAR | Stand-Alone-Restore | SAS | Slow Access Store |
| SAR | Storage Address Register | SAS | Speicher- und Anforderungssteuerung |
| SAR | Store Address Register | | |
| SAR | Successive Approximation Register | SAS | Speicheranschlußsteuerung |
| | | SAS | Staff Activity System |
| SAR | Sum Array Rows | SAS | Steuerwertausgabesystem |
| SAR | Symbol Acquisition Routine | SAS | Storage Address Switch |
| | | SAS | Stücklisten-, Arbeitsplan/ Arbeitsplatz-System |
| SAR | Sythetic Aperture Radar | | |
| SARA | Semi-Automatic Registration Analyzer | SAS | Surface Active Substances |
| | | SAS | System Analysis Study |
| SARA | Sequential Automatic Recorder and Annunciator | SASE | Statistical Analysis of Series of Events |
| SARA | Struktur-Analyse, Rechnung und Ausgabe | SASI | Shugart Associates System Interface |
| SARA | Student Admission Records Administration | SASI | Shugart Association Standard Interface |
| SARAH | Search And Rescue And Homing | SASM | Society or Automation in Science and Mathematics |
| SARD | Simulated Aircraft Radar Data | SASPA | Subassembly Staging Pre-Audit |
| SAREP | Speech And Reading Enrichment Program | SASR | Storage Address Select Register |
| SARIE | Selective Automatic Radar Identification Equipment | SAST | Systemablaufsteuerung |
| | | SASTO | Signal Amplitude Sampler and Totalizing |
| SARM | Set Asynchronous Response Mode | SAT | Satellite |
| SARO | Spezielle Anwenderroutine | SAT | Saturation |
| SAROAD | Storage And Retrieval Of Aerometric Data | SAT | Silicon Annular Transistor |

# S

| | | | |
|---|---|---|---|
| SAT | Societé Anonyme de Télécommunications | SAVI | Student Audio-Visual Interface |
| SAT | Solar Atmospheric Tide | SAVIC | Services Après-Vente Industriels et Commerciaux |
| SAT | Stabilization Assurance Test | | |
| SAT | Stepped Atomic Time | SAVIMAB | System Analysis of Variables of the Impact Man And Biosphere |
| SAT | Structured Analysis Tools | | |
| SAT | Surface Alloy Transistor | | |
| SAT | System Acceptance Test | SAVS | Status And Verification System |
| SAT | System Access Technique | | |
| SAT | System Analysis Table | SAVT | Save area Table |
| SAT | System Audit Table | SAVT | Secondary Address Vector Table |
| SAT | Systematische Arbeitstechnik | | |
| | | SAW | Surface Acoustic Waves |
| SATAN | Satellite Automatic Tracking Antenna | SAWI | Speichern und Automatisches Wiederfinden von Informationen |
| SATAN | Sensor for Airborne Terrain Analysis | | |
| SATAN | Storage Array Tester and Analyzer | SAWI | System zum Abspeichern und Wiederauffinden |
| | | SAWMARCS | Standard Aircraft Weapon Monitor And Release Control System |
| SATANAS | Semi-Automatic Analog Setting | | |
| SATCO | Signal automatic Air-Traffic Control | SAX | Small Automatic Exchange |
| | | SAYE | Save As You Earn |
| SATF | Shortest Access Time First | SAYTD | Sales Amount Year-To-Date |
| SATI | Selective Access to Tactical Information | | |
| | | SB | Schlußbestand |
| SATI | Shugart Associates System Interface | SB | Secondary Battery |
| | | SB | Sense Bit |
| SATIN | SAC Automated Total Information Network | SB | Sense Byte |
| | | SB | Separate Bit |
| SATIN | SAGE Air Traffic Integration | SB | Serial Binary |
| | | SB | Service Bureau |
| SATIN | System Automatic Teletypewriter Interfaces | SB | Set Binary |
| | | SB | Sideband |
| SATIR | System zur Auswertung taktischer Informationen auf Raketenzerstörern | SB | Sign Bit |
| | | SB | Sleeve Bearing |
| | | SB | Slow Blowing |
| SATIRE | Semi-Automatic Technical Information Retrieval | SB | Speicherbank |
| | | SB | Stabilized Breakdown |
| SATIRES | Semi-Automatic Technical Information Retrieval System | SB | Steuerbereich |
| | | SB | Store Bank |
| | | SB | Straight Binary |
| SATO | Self Aligned Thick Oxide | SB | Sum Byte |
| SATT | Strowger Automatic Toll Ticketing | SB | Sustained Breakdown |
| | | SB | Synchronization Bit |
| SAU | Standard Advertising Unit | SB | Systembeauftragter |
| SAUG | Swiss APL User Group | SB | Systemberater |
| SAUL | Seismic Application Users Language | SB | Systemberatung |
| | | SB | Systembereich |
| SAV | Satellitenvermittler | SBA | Secondary Boolean Analyzer |
| SAV | Save | | |
| SAVE | System Analysis of Vulnerability and Effectiveness | SBA | Set Buffer Address |
| | | SBA | Shared Batch Area |
| | | SBA | Siemens-Büro-Architektur |

# S

| | | | |
|---|---|---|---|
| SBA | Small Business Administration | SBR | Statistisches Betriebsregister |
| SBA | Standard Beam Approach | SBR | Storage Buffer Register |
| SBA | System for Business Automation | SBS | Satellite Business System |
| | | SBS | Sensor Based System |
| SBB | Silicon Borne Bond | SBS | Shared Business System |
| SBC | Simple Binary Computer | SBS | Silicon Bidirectional Switch |
| SBC | Single Board Computer | | |
| SBC | Small Bayonet Cap | SBS | Silicon Bilateral Switch |
| SBC | Small Binary Computer | SBS | Single Bit Store |
| SBC | Small Business Computer | SBS | Single Business Service |
| SBC | Standard Buried Collector | SBS | Small Business Switch |
| SBC... | Service Bureau Corporation | SBS | Small Business System |
| | | SBS | Speicherbereichsschutz |
| SBCA | Sensor Based Control Adapter | SBS | Subscript character |
| | | SBS | Subsystem |
| SBCT | Schottky-Barrier Collector Transistor | SBSD | Subsystem Description |
| | | SBSSC | Sensor Based Systems Support Center |
| SBD | Schottky-Barrier Diode | | |
| SBD | Selbstbedienungsdrucker | SBT | Single Byte Transfer |
| SBD | Sendebezugsdämpfung | SBT | Six-Bit Transcode |
| SBD | Service Bureau Division | SBT | Small Business Terminal |
| SBD | Standard Bibliographic Description | SBT | Subtract |
| | | SBT | Surface Barrier Transistor |
| SBDT | Schottky-Barrier Diode Transistor | SBTAM | Sensor Based Terminal Access Method |
| SBDT | Surface-Barrier Diffused Transistor | SBTC | System Binary Transcode |
| | | SBTTL | Schottky-Barrier TTL |
| SBE | Simple Boolean Expression | SBU | Schwachstrom-Betriebsunterbrechungsversicherung |
| SBED | Serial Bit Error Detector | | |
| SBFET | Schottky Barrier Field-Effect Transistor | | |
| | | SBUE | Switch Back-Up Entry |
| SBFET | Schottky-Barrier gate FET | SBW | Space-Bandwidth product |
| SBFM | Silver-Band Frequency Modulation | SC | Sample Clock |
| | | SC | Satellite Carriers |
| SBG GEDD | Schottky-Barrier-Gate Gun-Effect Digital-Device | SC | Satellite Computer |
| | | SC | Saturable Core |
| | | SC | Scaling Circuit |
| SBI | Single Byte Interleaved | SC | Scanner |
| SBJ | Schottky Barrier Junction | SC | Scanning |
| SBK | Schlußbilanzkonto | SC | Search Command |
| SBK | Single Beam Klystron | SC | Search Control |
| SBL | Structure Building Language | SC | Security Code |
| | | SC | See Copy |
| SBM | Small Business Machines | SC | Seek Command |
| SBM | Submit | SC | Selective Code |
| SBM | Subtract Memory | SC | Selector Card |
| SBM | System Balance Measure | SC | Selector Channel |
| SBN | Strong Base Number | SC | Selector Code |
| SBN | Standard Book Number | SC | Semiconductor |
| SBN | Standard-Buchnummer | SC | Sense Command |
| SBO | Sidebands Only | SC | Sequence Control |
| SBOS | Silicon Borne Oxygen System | SC | Sequence Counter |
| | | SC | Sequential Computer |
| SBP | Special Boiling Point | SC | Serial Computer |

# S

| | | | |
|---|---|---|---|
| SC | Serial Computing | SC/MP | Simple Cost effective Microprocessor |
| SC | Serial Counter | | |
| SC | Service | SCA | Selectivity Clear Accumulator |
| SC | Session Control | | |
| SC | Set Character | SCA | Sequence Chart Analyzer |
| SC | Shaped Charge | SCA | Sequence Control Area |
| SC | Shift Control | SCA | Software Control Authorization |
| SC | Short Circuit | | |
| SC | Short Circuiting | SCA | Synchronous Communication Adapter |
| SC | Shunt Capacitor | | |
| SC | Sign Code | SCA | System Control Adapter |
| SC | Signal Code | SCA | System Control Area |
| SC | Significant Comma | SCAD | Small Current Amplifying Device |
| SC | Silk Covered | | |
| SC | Silvered Copper | SCADA | Supervisory Control And Data |
| SC | Simultaneous Computer | | |
| SC | Sine Cosine | SCADA | Supervisory Control And Data Acquisition |
| SC | Single Contact | | |
| SC | Single-Current | SCADAR | Scatter Detection And Ranging |
| SC | Small Card | | |
| SC | Small Cluster | SCADS | Scanning Celestial Attitude Determination System |
| SC | Solar Coil | | |
| SC | Solar Constant | | |
| SC | Source Card | SCADS | Simulation of Combined Analog Digital Systems |
| SC | Source Computer | | |
| SC | Speach Communication | SCAL | STAR Computer Assembly Language |
| SC | Specific Coding | | |
| SC | Standard Channel | SCALE | Space Checkout And Launch Equipment |
| SC | Standard Counter | | |
| SC | Steel-Cored | SCALE | Syllabically Companded And Logically Encoded |
| SC | Stop-Continue register | | |
| SC | Storage Circuit | SCALO | Scanning Local Oscillator |
| SC | Storage Control | SCALP | Small Card Automated Layout Program |
| SC | Store Character | | |
| SC | Store Control | SCAM | Subcarrier Amplitude Modulation |
| SC | Subchannel | | |
| SC | Subcommittee | SCAMP | Scientific Computer And Modular Processor |
| SC | Subtract Carry | | |
| SC | Summary Card | SCAMP | Signal Conditioning Amplifier |
| SC | Super Calandered | | |
| SC | Super Computer | SCAMP | Sperry Computer Aided Message Processor |
| SC | Superimposed Coding | | |
| SC | Superimposed Current | SCAMP | System Compiler Assembly Program |
| SC | Supervisor Call | | |
| SC | Supervisory Control | SCAMPS | Small Computer Analytical and Mathematical Programming System |
| SC | Suppressed Carrier | | |
| SC | Switched Capacitor | | |
| SC | Switching Cell | SCAN | Schedule Analysis |
| SC | Symbol Checking | SCAN | Selective Current Awareness Notification |
| SC | Symbol Code | | |
| SC | Symbolcode | SCAN | Self-Correcting Automatic Navigation |
| SC | Symbolic Code | | |
| SC | Symbolic Coding | SCAN | Semiconductor Component Analysis Network |
| SC | Symbolic Compiler | | |
| SC | System Controller | | |

# S

| | | | |
|---|---|---|---|
| SCAN | Southern California Answering Network | SCATT | Shared Catalog Accessed Through Terminals |
| SCAN | Stockmarket Computer Answering Network | SCAX | Small County Automatic Exchange |
| SCAN | Switched Circuit Automatic Network | SCB | Seek Check Bit |
| | | SCB | Service Control Block |
| SCANIT | SCAN-only Intelligent Terminal | SCB | Shallow Cathode Barrier |
| | | SCB | Software Control Board |
| SCANS | Scheduling and Control by Automated Network System | SCB | Station Control Block |
| | | SCB | Store Check Bit |
| | | SCB | String Control Byte |
| SCANS | Stanford Computer for Analysis of Nuclear Structure | SCB | Supervisory Circuit Breaker |
| | | SCB | System Control Block |
| SCAP | Silent Compact Auxiliary Power | SCBAR | System Control Block Address Register |
| SCAR | Satellite Capture And Retrieval | SCC | Schweizer Computer Club |
| | | SCC | Self-Checking Code |
| SCAR | Submarine Celestial Altitude Recorder | SCC | Self-Correcting Code |
| | | SCC | Sequence Controlled Calculator |
| SCARD | Signal Conditioning And Recording Device | SCC | Serial Communications Controller |
| SCAT | Share Compiler, Assembler and Translator | SCC | Serial Correlation Coefficient |
| SCAT | Space Communication And Tracking | SCC | Signal Channel Controller |
| | | SCC | Simplified Computer Code |
| SCAT | Speed Command of Attitude and Thrust | SCC | Simulation Control Center |
| | | SCC | Single Card Checking |
| SCAT | Sperry Canada Automatic Tester | SCC | Single-Conductor Cable |
| | | SCC | Single-Cotton Covered |
| SCAT | Statistical Communications Analysis Technique | SCC | Slidell Computer Complex |
| | | SCC | Small Center Contact |
| SCAT | Supersonic Commerical Air Transport | SCC | Special Character Conversion |
| SCAT | Surface-Controlled Avalanche Transistor | SCC | Special Computer Center |
| | | SCC | Specialized Common Carriers |
| SCAT | System Configuration Acceptance Test | SCC | Speed Call Controller |
| | | SCC | Status Change Character |
| SCAT | System Configuration Audit Table | SCC | Storage Connecting Circuit |
| | | SCCD | Surface Charge Coupled Device |
| SCATE | Self Checking Automatic Test Equipment | SCCM | Short Circuit Conductance Matrix |
| SCATE | Stromberg-Carlson Automatic Test Equipment | SCCRD | Special Charge/Credit Description |
| SCATER | Security Control of Air Traffic and Electromagnetic Radiation | SCCS | Software Controlled Communication Service |
| SCATS | Sequentially Controlled Automatic Test Equipment | SCCS | Source Code Control System |
| SCATS | Simulation Checkout And Training System | SCCS | Straight-Cut Control System |
| SCATT | Scientific Communication And Technology Transfer | SCD | Schedule |

# S

| | | | |
|---|---|---|---|
| SCD | Screwed | SCFG | Stochastic Context Free Grammar |
| SCD | Semiconductor Device | | |
| SCD | Short-Code Dialling | SCFM | Standard Cubic Feet per Minute |
| SCD | Source Control Drawings | | |
| SCD | Space Control Document | SCFM | Subcarrier Frequency Modulation |
| SCD | Stored Charge Diode | | |
| SCD | System Contents Directory | SCFRPAC | Symposium on Computer Films for Research in Physics And Chemistry |
| SCD | System Control Data | | |
| SCDA | Small Card Design Automation | | |
| | | SCFS | Subcarrier Frequency Shift |
| SCDC | Service Code and Data Collection | SCFTS | SLT Card Final Test System |
| SCDC | Source Code and Data Collection | SCFTS | Small Card Facility Test System |
| SCDDS | Switched Circuit Digital Data Service | SCG | Software Concepts Group |
| | | SCH | Schalter |
| SCDG | Self-Checking Digit Generator | SCH | Schedule |
| | | SCH | Search |
| SCDL | Saturated Current Demand Logic | SCH | Special Character |
| | | SCHDL | Schedule |
| SCDP | Systems/Computer Development Program | SCHDLR | Scheduler |
| | | SCHDR | Schnelldrucker |
| SCDR | Subsystem Controller Definition Record | SCHED | Schedule |
| | | SCHM | Set Channel Monitor |
| SCDSB | Suppressed Carrier Double Sideband | SCHO | Standard Controlled Heterodyne Oscillator |
| SCE | Short-Channel Effect | SCHOLE | Schreibmaschinen-orientierte Leistungs-kontrolle |
| SCE | Signal Conversion Equipment | | |
| SCE | Single Cycle Execute | SCHREG | Schieberegister |
| SCE | Single-Cotton Enamelled | SCHT | Schalttafel |
| SCE | Solder Circuit Etch | SCHULIS | Schulinformationssystem |
| SCEA | Signal Conditioning Electronic Assembly | SCI | Science Citation Index |
| | | SCI | Sign Check Indicator |
| SCEC | Small Card Engineering Change | SCI | Single Column Inch |
| | | SCI | Soft Cast Iron |
| SCEI | Serial Carry Enable Input | SCI | Stock Card Index |
| SCEPTRE | Software-Controlled Electronic Processing Traffic Recording Equipment | SCI | Supervisor Call Instruction |
| | | SCI | Switched Collector Impedance |
| | | SCI | System Command Interpreter |
| SCERT | System and Computer Evaluation and Review Technique | | |
| | | SCI... | Scientific Computer Inc. |
| | | SCIB | Salon des services, de la Communication, de l'In-formatique et du Bureau |
| SCF | Satellite Control Facility | | |
| SCF | Scientific Computing Facility | | |
| | | SCIC | Semiconductor Integrated Circuit |
| SCF | Secondary Control Field | | |
| SCF | Self-Consistent Field | SCIL | System Core Image Library |
| SCF | Sequence Compatibility Firing | SCIM | Speech Communication Index Meter |
| SCF | System Control Facility | SCIMP | Self-Contained Imaging Micro-Profiler |
| SCFA | Self Consistent Field Approximation | | |
| | | SCIP | Scanning for Information Parameter |

## S

| | | | |
|---|---|---|---|
| SCIP | Self-Contained Instrument Package | SCM | Smith Corona Marchant Co. |
| SCIP | Stanford Center for Information Processing | SCM | Society for Computer Medicine |
| SCIP | Students Chemical Information Project | SCM | Stratified Charge Memory |
| | | SCM | Superimposed Coding Method |
| SCIPP | Silicon-Computing Instrument Patch-Programmed | SCM | Switch Core Matrix |
| | | SCM | System Control Manager |
| SCIRT | Supplier Capability Information Retrieval Technique | SCMP | Single Chip Microprocessor |
| | | SCN | Satellite Control Network |
| | | SCN | Scan |
| SCIRT | System Control In Real Time | SCN | Sensitive Command Network |
| | | SCN | Single Call Non-ringing |
| SCISRS | Stigma Center Information Storage and Retrieval System | SCN | Specific Control Number |
| | | SCND | Scanned |
| | | SCND | Self-Checking Number Device |
| SCK | Set Clock | | |
| SCK | Special Character Key | SCNG | Scanning |
| SCL | Scale | SCNG | Self-Checking Number Generator |
| SCL | Schedule | | |
| SCL | Simulation Coding Language | SCNR | Scanner |
| | | SCO | Subcarrier Oscillator |
| SCL | Space Charge Limited | SCOCLIS | Standing Conference Of Cooperative Library Information Services |
| SCL | Speed Call List | | |
| SCL | Static Complementary Logic | | |
| | | SCODA | Scan Coherent Doppler Attachment |
| SCL | Symbolic Correction Loader | SCODS | Standing Committee of Ocean Data Stations |
| SCL | Symmetric Clipper | | |
| SCL | System Chart Language | SCOLCAP | Scottish Libraries Co-operative Automation Project |
| SCL | System Consultants Limited | | |
| | | SCOLD | Small Company On-Line Data |
| SCL | System Control Language | | |
| SCL... | Systems Consultants Ltd. | SCOLDS | Spark Chamber On-Line Data System |
| SCLC | Space-Charge-Limited Current | | |
| | | SCOM | Service Central d'Organi-sation et de Méthodes |
| SCLD | Space Charge Limited Diode | | |
| | | SCOMO | Satellite Collection Of Meteorological Observation |
| SCLIGFET | Space-Charge-Limited Insulated-Gate Field-Effect Transistor | | |
| | | SCOOP | Scientific Computation Of Optimal Programs |
| SCLP | Security Command Language Processor | | |
| | | SCOOP | Scientific Computation Of Optimum Procurement |
| SCLWR | Scientific Computing Laboratory Work Request | | |
| | | SCOPE | Schedule-Cost-Performance |
| SCM | Secondary Core Memory | | |
| SCM | Segment Control Module | SCOPE | Sequential Customer Order Processing Electronically |
| SCM | Self-Correcting Memory | | |
| SCM | Serial Core Memory | | |
| SCM | Service Command Module | | |
| SCM | Signal Conditioning Module | SCOPE | Status Concept Of Program Evaluation |
| SCM | Single Chip Module | | |
| SCM | Small Capacity Memory | SCOPE | Supervisor Control Of Program Execution |
| SCM | Small Core Memory | | |

# S

| | | | |
|---|---|---|---|
| SCOPE | System for Computing Operational Probability Equations | SCR | Series Control Relay |
| | | SCR | Shift Count Register |
| | | SCR | Short Circuit Ratio |
| SCOPL | Simple Checkout-Oriented Programming Language | SCR | Silicon Controlled Rectifier |
| SCOPT | Subcommittee On Programming Terminology | SCR | Single Call Ringing |
| | | SCR | Single Card Reader |
| SCOR | Self-Calibration Omnirange | SCR | Small Card Reader |
| SCORE | Satellite Computer-Operated Readiness Equipment | SCR | Software Change Request |
| | | SCR | Space-Charge Recombination |
| SCORPIO | Subject Content Oriented Retriever for Processing Information Online | SCR | Split Cycle Random |
| | | SCR | Static Card Reader |
| | | SCR | Strip Chart Recorder |
| SCOT | Semi-automated Computer Oriented Text | SCR | System Control Routine |
| | | SCRAM | Strip Cylindrical Random Access Memory |
| SCOT | Standby Compatible One-Tape | SCRAP | Series Computation of Reliability And Probability |
| SCOUT | Surface-Controlled Oxide Unipolar Transistor | | |
| SCP | SAGE Computer Program | SCRIB | Salon de la Communication, Reprographie, de l'Informatique, de la Bureautique et du matériel de bureau |
| SCP | SAGE Computer Project | | |
| SCP | Safety Control Program | | |
| SCP | Secondary Control Program | | |
| SCP | Semiconductor Products | SCRID | Silicon Controlled Rectifier Indicator Driver |
| SCP | Sequence Checking Program | | |
| SCP | Special Character Printing | SCRIPT | Stanford Computerized Research Information Profile Technique |
| SCP | Storage Control Program | | |
| SCP | Support Control Program | | |
| SCP | Symbolic Conversion Program | SCRN | Screen |
| | | SCROLL | String and Character Recording Oriented Logogrammatic Language |
| SCP | System Communication Pamphlet | | |
| SCP | System Control Panel | SCRP | Small Card Release Processing |
| SCP | System Control Processor | | |
| SCP | System Control Program | SCRS | Single Character Recognition System |
| SCP | System Control Programming | | |
| | | SCRS | Strip Chart Recorder System |
| SCPC | Single Channel Per Carrier | | |
| SCPE | System Control Program Extended | SCS | Schedule Control System |
| | | SCS | Security Control System |
| SCPN | Small Card Part Number | SCS | Select Character Set |
| SCPT | SAGE Computer Programming Training | SCS | Selective Character Set |
| | | SCS | Serial Core Store |
| SCR | Scanning Control Register | SCS | Servo Controlled System |
| SCR | Screen | SCS | Short Circuit Stable |
| SCR | Selective Chopper Radiometer | SCS | Signal Communication System |
| SCR | Semiconductor-Controlled Rectifier | SCS | Silicon-Controlled Switch |
| | | SCS | Simulation Control Subsystem |
| SCR | Sequence Checking Routine | | |
| | | SCS | Single Channel Simplex |
| SCR | Sequence Control Register | SCS | Slow Code Scanner |

# S

| | | | |
|---|---|---|---|
| SCS | Small Commercial System | SCTY | Security |
| SCS | Small Computer System | SCU | S-band Cassegrain Ultra |
| SCS | SNA Character String | SCU | Scan Control Unit |
| SCS | Society for Computer Simulation | SCU | Secondary Control Unit |
| SCS | Space Cabin Simulator | SCU | Shared Control Unit |
| SCS | Space Communication System | SCU | Signal Conditioning Unit |
| SCS | Special Computer Service | SCU | Source Control Unit |
| SCS | Standard Character Set | SCU | Speed Call User |
| SCS | Standard Coordinate System | SCU | Storage Control Unit |
| SCS | Supervisory Control System | SCU | Subscriber Channel Unit |
| SCS... | Scientific Control Systems GmbH | SCUBA | Small Card Unit Block Analysis |
| SCSC | Summer Computer Simulation Conference | SCUG | Start of Closed User Group character |
| SCSCLC | Single-Carrier Space-Charge-Limited Current | SCUP | School Computer Use Plan |
| SCSCP | System Coordination for SAGE Computer Programming | SCV | Subsclutter Visibility |
| | | SCW | Search Control Word |
| | | SCW | Segment Control Word |
| | | SCW | Silk Covered Wire |
| | | SCW | Slow-Cyclotron Wave |
| | | SCW | Subchannel Control Word |
| SCSI | Small Computer Standard Interface | SCY | Successive Cycles |
| SCSI | Small Computer System Interface | SD | Sample Data |
| | | SD | Sample Delay |
| SCSL | Scientific Continuous Simulation Language | SD | Scan Data |
| | | SD | Schnelldrucker |
| SCT | Scanning Telescope | SD | Schottky Diode |
| SCT | Schottky Clamped Transistor | SD | Section Definition |
| | | SD | Selenium Diode |
| SCT | Service de Calcul par Téléphone | SD | Sendediode |
| | | SD | Sequential Disk |
| SCT | Service de Consultation Téléphonique | SD | Serial Data |
| | | SD | Serial Disc |
| | | SD | Seriendrucker |
| SCT | Single Channel Transponder | SD | Signal Data |
| SCT | Special Characters Table | SD | Signal Digit |
| SCT | Step Control Table | SD | Signal-to-Distortion |
| SCT | Subroutine Call Table | SD | Significant Digit |
| SCT | Surface Controlled Transistor | SD | Single Data |
| | | SD | Solenoid Driver |
| | | SD | Spectral Distribution |
| SCT | Surface-Charge Transistor | SD | Standard Deviation |
| SCT | System Component Test | SD | Storage and Distribution |
| SCT | System Configuration Table | SD | Streifendrucker |
| | | SD | Stücklistendatei |
| SCT | Système de Calcul par Téléphone | SD | Subtract Decimal |
| | | SD | Sweep Driver |
| | | SD | System Director |
| SCTL | Schottky Coupled Transistor Logic | SD | Systems Development Corp. |
| SCTL | Short Circuited Transmission Line | SDA | Satellite Data Area |
| | | SDA | Screen Design Aid |
| SCTP | Straight Channel Tape Print | SDA | Sélection Directe à l'Arrivée |
| SCTR | Sector | SDA | Shaft Drive Axis |

# S

| | | | |
|---|---|---|---|
| SDA | Share Distribution Agency | SDC | System Development Corporation |
| SDA | Shut Down Amplifier | | |
| SDA | Significant Digit Arithmetic | SDCC | Simulation Data Conversion Center |
| SDA | Source Data Acquisition | SDCCU | Synchronous Data Communication Control Unit |
| SDA | Source Data Automation | | |
| SDA | Standard Data Adapter | | |
| SDA | Statistical Deconvolution Algorithm | SDCF | Sampled Data Channel Filter |
| SDA | Supporting Data Analysis | SDCS | Science Data Conditioning System |
| SDA | Symbolic Disk Address | | |
| SDA | Symbols, Digits, Alphabetics | SDCS | Simulation Data Conversion System |
| SDA | Synchrondatenanschluß | SDCS | Space-borne Data Conditioning System |
| SDA | Synchronous Data Adapter | | |
| SDA | Systems Data Analysis | SDCS | Station Digital Command System |
| SDAC | Seismology Data Analysis Center | SDD | Selected Dissemination of Documents |
| SDAD | Satellite Digital and Analog Display | SDD | Service Data Description |
| SDADS | Satellite Digital And Display System | SDD | Signal Data Demodulator |
| | | SDD | Spécification de Description des Données |
| SDAIDS | System Debugging Aids | | |
| SDAP | Systems Development Analysis Program | SDD | Synthetic Data Display |
| | | SDD | System Defined Data |
| SDAS | Scientific Data Automation System | SDDLL | Simpled-Data Delay-Lock Loop |
| SDAS | Source Data Automation System | SDDS | Signal Data Demodulation Set |
| SDAS | Systems Data Analysis Section | SDDTTG | Stored Data Definition and Translation Task Group |
| SDAT | Symbolic Device Address Table | SDDU | Simplex Data Distribution Unit |
| SDAZ | Sonderdienstausscheidungs-ziffer | SDE | Selective Digit Emitter |
| | | SDE | Society of Data Educators |
| SDB | Segment Descriptor Block | SDE | Standard Data Element |
| SDB | Sélection de Débit Binaire | SDE | Storage Distribution Element |
| SDB | Standard Device Byte | | |
| SDB | Storage Data Buffer | SDE | Storage Distributor Element |
| SDB | Store Data Buffer | | |
| SDBS | Shared Data Bank System | SDE | Submission and Delivery Entity |
| SDC | Sampled Data Control | | |
| SDC | Scientific Data Center | SDF | Screen Definition Facility |
| SDC | Seismological Data Center | SDF | Serial Data Field |
| SDC | Send Data Condition | SDF | Single Disk File |
| SDC | Serial Digital Computer | SDF | Spectral Density Function |
| SDC | Setpoint Digital Control | SDF | Standard Data Format |
| SDC | Signal Data Converter | SDF | Supergroup Distribution Frame |
| SDC | Source of Demand Category | | |
| | | SDF | System Data File |
| SDC | Source of Demand Code | SDF | System Dialog Facility |
| SDC | Space Digital Computer | SDF-A | System Dialog Facility - Administration |
| SDC | Stabilization Data Computer | | |
| | | SDFD | System Data Flow Diagram |
| SDC | Standard Data Card | SDFL | Schottky Diode FET Logic |

# S

| | | | |
|---|---|---|---|
| SDG | Simulated Data Generation | SDM | Standardization Design Memoranda |
| SDG | Simulated Data Generator | | |
| SDG | Steuerdifferentialgeber | SDM | Statistical Delta Modulation |
| SDHE | Spacecraft Data-Handling Equipment | SDM | System Decision Manager |
| SDI | Schéma Directeur d'Informatisation | SDMA | Space Division Multiple Access |
| SDI | Selective Dissemination of Information | SDMD | Sequential Decision-Making Device |
| SDI | Serial Data In | SDMS | Shipboard Data Multiplex System |
| SDI | Serial Data Interface | | |
| SDI | Source Data Information | SDN | Sonderdienstnummer |
| SDI | Source Data Item | SDNM | Sampled-Data Nonlinearity Matrix |
| SDI | Spares Data Information | | |
| SDI | Standard Data Interface | SDO | Scan Data Out |
| SDI | Switch Discrete In | SDO | Software Distribution Operation |
| SDI | System Diagram Index | | |
| SDI | Systems Design and Installation | SDO | Spezielle Digitale Output |
| SDID | Supplier Data Item Description | SDOS | Source Data Operating System |
| SDIM | System of Documentation and Information for Metallurgy | SDP | Selective Data Processing |
| | | SDP | Signal Data Processor |
| | | SDP | Silicon Diode Pellet |
| SDK | Store Dump Key | SDP | Single Dry Plate |
| SDKZ | Sonderdienstkennzahl | SDP | Sinnbilder für Datenflußpläne |
| SDL | Screen Description Language | SDP | Site Data Processor |
| SDL | Second Level Directory | SDP | Standard Device Protocol |
| SDL | Specification and Description Language | SDP | Standards Development Program |
| SDL | Structure Definition Language | SDP | Station Data Processing |
| | | SDP | Survey Data Processing |
| SDL | System Descriptive Language | SDP | Systems and Data Processing |
| SDL | System Design Language | SDPL | Safeguard Data Processing Laboratory |
| SDL | System Directory List | | |
| SDL | Systematic Design Language | SDPL | Servomechanisms and Data Processing Laboratory |
| SDLC | Single-level Data Link Control | SDPS | Signal Data Processing System |
| SDLC | Synchronous Data Line Control | SDR | Schnelldrucker |
| | | SDR | Scientific Data Recorder |
| | | SDR | Self-Decoding Readout |
| SDLC | Synchronous Data Link Communications | SDR | Sender |
| | | SDR | Signal Data Recorder |
| SDLC | Synchronous Data Link Control | SDR | Single-Drift-Region |
| | | SDR | Sonar Data Recorder |
| SDM | Schnelldruckermeldung | SDR | Speicherdatenregister |
| SDM | Selective Dissemination of Microfiche | SDR | Statistical Data Recorder |
| | | SDR | Storage Data Register |
| SDM | Situation Display Matrix | SDR | Synchron-Duplex-Rechner |
| SDM | Software Development Methodology | SDR | System Definition Record |
| | | SDR | System Design Review |
| SDM | Source Data Management | SDR | System Direct Routine |

# S

| | | | |
|---|---|---|---|
| SDRC | Structural Dynamics Research Corporation | SDTP | Startover Data Transfer and Processing |
| SDRL | Subcontractor Data Requirements List | SDTRL | Saturating Drift Transistor Register Logic |
| SDRN | Sonderdienstrufnummer | SDTS | Satellite Data Transmission System |
| SDRONL | Software Development Realized On Natural Language | SDÜ | Schnelle Datenübertragung |
| | | SDU | Service Data Unit |
| SDRP | Simulated Data Reduction Program | SDU | Signal Display Unit |
| | | SDU | Simple Data Unit |
| SDS | Safety Data Sheet | SDU | Spectrum Display Unit |
| SDS | Sampled Data System | SDU | Storage Distribution Unit |
| SDS | Scientific Data Systems | SDU | Subcarrier Delay Unit |
| SDS | Scientific Data Systems Inc. | SDV | Slowed-Down Video |
| | | SDV | Start Device |
| SDS | Sequential Data Set | SDW | Segment Description Word |
| SDS | Service Data Sheet | SDW | Standing Detonation Wave |
| SDS | Share Data Set | SDX | Satellite Data Exchange |
| SDS | Shared Database System | SE | Schaltelement |
| SDS | Significant Digit Scanner | SE | Secondary Electron |
| SDS | Significant Digits | SE | Secondary Emission |
| SDS | Simulation Data Subsystems | SE | Select |
| | | SE | Self-Extinguishing |
| SDS | Simulation Data System | SE | Set |
| SDS | Single Disk Storage | SE | Shielding Effectiveness |
| SDS | Stammdatenspeicher | SE | Sign Extended |
| SDS | Status Display Support | SE | Single Entry |
| SDS | Summarized Demand State | SE | Software Engineer |
| SDS | System Data Synthesizer | SE | Sortiereinheit |
| SDSB | Satellite Data Services Branch | SE | Special Equipment |
| | | SE | Speichereinheit |
| SDSD | Single Disk Storage Device | SE | Starter Electrode |
| | | SE | Steuereinheit |
| SDSI... | Scientific Data Systems Israel Ltd. | SE | Steuereinrichtung |
| | | SE | Steuerteil für Einzelbetrieb |
| SDSS | Satellite Data System Spacecraft | SE | Storage Element |
| | | SE | Store Element |
| SDSSE | Science Data System Support Equipment | SE | Strukturelement |
| | | SE | Summary Error |
| SDT | Sequential Decision Tree | SE | System Equalizer |
| SDT | Serial Data Transmission | SE | Systemeinheit |
| SDT | Simulated Data Tape | SE | Systems Engineer |
| SDT | Start Data Traffic | SE | Systems Engineering |
| SDT | Start Data Transfer | SEA | Schneller Einsteller/Abtaster |
| SDT | Start Descriptor Table | | |
| SDT | Step Down Transformer | SEA | Société Européenne Automatique |
| SDT | Surveillance Data Transmission | | |
| | | SEA | Société d'Electronique et d'Automatisme |
| SDT | System Downtime | | |
| SDTDL | Saturated Drift Transistor Diode Logic | SEA | System Engineering Activity |
| | | SEA | Systems Effectiveness Analyzer |
| SDTK | Support Drift Tube Klystron | | |
| | | SEA | Systems Error Analysis |
| SDTL | Schottky-Diode-Transistor Logic | | |

# S

| | |
|---|---|
| SEAC | Standard Eastern Automatic Computer |
| SEAC | Standards Electronic Automatic Computer |
| SEAC | Statistics and Extended Access Control |
| SEADAC | Seakeeping Data Analysis Center |
| SEAL | Simulation, Evaluation and Analysis Language |
| SEALS | Stored Energy Actuated Lift System |
| SEAM | Systems Error Analysis Machine |
| SEAMIC | South-East Asia Management Information Center |
| SEAP | Selektor-Ein-Ausgabe-Prozessor |
| SEARCC | South-East Asia Regional Computer Conference |
| SEARCH | System Evaluation And Reliability Checker |
| SEARCH | System for Electronic Analysis and Retrieval of Criminal Histories |
| SEAS | Share European Association |
| SEAS | Speicher-Eingabe/Ausgabe-Steuerung |
| SEBIS | System zum Entwurf Betrieblicher Informationssysteme |
| SEC | Second |
| SEC | Secondary |
| SEC | Secondary Electron Conduction |
| SEC | Secondary Emission Conductivity |
| SEC | Securities and Exchange Commission |
| SEC | Service Entretien Clients |
| SEC | Simple Electronic Computer |
| SEC | Single Engineering Control |
| SEC | Single Error Correction |
| SEC | Standard Execute Card |
| SEC SYS | Securities Systems |
| SECAM | Sequential Colour And Memory |
| SECAP | System Experience Correlation and Analysis Program |
| SECC | Single Error Correction Circuitry |
| SECDED | Single Error Correction, Double Error Detection |
| SECIR | Semiautomatic Encoding of Chemistry for Information Retrieval |
| SECL | Sequential Emitter Coupled Logic |
| SECL | Symmetrical Emitter Coupled Logic |
| SECMA | Stock Exchange Computer Managers Association |
| SECO | Sequential Coding |
| SECO | Sequential Control |
| SECO | Sequential Encoder-decoder |
| SECOM | Systems Engineering Communication |
| SECOR | Sequential Correlation Range |
| SECPS | Secondary Propulsion System |
| SECRE | Société d'Etudes et de Construction Electroniques |
| SECS | Sequential Events Control System |
| SECS | Small Engineering Computer System |
| SECT | Section |
| SECT | Skin Electric Tracing |
| SECURE | Systems Evaluation Code Under Radiation Environment |
| SED | Spectral Energy Distribution |
| SED | Suppressed Electrical Discharge |
| SED | System Engineering Development program |
| SED | Système d'Enregistrement des Données |
| SEDAB | Systems Engineering Design And Build |
| SEDAC | Seakeeping Data Analysis Center |
| SEDIT | Sophisticated string Editor |
| SEDIX | Selected Dissemination of Index |
| SEDM | Sonar Evaluation Demonstration Model |
| SEDPC | Scientific and Engineering Data Processing Center |
| SEDR | System Effective Data Rate |
| SEDS | Space Electronics Detection System |

# S

| | | | |
|---|---|---|---|
| SEDS | System Effectiveness Data System | SEL | Schreibmaschine, Elektrisch, mit Lochstreifenstanzer |
| SEE | Special Equipment Engineering | SEL | Select |
| SEEDCON | Software Evaluation, Exchange and Development for Contractors | SEL | Selector |
| | | SEL | Selektor |
| | | SEL... | Standard Elektrik Lorenz |
| SEEK | Systems Evaluation and Exchange of Knowledge | SEL... | Systems Engineering Laboratories Inc. |
| SEER | System for Electronic Evaluation and Retrieval | SELAP | Sendelaufplan |
| | | SELAS | Sortiments-Erfolgs-Analyse-System |
| SEER | System for Event Evaluation and Review | SELCAL | Selective Calling |
| SEF | Shielding Effectiveness Factor | SELCH | Selector Channel |
| | | SELD | Selected |
| SEF | Shock Excited Filter | SELDAM | Selective Data Management |
| SEF | Simple Environment Factor | | |
| SEFI | Service Formation Information | SELDOM | Selective Dissemination Of MARC |
| SEG | Segment | SELEAC | Standard Elementary Abstract Computer |
| SEG | Sende- und Empfangsgerät | | |
| SEG | Simulation Event Generator | SELECT | Search, Extract, List, Edit, Count and Total |
| SEG | Systemerweiterungsgruppe | SELECT | Selectivity |
| SEG | Systems Engineering Group | SELFIC | Self-Featuring Information Compression |
| SEG C | Systemerweiterungsgruppe C | SELG | Selecting |
| | | SELMA | Systems Engineering Laboratory's Markovian Analyzer |
| SEGM | Segment | | |
| SEGMNT | Segment | | |
| SEGMOS | Service Goods Movement System | SELN | Selection |
| | | SELR | Selector |
| SEGTAB | Segment Table | SELRECT | Selenium Rectifier |
| SEGWA | System der Elektronisch Gesteuerten und geregelten Warenbewegung | SELT | SAGE Evaluation Library Tape |
| | | SELV | Selective |
| SEI | Systems Engineering and Integration | SEM | Scanning Electron Microscope |
| SEIAC | Science Education Information Analysis Center | SEM | Sequence of Events Monitor |
| SEIC | Solar Energy Information Center | SEM | Simple Electronic Multiplier |
| SEIC | System Effectiveness Information Center | SEM | Speichereingabemeldung |
| | | SEM | Stochastisch-Ergodische Messelektronik |
| SEINA | Société Européenne d'Instruments Numériques et Analogiques | SEM | Subarray Electronics Module |
| SEIP | Systems Engineering Implementation Plan | SEM | Superimposed Encoding Method |
| SEIS | Simulator für Echtzeit-Informationssysteme | SEM | Systems Engineering Management |
| SEIT | Satellite Educational and Informational Television | SEMA | Société d'Economie et de Mathématiques Appliquées |
| SEK | Sekunde | | |

# S

| | | | |
|---|---|---|---|
| SEMCAP | Specification for Electromagnetic Capability Analysis Program | SEPS | Service module Electrical Power System |
| SEMCOR | Semantic Correlation | SEPS | Severe Environment Power System |
| SEMICON | Semiconductor | SEPT | Silicon Epitaxial Planar Transistor |
| SEMICOND | Semiconductor | | |
| SEMIRAD | Secondary Electron-Mixed Radiation Dosimeter | SEQ | Sequence |
| | | SEQNO | Sequence Number |
| SEMLAM | Semiconductor Laser Amplifier | SEQR | Sequencer |
| | | SEQUIP | Study of Environmental Quality Information Programs |
| SEMLAT | Semiconductor Laser Array Technique | | |
| SEMM | Scanning Electron Mirror Microscope | SEQUL | Sequential |
| | | SER | Serial |
| SEMO | Systems Engineering Management Organization | SER | Standard Error |
| | | SER | System Environment Recording |
| SEMS | Severe Environment Memory Series | SERB | Study of Enhanced Radiation Belt |
| SEMS | Severe Environment Memory System | SERC | Science and Engineering Research Council |
| SEMS | Société Européenne de Mini-informatique et de Systèmes | SERDES | Serializer-Deserializer |
| | | SERDESCRC | Serializer-Deserializer Cyclic Redundancy Check |
| SEN | Scanner Encoder | SERDEX | Serial Data Exchange |
| SEN | Sense | SERE | Systems Error Record and Entry |
| SEN | Steam Emulsion Number | | |
| SENG | Sensing | SEREP | System Environment Recording and Edit Program |
| SENL | Standard Equipment Nomenclature List | | |
| SENS | Sense information | SEREP | System Error Record Editing Program |
| SENSE | Semantic Network Storage Experiment | | |
| | | SERLINE | Serials online |
| SENT | Scanner-Encoder-Transmitter | SERME | Sign Error Root Modulus Error |
| SENTOS | Sentinel Operating System | | |
| SEON | Send Only | SERPS | Service Propulsion System |
| SEOPSN | Select-Operate-Sense | SERR | Systems Error Record and Retry |
| SEP | Separate Element Pricing | | |
| SEP | Separating character | SERT | Système d'Enregistreurs sur Réseau Téléphonique |
| SEP | Separation | | |
| SEP | Separator | SERTI | Société d'Etudes et de Réalisations pour le Traitement de l'Information |
| SEP | Simulator Event Processor | | |
| SEP | Space Electronic Package | | |
| SEP | Standard Electronic Package | | |
| | | SERV | Service |
| SEP | Symbolic Equations Program | SERVO | Servomechanism |
| | | SES | Sende/Empfangs-Synchronisationseinrichtung |
| SEPAC | Système d'Evolution Progressive et Automatisée des Connaissances | | |
| | | SES | System Evaluation System |
| | | SESA | Société d'Etudes des Systèmes d'Automation |
| SEPOL | Settlement Problem-Oriented Language | | |
| | | SESA | Software et Engineering des Systèmes d'informatique et d'Automatique |
| SEPOL | Soil Engineering Problem-Oriented Language | | |
| SEPR | Separation | | |

# S

| | | | |
|---|---|---|---|
| SESAM | Symbolische Eingabesprache für Automatische Mess-Systeme | SEU | Sende-Empfangs-Umschalter |
| SESAM | Symbolisches Eingabesystem für Anweisungen bei Multiprogramming | SEU | Sende-Empfangs-Umsetzer |
| | | SEU | Sender-Empfänger-Umsetzer |
| SESAM | System zur Elektronischen Speicherung Alphanumerischer Markmale | SEU | Small End Up |
| | | SEU | Source Entry Utility |
| | | SEUGI | SAS European User Group International |
| SESAME | Service Sort And Merge | SEURE | Systems Evaluation code Under Radiation Environment |
| SESAME | Supermarket Electronic Scanning for Automatic Merchandise Entry | | |
| | | SEV | Severity |
| SESAME | Système Electronique de Saisie et d'Aiguillage des Messages | SEVA | System Evaluation program |
| | | SEVAS | Secure Voice Access System |
| SESAR | Systems Engineering Services Activity Record | SEW | Silicon Epitaxial Wafer |
| SESE | Secure Echo Sounding Equipment | SF | Safety |
| | | SF | Safty Factor |
| SESIP | Systems Engineering Summary of Installation and Program | SF | Sampled Filter |
| | | SF | Save user Files |
| | | SF | Scalar Function |
| SESIPP | Systems Engineering Summary of Installations and Program Planning | SF | Scale Factor |
| | | SF | Scaling Factor |
| | | SF | Schlüsselfeld |
| SESOME | Service, Sort and Merge | SF | Scratch File |
| SESR | System Equipment Status Report | SF | Secondary File |
| | | SF | Selective Filter |
| SET | Selective Employment Tax | SF | Selektive Fehlerabschaltung |
| SET | Self-Extending Translator | | |
| SET | Service Evaluation Telemetry | SF | Shared File |
| | | SF | Shift Forward |
| SET | Set of parameters | SF | Side Frequency |
| SET | Solar Energy Thermionic | SF | Signal Frequency |
| SET | System Entwicklungs-Techniken | SF | Signalformer |
| | | SF | Signalfrequenz |
| SET | System Evaluation Technique | SF | Single Frequency |
| | | SF | Standard File |
| SETAB | Sets Tabular material | SF | Standard Frequency |
| SETAR | Serial Event Time And Recorder | SF | Start Field |
| | | SF | Statement Function |
| SETC | Solid Electrolyte Tantalum Capacitor | SF | Steuer-Flipflop |
| | | SF | Store Field |
| SETDF | Set and/or reset Defaults | SF | System Facility |
| SETI | Société Européenne pour le Traitement de l'Information | SFAR | System Failure Analysis Report |
| | | SFB | Semiconductor Functional Block |
| SETN | Second Terminal Number | | |
| SETR | Setter | SFB | Solid-state Functional Block |
| SETRA | Simplified Electronic Tracking | | |
| | | SFC | S-band Frequency Converter |
| SETRAN | Selectable Element Translator | SFC | Sectored File Controller |

## S

| | | | |
|---|---|---|---|
| SFC | Shop Floor Control | SFOLDS | Ship Form On-Line Design System |
| SFCSIP | Special Foreign Currency Science Information Program | SFS | Service Fixé par Satellite |
| | | SFS | Sindelfinger Fertigungssteuerung |
| SFCU | Serial File Control Unit | | |
| SFD | Scale Factor Designator | SFS | Step Function Solution |
| SFD | Signal Flow Diagram | SFSCL | Shunt-Feedback Schottky Clamped Logic |
| SFD | Successive Feed | | |
| SFD | System Function Description | SFT | Schnelle Fourier-Transformation |
| SFD | System Functional Drawing | SFT | Semiconductor Filmstrain Transducer |
| SFE | Societe Français des Electriciens | | |
| | | SFT | Simulated Flight Test |
| SFE | Start Field Extended | SFT | Source Fetch Trigger |
| SFET | Sperrschichtfeldeffekttransistor | SFTS | Standard Frequency and Time Signal |
| SFET | Surface FET | SFTWR | Software |
| SFF | Standard File Format | SFU | Special Function Unit |
| SFG | Screen Format Generator | SFU | Synchronized Forms Unit |
| SFG | Signal Flow Graph | SG | Sawtooth Generator |
| SFG | Staircase Function Generator | SG | Scanning Gate |
| | | SG | Screen-Grid |
| SFGA | Single Floating - Gate Amplifier | SG | Set Gate |
| | | SG | Signal |
| SFH | Speicher-Fehlerhalt | SG | Signal Generator |
| SFI | Selected Feature Index | SG | Signal Ground |
| SFI | Special Feature Index | SG | Single Groove |
| SFI | Standard Feature Index | SG | Solar Generator |
| SFIB | Syndicat national des Fabricants d'ensembles d'Informatique et de machines de Bureau | SG | Specific Gravity |
| | | SG | Standing Group |
| | | SG | Steuergenerator |
| | | SG | Summierungsgerät |
| SFIC | San Francisco Information Center | SG | Sweep Generator |
| | | SG | Switched Gain |
| SFID | Supplementary Flight Information Documentation | SG | Symbol Generator |
| | | SG | Synchronous Generator |
| SFIM | Société de Fabrication d'Instruments de Mesure | SGA | Self-Gating AND |
| | | SGBD | Système de Gestion de Base de Données |
| SFIS | Small Firms Information Service | SGBDR | Système de Gestion de Bases de Données Relationnelles |
| SFK | Satelliten Füllfaktor Klausel | | |
| SFL | Subfile | SGC | Simulated Generation Control |
| SFL | Substrate FED Logic | | |
| SFL | Symbolic Flowchart Language | SGC | Space Guidance Computer |
| | | SGC | Spartan Guidance Computer |
| SFM | Société Française des Mécaniciens | | |
| | | SGC | Storing Gate-Controlled diode |
| SFM | Split-Field Motor | | |
| SFM | Surface Feet per Minute | SGCN | System Generated Change Number |
| SFM | Swept Frequency Modulation | | |
| | | SGCS | Silicon Gate Controlled Switch |
| SFMS | Store and Forward Message | | |
| SFN | Sort File Name | SGD | Silicon Grown Diffused |
| SFO | Special Factory Order | SGD | Solar-Geophysical Data |

# S

| | | | |
|---|---|---|---|
| SGDE | System Ground Data Equipment | SH | Single-Heterostructure |
| SGE | Slow Glass Etch | SH | Source Handshake |
| SGF | Système de Gestion de Fichiers | SH | Store Halfword |
| | | SH | Subharmonic |
| SGGD | Speichernde Gate-gesteuerte Diode | SHA | Sidereal Hour Angle |
| | | SHA | Software Houses Association |
| SGJP | Satellite Graphic Job Processor | SHACO | Shorthand Coding system |
| SGL | Signal | SHADRAC | Shelter Housed Automatic Digital Random Access |
| SGL | System Generation Language | SHARE | Society of Help to Avoid Redundant Efforts |
| SGLS | Space-to-Ground Link Subsystem | SHARES | Shared Acquisitions and Retention System |
| SGM | Spannungsgesteuerter Multivibrator | SHARP | Ships Analysis and Retrieval Program |
| SGM | Spark Gap Modulation | SHARP | Ships Analysis and Retrieval Project |
| SGM | Système de Gestion du Multitasking | SHAS | Shared Hospital Accounting System |
| SGMT | Subgroup MODEM Terminal | SHB | Scheibe |
| SGN | Scan Gate Number | SHD | Second Harmonic Distortion |
| SGO | Spannungsgesteuerter Oszillator | SHD | Shifted |
| SGOS | Silicon Gate Oxide Semiconductor | SHE | Sheet |
| | | SHE | Signal Handling Equipment |
| SGP | Statistics Generating Package | SHE | Standard Hydrogen Electrode |
| SGP | Statistics Generation Program | SHE | Substrate Hot-Electron |
| | | SHF | Set Horizontal Format |
| SGP | System Generation Program | SHF | Super-High Frequency |
| | | SHG | Self-Holding Gate |
| SGR | Select Graphic Rendition | SHG | Shifting |
| SGS | Simultaneous Graphics System | SHI | Select High Intensity |
| | | SHI | Sheet Iron |
| SGS | Single Green Silk | SHIEF | Shared Information Elicitation Facility |
| SGS | Societa Generale Semiconduttori | SHIMMS | Shipboard Integrated Man Machine System |
| SGS | Statistical Gathering System | SHINS | Shipping Instruction |
| | | SHIP | Simplified-Helmholtz-Integral Program |
| SGS | Symbol Generator and Storage | SHIPDA | Shipping Data |
| SGSP | Single-Groove Single-Petticoat insulator | SHIPDAFOL | Shipping Data Follows |
| | | SHIRTDIF | Storage, Handling and Retrieval of Technical Data in Image Formation |
| SGT | Segment Table | | |
| SGT | Sichtgerät | | |
| SGT | Silicon Gate Technology | | |
| SGT | Silicon Gate Transistor | SHIS | Software-Hardware-Informationsschau |
| SGT | Système de Gestion de Transmission | SHLD | Shield |
| SGU | Symbol Generating Unit | SHM | Simple Harmonic Motion |
| SGV | Screen Grid Voltage | SHO | Super High Output |
| SH | Sample and Hold | SHOAP | Symbolic Horribly Optimizing Assembly Program |
| SH | Shield | | |
| SH | Shunt | SHOCAD | Show CADAM Drawings |

# S

| | | | |
|---|---|---|---|
| SHOCON | Short and Continuity | SI | Status Indicator |
| SHODOP | Short range Doppler | SI | Storage Immediate |
| SHORAN | Short-Range Aid to Navigation | SI | Store Information |
| | | SI | Store Instruction |
| SHORT | Shared Hospital Online/ Realtime Time-sharing | SI | Suppress Index |
| | | SI | Symbolic Instruction |
| SHP | Shaft Horsepower | SI | Symptom Index |
| SHP | Single Highest Peak | SI | Système International |
| SHP | Standard Hardware Program | SI | Systems Integration |
| SHPC | Six Hour Pseudo Clock | SI | Systems Integrity |
| SHPDT | Shipping Date | SI/OC | Serial Input/Output Channel |
| SHPNM | Ship to Name | | |
| SHPO | Subharmonic Parametric Oscillator | SI/PO | Serial-In/Parallel-Out |
| | | SIA | Semiconductor Industry Association |
| SHR | Shift Register | | |
| SHR | Shift Right | SIA | Sense Information Address |
| SHREWD | System for Holding and Retrieving Wanted Data | SIA | Sequence Instruction Address |
| SHS | Select Horizontal Spacing | SIA | Serial Interface Adapter |
| SHS | Sheet Steel | SIA | Software Industry Association |
| SHSIC | Super High Speed Integrated Circuit | SIA | Standard-Interface Anschluß |
| SHT | Short | | |
| SHTC | Short Time Constant | SIA | Subminiature Integrated Antenna |
| SHW | Short Wave | | |
| SHY | Syllable Hyphen character | SIA | Subsequent Instruction Address |
| SI | Sample Interval | | |
| SI | Scheduled Interruption | SIA | System Integration Address |
| SI | Screen grid input | | |
| SI | Select Instruction | SIAD | Système Interactif d'Aide à la Décision |
| SI | Self-Induction | | |
| SI | Semi-Insulating | SIAG | Signalausgabe |
| SI | Sense Indicator | SIAM | Signal Information And Monitoring |
| SI | Sense Information | | |
| SI | Sequence Instruction | SIAM | Society for Industrial and Applied Mathematics |
| SI | Set Instruction | | |
| SI | Shift Instruction | SIAM | System Integrated Access Method |
| SI | Shift-In | | |
| SI | Shipping Instruction | SIAP | Standardinstallations- ablaufplan |
| SI | Sicherung | | |
| SI | Sign Indication | SIAS | Siemens Ablaufsimulator |
| SI | Signal Instruction | SIB | Session Information Block |
| SI | Signal Interface | SIBE | Sequential In-Basket Exercise |
| SI | Signal-to-Interference | | |
| SI | Signal-to-Intermodulation | SIBOL | Sweden Integrated Banking On-Line |
| SI | Signalinformation | | |
| SI | Signalleitung | SIC | Science Information Council |
| SI | Simulationsroutine | | |
| SI | Single Instruction | SIC | Self-Instructed Carry |
| SI | Skip Instruction | SIC | Semiconductor Integrated Circuit |
| SI | Software Instruction | | |
| SI | Source Input | SIC | Separately Instructed Carry |
| SI | Specific Impulse | | |
| SI | Standard Interface | SIC | Silicon Integrated Circuit |
| SI | Standing Instruction | | |

# S

| | | | |
|---|---|---|---|
| SIC | Simulation operation Computer | SID | Systèmes d'Informatique Distribuée |
| SIC | Single Input Change | SIDASE | Significant Data Selection |
| SIC | Specific Inductive Capacity | SIDEB | Sideband |
| SIC | Standard Industrial Classification | SIDIAS | Siemens-Dialogsteuer-system |
| SIC | Système Informatique pour la Conjoncture | SIDIS | Siemens-Direktbuchungs-Informationssystem |
| SICA | Society of Industrial and Cost Accountants of Canada | SIDL | System Identification Data List |
| | | SIDS | Spares Integrated Data System |
| SICAD | Siemens Computer Aided Design | SIDS | Speech Identification System |
| SICB | Subinterrupt Control Block | SIDS | Stellar Inertial Doppler System |
| SICC | Ship Inventory Consumption Claim | SIDT | Silicon Integrated Device Technology |
| SICIS | Strategic Issue Competitive Information System | SIE | Science Information Exchange |
| SICL | Short Interrupt Class Lists | SIE | Shift Instruction Execution |
| SICLOPS | Simplified Interpretive COBOL Operating System | SIE | Single Instruction Execute |
| | | SIE | Start Interpretative Execution |
| SICM | Simultaneous Insertion of Circuit Modules | SIEG | Signaleingabe |
| SICO | Switched In for Checkout | SIEP | Static Instruction Executed Plotter |
| SICO | Systèmes Informatique de la Connaissance | SIF | Selective Identification Feature |
| SICO | Systems Integration and Checkout | SIF | Sound Intermediate Frequency |
| SICOB | Salon international de l'Informatique, de la Communication et de l'Organisation de Bureau | SIF | Standard Interface |
| | | SIF | System Input File |
| | | SIF ESER | Standard Interface Einheitssystem Elektronischer Rechner |
| SICPLAN | Special Interest Committee on Program Languages | SIFCS | Sideband Intermediate Frequency Communications System |
| SICRO | Société d'Informatique de Conseil et de Recherche Operationnelle | |  |
| | | SIFDARO | Standard Interface Datenerfassung, -Aufbereitung, Rationalisierung, Organisation |
| SICS | Semiconductor Integrated Circuits | | |
| SICSOFT | Special Interest Committee on Software | SIFIB | Siemens-Finanzbuchhaltung |
| SID | Silicon Imaging Device | SIFT | Share Internal FORTRAN Translator |
| SID | Society for Information Display | SIFT | Software Implemented Fault Tolerance |
| SID | Speech Input Device | SIG | Sichtgerät |
| SID | Storage Image Dump | SIG | Signal |
| SID | Stroboscopic Indicator Display | SIG | Signature |
| | | SIG | Significance Testing |
| SID | Sudden Ionospheric Disturbance | SIG | Significant |
| SID | Synthax Improving Device | SIG | Silicon Insulated Gate |
| SID | System Integrational Diagnostic | SIG | Special Interest Group |

# S

| | |
|---|---|
| SIG | Système Informatique de Gestion |
| SIG DEST | Signal Destination |
| SIG SRC | Signal Source |
| SIGACT | Special Interest Group on Automation and Computability Theory |
| SIGALP | Special Interest Group on Automated Language Processing |
| SIGAP | Societé d'Information et de Gestion d'Analyse et de Programmation |
| SIGARCH | Special Interest Group on Architecture of computer systems |
| SIGART | Special Interest Group on Artificial intelligence |
| SIGBDP | Special Interest Group on Business Data Processing |
| SIGBIO | Special Interest Group on Biomedical computing |
| SIGBIP | Silicon Gate Bipolar |
| SIGCAI | Special Interest Group on Computer Assisted Instruction |
| SIGCAPH | Special Interest Group on Computers And the Physically Handicapped |
| SIGCIS | Special Interest Group on Community Information Services |
| SIGCOMM | Special Interest Group on data Communication |
| SIGCOSIM | Special Interest Group on Computer Systems Installation Management |
| SIGCPR | Special Interest Group on Computer Personnel Research |
| SIGCR | Special Interest Group on Classification Research |
| SIGCRS | Special Interest Group on Computerized Retrieval Services |
| SIGCSE | Special Interest Group on Computer Science Education |
| SIGCUE | Special Interest Group on Computer Uses in Education |
| SIGDA | Special Interest Group on Design Automation |
| SIGDOC | Special Interest Group on Documentation |
| SIGE | Silicon-Germanium |
| SIGED | Special Interest Group on Education for information science |
| SIGFET | Semi-Insulated Gate Field Effect Transistor |
| SIGFET | Silicon Gate FET |
| SIGFIS | Special Interest Group on Foundations of Information Science |
| SIGGAS | Special Interest Group on Computers And Society |
| SIGGEN | Signal Generator |
| SIGGRAPH | Special Interest Group on computer Graphics |
| SIGIAC | Special Interest Group on Information Analysis Centers |
| SIGINT | Signal Intelligence |
| SIGIP | Special Interest Group on Information Publishing |
| SIGIR | Special Interest Group on Information Retrieval |
| SIGLA | SIGMA Language |
| SIGLAN | Special Interest Group on Library Automation and Networks |
| SIGLASH | Special Interest Group on Language Analysis and Studies in Humanities |
| SIGMALOG | Simulation and Gaming Methods for the Analysis of Logistics |
| SIGMAP | Special Interest Group on Mathematical Programming |
| SIGMICRO | Special Interest Group on Microprogramming |
| SIGMINI | Special Interest Group on Minicomputers |
| SIGMOD | Special Interest Group on Management Of Data |
| SIGMR | Special Interest Group on Medical Records |
| SIGNUM | Special Interest Group on Numerical Mathematics |
| SIGOPS | Special Interest Group on Operation Systems |
| SIGPC | Special Interest Group on Personal Computing |
| SIGPIP | Signal Peripheral Interchange Program |
| SIGPLAN | Special Interest Group on Programming Languages |
| SIGPPI | Special Interest Group on Public-Private Interface |

# S

| | | | |
|---|---|---|---|
| SIGSAM | Special Interest Group on Symbolic and Algebraic Manipulation | SIM | Simulation |
| | | SIM | Simulator |
| SIGSIM | Special Interest Group on Simulation | SIM | Synthetisches Informationsmodell |
| SIGSOC | Special Interest Group on Social and behavioural science computing | SIM | System Information Management |
| | | SIM | System Integration Module |
| | | SIMA | Scientific Instrument Manufacturer Association of Great Britain |
| SIGSOFT | Special Interest group on Software engineering | | |
| SIGTIS | Special Interest Group on Technology, Information, and Society | SIMA | Simulations-Algorithmen |
| | | SIMAJ | Scientific Instrument Manufacturer Association of Japan |
| SIGUCC | Special Interest Group on University Computing Centers | | |
| | | SIMAL | Simplified Accountancy Language |
| SIGUOI | Special Interest Group on User Online Interaction | SIMAL | Simulated All-purpose Language |
| SIHB | Société Industrielle Honeywell Bull | SIMALE | Super Integral Microprogrammed Arithmetic Logic Expediter |
| SII | Short Interval Identification | | |
| | | SIMANNE | Simulation of Analogical Network |
| SII | Standard Individual Identifier | | |
| | | SIMBAT | Sequential Independent Model Block Analytical Triangulation |
| SIIRS | Smithsonian Institution Information Retrieval System | | |
| | | SIMBOL | Simulated Boolean Oriented Language |
| SIIS | Submission Index and Information System | | |
| | | SIMC | Silicon Integrated Monolithic Circuit |
| SIKOS | Simulation Kontinuierlicher Systeme | | |
| | | SIMCHE | Simulation and Checkout Equipment |
| SIL | Service Information Letter | | |
| SIL | Single-In-Line | SIMCOM | Simulation and Computer |
| SIL | Speech Interference Level | SIMCOM | Simulator Compiler |
| SIL | Surge Impedance Loading | SIMCOM | Simulator Computer |
| SIL | System Implementation Language | SIMCON | Scientific Inventory Management Control |
| SILC | System for Inter-Library Communication | SIMCON | Simplified Control |
| | | SIMD | Single Instruction Multiple Data |
| SILK | System für Integrierte Lokale Kommunikation | | |
| | | SIMDIS | Simulation, Discrete |
| SILON | Siemens-Programmbausteinserie Lohn und Gehalt | SIMDS | Single Instruction Multiple Data Stream |
| | | SIMICORE | Simultaneous Multiple Image Correlation |
| SILS | School of Information and Library Studies | | |
| | | SIMILE | Simulator of Immediate Memory In Learning Experiments |
| SILS | Silver Solder | | |
| SILS | Site-Initiated Line Switching | | |
| | | SIMM | Symbolic Integrated Maintenance Manual |
| SIM | Scientific Instrument Module | | |
| | | SIMMPS | Simulator of a Multiprocessor |
| sim | Sequential Inference Machine | | |
| | | SIMON | Simple Instructional Monitor |
| SIM | Set Initialization Mode | | |
| SIM | Simulate | | |

# S

| | | | |
|---|---|---|---|
| SIMOS | Stacked gate Injection MOS | SINAD | Signal-to-Noise ratio And Distortion |
| SIMOSC | System Independent Method of Operator/System Communication | SINAP | Satellite Input to Numerical Analysis and Procedure |
| SIMP | Satellite Interface Message Processor | SINAP | Siemens-Netzwerk-Analyse-Programmsystem |
| SIMP | Simulationsprogramm | SINEC | Siemens Netzwerk für Minicomputer |
| SIMPAC | Simplified Programming for Acquisition and Control | SINET | System für Interaktive Netzplantechnik |
| SIMPACS | Simulation In Multi-processor Accelerated Computer System | SINETIK | Siemens-Netzplantechnik |
| | | SINPO | Signal strength, Interference, Noise, Propagation disturbance, Overall merit |
| SIMPL | Simulation Implementation Machine Programming Language | SINS | Ship Inertial Navigation System |
| SIMPL | Single Identity Micro-Programming Language | SIO | Serial Input/Output |
| | | SIO | Start Input/Output |
| SIMPLE | Simulation Programming Language | SIOA | Serial Input/Output Adapter |
| SIMPLER | System for Information Management and Program Logic for Education and Research | SIOC | Serial Input/Output Channel |
| | | SIOF | Start Input/Output Fast release |
| SIMPRO | Simulation Program | SIOP | Selectro Input/Output Processor |
| SIMPS | Simultane Produktionssteuerung | SIOP | Single Integrated Operations |
| SIMPU | Simulation Punch | | |
| SIMR | Simulator | SIOUX | Sequential Iterative Operation Unit X |
| SIMS | School Information Management System | SIOV | Siemens metal Oxide Varistor |
| SIMS | Sekundäre Ionenmassenspektrometrie | SIP | Selbstinterpretierende Programme |
| SIMS | Shared Interconnect Modem Service | SIP | Selbstinterpretierender Programmgenerator |
| SIMS | Single-Item Multisource | | |
| SIMS | Symbolic Integrated Maintenance System | SIP | Semidirect Iterative Procedures |
| SIMSI | Selective Inventory Management of Secondary Items | SIP | Shipment In Process |
| | | SIP | Short Irregular Pulse |
| SIMTRAN | Simple Translation | SIP | Simulated Input Processor |
| SIMU | Simulation | SIP | Single In-line Package |
| SIMULA | Simulation Language | SIP | Single Item Punching |
| SIMULACRE | Standard Image for Multi-unit Laminar Circuit Representation | SIP | Solar Instrument Probe |
| | | SIP | SONAR Instrumentation Probe |
| SIN | Security Information Network | SIP | Standardized Interface Package |
| SIN | Sensitive Information Network | SIP | Stock In Process |
| | | SIP | Symbolic Input Program |
| SIN | Support Information Network | SIP | System Initialize Program |
| SIN | Symbolic Integrator | SIP | System Integration Program |

# S

| | | | |
|---|---|---|---|
| SIPASS | Siemens-Personen-Ausweissystem | SIR | System Initialization Routine |
| SIPE | Systems Internal Performance Evaluator | SIR | Systemintegriertes Rechnungswesen |
| SIPMOS | Siemens Power MOS | SIRB | System Interruption Request Block |
| SIPO | Significantly Improved Printer Output | SIRC | Standards Information Retrieval Center |
| SIPO | Systems Installation Productivity Option | SIRE | Simulationssystem zur Reihenfolgeplanung |
| SIPOP | Satellite Information Processor Operational Program | SIRE | Symbolic Information Retrieval |
| SIPPS | System of Information Processing for Professional Societies | SIRE | Syracuse Information Retrieval System |
| SIPROS | Simultaneous Processing Operating System | SIRENE | Système Informatique du Répertoire des Entreprises et des Etablissements |
| SIPS | SAC Intelligence Processing System | SIRF | Subsystem Information Retrieval Facility |
| SIPS | Satellite Instrumentation Processor System | SIRMI | Societa Italiana Ricerche del Mercator Informatica |
| SIPSDE | Society of Independent and Private School Data Education | SIRS | Satellite Infrared Spectrometer |
| SIR | Salon normand de l'Informatique et de la Robotique | SIRS | Selective Information Retrieval Systems |
| SIR | Scientific Information Retrieval | SIRS | Standards Information Retrieval System |
| SIR | Selective Information Retrieval | SIRS | Student Information Record System |
| SIR | Selektiver Informations-Ringtausch | SIRU | Strapdown Inertial Reference Unit |
| SIR | Semantic Information Retrieval | SIS | SAGE Interceptor Simulator |
| SIR | Sequential Information Retrieval | SIS | Satellite Interceptor System |
| SIR | Signal-to-Interference Ratio | SIS | Scheduling Information System |
| SIR | Signal-to-Intermodulation Ratio | SIS | School of Information Studies |
| SIR | Simplified Information Retrieval | SIS | Scientific Information System |
| SIR | Simultaneous Impact Rate | SIS | Semiconductor-Insulator-Semiconductor |
| SIR | Special Information Retrieval | SIS | Set of Identifying Sequences |
| SIR | Specification Information Retrieval | SIS | Shared Information System |
| SIR | Statistical Information Retrieval | SIS | Shorter Interval Scheduling |
| SIR | Stratified Indexing and Retrieval | SIS | Simulation Interface Subsystem |
| SIR | Subcontractor Information Request | SIS | Single Image Software |
| SIR | Symbolic Input Routine | SIS | Single Image System |
| | | SIS | Société d'Informatique et de Systèmes |
| | | SIS | Sound In Sync |

# S

| | | | |
|---|---|---|---|
| SIS | Specialized Information Services | SITOK | Siemens-Tool-Konzept |
| SIS | Specification Information System | SITS | SAGE Intercept Target Simulation |
| SIS | Standard Instruction Set | SIU | Storage Interface Unit |
| SIS | Station Identification Store | SIU | System Input Unit |
| SIS | Statistical Information System | SIU | System Integration Unit |
| SIS | STEP Information Subsystem | SIU | System Interface Unit |
| SIS | Stored Information System | SIV | Selektive Informationsverbreitung |
| SIS | Successor Instruction Set | SIW | Single Instruction Word |
| SIS | System Interrupt Supervisor | SIWIS | Siemens-Werkstätten-Informations-System |
| SIS | Systèmes d'Information et Statistiques | SIZ | Size |
| SISCO... | Singer Information Services Co. | SIZSOZ | Software-Informationszentrale für Sozialwissenschaften/Statistik |
| SISD | Single-Instruction Single-Data stream | SJCC | Spring Joint Computer Conference |
| SISO | Single-Input/Single-Output | SJCL | Standardized Job Control Language |
| SISS | Semiconductor-Insulator Semiconductor System | SJE | Systems Job Executive |
| SISS | Single Item, Single Source | SJP | Stacked Job Processing |
| SISS | Submarine Integrated Sonar System | SJQ | Selected Job Queue |
| SISSC | Shared Information System Support Center | SJS | Search Jam System |
| SIT | Semulation Input Tape | SJS | Sequential Job Scheduling |
| SIT | Sequential Interval Timer | SJS | Single Job Scheduling |
| SIT | Silicon Intensifier Target | SK | Satzkennzeichen |
| SIT | Software Integration Test | SK | Schaltkontakt |
| SIT | Spontaneous Ignition Temperature | SK | Schnellkanal |
| SIT | Static Induction Transistor | SK | Seek command |
| SIT | Stepped Impedance Transformer | SK | Sekundärgruppen-Koder |
| SIT | Storage Inspection Test | SK | Selection Key |
| SIT | Storage In Transit | SK | Selektorkanal |
| SIT | System Initialization Table | SK | Senderkennung |
| SIT | Systeminitialisierungstabelle | SK | Sichtlochkarte |
| SIT-REP | Situation Report | SK | Sichtlochkartei |
| SITA | Société Internationale de Télécommunications Aéronautiques | SK | Skip |
| | | SK | Sortierkriterium |
| | | SK | Standardkanal |
| SITAR | System for Interactive Text editing, Analysis and Retrieval | SK | Symbolic Key |
| | | SK | Synchrokomparator |
| | | SKC | Seek Check |
| SITE | Search Information Tape Equipment | SKC | Space Key Code |
| | | SKED | Schedule |
| SITE | Spacecraft Instrumentation Test Equipment | SKED | Sort Key Edit |
| | | SKIPA | Skip After |
| SITL | Static Induction Transistor Logic | SKIPB | Skip Before |
| | | SKL | Skip Lister |
| | | SKM | Sine-Kosine Multiplier |
| | | SKOR | Sperry Kalman Optimum Reset |
| | | SKP | Skip Line Printer |
| | | SKR | System der Kleinrechentechnik |
| | | SKR | System der Kleinrechner |

# S

| | | | |
|---|---|---|---|
| SKU | Schnellkanalumsetzer | SLAMPET | Solid Logic Automatic Module Production Evaluation Tester |
| SKU | Stock-Keeping Unit | | |
| SKW | Steuern Keine Wirkung | | |
| SKZ | Satzkennzeichen | SLAMS | Simplified Language for Abstract Mathematical Structures |
| SKZ | Schnellkanalzusatz | | |
| SL | Saturated Logic | | |
| SL | Satzlänge | SLAMS | Stored Logic Adaptive Microcircuits |
| SL | Schutzleitung | | |
| SL | Segmented Library | SLANG | Systems Language |
| SL | Sensation Level | SLANT | Simulator Landing Attachment for Night landing Training |
| SL | Separate Lead | | |
| SL | Sequential Logic | | |
| SL | Signallampe | SLAP | Simulation Language Assembly Program |
| SL | Signalleitung | | |
| SL | Simulation Language | SLAP | Small-signal Linear Analysis Program |
| SL | Single Lead | | |
| SL | Slave station | SLAP | Subscriber Line Access Protocol |
| SL | Solid Logic | | |
| SL | Sound Locator | SLAP | Symbolic Language Assembly Program |
| SL | Source Language | | |
| SL | Source Library | SLAR | Side Looking Aerial Radar |
| SL | Standard Label | SLAR | Side Looking Airborne Radar |
| SL | Statement Label | | |
| SL | Static Logic | SLASH | Seiler Laboratory ALGOL Simulated Hybrid |
| SL | Steuerlogik | | |
| SL | Streifenleser | SLATE | Small Lightweight Altitude Transmission Equipment |
| SL | Streifenlocher | | |
| SL | Subtract Logical | | |
| SL | Symbolic Language | SLATE | Stimulated Learning by Automated Typewriter Environment |
| SL | Symbolic Logic | | |
| SL | System Librarian | | |
| SL | System Loader | SLATE | Structural Linguistic Analysis and Text Evaluation |
| SL3 | System Language No. 3 | | |
| SLA | Satellite Link Adapter | | |
| SLA | Sound Line Alarm | SLATM | Sales Amount This Month |
| SLA | Special Libraries Association | SLB | Side-Lobe Blanking |
| | | SLC | Selective List Control |
| SLA | Standard Label Area | SLC | Set Location Counter |
| SLA | Sum-Line Algorithm | SLC | Shared Language Component |
| SLA | Synchronous Line Adapter | | |
| SLAC | Significance and Location Analysis Computer | SLC | Shift Left and Count instructions |
| SLADO | System Library Activity Dynamic Optimizer | SLC | Shop Load and Control |
| | | SLC | Side-Lobe Cancellation |
| SLAE | Systems of Linear Algebraic Equations | SLC | Simulated Linguistic Computer |
| SLAM | Simulation Language for Analog Modelling | SLC | Single Line Controller |
| | | SLC | Single-Lead Covered |
| SLAM | Single Layer Metallization | SLC | Specific Line Capacitance |
| | | SLC | Straight-Line Capacitance |
| SLAM | Stored Logic Adaptable Metal oxide semiconductor transistor | SLC | Synchronous Line with Clock |
| | | SLCB | Single-Line Colour Bar |
| SLAM | Stored Logic Adaptive Microcircuit | SLCC | Saturn Launch Control Computer |

# S

| | | | |
|---|---|---|---|
| SLCC | Saturn Launcher Computer Complex | SLM | Solid Logic Module |
| SLD | Second Level-Directory | SLM | Statistical Learning Model |
| SLD | Second Logic Diagram | SLM | Subscriber Line Multiplexer |
| SLD | Set Line Density | SLM | Subscriber Loop Multiplexer |
| SLD | Simplified Logic Diagram | SLMA | Subscriber Line Module Analog |
| SLD | Simulated Launch Demonstration | SLMD | Subscriber Line Module Digital |
| SLD | Solid | SLMP | Self-Loading Memory Print |
| SLD | Solid Logic Dense | SLN | Selection |
| SLD | Straight-Line Depreciation | SLO | Slow |
| SLD | Superluminescent Diode | SLO | Swept Local Oscillator |
| SLD | Superlumineszensdiode | SLOA | Starting Location of Output Area |
| SLDA | Solid Logic Design Automation | SLOMAR | Space Logistics Maintenance And Rescue |
| SLED | Solid Logic Edit | SLOP | Standard Lists Output Program |
| SLED | Synchronous Logic Element Display | SLP | Second Level Package |
| SLEM | State Local Education and Medical | SLP | Segmented Level Programming |
| SLEW | Static Load Error Washout | SLP | Selective Line Printing |
| SLF | Straight-Line Frequency | SLP | Self Loading Program |
| SLFGEN | Self-Generating | SLP | Single Link Procedure |
| SLFIND | Self-Indicating | SLP | Source Language Processor |
| SLG | Selecting | SLP | Standard Line Printer |
| SLG | Single Line-to-Ground | SLPA | Solid Logic Process Automation |
| SLG | Synchronous Line-Group | SLPC | Second Level Product Commitment |
| SLI | Sea Level Indicator | SLQTM | Sales Quantity This Month |
| SLI | Select Low Intensity | SLR | Segment Load Routine |
| SLI | Socket List Interface | SLR | Service Level Reporter |
| SLI | Standard Label Information | SLR | Short Length Record |
| SLI | Suppress Length Indication | SLR | Side-Looking Radar |
| SLIB | Subsystem Library | SLR | Single Lens Reflex camera |
| SLIC | Selective Letters In Combination | SLR | Stepped Load Resistor |
| SLIC | Subcriber Line Interface Circuits | SLR | Storage Limits Register |
| SLIM | Special Language Interpreting Matrix | SLRAP | Standard Low frequency Range Approach |
| SLIM | Standards Laboratory Information Manual | SLRE | Self-Loading Random-access Edit |
| SLIM | Stock Line Inventory Management | SLREG | Schrittweise Lineare Regression |
| SLIM | Store Labour and Inventory Management | SLRN | Select Read Numerically |
| SLIP | Serviceability Level Indicator Processing | SLRT | Sequential Likelihood Ratio Test |
| SLIP | Symmetric List Interpretive Program | SLS | Schrift-Lese-System |
| SLIP | Symmetric List Processor | SLS | Shop Load Scheduler |
| SLIS | Shared Laboratory Information System | SLS | Side Lobe Suppression |
| SLK | Sichtlochkarte | SLS | Side Looking Sonar |
| SLK | Sichtlochkartei | SLS | Source Language Statement |
| SLL | Synchronous-line Low Load | | |

# S

| | | | |
|---|---|---|---|
| SLSAP | Source Link Service Access Point | SM | Storage Module |
| SLSI | Super Large Scale Integration | SM | Subminiatur |
| | | SM | Synchronous Modem |
| | | SM | System Manager |
| SLSS | System Library Subscription Service | SM | System Manual |
| | | SM | Système Multipose |
| SLT | Searchlight | SM | Systems Manager |
| SLT | Select | SMA | Satzmarke |
| SLT | Self Loading Tape | SMA | Sequential Multiple Analyzer |
| SLT | Signalling Line Terminal | | |
| SLT | Simulated Launch Test | SMA | Simulated Machine Analysis |
| SLT | Solid Logic Technique | | |
| SLT | Solid Logic Technology | SMA | Synchronous Mode Adapter |
| SLT | Solid Logic Transistor | SMAC | Sequential Multiple Analyzer and Computer |
| SLT | Standard Light source | | |
| SLTE | Self-Loading Tape Edit | SMAC | Serial Memory Address Counter |
| SLTR | Service Life Test Report | | |
| SLU | Secondary Logical Unit | SMAC | Simulation Model of Automobile Collisions |
| SLU | Subscriber's Line Unit | | |
| SLU | Synchronous Line Unit | SMAC | Simulation, Manual And Computerized |
| SLUNT | Spoken Language Universal Numeric Translation | | |
| | | SMAC | Simultaneous Multichannel Analyzer and Computer |
| SLV | Slave | | |
| SLW | Store Logical Word | SMAC | Space Missiles Aircraft Computer |
| SLWL | Straight Line Wavelength | | |
| SM | Satzmarke | SMAC | Special Mission Attack Computer |
| SM | Scan Matrix | | |
| SM | Scan Mode | SMACC | Scheduling, Manpower Allocation and Cost Control |
| SM | Scheduled Maintenance | | |
| SM | Schreibmaschine | | |
| SM | Searching Machine | SMACS | Scheduled Machine Assembly Control System |
| SM | Searching Method | | |
| SM | Secondary Memory | SMAL | Structured Macro Assembly Language |
| SM | Segment Mark | | |
| SM | Selector Matrix | SMALGOL | Small computer Algorithmic Language |
| SM | Semi-Mat | | |
| SM | Sensing Method | SMALL | Selenium diode Matrix Alloy Logic |
| SM | Sequence and Monitor | | |
| SM | Sequential Machine | SMARI | Scalar Multiplay Array Rows by Itself |
| SM | Service Module | | |
| SM | Servomechanism | SMARR | Scalar Multiply Arrays Row by Row |
| SM | Servomotor | | |
| SM | Set Mode | SMART | Salton's Magical Automatic Retrieval Technique |
| SM | Shared Memory | | |
| SM | Short Memory | SMART | Satellite Maintenance And Repair Techniques |
| SM | Simulator | | |
| SM | Slow Memory | SMART | Scheduler Manager And Resource Translator |
| SM | Sortiermaschine | | |
| SM | Source Machine | SMART | Storage, Modification And Retrieval Transaction |
| SM | Speicherschreibmaschine | | |
| SM | Stack Mark | SMART | Supermarket Allocation and Recorder Technique |
| SM | Static Memory | | |
| SM | Status Modifier | SMART | Symposium on Mechanical And Related Technologies |
| SM | Storage Mark | | |
| SM | Storage Mask | | |

- 559 -

## S

| | | | |
|---|---|---|---|
| SMART | System Memory Automatic Recovery Technique | SME | Suboptimierung Mit Eignungsmatrizen |
| SMART | Systematic Master Receiver Tabulating | SMEI | Sales and Marketing Executives International |
| SMART | Systems Management Analysis, Research and Test | SMEK | Summary Massage Enable Keyboard |
| SMARTI | Simple Minded Artificial Intelligence | SMF | Solar Magnetic Field |
| | | SMF | Stable Matrix Form |
| SMARTS | Status Memory And Real Time System | SMF | Super-Microfiche |
| | | SMF | Symbolic Memory Formatter |
| SMAS | Switched Maintenance Access System | SMF | System Management Facility |
| SMAT | Société de Machines et Appareils Techniques | SMF | System Measurement Facility |
| SMB | Schedule Message Block | SMF | System Measuring Facility |
| SMB | Set Memory Bit | SMG | Sort/Merge Generator |
| SMB | Speed Matching Buffer | SMG | Sortier-Mischgenerator |
| SMBL | Semi-Mobile | SMI | Simulated Machine Indexing |
| SMC | Scientific Manpower Commission | SMI | Simulation of Machine Indexing |
| SMC | Set MAMO Counter | | |
| SMC | Shunt Mounted Chip | SMI | Start Manual Input |
| SMC | Silicon Monolithic Circuit | SMI | Start of Message Indicator |
| SMC | Single Memory Cycle | SMI | System Macro Instruction |
| SMC | Standard Microsystems Corporation | SMI | Système des Méthodes Intégrées |
| SMC | Station Monitor and Control | SMIAC | Sail Mechanics Information Analysis Center |
| SMC | Systems Management Committee | SMID | Semiconductor Memory Integrated Device |
| SMCC | Simulation Monitor and Control Console | SMIOP | Semiconductor Manu-facturing Internal Operating Procedure |
| SMD | Semiconductor Magnetic field Detector | SMIPS | Small interactive Image Processing System |
| SMD | Service-Mounted-Devices | | |
| SMD | Short Memory Dump | SMIRS | School Management Information Retrieval System |
| SMD | Sony's Magneto-Diode | | |
| SMD | Storage Module Drive | | |
| SMD | Surface Mounted Devices | SMIS | Sequential Multilayer Interconnection System |
| SMD | Systems Maintenance Design | SMIS | Society for Management Information Systems |
| SMD | Systems Measuring Device | | |
| SMD | Systems Monitor Display | SMIS | Supply Management Information System |
| SMDC | Superconductive Materials Data Center | SMIS | Surface Metal Insulator Semiconductor |
| SMDL | Spares Master Data Log | | |
| SME | Sekundärmultiplex-einrichtung | SMISOP | Safeguard Management Information System Operating Program |
| SME | Shop Maintenance Equipment | SML | Screen Manipulation Language |
| SME | Siemens Mikrocomputer Entwicklungssystem | SML | Search Mode Logic |
| SME | Society of Manufacturing Engineers | SML | Semantic Metal Language |
| | | SML | Spool Multi-Leaving |

# S

| | | | |
|---|---|---|---|
| SML | Symbolic Machine Language | SMPDU | Service Message Protocol Data Unit |
| SMLM | Simple-Minded Learning Machine | SMPS | Simplified Message Processing Simulation |
| SMM | Schreibmaschinenmeldung | SMPS | Switched Mode Power Supply |
| SMM | Standard Method of Measurement | SMQ | Save/restore Message Queue |
| SMM | Start Manual Mode | | |
| SMM | Static Magnetic Memory | SMRB | Signed Modified Reflected Binary |
| SMM | System Management Monitor | SMRD | Spin Motor Rate Detector |
| SMM | Systems Maintenance Management | SMS | Sammelmeldespeicher |
| | | SMS | Satellite Multi Services |
| SMM | Systems Maintenance Monitor | SMS | Semiconductor-Metal-Semiconductor |
| SMMA | Systems Maintenance Management Association | SMS | Shadow Mapping Support |
| | | SMS | Shared Multi-System |
| SMMIP | Strategic Material Management Information Program | SMS | Software Monitoring System |
| | | SMS | Standard Modular System |
| SMMIS | Ship Management Maintenance Information System | SMS | Standard Module System |
| | | SMS | Static Magnetic Store |
| SMMP | Standard Methods of Measuring Performance | SMS | Synchronous-altitude Meteorological Satellite |
| SMO | Stabilized Master Oscillator | SMS | System Management Service |
| SMOCIC | SLT Manufacturing Order Card Information Control | SMS | System Measurement Software |
| SMODOS | Self-Modulating Derivate Optical Spectrometer | SMS | Système Modulaire Standard |
| SMOG | Special Monitor Output Generator | SMSM | Shared Main Storage Multiprocessing |
| SMOOTH | Spectra Mode Of Operation Through Hardware | SMT | Service Module Technician |
| | | SMT | Set MAMO Timer |
| SMOS | Small Metal Oxide Semiconductor | SMT | Small Machines Technology |
| | | SMT | Software Measurement Tool |
| SMOS | Submicrometer MOS | | |
| SMP | Sample | SMT | Square Mesh Tracking |
| SMP | Sampler | SMT | System Master Tape |
| SMP | Site Management Program | SMT | Systems Maintenance Time |
| SMP | Sort-Merge Program | SMTCD | Statement Code |
| SMP | Space Management Page | SMTD | System Marketing Technique Development |
| SMP | Synthesis Measurement Plan | SMTE | Segment Map Table Entry |
| SMP | System Maintenance Program | SMTI | Selective Moving Target Indicator |
| SMP | System Management Processor | SMU | Self-Maneuvering Unit |
| | | SMU | Stimulus Measurement Unit |
| SMP | System Management Program | SMV | Selektives Mikrovoltmeter |
| SMP | System Modification Program | SMW | Selection Mask Word |
| | | SMX | Semi Micro Xerography |
| SMP | Systemmodifikations-programm | SMX | Submultiplex |
| | | SMX | Submultiplexer |
| SMPD | Sampled | SN | Semiconductor Network |

# S

| | | | |
|---|---|---|---|
| SN | Sign | SNE | Single Nylon Enamelled |
| SN | Signal to Noise | SNE | Suppress Normal End |
| SN | Sound Negative | SNEPIA | Syndicat National des Ecoles Privées d'Informatique et d'Automatique |
| SN | Sub-Nanosecond | | |
| SN | Subnetwork | | |
| SN | Symbolic Name | | |
| SN | Synchronizer | SNF | Sampled N-path Filter |
| SN | Systemnormausschuß | SNF | Sequence Number Field |
| SNA | Single Network Architecture | SNF | Signal-to-Noise Factor |
| | | SNF | System Noise Figure |
| SNA | Standard Numerical Attributes | SNG | Single |
| | | SNG | Synthetic Natural Gas |
| SNA | System Network Architecture | SNGL | Single |
| | | SNI | Sequence-Number Indicator |
| SNA | System Numerical Attributes | | |
| | | SNI | Serielles Netzwerk-Interface |
| SNACP | Subnetwork Access Protocol | SNI | SNA-Network Interconnection |
| SNACS | Share News on Automatic Coding Systems | SNICP | Subnetwork Independet Convergence Protocol |
| SNAP | Sharp Numeric Assembler Program | SNIF | Signal-to-Noise Improvement Factor |
| SNAP | Simplified Numerical Automatic Programmer | SNIMA | Service de la Normalisation Industrielle Marocaine |
| SNAP | Subroutines for Natural Actuarial Processing | | |
| SNAP | System for Natural Programming | SNIMAB | Syndicat National des Importateurs de Matériels de Bureau et d'informatique |
| SNAPS | Switched Network Automatic Profile System | | |
| SNARC | Short Nickel-line Accumulating Register Calculator | SNL | Sample Noise Level |
| | | SNL | Standard Nomenclature List |
| SNASC | Symbolic Network Analysis on a Small Computer | SNLG | Signalling |
| | | SNM | Signal-to-Noise Merit |
| SNATCH | SNA and Transdata Coupling of Hosts | SNMMMIS | Standard Navy Maintenace and Material Management Information System |
| SNBU | Switched Network Backup | | |
| SNC | Sequence Number Check | SNOBI | Salon Normand de l'Organisation de Bureau, de l'Informatique |
| SNC | Standard Navigation Computer | | |
| SNC | Stored-program Numeric Control | SNOBOL | String Oriented symbolic Language |
| SND | Send | SNOP | Start of Normal Production |
| SND | Send Next Digit | SNORE | Signal-to-Noise Ratio Estimator |
| SND | Sound | | |
| SNDCP | Subnetwork Dependent Convergence Protocol | SNOS | Selicon-Nitride-Oxide-Silicon |
| SNDG | Sending | SNOSFET | Silicon-Nitride-Oxide-Silicon Field-Effect Transistor |
| SNDO | Standard Nomenclature of Diseases and Operations | | |
| | | SNP | Serial Number Printing |
| SNDR | Signal-to-Noise Density Ratio | SNP | Synchro Null Pulse |
| | | SNR | Satznummer |
| SNDS | Stock Number Data Section | SNR | Signal-to-Noise Ratio |

# S

| | | | |
|---|---|---|---|
| SNR-CN | Signal-to-Noise Ratio due to Channel Noise | SOAP | Symbolic Optimum Assembly Programming |
| SNRM | Set Normal Response Mode | SOAR | Safe Operating Area |
| | | SOAR | Saturn Oriented Assembly Routine |
| SNRV | Signal-to-Noise Ratio-Video | SOAV | Solenoid Operated Air Valve |
| SNRZ | Staatliches Netz der Rechenzentren | SOB | Software Organisation Bornemann |
| SNS | Simulated Network Simulations | SOB | Start Of Block |
| SNSL | Stock Number Sequence Listing | SOBLIN | Self-Organizing Binary Logical Network |
| SNT | Schaltnetzteil | SOC | Schedule of Organizational Change |
| SNT | Sign-on Table | | |
| SNTCC | Simplified Neutron Transport Computer Code | SOC | Self-Organizing Control |
| | | SOC | Separated Orbit Cyclotron |
| SNV | Schweizerische Normen Vereinigung | SOC | Set Overrides Clear |
| | | SOC | Shift-Out Character |
| SNZ | Sum Not Zero | SOC | Simulation Operations Center |
| SO | Scanning Operation | | |
| SO | Seek Operation | SOC | Specific Optimal Controller |
| SO | Send Only | | |
| SO | Sequential Operator | SOC | Système d'Ordinateurs Connectés |
| SO | Service-Oszillograf | | |
| SO | Shift Order | SOCC | Self-Orthogonal Convolutional Code |
| SO | Shift-Out | | |
| SO | Shop Order | SOCKO | Systems Operational Checkout |
| SO | Sign Operator | | |
| SO | Sistema Operativa | SOCMA | Second Order Coherent Multiple Access |
| SO | Slow Operate | | |
| SO | Small Outline | SOCN | Source Control Number |
| SO | Socket | SOCO | Switched Out for Checkout |
| SO | Sondersysteme GmbH | SOCOM | Solar Communications |
| SO | Sortierer | SOCR | Sustained Operations Control |
| SO | Source | | |
| SO | Speicherorganisation | SOCRATES | Scope's Own Conditioned-Reflex, Automatic Trainable Electronic System |
| SO | Store Operation | | |
| SO | Substitution Oscillator | | |
| SO | Symbolic Operand | SOCRATES | System for Organizing Content to Review And Teach Educational Subjects |
| SOA | Safe Operating Area | | |
| SOA | Self-Optimizing and Adaptive | | |
| SOA | Start Of Address | SOD | Small Object Detector |
| SOA | Start Of Assembly | SOD | Small Oriented Diode |
| SOA | State Of the Art | SOD | Sound-On-Disk |
| SOA | Subsequent Order Address | SOD | Standard Outline of Diode |
| SOALM | Scanned Optically Addressed Light Modulators | SOD | Sum-Of-the-years Digit |
| | | SOD | Surface Oriented Diode |
| | | SOD | System Output Data |
| SOAP | SAGE Operation Analysis Project | SODA | Source Data Automation |
| | | SODA | Source Oriented Data Acquisition |
| SOAP | Self-Optimizing Automatic Pilot | | |
| | | SODA | System Optimisation and Design Algorithm |
| SOAP | Simplify Obscure ALGOL Program | | |
| | | SODAC | Source Data Collection |

# S

| | | | |
|---|---|---|---|
| SODAR | Sound Detection And Ranging | SOH | Start Of Header |
| SODAS | Structure Oriented Description And Simulation | SOH | Start Of Heading |
| | | SOI | Silicon-On-Insulator |
| | | SOI | Specific Operating Instruction |
| SODAS | Synoptic Oceanographic Data Assimilation System | SOI | Standard Operation Instruction |
| SODET | Sound Detector | SOIS | Ship Operating Information System |
| SODIS | Sofortdispositions- und Informations-System | SOIS | Shipping Operations Information System |
| SODS | Subordinate Operations Data System | SOIS | Silicon On Insulating Substrate |
| SODT | Scope Octal Debugging Tape | SOIS | Silicon-On-sapphire Integrated Semiconductor |
| SOE | Shift Order Execution | | |
| SOE | Silicon Overlay Epitaxial | SOJUS | Softwaresystem zur Unterstützung operativer Hilfsaufgaben in der Justiz |
| SOE | Start Of Entry | | |
| SOE | Stripline Opposed Emitter | | |
| SOERO | Small Orbiting Earth Resource Observatory | | |
| | | SOL | Schalter Online |
| SOF | Sound-On-Film | SOL | Simulation Oriented Language |
| SOF | Sprachoberfläche | | |
| SOF | Stage Order File | SOL | Solar |
| SOF | Start-Of-Format control | SOL | Solenoid |
| SOF | System Output File | SOL | Solid |
| SOFAR | Sound Fixing And Ranging | SOL | Systems Oriented Language |
| SOFAR | Sound Fusing And Ranging | | |
| SOFCS | Self-Organizing Flight Control System | SOLACE | Sales Order and Ledger Accounting using the Computerline Environment |
| SOFE | Stop On First Error | | |
| SOFI | Software Information | | |
| SOFIA | Système d'Ordinateurs pour le Frêt International Aérien | SOLAPIC | Solar Applications Information Center |
| | | SOLAR | Serialized On-Line Automatic Recording |
| SOFIM | Service d'Ordinateurs pour le Frêt International Maritime | SOLAR | Shared On-Line Airline Reservations |
| | | SOLAR | Shared On-Line Automated Reservation |
| SOFIX | Stoftware Fix | | |
| SOFNET | Solar Observing and Forecasting Network | SOLAR | Storage and On-Line Automatic Retrieval |
| SOFO | Sortierfolge- und Satzlängenprüfprogramm | SOLD | Simulation Of Logic Design |
| | | SOLD | Soft Option in Logic Design |
| SOFT | Simple Output Format Translator | | |
| | | SOLD | System On Line Diagnosis |
| SOFTLAB | Softwarelabor | SOLID | Self-Organizing Large Information Dissemination |
| SOFTMARK | Softwarevermarktung | | |
| SOG | Same Output Gate | | |
| SOGAMMIS | South Gate city Municipal Management Information System | SOLIS | Symbionics On-Line Information System |
| | | SOLMIS | Supply On-Line Management Information System |
| SOGET | Software Gestione Terminali | | |
| | | SOLN | Solution |
| SOGREP | Société Générale de Recherche et Programmation | SOLO | SAMI On-Line Operations |
| | | SOLO | Selective Optical Lock-On |

# S

| | | | |
|---|---|---|---|
| SOLO | System for On-Line Optimization | SORC | Source |
| SOLOMON | Simultaneous Operation Linked Ordinal Modular Network | SORC | Systems Objectives and Requirements Committee |
| | | SORCS | Shipboard Ordnance Requirement Computer System |
| SOLRAD | Solar Radiation | | |
| SOLV | Solenoid Valve | SOREL | Système Oscilloperturbo-grahique Rapide Electronique |
| SOM | Small Office Microfilm | | |
| SOM | Start Of Message | | |
| SOMA | Software-Machine | SORTI | Satellite Orbital Track and Intercept |
| SOMADA | Self Organizing Multiple Access Discrete Address | | |
| | | SORTIE | Supercircular Orbital Reentry Test Integrated Environment |
| SOMIS | Source Oriented Medical Information System | | |
| SOMP | Start-Of-Message Priority | SORTRAN | Syntax Oriented Translator |
| SONAR | Sound Navigation And Ranging | SOS | Self-Organizing System |
| | | SOS | Share Operating System |
| SONIC | Simultaneously Operating Numerical Integration Computer | SOS | Silicon-On-Sapphire |
| | | SOS | Silicon-On-Spinel |
| | | SOS | Simulator Operating System |
| SONIC | System-wide On-line Network for Informational Control | | |
| | | SOS | Sophisticated Operation System |
| SONOAN | Sonic Noise Analyzer | SOS | Sound-On Sync |
| SOP | Signal-Operating Procedure | SOS | Special Ordered Sets |
| | | SOS | Student-Operationssystem |
| SOP | Simulated Output Program | SOS | Sum-Of-the Squares |
| SOP | Simulation Operations Plan | SOS | Symbolic Operating System |
| SOP | Solution Output Processor | SOSI | Shift Out, Shift In |
| SOP | Sortierprogramm | SOSOFT | Software System Oriented to Fuse Testing |
| SOP | Standard Operating Procedure | | |
| | | SOSP | Silicon On Spinel |
| SOP | Study Organization Plan | SOSTEL | Solid State Electric Logic |
| SOP | Sum Of Products | SOSUS | Sound Surveillance System |
| SOP | Symbolic Optimum Program | SOT | Scanning Oscillator Technique |
| SOP | System Operator's manual | SOT | Short-Open Test |
| SOPC | Speicheroperationscode | SOT | Sound On Tape |
| SOPHOMATION | Synergetic Open Philips Office Automation | SOT | Standard Outline of Transistor |
| | | SOT | Start Of Tape |
| SOPM | Speicheroperationsmodus | SOT | Syntax-Oriented Translator |
| SOPP | Sachgebietsorientiertes Programmpaket | SOT | System Order Tape |
| | | SOT | Systems Operation Test |
| SOPS | Sachgebietsorientiertes Programmiersystem | SOTEL | Société de Télé-informatique |
| SOPS | Speicher-Operations-steuerung | SOTUS | Sequentially Operated Teletypewriter Universal Selector |
| SOR | Sampling Oscilloscope Recorder | | |
| | | SOU | System Output Unit |
| SOR | Single Operator Responsibility | SOUSY | Sounding System |
| | | SOV | Sound On Vision |
| SOR | Slow Operating Relay | SOW | Start Of Word |
| SOR | Specific Operations Requirements | SOW | System Output Writer |
| | | SP | Sample |
| SOR | Start Of Record | | |

# S

| | | | |
|---|---|---|---|
| SP | Sample Program | SP | Speicherung |
| SP | Satellite Processor | SP | Sperrprogrammspeicher |
| SP | Scaling Position | SP | Spool |
| SP | Scanning Program | SP | Square Punch |
| SP | Schnittstelle, Parallel | SP | Stack Pointer |
| SP | Scratch Pad | SP | Standard Program |
| SP | Search Problem | SP | Standardperipherie |
| SP | Search Procedure | SP | Steering Program |
| SP | Search Process | SP | Stick Printer |
| SP | Secondary Program | SP | Storage Process |
| SP | SEGWA Programm | SP | Storage Protect |
| SP | Select by light Pen | SP | Stored Program |
| SP | Self-Powered | SP | Structured Programming |
| SP | Self-Programming | SP | Strukturierte Programmierung |
| SP | Self-Propelled | | |
| SP | Sensing Program | SP | Subliminal Perception |
| SP | Separable Programming | SP | Subprogram |
| SP | Sequence Programmer | SP | Subtract decimal Packed |
| SP | Sequential Processing | SP | Summary Plotter |
| SP | Sequential Programming | SP | Summary Punch |
| SP | Serial Printer | SP | Summating Potential |
| SP | Serial Programming | SP | Superprogramm |
| SP | Serial-to-Parallel | SP | Support |
| SP | Service Program | SP | Symbol Programmer |
| SP | Set Pulse | SP | Symbolic Package |
| SP | Shift Pulse | SP | Symbolic Programming |
| SP | Sign Part | SP | Synthesis Programming |
| SP | Sign Printing | SP | System Processor |
| SP | Signal Processor | SP | System Product |
| SP | Silver Plated | SP | System Program |
| SP | Simple Printing | SP | System Programming |
| SP | Simple Programming | SP | Systemplattenspeicher |
| SP | Simulation Program | SP | Systemprogrammierer |
| SP | Single Phase | SP | Systemprozeß |
| SP | Single Pole | SP | Systems and Procedures |
| SP | Single Precision | SP/GR | Specific Gravity |
| SP | Single Program | SPA | S-band Power Amplifier |
| SP | Single Programmer | SPA | Scratchpad Area |
| SP | Software Package | SPA | Serielle Port Applikationen |
| SP | Software Program | SPA | Servo Power Assembly |
| SP | Sortierprogramm | SPA | Spectrum Analyzer |
| SP | Sound Positive | SPA | Speicherausgang |
| SP | Sound-Powered telephone | SPA | System Parameter Address |
| SP | Source Program | SPA | System Performance Analysis |
| SP | Sousprogramme | | |
| SP | Space | SPAA | Systems and Procedures Association of America |
| SP | Space Character | | |
| SP | Specific | SPAC | Signal Programmer And Conditioner |
| SP | Specific Program | | |
| SP | Specific Programming | SPAC | Spatial Computer |
| SP | Specitication | SPACE | Self-Programming Automatic Circuit Evaluator |
| SP | Specified | | |
| SP | Specify | SPACE | Self-Programming Automatic Checkout Equipment |
| SP | Speicher | | |
| SP | Speicherplatz | | |

# S

| | | | |
|---|---|---|---|
| SPACE | Sequential Position And Covariance Estimation | SPAN | System Performance Analysis |
| SPACE | Serial-Programming by Associative Coordinate Execution | SPANRAD | Superimposed Panoramic Radar Display |
| SPACE | Sidereal Polar Axis Celestial Equipment | SPAQUA | Sealed Package Quality Assurance |
| SPACE | Stored Program Accounting and Calculating Equipment | SPAR | Sea-going Platform for Acoustic Research |
| SPACE | Symbolic Programming Anyone Can Enjoy | SPAR | Selection Program for ADMIRAL Runs |
| SPACE | System Precision Automatic Checkout Equipment | SPAR | Standardprogramm-ablaufroutine |
| SPACEA | Space After | SPAR | Store Port Allocation Register |
| SPACEB | Space Before | SPAR | Superprecision Approach Radar |
| SPACELOOP | Speech Analog Compression and Editing Loop | SPAR | Symbolic Program Assembly Routine |
| SPACES | Scheduling Package And Computer Evaluation Schools | SPAR | System Performance Activity Recorder |
| SPACON | Space Control | SPAR | System Performance Analysis and Reporting |
| SPAD | Satellite Position predictor And Display | SPARC | Spectral Analyzer and Recognition Computer |
| SPAD | Satellite Protection for Area Defence | SPARC | Steam Plant Automation and Results Computer |
| SPAD | Sundstrand Performance Advisory Display | SPARS | Space Precision Attitude Reference System |
| SPADATS | Space Detection And Tracking System | SPARSA | Spherics Pulse, Azimuth, Rate, and Spectrum Analyzer |
| SPADE | Signal Processing And Display Equipment | SPARTA | Sequential Programmed Automatic Recording Transistor Analyzer |
| SPADE | Single-channel-per carrier PCM multiple Access Demand assignment Equipment | SPARTAN | Scheduling Program for Allocating Resources To Alternative Networks |
| SPADE | Sparta Acquisition Digital Equipment | SPAS | Serial Poll Active State |
| SPADE | Sperry Air Data Equipment | SPASM | Special Purpose Application Service Module |
| SPADL | Spare Parts Application Data List | SPASM | System Performance and Activity Software Monitor |
| SPADU | Signal Processing And Display Unit | SPAT | Silicon Precision Alloy Transistor |
| SPAG | Standard Promotion and Application Group | SPATA | Systems Performance And Technical Analysis |
| SPAIS | Suburban Police Automated Information System | SPATS | Semiconductor Process Area Test System |
| SPAN | Solar Particle Alert Network | SPAU | Signal-Processing Arithmetic Unit |
| SPAN | Statistical Processing and Analysis | SPAZ | Speicherabzugprogramm |
| SPAN | Stored Program Alphanumerics | SPAZ | System zum Speichern und Auffinden Zeitlich gegliederter Daten |

- 567 -

# S

| | | | |
|---|---|---|---|
| SPB | Speiseblock | SPDC | Stored Program Digital Computer |
| SPB | Strategische Problembeschreibung | SPDCU | Subsurface Probe Data and Control Unit |
| SPC | Set Point Control | SPDD | Selectable Parameter Digital Display |
| SPC | Set Point Controller | | |
| SPC | Silver-Plated Copper | SPDE | Special Purpose Difference Equation |
| SPC | Single Paper Covered | | |
| SPC | Single Purpose Computer | SPDP | Society of Professional Data Processors |
| SPC | Site Programmer Course | | |
| SPC | Small Punched Card | SPDS | Safe-Practice Data Sheet |
| SPC | Software Program Counter | SPDT | Single-Pole Double Throw |
| SPC | Special | SPDTDB | Single-Pole, Double-Throw, Double-Break |
| SPC | Special Program Code | | |
| SPC | Starting Point Counter | SPDTNCDB | Single-Pole, Double-Throw, Normally Closed, Double-Break |
| SPC | Storage Programmed Computer | | |
| SPC | Stored Program Computer | SPDTNO | Single-Pole, Double-Throw, Normally Open |
| SPC | Stored Program Control | | |
| SPC | Stored Program Controlled | SPDTNODB | Single-Pole, Double-Throw, Normally Open, Double-Break |
| SPC | Stored Program Controller system | | |
| SPC | Stored Programmed Command | SPE | Signal Processing Element |
| | | SPE | Silicon Planar Epitaxial |
| SPC | Summary Punch Control | SPE | Speichereinheit |
| SPCB | Systems Planning and Computing Board | SPE | Speichererweiterung |
| | | SPE | Stored Program Element |
| SPCC | Staggered Phase Carrier Cancellation | SPE | Summary Punch Entry |
| | | SPE | Systems Performance Effectiveness |
| SPCC | Stored Program CAMA and Control channel | | |
| | | SPEAL | Special Purpose Engineering Analysis Language |
| SPCFY | Specify | | |
| SPCHC | Special Charge Code | | |
| SPCL | Self Propagating Core Logic | SPEARS | Satellite Photo-Electronic Analog Rectification System |
| SPCL | Special | | |
| SPCR | Scratch Pad Control Register | SPEC | Specification |
| | | SPEC | Specify |
| SPCR | Silicon Planar Controlled Rectifier | SPEC | Speech Predictive Encoded Communications |
| SPD | Sample Pulse Driver | | |
| SPD | Serial/Parallel Decoder | SPEC | Speech Predictive Encoding |
| SPD | Shareable Private Disk | | |
| SPD | Single Path Doppler | SPEC | Stored Program Educational Computer |
| SPD | Situation Projected Display | | |
| | | SPEC | Student Performance Evaluation by Computer |
| SPD | Speech Processing Device | | |
| SPD | Stored Program Decoder | SPECOL | Special Customer Oriented Language |
| SPD | Stored Program Decommutation | | |
| | | SPECS | Specifications |
| SPD | Synchronizer for Peripheral Devices | SPED | Supersonic Planetary Entry Decelerator |
| SPD | Systems Program Documentation | SPEDAC | Solid-state Parallel Expandable Differential Analyzer Computer |
| SPDC | Stored Program Data Compressor | | |

# S

| | | | |
|---|---|---|---|
| SPEDAS | Speditionsabfertigungs- und Abrechnungssystem | SPF | System Performance Factor |
| SPEDE | State system for Processing Educational Data Electronically | SPF | System Productivity Facility |
| SPEDE | System for Processing Educational Data Electronically | SPFP | Single Point Failure Potential |
| | | SPFW | Single-Phase Full-Wave |
| SPEDTAC | Stored Program Educational Transistorized Automatic Computer | SPG | Scan Pattern Generator |
| | | SPG | Simple Phrase Grammar |
| | | SPG | Single Point Ground |
| | | SPG | Sort Program Generator |
| SPEED | SEL Programmed Electronic Equation Delineator | SPG | Steuerpulsgenerator |
| | | SPG | Synchronization Pulse Generator |
| SPEED | Self-Programmed Electronic Equation Delineator | SPG | System Programmers Guide |
| | | SPHW | Single-Phase Half-Wave |
| SPEED | Signal Processing in Evacuated Electronic Device | SPI | Semi-Permanent Information |
| | | SPI | Services et Progiciels Informatiques |
| SPEED | Subsistence Preparation by Electronic Energy Diffusion | SPI | Shared Peripheral Interface |
| | | SPI | Signal Point Identification |
| SPEED | Systematic Plotting and Evaluation of Enumerated Data | SPI | Single Program Initiated |
| | | SPI | Single Program Initiation |
| | | SPI | Single Program Initiator |
| SPELA | Special Purpose Engineering Language | SPI | Software Products International |
| SPENT | Summary Punch Entry | | |
| SPER | Syndicat des industries de matériels Professionnels Electroniques et Radioélectriques | SPI | Special Position Identification pulse |
| | | SPI | Specific Productivity Index |
| SPERT | Schedule Performance Evaluation and Review Technique | SPI | Standard Practice Instruction |
| | | SPI | Symbolic Pictorial Indicator |
| SPERT | Simplified Program Evaluation and Review Technique | SPIC | Spare Parts Inventory Control |
| SPES | Simple Plant Economic Simulator | SPIC | Ship's Position Interpolation Computer |
| SPES | Sozialpolitisches Entscheidungssystem | SPICE | Sales Point Information Computing Equipment |
| SPES | Stored Program Element System | SPICE | Simulation Program with Integrated Circuit Emphasis |
| SPESS | Stored Program Electronic Switching System | SPIDAC | Speciment Input to Digital Automatic Computer |
| SPET | Solid Propellant Electrical Thruster | SPIDER | Sonic Pulse-echo instrument Designed for Extreme Resolution |
| SPEX | Summary Punch Exit | | |
| SPF | Sequential Processing Facility | SPIE | Scavenging-Precipitation-Ion Exchange |
| SPF | Spezieller Prioritätsfehler | | |
| SPF | Structured Programming Facility | SPIE | Scientifically Programmed Individualized Education |

# S

| | | | |
|---|---|---|---|
| SPIE | Self-Programmed Individualized Education | SPL | South Pacific program Library |
| SPIE | Simulated Problem Input Evaluation | SPL | Space Programming Language |
| SPIF | Sequential Prime Implicant Form | SPL | Special Purpose Language |
| | | SPL | Speed Phase Lock |
| SPIF | Special Interface | SPL | Spooled |
| SPIL | Systems Programming Implementation Language | SPL | Standard-Programmier-Logik |
| SPIN | Searchable Physics Information Notices | SPL | Steuerprogramm Laden |
| | | SPL | Subrecursive Programming Language |
| SPIN | Set Pin | | |
| SPIN | Strategies and Policies in Informatics | SPL | Survey Processing Language |
| SPINDEX | Selective Permutation Indexing | SPL | Symbolic Programming Language |
| SPINE | Simulated Program for Investigation of Nuclear Effects | SPL | Systems Programming Language |
| | | SPL | Systems Programming Limited |
| SPINES | Science and technology Policies Information Exchange System | SPLICE | Shorthand Programming Language In COBOL Environment |
| SPIO | Speech Input-Output system | SPLIS | Source Program Library System |
| SPIRAL | Sandia's Program for Information Retrieval | SPLIT | Space Program Language Implementation Tool |
| SPIRES | Standard Personnel Information Retrieval System | SPLIT | Sundstrand Processing Language Internally Translated |
| SPIRES | Standard Public Information Retrieval System | SPLM | Space Programming Language Machine |
| SPIRES | Stanford Physics Information Retrieval System | SPLML | Space Programming Language Machine Language |
| SPIRIT | Sales Processing Interactive Realtime Inventory Technique | SPLS | Storage Protect Local Store |
| SPIRT | Special Program for Instant Registration Testing | SPLSM | Single Position Letter Sorting Machine |
| | | SPM | Scratch Pad Memory |
| SPITBOL | Speedy Implementation of SNOBOL | SPM | Scratch Pad Module |
| | | SPM | Self-Propelled Mount |
| SPIX | Spooler für Druckfiles unter Unix | SPM | Semi-Permanent Memory |
| | | SPM | Sequential Processing Machine |
| SPK | Storage Protection Key | | |
| SPKR | Speaker | SPM | Serial-Parallel Multiplier |
| SPL | Signal Processing Language | SPM | Set Program Mask |
| SPL | Simple Phrase Language | SPM | Single Program Mode |
| SPL | Simple Programming Language | SPM | Source Program Maintenance |
| SPL | Simulation Programming Language | SPM | Special Purpose Multiplexor |
| SPL | Software Programming Language | SPM | Standard Practice Memo |
| | | SPM | Storage Protect Memory |
| SPL | Sound-Pressure Level | SPM | Symbol Processing Machine |
| SPL | Source Program Library | | |

# S

| | | | |
|---|---|---|---|
| SPM | System Preventive Maintenance | SPPC | Spare Parts Provisioning Card |
| SPM | Systems Program Manager | SPPL | Serial Printer Product Line |
| SPMMS | Software Production and Maintenance Management Systems | SPPL | South Pacific Program Library |
| SPMS | Solar Particle Monitoring System | SPPM | Serial-Parallel Pipeline Multiplier |
| SPMS | System Program Management Survey | SPPPA | Spartan Production Program Producibility Analysis |
| SPN | Separation Program Number | SPPS | Subsystem Program Preparation Support |
| SPN | Series-Parallel Network | SPPU | Summary Punch Pickup |
| SPN | Standard Printable Name | SPQ | Special Product Quotation |
| SPN | Switched Public Network | SPQE | Sub-Pool Queue Element |
| SPNC | Stored Program Numerical Control | SPR | Sense Printer |
| SPNS | Self-Programmed Number Selector | SPR | Sequential Pattern Recognition |
| SPO | Short-Period Oscillation | SPR | Serial Printer |
| SPO | Single Program Operation | SPR | Short-Pulse Radar |
| SPO | Subprogrammorganisation | SPR | Silicon Power Rectifier |
| SPO | System and Programming Organisation | SPR | Speicherprüfroutine |
| | | SPR | Sprache |
| SPOC | Single-Point Orbit Calculator | SPR | Sprung |
| | | SPR | Sprungbefehl |
| SPOC | Splicing Of Cross | SPR | Sudden Pressure Relay |
| SPODP | Single Precision Orbit Determination Program | SPR | System Parameter Record |
| | | SPR | Systemprogramm |
| SPOOK | Supervisor Program Over Other Kinds | SPRA | Space Probe Radar Altimeter |
| SPOOL | Simultaneous Peripheral Operations On-Line | SPRC | Self-Propelled Robot Craft |
| | | SPRE | Special Prefix code |
| SPOOL | Spontaneous Peripheral Operations On-Line | SPRESI | Speicherung und Recherche Strukturchemischer Informationen |
| SPOOL | Spooling | | |
| SPOT | Steel Plate Ordering Technique | SPRINT | Selective Printing |
| | | SPRINT | Simultaneous Print |
| SPOT | Systems Programmers and Operators Transaction | SPRINT | Special Police Radio Inquiry Network |
| SPP | Solar Photometry Probe | SPROM | Switched Programmable Read-Only Memory |
| SPP | Sound-Powered Phone | | |
| SPP | Speed Power Product | SPROSS | Simulation Program for Sequential Systems |
| SPP | Structured Programming Processor | SPRS | Single Passenger Reservation System |
| SPP | Strukturierte Prozessor Programmierung | SPRT | Sequential Probability Ratio Test |
| SPP | System Package Plan | | |
| SPP | System Package Program | SPRTAP | Specially Prepared Tape Program |
| SPPA | Satellite Purchasing Programs Administrator | SPS | Sample Per Second |
| | | SPS | Secondary Propulsion System |
| SPPB | Système de Planification, Programmation, Budgétisation | SPS | Segment-Programmsystem |

# S

| | | | |
|---|---|---|---|
| SPS | Semi-Permanent Storage | SPT | Silicon Planar Transistor |
| SPS | Semi-Permanent Store | SPT | Silicon Powered Transistor |
| SPS | Sequential Partitional Scheduler | SPT | Symbolic Program Tape |
| SPS | Sequential Partitioned System | SPT | Symbolic Program Translator |
| SPS | Serial-Parallel-Serial | SPT | System Parameter Table |
| SPS | Serial/Parallel Storage | SPTC | Specified Period of Time Contact |
| SPS | Service Propulsion System | | |
| SPS | Shared Processor System | SPTD | Sprechtext der Telefoninformationsdienste |
| SPS | Solar Probe Spacecraft | | |
| SPS | Special Processor System | SPTF | Signal Processing Test Facility |
| SPS | Speicherprogrammierbare Steuerung | SPTS | System Performance Test Set |
| SPS | Speicherprogrammierte Steuerung | SPTS | System Programmers Tool Set |
| SPS | Spezielle Prioritätsschaltung | SPU | Select Printed Unit |
| | | SPU | Sense Punch |
| SPS | Steuerprogrammsystem | SPU | Serien-Parallel-Umsetzer |
| SPS | Stored Program Simulator | SPU | Signal Processing Unit |
| SPS | Summary Punch Switch | SPU | Small Peripheral Unit |
| SPS | Superscript character | SPU | Software-Produktionsumgebung |
| SPS | Supplementary Power Supply | | |
| | | SPU | Sprung ins Unterprogramm |
| SPS | Support Programming System | SPU | Standard Propulsion Unit |
| | | SPU | System Processing Unit |
| SPS | Symbol-Programmsystem | SPUD | Stored Program Universal Demonstrator |
| SPS | Symbolic Programming System | | |
| SPS | Symbolisches Programmiersystem | SPUR | Single Precision Unpacked Rounded floating point package |
| SPS | Symbols Per Second | SPUR | System for Project Updating and Reporting |
| SPS | Synchronous Program Supervisor | | |
| | | SPURM | Special Purpose Unilateral Repetitive Modulation |
| SPSELIM | Space Shift Elimination | | |
| SPSR | Speicherschlüsselregister | SPURT | Spinning Unguided Rocket Trajectory |
| SPSS | Statistical Package for Social Sciences | | |
| | | SPW | Speicherwerk |
| SPSS | Statistical Package for the Social Sciences | SPWM | Sine Pulse Width Modulation |
| SPST | Speicherstelle | SPZ | Speicherzelle |
| SPST | Single-Pole Single-Throw | SQ | Squint Quoin |
| SPSTNC | Single-Pole Single-Throw, Normally Closed | SQ | Superquick |
| | | SQ-PCM | Slope-Quantized Pulse Code Modulation |
| SPSTNO | Single-Pole Single-Throw, Normally Open | SQA | Squaring Amplifier |
| | | SQA | System Queue Area |
| SPSW | Single-Pole Switch | SQC | Self Quenching Counter |
| SPSW | Statistische Programmiersprache Würzburg | SQC | Statistical Quality Control |
| | | SQF | Shortest Queue First |
| SPSW | Steuerndes Programmstatuswort | SQIN | Sequential Quadrature Inband |
| SPT | Shorted Processing Time | | |
| SPT | Signal Processing Technique | SQIRE | System for Quick ultrafiche-based Information Retrieval |
| SPT | Silicon Planar Thyristor | | |

- 572 -

# S

| | | | |
|---|---|---|---|
| SQL | Structured Query Language | SR | Speed Regulator |
| SQL/DS | Structured Query Language/ Data System | SR | Speicherregister |
| | | SR | Split Ring |
| SQP | Supplier Quality Program | SR | Spur |
| SQR | Sequence Relay | SR | Standard Resistor |
| SQR | Square Root | SR | Standard Routine |
| SQS | Stoachiastic Queuing System | SR | Start Routine |
| | | SR | Starting Relay |
| SQS | System Queue Space | SR | Static Register |
| SQT | Sequential-Quotiententest | SR | Stimulus-Response |
| SQT | Square rooter | SR | Storage Register |
| SQUID | Sperry Quick Updating of Internal Documentation | SR | Storage Ring |
| | | SR | Storage and Retrieval |
| SQUID | Superconducting Quantum Interference Device | SR | Store Register |
| | | SR | Study Requirement |
| SQW | Square Wave | SR | Subroutine |
| SQYTD | Sales Quantity Year-To-Date | SR | Summary Recorder |
| | | SR | Surveillance Radar |
| SR | Sampling Rate | SRA | Shift Register/Adder |
| SR | Satellitenrechner | SRAM | Semoconductor Random Access Memory |
| SR | Save/Restore | | |
| SR | Scan Routine | SRB | Service Request Block |
| SR | Schwenkrahmen | SRBI | Smooth and Rotate Base Index |
| SR | Scientific Report | | |
| SR | Secondary Radar | SRBP | Synthetic-Resin-Bonded Paper |
| SR | Seek Routine | | |
| SR | Segment Root | SRC | Scan Request Channel |
| SR | Selective Reading | SRC | Send Register Control |
| SR | Selective Ringing | SRC | Send Request Circuit |
| SR | Selenium Rectifier | SRC | Shared-Resource-Computer |
| SR | Send-Receive | | |
| SR | Sending/Receiving | SRC | Shift Register Counter |
| SR | Sequence Register | SRC | Single Reflex Camera |
| SR | Series Relay | SRC | Sound Ranging Control |
| SR | Service Routine | SRC | Source |
| SR | Shift Register | SRC | Standard Requirements Code |
| SR | Shift Reverse | | |
| SR | Short Range | SRC | Stock Record Card |
| SR | Sign Register | SRC | Sub-Routine Call |
| SR | Silicon Rectifier | SRC | Subject-field Reference Code |
| SR | Simple Register | | |
| SR | Simulation Routine | SRCB | Sentence Record Control Byte |
| SR | Slip Ring | | |
| SR | Slow Running | SRCC | Shift, Rotate, Check, Control |
| SR | Slow-release Relay | | |
| SR | Software Requirements | SRCD | Set-Rest Clocked Data |
| SR | Solid Rocket | SRCDL | Survey Research Center Data Library |
| SR | Sorter-Reader | | |
| SR | Sound Ranging | SRCH | Search |
| SR | Sound Rating | SRCL | Siemens-Robot-Control-Language |
| SR | Source | | |
| SR | Sousroutine | SRCU | Shared Remote Control Unit |
| SR | Specific Resistance | | |
| SR | Specific Routine | SRD | Secret Restricted Data |
| SR | Speed Recorder | SRD | Selected Read Data |

# S

| | | | |
|---|---|---|---|
| SRD | Shift Register Drive | SRIS | Safety Research Information Service |
| SRD | Signal Receiver and Distributor | SRJE | SNA Remote Job Entry |
| SRD | Software Requirements Document | SRL | Shift Register Latch |
| | | SRL | Sub-Routine Library |
| SRD | Standard Rate and Data | SRL | System Reference Library |
| SRD | Standard Reference Data | SRLR | Schieberegister mit Linearer Rückkopplung |
| SRD | Step Recovery Diode | | |
| SRD | Swing Rate Discriminator | SRLY | Series Relay |
| SRD | SW-Requirements Document | SRM | Shared Resource Management |
| SRDAS | Service Recording and Data Analysis System | SRM | Shared Resource Manager |
| SRDC | Standard Reference Data Center | SRM | Subarea Routing Manager |
| | | SRM | System Resources Manager |
| SRDS | Standard Reference Data System | SRME | Submerged Repeater Monitoring Equipment |
| SRE | Search Radar Element | SRNH | Service Request Not Honoured |
| SRE | Selective Reject | | |
| SRE | Spannungsregeleinrichtung | SRO | Single Resonant Oscillator |
| SRE | Surveillance Radar Equipment | SROB | Short Range Omni-directional Beacon |
| SREJ | Selective Reject | SROM | Static Read-only Memory |
| SREM | System Requirements Engineering Methodology | SRP | Sales Record Performance |
| | | SRP | Serial Reader Punch |
| SRETL | Screened Resistor Etched Transistor Logic | SRP | Shift Register Partition |
| | | SRP | Station Readout Pickup |
| SRETL | Screened Resistor Evaporated Transistor Logic | SRP | Status Response Field |
| | | SRP | Storage Recovery Program |
| | | SRP | System Recovery Program |
| SRF | Self-Resonant Frequency | SRP | System Routine Program |
| SRF | Service Record File | SRPM | Single Reversal Permanent Magnet |
| SRF | Software Recovery Facility | SRPP | Serial Reader Parallel Punch |
| SRF | Spectral Redistribution Function | SRPS | Synchronous Random Pulse Sequence |
| SRF | Storage Reconfiguration Facility | SRPT | Systems Reliability Prediction Technique |
| SRF | Strength of Radio Frequency | SRQ | Sales Record Quota |
| SRG | Shift-Register Generator | SRQ | Service Request |
| SRG | Standard Requirement Generator | SRQ | Status Request field |
| | | SRR | Serially Re-usable Resource |
| SRH | Shockley-Read-Hall | | |
| SRI | Servo Repeater Indicator | SRR | Shift Register Realization |
| SRI | Standby Request for Information | SRR | Shift Register Recognizer |
| | | SRR | Short Range Radar |
| SRI | Standard Runtime Interface | SRR | Sound Recorder Reproducer |
| SRI | Stanford Research Institute | SRR | Space Request Routine |
| | | SRS | Seat Reservations System |
| SRI | Systems Research Institute | SRS | Selective Recording System |
| SRIBA | Salon Régional de l'Informatique, de la Bureautique et de l'Automation | | |
| | | SRS | Send-Receive Switch |
| | | SRS | Shipping Research Services |

# S

| | | | |
|---|---|---|---|
| SRS | Simulated Remote Sites | SS | Single Shift |
| SRS | Simultaneous Reporting System | SS | Single Shot |
| | | SS | Single Sideband |
| SRS | Substitute Route Structure | SS | Single Signal |
| SRSK | Short-Range Station Keeping | SS | Single Silk |
| | | SS | Single System |
| SRSS | Simulated Remote Sites Subsystem | SS | Slow Storage |
| | | SS | Small Signal |
| SRST | System Resource and Status Table | SS | Small System |
| | | SS | Solar System |
| SRT | Segmentation Register Table | SS | Solid State |
| | | SS | Source Statement |
| SRT | Set-Reset Trigger | SS | Space Simulator |
| SRT | Single Requestor Terminal | SS | Special Symbol |
| SRT | Single Run Time | SS | Specification Statement |
| SRT | Step Recovery Transistor | SS | Speicher-Speicherbefehl |
| SRT | Supporting Research and Technology | SS | Spin Stabilized |
| | | SS | Start/Stop |
| SRT | System Recovery Table | SS | Statement Storage |
| SRT | System Resource Table | SS | Static Subroutine |
| SRT | Systems Readiness Test | SS | Statistical Standards |
| SRTOS | Special Real Time Operating System | SS | Steady State |
| | | SS | Step Size |
| SRU | Schwarz/Rot-Umschaltung | SS | Steuerschalter |
| SRU | Session Recover Unit | SS | Storage-to-Storage |
| SRU | Shop Replacement Unit | SS | Subsystem |
| SRU | Subscriber Response Unit | SS | Summing Selector |
| SRV | Service | SS | System Service |
| SRV | Step Recovery Vector | SS | System Status |
| SRV AMPL | Servo Amplifier | SS | Systems Support |
| SRVAR | Sum Row Values for Array Rows | SSA | Segment Search Argument |
| | | SSA | Slave Service Area |
| SRZ | Satz-Rechenzentrum | SSA | Solid State Amplifier |
| SS | Samples per Second | SSA | Status Save Area |
| SS | Schedule Status | SSA | Store System Arrangement |
| SS | Score Storage | SSA | Structured Systems Analysis |
| SS | Secondary Storage | | |
| SS | Secondary Store | SSA | Symbol Synchronizer Assembly |
| SS | Select Subroutine | | |
| SS | Selection Sequence | SSA | Synchro Signal Amplifier |
| SS | Selective Signalling | SSA | System-Service-Anwendung |
| SS | Selector Switch | | |
| SS | Sensing Station | SSAC | Space Science Analysis and Command |
| SS | Sequence Switch | | |
| SS | Sequential Scheduler | SSAD | Switching System Application Dispatcher |
| SS | Sequential Store | | |
| SS | Serial Store | SSAM | Skip Sequential Access Method |
| SS | Share Storage | | |
| SS | Shared Segment | SSAM | Slave Service Area Module |
| SS | Siemens System | | |
| SS | Signal Selector | SSAP | Statement of Standard Accounting Practice |
| SS | Signal Strength | | |
| SS | Simple Statement | SSAR | Special Save Register |
| SS | Simplified Spelling | SSAS | Special Signal Analysis System |
| SS | Single Segment | | |

- 575 -

# S

| | | | |
|---|---|---|---|
| SSAS | Sub-System Announcement Summary | SSDA | Synchronous Serial Data Adapter |
| SSB | Single-Sideband | SSDC | Space Science Data Center |
| SSBAM | Single Sideband Amplitude Modulation | SSDD | Single Sided Double Density |
| SSBD | Single-Sideboard | SSDPS | Solar System Data Processing System |
| SSBFM | Single Sideband Frequency Modulation | SSDR | Supermarket Subsystem Definition Record |
| SSBM | Single Sideband Modulation | SSDS | Small Ship Data System |
| SSBO | Single Swing Blocking Oscillator | SSDS | Solutions Development System |
| SSBSC | Single Sideband with Suppressed Carrier | SSE | Single-Silk Enamelled |
| SSBSC-AM | Single Sideband with Suppressed Carrier, Amplitude-Modulated | SSE | Solid State Electronics |
| | | SSE | Solid State Electrolyte |
| | | SSE | Solid State Element |
| SSBSCOM | Single Sideband, Suppressed Carrier Optical Modulator | SSE | Space Shift Elimination |
| | | SSE | Sum Square Error |
| | | SSE | Switching System Engineer |
| SSBWC | Single Sideband With Carrier | SSEC | Selective Sequence Electronic Calculator |
| SSC | Second Search Character | SSEC | Static Source Error Correction |
| SSC | Self-Scheduling Channel | | |
| SSC | Serial Shift Counter | SSEP | System Safety Engineering Plan |
| SSC | Single Silk Covered | | |
| SSC | Small Scientific Computer | SSESM | Spent Stage Experimental Support Module |
| SSC | Software Support Center | | |
| SSC | Solid State Circuit | SSF | Signal Speicherfreigabe |
| SSC | Solid State Component | SSF | Substitution Selector F |
| SSC | Station Selection Code | SSF | Supersonic Frequency |
| SSCDS | Small Ship Combat Data System | SSFB | Special Systems Feature Bulletin |
| SSCF | Secondary System Control Facility | SSFC | Sequential Single Frequency Code |
| SSCH | Start Subchannel | SSFL | Steady State Fermi Level |
| SSCI | Socieda de Servicios y Consulta en Informatica | SSFM | Single Sideband Frequency Modulation |
| SSCI | Société de Services et de Conseils en Informatique | SSG | Small Single Gain |
| | | SSG | Standard Signal Generator |
| SSCP | System Services Control Point | SSG | Surface discharge Spark Gap |
| SSCS | Symposium on the Simulation of Computer Systems | SSG | Sweep Signal Generator |
| | | SSGS | Standard Space Guidance System |
| SSCT | Subsystem Control Table | SSGS | Standardized Space Guidance System |
| SSCW | Single-Silk Covered Wire | | |
| SSD | Sequence Switch Driver | SSI | Separate Shifting Instruction |
| SSD | Sequential Stored Data | | |
| SSD | Silicon Single Diffused | SSI | Single Scale Integration |
| SSD | Software System Design | SSI | Small-Scale Integration |
| SSD | Solid State Device | SSI | System Standard Interface |
| SSD | Solid State storage Device | SSI | System Status Index |
| SSD | Solid-State Detector | SSI | System Status Information |
| SSDA | Sequential Similarity Detection Algorithm | SSIA | Subschema Information Area |

# S

| | | | |
|---|---|---|---|
| SSID | Subsystem Identification | SSN | Social Security Number |
| SSIE | Smithsonian Institutions Science Information Exchange | SSN | Specification Serial Number |
| | | SSN | System Segment Name |
| SSIG | Single Signal | SSO | Steady State Oscillator |
| SSII | Société de Services et d'Ingénierie Informatique | SSOCR | Super-Scale Optical Character Reader |
| | | SSOU1 | System Output Unit 1 |
| SSIS | Social Science Information System | SSP | Scientific Subroutine Package |
| SSIS | Squib Science Information System | SSP | Simultanspeicher |
| | | SSP | Solid State Preamplifier |
| SSIT | Shared Segment Index Table | SSP | Steady State Pulse |
| | | SSP | System Service Program |
| SSIXS | Submarine Satellite Information Exchange System | SSP | System Status Panel |
| | | SSP | System Support Processor |
| | | SSP | System Support Program |
| SSK | Set Storage Key | SSPC | Système de Simulation de Processus Continu |
| SSKA | Schweizerische Studiengesellschaft für Kommunikation und Administration | SSPDA | Surface Sampler Processing and Distribution Assembly |
| SSL | Shift and Select | SSPM | Single Sideband Phase Modulation |
| SSL | SODA Statement Language | | |
| SSL | Solid-State Lamp | SSPS | Satellite Solar Power Station |
| SSL | Source Statement Library | | |
| SSL | Storage Structure Language | SSQ | Sum of the Squares |
| SSL | Super Speed Logic | SSQD | Single Sided Quad Density |
| SSL | Support System Language | SSR | Schutzschlüsselregister |
| SSL | System Simulation Language | SSR | Secondary Surveillance Radar |
| SSLC | Synchronous Single Line Controller | SSR | Sicherungssteuerrechner |
| | | SSR | Single Signal Receiver |
| SSM | Semiconductor Storage Module | SSR | Solid-State Relay |
| | | SSR | Source/Sink Request |
| SSM | Single Sideband Modulation | SSR | Standby Supply Relay |
| SSM | Solid State Materials | SSR | Stationary Stores Requisition |
| SSM | Spred Spectrum Modulation | | |
| SSM | Stochastic Sequential Machine | SSR | Stock Status Report |
| | | SSR | Storage Select Register |
| SSM | Subsystem Simulation Model | SSR | Store Search Register |
| | | SSR | Switching Selector Repeater |
| SSM | System-Software-Mitteilung | SSR | Synchronous Stabel Relaying |
| SSMA | Spred Spectrum Multiple Access | SSRB | Sequential Scan Request Block |
| SSMD | Silicon Stud-Mounted Diode | SSRC | Single-Sideband Reduced |
| SSMIS | Support Services Management Information System | SSRD | Secondary Surveillance Radar Digitzer |
| SSMS | Solid State Mass Spectrometer | SSRG | Simple Shift Register Generator |
| SSMTG | Solid-State and Molecular Theory Group | SSRS | Start-Stop-Restart System |
| SSMV | Single Shot Multivibrator | SSRT | Subsystem Readiness Test |

# S

| | | | |
|---|---|---|---|
| SSRU | Standard Speech Reproducing Unit | SSX | Small System Executive |
| SSS | Scientific Subroutine System | SSX | Small System Extended |
| | | SSX/VSE | Small System Executive/ Virtual Storage Extended |
| SSS | Self-Shifting Synchronizing | SSZ | Setzen Speicherplatzzähler |
| SSS | Sequential Scheduling System | ST | Sampling Time |
| | | ST | Sawtooth |
| SSS | Signal Storage System | ST | Scan Time |
| SSS | Simulation Study Series | ST | Schlußtaste |
| SSS | Single-Signal Superheterodyne | ST | Schmitt-Trigger |
| | | ST | Scientific and Technical |
| SSS | Small Scientific Satellite | ST | Searching Technique |
| SSS | Software Specification Sheet | ST | Segment Table |
| | | ST | Select Time |
| SSS | Software Subsription Service. | ST | Sending Time |
| | | ST | Serial Tasking |
| SSS | Solid State Scientific | ST | Service-Techniker |
| SSS | Solid State System | ST | Set Trigger |
| SSS | Speech Signal Storage | ST | Settling Time |
| SSS | Subsystem Support Services | ST | Short Ton |
| | | ST | Single Throw |
| SSS | Symbolic Shorthand System | ST | Sort Time |
| SSS | Synchronous Self-Shifting | ST | Sound Telegraphy |
| SSSC | Single-Sideband Suppressed Carrier | ST | Sous-Tension |
| | | ST | Standard Tape |
| SSSD | Single Sided Single Density | ST | Standard Time |
| SSSG | Scientific System Support Group | ST | Stanzer |
| | | ST | Star Technologies |
| SSSTFR | Share Software Service Task Force Report | ST | Start |
| | | ST | Start Timing |
| SST | Simple Secure Transfer | ST | Startsignal |
| SST | Simulated Structural Test | ST | Statement |
| SST | Single Step | ST | Steuerung |
| SST | Solid State Technology | ST | Steuerwerk |
| SST | Solid State Transmitter | ST | Storage Time |
| SST | Step-by-Step Test | ST | Store |
| SST | Streifenstanzer | ST | Store Technique |
| SST | Subsystem Test | ST | Strahlteiler |
| SST | Supersonic Telegraphy | ST | Straight Time |
| SST | Supersonic Transport | ST | Studio-to-Transmitter |
| SST | System Scheduler Table | ST | Surface Tension |
| SSTC | Single-Sideband Transmitted Carrier | ST | Symbol Table |
| | | ST | Synchronization Table |
| SSTG | Subschema Task Group | ST | System Table |
| SSTO | Second Stage Tail-Off | ST | Systemtechnik |
| SSTP | Subsystem Test Procedure | STA | Segment Table Address |
| SSTR | Solid State Track Recorder | STA | Startimpuls |
| SSTV | Slow Scan Television | STA | Station |
| SSU | Semiconductor Storage Unit | STA | Steel-Tape-Armoured |
| | | STA | Steueranweisung |
| SSW | Safety Switch | STA | Store Address |
| SSW | Standard Software | STAB | Stabilization |
| SSW | Synchro Switch | STAB AMP | Stabilizing Amplifier |
| SSWAM | Single-Sided Wideband Analog Modulation | STAC | Shell Terminal Automation Computerization |

# S

| | | | |
|---|---|---|---|
| STAC | System Test Adapter Complex | STAN | Standardization |
| STACOM | Standard Airborne Computer | STANTEC | Standard Telephones Electronic Computer |
| STACS | Satellite Telemetry And Computer System | STAP | Standardablaufplan |
| STAD | Société de Traitement Automatique des Données | STAP | Start des Applikationsprogramms |
| STAD | Système de Test Analogique et Digital | STAP | Steuerungsablaufplan |
| STADAN | Satellite Tracking And Data Acquisition Network | STAPP | Simulation Tape Print Program |
| STADAN | Space Tracking And Data Acquisition Network | STAPP | Standard Tape Print Program |
| STADAR | Servo Tester with Automatic Data Acquisition and Reduction | STAPRO | Saison-Trend-Analyse- und Prognosesystem |
| STADES | Standard Data Element System | STAR | Segment Table Address Register |
| STAE | Second-Time-Around Echo | STAR | Self-Testing And Repairing |
| STAE | Specify Task Asynchronous Exit | STAR | Site Trunk Analysis Routine |
| STAEN | Statistische Analyse Elektrischer Schaltungen | STAR | Standard Routine |
| STAF | Scientific and Technological Applications Forecast | STAR | Standard Telecommunications Automatic Recognizer |
| STAF | Statistical Analysis of Files | STAR | Statistical Analysis Routine |
| STAFF | System To Analyze FORTRAN Four | STAR | Statistical Table Assembly and Retrieval |
| STAG | Self Teaching Assistance Group | STAR | Storage Address Register |
| STAIAT | Service de Traitement Automatique de l'Information de l'Armée de Terre | STAR | System Training Analysis Report |
| | | STAR | System for Telephone Administrative Response |
| | | STARE | Steerable Telemetry Antenna Receiving Equipment |
| STAIR | Structural Analysis Interpretive Routine | STARFIRE | System To Accumulate and Retrieve Financial Information with Random Extraction |
| STAIRS | Storage And Information Retrieval System | STARR | State-of-the-Art Recorder/Reproducer |
| STAK | Stammdatei Arbeitskräfte | STARS | Satellite Telemetry Automatic Reduction System |
| STAKT | Schiebetakt | | |
| STALO | Stabilized Local Oscillator | | |
| STAM | Single Terminal Access Method | STARS | Services and Techniques for Advanced Real-time Systems |
| STAM | Statistical Analog Monitor | | |
| STAMO | Stabilized Master Oscillator | STARS | Synchronized Time, Automated Reporting System |
| STAMOS | Sortie Turn-Around Maintenance Operations Simulation | START | Selections To Activate Random Testing |
| STAMP | Systems Tape Addition and Maintenance Program | START | Status And Reporting Technique |
| STAN | Standard | START | Story-Telling Automatic Reading Tutor |

## S

| | | | |
|---|---|---|---|
| START | Studiengesellschaft zur Automatisierung für Reise und Touristik GmbH | STD | Semiconductor on Thermoplastic on Dielectric |
| START | Summary Tape Assistance Research and Training | STD | Silicon Triple Diffused |
| | | STD | Sledborne Time Digitizer |
| START | Systematic Tabular Analysis of Requirements Technique | STD | Spectral Theory of Diffraction |
| | | STD | Standard |
| | | STD | Storage Tube Display |
| STASYS | Standards zur Systementwicklung | STD | Stored |
| | | STD | Störungsdienst |
| STAT | Status | STD | Stream Tree Data |
| STATICE | Statistics in the Computerline Environment | STD | Stripline Tunnel Diode |
| | | STD | Subscriber Trunk Dialling |
| STATPAC | Statistics Package | STD | Superconductive Tunnelling Device |
| STATPK | Statistical Package | | |
| STB | Segment Table Base | STD | SW-Transfer-Document |
| STB | Selective Top-to-Bottom | STDA | Stripline Tunnel Diode Amplifier |
| STB | Start To Build | | |
| STB | Subsystem Test Bed | STDBY | Stand-By |
| STBA | Selective Top-to-Bottom Algorithm | STDM | Statistical Time Division Multiplexer |
| STBY | Stand-By | STDM | Synchronous Time Division Multiplexing |
| STC | Satellite Test Center | | |
| STC | Schmitt Trigger Circuit | STDMA | Space Time Division Multiple Access |
| STC | Sensitivity Time Control | | |
| STC | Short Time Constant | STDN | Spaceflight Tracking and Data Network |
| STC | Simulation Tape Conversion | | |
| | | STDP | Single-Throw, Double-Pole |
| STC | Stacked-Capacitor cell | STDS | Set Theoretic Data Structure |
| STC | Standard Transmission Code | | |
| | | STE | Segment Table Entry |
| STC | Storage Test Control | STE | Service Technique Externe |
| STC | Store Characters | STE | Shop Test Equipment |
| STC | Stored Time Command | STE | Signalling Terminal |
| STC | Symbol Table Counter | STE | Single-Threshold Element |
| STC | System Test Complex | STE | Steckeinheit |
| STC | System Test Coordinator | STE | Stelle |
| STC | System Transfer Constant | STE | Steuereinheit |
| STC... | Standard Telephones and Cables Ltd. | STE | Steuereinheitsende |
| | | STE | Steuereinrichtung |
| STC... | Storage Technology Corporation | STE | System Timing Element |
| | | STEAP | Simulated Trajectories Error Analysis Program |
| STCB | Sub-Task Control Block | | |
| STCDS | System Test Complex Data System | STEAP | Space Trajectory Error Analysis Program |
| STCE | System Test Complex Equipment | STEC | Solar-to-Thermal Energy Conversion |
| STCL | Storage Control | STEC | Store Exception Condition |
| STCPS | Store Channel Path Status | STEC | Study of Trends and Escalation of Costs |
| STCR | System Test Configuration Requirements | | |
| | | STEDMIS | Ships Technical Data Management Information System |
| STCRW | Store Channel Report Word | | |
| STCW | System Time Code Word | | |
| STD | Salinity Temperature Depth | STEDR | Staging Effective Data Rate |

# S

| | | | |
|---|---|---|---|
| STEEL | Structural Engineers Easy Language | STERILE | System of Terminology for Retrieval of Information through Language Engineering |
| STEG | Simulated Timebase and Echo Generator | | |
| STEIL | Steuerteil | STET | Specialized Technique for Efficient Types |
| STELLA | Satellite Transmission Experiment Linking Laboratories | STEU | Steuerung |
| | | STEV | Softwaretest e.V. |
| STELLA | System Ten European Language Ledger Accounting | STF | Service Tabulating Form |
| | | STF | Standardisiertes Trägerfrequenzsystem |
| STEM | Scanning Transmission Electron Microscope | STG | Stage |
| | | STG | Starting |
| STEM | Self-storing Tubular Extensionable Member | STG | Storage |
| | | STGE | Storage |
| STEM | Shaped Tube Electrolytic Machining | STI | Scientific Technical Information |
| STEM | Stay Time Extension Module | STI | Service du Traitement de l'Information |
| STEM | Storable Tubular Extendable Member | STI | Special Test Instruction |
| | | STI | Speech Transmission Index |
| STEP | Safeguard Test and Evaluation Program | STIBCO | Salon Tarnais de l'Informatique, de la Bureautique et de la Comptabilité |
| STEP | Safety Test Engineering Program | | |
| STEP | Scientific and Technical Exploitation Program | STIC | Space Technical Information Control |
| STEP | Simple Transition to Electronic Processing | STICO | Standard Interpretation and Compiling system |
| STEP | Standard Equipment Practice | STICO | Standard Interpretationsund Compilierungs-System |
| STEP | Standard Tape Executive Package | | |
| STEP | Standard Tape Executive Program | STID | Scientific and Technical Information Dissemination |
| STEP | Standard Terminal Program | STIDAS | Speech Transmission Index Device using Artificial Signals |
| STEP | Steuerungssystem for Echtzeit-Programme | STIF | Scientific and Technical Information Facilities |
| STEP | Supervisory Tape Executive Program | STIL | Statistical Interpretive Language |
| STEP | System for Test and Plug | STINFO | Scientific and Technical Information |
| STEP | Systematisches Trainingsund Entscheidungsprogramm | | |
| | | STINGS | Stellar Inertial Guidance System |
| STEPS | Solar Thermionic Electric Power System | STIO | Store Input/Output |
| | | STIPIS | Scientific; Technical, Intelligence and Program Information System |
| STEPS | Strategisches Evaluierungs- und Planungssystem | | |
| | | STIR | Scientific and Technical Intelligence Register |
| STEPS | Strategy Evaluation and Planning System | | |
| | | STIR | Statistic Indexing and Retrieval |
| STERIA | Société de Réalisations en Informatique et Automatisme | | |
| | | STIRE | Service Time Requirements |

- 581 -

# S

| | | | |
|---|---|---|---|
| STIRS | Self-Training Interpretive and Retrieval System | STOCS | Small Terminal Oriented Computer System |
| STISEC | Scientific and Technological Information Services Enquiry Committee | STOKPAC | Stock control Package |
| | | STOL | Saturn Test Oriented Language |
| STIWEX | Stichwortindex | STOL | Short Takeoff and Landing |
| STK | Steuerkarte | STOL | Systems Test and Operation Language |
| STK | Stock | | |
| STKFA | Stock Fund Accounting | STOP | Selected Test Optimization Program |
| STL | Schottky Transistor Logic | | |
| STL | Selective Tape Listing | STOP | Storage Protection |
| STL | Sequential Table Lookup | STOP | Storage Protector |
| STL | Simulated Tape Load | STOP THIEF | Stop The Human Initiated Equipment Failure |
| STL | Space-To-Letters | | |
| STL | Standard Telecommunications Laboratories | STOR | Segment Table Origin Register |
| STL | Steuerloch | STOR | Storage |
| STL | Structured Test Language | STOR | Store |
| STL | Studio Transmitter Link | STOR | Summary Tape Operations Rental |
| STL | Synchronous Transistor Logic | | |
| | | STORES | Syntactic Trace Organized Retrospective Enquiry System |
| STLB | Standardleistungsbuch | | |
| STLI | Stockage List Item | | |
| STLS | Stream Load and Store | STORET | Storage and Retrieval |
| STLV | Standardleistungsverzeichnis | STORM | Statistically Oriented Matrix programming |
| STM | Schmitt Trigger Module | STOS | Softwaretrommel-Organisations-System |
| STM | Send Test Message | | |
| STM | Service Test Module | STP | Selective Tape Print |
| STM | Short-Term Memory | STP | Self Triggering Program |
| STM | Statement | STP | Sequenztiefpaß |
| STM | Stellenmaschine | STP | Signal Transfer Point |
| STM | Store Multiple | STP | Signalling Transfer Point |
| STM | Structural Test Model | STP | Simultaneous Track Processor |
| STM | Système Télématique Multifonction | | |
| | | STP | Source Term Program |
| STMC | Store MAMO Counter | STP | Standard Temperature and Pressure |
| STMGR | Station Manager | | |
| STMIS | System Test Manufacturing Information System | STP | Standardprogramm |
| | | STP | Steuerprogramm |
| | | STP | Steuerpult |
| STMNT | Statement | STP | Stop Character |
| STMP | Single Track MORT Processing | STP | Storage Tube Processor |
| | | STP | System Terminal Programmable |
| STMT | Statement | | |
| STMT | Store MAMO Timer | STP | System Test Plan |
| STMU | Special Test and Maintenance Unit | STPG | Stepping |
| | | STPMU | Software-Technologie, Produkt, Markt-Untersuchung |
| STN | Station | | |
| STO | Storage | | |
| STO | System Test Objectives | STPR | Steuerprogramm |
| STOC | Stock Transfer Online Control | STPS | Series-Tuned Parallel Stabilized |
| STOC | Symposium on the Theory Of Computing | STR | Serial Transmit-Receive |
| | | STR | Spannungs-Testregister |

- 582 -

# S

| | | | |
|---|---|---|---|
| STR | Start | STS | Secure Teletypewriter System |
| STR | Startadreßregister | STS | Selective Two-Step |
| STR | Storage Test Routine | SIS | Self-Test Select |
| STR | Store | STS | Sequential Transistor Switch |
| STR | Strobe | | |
| STR | Synchronous Transmit/Receive | STS | Set Transmit State |
| STR | Synchronous Transmitter/Receiver | STS | Speicher-Test-Steuerung |
| | | STS | Static Test Stand |
| STR... | Standard Telephon und Radio AG | SIS | Status |
| | | STS | Structural Transition Section |
| STRAD | Signal Transmission, Reception And Distribution | STS | System Trouble Shooting |
| STRADAP | Storm Radar Data Processor | STSCH | Store Subchannel |
| | | STSN | Set-and-Test-Sequence-Number |
| STRAM | Synchronous Transmit Receive Access Method | STST | System Task Set Table |
| STRAP | Simplified Transient Radiation Analysis Program | STT | Schautisch-Terminals |
| | | STT | Sequence Test Trigger |
| | | STT | Service de Téléinformatique Touristique |
| STRAPP | Structural Analysis Program Package | STT | Short-Time Test |
| STRAW | Simultaneous Tape Read And Write | STT | Single Track Table |
| | | STT | Sortieren und Trennen |
| STRB | Strobe | STT | Start Timing |
| STRENA | Straßenentwurf im Aufriß | STT | Système de Traitement de Texte |
| STRESS | Statistical Reliability Evaluation by Synthetic Sampling | STTC | Start of Transit Through-Connect-signal |
| STRESS | Structural Engineering System Solver | STTD | Started |
| | | STTL | Schottky Transistor-Transistor Logic |
| STRG | Steuerung | | |
| STRIP | Standard Taped Routines or Image Processing | STU | Segment Time Unit |
| | | STU | Store-to-store Transfer Unit |
| STRIP | String Processing | | |
| STRIVE | Standard Techniques for Reporting Information on Value Engineering | STU | Systems Test Unit |
| | | STUFF | Sixteen Twenty, Universal Function Filter |
| STRL | Schottky Transistor-Resistor Logic | STV | Sondercode Textverarbeitung |
| STRLD | Start Load | STV | Stapelverarbeitung |
| STRN | Standard Technical Report Number | STV | Stromversorgung |
| | | STV | Surveillance Television |
| STROBE | Storage Read-Out Bias Eliminate | STW | Steuerwerk |
| | | STW | Store Word |
| STROBES | Shared Time Repair Of Big Electronic Systems | STW | System Tape Writer |
| | | STX | Start of Text |
| STRUDEL | Structural Design Language | STZ | Store Zero |
| | | SU | Schnittstellenumsetzer |
| STRUDL | Structural Design Language | SU | Schulungsunterlage |
| | | SU | Selectable Unit |
| STRUM | Structured Microprogramming language | SU | Sensation Unit |
| | | SU | Service Unit |
| STS | Satellite Tracking Station | SU | Servo Unit |
| STS | Scientific Terminal System | SU | Set Up |

# S

| | | | |
|---|---|---|---|
| SU | Signal Unit | SUMB | Schnelle Umbuchung |
| SU | Storage Unit | SUMC | Space Ultrareliable Modular Computer |
| SU | Store Unit | | |
| SU | Support | SUMIT | Standard Utility Means for Information Transformation |
| SU | Suspended status | | |
| SU | Symbolic Unit | | |
| SU | Systems Usage | SUMM | Summarize |
| SU | Systemunterstützung | SUMMIT | Supervisor of Multiprogramming Multiprocessing, Interactive Timesharing |
| SUADPS | Shipboard Uniform Automatic Data Processing System | | |
| SUAS | System for Upper Atmospheric Sounding | SUMP | Sum of Products |
| | | SUMS | Sperry Univac Material System |
| SUB | Substitute | | |
| SUB | Substitution | SUMT | Sequential Unconstraine Minization Technique |
| SUB | Subtract | | |
| SUB | Subtrahieren | SUN | Symbols, Units, Nomenclature |
| SUB | Subtraktion | | |
| SUBIRS | Submarine Installed RADIAC System | SUP | Supply |
| | | SUP | Suppress |
| SUBR | Sub-Routine | SUP | Suppressor |
| SUBS | Subsystem | SUP | System Utilisation Procedure |
| SUBST | Substitute | | |
| SUBST | Substitution | SUPD | Suppressed |
| SUBT | Subtract | SUPER | Superheterodyne |
| SUBTIL | Synthesized User Based Terminology Index Language | SUPERB | Supervisor B |
| | | SUPFID | Supplementary Flight Information Document |
| SUBTR | Subtractor | SUPIR | Supplementary Photographic Interpretation Report |
| SUBUPOS | Subtract Units Position | | |
| SUC | Single Use Charge | | |
| SUCHG | Setup Change | SUPO | Superpower |
| SUD | Schuldatei | SUPP | Support |
| SUD | Structural Unit Descriptor | SUPROX | Successive approximation |
| SUDT | Silicon Unilateral Diffused Transistor | SUPV | Supervisory |
| | | SUR | Surface |
| SUE | System User Engineered | SURANO | Surface Radar And Navigation Operation |
| SUHL | Sylvania Universal High Level logic | | |
| | | SURCAL | Surveillance Calibration |
| SUHL | Sylvania Ultrahigh Level logic | SURE | Symbolic Utility Revenue Environment |
| SUIAP | Simplified Unit Invoice Accounting Plan | SURF | Selective Unit Record File |
| | | SURF | System Utilization Reporting Facility |
| SUIS | Ship Upkeep Information System | | |
| | | SURGE | Sorting, Updating, Report Generating |
| SUKA | Suchkarte | | |
| SUL | Standard and User Label | SURGE | Sorting, Updating, Report Generator |
| SUL | Systemunterlage | | |
| SULIS | Sulzer Literaturverteilung und Sortierung | SURIC | Surface ship Integrated Control system |
| | | SURISS | Sheffield Urban and Regional Instructional Simulation System |
| SULK | Signs Unlike | | |
| SUM | Summary | | |
| SUM | SW-User Manual | | |
| SUM | System Utilisation Monitor | SURWAC | Surface Water Automatic Computer |

# S

| | | | |
|---|---|---|---|
| SUS | Silicon Unidirectional Switch | SVI | System de Visualisation et Impression |
| SUS | Silicon Unilateral Switch | SVIP | Swiss-Viewdata Information Providers Association |
| SUS | Single Underwater Sound | | |
| SUSFD | Successive Feed | SVIPA | Swiss Videotext Information Providers Association |
| SUSIE | Stock Updating Sales Invoicing Electronically | | |
| SUSY | Saarbrücker Übersetzungssystem | SVM | Supervisor Virtual Machine |
| | | SVM | System Virtueller Maschinen |
| SUSY | Subsystem | | |
| SUSY | Suchsystem | SVOR | Schweizerische Vereinigung für Operations Research |
| SUSY | Survey System | | |
| SUT | System Under Test | SVP | Service Processor |
| SUTIL | Short Utility | SVP | Serviceprozessor |
| SUU | Subsystem Unit Unusable | SVP | Software-Verification Plan |
| SV | Safety Valve | SVR | Servicevertrag für Rechenzentrumsarbeiten |
| SV | Saponification Value | | |
| SV | Scalar Variable | SVR | Squelette de Vecteur de Renseignement |
| SV | Schreibverstärker | | |
| SV | Simultanverarbeitung | SVR | Supply-Voltage Rejection |
| SV | Single-silk Varnish | SVRB | Supervisor Request block |
| SV | Steuerungsverfahren | SVS | Select Vertical Spacing |
| SV | Stop Valve | SVS | Servicevertrag für Systemberatung |
| SV | Stromversorgung | | |
| SV | Supervisor | SVS | Single Virtual Storage |
| SV | Systeme und Verfahren | SVS | Structural Verification Simulator |
| SVA | Sampled Voltage Analysis | | |
| SVA | Shared Virtual Area | SVS | Supervisory Signal |
| SVA | Spezielle Vertrags-Angebote | SVT | System Variable Table |
| | | SVTP | Sound, Velocity, Temperature, Pressure |
| SVB | Statischer Verständigungsbereich | | |
| | | SVU | Select Vertical format Unit |
| SVC | Service | | |
| SVC | Solid-state Voltage Control | SVV | Schnittstellenvervielfacher |
| | | SW | Schichtwiderstand |
| SVC | Special Vendor Code | SW | Schreibwerk |
| SVC | Supervisor Call | SW | Schrittschaltwerk |
| SVC | Switched Virtual Call | SW | Semi-Word |
| SVC | Switched Virtual Circuit | SW | Shock Wave |
| SVCT | Supervisor Call address Table | SW | Short Wave |
| | | SW | Single Weight |
| SVD | Schweizerische Vereinigung für Datenverarbeitung | SW | Single Word |
| | | SW | Software |
| SVD | Simultaneous Voice/Data | SW | Sollwert |
| SVDSS | Space Vehicle Data Systems Synthesizer | SW | Specific Weight |
| | | SW | Standing Wave |
| SVE | Stromversorgungseinheit | SW | Status Word |
| SVF | Set Vertical Format | SW | Steel Wire |
| SVF | Single Volume File | SW | Steuerwerk |
| SVFLIH | Supervisor First Level Interrupt Handler | SW | Storage Word |
| | | SW | Store Word |
| SVG | Stromversorgungsgerät | SW | Switch |
| SVGR | Stromversorgungsgerät | SW | Switchband Wound |
| SVI | Schweizerische Vereinigung für Informatik | SW | Switched line |
| | | SWA | Scheduler Work Area |

# S

| | | | |
|---|---|---|---|
| SWA | Speicherwortausgabe | SWI | Short-Wave Interference |
| SWAC | Standards Western Automatic Computer | SWI | Standing Wave Indicator |
| | | SWI | Store Write Instruction |
| SWAD | Speicherwortadresse | SWI | Switch |
| SWADS | Scheduler Work Area Data Set | SWIFR | Slow Writing-Fast Reading |
| | | SWIFT | Selected Words in Full Title |
| SWALCAP | South West Academic Libraries Cooperative Automation Project | SWIFT | Sequential Weight Increasing Factor Technique |
| SWALM | Switch Alarm | | |
| SWAMI | Software-Aided Multifont Input | SWIFT | Signal Word Index of Field and Title |
| SWAMI | Software-Aided Multiform Input | SWIFT | Society for Worldwide Interbank Financial Telecommunications |
| SWAMI | Software-Aided Multipoint Input | SWIFT | Software Implemented Friden Translator |
| SWAMI | Stanford Worldwide Acquisition of Meteorological Information | SWIFT-LASS | Signal Word Index of Field and Title-Literature Abstract Specialized Search |
| SWAP | Society for Wang Applications and Programs | | |
| SWAP | Stewart Warner Array Program | SWIFT-SIR | Signal Word Index of Field and Title-Scientific Information Retrieval |
| SWAP | Stone and Webster Automatic Program | SWIMS | Serialized Weapons Information Management System |
| SWAP | Switching Assembly Program | | |
| SWAT | Sidewinder IC Acquisition Track | SWINC | Soft-Wired Integrated Numerical Controller |
| SWAT | Switching and Automata Theory | SWINGR | Sweep Integrator |
| | | SWIRS | Solid Waste Information Retrieval System |
| SWB | Short Wheelbase | | |
| SWBD | Switchboard | SWITT | Surface Wave Independent Tap Transducer |
| SWC | Semi-Word Command | | |
| SWC | Short Word Computer | SWL | Short-Wave Listener |
| SWC | Soft-Wired Control | SWL | Short Wavelength Limit |
| SWCS | Space Warning and Control System | SWM | Single Wire Memory |
| | | SWN | Significant Word Number |
| SWD | Serial Write Data | SWN | Switched Network |
| SWD | Smaller Word | SWNG | Switching |
| SWE | Society for Women Engineers | SWO | Semi-Word Order |
| | | SWOC | Subject Word Out-of-Context |
| SWE | Softwareentwicklung | | |
| SWE | Speicherworteingabe | SWOP | Structural Weight Optimization Program |
| SWEDIS | Swedish Drug Information System | | |
| | | SWORCC | Southwestern Ohio Regional Computer Center |
| SWEDNET | Swedish packet Network | | |
| SWF | Selbstwähl-Fernnetz | SWORD | Shallow Water Oceanographic Research Data |
| SWF | Short Wave Fade-out | | |
| SWF | Simulation Work File | SWORDS | Standard Work Order Recording and Data System |
| SWF | Sudden Wave Fade-out | | |
| SWFR | Slow Write, Fast Read | | |
| SWG | Standard Wire Gauge | SWP | Safe Working Pressure |
| SWGR | Switchgear | SWP | Selected Word Position |
| SWI | Semi-Word Instruction | SWP | Subscriber With Priority |

# S

| | | | |
|---|---|---|---|
| SWR | Standing Wave Ratio | SYLT | Synchronous Line Terminator |
| SWR | Stepwise Refinement | | |
| SWROM | Standing-Wave Read-Only Memory | SYLT | System-Leitungsschalten |
| | | SYM | Symbol |
| SWRSIC | Southern Water Resources Scientific Information Center | SYM | Symmetrical |
| | | SYM | System |
| | | SYMAP | Symbol Manipulation Program |
| SWS | Sendewartespeicher | | |
| SWS | Shift Word, Substituting | SYMAP | Symbolsprache zur Maschinellen Programmierung |
| SWS | Single White Silk | | |
| SWS | Stripline With Stud | SYMB | Symbol |
| SWS | System Work Sheet | SYMBAL | Symbolic Algebra |
| SWSR | Standing Wave Signal Ratio | SYMBAL | Symbolic Algebra Language |
| SWT | Supersonic Wind Tunnel | | |
| SWU | Switching Unit | SYMBIOSIS | System for Medical and Biological Sciences Information Searching |
| SWULSCP | South West University Libraries Systems Cooperation Project | | |
| | | SYMBOL | System for Mass Balancing in Off-Line |
| SWVR | Standing Wave Voltage Ratio | | |
| | | SYMBUG | Symbolic debugging |
| SWW | Severe Weather Warning | SYMOB | Système Modulaire Bull |
| SX | Scientific Extension | SYMPAC | Symbolic Programming for Automatic Controls |
| SX | Simplex | | |
| SXA | Store Index in Address | SYMPLE | Syntax Macro Preprocessor for Language Evaluation |
| SXA | Stored Index to Address | | |
| SXD | Store Index in Decrement | SYMRAP | Symbolic Reliability Analysis Program |
| SXP | Scientific Extension Processor | | |
| | | SYN | Synchronisierung |
| SXPU | Secondary X Pickup | SYN | Synchronisierzeichen |
| SXS | Step-by-Step | SYN | Synchronization |
| SY | Security | SYN | Synchronize |
| SY | Symbol | SYN | Synchronized |
| SY | Synchronized | SYN | Synchronizer |
| SY | System | SYN | Synchronous |
| SYC | Symbolic Corrector | SYN IND | Synchronization Indicator |
| SYCOM | Synchronous Communications | SYNAME | Syndicat National de la Mesure Electrique et électronique |
| SYCOP | System für Computer-gestützte Programm-umstellung, Programm-entwicklung und Programmpflege | | |
| | | SYNC | Synchronization |
| | | SYNC | Synchronize |
| | | SYNC | Synchronizer |
| | | SYNC | Synchronizing |
| SYCR | Synchronize | SYNC | Synchronous |
| SYDAS | System Data Acquisition System | SYNC SEP | Synchronization Separator |
| | | SYNCOM | Synchronous-orbiting Communications satellite |
| SYDONI | Système de Documentation National Informatisé | | |
| | | SYNCR | Synchronizer |
| SYDONI | Système de Documentation Notariale Informatique | SYNSEM | Syntax and Semantics |
| | | SYNTOL | Syntagmatic Organization Language |
| SYEPAC | Systèmes Et Périphe-riques Associés aux Calculateurs | | |
| | | SYNTRAN | Syntax Translation |
| | | SYNUS | System-Netzknoten Und Stapelstation |
| SYFA | System For Access | | |
| SYGEBRE | Système de Gestion documentaire des Brevets | SYP | Systemprogramm |

# S

| | | | |
|---|---|---|---|
| SYPS | Symbolische Programmiersprache | SYSRES | System Residence |
| SYS | System | SYSRES | Systemresidenz-Speicher |
| SYS-CSL | System Console | SYST | System |
| SYSCAP | System of Circuit Analysis Program | SYSTOD | System Time Of Day |
| | | SYSTRAN | Systems analysis Translator |
| SYSCMA | System Core image library Maintenance program | SYSTRAN | Systems Translator |
| | | SYSX... | Systems Exchange Co. |
| SYSCR | System Control Register | SYTPHYDATA | System for the Acquisition Transmission and Processing of Hydrological Data |
| SYSDA | System-Designanalyse | | |
| SYSDFT RPY | System Default Reply | | |
| SYSEX | System Executive | | |
| SYSGEN | System Generation | SZ | Satzanweisung |
| SYSGEN | System Generator | SZ | Satzzeichen |
| SYSIN | System Input | SZ | Servicezentrum |
| SYSIPT | System Input | SZ | Size |
| SYSLIB | System Library | SZ | Spuren/Zylinder |
| SYSLIST | System List | SZ | Steuerzentrale |
| SYSLNK | System Link | SZ | Storage Zone |
| SYSLOG | System Log | SZ | Store Zone |
| SYSMSG | System Message | SZ | Suchzeit |
| SYSOUT | System Output | SZ | Synchronisierungszeichen |
| SYSPCH | System Punch | SZA | Speicherzyklusanforderung |
| SYSPOP | System Programmed Operator | SZL | Stör- und Zerstörfestigkeit der Logik |
| SYSPRO | Systematik der Programmvorgaben | SZL | Stör- und Zerstörsichere Logik |
| SYSRDR | System Reader | SZVR | Silicon Zener Voltage Regulator |
| SYSREC | System Recorder | | |

# T

| | | | |
|---|---|---|---|
| T | Tabelle | TAA | Transferable Account Area |
| T | Tabulated | TAA | Treudata-Programmsystem zur Automatischen Abstimmung |
| T | Tank | | |
| T | Tape | | |
| T | Tastatur | TAABS | The Army Automated Budget System |
| T | Tausend | | |
| T | Telefunken | TAADS | The Army Authorized Document System |
| T | Telephone | | |
| T | Temperature | TAAP | Transient Analysis Array Program |
| T | Tera | | |
| T | Terminal | TAAR | Target Area Analysis Radar |
| T | Tesla | | |
| T | Time | TAAS | Three-Axis Attitude Sensor |
| T | Torque | TAB | Tabelle |
| T | Track | TAB | Tabelliermaschine |
| T | Transaction | TAB | Table |
| T | Transfer | TAB | Tabulate |
| T | Transformer | TAB | Tabulating Machine |
| T | Transistor | TAB | Tabulation |
| T | Translation | TAB | Tabulator |
| T | Transmission | TAB | Tape Automated Bonding |
| T | Transmit | TAB | Technical Abstract Bulletin |
| T | Transmitter | | |
| T | Trigger | TAB | Technical Administration Bulletin |
| T | Trimmer | | |
| T | Triode | TAB | Technischer Arbeitsbericht |
| T | Tritium | TAB | Technologischer Auftragsbelegsatz |
| T | Trommel | | |
| T... | Telefunken AG | TAB | Tone Answer-Back |
| T... | Télémecanique | TAB | Totalizer Agency Boards |
| T & M | Time & Materials | TABC | Tabulator Character |
| T&D | Transmission and Distribution | TABL | Tabling |
| | | TABL | Tabulator |
| T&O | Test and Operation | TABL | Taylor Advanced Batch Language |
| TA | Table Argument | | |
| TA | Tape Adapter | TABS | Tabulator Stop |
| TA | Tape Advance | TABS | Tailored Abstracts Service |
| TA | Target | TABS | Terminal Access to Batch Service |
| TA | Tastatur | | |
| TA | Technischer Außendienst | TABSIM | Tabulator Simulator |
| TA | Teilantwort | TABSOL | Tabular Systems Oriented Language |
| TA | Teilnehmeranschluss | | |
| TA | Terme Associé | TABSTONE | Target And Background Signal-To-Noise Evaluation |
| TA | Terminal Adaptor | | |
| TA | Terminal Address | | |
| TA | Track Address | TABT | Total Assembly Build Time |
| TA | Track Arrangement | TABTRAN | Table Transiator |
| TA | Trailer Address | TAC | Tape Adapter Cabinet |
| TA | Trank Amplifier | TAC | Technical Assistance Center |
| TA | Transactional Analysis | | |
| TA | Tschebyscheff-Approximation | TAC | Terminal Access Controller |
| | | TAC | Terrain Avoidance Computer |
| TA | Turbulence Amplifier | | |
| TA... | Triumpf Adler | TAC | Three Address Code |
| TA/DK | Tape/Diskette | TAC | Three Address Command |

# T

| | | | | |
|---|---|---|---|---|
| TAC | Time Analysis Computer | | TACS | Tactical Air Control System |
| TAC | Time Average Computer | | TACS | Television Automatic Control System |
| TAC | Time-to-Amplitude Conversion | | TACS | Total Access Communication System |
| TAC | Time-to-Amplitude Converter | | TACSAT | Tactical Communications Satellite |
| TAC | Token Access Controller | | TACT | Traffic Administered by Computer and Teletypewriter |
| TAC | Tokyo Automatic Computer | | | |
| TAC | TRANSAC Assembler Compiler | | TACT | Transient Area Control Table |
| TAC | Transformer Analog Computer | | TACT | Transistor And Component Tester |
| TAC | Transistorized Automatic Control | | TACTIC | Totally Applied Computerized Tariff Information Center |
| TAC | Transistorized Automatic Computer | | TACTICS | Transportation And Computer Teamed to Integrate Carriers and Shippers |
| TAC | Translator-Assembler-Complier | | | |
| TAC | Transmitter, Assembler, Compiler | | | |
| TAC | Trapped Air Cushion | | TAD | Tagesdatei |
| TAC | Triumph-Adler-Centren | | TAD | Target Acquisition Data |
| TAC | Triumph-Adler Computer-vertriebs GmbH | | TAD | Telemetry Analog-to-Digital |
| TAC | Two Address Command | | TAD | Top Assembly Drawing |
| TACADS | Tactical Automated Data processing System | | TAD | Traffic Analysis and Display |
| TACAID | Tactical Airborne Information Document | | TAD | Traitement Automatique des Documents |
| TACAN | Tactical Air Navigation | | | |
| TACCAR | Time-Averaged Clutter Coherent Airborne Radar | | TAD | Transient Area Descriptor |
| | | | TAD | Transmission Automatique des Données |
| TACDACS | Target Acquisition and Data Collection System | | TADARS | Tropo Automated Data Analysis Recorder System |
| TACDEN | Tactical Data Entry | | | |
| TACL | Teaching-And-Course writing computer Language | | TADDS | Target Alert Data Display Set |
| | | | TADIC | Telemetry Analogue Digital Information Converter |
| TACL | Time And Cycle Log | | | |
| TACLE | Terminal Abnormal Condition Line Entry | | TADIL | Tactical Digital Information Link |
| TACMAR | Tactical Memory Address Register | | TADOR | Table Data Organization and Reduction |
| TACMAR | Tactical Multifunction Array Radar | | TADR | Test Answer Document Reader |
| TACMOD | Tactical Modular Display | | TADS | Tactical Automatic Digital Switch |
| TACODA | Target Coordinate Data | | | |
| TACOL | Thinned Aperture Computed Lens | | TADS | Teletypewriter Automatic Dispatch System |
| TACP | Terminal Abnormal Condition Program | | TADS | Transportable Automatic Digital Switch |
| TACPOL | Tactical Procedure Oriented Language | | TADS | Type Automated Data System |
| TACR | Time And Cycle Record | | | |

# T

| | | | |
|---|---|---|---|
| TADSS | Tactical Automatic Digital Switching System | TALK | Titles Alphabetically Listed by Keyword |
| TAE | Technische Akademie e.V. Esslingen | TALK | Tradeoff Analysis based on Linecast and Knowhow |
| TAERS | The Army Equipment Record System | TAM | Tag Addressed Memory |
| | | TAM | Teilnehmeranschlußmodem |
| TAF | Time And Frequency | TAM | Teilnehmeranschlußmodul |
| TAF | Trans-Axle Fluid | TAM | Telecommunication Access Method |
| TAFAS | Trunk Answer From Any Station | TAM | Telephone Answering Machine |
| TAFIIS | Tactical Air Force Integrated Information System | TAM | Teleprocessing Access Method |
| TAFUBAR | Things Are Fouled Up Beyond All Recognition | TAM | Terminal Access Method |
| | | TAM | The Access Method |
| TAG | Teilnehmeranschlußgerät | TAM | Three Address Machine |
| TAG | Teilnehmeranschlußgruppe | TAM | Two Address Machine |
| TAG | Telecomputer Application Group | TAMCO | Training Aid for MOBIDIC Console Operators |
| TAG | Telexteilnehmer-Anschaltgerät | TAME | Television Automatic Monitoring Equipment |
| TAG | The Acronym Generator | TAMIS | Telemetric Automated Microbial Identification System |
| TAG | Time Automated Grid | | |
| TAG | Transient Analysis Generator | TAMOS | Transaktions-Monitor-System |
| TAGDAT | Tagesdaten | | |
| TAGS | Tactical Aircraft Guidance System | TAN | Total Acid Number |
| | | TAN | Transaktionsnummer |
| TAHA | Tapered Aperture Horn Antenna | TAO | Three Address Order |
| | | TAO | Traduction Assistée par Ordinateur |
| TAI | Technischer Assistent Informatik | TAO | Two Address Order |
| TAI | Three Address Instruction | TAP | TAG Assisted Programming |
| TAI | Time to Autoignition | TAP | Task Analysis Procedure |
| TAI | Traitement Automatique de l'Information | TAP | Technical Administration Practice |
| TAI | Two Address Instruction | TAP | Technologenarbeitsplatz |
| TAICH | Technical Assistance Information Clearing House | TAP | Term Availability Plan |
| | | TAP | Terminal Applications Package |
| TAL | Technical Administration List | TAP | Terminal Assistance Package |
| TAL | Terminal Application Language | TAP | Terminal-Anpassungs-Prozessor |
| TALAB | Tape Label | TAP | Terminal-Anschluß-Prozessor |
| TALAR | Tactical Landing Approach Radar | | |
| | | TAP | Terminalanschlußpunkt |
| TALES | Test Analyzer Logic Evaluation System | TAP | Time-sharing Accounting Package |
| TALINET | Telecommunications Library Information Network | TAP | Time-sharing Assembly Program |
| | | TAP | Timing Analysis Program |
| TALISMAN | Transfer Accounting and Lodgement for Investors, Stock Management | TAP | Transfer und Archivierung Produktdefinierender Daten |

# T

| | | | |
|---|---|---|---|
| TAP | Transient Analysis Program | TARE | Telemetry Automatic Reduction Equipment |
| TAP | Transistor Analysis Program | TAREF | TAG Reference |
| TAP | Turn Around Point | TARFU | Things Are Really Fouled Up |
| TAPAC | Tape Automatic Positioning And Control | TARIF | Telegraph Automatic Routing In the Field |
| TAPE | Tape Automatic Preparation Equipment | TARMAC | Terminal Area Radar Moving Aircraft |
| TAPE | Totally Automated Programming Equipment | TARP | Test-And-Repair Processor |
| TAPER | Task Assignment Performance Evaluation Report | TARS | Technical Aircraft Reliability Statistics |
| TAPES | Transformer Analog Polynomial Equation Solver | TARS | Terrain And Radar Simulator |
| TAPGEN | Terminal Applications Program Generator | TARS | Three-Axis Reference System |
| TAPITS | Tactical Airborne Processing Interpretation and Transmission System | TARSC | Terrain Avoidance Radar Scan Converter |
| TAPLO | Triumph-Adler Programm Logikkonstruktor On-Line | TART | Twin Accelerator Ring Transfer |
| TAPMC | Term Availability Plan Monthly Charge | TAS | Tastatur |
| TAPP | Two-Axis Pneumatic Pickup | TAS | Technical Administration Standard |
| TAPS | Tactical Area Positioning System | TAS | Telefunken Assembler |
| TAPS | Terminal Application Processing System | TAS | Telegraphy with Automatic Switching |
| TAPS | Texas Automated Plotting System | TAS | Telephone Answering Service |
| TAPS | Transform Adaptable Processing System | TAS | Teleprogrammer Assembly System |
| TAPS | Two-dimensional Alphanumeric Picture System | TAS | Terminabrufsystem |
| TAR | Temporäres Adreßregister | TAS | Terminal Address Selector |
| TAR | Temporary Accumulator Register | TAS | Three Address System |
| TAR | Temporary Address Register | TAS | Total Application Solution |
| TAR | Terminal-Anpassungsrechner | TAS | Transaktionsorientiertes Anwendungssystem |
| TAR | Terrain Avoidance Radar | TAS | Treudata Abrechnungssystem |
| TAR | Thrust-Augment Rocket | TASAS | Transformer Analog Servo Analyzer and Synthesizer |
| TAR | Track Address Register | TASC | Tabular Sequence Control |
| TAR | Trajected Analysis Room | TASC | Technology for Aerospace Computers |
| TAR | Transaction Area | TASC | Terminal Area Sequence and Control |
| TAR | Travelling Advance Receipt | TASC | Translator Auto-Scaler and Coder |
| TARAN | Tactical Attack Radar And Navigator | TASCON | Television Automatic Sequence Control |
| TARE | Telegraph Automatic Relay Equipment | TASD | Tactical Action Situation Display |
| | | TASI | Time-Assigned Speech Interpolation system |
| | | TASI | Time Assignment Speech Interpolation |

# T

| | | | |
|---|---|---|---|
| TASK | Temporary Assembled Skeleton | TBR | Temporary Base Register |
| TASO | Taktil-Akustische Seiten-orientierung | TBRL | Transmitter Buffer Register Load |
| TASS | Tactical Automatic Switching System | TBS | Tape and Buffer System |
| | | TBS | Teilnehmerbetriebssystem |
| TASS | Tactical Avionics System Simulator | TBS | Terminal Business System |
| | | TBS | Test Bit Store |
| TASS | Tech Assembly System | TBS | Tonbildschau |
| TAT | Tape Automatic Testing | TBT | Teilnehmerbesetzton |
| TAT | Track Allocation Table | TBU | Time Base Unit |
| TAT | Tuned-Aperiodic Tuned | TBW | Time Bandwidth |
| TATC | Terminal Air-Traffic Control | TBWP | Triple-Braid Weatherproof |
| | | TC | Tab Card |
| TATC | Trans-Atlantic Telephone Cable | TC | Tabulating Card |
| | | TC | Tabulation Character |
| TATDL | Tabulated Assembly Technical Data List | TC | Tactical Computer |
| | | TC | Tantalum Capacitor |
| TAU | Tape Adapter Unit | TC | Tape Card |
| TAU | Temps Actif Unitaire | TC | Tape Channel |
| TAVET | Temperature, Acceleration, Vibration Environmental Tester | TC | Tape Control |
| | | TC | Tape Copy |
| | | TC | Tape Core |
| TAWS | Terrain Avoidance Warning Subassembly | TC | Tape Cutter |
| | | TC | Tape-to-Card |
| | | TC | Technical Commitee |
| TB | Tabelle | TC | Technical Control |
| TB | Tape Block | TC | Telecommunication |
| TB | Technical Bulletin | TC | Telefunken Computer AG |
| TB | Technische Beschreibung | TC | Temperature Coefficient |
| TB | Terminal Block | TC | Temperature Compensation |
| TB | Terminal Board | | |
| TB | Test Bit | TC | Tera-Cycle |
| TB | Time Base | TC | Terminal Computer |
| TB | Time-Bandwidth | TC | Terminal Control |
| TB | Tonbandgerät | TC | Termination Code |
| TB | Transmitter Blocker | TC | Ternary Code |
| TB | Transmitter Buffer | TC | Test Card |
| TB | Triple Braid | TC | Test Conductor |
| TBA | Table Base Address | TC | Test Console |
| TBAX | Tube Axial | TC | Text Card |
| TBB | Tabellenberechnungen | TC | Thermocouple |
| TBC | Tabulation Clear | TC | Thermocurrent |
| TBC | Toss Bomb Computer | TC | Thrust Chamber |
| TBD | To Be Determined | TC | Time Card |
| TBDF | Trans Border Data Flow | TC | Time Closing |
| TBE | Time Base Error | TC | Time Constant |
| TBG | Testbaugruppe | TC | Time Controlled |
| TBG | Time Base Generator | TC | Time to Computation |
| TBL | Table | TC | Timing Chart |
| TBM | Terabit Memory | TC | Timing Circuit |
| TBO | Time Between Overhauls | TC | Toll Center |
| TBP | Transaction Backout Program | TC | Toll Completing |
| | | TC | Track Check |
| TBP | Twisted Bonded Pair | TC | Tracking Camera |
| TBR | Tape Bootstrap Routine | TC | Trailer Card |

# T

| | | | |
|---|---|---|---|
| TC | Transfer Check | TCC | Total COBOL Capability |
| TC | Transfer Command | TCC | Total Card Count |
| TC | Transform Coding | TCC | Tracking and Control Center |
| TC | Transistorized Carrier | | |
| TC | Transmission Check | TCC | Traffic Control Center |
| TC | Transmission Channel | TCC | Transfer Channel Control |
| TC | Transmission Code | TCC | Transfer of Control Card |
| TC | Transmission Control | TCC | Transmission Control Character |
| TC | Transmitter Clock | | |
| TC | Tuned Circuit | TCC | Transportable Cassette Converter |
| TC | Twin Capacity | | |
| TCA | Task Control Area | TCC | Triple-Cotton Covered |
| TCA | Telecommunications Association | TCCA | Technical Committee on Computer Architecture |
| TCA | Temperature Control Amplifier | TCCC | Technical Commitee for Computer Communication |
| TCA | Ternary Coded Asynchronous | TCCN | Trans-Canada computer Communications Network |
| TCA | Time Cost Analyzer | TCCP | Tape Controlled Card Punch |
| TCAC | Tone Count Audiometric Computer | TCCS | Teletex Computer Communications Service |
| TCAI | Tutorial Computer-Assisted Instruction | TCCS | Telex Computer Communications Service |
| TCAM | Telecommunications Access Method | TCD | Telemetry and Command Data |
| TCARS | Test Call Answer Relay Set | TCD | Temperature Control Device for crystal units |
| TCAS | Terminal Control Address Space | TCD | Thermal Conductivity Detector |
| TCAT | Tape-Controlled Automatic Testing | TCD | Thyratron Core Driver |
| TCB | Task Control Block | TCD | Time-Correlation Data |
| TCB | Technical Coordinator Bulletin | TCD | Transistor Controlled Delay |
| TCB | Terminal Control Block | TCDS | Test Case Development System |
| TCB | The Computer Bulletin | | |
| TCB | Thread Control Block | TCE | Telemetry Checkout Equipment |
| TCB | Time Correlation Buffer | | |
| TCBV | Temperature Coefficient of Breakdown Voltage | TCE | Total Composite Error |
| | | TCED | Thrust Control Exploratory Development |
| TCC | Tactical Control Computer | | |
| TCC | Tape Controlled Calculating | TCF | Terminal Configuration Facility |
| TCC | Tape Controlled Carriage | TCF | Terminal Control Firmware |
| TCC | Tape Controlled Computer | | |
| TCC | Tape-to-Card Conversion | TCG | Time Code Generator |
| TCC | Tape-to-Card Converter | TCG | Time Controlled Gain |
| TCC | Technical Computing Center | TCG | Tune Controlled Gain |
| | | TCH | Test Channel |
| TCC | Television Control Center | TCH WKING | Test Channel Working |
| TCC | Temperature Coefficient of Capacitance | TCI | Telemetry Components Information |
| TCC | Test Control Center | TCI | Terrain Clearance Indicator |
| TCC | Test Controller Console | | |
| TCC | Thermo-Carbon-Copy | TCJ | The Computer Journal |

# T

| | | | |
|---|---|---|---|
| TCL | Terminal Command Language | TCP/IP | Transmission Control Protocol/Internet Protocol |
| TCL | Time and Cycle Log | TCPC | Tab Card Punch Control |
| TCL | Timeshare Conversational Language | TCPP | Tape-to-Card Printing Punch |
| TCL | Transistor-Coupled Logic | TCR | Tab Card Reader |
| TCL | Transmit Clock | TCR | Tape Cartridge Reader |
| TCM | Tape Controlled Machine | TCR | Television Cathode Ray |
| TCM | Telemetry Code Modulation | TCR | Temperatur Coefficient of Resistor |
| TCM | Terminal-to-Computer Multiplexer | TCR | Temperature Coefficient of Resistivity |
| TCM | Test Control Module | | |
| TCM | Thermal Conduction Module | TCR | Thermal Coefficient of Resistance |
| TCM | Thermally-Controlled Module | TCR | Thermo-Carbon-Ribbon |
| TCM | Time Compression Multiplex | TCR | Time Code Reader |
| | | TCR | Transfer Control Register |
| TCM | Tone Code Modulation | TCR | Transportable Cassette Recorder |
| TCM | Trellis-Coded Modulation | TCRC | Time and Cycle Record Card |
| TCMA | Tabulating Card Manufacturers Association | TCS | Tactical Channel Simulator |
| | | TCS | Tape Controlled System |
| TCMF | Touch Calling Multi-frequency | TCS | Telecommunications Control System |
| TCMP | Tightly Coupled Multi-processor | TCS | Terminal Control System |
| | | TCS | Terminal Count Sequence |
| TCMS | Transistorized Computer Machine Switch | TCS | Terminal Countdown Sequencer |
| TCO | Temperature Coefficient of Offset | TCS | Ternary Compound Semiconductor |
| TCO | Trunk Cut-Off | TCS | Test Customization System |
| TCOA | Translational Control A | TCS | Text Composition System |
| TCOB | Translational Control B | TCS | Thermal Conditioning Service |
| TCOP | Teleprocessing Control Program | | |
| | | TCS | Traffic Control Station |
| TCP | TAG Converter Program | TCS | Transfer Carry for Subtraction |
| TCP | Tape Controlled Printer | | |
| TCP | Tape Controlled Punch | TCS | Transportation and Communication Service |
| TCP | Tape-to-Card Punch | | |
| TCP | Telecommunications Processor | TCSC | The Computer Software Company |
| TCP | Telemetry and Command Processor | TCSC | Trainer Control and Simulation Computer |
| TCP | Terminal Control Program | TCSP | Telecommunications Special Product |
| TCP | Terminal-Control-Process | | |
| TCP | Test Checkout Procedure | TCT | Tape Controlled Typewriter |
| TCP | Thermo-Carbon-Paper | | |
| TCP | Thrust Chamber Pressure | TCT | Terminal Control Table |
| TCP | Traffic Control Post | TCT | Time Code Translator |
| TCP | Transaction Control Program | TCT | Transaction Class Table |
| | | TCT | Transaction Code Table |
| TCP | Typewriter Card Punch | TCT | Transfer Control Table |

# T

| | | | |
|---|---|---|---|
| TCT | Translator and Code Treatment frame | TD | Time Distribution |
| TCTAP | Transistor Circuit Transient Analysis Program | TD | Time Division |
| | | TD | Timing Device |
| | | TD | Track Data |
| | | TD | Transaction Driven |
| TCTS | Trans Canadian Telephone System | TD | Transducer |
| | | TD | Transformation Description |
| TCTS | Transcanada-Telefonsystem | TD | Transient Data |
| | | TD | Translating Device |
| TCTTE | Terminal Control Table Terminal Entry | TD | Transmit Data |
| | | TD | Transmitted Data |
| TCU | Tape Control Unit | TD | Transmitter-Distributor |
| TCU | Tele-Communication Unit | TD | Trapped Domain |
| TCU | Telecommunication Control Unit | TD | Tunnel Diode |
| | | TD | Tunneldiode |
| TCU | Terminal Control Unit | TDA | Target Docking Adapter |
| TCU | Test Control Unit | TDA | Telemetric Data Analyzer |
| TCU | Time Code Unit | TDA | Today |
| TCU | Timing Control Unit | TDA | Tracking Data Analysis |
| TCU | Transmission Control Unit | TDA | Tracking and Data Acquisition |
| TCUI | Transmission Control Unit Interface | TDA | Transistorized Drum Assembly |
| TCV | Text Computer Vertriebs-GmbH | TDA | Tunnel Diode Amplifier |
| TCVFU | Tape Controlled Vertical Format Unit | TDAS | Tactical Data Automation System |
| TCVR | Transceiver | TDAS | Thermocouple Data Acquisition System |
| TCW | Time Code Word | | |
| TCW | Track Confirmation Word | TDAS | Tracking and Data Acquisition System |
| TCWG | Telecommunications Working Group | TDB | Toxicology Data Bank |
| TCXO | Temperature-Compensated Crystal Oscillator | TDC | Tactical Data Converter |
| | | TDC | Target Data Collection |
| TCXO | Temperature-Controlled Crystal Oszillator | TDC | Technical Data Center |
| | | TDC | Technical Development Capital |
| TCZD | Temperature-Compensated Z-Diode | TDC | Telemetry Data Center |
| TD | Tabular Data | TDC | Telex Destination Code |
| TD | Tape Deck | TDC | Test Data Carrier |
| TD | Tape Drive | TDC | Test Data Control |
| TD | Tape Dump | TDC | Time Delay Closing |
| TD | Tape-to-Disk | TDC | Time of Day Clock |
| TD | Telemetry Data | TDC | Ton Digital Command |
| TD | Teletype Digit | TDC | Top Dead Centre |
| TD | Temperature Differential | TDC | Top Desk Computer |
| TD | Terminal Distributor | TDC | Track Data Central |
| TD | Test Data | TDC | Transistor Digital Circuit |
| TD | Testdaten | TDC | Transistor Digital Control |
| TD | Testing Data | TDC | Transistorized Digital Circuit |
| TD | Testing Device | | |
| TD | Tests and Diagnostics | TDC... | Technical Development Corporation |
| TD | Text- und Datensysteme | | |
| TD | Time Delay | TDCC | Tactical Data Communications Center |
| TD | Time Device | | |
| TD | Time Difference | | |

# T

| | | | |
|---|---|---|---|
| TDCC | Tactical Data Communications Central | TDL | Telemetry Data Link |
| TDCC | Transportation Data Coordinating Committee | TDL | Terminal Display Language |
| | | TDL | Test and Diagnostic Language |
| TDCM | Transistor Driver Core Memory | TDL | Transistor Diode Logic |
| | | TDL | Tunnel-Diode Logic |
| TDCO | Torpedo Data Computer Operator | TDLS | Topographic Data Library System |
| TDCR | Technical Data Change Request | TDM | Telemetric Data Monitor |
| | | TDM | Test Data Memorandum |
| TDCS | Test Data Control System | TDM | Time Division Multiplex |
| TDCT | Track Data Central Table | TDM | Time Division Multiplexing |
| TDCU | Target Data Control Unit | TDM | Time Division Multiplexor |
| TDD | Target Detection Device | TDM | Tunnel Diode Memory |
| TDD | Technical Data Digest | TDMA | Time-Distributed Multiple-Access |
| TDD | Telemetry Data Digitizer | | |
| TDD | Time Decoding Device | TDMA | Time Division Multiple Access |
| TDD | Timing Data Distributor | | |
| TDDL | Time Division Data Link | TDMAS | Teletype/Data Multiplexer Address System |
| TDDLPO | Time Division Data Link Print-Out | | |
| | | TDMD | Time Division Multiplex Device |
| TDDR | Technical Data Department Report | TDMF | Time Division Multiplex Frame |
| TDE | Technical Data Engineer | | |
| TDE | Technical Data Evaluation | TDMG | Telegraph and Data Message Generator |
| TDEP | Tracking Data Editing Program | | |
| | | TDMN | Time Division Multiplex Network |
| TDF | Table de Description des Fichiers | | |
| | | TDMS | Tele-Diagnostic-Maintenance-System |
| TDF | Tape Data Family | | |
| TDF | Télédiffusion de France | TDMS | Telegraphic Distortion Measuring Set |
| TDF | Test Data File | | |
| TDF | Transborder Data Flow | TDMS | Telemetry Data Monitor Set |
| TDF | Two Degrees of Freedom | | |
| TDFG | Test Data File Generator | TDMS | Teleprocessing Data Management System |
| TDFL | Tunnel Diode FET Logic | | |
| TDG | Test Data Generator | TDMS | Time Division Multiplexing System |
| TDG | Test Data Generation | | |
| TDG | Testdatengenerator | TDMS | Time-shared Data Management System |
| TDH | Tracking Data Handling | | |
| TDHS | Tape Data Handling System | TDMT | Time Division Multiplex Terminal |
| TDI | Target Data Inventory | TDMU | Time Division Multiplex Unit |
| TDI | Technical Data Interface | | |
| TDI | Test Data Interpolation | TDN | Target Doppler Nullifier |
| TDI | Time-Delay-and-Integration | TDO | Time Delay Opening |
| | | TDO | Transistor Dip Oscillator |
| TDIA | Transient Data Input Area | TDOA | Transient Data Output Area |
| TDIC | Target Data Input Computer | | |
| | | TDOS | Tape Disk Operating System |
| TDIO | Terminal Data Input/Output system | | |
| | | TDOS | Test Data Output System |
| TDIO | Timing Data Input-Output | TDP | Tape Data Processing |
| TDL | Tactical Data Link | TDP | Technical Data Package |
| TDL | Task Description Library | | |

- 597 -

# T

| | | | |
|---|---|---|---|
| TDP | Technical Development Plan | TDS | Translation and Docking Simulator |
| TDP | Teledata Processing | TDS | Tunnel Diode Store |
| TDP | Terminal de Données Prêt | TDSA | Telegraph and Data Signal Analyser |
| TDP | Track Data Processor | | |
| TDP | Traffic Data Processor | TDSDT | Tactical Data System Development Testbed |
| TDP | Transient Data Program | | |
| TDP | Transistorized Data Printer | TDT | Target Designation Transmitter |
| TDPM | Time-Domain Prony Method | TDT | Telemetering Data Transmission |
| TDPS | Tactical Data Processing System | TDT | Transfer Data Test |
| | | TDT | Tunnel Diode Transducer |
| TDPSK | Time Differential Phase Shift Keying | TDTL | Tunnel Diode Transistor Logic |
| TDR | Target Discrimination Radar | TDU | Topographical Display Unit |
| | | TDV | Test Device |
| TDR | Technical Data Relay | TDX | Thermal Demand Transmitter |
| TDR | Technical Data Report | | |
| TDR | Test Data Recorder | TDX | Time Division Exchange |
| TDR | Test Data Reduction | TDX | Torque Differential Transmitter |
| TDR | Test Data Report | | |
| TDR | Time Delay Relay | TE | Table of Equipment |
| TDR | Time Domain Reflectometer | TE | Tabulating Equipment |
| | | TE | Takteinheit |
| TDR | Torque Differential Receiver | TE | Takterzeugungseinheit |
| | | TE | Tape Edit |
| TDR | Track Description Record | TE | Tape Error |
| TDR | Tracking and Data Relay | TE | Technicien d'Entretien |
| TDRE | Transmit Data Register Empty | TE | Telecommunication |
| | | TE | Terminal Equipment |
| TDRS | Tracking and Data Relay Satellite | TE | Test Equipment |
| | | TE | Testing |
| TDRSS | Tracking and Data Relay Satellite System | TE | Thermal Element |
| | | TE | Thermoelectric |
| TDS | Tactical Data System | TE | Time Equipment |
| TDS | Tactical Display System | TE | Timing Error |
| TDS | Tape Data Selector | TE | Totally Enclosed |
| TDS | Target Designation System | TE | Track Element |
| TDS | Technical Data System | TE | Track End |
| TDS | Tele-Data-Service | TE | Track Error |
| TDS | Telegramm-Dienst-System | TE | Trailing Edge |
| TDS | Television Display System | TE | Transistor Equipment |
| TDS | Test Data Sheet | TE | Transverse Electric |
| TDS | Test Data Specification | TEA | Task Equipment Analysis |
| TDS | Test Data System | TEA | Total-Energieanlage |
| TDS | Text- und Datensystem | TEA | Transferred Electron Amplifier |
| TDS | Time Division Switch | | |
| TDS | Track Data Simulator | TEA | Tunnel Emission Amplifier |
| TDS | Track Data Storage | TEACHTRAN | Teaching-logic Translator |
| TDS | Tracking and Data System | | |
| TDS | Transaction Data Set | TEADDA | Teledyne Electrically Alterable Digital Differential Analyzer |
| TDS | Transaction Driven System | | |
| TDS | Transistor play and Data handling System | | |

- 598 -

# T

| | | | |
|---|---|---|---|
| TEAM | Technique for Evaluation and Analysis of Maintainability | TEF | Terminal Error Funtion |
| | | TEF | Transfer on End of File |
| TEAM | TEDIS für Auftragsabwicklung und Materialdisposition | TEF | Transfert Electronique de Fonds |
| | | TEFKTN | Text für Funktionsbezeichnungen |
| TEAM | Terminology Evaluation and Acquisition Method | TEFRA | Tax Equity and Fiscal Responsibility Act |
| TEAMS | Test Evaluation And Monitoring System | TEG | Thermoelectric Generator |
| | | TEHI | Testhilfsprogramm |
| TEAWC | Totally Enclosed Air-Water-Cooled | TEI | Technical and Economic Information |
| TEB | Task Entry Block | TEI | Terminal Endpoint Identifier |
| TEB | Tape Error Block | | |
| TEBER | Teilebedarfsrechnung | TEI | Transfer on Error Indication |
| TEBERU | Text für Berufsbezeichnungen | TEIC | Tissue Equivalent Ionization Chamber |
| TEC | Tactical Electromagnetic Coordinator | TEK | Termineingabekarten |
| TEC | Test, Evaluation, and Control | TEKTEST | Tektronik Test Programming Language |
| TEC | Thermoelectric Cooler | TEL | Telegraph |
| TEC | Thermonic Energy Conversion | TEL | Telephone |
| | | TEL | Telephony |
| TEC | Transistor à Effet de Champ | TEL | Teleprocessing |
| | | TEL | Teletypewriter |
| TEC... | Tokyo Electric Co. | TEL... | Tokyo Electron Ltd. |
| TECE | Teleprinter Error Correction Equipment | TELAS | Telefunken-Laborautomatisierungs-System |
| TECMT | Test Engineering Circuit Master Tape | TELCO | Telephone Company |
| | | TELD | Transferred-Electron Logic Device |
| TECO | Text und Communication | | |
| TECOS | Telecommunications System | TELDOK | Telefunken Dokumentationssystem |
| TED | Teleprinter Error Detector | TELECAUSE | Telecommunications Competitive Alternatives for User Services and Equipment |
| TED | Tender Electronic Daily | | |
| TED | Time Encoding Device | | |
| TED | Transferred Electron Devices | TELECOM | Telecommunications |
| TED | Transferred Electron-effect Device | TELEDAC | Telefunken Dial-radio-telephone with Automatic Channel-access |
| TED | Translation Error Detector | | |
| TEDAR | Telemetered Data Reduction | TELEDAC | Telemetric Data Converter |
| | | TELEPAK | Telemetering Package |
| TEDES | Telemetry Data Evaluation System | TELEPERT | Telefunken PERT |
| | | TELERAN | Television and Radar Navigation |
| TEDIS | Tele-Dateninformationsdienst | | |
| | | TELESAT | Telecommunications Satellite |
| TEDIT | Tape Edit | | |
| TEDS | Time Encoded Digital Speech | TELESIM | Teletypewriter Simulator |
| | | TELETEL | Téléphone et Télévision |
| TEE | Test Equipment Engineering | TELEX | Teleprinter Exchange |
| | | TELEX | Teleprocessing Executive |
| TEED | Transferred Electron Effect Diode | TELI | Technisch-Literarische Gesellschaft e.V. |

# T

| | | | |
|---|---|---|---|
| TELL | Teacher-aiding Electronic Learning Links | TERMS | Terminal Management System |
| TELOBE | Text für Lohnbestandteile | TERMTRAN | Terminal Translator |
| TELOPS | Telemetry On-line Processing System | TERP | Terrain Elevation Retrieval Program |
| TELRY | Telegraph Reply | TERPE | Tactical Electronic Reconnaissance Processing and Evaluation |
| TELSCOM | Telemetry Surveillance Communications | | |
| TELSIM | Teletypewriter Simulator | TERPES | Tactical Electronic Reconnaissance Processing and Evaluation System |
| TELUS | Telemetric Universal Sensor | | |
| TEM | Telex-Extended Memories | TERPS | Terminal Enquiry Response Programming System |
| TEM | Template | | |
| TEM | Transmission Electron Microscope | TERS | Tactical Electronic Reconnaissance System |
| TEM | Transverse Electromagnetic Mode | TERSI | Termineurs Signaleurs |
| | | TES | Technical Engineering Standard |
| TEMA | Testmakro | | |
| TEMCO | Terminal d'Encaissement Multi-Commerce | TES | Teilnehmereinrichtungsschaltung |
| TEMEX | Telemetric Exchange | TES | Temperatur-Schätz-System |
| TEMEX | Telemetry Exchange | TES | Testendsteuerung |
| TEMOD | Terminal Environment Module | TES | Text Editing System |
| | | TESA | Television and Electronic Service Association |
| TEO | Transferred Electron Oscillator | | |
| TEOM | Transformer Environment Overcurrent Monitor | TESE | Tactical Exercise Simulator and Evaluator |
| | | TESLA | Technical Standards for Library Automation |
| TEP | Technical Engineering Practice | | |
| | | TESPOS | Testprogrammsystem |
| TEP | Terminal Error Program | TESS | Tactical Electromagnetic Systems Study |
| TEPG | Thermionic Electrical Power Generator | | |
| | | TESS | Thermal Expansion Shear Separation |
| TEPI | Technical Equipment Planning Information | | |
| | | TEST | Teleprocessing Environmental Simulator Testing |
| TEPOS | Testprogrammsystem | | |
| TEPPS | Technique for Establishing Personnel Performance Standard | TEST MSG | Test Message |
| | | TESTDAT | Testdatengenerator |
| | | TESTRAN | Test Translator |
| TER | Tape Edit Routine | TESTSYS | Testsystem |
| TER | Terminal | TESY | Terminal Editing System |
| TER | Terminate | TESY | Testauswertungssystem |
| TER | Termination | TESY | Testsystem |
| TER | Test Row | TET | Total Elapsed Time |
| TER | Transmission Equivalent Resistance | TETAET | Text für Tätigkeitsbezeichnungen |
| TER | Triple Ejection Rack | TETFT | Test Engineering Translate Functions Tape |
| TERCO | Telefonrationalisierung mit Computern | | |
| | | TETRA | Terminal Tracking telescope |
| TERCO | Telephone Rationalization by Computer | | |
| | | TEWC | Totally Enclosed, Water-Cooled |
| TEREC | Tactical Electromagnetic Reconnaissance | | |
| | | TEX | Teleprinter Exchange |
| TERM | Terminal | TEX | Telex |
| TERMA | Terminator Assignment | TEXTFAX | Text und Faksimile |

# T

| | | | |
|---|---|---|---|
| TEXTIR | Text Indexing and Retrieval | TFFT | Thin-Film Field-Effect Transform |
| TF | Table Function | TFFT | Truly Fast Fourier Transform |
| TF | Tabulating Form | TFG | Transmit Format Generator |
| TF | Tape Feed | | |
| TF | Tape File | TFHC | Thick-Film Hybrid Circuit |
| TF | Telefunken | TFIC | Thin-Film Integrated Circuit |
| TF | Terminal Funktion | | |
| TF | Terminate Flag | TFIE | Thin-Film Integrated Electronics |
| TF | Test Fixture | | |
| TF | Thin Film | TFIO | Thin-Film Integrated Optics |
| TF | Threshold Function | | |
| TF | Ticket File | TFL | Transformerless |
| TF | Time Factor | TFL | Transient Fault Locator |
| TF | Time Frequency | TFM | Thin-Film Memory |
| TF | Title Format | TFM | Thin-Film Microelectronics |
| TF | Track Format | TFM | Time-quantized Frequency Modulation |
| TF | Trägerfrequenz | | |
| TF | Transaction File | TFO | Test For Overflow |
| TF | Transfer Function | TFO | Tuning Fork Oscillator |
| TF | Transformer | TFOL | Tape File Octal Load |
| TF | Transition Function | TFR | Terrain-Following Radar |
| TF | Transversal Filter | TFR | Thin-Film Resist |
| TF-FET | Thin-Film FET | TFR | Transfer |
| TFA | Telex File Adapter | TFR | Transfer Function Response |
| TFA | Transfer Function Analyzer | TFS | Technical Facilities Standard |
| TFAD | Thin-Film Active Device | | |
| TFB | Technology for Business | TFS | Text- und Faksimile-Server |
| TFB | Trailer File Block | | |
| TFC | Thin-Film Circuit | TFS | Thin-Film Storage |
| TFC | Transfer Function Compensation | TFS | Thin-Film Store |
| | | TFSF | Time to First System Failure |
| TFC | Transfer Function, Cumulative | TFSK | Time Frequency Shift Keying |
| TFC | Trigonometric Function Computer | TFT | Thin-Film Technology |
| TFCC | Tank Fire Combat Computer | TFT | Thin-Film Transistor |
| | | TFT | Thin-film FET |
| TFCS | Torpedo Fire Control System | TFT | Threshold Failure Temperatures |
| TFD | Tape Feeding Device | TFT | Time-to-Frequency Transformation |
| TFD | Time and Frequency Dissemination | TFT | Translate Functions Tape |
| TFD | Total Frequency Deviation | TFZ | Transfer Zone |
| TFDS | Tactical Flag Data System | TG | Taktgeber |
| TFE | Thermal Field Emission | TG | Taktgenerator |
| TFEL | Thin-Film Electro-Luminescent | TG | Tape Generator |
| | | TG | Terminator Group |
| TFET | Thin-film Field Effect Transistor | TG | Tochtergesellschaft |
| | | TG | Transfer Gate |
| TFF | Toggle Flip-Flop | TG | Transmission Group |
| TFF | Triggered Flip-Flop | TG | Trigger |
| TFFET | Thin-Film Field Effect Transistor | TG | Tuned Grid |
| | | TG | Tuning |

- 601 -

# T

| | | | |
|---|---|---|---|
| TGA | Table Générale d'Allocation | THERM | Thermostat |
| TGA | Télégestion des Abonnés | THERMISTOR | Thermal resistor |
| TGA | Thermogravimetric Analysis | THERP | Technique for Human Error Rate Prediction |
| TGAO | Technologie de Groupe Assitée par Ordinateur | THG | Third Harmonic Generation |
| TGAR | Trunk Group Access Restriction | THI | Temperature Humidity Index |
| TGC | Terminator Group Controller | THIR | Temperature Humidity Infrared Radiometer |
| TGC | Transmit Gain Control | THIS | Total Hospital Information System |
| TGD | Télécopieur Grande Diffusion | THOMIS | Total Hospital Operating and Medical Information System |
| TGE | Tape Generator and Editor | | |
| TGF | Test Generating Function | THOPS | Tape Handling Operational System |
| TGID | Transmission Group Identifier | THOR | Tape-Handling Option Routine |
| TGR | Trigger | | |
| TGS | Technisches Grunddaten-System | THOR | Transistorized High-speed Operations Recorder |
| TGS | Transfer Generator System | THP | Terminal Handling Processor |
| TGS | Translator Generator System | THS | Thermostat Switch |
| TGSE | Telemetry Ground Support Equipment | THSS | Teilhabersystem-Steuersystem |
| TGT | Table Générale des Travaux | THSSTR | Teilhabersystem-Startroutine |
| TGT | Task Global Table | THT | Très Haute Tension |
| TGT | Transformational Grammar Tester | THU | Tape Handling Unit |
| | | THY | Thyratron |
| TGTP | Tuned-Grid Tuned-Plate circuit | THY | Thyristor |
| | | THYR | Thyristor |
| TGZMP | Temperature Gradient Zone Melting Process | THz | Terahertz |
| | | TI | Tape Indicator |
| TH | Tape Handler | TI | Tape Input |
| TH | Temporary Hold | TI | Tape Instruction |
| TH | Track Head | TI | Tape Inverter |
| TH | Transmission Header | TI | Technischer Inspektor |
| TH/P | Thousands Position | TI | Technologies de l'Information |
| THAT | Twenty-four Hour Automatic Teller | | |
| | | TI | Technology Innovation |
| THC | Thermal Converter | TI | Terminal Interchange |
| THC | Thrid Harmonic | TI | Termination Interrupt |
| THC | Thrust Hand Controller | TI | Terminator Interrupt |
| THC | Total Harmonic | TI | Test Indicator |
| THD | Total Harmonic Distortion | TI | Test Instruction |
| THE | Tape Handling Equipment | TI | Thallium |
| THE BRAIN | The Harvard Experimental Basic Reckoning And Instructional Network | TI | Time Interval |
| | | TI | Title Information |
| | | TI | Traffic Identification |
| THEMIS | Three Hole Element Memory with Integrated Selection | TI | Training Instructions |
| | | TI | Traitement de l'Information |
| THERM | Thermal | TI | Transfer Impedance |
| THERM | Thermometer | TI | Transfer Instruction |

# T

| | | | |
|---|---|---|---|
| TI | Transmission Identification | TICCIT | Time-shared, Interactive, Computer-Controlled Information Television |
| TI | Transmitted Information | | |
| TI | Tuning Inductance | TICE | Time Integral Cost Effectiveness |
| TI... | Texas Instruments Corporation | TICES | Type-In Coding and Editing System |
| TIA | Table Interrupt Address | | |
| TIA | Tactical Identificaton and Acquisition | TICLER | Technical Input Check List/Evaluation Report |
| TIA | Target Identification and Acquisition | TICOL | Texas Instruments Cassette Operating Language |
| TIA | Three Input Adder | | |
| TIA | Two Input Adder | TICOM | Texas Institute for Computational Mechanics |
| TIAC | Technical Information and Analysis Center | TICS | Technical Information and Control System |
| TIAC | Texas Instruments Automatic Computer | TICS | Terminal Interface Control System |
| TIAM | Terminal Interactive Access Method | TICTAC | Terminal Intégré Comportant un Téléviseur et l'Appel au Clavier |
| TIARA | Target Illumination And Recovery Aid | | |
| TIAS | Target Identification and Aquisition System | TICTAC | Time Compression Tactical Communications |
| TIAS | Train Initial Avoidance System | TID | Tactical Information Display |
| TIB | Technical Information Bulletin | TID | Target Information Display |
| TIB | Technische Informationsbibliothek | TID | Technical Information Division |
| TIB | Transparent Interleaved Bipolar | TID | Telephone Inquiry Device |
| | | TID | Texas Instruments Deutschland |
| TIBOE | Transmitting Information By Optical Electronics | TID | Touch Input Device |
| TIBOL | Texas Instrument Bubble Operating Language | TIDAR | Texas Instruments Digital Analog Readout |
| TIC | Tantalum Integrated Circuit | TIDAR | Time Delay Array Radar |
| | | TIDAS | Totally Integrated Data System |
| TIC | Tape Identification Card | | |
| TIC | Tape Intersystem Connection | TIDB | Technical Information Dissemination Bureau |
| TIC | Target Intercept Computer | TIDDAC | Time In Deadband Digital Attitude Control |
| TIC | Technical Information Center | TIDE | Tactical International Data Exchange |
| TIC | Technology Information Center | TIDE | Transponder Interrogation and Decoding Equipment |
| TIC | Temperature Indicating Controller | TIDEDA | Time Dependent Data Analysis |
| TIC | Time Interval Counter | TIDES | Time Division Electronics Switching |
| TIC | Time Issue Control | | |
| TIC | Transfer-In Channel | TIDESS | Time Division Electronics Switching System |
| TIC | Tuned Integrated Circuit | | |
| TICCET | Time-shared Interactive Computer-Controlled Educational Television | TIDG | Taper-Isolated Dynamic-Gain |
| | | TIDIC | Time-Interval Distribution Computer |

# T

| | | | |
|---|---|---|---|
| TIDOS | Table and Item Documentation System | TIM | Transistor Information Microfile |
| TIDP | Telemetry and Image Data Processing | TIMARC | Time Multiplexed Analog Radio Control |
| TIDU | Technical Information and Documents Unit | TIME | Telecommunication Information Management Executive |
| TIE | Technical Information Exchange | TIMES | Time Interval Measuring System |
| TIE | Technical Integration and Evaluation | TIMIC | Time Interval Modulation Information Code |
| TIE | Texas Information Exchange | TIMINT | Time Interval |
| TIE | Track-In Error | TIMIS | Totally Integrated Management Information System |
| TIES | Tactical Information Exchange System | TIMM | Thermionic Integrated Micro-Modules |
| TIES | Textbook Information and Exchange Service | TIMMS | Total Integrated Manpower Management System |
| TIES | Total Information for Educational Systems | TIMOC | Time-dependent Monte-Carlo code |
| TIES | Transmission and Information Exchange System | TIMOS | Texas Instruments Metal Oxide Semiconductor |
| TIF | Telephone Influence Factor | TIMOS | Total Implanted Metal Oxide Semiconductor |
| TIF | Telephone interference Factor | TIMP | Texas Instructional Media Project |
| TIFRAC | Tata Institute of Fundamental Research Automatic Computer | TIMS | Tape Inventory Management System |
| TIFT | Truncated Inverse Fourier Transform | TIMS | Telecommunications Instruction Module System |
| TIG | Teletype Input Generator | | |
| TIGER | Telephone Information Gathering for Evaluation and Review | TIMS | Teleprocessing Interface Macro System |
| TIH | Technical Information Handbook | TIMS | Textile Industry Monitoring System |
| TIH | Texas Instruments Hybrids | TIMS | The Information Management System |
| TIH | Time In Hold | | |
| TIIAL | The International Institute of Applied Linguistics | TIMS | The Institute of Management Sciences |
| TIIS | Test Instrument Industries | TIMS | Training Information Management System |
| TIKI... | Tiki-Data-Inc. | | |
| TILS | Terminal Initiated Line Switching | TIN | Technical Information Notice |
| TILT | Texas Instruments Language Translator | TIN | Temperature Independent |
| | | TINT | Teletype Interpreter |
| TIM | Technical Information on Microfilm | TIO | Test Input/Output |
| | | TIO | Time Interval Optimization |
| TIM | Terminal Independent Module | TIO | Transistorized Image Orthicon camera |
| TIM | The Inventory Machine | TIOA | Tape Input/Output Adapter |
| TIM | Time Interval Meter | TIOA | Terminal Input/Output Area |
| TIM | Time Meter | | |
| TIM | Topic Indexing Matrix | TIOB | Terminal Input/Output Block |
| TIM | Tracking Information Memorandum | | |

# T

| | | | |
|---|---|---|---|
| TIOB | Test Input Output and Branch | TIPS | Tactical Information about Perilous Situations |
| TIOC | Terminal Input/Output Coordinator | TIPS | Teaching Information Processing System |
| TIOM | Terminal Input/Output Manager | TIPS | Technical Information Processing System |
| TIOM | Terminal Input/Output Module | TIPS | Technology Information Processing System |
| TIOPTO | Texas Instruments Optoelectronics | TIPS | Telemetry Integrated Processing System |
| TIOS | Tactical Information Organization System | TIPS | Test Information Processing System |
| TIOT | Task Input/Output Table | TIPS | Total Information Processing System |
| TIOT | Terminal Input/Output Task | TIPS | Transportation Integrated Processing System |
| TIP | Tactical Information Presentation | TIPSY | Task Input Parameter Synthesizer |
| TIP | Technical Information Processing | TIPTOP | Tape Input, Tape Output |
| TIP | Technical Information Project | TIQ | Task Input Queue |
| TIP | Technical Information Program | TIR | Technical Information Report |
| TIP | Technology In Production | TIR | Total Indicator Reading |
| TIP | Telephone Information Processing | TIRAS | Technical Information Retrieval and Analysis System |
| TIP | Teletype Input Processing | TIRC | Technical Information Retrieval Center |
| TIP | Terminal Interface Processor | TIRKS | Trunks Integrated Record Keeping System |
| TIP | Terminal Interface message Processor | TIROS | Television and Infrared Observation Satellite |
| TIP | Tests Interactive Program | TIRP | Total Internal Reflection Prism |
| TIP | Total Information Processing | TIRSS | Technical Information Retrieval and Storage System |
| TIP | Toxicology Information Program | TIS | Tabular Interpretive Scheme |
| TIP | Transaction Interface Package | TIS | Tape Information Sheet |
| TIP | Transponder Interrogator Processor | TIS | Target Information System |
| TIPAC | Texas Instruments Programming And Control | TIS | Team Integrating System |
| TIPACS | Texas Instruments Planning And Control System | TIS | Technical Information Service |
| TIPC | Texas Instruments Professional-Computer | TIS | Technisches Informationssystem |
| TIPI | Tactical Information Processing and Interpretation | TIS | Technology Information System |
| TIPL | Teach Information Processing Language | TIS | Telecommunication Information System |
| TIPP | Time-Phasing Program | TIS | Telemetry Input System |
| TIPPC | Texas Instruments Portable Professional Computer | TIS | Temperature Indicating Switch |
| | | TIS | Textinformationssystem |
| | | TIS | Total Information System |

# T

| | | | |
|---|---|---|---|
| TIS | Total-Informationssystem | TL | Tape Label |
| TIS | Transportation Information System | TL | Tape Library |
| | | TL | Target Language |
| TIS | True Input Signal | TL | Terminology Library |
| TISA | Technical Information Systems Activities | TL | Test Link |
| | | TL | Threshold Logic |
| TISAP | Technical Information Support Activities Project | TL | Tie Line |
| | | TL | Time Limit |
| | | TL | Time Loss |
| TISC | Technical Information Sources Center | TL | Trailer Label |
| | | TL | Transistor Logic |
| TISCO | Technical Information Systems Committee | TL | Transistorlogik |
| | | TL | Transit Lock |
| TISEO | Target Identification System, Electro-Optical | TL | Transmission Level |
| | | TL | Transmission Line |
| TIT | Total Information Management | TL | Transmission Loss |
| | | TL | Trigger Logic |
| TIT | Transmission Identification Tape | TLA | Telex Line Adapter |
| | | TLAB | Tape Label |
| TITAN | Teamster's International Terminal and Accounting Network | TLAB | Translation Look-Aside Buffer |
| | | TLB | Translation Lookaside Buffer |
| TITAN | Terminal Interactif de Télétexte à Appel par Numérotation | TLBL | Tape Label |
| | | TLC | Tangent Latitude Computer |
| TITES | Technology Independent Test Engineering System | TLC | Teachable Language Comprehender |
| TITN | Traitement de l'Information, Technique Nouvelle | TLC | Temperature Level Control |
| TITTL | Texas Instruments Transistor-Transistor Logic | TLC | Thin Layer Chromatography |
| | | TLCA | Tangent Latitude Computer Amplifier |
| TITUS | Textile Information Treatment Users Service | TLCAP | Transmission Line Circuit Analysis Program |
| TIU | Tape Identification Unit | | |
| TIU | Typesetter-Input Unit | TLD | Technical Logistics Data |
| TIX | Transfer on Index | TLD | Transmission Line Driver |
| TJB | Time sharing Job control Block | TLDI | Technical Logistics Data and Information |
| TJC | Trajectory Chart | TLDIP | Technical Logistics Data Information Program |
| TJD | Trajectory Diagram | | |
| TJE | Terminal Job Entry | TLE | Tracking Light Electronics |
| TJF | Test Jack Field | TLE | Thyristorleitungselektronik |
| TJF | Time-to-Jitter Flag | TLF | Table Linkage Field |
| TJID | Terminal Job Identification | TLG | Timing Level Generator |
| TJS | Transverse Junction Stripe | TLI | Table Lookup Instruction |
| TJT | Tri-Junction Transistor | TLI | Telephone Line Interface |
| TK | Terminkarte | TLIB | Tape Library |
| TK | Typenkennung | TLK | Test Link |
| TKD | Technischer Kundendienst | TLM | Telemeter |
| TKP | Tabellenkalkulationsprogramm | TLM | Telemetry |
| | | TLMG | Telemetering |
| TL | Table Lookup | TLMS | Tape Library Management System |
| TL | Talk Listen | | |
| | | TLMY | Telemetry |

# T

| | | | |
|---|---|---|---|
| TLP | Tactical Line Printer | TMA | Telecommunications Manager Association |
| TLP | Term Lease Plan | | |
| TLP | Threshold Learning Process | TMA | Territory Maintenance Analysis |
| TLP | Total Language Processor | | |
| TLR | Tape Loop Recorder | TMACS | Tone Multiplex Apollo Command System |
| TLR | Toll Line Release | | |
| TLS | Terminal Landing System | TMARK | Tape Mark |
| TLS | Thesaurus and Linguistic integrated System | TMB | Technical Manufacturing Bulletin |
| TLS | Total List Speed | TMCC | Time-Multiplexed Communication Channel |
| TLT | Telecommunications Translator | TMCOMP | Telemetry Computation |
| TLT | Terminal List Table | TMD | Tactical Mission Data |
| TLT | Transmission Line Terminator | TMD | Technical Manual Data list |
| TLT | Transportable Link Terminal | TMD | Telemetered Data |
| | | TMDCS | Transaktionsorientiertes Maschinenüberwachungs-, Datenerfassungs- und Communications-System |
| TLTP | Teletype | | |
| TLTR | Translator | | |
| TLU | Table Look-Up | | |
| TLU | Terminal Logic Unit | TMDT | Total Mean Downtime |
| TLU | Threshold Logic Unit | TMF | Television Multiplex Facility |
| TLV | Threshold Limit Value | | |
| TLX | Telex | TMF | Time Marker Frequency |
| TLZ | Transfer on Less than Zero | TMF | Tonfrequenz Multiplex Fernsteuerung |
| TM | Tabulated Mesage | | |
| TM | Tabulating Machine | TMF | Tonfrequenz Multiplex Fernübertragung |
| TM | Tape Mark | | |
| TM | Tape Memory | TMG | Thermal Meteoroid Garment |
| TM | Tape Module | | |
| TM | Task Master | TMG | Time Mark Generator |
| TM | Task Memory | TMG | Timing |
| TM | Teaching Machine | TMGE | Thermo-Magneto-Galvanic Effect |
| TM | Technical Manual | | |
| TM | Teilnehmermodul | TMI | Tuning Meter Indicator |
| TM | Telemetering | TMIMIS | Technical Manual Integrated Management Information System |
| TM | Telemetry | | |
| TM | Temperature Meter | | |
| TM | Temps de Montée | TMIS | Television Management Information System |
| TM | Terminal Multiplexer | | |
| TM | Terminalmodus | TMIS | Total Management Information System |
| TM | Termination Module | | |
| TM | Test Mode | TML | Technical Manufacturing List |
| TM | Time Modulation | | |
| TM | Timing Mark | TML | Teradyne Modelling Language |
| TM | Tone Modulation | | |
| TM | Top Management | TMM | Telex Main Memories |
| TM | Traffic Manager | TMM | Transmit Mode Message |
| TM | Transaction Mode | TMM | Transmission en Mode Message |
| TM | Transfer Matrix | | |
| TM | Translation Memory | TMMD | Tactical Moving Map Display |
| TM | Transmission Matrix | | |
| TM | Transverse Magnetic | TMN | Technical and Management Note |
| TM | Tuning Meter | | |
| TM | Touring Machine | TMN | Transmission |

- 607 -

# T

| | | | |
|---|---|---|---|
| TMP | Teaching Machine Program | TN | Transport Network |
| TMP | Temperature | TN | Transport-Netzwerk |
| TMP | Temporary | TN | Tuning |
| TMP | Terminal Message Program | TN-LCD | Twisted Nematic LCD |
| TMP | Terminal Monitor Program | TNA | Teilnehmeranschluss |
| TMPP | Test Message Processing Program | TNA | Transient Network Analyzer |
| TMPRLY | Temporarily | TNA | Transistor Noise Analyzer |
| TMPROC | Telemetry Processing | TNAME | Terminal Name |
| TMR | Temps Moyen de Réparation | TNBA | Teilnehmerbündelanschluss |
| | | TNC | Track Navigation Computer |
| TMR | Time Meter Reading | | |
| TMR | Timer | TNL | Technical Newsletter |
| TMR | Transmitter | TNL | Teilenummernliste |
| TMR | Triple Modular Redundancy | TNL | Terminal Net Loss |
| TMRVDP | Terminal-Modified Radar Video Data Processor | TNLDIO | Tunnel Diode |
| | | TNM | Theoretisch Notwendiger Multiplexer |
| TMS | Tape Management Software | | |
| | | TNM | Twisted Nematic Mode |
| TMS | Tape Mangement System | TNO | Transfer on No Overflow |
| TMS | Telemetry Modulation System | TNRIS | Texas Natural Resources Information System |
| TMS | Teletex Mailing System | TNS | Tandem Non-Stop |
| TMS | Terminal Management System | TNS | Tandem Non-stop System |
| | | TNS | Telefon-Nachrichten- steuerung |
| TMS | Test and Monitoring Station | | |
| | | TNS | Text- und Nachrichten- system |
| TMS | The Manufacturing System | | |
| TMS | Time-shared Monitor System | TNTDL | Tabulated Numerical Technical Data List |
| TMS | Tonfrequenz-Multiplex- system | TNX | Transfer on No Index |
| | | TNXCD | Transaction Type Code |
| TMS | Transmission Measuring Set | TNZ | Transfer on Nor-Zero |
| | | TO | Take-Off |
| TMS | Touring Machine System | TO | Tape Operated |
| TMT | Transmit | TO | Tape Oriented |
| TMTC | Tri-Mode Tape Converter | TO | Tape Output |
| TMTR | Transmitter | TO | Technical Order |
| TMU | Temps de Montée Utile | TO | Telemetry Oscillator |
| TMU | Time Measurement Unit | TO | Terminal Ordinaire |
| TMU | Time Multiplexer Unit | TO | Time Open |
| TMUX | Terminal Multiplexer | TO | Time Out |
| TMW | Tomorrow | TO | Time Over |
| TMX | Taylor Multiprogramming Executive | TO | Transfer Operation |
| | | TO | Transfer Order |
| TMX | Telemeter Transmitter | TO | Transistor Outline |
| TMX | Tertiary Matrix | TO | Trigger Output |
| TN | Tape Number | TO | Turn Over |
| TN | Task Number | TO | Type d'Opération |
| TN | Technical Note | TOA | Terz-Oktav-Analysator |
| TN | Teilnehmer | TOADS | Terminal-Oriented Administrative Data Systems |
| TN | Telefon und Normalzeit | | |
| TN | Telenorma | | |
| TN | Terminal Number | TOAF | TCAM Origin Address Field |
| TN | Total Numerical control | | |

# T

| | | | |
|---|---|---|---|
| TOAKE | Tape Oriented Advanced Key Entry | TOM | Teleprinting On Multiplex |
| TOALS | Time Of Arrival Location System | TOM | Toolmanager |
| TOB | Take-Off Boost | TOM | Transistor Oscillator Multiplier |
| TOB | Telemetry Output Buffer | TOM | Translator Octal Mnemonic |
| TOC | Table Of Contents | TOM | Transparent Office Manager |
| TOC | Television Operating Center | TOMAL | Task Oriented Microprocessor Applications Language |
| TOCAP | Terminal Oriented Control Applications Program | TOMB | Technical Organizational Memory Bank |
| TOCC | Transfer Of Control Card | TOMCAT | Telemetry On-line Monitoring Compression And Transmission |
| TOCS | Terminal Operations Control System | | |
| TOCS | Term-Oriented Classification System | TOMCIS | Test Of Multiple Corridor Identification System |
| TOCT-TOU | Time Of Check To Time Of Use | TOMS | Transactions On Mathematical Software |
| TOD | Technical Objective Directive | TOMSI | Transfer Of Master Scheduled Item |
| TOD | Technical Objective Documents | TONLAR | Tone-Operated Net Loss Adjusted Receiving |
| TOD | Time Of Day | TOO | Time Of Origin |
| TOD | Time Of Delivery | TOOL | Test Oriented Onboard Language |
| TODA | Third-Octave Digital Analyzer | TOOL | Transaction-Oriented Operating System |
| TODARS | Terminal Oriented Data Analysis and Retrieval System | TOOT | Three Out Of Twelve |
| TODAS | Typewriter-Oriented Documentation Aid System | TOP | Tape Operated Printer |
| | | TOP | Technical Orientation Program |
| TODS | Test Oriented Disc System | TOP | Technik, Organisation, Planung |
| TOE | Tape Overlap Emulator | | |
| TOE | Total Operating Expense | TOP | Terminal Ordoprocesseur Procédure |
| TOEFL | Test Of English as a Foreign Language | TOP | The Option Process |
| TOF | Terz-Oktav-Filter | TOP | Tool Package |
| TOF | Time Of Filing | TOP | Training for Opportunities in Programming |
| TOI | Task Oriented Instruction | | |
| TOI | Technical Operation Instruction | TOP | Transaktionsorientierte Programmierung |
| TOIL | Test-Oriented Interactive Language | TOP | Transport-Optimierungs-Programm |
| TOJ | Track On Jamming | TOP | Tube à Ondes Progressives |
| TOL | Test Oriented Language | TOPC | Test and Operational Program Console |
| TOLCCS | Trends in On-Line Computer Control Systems | TOPCOPS | The Ottawa Police Computerized Online Processing System |
| TOLIP | Trajectory Optimization and Linearized Pitch | | |
| TOLTEP | Teleprocessing On-Line Test Executive Program | TOPI-TOPO | Tons Of Paper In, Tons Of Paper Out |
| TOLTS | Total On-Line Test System | TOPIC | Time Ordered Programmer Integrated Circuit |
| TOLTS | Totales Online Testsystem | | |
| TOM | Teleprinter On Multiplex | | |

# T

| | | | |
|---|---|---|---|
| TOPICS | Table Oriented Process and Information Control System | TOS | Time Operation System |
| TOPICS | Total On-line Program Information and Control System | TOS | Time Ordered System |
| | | TOS | Time-sharing Operating System |
| | | TOS | True Output Signal |
| TOPICS | Traffic Operations Program for Increasing Capacity and Safety | TOSAR | Topologische Wiedergabe von Synthetischen und Analytischen Relationen von Begriffen |
| TOPL | Terminal Operated Production Language | TOSBAC | Toshiba Computer |
| | | TOSBAC | Toshiba Scientific and Business Automatic Computer |
| TOPOS | Topologically Oriented Simulator | | |
| TOPR | Thermoplastic Optical Phase Recoder | TOSHIBA... | Tokyo Shibaura Electric Co. Ltd. |
| TOPS | Task Oriented Processing System | TOSMA | Topological Symbolic Macromodelling Algorithm |
| TOPS | Tele-center Omni-Processing System | TOSNUC.. | Toshiba Numerical Control |
| TOPS | Telemetry Online Processing System | TOSSA | Transient Or Steady-State Analysis |
| TOPS | Teleregister Omni-Processing and Switching | TOT | Time Of Tape |
| | | TOT | Time Of Transmission |
| TOPS | Test Oriented Programming System | TOT | Time On Tape |
| | | TOT | Time Out |
| TOPS | Testing and Operating System | TOT | Total |
| | | TOT | Total Outage Time |
| TOPS | The Operating Planning System | TOTE | Tape Online Test Execute |
| | | TOTE | Tape Online Test Executive |
| TOPS | Total Operations Processing System | TOTE | Teleprocessing Online Test Executive |
| TOPS | Total Planning System | | |
| TOPTS | Test Oriented Paper Tape System | TOTES | Time-Ordered Techniques Experiment System |
| TOR | Telephone Order Register | TOTLZ | Totalize |
| TOR | Teleprinter-On-Radio | TOTN | To Terminal Number |
| TOR | Teleprinting Over Radio | TOTRAD | Tape Output Test Rack Autonetics Diode |
| TOR | Teletype On Radio | | |
| TOR | Thermal Overload Relay | TOU | Technologieorientierte Unternehmungsgründung |
| TOR | Time Of Receipt | | |
| TOR | Torungsimpuls | TOV | Transfer on Overflow |
| TOROS | Tantalum Oxide Read-Only Store | TOXICON | Toxicology Information Conversational Online Network |
| TORQUE | Technology Or Research Quantitative Utility Evaluation | | |
| | | TOXLINE | Toxicology information online |
| TORS | Time Order Reporting System | TP | Tape |
| | | TP | Tape Perforator |
| TORTOS | Terminal-Oriented Real-Time Operating System | TP | Tape Positioning |
| | | TP | Tape Print |
| TOS | TIROS Operational System | TP | Tape Punch |
| TOS | Tactical Operating System | TP | Tape-to-Printer |
| TOS | Tape Operating System | TP | Technical Publication |
| TOS | Terminal-Oriented System | TP | Teilprozeß |
| TOS | Text Organizing System | TP | Telegraph Printer |

# T

| | | | |
|---|---|---|---|
| TP | Telemetry Processor | TPB | Technical Programming Bulletin |
| TP | Teleprinter | | |
| TP | Teleprocess | TPB | Turn-Push Button |
| TP | Teleprocessing | TPBV | Two-Point Boundary-Value |
| TP | Terminal Portable | TPBVP | Two-Point Boundary-Value Problem |
| TP | Terminal Printer | | |
| TP | Terminal Processing | TPC | Teleprinter Code |
| TP | Terre de Protection | TPC | Test Program Control |
| TP | Test Panel | TPC | Total Print Control |
| TP | Test Point | TPC | Triple-Paper-Covered cable |
| TP | Test Procedure | | |
| TP | Testprogramm | TPCB | Tens Position C Bit |
| TP | Text Processing | TPCOMP | Tape Compare |
| TP | Three-Pole | TPCU | Test Power Control Unit |
| TP | Tiefpass-Filter | TPD | Tape Playback Discriminator |
| TP | Time Pulse | | |
| TP | Timing Point | TPD | Test Point Data |
| TP | Timing Pulse | TPD | Test Procedure Drawing |
| TP | Total Printing | TPD | Time Pulse Distributer |
| TP | Trace Program | TPD | Time Pulse Distribution |
| TP | Tracing Program | TPD | Total Program Diagnostic |
| TP | Track Pitch | TPD | Transaction Processing Description |
| TP | Tracking Program | | |
| TP | Train Printer | TPD | Trivial Problem Discriminator |
| TP | Training Program | | |
| TP | Transaction Processing | TPDS | Tape Playback Discriminator System |
| TP | Transaction Processor | | |
| TP | Transfer Printing | TPDT | Triple-Pole, Double-Throw |
| TP | Transfer Process | TPDUP | Tape Duplicate |
| TP | Translating Program | TPE | Text Processing Equipment |
| TP | Trigger Pulse | TPE | Transfer Print Entry |
| TP | Triple-Play tape | TPE | Transmission Parity Error |
| TP | True Positioning | TPEDT | Tape Edit |
| TP | Tuned Plate | TPF | Terminal Phase Finalization |
| TP | Turning Point | | |
| TP | Type Printer | TPF | Two-Photon Fluorescence |
| TP | Type Printing | TPFW | Three-Phase Full Wave |
| TP-BP | Tiefpass-Bandpass | TPG | Test Pattern Generator |
| TPA | Tape Pulse Amplifier | TPG | Test Program Generator |
| TPA | Telemetry Power Amplifier | TPG | Timing Pulse Generator |
| TPA | Test Point Access | TPH | Telephone |
| TPA | Test Point Address | TPH | Through Plated Hole |
| TPA | Transfer of Pay Account | TPHC | Time-to-Pulse Height Converter |
| TPA | Transient Program Area | | |
| TPACS | Total Product Auto Control System | TPHW | Three Phase, Half-Wave |
| | | TPI | Tape Phase Inverter |
| TPAD | Teleprocessing Analysis and Design program | TPI | Terminal Phase Initiate |
| | | TPI | Test Pending Interruption |
| TPAM | Tele-Processing Access Method | TPI | Threads Per Inch |
| | | TPI | Tracks Per Inch |
| TPAS | Traffic Profile Analysis System | TPI | Trim Position Indicator |
| | | TPI | Turns Per Inch |
| TPAT | Thermoplastischer Aufzeichnungsträger | TPINIT | Tape Initializer |
| | | TPL | Tabular Program Language |

# T

| | | | |
|---|---|---|---|
| TPL | Teacher Programming Language | TPR | Technical Proposal Requirements |
| TPL | Technical Programming List | TPR | Teilprogramm |
| | | TPR | Tele-Processing Region |
| TPL | Telecommunications Programming Language | TPR | Teleprinter |
| | | TPR | Telescopic Photograph Recorder |
| TPL | Terminal Programming Language | TPR | Test Performance Recorder |
| TPL | Test Parts List | | |
| TPL | Test Point Logic | TPR | Thermoplastic Recording |
| TPL | Total Peak Loss | TPR | Timing Pulse Rate |
| TPL | Transaction Programming Language | TPR | Transaction Processing Routine |
| TPL | Transfer on Plus | TPR | Transmitter Power Rating |
| TPLAB | Tape Label | TPRA | Tape to Random Access |
| TPLH | Teleprocessing Line Handling | TPRV | Transient Peak Reverse Voltage |
| TPLIB | Transient Program Library | TPS | Tape Plotting System |
| | | TPS | Tape Processing System |
| TPLL | Threshold Phase-Locked Loop | TPS | Tape Programming System |
| | | TPS | Tape Punch Subassembly |
| TPM | Tape Preventive Maintenance | TPS | Task Parameter Synthesizer |
| TPM | Tape Processing Machine | TPS | Technical Programming Standard |
| TPM | Tape Punch Method | | |
| TPM | Telemetry Processor Module | TPS | Tele-Processing Supervisor |
| | | TPS | Telecommunication Programming System |
| TPM | Teleprinter Message | | |
| TPM | Third Party computer Maintenance | TPS | Telemetry Processing Station |
| TPM | Third Party Maintenance | TPS | Terminals Per Station |
| TPM | Transmission and Processing Model | TPS | Test Program Set |
| | | TPS | Thermal Protection System |
| TPMA | Thermodynamics Properties of Metals and Alloys | TPS | Thyristor Power Supply |
| | | TPS | Tracking antenna Pedestal System |
| TPMF | Tele-Processing Multiplex Feature | TPS | Training-Package-System-planung |
| TPMM | Tele-Processing Multiplexer Module | TPS | Transactional Processing System |
| TPMS | Transaction Processing Management Software | TPS | Transportation Programming System |
| TPNL | Test Panel | | |
| TPNS | Teleprocessing Network Simulator | TPSB | Telemetry Processing System Buffer |
| TPO | Teilprogrammorganisation | TPSI | Torque Pressure in pounds per Square Inch |
| TPP | Technical Programming Practice | TPSIS | Transportation Planning Support Information System |
| TPP | Test Point Pace | | |
| TPP | Theorem Proving Program | | |
| TPP | Transducer Power Programmer | TPSP | Tape Punch Subassembly Panel |
| TPPR | Tape to Printer | TPST | Test Program Symbol Table |
| TPR | T-Pulse Response | | |
| TPR | Tape Programmed Row | TPST | Triple-Pole, Single-Throw |
| | | TPT | Teleprinter Tape |

# T

| | | | |
|---|---|---|---|
| TPT | Teletype Punched Tape | TR | Transition |
| TPTC | Temperature Pressure | TR | Translate |
| | Test Chamber | TR | Translating Routine |
| TPTG | Tuned Plate, Tuned Grid | TR | Translation |
| TPTP | Tape to Tape | TR | Translator |
| TPU | Tape Preparation Unit | TR | Transmission |
| TPU | Task Processor Unit | TR | Transmit-Receive |
| TPU | Temperature Preparation | TR | Transmitter |
| | Unit | TR | Transmitter Receiver |
| TPU | Terminal Processing Unit | TR | Trigger |
| TPU | Test Peripheral Unit | TR | Tunnel Rectifier |
| TPV | Terminal Point de Vente | TR | Type of Request |
| TPV | Terminale Punto de Venta | TRA | Tape Read Alpha |
| TPV | Thermophotovoltaic | TRA | Tape Recorder Amplifier |
| TQE | Timer Queue Element | TRA | Transit-Amt |
| TQF | Terminal Query Facility | TRAAC | Transit Research And |
| TQTP | Transistor Qualification | | Attitude Control |
| | Test Program | TRAACS | Transit Research And |
| TR | Tally Register | | Attitude Control |
| TR | Tape Reader | | Satellite |
| TR | Tape Reading | TRAB | Transcribe |
| TR | Tape Recorder | TRAB | Transcriber |
| TR | Tape Reel | TRAB-AS | Transportbeton- |
| TR | Tape Register | | Abrechnungs-System |
| TR | Tape Reperforator | TRAC | Telecommunication |
| TR | Tape Resident | | Research's Analysis |
| TR | Taschenrechner | | Center |
| TR | Tätigkeitsregister | TRAC | Test Reckoning And |
| TR | Technical Report | | Compiling |
| TR | Technische Registratur | TRAC | Texas Reconfigurable |
| TR | Teilnehmerrechner | | Array Computer |
| TR | Telefunken Rechensystem | TRAC | Tool Record Adjustment |
| TR | Temporary Routing | | Card |
| TR | Terminal Repeater | TRAC | Tracing |
| TR | Test Request | TRAC | Tracking Reporting |
| TR | Test Run | | Analysis and Control |
| TR | Thermal Resistance | TRAC | Transient Radiation |
| TR | Time Routine | | Analysis by Computer |
| TR | Time-delay Relay | TRACAL | Tracking Calculator |
| TR | Timer Register | TRACE | Tactical Readiness And |
| TR | Tischrechner | | Checkout Equipment |
| TR | Torque Receiver | TRACE | Tape-controlled Recording |
| TR | Torque Repeater | | Automatic Checkout |
| TR | Trabantenstation | | Equipment |
| TR | Trace | TRACE | Teleprocessing Recording |
| TR | Trace Routine | | for Analysis by the |
| TR | Tracing Routine | | Customer Engineer |
| TR | Track | TRACE | Test-equipment for Rapid |
| TR | Transaction Routine | | Automatic Checkout and |
| TR | Transfer | | Evaluation |
| TR | Transfer Register | TRACE | Time Repetitive Analog |
| TR | Transformation Ratio | | Contour Equipment |
| TR | Transformer | TRACE | Time-shared Routiness for |
| TR | Transient Response | | Analysis Classification |
| TR | Transistor | | and Evaluation |

# T

| | | | |
|---|---|---|---|
| TRACE | Tolls Recording And Computing Equipment | TRAM | Ternary Random Access Memory |
| TRACE | Total Remote Assistance Center | TRAMMS | Transportation Automated Material Movements System |
| TRACE | Tracking Retrieval, and Analysis of Criminal Events | TRAMP | Test Retrieval And Memory Print |
| TRACE | Transaction Accounting Control and Endorsing | TRAMP | Time-shared Relational Associative Memory Program |
| TRACE | Transaction Control and Encoding | TRAMPS | Temperature Regulator And Missile Power Supply |
| TRACE | Transistor Radio Automatic Circuit Evaluator | TRAMPS | Text information Retrieval And Management Program System |
| TRACE | Transportable Automate Control Environment | TRAN | Transmit |
| TRACIS | Traffic Records And Criminal justice Information System | TRANDIR | Translation Director |
| | | TRANET | Tracking Network |
| TRACOMP | Tracking Comparator | TRANET | Transit Network |
| TRACOMP | Tracking Comparison | TRANEX | Transaction Executive |
| TRACON | Terminal Radar Approach Control facility | TRANS | Telemetry Redundacy Analyzer System |
| TRACON | Terminal Radar Control | TRANS | Traffic Network Simulator |
| TRACS | Total store Reporting And Communication System | TRANS | Transaction |
| | | TRANS | Transfer |
| TRACS | Traffic Reporting And Control System | TRANS | Transformation |
| | | TRANS | Transformer |
| TRACUT | Transformation of Cutter | TRANS | Transition |
| TRAD | Traductrice | TRANS | Translation |
| TRADAR | Transaction Data Recorder | TRANS | Translator |
| TRADES | Transaction Reporting, Analysis, Documentation, and Evaluation System | TRANS | Transmission |
| | | TRANS | Transmitter |
| | | TRANSAC | Transistorized Automatic Computer |
| TRADEX | Target Resolution And Discrimination Experiment | TRANSC | Transcribe |
| | | TRANSC | Transcription |
| TRADIC | Transistor Digital Computer | TRANSCAP | Transient Circuit Analysis Program |
| TRADIC | Transistorized Airborne Digital Computer | TRANSDUMP | Transparent Dump |
| | | TRANSEC | Transmission Security |
| TRADIS | Tape Repeating Automatic Data Integration System | TRANSF | Transfer |
| | | TRANSISTOR | Transistor transfer resistor |
| TRAE | Trommelausgabe/-eingabe | | |
| TRAFIC | Transportoptimierung und Fuhrparkeinsatzplanung mit dem Computer | TRANSL | Translate |
| | | TRANSL | Translation |
| | | TRANSL | Translator |
| TRAIL | Tactical Reconnaissance Airborne Imaging Laser | TRANSLANG | Translator Language |
| | | TRAP | Tape Recorder Action Plan |
| TRAIN | Telerail Automated Information Network | TRAP | Terminal Radiation Airborne Program |
| TRAIS | Transportation Research Activities Information Service | TRAP | Test and Repair Processor |
| | | TRAP | Tracker Analysis Program |
| | | TRAP | Trajectory Analysis Program |
| TRAM | Target Recognition and Attack Multisensor | | |

# T

| | | | |
|---|---|---|---|
| TRASS | Test Results Analysis Standard System | TRI | Transmission Interface converter |
| TRAWL | Tape Read And Write Library | TRI | Triode |
| | | TRIAC | Triode Alternating Current |
| TRAY | Translation Array | TRIAL | Technique for Retrieving Information of Abstracts of Literature |
| TRB | Technical Records Bulletin | | |
| TRC | Table Reference Character | | |
| TRC | Tape Reader Calibrator | TRIAL | Technique to Retrieve Information from Abstracts of Literature |
| TRC | Tape Reader Control | | |
| TRC | Tape Record Coordinator | | |
| TRC | Temperature Recording Controller | TRIASIS | Triumph/Adler Software-paket Integriertes Rechnungswesen mit Kennzahlen Informations-System |
| TRC | Time Ratio Control | | |
| TRC | Timed Readout Control | | |
| TRC | Trace | | |
| TRC | Transit to Customer | TRIASS | Triumph-Adler-Assembler |
| TRC | Transmitter Circuit | TRIB | Transfer Rate of Information Bits |
| TRC | Transverse Redundacy Check | | |
| | | TRIC | Therapeutic Recreation Information Center |
| TRC | Tube à Rayon Cathodique | | |
| TRCC | Tracking Radar Central Control | TRICE | Transistorized Real-time Incremental Computer Engine |
| TRCP | Technology Release Components Procedure | | |
| | | TRICE | Transistorized Real-time Incremental Computer, Expandable |
| TRCP | Technology Release and Change Procedure | | |
| TRD | Tape Reading Device | TRICO | Transistorized Real-time Incremental Computer |
| TRD | Typenraddrucker | | |
| TRDL | Translator Rule Description Language | TRIDAC | Three Dimensional Analog Computer |
| TRDM | Tactical Reconnaissance Data Marking | TRIM | Technical Requirements Identification Matrix |
| TRDPS | Telegraphic Retrieval and Data Presentation System | TRIM | Technique for Responsive Inventory Management |
| TRDTO | Tracking Radar Data Take-Off | TRIM | Terminal Reader In Magnetics |
| TRE | Telecommunication Research Establishment | TRIM | Test Rules for Inventory Management |
| TRE | Time Request Element | TRIM IC | Tri-Mask Integrated Circuit |
| TRE | Timing Read Error | | |
| TREAT | Transient Radiation Effects Automated Tabulation | TRIMIS | Tri-service Medical Information System |
| | | TRIMS | Transportation Integrated Management System |
| TREE | Transient Radiation Effects on Electronics | TRIP | Technical Reports Indexing Project |
| TREND | Tropical Environmental Data | TRIP | Truck Routing Improvement Program |
| TRF | Thermal Radiation at microwave Frequencies | TRIPS | Technical Reports Integrated Processing System |
| TRF | Transfer | | |
| TRF | Tuned Radio Frequency | TRIS | Transportation Research Information System |
| TRG | Trigger | | |
| TRH | Tape Reading Head | TRISEC | Total Reconnaissance Intelligence System Evaluation & Comparison |
| TRH | Tape Relay Heading | | |

# T

| | | | | |
|---|---|---|---|---|
| TRK | Track | | TRS | Tape Recorder Subsystem |
| TRL | Technical Records List | | TRS | Tape Rewind Speed |
| TRL | Time Request List | | TRS | Technology Record System |
| TRL | Transistor-Resistor Logic | | TRS | Technology Reporting System |
| TRM | Terminate | | | |
| TRM | Test Request Message | | TRS | Téléinformatique et Réseaux Spécialisés |
| TRM | Thermal Permanent Magnetization | | | |
| TRM | Time Ratio Modulation | | TRS | Test Response Spectrum |
| TRMBDR | Trommel-Magnetbanddatei als Druckdatei | | TRS | Time Reference System |
| | | | TRS | Track and Store |
| | | | TRS | Transkription |
| TRML | Terminal | | TRS | Transmit-Receive Switch |
| TRMNTR | Terminator | | TRS | Transmitter |
| TRMS | True Root Mean Square | | TRSB | Time Reference Scanning Beam |
| TRMT | Terminate | | | |
| TRN | Tape Relay Network | | TRSBG | Transcribing |
| TRN | Technical Research Note | | TRSBR | Transcriber |
| TRN | Transfer | | TRSFR | Transfer |
| TRN | Transfer on Negative | | TRSL | Translate |
| TRN | Translate | | TRSN | Transaction |
| TRN | Transparent | | TRSP | Transport |
| TRNS | Transition | | TRST | Transit |
| TRNT | Transient | | TRSTN | Transition |
| TRO | Tape Relay Operation | | TRT | Télécommunication Radioélectrique et Téléphonique |
| TRO | Timer Run Out | | | |
| TROM | Ternary Read Only Memory | | | |
| | | | TRT | Trace Table |
| TROM | Testable Read Only Memory | | TRT | Translate and Test |
| | | | TRTL | Transistor-Resistor-Transistor Logic |
| TROM | Transformer Read Only Memory | | | |
| | | | TRU | Transfer Unconditional |
| TROMP | Testable Read Only Memory, Programmable | | TRU | Transmit-Receive Unit |
| | | | TRU | Transportable Radio Unit |
| TROPICS | Tour Operators Integrated Computer System | | TRUMP | Teller Register Unit Monitoring Program |
| TROS | Tape Read Only Storage | | TRV | Telefon-Rechner-Verbund |
| TROS | Tape Resident Operating System | | TRV | Transient Recovery Voltage |
| TROS | Timesharing Realtime Operating System | | TRVM | Transistorized Voltmeter |
| | | | TRW... | Thompson Ramo Wolldrige Inc. |
| TROS | Transducer Read-Only Storage | | | |
| | | | TRX | Transaction |
| TROS | Transformer Read-Only Storage | | TRX | Transmitter |
| | | | TRXRX | Transmitter/Receiver |
| TRP | Technical Records Practice | | TRZ | Transfer on Zero |
| | | | TS | Tape Speed |
| TRP | Trace control Program | | TS | Tape Start |
| TRP | Transfert d'informations Prioritaires | | TS | Tape Station |
| | | | TS | Tape Stop |
| TRP | TV Remote Pickup | | TS | Tape Store |
| TRR | Take Read Result | | TS | Tape Supply |
| TRR | Tape Read Routine | | TS | Tape System |
| TRR | Target Ranging Radar | | TS | Teilnehmerschaltung |
| TRR | Trouble Recorder | | TS | Temperature Switch |
| TRS | Tape Reading System | | TS | Temporary Storage |

# T

| | | | |
|---|---|---|---|
| TS | Tensile Strength | TSAC | Title, Subtitle, And Caption |
| TS | Terminal Series | | |
| TS | Terminal Statement | TSAR | Telemetry Systems Application Requirements |
| TS | Terminal Station | | |
| TS | Terminal Strip | TSAR | Time-Sharing Activity Report system |
| TS | Terminal Supervisor | | |
| TS | Terminate Statement | TSAS | Time Sharing Accounting System |
| TS | Terminating Symbol | | |
| TS | Terminating System | TSB | Technical Systems Bulletin |
| TS | Termination Set | TSB | Terminal Status Block |
| TS | Termination System | TSB | Twin Sideband |
| TS | Terre de Signalisation | TSBP | Time-Sharing Business Package |
| TS | Tertiärspeicher | | |
| TS | Test Set | TSC | Technical Service Center |
| TS | Test Solution | TSC | Technical Subcommittee |
| TS | Test Specification | TSC | Test Set Computer |
| TS | Test Switch | TSC | Time Slot Code |
| TS | Test and Set | TSC | Time-Sharing Control |
| TS | Testing State | TSC | Total System Control |
| TS | Textsystem | TSC | Totally Self-Check |
| TS | Threaded Studs | TSC | Transfer System C |
| TS | Three-State | TSC | Transmitter Start Code |
| TS | Time Service | TSC | Transmitting Switch Control |
| TS | Time Shared | | |
| TS | Time Switch | TSC | Tristate Control |
| TS | Time System | TSCB | Task Set Control Block |
| TS | Time-Sharing | TSCC | Telemetry Standards Coordination Committee |
| TS | Timing Selector | | |
| TS | Tool Steel | TSCH | Test Subchannel |
| TS | Trace Statement | TSCLT | Transportable Satellite Communications Link Terminal |
| TS | Track Selection | | |
| TS | Trailer Statement | | |
| TS | Transfer Set | TSCP | Temporary Storage Control Program |
| TS | Transfer Signal | | |
| TS | Transit Storage | TSCP | Top Secret Control Proceeding |
| TS | Translation Store | | |
| TS | Translation System | TSCTL | Temporary Storage Control |
| TS | Transmission Services | | |
| TS | Transmission Subsystem | TSCU | Telemetry Signal Conditioning Unit |
| TS | Transmit Station | | |
| TS | Transmitting Station | TSD | Temporäre Sicherungsdatei |
| TS | Tristate | TSD | Time Sharing Driver |
| TS | Type Statement | TSD | Time System Division |
| TSA | Task Scheduling Algorithm | TSD | Time-Sharing Data acquisition |
| TSA | Telegraph System Analyzer | | |
| TSA | Time Series Analysis | TSD | Traffic Situation Display |
| TSA | Total System Analyzer | TSD | Traffic Status Display |
| TSA | Transfer System A | TSDD | Temperature-Salinity-Density-Depth |
| TSA | Tree-Structured Attribute | | |
| TSA | Two-Step Antenna | TSDF | Target System Data File |
| TSA/PPE | Total System Analyzer/ Problem Program Evaluator | TSDI | Tactical Situation Display Indicator |
| | | TSDM | Time-Shared Data Management system |
| TSAC | Time Slot Assignment Circuit | TSDM | Tri-State Delta Modulation |

- 617 -

# T

| | | | |
|---|---|---|---|
| TSDOS | Time-Shared Disk Operating System | TSL | Translator |
| TSDS | Time Sharing Disk Supervisor | TSL | Tree Searching Language |
| | | TSL | Tri-State Logic |
| TSDU | Target System Data Update | TSLS | Two Stage Least Squares |
| | | TSLT | Translate |
| TSE | Telemetry Support Equipment | TSLTR | Translator |
| | | TSM | Time Switching Memory |
| TSE | Temperaturschreiber, Elektronischer | TSM | Time Switching Module |
| | | TSM | Time-Sharing Mode |
| | | TSM | Time-Sharing Monitor |
| TSE | Terminalsteuereinheit | TSM | Time-Sharing Multiplex |
| TSE | Test- und Simuliereinrichtung | TSM | Track Switching Matrix |
| | | TSM | Transmit |
| TSEL | Tape Select | TSM | Troubleshooting Manual |
| TSEQ | Time Sequence | TSMT | Transmit |
| TSES | Technical Simulation and Evaluation System | TSMU | Time-Share Multiplex Unit |
| | | TSN | Task Sequence Number |
| TSET | Transmitter Signal Element Timing | TSNC | Time Shared Numerical Control |
| TSF | Ten-Statement FORTRAN | TSO | Terminator Sensor Output |
| TSF | Thin Solid Films | TSO | Time Shared Operation |
| TSF | Through Supergroup Filter | TSO | Time Slot zero |
| TSF | Time Setting Filter | TSO | Time-Sharing Option |
| TSFF | Transition Sensitive Flip Flop | TSOC | Tape System Output Converter |
| TSFP | Time-to-System Failure Period | TSOC | Time-Sharing Operating Control |
| TSFR | Transfer | TSOS | Time-Sharing Operating System |
| TSG | Test Signal Generator | | |
| TSG | Time Signal Generator | TSP | Technical Systems Practice |
| TSG | Track System Generator | | |
| TSG | Tracking Signal Generator | TSP | Telemetry Simulation Program |
| TSG | Transaction Generator | | |
| TSG | Triggered Spark Gap | TSP | Temporary Storage Program |
| TSGID | Temporary Storage Group Identification | TSP | Terminal Support Processor |
| TSI | Table Search Instruction | | |
| TSI | Threshold Signal-to-Interference ratio | TSP | Testsperre |
| | | TSP | Time Separation Pitch |
| TSI | Time Sharing Input | TSP | Time Sorting Program |
| TSI | Time Slot Input | TSP | Transfer and Store the Program |
| TSI | Time Slot Interchange | | |
| TSI | Total System Integration | TSP | Transponder |
| TSIC | Time Slot Interchange Circuit | TSP | Triggering System Pulse |
| | | TSP | Trommelspeicher |
| TSIMS | Telemetry Simulation Submodule | TSPAK | Time Series Package |
| | | TSPL | Telephone System Programming Language |
| TSIOA | Temporary Storage Input/Output Area | TSPS | Telecommunications Support Processing System |
| TSK | Time-Shift Keyed | | |
| TSK | Time-Shift-Keying | | |
| TSL | Technical Service Letter | TSPS | Time-Sharing Programming System |
| TSL | Technical Systems List | | |
| TSL | Test Set Logic | TSPS | Traffic Service Position System |
| TSL | Total Signal Loss | | |

# T

| | | | |
|---|---|---|---|
| TSPS | Trommelspeichersteuerung | TSU | Technical Support Unit |
| TSR | Temperature Sensitive Resistor | TSU | Time Standard Unit |
| | | TSU | Transfer Switch Unit |
| TSR | Time Signal Recorder | TSUT | Temporary Storage Unit |
| TSR | Time Status Register | TSW | Test Switch |
| TSR | Transistorized Switching Regulator | TSW | Transfer Switch |
| | | TSX | Time-Sharing Executive |
| TSRS | Time Synchronized Ranging System | TSX | Time-Sharing Execution |
| | | TSX | Transfer and Set index |
| TSRT | Teacher Situation Reaction Test | TT | Tape Telemetry |
| | | TT | Tape Test |
| TSS | Tape Search Standard | TT | Tape Threading |
| TSS | Teilestammsatz | TT | Tape Transmitter |
| TSS | Telecommunication Switching System | TT | Tape Transport |
| | | TT | Tape Typewriter |
| TSS | Teletex-Steuersystem | TT | Tape-to-Tape |
| TSS | Teletype Switching Subsystem | TT | Teleterminal |
| | | TT | Teletypewriter |
| TSS | Teststartsteuerung | TT | Temporarily Transferred |
| TSS | Time-Shared System | TT | Terminal Timing |
| TSS | Time-Sharing Support | TT | Test Tape |
| TSS | Time-Sharing System | TT | Test Terminator |
| TSS | Time-shared Supervisory System | TT | Test Time |
| | | TT | Thermally Tuned |
| TSS | Transmission Surveillance System | TT | Thermostat switch |
| | | TT | Ticker Tape |
| TSSA | Telemetry Subcarrier Spectrum Analyzer | TT | Timing and Telemetry |
| | | TT | Top to Top |
| TSSA | Test Scorer and Statistical Analyzer | TT | Touch Tone |
| | | TT | Tracking Telescope |
| TSSCS | Tactical Synchronous Satellite Communication System | TT | Transaction Tape |
| | | TT | Transfer Time |
| | | TT | Transistortechnik |
| TSSP | Tactical Satellite Signal Processor | TT | Transit Time |
| | | TT | Transmitting Typewriter |
| TSSS | Time Sharing Support System | TT&C | Telemetry Tracking and Control |
| TST | Telemetry Simulation Terminal | TTA | Teletex Adapter |
| | | TTAC | Telemetry, Tracking And Command |
| TST | Test | | |
| TST | Threshold Setting Tracer | TTB | Test Two Bits |
| TST | Time-Shared Terminal | TTC | Tape To Card |
| TST | Transaction Status Table | TTC | Tape-to-Tape Converter |
| TST | Transportsteuerwerk | TTC | Telecommunication Trainings-Center |
| TST CSL | Test Console | | |
| TSTA | Transmission, Signalling, and Test Access | TTC | Teletype Code |
| | | TTC | Teletype-message Converter |
| TSTFLT | Test Set Fault | | |
| TSTR | Tester | TTC | Test Table of Contents |
| TSTR | Transistor | TTC | Tight Tape Contact |
| TSTRZ | Transistorize | TTC | Total Time Constant |
| TSTS | Tracking System Test Set | TTC | Transit Through-Connect signal |
| TSTS | Tracking System Test Stand | | |
| | | TTC... | TRAN Telecommunications Corporation |
| TSU | Technical Service Unit | | |

- 619 -

# T

| | | | |
|---|---|---|---|
| TTCP | Transmitting Typewriter with Card Punch | TTR | Target Tracking Radar |
| TTCU | Teletypewriter Control Unit | TTR | Teletype Translator |
| | | TTR | Test Technology Report |
| TTCV | Tracking, Telemetry, Command, and Voice | TTR | Time To Repair |
| | | TTRC | Transistorized Thyratron Ring Counter |
| TTD | Temporary Text Delay | TTS | Takt- und Träger- synchronisierung |
| TTDB | Textile Technology Data Base | | |
| | | TTS | Telemetry Transmission System |
| TTDR | Tracking Telemetry Data Receiver | | |
| | | TTS | Teletype Setter |
| TTDT | Tactical Test Data Translator | TTS | Teletypesetting |
| | | TTS | Teletypewriter System |
| TTE | Text Terminal Equipment | TTS | Temporary Threshold Shift |
| TTE | Time-To-Event | TTS | Three-state Transceiver |
| TTF | Tabular Test Format | TTS | Transistor-Transistor logic Schottky barrier |
| TTF | Terminal Transaction Facility | | |
| | | TTS | Transmission Test Set |
| TTF | Test-To-Failure | TTS | Transportable Telemetry Set |
| TTF | Thoriated Tungsten Filament | | |
| | | TTTL | Transistor-Transistor- Transistor Logic |
| TTF | Time To Failure | | |
| TTG | Takt- und Trägergenerator | TTTLS | Transistor-Transistor- Transistor Logik mit Schottky-Diode |
| TTG | Technical Translation Group | | |
| | | TTTP | Transmitting Typewriter with Tape Punch |
| TTG | Time-To-Go | | |
| TTI | Telecommunication Trainings-Institut | TTU | Teletex-Telex-Umsetzer |
| | | TTU | Teletype Terminal Unit |
| TTI | Teletype Input | TTU | Terminal Timing Unit |
| TTI | Teletype Test Instruction | TTUS | Teletex-Telex Umsetzersatz |
| TTI | Time Temperature Indicator | | |
| | | TTW | Tontastenwahl |
| TTK | Two Tone Keying | TTY | Teletype |
| TTL | Transistor-Transistor Logic | TTY | Teletypewriter |
| | | TTYA | Teletypewriter Assembly |
| TTL | Transistor-Transistor Logikschaltkreis | TTYL | Teletype Link |
| | | TTZ | Technologie Transfer- Zentrum |
| TTL | Transistor-Transistor- Logik | | |
| | | TTuL | Transistor-Transistor- Micrologic |
| TTLIC | Transistor-Transistor- Logic Integrated Circuit | | |
| | | TU | Take-Up |
| TTLS | Transistor-Transistor Logik durch Schottky- Dioden verschnellert | TU | Tape Unit |
| | | TU | Teilkanalunterbrechung |
| | | TU | Terminal Unit |
| TTM | Tactical Telemetry | TÜ | Terminalübersicht |
| TTM | Two-Tone Modulation | TU | Thermal Unit |
| TTMS | Telephoto Transmission Measuring Set | TU | Timing Unit |
| | | TU | Traffic Unit |
| TTO | Teletype Output | TU | Translator Unit |
| TTO | Transmitter Turn-Off | TU | Transmitting Unit |
| TTP | Tabular Tape Processor | TUC | Technical Usage Code |
| TTP | Tape To Print | TUC | Triangle University Computing |
| TTP | Teletype Tape Punch | | |
| TTP | Teletype Telegraph Printer | | |
| TTR | TRAP Translator | | |

# T

| | | | |
|---|---|---|---|
| TUDAT | Tunnel Diode Arithmetic Tester | TVIS | Television Information Storage |
| TUEP | Tape-Überwachungsprozedur | TVIST | Television Information Storage Tube |
| TUFA | Teletexumsetzer für Fernsprech-Nebenstellenanlagen | TVM | Tachometer Voltmeter |
| | | TVM | Transistor Voltmeter |
| | | TVM | Transistorized Voltmeter |
| TUFF | Tape Updater for Formatted Files | TVOC | Television Operatings Center |
| TUFI | Teletex-Umsetzer Fernsprechnebenanlage-IDN | TVOM | Transistorized VOM |
| | | TVOR | Terminal Very high frequency Omnirange |
| TUG | Tape Updater and Generator | TVP | Telex-Verschlüsselungs-Paket |
| TUG | TRANSAC Users Group | TVP | Time Variable Parameter |
| TUI | Tape Unit Indicator | TVS | Tactical VOCODER System |
| TULE | Transistorized Universal Logic Elements | TVS | Taktversorgung |
| TULIPS | Telemetered Ultrasonic Liquid Interface Plotting System | TVS | Taktversorgung Senderichtung |
| | | TVS | Television Viewing System |
| TULPE | Terminal-Unterstützende-Lokale Prozessor-Einheit | TVS | Textverarbeitungssekretariat |
| TUM | Test Under Mask | TVSM | Time-Varying Sequential Measuring |
| TUM | Tuning Unit Member | | |
| TUMI | Terminal Users Manual of Instruction | TVSM | Time-Varying Signal Measurement |
| TUNNET | Tunnel Transit-time | TW | Tabular Work |
| TUP | Telephone User Part | TW | Technisch-Wissenschaftlich |
| TUP | Titre Universel de Paiement | TW | Technische Wartung |
| | | TW | Thermal Wire |
| TUP | Trommelunterprogramm | TW | Time Word |
| TUR | Take-Up Reel | TW | Track Width |
| TUR | Traffic Usage Recorder | TW | Travelling Wave |
| TUT | Transistor Under Test | TW | Typewriter |
| TV | Taktverstärker | TWA | Task Work Area |
| TV | Tape Version | TWA | Technische Wissenschaftliche Anwendung |
| TV | Teilnehmerverbinder | | |
| TV | Television | TWA | Terminal Working Area |
| TV | Test Voltage | TWA | Transaction Work Area |
| TV | Textverarbeitung | TWA | Travelling Wave Amplifier |
| TV | Thermal Vacuum | TWA | Two-Way Alternate communication |
| TV | Transfer Vector | | |
| TV | Transistorverstärker | TWADL | Two-Way Air Data Link |
| TV | Transitverkehr | TWAIT | Terminal Wait |
| TV | Tube Voltmeter | TWAP | Thin Wire Analysis Program |
| TV/TA | Textverarbeitung/ Textautomation | TWCRT | Travelling Wave Cathode Ray Tube |
| TVG | Tiold Voltage Generator | | |
| TVGDHS | Television Ground Data Handling System | TWE | Technisch-Wissenschaftlicher Einsatz |
| TVI | Television Interference | TWICE | Test Ware In-Circuit Emulator |
| TVID | Television frame Identification Data | | |
| | | TWK | Travelling Wave Klystron |
| | | TWK | Typewriter Keyboard |

# T

| | | | |
|---|---|---|---|
| TWLC | Two Way Logic Circuit | TX | Transmitter |
| TWM | Travelling Wave Magnetron | TXA | Task Extension Area |
| TWMBK | Travelling Wave Multiple-Beam Klystron | TXC | Transaction Code |
| | | TXE | Telephone Exchange Electronics |
| TWO | Teilworte | | |
| TWPA | Travelling Wave Parametric Amplifier | TXH | Transfer on Index High |
| | | TXI | Transfer with Index Incremented |
| TWR | Tastwahlregister | | |
| TWR | Tower | TXL | Transfer on Index Low |
| TWR | Travelling Wave Resonator | TXR | Transistor |
| TWS | Technisch-Wissenschaftliches Software-Zentrum | TXRX | Transmit-Receive |
| | | TXRX | Transmitter-Receiver |
| TWS | Teletypewriter Exchange Service | TXT | Text |
| | | TYDAC | Typical Digital Automatic Computer |
| TWS | Track While Scan | | |
| TWS | Translator Writing System | TYP | Typewriter |
| TWS | Two-Way Simultaneous | TYPE | Typewriter |
| TWSRO | Track While Scan on Receive Only | TYPOUT | Typewriter Output |
| | | TYPR | Typewritten |
| TWSRS | Track While Scan Radar Simulator | TYPW | Typewriter |
| | | TYPW | Typewriting |
| TWT | Travelling Wave Tube | TYPW | Typewritten |
| TWTA | Travelling Wave Tube Amplifier | TYPWRT | Typewriter |
| | | TYPX | Type Text |
| TWX | Telegraph | TZ | Taktzentrale |
| TWX | Teletype Message | TZ | Tischzentrale |
| TWX | Teletypewriter Exchange | TZ | Transitzentrale |
| TX | Television receiver | TZE | Terminalzentraleinheit |
| TX | Torque synchro transmitter | TZE | Transfer on Zero |
| TX | Torque transmitter | TZP | Time Zero Pulse |
| TX | Transistor | TZR | Tafelzeigeregister |
| TX | Transmit | | |

# U

| | | | |
|---|---|---|---|
| Ü | Überlauf | UATCS | Universal Air Traffic Control Simulator |
| Ü | Übertrager | | |
| Ü | Übertragung | UATE | Universal Automatic Test Equipment |
| U | Umdrehung | | |
| U | Umschalter | UATS | Universal Assembly Translator System |
| U | Unclassified | | |
| U | Undefined | UAX | Unit Automatic Exchange |
| U | Unit | UB | Umschaltbaugruppe |
| U | Unload | UB | Unternehmensbereich |
| U | Up | UBB | Universal Building Block |
| U FRAME | Unnumbered control Frame | UBC | Universal Buffer Controller |
| U/MIN | Umdrehungen pro Minute | UBD | Unternehmensbereich Datentechnik |
| UA | Unassigned | | |
| UA | UND-Ausgang | UBD | Utility Binary Dump |
| UA | Unnumbered Acknowledge | UBHR | User Block Handling Routine |
| UA | User Agent | | |
| UAA | Unité d'Appel Automatique | UBI | Unibus Interface |
| UAA | User Action Analyzer | UBLK | Unblank |
| UAC | Upper Air Control | UBLK | Universal Block |
| UACTE | Universal Automatic Control and Test Equipment | UBR | Unterbrechbarkeitsroutine |
| | | UBS | Unit Backspace Character |
| | | UBS | Utility Billing System |
| UAD | User Attribute Definition | UC | Unichannel |
| UADPS | Uniform Automated Data Processing System | UC | Unit Call |
| | | UC | Unit Cell |
| UADS | User Attribute Data Set | UC | Unit Check |
| UAE | User Agent Entity | UC | Unité Centrale |
| UAID | User Automated Interface Data | UC | Universal Controller |
| | | UC | Unoperated Control |
| UAIDE | Users of Automatic Information Display Equipment | UC | Upper Case |
| | | UC | Upper Characters |
| | | UC | Upper Control |
| UAIMS | United Aircraft Information Management System | UC | Usable Control |
| | | UC | Usage Code |
| UAL | Unité Arithmétique et Logique | UC | User Class character |
| | | UCA | Unitized Component Assembly |
| UAL | Universal Assembly Language | UCA | Universal Cable Adapter |
| UAL | Upper Acceptance Limit | UCAS | Uniform Cost Accounting Standards |
| UAL | User Adaptive Language | | |
| UAL | User Agent Layer | UCB | Unit Control Block |
| UAN | UND-Ausgang Negiert | UCB | Universal Character Buffer |
| UAR | Unterbrechungsadreß-register | UCBT | Universal Circuit Board Tester |
| UAR | Upper Atmosphere Research | UCC | Uniform Commercial Code |
| | | UCC | Uniform Credit Code |
| UART | Universal Asynchronous Receiver Terminal | UCC | Unit Communications Control |
| UART | Universal Asynchronous Receiver Transmitter | UCC | Universal Commercial Code |
| ÜAS | Übertragungsablaufsteuerung | UCC | Universal Communication Controller |
| UAT | Uniform Asymptotic Theory | UCC | University Computing Center |

- 623 -

# U

| | | | |
|---|---|---|---|
| UCC... | University Computing Company | UCS | Universal Character Set |
| UCCC | Uniform Consumer Credit Code | UCS | Universal Classification System |
| UCCRS | Underwater Coded Command Release System | UCS | University Computer System |
| UCCS | Universal Camera Control System | UCS | Users Control System |
| UCDP | Uncorrected Data Processor | UCSAR | Universal Character Set Address Register |
| UCDP | Uncorrelated Data Processor | UCSB | Universal Character Set Buffer |
| UCE | Unit Checkout Equipment | UCSD | Universal Communications Switching Device |
| UCE | Unit Control Error | UCSD | University of California, San Diego |
| UCE | Unité de Calcul Electronique | UCSTR | Universal Code Synchronous Transmitter/Receiver |
| UCF | Unit Control File | UCT | Unité de Contrôle de Transmission |
| UCF | Universal Communications Facility | UCW | Unit Control Word |
| UCF | Utility Control Facility | ÜD | Überspringen von Daten |
| UCG | Ultrasound Cardiogram | UD | Underground Distribution |
| UCHCIS | Urban Comprehensive Health Care Information System | UD | Universal Dipole |
| | | UD | Up-Down |
| UCI | Unit Construction Index | UD | Usage Data |
| UCI | Upper Constant Impulse | UDAC | Uppsala Data Center |
| UCI | Upper Control Impulse | UDAM | Universal Digital of Avionics Module |
| UCI | Utility Card Input | UDAR | Universal Digital Adaptive Recognizer |
| UCIS | Uprange Computer Input System | UDAS | Unified Direct Access Standards |
| UCK | Unit Check | UDB | Universal Data Base |
| UCL | Upper Confidence Limit | UDB | Universelle Datenbank |
| UCL | Upper Control Limit | UDB | Universeller Datenbetrieb |
| UCLA | Universal Communication Line Adaptor | UDB | Up Data Buffer |
| UCM | Unité Controle Multifonction | UDC | Unidirectional Current |
| | | UDC | Universal Decimal Classification |
| UCMF | Utilitaire de Création Maintenance de Fichiers | UDC | Universal Decimal Code |
| UCMS | Utilitaire de Création Maintenance de language Source | UDC | Upper Dead Center |
| | | UDC | User Designation Code |
| | | UDC | User-Defined Command |
| UCN | Uniform Control Number | UDCCS | Uniform Data Classification Code Structure |
| UCOP | User Controller Process | | |
| UCOS | Uprange Computer Output System | UDCD | Unit Data and Control Diagram |
| UCP | Uninterruptable Computer Power | UDEC | Unitized Digital Electronic Calculator |
| UCP | Unit Construction Principle | UDEC | Unitized Digital Electronic Computer |
| UCP | Users Control Program | UDF | UHF Direction Finding |
| UCRL | Upper Control Limit | UDI | Universal Development Interface |
| UCS | United Computing Systems | | |
| UCS | Universal Card Scanner | | |

# U

| | | | |
|---|---|---|---|
| UDI | Universal Digital Instrument | UEAS | Übertragungsablaufsteuerung |
| UDI | Update Information | UED | Unité d'Echange Directe |
| UDITS | Universal Digital Test Set | UEIS | United Engineering Information Service |
| UDK | Universelle Dezimalklassifikation | UEJ | Unchanged Eject |
| UDL | Undersea Data Link | UEM | Unité d'Echanges Multiples |
| UDL | Uniform Data Link | UEN | UND-Eingang Negiert |
| UDL | Up Data Link | UEP | Unité d'Echanges Programmées |
| UDLC | Universal Data Link Control | UEPB | Universal Electronic Program Board |
| UDO | Untergliederte Datenspeicherung für Online-Verarbeitung | UER | Universal-Einfachrepeater |
| | | UER | Unsatisfactory Equipment Report |
| UDOP | Ultra high frequency Doppler | UERMWA | United Electrical-Radio Machine Workers of America |
| UDP | Update Program | | |
| UDR | Universal Data Report | | |
| UDR | Universal Digital Readout | UERS | Universal Event Recording System |
| UDR | Universal Document Reader | UERS | Unusual Event Recording System |
| UDR | Unterdrücken | | |
| UDR | Update Routine | UET | Unattended Earth Terminal |
| UDR | Usage Data Report | UEW | United Electrical Workers |
| UDR | Utility Data Reduction | UEX | Unit Exception |
| UDRC | Utility Data Reduction Control | UF | Ultrasonic Frequency |
| | | UF | Unternehmensforschung |
| UDRO | Utility Data Reduction Output | UFAED | Unit Forecast Authorization Equipment Data |
| UDS | Ultronic Data Systems | UFB | Übertragungsfrequenzbereich |
| UDS | United Data Set | | |
| UDS | Universal Data Set | UFC | Universal Flight Computer |
| UDS | Universal Documentation System | UFCB | Unit File Control Block |
| | | UFD | Unit Functional Diagram |
| UDS | Universelles Datenbanksystem | UFD | User File Directory |
| | | UFDC | Universal Flight Director Computer |
| UDS | Utility Definition Statement | UFET | Unipolar Field-Effect Transistor |
| UDT | Unidirectional Transducer | | |
| UDT | Universal Data Transcriber | UFF | Universal Flip-Flop |
| UDT | Universal Data Transfer | UFI | User Friendly Interface |
| UDT | Untere Datentechnik | UFM | Universal Function Module |
| UDT | User Display Terminal | | |
| UDTI | Universal Digital Transducer Indicator | UFN | Until Further Notice |
| | | UFO | User File On-line |
| UDTS | Universal Data Transfer Service | UFP | Utility Facilities Program |
| | | UFR | Underfrequency Relay |
| UDU | Updata Data Unit | UFS | Uniform Filing System |
| ÜE | Übermittlungseinheit | UFT | Unified File Transfer facility |
| ÜE | Übertragungseinheit | | |
| ÜE | Übertragungseinrichtung | UG | Union Guide |
| ÜE | Überwachungseinheit | UGL | Ungleich |
| UE | Unité Externe | UGLI | Universal Gate for Logic Implementation |
| UE | Unité d'Echange | | |

# U

| | | | |
|---|---|---|---|
| UGLIAC | United Gas Laboratory Internally-programmed Automatic Computer | UKHIS | United Kingdom Hazard Information Service |
| UGP | Unité de Gestion de Postes | UKOLUG | United Kingdom On-Line User Group |
| ÜGU | Übergruppenumsetzer | UKPO | United Kingdom Post Office |
| UH | Unit Heater | UKTG | Universal Keyboard Test Generator |
| UHCS | Ultra-High Capacity Storage | ÜL | Überlappung |
| UHELP | University of Houston Easy Linear Programming | UL | Ultralinear |
| | | UL | Uncoded Language |
| UHF | Ultra-High Frequency | UL | Underline |
| UHF | Ultrahohe Frequenz | UL | Underwriters Laboratories |
| UHFM | University of Houston Formula Manipulation | UL | Unité de Liaison |
| | | UL | Urladung |
| UHGROUP | User Home Group | UL | User Language |
| UHL | User Header Label | UL/1 | User Language 1 |
| UHR | Ultra-High Resistance | ULA | Uncommitted Logic Array |
| UHSIC | Ultra High Speed Integrated Circuit | ULA | Universal Logic Array |
| | | ULA | Upper Layer Architecture |
| UHT | Ultra-High Temperature | ULANG | Update Language |
| UHTSS | University of Hawaii Time Sharing System | ULATTR | User Local Attributes |
| | | ULB | Universal Logic Block |
| UHV | Ultra-High Vacuum | ULC | Universal Logic Circuit |
| UHV | Ultra-High Voltage | ULC | Upper and Lower Case |
| UI | Unnumbered Information | ULCB | User Local Control Block |
| UI | Unscheduled Interruption | ULCC | University of London Computer Center |
| UI | User Interface | | |
| UIC | Unit Identification Code | ULCER | Underwater Launch Current and Energy Recorder |
| UIC | Unrestricted Input Change | | |
| UICPS | Uniform Inventory Control Points System | ULD | Unit Logic Device |
| UID | Universal Identifier | ULD | Universal Language Description |
| UID | Universal individual Identifier | ULE | Universelle Logische Einheit |
| UIF | Unsigned Integer Format | | |
| UIL | UNIVAC Interactive Language | ULF | Ultra-Low Frequency |
| | | ULF | Upper Limiting Frequency |
| UIM | Ultra Intelligent Machine | ULI | Universal Logic Implementer |
| UIO | Utility Iterative Operation | | |
| | | ULICP | Universal Log Interpretation Computer Program |
| UIR | Upper Information Region | | |
| UIRC | Universal Interline Reservations Code | ULICS | University of London Institute of Computer Science |
| UIS | Universal Information Service | | |
| | | ULM | Universal Logic Module |
| UIT | Union Internationale des Télécommunications | ULP | Universal Logic Primitive |
| | | ULS | Universale Logikschaltung |
| UJ | Unconditional Jump | ULSI | Ultra Large Systems Integration |
| UJT | Unijunction Transistor | | |
| UJTO | Unijunction Transistor Oscillator | ULSI | Upper Large Scale Integration |
| UK | Unterkanal | ULT | Uniform Low frequency Technique |
| UKCIS | United Kingdom Chemical Information Service | | |

# U

| | | | |
|---|---|---|---|
| ULTRA | Universal Language for Typographic Reproduction Applications | UMX | User Microroutine Execution |
| UM | Unit of Measure | UN | Unit |
| UM | Unscheduled Maintenance | UNACOM | Universal Army Communication system |
| UM | Unteres Management | UNAMACE | Universal Automatic Map Compilation Equipment |
| UMA | Universal Measuring Amplifier | UNBAL | Unbalanced |
| UMAS | Universal Meß-Auswerte- und Steuersprache | UNC | Undercurrent |
| | | UNC | Unified Coarse thread |
| UMASS | Unlimited Machine Access from Scattered Sites | UNC | Universal Navigation Computer |
| UMC | User Microinstruction Cycle | UNC | Unusual Command |
| | | UNCDRP | Universal Card Read-in Program |
| UMF | Ultra-Microfiche | | |
| UMF | Users Master File | UNCL | Unified Numerical Control Language |
| UMFC | Unit of Measure Family Code | UNCOL | Universal Computer Oriented Language |
| UMIS | Urban Management Information System | UNCP | Universal Network Communication Processor |
| UML | User Microroutine Length | | |
| UMLA | Universal Multi-Line Adaptor | UNCTAD | United Nations Conference on Trade And Development |
| UMLC | Universal Multi-Line Controller | UND | Unterrichtdeskriptor |
| UMLER | Universal Machine Language Equipment Register | UNEJ | Unchanged Eject |
| | | UNESCO | United Nations Educational, Scientific and Cultural Organization |
| UMO | User Microroutine Overhead | UNF | Unified Fine thread |
| UMOS | U-groove Metal Oxide Semiconductor | UNFET | Unipolar Field Effect Transistor |
| UMOST | U-groove power MOSFET | UNI | User Node Interface |
| UMP | Uniformly Most Powerful | UNI FREDI | Universal Flight Range and Endurance Data Indicator |
| UMP | Universal Macro Processor | | |
| UMPDU | User Message Protocol Data Unit | UNIBI | Unipolar Bipolar |
| UMPIRE | Universal Mathematical Programming system Incorporating Refinements and Extensions | UNIBIS | Universelles Bilanzierungs- und Informationssystem |
| | | UNIBIS | Universelles Bilanzierungssystem |
| UMPLIS | Umwelt-Planungs- Informations-System | UNIBORS | UNIVAC Bill Of material processor Random System |
| UMR | Umrichtermodul | | |
| UMRECC | University of Manchester Regional Computer Centre | UNIBOSS | UNIVAC Bill Of material processor Sequential System |
| UMSES | Universelles Mikroprozessor Software Engineering System | UNICOL | Universal Computer Oriented Language |
| UMT | Unlabeled Magnetic Tape | UNICOM | Universal Integrated Communications |
| UMVUE | Uniformly Minimum Variance Unbiased Estimator | UNICOMP | Universal Compiler |
| | | UNICON | Unidensity Coherent light recording |
| UMW | Ultramicrowaves | | |

# U

| | | | |
|---|---|---|---|
| UNIDATS | Unified Data Transmission System | UO | Umdruckoriginal |
| UNIDAV | Universelle Dateiverwaltung | UOC | Ultimate Operating Capability |
| UNIDEB | Universelle Debitorenbuchhaltung | UODL | User-Oriented Data-display Language |
| UNIFET | Unipolar Field Effect Transistor | UOV | Units Of Variance |
| | | ÜP | Übersetzungsprogramm |
| UNILOG | Universelle Lohn- und Gehaltsabrechnung | UP | Unabhängige Pufferzeit |
| | | UP | Unabhängiger Puffer |
| UNIMS | UNIVAC Information Management System | UP | Uniprozessor |
| | | UP | Units Position |
| UNIPOL | Universal Procedures Oriented Language | UP | Unterprogramm |
| | | UP | Untersuchungsprogramm |
| UNIPRO | Universal Processor | UP | User Part |
| UNIRAS | Universal Raster System | UP | User Program |
| UNIREB | UNIVAC Rechnungswesen Betriebsabrechnung | UP | User Programmer |
| | | UP | Utility Path |
| UNIREF | UNIVAC Rechnungswesen Finanzbuchhaltung | UP | Utility Program |
| | | UPACS | UNIVAC Patient Accounting and Control System |
| UNIRES | UNIVAC Rechnungswesen-System | UPADI | Union Panamericana de Associaciones De Ingenieros |
| UNIS | UNIVAC Industrie System | | |
| UNISAP | UNIVAC Share Assembly Program | UPAM | User's Primary Access Method |
| UNISIST | Universal System for Information in Science and Technology | UPAS | Universelles Programm- und Analysesystem |
| UNISTAR | User Network for Information Storage, Transfer Acquisition, and Retrieval | UPASS | User Password |
| | | UPC | Unit Processing Code |
| | | UPC | Universal Product Code |
| | | UPCC | Uniform Product Code Council |
| UNIT | Universal Numerical Interchange Terminal | UPD | Universally Programmable Digitizer |
| UNITRAC | Universal Trajector Compiler | UPD | Update |
| | | UPE | Universal Processing Element |
| UNITS | Unit Inventory Technique System | | |
| UNIV | Universal | UPF | Ultraspherical Polynomial Filter |
| UNIVAC | Universal Automatic Computer | UPIC | Universal Personal Identification Code |
| UNL | Unlatch | | |
| UNLD | Unload | UPL | Universal Programming Language |
| UNLK | Unlock | | |
| UNOPAR | Universal Operator Performance Analyzer and Recorder | UPL | User Programming Language |
| | | UPN | Umgekehrte Polische Notation |
| UNPK | Unpack | | |
| UNPKD | Unpacked | UPO | Undistorted Power Output |
| UNPRT | Unprintable | UPOS | Utility Program Operating System |
| UNPS | Universal Power Supply | | |
| UNRAU | Unified Numeric Representation Arithmetic Unit | UPR | Ultrasonic Paramagnetic Resonance |
| UNS | Unified Numbering System | UPRO | Unterprogramm |

- 628 -

# U

| | | | |
|---|---|---|---|
| UPRP | Used Parts Returnable Program | URS | Universal Regulating System |
| UPS | Uninterruptible Power Supply | URS | Universelles Regelungs- und Steuerungssystem |
| UPS | Uninterruptible Power System | URSP | Universal Radar Signal Processor |
| UPS | United Parcel Service | ÜRTL | Überwachbare Resistance- Transistor-Logik |
| UPS | Unterprogrammsprung | | |
| UPSG | Unique Phrase Structure Grammar | URV | Unité à Réponse Vocale |
| | | URZ | Universitätsrechenzentrum |
| UPSI | User Program Switch Indicator | ÜS | Überoperativer Speicher |
| | | US | Unconditional Selection |
| UR | Ultra-Red | US | Unconditional Stop |
| UR | Unformatted Record | US | Underwater-to-Surface |
| UR | Unit Record | US | Undistorted Signal |
| UR | Unterreihe | US | Unit Separator |
| UR | User Record | US | Unterbrechungssystem |
| UR | User Requirements | US | Unteres Seitenband |
| UR | Utility Register | US | Untersystem |
| URBS | UNIVAC Random Beratung Serie 9000 | US/U.S. | United States |
| | | USACIU | United States Army Command Information Unit |
| URC | Uniform Resistance- Capacitance | | |
| URC | Unit Record Card | USACSC | United States Army Computer Service Center |
| URC | Unit Record Controller | | |
| URCLK | Universal Receiver Clock | USACSEC | United States Army Computer Systems Evaluation Command |
| URD | User Record Dictionary | | |
| URIPS | Undersea Radioisotope Power Supply | USAD | Untersätze-Adressensatz |
| | | USADC | United States Army Data support Command |
| URIR | Unified Radioactive Isodromic Regulator | | |
| | | USADSC | United States Army Data Services and administra- tive systems Command |
| URIS | Universal Resources Information Symposium | | |
| URISA | Urban & Regional Information Systems Association | USAEC | United States Atomic Energy Commission |
| | | USAIDSCOM | United States Army Information and Data Systems Command |
| URL | User Requirements Language | | |
| URM | Unlimited Register Machine | USAM | Unique Sequential Access Method |
| URMS | Universal Reproducing Matrix System | USAP | Unternehmensspezifisches Absatzpotential |
| URR | Unite Row and Row | | |
| ÜRS | Überwachung, Regelung, Steuerung | USAPDSC | United States Army Personnel Data Support Center |
| URS | Unite Ringe Sum | | |
| URS | Unformatted Read Statement | USART | Universal Synchronous/ Asynchronous Receiver/ Transmitter |
| URS | Uniform Reporting System | | |
| | | USASCII | USA Standard Code for Information Interchange |
| URS | Uniformly Reflexive Structure | | |
| | | USASCSOCR | United States Army Standard Character Set for Optical Character Recognition |
| URS | Unit Record Systems | | |
| URS | Universal Reference System | | |

# U

| | | | |
|---|---|---|---|
| USASI | USA Standards Institute | USTT | Unicode Single Transition Time |
| USB | Unified S-Band | | |
| USB | Upper-Sideband | USV | Unterbrechungsfreie Stromversorgung |
| USC | University of Southern California | USVA | Unterbrechungsfreie Stromversorgungsanlage |
| USCHI | Umweltschutz-Informations- und Steuerungssystem | USW | Ultra Short Wave |
| | | UT | Unconditional Transfer |
| USCMI | United States Commission on Mathematical Instruction | UT | Unité de Traitement |
| | | UT | Units Tens |
| | | UT | Universal Time |
| USD | Ultimate Strength Design | UT | Universal Tube |
| USD | Universal Standard Data | UT | User Terminal |
| USE | Unit Support Equipment | UT | Utility |
| USE | UNIVAC Scientific Exchange | UT... | Unitech Inc. |
| | | UTA | Universal-Telex-Adapter |
| USEC | United System of Electronic Computers | UTA | Universeller Telex-Adapter |
| | | ÜTB | Übertragungsblock |
| USER ID | User Identification | UTC | Ultra-Thin Copper |
| USF | Universal Source File | UTC | Unit Time Coding |
| ÜSG | Überwachungs- und Steuergerät | UTC | Universal Terminal Controller |
| USIC | United States Information Center | UTC | Universal Time Code |
| | | UTC | Universeller Teletex Controller |
| USIS | United States Information Service | UTC | Universeller Telex-Controller |
| USISL | United States Information Service Library | UTD | Uniform Theory of Diffraction |
| USL | Underwater Sound Laboratory | UTEC | University of Toronto Electronic Computer |
| USL | Upper Square Law limit | | |
| USN | Update Sequence Number | UTI | Unconditional Transfer |
| USNDC | United States Nuclear Data Committee | UTIL | Utility |
| | | UTL | User Trailer Label |
| ÜSP | Übertragungsspeicher | UTLAS | University of Toronto Library Automation System |
| USP | Universal Signal Processor | | |
| USP | Unterprogrammsprung | | |
| USPS | US Postal Service | UTM | Universal Test Message |
| USR | Universal Series Regulator | UTM | Universal Transverse Mercator |
| USRT | Universal Synchronous Receiver/Transmitter | | |
| | | UTM | Universeller Transaktionsmonitor |
| USS | Unformatted System Services | | |
| | | UTP | Universal Tape Processor |
| USS | Unified Software System | UTP | User Test Program |
| USS | Unifiziertes Software-System | UTP | Utility Tape Processor |
| | | UTR | Unprogrammed Transfer Register |
| USS | United States Standard | | |
| USS | Universal Scheduling System | UTR | Up-Time Ratio |
| | | UTS | Ultimate Tensile Strength |
| USS | User Support System | UTS | Unbound Task Set |
| ÜST | Übertragungssteuerung | UTS | Unified Transfer System |
| UST | Usage Structure Tape | UTS | Universal Terminal System |
| USTIS | Ubiquitous Scientific and Technical Information System | UTS | Universal Test Station |
| | | UTS | Universal Time Sharing |

# U

| | | | |
|---|---|---|---|
| UTT | Universal Teleprocessing Tester | UVD | Undervoltage Device |
| UTTC | Universal Tape-to-Type Converter | UVL | Ultra-Violet Light |
| | | UVS | Universal Versaplot Software |
| UUA | UNIVAC Users Association | Üw | Überwachung |
| UUD | Unit Under Development | UW | Ultrasonic Wave |
| UUT | Unit Under Test | UW | Unique Word |
| UV | Ultra-Violet | UWBIC | University of Washington Basic Interpretative Compiler |
| UV | Unabhängige Variable | | |
| UV | Unbemanntes Verstärkeramt | UWS | Überwachungssignal |
| UV | Under Voltage | UWS | Unformatted Write Statement |
| UV | Univibrator | | |
| UV | Use Volumes | UZ | Universalzähler |
| UV ROM | Ultra-Violet Read-Only Memory | UZ | Unterzentrale |
| | | ÜZR | Überwachungszählregister |
| UVASER | Ultra-Violet Amplification by Stimulated Emission of Radiation | | |

# V

| | | | |
|---|---|---|---|
| V | Vacuum | VAI | Video-Assisted Instruction |
| V | Valve | VAL | Validity |
| V | Variabel | VAL | Value |
| V | Variante | VAL | Verbale Aspektnamenliste |
| V | Vartan | VALSAS | Variable Length-word Symbolic Assembly System |
| V | Verbindung | | |
| V | Verkehr | | |
| V | Verstärker | VAM | Vector Airborne Magnetometer |
| V | Verstärkung | | |
| V | Vertical | VAM | Virtual Access Method |
| V | Video | VAM | Voltammeter |
| V | Visual | VAMIS | Virginia Medical Information System |
| V | Voice | | |
| V | Volt | VAMP | Vector Arithmetic Multiprocessor |
| V | Voltage | | |
| V | Voltmeter | VAMP | Virtual Access Method of Processing |
| V | Volume | | |
| V | Vorzeichen | VAMP | Visual-Acoustic-Magnetic Pressure |
| V-MOS | Vertical Metal Oxide Semiconductor | | |
| | | VAN | Value Added Network |
| V-V | Velocity Volume | VANS | Value Added Network Services |
| V-to-F | Voltage-to-Frequency | | |
| V/ATE | Vertical Anisotropic Etch | VANT | Vibration And Noise Tester |
| V/RMS | Volt Root Mean Square | VAPOX | Vapor deposite Oxide |
| VA | Value | VAPT | Variable Automatic Pulse Tester |
| VA | Value Analysis | | |
| VA | Value Assignment | VAR | Value Added Resellers |
| VA | Variable Address | VAR | Variable |
| VA | Variometer | VAR | Varistor |
| VA | Vertical Amplifier | VAR | Visual Aural Range |
| VA | Video Amplifier | VAR | Volt-Ampère Réactif |
| VA | Virtual Addressing | VARAD | Varying Radiation |
| VA | Volt Ampere | VARHM | VAR-Hour Meter |
| VA | Voltage Amplifier | VARIAC | Variable Capacitor |
| VA | Vorsatzadresse | VARISTOR | Variable Resistor |
| VAA | Verkaufs-Auftrags-abwicklung | VARITRAN | Variable-voltage Transformer |
| VAB | Van Allen Belt | VARR | Variable Range Reflector |
| VAB | Voice Answer-Back | VARR | Visual Aural Radio Range |
| VAC | Vacuum | VARS | Variable Attribute Raster Scan System |
| VAC | Value-Added Carrier | | |
| VAC | Vector Analog Computer | VARS | Vertical Azimuth Reference System |
| VAC | Video Amplifier Chain | | |
| VAC | Volt Alternating Current | VARTAB | Variable Tabellen |
| VADE | Vandenberg Automatic Data Evaluation | VAS | Vierstellige Ausführliche Systematik |
| VADE | Versatile Auto Data Exchange | VASCAR | Visual Average Speed Computer And Recorder |
| VADIS | Voice And Data Integrated System | VASI | Visual Approach Slope Indicator |
| VADS | Viking Automated Data System | VASIS | Visual Approach Slope Indicator System |
| VAEP | Variable, Attributes, Error Propagation | VASP | Variable Automatic Synthesis Program |
| VAI | Video Aided Instruction | VASS | Visual Analysis Subsystem |

# V

| | | | |
|---|---|---|---|
| VAST | Versatile Automatic Specification Tester | VCAD | Vertical Contact Analog Display |
| VAST | Versatile Avionics Ship Test | VCAM | Virtual Communication Access Method |
| VASTL | Variable Strukturlisten | VCBA | Variable Control Block Area |
| VAT | Value Added Tax | | |
| VAT | Variable Auto Transformer | VCC | Video-Colour-Copier |
| VAT | Virtual Address Translation | VCC | Visual Communications Congress |
| VAT | Virtual Address Translator | | |
| VAT | Visual Automation Technique | VCC | Voice Control Center |
| | | VCC | Voice-Controlled Carrier |
| VATE | Versatile Automatic Test Equipment | VCC | Void Compensation Check |
| | | VCC | Voltage-Controlled Clock |
| VATLS | Visual Airborne Target Locator System | VCCO | Voltage-Controlled Crystal Oscillator |
| VATS | Vehicle Automatic Test System | VCD | Variable Capacitance Diode |
| VAU | Vertical Arithmetic Unit | VCF | Variable Crystal Filter |
| VAZ | Verkehrsausscheidungsziffer | VCF | Voltage-Controlled Frequency |
| VB | Vacancy Bit | VCG | Vertical line through Centre of Gravity |
| VB | Valence bond | | |
| VB | Valve Box | VCG | Video Command Generator |
| VB | Verkaufsbeauftragter | VCI | Volatile Corrosion Inhibitor |
| VB | Vertriebsbeauftragter | | |
| VB | Vibration | VCL | Vertical Center Line |
| VB | Vibrator | VCLO | Voltage-Controlled Local Oscillator |
| VB | Voltage Board | | |
| VBD | Voice Band Data | VCM | Verification Comparison Matrix |
| VBO | Voltage, Breakover | | |
| VBS | Visual Business System | VCM | Vibrating Coil Magnetometer |
| VBS | Vocabulary Building System | VCMIP | Videotext Communication Monitor for Information Providers |
| VC | Validity Check | | |
| VC | Variable Capacitor | | |
| VC | Vector Control | VCMV | Voltage Controlled Multivibrator |
| VC | Versatility Code | | |
| VC | Video Correlation | VCNA | Virtual Communications Network Application |
| VC | Video Correlator | | |
| VC | Virtual Circuit | VCNA | VTAM Communications Network Application |
| VC | Voice Call | | |
| VC | Voice Coil | VCNC | Voltage Controlled Negative Capacitance |
| VC | Volkscomputer | | |
| VC | Voltage Changer | VCNR | Voltage Controlled Negative Resistance |
| VC | Voltage Comparator | | |
| VC | Volume Class | VCO | Vocoder |
| VCA | Valve Control Amplifier | VCO | Voice Coder |
| VCA | Voice-Connecting Arrangements | VCO | Voltage-Controlled Oscillator |
| VCA | Voice-controlled Carrier | VCORE | Variable Core |
| VCA | Voltage Current Adapter | VCP | Velocity Control Programmer |
| VCA | Voltage-Controlled Amplifier | VCP | Virtual Communication Path |

# V

| | | | |
|---|---|---|---|
| VCP | Virtual Control Processor | VDC | Voltage-to-Digital Converter |
| VCR | Video Cartridge Recorder | | |
| VCR | Video Cassette Recorder | VDC | Volume Description Card |
| VCR | Video Cassette Recording | VDCP | Video Data Collection Program |
| VCR | Voltage Control Resistor | | |
| VCR | Voltage-Controlled Resistor | VDD | Visual Display Data |
| | | VDD | Visual Display Device |
| VCS | Vacuum actuated Control Switch | VDD | Voice Digital Display |
| | | VDDI | Voyager Data Detailed Index |
| VCS | Vertical Channel Select | | |
| VCS | Video Communications System | VDDL | Virtual Data Description Language |
| VCS | Virtual Circuit Service | VDDL | Voyager Data Distribution List |
| VCS | Visually Coupled System | | |
| VCSIP | Videotext Communication System for Information Providers | VDDS | Voyager Data Description Standards |
| | | VDE | Verband Deutscher Elektrotechniker |
| VCSR | Voltage-Controlled Shift Register | VDE | Vorschriftenwerk Deutscher Elektrotechniker |
| VCT | Voice Code Translation | | |
| VCT | Voice Coded Translator | | |
| VCT | Voltage Clock Trigger | VDES | Voice Data Encoding System |
| VCT | Voltage-Controlled Transfer | VDET | Voltage Detector |
| VCTD | Vender Contract Technical Data | VDF | Verband der Datenverarbeitungsfachleute |
| VCU | Variable Correction Unit | VDF | Very-high-frequency Direction Finder |
| VCU | Video Combiner Unit | | |
| VCVS | Voltage-Controlled Voltage Source | VDF | Video Disk File |
| | | VDF | Video Frequency |
| VCXO | Voltage-Controlled Crystal-Oscillator | VDFG | Variable Diode Function Generator |
| VD | Vapour Density | VDG | Vehicle Data Guide |
| VD | Verdahtung | VDG | Video Display Generator |
| VD | Video Display | VDH | Variable-length Divide or Halt |
| VD | Voice Data | | |
| VD | Voltage Detector | VDI | Verein Deutscher Ingenieure |
| VD | Voltage Drop | | |
| VDA | Variable Data Area | VDI | Vertical Display Indicator |
| VDA | Vendor Data Article | VDI | Video Display |
| VDA | Verband der Automobilindustrie | VDI | Virtual Device Interface |
| | | VDI | Visual Doppler Indicator |
| VDA | Vision Distribution Amplifier | VDI | Voluntary Data Inquiry |
| | | VDID | Verzeichnis Deutscher Informations- und Dokumentationsstellen |
| VDAC | Vendor Data Article Control | | |
| VDAFS | Verband der Automobilhersteller-Flächen-Schnittstelle | VDL | Variable Delay Line |
| | | VDL | Vienna Definition Language |
| VDAL | Variable Datalength Assembly Language | VDM | Varian Data Machines |
| | | VDM | Video Delta Modulation |
| VDAS | Vibration Data Acquisition System | VDM | Virtual Device Metafile |
| | | VDMA | Verein Deutscher Maschinenbauanstalten |
| VDC | Volt Direct Current | | |

# V

| | | | |
|---|---|---|---|
| VDMOS | Vertical-planar Double-diffused Metal Oxide Semiconductor | VECO | Vernier Engine Cut-Off |
| VDMOST | Vertical DMOST | VECOS | Vehicle Checkout Set |
| VDMS | Video Data Modulation System | VECP | Value Engineering Change Proposal |
| VDN | Verteilte Datenbank Nixdorf | VEDAC | Vehicle-borne Data Converter |
| VDP | Variable-length Divide or Proceed | VEIS | Vocational Education Information System |
| VDP | Vertical Data Processing | VEL | Velocity |
| VDP | Video-Display Processor | VELF | Velocity Filter |
| VDP | Video-Display-Prozessor | VENUS | Variable and Efficient Network Utility Service |
| VDP | Virtual Device Protocol | VENUS | Vermietungsgeschäft einschließlich Nebengebiete Und Statistik |
| VDPI | Voyager Data Processing Instruction | VEP | Vorrangentschlüsselungsprogramm |
| VDPS | Voice Data Processor System | VEPIS | Vocational Education Program Information System |
| VDR | Validated Data Record | | |
| VDR | Vendor Data Request | VEPRO | Versorgungsprogramm |
| VDR | Video Disk Recording | VER | Verify |
| VDR | Voltage Dependent Resistor | VER | Versions |
| VDRA | Voice and Data Recording Auxiliary | VERA | Vision Electronic Recording Apparatus |
| VDRZ | Verband Deutscher Rechenzentren | VERDAN | Versatile Differential Analyzer |
| VDS | Variable Depth SONAR | VERDIS | Verlags-Dialog-Informations-System |
| VDS | Vereinigung Deutscher Software-Hersteller e.V. | VERKDB | Vermessungsprogrammsystem einschließlich Koordinatendatenbank |
| VDS | Vertical Display System | | |
| VDS | Video Display System | | |
| VDS | Video-Display-Signal | VEST | Vertical Earth Scanning Test |
| VDS | Visual Data System | | |
| VDT | Validate | VETRAS | Vehicle Traffic Simulator |
| VDT | Video Data Terminal | VEV | Voice-Excited Vocoder |
| VDT | Video Display Terminal | VEWS | Very Early Warning System |
| VDT | Visual Display Terminal | VF | Variable Frequency |
| VDU | Video Display Unit | VF | Vector Field |
| VDU | Visual Display Unit | VF | Video Frequency |
| VE | Value Engineering | VF | Visible File |
| VE | Verarbeitungseinheit | VF | Voice Frequency |
| VE | Verkehrseinheit | VF | Voltage-Frequency |
| VE | Vernier Engine | VFAP | Valley Forge Assembly Program |
| VE | Virtual Environment | | |
| VEB | Variable Elevation Beam | VFB | Vertical Format Buffer |
| VEB DVZ | Volkseigener Betrieb Datenverarbeitungszentrum | VFC | Variable Frequency Clock |
| | | VFC | Vertical Format Control |
| | | VFC | Video Frequency Carrier |
| VEB MR | Volkseigener Betrieb Maschinelles Rechnen | VFC | Voice Frequency Carrier |
| | | VFC | Voice Frequency Channel |
| VECI | Vehicular Equipment Complement Index | VFC | Voltage Frequency Converter |
| VECO | Verification et Correction des rubans perforés | VFCT | Voice-Frequency Carrier Telegraphy |

# V

| | | | |
|---|---|---|---|
| VFD | Voltage Fault Detector | VHSIC | Very High Speed Integrated Circuit |
| VFET | V-groove FET | VHV | Very High Voltage |
| VFET | Vertical Field Effect Transistor | VI | Video Integrator |
| | | VI | Viscosity Index |
| VFET | Vertikal-Feldeffekt-transistor | VI | Visual Indicator |
| VFL | Variable Field Length | VI | Volume Indicator |
| VFLA | Volume Folding and Limiting Amplifier | VIA | Versatile Interface Adapter |
| VFMED | Variable Format Message Entry Device | VIAS | Voice Interference Analysis Set |
| VFO | Variable Frequency Oscillator | VIBS | Vocabulary, Information, Block design, Similarities |
| VFP | Variable Factor Programming | VIC | Variable Instruction Computer |
| VFP | Variable Floating Point | | |
| VFR | Visual Flight Rules | VIC | Vision Information Center |
| VFT | Voice Frequency Telegraphy | VICC | Visual Information Control Console |
| VFU | Vertical Format Unit | VID | Video |
| VFX | Variable Frequency Crystal oscillator | VID | Video Image Display |
| | | VID | Volume Information Density |
| VFsDx | Verordnung für den Fernschreib- und Datexdienst | VIDAC | Visual Information Display And Control |
| VG | Voice Grade | | |
| VG | Voltage Gain | VIDAMP | Video Amplifier |
| VGA | Variable Gain Amplifier | VIDAP | Vibration Data Accuracy Program |
| VGC | Viscosity-Gravity Constant | | |
| VGF | Vergleichsfehler | VIDAT | Visual Data |
| VGP | Vertex Generating Program | VIDEO | Visual Data Entry Online |
| | | VIDF | Video Frequency |
| VGPI | Visual Glide Path Indicator | VIDIAC | Visual Information Display And Retrieval |
| VH | Very Hard | VIDT | Vertical Interval Data Transmission |
| VHAA | Very High Altitude Abort | | |
| VHF | Very High Frequency | VIE | Visual Indicator Equipment |
| VHIC | Very High-speed Integrated Circuit | VIF | Visible Index File |
| | | VIF | Voice Interface Frame |
| VHLL | Very High Level Languages | VIFI | Voyager Information Flow Instructions |
| VHM | Virtual Hardware Monitor | | |
| VHO | Very High Output | VIG | Video Integrating Group |
| VHOICE | Vocal Human Oriented Information Consultative Equipment | VIL | Vertical Injection Logic |
| | | VIL | Vertikale Informationsleitung |
| VHP | Very High Performance | VIL | Vertikale Injektionslogik |
| VHPIC | Very High Performance Integrated Circuit | VILP | Victor Impedance Locus Plotter |
| VHR | Video-to-Hardware Recorder | VIM | Verallgemeinerte Indexmethode |
| VHRR | Very High Resolution Radiometer | VIM | Vereinfachte Indexsequentielle Methode |
| VHSI | Very High Speed Integration | VIM | Verkaufs- und Informationssystem Möbel |
| VHSIC | Very High Scale Integrated Circuit | VINRAM | Virtually Nonvolatile Random Access Memory |

# V

| | | | |
|---|---|---|---|
| VINS | Velocity Inertia Navigation System | VIS | Volkswirtschaftliches Informationssystem |
| VINT | Video Integration | VIS | Voltage Inverter Switch |
| VIO | Virtual Input/Output | VIS | Vorstands-Informations-System |
| VIOC | Variable Input/Output Code | VISAM | Virtual Index Sequential Access Method |
| VIP | V-Insulation with Polysilicon | VISSR | Visible Infrared Spin-Scan Radiometer |
| VIP | Variable Information Processor | VISTA | Visual Information for Satellite Telemetry Analysis |
| VIP | Vendor Involvemen Programme | VIT | Very Intelligent Terminal |
| VIP | Verbraucher-Informationsprogramm | VITAL | Variably Initialized Translator for Algorithmic Languages |
| VIP | Verifying Interpreting Punch | VITAL | VAST Interface Test Application Language |
| VIP | Versatile Information Processor | VITS | Vertical Interval Test Signal |
| VIP | Video Information Panel | VIU | Voice Intercommunication Unit |
| VIP | Video Instructional Program | VK | Verriegelungskreis |
| VIP | Video Integrator and Processor | VK | Vielkanalanalysator |
| VIP | Video Interface Processor | VKA | Vielkanalanalysator |
| VIP | Virtual Instruction Package | VKL | Vielfachklinke |
| VIP | Visual Image Processor | VKN | Vorgangsknotennetz |
| VIP | Visual Indicator Panel | VKN | Vorgangsknotennetzplan |
| VIP | Visual Information Processor | VKR | Videokonferenzraum |
| VIP | Visual Information Project | VKS | Visuelles Kommunikationssystem |
| VIP | Visual Information Projection | VL | Verbindungsleitung |
| VIP | Voltage Impulse Protection | VL | Verknüpfungslogik |
| VIPER | Video Processing and Electronic Reduction | VL | Very Large |
| | | VL | Video Logic |
| VIPP | Variable Information Processing Package | VL | Vorwärtslesen |
| VIPS | Voice Interruption Priority System | VLA | Verband für Lochkarten- und Automatenfachleute |
| | | VLA | Very Large Antenna |
| VIR | Vendor Information Request | VLA | Very Large Array |
| | | VLA | Very Low Altitude |
| VIR | Vertical Interval Retrace | VLAM | Variable Level Access Method |
| VIR | Virtual | VLAN | Very Local Area Network |
| VIRNS | Velocity Inertia Radar Navigation System | VLC | Variable Length Computer |
| | | VLC | Virtual Local Controller |
| VIRS | Vertical Interval Reference Signal | VLCBX | Very Large Computerized Branch Exchange |
| VIRTDSK | Virtual Disk | VLCC | Very Large Crude Carrier |
| VIS | Video Information System | VLCD | Very Low Cost Display |
| VIS | Video-Informationssystem | VLCM | Very Large Capacity Memory |
| VIS | Visual Information System | | |
| VIS | Visual Instrumentation Subsystem | VLCM | Very Low Cost Memory |
| VIS | Visuelles Informationssystem | VLCR | Variable Length Cavity Resonance |

# V

| | | | |
|---|---|---|---|
| VLCS | Very Large Computer System | VMACS | Vehicle Monitoring and Action Control System |
| VLCS | Voltage-Logic, Current-Switching | VMC | Variable Message Cycle |
| VLD | Valid | VMC | Vertical Microcode |
| VLDR | Very Low Data Rate | VMCB | Virtual Machine Control Block |
| VLE | Very Large Enhanced | | |
| VLE | Voice Line Expansion | VMD | Vertical Magnetic Dipole |
| VLED | Visible Light-Emitting Diode | VME | Verkehrsmesseinrichtung |
| | | VME | Versa Module Eurocard |
| VLF | Vertical Launch Facility | VME | Virtual Machine Environment |
| VLF | Very Low Frequency | | |
| VLFS | Variable Low Frequency Standard | VMID | Virtual Machine Identification |
| VLI | Very Low Impedance | VMM | Virtual Machine Manager |
| VLM | Variable Length Multiply | VMM | Virtual Machine Monitor |
| VLN | Variable Length | VMOS | V-groove Metal Oxide Semiconductor |
| VLOG | VMC error Log | | |
| VLP | Video Langspielplatte | VMOS | Virtual Memory Operating System |
| VLP | Video Long Play | | |
| VLR | Very Long Range | VMOS | Virtual Memory Operating Software |
| VLS | Vapor-Liquid-Solid | | |
| VLS | Vehicle Locator System | VMP | Virtual Multiprocessor |
| VLSI | Very Large Scale Integration | VMRS | Virtuelles Mehrrechnersystem |
| VLVS | Voltage Logic, Voltage-Switching | VMS | Variable Magnetic Shunt |
| | | VMS | Variable Memory System |
| VLW-PCM | Variable Length Word - Pulse Code Modulation | VMS | Variable Mesh Simulator |
| | | VMS | Verarbeitungsmaschinensystem |
| VM | Velocity Modulation | | |
| VM | Verkehrsmessung | VMS | Vermittlungssystem |
| VM | Virtual Machine | VMS | Video Motion Sampler |
| VM | Virtual Memory | VMS | Videofile Microwave System |
| VM | Virtual Multi-access | | |
| VM | Virtuelle Maschine | VMS | Virtual Memory System |
| VM | Voice Modulation | VMS | Visual Memory Span |
| VM | Volatile Memory | VMS | Voice Mail Server |
| VM | Voltage Memory | VMS | Voice Mail System |
| VM | Voltage Meter | VMT | Validate Master Tape |
| VM | Voltmeter | VMT | Video Matrix Terminal |
| VM-ESX | VM Extended Systems Executive | VMT | Virtual Memory Technique |
| | | VMTL | Voltage Mode Transistor Logic |
| VM-ESN | Virtual Machine Extended Systems Networking | VMTSS | Virtual Machine Time Sharing System |
| VM/BSE | VM/Basic System Extensions | VN | Valid Name |
| VM/IFS | VM/Interactive File Sharing | VN | Verknüpfungsnetzwerk |
| | | VN | Verteilernetzwerk |
| VM/PC | Virtual Machine/Personal Computer | VNET | Virtuelles Netz |
| | | VNL | Via Net Loss |
| VM/SP | Virtual Machine/System Product | VNR | Verband Norddeutscher Rechenzentren e.V. |
| VM/XA | Virtual Machine/Extended Architecture | VO | Vacuum-tube Oscillator |
| | | VO | Valve Oscillator |
| VMA | Valid Memory Address | VO | Verbal Orders |
| VMA | Virtual Machine Assist | VO | Vertical Output |

# V

| | | | | |
|---|---|---|---|---|
| VOC | Variable Output Circuit | VOTEM | Voice Operated Typewriter Employing Morse |
| VOC | Voice-Operated Coder | VOX | Voice Operated |
| VOCA | Voice Communications Assembly | VP | Vapour Pressure |
| VOCODER | Voice Coder | VP | Vektor Prozessor |
| VOCOM | Voice Communications | VP | Verarbeitungsperiode |
| VODACOM | Voice Data Communications | VP | Verarbeitungsprogramm |
| | | VP | Verifying Punch |
| VODACTOR | Voice Data Compactor | VP | Versuchsprogramm |
| VODAT | Voice-Operated Device for Automatic Transmission | VP | Vertical Polarization |
| | | VP | Video Processor |
| VODER | Voice Coder | VP | Virtual Processor |
| VODER | Voice Operation Demonstrator | VP | Virtual machine control Program |
| VOGAA | Voice-Operated Gain-Adjusting Amplifier | VP | Vulnerable Point |
| | | VPA | Voice Processing Algorithm |
| VOGAD | Voice-Operated Gain-Adjusting Device | VPAC | Video Processor And Controller |
| VOH | Verification Off Hook | | |
| VOICES | Voice Operated Identification Computer Entry System | VPAM | Virtual Partitioned Access Method |
| | | VPB | Virtually Pivoted Beam laser |
| VOIS | Visual Observation Instrumentation Subsystem | VPC | Vente Par Correspondance |
| | | VPC | Verge Perforated Card |
| VOL | Verdingungsordnung für Leistungen | VPC | Vertical Path Computer |
| | | VPC | Voltage-to-Probability Converter |
| VOL | Volume | | |
| VOL | Volume Label | VPC | Voltage-to-Pulse Converter |
| VOLCAS | Voice-Operated Loss Control And Suppressor | VPCB | Virtual Processor Control Block |
| VOLCAT | Volume Catalog | | |
| VOLSER | Volume Serial number | VPCDS | Video Prelaunch Command Data System |
| VOLT | Volume Table | | |
| VOLTAN | Voltage Amperage Normalizer | VPD | Vehicle Performance Data |
| | | VPE | Vapor Phase Epitaxial |
| VOM | Volt-Ohm-Milliammeter | VPE | Video Processing Equipment |
| VOM | Volt-Ohmmeter | | |
| VOPP | Verfahrensorientiertes Programmierpaket | VPE | Vulcanized Polyethylene |
| | | VPI | Vacuum Pressure Impregnation |
| VOPS | Verfahrensorientiertes Programmiersystem | | |
| | | VPIB | Virtual Processor Identificaton Block |
| VOR | Very high frequency Omnidirectional Range | | |
| | | VPID | Virtual Processor Identification |
| VORAG | Vorgabearbeitsgänge | | |
| VORELLE | Vorübersetzer für Entscheidungstabellen | VPM | Volts Per Meter |
| | | VPN | Vorgangspfeilnetz |
| VORTAC | VOR co-located with TACAN | VPP | Volts Peak to Peak |
| | | VPR | Variable Parameter Record |
| VORTEX | Varian Omnitaste Real-Time Executive | VPR | Vertical Position Relative |
| | | VPRF | Variable Pulse Repetition Frequency |
| VOS | Virtual Operating System | | |
| VOS | Vocational Orientation System | VPS | Verbindungsprogrammierte Steuerung |
| VOS | Voice Operated Switch | VPS | Vibrations Per Second |

# V

| | | | |
|---|---|---|---|
| VPS | Video Programm System | VS | Vector Scan |
| VPS | Video-Programm-Service | VS | Verarbeitungssystem |
| VR | Variable Resistance | VS | Verbindungssatz |
| VR | Verbundrechner | VS | Versus |
| VR | Verkehrsrechner | VS | Vertical Spacing |
| VR | Vermittlungsrechner | VS | Very Soft |
| VR | Verteilerregister | VS | Virtual Storage |
| VR | Vertical Redundancy | VS | Virtual System |
| VR | Virtual Record | VS | Virtueller Speicher |
| VR | Virtual Route | VS | Virtuelles Speichersystem |
| VR | Voltage Regulation | VS | Virtuelles System |
| VR | Voltage Regulator | VS | Visual Signalling |
| VR | Voltage Relay | VS | Volatile Storage |
| VR | Vorrechner | VS | Voltmeter Switch |
| VR | Vorregister | VS | Volume Set |
| VRAM | Video Random Access Memory | VS | Volumetric Solution |
| | | VS | Votrox Sprachsimulator |
| VRAP | Vertical Registration Analysis Program | VSA | Value Systems Analysis |
| | | VSAM | Variable Sequential Access Method |
| VRB | VHF Recovery Beacon | | |
| VRC | Vertical Redundancy Character | VSAM | Variable, Spanned- And undefined Mode |
| VRC | Vertical Redundancy Check | VSAM | Virtual Sequential Access Method |
| VRC | Video Recorder | VSAM | Virtual Storage Access Method |
| VRC | Visible Record Computer | | |
| VRC | Visual Record Computer | VSB | Very Small Business user |
| VRCR | Vertical Redundancy Check Register | VSC | Variable Speech Control |
| | | VSC | Vibration Safety Cutoff |
| VRCT | Vertical Redundancy Check-Track | VSC | Video Scan Converter |
| | | VSC | Voltage Saturated Capacitor |
| VRD | Variable Ratio Devider | | |
| VRE | Variable Record | VSCF | Variable Speed Constant Frequency |
| VRF | Verify | | |
| VRID | Virtual Route Identifier | VSCR | Virtual Storage Constraint Relief |
| VRM | Video Refresh Memory | | |
| VRPF | Voltage Regulated Plate-Filament | VSCS | Very Small Computer Systems |
| VRPS | Voltage Regulated Power Supply | VSD | Vertical Situation Display |
| | | VSE | Virtual Storage Extended |
| VRR | Visual Radio Range | VSE | Virtual Storage Extension |
| VRS | Visual Reference System | VSE/ICCF | VSE/Interactive Computing and Control Facility |
| VRSA | Voice Reporting Signal Assembly | | |
| VRSS | Voice Reporting Signal System | VSE/SP | Virtual Storage Extended/ System Package |
| VRU | Voice Readout Unit | VSFS | Voice Store and Forward messaging System |
| VRU | Voice Response Unit | | |
| VRX | Virtual Resource Executive | VSG | Versatile Symbol Generator |
| VRY | Vary | | |
| VRZ | Verkehrsrechenzentrum | VSI | Vertical Sideband |
| VRZ | Vor-Rückwärts-Zähler | VSI | Vertical Speed Indicator |
| VS | Vacuum Switch | VSL | Voltage Sense Level |
| VS | Variable Speed | VSM | Vestigial Sideband Modulation |
| VS | Variable Sweep | | |

# V

| | | | |
|---|---|---|---|
| VSM | Vibrating-Sample Magnetometer | VT | Videotext |
| VSM | Virtual Storage Management | VT | Virtual Terminal |
| | | VT | Voice Tube |
| | | VTA | Vacuum Tube Amplifier |
| VSM | Virtuelle Schaltmatrix | VTA | Virtual Terminal Agent |
| VSMF | Vendor Specifications Macrofilm File | VTAM | Virtual Telecommunications Access Method |
| VSMF | Visual Search Microfilm File | VTAM | Virtual Terminal Access Method |
| VSN | Volume Serial Number | VTAM | VORTEX Telecommunications Access Module |
| VSO | Very Stable Oscillator | | |
| VSO | Voltage Sensitive Oscillator | VTAMAP | VTAM-Anwendungsprogramme |
| VSP | Vehicle Scheduling Program | VTAME | VTAM Entry |
| | | VTAMPARS | VTAM Performance and Analysis Reporting System |
| VSP | Video Signal Processor | | |
| VSPC | Virtual Service Personal Computing | VTB | Voltage Time to Breakdown |
| VSPC | Virtual Storage Personal Computing | VTCS | Vehicular Traffic Control System |
| VSPT | Virtual Storage Performance Tool | VTD | Vacuum Tube Detector |
| | | VTD | Vertical Tape Display |
| VSPX | Vehicle Scheduling Program Extended | VTDM | Variable Time Division Multiplexer |
| VSR | Variable-length Shift Register | VTDV | Vermittlungstechnik für Datenverarbeitung |
| VSR | Very Short Range | VTF | Vertical Test Fixture |
| VSS | Variable Stability System | VTF | Voltage Transfer Function |
| VSS | Verbundsteuersystem | VTL | Variable Threshold Logic |
| VSS | Verkaufs-Service System | VTL | Vendor Transistor Logic |
| VSS | Video Storage System | VTM | Vacuum Tube Modulator |
| VSS | Virtual Support System | VTM | Virtual Task Manager |
| VSS | Visual Simulation System | VTM | Voltage Tunable Magnetron |
| VSS | Voice Storage System | VTO | Vacuum Tube Oscillator |
| VSSH | Video Signal Sample and Hold | VTO | Voltage Tuned Oscillator |
| VST | Vermittlungsstelle | VTOC | Volume Table Of Contents |
| VST | Visible Speech Translator | VTP | Video Tape |
| VSTOL | Vertical and Short Take-Off and Landing | VTPS | Videotext Terminal Protocol Support |
| VSTR | Volt Second Transfer Ratio | VTR | Video Tape Recorder |
| VSW | Very Short Wave | VTRAM | Variable Topology Random Access Memory |
| VSWR | Voltage Standing Wave Ratio | VTRS | Video Tape Recording System |
| VSX | Voice Switch | VTS | Vertical Test Stand |
| VT | Vacuum Tube | VTSU | Virtual Terminal Support |
| VT | Variable Time | VTV | Verband für Textverarbeitung e.V. |
| VT | Velocity/Time | | |
| VT | Verfahrenstechnik | VTVM | Vacuum Tube Voltmeter |
| VT | Vertical Tab | VTVS | Virtuelles Tabellen-Verarbeitungs-System |
| VT | Vertical Tabulation | | |
| VT | Vertical Tail | VTX | Videotext System |
| VT | Vertikaltabulation | VU | Vehicle Unit |
| VT | Video Tape | VU | Volume |
| VT | Video Terminal | | |

# V

| | | | |
|---|---|---|---|
| VU | Volume Unit | VWP | Variable Width Pulse |
| VUTS | Verfication Unit Test Set | VWSS | Vertical Wire Sky Screen |
| VUVM | Voluntary Universal Marking program | VXO | Variable Crystal Oscillator |
| | | VZ | Verarbeitungszeit |
| VV | Vorverstärker | VZ | Verhältniszähler |
| VVC | Voltage Variable Capacitance | VZ | Vermittlungszentrale |
| | | VZ | Verzweigung |
| VVC | Voltage Variable Capacitor | VZ | Vorzeichen |
| VVL | Variable Verzögerungslinie | VZE | Verzweigungseinheit |
| VVR | Variable Voltage Rectifier | VZR | Verbund-Zentralrechner |
| VVT | Verarbeitungs- und Verfahrenstechnik | VZS | Vielfachzugriffsystem |
| | | VZZ | Verzögerungszähler |
| VWL | Variable Word Length | | |

# W

| | | | |
|---|---|---|---|
| W | Wahlleitung | WAM | Words A Minute |
| W | Wattmeter | WAM | Work Analysis and Measurement |
| W | Watt | WAM | Worth Analysis Model |
| W | Waveform analyzer | WAMI | World Association for Medical Informatics |
| W | Waveguide | | |
| W | Weber | WAMIS | Water Management Information System |
| W | Wechselspannung | | |
| W | Wechselstrom | WAMOSCOPE | Wave-Modulated Oscilloscope |
| W | Width | | |
| W | Wire | WAN | Wide Area Network |
| W | Wireless | WAND | Westinghouse Alpha Numeric Display |
| W | Word | | |
| W | Wort | WANS | Wide Area Networks |
| W | Writer | WAO | Wissenschaftliche Arbeitsorganisation |
| W/L | Width-to-Length | | |
| WA | Wave Analyzer | WAP | Wissenschaftlicher Arbeitsprozeß |
| WA | Wide Angle | | |
| WA | Wire Armoured | WAP | Work Assignment Procedure |
| WA | Word Add | | |
| WA | Word After | WAP | Worst-case-circuit Analysis Program |
| WAA | Wide Angle Acquisition | | |
| WAAC | Working Amperes Alternating Current | WAPS | Wortausgabe-Puffersteuerung |
| WAC | Westdeutsches Auswertungs-Centrum | WAR | Work Acquisition Routine |
| | | WAR | Work Authorization Request |
| WAC | Work Assignment Code | | |
| WAC | Write Address Counter | WAR | Wortausgaberegister |
| WAC... | Wagner Computer | WARC | World Administrative Radio Conference |
| WACF | Weighted Average Cost File | | |
| | | WARLA | Wide Aperture Radio Location Array |
| WACK | Wait before receive positive Acknowledgement | | |
| | | WARN | Warning |
| | | WAS | Wiskom Accounting System |
| WACK | Wait and Acknowledge | WASCO | Wissenschaftliche Anwender von Siemens-Computer |
| WACM | Western Association of Circuit Manufacturers | | |
| WACO | Wire And Cable Company | WASP | Workshop Analysis and Scheduling Program |
| WACS | Wide-Area Computing Service | | |
| | | WAT | Weight, Altitude and Temperature |
| WACS | Workshop Attitude Control System | | |
| | | WATS | Wide Area Telephone Service |
| WADEX | Word and Author index | | |
| WADR | Weight Analysis Data Report | WAVE | Westinghouse Audio-Visual Electronics |
| WADS | Wide Area Data Service | WAVOR | Warenbewegung, Vorrats- und Reservewirtschaft |
| WAF | Wiring Around Frame | | |
| WAF | Word Address Format | WAZ | Wahlaufforderungszeichen |
| WAGIS | Waren-Genossenschaftliches Informations-System | | |
| | | WB | Wheel Base |
| | | WB | Wide Band |
| WAI | Work Area Information | WB | Word Before |
| WAL | Wiederanlauf | WB | Word Buffer |
| WALDO | Wichita Automatic Linear Data Output | WB | Write Buffer |
| | | WBCO | Waveguide Below Cut-Off |
| WALT | Write Ahead Log Tape | | |

# W

| | | | |
|---|---|---|---|
| WBCT | Wide Band Current Transformer | WD | Williams Domain |
| WBCV | Wide-Band Coherent Video | WD | Wiring Diagram |
| WBD | Wide-Band Data | WD | Word |
| WBD | Wire Bound | WD | Word Display |
| WBDA | Wide-Band Data Assembly | WDAG | Word Driver AND Gate |
| WBDL | Wide-Band Data Link | WDB | Werkstoffdatenbank |
| WBFM | Wide-Band Frequency Modulation | WDB | Wide Band |
| | | WDB | World Data Bank |
| WBGT | Wet Bulb Globe Thermometer | WDC | Working Device Code |
| | | WDC | World Data Center |
| WBIF | Wide-Band Intermediate Frequency | WDC | Write Data Channel |
| | | WDCNTO | Word Count Zero |
| WBIS | Wide-Band Information System | WDI | Weapon Data Index |
| | | WDL | Wireless Data Link |
| WBNL | Wide-Band Noise Limiting | WDPC | Western Data Processing Center |
| WBP | Weather- and Boilproof | | |
| WBP | Working Binary Program | WDS | Word Discrimination Score |
| WBR | Word Buffer Register | WDS | Write Disk Storage |
| WBRS | Wide-Band Remote Switch | WDSS | Workstation Dependent Segment Storage |
| WBS | Work Breakdown Structure | | |
| WBVTR | Wide-Band Video Tape Recorder | WDT | Weight Data Transmitter |
| | | WDV | Wissenschaftliche Datenverarbeitung |
| WC | Wire Cable | | |
| WC | Without Charge | WDV | Wissenschaftliche Daten- verarbeitung GmbH |
| WC | Word Count | | |
| WC | Work Control | WE | Western Electric |
| WC | Write and Compute | WE | Write Enable |
| WCATT | Worcester Country Association of Television Technicians | WEB | Wochenergebnisbericht |
| | | WEBU | Wechselbuchführung |
| | | WEDAC | Westinghouse Digital Airborne Computer |
| WCC | Word Count Cycle | | |
| WCC | Write Control Channel | WEDGE | Waterless Electrical Data Generating Effortless |
| WCC | Write Control Character | WEF | Wareneinkaufsformular |
| WCC | Write Control Code | WEFA | Werkstattfakturierung |
| WCD | Weather Card Data | WEFAX | Wetterfaksimilesystem |
| WCD | Worse Case Difference | WEMA | Western Electronic Manufacturers Association |
| WCDPC | War Control Data Processing Center | | |
| | | WEN | Write Enable |
| WCF | White Cathode Follower | WESCON | Western Electronics Show and Convention |
| WCGA | World Computer Graphics Association | | |
| | | WESDAC | Westinghouse Data Acquisition and Control |
| WCGM | Writable Character Generation Module | | |
| | | WEST | Wareneingangssteuerung |
| WCM | Wired Core Matrix | WESTI | Westinghouse Tele- processing Interface |
| WCM | Wired Core Memory | | |
| WCM | Word Combine and Multiplexer | WETAC | Westinghouse Electronic Tubeless Analog Computer |
| WCM | Writable Control Memory | | |
| WCR | Wire Contact Relay | WETARFAC | Work Element Timer And Recorder For Automatic Computing |
| WCR | Word Control Register | | |
| WCS | Writeable Control Storage | | |
| WCT | Water-Cooled Tube | WEX | Wortexpander |
| WD | Watt Demand | WEZ | Wahlendezeichen |
| WD | Waveform Distortion | WF | Walsh Function |
| | | WF | Waveform |

# W

| | | | |
|---|---|---|---|
| WF | Word Format | WIP | Work In Progress |
| WF | Write Forward | WIR | Wiring |
| WFA | Waveform Analyzer | WIRDS | Weather Information Reporting and Display System |
| WFG | Waveform Generator | | |
| WFRG | Wortfreigabe | | |
| WFT | Walsh-Fourier Transform | WIRKOSS | Wirkungsorientiertes Organisations- und Softwaresystem |
| WFTA | Winograd Fourier Transform Algorithm | | |
| WFW | Write Full Word | WIS | Wertpapierinformationssystem |
| WG | Wandel & Goltermann | | |
| WG | Water Gauge | WISARD | Wide-band System for Acquiring and Recording Data |
| WG | Waveguide | | |
| WG | Wire Gauge | | |
| WG | Working Group | WISC | Wisconsin Integrally Synchronized Computer |
| WGBC | Waveguide operating Below Cut-off | | |
| | | WISE | Wang Inter System Exchange |
| WGN | White Gaussian Noise | | |
| WGR | Wiedergaberegister | WISE | Water Information System for Enforcement |
| WGR | Wiedergeben, Rückwärts | | |
| WGS | Waveguide Glide Slope | WISE | Wehaton Information System for Education |
| WGV | Wiedergeben, Vorwärts | | |
| WH | Writing Head | WISL | Westinghouse Information System Laboratory |
| WH | Where used | | |
| WHDM | Watt-Hour Demand Meter | WISS | Wirtschaftsinformatikschule Schweiz |
| WHF | Walsh-Hadamard Function | | |
| WHL | Watt-Hour meter with Loss compensator | WISS | Workstation Independent Segment Storage |
| WHP | Wiederholungsprüfung | WIT | Weekly Information Tape |
| WHT | Walsh-Hadamard Transform | WITA | Wang Information Transfer Architecture |
| WI | Work In process | WITCH | Wolverhampton Instrument for Teaching Computation from Harwell |
| WI | Wrought Iron | | |
| WID | Wirtschaftlichkeit von Informations und Dokumentationseinrichtungen | | |
| | | WITS | Waterloo Interactive Terminal System |
| WIDE | Wiring Integration Design | WITS | Weather Information Telemetering System |
| WIF | Water Immersion Facility | | |
| WIL | White Indicator Lamp | WITS | Westinghouse Interactive Time Sharing |
| WILO | Wirtschaftliche Losgröße | | |
| WIN | Welfare Information Network | WIZ | Wechselinformationszeichen |
| WIN | Western Information Network | WJCC | Western Joint Computer Conference |
| WINC | Worldwide Integrated Communication | WK | Week |
| | | WL | Wave Length |
| WIND | Weather Information Network and Display | WL | Wire List |
| | | WL | Word Length |
| WINDEE | Wind tunnel Data Encoding and Evaluation | WL | Wortlänge |
| | | WLN | Wiswesser Line Notation |
| WINDS | Weather Information Network and Display System | WLR | Wrong Length Record |
| | | WLSI | Wafer Large Scale Integration |
| WIP | Ware In Process | WM | Wattmeter |
| WIP | Women in Information Processing | WM | Word Mark |
| | | WM | Working Memory |

# W

| | |
|---|---|
| WM | Wortmaschine |
| WM | Wortorganisierte Maschine |
| WMA | Wortmarke |
| WMO | World Meteorological Organization |
| WMS | Wire Matrix Switch |
| WMSS | Westinghouse Micro-Scan System |
| WNG | Wiring |
| WNK | Wink |
| WNS | Warennachschubsystem |
| WO | Write Out |
| WOA | Wang Office Assistant |
| WOC | Wafer Order Control |
| WOCG | Weather Outline Contour Generator |
| WODD | World Oceanographic Data Display |
| WOM | Word Organized Memory |
| WOM | Write Only Memory |
| WOM | Write Optional Memory |
| WOOD | Write One Optical Disk |
| WOOL | Words Out of Ordinary Language |
| WORDCOM | Word Computer |
| WOS | Word Organized Storage |
| WOS | Work Order Summary |
| WOT | Word Overlap Trigger |
| WOW | Who Owns Whom |
| WOW | Word On Way |
| WP | Wartungsprozessor |
| WP | Word Period |
| WP | Word Processing |
| WP | Word Punch |
| WP | Working Pressure |
| WP | Workstation Printer |
| WP | Worst Pattern |
| WP/AS | Word Processing/ Administrative Support |
| WP/OS | Word Processing/Office System |
| WPB | Write Printer Binary |
| WPC | Wired Program Computer |
| WPIS | Wafer Parameter Identification System |
| WPL | Wechselplatte |
| WPL | Word Processing Language |
| WPLOT | Wire Plot |
| WPM | Words Per Minute |
| WPS | Wechselplattenspeicher |
| WPS | Word Processing System |
| WPS | Words Per Second |
| WPU | Write Punch |
| WPWM | Wide Pulse Width Modulator |
| WQM | Write-circuit for Queueing Messages |
| WR | Wagenrücklauf |
| WR | Wall Receptacle |
| WR | Warehouse Receipt |
| WR | Workshop Reporting |
| WR | Write Record |
| WR CHK | Write Check |
| WR/ZL | Wagenrücklauf/ Zeilenvorschub |
| WRAP | Wayne Remote Access Processor |
| WRAP | Wire Routing And Packaging |
| WRAPS | Workload and Repair Activity Process Simulator |
| WRCALL | Write Call |
| WRCHK | Write Check |
| WRD | Word |
| WREDAC | Weapon Research Establishment Digital Automatic Computer |
| WRK | Work |
| WRKSTN | Workstation |
| WRL | Wagenrücklauf |
| WRM | Write into Memory |
| WRP | Write Peripheral |
| WRSTAT | Write Status |
| WRT | Write |
| WRU | Who is there? |
| WRU | Who Are You? |
| WS | Warteschlange |
| WS | Wiedergabespalt |
| WS | Word Separator |
| WS | Working Storage |
| WS | Workshop control |
| WS | Workspace |
| WS | Workstation |
| WS | Wort Select |
| WS | Write Statement |
| WS | Writing System |
| WSC | Workstation Controller |
| WSD | Wurzelsegmentdatei |
| WSDD | Weapons Status Digital Display |
| WSE | Word Size Entry |
| WSE | Work Station Entry |
| WSEN | Writing Speed Enhancer |
| WSF | Workstation Search Facility |
| WSI | Wafer Scale Integration |
| WSI | Workstation Interface |
| WSN | Wang System Network |
| WSN | Wang System Networking |

# W

| | | | |
|---|---|---|---|
| WSP | Wideband Signal Processor | WTO | Write-To-Operator |
| WSPACS | Weapon System Programming And Control System | WTOR | Write-To-Operator with Reply |
| | | WTR | Writer |
| WSPD | Weapon System Planning Data | WTS | Word Terminal Synchronous |
| | | WTZ | Wähltonzeichen |
| WSR | Wire Shift Register | WTZ | Wiedergabetaktzähler |
| WSR | Word Switch Register | WUC | Work Unit Code |
| WSS | Wahlschlußsignal | WUF | Where Used File |
| WSS | Word Structured Storage | WUI | Western Union International |
| WSSD | Weapons Status Situation Display | WUIS | Work Unit Information System |
| WST | Work Station Terminal | | |
| WST | Write Symbol Table | WUT... | Western Union Telegraph Co. |
| WSWS | Werkstückwechselsystem | | |
| WT | Wählton | WV | Wave |
| WT | Watt | WV | Werksvertretung |
| WT | Wechselstromtelegraphie | WV | Working Voltage |
| WT | Weight | WVAC | Working Volt Alternating Current |
| WT | Wireless Telegraphy | | |
| WT | World Trade | WVC | Write Validity Check |
| WT | Worttakt | WVDC | Working Volt, Direct Current |
| WT | Write | | |
| WTA | Warning Tone Allowed | WVL | Wave Length |
| WTB | Write Tape Binary | WW | Wire Wrap |
| WTC | World Trade Corporation | WW | Wire-Wound |
| WTD | Warning Tone Denied | WW | Wireway |
| WTD | Wind Tunnel Data | WWAM | World Wide Accounting Machine |
| WTD | World Telecommunications Directory | WWMCCS | World Wide Military Command and Control System |
| WTD | Write Tape Decimal | | |
| WTG | Wartung | | |
| WTI | Wissenschaftliche und Technische Information | WWP | Write Without Program |
| | | WWS | Warenwirtschaftssystem |
| WTIC | World Trade In Computers | WWw | World Weather Watch |
| WTID | Wissenschaftlich-Technische Information und Dokumentation | WX | Wireless |
| | | WXTRN | Weak External Reference |
| | | WZHS | Werkzeughandhabungssystem |
| WTKR | Wissenschaftlich-Technischer Kleinrechner | WZL | Werkzeugmaschinenlabor |
| WTM | Wiskom Tool Manager | WZW | Werkzeugwechsel |
| WTM | Write Tape Mark | | |

# X

| | | | |
|---|---|---|---|
| X | Exchange | XHIS | Extended Hospital Information System |
| X | Extension | | |
| X | Trans... | XHV | Extreme High Vacuum |
| X | X-ray tube | XIC | Transmission Interface Converter |
| X | Xenon | | |
| X-off | Transmitter off | XID | Exchange Identification |
| X-on | Transmitter on | XID | Xerox-Intel-Dec |
| X-ray | Roentgen Ray | XIO | Execute Input/Output |
| X-wave | Extraordinary wave | XIO | Transfer Input/Output |
| XA | Auxiliary Amplifier | XIS | Cross Interface Switch |
| XA | Extended Architecture | XITB | Transparent Intermediate Block |
| XA | Transmission Adapter | | |
| XACT | X Automatic Code Translation | XL | Extend List |
| | | XLT | Transaction List Table |
| XAR | Index Adder Register | XLT | Translate |
| XB | Crossbar | XLTR | Translator |
| XBAR | Crossbar | XMISSION | Transmission |
| XBT | Expendable Bath-Thermography | XMIT | Transmit |
| | | XMIT | Transmitter |
| XCD | Exceed | XMITTER | Transmitter |
| XCH | Exchange | XMOS | High-Speed Metal Oxide Semiconductor |
| XCL | Exclusive | | |
| XCON | Expert Configurer | XMSN | Transmission |
| XCONN | Cross Connection | XMSSN | Transmission |
| XCS | Xerox Computer Service | XMT | Transmit |
| XCSTP | Extended Code Segment Table Pointer | XMTD | Transmitted |
| | | XMTG | Transmitting |
| XCT | X-band Communications Transponder | XMTL | Transmittal |
| | | XMTR | Transmitter |
| XCTL | Transfer Control | XMTT | Transmitter |
| XCU | Transmission Control Unit | XNS | Xerox Network System |
| XCVR | Transceiver | XO | Cyrstal Oscillator |
| XDCR | Transducer | XOI | Exclusive Or Inverter |
| XDD | Exclude Digit Display | XOP | Extended Operation |
| XDER | Transducer | XOR | Exclusive OR |
| XDLE | Transparent DLE | XOVER | Crossover |
| XDP | X-ray Density Probe | XOVR | Crossover |
| XDR | Transducer | XPD | Cross Polar Decoupling |
| XDS | Xerox Data Systems | XPD | Cross Polar Discrimination |
| XE | Experimental Engine | XPDR | Transponder |
| XEG | X-ray Emission Gauge | XPL | Explain |
| XENQ | Transparent ENQ | XPL | Explanation |
| XETB | Transparent End of Transmission Block | XPLN | Explanation |
| | | XPN | External Priority Number |
| XETB | Transparent ETB | XPNDR | Transponder |
| XETX | Transparent End of Text | XPOND | Transponder |
| XETX | Transparent ETX | XPONDER | Transponder |
| XF | Extended Facility | XPT | Cross-Point |
| XFD | Crossed Field Discharge | XPT | External Page Table |
| XFER | Transfer | XPYB | X Position Y Bit |
| XFMR | Transformer | XR | Index Register |
| XFR | Transfer | XRCD | X-Ray Cyrstal Density |
| XGS | Extended Graphic Software | XREP | Auxiliary Report |
| XHAIR | Cross Hair | XRF | Extended Recovery Facility |

- 651 -

# X

| | | | |
|---|---|---|---|
| XRM | External ROM Mode | XTASI | Exchange of Technical Apollo Simulation Information |
| XRM | X-Ray Microanalyzer | | |
| XRPM | X-Ray Projection Microscope | XTEL | Cross Tell |
| XS | Extra Strong | XTEN | Xerox Telecommunications Network |
| XSCBR | Transcriber | | |
| XSECT | Cross Section | XTENT | Extent |
| XSIS | Xerox System Intergation Standard | XTLO | Crystal Oscillator |
| | | XTR | Transmitter |
| XST | External Segment Table | XTRAN | Experimental Translator |
| XST | External Symbol Table | XTS | Cross-Tell Simulator |
| XST | Transparent Start of Text | XTTD | Transparent TDD |
| XSTR | Transistor | XU | X Unit |
| XSTX | Transparent Start of Text | XUV | Extreme Ultraviolet |
| XSYN | Transparent Synchronous/idle | XVAR | External Variable |
| | | XVTR | Transverter |
| XT | Cross Talk | XXXXX | Error |
| XTALK | Crosstalk | XYP | X-Y Plotter |
| XTAM | Extended Telecommunications Access Method | XYR | X-Y Recorder |

# Y

| | | | |
|---|---|---|---|
| Y | Vertical deflection | YIL | Yellow Indicating Light |
| Y | Yard | YK | Yoke |
| Y | Yellow | YL | Yellow Lamp |
| Y | Yoke | YM | Your Message |
| Y | Yttrium | YMD | Year, Month, Day |
| Y-PUNCH | Perforation in Row 12 of Card | YP | Yield Point |
| | | YR | Year |
| YAG | Yttrium Aluminum Garnet | YRGB | Yellow-Red-Green-Blue |
| YAIG | Yttrium Aluminum Iron Garnet | YS | Yield Strength |
| | | YSF | Yield Safety Factor |
| YAMP | Vertical Amplifier | YSLF | Yield Strength Load Factor |
| YDC | Yaw Damper Computer | YTD | Year To Date |
| YE | Year End | YV | Yield Value |
| YIG | Yttrium Iron Garnet | | |

# Z

| | | | |
|---|---|---|---|
| Z | Impedance | ZD | Zentrale Daten-verarbeitung |
| Z | Zahl | ZD | Zero Defect |
| Z | Zähler | ZD | Zusatzdrucker |
| Z | Zeichen | ZD-SIB | Zentraldaten-Sicherungs-bestand |
| Z | Zentralregister | | |
| Z | Zero | ZD-ZUG | Zentraldaten-Zugangsdatei |
| Z | Ziffer | ZDB | Zentrale Datenbank |
| Z | Zone | ZDE | Zentralstelle Dokumenta-tion Elektrotechnik |
| Z | Zuverlässigkeit | | |
| Z | Zwischenresultat | ZDI | Zentralstelle für Dokumen-tation und Information |
| Z... | Zuse | | |
| ZA | Zahl | ZDM | Zentraler Datenmultiplexer |
| ZA | Zeilenart | ZDO | Zentrum für Datenverarbei-tung und Organisation |
| ZA | Zentrale Anzeigeeinheit | | |
| ZA | Zero Adjusted | ZDOK | Zeitschriftenverzeichnis des Dokumentations-zentrums |
| ZA | Zero and Add | | |
| ZA | Ziffernanzeige | | |
| ZA | Ziffernanzeigeeinheit | | |
| ZA | Ziffernauswertung | ZDP | Zero Delivery Pressure |
| ZAD | Zentrale Adreßdatei | ZDR | Zeichendrucker |
| ZAE | Zentrale Autragserfassung | ZDR | Zentraldaten auf Random-Speicher |
| ZAI | Zero Address Instruction | | |
| ZAL | Zeichenalarm | ZDR | Zentraler-Daten-Random-Bestand |
| ZAM | Zentrum für Angewandte Mikroelektronik e.V. | | |
| | | ZDT | Zero-Ductility Transition |
| ZAP | Zentralarbeitsplatz | ZDÜ | Zentrales Daten-übertragungsteil |
| ZAP | Zero Add Packed | | |
| ZAP | Zero and Add Packed | ZDV | Zentrale Daten-verarbeitung |
| ZAS | Zeichenausgabe, Seriell | | |
| ZAS | Zentrales Alarmsystem | ZDVA | Zentrale Daten-verarbeitungsanlage |
| ZAS | Zero Access Storage | | |
| ZAVI | Zero Array Values with given Index | ZE | Zeilenende |
| | | ZE | Zeiterfassung |
| ZB | Zap data Base | ZE | Zentraleinheit |
| ZB | Zero Beat | ZE | Zeros Extended |
| ZB | Zero-Based | ZEA | Zentral-Ein-Ausgabe |
| ZB | Zubehör | ZEA | Zentrales Ein/Ausgabe-gerät |
| ZBA | Zentralisierte Betriebs-ausrüstung | | |
| | | ZEA | Zero Energy Assembly |
| ZBB | Zero Base Budgeting | ZEBEDA | Zentrale Betriebs-Datei |
| ZBS | Zentrale Bus-Steuerung | ZED | Zentrale Einrichtung für direkte Datenfern-verarbeitung |
| ZBT | Zusatzbestelltext | | |
| ZBÜ | Zentrale Betriebs-überwachung | | |
| | | ZED | Zentralstelle für Elektro-nische Datenverarbeitung |
| ZC | Zero Check | | |
| ZCC | Zero Crossing Counter | ZEEP | Zero Energy Experimental file |
| ZCD | Zone-Controlled Deposition | | |
| | | ZEG | Zufallentscheidungs-generator |
| ZCI | Zero Crossing Interval | | |
| ZCR | Zone of Correct Reading | ZEILNR | Zeilennummer |
| ZCT | Zero Count Table | ZEK | Zentraler Elektronischer Komplex |
| ZD | Zahlendarstellung | | |
| ZD | Zener Diode | ZELASI | Zentrale Lagersimulation |
| ZD | Zentraldaten | ZEM | Zentrales Entscheidungs-modell |

# Z

| | | | |
|---|---|---|---|
| ZEP | Zeicheneingabe, Parallel | ZIPCD | Zip Code |
| ZES | Zeicheneingabe, Seriell | ZIS | Zentrales Informationssystem |
| ZES | Zero Energy System | ZIS | Zweiginformationssystem |
| ZESA | Zeicheneingabe/Sprachausgabe | ZIT | Zeitimpulstaxierung |
| ZEVIS | Zentrales Verkehrs-Informationssystem | ZIV | Zentrales Informationssystem Vertrieb |
| ZF | Zero Frequency | ZIZ | Zeit Impuls Zählung |
| ZFC | Zero Failure Criteria | ZKI | Zylinder für Kennsatzinformationen |
| ZFD | Zeitschrift Für Datenverarbeitung | ZKP | Zeit-Kosten-Planung |
| ZFS | Zero Field Splitting | ZL | Zählen/Löschen |
| ZFS | Zone Field Selection | ZL | Zeile |
| ZFT | Zero Fill Trigger | ZL | Zeilenvorschub |
| ZFV | Zwischenfrequenzverstärker | ZL | Zentralvermittlungsleitung |
| | | ZL | Ziffernlampe |
| ZG | Zahlengeber | ZLGID | Zentrale Leitung für Gesellschaftswissenschaftliche Information und Dokumentation |
| ZG | Zeichengeber | | |
| ZG | Zeichengenerator | | |
| ZG | Zeitgeber | | |
| ZG | Zero Gravity | ZLID | Zentrale Leitstelle für Information und Dokumentation |
| ZGE | Zero Gravity Effect | | |
| ZGS | Zero Gradient Synchroton | | |
| ZI | Zero Input | ZLMID | Zentrale Leitstelle für Medizinische Information und Dokumentation |
| ZI | Ziffer | | |
| ZIAS | Zentrales Informations- und Auskunftssystem | | |
| | | ZLV | Zeilenvorschub |
| ZIB | Zentrale Informationsbank | ZM | Impedance Meter |
| ZID | Zentrale Informations-Datei | ZM | Zap Module |
| | | ZM | Zählfrequenzmesser |
| ZID | Zentralinstitut für Information und Dokumentation | ZM | Zeitmarke |
| | | ZM | Zeitmultiplex |
| ZIDA | Zentrum für Information und Dokumentation der Außenwirtschaft | ZM | Zero Marker |
| | | ZM | Zone de Manoeuvre |
| | | ZM | Zustandsmodifizierer |
| ZIF | Zero Insertion Force | ZMA | Zink Meta-Arsenite |
| ZII | Zentralstelle für Information der Industrie | ZMD | Zentralstelle für Maschinelle Dokumentation |
| ZIG | Zählimpulsgeber | ZME | Zentrale Meßwerterfassungseinrichtung |
| ZIG | Zeitimpulsgeber | | |
| ZII | Zero Intersymbol Interference | ZMI | Zentrum für Mikroelektronik und Informationstechnik |
| ZIID | Zentralinstitut für Information und Dokumentation | ZMR | Zentrale Meßwertregistrierung |
| ZIK | Zeitimpulshöhenkonverter | ZN | Zone |
| ZIL | Zentrale Information Lesematerial | ZNK | Zentrale Namenkartei |
| | | ZNR | Zinc oxide-non-linear Resistance |
| ZIM | Zentrales Investitions-Modell | | |
| | | ZNT | Zentrale Netztaktaufbereitung |
| ZIOP | Zielgruppenoptimierung | | |
| ZIOP | Zieloptimierungsplan | ZODIAC | Zone Defense Integrated Active Capability |
| ZIP | Zinc Impurity Photodetector | | |
| | | ZOE | Zero Energy |
| ZIP | Zone Inter-Partitions | ZOH | Zero Order Hold |

- 656 -

# Z

| | | | |
|---|---|---|---|
| ZOI | Zero-Order Interpolator | ZSW | Zeichen-Spaltenwähler |
| ZOP | Zero-Order Predictor | ZSW | Zeitschaltwerk |
| ZP | Zentralprozessor | ZSY | Zeichensynchronisier- |
| ZP | Zone Punch | | einrichtung |
| ZP | Zykluspuffer | ZT | Zähltaste |
| ZPB | Zentrales Platzbuchungs- | ZT | Zähltor |
| | system | ZT | Zeittaktgeber |
| ZPC | Zero Print Control | ZT | Zieltext |
| ZPD | Zentralstelle für | ZT | Zifferntaste |
| | Primärdokumentation | ZT | Zone Time |
| ZPI | Zone Position Indicator | ZT | Zyklustakt |
| ZPL | Zentrale Projektleitung | ZTDI | Zentralstelle für Textil- |
| ZPRCTRL | Zero Print Control | | dokumentation und |
| ZPS | Zeroes Per Second | | -Information |
| ZPT | Zero Power Test | ZTE | Zeichentaktempfang |
| ZR | Zeichenregenerator | ZTE | Zentraleinheit |
| ZR | Zentralrechner | ZTG | Zeittaktgeber |
| ZR | Zero | ZTS | Zero-To-Space |
| ZR | Ziffernrechner | ZÜ | Zeichenübertragung |
| ZR | Zwischenraum | ZÜ | Zwischenüberträger |
| ZR | Zwischenregister | ZÜB | Zeichenübertragungs- |
| ZRA | Zeiss-Rechenautomat | | baustein |
| ZRA | Zentrale Rechenanlage | ZÜE | Zentrale Überrechnungs- |
| ZRA | Ziffern-Rechenautomat | | einheit |
| ZRD | Zeitreihendatei | ZÜE | Zentrale Überwachungs- |
| ZRE | Zentrale Recheneinheit | | einrichtung |
| ZRI | Zentraler Rücksetzimpuls | ZUG | Zugriffszeit |
| ZRI | Zentrales Recheninstitut | ZÜP | Zeitüberwachtes Programm |
| ZRP | Zeitreihenprozessor | ZÜR | Zugüberwachung, Rechner- |
| ZRP | Zentraler-Reservierungs- | | unterstützt |
| | Platz | ZUSI | Zufallssimulator |
| ZS | Zentrale Steuerung | ZV | Zeilenvorschub |
| ZS | Zero and Substract | ZV | Zustandsvariablenspeicher |
| ZS | Zustandsspeicher | ZV | Zustandsvektoren |
| ZS | Zwischenspeicher | ZVE | Zentrale Verarbeitungs- |
| ZSB | Zwischenspeicherbereich | | einheit |
| ZSC | Zahlensicherheitscode | ZVE | Zuverlässigkeit Elektri- |
| ZSC | Ziffernsicherungscode | | scher Einrichtungen |
| ZSD | Zentraler Schreibdienst | ZVEI | Zentralverband der |
| ZSE | Zero Suppress End | | Elektrotechnischen |
| ZSF | Zero Skip Frequency | | Industrie |
| ZSI | Zentraler Startimpuls | ZVIS | Zentralverwaltung |
| ZSK | Ziffernsicherungskode | | Informationssysteme |
| ZSK | Zusatzkernspeicher | ZVL | Zeichen Verloren |
| ZSP | Zählspeicher | ZVS | Zero Voltage Switching |
| ZSP | Zwischenspeicher | ZVST | Zentrale Vermittlungs- |
| ZSR | Zugsteuerrechner | | stelle |
| ZSR | Zustandsregister | ZVZ | Zentraler Verarbeitungs- |
| ZSS | Zusatzspeicher- | | einheit-Zusatz |
| | Steuergerät | ZW | Zählwerk |
| ZST | Zentralsteuerung | ZWC | Zone Wind Computer |
| ZST | Zentralsteuerwerk | ZWD | Zwischendatei |
| ZST | Zone Standard Time | ZWR | Zwischenraum |
| ZSTPR | Zentrales Steuerprogramm | ZWR | Zwischenraumzeichen |
| ZSUP | Zero Suppress | ZWR | Zwischenregister |

# Z

| | | | | |
|---|---|---|---|---|
| ZYF | Zyklusfehler | ZZF | Zentralamt für Zulassungen im Fernmeldewesen |
| ZYK | Zyklus | | |
| ZYK | Zykluszeit | ZZK | Zentraler Zeichenkanal |
| ZYL | Zylinder | ZZR | Zykluszählregister |
| ZZ | Zonenzähler | ZZZ | Zeitzonenzähler |